SOLVING PROBLEMS USING ELEMENTARY MATHEMATICS

SOLVING PROBLEMS USING ELEMENTARY MATHEMATICS

DAVID GAY

University of Arizona, Tucson

DELLEN PUBLISHING COMPANY

an imprint of

MACMILLAN PUBLISHING COMPANY

New York

MAXWELL MACMILLAN CANADA

Toronto

To
Lonie, Adam,
and Katie

On the cover: "Nine" is an oil painting by San Francisco Bay Area artist Deborah Oropallo. The work is from a series inspired by Veronica O'Neill's book *Teaching Arithmetic to Deaf Children.*

Deborah Oropallo's work was presented in the last Biennial Exhibition at New York's Whitney Museum. Her work may be seen in the collections of the Baltimore Museum of Art, Baltimore, Maryland; the La Jolla Museum of Contemporary Art, La Jolla, California; the Lannan Foundation, Los Angeles, California; and the Crocker Museum in Sacramento, California. Oropallo is represented by the Stephen Wirtz Gallery in San Francisco, California.

Technical illustrations and drawings by Barbara Barnett Illustrations and Associates. Cartoons by Tom Barnett. Computer generated illustrations by Alexander Productions.

Printed in the United States of America

Macmillan Publishing Company
866 Third Avenue, New York, New York 10022

Macmillan Publishing Company is
part of the Maxwell Communication
Group of Companies.

Maxwell Macmillan Canada, Inc.
1200 Eglinton Avenue East
Suite 200
Don Mills, Ontario M3C 3N1

Permissions: Dellen Publishing Company
               400 Pacific Avenue
               San Francisco, California   94133

Orders: Dellen Publishing Company   Collier Macmillan Canada, Inc.
               c/o Macmillan Publishing Company   1200 Eglinton Avenue East
               Front and Brown Streets   Suite 200
               Riverside, New Jersey   08075   Don Mills, Ontario M3C 3N1

Library of Congress Cataloging-in-Publication Data

Gay, David.
  Solving problems using elementary mathematics/David Gay.
    p. cm.
  Includes index.
  ISBN 0–02–341101–5
  1. Arithmetic—Study and teaching.   2. Problem solving.
I. Title.
QA135.5.G38   1991   90–21827
510—dc20   CIP

Printing: 1   2   3   4   5   6   7   8   9   Year: 0   1   2   3   4   5

ISBN 0-02-341101-5

CONTENTS

CHAPTER **3** ANSWERING QUESTIONS OF HOW MANY? 93
OUR SYSTEM OF WRITTEN NUMERALS

CHAPTER 6   DIVISION OF WHOLE NUMBERS   237

CHAPTER 7   MULTIPLES, DIVISORS AND PRIMES   273

CHAPTER **8** INTRODUCTION TO FRACTIONS AND RATIOS   309

CHAPTER 11   EXTENDING THE NUMBER LINE: POSITIVE AND NEGATIVE NUMBERS   429

CHAPTER 12   EXPONENTS, LARGE NUMBERS, AND THE ART OF ESTIMATION   463

CHAPTER *13*

INTRODUCTION TO MEASUREMENT: LENGTH, POSITION, AND SHAPE
505

CHAPTER *14*

GRAPHING
551

CHAPTER **15** MEASURING LENGTH INDIRECTLY   601

CHAPTER **16** CIRCLES AND ANGLES   669

FOREWORD

Mathematics is something that is meant to be done and enjoyed. It is a way to solve interesting problems that could not otherwise be solved, or to solve problems much more efficiently than they could otherwise be solved. It is not a spectator sport, nor is it a way to provide dreary, boring activities to keep children busy.

Unfortunately, much of school mathematics gives the impression that we teach it to keep children occupied so they won't have time to get into trouble: a sort of replacement for the nineteenth century practice of making samplers, except in the case of samplers the final product was beautiful and worth saving. A major goal of the National Council of Teachers of Mathematics *Standards for Teaching Mathematics,* and other similar reports, is to help students see that mathematics is exciting and useful by allowing them to actually do mathematics.

In this book David Gay makes the learner an active participant in doing mathematics. He helps the reader discover how mathematical thinking can be used to analyze and solve varied problems, some of which should be of interest to almost anybody, no matter what his or her previous background. He brings his extensive knowledge and creative imagination to elementary school mathematics and provides motivated and intellectually honest development of topics that should be taught to young children.

Prospective teachers who study this material and who do a reasonable number of the many problems and laboratory activities suggested in this book and its companion laboratory manual will derive a much better understanding of what mathematics is, why we teach it, and how they can teach it so children will learn and enjoy mathematics. Their pupils will think of mathematics as something to be done and enjoyed—as something they can figure out themselves (without memorizing formulas or procedures), and as something that is useful in solving problems that they wish to solve for their own benefit and for the benefit of others.

Stephen S. Willoughby

PREFACE

A compelling reason why mathematics holds a central position in our educational system is that it can be useful in solving problems. Everybody, at one time or another, solves problems using mathematics. The more skill you have at solving problems with mathematics, the more options are open to you. The success of an engineer or scientist depends heavily on an ability to solve problems with mathematics. Although not everyone becomes an engineer or scientist, the recent proliferation of high-speed, electronic computers means that there are fewer jobs available to those without mathematical problem-solving skills.

"Skill" does not refer here to a tool to be used routinely or mechanically, without thinking. In the real world, routine problems such as "multiply these two numbers" or "simplify this algebraic expression" do not often appear. A real problem usually must be carried through a number of stages before it can be solved by activities such as "divide this fraction by that one." Problem-solving skills for the real world involve thinking and active involvement. These are skills of survival, and their use is very human.

The purpose of this book is to get you actively involved in solving problems with mathematics. This will be done in several ways. First, you will be introduced to some useful problem-solving strategies and given the opportunity to work with them. Secondly, you will encounter problems that are not routine, but realistic problems, which I hope you will perceive as really needing solutions. Thirdly, solutions to several of these problems will appear in the text, demonstrating to you (in an informal way) processes that lead to a solution, including the meanderings and dead-ends characteristic of any real problem-solving situation. Finally, you will see how mathematical ideas and techniques develop out of this process: a new idea is usually a consequence of solving a problem (or several problems), a new technique comes about because there is a need for it.

You intend to teach mathematics in an elementary or middle school; the mathematics of this text is closely related to the mathematics taught in such a school. However, you will have seen much of this before opening this book. How do you become involved when the problems are easy (to you) and the mathematical idea or technique is one that you already know? How do you think about a technique whose use has become routine? How do you think about an idea you may not have been encouraged to think about? When you become a teacher, you will want to be able to put yourself in your students' shoes; you will want to know what it is like to solve problems with limited knowledge. To turn the difficulty of thinking about something routine into an advantage, the text will ask you to solve a "simple" problem as if you were a person with a certain limited knowledge. For example, to introduce multiplication of several-digit whole numbers, a problem will appear that (you and I know) can be solved by the usual method. You will be asked to assume that you don't know the method and then to solve the problem using only other skills of arithmetic (addition, subtraction, single-digit multiplication, . . .).

Solving a problem using limited knowledge has positive consequences. First, you will learn directly that there are many ways to solve a problem, that there may be "unsophisticated" yet successful ways of solving a problem, and that deciding on the best way to solve a problem may depend on the person solving it. Secondly, it should make you aware of things you already know but haven't thought about lately. Thirdly, it should give you an understanding of how one piece of mathematics follows from another. This approach also makes sense to a future teacher: to nurture a mathematical idea in the mind of a fourth grader, it might be good if it first thrived in the mind of her teacher.

Here is what I want from your use of this book. I want you to begin to own, personally, the mathematical ideas that you once knew unthinkingly or only peripherally (and sometimes anxiously). I want you to begin to believe that mathematics is useful and use it. I want you to become competent and confident using mathematical ideas and techniques. I want you to be ready to learn how to get other persons actively involved in problem solving. I want you to have a blast solving problems.

Learning to solve problems can be frustrating, like learning to swim. Until you get that stroke down, you feel awkward and out of place. But when you grasp it, it's as if you and the water are one machine working together. Until you get the hang of solving problems, you can feel pretty inept. But when you finally succeed in solving a problem you haven't solved before, you will have a wonderful feeling of satisfaction. I hope that you will experience the joy of discovering mathematical facts you never knew before and of understanding for the first time how certain mathematical ideas and techniques fit together. As you solve more problems and gain more confidence in your mathematical abilities, you will have these good experiences more and more often.

Good luck and happy problem solving!

HOW EACH CHAPTER IS ORGANIZED

First Part of the Chapter   Each chapter develops ideas and techniques that are related by a common theme. The first part of the chapter develops these in the following format: statement of a problem, solution of the problem, mathematical idea springing from the solution, exercises to try out the new idea. This format may repeat itself several times during a chapter. Each problem is chosen because it needs to be solved and because the techniques acquired up to that point for solving it are clumsy or inefficient. The solution to one problem will typically build on previous solutions and mathematical ideas.

The first part of the chapter is its core. Its style is informal, allowing ideas to germinate and evolve naturally.

Second Part of the Chapter   The second part of the chapter embellishes the first. Its style is less leisurely and more condensed. It contains one or more sections of the following types. (Many chapters contain all types.)

- *Looking back*   This section looks at the ideas of the first part of the chapter in a more rigorous or formal way than the first part does. It should provide you with a different perspective on the earlier material.

- *Looking ahead*   This section relates the ideas of the first part to themes developed later in the text.

- *Extending ideas*   This section carries some of the ideas of the first part further and puts them in a larger mathematical context. The ideas developed here will probably not be encountered later in the book.

- *Calculators and computers*   This section discusses how calculators or computers (or both) can illustrate an idea, carry out a technique, or solve a problem. Chapter 1 has an introduction to calculators as well as to programming a computer in BASIC. (I encourage you to use calculators and computers to help you solve all the problems in this book, especially those that require a lot of computation.)

END-OF-CHAPTER FEATURES

- *Important ideas and techniques*   This is a summary of the main concepts and techniques of the chapter. This should be useful for study and review.

- *Problem set*   This is a collection of problems to solve to test your understanding and hone your problem-solving skills. The ideas and techniques of the chapter should be useful here. The problem set has two parts. Most of the problems in **Practicing Skills** are routine, needing only one or two steps to solve. A problem here may be like a problem solved in the chapter itself—in order to solve, you mimic the solution given in the text. The problems in the **Using Ideas** sections are more involved and may require you to use the ideas and techniques of the chapter in new ways. Or, you may need to develop a new, related idea or technique.

- *Three-chapter review*   This is a set of problems for use as a "Sample Test" over the material of the previous three chapters. Solutions to the problems in these Reviews are in the back of the book.

OTHER FEATURES OF THE TEXT

STOP (Try this yourself)   The stop sign occurs in the text after a statement of a problem, followed by an exhortation to try the problem before reading the text's solution. This is an important message! You need to get actively involved in solving problems in order to get the most out of this text.

Italics   Key words appear in italics.

Boxes   Boxed material highlights important definitions, ideas, and techniques. This should be useful for reference and review.

Boldface Color   When a problem-solving strategy is used to solve a problem, its name will be printed in colored, boldface type. A list of all problem-solving strategies announced in this book is printed in the index under "Strategies for solving problems."

Exercises   These occur throughout the text so that you can test your understanding immediately after an idea or technique has been presented. The answers to these exercises are in the back of the book.

Hands-on Activities   Throughout the text you are encouraged to use objects to solve problems and enhance your understanding. Use these also to become acquainted with materials for teaching mathematics. Some of these items are readily available—stones, rulers, compasses, protractors. I may suggest that you trace others, cut them out, and tape them together.

Historical Comments   These boxed items are meant to add human interest to the text's development and enlighten its ideas, without interrupting its flow.

The *Lab Manual* is a workbook-sized paperback containing laboratory activities to accompany specific topics in the text. The activities are designed especially to be used with hands-on materials.

The manual also contains things to cut out and assemble. Some of these can be used to accompany the text; others can be used to carry out the laboratory activities. The pages are perforated for easy removal.

Three of the lab activities involve the use of a computer spreadsheet.

The *Solutions Manual* contains worked-out solutions to all exercises interspersed throughout the text and to many of the problems in the chapters' problem sets. This will provide you with more examples of problem solutions.

This Book and the NCTM Standards My selection of topics and My approach follow the recommendations made by the National Council of Teachers of Mathematics in its *Curriculum and Evaluation Standards for School Mathematics* (1989), commonly referred to as "The NCTM Standards." I feel that this text reinforces the goals of the Standards in the following particularly strong ways:

1. *Learning to value mathematics.* A strong attempt is made to connect the mathematics of this text with its uses in the real world. Real problems are presented that need to be solved. The mathematical ideas and techniques evolve from the need to create efficient solutions to these problems.

2. *Becoming confident in one's own ability.* To keep from overwhelming the reader with unnecessary terminology and symbolism, I try to introduce just those concepts and techniques that are needed and that emerge naturally from problem situations. I try to make the material appropriate for the reader's background and for how the reader will use it. The writing style is friendly and conversational; it is meant to help the reader become a participant in the development.

3. *Becoming a mathematical problem solver.* Problem solving is the heart of this book. The text integrates problem solving in its development: concepts emerge from problems and their solutions. I make every attempt to engage the reader in problem-solving activities and to provide all the aids I can for the reader to be successful in them.

4. *Learning to communicate mathematically.* Readers are encouraged to use certain strategies not only to solve problems but also to communicate ideas: draw a picture, make a model (use hands-on items), organize data in a table, make a graph, draw a histogram, and so on. These form part of a common language for users of this text. In part of each chapter's problem set (**Using Ideas**), the reader is asked to communicate his or her solution to each problem in the form of a written essay. In the *Lab Manual* are activities for several readers to work together solving problems and learning to communicate their ideas with each other.

5. *Learning to reason mathematically.* I make every effort to have the material make sense and hang together. Not only are there connections between the mathematics of the text and its real world uses, but also there are connections between mathematical ideas developed in the text itself. Making connections is an important aspect of reasoning. I provide arguments appropriate to the reader, plausible arguments that may not always be rigorous to a mathematician. I ask the readers to make similar connections and arguments in writing out the solutions to their problems.

Additional Themes Woven into the Text   Several topics occur in several chapters as subsidiary themes.

- *Number line*   This device is for visualizing the operations and the order relationships of numbers. Its use appears in chapters 3 through 11.
- *Algebra*   This topic occurs in chapters 4 through 11 to show the connections between elementary mathematics and algebra.
- *Graphing*   This theme is introduced in chapter 14 and is developed thereafter as a subtopic in the chapters on geometry, chapters 15 to 20.
- *Computational tools*   The use of calculators and computers is introduced in chapter 1 and recurs throughout the text. Which tool is appropriate for which problem is frequently discussed.

The use of computers is integrated in the text in a variety of ways. Just enough BASIC commands are introduced in chapter 1 to solve some of the problems there. Additional BASIC commands are introduced as needed in later chapters. A section on *Logo* occurs in chapter 16, an early geometry chapter. The *Lab Manual* contains several activities using a computer spreadsheet. One of these can be used as an alternative to BASIC in chapter 12; this same activity may also be adapted for earlier use with the text. Another can be used with the sections on graphing. A third can be used with chapter 22, which deals with organization of data.

Possible Courses Using This Book   You can use this text to design several different courses. There are two features of the book that can be particularly helpful to you in doing this.

First of all, the book contains material on a variety of topics, from chapters on whole number numeration and fractions to those on geometry and measurement, from chapters on estimation and graphing to those on probability and statistics.

Secondly, each chapter is designed so that you can choose the degree of informality or formality for treating the covered topics. The essential part of each chapter is the first part in which the main ideas are developed through solving many problems. In the second part there are many options for covering additional material. Some sections of this second part present the earlier material from a more formal or abstract viewpoint. Others present enrichment material. Still others present material that is developed through the themes mentioned above. Of course, you can select as many of these additional sections as you wish. If you want a more informal course, you may want to supplement the first part of the chapter with only one or two sections (or even none) of the second part. If you want a more formal course, you may want to supplement the first part with several sections of the second.

Here are some possible courses in which the first part of each chapter is covered plus an occasional section from the second part:

One semester (three hours per week) or one quarter (five hours per week) courses.

- Problem solving, whole numbers, fractions, and number theory: chapters 1–10.
- Problem solving, whole numbers, fractions, and probability: chapters 1–6, 8–10, 21.
- Problem solving, estimating, graphing, and geometry: chapters 1, 12–20.

Two semester (three hours each per week) or two quarter course (five hours each per week).

- First semester/quarter: problem solving, whole numbers, fractions, and integers: chapters 1–6, 8–11.
- Second semester/quarter: estimating, geometry, probability, and data presentation: chapters 12–13, 15–22.

Intense one semester course (four hours per week).

- Problem solving, whole numbers, fractions, and geometry: chapters 1–6, 8–10, 13, 15–20.

There are, of course, many other possibilities.

Instructor's Handbook   This is a paperback that contains answers to all exercises and problems in the text that do not already appear at the end of the book.

ACKNOWLEDGMENTS   This book is the result of twelve years of development. There were two stages. The first consisted of a lot of experimentation with materials for a mathematics course for prospective elementary school teachers at the University of Arizona. During this time, I can't remember having an inkling that a book might evolve from these materials. In the second stage, the text was prepared; it has been used in classes for four years and completely revised three times.

During both stages several persons made contributions to the final outcome of the project. My own students unwittingly encouraged me to experiment with new materials in the first place. I am particularly grateful to those who began their studies with me saying "I don't like mathematics and I was never any good at it" and left with "Hey! I *can* do it; math is neat!" Thanks also to the students who used the first versions of the text and put up with the misprints, omissions, and obscure explanations.

A second group to which I am indebted is the group of teaching assistants at the University of Arizona who worked with me in the experimental first stage or taught with the manuscript in the second stage. These persons were not only willing to try new ideas but also forced me to articulate mine better: Debi Anderson, Fernando Avila-Murillo, Teri Bennett, Jim Cain, Mirian Cuesta, Mark Dougan, Sil diGregorio, Steve Hammel, Gary Hudson, Steve Hughes, Grace Ikanaga, Jill Keller, Donna Krawczyk, Erich Kuball, Harry Miller, Burr Munsell, Diane Riggs, Steve Slonaker, Susan Taylor, Jon Thomsen, Steve Wheaton, and Mary Wheeler. I especially appreciate the assistance of Deborah Yoklic and James Abolt who are part of this group and who wrote new problems.

I am also grateful to those colleagues in the Mathematics Department of the University of Arizona who taught the course with me, who tolerated my sometimes outrageous ideas, and who in the end supported this project wholeheartedly: Fred Stevenson, Gail Konkle, Virginia Horak, and Rich Friedlander. I want to give special thanks to Art Steinbrenner, from whom I learned what teaching mathematics to future elementary school teachers is all about.

It may not be traditional to thank one's competitors. However, I have found that several good books have helped me to find out what works for me and what are the important ideas. These are *From Sticks and Stones* by Paul Johnson, *Mathematics for Elementary Teachers* by Eugene Krause, and *Mathematics, an Informal Approach* by Albert Bennett and Leonard Nelson.

A book on solving problems needs good problems to solve. Rich sources of these I have used are *The Math Workshop: Algebra* by Deborah Hughes Hallett, *Using Algebra* by Ethan Bolker, *Make It Simpler* by Carol Meyer and Tom Sallee, *Sourcebook of Applications of School Mathematics* by Donald Bushaw et al., and *When Are We Ever Gonna Have to Use This?* by Hal Saunders. A book that was invaluable to me in the development of chapter 3 is *Number Words and Number Symbols* by Karl Menninger.

I am grateful to these reviewers for their helpful comments:

Mary K. Alter, University of Maryland
Elton E. Beougher, Fort Hays State University
James R. Boone, Texas A & M University
Douglas K. Brumbach, University of Central Florida
Donald Buckeye, Eastern Michigan University
Jane Carr, McNeese State University
Helen Coulson, California State University Northridge
Georgia K. Eddy, student at University of Arizona
Adelaide T. Harmon-Elliott, California Polytechnic State University, San Luis Obispo
Patricia Henry, Weber State College
Diana Jordan, Cleveland State University
Martha C. Jordan, Okaloosa-Walton Jr. College
Alice J. Kelly, University of Santa Clara
Ben Lane, Eastern Kentucky University
Stanley M. Lukawecki, Clemson University
Robert Matulis, Millersville University
Curtis McKnight, University of Oklahoma
Ruth Ann Meyer. Western Michigan University
Philip Montgomery, University of Kansas
Barbara Moses, Bowling Green State University
Charles Nelson, University of Florida
Bernadette Perham, Ball State University
James Riley, Western Michigan University
Lee Saunders, Miami University
Ned Schillow, Lehigh County Community College
Tammy Sewell, student at University of Arizona
Lisa M. Stark, student at University of Arizona
Diane Thiessen, University of Northern Iowa
Barbara Wilmot, Illinois State University
James N. Younglove, University of Houston, University Park

and especially to Lawrence Feldman, University of Pennsylvania, Ben Lane, Eastern Kentucky University, and Steve Willoughby, University of Arizona, who read the entire manuscript.

I want to give a special thanks to Alice Kelly, who reviewed the manuscript at several stages, wrote some original problems, solved all of the exercises, and put together the Student's and Instructor's Manuals.

Finally, many persons at Dellen/Macmillan have given a lot of tender loving care to this project. I want to express my gratitude to them, especially to Janet Bollow, designer and production coordinator, and to Don Dellen, the boss of it all. It has been a pleasure and a privilege to work with you!

David Gay

PROBLEM-SOLVING STRATEGIES

C H A P T E R

In this chapter we will discuss several strategies for solving problems. To introduce each one, we will pose a problem, solve it, and then discuss the strategy (or strategies) we used. To benefit from our solutions, you must try the problem yourself. The aim is for you to become a better problem solver, and you learn from doing. When each problem is stated in the text, take pencil and paper and try to solve it. Spend time on it. Then, whether you solve the problem or not, read our solution. Incidentally, a solution includes an "answer" as well as the method of obtaining the answer. Method and answer are both important. Following our solution is a discussion of the strategies used.

When you solve one of these problems, compare your solution with ours. If your solution differs from ours, don't be surprised or dismayed. A given problem may have many different acceptable solutions. Compare your friends' solutions with yours as well. To give you a realistic idea of what is involved in solving a problem, some of our solutions may contain false starts, dead ends, or seemingly aimless wanderings, all normal occurrences when problems are being solved. Sometimes our solution won't be particularly polished or clever or even the shortest possible. Don't let the length of a solution scare you. Solving a problem can take a while.

So, get yourself lots of blank paper, a bunch of sharpened pencils, a cool drink, and dig in. Work the problems and the exercises as you read along. You are on your way to becoming a good problem solver!

**THE DITCH
DIGGING PROBLEM**

**Be sure to try this
problem yourself before
looking at our solution!**

**A Solution to the Ditch
Digging Problem**

You have just landed a job working on a ranch. Your first assignment is to help dig a ditch 720 ft long, which will be used to bring water to the ranch animals. You and two other people, Jack and Sarah, will be digging the ditch. The ranch foreman claims that if all of you keep digging steadily, the job can be completed in 3 days. You are now at the end of the first day. Sarah has hurt her back and will not be able to continue with the digging. Nevertheless, the foreman is in a hurry to get the ditch dug. You want to know how much longer it will take you and Jack to complete the job. You have noticed that all three of you seemed to dig at about the same rate.

You think: "Let me draw a picture of the ditch. That will give me a feeling for what the problem is about.

"We were supposed to have finished the ditch in 3 days. Let me mark each day's part of the ditch on my picture.

Day 1	Day 2	Day 3

There were three of us digging. I can divide the part of the ditch for each day into three equal pieces; I'll mark one of them M for me; another, J for Jack, and the third, S for Sarah.

Day 1			Day 2			Day 3		
M	J	S	M	J	S	M	J	S

That describes what we *were going* to do. Now to describe what we *will be* doing: The first day is the same, since we've completed it. Sarah won't be with us for the next 2 days. Let me cross out what she would have done.

Day 1			Day 2			Day 3		
M	J	S	M	J̶	S	M	J	S

If I do one of the parts that Sarah won't be able to do and Jack does the other, then we could finish the job in 1 extra day! Here's how the digging would go.

DAY 1			DAY 2			DAY 3		DAY 4	
M	J	S	M	J	J	M	J	M	

"It will take us 4 days in all. You know, I never used the fact that the ditch is 720 feet long. . . ."

Our solution to the ditch digging problem uses a device that will be useful in solving other problems. That device is *drawing a picture*. As we solve more and more problems in this book, you will see the sorts of pictures we use and the ways they are used, sometimes as an important part of a solution and sometimes just as a way to get a feeling for what the problem is about. You will also see how an initial picture can be made more useful by adding details (such as labels) or by altering it. Sometimes the first picture will be discarded in favor of a more appropriate one.

Another solution to the ditch digging problem might be quicker. Our solution involved drawing a picture, fiddling with it, looking at it this way and that—all activities that take time. Solving problems *will* take time.

1.2   PROBLEM SOLVING IN THIS BOOK

Practically every idea or technique discussed in this book will come about as the result of solving some problem or another; thus, the strategies we develop are an important feature of the book. You will see them used many times in this and later chapters. To emphasize their use as well as to point out where a given strategy is used, we will indicate its occurrence by printing its name in color, like this:

Draw a picture.

In later chapters, not only will we use the strategies developed in chapter 1 but we will also introduce new ones. We will announce each new strategy when it is first used and flag each use afterward by using color. Inside the back cover you will find a list of all the problem-solving strategies announced in this book with the page number on which the strategy is first used.

EXERCISES

1. Four bricklayers are laying the cement block for a new house. They all work at the same rate, and it is estimated that it will take them 5 days to do the job. At the end of 2 days on the job, two of the bricklayers become sick. With just the two workers, how many more days will it take to complete the job?

2. With the increased use of economy cars, parking lots find that they can reduce the size of their spaces and use the resulting area for other things. Downtown Parking Lot plans to take advantage of this to comply with a recent greenery ordinance for downtown establishments. Each row of Downtown Parking Lot consists of six spaces for parking cars side by side (versus front to back). Each space is 12 ft long and 7 ft wide. The lot owner wants to use one end of each row for greenery that she plans to plant. She wants this garden area to be 12 ft long and 8 ft wide. She wants to know how many inches each parking space will have to be reduced to allow room for the same number of spaces in each row and for the planting. Help her solve this problem.

THE PROBLEM OF WHERE TO CATCH THE BUS

You live on a bus line 21 mi from your work. In the morning you plan to leave your home, walk along the bus line to a bus stop, and get on a bus that will drop you off at work an hour later. Your walk to the bus is an important part of your day's exercise and you would like your walk to the bus to give you as lengthy an exercise period as possible. You also don't want to be late for work; you want to get there within an hour of leaving your home. Where along the line should you catch the bus? Some clues that may help:

Try the problem
yourself first!

- You walk at the rate of 4 mph.
- The buses on this route average 30 mph and pass by every 5 min.
- It is possible to catch a bus anywhere along the way.

What is your solution to this problem?

A Solution to the Problem of Where to Catch the Bus

You might solve the problem this way: "Let me draw a picture of the bus line.

Then let me label one end Home and the other end Work.

Home •————————————————• Work

The point to catch the bus is between Home and Work.

Let me guess where the point is. I walk at the rate of 4 mph. Let me try a point 4 miles from Home.

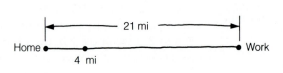

If I got on the bus there, I'd use up the whole hour walking! That guess is not the right answer, but it tells me that I would have to get on the bus somewhere between Home and the 4-mile point. Let me try the 2-mile point.

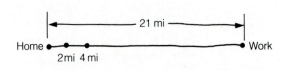

It would take me half an hour to walk that, plus another 5 minutes to wait for the bus. How long would it take the bus to go the rest of the way? The bus has to go 19 miles at 30 miles per hour. If the bus goes 30 miles in an hour, it would go 10 miles in 19 minutes. So it would take more than half an hour to go 19 miles. That's too long. But now I know that the point to get on the bus is between Home and the 2-mile point. Let me try 1 mile from home.

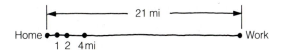

How long will it take me to walk that 1 mile? I walk 4 miles in 60 minutes, so I walk 1 mile in 15 minutes. Allowing 5 minutes to wait for the bus would leave 40 minutes for riding on the bus. The bus can go 10 miles in 20 minutes and 20 miles in 40 minutes. I'd be traveling on the bus for 20 miles. That's just right!"

Strategy 2: Make a Guess

Our solution to the problem of where to catch the bus used several devices. We used one of these before, drawing a picture. The picture in the bus problem helped to keep us focused on the heart of the problem: to find the best *point* for boarding the bus.

Another device used is called *making a guess.* Students in mathematics classes are frequently discouraged from guessing. But there are many advantages to this approach. First of all, permitting yourself (the problem solver) to make a guess frees you from any hesitation you might have in getting started. You are allowed to jump in and try something. Second of all, making a guess will tell you something about the problem. If your initial guess doesn't work, maybe you'll learn something from your mistake and try another guess that will be better. The solver of the bus problem learned a lot about the first guess: "If I were to get on the bus at the 4-mile point, then I would use up a whole hour. There would be no time for the bus trip and I'd be late for work." Not only does the solver learn that 4 miles is *not* the answer, but also he learns that the true answer has to be a distance between 0 and 4 miles. The answer cannot be 12 miles or 20 miles or even 100 miles. The possibilities for the answer have been narrowed down. After the initial guess, more guesses were made. After each guess, the search was narrowed even more: The second guess was 2 miles; the consequences of this guess narrowed the search to distances between 0 and 2 miles. The third guess was right on target.

As with drawing a picture, you notice that making a guess (and following through on its implications) can take time. But frequently, this strategy is just what you need to solve a problem.

The problems we have dealt with so far have neat, whole number solutions. Not all problems are like this. Watch for problems with "messier" (and more interesting) solutions.

EXERCISE

3. You live on a bus line 30 mi from work. You want to take 1 hour to go to work, and you want to combine walking with riding the bus. The bus travels at 45 mph, and comes by every 5 min; your walking rate is 3 mph. Where along the route should you get on the bus in order to spend the least amount of time on the bus? (This problem may not come out "even" as in the problems above. Find the answer to the nearest half mile. But don't be late to work!)

THE PROBLEM OF THE MISSING TIME

You just read the results of the 200-yd backstroke event in the local paper, but one of the times was missing. It said that the three swimmers from State had times of

Don't forget to try the problem yourself.

2:12.43, 2:14.09, and 2:19.66, while from your school, Garcia had a time of 2:11.93 and Hersch a time of 2:17.59. You know that Pepper also swam, but her time was not mentioned. The article did say that your team scored a total of 9 points in the event (in which first place gets 6 points, second gets 4 points, third gets 3 points, fourth gets 2 points, and fifth gets 1 point). You want to know where Pepper finished.*

A Solution to the Problem of the Missing Time

You feel that it might be useful to organize the information you read in the paper. You decide to arrange the times in order of finish together with the names of the swimmers having those times.

2:11.93   Garcia
2:12.43   A
2:14.09   B
2:17.59   Hersch
2:19.66   C

(You call the unknown State swimmers A, B, and C.) You think: "I need to figure out where Pepper fits in. It might be useful to know that our team got 9 points. Let me write down the point system.

PLACE	POINTS
1st	6
2d	4
3d	3
4th	2
5th	1
6th	0

Pepper finished in one of the six places. Let me make a guess: Suppose that Pepper finished in first place. That would mean the following finishing order.

          Pepper
2:11.93   Garcia
2:12.43   A
2:14.09   B
2:17.59   Hersch
2:19.66   C

With this finishing order, our team would have gotten these points.

PLACE	POINTS	
1st	6	×
2d	4	×
3d	3	
4th	2	
5th	1	×
6th	0	
	Total points: > 11	

---

* Adapted from Carol Meyer and Tom Sallee, *Make It Simpler*, Addison-Wesley, Reading, MA, 1983, p. 276. (All further references to this work indicate adaptations from it.)

"Eleven points is too many. Let me make another guess: Suppose Pepper finished in second place. Again our team would get more points than the newspaper article claimed. I should try Pepper in third place. Before doing that, let me extend my chart to keep track of the information I'm gathering. Then I can figure out the total number of points for Pepper's finishing in fourth, fifth, and sixth place, too.

		PEPPER'S POSITION					
Place	Points	1st	2d	3d	4th	5th	6th
1st	6	×	×	×	×	×	×
2d	4	×	×				
3d	3			×			
4th	2				×	×	×
5th	1	×	×	×	×	×	
6th	0						×
Total points for us: →		11	11	10	9	9	8

The only way we can get 9 points for the event is if Pepper finishes in fourth or fifth position! So, the finishing times look like this.

2:11.93 Garcia
2:12.43 A
2:14.09 B
2:17.59 Hersch Pepper
2:19.66 C

"When I see her again, I'll have to ask Pepper which position it was exactly. One thing is for certain: State got only 7 points in the backstroke event."

Strategy 3: Organizing the Data

One feature of the solution of the missing time problem is how it handled all the bits of information given in the statement of the problem. There were several times and names and a point scoring scheme. To use all of this, you *organize the data.* Since it is not always clear how to do this, you jump in and try. You start with the obvious. What kinds of data are there? For this problem there are times, names, and scoring points. You start with the times and make a list, fastest to slowest. To handle the names, you tack them on to the first list. For the points, you make a chart from the scoring scheme. The list and chart help you to focus on the problem; they help you think of possible positions for Pepper. You are ready for a guess. You make one and several more. It is the last bit of information—the total score for your team—that tells you which guesses work.

Another interesting feature of our solution to the missing time problem is that there are two correct answers. Some problems are like that.

EXERCISE 4. Our volleyball team had just finished playing in a tournament, and the 20 of us decided to go to the yogurt shop across the street for a snack before heading home. Each of us ordered either a small cone (for $ .50), a large cone (for $ .70), or a large dish with nuts and carob chips (for $1.30). After everyone had ordered, the bill came to exactly $19.00. On the way home, I was trying to remember what people had ordered, but I finally had to give up. I decided to figure out how many people might have ordered large dishes. Help me.*

THE BIRDSEED PROBLEM

Don't forget, try this yourself.

The zoo is ordering birdseed. The keeper of the bird cages knows that two crested cockatoos will eat 2 lb of birdseed every 2 wk; that three Peruvian parrots will eat 3 lb of birdseed every 3 wk; and that four Mexican macaws will eat 4 lb of birdseed every 4 wk. How much birdseed should the zoo order for its twelve crested cockatoos, twelve Peruvian parrots, and twelve Mexican macaws for 12 wk?[†]

A Solution to the Birdseed Problem

You decide that this problem calls for some organization of data.

These birds	eat this amount	in this time
2 CC	2 lb	2 wk
3 PP	3 lb	3 wk
4 MM	4 lb	4 wk

"I want to find out what 12 crested cockatoos, 12 Peruvian parrots, and 12 Mexican macaws will eat in 12 weeks. Let me fit those questions into my chart.

These birds	eat this amount	in this time
2 CC	2 lb	2 wk
3 PP	3 lb	3 wk
4 MM	4 lb	4 wk
12 CC	?	12 wk
12 PP	?	12 wk
12 MM	?	12 wk

It looks like a lot to figure out all at once. But I don't have to do it all at once. Let me figure out what the 12 cockatoos need first. Then I can figure out what the 12 parrots need; and after that, I can deal with the 12 macaws. Those are smaller problems. After solving them, I can add the three answers together to get the solution to the big problem.

"Here is the beginning of my chart again.

These birds	eat this amount	in this time
2 CC	2 lb	2 wk

I want to know about birdseed for 12 cockatoos for 12 weeks. A simpler problem would be 12 cockatoos in 2 weeks. If 2 cockatoos eat 2 pounds in 2 weeks, 1 cockatoo would eat 1 pound in 2 weeks.

These birds	eat this amount	in this time
2 CC	2 lb	2 wk
1 CC	1 lb	2 wk

---

* *Make It Simpler,* p. 361.
[†] *Make It Simpler,* p. 37.

It follows that 12 cockatoos would eat 12 times as much in the same amount of time.

These birds	eat this amount	in this time
2 CC	2 lb	2 wk
1 CC	1 lb	2 wk
12 CC	12 lb	2 wk

If they eat that much in 2 weeks, then they'd eat 6 times that much in 12 weeks.

These birds	eat this amount	in this time
2 CC	2 lb	2 wk
1 CC	1 lb	2 wk
12 CC	12 lb	2 wk
12 CC	*72 lb*	12 wk

That solves the problem with the cockatoos. I can use the same procedure with the parrots.

These birds	eat this amount	in this time
3 PP	3 lb	3 wk
1 PP	1 lb	3 wk
12 PP	12 lb	3 wk

If 12 parrots eat 12 pounds in 3 weeks, they'd eat 4 times that much in 12 weeks.

These birds	eat this amount	in this time
3 PP	3 lb	3 wk
1 PP	1 lb	3 wk
12 PP	12 lb	3 wk
12 PP	*48 lb*	12 wk

"Now let's deal with the macaws.

These birds	eat this amount	in this time
4 MM	4 lb	4 wk
1 MM	1 lb	4 wk
12 MM	12 lb	4 wk
12 MM	*36 lb*	12 wk

"I've solved the three smaller problems: 12 crested cockatoos eat 72 pounds in 12 weeks, 12 Peruvian parrots eat 48 pounds in 12 weeks, and 12 Mexican macaws eat 36 pounds in 12 weeks. The solution to the big problem is the sum of the three amounts of birdseed: 72 lb + 48 lb + 36 lb = 156 lb. The zoo should order 156 pounds of birdseed."

Strategy 4: Break the Problem Up into Smaller Problems

Strategy 5: Solve a Simpler, Similar Problem

Being overwhelmed by a large amount of data and a large number of anticipated steps for solving the problem can put you on a road to failure. The person who solved the birdseed problem above used several devices to avoid this. We have already discussed one of these, organizing the data.

The person solving the birdseed problem discovered that the whole problem could be solved by solving three smaller problems: find the amount of birdseed needed for (1) the cockatoos, (2) the parrots, and (3) the macaws. This device is called *breaking the big problem up into smaller problems.*

A third device was introduced in trying to figure out how much birdseed would be needed for 12 cockatoos in 12 wk. The solver might have asked: "Is there a simpler, similar problem I can solve? Maybe solving such a problem will give me a clue." He then went on to solve these simpler problems: (1) How much birdseed is needed for 1 cockatoo in 2 wk? (2) How much birdseed is needed for 12 cockatoos in 2 wk? From there he went on to complete a solution to the problem of the cockatoos; he attacked the problems for the parrots and the macaws similarly. This is called *solving simpler, similar problems.*

EXERCISE

5. Two women were complaining about their teenagers' preoccupation with clean hair. One moaned, "My four boys will use up 3 bottles of shampoo in 2 weeks." The other replied, "My five girls will use up 4 bottles of shampoo in 3 weeks." Who uses the most shampoo in a week, one of the boys or one of the girls? How much more?*

1.3 GETTING OUT OF A RUT

THE SWITCHING PROBLEM

You are the engineer of a switching locomotive in a railroad yard. Your job today is to interchange the positions of the two coal cars shown below, a Santa Fe car and a Southern Pacific car, and return the locomotive to its original position.

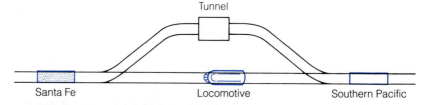

Tunnel

Santa Fe   Locomotive   Southern Pacific

Try it, please.

The cars and the locomotive can hook together in any combination, and the locomotive can push or pull either car or both cars simultaneously. You can use the side track with the tunnel. However, although the tunnel is big enough to allow each car to pass through, it is not big enough for the locomotive. Each car is longer than the tunnel so that when it is in the tunnel it can be accessible to the locomotive from either end. How can you manage to exchange the positions of the two coal cars?†

---

* *Make It Simpler,* p. 163.

† From Bonnie Averbach and Orin Chein, *Mathematics: problem solving through recreational mathematics,* W. H. Freeman, San Francisco, 1980, p. 3, problem 1.6.

You draw a large picture of the track, switches, and tunnel, and you select a penny, a dime, and a nickel to play the roles of the two cars and engine. You can move these objects around on your picture using the restrictions described in the problem. After moving the "engine" and these two "cars" around a bit without success, you stop and ask, "Is there a simpler problem?"

You think: "If there were fewer objects to move around, the problem would be simpler. Is there a problem I can solve with just the locomotive and *one* car? Let me take the locomotive and the Santa Fe car and try to exchange their positions.

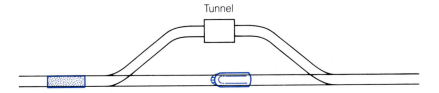

"The locomotive pulls the Santa Fe car to the right.

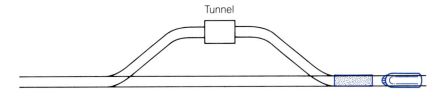

"The locomotive pushes the Santa Fe car into the tunnel.

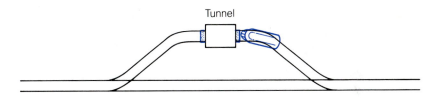

"The locomotive returns to the main track, then moves left.

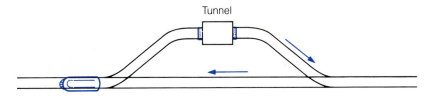

"The locomotive picks up the Santa Fe car at the tunnel and pulls it back to the main track.

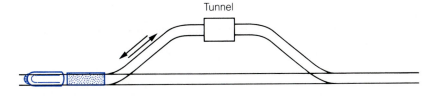

"The locomotive pushes the Santa Fe car to the right, then returns to where the Santa Fe car started.

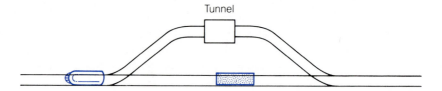

"That solves a problem with one coal car. Will this help me?"

You move the "cars" around some more. You exchange the positions of L (locomotive) and SF (Santa Fe car). You try shunting SF, then exchanging the positions of L and SP (Southern Pacific car). You are frustrated: SF gets in the way. You think: "So far, no success. One thing I haven't done is to hitch all three together. Can I use this capability and the solution to the simpler problem to solve the big problem?

"Here's an idea. Hook up SP and L together and treat the two in combination as if they were just the locomotive. If the locomotive can't get through the tunnel, neither can the combination of the two together. I'd have only two things to switch: SF and the combination. I could use the solution to the simpler problem to exchange the positions of the combination and the SF. We start out as before.

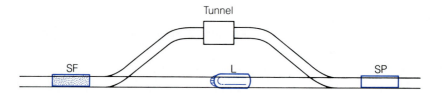

Then hook up L with SP to make the combination. Exchange the combination with SF to get this.

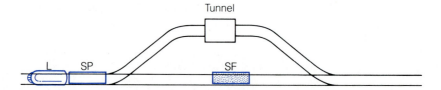

Now all I have to do is push SF to the right, dismantle the combination, and exchange the positions of SP and L. That's the simpler problem again, only in reverse. It should work.

"Combination pushes SF to the right.

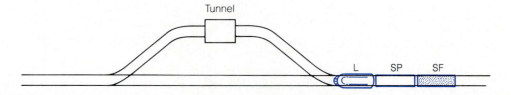

"To exchange positions of L and SP, L pulls SP to the left, then pushes it into the tunnel.

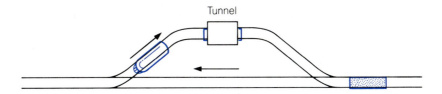

"L returns to the main track and moves right.

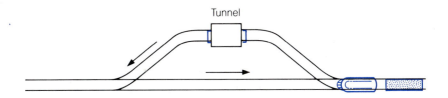

"L picks up SP in the tunnel at right and moves back to the main track.

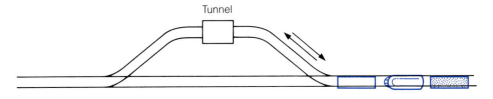

"That does it!"

Strategy 6: Building a Model

Strategy 7: Getting Out of a Rut

In the solution just presented, the solver did more than draw a picture; she *built a model* of the tracks, switches, cars, and locomotive. It was crude but useful.

Another feature of the solution is a strategy discussed before: Solve a simpler problem. In the solution to the switching problem, the simpler problem was switching one of the cars with the locomotive. The solution to the simpler problem turned out to be an important ingredient in the final solution. Things do not always work out as nicely as this. The solution to a simpler problem may simply get you started and give you insight. It's a valuable investment of time in any case.

A third feature of the solution is finding a new way to look at a problem after you are frustrated in your original approach. Finding a radically new way to look at a problem is called *getting out of a rut,* and it means breaking out of set ways of thinking. In the solution to the switching problem, the solver tried everything involving exchanging positions of a pair—a locomotive with a car, a car with a car—and got nowhere. The rut was in thinking that this was the only way. The insight that broke down this mental block—and eventually led to a solution—was the idea that a locomotive hitched to a car could be treated as *one thing* to exchange positions with the remaining car.

Incidentally, not everybody experiences the rut that occurred in our solution to the switching problem. As a person solves more and more problems, many mental blocks disappear.

EXERCISES **6.** Below is a picture of the same railroad yard that appeared in the switching problem.

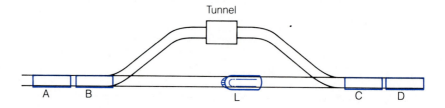

This time there are four railroad cars, A, B, C, and D, in addition to L, the locomotive. They are arranged in the order A B L C D. Using the side track and the conditions given in the switching problem, rearrange the cars in this order: C D L A B, as shown in the next figure.

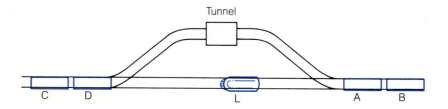

7. Starting again with order A B L C D, rearrange the cars in this order: D C L B A.

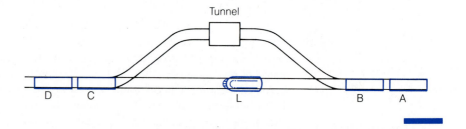

1.4   THE "12 MATH MYTHS"

In case you feel frustrated or anxious or angry while you are working on the problems in the text or at the end of this chapter, you might want to take a peek at what Stanley Kogelman and Joseph Warren call the "12 math myths."

1. Men are better in math than women.

2. Math requires logic, not intuition.

3. You must always know how you got the answer.
4. Math is not creative.
5. There is a best way to do a math problem.
6. It's always important to get the answer exactly right.
7. It's bad to count on your fingers.
8. Mathematicians do problems quickly, in their heads.
9. Math requires a good memory.
10. Math is done by working intensely until the problem is solved.
11. Some people have a "math mind" and some don't.
12. There is a magic key to doing math.*

Perhaps a better name for these "myths" would be the "12 Math Misconceptions"!

1.5   USING SEVERAL STRATEGIES

In the remainder of the chapter we will solve problems using the strategies we've introduced in new ways. Some strategies combined will be so useful that we will identify the combination as a new strategy. Organizing guesses in a chart is a good example of one of these useful combinations.

The solutions to the remaining problems are long and involve the use of many strategies. You will not always know this in advance, but it is helpful to make an initial plan of attack with the idea that you can revise it when necessary. Being in the middle of a lengthy solution is like trying to find a path through a jungle without having any idea of where you are going. Making a plan is one way to deal with unknown territory. Sometimes when you are in a jungle, unexpected things come up; you find that your original plan is not working and you must alter it. Unexpected things may come up in solving a problem. You may have to revise your original plan.

THE COFFEE BLEND PROBLEM

Have you tried the problem yet?

Max's Coffee Mill sells coffee by the pound. At the moment, Max sells inexpensive Costa Rican coffee for $4.50/lb and expensive mocha coffee for $7.00/lb. Because of the expense, most customers avoid the mocha. Max feels that his customers would be interested in a blend of Costa Rican and mocha that is richer in flavor than the Costa Rican but not as expensive as the mocha. He thinks that a blend costing $5.20/lb would be priced just about right. To try out the new blend, he plans to have 50 lb of it on hand to sell. He needs to know how many pounds of Costa Rican and how many pounds of mocha he will need to do this.

A Solution to the Coffee Blend Problem

Max decides to make a guess: "Suppose I were to try 30 pounds of Costa Rican in the blend. That would mean $50 - 30 = 20$ pounds of mocha. Thirty pounds of Costa Rican would cost $30 \times \$4.50 = \$135$, and 20 pounds of mocha would cost $20 \times \$7 = \$140$. The total cost would be $\$135 + \$140 = \$275$. How does that figure compare with what I *want* the blend to cost? A blend of 50 pounds at $5.20/lb would cost $50 \times \$5.20 = \$260$. That is my target cost. My guess would result in a blend that is too expensive ($275). It looks as if I should have more of the inexpensive Costa

---

* From Stanley Kogelman and Joseph Warren, *Mind over Math,* Dial, New York, 1978, pp. 31ff.

Rican in my blend and less mocha. I should make another guess. Let me organize what I've got.

COSTA RICAN (POUNDS)	MOCHA (POUNDS)	COST—COSTA RICAN	COST—MOCHA	TOTAL COST	TARGET COST OF BLEND
30	20	$135	$140	$275	$260

"Let me try a guess of 40 pounds of Costa Rican. Here is what would happen.

COSTA RICAN (POUNDS)	MOCHA (POUNDS)	COST—COSTA RICAN	COST—MOCHA	TOTAL COST	TARGET COST OF BLEND
30	20	$135	$140	$275	$260
40	10	$180	$70	$250	
35	15	$157.50	$105	$262.50	
36	14	$162	$98	$260	

This amount is too small. Try something between 30 and 40.

This is closer but still too high. Try a bit more Costa Rican in the blend.

Just right!

The blend I want will consist of 36 pounds of Costa Rican and 14 pounds of mocha."

Strategy 8: Organize Your Guesses in a Chart

The method of solving the coffee blend problem involves a combination of two strategies we have seen before. One strategy is guessing; the other is organizing the data. In our solution, Max began with a guess and then calculated the consequences of this guess. On the basis of those consequences, he made his next guess, hoping by that to zero in on the target cost: the cost of the desired blend. To help him make subsequent guesses, he decided to use another strategy we've seen, organization of data. Strictly speaking, the data he organized were not data contained in the original problem but data generated by the guesses he made. We call this combination of strategies *organize your guesses in a chart.* It is so useful that we will illustrate its use in a solution to the next problem.

You might be tempted to solve the following problem using algebra. (You might have been tempted that way with the coffee blend problem too!) Organizing guesses in a chart is a problem-solving tool accessible to people with few or no algebra skills. It is a tool that helps you focus on the problem and gain an understanding of it; it may lead to success where algebra fails. It may also help you figure out how to solve it with algebra. If you like, try solving the problems both ways—using algebra and by organizing guesses in a chart. Then compare the solutions.

THE SUITCASE PROBLEM

No peeking at the solution until *you* try it!

Half an hour ago Susan left town on a business trip. Her husband, Robert, has just discovered that she left her packed suitcase behind. He decides to get in his car with the suitcase and overtake her. She is driving her own car, and Robert figures that she will be traveling at an average of 50 mph. He also figures that he can travel at an average of 60 mph. As he pulls away from the curb, he looks nervously at his watch and starts to figure out how long it will take him to reach her. Help him to figure out how long.

A Solution to the Suitcase Problem

To get started with the problem, let's *make a guess* of 1 hr as the time it will take for Robert to reach Susan. We need to figure out some consequences of this guess.

One hour after Robert leaves, Susan will have been traveling for $1\frac{1}{2}$ hr. At 50 mph, that puts her 75 mi from town. Robert will have been traveling for 1 hr at 60 mph. That puts him 60 mi from town. At this point, we make a chart to organize these and subsequent data.

	TIME FROM ROBERT'S DEPARTURE	SUSAN'S DISTANCE FROM TOWN	ROBERT'S DISTANCE FROM TOWN
Guess 1	1 hr	75 mi	60 mi
Guess 2	2 hr	125 mi	120 mi
Guess 3	3 hr	175 mi	180 mi
Guess 4	$2\frac{1}{2}$ hr	150 mi	150 mi

Robert has passed Susan!

This is it!

EXERCISES

8. You want to prepare a 70-lb mixture of peanuts and cashews that will cost $1.95/lb. Here is what you know:
   ■ Peanuts cost $1.37/lb.
   ■ Cashews cost $3.13/lb.
   You want to know how many pounds of each nut should go into the mixture. Solve this problem by making guesses and organizing the consequences in a chart.

9. To entice customers, a department store advertises black and white television sets on sale at a price that causes them a loss of $18 per set. When the customers come in, the store hopes they will buy color instead, on which the profit is $81 per set. In a typical day, 30 TVs are sold. How many of these must be color sets for the store to show a net profit? (Solve this problem by making guesses and organizing the consequences in a chart.)

10. At 8:17 P.M. a known criminal is seen passing the city limits of Winslow in a car going 70 mph. At 8:32 P.M., a policeman in pursuit of the criminal is seen passing

the same point going in the same direction at 80 mph. Assuming that they both continue in the same direction and at the same speed, find the time that the policeman overtakes the criminal. (Make guesses and organize them in a chart.)

1.6

MAKING A PLAN

THE MOUNTAIN
CLIMB PROBLEM

Tomorrow you are going to climb to the top of Mt. Massive, leaving from your home in Half Moon Gulch. A profile of the trail you will follow, as seen from a nearby valley, is shown in the picture.

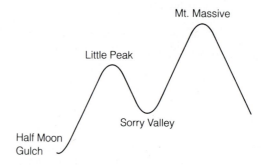

You have a dinner date tomorrow night at 7 P.M. in Half Moon Gulch. You want to know what's the latest time tomorrow morning you can leave on the hike and still make your date on time. To help you determine this, you have made the following list:

■ From past experience in climbing mountains, you know that your climbing rate averages 1000 ft of altitude gain each hour.

■ Also from past experience, you know that your descending rate is a steady 1500 ft of altitude loss each hour.

■ The altitude of Mt. Massive is 14,420 ft.

■ The altitude of Half Moon Gulch is 10,050 ft.

■ There is an altitude loss of 315 ft from Little Peak to Sorry Valley; otherwise, the climb is steadily upward.

■ When you reach the top of Mt. Massive, you will spend an hour resting.

■ When you get back home from the climb, you will need an hour to get cleaned up and dressed for dinner.

Don't forget to try the problem first.

What time should you leave in the morning?

A Solution to the Mountain Climb Problem

To get some feeling for the problem, you decide to draw a time line, a picture of how time will pass tomorrow.

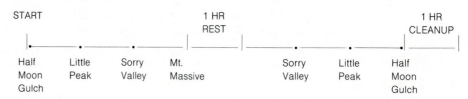

To this picture you decide to add information about altitudes and altitude gains and losses:

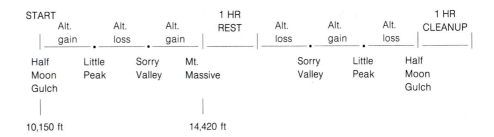

You figure that if you knew how long each of the little stretches would take, you could add all these times up. You know about two of those times already: the 1-hr rest at the top and the 1-hr cleanup. To figure the times for altitude gains and losses, you plan first to determine the altitude gain for each stretch; from that you will calculate the time for that stretch using the rate for climbing or the rate for descending.

When you start off to determine the altitude gain for the first stretch, you notice that the altitude of Little Peak is not given. You realize that there is no way to figure out the altitude of Little Peak with the information given. So much for your first plan.

You look at your time line again. You think: "There is a simpler problem to solve. If there were no Little Peak, figuring out the altitude gain would be easy. Putting Little Peak back would introduce some altitude loss and some altitude gain. I know how much the loss is. But how much is the gain? Here's a picture.

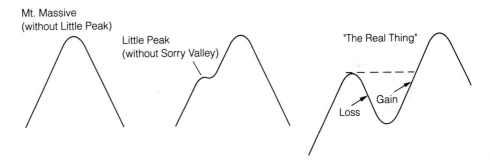

"The altitude gain added by Little Peak is the same as the altitude loss added. Now I can figure out the total amount of altitude gain on my ascent. In fact, why not figure out the *total* amount of altitude gain in the ascent *and* descent. Here is my plan for solving the problem.

PLAN

1. Figure total amount of altitude gain.
   Trip up:
   Trip down:
   Total:

2. Figure total amount of altitude loss.
   Trip up:
   Trip down:
   Total:

3. Figure time for total altitude gain.

4. Figure time for total altitude loss.

5. Add up the following times:
   Time for altitude gain:
   Time for altitude loss:
   Time for rest at top: 1 hr
   Time for cleanup at bottom: 1 hr
   _____
   Total time:

6. Figure out when I should leave in the morning.

"The plan breaks the big problem into a lot of smaller problems. What's more, my total altitude gain must be equal to my total altitude loss.

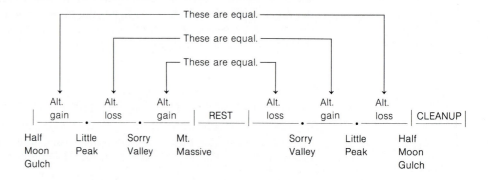

"Solving part 1 of my plan would solve part 2!
"Let me solve part 1. The altitude gain on trip up is this much.

Gain for these two pieces is:

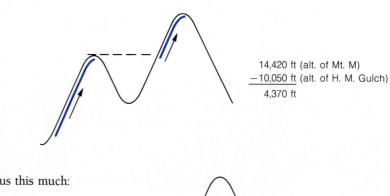

14,420 ft (alt. of Mt. M)
−10,050 ft (alt. of H. M. Gulch)
_____
4,370 ft

plus this much:

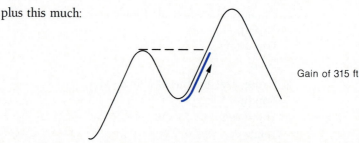

Gain of 315 ft

On the trip down, the only altitude gain is this:

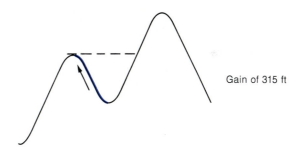

Gain of 315 ft

"Adding up these amounts, I get:

1. Altitude gain on trip up: 4370 ft
                                  +315 ft
   Altitude gain on trip down: 315 ft
   Total altitude gain: 5000 ft

2. Total altitude loss: 5000 ft

"Since I gain altitude at the rate of 1000 feet per hour, I have this:

3. Time spent in gaining altitude is 5 hours.

"That takes care of parts 1, 2, and 3 of my plan. Since the total amount of altitude loss is also 5000 feet, 1 should be able to figure out the total amount of time spent losing altitude. The rate at which I lose altitude is 1500 feet per hour. In 3 hours I'd lose 3×1500 feet = 4500 feet in altitude. How long would it take me to lose 500 feet? It would take a third of an hour, or 20 minutes. So I can conclude:

4. Time spent in losing altitude is 3 hours, 20 minutes.

"That takes care of part 4. Now for part 5 of the plan:

5. Add up the following times:
   Time for altitude gain: 5 hr
   Time for altitude loss: 3 hr, 20 min
   Time for rest at top: 1 hr
   Time for cleanup at bottom: 1 hr
   Total time: 10 hr, 20 min

"Finally, to figure out when I leave in the morning, I know that I leave 10 hours and 20 minutes before dinner time at 7 P.M. That's 3 hours and 20 minutes before noon or 20 minutes before 9 A.M. or

6. I leave on my hike at 8:40 A.M."

Strategy 9: Making a Plan

The solution to the mountain climb problem involved the use of several strategies: drawing pictures, organizing data, and solving simpler problems. Furthermore, the solution has a feature that appeared before but is more evident this time. We call this feature *making a plan*. This feature should be more prominent when a problem contains a variety of data and when it appears that a variety of strategies will be used. Let's see how this device was used in your solution to the mountain climb problem.

1. You drew a time line and labeled it using given information. This *initial plan* uses the strategies drawing a picture and organizing data.

2. You decide to figure out times for the individual stretches, then add them up. This *second plan* for the remainder of the solution uses the strategy break the problem up into small problems.

3. Since the second plan wouldn't work, you needed to revise it. You figured out the effect of Little Peak on altitude gain and replaced the second plan with a *third plan* by breaking the problem up into small problems in a different way.

In the coffee blend problem, the strategy making a plan was used in the following way:

1. Your initial plan was to make a guess, calculate its consequences, and make a second plan based on what happened.

2. Your second plan was to make more guesses, organize the consequences in a chart, and zero in on a solution.

The mountain climb problem also illustrates the need for *revising the plan* if the previous one doesn't work. In the coffee blend problem, there was no need to revise the second plan.

Knowing that you can revise an initial plan may help you to jump into a problem without knowing the eventual outcome at the start. It enables you to keep going in the middle of a problem when you still don't know where and when and what the end will be. Beginning to solve a problem is like entering uncharted territory. The strategies help you to explore this territory; organizing these strategies into a plan of action keeps you focused on finding what you are looking for.

EXERCISE

11. Just behind Mt. Massive is a ridge that leads to Big Peak, at the same elevation as Mt. Massive. Suppose that in addition to hiking to Mt. Massive you decide to include the hike along the ridge to the top of Big Peak and back. When should you leave in the morning for this trip? (Again, you want to be back in time for your date.) A silhouette of the ridge is shown.

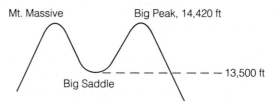

1.7   LOOKING FOR A PATTERN

THE PROBLEM OF THE EMPTY ENVELOPE

A secretary was sending out promotional brochures to the firm's prospective clients. After counting out eight brochures, typing addresses on eight envelopes, and stuffing the brochures into the envelopes and sealing them, the secretary discovered one brochure on the floor. Since he did not want to retype all the envelopes, he decided to use a pan balance scale (shown) to determine which envelope was missing a brochure. How can he use the balance scale to do this?

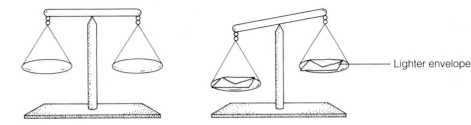

Lighter envelope

A Solution to the Empty Envelope Problem

All eight sealed envelopes weigh the same, except for the one with the missing brochure. The problem is to identify the lighter envelope. One way to solve it is to take one of the envelopes and put it in the left-hand pan. Then, keeping that envelope in the left-hand pan, place each of the other envelopes in turn in the right-hand pan until the empty envelope is found. The empty envelope can be found in at most seven weighings.

A Second Solution to the Empty Envelope Problem

The secretary says, "I've got a better solution than that. Divide the envelopes up into pairs.

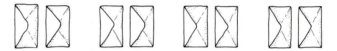

The empty envelope will be in one of the pairs. Take the envelopes in the first pair and compare them using the pan balance, one in one pan, the other in the other pan. If the pans don't balance, I have located the empty envelope: It's on the upper pan. Then I'm finished. If the pans do balance, I haven't located the empty envelope, so I move to the next pair and try the same thing. After, at most, four weighings, I locate the empty envelope. That's better than seven weighings."

THE SECOND EMPTY ENVELOPE PROBLEM

Is there a method that guarantees finding the empty envelope in fewer than four moves? In fact, what is the SMALLEST number of moves?

A Solution to the Second Empty Envelope Problem

Place four envelopes on one pan and the remaining four in the other. The empty envelope must be on the pan that is higher.

Remove the four envelopes from the lower pan. Of the four envelopes in the higher pan place two on one pan and two in the other. Again, the empty envelope is in the higher pan.

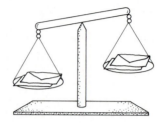

Finally, compare the weights of the last two envelopes using the pan balance. You have found the empty envelope in three moves.

Is this the best we can do? Is there a method for weighing the envelopes that will identify the empty envelope in no more than two weighings? Let's see if we can find simpler, similar problems whose solutions could give us some clues. How about if there are seven envelopes equal in weight except for one empty envelope, which we want to find? Or six envelopes, one of them empty? Or the very simple problem of two envelopes, one of them empty? There is a whole collection of simpler problems:

- Two envelopes of which one is empty. Find it.
- Three envelopes equal in weight except an empty one. Find it.
- Four envelopes equal in weight except an empty one. Find it.
- Five envelopes equal in weight except an empty one. Find it.
- Six envelopes equal in weight except an empty one. Find it.
- Seven envelopes equal in weight except an empty one. Find it.

Let's solve these. Maybe we'll notice a pattern.

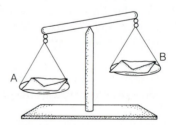

2 envelopes, labeled A and B: Weigh A against B. The lighter one is the one you're looking for. *One* weighing is sufficient.

3 envelopes labeled A, B and, C: Weigh A against B. If one is lighter, that's the empty one; if they are the same weight, the empty one must be C. At most, *one* weighing is necessary.

4 envelopes labeled A, B, C, and D: Weigh A and B against C and D. The lighter pair must contain the empty envelope. Using the lighter pair, follow the same procedure as with the two-envelope procedure. At most, *two* weighings are necessary.

5 *envelopes labeled A, B, C, D, and E:* Weigh A and B against C and D, as with four envelopes. If the empty one is not among A, B, C, and D, then it must be E. At most, *two* weighings are necessary.

6 *envelopes labeled A, B, C, D, E, and F:* Weigh A, B, and C against D, E, and F. The lighter of the two groups must contain the empty envelope. Using the lighter group, proceed as with the three-envelope procedure. At most, *two* weighings are necessary.

7 *envelopes labeled A, B, C, D, E, F, and G:* Weigh A, B, and C against D, E, and F as with six envelopes. If the empty one is not among A, B, C, D, E, and F, it must be G. At most, *two* weighings are necessary.

Now let's look at the problem with eight envelopes and consider what the choices are for the first weighing:

> FOUR against four
> THREE against three
> TWO against two
> ONE against one

We used the first choice earlier. Our first weighing in the six- and seven-envelope procedures consisted of weighing three envelopes against three envelopes. For both of those, we needed at most two weighings. Let's try this choice for the first weighing in the eight envelopes problem.

8 *envelopes labeled A, B, C, D, E, F, G, and H:* Weigh A, B, and C against D, E, and F as with the six-envelope procedure.

If the empty envelope were in neither pan, then the empty envelope would be among G and H. To identify the empty one in this case requires one more weighing for a total of two weighings. If the empty envelope were in one of the pans, then according to the six-envelope procedure, it would take two weighings in all to identify the empty one. Two weighings for eight envelopes is sufficient.

EXERCISES

12. What is the fewest number of weighings you will need for nine envelopes, and what is your method?

13. What is the fewest number of weighings you will need for ten envelopes and what is your method?

Strategy 10: Looking for a Pattern

In solving the second empty envelope problem, we thought of a natural line-up of simpler and similar problems, from the simplest (two envelopes) to the most complex (seven envelopes). We had a feeling that solving all of them in that order might reveal a pattern giving us strong clues about what to do with eight envelopes. This strategy is called *looking for a pattern.*

14. Suppose this time you have eighteen envelopes equal in weight except for one empty one. What is the fewest number of weighings you will need to find the empty one? What is your method?

THE BEST-PRICE PROBLEM

A gift shop chain in the Southwest presently sells miniature cactus gardens for $20 each. It costs the chain $10 per garden for materials, assembling, and packaging. The chain's management is considering changing the price per garden to improve total profits from the gardens. At the present price the chain sells 200/wk. Marketing consultants have told the chain that for each decrease of $1 in the present selling price, the chain can sell 5 additional gardens above the 200. Similarly, for each $1 increase in the selling price, the chain will sell 5 gardens fewer than the 200. (For example, at a price of $21 each, the chain will sell 195; at a price of $22 each, the chain will sell 190; and so on.) Management wants to know whether it should raise or lower the selling price and by how much in order that its total income from the gardens be as large as possible.

Try it!

A Solution to the Best-Price Problem

Management suggests: "Let's make a guess. What would happen if we were to lower the price by $1? The price of each garden would be $19, we would sell 205 of them, and we would have a total profit of 205 × $9 = $1845.

"How does that compare with what we're doing now? Right now we sell 200 gardens at $20 each with a total profit of 200 × $10 = $2000. Lowering the price $1 won't do us any good! Let's look at this a little more closely and try some more numbers. First, let's get organized and make a chart."

PRICE EACH	NUMBER SOLD	TOTAL DOLLAR PROFITS
20	200	2000
19	205	1845

What would happen if we were to lower the price to $18?

PRICE EACH	NUMBER SOLD	TOTAL DOLLAR PROFITS
20	200	2000
19	205	1845
18	210	1680

This is even worse.

"Let's try a price increase.

PRICE EACH	NUMBER SOLD	TOTAL DOLLAR PROFITS
20	200	2000
21	195	2145

That looks promising. Let's try more figures.

PRICE EACH	NUMBER SOLD	TOTAL DOLLAR PROFITS
20	200	2000
21	195	2145
22	190	2280
23	185	2405
24	180	2520
25	175	2625
26	170	2720

Profits keep going up. Let's try $30, $40, and $50.

PRICE EACH	NUMBER SOLD	TOTAL DOLLAR PROFITS
20	200	2000
21	195	2145
22	190	2280
23	185	2405
24	180	2520
25	175	2625
26	170	2720
⋮		
30	150	3000
⋮		
40	100	3000
⋮		
50	50	2000

"At a price of $50, we make just what we're making now. Both $30 and $40 are the best prices so far. Let's check the total profits for a price between $30 and $40.

PRICE EACH	NUMBER SOLD	TOTAL DOLLAR PROFITS
20	200	2000
21	195	2145
22	190	2280
23	185	2405
24	180	2520
25	175	2625
26	170	2720
⋮		
30	150	3000
⋮		
35	125	3125
⋮		
40	100	3000
⋮		
50	50	2000

The best price is $35 so far. Let's check prices on either side of $35.

PRICE EACH	NUMBER SOLD	TOTAL DOLLAR PROFITS
20	200	2000
21	195	2145
22	190	2280
23	185	2405
24	180	2520
25	175	2625
26	170	2720
⋮		
30	150	3000
⋮		
34	130	3120
35	125	3125
36	120	3120
⋮		
40	100	3000
⋮		
50	50	2000

It looks as if total profits go up as the price increases from $20 to $35 and go down as the price increases from $35. Total profits seem to peak at $35."

1.8 COMBINING STRATEGIES ONCE AGAIN: GUESSES, CHARTS, AND PATTERNS

The solution to the best-price problem involved making guesses, organizing their consequences in a chart, and observing a pattern in the chart. Management observed that total profits increase from $2000 to $3125 as the price increases from $20 to $35 and total profits *decrease* from $3125 to $2000 as the price *increases* from $35 to $50. Observing this pattern enabled management to solve the problem.

EXERCISES

15. Is it possible that if the price in the best-price problem were increased to some figure in excess of $50, the total profits might increase again—to some figure above $3125? Is it possible that if the price were lowered *enough,* the total profits might get bigger?

16. The chain will be opening a branch in the Northeast, where the market for cactus gardens is different. There, a marketing consultant estimates that at a price of $26 the branch can sell 60/wk, that each $1 increase in price will decrease sales by 10 gardens/wk, and that each $1 decrease in price will increase sales by 10 gardens/wk. Because of shipping costs, the cost per garden to the chain has increased to $14. What should the price per garden be so that the chain's profits for the branch is greatest?

1.9 LOOKING BACK: POLYA AND THE ART OF SOLVING PROBLEMS

George Polya (1887–1985), perhaps more than anyone else, was responsible for the present concern among mathematics educators with problem solving. It was his belief that we should be spending time in school solving nonroutine problems and that we should be teaching ways to approach such problems. Polya was born in Hungary and came to this country in 1940. He was a research mathematician and a university professor at Stanford and at the Swiss Technical Institute in Zurich. As a teacher, he wanted to convey to his students what is involved in solving problems. In 1945, he wrote his first of several books on problem solving, *How to Solve It.* In that book, his outline for "how to solve it" has the following main parts:

Understanding the problem
Devising a plan
Carrying out the plan
Looking back*

All of the strategies we have been discussing fit somewhere into this comprehensive scheme:

- Understanding the Problem
  Draw a picture
  Organize the data
  Make a guess
  Make a model

- Devising a plan
  Break the problem down into simpler problems
  Solve a similar problem
  Organize your guesses in a chart
  Look for a pattern

- Carrying out the plan
  Revise your plan if necessary
  Get out of a rut

- Looking back

Here is a paraphrase of what Polya has to say about looking back:

Can you *check your answer to the problem?* Can you check the steps you took in coming up with the answer? Can you get your answer by another method, another series of steps? Is your answer to the problem now clear and obvious to you? Can you use your answer or the method of solution for some other problem?

Polya is interested in having us learn something about our solution to a problem not only so that we can be ready for the next problem that comes up but also so that we can think of new problems while we're waiting. Posing problems is almost as important as solving them. Solving a problem frequently involves changing course and solving a related one that you pose. Besides, a problem that you've posed yourself is more exciting to solve—you've got more at stake!

---

* George Polya, *How to Solve It,* 2d ed., Doubleday, Garden City, N.Y., pp. xvi–xvii.

1.10 USING CALCULATORS TO SOLVE PROBLEMS

Many of the problems in this book are easier to solve with a calculator than without. This is especially true for a solution involving a lot of arithmetical calculations. For example, in the coffee blend problem, we made a lot of guesses, determined consequences for each guess, and organized guesses and consequences in a chart. To figure out the consequences for each guess, we had to make some calculations. While it turns out that we made only four guesses, other problems may have solutions that require more. The amount of arithmetic would get to be too much, unless, of course, you use a calculator.

Following are some tips on how to use a calculator. There are two parts to the discussion: keying in numbers and the order of operations; and the constant feature. We will elaborate on these in later chapters.

Keying in Numbers and the Order of Operations

No doubt you have already used a calculator and are familiar with the four keys of the calculator that perform the operations of arithmetic:

The [+] key adds two numbers.
The [−] key subtracts one number from another.
The [×] key multiplies two numbers.
The [÷] key divides one number by another.

We will be discussing calculators that perform multiplication and division in order, left to right, before performing addition and subtraction. This is the same order that is used in interpreting written mathematical expressions. A calculator that follows this order has *hierarchy*.

For example, key the following sequence into the calculator and watch the display as you do it.

Key sequence: [2] [+] [3] [×] [4] [−] [6] [=]
Display: 2   2   3   3   4   14   6   8

A calculator with hierarchy does not compute $2 + 3$ when you punch in the first three keys (other calculators will, however). When the [−] key is pressed, the calculator first multiplies 3 times 4 and then adds 2 to that product to get 14. The answer 8 is what we would normally get if we carry out the calculation $2 + 3 \times 4 - 6$; that is, $2 + 3 \times 4 - 6 = 8$.

If we want to perform the addition $2 + 3$ first and then multiply that sum by 4, we use parentheses, thus, $(2 + 3) \times 4 - 6$. The rule for written mathematical expressions is that operations in parentheses are performed first. The same is true for the calculator with hierarchy. To calculate the same expression on the calculator, we key in the sequence

Keying sequence: [(] [2] [+] [3] [)] [×] [4] [−] [6] [=]
Display: 0   2   2   3   5   5   4   20   6   14

which is consistent with the equation $(2 + 3) \times 4 - 6 = 14$.

EXERCISE   17. Write keying sequences for the mathematical expressions in the following exercises. Use your calculator to evaluate these expressions.

(a) $2 + 5 \times 20$ (b) $(2 + 5) \times 20$ (c) $2 + 5 \times 20 + 3$
(d) $(2 + 5) \times 20 + 3$ (e) $(2 + 5) \times (20 + 3)$ (f) $2 + 5 \times (20 + 3)$

So far the sequence of keys to be pressed corresponds closely to the symbols that occur in the mathematical expression that we want to calculate. Let's look at an example that might create a difficulty.

$$\frac{5 + 7 + 9}{3}$$

The horizontal line in this expression calls for division. We might try the following sequence to calculate it.

Keying sequence: [5] [+] [7] [+] [9] [÷] [3] [=]

The display on the calculator will calculate the answer to $5 + 7 + 9 \div 3$; that is, divide 9 by 3 and add this to the sum of 5 and 7. This gives you 15. But to evaluate

$$\frac{5 + 7 + 9}{3}$$

you want to calculate the sum of 5, 7, and 9 first and divide the sum by 3. Another way of writing this mathematical expression is $(5 + 7 + 9) \div 3$, which suggests how to key it into the calculator.

Key sequence: [(] [5] [+] [7] [+] [9] [)] [÷] [3] [=]

Try that sequence on your calculator and you will get the correct answer: $(5 + 7 + 9) \div 3 = 7$.

EXERCISES   18. For each of the following mathematical expressions, write a keying sequence that will give the value of the expression on the calculator.

(a) $\dfrac{4 + 5 + 6}{3}$ (b) $\dfrac{20}{4 + 6}$ (c) $\dfrac{10 + 12 + 16}{9 + 10}$

19. Use the calculator to evaluate the following mathematical expressions.

(a) $17 \times (13 + 3 \times (23 + 59) - 57) + 29$

(b) $\dfrac{12 \times 14 + 24 \times 33}{37 \times 42 + 57}$ (c) $\dfrac{7 \times (52 - 17) + 13}{83 - 35}$

The K Key or Other Constant Feature of Calculators

There are many situations where you might want to multiply a bunch of different numbers by a single number. (Filling in a table of numbers is one such.) For example, suppose you want to multiply each of the numbers 23, 47, 107, and 97 by 53. There is a feature on most calculators that enables you to do this without having to key in the [×] [5][3] four times. On some calculators you use a [K] key; on others you press the [×] key twice; and on others there are no special key presses, but you have to follow a certain sequence.

To simplify things in what follows, we will write the numbers in the keying sequences without brackets, thus, 7 [×] 5 for [7] [×] [5].

For a calculator with [K] key, the keying sequence for multiplying 23, 47, 107, and 97 by 53 would be

KEYING SEQUENCE	DISPLAY	MATHEMATICAL EXPRESSION
53 [×] [K] 23 [=]	1219	53 × 23
47 [=]	2491	53 × 47
107 [=]	5671	53 × 107
97 [=]	5141	53 × 97

For other calculators, the keying sequence for doing this will be

KEYING SEQUENCE	DISPLAY	MATHEMATICAL EXPRESSION
53 [×] [×] 23 [=]	1219	53 × 23
47 [=]	2491	53 × 47
107 [=]	5671	53 × 107
97 [=]	5141	53 × 97

For still other calculators, the keying sequence will be

KEYING SEQUENCE	DISPLAY	MATHEMATICAL EXPRESSION
23 [×] 53 [=]	1219	53 × 23
47 [=]	2491	53 × 47
107 [=]	5671	53 × 107
97 [=]	5141	53 × 97

Notice in the latter case that the factor that remains the same is keyed in second in the initial keying sequence.

You will have to experiment to find out which of the above procedures (or possibly some other procedure) is appropriate for your calculator.

EXERCISES

20. The procedure for *adding* 53 to each of the numbers 23, 47, 107, and 97 is similar: You replace [×] by [+]. Try this out with your calculator.

21. In a recent inventory of their branch stores, Safeland Supermarkets counted the quantities of jars of Sticky Peanut Butter shown in the table.

BRANCH STORE	NO. OF 8 OZ JARS STICKY	WHOLESALE VALUE
Lakeland	54	$64.80
Payson	89	
Verde Valley	123	
Los Alamos	65	
Lukeville	47	

Each jar of Sticky has a wholesale value of $1.20. Use your calculator to complete the Wholesale Value column in the table.

USING COMPUTERS TO SOLVE PROBLEMS

A computer, like a calculator, is tool that can be used to solve problems. A computer can do calculations, but one difference is that you can tell it to do a whole bunch of calculations in sequence. When I say "a whole bunch," I mean it. Tens, hundreds, thousands of calculations . . . while you watch. A computer is much more powerful than a calculator, but it takes a little longer to learn how to use one. You will need to learn a little bit of a computer *language,* the vehicle through which you tell a computer to carry out a sequence of calculations. Of several computer languages, the one we will learn here is called BASIC, perhaps the most popular computer language.

THE MICROCOMPUTER SETUP   A microcomputer looks like a fancy typewriter keyboard hooked up to a TV. There is more to a microcomputer than this, but this is pretty much what a user comes in contact with. That's about all you need to know in order to *use* it now. Of course, you should get somebody knowledgeable about computers (referred to later as your "expert") to show you how to turn it on, to hang around as you try the tasks described in this section, and later to tell you about some of the computer's peripheral equipment, such as floppy discs, disc drives, and printers. To get the most out of this section, you should be seated in front of a microcomputer that is turned on, working, and ready to do BASIC (check with your expert on this).

USING A MICROCOMPUTER AS A CALCULATOR   Let's start with some simple calculations that a computer can do. (First, "load" BASIC. You will see a symbol blinking on and off at the left of your screen, possibly looking like: >. This blinking symbol is called a *prompt.*) When you are asked to type something onto the keyboard in the following discussion, type verbatim the part printed in color.

Addition   To add 5 and 8, do the following:

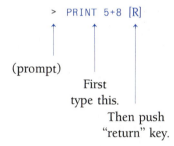

```
>  PRINT 5+8 [R]
```

(prompt)

First
type this.

Then push
"return" key.

Here is what you should see on the screen:

```
>  PRINT 5+8      What you typed in.
   13      The answer to your calculation.
>      Prompt again, ready for the next task!
```

Multiplication   To multiply 5 by 8, do the following:

```
>  PRINT 5*8 [R]      What you type in, followed by a push of return key.
   40      The answer appears.
>
```

Division   To divide 5280 by 12, do the following:

```
>  PRINT 5280/12 [R]      What you type in, followed by return key.
   440      The answer.
>
```

Subtraction

```
> PRINT 235-47 [R]
  188
>
```

Combining Operations   Several operations can be combined in one calculation. For example, try the following:

```
> PRINT 4*5+24-13 [R]
  31
>
```

The operations in BASIC are performed in the same order that is used in interpreting written mathematical expressions: Multiplications and divisions are performed in order, left to right, before additions and subtractions are performed. This is just like a calculator with hierarchy. Parentheses can also be used in BASIC and, again, the rules are the same as for written expressions: Operations in parentheses are performed first. For example, try

```
> PRINT 4*(5+24)-13 [R]
  103
>
```

Also try the following two calculations and compare the results.

```
1. > PRINT (4+5+6)/3 [R]
     5
   >
```

```
2. > PRINT 4+5+6/3 [R]
     11
   >
```

From these two examples you can see that in order to calculate

$$\frac{4+5+6}{3},$$

you must use parentheses and type $(4+5+6)/3$, not $4+5+6/3$.

So far we have not described anything a computer can do that a calculator can't. However, at least one advantage of a microcomputer over most calculators should be clear: You can see on the screen the expression that you have keyed into the computer.

EXERCISE   22. Use a microcomputer to calculate the following expressions.

(a) $23 + 47$	(b) 23×47	(c) $6786 \div 9$
(d) $7 + 14 \times 12$	(e) $(7 + 14) \times 12$	(f) $7 + 14 \times (12 - 7)$
(g) $(7 + 14) \times (12 - 7)$	(h) $\dfrac{7 + 14 \times 12}{5}$	(i) $\left(7 + \dfrac{150}{3}\right) \times 8$

MICROCOMPUTER PROGRAMS   To illustrate what a computer can do that a calculator can't (unless the calculator happens to be a computer in disguise), we will show how a computer can be used to solve the coffee blend problem. We will do this in a few stages. In the first stage, we will get the computer to do what a calculator does with a K key or other constant feature. In the second, we will show how a microcomputer can print out an entire table of guesses for the quantity of Costa Rican in the blend along with consequences of each guess. In the third stage, we will show how to get the computer to solve the whole problem. For each stage we will want the computer to carry out several tasks. And, for carrying out several tasks, we will have to write a *program*.

To have the computer make a single calculation that may involve the use of more than one operation, such as $43 \times 72 + 1235$, we type (after the prompt) the *command* PRINT 43*72+1235. To have the computer do several things, we build a *program*: We will type in several commands on several lines, one command to a line, and each line beginning with a different number. The computer will carry out first the command with the smallest line number, then carry out the command with the next largest line number, and so on. Here is a simple program to type into your computer:

```
10 INPUT P
20 PRINT 4.5*P
100 END
```

Each line of the program should end with [R] in order to start a new line. The last line of each program should contain the simple command END.

You may already recognize part of the program from what we have already done. Line 20 says PRINT 4.5*P, that is, calculate $4.5 \times P$, and print it on the screen. The letter *P* is the name of a *variable,* a location in the computer's memory for storing a number. When the computer sees 4.5*P, it will take the number in the location whose name is *P* and multiply it by 4.5. What number is in location *P*? The answer to this is related to line 10 of the program and will be revealed in the following discussion.

After you have typed in the program, what happens? Nothing! The computer just sits there. To get it to do something, you must type RUN:

```
10 INPUT P
20 PRINT 4.5*P
100 END
RUN
```

When you type RUN, then [R], the following will happen:

```
10 INPUT P
20 PRINT 4.5*P
100 END
RUN
?        Computer types a ?.
```

The ? means that the computer is asking you to put a number in the location named *P.* (You are being asked to "assign a value to the variable *P*.") So you type in a number for *P*—you "input" *P*—followed by [R].

```
10 INPUT P
20 PRINT 4.5*P
100 END
RUN
? 30      You type 30 followed by [R].
135       Computer responds with this.
```

Here is what happened: the computer assigned the value 30 to *P,* calculated 4.5×30, and printed the answer, 135, on the screen.

Having typed in the program, we can run it again:

```
10 INPUT P
20 PRINT 4.5*P
100 END
RUN
? 30
135
RUN        You type this in again, followed by [R].
? 40       Computer types ?; you type 40, followed by [R].
180        Computer calculates 4.5 × 40, prints it on screen.
```

The little program we have written accepts a number (which we "input" on request), multiplies it by 4.5, and prints it on the screen. The program is doing what the constant feature of a calculator does! Since $4.50 is the price of a pound of Costa Rican, $4.5 × P is the cost of P 1b of Costa Rican. We could use our program to fill in the third column of our table:

COSTA RICAN (POUNDS) (P)	MOCHA (POUNDS)	COST—COSTA RICAN ($4.5 × P)	COST—MOCHA	TOTAL COST
30		135		
40		180		

Now we are at a point where we can get the computer to do more than a calculator. With a few adjustments to our original program, we will write a program that will ask for input P (number of pounds of Costa Rican) and then print out a whole line of the coffee blend chart. To do this, we need to be able to write an expression for the number in each column in terms of P. For example, if P is the number of pounds of Costa Rican, then the number of pounds of Mocha is 50-P. Here are the expressions for all the columns in terms of P:

COSTA RICAN (POUNDS)	MOCHA (POUNDS)	COST—COSTA RICAN	COST—MOCHA	TOTAL COST
P	50-P	4.5*P	7*(50-P)	4.5*P+7*(50-P)

And here is the new program to type in.

```
10 INPUT P
20 PRINT P, 50-P, 4.5*P, 7*(50-P), 4.5*P+7*(50-P)
100 END
```

Notice that the several items to be printed are separated by a comma. Now, here is what happens when we run the program:

```
10 INPUT P
20 PRINT P, 50-P, 4.5*P, 7*(50-P), 4.5*P+7*(50-P)
100 END
RUN
? 30
30    20    135    140    275
```

This last row of numbers corresponds to the row that begins with 30 1b in our table.

COSTA RICAN (POUNDS)	MOCHA (POUNDS)	COST—COSTA RICAN	COST—MOCHA	TOTAL COST
30	20	135	140	275

Of course, we can run the program again using a different input.

```
10 INPUT P
20 PRINT P, 50-P, 4.5*P, 7*(50-P), 4.5*P+7*(50-P)
100 END
RUN
? 30
30    20    135    140    275
RUN
? 40
40    10    180    70    250
```

Thus, we can fill in the line for 40 lb in our table.

COSTA RICAN (POUNDS)	MOCHA (POUNDS)	COST—COSTA RICAN	COST—MOCHA	TOTAL COST
30	20	135	140	275
40	10	180	70	250

PROGRAM WITH A LOOP   With the preceding program we get the computer to produce a row of the coffee blend chart, one row at a time, a row for the value we assign to P each time we run the program. By changing the program once again we can create a program that will produce the entire chart. Essentially, what we do is write a program that tells the computer to assign to P a string of consecutive numbers, all of them numbers that we might assign one by one. For example, we might want to assign to P (the number of pounds of Costa Rican) all the whole numbers from 30 to 40. The following is a program that does this.

```
10 FOR P=30 TO 40
20 PRINT P, 50-P, 4.5*P, 7*(50-P), 4.5*P+7*(50-P)
30 NEXT P
100 END
```

What happens when you run it?

```
RUN

30    20    135      140    275
31    19    139.5    133    272.5
32    18    144      126    270
33    17    148.5    119    267.5
34    16    153      112    265
35    15    157.5    105    262.5
36    14    162       98    260
37    13    166.5     91    257.5
38    12    171       84    255
39    11    175.5     77    252.5
40    10    180       70    250
```

The rightmost column gives the total cost of the blend. So you can look there to find the target price—$260. You find it in the row with P = 36, and, of course, 36 lb of Costa Rican and 14 lb of mocha is the solution.

To understand how this last program works, let's compare it (2) with the previous program (1):

PROGRAM 1

```
10 INPUT P
20 PRINT P, 50-P, 4.5*P, 7*(50-P), 4.5*P+7*(50-P)
100 END
```

PROGRAM 2

```
10 FOR P=30 TO 40
20 PRINT P, 50-P, 4.5*P, 7*(50-P), 4.5*P+7*(50-P)
30 NEXT P
100 END
```

You notice that line 20 of both programs is the same. In program 2 the INPUT statement has been deleted and two new lines have been inserted in its place, one above and one below line 20. Program 2 works in the following way:

1. As the computer begins to carry out program 2, it looks at line 10. It assigns the number 30 to the variable P.

2. The computer moves on to line 20 and does what it is told to do there (calculates and prints a line of the chart for P=30).

3. Then the computer moves on to line 30, which tells it to increase the number assigned to P by 1, making it 31.

4. Again the computer moves to line 20 and does what it says there for P=31.

5. Moves to line 30, increases value of P by 1. Carries out line 20. And so on.

6. Each time the computer moves to line 30, it checks to see whether the value of P is equal to 40. (It must look at line 10 for the 40, the top value of P.) If it isn't, it proceeds as above and increases the value of P by 1. If it is equal to 40, the computer goes on to line 100 and ends.

The following flowchart shows more graphically what is happening.

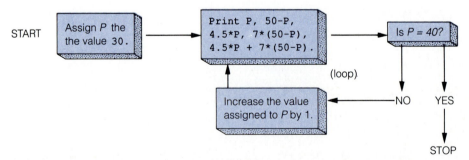

Program 2 is called a *loop* because of the "loop" that occurs in the flowchart above. A loop in BASIC begins with a line in the form.

FOR _____ = _____ TO _____

This is followed by one or more lines to execute and ends with a line in the form

NEXT _____ .

The blank in the NEXT statement must contain the name of a variable. The first blank in the FOR statement must contain the same name (for the same variable). In the second and third blanks of the FOR statement you write the lowest and highest values you want to have assigned to the variable.

Here is program 2 altered slightly and what happens when it is run.

```
10 FOR P=1 TO 15
20 PRINT P, 50-P, 4.5*P, 7*(50-P), 4.5*P+7*(50-P)
30 NEXT P
100 END
RUN
```

1	49	4.5	343	347.5
2	48	9	336	345
3	47	13.5	329	342.5
4	46	18	322	340
5	45	22.5	315	337.5
6	44	27	308	335
7	43	31.5	301	332.5
8	42	36	294	330
9	41	40.5	287	327.5
10	40	45	280	325
11	39	49.5	273	322.5
12	38	54	266	320
13	37	58.5	259	317.5
14	36	63	252	315
15	35	67.5	245	312.5

EDITING AND LIST   Program 1 and program 2 are quite similar. If you have already typed in and run program 1 and want to type and run program 2, you don't have to type program 2 from scratch. You can revise program 1: Keep those lines of program 1 that are the same for program 2 and change the others. For example, line 20 of program 1 is also a line of program 2, so you keep it. Line 10 of program 2 is different, so you retype it as if it were a new line. Line 30 of program 2 is new, so you just type that in. Here is what your work might look like:

Program 1 already typed in:

```
10 INPUT P
20 PRINT P, 50-P, 4.5*P, 7*(50-P), 4.5*P+7*(50-P)
100 END
```

Then you type:

```
10 FOR P = 30 TO 40
30 NEXT P
```

If you want to see what your revised program looks like, with the lines printed in order, you type LIST (just as you would type RUN). What happens?

```
LIST
10 FOR P=30 TO 40
20 PRINT P, 50-P, 4.5*P, 7*(50-P), 4.5*P+7*(50-P)
30 NEXT P
100 END
```

Here are some more rules for revising a program:

- To delete a line, simply type the line number, then [R]. For example, to delete line 10, you type the following:

  10 [R]

- To add a new line, assign it a line number not already in use but one that will cause the commands in the lines of the revised program to be carried out in the correct order. For example, to program 1 you wanted to add the line NEXT P. Since you want it to be read after line 20, you must assign it a number bigger than 20. (We gave it number 30.) Incidentally, you may have noticed that we have been numbering the lines of the program in increments of 10. This is to allow for possible insertions should the program have to be revised later. (Most programs have to be revised!)

- To replace a line by another line, type in the new line using the same line number as the line being replaced. For example, to replace 10 INPUT P with 10 FOR P=30 TO 40, simply type the latter.

SAVE, LOAD, and NEW   PRINT, INPUT, and FOR . . . NEXT are called *program commands*. These commands are internal to a program. RUN and LIST are what are called *system commands* and are instructions that are external to a program. Here are some additional system commands that will be useful.

SAVE   If you have been working on a program that you want to come back to at a later time—perhaps after turning off the computer—then you can save your program using the SAVE command. The SAVE command will make a copy of your program on a floppy disc that has been inserted in one of the computer's disc drives. (At this point, you may want to ask your expert about the computer's disc drives, floppy discs, how to *format* a floppy disc, how to insert a floppy into the drive, and so on.) To use the SAVE command you will also need a name for your program. You type SAVE followed by a space, then the program's name. For example, suppose you are saving program 2, which you want to call BLEND. You type

  SAVE BLEND

If you return to the computer at a later time and want to retrieve the program named BLEND, you type the following:

  LOAD BLEND

Having done this, your computer will understand that you are working on the BLEND program. To remind yourself what this program is you can type LIST.

NEW   If you have been working on one program and want to start on a second program, you can type NEW. This provides you with a clean slate, and you can start typing in your second program. Everything about the first program will have been erased. (If you want to be able to return to the first program at a later time, then you should go through the SAVE routine I have described, then use LOAD when you want to return.)

Warning: There are many dialects to BASIC. The version that you are using is just one of those dialects. In this discussion I have tried to use parts of BASIC that are common to most dialects. I may not have succeeded completely in your case. Check with your expert.

23. Type and run each of the following programs and describe what each one does.

(a)
```
10 INPUT N
20 PRINT N*N
100 END
```

(b) Revision of (a):
```
5  PRINT "THIS PROGRAM WILL SQUARE A NUMBER."
7  PRINT "WHAT NUMBER DO YOU WANT TO SQUARE?"
10 INPUT N
20 PRINT N*N
100 END
```

Program (b) has a feature that you haven't seen before. What is it and how does it work?

(c)
```
10 FOR I=1 TO 10
20 PRINT I*I
30 NEXT I
100 END
```

(d) Revision of (c):
```
10 FOR I=1 TO 10
20 PRINT I, I*I
30 NEXT I
100 END
```

How does the output (what the computer prints out after you type RUN) of program (d) differ from that of program (c)? What part of the program makes this difference?

(e) Revision of (d):
```
10 FOR I=1 TO 10
20 PRINT I, I*I
25 PRINT
30 NEXT I
100 END
```

How does the output of program (e) differ from that of program (d). Why?

(f) Revision of (c):
```
5  INPUT L
10 FOR I=1 TO L
20 PRINT I*I
30 NEXT I
100 END
```

This program has a feature that you haven't seen before. What is it?

(g) Revision of program 2:
```
10 FOR P=30 TO 40 STEP 2
20 PRINT P, 50-P, 4.5*P, 7*(50-P), 4.5*P+7*(50-P)
30 NEXT P
100 END
```

This program also has a feature that you haven't seen before. What is it?

(h) Revision of (g):
```
5  PRINT "C.R./LB", "MOCHA/LB", "COST C.R.", "COST M.",
6  PRINT "COST BLEND"
10 FOR P=30 TO 40 STEP 2
20 PRINT P, 50-P, 4.5*P, 7*(50-P), 4.5*P+7*(50-P)
30 NEXT P
100 END
```

24. Our Greasy Spoon Cafe sells quarter-pound burgers. But, unlike those in other fastfood establishments, ours are not all beef. In fact, our burgers are a mixture of Beeftane (a soy product) and Crd-Brd-2 (a cellulose derivative). We make up our mixture in batches of 150 lb, and we want our final product to cost $ .25/lb. Beeftane costs $ .45/lb; Crd-Brd-2 costs $ .21/lb. We want to know how many pounds of Beeftane and how many pounds of Crd-Brd-2 should be in the mixture. To solve this problem, we calculate the target cost of the mixture as $150 \times \$ .25 = \$37.50$. Then we could set up a chart.

BEEFTANE (POUNDS)	Crd-Brd-2 (POUNDS)	COST— BEEFTANE	COST— Crd-Brd-2	TOTAL COST OF MIXTURE	TARGET COST
10	140				$37.50
20	130				
30	120				
40	110				
50	100				
60	90				
⋮	⋮				

Instead, modify program 2 to print on the screen a completed version of this chart, including the third, fourth, and fifth columns. Use this to solve the problem.

25. Modify program 2 to solve exercise 8 following the coffee blend problem.

26. Modify program 2 to solve the best-price problem.

1.12   SUMMARY OF IMPORTANT IDEAS AND TECHNIQUES

- Using strategies to solve problems
  Drawing a picture
  Making a guess
  Organizing the data
  Breaking the big problem up into simpler problems
  Solving simpler, similar problems
  Making a model
  Getting out of a rut
- Combining strategies
  Organizing the consequences of guesses in a chart
  Making a plan; revising the plan if necessary
  Looking for a pattern
- Simplifying the labor of problem solving using calculators and computers

PROBLEM SET

PRACTICING
SKILLS

1. Mr. Lovejoy hired the twins to rake his yard, front and back, for $6. It was a large yard, but the front and back were about the same size. When the time came to start, Bill was not home from his music lesson, so Bryan started alone. Bryan was finished with the whole front before Bill

showed up; he had forgotten about the job and stopped at a friend's house. The two of them raked the back together. How should they split the money?*

2. A digger starts digging a hole at 8 A.M. on Monday and continues digging from 8 A.M. to 1 P.M. each day until the job is finished. She digs a depth of 5 ft each day, and the hole is to be 30 ft deep. However, due to the condition of the soil, 2 ft of dirt falls back in the hole each night while she is not working. When will she finish the hole?

3. You wake up in the morning. You look at your electric digital clock and notice that it is blinking. The time on the clock shows 5:00. "Hmm. The electricity went off during the night. I wonder when? I know that when the electricity goes off and then comes back on, the clock resets itself to 12:00." You notice that your wristwatch reads 8:30 (the correct time), and the conventional electric clock in the kitchen reads 6:00. How long was the electricity off and when did it go off?

4. You are planning to have champagne for your wedding reception and figure you will need 20 bottles. A special French brand costs $15 per bottle while an acceptable (but cheap) domestic brand costs $7 per bottle. You would like to buy only the French brand, but you can't since you have no more than $200 to spend on champagne. So you figure you will buy French champagne for serving early in the reception and the cheap kind for serving later. What is the largest number of French bottles you can buy, keeping to your budget of $200 and buying a total of 20 bottles?

5.
June 30, 1989

I really can't stand the heat today. It must be around 90° right now. Just a few days ago it was only 63°. I remember the heat wave we had in April; one day the temperature was 2° below freezing, and the next, it jumped to 95°.

I had some errands to run this morning before driving into Manhattan from Queens. We had run out of stamps, so I went to the post office and bought two rolls of 25¢ stamps, 100 to a roll, and a dispenser for 49¢. I also went to the Fast Copy Center to get 10 copies made of a recent newspaper article. They were 7¢ for the first 5 copies and 6¢ for each additional copy.

I had to stop for gas and only needed 4.8 gallons, which cost $4.15. I realized I had gotten pretty good mileage on my VW since I had gone 144 miles since my last fill up.

Joe and I met for lunch at La Garbage. Joe ordered a rare steak for $7.85 and coffee for $ .65. I had a chicken salad plate for $5.25 and coffee as well. The waiter put everything on one check, but we decided we would each pay for what we had ordered. We each left about a 15 percent tip.

At that point, I thought to myself, "Gee, I've spent a lot of money so far today. I wonder how much?"

How much did I spend?†

6. The Health Food Shop sells raisins at $3.70/lb and granola at $2.50/lb. The owner wants to make 90 lb of a hike mix consisting of granola and raisins and costing $3.50/lb. To figure out how many pounds of raisins and how many pounds of granola should go into the mix, the owner decides to make some guesses and organize them in a chart—with the hope that he can zero in on a solution. Here is the beginning of his chart, his first guess, and some consequences of his first guess.

---

* *Make It Simpler*, p. 71.
† *Mind over Math*, p. 61.

RAISINS (POUNDS)	COST—RAISINS	GRANOLA (POUNDS)	COST—GRANOLA	TOTAL COST OF MIX	TARGET COST OF MIX
45	$166.50	45	$112.50	$279.00	

What should the target cost of the mix be?

7. In problem 6, is the cost of the mix of 45 lb raisins and 45 lb granola bigger or smaller than the target cost? Choose the most reasonable of the following possible next guesses: (a) 50 lb raisins and 40 lb granola; (b) 40 lb raisins and 50 lb granola. What are the consequences of the guess you chose?

8. You are the same engineer of a switching locomotive as in the switching problem. Today three railroad cars are arranged as in the top picture. You want to interchange them so that they will be arranged as in the bottom picture. As before, the cars and locomotive can hook together in any combination so that locomotive can push or pull one, two, or three cars at once; the tunnel is big enough for each car but not for the locomotive; and each car is longer than the tunnel. How can you do the switching?

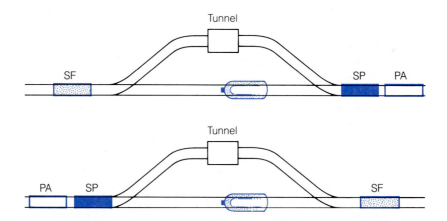

9. On my home's electric meter there is a little dial that goes around once for each 10 Wh (watthour, watthours) of electricity used. I wanted to figure out how much it costs to bake cookies. First of all, the oven is on for 20 min when I bake cookies. Also I discovered that 1000 Wh cost $ .13. To figure out how many watthours are used to bake cookies, I found that, with the oven off, the little dial on the meter took 10 sec to go around once. With the oven on, it took the little dial only 6 sec to go around once. With this information, I was able to solve my problem. How? How much does it cost me to bake cookies?

10. A team of five asphalt-spreading machines is laying asphalt on 21 mi of city streets. City Transportation figures it will take the team 30 working days to complete the work. At the end of 10 working days, one of the machines breaks down and will be in the shop for quite a while waiting for replacement parts. How much longer will it take the remaining four machines to complete the job?

11. Tomorrow you are planning a bike trip to Picacho Peak, leaving from your home in Tucson. Tomorrow night at 8 o'clock you have an appointment in Tucson, so you would like to know what's the latest time you can leave tomorrow morning to be back in time for your appointment.

You make the following list of facts to help you decide:

- Average biking speed from Tucson to Picacho Peak is 12 mph.
- Average biking speed from Picacho Peak to Tucson is 10 mph. (It's uphill from the peak to Tucson.)
- Distance from house to Picacho Peak is 60 mi.
- Spend an hour at Picacho Peak eating, resting, and enjoying the scenery.
- On return to Tucson, need 1 hr to eat and get cleaned up and dressed for appointment. Need 20 min to get from house to appointment.

When should you leave in the morning?

12. There are 15 people at a party and everybody shakes hands exactly once with each person present. How many handshakes will have taken place?

13. You want to figure out the occupations of Andres, Brown, and Cohen. You know the following facts:

- One is a bank teller, one a farmer, and one a chef.
- Andres is neither the teller nor the farmer.
- Cohen is not the teller.

What are the occupations of the three women?

14. The Southwestern gift shop chain mentioned in the best-price problem also sells herbariums for $20 each. At this price the chain sells 100 of them each week. Marketing consultants have told the chain management that for each decrease of $1 in the price, the chain can sell 10 additional herbariums each week. Should management lower the selling price to increase its income from herbariums? What should the price be so that its income from herbariums is as large as possible? The cost to the chain for each herbarium is $5.

15. If you have a chain saw with a blade 18 in. long, can you cut a log that is 16 ft long and 8 in. in diameter into 4-ft pieces by making only two cuts?

16. Modify BASIC program 2 from section 1.11 to figure out how many pounds of raisins and how many pounds of granola should be in the hike mix of problem 6 in order that the mix costs $3.50/lb.

USING IDEAS *For each remaining problem in this problem set, write an essay explaining as clearly and completely as you can your solution to the problem. In your essay, describe the steps you take to solve the problem, mention the problems or solutions from the text that gave you ideas, and include the problem-solving strategies you used. You may want to outline and organise your work before writing your final essay.*

17. A bunch of students on a field trip to a local bottling plant were watching the machine that puts the tops on bottles. It was a circular device holding 36 bottles equally spaced around the outside. The students were trying to figure out how long it would take to cap all 36 bottles. One student started timing right after the top was put on the first bottle and found that it took 10 sec until the ninth bottle was completely capped. At that point, the students were dragged off to another part of the plant. How long would it have taken for the machine to cap all 36 bottles?*

18. Inspector Lee looked once again at the dead body of Horace Rimple and noted the time on the shattered watch: 1:10. The watch had undoubtedly been shattered by the bullet that killed old Mr. Rimple as he lay asleep in his bed.

---

* *Make It Simpler,* p. 165.

"Tell me what happened today," he instructed the butler.

"As always, on Sunday, it was Mr. Rimple's wish to have the family gather for the afternoon. On days such as today, when he was feeling unwell, the members of the family were to go in and sit by his bed to talk, even if he looked asleep. He could still hear them even if he did not make the effort to open his eyes.

"Today, as customary, Robert spent the time from 1:00 to 1:03 in the afternoon with him; Susan the time from 1:03 to 1:06; James, the time from 1:06 to 1:09; William, the time from 1:09 to 1:12; Lawrence, the time from 1:12 to 1:15; and Mary, the youngest, the time from 1:15 to 1:18. Mr. Rimple was very particular about those times. Each of them said he seemed to be asleep."

"Well," said Inspector Lee, "it seems very clear that William is the murderer."

"Unfortunately," said the butler, "it is not quite that simple. While Mr. Rimple loved that watch, it did not keep very good time. It lost exactly 6 minutes every 24 hours. I would set it correctly each night at 11:00 before going to bed. Thus, the watch was always incorrect."

"Ah." said Inspector Lee. "Then the murderer must be . . ."
Who?*

19. On the track in the accompanying diagram, interchange the position of cars A and B and return the engine to its starting position. Only the engine can pass through the tunnel; the railroad cars are too big.

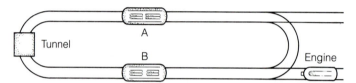

20. Ann, Becky, and Jane live in adjacent apartments. Becky has the middle apartment. They work as a chemist, a radio announcer, and a plumber, but not necessarily in that order. The radio announcer feeds Jane's cat when she goes away for the weekend. The chemist taps on Ann's wall when she wants to go jogging. What occupation does each woman have? (*Hint:* It might be useful to organize data and keep track of progress in a chart such as is shown.)

	CHEMIST	ANNOUNCER	PLUMBER
Ann			
Becky			
Jane			

21. Three singers, Conrad, Darlene, and Letha, met at the rehearsal of the Long Beach Choral Society. Their last names were Jacobs, Kaufman, and Nishio, not necessarily in that order, and their professions were accountant, plasterer, and teacher, again not necessarily in that order. Here are some things that you know about these people.

■ The plasterer, who was starting her own solar installation firm, offered to design a sauna for Nishio.

■ Kaufman jogged every morning on the beach, which was one block from his condo.

■ Darlene's last name was not Nishio.

■ Conrad was not the accountant.

---

* *Make It Simpler*, p. 223.

Match the singers' first names with their last names and professions. You may find the charts useful.*

	Jacobs	Kaufman	Nishio	Accountant	Plasterer	Teacher
Conrad						
Darlene						
Letha						
Accountant						
Plasterer						
Teacher						

	Last Name	Profession
Conrad		
Darlene		
Letha		

22. You have two egg timers: an 11-min and a 7-min timer. How can you time the boiling of vegetables for 15 min using these two timers?

7-min egg timer

11-min egg timer

23. *Problems for the Quickening of the Mind,* a collection of problems dating from the Dark Ages, contains the following question:

If 100 bushels of corn are distributed among 100 people in such a manner that each man receives 3 bushels, each woman 2 bushels, and each child half a bushel, how many men, women, and children are there?

(*Hint:* There are several solutions. Try to find as many as you can.)

---

* Problem and charts from Ruth Afflack, *Beyond EQUALS*, Math/Science Network, Mills College, Oakland, Calif., 1982, prob. 2, p. 108.

24. Your French vineyard produces two types of champagne: dry and brut. This season you plan to create a third type, extra dry, as a mixture of brut and dry. You want the retail price of extra dry to be 53 francs per liter. You know that the retail price of brut is 55 francs/l and that the retail price of dry is 47 francs/l. Furthermore, you anticipate being able to sell the following amounts of each type:

   ■ 800 liters extra dry
   ■ 400 liters dry
   ■ 300 liters brut

   How many liters of dry and how many liters of brut should your vineyard produce?

25. You have 12 coins that are identical except for the fact that 1 of them is counterfeit and therefore heavier or lighter than the others. Using a balance scale, how can you find the counterfeit coin and also tell whether it is lighter or heavier than the others? What is the fewest number of tries that you need?

26. Quabbin Reservoir, located in the western part of Massachusetts, supplies most of the water for the Boston area. The water from Quabbin is pumped into several holding reservoirs in the immediate vicinity of Boston, and Boston and its suburbs draw water from these holding reservoirs. At the end of each day, Quabbin refills the holding reservoirs to replace exactly the water drawn during the day. You work for Quabbin Reservoir and need to know the contents of the reservoir at the end of today's activities. Here is what you know:

   ■ There are three holding reservoirs.
   ■ Holding reservoir A starts with 300 million gal each day.
   ■ Holding reservoir B starts with 250 million gal each day.
   ■ Holding reservoir C starts with 150 million gal each day.
   ■ Boston takes 137 million gal each day from C.
   ■ Cambridge and Watertown each take 125 million gal daily from A.
   ■ Newton, Roxbury, and Waltham each take 25 million gal from B daily.
   ■ Quabbin Reservoir started yesterday morning with 700 million gal.
   ■ It rained this morning and Quabbin Reservoir received 400 million gal additional water.

   What is the solution to your problem?*

27. La Dolce Vita apartment house has 100 identical apartments. The owner wants to know what the rent for each apartment should be so that her total profit from the whole building is largest. Local rental trends indicate that if the rent on each apartment is $200, then she can keep all apartments rented and that for each $10 increase in the monthly rent the number of vacancies will increase by two. For example, if the rent is $210, then there will be two vacancies. The cost (upkeep and mortgage) per apartment is $50/mo. What should the rent be so that total profit is largest?

28. There are five houses in a row. Each is occupied by a person of different nationality. You'd like to find out who drinks brandy and who owns a skunk. Here are some clues.

   ■ The Spaniard owns a dog.
   ■ The person who is English lives in the red house.
   ■ Coffee is drunk in the green house.
   ■ The Ukrainian drinks tea.
   ■ The green house is immediately to the right of the ivory house.

---

*Adapted from Deborah Hughes Hallett, *The Math Workshop Algebra*, W. W. Norton & Company, New York, 1980, p. 18, problem 116.

- The doctor owns snails.
- The mathematician lives in the yellow house.
- Milk is drunk in the middle house.
- The Norwegian lives in the first house.
- The stockbroker lives next door to the person with the fox.
- The mathematician lives next to the house where horses are kept.
- The carpenter drinks orange juice.
- The Japanese is a salesperson.
- The Norwegian lives next door to the blue house.
- Each person has one home, one pet, one occupation, one nationality, and one drink.

SOLVING PROBLEMS USING SETS

C H A P T E R

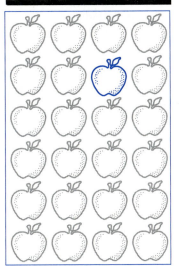

Our goal in this chapter is to enlarge our repertoire of problemsolving techniques by introducing a new kind of picture, the Venn diagram. The Venn diagram is particularly helpful in organizing data for problems having to do with surveys and inventories and other situations in which classifications are impor-tant. Sets are useful for such problems also, and we will discuss the relationship of the diagram and sets. One outcome of the use of a Venn diagram is that it enables us to determine the number of objects in one set given that the number of objects in other related sets are known.

2.1   VENN DIAGRAMS

THE LEMONMOBILE PROBLEM

Lemonmobiles are available with two possible options: radio and air conditioning. The owner of the Lemonmobile Emporium is studying a recent inventory of his lot, which shows

    50 Lemonmobiles on hand in all
    25 Lemonmobiles have radios
    13 have both options, radios and air conditioning
    15 have neither option

Try this problem yourself before looking at the solution below.

The owner wants to know two things: How many of the Lemonmobiles on hand have air conditioning? How many of the Lemonmobiles on hand have radios but no air conditioning?

How can he solve this problem?

A Solution to the Lemonmobile Problem

The owner decides to *draw a picture* of the lot in which his Lemonmobiles are parked.

He thinks: "There are 50 Lemonmobiles in the whole lot. There are 25 with radios. Let me designate a special area of the parking lot in which to park the cars with radios.

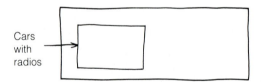

Let me designate another area of the lot in which to park the cars with air conditioning.

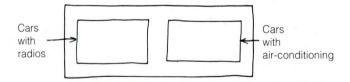

Where will I park a car that has both options? Instead of what I just drew, my picture should be

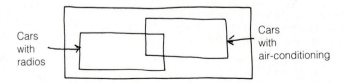

The part of the picture where the two smaller rectangles overlap is where the cars with both options should be parked. There are 13 of those.

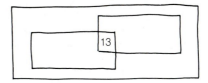

Of course, the 15 cars with no options must be parked outside both smaller rectangles.

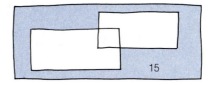

There are 25 cars that have radios. They should be parked inside the first smaller rectangle I drew.

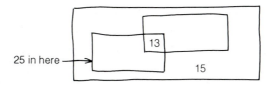

But 13 are already there—the cars with radios *and* air conditioning. The others, 12 of them, must have radios but no air conditioning.

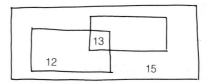

"I have accounted for all the cars in the lot except the ones that belong in the part of the drawing that has been shaded.

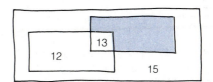

Cars parked here should have air conditioning but no radios. I don't see any clues about how many of these there might be. But I haven't used the fact that there are 50 Lemonmobiles in all. All the quantities in the picture—including the missing one—must add up to 50.

$$15 + 12 + 13 + ? = 50 \qquad \text{or} \qquad 40 + ? = 50.$$

The missing number is 10.

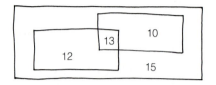

"Now to answer the questions. (1) The Lemonmobiles with air conditioning are in the shaded part of the following drawing.

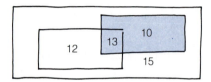

There are $10 + 13 = 23$ of them. (2) The Lemonmobiles with radios but no air conditioning are in the shaded part of the next drawing.

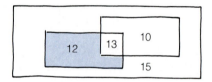

There are 12 of them."

The Mathematical Idea: Venn Diagrams and Sets

The information given in the Lemonmobile problem suggested a classification of Lemonmobiles according to certain attributes: Each Lemonmobile either has a radio or it doesn't; each Lemonmobile either has air conditioning or it doesn't. Such classifications are inherent to inventories and surveys. In solving a problem associated with such a classification there is a special picture that one can draw that helps to organize the data and solve the problem. To begin solving the Lemonmobile problem, the owner drew a picture.

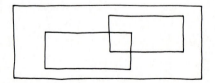

The picture is a version of a Venn diagram. A Venn diagram is frequently drawn in the following way.

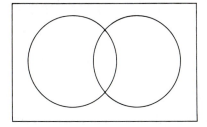

The diagram is so useful that special terminology and symbols are available for describing and labeling its parts: the terminology and symbols of sets.

A *set* is a collection of objects. The collection of all Lemonmobiles in the lot is a set. Let C denote this set. The objects that make up the set are called its elements, or members. Thus, a Lemonmobile on the lot is a member of C. In the Lemonmobile problem, two attributes are important: having a radio (or not) and having air conditioning (or not). So we introduce the following additional sets.

C = the set of all Lemonmobiles in the lot

R = the set of all Lemonmobiles in the lot with radios

A = the set of all Lemonmobiles in the lot with air conditioning

We use these symbols to label the Venn diagram associated with the Lemonmobile problem.

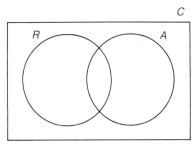

The set A is also called a *subset* of C, meaning that every element of A is also an element of C. Similarly, R is a subset of C.

If we are interested in the set of all Lemonmobiles in the lot with radios *and* air conditioning, then we are interested in those objects common to both sets R and A. This new set is called the *intersection of R with A* and is denoted $R \cap A$. The set $R \cap A$ corresponds to the shaded portion of the following drawing.

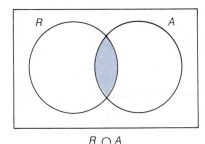

$R \cap A$

If we are interested in the set of all Lemonmobiles in the lot with radio or air conditioning or both, that is, a car with some option, then we are interested in the objects in sets R and A combined. This new set is called the *union of R with A* and is denoted $R \cup A$. The set $R \cup A$ corresponds to the shaded portion of the next drawing.

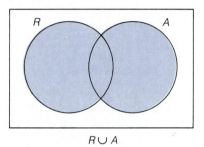

$R \cup A$

The Venn diagram is a powerful tool. To use it, one must be able to match parts of the diagram with verbal descriptions. Here are some matchings.

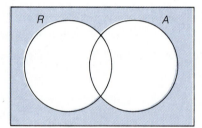

Cars that have neither
radio nor air-conditioning

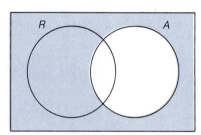

Cars that have
no air-conditioning

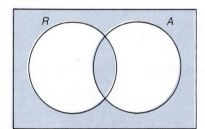

Cars that have no
option or both options

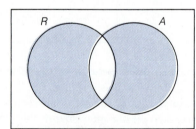

Cars that have exactly
one option

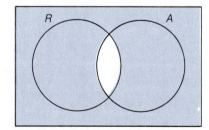

Cars that have at
most one option

EXERCISES 1. For each verbal description, draw a Venn diagram and shade in the region matching the description.
 (a) All cars that have air conditioning but no radio
 (b) All cars that have at least one option
 (c) All cars that have no radio
 (d) All cars that have either a radio or nothing at all

2. At a local TV appliance store you can purchase a TV in two sizes: large (20 in. diagonal) or small (10 in. diagonal). Each TV has either a black and white or a color screen. The owner of the store has checked her stock and found out that she has

23 large TVs
6 small black and white TVs
19 color TVs
21 black and white TVs

(a) Let A denote the set of all TVs in stock, L the set of large TVs in stock, and C the set of color TVs in stock. Following are Venn diagrams that go with these sets. For each one write a verbal description of the set of TVs that matches the shaded part of the diagram.

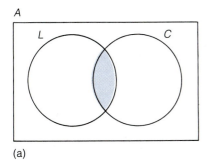

(a)

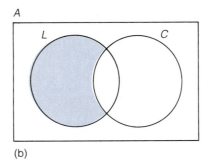

(b)

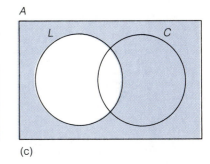

(c)

(b) For each of the following verbal descriptions draw a Venn diagram with sets A, L, and C and shade in the region that matches the description.
   (i) The set of all black and white TVs
   (ii) The set of all large black and white TVs
   (iii) The set of all large and color TVs
   (iv) The set of all TVs that are either color or large (or both)

(c) Draw a Venn diagram and use it to answer the following questions based on what the owner knows about her stock of TVs.

How many large color TVs are there?
How many small TVs are there?
How many TVs are there in all?

THE ENROLLMENT
PROBLEM

A survey was taken of students at the university concerning their enrollment in liberal arts courses. Each of 600 students was asked to answer yes or no to each of the questions

Are you enrolled in a humanities course?
Are you enrolled in a natural science course?
Are you enrolled in a social science course?

So far the following data from the survey have been tabulated.

250 of the students surveyed are enrolled in natural science courses
100 are enrolled both in a humanities course and a social science course
130 are enrolled in a natural science course but not in a humanities course
120 are enrolled only in a social science course
 30 are enrolled in all three course areas
270 are enrolled in a social science course
300 are enrolled in only one of the three areas

The dean of liberal arts is interested in knowing the answers to the questions

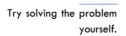

1. How many of the students surveyed are enrolled in none of these three areas?
2. How many of the students surveyed are enrolled in at least one of the three areas?
3. How many of the students surveyed are enrolled in at least two of the three areas?
4. How many of the students surveyed are enrolled in a humanities course?

Try solving the problem
yourself.

Help the dean answer these questions.

A Solution to the
Environment Problem

The dean solves the problem this way: "First, let me draw a rectangle designating the set of all students surveyed.

Next, let N be the set of all students enrolled in natural science courses; S, the set of students enrolled in social science courses; and H, the set of those in humanities courses. I'll draw circles for all three sets inside the rectangle. These circles will have to overlap each other to account for students enrolled in more than one area.

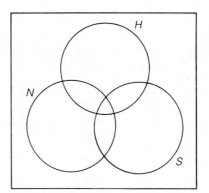

"Now I can use this picture to *organize the data* that I have from the survey. Let me identify the region that corresponds to each piece of data.

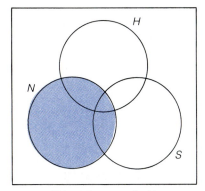

250 students enrolled in natural science courses

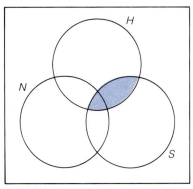

100 simultaneously enrolled in humanities course and in a social science course

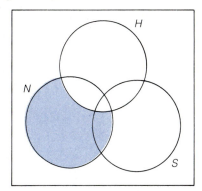

130 students enrolled in a natural science course but not in a humanities course

Now, I want the region for those taking *only* social science courses. These must be *inside* the S circle, *outside* the N circle, and *outside* the H circle.

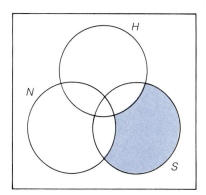

120 students enrolled only in a social science course

Here are the regions for the rest.

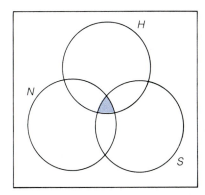

30 enrolled in all three

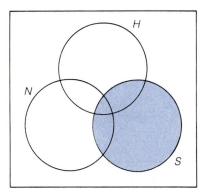

270 enrolled in a social science course

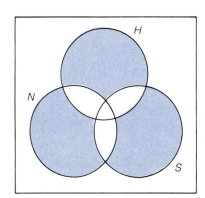

300 enrolled in only one of the three areas

"Finally, here are drawings of the sets I want to know about.

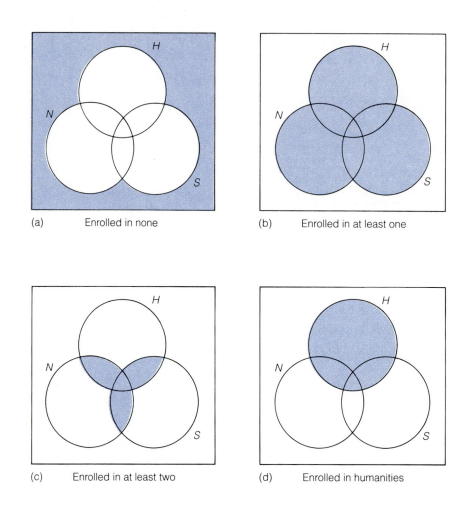

(a)   Enrolled in none

(b)   Enrolled in at least one

(c)   Enrolled in at least two

(d)   Enrolled in humanities

"To figure out the number of students enrolled in at least two areas—the set shaded in (c)—I should *break the problem into simpler problems,* that is, figure out the number of students in each of the following small sets, then add them up.

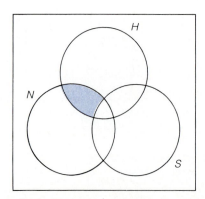

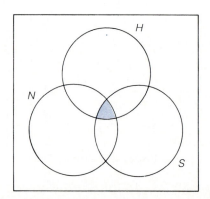

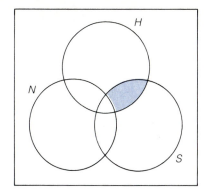
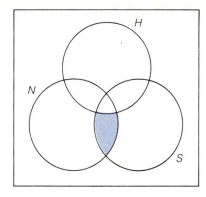

I can do the same for each of the other sets—break it up into the small parts of the Venn diagram, figure out how many students are in each of the small parts, then add them up. Now I must figure out how many students in each small set.

"From the data I can figure out directly the number of students in the following two small sets.

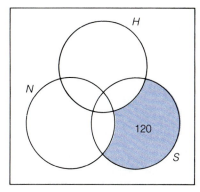

120 students enrolled in
social science courses only.

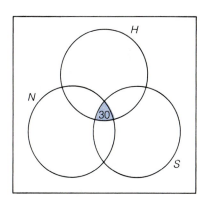

30 students enrolled in
all three areas.

"I also know that

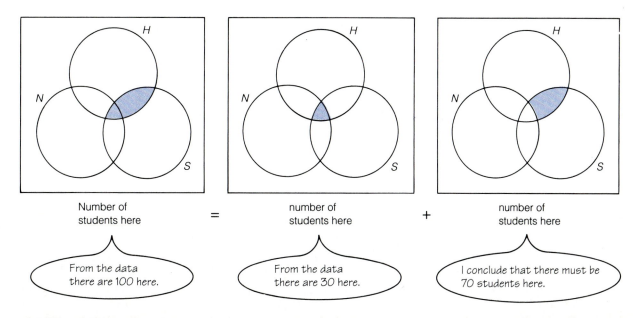

Number of
students here

=

number of
students here

+

number of
students here

From the data
there are 100 here.

From the data
there are 30 here.

I conclude that there must be
70 students here.

So I know

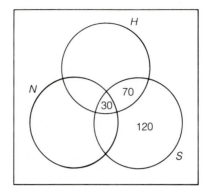

"I can use the same idea again.

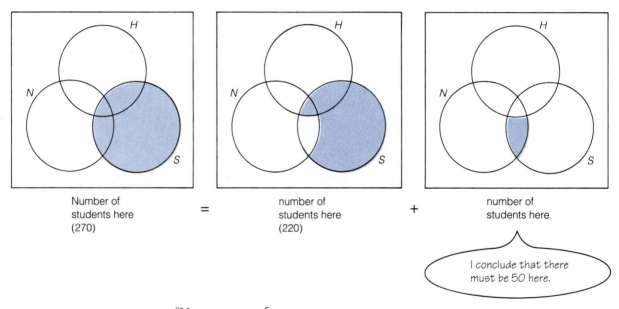

| Number of students here (270) | = | number of students here (220) | + | number of students here |

I conclude that there must be 50 here.

"My progress so far:

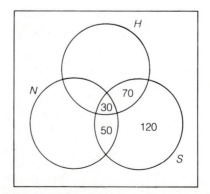

"Once again,

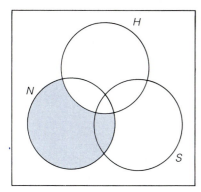
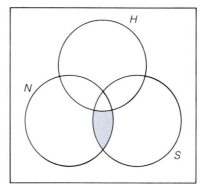
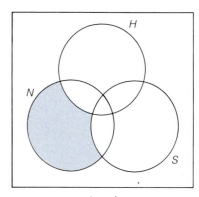

Number of students here (130)   =   number of students here (50)   +   number of students here

I conclude that there must be 80 here.

"Here's what I know now:

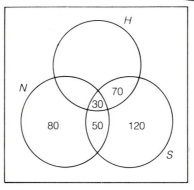

N 80 | 30 | 50 | 70 | 120 | H | S

"Now I'll use the same idea again.

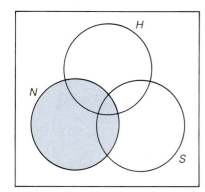
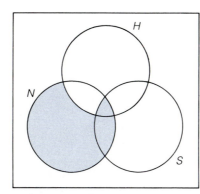
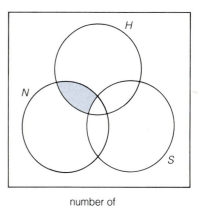

Number of students here (250)   =   number of students here (160)   +   number of students here

There must be 90 here.

"Now I know

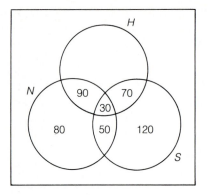

"Finally, I can use the last piece of data.

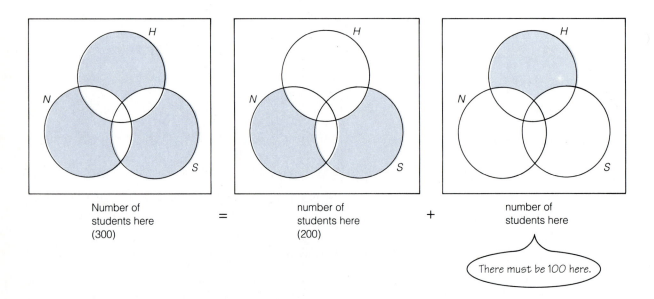

| Number of students here (300) | = | number of students here (200) | + | number of students here |

There must be 100 here.

"I get

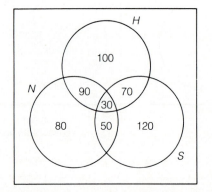

"There is still one part of the diagram for which I lack a number.

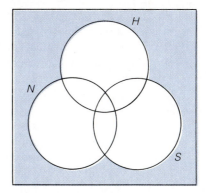

"And there is still one piece of information that has been given that I haven't used: 600 students were involved in the survey altogether. So, from what I know,

$$80 + 90 + 100 + 30 + 70 + 50 + 120 + ? = 600 \quad \text{or} \quad 540 + ? = 600.$$

The missing number is 60 and I have

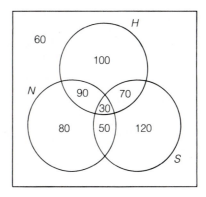

"I have found a number for each small part of the diagram. Now I can answer all the questions:

1. 60 students are enrolled in neither of the three areas.

2. The number of students taking courses in at least one of the three areas is equal to

$$80 + 90 + 100 + 30 + 70 + 50 + 120 = 540.$$

3. The number of students taking courses in at least two of the three areas is equal to

$$90 + 30 + 70 + 50 = 240.$$

4. The number of students enrolled in a humanities course is equal to

$$100 + 70 + 30 + 90 = 290.$$

"That's it!"

The Mathematical Idea: The Three-Circle Venn Diagram

In the enrollment problem every student in the set of those surveyed could be classified in three ways: (1) He or she is or is not a member of H, (2) he or she is or is not a member of S, and (3) he or she is or is not a member of N. Whenever you can classify the members of a set this way, using three of its subsets, then a three-circle Venn diagram can be useful, as in the solution to the enrollment problem.

In the Lemonmobile problem, each member of the set L of all Lemonmobiles on the lot could be classified in two ways: (1) It is or is not a member of A (set of cars with air conditioning), and (2) it is or is not a member of R (set of cars with radios). A two-circle Venn diagram was sufficient for solving this problem.

There are potential difficulties in using sets and a Venn diagram to solve a problem. One has to do with how we interpret English sentences. For example, in the solution to the enrollment problem, the dean felt that the set X of students enrolled in a natural science course but not a humanities course corresponded to the shaded portion of the diagram

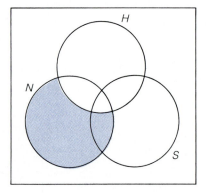

Why should the shaded portion of the following diagram be included in the set X?

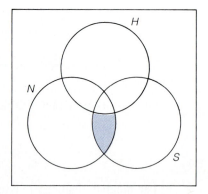

A student in the shaded region is also taking a social science course. Since the description of the set X says nothing about taking social science courses, can such an element be allowed in the set X? The answer is yes. A student in the shaded portion of the diagram satisfies the requirement for membership in the set X: The student is enrolled in a natural science course and not enrolled in a humanities course. That's all there is to it.

Another potential difficulty is concerned with recording and interpreting numerical information on a Venn diagram. Here are some examples from the enrollment problem of how numerical information on a Venn diagram is to be interpreted.

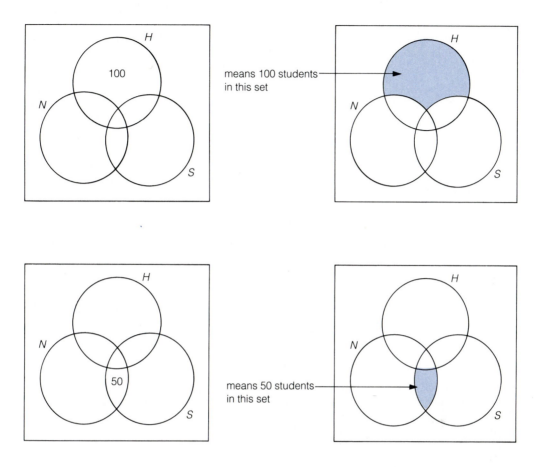

means 100 students in this set

means 50 students in this set

On the other hand, how can we record on the Venn diagram that 250 students are enrolled in natural science courses? If we were to label the diagram,

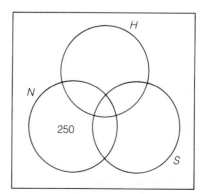

we would interpret the labeling to mean that there are 250 students in the following set.

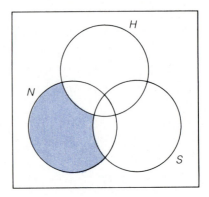

This is not what we intend. To avoid misunderstanding, a number recorded on a diagram refers to the smallest part of the diagram in which it is contained. We postpone recording the information "250 students are enrolled in natural science courses" until we can use it without introducing ambiguity.

EXERCISES   3. A public opinion survey was conducted to determine how much support there is for the president's policies. People were asked three questions.

Do you support the president's economic policy?
Do you support the president's foreign policy?
Do you support the president's social policy?

Let E, F, and S denote the sets of persons responding yes to the first, second, and third questions, respectively. The results of the survey are shown in the next Venn diagram.

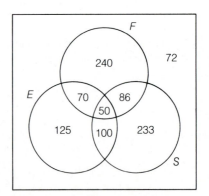

Using this diagram, answer the following questions: How many people participated in the survey? How many people agree with his economic policy? How many people disagree with all three policies? How many people disagree with just one of his policies?

4. When receiving a blood transfusion, the recipient's blood must have all the antigens of the donor's blood. A person's blood may have one or more of the three antigens A, B, and Rh or none at all. Depending on which antigens it contains, blood can

be classified into eight types as shown in the Venn diagram below, where *U* is the set of all people.

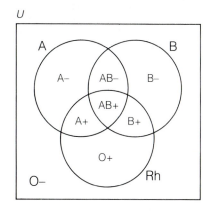

BLOOD TYPES

A–	A+
B–	B+
AB–	AB+
O–	O+

An A− person has blood with A antigens but no B or Rh; an O+ person has Rh but neither A nor B; an AB− person has A and B antigens but no Rh; and so on.

Using this diagram, indicate which of the eight blood types are included in each set.

(a) The set of all people with antigens A and Rh
(b) The set of all people with antigen A or Rh or both
(c) The set of all people with neither B nor A
(d) The set of all people who don't have A but do have Rh

5. At an election 100 voters voted on three propositions, A, B, and C. The results from the election have been tabulated.

Ten did not vote yes on any proposition.
Fifty voted yes on C but no on A.
Thirty voted yes on both B and C.
Twenty voted no on A but yes on B.
Twelve voted yes on all three.

How many people voted yes on A?

2.2   SURVEY AND INVENTORY PROBLEMS WITH NO EXACT ANSWER

THE DESK PROBLEM

Try the problem first.

The Desk Depot sells office desks. The desks are either three-drawer or six-drawer and either metal or wooden. Jack, a salesman for the Desk Depot, is out of town talking with a client. The client is considering placing a large order, perhaps buying all the desks that the Depot has in its warehouse. Jack needs to know roughly how many desks there are in all. He does remember that there are 30 three-drawer desks, 40 metal desks, and no six-drawer wooden desks. Help Jack use this information to make the best possible estimate of the total number of desks in the warehouse.

A Solution to the Desk Problem

Jack decides to *draw a Venn diagram* to *organize the data* he has about the number of desks in the warehouse. Here is how he proceeds.

"Let *A* be the set of all desks in the warehouse, *T* the set of all three-drawer desks in the warehouse, and *M* the set of all metal desks.

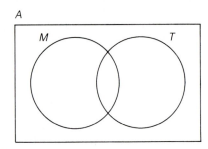

Since every desk is either three-drawer or six-drawer, the six-drawer desks are in the shaded part of the rectangle.

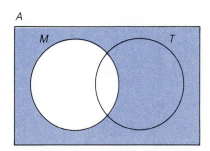

The wooden desks are in the shaded part below.

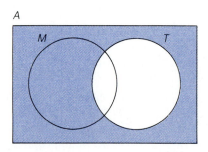

The set of six-drawer wooden desks corresponds to the shaded part in the next drawing.

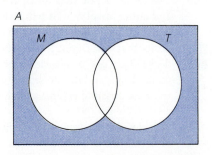

Since there are *no* six-drawer wooden desks, all the desks must be in the part shaded now.

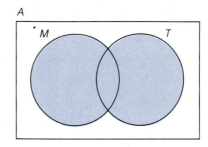

"There are 30 three-drawer desks . . . and 40 metal desks.

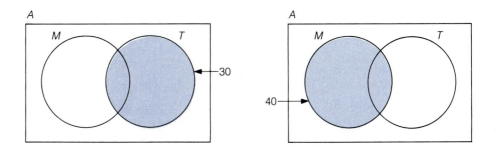

"If I knew the number of three-drawer metal desks,

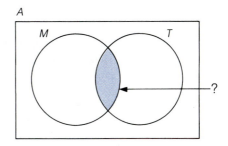

then I could figure out everything. Let me *make a guess.* If there were exactly 5 three-drawer metal desks, then I'd know

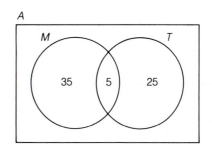

There would be a total of 65 desks in the warehouse. But in reality I know very little about the number of three-drawer metal desks. What are the possibilities for the number of desks in $T \cap M$? What is the smallest that this number can be? If I were to *guess* that there were no desks at all in $T \cap M$, I'd have

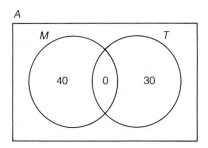

In this case, the total number of desks in the warehouse would be 70. Let me consider some other guesses and *make a chart to organize their consequences.*

NUMBER OF THREE-DRAWER METAL DESKS	NUMBER OF DESKS IN WAREHOUSE
0	70
1	69
2	68
3	67
4	66
5	65

"Now I *look for a pattern.* It seems that the largest number of desks possible in the warehouse is 70. Next, I should find out what the smallest possible number is. To do this, I should figure out the *largest* possible number of three-drawer metal desks. Let me try more numbers in the chart.

NUMBER OF THREE-DRAWER METAL DESKS	NUMBER OF DESKS IN WAREHOUSE
0	70
1	69
2	68
3	67
4	66
5	65
10	60
20	50
30	40

"A picture for the last entry in the chart would look like

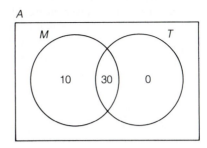

It's strange but consistent with what I know. This must be the end of the chart of possibilities, inasmuch as 30 is the largest number of three-drawer metal desks there can be: There are no more than 30 three-drawer desks in all, both metal and wooden.

"To sum up: In the entire warehouse there are at least 40 and no more than 70 desks."

EXERCISES

6. A car shop has 12 mechanics, of whom 8 can work on transmissions and 7 can work on brakes. What can you say about the number who can do both? What can you say about the number who can do neither?

7. A paper carrier delivers 21 copies of the *Citizen* and 27 copies of the *Daily Star* to a subdivision having 40 houses. No house receives 2 copies of the same paper. What is the least number of houses to which 2 papers could be delivered? The greatest number?

2.3 LOOKING BACK

The Language and Symbols of Sets

Venn diagrams help us to solve certain kinds of problems. For historical reasons and because of its unambiguity, simplicity, and flexibility, the language of sets is an accepted part of the common discourse of present-day mathematicians. To read most mathematics textbooks with ease, one should feel comfortable with the language and notation of sets. We will use sets in later chapters, especially when we want to be careful and precise. In this section, we will describe some additional notation and terminology related to sets.

The theory of sets originated in the 1890s with the German mathematician Georg Cantor. An important point of Cantor's notion is that a collection of objects (a set) is to be regarded as a single entity, so that attention is transferred from individual objects to a collection of objects. This is not such a new idea, for consider the phrases "a *school* of fish," "a *flock* of sheep," "a *gaggle* of geese," "a *multitude* of the heavenly hosts," "a *pack* of lies," and "an *army* of ants." The words *school, flock, gaggle, multitude, pack,* and *army* are all historical names for sets.

Description of a Set

Perhaps the simplest way to describe a set is by listing its members. For example, the set of standard vowels in the English alphabet can be written as $\{a,e,i,o,u\}$ (read "the set consisting of a, e, i, o, u as members"). The set of whole numbers between 17 and 22 can be written as $\{18,19,20,21\}$. The set of presidents of the United States in 1989 can be written as $\{$George Bush$\}$.

Using curly braces—$\{$and$\}$—to enclose the elements of a set is called the *listing method* and is a typical way to describe a set. The set of all even natural numbers up to and including 100 can be written as $\{2,4,6,8,\ldots,100\}$ using the listing method and three dots—$\ldots$—or *ellipsis,* which means to "continue in the same fashion." Even some infinite sets, or sets without limit, can be described this way. For example, the set of natural numbers can be written as $\{1,2,3,4,\ldots\}$ and the set of even natural numbers as $\{2,4,6,8,\ldots\}$.

By contrast, a set that is limited—not infinite—is called *finite.* The sets $\{a,e,i,o,u\}$, $\{$George Bush$\}$, and $\{2,4,6,8,\ldots,100\}$ are examples of finite sets.

A second method of describing a set uses *set builder notation.* The symbols $\{x:\underline{\hspace{1cm}}\}$ are to be read "the set of all x such that $\underline{\hspace{1cm}}$," where the dash is replaced by a condition that specifies the circumstances under which an element x is to be a member of the set in question.

For example, the three descriptions

$\{x : x = 2n$ where $n = 1, 2, \ldots, 50\}$
$\{x : x$ is an even natural number between 2 and 100 inclusive$\}$
$\{x : x$ is an even natural number such that $2 \leq x \leq 100\}$

all describe the set $\{2,4,6,8,\ldots,100\}$.

Another example is $\{x : x$ has a radio and x is a Lemonmobile on the Lemonmobile Emporium's lot$\}$, which would describe the set R, used earlier. Of course, a *verbal description* of a set is also acceptable.

Another useful method for describing a set is in terms of other, possibly simpler, sets using set union and set intersection. We will take another look at this later in this section.

Set Membership

We use capital letters as abbreviations for sets and small letters as abbreviations for elements of sets. Special notation is commonly used to express the membership of an element in a given set.

MEMBERSHIP IN A SET

If S is a set and x is member of S, then we write $x \in S$. If x represents an object that is *not* a member of S, then we write $x \notin S$.

Some examples of the use of set membership notation are:

$10 \in \{2,4,6,\ldots,100\}$
$7 \notin \{2,4,6,\ldots,100\}$
$a \in \{t,e,a,c,h,r\}$
$b \notin \{t,e,a,c,h,r\}$

8. Which of the following are true statements about objects and the set $A = \{t,e,a,c,h,r\}$?
   (a) $f \in A$ (b) $7 \notin A$ (c) $g \notin A$ (d) $3 \in A$

Set Equality and Subsets

SET EQUALITY

If S and T are sets and S and T have the same members, then the two sets are called *equal*; and we write $S = T$.

For example, if $A = \{x: x$ is a letter of the word *teacher*$\}$ and $B = \{x : x$ is a letter of the word *cheater*$\}$, then $A = \{t,e,a,c,h,r\}$ and $B = \{c,h,e,a,t,r\}$. Furthermore, $A = B$, since the elements of two sets are exactly the same.
   If

$$C = \{x : x \text{ is a letter of the word } theater\}$$

and

$$D = \{x : x \text{ is a letter of the word } head\},$$

then

$$C = \{t,h,e,a,r\} \quad \text{and} \quad D = \{h,e,a,d\}.$$

But $C \neq A$ because $c \in A$ but $c \notin C$; that is, the two sets are not equal. Also, $D \neq A$ and $D \neq C$.
   However, every element of C is also an element of A so that C is a *subset* of A. In general,

---

DEFINITION OF SUBSET

If S and T are two sets and every element of S is an element of T, then S is a *subset* of T; and we write $S \subset T$.

The expression "$S \subset T$" is read "S is a subset of T." Thus, $C \subset A$.

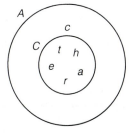
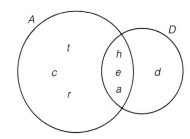

Not every element of D is an element of A so D is *not* a subset of A and we write $D \not\subset A$. This expression is read "D is not a subset of A."

The set A is equal to $\{t,e,a,c,h,r\}$. The set $\{t\}$ is a subset of A. So is $\{a\}$. A set, such as $\{t\}$ or $\{a\}$, having exactly one element is called a *singleton* set.

The following also describes a subset of A: $E = \{x: x \in A$ and x is a letter of the word *look*$\}$. Since there are *no* letters in A that are also letters of the word *look*, the set E has no elements! The set with no elements is called the *empty set* and is denoted $\emptyset$. So $E = \emptyset$. Other sets equal to the empty set:

$$\emptyset = \{x: x \text{ is a whole number and } x = x + 1\}$$
$$\emptyset = \{\,\}$$
$$\emptyset = \{x: x \text{ is a green cow in the San Diego Zoo}\}$$

The empty set is a subset of every set.

EXERCISES

9. Using the definitions of the sets A, B, C, and D previously given, decide which of the following statements are true.
   (a) $A \subset B$ (b) $D \subset C$ (c) $B \subset D$
   (d) $B \not\subset C$ (e) $\emptyset \subset D$ (f) $d \in D$
   (g) $\{d\} \subset D$ (h) $k \in C$ (i) $\{k\} \not\subset C$

10. Translate each of the following verbal expressions into a symbolic expression of the form $A \subset B$.
    Example: All men are mortal. (Let M be the set of men and D the set of mortals. Then the statement translates into $M \subset D$.)
    (a) All babies are illogical.
    (b) All politicians are dishonest.
    (c) Every square is a rectangle.
    (d) Every equilateral triangle is an isosceles triangle.

11. What can you say about two sets A and B if you know that $A \subset B$ and that $B \subset A$?

12. What can you say about two sets A and B if you know that there is a third set D such that $A \subset D$ and $D \subset B$?

13. List all the subsets of the set $\{h,e,a,t\}$.

Operations

If S and T are sets, then earlier we described ways to build new sets from them using the intersection and the union of S and T. These can be described using our new notation.

DEFINITION OF SET INTERSECTION AND UNION USING SET BUILDER NOTATION

Suppose that S and T are sets. Then the *intersection* of S and T is the set

$$S \cap T = \{x: x \in S \text{ and } x \in T\}.$$

The *union* of S and T is the set

$$S \cup T = \{x: x \in S, \text{ or } x \in T, \text{ or both}\}.$$

For example, if $A = \{t,e,a,c,h,r\}$ and $D = \{h,e,a,d\}$, then $A \cap D = \{h,e,a\}$ and $A \cup D = \{t,e,a,c,h,r,d\}$.

In mathematical discourse, the statement $x \in S$ or $x \in T$ includes the possibility that x might be an element of both sets. The *or* in mathematics is the inclusive *or*. The *or* frequently used in English is the exclusive *or*. For example, if a person were to say, "I will drink tea or coffee after dinner tonight," the person usually means that she will drink one or the other but not both.

EXERCISES
14. Suppose that $S = \{1,2,3,4,5\}$ and $T = \{1,3,5,7,9\}$. As in the previous example, describe the sets $S \cap T$ and $S \cup T$ using the listing method.

15. Let T denote the set of all students at the university who are over 25 years of age and let S denote the set of all students at the university who smoke cigarettes. Give verbal descriptions for the sets $S \cap T$ and $S \cup T$.

Set Complement

In a typical discussion where sets are used, there is usually a large set of which all the sets mentioned are subsets. This large set is a *universal set*. For example, in the Lemonmobile problem, every set in the discussion is a subset of L, the set of all Lemonmobiles in the Lemonmobile Emporium. For this problem, L is the universal set. The choice of a universal set for a given discussion is a matter of discretion, but it is usually just big enough that all sets mentioned are subsets. For the sets A, B, C, and D enumerated earlier, a good choice for a universal set is the set

$$U = \{a,b,c,d,e,f,g,h,i,j,k,l,m,n,o,p,q,r,s,t,u,v,w,x,y,z\}.$$

DEFINITION OF SET COMPLEMENT

Suppose that S is a subset of a universal set U.
 Then the *complement* (*of S in U*) is the set $U \backslash S = S' = \{x : x \in U \text{ and } x \notin S\}$.
In words, the set S' is the set of all elements of U that are *not* elements of S.

EXERCISE
16. Suppose that A is the set of all people in the state of Arizona who own a personal computer and B the set of all 22-year-olds in the state of Arizona. The universal set U is the set of all persons in the state of Arizona. What can you say about k if

(a) $k \in A$ (b) $k \in B$ (c) $k \in A'$ (d) $k \in A \cap B$
(e) $k \in A \cup B$ (f) $k \in A' \cap B'$ (g) $k \in (A \cap B)'$

Pictures and Symbols

We can use what we have developed to give concise, symbolic names to the regions of a Venn diagram. Suppose that U is the universal set and that A and B are two subsets of U. Then the shaded portion of each of the following Venn diagrams corresponds to the symbolic expression written with the diagram.

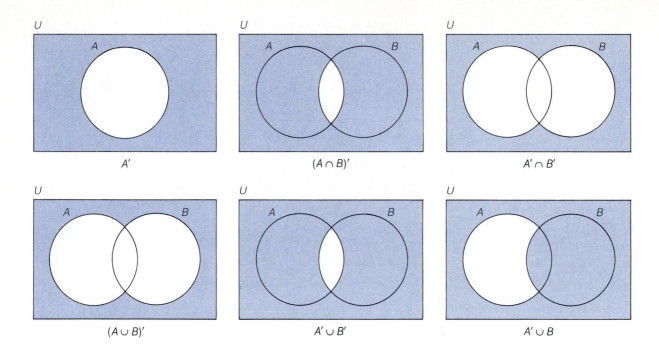

A' $(A \cap B)'$ $A' \cap B'$

$(A \cup B)'$ $A' \cup B'$ $A' \cup B$

EXERCISE   17. For each Venn diagram, write a symbolic expression that corresponds to the shaded part of the diagram.

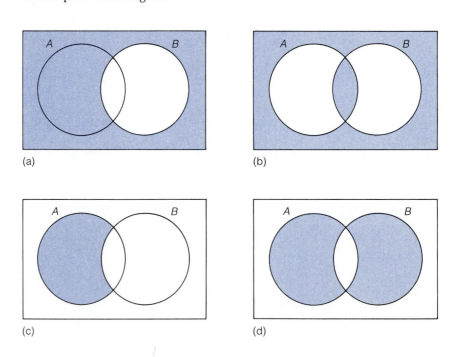

(a)   (b)

(c)   (d)

Parentheses and Order of Operations

When more than two operations are involved in a symbolic expression for a set, we need a way of specifying which operation is to be carried out first. A pair of parentheses does this. There is a rule for dealing with expressions involving parentheses.

RULE FOR THE ORDER OF OPERATIONS

When a pair of parentheses occurs in an expression, the operation inside the parentheses should be carried out first. If one pair of parentheses occurs inside another, the operation in innermost parentheses should be carried out first.

For example, in the expression $A \cup (B \cap C)$ the intersection is carried out first, then the union. The set $A \cup (B \cap C)$ corresponds to the shaded portion of the Venn diagram.

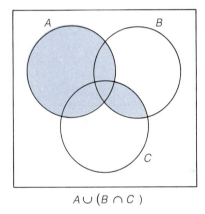

$$A \cup (B \cap C)$$

On the other hand, in the expression $(A \cup B) \cap C$ the union is done first and the intersection second. This set corresponds to the new shaded portion of the Venn diagram.

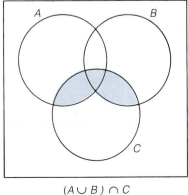

$$(A \cup B) \cap C$$

The expression $A \cup B \cap C$ is ambiguous without parentheses. Does it mean $(A \cup B) \cap C$ or does it mean $A \cup (B \cap C)$? It can't mean both, because it can be seen from the diagrams that the two sets are different.

EXERCISES 18. Let the universal set be $U = \{1,2,3,4,5, \ldots\}$ and let $A = \{2,4,6,8\}$, $B = \{1,3,5,7,9\}$, and $C = \{1,2,3,4,5,6\}$. Describe each of the following sets using the listing method.

(a) $A \cap B$ (b) $(A \cap B) \cup C$ (c) $(A \cup C) \cap B$ (d) $A' \cap C$

(e) $(A \cup B)'$ (f) $[(A' \cup C) \cap B]'$ (g) $A \cap A'$ (h) $A \cup A'$

19. In each of the following Venn diagrams, shade in the set whose symbolic expression appears with the diagram.

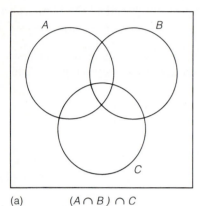

(a) $(A \cap B) \cap C$

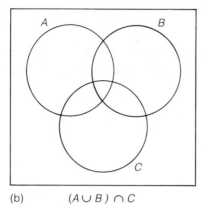

(b) $(A \cup B) \cap C$

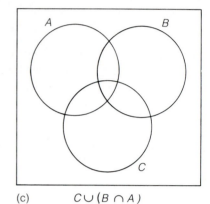

(c) $C \cup (B \cap A)$

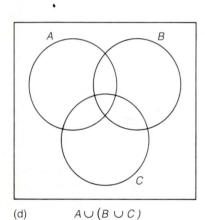

(d) $A \cup (B \cup C)$

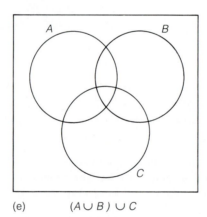

(e) $(A \cup B) \cup C$

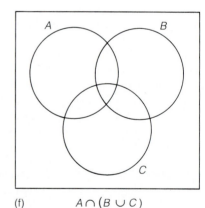

(f) $A \cap (B \cup C)$

20. The following statements are assumed to be related, and they can all be rewritten in the language of sets. Let the set of all persons be the universal set U. Assign letters to the subsets of U suggested by the statements. Translate each statement into a symbolic expression of the form $A \subset B$, as in exercise 10. Then draw and label a diagram of sets that captures the statement.

(a) All babies are illogical.

(b) Nobody is despised who can manage a crocodile.

(c) All illogical persons are despised.

     Assume that the statements above are true. Use the diagrams and what you know about sets to conclude that

(d) Babies cannot manage crocodiles.

2.4 LOOKING AHEAD: ALGEBRAIC PROPERTIES OF SET OPERATIONS

Working with symbols that represent sets and set operations can be more efficient than working with verbal descriptions or pictures. However, what I gain in efficiency may be lost in understanding, at least until I have some facility manipulating the symbols. Symbolic expressions are abstract, whereas pictures and verbal expressions seem more concrete. Which of these three representations of sets should I use? I should use whichever helps me solve the problem at hand. Ultimately, I should feel comfortable with all three, because then I may have *three* ways of dealing with a problem. That gives me a lot of power. If one way doesn't work, I can use another. Also, if I solve it one way, I can use another to check my solution.

To make using symbols for sets most efficient, I need to know when two symbolic expressions represent the same set; I need to know when a set inclusion or equation follows from other set inclusions or equations. Since I am not relying on pictures and verbal descriptions that yield conclusions I feel comfortable with, I am going to need rules that give me confidence and certainty and also help me solve the problem. Such rules, listed below, may be useful in working with sets as they come up in other books or contexts. They are similar to rules for manipulating symbolic expressions involving numbers—the rules of algebra—which we will take up later.

RULES FOR SETS

Suppose that A, B, and C are sets and that the universal set is U. The following are true statements about these sets.

INCLUSION

1. If we know that $A \subset B$ and $B \subset A$, then we can conclude that $A = B$ (*antisymmetry*).
2. $A \subset A$ (*reflexivity*).
3. If we know that $A \subset B$ and $B \subset C$, we can conclude that $A \subset C$ (*transitivity*).
4. If we know that $A \subset B$, we can conclude that $B' \subset A'$.

COMPLEMENT

5. $(A')' = A$.

UNION AND INTERSECTION

6. $A \cup B = B \cup A$ and $A \cap B = B \cap A$ (*commutativity*).
7. $(A \cup B) \cup C = A \cup (B \cup C)$ and $(A \cap B) \cap C = A \cap (B \cap C)$ (*associativity*).
8. $A \cup (B \cap C) = (A \cup B) \cap (A \cup C)$ and
   $A \cap (B \cup C) = (A \cap B) \cup (A \cap C)$ (*distributivity of $\cup$ over $\cap$ and of $\cap$ over $\cup$*).

$\varnothing$ AND U

9. $\varnothing \cup A = A$ and $U \cap A = A$ (*identities with respect to $\cup$ and $\cap$*).

DUALITY

10. $(A \cup B)' = A' \cap B'$ and $(A \cap B)' = A' \cup B'$ (*De Morgan's laws*).

It is clear why many of the properties are true. For example, $A \cup B = B \cup A$ seems to follow directly from the definition of set union. Other properties appear to be true when checked against a picture. For example, in property 3, pictures for $A \subset B$ and $B \subset C$ are

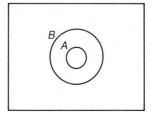 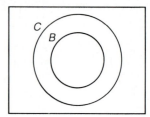

or, combining the two pictures,

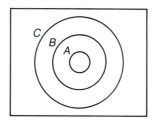

From this last picture, it is easy to conclude that $A \subset C$, which shows why property 3 holds.

As another example, consider property 5: $(A')' = A$. To show this, note that the shaded portion of the following diagram is A'.

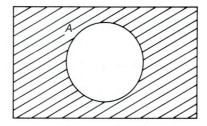

Now $(A')'$ is the complement of the shaded portion of the diagram. So the set $(A')'$ is the doubly shaded portion of the diagram.

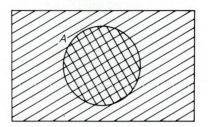

Thus, $(A')' = A$.

Arguments for the other properties can be more involved. For example, take the first statement of property 8: $A \cup (B \cap C) = (A \cup B) \cap (A \cup C)$. To show why this is true, we will analyze both sides of the equation using Venn diagrams. We start with the left-hand side.

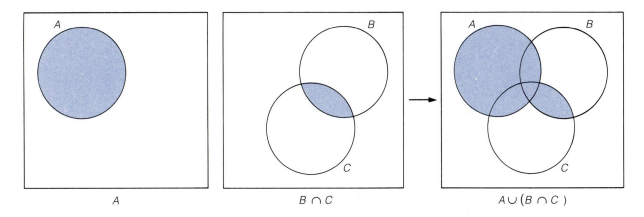

Now for the right-hand side.

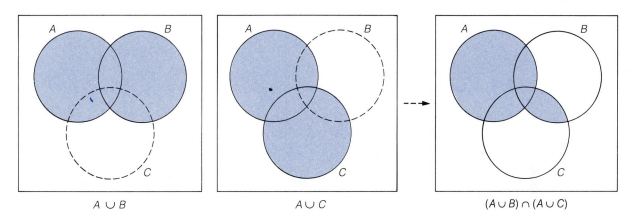

From the pictures it should be clear that the two sets $A \cup (B \cap C)$ and $(A \cup B) \cap (A \cup C)$ are the same.

Picture arguments justifying the rules are adequate for us. In other treatments of the subject, more formal arguments are given.

EXERCISES

21. Give a picture argument showing why the second statement of rule 8 is true.

22. Give a picture argument showing why rule 4 is true.

23. Give a picture argument showing why the first statement of rule 10 is true.

24. Use the rules given (*not* pictures!) to show that the statements are true.
    (a) For any sets A, B, and C, you can conclude that $A \cup (B \cap C) = (C \cap B) \cup A$.
    (b) If you know that $A \subset B$, you also know that $A \cap (B \cup C) = A$.
    (c) For any sets A and B, you can conclude that $A \cup B = (A' \cap B')'$.
    (d) For any sets A, B, and C, you can conclude that
    $A' \cup (B \cap C') = (A \cap B')' \cap (A \cap C)'$.

- Set; how the idea is used in solving certain problems
- Basic terminology associated with sets
  Element, or member of a set
  Subset of a set
  Union of two sets
  Intersection of two sets
  A universal set for a specific context
  Complement of a set (in a universal set)
- Venn diagrams in solving problems of inventories and surveys and in situations where an exact answer is not possible
- Methods for describing a set
  Venn diagram (a picture of a set)
  Verbal description
  Listing method
  Set builder notation
  Using set operations, other sets, and symbols
- Requirements for working with sets effectively
- Additional terminology for sets
  Empty set
  Infinite/finite set
  Singleton set
- Rules for manipulating symbolic expressions involving sets and their operations

PROBLEM SET

PRACTICING SKILLS   *The following information is used for exercises 1 through 4. Calvin's Clock Company makes clocks. Each clock that the company makes is either chiming or nonchiming and either digital or nondigital.*

1. Let U be the set of all clocks that the company has in stock, C the set of all clocks in stock that chime, and D the set of all clocks in stock that are digital. For each of the following Venn diagrams write a sentence describing the set of clocks that corresponds to the shaded portion.

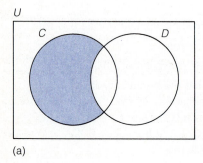

(a)

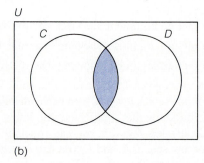

(b)

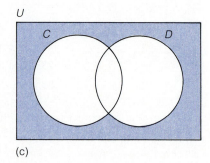

(c)

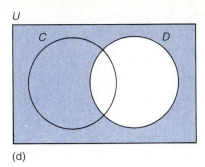

(d)

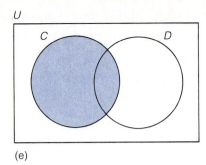

(e)

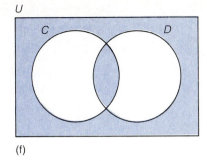

(f)

2. Below is a Venn diagram using the sets U, C, and D from exercise 1.

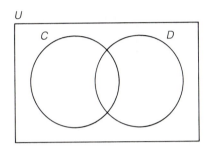

For each of the following phrases copy this Venn diagram and shade in the region corresponding to the set being described:
(a) The set of nonchiming clocks
(b) The set of nonchiming digital clocks
(c) The set of clocks that are chiming, or are digital, or both
(d) The set of clocks that are chiming or digital but not both

3. Calvin has gathered the following information about the clocks he has in stock:

14 clocks are chiming
33 clocks are digital
 8 clocks are chiming and digital
46 clocks are neither chiming nor digital

Use this information to answer the questions.
(a) How many clocks are chiming but not digital?
(b) How many clocks are nonchiming and also digital?
(c) How many clocks have at least one of these two features: chiming and digital?
(d) How many clocks does Calvin have in stock altogether?

4. A clock case may be made out of plastic, wood, or aluminum, or any combination of the three materials. Calvin's Clock Company has received orders for a number of clocks. Calvin gave the production manager the following information about the cases for these clocks.

70 clocks have been ordered.
23 are to have cases containing plastic but no wood.
15 are to have cases containing aluminum but no wood.
 5 are to have cases containing all three materials.
15 are to have cases containing plastic and aluminum.
12 are to have cases containing plastic and wood.

Draw a Venn diagram and help the production manager answer the questions.
(a) How many of the clocks ordered will have cases containing plastic and aluminum but no wood?
(b) How many of the clocks ordered will have cases made of plastic only?
(c) How many of the clocks ordered will have cases made of aluminum only?
(d) How many of the clocks ordered will have cases containing plastic and wood but no aluminum?
(e) How many clocks will have cases containing aluminum?

5. Washington School's Parent Association sold books at the Washington School Fair. Each book sold was either fiction or nonfiction and was either a hardback or a paperback. Hardback books of fiction bring in the most money. The chairperson of the book-selling committee can't remember exactly how many of these were sold, but he does remember that

> 30 books were sold in all.
> 20 hardcover books were sold.
> 15 books of fiction were sold.

Based on this information,
(a) What is the smallest possible number of hardback books of fiction sold?
(b) What is the largest possible number of hardback books of fiction sold?

For exercises 6 through 8 use the following sets:

$$A = \{a,b,c,d,e\}$$
$$B = \{2,d,a,4\}$$
$$C = \{4,1,5,2\}$$
$$D = \{5,3,2,1,4\}$$
$$E = \{e,a\}$$

6. Do the following problems.
(a) Name the sets above for which 2 is an element.
(b) Name the sets above for which e is an element.
(c) Name the sets above for which c is an element.
(d) Name the sets above for which 1 is an element.

7. Do the following problems.
(a) Name the sets above for which $\{c,e\}$ is a subset.
(b) Name the sets above for which $\{1,2,4,5\}$ is a subset.
(c) Name the sets above for which $\{e\}$ is a subset.
(d) Name the sets above for which $\{2,4\}$ is a subset.
(e) Name the sets above for which $\{d,4\}$ is a subset.
(f) Name the sets above for which $\{d,5\}$ is a subset.

8. Using $\{a,b,c,d,e,1,2,3,4,5\}$ as the universal set, list the elements for each of the sets.
(a) $A \cup B$ (b) $E \cup B$ (c) $C \cup D$
(d) $B \cap C$ (e) $C \cap D$ (f) $E \cap D$
(g) E' (h) $E' \cap D'$ (i) $A \cup B'$

9. Name the subsets of $\{C,3,P,O\}$.

10. Many verbal statements can be rewritten symbolically using letters for sets and the symbols for set membership, inclusion, and operations. For example, "All men are mortal" can be rewritten as $M \subset D$, where M is the set of men and D is the set of mortals. Do this for the following statements, using letters to abbreviate the sets.

(a)   Piano players are musicians.
(b)   Computers are not intelligent.
(c)   Susan is a brunette.
(d)   There are no purple cows.

11.   Let U—the universal set—be the set of children at Adam Smith Elementary School, W the set of children in Ms. Wilson's first-grade class, and S the set of children (at Adam Smith Elementary School) who are at least 7 years old. For each of the following, use an English sentence to describe a child k if

(a) $k \in W$ (b) $k \in S \cap W'$ (c) $k \in S \cup W'$
(d) $k \in (S \cup W')'$ (e) $k \in S' \cap W$ (f) $k \in S' \cup W'$

12.   Below is the Venn diagram for subsets A and B of a universal set U.

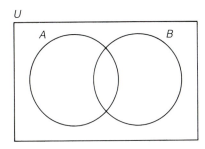

For each of the following sets copy this Venn diagram and shade in the region corresponding to the set.

(a) A' (b) $A \cup B'$ (c) $A' \cap B$
(d) $(A \cup B') \cap A'$ (e) $(A \cup B) \cap A'$ (f) $(A' \cap B) \cup (A \cap B')$

13.   Give a picture argument showing why the second part of rule 10 (sec. 2.4) for sets is true.

14.   Suppose U is the universal set and A a subset of U. Answer each of the following questions and give an argument to support your answer.
(a)   What is $\varnothing'$?
(b)   What is U'?
(c)   What is $A \cap A'$?
(d)   What is $A \cup A'$?

15.   Use the rules for sets in section 2.4 (*not* pictures) to show why each of the following statements about sets is true.
(a) $A \cap B = (A' \cup B')'$ (b) $(A \cup B)' = (A \cup B') \cap A'$

USING IDEAS   *For each remaining problem in this problem set, write an essay explaining as clearly and completely as you can your solution to the problem. In your essay, describe the steps you took to solve the problem, mention the problems or solutions from the text that gave you ideas, and include the problem-solving strategies you used. You may want to outline and organize your work before writing your final essay.*

16.   Mountain Telephone can offer you a phone with two options—the push-button option and the decorator color option. Of course, one can obtain a phone with both of these options or neither of them. The standard model (no options) is black with the "old-fashioned" dial. Mountain Telephone wants to know how many phones in decorator colors it has in stock. Here are some clues found on the latest inventory sheet.

There are 50 push-button phones in stock.
30 phones have both special options.
25 of the phones in stock are the standard model.
There are a total of 90 phones in stock.

Use the diagram to help you organize this information and solve the problem. *P* is the set of all push-button models, and *D* is the set of phones in decorator colors.

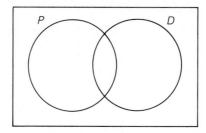

17. A sociologist is doing a study on the affluence of college students. She has surveyed 100 college students and has found that

   75 students own a stereo.
   45 own cars.
   36 own only one of the two items.

   Her questions are
   (a) How many students own both items?
   (b) How many students own neither item?
   Help her to answer these questions.

18. A second sociologist did his own survey of another set of 100 college students and came up with these data:

   72 own cars.
   60 own stereos.
   20 own both items.

   On seeing these results, the first sociologist claimed that the second sociologist was either a fraud or incompetent (or both). Was she right? Why or why not?

19. A third sociologist has conducted the same survey (with a third set of 100 students) as the two in problems 17 and 18 but has misplaced her data. However, she does remember that, according to her survey, 40 own cars and 60 own stereos.
   Using this information, what can she say about the number of students who own both? Neither?

20. A mattress manufacturer makes several kinds of mattresses. In particular, he makes king-size and standard-size, with foam or innerspring interiors, and with either plastic or cloth covers. A clerk has recorded the following information concerning the mattresses in stock.

   50 mattresses in stock
   14 king-size
   21 foam interiors
   22 plastic-covered
    6 king-size with plastic covers
    7 king-size with foam interiors
    8 foam with plastic covers
    2 king-size with foam interiors and with plastic covers

The manufacturer wants to know how many cloth-covered, standard-size, innerspring mattresses he has in stock. Help him find out.*

21. Here are the results of a survey of 120 people indicating the television networks they watched on a certain evening. You want to know how many people did not watch any of these three networks on that evening.

NETWORKS	NUMBER OF PEOPLE WHO WATCHED
ABC	55
NBC	30
CBS	40
ABC and CBS	10
ABC and NBC	12
NBC and CBS	8
ABC, CBS, and NBC	5

22. In a survey of faculty members at a small liberal arts college, 35 were asked
    (a) Have you had more than 10 years of teaching experience?
    (b) Have you taught at another college sometime in your career?
    (c) Do you have a Ph.D.?
    The college president wants to know how many answered yes to all three questions, how many answered yes to both questions (a) and (b), and how many answered yes only to question (c). He has already determined from the survey that

    15 answered yes to question (a).
    28 answered yes to question (b).
    3 answered yes to both questions (a) and (b) and no to question (c).
    Only one person answered yes to both questions (a) and (c) and no to question (b).
    2 answered yes to question (a) and no to the rest.
    11 answered yes to question (b) and no to the rest.

23. A market survey is being made of 100 households. According to the survey,

    70 of the households have children.
    80 households have incomes over $15,000.
    65 households have washing machines.

    A market specialist wants to estimate from this information the number of households in the survey that have children, incomes over $15,000, and washing machines. Help him to do this.

24. Roga, who lived in a village of long ago when no one could count as we do today, sold coconuts. She classified them as large (versus small), hairy (versus smooth), and thick skinned (versus thin skinned). She had three hemp loops and placed the subset *L* of large coconuts inside one loop, the subset *H* of hairy coconuts inside a second loop, and the subset *T* of thick-skinned coconuts inside a third loop.

---

* Adapted from Paul B. Johnson, *From Sticks and Stones,* SRA, Chicago, 1975, p. 49.

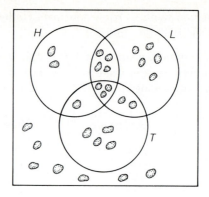

Inside the balloon is a set of stones whose elements match with the elements of the set of coconuts that are both large and hairy.

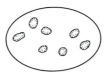

On the left, following, are verbal descriptions of subsets of Roga's coconuts. Inside the corresponding balloon on the right draw a set of stones whose elements can be matched with those of the subset.

- Coconuts that are hairy and thick skinned

- Coconuts that are large but not thick skinned

- Coconuts that are hairy and small

- Coconuts that are hairy, thick skinned, and large

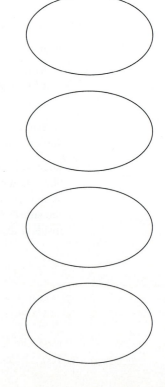

■ Coconuts that are hairy or thick skinned or both

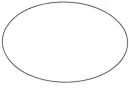

■ Coconuts that are large, smooth, and thin skinned

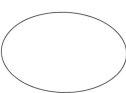

25. Norum tends the sheep in the same village where Roga lives. He has classified the set X of these sheep into those that are black (versus white) and those that are long-haired (versus short-haired). He has found that *the following*:

■ The set B of black sheep matches with the set (of stones)

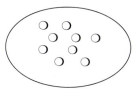

■ The set L of long-haired sheep matches with the set

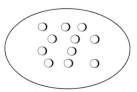

■ The set of sheep that are both short haired and white matches with the set

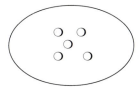

■ The set of sheep that are both short haired and black matches with the set

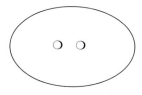

Norum made a big rectangle on the ground out of a rope loop. Into this rectangle he placed stones representing all his sheep. Two other smaller loops he made into circles. Inside the rectangle with one of these small loops he surrounded the stones that match with the elements of B; likewise, with the other loop he surrounded the stones that match with the elements of L. In the picture of the loops draw in the stones as they should be.

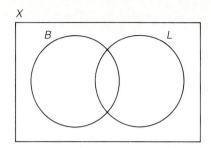

Use this picture to fill each empty balloon with stones that can be matched with the subset of X described verbally to its left.

(a)   Sheep that are both black and long haired

(b)   Sheep that are either black or short haired or both

(c)   All the sheep that Norum tends

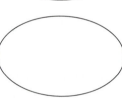

(d)   Sheep that are both long haired and white

26.   How many subsets does the following set have?

$\{a,b,c,d,e,f,g,h,i,j,k,l,m,n,o,p,q,r,s,t,u,v,w,x,y,z\}$

(*Hint:* Look for a pattern. For a start, list the subsets of each of the sets $\{a\}$, $\{a,b\}$, $\{a,b,c\}$, $\{a,b,c,d\}$ and count how many subsets each has. The answer to exercise 13 in the text may help.)

27.   As in exercise 20 of the text, translate each of the following statements into the language of sets using letters and symbols.
(a)   There are no pencils of mine in this box.
(b)   No sugar plums of mine are cigars.
(c)   The whole of my property that is not in this box consists of cigars.
     What is an appropriate universal set for these statements?
     As before, draw a diagram of sets corresponding to each of the three statements. Combine these pictures to conclude that
(d)   No pencils of mine are sugar plums.

ANSWERING QUESTIONS OF HOW MANY? OUR SYSTEM OF WRITTEN NUMERALS

C H A P T E R

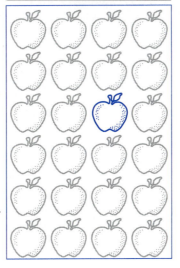

The goal of this chapter is to describe how our system of written numerals works. In subsequent chapters we will be discussing the methods we normally use for adding, subtracting, multiplying, and dividing whole numbers. Understanding these methods depends very much on how we represent numbers with written numerals. We show how this system of written numerals might have developed from basic needs and primitive solutions. We also look at other systems that have features in common with our own and can be used to illustrate how our methods for calculating work. Using these other systems will give us experiences similar to those of small children when they begin to use our own system.

The development begins with simple problems involving questions of How many? and with solutions to these that do not involve our number system but instead involve simpler systems based more directly on pairing and one-to-one correspondence. These "primitive" solutions could have been created either by young children or by people in a primitive culture. As we look at more complex problems in this development, it becomes apparent that more sophisticated tools are needed. In this hypothetical history these "more sophisticated tools" evolve into our number system.

At the same time we will see that some problems that we normally solve with our sophisticated tools can also be solved with primitive ones. A primitive solution may be more accessible, more natural, and more appropriate for a given child at his or her stage of development than the more sophisticated one.

ANSWERING QUESTIONS OF HOW MANY?

THE PENCIL PROBLEM

Katie is in kindergarten. She has been asked to hand out pencils to the students in her class: a pencil for each student. She wants to know the answers to these questions: Will there be enough pencils for everybody? (Will there be more people than pencils?) Will there be more pencils than people? Will there be the same number of pencils as people?

How can Katie answer these questions?

The typical adult response to this problem is to count the pencils, count the students, and compare the two numbers. Katie can count a little. But her experience with numbers is minimal. It is unlikely that the adult solution is available to her. There is an alternative solution that doesn't involve counting.

She takes the box of pencils and hands them out to all the members of the class, a pencil for each student. If she runs out of pencils before everybody gets one, then there are not enough pencils for everybody: There are more people than pencils. If she has pencils left over after everybody gets one, there are more pencils than people. If everybody gets a pencil and there are no pencils left over, then there are the same number of pencils as people.

The Mathematical Idea: Questions of How Many? Decided by Pairing

Katie was able to answer the questions Which are there more of, pencils or people? or Is there the same number of both? by *pairing* the pencils with the people in her class.

She was trying to make what is called a *one-to-one correspondence* between the set of pencils and the set of people.

PAIRING AND ONE-TO-ONE CORRESPONDENCE

Suppose you have two sets A and B. You select an element of A and *pair* it up with an element of B. Only one element of B can be paired with an element of A; only one element of A can be paired with an element of B. When all the elements of one of the two sets are used up, you have a *pairing* of A and B.

A *one-to-one correspondence* between sets A and B is a pairing of the elements of A with the elements of B so that each element of A is paired with an element of B and each element of B is paired with an element of A. No elements of A or B are unpaired. In this case you say that *A and B have the same number of elements.*

If you have a pairing of A and B in which every element of A is paired with one element of B and there are elements of B that have not been paired, then there are *more elements of B than elements of A.* If you have a pairing in which every element of B is paired with an element of A and there are elements of A that have not been paired, then there are *more elements of A than elements of B.*

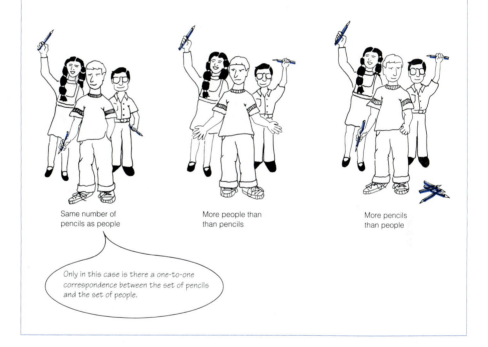

Same number of
pencils as people

More people than
than pencils

More pencils
than people

Only in this case is there a one-to-one
correspondence between the set of pencils
and the set of people.

EXERCISE 1. You live in a civilization that hasn't learned to count yet. You are responsible for supplying a horse to each adult in the village. You have gathered a lot of horses into your corral. How do you find out if you have enough?

Katie will be celebrating her fifth birthday soon. She wants to give each of her guests a birthday hat. Will she have enough? (Though she can count to 10 or so, that won't help. To her, counting is just a series of sounds she has memorized.) How can she decide if she has enough before the guests arrive?

A Solution to the Birthday Hat Problem

Katie could wait until her guests arrive, place a hat on each guest, and see if there are more guests than hats, more hats than guests, or the same number of hats as guests. However, Katie doesn't want to be caught short when her guests arrive; she wants to know *ahead of time* whether she has enough hats. She does know the names of her guests. As she says the name of each guest, she puts a hat aside. If she has used up all the hats before all the names have been spoken, there are not enough hats. If all the names have been spoken and a hat has been put aside for each, there are enough hats.

The Mathematical Idea: Pairing Using an Intermediary Set

To decide whether there are enough hats, Katie—unable to pair each hat with a guest in person—tried to pair each hat with the name of a guest. Katie knows something like the following: There is a one-to-one correspondence between the names of the guests and the guests themselves. She knows that if there is a one-to-one correspondence between hats and names, then there is a one-to-one correspondence between hats and guests; if there are more hats than names, then there are more hats than guests. In either case, there will be enough hats. By the same reasoning, she knows that if there are more names than hats, then there are more guests than hats. This kind of reasoning is valuable to Katie, since it is a lot more convenient to try to pair hats with names than to pair hats with guests.

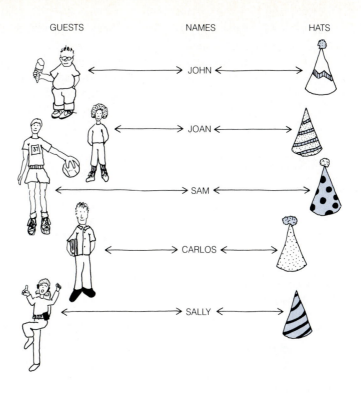

GUESTS	NAMES	HATS

JOHN

JOAN

SAM

CARLOS

SALLY

Erase **names** and get this pairing:

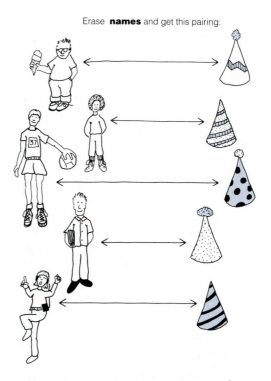

THE ERASER PROBLEM Katie's teacher has asked her to go to the school storeroom and get erasers for all the students in her class. The teacher wants each student to have just one eraser, with no erasers left over. How can Katie solve this problem?

Katie suggests to the teacher that she take all the students to the storeroom and pair each student with an eraser. The teacher frowns at this idea, so Katie must think of something else. Katie also considers pairing the students' names with erasers, but there are too many names for her to remember. She thinks: "I could carry something belonging to each person, such as a shoe or a sock ... Better yet, everybody can get a bead from the bead bin and give it to me. I'll take the beads to the storeroom and pair beads with erasers."

EXERCISE

2. The warriors in my primitive village need new spearheads, a spearhead for each warrior. Spearheads are made in the next village, and I plan a trip there to trade sheepskins for spearheads, one sheepskin for one spearhead. I want to be sure that I carry the right amount of sheepskins with me and I want to be sure that I bring back just the right amount of spearheads. How can I do this? (Remember, the people in my village can't count.)

THE RANCHERS' TRADE PROBLEM

Try this problem first!

Rancher Zor raises horses and Rancher Moq raises cattle. They meet in the village market to discuss a trade. They agree to trade some cattle for some horses, one cow for one horse. Zor doesn't want to bring to the village all the horses he wants to trade, because he may want to trade more horses than Moq has cattle to trade. And Moq doesn't want to bring all his cattle to the village for the same reason. But since they can't count, they need some way to compare the collection of cattle Moq wants to trade with the collection of horses Zor wants to trade. Help them solve this problem using pairing.

A Solution to the Ranchers'
Trade Problem

Zor says aloud: "What if I pair each horse I want to trade with a stone, one stone for one horse?" And Moq says: "What if I pair one cow I want to trade with a stone, one stone for one cow? Then we could try to pair my stones with your stones, stone for stone. If we pair all my stones with your stones and some of your stones are unpaired, then you will have some horses I cannot trade for. If we pair my stones with all your stones and some of my stones are left over, then I will have cattle that I cannot trade with you. If neither of these happens, then both of us will be able to trade all the cattle and horses we want to."

The Mathematical Idea: Convenient Sets for Pairing

The problems we have discussed so far in this chapter are ones of comparing the sizes of two sets using pairing. In the birthday problem, the eraser problem, and the ranchers' trade problem it was not convenient to pair the two sets directly. In each situation at least one of the sets to be compared was replaced by a convenient, intermediate set having the same number of elements. The intermediate set was used to make the comparison.

As the sets to be compared get bigger, another difficulty appears. The intermediate sets themselves become cumbersome. If Zor and Moq had had several hundred cattle and horses to trade, then the weight of the stones and the amount of work involved in pairing the two sets would have been too much. Something new is needed.

A natural response to this new problem would be to group stones together systematically and replace each group by another object. For example, Zor and Moq could group 10 stones together and replace the bunch of 10 stones by a stick. Every time they see a stick used in an intermediate set, they can pair it with another stick or with 10 stones.

EXERCISE **3.** Ugboo is trading sheepskins for Lagor's spears, one sheepskin for each spear. The collection of sticks and stones in the left-hand drawing is an intermediate set representing the sheepskins that Ugboo wants to trade. Each stone represents 1 sheepskin; each stick represents 10 stones. The collection of sticks and stones in the right-hand drawing represents the spears that Lagor wants to trade. Again, each stone represents 1 spear, and each stick represents 10 stones. By comparing the two collections, decide which set is biggest, the set of sheepskins or the set of spears.

The Mathematical Idea: Grouping

In exercise 3, a group of 10 stones is replaced by a stick. In this system, to compare two sets *A* and *B*, you first create two intermediate sets of stones, the first set in one-to-one correspondence with *A*, the second set in one-to-one correspondence with *B*. Second, in each of the two intermediate sets, group the stones into bunches of 10 and replace each bunch with a stick. (This grouping can be done while you form the one-to-one correspondence, much as we do when we tally: |||| |||| |||| |||| ||| . . ..) Each intermediate set has been replaced by a collection of sticks and stones. Finally, you make a pairing of the sticks and stones in one collection with the sticks and stones in the other. Pairing has become a bit more sophisticated.

REPLACEMENT NUMBERS

The scheme that we have described in which 10 stones can be replaced by a stick could be extended by allowing 10 sticks to be replaced by an arrowhead, and 10 arrowheads by something else, and so on.

In this system, 10 objects of lesser value can be exchanged for a single object of the next higher value, and vice versa. The number 10 is not special here: One civilization might use the number 12 and another might use the number 5. Historically, however, the numbers 5, 10, and 20 occur most often in this context because a person has 5 fingers on a hand, 10 fingers in all, and 20 digits in all on hands and feet.

In some systems of this kind, the numbers for replacement and exchange are not the same at all levels. For example, a twentieth-century coinage system used the "replacement" numbers: 4, 12, 5, 4. These are the replacement numbers for the old British farthing, pence, shilling, crown, pound system, in which

    1 pence = 4 farthings
    1 shilling = 12 pence
    1 crown = 5 shillings
    1 pound = 4 crowns

Citizens of the United States use a system of measuring for which the replacement numbers are 12, 3, 220, 8, and 3. These are the replacement numbers for our inch-foot-yard-furlong-mile-league system for linear measurement.

4. A common system of measurement in use throughout the world uses the replacement numbers 60, 60, 24, 7, and 52. What is the system of measurement, and what do the replacement numbers stand for?

5. What are the replacement numbers for the system of liquid measurement traditionally used in the United States?

3.2 THE DEVELOPMENT OF OUR HINDU-ARABIC, DECIMAL NUMERAL SYSTEM

The Counting Board

As an alternative to the stick-and-stone system, suppose that instead of replacing each group of 10 stones from your main pile of stones with a stick, you replace each group of 10 stones from the main pile with another stone placed in a second pile. In this system each set to be compared will have two piles associated with it, a "10s" pile and a main pile. You may want to separate the two piles with a line.

10s pile   Main pile

When the 10s pile gets large, you can create a third pile: You can replace each group of 10 stones from the 10s pile by putting a stone in a third pile, the "10s of 10s" (or "100s") pile. When the 10s of 10s pile gets large, you can replace each group of 10s of 10s stones in it with a stone placed in the "10s of 10s of 10s" (or "1000s") pile. And so on.

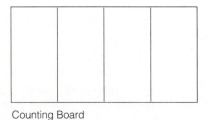

Counting Board

This system could easily have evolved into a *counting board*, a flat surface divided by parallel lines into separate spaces called *columns*. Stones are placed on the counting board between the lines, in the columns; the different columns correspond to the different piles in the system above. The main pile is the right-most column, the 10s pile goes in the column just to its left, and so on.

RULES FOR A COUNTING BOARD

A stone in the right-most column represents a single element. (Such a stone is called a *unit*.) A stone in any other column is worth 10 stones in the column just to its right. For example:

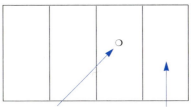

The stone here is worth 10 stones here.

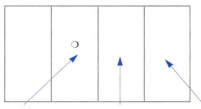

The stone here is worth 10 stones here or 100 stones here.

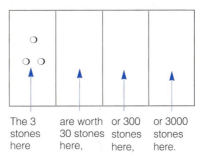

The 3 stones here   are worth 30 stones here,   or 300 stones here,   or 3000 stones here.

EXERCISE   6. Farida wants to trade her wheat for Milor's sheep—1 bushel of wheat for 1 sheep. Farida wants to know if she has enough wheat to obtain all Milor's sheep. Here are some clues.

Farida has this many bushels of wheat:

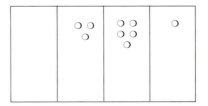

Milor has this many sheep:

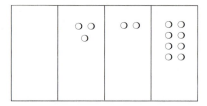

Solve this problem using the rules of the counting board.

Numbers and Numerals

Two sets that can be put in one-to-one correspondence have the same number of elements. What do we mean by the phrase "the number of elements in a set"? (A phrase that has the same meaning is "the number of a set.") When we say that the number of elements in a set A is 3, we mean that there is a one-to-one correspondence between A and the set $\{a,b,c\}$. The number 3 is the attribute in common to all sets for which there is a one-to-one correspondence with the set $\{a,b,c\}$. The number of a set S is the attribute in common to all sets for which there is a one-to-one correspondence with the set S.

We normally use the symbol 3 to represent the number 3. This symbol is called a *numeral* in our standard system of numerals, the Hindu-Arabic system. In any system of numerals there is a numeral for each number, and different numbers must be represented by different numerals.

A requirement for a good system of numerals is that given a set, you can easily figure out the numeral that represents the number of the set. One crude system of numerals is the one that represents a set by a set of stones in one-to-one correspondence with it.

Representing a Number Uniquely on a Counting Board

Another system of numerals involves representing a number by a collection of stones on a counting board, as we have just been discussing. For a counting board there are rules for passing from a set to the numeral that represents its number. Another requirement of a good system of numerals is that you can use it to compare numbers. Let's see how we can compare numbers using a counting board. Consider three numbers represented by the following counting board numerals:

Which numeral represents the largest number? You notice that in (a) and (c) there are columns in which there are more than 10 stones. You decide to reduce the number of stones used in the numerals as shown.

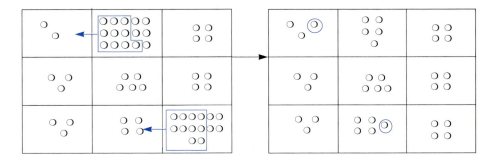

Thus all three numerals represent the same numbers! To tell at a glance which of two numerals represents the largest number, it might be useful to require that

- There be only one numeral representing a given number.
- Each numeral use the fewest possible number of stones.

The counting board system of numerals will satisfy these requirements if we adopt a rule.

NEW RULE FOR A COUNTING BOARD

The largest number of stones allowable in any column is 9.

As we mentioned earlier, a good system of numerals should have the ability to represent a given number without too much difficulty. To use a counting board to record a given number directly, suppose that you have a set of bushels (of wheat) and you want to represent its number on the counting board. You start with the right-hand column of the counting board and place a stone on the board, 1 for each bushel, as if you were pairing stones with bushels. When you have 10 stones in the right-hand column, you remove them and place 1 stone in the next column to the left. You keep doing this: For each bushel you place a stone in the right-hand column until you get 10, which you then remove and replace by a single stone in the column to its left. Whenever you accumulate 10 stones in *any* column, you immediately remove them and replace them with a single stone in the column just to its left.

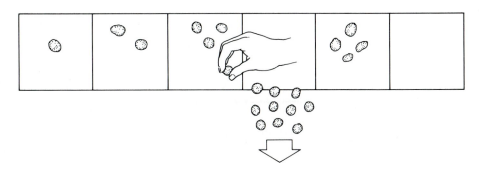

This rule works like an odometer in an automobile.

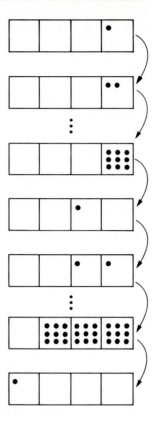

In the end you have represented the number so that there are no more than 9 stones in a column: The fewest possible stones are used (within the context of the original rules of the counting board), and this way of representing the quantity is unique: Two distinct numerals represent different numbers. You have also "counted" the bushels of wheat one by one, from whence the name, counting board.

FARIDA'S WHEAT PROBLEM Farida now has this many bushels of wheat:

Milor has this many sheep:

Farida wants to trade wheat for sheep—1 bushel for 1 sheep. Does she have enough wheat to buy all Milor's sheep?

A Solution to Farida's Farida thinks: "Knowing how to represent a number directly on the counting board
Wheat Problem by 'counting' also tells me which of two counting board numerals represents the larger number.

"As I count a number on the counting board, stones begin to occupy more and more of the columns to the left.

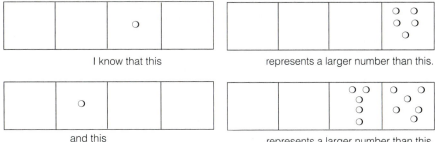

I know that this   represents a larger number than this.

and this   represents a larger number than this.

In fact, to decide which of two numerals represents the larger number, I start with the left-most column and compare the stones in that column from the two numerals. If they are the same, I move to the next column to the right. I keep doing this until I reach a column where the number of stones differs for the two numerals. The numeral with more stones there represents the larger number.

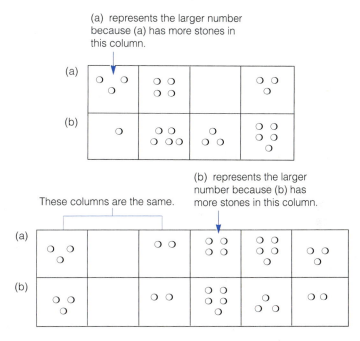

(a) represents the larger number because (a) has more stones in this column.

(b) represents the larger number because (b) has more stones in this column.

These columns are the same.

"Let's try this method with my bushels and Milor's sheep. Here they are, represented on a counting board.

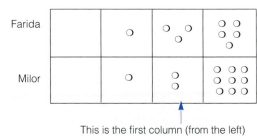

This is the first column (from the left) where the two numerals differ. Farida has more wheat because her numeral has more stones in this column.

Written Numerals Corresponding to Counting Board Numerals

The ancient Egyptian system of numerals is very close to the system of counting board numerals. The chart shows the system.

Unit = |

∩ = 10 | = 10 units

𝟗 = 10 ∩ = 100 units

↑ = 10 𝟗 = 1000 units

𝄞 = 10 ↑ = 10,000 units

◝ = 10 𝄞 = 100,000 units

👤 = 10 ◝ = 1,000,000 units

Take a look at some sample numerals and their Hindu-Arabic equivalents.

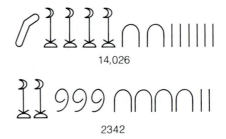

14,026

2342

A numeral in this system is called an *Egyptian numeral*.

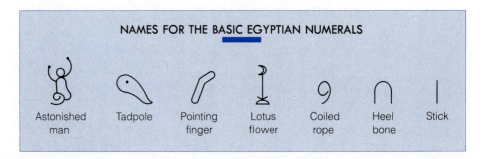

NAMES FOR THE BASIC EGYPTIAN NUMERALS

Astonished man	Tadpole	Pointing finger	Lotus flower	Coiled rope	Heel bone	Stick

It is easy to convert a counting board numeral to the Egyptian numeral representing the same number. (Two numerals, one from one numeral system and the other from another system, are *equivalent* if they represent the same number.) In fact, each of the columns of the counting board can be labeled with an Egyptian symbol so that each stone in that column represents the same number as the symbol.

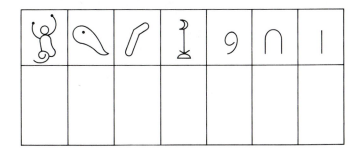

A counting board numeral consists of stones placed on a counting board. An Egyptian numeral is written. There are advantages to the latter. A written numeral is portable. You can use written numerals to keep permanent records of the numbers.

You may want to calculate with your numeral system. The Egyptian system is not very convenient for this. For example, multiplication of Egyptian numerals (using methods we use with our Hindu-Arabic numerals) would involve a lot of writing with a stylus on papyrus, a slow and tedious process. The Egyptian system was designed to record the outcomes of calculations, not to do the calculations. To calculate, Egyptians would have used a counting board, or something like it, by converting the Egyptian numerals to stones on the counting board, calculating there, then converting the counting board answer to the equivalent Egyptian numeral. The illustration shows two examples of the conversion of an Egyptian numeral to a counting board numeral.

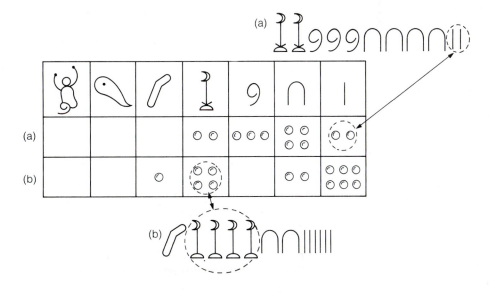

7. Write the Egyptian numeral equivalent to the following counting board numeral.

8. Two Egyptian numerals are shown. Draw pictures of the equivalent counting board numerals to decide which represents the larger number.

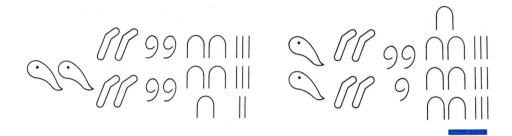

The Mathematical Idea: Egyptian Numerals, the Counting Board, and Our Own Decimal Numerals

The way an Egyptian might have used a counting board is similar to the way we use a calculator: We transfer our numerals to the calculator (we "punch in the numbers"), carry out calculations there, and, if we need to remember the results, we save the written numerals somehow. The counting board is an ancient calculator.

We do not normally use a counting board for making computations, but it can be useful for describing and understanding how our own system of written numerals works. It's easy for us to write the numeral in our system that corresponds to a quantity represented by stones on a counting board. For example, consider the following counting board setup.

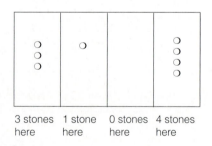

3 stones here   1 stone here   0 stones here   4 stones here

This counting board numeral is equivalent to the *decimal numeral* 3104. To go the other way, the counting board numeral equivalent to the decimal numeral 7065 is

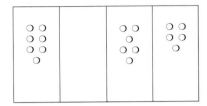

Going back and forth between counting board numerals and decimal numerals is so easy that it seems as if they were designed for each other. For an Egyptian to convert stones on a counting board into an Egyptian numeral, she has to remember which symbol goes with which column of the counting board: A stone in the third column from the right converts to φ; a stone in the sixth column converts to $\mathscr{C}$, and so on. For us, we have to remember the 10 digits to which each configuration of stones in a column converts.

STONES IN COLUMN	DECIMAL CONVERSION
	0
○	1
○ ○	2
○ ○ ○	3
•	•
•	•
•	•

A typical decimal numeral consists of a row of digits. In converting a counting board numeral to the equivalent decimal numeral and back, the columns of the counting board correspond to *places* (or positions) in this row of digits. Thus, if the fourth column from the right of the counting board has 5 stones in it, then the converted decimal numeral has a 5 in the fourth place from the right.

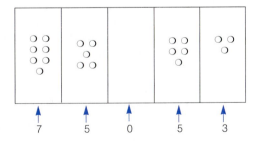

Each stone in the fourth column (from the right) represents the number one thousand. So 5 stones in the fourth column represents the number five thousand. However, 5 stones in the second column represents the number 5 tens (fifty). The symbol 5 in the numeral 75053 occurs at two different positions. It represents different numbers for each of the two occurrences. Because a given digit in a numeral represents a different number depending on its place in the row of digits, our system is called a *place value* system. The Egyptian system is not a place value system. For an Egyptian, the two symbols shown represent the same quantity.

The Egyptian digit 9 represents the number one hundred no matter what position it holds in the entire numeral. Furthermore, as a new column is added on the left of the counting board, a new Egyptian digit must be created to which a stone in that column can be converted. For a place value system, all that is needed is an additional place.

Our number words (or spoken numerals) correspond nicely to counting board numerals. In fact, if we label a column of the counting board with our word for the value of a stone occurring in that column, we would have

TEN THOUSANDS (10,000s)	THOUSANDS (1000s)	HUNDREDS (100s)	TENS (10s)	UNITS (1s)

These labels are also the names of the places of the digits in one of our written numerals. For example, 3154 is spoken as "three thousand, one hundred, five tens, four units." We don't quite say this, however. The word "unit" is dropped, and "five tens" has been condensed over the years to "fif-ty." So the spoken numeral equivalent to the written numeral 3154 is "three thousand one hundred fifty-four."

When there are no stones in a given column of the counting board, the digit 0 (zero) is placed in the corresponding position in the decimal numeral. In a place value system, it is important to have a symbol indicating no stones in a column of the counting board. In the Egyptian system there is no analogue to our written 0. There is no need for it. In our spoken numeral, no stones in a column is indicated by omitting the name of the column. We say "three thousand one hundred four" for 3104—and understand by omission that there are no tens. We say "three thousand one hundred forty" for 3140—and understand by omission that there are no units. The Egyptians write

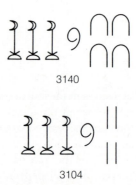

3140

3104

Our decimal system of numerals originated in India, was used in Arabic countries beginning in the eleventh century A.D. and was introduced into Western Europe by Fibonacci, a thirteenth-century Italian. The system is sometimes referred to as the *Hindu-Arabic system*.

We all know that the decimal numeral 3104 can be rewritten, using our symbols for addition and multiplication as $3104 = 3 \times 1000 + 1 \times 100 + 0 \times 10 + 4$. Similarly, $5673 = 5 \times 1000 + 6 \times 100 + 7 \times 10 + 3$.

These are examples of *expanded form* for a decimal numeral. They are possible because decimal numerals are a place value system and show in symbolic form the close connection of decimal numerals and counting board numerals. The standard methods we use for adding, subtracting, multiplying, and dividing depend heavily on being able to write decimal numerals in expanded form. Thus we will be able to use counting board numerals to show how these operations work in a tangible way, using stones instead of the decimal digits.

We will also use *expanded form on a counting board*, in which the digits of a numeral are written directly on a counting board.

	10,000s	1000s	100s	10s	1s
5673 =		5	6	7	3

EXERCISE

9. Write the expanded form for each of these decimal numerals:
   (a) 165   (b) 4073   (c) 17,078   (d) 245,673

Place Value Blocks

Another system for representing numbers that is close to our written numerals and that we will use in subsequent chapters uses a set of blocks of different sizes. These are called *place value blocks* and are related as follows:

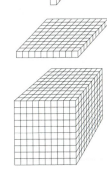

The unit is a centimeter cube:

A *long* is equal to 10 units:

A *flat* is equal to 10 longs:

A *cube* is equal to 10 flats:

The following table shows conversions of place value blocks and our numerals.

PLACE VALUE BLOCK	DECIMAL NUMERAL

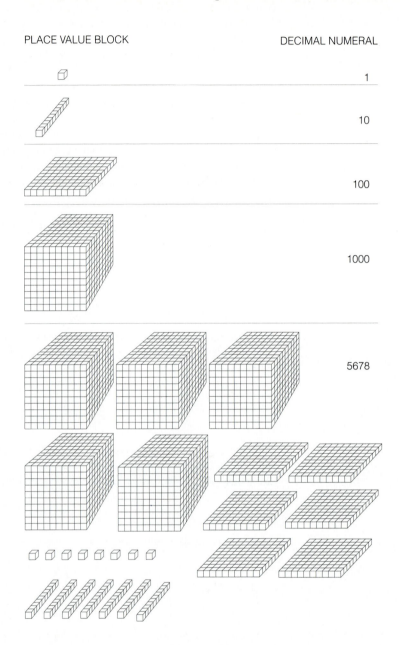

10. Write the decimal numeral equivalent to the collection of place value blocks shown below.

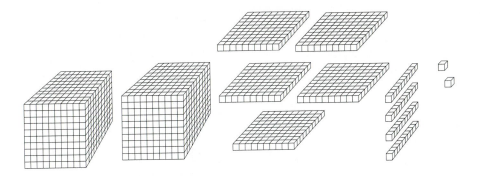

11. Draw the place value blocks equivalent to each of the following decimal numerals.
(a) 27   (b) 270   (c) 207   (d) 456   (e) 5063

The Abacus

The *abacus* is a device closely related to the counting board. There are many types of abaci; we shall describe a particularly simple version. Instead of the columns of the counting board, this abacus has wires or rods attached vertically to a board. The base of the board rests flat on the ground.

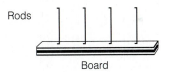

Beads are used instead of stones, and these slide on the rods.

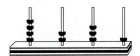

The first rod (on the right) of the abacus corresponds to the first column (on the right) of the counting board. The second rod corresponds to the second column, and so on. Thus, the counting board numeral and the abacus numeral shown in the illustration are equivalent.

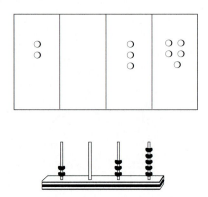

THE RUSSIAN ABACUS

This Russian abacus consists of beads on wires stretched from the top side of a frame to the bottom. There are 10 beads on each wire. The illustration shows how to "set" the decimal number 5,123,012 on the abacus.

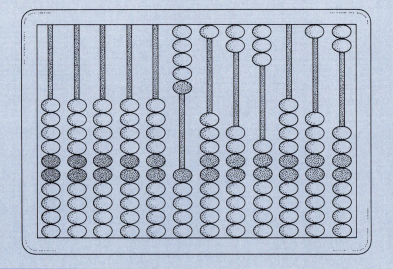

A GALLERY OF COMPUTATIONAL DEVICES

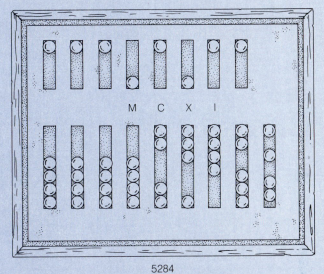

5284
A Roman abacus

Stones (*calculi*) slide in grooves carved on a board, making the Roman abacus as much a counting board as an abacus. (The two right-most grooves are reserved for fractions.)

European counting boards of the Renaissance

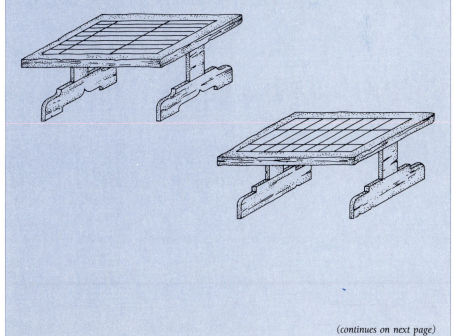

(continues on next page)

(continued from page 115)

The woodcut from the Renaissance shows two people calculating, one using a counting board, the other using written numerals. The female figure in the background personifies Arithmetic and appears to be deciding the debate between those on the one hand who think the abacus is the best way to calculate and those on the other hand who think the newly introduced (into Western Europe) Arabic numerals with pencil and paper are the way to go.

(Cartoon drawn by Ellen Champagne.)

In the cartoon, a takeoff on the Renaissance woodcut, the debate is between those who think the personal computer or electric calculator (modern-day abacus) is the best way to calculate and those who think Arabic numerals with pencil and paper are the way to go.

Japanese abacus (twentieth century)

For addition and subtraction, it is faster for experienced operators to use a modern abacus than it is to use either standard paper and pencil methods or a hand-held calculator.

EXERCISES

12. Write the decimal numeral equivalent to the following abacus numeral.

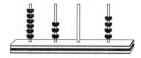

13. Draw the abacus numeral equivalent to the decimal numeral 3506.

Base Systems

For our counting board a stone in a given column is worth 10 stones in the column just to its right. This is called a *base 10* counting board. One can imagine another counting board for which a stone in a given column is worth *B* stones in the column just to its right. Such a counting board is called a *base B* counting board. One can also have a base *B* abacus. (The abacus described above is, of course, a base 10 abacus.) A system of numerals closely tied to such a counting board is called a *base system*. The base of the corresponding counting board is called the *base* of the system of numerals. The common base of the Egyptian system, our numeral system, and place value blocks is 10.*

Our system of written numerals is called a *decimal* system because it is a base 10 system. (*Decem* is the Latin word for "ten.")

Stick Numerals

Besides working with the counting board, expanded form on a counting board, place value blocks, and an abacus, we will also work with another numeral system.

Imagine a base 5 abacus. For this abacus

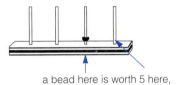

a bead here is worth 5 here,

a bead here is worth 5 here, and

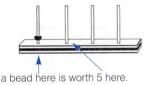

a bead here is worth 5 here.

Each bead on the first rod corresponds to an element of the set; each bead on any other rod is worth 5 beads on the rod just to its right. For example,

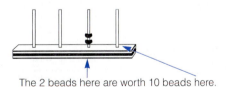

The 2 beads here are worth 10 beads here.

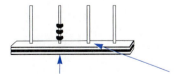

The 3 beads here are worth 15 beads here.

---

* There are place value blocks for bases other than 10. In the lab manual designed to accompany this text, there are base 5, 6, and 10 place value blocks to cut out and assemble.

Let us create a place value system of written numerals closely related to these base 5 abacus numerals. A written numeral will look very much like the equivalent abacus numeral. The table gives the "digits":

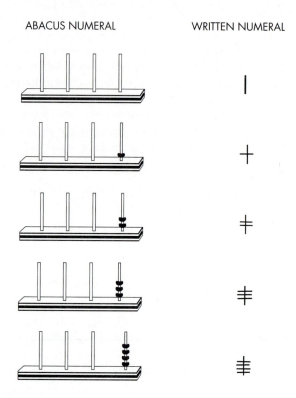

ABACUS NUMERAL · WRITTEN NUMERAL

The next table gives some equivalents.

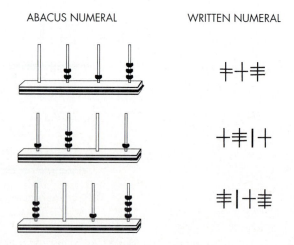

ABACUS NUMERAL · WRITTEN NUMERAL

We will call these written numerals *stick numerals*.

Why Stick Numerals?

In the next few chapters we will be discussing methods for adding, subtracting, multiplying, and dividing whole numbers. In these discussions we will use stick numerals in addition to counting boards and our own numerals. We will use stick numerals because they are very much like our own. We will discuss methods for computing with stick numerals that are very much like standard methods for computing with our own numerals. Although stick numerals and the methods for working with them will seem strange, there is a purpose to using them. Their use will enable us to experience feelings similar to those felt by small children when they begin to work with our standard numerals—a system that feels strange to *them*.

In working with stick numerals it is important to remember that like the base 5 abacus from which they came, the system of stick numerals is a base 5 place value system. There are some important facts to remember.

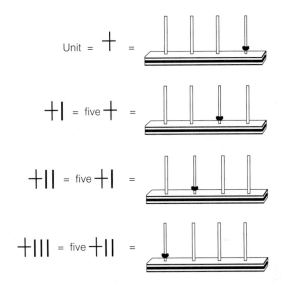

To get a feel for stick numerals and how they work, look at the following equivalents between stick numerals and decimal numerals.

0	1	2	3	4	5	6	7	8	9
│	┼	╪	╪	╪	┼│	┼┼	┼╪	┼╪	┼╪

Each bead on the second rod is worth 5, so the following number is equivalent to 10.

A bead on the third rod is worth 5 on the second rod and each bead on the second rod is worth 5. So a bead on the third rod is worth $5 \times 5 = 25$. Thus, the following numeral is equivalent to 75.

The following numeral is equivalent to $75 + 10 + 4 = 89$.

$$\text{≢╪≢}$$

The numeral ╪≢╪ is equivalent to $2 \times 25 + 3 \times 5 + 2 = 50 + 15 + 2 = 67$. Note the similarity to expanded form for our numerals.

Converting stick numerals to decimal numerals may help in understanding stick numerals. However, frequently we will work entirely within the stick numeral system and not resort to conversion from that system to ours.

Counting with stick numerals, like counting on a counting board and counting with our own numerals, works like an automobile odometer.

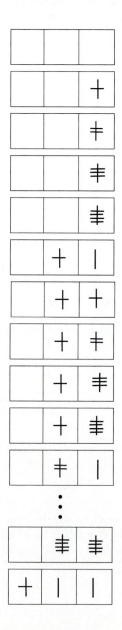

14. The picture below shows a farmer's calendar from the city of Styria (now in Austria) in the late Middle Ages.

The letters stand for days of the week. The symbols along the very bottom are numerals equivalent to

2 10 18 5 15 4 12 1 9 3 11 21 8 16 5 13

How does this numeral system work?

15. Represent the following collection of stones as a stick numeral. (No fair using decimal numerals as an crutch! Count using stick numerals as described in the text.)

16. For each of the following pairs of stick numerals, decide which of the two numerals represents the larger number. (No fair converting to decimal numerals! Refer to the method of comparing with base 10 counting board numerals.)

╪╪|╪ vs. ╪╪╪| ╪‖╪ vs. ╪╪╪╪

╪╪|╪ vs. ╪╪╪|

Modeling Standard Numerals

Counting boards, abaci, and place value blocks make the standard numeral system concrete and tangible and thus help us to understand how it works. These tangible systems are models for ours and will enable us later to use the problem-solving strategy, *make a model,* when working with our numerals.

When we say that the number of elements in a set S is 3, we mean that there is a one-to-one correspondence between S and the set $\{1,2,3\}$. We write $n(S) = 3$ to express this fact. Thus $n(\{a,b,c\}) = n(\{@, \#, \&\}) = n(\{1,2,3\}) = 3$. Following are some definitions related to this notation.

DEFINITIONS RELATED TO NUMBERS

If S is a set, then $n(S)$ denotes the *number of S,* or the *number of elements in S.* If S is in one-to-one correspondence with the set $\{1,2,\ldots,N\}$, then we write $n(S) = N$.

   If ϕ is the empty set, the set with no elements, then we say that the number of elements in ϕ is zero and write $n(\phi) = 0$.

   A *natural number* is any member of the set $\{1,2,3,\ldots\}$.

   A *whole number* is any member of the set $\{0,1,2,3,\ldots\}$.

Exponential Notation

The numbers 10, 100, 1000, 10,000, ... are important to our system of numerals. They are related as shown.

$$100 = \text{ten 10s} = 10 \times 10$$
$$1000 = \text{ten 100s} = 10 \times 100$$
$$10,000 = \text{ten 1000s} = 10 \times 1000$$
$$100,000 = \text{ten 10,000s} = 10 \times 10000$$

And so on.

We can also write them this way.

$$100 = 10 \times 10$$
$$1000 = 10 \times 10 \times 10$$
$$10,000 = 10 \times 10 \times 10 \times 10$$
$$100,000 = 10 \times 10 \times 10 \times 10 \times 10$$

And so on.

There is a shorthand way to write these numbers using the convention of exponential notation.

EXPONENTIAL NOTATION

For any number N,

$$\underbrace{N \times N \times \cdots \times N}_{p \text{ times}} = N^p.$$

The number p is called the *exponent* of N^p.

Using exponential notation, we can write

$$10 = 10^1$$
$$100 = 10^2$$
$$1000 = 10^3$$
$$10000 = 10^4$$
$$100000 = 10^5$$

and, in general,

$$\underbrace{100\ldots00}_{n\text{ zeros}} = 10^n.$$

The numbers 10^n are called the *powers of 10*. Note the economy of symbols achieved using exponential notation.

How does expanded form for a whole number look when exponential notation is used?

$$5843 = 5 \times 10^3 + 8 \times 10^2 + 4 \times 10^1 + 3.$$
$$9{,}234{,}705 = 9 \times 10^6 + 2 \times 10^5 + 3 \times 10^4 + 4 \times 10^3 + 7 \times 10^2 + 0 \times 10^1 + 5.$$

EXERCISES

17. Write the numbers in exponential notation as powers of 10:
   (a) 1 million (b) 1 billion (c) 1 trillion

18. Write the numbers in expanded form using exponential notation:
   (a) 12,378 (b) 508,122 (c) 89,142,693

3.4   EXTENDING THE IDEAS: OTHER NUMERAL SYSTEMS

Bases Other than 10

Recall the stick numerals and their equivalents, shown in the table.

STICK NUMERAL	DECIMAL NUMERAL	DECIMAL NUMERAL IN EXPONENTIAL NOTATION
+I	5	5^1
+II	25	5^2
+III	125	5^3
+IIII	625	5^4
+IIIII	3125	5^5
+IIIIII	15,625	5^6
$\vdots$	$\vdots$	$\vdots$

The stick numeral ⫢⫲|⫢† converts to a decimal numeral as shown.

$$⫢⫲|⫢† = 3 \times 5^4 + 2 \times 5^3 + 0 \times 5^2 + 4 \times 5^1 + 1.$$

The expression on the right-hand side, using exponential notation, allows you to determine the equivalent decimal numeral.

Commonly, the expression $3 \times 5^4 + 2 \times 5^3 + 0 \times 5^2 + 4 \times 5^1 + 1$ is written 32041_{five}. The numeral 32041_{five} is called a *standard* base 5 numeral. Of course, a stick numeral is also a base 5 numeral. However, the standard base 5 numerals are the ones you are most likely to encounter in other sources. Incidentally, 34_{five} is read as "three four, base five," *not* "thirty-four, base five." Thirty-four means three 10s and 4, not three 5s and 4. Likewise, 201_{five} is read as "two zero one, base five" (and also as "two oh one, base five").

The notation for standard base 5 numerals is commonly used for other bases. For example,

$$57032_{\text{eight}} = 5 \times 8^4 + 7 \times 8^3 + 0 \times 8^2 + 3 \times 8^1 + 2.$$

The numeral on the left is pronounced "five seven zero three two, base eight." The $5, 7, 0, 3,$ and 2 are the *digits* of this base 8 numeral. The possible digits of a standard base 8 numeral are 0, 1, 2, 3, 4, 5, 6, and 7, just as the possible digits of a standard base 5 numeral are 0, 1, 2, 3, and 4.

Notice that if you multiply out the right-hand side of the 57032_{eight} equation, you get

$$5 \times 8^4 + 7 \times 8^3 + 0 \times 8^2 + 3 \times 8^1 + 2$$
$$= 5 \times 4096 + 7 \times 512 + 0 \times 64 + 3 \times 8 + 2$$
$$= 20{,}480 + 3584 + 0 + 24 + 2$$
$$= 24{,}090.$$

Thus, $57032_{\text{eight}} = 24090_{\text{ten}}$. The $_{\text{ten}}$ usually is omitted from a base 10 numeral.

Another example is

$$100101_{\text{two}} = 1 \times 2^5 + 0 \times 2^4 + 0 \times 2^3 + 1 \times 2^2 + 0 \times 2^1 + 1.$$

Multiplying out the right-hand side of this equation, we get

$$1 \times 2^5 + 0 \times 2^4 + 0 \times 2^3 + 1 \times 2^2 + 0 \times 2^1 + 1$$
$$= 1 \times 32 + 0 \times 16 + 0 \times 8 + 1 \times 4 + 0 \times 2 + 1$$
$$= 32 + 4 + 1$$
$$= 37.$$

That is, $100101_{\text{two}} = 37$. Notice that the digits of a standard base 2 numeral are 0 and 1.

Both base 8 and base 2 numerals are used internally in computers. Another base used by computers is base 16. Since a base 16 system of numerals needs 16 digits, we will need some additional digits in addition to the traditional ones. The digits commonly used for base 16 numerals are 0, 1, 2, 3, 4, 5, 6, 7, 8, 9, A, B, C, D, E, and F. In this system $A_{\text{sixteen}} = 10$, $B_{\text{sixteen}} = 11$, $C_{\text{sixteen}} = 12$, and so on, for example,

$$7 \times 16^4 + 11 \times 16^3 + 0 \times 16^2 + 14 \times 16^1 + 5 = 7B0E5_{\text{sixteen}}.$$

19. Find the base 10 numeral equivalent to $9A3F_{sixteen}$.

20. Find the base 10 numeral equivalent to 11001011_{two}.

21. Find the base 10 numeral equivalent to 605_{seven}.

EXAMPLES OF SPOKEN SYSTEMS OF NUMERALS

	WORD	MEANING
1	tai	
2	lua	
3	tolu	
4	vari	
5	luna	hand
6	otai	other one
7	olua	other two
8	otolu	other three
9	ovair	other four
10	lua luna	two hands

A base 5 spoken system of numerals: the Api language of the New Hebrides.

1	urapun	3	okosa-urapun	5	okosa-okosa-urapun
2	okosa	4	okosa-okosa	6	okosa-okosa-okosa

A base 2 spoken system of numerals: a western tribe of Torres Straits.

Converting from One Base to Another

As you can see from the previous discussion, it is easy to convert a numeral in a base other than 10 to a standard base 10 numeral. It is also easy to convert from a base 10 numeral. Let's do an example.

Let's write the base 6 numeral for 967 (base 10 numeral). First divide 967 by 6 getting a quotient and remainder.

$$\begin{array}{r} 161 \text{ R}1 \\ 6 \overline{)967} \end{array}$$

(If you have 967 unit place value blocks and convert as many of them as you can into base 6 *longs*, you get 161 longs with 1 unit left over.) Then do the same thing with 161: Divide it by 6 getting a quotient and remainder.

$$\frac{26 \text{ R}5}{6 \overline{\smash{)}161}}$$

$$\frac{\text{R}1}{6 \overline{\smash{)}967}}$$

If you convert the 161 base 6 *longs* into base 6 *flats*, you get 26 flats with 5 longs left over. Then do the same thing with 26: Divide it by 6 getting a quotient and a remainder.

$$\frac{4 \text{ R}2}{6 \overline{\smash{)}26}}$$

$$\frac{\text{R}5}{6 \overline{\smash{)}161}}$$

$$\frac{\text{R}1}{6 \overline{\smash{)}967}}$$

If you convert the base 6 flats into base 6 *cubes*, you get 4 cubes with 2 flats left over. Since the last quotient you get is less than the base, you are finished. This last quotient and the previous remainders are your digits.

$$967_{\text{ten}} = 4251_{\text{six}}.$$

EXERCISES

22. Find the base 6 numeral equivalent to 1425.

23. Find the base 8 numeral equivalent to 967.

24. Find the base 2 numeral equivalent to 967.

Numeral Systems of Historical Importance

The chart on page 127 illustrates several examples of different numeral systems used historically.

EQUIVALENT HISTORICAL NUMERALS

HINDU-ARABIC	GREEK	ROMAN	CHINESE	EGYPTIAN	BABYLONIAN	HINDU-ARABIC	GREEK	ROMAN	CHINESE	EGYPTIAN	BABYLONIAN
1	α	I				70	ο	LXX			
2	β	II				80	π	LXXX			
3	γ	III				90	ϟ	XC			
4	δ	IV				100	ρ	C			
5	ε	V				200	σ	CC			
6	ϛ	VI				300	τ	CCC			
7	ζ	VII				400	υ	CD			
8	η	VIII				500	φ	D			
9	θ	IX				600	χ	DC			
10	ι	X				700	ψ	DCC			
20	κ	XX				800	ω	DCCC			
30	λ	XXX				1000	‚α	M			
40	μ	XL									
50	ν	L									
60	ξ	LX									

Babylonian Numerals

The Babylonian system, in use before 2000 B.C., is of particular interest and is worthy of more explanation. It is a base 60 place value system. There are 59 "digits," each one made of the two symbols ⟨ and ⟨. Some examples are shown in the chart of equivalent historical numerals. Here are some more.

BABYLONIAN "DIGIT"	EQUIVALENT DECIMAL NUMERAL
⟨𐎝	13
⟨ 𐎝 ⟨ 𐎝 𐎝	37
⟨ 𐎝 ⟨ 𐎝 ⟨ 𐎝	59

The Babylonian digit 𐎝 is equivalent to 1, and the digit ⟨ is equivalent to 10. The other 57 nonzero digits are constructed from these. For example, to construct the Babylonian digit equivalent to the decimal numeral 48, take 4 Babylonian digits for 10 and 8 Babylonian digits for 1 and put them together in the following way.

To construct the Babylonian digit equivalent to the decimal numeral 25, take 2 Babylonian digits for 10 and 5 Babylonian digits for 1 and put them together in the following manner.

These two examples and the other Babylonian digits that appear in the chart should give you a good idea of what the pattern is.

A typical Babylonian numeral will be a sequence of these digits. For example, the Babylonian numeral has the digits [cuneiform digits]

in succession. The decimal equivalents, in succession, are 17, 34, 42.

The Babylonian numeral [cuneiform numeral]

has the digits   [cuneiform digits], [cuneiform], [cuneiform], and [cuneiform]

in succession. The decimal equivalents, in succession, are 7, 23, 5, and 38.

Here are two examples of conversions of Babylonian numerals to our standard base 10 numerals.

[cuneiform numeral]

$$= 17 \times 60^2 + 34 \times 60^1 + 42.$$

[cuneiform numeral]

$$= 7 \times 600^3 + 23 \times 60^2 + 5 \times 60^1 + 38.$$

In early uses of Babylonian numerals there was no symbol equivalent to our zero to "hold a place." One would have had to decide from the context which was meant by the symbol ⟨cuneiform⟩. However, around 400 B.C. the Greeks began to use the symbol o (this is the Greek letter *omicron*) as a place holder. Thus 60 would be written ⟨cuneiform⟩o and 1 would be written ⟨cuneiform⟩. Moreover,

[cuneiform numeral] o [cuneiform]

$$= 23 \times 60^2 + 0 \times 60^1 + 11.$$

As you can see from the chart of equivalent historical numerals, the Greeks of classical time had their own system of written numerals. However, whenever involved calculations had to be made, the Greeks used the Babylonian system because it was much more efficient. This is what the mathematician Archimedes (287–212 B.C.) and the astronomer Ptolemy (2d century A.D.) did. It is likely that the Babylonian system was developed because of the need to make large numbers of astronomical calculations. The number of minutes in an hour (60), the number of seconds in a minute (60), and the number of angle degrees in a circle (360) are all vestiges within our own measurement systems of the Babylonian base 60 system.

THE EVOLUTION OF WRITTEN DIGITS IN THE HINDU-ARABIC NUMERAL SYSTEM

The chart* shows the evolution of the written forms of digits for the Hindu-Arabic system of numerals. The changes are due mostly to the fact that they were written by hand. In the sixteenth century, just after the invention of the printing press, the forms of the digits stabilized to forms very much like what they are today. The symbol for zero (a place holder) is presumably of Greek origin from around 400 B.C.

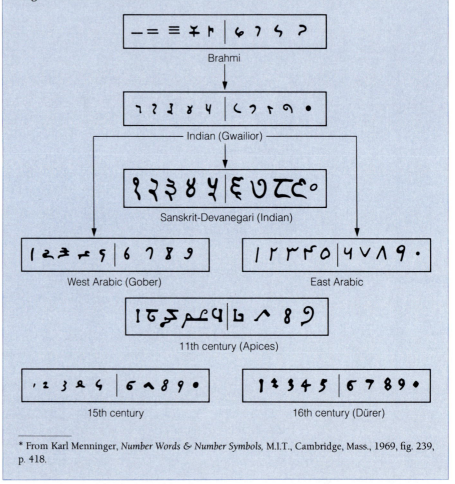

* From Karl Menninger, *Number Words & Number Symbols*, M.I.T., Cambridge, Mass., 1969, fig. 239, p. 418.

EXERCISES

25. Convert the following Babylonian numerals into standard decimal numerals.

(a)   (b)   (c)

(d)   (e)

26. Convert the expressions in decimal numerals to Babylonian numerals.
    (a) $12 \times 60 + 32$ (b) $23 \times 60^2 + 44 \times 60 + 7$
    (c) $7 \times 60^3 + 15 \times 60^2 + 39$

LOOKING AHEAD: THE NUMBER LINE
AND ORDER PROPERTIES OF THE WHOLE NUMBERS

The Comparison Problem

The children in the third grade were comparing the number of marbles owned by different students in the class. They had gathered the following data.

PERSON	NUMBER OF MARBLES OWNED
John	16
Amy	21
Carlos	33
Sally	28
Abe	19
Sonya	40

The students could rank the people according to how many marbles they owned. But they wanted a way to *visualize* these numbers; they wanted to *draw a picture* showing how much more one person had than another.

After some thought, the students came up with an idea. Along the bottom of a large piece of paper they drew a line and marked equally spaced dots, which they labeled with numerals in order from left to right.

16 17 18 19 20 21 22 23 24 25 26 27 28 29 30 31 32 33 34 35 36 37 38 39 40

Then, above the numeral representing the number of marbles that a person owned, they wrote the owner's name.

John . . . . Abe . . . Amy . . . . Sally . . . . . Carlos . . . . Sonya
16 17 18 19 20 21 22 23 24 25 26 27 28 29 30 31 32 33 34 35 36 37 38 39 40

This device gave them a visual way to compare the number of marbles different people owned. For example, of two people, the one whose name appeared on the right was the one with more marbles. Also, reading the names from right to left gave them a ranking of people according to how many marbles each owned, the person with the most marbles first. Finally, they could see that certain pairs in this ranking were closer than others. For example, Abe and Amy ranked next to each other but were "closer" than Sonya and Carlos who also ranked next to each other.

The Mathematical Idea: The Number Line

The students in the third grade created a useful device for visualizing whole numbers and for comparing a collection of them. What the students constructed is a piece of the *number line*.

0 1 2 3 4 5 6 7 8 9 10 11 12 13 14 15

A line is drawn; equally spaced dots are placed on the line and are labeled successively with the numbers 0, 1, 2, 3, ...

Every whole number corresponds to a point on the number line. (At least this is theoretically so, given that the line you have drawn can be extended indefinitely to the right.) Given a pair of whole numbers A and B on the number line, it is easy to tell which is bigger: The one on the right is bigger.

We will use the number line in later chapters in order to visualize whole numbers and the operations on them.

EXERCISES

27. Here is a table giving the distances (in millions of miles) from the Sun to each of the planets in the solar system.

PLANET	DISTANCE FROM SUN
Mercury	36
Venus	67
Earth	93
Mars	142
Jupiter	483
Saturn	887
Uranus	1783
Neptune	2794
Pluto	3666

Arrange these numbers on a number line. [You will have to decide on a *scale,* a length that represents 1 (million miles), in order to get all the distances on the line and in the right place.]

28. Draw a number line on which to place the numbers 1, 10^1, 10^2, 10^3, and 10^4. (As in exercise 27, you will have to decide on a scale.)

Order of Whole Numbers

As we have seen, given two numbers, it is frequently important to know whether they are equal and if they aren't equal which of the two is bigger. This is an issue of what is called the *order* of the whole numbers. Underlying this is a fundamental fact that we all know.

TRICHOTOMY OF ORDER FOR WHOLE NUMBERS

Given two whole numbers A and B, one and only one of the following assertions is true:

A is equal to B.
A is bigger than B.
B is bigger than A.

Given two whole numbers, we have several methods for deciding which of the three assertions is true. First, if we know the points on the number line corresponding to the two numbers, then the discussion in the previous paragraph tells us how to settle the issue. Second, earlier in this chapter we discussed how, given the decimal numerals representing the numbers, to decide whether they were equal and, if different, which represented the larger quantity. Third, if the two numbers are the number of elements in two sets, then we can decide by pairing the elements of the two sets. Because the order of a pair of whole numbers is such an important concept, we frequently use symbolic abbreviations.

ABBREVIATIONS FOR ORDER OF WHOLE NUMBERS

For whole numbers A and B

$$A = B$$

means that A *is equal to B.*

$$A > B$$

means that A *is greater than B.*

$$A < B$$

means that A *is less than B.*

$$A \geq B$$

means that A *is greater than or equal to B.*

$$A \leq B$$

means that A *is less than or equal to B.*

Trichotomy now has the following look.

TRICHOTOMY USING SYMBOLS

Given whole numbers A and B, one and only one of the following assertions must be true:

$$A = B.$$
$$A > B.$$
$$A < B.$$

An important property of order is transivity.

TRANSITIVITY OF ORDER FOR WHOLE NUMBERS

Suppose that A, B, and C are whole numbers and you know that $A > B$ and $B > C$. You can conclude that $A > C$.

If D, E, and F are whole numbers and you know that $D > E$ and $E > F$, the two facts are frequently summarized $D > E > F$.

Following are some examples of the use of these symbol abbreviations.

1. If A is the number of automobile steering wheels and B is the number of ordinary working automobiles, then $A \geq B$. (You may also write $B \leq A$ to mean the same thing.)

2. Smithtown School District mandates that no classroom have more than 30 students. If Mr. Bailey's class has A students and his class is not in violation of the mandate, then $A \leq 30$. If Mrs. Jones's class has C students and her class is in violation of the mandate, then $C > 30$. If the maximum number of allowable students in a class is B, then $B = 30$.

3. $12{,}340 > 12{,}304 > 12{,}034 > 10{,}234 > 1{,}234$.

EXERCISE

29. For each of the following statements about a pair of numbers A and B, decide which is most appropriate: $A = B$, $A < B$, $A \leq B$, $A > B$, or $A \geq B$.
   (a) $A =$ number of lived-in houses in Central City; $B =$ number of people in Central City
   (b) $A =$ number of baby buggies in Central City; $B =$ number of children under 4 in Central City
   (c) $A =$ number of toothbrushes in Central City; $B =$ number of people in Central City
   (d) $A =$ number of post offices in Central City; $B =$ number of post office employees in Central City

3.6   SUMMARY OF IMPORTANT IDEAS AND TECHNIQUES

- Evolution of our number system from primitive methods of pairing the elements of two sets

- Pairing the elements of two sets and one-to-one correspondence between two sets

- How to decide by pairing the elements of two sets whether one of the sets has more elements than, the same number of elements as, or fewer elements than the other

- Stages for making pairing of the elements of two sets easier
   Using convenient, intermediate sets
   Grouping the elements of an intermediate set
   Creation of a numeral system, a device for representing the numbers of elements in sets

- Different kinds of numeral systems
   Stones on a counting board
   Egyptian numerals
   Beads on an abacus
   Place value blocks
   Hindu-Arabic numerals
   Stick numerals

- Features of numeral systems
   Comparing sizes of numbers using numerals
   Each number having a unique numeral
   Counting using a numeral system

Place value numeral systems: counting board; abacus; Hindu-Arabic numerals; stick numerals; base B numeral systems; standard base B numerals; expanded form (for standard base B numerals); and expanded form on a counting board

- Definitions of whole number and natural number
- For set S, $n(S)$ as the number of elements in S
- Exponential notation; expanded form using exponential notation
- Converting standard numerals from one base to another
- Numeral systems of historical interest—Babylonian numerals
- Visualizing whole numbers using the number line; some order properties of whole numbers

PROBLEM SET

PRACTICING
SKILLS

1. A certain shepherd wants to be sure that he has the same number of sheep when he brings them in from pasture in the evening as he had when he let them out for pasture in the morning. How can he do this even though he knows nothing about counting?

2. Here are some pairs of (base 10) counting boards. The stones on each counting board represent a number. Some boards do not satisfy the "new" rule: There are columns with more than 9 stones in them. Put each board in compliance with the rule but make sure that it still represents the same number as before. Indicate which board of the pair represents the larger number.

(a)

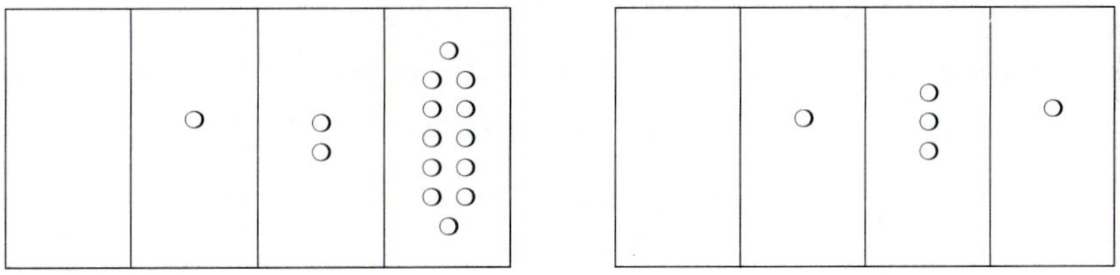

(b)

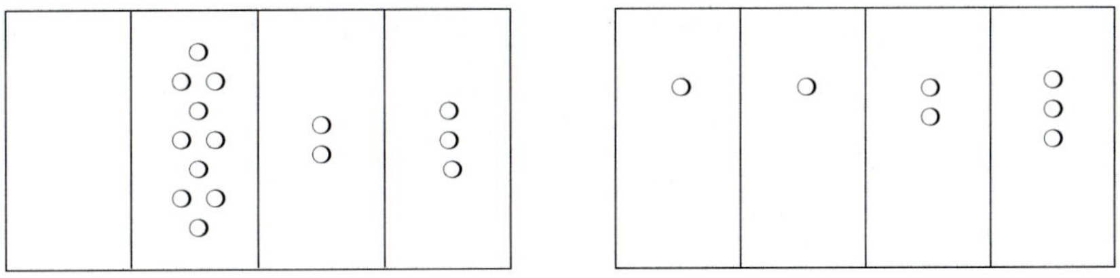

(c)

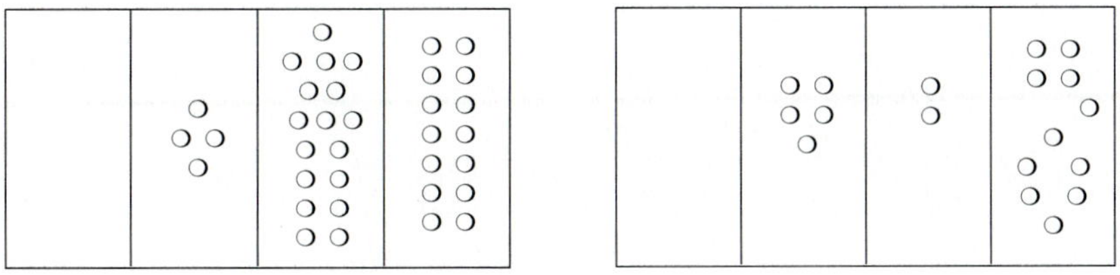

3. Several counting board numerals are shown below. Find the standard numeral equivalent to each.

(a)

(b)

(c)

(d)

4. Draw the counting board numerals equivalent to the standard numerals
   (a) 68   (b) 4057   (c) 4507   (d) 4570   (e) 70,000

5. Here are two Egyptian numerals. Decide which represents the larger number.

(a)

(b)

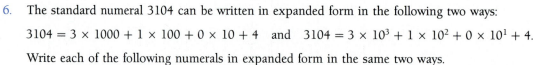

6. The standard numeral 3104 can be written in expanded form in the following two ways:

$3104 = 3 \times 1000 + 1 \times 100 + 0 \times 10 + 4$ and $3104 = 3 \times 10^3 + 1 \times 10^2 + 0 \times 10^1 + 4.$

Write each of the following numerals in expanded form in the same two ways.
   (a) 452   (b) 31   (c) 701   (d) 89,425   (e) 30,016   (f) 2,708,280

7. For each pile of place value blocks shown below write the standard numeral equivalent to it.

(a)

(b)

(c)

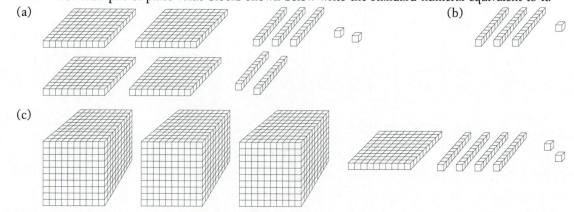

8. For each of the standard numerals, draw a pile of place value blocks equivalent to it.
   (a) 17   (b) 3172   (c) 2003   (d) 513

9. Here are base 10 abaci with beads on them. For each abacus write the equivalent standard numeral.
   (a)   (b)

10. For each of the standard numerals, draw the equivalent base 10 abacus numeral.
    (a) 5690   (b) 90,073

11. For each of the stick numerals write the next largest stick numeral.
    (a)   (b)   (c)
    (d)   (e)   (f)

12. Write each of the stick numerals in expanded form (write "plus" in place of a plus sign, +).
    (a)   (b)   (c)
    (d)   (e)   (f)

13. For each pair of stick numerals, decide which represents the larger number.
    (a)
    (b)

14. Write the following standard decimal numerals in expanded form using exponential notation.
    (a) 37,153   (b) 498,000   (c) 17,320,508   (d) 223,606,798

15. For each of the following numerals, find the base 10 numeral equivalent to it.
    (a) $CAB_{sixteen}$ (b) 110110101_{two} (c) 430_{five} (d) 873_{nine}

16. Find the standard numeral equivalent to 377 in each base.
    (a) base 16   (b) base 2   (c) base 5   (d) base 9

17. Find the standard base 10 numeral equivalent to each Babylonian numeral.
    (a)   (b)

18. Draw a number line to include the numbers from zero to 100. Mark on this number line the powers of 2, 3, 5, and 10 that are between zero and 100 inclusive. Distinguish the different sets of powers in some way, perhaps by using different colors. Use what you have done to determine the number of digits needed to represent 100 in each of these different bases.

For each problem remaining, document as clearly and completely as you can your solution to the problem. Include the steps you took to solve the problem, mention the problems or solutions from the text that gave you ideas, and include the problem-solving strategies you used. Outline and organize your work before writing your final report in essay form.

Problems 19–22 are ones that people in an innumerate society may have encountered. Solve them as they might have—by pairing elements of sets, but without our numerals, our methods of counting, and our sophisticated operations on whole numbers.

19. The citizens of Dotta represent a number by making dot marks on sheepskin, one dot for each element of a set. The law of Dotta requires that each business negotiation be recorded by a pair of these Dotta numerals. A copy of the document for one day's business activities is provided. The numeral on the left is either the offer or the asking price (in dottas, the monetary unit), depending on who began the negotiations, the buyer or the seller. The numeral on the right is the actual price paid. A Dotta buyer never pays more than the seller asks, and a Dotta seller never asks less than a buyer offers. Determine who initiated each negotiation and describe how you figured it out.

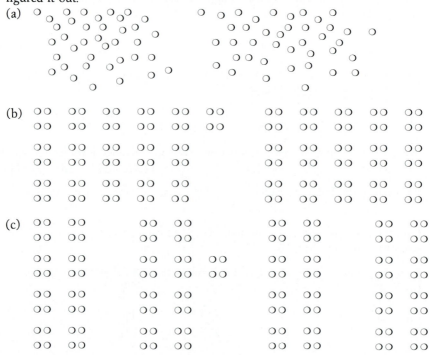

20. Ugboo, his mother and father, his brother Nip, his sisters Snip and Snap, and little brother Norum are planning a trip to a faraway village of Dom. Ugboo's friend Lagor once took a trip to Dom and kept track of it by bringing back a pile of sticks, one for each day of traveling. These are shown on the left. On the right is a pile of stones, one for each loaf of bread Ugboo's mother has baked for the trip. In the middle is a pile of square tiles, one for each member of Ugboo's family.

Lagor has told Ugboo that each person must have one loaf of bread for each day of travel. Make a copy of the items in the picture above and do (a) or (b), whichever is appropriate.

(a) On the copy of the picture, circle the stones representing the loaves that will be left over from the trip.

(b) Draw a balloon and in it draw pictures of stones representing the loaves of bread that yet must be baked if there is to be enough bread for the trip.

21. On the left in the illustration is a pile of sticks, 1 for each blanket that Lagor has. On the right is a pile of stones, 1 for each sheep Ugboo has. Lagor wants to trade all the blankets for sheep. Ugboo has said, | | | blankets for each sheep. Lagor agrees to this.

On a copy of the items in the illustration, either circle the sticks representing the blankets Lagor has left over (after "buying") all of Ugboo's sheep or circle the sheep Lagor cannot buy after he has used up all his blankets.

22. Lagor now wants to buy horses and cows from Gorul. Again, Lagor has blankets to trade as represented by the sticks on the left in the illustration, 1 stick for each blanket. Gorul's horses are represented by the pile of square tiles, 1 tile for each horse; his cows are represented by stones, 1 stone for each cow. Gorul and Lagor agree that the prices are | | | for each cow and | | | | for each horse. Lagor will trade blankets for all of Gorul's cows and buy as many horses as he can with the remaining blankets. On a copy of the illustration, circle a set of stones in one-to-one correspondence with the horses Lagor can buy and circle the set of sticks in one-to-one correspondence with the blankets Lagor uses to buy cows and horses.

23. Farida wants to trade wheat for Milor's sheep—1 bushel of wheat for 1 sheep. Farida wants to know if she has enough wheat. Here are some clues:

■ Farida has this many bushels of wheat:

■ Milor has this many sheep:

Help Farida solve this problem. Don't convert Egyptian numerals to standard numerals; work completely within the Egyptian system.

24. Ruut grows barley and Pilan raises goats. Ruut wants to trade the barley he has raised this month and last month for goats, 1 bushel of barley for 1 goat. Ruut wants to know whether he has enough barley to buy all the goats. Here are some clues.

■ Ruut harvested this many bushels of barley last month:

■ Ruut harvested this many bushels of barley this month:

■ Pilan has this many goats for trade:

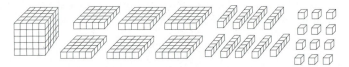

Help Ruut solve this problem. As in problem 21, work completely within the Egyptian system.

25. Convert the collection of base 5 place value blocks into an equivalent one in which there are no more than 4 blocks of one type.

26. Decide which of the following two collections of base 5 place value blocks represents the larger number. Stay within the system of place value blocks while you do this.

(a)   (b)

27. Mina, a child in Ugboo's village many generations later, is learning about stick numerals in school. Below are shown homework sheets in which she is being asked to convert some bunches of stones to stick numerals and vice versa. Help her finish her homework.

(a) | (b) |

28. Three prosperous chicken farmers from Glapora have decided to trade in the market of Mina's village. Each comes with a bag of stones, a stone for each chicken he wants to sell. To trade in the village market, the farmers from Glapora must convert their stones to the village's stick numeral system. Help them do this. Here are the stones from each farmer's bag.

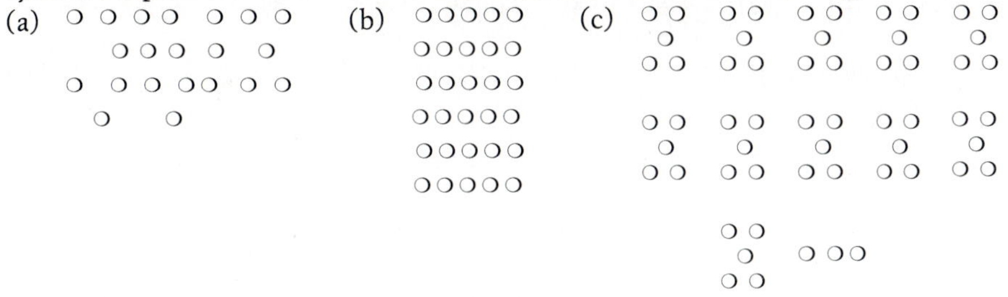

(a)
```
O O O O   O O O
   O O O O   O O
O  O O O O O  O O
     O     O
```
(b)
```
O O O O O
O O O O O
O O O O O
O O O O O
O O O O O
O O O O O
```
(c)
```
O O   O O   O O   O O   O O
  O      O      O      O      O
O O   O O   O O   O O   O O

O O   O O   O O   O O   O O
  O      O      O      O      O
O O   O O   O O   O O   O O

   O O
   O      O O O
   O O
```

29. On the homework sheet below, Mina is being asked—for various pairs of stick numerals—to determine which represents the larger number. Help her.

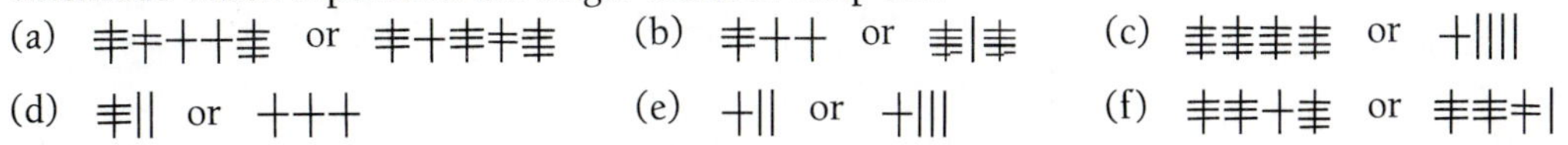

(a) ≢≢++≢ or ≢+≢+≢   (b) ≢++ or ≢|≢   (c) ≢≢≢≢ or +||||

(d) ≢|| or +++   (e) +|| or +||| (f) ≢≢+≢ or ≢≢+|

30. To help her learn about stick numerals, Mina is using base 5 place value blocks and a base 5 counting board. Help her fill in the blanks in the table.

STICK NUMERAL	PLACE VALUE BLOCKS	COUNTING BOARD NUMERAL
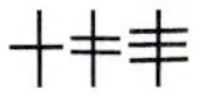 ++≢	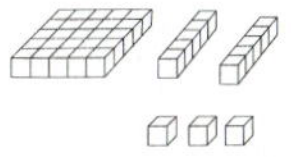	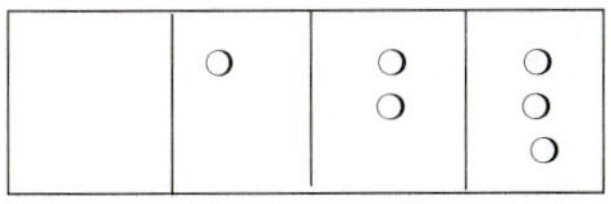
	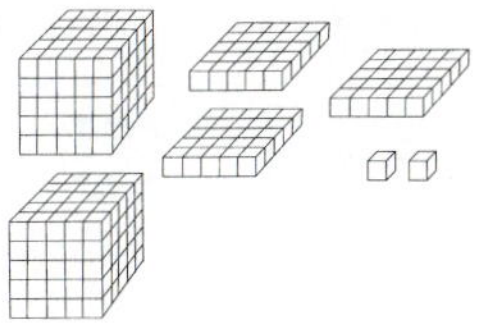	
		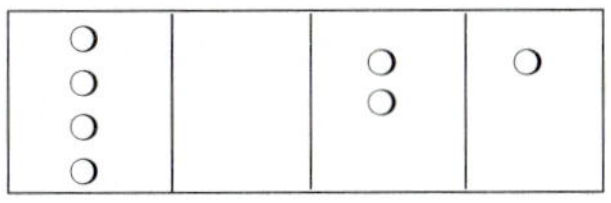
≢|≢|		

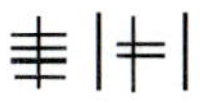

31. Archaeologists are studying a scroll discovered on the site of Mina's ancient village. They found some stick numerals on the scroll.

(a) +| (b) +|| (c) +||| (d) +|||| (e) ‡‡

(f) ‡+| (g) +‡ (h) +‡|‡ (i) +‡+ (j) +|‡‡|

To complete their study, they must convert these numerals to standard numerals. Help them do this.

32. You have come across a copy of a Mayan "manuscript" showing a list of numerals in the Mayan system.

(a) You suspect that this list has a purpose and want to figure out what it is. You have heard that the Mayan numeral system is a place value system with a base. You wonder: What is the base of the system? What are the digits? What is the symbol for zero? Answer these questions as you break the puzzle of the list.

(b) Based on what you learned in (a), determine which Mayan numeral in each pair represents the larger number.

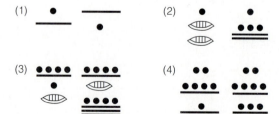

(c) Convert the following sets of stones into Mayan numerals.

(1)

(2)

(d) As an archaeologist, you need to convert Mayan numerals into standard decimal numerals. Do this for the numerals shown.

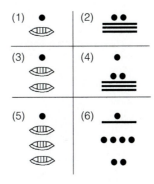

Several possible answers are given for each question. Choose the item that answers the question best.

1. Table Top sells kitchen table tops that are either round or square and either plastic or wooden. The manager denotes the set of all table tops she has on hand by *T*, the set of round table tops by *R*, and the set of plastic table tops by *P*. Then she draws a diagram:

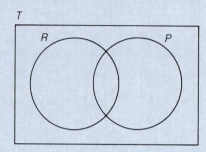

Consider the set of table tops corresponding to the shaded portion of the next diagram:

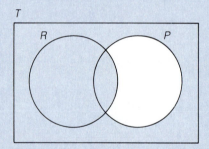

The best description of this set is
(a) The set of tops that are round but not plastic
(b) The set of tops that are round and wooden
(c) The set of tops that are either wooden or square but not both
(d) The set of tops that are both round and plastic
(e) The set of tops that are round or wooden or both

2. Table Top is having a sale. In its advertisement you read that in the sale there will be 22 round table tops and 15 wooden table tops. You are opening a cafè, need to buy a large quantity of table tops, and are considering buying your table tops at the Table Top sale. Based on the information in the ad, the most accurate conclusion you can reach concerning the total number of table tops for sale is
(a) A minimum of 15 and a maximum of 22
(b) A minimum of 7 and a maximum of 15
(c) A minimum of 22 and a maximum of 37
(d) A minimum of 15 and a maximum of 37
(e) A minimum of 7 and a maximum of 22

3. A clothing factory inspector examines shirts for the following types of defects: buttons missing, defects in the cloth, and defects in the stitching. He has examined a 100 shirt lot and tabulated his results in a Venn diagram:

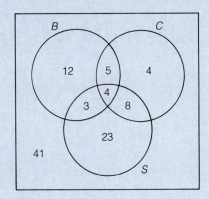

Here B = set of shirts with buttons missing, C = set of shirts with defects in the cloth, and S = set of shirts with defects in the stitching.

The number of shirts with no buttons missing but with a defect in stitching is
(a) 26 (b) 31 (c) 38 (d) 76 (e) 7

4. Shown is a collection of base 4 place value blocks. This is equivalent to which standard decimal numeral?

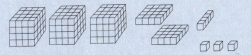

(a) 135 (b) 231 (c) 3213 (d) 9 (e) 59

5. The Health Food Shop sells raisins at \$3.65/lb and granola at \$2.35/lb. The owner wants to make 80 lb of a hike mix consisting of granola and raisins and costing \$3.30/lb. To figure out how many pounds of raisins and how many pounds of granola should go into the mix, the owner decides to make some guesses and organize them into a chart, hoping that he can zero in on a solution. Here is the beginning of his chart and his first guess:

RAISINS IN HIKE MIX (POUNDS)	GRANOLA IN HIKE MIX (POUNDS)	COST OF RAISINS IN MIX	COST OF GRANOLA IN MIX	TOTAL COST OF MIX	TARGET COST OF MIX
30	50	\$109.50	\$117.50	\$227.00	

The target cost of the mix is
(a) \$240 (b) \$227 (c) \$292 (d) \$188 (e) \$264

6. The owner makes another guess and continues to fill in the chart.

RAISINS IN HIKE MIX (POUNDS)	GRANOLA IN HIKE MIX (POUNDS)	COST OF RAISINS IN MIX	COST OF GRANOLA IN MIX	TOTAL COST OF MIX	TARGET COST OF MIX
30	50	$109.50	$117.50	$227.00	
45	35	?			

The amount that should go in the space marked "?" is
(a) $246.50   (b) $105.75   (c) $127.75   (d) $164.25   (e) $82.25

7. The collection of stones on a (base 10) counting board is equivalent to which standard decimal numeral?

(a) 4125   (b) 3025   (c) 3026   (d) 3036   (e) 4025

8. Ugboo wants to trade as many blankets as he can for Lagor's sheep. This many blankets (III) are to be traded for this many sheep (○○○○). Here are Ugboo's blankets

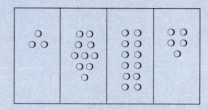

and here are Lagor's sheep

What will be left over after all the trading has taken place?
(a) IIOO   (b) OO   (c) IIOO   (d) II   (e) IOOO

9. This quantity of stones

converted to stick numbers is
(a)    (b)   (c)   (d)   (e)

10. A universal set U has subsets A and B. The subset $A' \cap B$ corresponds to the shaded portion of which diagram below?

(a) U

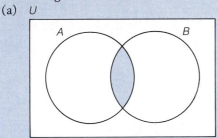

(b) U

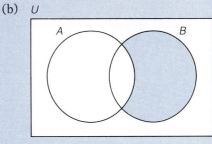

(c) U

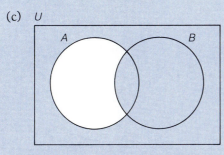

(d) U

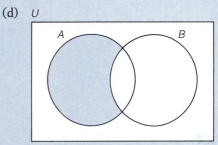

(e) U

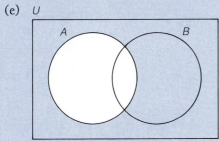

ESSAY QUESTIONS *For each of the remaining problems, document your solution carefully in the form of an essay.*

11. A personnel director is trying to narrow the selection process in hiring a new computer specialist. Of the 80 applicants, he wants to know how many have both a college education as well as at least four years of work experience with computers. He has tabulated the following information so far:

42 have a college education.

37 have had at least four years of work experience with computers.

13 have had no college education and have less than four years of work experience with computers.

Use the information to help him solve his problem.

12. You are hiking from the bottom of Death Valley (at 289 ft below sea level) to the top of Telescope Peak (at 10,811 ft above sea level), a mountain at the edge of the Valley.

    When you leave on your hike the temperature at the bottom of Death Valley is 50°C and drops by 1°C for every 300 ft in elevation gain. What will the temperature be when you reach the top of the mountain?

13. In the country of Xoran the money system is as follows:

    Yellow Ⓨ is the basic coin.
    Green Ⓖ is worth ⓎⓎⓎⓎ.
    Red Ⓡ is worth ⓖⓖ.
    Blue Ⓑ is worth ⓇⓇⓇ.

    You wish to buy a camel whose price is

    ⒷⒷⒷⒷ Ⓡ ⒼⒼⒼ ⓎⓎ.

    With you, you have

    ⒼⒼ ⓎⓎⓎⓎⓎⓎⓎ
    Ⓑ ⓇⓇⓇⓇⓇ.

    Can you buy the camel? Why or why not?

14. We were driving across the desert, but my father refused to turn on the air conditioning. "You know that if I turn on the air conditioning, we only get 16 miles to the gallon. Right now we're getting 18." I began to figure just how much it would cost us to keep cool. We were going 55 mph out there in the desert, and gas cost $1.20 gal. Just how much would it cost us to keep cool?*

---

* From Carol Meyer and Tom Sallee, *Make It Simpler,* Addison-Wesley, Reading, Mass., 1983, p. 261.

ADDITION AND SUBTRACTION OF WHOLE NUMBERS

CHAPTER 4

In the previous chapter we considered the development of our system of written numerals. In this and the next two chapters we will discuss the standard operations with whole numbers. We devote this chapter to addition and subtraction. In this context, an *operation* takes a pair of numbers and associates with the pair a third number, the *sum* of two numbers in the case of addition, the *difference* of two numbers in the case of subtraction. Our aim is to describe what the operations mean at a primitive level (of sets) and to show how and why the standard methods for computing the sum and difference work. We will start with simple problems and work up to more complicated ones. The solutions to the problems will build on each other.

As in chapter 3, we will try to put ourselves in the shoes of children and solve these problems from their point of view. As adults, we have computed so much and for so long that we can do these operations with ease and without thinking. This is not so for people just learning. Solving problems from their point of view will show us how the standard methods evolved, how they work and what mathematical stages one must go through to learn, use, and understand them. We will use the various devices introduced in chapter 3 for *making concrete models* of numbers such as counting boards and place value blocks. We will also use expanded notation as well as the standard decimal numerals.

Ugboo has this many sheep

● ● ● ● ● ● ● ● ●

and Lagor has this many

● ● ● ● ● ● ● ● ● ● ●

Do they have enough sheep together to buy this many blankets

● ●,

Try this problem yourself first.

1 sheep for 1 blanket? Help them solve their problem using the fact that the only technique they have for comparing quantities is pairing the elements of a set. They do not have our decimal numerals to work with.

A Solution to Ugboo and
Lagor's Problem

Take the set S of stones representing Ugboo's sheep and the set L of stones representing Lagor's sheep and form the union $S \cup L$ of the two sets. Then pair the elements of $S \cup L$ with the set B of stones representing the blankets.

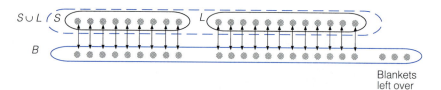

Blankets
left over

Every element of $S \cup L$ has been paired with an element of B, and there are elements of B left over. Ugboo and Lagor have enough sheep to buy the blankets.

The Mathematical Idea: Primitive Addition

Ugboo and Lagor know how to compare one set with another by pairing the elements. In this problem they want to compare two sets: $S \cup L$ and B. The set $S \cup L$ is a union of the sets S and L. Since Ugboo and Lagor do not have numerals to represent numbers, addition for them means forming the union of two sets having no elements in common.

DEFINITION OF DISJOINT SETS

Sets A and B having no elements in common are called *disjoint*. A and B disjoint means

$$A \cap B = \emptyset.$$

For example, if A is the set of letters of the word *heat*, B is the set of letters of the word *song*, and C is the set of letters of the word *chime*, then A and B are disjoint while A and C are not disjoint.

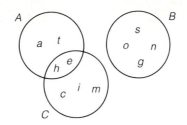

 EXERCISE 1. In the circles are stones representing, from left to right, the camels that Roga has, the camels that Luxora has, and people requesting camels for a caravan leaving this weekend. Are there enough camels for people? Solve this without counting.

THE BIRTHDAY FAVOR PROBLEM

Solve this yourself!

John is having a birthday party. He wants to give each of his 10 guests a favor. He has saved up money and bought 5 hats; his mom gave him 7 more hats. Will he have enough? John is in the first grade; he can count to 50 and knows how to compare numbers by counting. How would he solve this?

A Solution to the Birthday Favor Problem

"Let me take the favors I bought and the favors Mom gave me. I'll put the two bunches together. Then I'll count the whole bunch. I get 12 altogether. I know that 12 is bigger than 10, the number of guests. So I'll have enough!"

The Mathematical Ideas: Addition and Addition Facts

In chapter 3 we learned that it is more efficient to compare two "large" sets by comparing the numbers of the sets (using the numerals that represent them) than it is to compare them by pairing elements. When we have two sets that we want to compare, then, we count the two sets, obtain their numbers, and compare them. We do the same when one of the sets S is a union of two other disjoint sets A and B: $S = A \cup B$, $A \cap B = \varnothing$. Finding the number that corresponds to $n(A \cup B)$ is called *addition*. The number $n(A \cup B)$ is the *sum* of the addends $n(A)$ and $n(B)$ and is written $n(A \cup B) = n(A) + n(B)$.

After solving a lot of addition problems like the one above, where each set has fewer than 10 items in it, young John will begin to remember the answers to them. He will remember that the disjoint union of a set with 5 items and a set with 7 items in it is a set with 12 items in it; he will say "7 plus 5 is 12" and will write $7 + 5 = 12$ for this fact. In other words, he will begin to learn his addition tables and to write these elementary addition facts in symbols.

The two second grade classes at George Washington Elementary School have received a shipment of new math books. Sam and Carlotta have been assigned the task of determining whether there are enough books for the two classes, 58 students in all. Sam has a box of 24 books and Carlotta has a box of 38 books. The two of them have had lots of experience adding numbers less than 10 but no experience adding larger numbers. How can they figure out whether there will be enough books?

A Solution to the Math Book Problem

Sam and Carlotta realize that they must figure out the number of books in the two boxes combined. They consider forming the union of the two sets and counting the new set from scratch.

"You know," Carlotta says, "there might be a way easier than counting to figure out what we would get. Let's try *making a model* of the two numbers using place value blocks."

"Sure," Sam responds, "do you remember how they work?"

"Well, each little cube is a unit. Each long stands for 10 units. Do you see, if you glued 10 units together, you'd get a long? Here are 38 and 24 in place value blocks.

38   24

If you put all the blocks together, you'd have

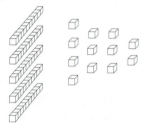

There are 5 longs and 12 units. Trade 10 units for 1 long.

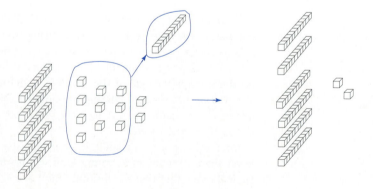

Now you have 6 longs and 2 units. That's 6 tens and 2 units. That makes 62, which is more than 58. There will be enough books for everybody."

2. Find the following sum using place value blocks and the solution to the math book problem as a plan: 46 + 38 = .

3. Find the sum of the stick numbers ╪╪ and ┼╪ using base 5 place value blocks.

THE PTA PROBLEM

The PTA has an annual fair to raise money for special school needs. Each classroom sponsors a booth. The booth for one third grade class raised $376 while the booth for the other third grade class raised $548. Third graders Adam and Samantha have been given the job of figuring out how much the two third grades raised together. They have decided to *make models* of the numbers and use place value blocks. They've had experience adding two-digit numbers with place value blocks but no experience adding three-digit numbers. Help them solve the problem using place value blocks.

A Solution to the PTA Problem

Adam and Samantha set up the place value blocks for the two numbers as shown.

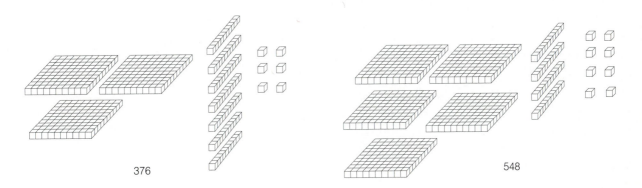

376   548

Samantha: "We've *solved similar problems* with two-digit numbers. Let's do what we did there and put all the flats together, all the longs together, and all the units together from the two piles. The new pile of place value blocks represents the sum of the two numbers."

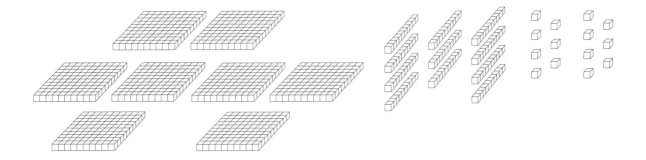

Adam: "There are 8 flats, 11 longs, and 14 units. What number corresponds to that? Wait, you just told me that I can trade 10 longs for a flat.

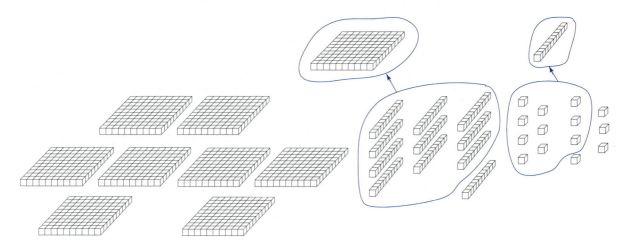

That makes 9 flats, 1 long, and 14 units."

Samantha: "I can trade 10 of the 14 units for a long. Then we would have 9 flats, 2 longs, and 4 units. That's 9 hundreds, 2 tens, and 4. Nine hundred twenty-four dollars. The two classes together raised $924."

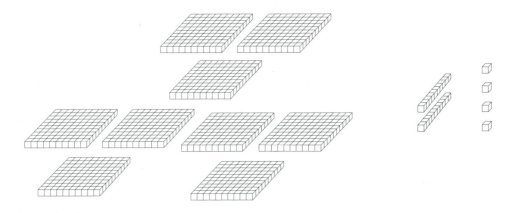

EXERCISES 4. Solve the addition problems using place value blocks:
(a) $357 + 486$ (b) $746 + 569$

5. Solve the problem of adding ╪╪╪ to ╪│╪ using base 5 place value blocks.

The Mathematical Idea: From the Concrete to the Abstract

Since place value blocks consist of unit blocks glued together in convenient combinations, the solution to the PTA problem using place value blocks is very concrete. You can see and feel the union of the two sets being formed when the two collections of place value blocks are shoved together. A certain amount of trading then occurs to determine the number associated with the union.

We will look at three more solutions to the PTA problem. Each solution will use a different device, and each succeeding solution will be slightly more abstract than the one that precedes it. The third solution will use the standard method.

A Solution to the PTA Problem Using a Counting Board

Make models of 376 and 548 on a counting board.

100s	10s	1s	
○ ○ ○	○ ○ ○ ○ ○ ○ ○	○ ○ ○ ○ ○ ○	376
○ ○ ○ ○ ○	○ ○ ○ ○	○ ○ ○ ○ ○ ○ ○ ○	548

To find the sum, in each column lump the stones from the two numbers together.

100s	10s	1s
○ ○ ○ ○ ○ ○ ○ ○	○ ○ ○ ○ ○ ○ ○ ○ ○ ○ ○	○ ○ ○ ○ ○ ○ ○ ○ ○ ○ ○ ○ ○ ○

There are 14 stones in the 1s column, 11 stones in the 10s column, and 8 stones in the 100s column. There must be fewer than 10 stones in each column. Start with the units column and replace 10 stones there by another stone in the 10s column.

100s	10s	1s
○ ○ ○ ○ ○ ○ ○ ○	○ ○ ○ ○ ○ ○ ○ ○ ○ ○ ○	○ ○ ○ ○ ○ ○ ○ ○ ○ ○ ○ ○ ○ ○

100s	10s	1s
○ ○ ○ ○ ○ ○ ○ ○	○ ○ ○ ○ ○ ○ ○ ○ ○ ○ ○ ○	○ ○ ○ ○

Now there are 4 stones in the 1s column, 12 in the 10s column, and 8 in the 100s column. The units column is satisfactory.

Move to the 10s column where there are now 12 stones. Replace 10 of those stones by a stone in the 100s column.

100s	10s	1s
○ ○ ○ ○ ○ ○ ○ ○	○ ○ ○ ○ ○ ○ ○ ○ ○ ○ ○ ○	○ ○ ○ ○

The result is

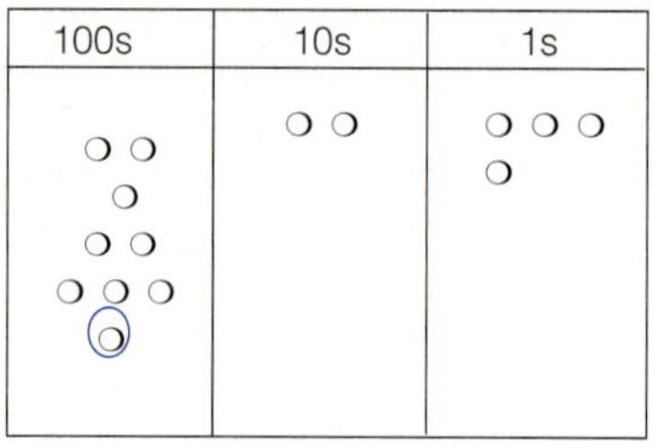

100s	10s	1s
○ ○ ○ ○ ○ ○ ○ ○ ⊚	○ ○	○ ○ ○ ○

That makes 4 stones in the 1s column, 2 in the 10s column, and 9 in the 100s column. There are now fewer than 10 stones in each column. The number represented on the counting board is 9 hundreds, 2 tens, and 4, or 924.

EXERCISES

6. Solve the problems using stones on a counting board:
   (a) 357 + 486   (b) 746 + 569

7. Add the stick numerals ≢╪≢ and ╪│≢ using a base 5 counting board.

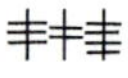

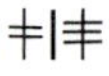

A Solution to the PTA Problem Using Expanded Notation on a Counting Board

Expand 376 and 548 on a counting board:

100s	10s	1s
3	7	6
5	4	8

Add the two quantities in the units column and get $6 + 8 = 14$. Do the same thing in each of the other columns: In the 10s column, $7 + 4 = 11$; in the 100s column, $3 + 5 = 8$.

100s	10s	1s
3	7	6
5	4	8
8	11	14

To interpret the numbers in the bottom row, each must be 9 or less. In the first column you notice that $14 = 10 + 4$. You can exchange 10 in the units column with a 1 in the second column. So you replace the 14 by 4 in the units column and add 1 to the 10s column.

100s	10s	1s
3 5	7 4	6 8
8	~~11~~ 12	~~14~~ 4

Finally, you notice in the 10s column that $12 = 10 + 2$. That means 10 tens (or 1 hundred) plus 2 tens. You can exchange the 10 for a 1 in the 100s column. So replace the 12 by 2 in the 10s column and add 1 to the 100s column.

100s	10s	1s
3 5	7 4	6 8
~~8~~ 9	~~11~~ ~~12~~ 2	~~14~~ 4

Now you have 9 in the 100s column, 2 in the 10s column, and 4 in the units column. That's 924.

EXERCISES 8. Use expanded notation on a counting board to solve the addition problems.

   (a) $357 + 486$ (b) $746 + 569$

9. Use expanded notation on a base 5 counting board to add ≢╪≢ to ╪│≢ .

A Solution to the PTA Problem Using the Standard Method

Here is another solution using expanded notation on a counting board. This time we do the trading as we go, column by column. We start with the units column, add the numbers in that column, and, if the sum is greater than 9, trade 10 from that column for 1 in the column just to its left; then we move to the 10s column and do the same thing there; then to the 100s column; and so on.

This solution is so close to the standard method that we show the two methods in parallel, with the standard method on the right. The word for *trade* in the standard method has traditionally been *carry*, literally from the act of carrying a stone to the next column of the counting board.

	100s	10s	1s
Add in units column	3 5	7 4	6 8
		1	4

1 ←— "Carry" 1
376
548
———
4

	100s	10s	1s	
				"Carry" 1
Add everything in 10s column	3	7	6	1 1 376
	5	4	8	48
	1	1	4	24
		2		

	100s	10s	1s	
Add everything in 100s column	3	7	6	1 1 376
	5	4	8	548
	1	1	4	924
	9	2		

EXERCISE

10. Use the standard method to add to 𐄞𐄞𐄞.

4.2 SUBTRACTION OF WHOLE NUMBERS

We now turn to subtraction. As with addition, we begin with primitive subtraction, build on that, and wind up eventually with the standard method of subtraction.

UGBOO'S HORSE PROBLEM

Ugboo has this many stones

○○○○○○○○○○○○○○○○○○○○○○○○○○○○○○○○○○○○

He wants to buy a horse from Neevil, who will sell the horse for this many stones

○○○○○○○○○○○○○○○

STOP

Try this first.

Ugboo needs to know what will be left over after paying for the horse because he wants to buy a saddle for the horse, too. How can Ugboo find out what he'll have left? Remember that Ugboo does not have our numerals to work with; his only technique for deciding how many is pairing the elements of two sets.

A Solution to Ugboo's Horse Problem

Let U be the set of stones Ugboo has. Find a subset S of U that is in one-to-one correspondence with the set representing Neevil's price. With U as the universal set, what Ugboo would have left over after buying Neevil's horse is S', the complement of S in U.

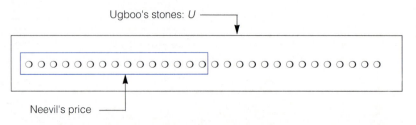

The Mathematical Idea: Primitive Subtraction

In Ugboo's horse problem Ugboo wants to find the set S', where $S \subset U$ and S represents Neevil's price. Finding the number of S' is called *subtraction of $n(S)$ from $n(U)$*, and we write $n(S') = n(U) - n(S)$.

U

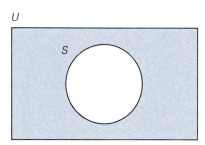

Shaded part is S'

THE TOY PROBLEM

Solve this first!

Miguel is in the first grade and has been given a gift of $8 (in single dollar bills) for his birthday. With $5 of this money he plans to buy a toy. He wants to know how much he will have left. Help him solve this. Miguel has had a lot of experience adding single-digit numbers. He has not yet learned about subtraction.

A Solution to the Toy Problem

From the eight dollar bills, Miguel counts out five dollar bills for the toy. He counts what is left and gets three dollar bills.

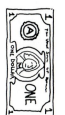       

Price   The rest

The Mathematical Ideas: Subtraction and Subtraction Facts

Start with a set U. Identify a subset S. If you know the standard decimal numbers $n(U)$ and $n(S)$, you would like an efficient way to find the standard decimal number $n(S') = n(U) - n(S)$.

After solving a lot of subtraction problems like the toy problem—in which the number of the larger set is no bigger than 19 and the number of the subset to be identified is no bigger than 10—Miguel will begin to remember the answers to these problems. He will remember that a 5-element subset of an 8-element set has a complement of 3 elements. At the same time, he will begin to say "5 subtracted from 8 is 3" and write $8 - 5 = 3$ for this fact. Such a fact is called an *elementary subtraction fact*.

EXERCISE

11. What are the basic addition facts and the basic subtraction facts for standard base 6 numerals?

THE PAPER PAD PROBLEM

Try this yourself, first!

The school secretary has given Adam and Samantha's class 57 paper writing pads for use in the next two months. The students know that they use up about 23 pads per month. They want to know if, after going through 23 pads this month, there will be enough for the following month. The students have had experience subtracting single-digit numbers but have not had experience subtracting two-digit numbers. The students in the class decide to solve this by *making models* of standard numerals and using place value blocks. Help them do this.

A Solution to the Paper Pad Problem

The students set up the place value blocks corresponding to 57.

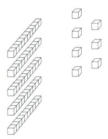

They think: "There are 5 longs (tens) and 7 units. In those blocks we want to identify the number 23—2 longs and 3 units. We identify 3 units in the 7 units, with 4 units remaining. We identify 2 longs in the 5 longs, with 3 longs remaining. What makes up the difference (the complement) after identifying 23 is 3 longs and 4 units. That's 34. There will be enough pads left over for another month."

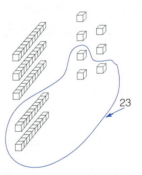

23

EXERCISES

12. Solve the paper pad problem using stones on a counting board, assuming no previous experience with two-digit subtraction.

13. Solve 89 − 42 in two ways: (a) using place value blocks and (b) using stones on a counting board.

14. Subtract ⧺ from ⧻ in two ways: (a) using base 5 place value blocks and (b) using stones on a base 5 counting board.

Willow Elementary School will have an assembly, primarily for the students; but it would like to issue tickets for parents and others according to the availability of seats. The auditorium will seat 542 people. The number of students, teachers, and school staff who will be attending is 375. The students of Adam's and Samantha's class have been given the task of finding out how many tickets can be issued for parents and others. The students in Adam's and Samantha's class are feeling good about having *solved a simpler, similar problem,* the paper pad problem. So they decide to tackle this problem with place value blocks also. Help them do this.

First, try it yourself!

A Solution to the Assembly
Ticket Problem

The students *make a model* of 542 in place value blocks.

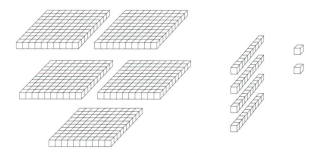

In this collection they want to identify 375: 3 flats, 7 longs, and 5 units. They notice right away that things are not quite as nice as they were for the paper pad problem. For one thing, there are 2 unit blocks in the 542 collection and 5 unit blocks in the 375 collection. "How can we identify a subset having 5 units when there are only 2 units in the large set?" they ask.

Somebody suggests, "Why don't we do some trading so that we *can* find 5 unit blocks? Trade one of the 4 longs of 542 for 10 unit blocks. That gives us 5 flats, 3 longs, and 12 units."

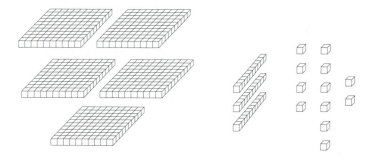

"Now we can identify a subset of 5 units. Now for the longs. We want to identify a subset with 7 longs, but there are only 3 there," another says. "We can trade one of the 5 flats in 542 for 10 longs. The collection of blocks representing 542 now has 4 flats, 13 longs, and 12 unit blocks. Now we can identify a subset—consisting of 3 flats, 7 longs, and 5 units—in the set of blocks for 542."

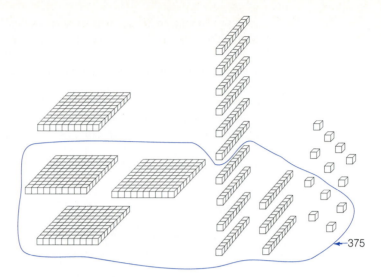

←375

What's left in 542 is 1 flat, 6 longs, and 7 units. The number is 167."

EXERCISES

15. Solve the assembly ticket problem using stones on a counting board. Use the same idea as in the solution using place value blocks: Make a model of 542 on a counting board and trade until you can identify a subset of stones corresponding to 375. Then figure out what's left.

16. Solve the problem using place value blocks: $735 - 468$.

17. Subtract ┼╪╪ from ╪┼╫ using base 5 place value blocks.

The Mathematical Idea: Trading Systematically

In the paper pad and assembly ticket problems the trick is to identify a certain subset in a set of blocks. If this is not possible at first, you trade blocks in the set until it is possible.

To be systematic, you do this one block size at a time, starting with the smallest block size. You want to identify the units of the number you are subtracting as a subset of the unit blocks; if you can't do this, trade a long for 10 units. Then you should be able to identify a subset of the unit blocks equal to the units of the number you are subtracting. Next, you move to the longs; if you can, identify the 10s of the number you are subtracting with the longs; if you can't, trade a flat for 10 longs. There will now be enough longs. Then move to the flats, and so on.

A Solution to the Assembly Ticket Problem Using the Counting Board

First we place 542 on the counting board.

100s	10s	1s
○ ○	○ ○	○ ○
○	○ ○	
○ ○		

We want to identify a subset of these stones corresponding to 375. We do it one place at a time starting with the units. There are only 2 unit stones on the counting board, and we need at least 5. On the counting board we trade a stone from the 10s column for 10 stones in the units column.

100s	10s	1s

Then we identify 5 stones in the units column of the counting board:

100s	10s	1s

Next, the 10s column. We need to identify a subset of 7 stones here, but there are only 3 there now. Again, we exchange 1 stone from the 100s column for 10 stones in the 10s column.

100s	10s	1s

Then we identify 7 stones in the 10s column.

100s	10s	1s

Finally we identify 3 stones in the 100s column.

The remaining stones are our answer.

100s	10s	1s

A Solution to the Assembly Ticket Problem Using Expanded Form on a Counting Board and the Standard Method

What follows is a solution similar to the previous one. The difference is that we use expanded form on a counting board, and we determine what is left in each column as we go. (Identifying a subset and determining what is left in a column is called *subtracting in such and such a place* in the standard method.) On the left below is the solution using expanded form and in parallel, on the right, the solution using the standard method. Traditionally, the word *borrow* has been used in place of *trade*. Thus, in place of "trade 1 long for 10 units," one might say "borrow 1 long for 10 units."

Can't subtract in 1s column.

100s	10s	1s
5	4	2
(3	7	5)

```
  5 4 2
  3 7 5
```

Trade 1 in 10s column
for 10 in 1s column.

100s	10s	1s
5	⁴̸3	12
(3	7	5)

```
     3
  5 4̸¹2
  3 7 5
```

Subtract in 1s column.
Can't subtract in 10s column.

100s	10s	1s
5	⁴̸3	12
(3	7	5)
		7

```
     3
  5 4̸¹2
  3 7 5
      7
```

Trade 1 in 100s column
for 10 in 10s column.

100s	10s	1s
5̸ 4	⁴̸13	12
(3	7	5)
		7

```
   4 ¹3
  5̸ 4̸¹2
  3 7 5
      7
```

Subtract in 10s column

100s	10s	1s
5̸4	⁴̸13	12
(3	7	5)
	6	7

```
   4 ¹3
  5̸ 4̸¹2
  3 7 5
    6 7
```

Subtract in 100s column

100s	10s	1s
5̸4	⁴̸13	12
(3	7	5)
1	6	7

```
   4 ¹3
  5̸ 4̸¹2
  3 7 5
  1 6 7
```

Notice that to use these techniques with ease, you must know the elementary subtraction facts.

EXERCISES

18. Solve the subtraction problems
    (a) $804 - 456$ (b) $5641 - 2825$
    using each of the following devices: (i) place value blocks, (ii) stones on a counting board, and (iii) expanded form on a counting board. (For the latter, subtract at each place value before moving on to the next.)

19. Solve the subtraction problems
    (a) $403_{six} - 345_{six}$ (b) $3210_{six} - 1542_{six}$
    using each of the following devices: (i) base 6 place value blocks, (ii) a base 6 counting board, and (iii) expanded form on a base 6 counting board. (For the latter, subtract at each place value before moving on to the next.)

A Solution to the Assembly Ticket Problem Using the Method of Equal Additions

There is another "standard" method for subtracting called the *method of equal additions*. It is commonly taught in European countries; as recently as the 1950s it was commonly taught in this country but now only rarely.

We will illustrate the method of equal additions by solving the problem $542 - 375$. The method is related to this observation: If a friend has $25 more than you and someone gives both of you $10, then your friend still has $25 more than you.

PRINCIPLE BEHIND METHOD OF EQUAL ADDITIONS

Suppose that A and B are whole numbers and $A > B$. Then

$$A - B = (A + S) - (B + S)$$

for any whole number S.

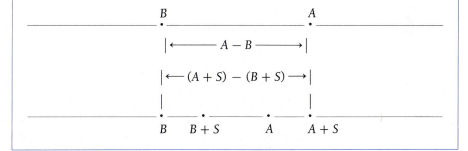

Here is the method of equal additions used to solve the problem $542 - 375$.

	100s	10s	1s
Can't subtract	5	4	2
in 1s column.	(3	7	5)

	100s	10s	1s
Add 10 to both 542 and 375	5	4	12
allowing subtraction in 1s column.	(3	7̸8	5)
			7

	100s	10s	1s
Can't subtract in 10s column.	5	14	12
Add 100 to both numbers allowing	(3̸4	7̸8	5)
subtraction in 10s column.		6	7

	100s	10s	1s
Subtract in 100s column.	5	14	12
	(3̸4	7̸8	5)
	1	6	7

EXERCISE

20. Solve the problems using the method of equal additions.
   (a) $804 - 456$ (b) $5641 - 2825$

We Know How to Subtract But When Do We Subtract?

THE EGG PROBLEM   Miguel plans to fix breakfast for his family. He will need 9 eggs. He has 5 eggs already. He has decided to borrow the rest from neighbors. How many eggs will he need to borrow? Remember, Miguel is in the first grade. He has solved the toy problem and is beginning to learn the elementary subtraction facts.

You know that the answer is the same as the answer to "5 subtracted from 9." But does Miguel know this? The toy problem feels different from the egg problem. Miguel might approach the latter in this way: "I've got 5 eggs. How many more do I need to make 9? I need to figure out what I add to 5 to get 9—$5 + ? = 9$."

Later, he might think: "Let me *draw a picture* of the 9 eggs that I need and of the 5 eggs that I have.

Need: O O O O O O O O O
Have: O O O O O

Let me cross off the 5 eggs that I have from the eggs that I need.

Need: Ø Ø Ø Ø Ø O O O O
Have: O O O O O

It's subtraction! The 4 eggs that remain I have to borrow from the neighbors."

The Mathematical Idea: Subtraction as Finding the Solution to a Missing Addend Problem

What Miguel has discovered here is that solving a subtraction problem $542 - 375$ is the same as solving the *missing addend* problem $375 + ? = 542$, and vice versa. Recall that the two numbers being added in an addition problem are called *addends*.

The egg problem is a simple problem; it is naturally a missing addend problem. For a person just learning to use subtraction, it takes a little bit of effort to show that it is a subtraction problem. The standard method of subtraction is based more on the method used to solve the toy problem. In section 4.4 we will describe a method of subtraction based on the idea of finding a missing addend.

More Problems in Which Subtraction Is Used to Find Solutions

Here are more problems that call for subtraction in their solutions. Note the language used in each situation.

- Washington Elementary PTA took in $4357 in their fund-raising; Jefferson Elementary PTA took in $3802. You are interested in knowing *how much more* Washington took in than Jefferson did. Answer: $4357 - $3802 = $555.
- The car trip from Tucson to Phoenix is 110 mi. You have already traveled 48 mi. You want to know *how much farther* you have to travel. Answer: $110 - 48 = 62$. You must travel 62 more miles.
- John's family has agreed to pay $55 toward the price of a new bike and John has agreed to pay the *difference*. The price of the bike is $129. John wants to know how much he will be paying. Answer: $129 - $55 = $74.

EXERCISE 21. Show that subtraction really does solve each of the preceding problems by showing how the original definition of subtraction given at the beginning of this chapter applies.

Why Do We Need to Do All This?

Imagine the following third grade scene:

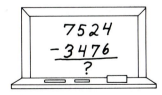

"Class, today we are going to learn how to subtract with large numbers. To illustrate the method, we will subtract 3476 from 7524. First, write down the larger number.

7524

Then subtract each digit of the smaller number 3476 from 9 and write your answers from left to right under the 7524.

$$7524$$
$$6523$$

Now add the two numbers together.

$$
\begin{array}{r}
7524 \\
+\,6523 \\
\hline
14{,}047
\end{array}
$$

Next cross out the 1, the leftmost digit of the sum, and add it underneath.

$$
\begin{array}{r}
7524 \\
+\,6523 \\
\hline
14{,}047 \\
+\,1 \\
\hline
4048
\end{array}
$$

This last number, 4048, is your answer.

$$
\begin{array}{r}
7524 \\
-\,3476 \\
\hline
4048"
\end{array}
$$

The Method of Complements for Subtraction

The method of subtraction we have just described is called the *method of complements*. You probably feel about our discussion of this method just as a third grader would feel if he were given the standard method without experiences and explanations leading up to it.

Here is another example of subtraction using the method of complements. To subtract 23,875 from 51,324, add

the larger of the two numbers	51,324
to the smaller number subtracted from 99,999	$+\,76{,}124$
and get this sum	127,448.

Cross out the leftmost digit of the sum (It will always be a 1. Why?) and add it to what's left.

$$
\begin{array}{r}
27{,}448 \\
+\,1 \\
\hline
27{,}449
\end{array}
$$

This most recent sum is the answer to your problem.

$$
\begin{array}{r}
51{,}324 \\
-\,23{,}875 \\
\hline
27{,}449
\end{array}
$$

EXERCISE 22. Use the method of complements to solve the subtraction problems.

    (a) $6407 - 2358$ (b) $75{,}432 - 43{,}094$

    (c) $5316 - 728$ (Careful with this one!)

4.3   LOOKING BACK: FORMAL PROPERTIES OF ADDITION AND SUBTRACTION

In this section we want to take a more formal look at the definitions and properties of addition and subtraction of whole numbers.

DEFINITION OF ADDITION OF WHOLE NUMBERS

Suppose that A and B are disjoint sets and that we know the numbers $n(A)$ and $n(B)$. *Addition* is the operation that assigns to the pair of whole numbers $n(A)$ and $n(B)$ the whole number $n(A \cup B)$, and we write

$$n(A) + n(B) = n(A \cup B).$$

$n(A) + n(B)$ is called the *sum*, and $n(A)$ and $n(B)$ are called *addends*.

DEFINITION OF SUBTRACTION OF WHOLE NUMBERS

Suppose that S and U are sets such that $S \subset U$ and that we know the numbers $n(S)$ and $n(U)$. Subtraction assigns to the pair of whole numbers $n(S)$ and $n(U)$ the whole number $n(S')$, and we write

$$n(U) - n(S) = n(S').$$

$n(U) - n(S)$ is called the *difference*.

Notice that, since $n(\emptyset) = 0$ and $\emptyset \cup A = A$ for any set A, we have

---

PROPERTIES OF ZERO IN ADDITION AND SUBTRACTION

$0 + N = N$ and $N - 0 = N$ for any whole number N. The number 0 is called the *identity for addition*.

Strictly speaking, subtraction is not an operation on the whole numbers, because there are ordered pairs of whole numbers for which subtraction has not been defined. For example, for the pair 3, 7 we have not defined $3 - 7$. (It makes no sense as a whole number.) For $\#$ to be an operation on a set S, $p \# q$ and $q \# p$ must both make sense, for all p and $q \in S$.

Commutative Property of Addition

Suppose a child is solving the problem $12 + 3$. She may think of getting the answer by counting three more numbers beyond 12: "thirteen, fourteen, fifteen." So $12 + 3 = 15$. Now suppose the same child is to solve the problem $3 + 12$. Again she may think of getting the answer by counting twelve more numbers beyond 3: "four, five, six, seven, eight, nine, ten, eleven, twelve, thirteen, fourteen, fifteen." So $3 + 12 = 15$. After solving a lot of addition problems, eventually she will notice that $3 + 12 = 12 + 3$ and $5 + 4 = 4 + 5$ and $8 + 6 = 6 + 8$. These are all instances of the commutative property of addition of whole numbers.

COMMUTATIVE PROPERTY OF ADDITION OF WHOLE NUMBERS

For all whole numbers N and M,

$$N + M = M + N.$$

The explanation for this formal rule is very reasonable. If you have a pair of disjoint sets, one with 12 elements and another with 3, and you want to "count" the union of the two sets, it doesn't matter where you start to count.

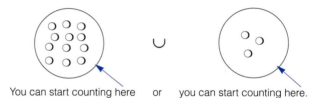

You can start counting here   or   you can start counting here.

Another way of putting it is this: $A \cup B = B \cup A$ (set union is commutative!) so that when $A \cap B = \varnothing$,

$$n(A) + n(B) = n(A \cup B) = n(B \cup A) = n(B) + n(A).$$

The question of whether subtraction has a commutative property doesn't arise. If $N \geq M$, then $N - M$ is defined and is a whole number; however, $M - N$ is not even defined (unless, of course, $M = N = 0$).

Associative Property of Addition

Suppose you are a second grader and you know your addition facts up to $10 + 10 = 20$ and you want to solve this addition problem: $13 + 6$. You know that if you took 3 from the 13 and added it to the 6, you would get 9. So the problem becomes $10 + 9$. You know the answer to this: $10 + 9 = 19$. Thus,

$$13 + 6 = (10 + 3) + 6 = 10 + (3 + 6) = 10 + 9 = 19.$$

(*Note:* In the expression $(10 + 3) + 6$ there are two additions to be performed. An operation in parentheses is performed first.) The fact $(10 + 3) + 6 = 10 + (3 + 6)$ is an instance of the associative property for addition of whole numbers.

ASSOCIATIVE PROPERTY FOR ADDITION OF WHOLE NUMBERS

For all whole numbers N, M, and P

$$(N + M) + P = N + (M + P).$$

Again, the associative property follows from the fact that if you have three sets A, B, and C, no matter how you put them together using set union, you will wind up with the same set.

$$A \cup (B \cup C) = (A \cup B) \cup C.$$

In other words, set union satisfies the associative property. Formally, if A, B, and C are disjoint sets in pairs,

$$\begin{aligned}
[n(A) + n(B)] + n(C) &= n(A \cup B) + n(C) \\
&= n((A \cup B) \cup C) \\
&= n(A \cup (B \cup C)) \\
&= n(A) + n(B \cup C) \\
&= n(A) + (n(B) + n(C))
\end{aligned}$$

Because of the associative property, when there are more than two numbers to add together, there is no need to use parentheses; it doesn't matter which addition you perform first. The expression $5 + 34 + 45 + 17$ is unambiguous. With the commutative property and the associative property together you can scramble the numbers up and add them in any order you want.

4.4   LOOKING AHEAD: ADDITION AND SUBTRACTION IN ALGEBRA

In this chapter we have used symbols and letters to describe properties of addition and subtraction and to solve problems. In this section we will look more carefully at the use of letters and symbols and discuss some rules governing their use. This is the first glimpse of algebra in this book.

In the previous section, in order to describe properties of whole numbers, we used letters to represent them. For example, the commutative law for addition can be stated "For all whole numbers N and M, the equation $N + M = M + N$ is true." We had previously observed that $7 + 3 = 3 + 7$, $8 + 6 = 6 + 8$, and other similar facts. On the one hand, these last two equations are *instances* of the commutative law. On the other hand, the law is a *generalization* of the two equations. The law says a great deal. Not only does it say that $7 + 3 = 3 + 7$ and $8 + 6 = 6 + 8$, but it also says that no matter what two whole numbers you take (call them N and M), it will always be the case that $N + M = M + N$. Using symbols enables one to make this generalization, to say something about *all* pairs of whole numbers.

We used symbols for whole numbers in yet another context. In our discussion we came across a problem of the sort "Find a whole number N such that $12 + N = 33$." We called this problem a *missing addend problem*; we know that its solution is $N = 33 - 12$. The problem is solved by subtraction of whole numbers.

The use of a symbol (letter) for a whole number in the missing addend problem is different from the use of a symbol for a whole number in the commutative law. In the missing addend problem the symbol stands for an *unknown* whole number—the symbol N acts as a *temporary name* for a whole number. In the commutative law a symbol stands for a *typical* whole number. The context should tell you how a given symbol for a whole number is being used. Both uses of symbols are very powerful, and we will employ them in subsequent chapters. In the meantime, we should agree on some rules to use when working with expressions involving symbols, including not only letter symbols but also numerals and $+$, $-$, and $=$.

We have already seen some rules dealing with the use of symbols in the definitions of the commutative and associative properties. More basic than these are rules relating to equality and these operations.

THE SUBSTITUTION PRINCIPLE

If A and B are (symbols for) whole numbers and $A = B$, then in any expression involving A we can replace any occurrence of the symbol A by the symbol B and obtain an expression equal to the first.

ADDITION AND SUBTRACTION PROPERTIES OF EQUALITY

If A, B, and C are whole numbers and $A = B$, then $A + C = B + C$. If $C \leq A$, then $A - C = B - C$.

These properties are frequently expressed this way: "If you add the same thing to both sides of an equation, then equality is maintained. If you subtract the same thing from both sides of an equation, then equality is maintained."

Finally, there is another rule related to the interaction of addition with equality.

CANCELLATION PROPERTY OF ADDITION

If A, B, and C are whole numbers and $A + C = B + C$, then also $A = B$.

The addition property of equality and the cancellation property of addition are not the same. However, one is called the *converse* of the other.

The Cashier Method of Subtraction

The cancellation property of addition is the basis for the following method of subtraction. (This is sometimes called the cashier method, a method based on finding a missing addend.) Suppose you buy something that costs $27 and you give the cashier a $50 bill. The amount of change that you get back is the solution N to the missing addend problem $27 + N = 50$.

The cashier solves the problem

"27 plus 3 is 30, plus *10* more is 40, plus *10* more is 50."

So you know that $27 + (3 + 10 + 10) = 50$ or $27 + 23 = 50$. You also know that $27 + N = 50$. Thus, $27 + 23 = 27 + N$. By the cancellation property of addition, $N = 23$.

EXERCISE 23. Use the cashier method of subtraction to solve the missing addend problems.
(a) $62 + P = 100$ (b) $133 + N = 500$ (c) $419 + M = 1000$

Parentheses and the Order of Operations

The operations in parentheses are to be performed before the other operations in an expression. The associative property of addition says that for all whole numbers A, B, and C the equation $(A + B) + C = A + (B + C)$ holds. In words this says, if you first add B to A and then to that add C, you get the same as if you had first added C to B and then added what you got to A. Which addition you carry out first doesn't matter, so the parentheses can be ignored. There are, however, expressions involving addition and subtraction of whole numbers where the parentheses are important.

Suppose you have whole numbers A, B, and C. You subtract B from A and to that you add C. You get $(A - B) + C$. Can the parentheses be ignored? Can you calculate the expression by first adding C to B and then subtracting that from A? In other words, we are asking whether the equation $(A - B) + C = A - (B + C)$ is valid for all whole numbers A, B, and C.

A quick check with some specific numbers $(A = 3, B = 2, C = 1)$ shows that this is not true for all A, B, and C. Parentheses and order of operation are important! However, an expression such as $A - B + C$, involving both addition and subtraction but without parentheses, usually has the following interpretation: You carry out the operations in order, from left to right.

EXERCISES 24. The following expressions involve whole numbers A, B, and C, the operations $+$ and $-$, and some parentheses. Write equations showing which pairs of expressions are equal for any choice of A, B, and C.
(a) $(A - B) + C$ (b) $(A + C) - B$ (c) $(A - B) - C$
(d) $A - (B + C)$ (e) $A - (B - C)$ (f) $(A + C) - B$
Use the set definitions of addition and subtraction to show why the equations you have made are true for any choice of A, B, and C.

25. Use the rules we have developed for working with symbols to solve the following problems.
(a) Find a whole number A so that $37 + A = 62$.
(b) Find a whole number B so that $137 - B = 69$.
(c) Find a whole number C so that $73 = C + 45$.
(d) Find whole numbers D and E so that $D = 2 + E$ and $D + E = 8$.
(e) Find whole numbers F and G so that $F = G + 75$ and $123 = F + G$.
(f) Find whole numbers H and J so that $H + J = 1371$ and $H - J = 513$.

4.5   EXTENDING THE IDEAS: ORDER, ADDITION, AND SUBTRACTION ON THE NUMBER LINE

In chapter 3 we introduced the number line, a way to visualize whole numbers and the order of whole numbers. The number line is also a vehicle for visualizing addition and subtraction of whole numbers and for visualizing relationships between order and addition and subtraction.

We begin this section by showing how to add and subtract on the number line using an *add-subtract slide rule.*

Make two copies of the number line with one copy just above the other.

Call the number line on the top the *top line* and the one on the bottom the *bottom line.* The top line will stay fixed and the bottom line will "slide." This is the add-subtract slide rule.

To add with the add-subtract slide rule, let A and B be two whole numbers. To find the sum $A + B$ on *top,* slide the *bottom line* so that 0 of the bottom line and A of the top line are in the same position:

```
0                    A                                    Top
•                    •

           ─────────────────────────────────────────────

                     •                    •
                     0                    B                Bottom
```

Look for B on the bottom line. The point on the top just above B is $A + B$.

```
0                    A                    A + B           Top
•                    •                    •

           ─────────────────────────────────────────────

                     •                    •
                     0                    B                Bottom
```

EXERCISES

26. Use an add-subtract slide rule to calculate
(a) $16 + 27$ (b) $25 + 38$.

27. Why does the add-subtract slide rule work in adding two whole numbers?

Now that we know how to add on the number line using the add-subtract slide rule, it should be easy to figure out how to subtract. Suppose that A and B are whole numbers and that $B \leq A$. Given A and B on the number line, we want to find the whole number $N = A - B$. We know that N is the solution to the missing addend problem $B + N = A$. We also know that to add N to B using the add-subtract slide rule, we place the 0 of the bottom line just below the B of the top line.

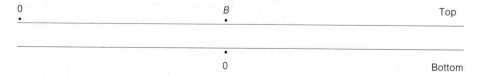

If we knew N, then the sum $B + N$ would be the point on the top line just above N on the bottom line.

| 0 | | B | | B + N | | Top |

| | | 0 | | N | | Bottom |

But we know the sum—it's A. So we look for A on the top line. The number N we are looking for is the point just below A on the bottom line:

| 0 | | B | | A | | Top |

| | | 0 | | $N = A - B$ | | Bottom |

Let's summarize the discussion.

HOW TO ADD AND SUBTRACT ON THE NUMBER LINE
USING THE ADD-SUBTRACT SLIDE RULE

Suppose that A and B are whole numbers. To find the sum $A + B$ on the number line, set the 0 of the *bottom line* and the A of the *top line* at the same position. Then the B of the bottom line and the $A + B$ of the top line will be in the same position.

If $B \leq A$, then to find the difference $A - B$ on the number line, set the 0 of the *bottom line* and the B of the *top line* at the same position. The A of the top line and the $A - B$ of the bottom line will be in the same position.*

With these ideas, we can define $A \leq B$ using only addition.

DEFINITION OF ORDER OF WHOLE NUMBERS USING ADDITION

Suppose that A and B are whole numbers. Then $A \leq B$ means that there is a whole number N such that $A + N = B$. Furthermore, $A < B$ means there is a whole number $N \neq 0$ such that $A + N = B$.

The order of whole numbers $A < B$ cooperates with addition and subtraction.

---

* The manual designed to be used with this text contains an add-subtract slide rule to cut out, assemble, and use.

Suppose that A, B, and C are whole numbers and that $A < B$. Then also $A + C < B + C$. If in addition to knowing $A < B$ we know that $C \leq A$, then $A - C < B - C$.

0			A	$A + C$		B	$B + C$

0	$A - C$	A			$B - C$	B	

The pictures show why these order properties are true. We can show these in another way using the fact that $A < B$ means there is a whole number $N \neq 0$ such that $A + N = B$. Indeed, if $A + N = B$, then $(A + N) + C = B + C$ by the addition property of equality. But $(A + N) + C = (A + C) + N$ by the commutative and associative properties of addition. Thus, $(A + C) + N = B + C$. This, in turn, means that $A + C < B + C$. This same argument shows—using the formal properties of addition—that the difference $B - A$ is the same as the difference $(B + C) - (A + C)$. This gives a formal justification of the equal additions method of subtraction.

EXERCISES

28. Use the subtraction property of equality to show that if $C < A$ and $A < B$, then $A - C < B - C$.

29. Suppose that A, B, C, and D are whole numbers and that $A < B$ and $C < D$. Can you use the order property of addition to say anything about which is larger, $A + C$ or $B + D$?

30. Suppose that A, B, C, and D are whole numbers and that $A < B$, $C < D$, and $D \leq A$. Can you use the order property of subtraction to say anything about which is larger, $A - D$ or $B - C$?

Using Order Properties of Addition and Subtraction to Estimate Answers or Check Their Reasonableness

The results of exercises 29 and 30 should lead you to the following properties.

If A, B, C, and D are whole numbers such that $A < B$ and $C < D$, then $A + C \leq B + D$. If in addition $D \leq A$, then $A - D < B - C$.

We can use these properties to check answers to addition and subtraction problems. For example, suppose you want to check your answer to the addition problem

$$\begin{array}{r} 582 \\ + 247 \\ \hline \end{array}$$

You know that $500 < 582$ and that $200 < 247$. Using the new order property of addition, you get $500 + 200 < 582 + 247$. Also, $582 < 600$ and $247 < 300$ so that $582 + 247 < 600 + 300$. These two inequalities together give you an estimation for the sum. It must lie between 700 and 900: $700 < 582 + 247 < 900$.

If you have calculated an "exact" answer and it lies outside this range, then you know you have made a mistake in your calculation.

As a second example, suppose you want to estimate or check your answer to the subtraction problem

$$\begin{array}{r} 582 \\ - 247 \\ \hline \end{array}$$

You know that $582 < 600$ and $200 < 247$. The new order property of subtraction then says that

$$(1) \quad 582 - 247 < 600 - 200.$$

You also know that $500 < 582$ and $247 < 300$. Again, the new order property of subtraction says that

$$(2) \quad 500 - 300 < 582 - 247.$$

Putting inequalities (1) and (2) together, you get $200 < 582 - 247 < 400$. So the answer to our problem is estimated to be between 200 and 400. If an "exact" answer we get to our problem doesn't lie in this range, then we must have made a mistake.

EXERCISE 31. Use the technique just described to estimate the answers.

(a) $\begin{array}{r} 673 \\ + 385 \\ \hline \end{array}$ (b) $\begin{array}{r} 3407 \\ + 923 \\ \hline \end{array}$ (c) $\begin{array}{r} 12{,}305 \\ + 47{,}831 \\ \hline \end{array}$

(d) $\begin{array}{r} 735 \\ - 286 \\ \hline \end{array}$ (e) $\begin{array}{r} 9703 \\ - 5678 \\ \hline \end{array}$ (f) $\begin{array}{r} 34{,}590 \\ - 17{,}803 \\ \hline \end{array}$

4.6 SUMMARY OF IMPORTANT IDEAS AND TECHNIQUES

- Primitive addition
- The definition of addition of whole numbers using the union of two disjoint sets
- Stages in the development of the standard method for addition
  Elementary addition facts
  Addition using place value blocks
  Addition using a counting board
  Addition using expanded form on a counting board
- Primitive subtraction
- The definition of subtraction for whole numbers using the complement of a set
- Stages in the development of the standard method for subtraction
  Elementary subtraction facts
  Subtraction using place value blocks
  Subtraction using stones on a counting board
  Subtraction using expanded form on a counting board

- Unusual methods of subtraction
  The method of equal additions
  The method of complements
  The cashier method
- Recognizing problem situations that call for subtraction
- Formal properties of addition
  Zero, an identity for addition
  Commutative property of addition
  Associative property of addition
- The use of symbols and letters: a glimpse at algebra
  Rules for working with symbols
  Substitution principle
  Addition and subtraction properties of equality
  Cancellation property of addition
- The relationship of order to addition and subtraction
  The add-subtract slide rule
  Definition of order using addition
  The order properties of addition and subtraction
  Using order properties to estimate solutions or check the reasonableness of solutions to addition and subtraction problems

PROBLEM SET

PRACTICING
SKILLS

1. Curious George, the irrepressible monkey, is going on a picnic with his relatives. Every monkey wants to wear a hat. George brings out his hats from his closet. He has this many hats:

   ◯ ◯ ◯ ◯ ◯

   His cousin Martha gets her hats from her closet. She has this many hats:

   ◯ ◯ ◯ ◯ ◯ ◯ ◯ ◯

   George and Martha and the rest of the monkeys line up to choose hats.

   ◯ ◯ ◯ ◯ ◯ ◯ ◯ ◯ ◯ ◯ ◯ ◯

   Will every monkey have a hat to wear? Solve this problem without counting.

2. Solve the addition problems using place value blocks.
   (a) 469 + 375   (b) 582 + 740

   Record your steps using ⬜ for a cube, ⬜ for a flat, ▭ for a long, and ▢ for a unit.

3. Solve the addition problems using stones on a counting board.
   (a) 683 + 299   (b) 756 + 849
   Record your steps by drawing pictures of counting boards with stones.

4. Use expanded form on a counting board to solve the addition problems.
   (a) $258 + 493$ (b) $954 + 867$

5. Max has counted 37 pieces of candy, all that he collected at Halloween. He wants to know how much will be left for himself if he gives 1 piece of candy to each student in his first grade class. He knows there are 26 students in his class. He has had a lot of experience with single-digit numbers, but he has not yet learned about subtraction. How could Max solve this problem?

6. Solve the following subtraction problems using (i) place value blocks and (ii) stones on a counting board.
   (a) $79 - 46$ (b) $685 - 423$ (c) $873 - 498$ (d) $4365 - 3896$

7. Use expanded form on a counting board to solve the subtraction problems.
   (a) $483 - 289$ (b) $8602 - 1953$

8. Use the method of equal additions to solve the subtraction problems.
   (a) $765 - 289$ (b) $6843 - 4788$

9. Use the method of complements to solve the subtraction problems.
   (a) $8213 - 3629$ (b) $7644 - 5087$

10. Use the rules developed for working with symbols to solve the problems.
    (a) Find a whole number A so that $A + 58 = 97$.
    (b) Find a whole number B so that $259 - B = 147$.

11. Use the rules developed for working with symbols to solve the problems.
    (a) Find whole numbers A and B so that $A = 35 + B$ and $241 = A + B$.
    (b) Find whole numbers C and D so that $C = 23 - D$ and $D = 57 + C$.

12. Use the order properties of addition and subtraction to estimate the answers.

(a)	(b)	(c)	(d)
5329	$74{,}618$	8971	$65{,}702$
$+\ 856$	$+\ 97{,}864$	$-\ 2089$	$-\ 28{,}738$

13. Complete the following addition table for stick numerals. This table should include all the elementary addition facts for stick numerals.

Plus	十	卉	韭	韮	十|
十					
卉					
韭		十|			
韮					
十|					

14. Use the table completed in problem 13 to solve the following stick numeral subtraction problems as missing addend problems.
    (a) 十韭 − 韮
    (b) 十韭 − 卉
    (c) 十韭 − 十\|
    (d) 十十 − 韭

For each problem remaining, document as clearly and completely as you can your solution to the problem. Include the steps you took to solve the problem, mention the problems or solutions from the text that gave you ideas, and include the problem-solving strategies you used. You might want to outline and organize these details before assembling your final report.

15. Find the sum of stick numerals ⵣⵏⵣ and ⵏⵣⵏ by *making models* of them in two different ways: (a) using base 5 place value blocks and (b) using a base 5 counting board. Record your solutions using pictures.

16. Subtract stick numeral ⵏⵣⵏ from ⵣⵏⵣ by making models of them in two different ways: (a) using base 5 place value blocks and (b) using a base 5 counting board. Record your solutions using pictures.

17. Find the sum of the base 7 place value block numerals shown, working entirely within the system of blocks. Record your steps in solving this with pictures.

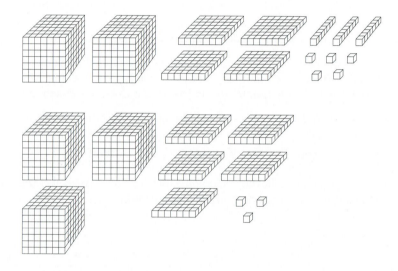

18. In problem 17, subtract the smaller place block numeral from the larger. Again, work entirely with the base 7 system of place value blocks. Record your steps with pictures.

19. Find the sum of the base 8 counting board numerals shown, working entirely within the counting board system. Record the steps of your solution with pictures of stones on counting boards.

(a)

8²s	8s	1s
O O O O	O O O O O	O O O O O

(b)

8²s	8s	1s
O O	O O O O O O O	O O O O O O

20. In problem 19, subtract the smaller counting board numeral from the larger. Work entirely within the base 8 counting board system and record your steps with pictures.

21. Addition of stick numerals can also be carried out using a base 5 abacus, which allows in the early steps of a solution an unlimited number of beads on a post. First, go through a sample problem and solution.

   Problem: Add the stick numerals 丰丰丰 and 十十丰.
   Solution: Convert the first numeral to beads on an abacus.

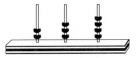

   Post by post, from the second numeral add beads to the abacus equal to the number of horizontal cross bars of the numeral.

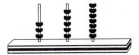

   Trade 5 beads on any post for a single bead on the post just to its left. Do this until there are no more than 4 beads on any post.

   (a) 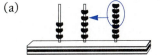 (b) 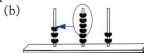 (c)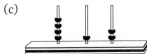

   Use this method to add these stick numerals: 丰|丰 and 十丰十.
   Record the steps you take with pictures of beads on abaci.

22. The method of problem 21 can be altered so that at any stage no more than 4 beads on a post are allowed. For example, to add the stick numerals 丰丰丰 and 十十丰, convert one of them to an abacus as before.

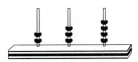

   Then add the other numeral to it, post by post, as follows.

   (i) *First post:* The abacus has 丰 here. The other numeral has 丰. The sum of these is the stick numeral 十丰. So, on the abacus you remove 2 beads from the first post, leaving 2, and add 1 to the second.

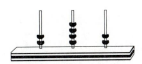

(ii) *Second post:* The abacus now has 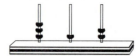 on this post; the numeral has ⊥. The sum of these is the stick numeral ⊥⊥. So, on the abacus you remove 3 beads from the second post, leaving 1, and add 1 to the third:

(iii) *Third post:* The abacus has 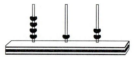 on this post and the numeral has ⊥. The sum is the numeral ≢. Thus, you add 1 to the fourth:

(a) Use this method to add the stick numerals

≢ ⊥ ≢ and ⊥ ≢ ≢

(b) Try this method with the stick numerals

⊥ ≢ ≢ and ⊥ ≢ ⊥

What happens with this pair that didn't happen with the worked out example above and that creates a problem? What do you do to resolve this problem?

23. A base 5 abacus can also be used to subtract stick numerals.
   (a) In the manner of problem 21, outline a method of subtracting one stick numeral from another on a base 5 abacus that allows an unlimited number of beads on each post in the early stages of the solution. Illustrate your method by subtracting ⊥ ≢ ≢ from ≢ ⊥ ≢ and ⊥ ≢ ≢ from ≢ | ≢.
   (b) In the manner of problem 22, alter the method of problem 23(a) so that at most 4 beads are allowed on a post at any stage of the solution. Illustrate your method with the same pairs of stick numerals as in (a).

24. How you would adapt the standard method of addition for decimal numerals to one for stick numerals? (*Suggestions:* One way you might answer this is to display an annotated solution using expanded notation on a counting board, in parallel with the standard method, as was done in the text. The particular numerals in your illustration should be chosen carefully so that the solution contains all variations of your method. For instance, numerals that don't involve trading would not be a good choice.)

25. How would you adapt the standard method of subtraction for decimal numerals to one for stick numerals? (See suggestions in prob. 24.)

26. Find the missing digits in the following stick numeral addition and subtraction problems.
   (a) ☐ ≢ ≢ ☐   (b) ⊥ ☐ | ≢   (c) ⊥ | ☐ ⊥   (d) ☐ ⊥ ☐ ⊥
   (plus) ≢ ☐ ≢   (plus) ≢ ⊥ ☐ ☐   (minus) ☐ ⊥ ≢   (minus) ⊥ ≢ ⊥ ☐
   ‾‾‾‾‾‾‾‾‾   ‾‾‾‾‾‾‾‾‾   ‾‾‾‾‾‾‾‾‾   ‾‾‾‾‾‾‾‾‾
   ≢ ☐ | ≢   ☐ ⊥ | ⊥   ≢ ☐   ⊥ ☐ | ⊥

27. Here is a stick number addition problem in code. Each letter stands for one of the stick digits │, ┼, ╪, ╪, or ╪. Different letters stand for different digits. (Obviously, the left-most digit in any stick numeral can't be │.) Decode the problem by finding X, B, and A.

$$
\begin{array}{r}
X\ X\ X \\
B \\
\hline
B\ A\ A\ A
\end{array}
$$

28. Jatora lives in the kingdom of Xapho, where the basic monetary unit is the xaph. She uses a base 6 counting board having four columns as shown on the far left below. Each pebble in the right-most column (marked with an X) is worth 1 xaph. Jatora wants to buy a camel that costs the amount indicated in the diagram below; she also wants to buy a saddle that costs the amount indicated second from the right. Jatora has the amount also indicated in the diagram. Figure out how much Jatora will have left after she pays for the camel and the saddle.

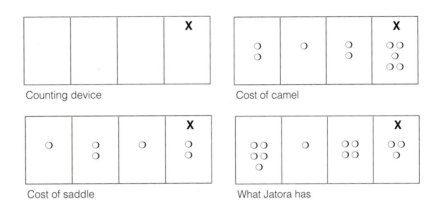

Counting device

Cost of camel

Cost of saddle

What Jatora has

Use only the base 6 counting board system to solve this problem. Draw pictures of counting boards showing how you solved it.

29. You are in charge of ordering emergency phone boxes to go along the interstate from Tucson to Nogales. How many should you order? You know that

The phones are to be placed every 1056 ft on both sides of the road.
The length of the road to be covered is 55 mi.
No phones are needed at either end of the road to be covered.
1 mi = 5280 ft.

30. Here is an addition problem in code for decimal numerals. Each letter stands for one of the digits 0 through 9. Different letters stand for different digits. Each letter stands for the same digit for all its occurrences. For example, if the E in MORE stands for 3, then the E in MONEY also stands for 3. (By convention, the left-most digit of any decimal numeral cannot be 0.)

$$
\begin{array}{r}
S\ E\ N\ D \\
+\ M\ O\ R\ E \\
\hline
M\ O\ N\ E\ Y
\end{array}
$$

Decode the problem by finding out what digit each letter stands for. (You might want to make a guess or two to get started.)

31. Here is a subtraction problem in code. Each letter stands for one of the digits 0 through 9. Different letters stand for different digits. (The rules are the same as for prob. 30.)

$$
\begin{array}{r}
S\ P\ E\ N\ D \\
-\ M\ O\ R\ E \\
\hline
M\ O\ N\ E\ Y
\end{array}
$$

Find out what each letter stands for. (*Hint:* More than one answer is possible. For a start, make a guess for *M* from among 1, 2, 3, 4, 5, 6, 7, 8, 9 and see what the consequences are.)

32. Explain why the method of complements, as a method for subtraction, always works.

33. Consider the expression $97 + 42 - 24 + 12 - 37$. (You recall that in an expression involving additions and subtractions, you perform the operations from left to right.) To calculate this number using a calculator, you use the key sequence

$$97\ [+]\ 42\ [-]\ 24\ [+]\ 12\ [-]\ 37\ [=].$$

(a) Here is a list of your checking account transactions for the month of November:

Nov. 1: Balance from October	$573
Nov. 5: Check for rent	$275
Nov. 7: Deposit	$435
Nov. 13: Check for food	$72
Nov. 17: Check for car payment	$135
Nov. 20: Check for clothing	$110
Nov. 22: Check for insurance	$153
Nov. 25: Deposit	$127
Nov. 29: Check for food	$84

Use a calculator to determine the balance at the end of the month.

(b) Below is a table of annual 1988 budgets for the major zoological parks in the Southwest.

Arizona-Sonora Desert Museum	$2,500,000
Dallas Zoo	2,400,000
Houston Zoo	2,600,000
Los Angeles Zoo	1,400,000
Phoenix Zoo	2,600,000
San Antonio Zoo	5,700,000
San Diego Zoo	28,000,000
San Diego Wild Animal Park	16,000,000

Use your calculator to determine the total amount spent by these parks in 1988.

MULTIPLICATION OF WHOLE NUMBERS

CHAPTER

In this chapter we will discuss the multiplication of whole numbers. Our goal is to understand what multiplication is, where it is used, and why the familiar methods we use for multiplication actually do what they are supposed to. The main part of the chapter consists of a series of problems each of which can be solved by multiplying two whole numbers and which progresses from simple problems involving single-digit numbers to problems containing several-digit numbers. We will solve the problems from the point of view of a person who has had no previous experience with multiplication but who has had a lot of experience with addition and subtraction. As the problems increase in complexity, this person gains experience, and we are able to see just what new mathematical skills are needed for solving the new problems. In this way we will experience for ourselves the evolution of the standard method for multiplying several-digit numbers and understand how it works. Since the method evolves from real problems and their solutions, the person will gain the ability to recognize many situations where the method can be used and believe that it does the job it is supposed to.

A discussion of some formal properties of multiplication follows, which, in turn, leads to rules for solving equations with unknowns. We will also discuss the relationship of multiplication to order and its use in estimating products of large numbers.

In the early parts of the chapter, we think of multiplication first as repeated addition and then as counting the number of items in an array. Later in the chapter, we look at two additional ways of thinking about multiplication: (1) as counting the number of branch ends in certain *tree diagrams* and (2) as counting the number of elements in the *cartesian product* of two sets.

We begin the chapter with a problem that involves large numbers in order to show that a person can solve a complicated multiplication problem without knowing anything about multiplication and—since the nontraditional solution we offer involves a lot of work—to motivate the development of a more systematic method for multiplying two numbers.

THE HOTEL PROBLEM

Try this yourself before reading on.

You run a hotel. All the rooms in Our Hotel are filled for the evening. You'd like to know what your receipts for the night should be. (For one thing, you'd like to know whether the amount of money you have in your cash register matches the amount of money you ought to have taken in.) Here are some clues:

The charge for each room is $45.
Your hotel has 68 rooms.

You are also a person who knows how to add and subtract two- and three-digit numbers. But you don't know about multiplication. How would you solve this?

Solution to the Hotel Problem

You might think like this: "One room costs $45. Two rooms would cost

$$
\begin{array}{r}
\$45 \\
+\ 45 \\
\hline
\$90
\end{array}
$$

Three rooms would cost $45 more than that.

$$
\begin{array}{r}
\$90 \\
+\ 45 \\
\hline
\$135
\end{array}
$$

Hey, I get it. For 68 rooms, just add $45 consecutively 68 times.

$45
$45
$45
$45
$45
$45
$45
$45
$45
$45
$\vdots$

Wait a minute. SIXTY-EIGHT TIMES? I can't get that all on one page. Suppose I were to add the $45s up in bunches of 10 at a time.

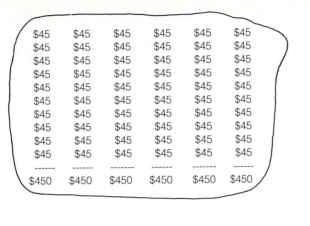

$45 \quad $45 \quad $45 \quad $45 \quad $45 \quad $45
$45 \quad $45 \quad $45 \quad $45 \quad $45 \quad $45
$45 \quad $45 \quad $45 \quad $45 \quad $45 \quad $45
$45 \quad $45 \quad $45 \quad $45 \quad $45 \quad $45
$45 \quad $45 \quad $45 \quad $45 \quad $45 \quad $45
$45 \quad $45 \quad $45 \quad $45 \quad $45 \quad $45
$45 \quad $45 \quad $45 \quad $45 \quad $45 \quad $45
$45 \quad $45 \quad $45 \quad $45 \quad $45 \quad $45
$45 \quad $45 \quad $45 \quad $45 \quad $45 \quad $45
$45 \quad $45 \quad $45 \quad $45 \quad $45 \quad $45

------ ------ ------- ------ ------- ------
$450 $450 $450 $450 $450 $450

"I wouldn't have to total all of the columns; I'd only have to do one of them. The others would add to the same thing—$450. Let me add up the amounts for the six columns.

$$
\begin{array}{r}
\$450 \\
\$450 \\
\$450 \\
\$450 \\
\$450 \\
\$450 \\
\hline
\$2700
\end{array}
$$

"That accounts for the receipts for the first 60 rooms. There are 8 more rooms to account for.

$$
\begin{array}{r}
\$45 \\
\$45 \\
\$45 \\
\$45 \\
\$45 \\
\$45 \\
\$45 \\
\$45 \\
\hline
\$360
\end{array}
$$

"That's it. All I have to do is add the $2700 to the $360.

$$
\begin{array}{r}
\$360 \\
\$2700 \\
\hline
\$3060
\end{array}
$$

"That does it!"

Too Much Work to Solve the Problem?

The solution to the hotel problem seems like a lot of work, especially since you know that it can be solved easily with the standard method for multiplication of two-digit numbers.

Nevertheless, it is an appropriate solution for someone who isn't acquainted with the standard method. After working a few such problems this long way, this person will feel the need for a "better way." When he is acquainted with the better way, he will know and appreciate what is being accomplished when he uses it. Now, let's build up to the method by considering problems with smaller numbers.

EXERCISE

1. You own the wheat field shown below. You know that each of the little squares in the picture produces a bushel of wheat. You'd like to know how much wheat the whole field produces. You have solved the hotel problem, so you know how to add three- and four-digit numbers. But you know nothing about multiplication. How would you solve this?

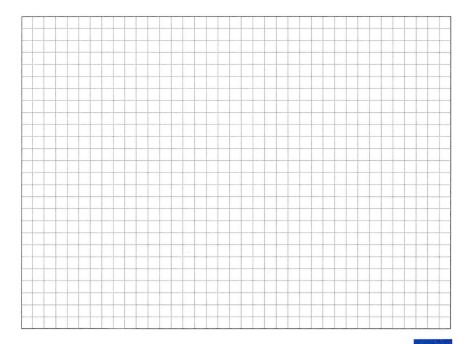

THE BOOK PROBLEM

Try this.

Sarah is in the third grade. She knows nothing about multiplication. She plans to sell 7 books at $8 each and wants to know what her total receipts will be from this sale. How could she solve this?

A Solution to the Book Problem

You, Sarah, add up $8 seven times: $8 + $8 + $8 + $8 + $8 + $8 + $8 = $56.

The Mathematical Idea: Multiplication as Repeated Addition

Sarah solved the book problem by adding $8 to itself repeatedly. You solved the hotel problem by adding 45 repeatedly: there were 68 addends, and each addend was the whole number 45. This method of solution is called repeated addition and leads to the following definition.

DEFINITION OF *MULTIPLICATION*

For any whole numbers A and B,

$$A \times B = \underbrace{B + B + B + \ldots + B.}_{A \text{ addends}}$$

The whole number $A \times B$ is called the *product* of A with B. The whole numbers A and B are called the *factors* of $A \times B$. Given A and B, finding the whole number $A \times B$ is called *multiplication*. In particular, for $1 \times B$ there is one addend so that $1 \times B = B$, and for $0 \times B$ there are *no* addends so that $0 \times B = 0$.

At some point Sarah will be told that 7×8 is shorthand for "7 times 8," which is shorthand for adding 8 repeatedly with 7 addends. After solving many such problems in this way, Sarah will begin to remember the answers to them and would be able to solve the book problem by thinking "$8 added to itself 7 times is $7 \times \$8$ or $56." She will begin to memorize the multiplication tables, the *elementary multiplication facts.*

In earlier grades Sarah and her friends will have had lots of experience with repeated addition when the number to be repeated is 2 or 5 or 10. This occurs in what is called skip counting.

2, 4, 6, 8, 10, . . . (skip counting by 2s)
5, 10, 15, 20, 25, . . . (skip counting by 5s)
10, 20, 30, 40, . . . (skip counting by 10s)

For example, to figure out 4×5, you skip count: 5, 10, 15, 20. The fourth number in the sequence, 20, is the answer.

EXERCISES

2. Mina uses (base 5) stick numerals and doesn't know her multiplication tables. How would she solve ╪ × ╪ ?

3. Suppose that your system of numerals is the base 8 system and that you don't know the base 8 multiplication tables. How would you solve $7_{\text{eight}} \times 5_{\text{eight}}$ completely within the base 8 system? How about $5_{\text{eight}} \times 7_{\text{eight}}$?

4. Make a multiplication table for the base 8 system.

DEVELOPMENT OF THE STANDARD METHOD FOR MULTIPLICATION

THE CLASSROOM SEAT PROBLEM

The seats in John's classroom are arranged as shown.

U U U U U U U U
U U U U U U U U
U U U U U U U U
U U U U U U U U
U U U U U U U U
U U U U U U U U
U U U U U U U U

Try this yourself, first!

John, in the third grade, wants to know how many seats there are. He knows that multiplication is repeated addition and has just learned his multiplication tables. How could he figure out many seats there are?

A Solution to The Classroom Seat Problem

John thinks: "I could count the seats one by one. But maybe there is an easier way. Let me count the seats in the first row: There are 8 of them. All the other rows have 8 seats too. Then, 8 in the first plus 8 in the second, plus 8 in the third . . . Wait! To figure out the number of seats, all I have to do is add 8 to itself as many times as there are rows. Let's see: I count 7 rows. So the answer is 8 added to itself 7 times. Hey, that's just $7 \times 8 = 56$. The answer is 56 seats!"

The Mathematical Idea: Arrays and Multiplication

A bunch of objects arranged in a rectangular formation such as in the illustration of the seats in John's classroom or in that of the marching band, following, is called an *array*.

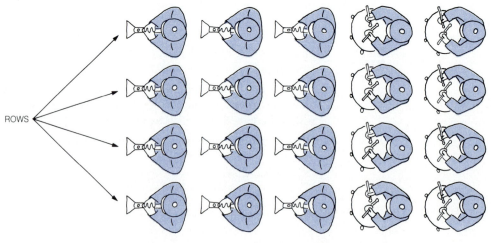

ROWS

A 4 BY 5 ARRAY

The horizontal lines of the array are called *rows*. One row must have the same number of objects as any other. In the case of the array of seats, there are 7 rows and each row has 8 seats. In the case of the marching band, there are 4 rows with 5 players in each row.

John made the connection between the number of items in an array having 7 rows with 8 in a row and the number gotten by adding 8 to itself 7 times. (He knew that this number is the product 7 × 8, which is equal to 56.) This may be an obvious connection for us, but it isn't for someone making it for the first time. We can make a general statement connecting arrays with multiplication.

THE NUMBER OF ITEMS IN AN ARRAY

A certain array has *R* rows with *C* items in each row.

This is called an *R by C* array. The total number of items in an *R by C* array is *R* × *C*.

Let's look at another example where you want to find the number of items in an array. You are purchasing a rectangular rug that is 10 ft long and 12 ft wide.

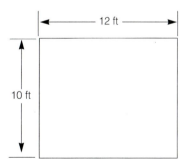

You pay for a rug according to how many square feet it contains. To determine how many square feet in the rug in this example, you superimpose a grid on the rug so that each square is a foot on a side.

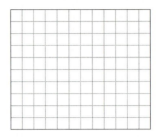

This gives you a 10 by 12 array of squares. As you know, 120, the number of squares (each square a square foot) in this array is the *area* of the rug. We will discuss area in more detail beginning in chapter 17.

EXERCISE

5. Here is a picture of the vines in a vineyard.

John wants to know how many vines there are in this vineyard. How would John figure this out?

THE MOTEL PROBLEM

John runs a motel, Our Motel. All rooms are booked for the night. How much money will this bring him? He knows that

The charge for each room is $68.
The motel has 45 rooms.

Don't forget. Try it!

John solved the hotel problem at the beginning of the chapter. John has also solved the classroom seat problem and knows the connection between repeated addition (multiplication) and arrays. All he knows about multiplication is the tables. Help John solve this problem.

A Solution to the Motel Problem

Here is one way John might go about solving the problem. "In the hotel problem there were 68 rooms, and the charge for each was $45. We *solved that similar problem* by adding $45 to itself 68 times. For the motel problem I should add $68 to itself 45 times. That's a lot of work. Is there another way? I wonder if it means anything that the pairs of numbers are the same—$45 and 68 in one, $68 and 45 in the other. Let me *look at a simpler and similar problem.*

"Suppose I have Cheap Hotel with 7 rooms at $9 a room and Cheap Motel with 9 rooms at $7 a room. All the rooms are filled in Cheap Hotel and in Cheap Motel. I know that the total amount of money taken in for Cheap Hotel is $9 + $9 + $9 + $9 + $9 + $9 + $9 = $9 × 7 = $63 and that the amount of money taken in for Cheap Motel is $7 + $7 + $7 + $7 + $7 + $7 + $7 + $7 + $7 = $7 × 9 = $63. Is it a coincidence that these two totals are the same? Will the same thing happen with the big numbers? I just solved the classroom seat problem. Let me arrange the dollars for Cheap Hotel in an array like this,

$ $ $ $ $ $ $ $ $
$ $ $ $ $ $ $ $ $
$ $ $ $ $ $ $ $ $
$ $ $ $ $ $ $ $ $
$ $ $ $ $ $ $ $ $
$ $ $ $ $ $ $ $ $
$ $ $ $ $ $ $ $ $

with 7 rows (the 7 rooms) and 9 dollar signs in each row (the charge for each room). The total number of dollars in that array is $9 × 7 or $63. If I turn Cheap Hotel's array on its side, I'll get the array for Cheap Motel:

$ $ $ $ $ $ $
$ $ $ $ $ $ $
$ $ $ $ $ $ $
$ $ $ $ $ $ $
$ $ $ $ $ $ $
$ $ $ $ $ $ $
$ $ $ $ $ $ $
$ $ $ $ $ $ $
$ $ $ $ $ $ $

"The same thing would work for Our Hotel and Our Motel! For Our Hotel, let me make an array of little squares with 68 rows (a row for each room) and with 45 squares in each row (a square for each dollar of a room's price).

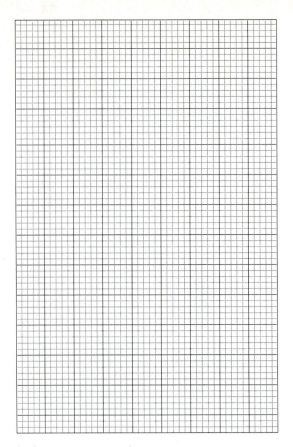

"Then let me tilt this array on its side.

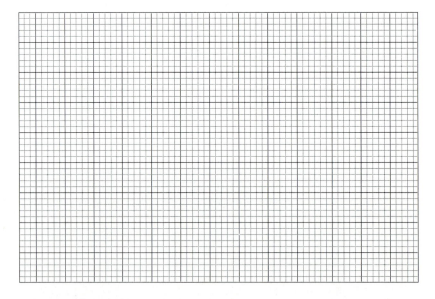

"The array tilted on its side is an array with 45 rows (one row for each room in Our Motel) and 68 squares in each row (the price for a room in Our Motel). The number of dollars for the hotel and the motel problem is the same! The answer to the hotel problem was $3060. The answer to the motel problem is also $3060."

The Mathematical Idea: Multiplication as Commutative

John solved the motel problem first by relating it to the hotel problem and then by looking at a pair of simpler problems, Cheap Hotel and Cheap Motel. He noticed that a 7 by 9 array has the same number of elements as a 9 by 7 array, or, in terms of multiplication, that $7 \times 9 = 9 \times 7$. Children learning their multiplication tables will notice that $3 \times 4 = 4 \times 3$, that $7 \times 9 = 9 \times 7, \ldots$ and be amazed. It is not surprising that they are amazed because the *problems* that give rise to the products 7×9 and 9×7 can be quite different, as we saw with Cheap Hotel and Cheap Motel. However, by viewing a product as the number of objects in a suitable array, we see that $7 \times 9 = 9 \times 7$ and $4 \times 8 = 8 \times 4$ are not coincidences and that this sort of thing works for the product of any pair of whole numbers, no matter how big they might be. An array with A rows of B items each (having a total of $A \times B$ items in the whole array) that is tilted on its side becomes an array with B rows of A items each (having a total of $B \times A$ items in the whole array). This demonstrates the *commutative* property of multiplication.

COMMUTATIVE PROPERTY OF MULTIPLICATION

For every pair of whole numbers A and B, $A \times B = B \times A$. The whole number $\underbrace{B + B + \cdots + B}_{A \text{ addends}}$ is the same as the whole number $\underbrace{A + A + \cdots + A}_{B \text{ addends}}$.

The commutative property of multiplication can be used to help organize the *elementary multiplication facts*. Once you know that $5 \times 9 = 45$, then by the commutative property you also know that $9 \times 5 = 45$.

EXERCISES

6. John knows that the answer to the wheat field problem (exercise 1) is 962 bushels of wheat. Help him solve the corresponding problem for another wheat field.

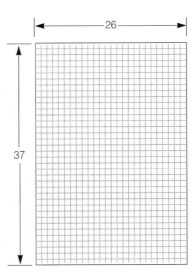

7. Mina's friend Ila has a field of cabbages.

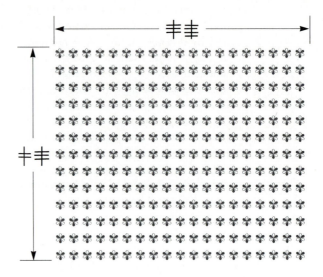

Ila knows that there are 十丰丰十 cabbages in the field and has told Mina that. Mina has a field of cauliflowers.

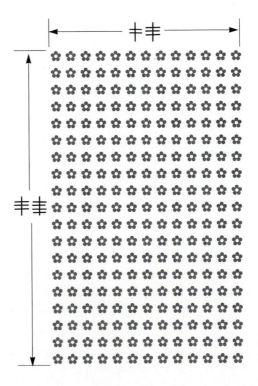

Mina wants to know how many cauliflowers she has. Help her find out. (Mina and Ila both use stick numerals to represent numbers.)

Maria is trying to find out how many linoleum tiles will be needed to tile the family room in her house. She has figured out that the tiles will look like this when placed on the family room floor.

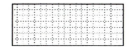

Maria knows her multiplication tables up through the 10s, and she knows the connection between multiplication and the number of objects in an array. But that's all. If you were Maria, how would you solve the problem?

A Solution to the Floor Tile Problem

Maria thinks: "This is an array of tiles. There are 7 rows and 19 tiles in each row. If it were smaller—such as a 7 by 9 array—then I could solve it. A 7 by 9 array would have $7 \times 9 = 63$ tiles in all. My array has too many tiles in each row. Wait! What if I were to cut up the array into two smaller arrays?"

"Now I have two arrays of tiles. One is a 7 by 10 array; the other is a 7 by 9 array. I can figure out the number of tiles in each of the two small arrays: $7 \times 10 = 70$ in one and $7 \times 9 = 63$ in the other. I could add the two answers together to get the total number of tiles in the 7 by 19 array: $7 \times 19 = 70 + 63 = 133$ tiles."

The Mathematical Idea: Multiplication as Distributive over Addition

Maria solved the floor tile problem by *breaking the main problem into smaller problems* that she could solve. She did this by breaking the large array into two smaller arrays.

What does this look like in symbols? You want to find the product 7×19. You know that $19 = 10 + 9$. So $7 \times 19 = 7 \times (10 + 9)$. You find 7×19 by first finding 7×10, then 7×9, and finally adding the two quantities together: $7 \times 19 = 7 \times (10 + 9) = 7 \times 10 + 7 \times 9$. This is an instance of a general property of multiplication and addition.

DISTRIBUTIVE PROPERTY OF MULTIPLICATION OVER ADDITION

$$A \times (B + C) = (A \times B) + (A \times C)$$

for all whole numbers A, B, C. Also, since multiplication is commutative,

$$(A + B) \times C = (A \times C) + (B \times C).$$

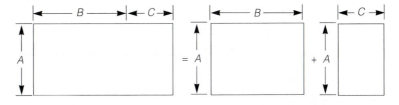

The distributive property can be used to figure out the elementary multiplication facts for "larger" numbers if you know them for "smaller" numbers. For example, suppose you want to figure out 6×9. You can write 9 as $9 = 4 + 5$ and use the distributive law: $6 \times 9 = 6 \times (4 + 5) = 6 \times 4 + 6 \times 5$. Because you know the multiplication tables for smaller numbers, you can calculate the right-hand side. It's $24 + 30 = 54$. So $6 \times 9 = 54$.

EXERCISES

8. Maria must figure out the number of trees in her uncle's orchard.

All Maria knows about multiplication is the tables. Help Maria solve this problem using the distributive law.

9. Your system of numerals is the base 8 system, and now you know the base 8 multiplication tables; but that's all you know about multiplication. Use what you know and the distributive law to figure out the number of vines in the vineyard across the road.

THE SECOND FLOOR TILE PROBLEM

Maria now has the problem of figuring out the number of parquet tiles needed for her living room. She has figured out that the tiles will be arranged as shown.

Try it, please!

If you were Maria how would you solve this new problem?

Maria thinks: "It's another array. This time, the number of tiles in each row and the number of rows are *both* too big! Before I give up why don't I do what I did before and cut down on the number of objects in each row. I'll try this.

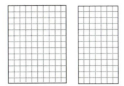

That's a little better. Now I need to cut down on the number of rows. But that's no problem. Let me try this.

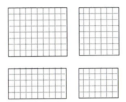

I have *broken the problem up into simpler problems.* Now there are four arrays, each of a size I can handle. I can figure out the number of tiles in each one, then add them all up to get the answer."

The Mathematical Idea: Using the Distributive Law Several Times

Maria used the distributive law several times. Here's what her solution looks like in symbols and pictures.

$$13 \times 17 = 13 \times (10 + 7)$$
$$= 13 \times 10 + 13 \times 7$$
$$= (8 + 5) \times 10 + (8 + 5) \times 7$$
$$= 8 \times 10 + 5 \times 10 + 8 \times 7 + 5 \times 7$$
$$= 80 + 50 + 56 + 35$$
$$= 221.$$

	17			10	7
13	13 X 17	=	8	8 X 10	8 X 7
			5	5 X 10	5 X 7

10. Help Maria find the number of trees in *this* orchard.

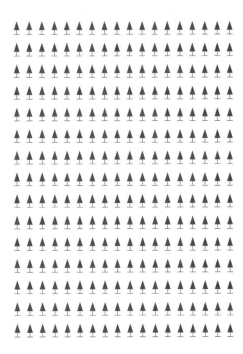

11. Your system of numerals is the base 8 system, and now you know the base 8 multiplication tables; but that's all you know about multiplication. Use what you know and the distributive law to figure out the number of vines in the vineyard on the edge of town.

THE COMPUTER HANDBOOK
PROMBLEM

Please try it yourself first.

At Saul's school, the PTA plans to raise enough money to buy a computer handbook for every student in the school. Saul would like to know how much the PTA will have to raise. He knows that there are about 325 students in his school and that each handbook costs about $10. Saul knows his multiplication table (through the 10s), has solved many different multiplication problems—such as the classroom seat problem, the hotel and motel problems, and the floor tile problem—using the commutative and distributive properties of multiplication, but he doesn't know the standard method for multiplying many-digit numbers.

A Solution to the Computer
Handbook Problem

Saul thinks: "I can find the answer by adding up $10 to itself 325 times. Let's see. I know that ten 10s is 100. So twenty 10s would be 200. And five more 10s would make 250. Twenty-five 10s is 250. Now what about three hundred 10s? That's a lot more work. All these 10s make me think of a counting board. Let me *make a model* of 300 on a counting board.

Three stones are in the 100s column. Repeated addition of that 10 times yields 30 stones in the 100s column. Each 10 of the stones is worth a single stone in the column to the left. That gives me 3 stones in the 1000s column.

So $10 \times 300 = 3000$. Putting all that I know together, I get $10 \times 325 = 3000 + 250$."

The Mathematical Idea: Multiplication by 10

If a person can skip count by 10 or has a good knowledge of place value, then it is easy for that person to learn the 10s multiplication table: $1 \times 10 = 10$, $2 \times 10 = 20, \ldots, 10 \times 10 = 100$. A next step might be to learn how to multiply 10 by any number.

Saul's solution to the problem of finding 10×300 involved a counting board. Let's look at another multiplication problem using this device. Consider the problem 10×457. Here is 457 on the counting board.

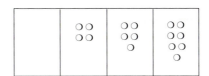

Multiplication of this by 10 (using repeated addition) means replacing each stone by 10 stones, then replacing each of those 10 stones by a stone in the column to its left. The net effect is to move each original stone one column to its left.

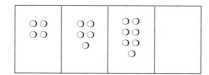

In terms of written numerals, multiplication by 10 amounts to placing a zero to the right of the numeral! (*You* knew that, of course, but did Saul?)

Here is another way to see that $10 \times 325 = 3250$ by *making a model* of 325 with place value blocks.

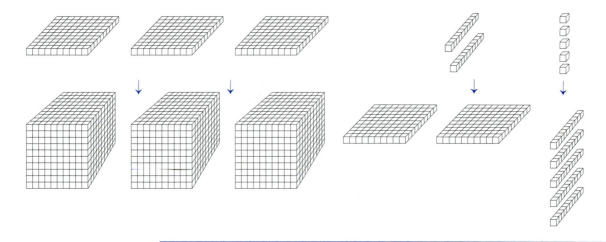

MULTIPLICATION BY 10

To multiply a decimal numeral by 10, place a 0 to the right of the numeral.

EXERCISES

12. Find a rule for multiplication of a stick numeral by $+|$ and justify your rule.

13. Find a rule for multiplication of a base 8 numeral by 10_{eight} and justify your rule.

THE AUDITORIUM SEAT PROBLEM

The seating arrangement of the auditorium in Sarah's school looks like the picture.

∩∩∩∩∩∩∩∩∩∩∩∩∩∩∩∩∩∩∩∩∩∩∩∩∩∩∩∩∩∩∩∩∩∩∩
∩∩∩∩∩∩∩∩∩∩∩∩∩∩∩∩∩∩∩∩∩∩∩∩∩∩∩∩∩∩∩∩∩∩∩
∩∩∩∩∩∩∩∩∩∩∩∩∩∩∩∩∩∩∩∩∩∩∩∩∩∩∩∩∩∩∩∩∩∩∩
∩∩∩∩∩∩∩∩∩∩∩∩∩∩∩∩∩∩∩∩∩∩∩∩∩∩∩∩∩∩∩∩∩∩∩
∩∩∩∩∩∩∩∩∩∩∩∩∩∩∩∩∩∩∩∩∩∩∩∩∩∩∩∩∩∩∩∩∩∩∩
∩∩∩∩∩∩∩∩∩∩∩∩∩∩∩∩∩∩∩∩∩∩∩∩∩∩∩∩∩∩∩∩∩∩∩
∩∩∩∩∩∩∩∩∩∩∩∩∩∩∩∩∩∩∩∩∩∩∩∩∩∩∩∩∩∩∩∩∩∩∩
∩∩∩∩∩∩∩∩∩∩∩∩∩∩∩∩∩∩∩∩∩∩∩∩∩∩∩∩∩∩∩∩∩∩∩
∩∩∩∩∩∩∩∩∩∩∩∩∩∩∩∩∩∩∩∩∩∩∩∩∩∩∩∩∩∩∩∩∩∩∩

Sarah wants to know the number of seats in the auditorium (so she'll know whether or not extra seats have to be brought in for the assembly). Sarah now knows the multiplication tables, the connection between repeated addition and arrays, how to multiply any number by 10, and the commutative and distributive properties of multiplication—at least as they relate to arrays. Help Sarah solve this problem.

A Solution to the Auditorium Seat Problem

Sarah thinks: "There are 9 rows with 30 in each row. I can organize the seats this way.

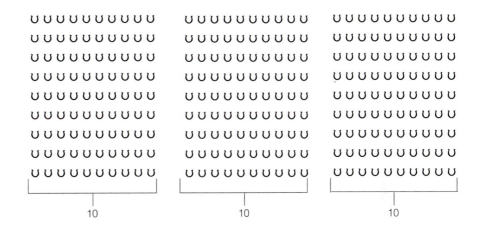

"This breaks the big array up into three smaller arrays. A row in each of the small arrays has 10 seats in it. If I replace each row in the small arrays with a dash, I'd get something like this:

This is an array of dashes. The array has 9 rows with 3 dashes in each row. So this array has $9 \times 3 = 27$ dashes. Since each dash represents 10 seats, there are $27 \times 10 = 270$ seats in all."

The Mathematical Idea: Multiplication as Associative

To figure out 9×30, Sarah first noticed that $30 = 3 \times 10$ and split each row of 30 into three 10s. Replacing each 10 by a dash gave her a 9 by 3 array of dashes. She multiplied 9 times 3 to get 27. Then she multiplied 27 times 10 to get 270. In symbols, this is $9 \times 30 = 9 \times (3 \times 10) = (9 \times 3) \times 10$. The equation says that multiplying 3 by 10 and then multiplying the answer by 9 is the same as multiplying 9 by 3 and then multiplying the answer by 10. This is an instance of the *associative* property of multiplication of whole numbers.

ASSOCIATIVE PROPERTY OF MULTIPLICATION

$$A \times (B \times C) = (A \times B) \times C$$

for all whole numbers A, B, and C.

Together with the commutative property of multiplication, the associative property can be used to help organize the elementary multiplication facts. For example, if a person knows multiplication tables for "small" numbers, she can figure out the product 3×8 this way: $3 \times 8 = 3 \times (2 \times 4) = (3 \times 2) \times 4 = 6 \times 4 = 24$.

EXERCISE

14. Use the associative law to help John find the product 8×70.

THE SCHOOL CAFETERIA FLOOR PROBLEM

Maria is looking at a picture of her school cafeteria floor.

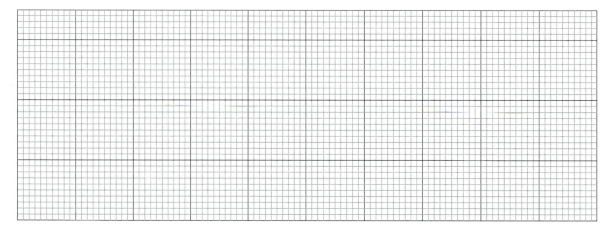

Try it!

The picture shows an array of linoleum tiles that has 35 rows with 100 in each row. Maria wants to know how much all the tiles will cost. Since each tile costs $1, she needs to know how many tiles there are. Maria knows her multiplication tables, knows about arrays, has experience with the commutative, associative, and distributive properties of multiplication, and can multiply any number by 10—and that's all. Help Maria solve this problem.

A Solution to the School Cafeteria Problem

Maria thinks about *simpler problems she has solved*. She thinks: "I want to figure out 35×100. I know that $100 = 10 \times 10$ so that $35 \times 100 = 35 \times (10 \times 10)$. I know how to multiply by 10, and I know the associative property. So

$$35 \times 100 = 35 \times (10 \times 10) = (35 \times 10) \times 10$$
$$= 350 \times 10$$
$$= 3500.$$

That's 3500—35 with two zeros placed to the right of the numeral."

The Mathematical Idea: Multiplication by 100, 1000, . . .

Maria just figured out an instance of the rule for multiplication by 100.

MULTIPLICATION BY 100

To multiply a decimal numeral times 100, you place two zeros to the right of the numeral.

Why it works is that to multiply 100 times 4567 means that you first think of 100 as 10×10; then you use the associative property of multiplication.

$$4567 \times 100 = 4567 \times (10 \times 10) = (4567 \times 10) \times 10 = 45{,}670 \times 10 = 456{,}700.$$

↑   ↑

Place one   Place
zero.   a second
zero.

Multiplication by 1000 can be dealt with in the same way. For example, to multiply 1000 times 1234, we think $1000 = 10 \times 100$ and use associativity. Then

$$1234 \times 1000 = 1234 \times (10 \times 100) = (1234 \times 10) \times 100$$
$$= 12{,}340 \times 100 = 1{,}234{,}000.$$

↑   ↑

Place a new zero   Place two more
(from 10).   zeros (from 100).

Here is the general rule.

MULTIPLICATION OF A DECIMAL NUMERAL BY 10^n

To multiply a decimal numeral by 10^n, place n zeros to the right of the numeral. For example, $10^5 \times 1234 = 123{,}400{,}000.$

↑   ↑

Exponent 5   5 zeros

EXERCISES

15. Maria must figure out the answer to this multiplication problem: $10{,}000 \times 472$. *You* know that the answer is 4,720,000. Explain this to Maria so that she will know and understand how to multiply any number by 10,000. Use the ideas just presented but not the general rule for multiplication by 10^n.

16. Find and justify a rule for multiplication of a stick numeral by $+||$. Do the same for $+|||$.

17. Find and justify a rule for multiplication of a standard base 8 numeral by 100_{eight}. Do the same for 1000_{eight}.

A HARDER PROBLEM

Try it first!

Third graders Sarah, John, Maria, and Saul have solved the multiplication problems that we have seen, starting with the book problem and ending with the school cafeteria floor tile problem. They haven't yet learned the standard method for multiplying two-digit numbers. They need to solve the problem 34 × 57. With their knowledge and experience how might they solve it?

A Solution to a Harder Problem

They sketch a 34 by 57 array.

They think of using the distributive law to break up the 34 by 57 array into smaller arrays. Expanded form suggests to them where to make the break.

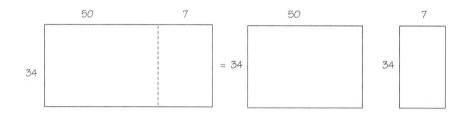

And again:

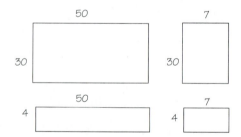

They now have four sub-arrays to deal with. They notice that the one in the lower right-hand corner is easy: There are 4 × 7 = 28 items in the array.

John says: "The array in the lower left-hand corner, 4 × 50, is also easy! We can *use a solution to another problem,* the auditorium seat problem, and organize it like this.

Each dash represents 10 items, making a 4 by 5 array of dashes. The array has 4 × 5 = 20 dashes. That's 20 × 10 = 200 original items."

Sarah says: "The upper right-hand corner can be handled in the same way. Organize its array this way.

Once again, each dash represents 10 items. It's a 3 by 7 array of dashes. So $3 \times 7 = 21$ dashes, and $21 \times 10 = 210$ items."

To handle the 30 by 50 sub-array in the upper left-hand corner, Maria suggests that they use the distributive law again and organize it to look like this.

Every big square represents a 10 by 10 array or $10 \times 10 = 100$ original items.

Maria says: "We have a 3 by 5 array of large squares. So there are $3 \times 5 = 15$ large squares or $15 \times 100 = 1500$ original items in the 30 by 50 sub-array."

Finally, they put all this together in one picture, wrote down the numbers they calculated from various parts of the picture, and added them up.

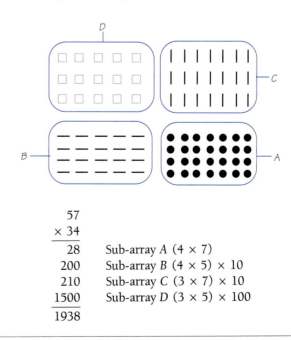

$$
\begin{array}{r}
57 \\
\times\ 34 \\
\hline
28 \\
200 \\
210 \\
1500 \\
\hline
1938
\end{array}
$$

Sub-array A (4×7)
Sub-array B $(4 \times 5) \times 10$
Sub-array C $(3 \times 7) \times 10$
Sub-array D $(3 \times 5) \times 100$

The Mathematical Idea: Organizing the Array into Sub-Arrays of Dots, Dashes, and Squares

Sarah, John, Maria, and Saul solved the problem 34×57 first by *drawing a picture* of the product as an array (of dots, say). Then they organized the array into sub-arrays of dots, dashes, and squares. Let's solve exercise 1 (the wheat field problem) in the same way.

First *draw a picture* of the wheat field as an array of squares on a piece of graph paper.

Using the grid as a guide, set out the length and width of the wheat field along two sides of its periphery with dashes and dots, where a dash is 10 and a dot is 1.

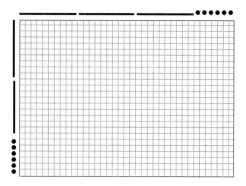

Then, in the array of squares, mark off 10 by 10 squares, dashes, and dots.

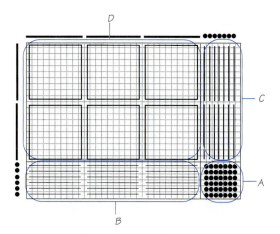

Finally, after labeling the sub-arrays, compute the products corresponding to each of them (called *partial products*) and add them up.

$$
\begin{array}{r}
37 \\
\times\ 26 \\
\hline
42 \\
180 \\
140 \\
600 \\
\hline
962
\end{array}
$$

Sub-array A (6×7)
Sub-array B $(6 \times 3) \times 10$
Sub-array C $(2 \times 7) \times 10$
Sub-array D $(2 \times 3) \times 100$

18. Use graph paper and organizing the array into sub-arrays of dots, dashes, and squares to find the product 45 × 32, as in the solution to the wheat field problem.

19. One way to make a model of a product is to use place value blocks. In a way similar to organizing an array into sub-arrays of dots, dashes, and squares, you make a rectangular layout with place value blocks, with unit cubes in place of dots, longs in place of dashes, and flats in place of squares. Use this method with place value blocks to find 27 × 34.

20. As in exercise 19, use base 5 place value blocks to make a model of the product ╪╪ × ╪╪ . Find the partial products as stick numerals and add them up to calculate the full product.

The Method of Sub-Arrays with Expanded Form, the Method of Partial Products with Zeros, and the Standard Method

The method of multiplying used in the solution to a harder problem used the following ideas and techniques.

- Expanded form and the distributive property to establish sub-arrays
- Calculation of the partial products corresponding to the sub-arrays
- Adding up the partial products to get the final answer

A more abstract version of the solution, without using dots, dashes, and squares, might go like this. Break up the big array as before.

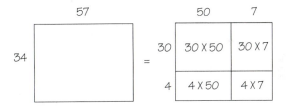

This time each partial product can be calculated using the associative and commutative properties of multiplication.

$$
\begin{aligned}
30 \times 50 &= (3 \times 5) \times 100 = 15 \times 100 = 1500 \\
30 \times 7 \ &= (3 \times 7) \times 10 \ = 21 \times 10 \ = \ 210 \\
4 \times 50 \ &= (4 \times 5) \times 10 \ = 20 \times 10 \ = \ 200 \\
4 \times 7 \ &\hspace{4.7cm} = \ \ 28 \\
\hline
\text{Total} &\hspace{4.5cm} 1938
\end{aligned}
$$

Notice that each partial product is calculated by combining an elementary multiplication fact with multiplication by a power of 10.

An even more abstract version is like the one just completed but avoids the drawing of an array.

$$
\begin{array}{r}
57 \\
\times\ 34 \\
\hline
1500 \\
210 \\
200 \\
28 \\
\hline
1938
\end{array}
$$

It is called the method of *partial products with zeros*.

The thinking for a streamlined version of the method of partial products with zeros might go this way: "Consider the array for 34 × 57.

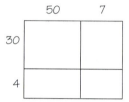

Instead of calculating the four partial products separately, we ought to be able to make some shortcuts. Let's calculate together the sum of the two lower partial products (the two bottom segments of the rectangle). This sum is actually the product 4 × 57. First, to calculate the partial product on the lower right, we multiply 4 times 7 and get 28. We write down the 8 and carry the 2 (tens). Then to calculate the partial product on the lower left, multiply 4 times 5 (tens) getting 20 (tens) and add on the carried 2 (tens) to make 22 (tens). Write 22 down just to the left of the 8 to get 228 (the sum of 22 tens plus 8). This is actually the product 4 × 57."

$$
\begin{array}{r}
57 \\
\times\ 34 \\
\hline
228
\end{array}
$$

(Notice that there is no actual need to draw the array; you just need to keep an image of it in mind.) "Next let's calculate the sum of the two upper partial products (the two segments at the top of the drawing). This sum should be the product 30 × 57. This should be the same as (3 × 57) × 10. So put down a zero right under the 8 of the 228 (for the "10" of the product). Then we write down just to the left of this zero what we get from computing 3 × 57. We calculate 3 × 57 just as we calculated 4 × 57 and get 171."

$$
\begin{array}{r}
57 \\
\times\ 34 \\
\hline
228 \\
1710
\end{array}
$$

A final stage would be to "suppress" the zero we have written under the 8 of 228 and begin writing the product 3×57 one digit to the left.

$$
\begin{array}{r}
57 \\
\times\ 34 \\
\hline
228 \\
171 \\
\hline
1938
\end{array}
$$

This is the *standard method* for multiplication.

An Anatomy of a Multiplication Problem

A more difficult multiplication problem is 38×567. We will solve this problem first by organizing the array into sub-arrays, then by partial products with zeros, and finally by the standard method. In this anatomy we will point out the skills needed at each stage.

METHOD 1, ORGANIZING THE ARRAY INTO SUB-ARRAYS We organize the solution into three steps.

Step 1 Sketch the array and organize it into sub-arrays using expanded notation and the distributive law.

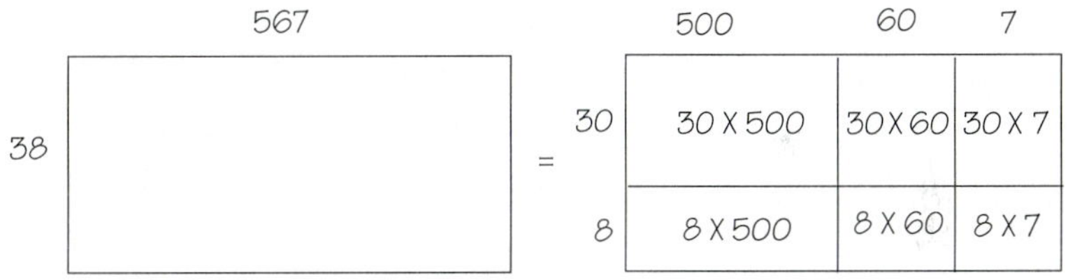

	500	60	7
30	30 X 500	30 X 60	30 X 7
8	8 X 500	8 X 60	8 X 7

(array labeled 567 by 38, equals the table with columns 500, 60, 7 and rows 30, 8)

Step 2 Calculate each partial product using elementary multiplication facts, the associative property of multiplication, and the rule for multiplication of a decimal numeral by a power of 10.

F	E	D
(3 X 5) X 1000	(3 X 6) X 100	(3 X 7) X 10
C	B	A
(8 X 5) X 100	(8 X 6) X 10	8 x 7

	567
	× 38

SUB-ARRAY	PARTIAL PRODUCTS		
A	8×7	$= 56$	$= 56$
B	$(8 \times 6) \times 10$	$= 48 \times 10$	$= 480$
C	$(8 \times 5) \times 100$	$= 40 \times 100$	$= 4000$
D	$(3 \times 7) \times 10$	$= 21 \times 10$	$= 210$
E	$(3 \times 6) \times 100$	$= 18 \times 100$	$= 1800$
F	$(3 \times 5) \times 1000$	$= 15 \times 1000$	$= 15{,}000$

Add these.

$$\underline{21{,}546} \quad \text{Sum}$$

METHOD 2, PARTIAL PRODUCTS WITH ZEROS The method of partial products with zeros consists of writing down the set of partial products and adding them up. All the other steps of the method of organizing the array into sub-arrays are carried out mentally. Otherwise, method 2 is identical to method 1.

$$
\begin{array}{r}
567 \\
\times\ 38 \\
\hline
56 \\
480 \\
4000 \\
210 \\
1800 \\
15{,}000 \\
\hline
21{,}546
\end{array}
$$

Add these.

Sum

METHOD 3, THE STANDARD METHOD

PARTIAL PRODUCTS WITH ZEROS

$$
\begin{array}{r}
567 \\
\times\ 38 \\
\hline
56 \\
480 \\
4000 \\
210 \\
1800 \\
15{,}000 \\
\hline
21{,}546
\end{array}
$$

Add these. → 4536

Add these. → 17,010 Suppress zeros. →

$$
\begin{array}{r}
567 \\
\times\ 38 \\
\hline
 \\
4536 \\
\\
21{,}546
\end{array}
$$

STANDARD METHOD

$$
\begin{array}{r}
567 \\
\times\ 38 \\
\hline
4536 \\
1701 \\
\hline
21{,}546
\end{array}
$$

→ 4536

→ 1701

EXERCISES

21. Solve the multiplication problem 476×53 using the three methods just shown.

22. Solve the stick numeral multiplication problem ╪╪╪ × ╪╪ using the three methods just shown. Remember that stick numerals are base 5 and that expanded form is an important part of the methods.

23. Solve the base 8 multiplication problems using the three methods just shown. Explain your steps carefully.
    (a) $45_{\text{eight}} \times 32_{\text{eight}}$ (b) $476_{\text{eight}} \times 53_{\text{eight}}$

Why Do We Need to Do All This?

Imagine the following fourth grade classroom scene.

"Ladies and gentlemen of the fourth grade, we want to find out how many seats are in this auditorium.

"You can see that the answer is the same as what you get when you add 38 together to itself 23 times. That is a lot of work. There's an easier way.

1. Write down 23 and 38:   23   38
2. Double 23, write it here.   46   19   **3.** Halve 38; write it here.
4. Double 46, write it here.   92   9   **5.** Halve 19, throw away the remainder, and write it here.

6. Keep doing this (doubling the numbers in the left-hand column and halving the numbers in the right-hand column) until you get a 1 in the right-hand column.

     184   4
     368   2
     736   1

7. Here is your work written out again. Look for the numbers in the right-hand column that are even. Cross out the numbers in those rows.

     ~~23~~   ~~38~~
     46   19
     92   9
     ~~184~~   ~~4~~

8. Add up the numbers in the left-hand column that haven't been crossed out. The resulting sum is your answer!

     ~~368~~   ~~2~~
     736   1
     ‾‾‾‾
     874

"There are 874 seats in the auditorium! It works! (It always works.) Check it out."

The Mathematical Idea: The Egyptian Method for Multiplication

Here is another multiplication problem (43 × 67) solved by the method just described.

$$
\begin{array}{cc}
43 & 67 \\
86 & 33 \\
\text{---}172\text{---} & 16 \\
\text{---}344\text{---} & 8 \\
688\text{---} & 4 \\
\text{---}1376\text{---} & 2 \\
\underline{2752} & 1 \\
2881 &
\end{array}
$$

Talk about magic! If you had been taught to multiply this way with no other background (except learning how to double and how to halve), would you have been very happy with multiplication? I suspect that a fourth grader, taught the standard method without any background or explanation, would feel like you do right now, having been shown the method above. Things a person learns can and should make sense. Making sense takes time and care.

The method of multiplying by doubling and halving was used by the ancient Egyptians and is sometimes called the Egyptian method. It was also used in parts of Europe in the Middle Ages.

EXERCISE 24. Solve the multiplication problem 68 × 57 using the Egyptian method.

5.3 LOOKING BACK: PARADIGMS FOR MULTIPLICATION

Originally, we defined the product $A \times B$ of two whole numbers A and B as the solution to the repeated addition

$$
\underbrace{B + B + \cdots + B.}_{A \text{ times}}
$$

Later, we showed that an array of items with A rows and B items in each row has a total of $A \times B$ items in it. Eventually, we thought of multiplication as the number of items in an array as much as we thought of it as the solution to a repeated addition. Both ways of thinking about multiplication are *paradigms for multiplication.* Other useful paradigms for multiplication are related to *the tree diagram* and *the cartesian product of two sets.* Knowledge of these new ways of thinking about multiplication will increase our problem-solving abilities by increasing the range of problems for which multiplication is a solution. We will introduce both ways through a problem.

At the City Diner, when you order a sandwich, you have a choice of four fillings: turkey, tuna fish salad, cheese, and egg salad. You also have a choice of five kinds of bread: white, French, onion roll, rye, and whole wheat. You want to know how many different kinds of sandwiches you can order.

A Solution to the Sandwich Problem Using Tree Diagrams

One way to solve the problem is to make a list of the possibilities and then count the number of items in the list. However, if you do not make a list in an organized fashion, you might miss a few of the possibilities or you might list a certain sandwich more than once (or you might commit both of these errors). Here is an organized way of making a list.

It's likely that you make a choice of sandwich in stages. First you choose a filling; then you choose the kind of bread. You can organize the possible outcomes of the first choice in the following *tree diagram.*

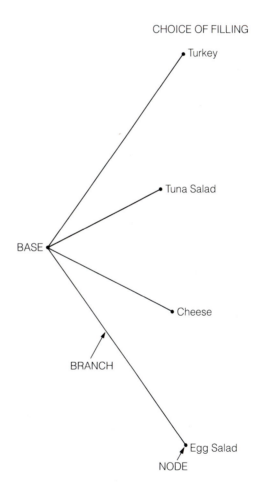

CHOICE OF FILLING

• Turkey

• Tuna Salad

BASE

• Cheese

BRANCH

• Egg Salad

NODE

In this diagram (a "tree" on its side), the point on the left is the *base* of the tree, the lines are *branches,* and the points at which the outcomes of the choice are written are called *nodes* of the tree.

Now you are ready for the second choice, selecting the type of bread. We will extend the tree diagram to the right to show the outcomes of this choice. If the outcome of your first choice was turkey, then the possible outcomes for the second choice are white, French, onion roll, rye, and whole wheat. We indicate this by drawing branches to the right beginning at the "Turkey" node.

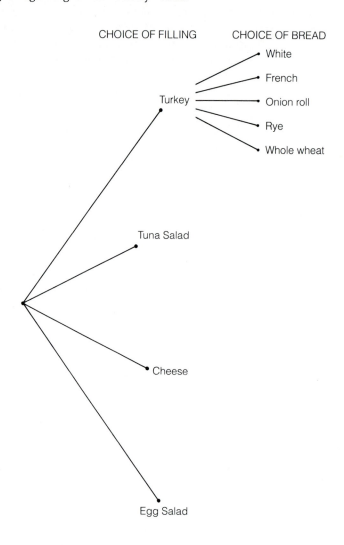

For every other outcome of the first choice, we do the same: draw branches from the outcome and at the tips write the choice of bread.

CHOICE OF FILLING   CHOICE OF BREAD

Turkey — White, French, Onion roll, Rye, Whole wheat

Tuna Salad — White, French, Onion roll, Rye, Whole wheat

Cheese — White, French, Onion roll, Rye, Whole wheat

Egg Salad — White, French, Onion roll, Rye, Whole wheat

The end of each of these latter branches corresponds to a choice of sandwich.

CHOICE OF FILLING	CHOICE OF BREAD	CHOICE OF SANDWICH
Turkey	White	Turkey on white
	French	Turkey on French
	Onion roll	Turkey on onion roll
	Rye	Turkey on rye
	Whole wheat	Turkey on whole wheat
Tuna Salad	White	Tuna on white
	French	Tuna on French
	Onion roll	Tuna on onion roll
	Rye	Tuna on rye
	Whole wheat	Tuna on whole wheat
Cheese	White	Cheese on white
	French	Cheese on French
	Onion roll	Cheese on onion roll
	Rye	Cheese on rye
	Whole wheat	Cheese on whole wheat
Egg Salad	White	Egg salad on white
	French	Egg salad on French
	Onion roll	Egg salad on onion roll
	Rye	Egg salad on rye
	Whole wheat	Egg salad on whole wheat

The items under the heading "Choice of Sandwich" constitute a complete list of all the possible sandwiches City Diner sells. Moreover, they are all different. So the number of sandwich choices is equal to the number of branch ends the tree has. Five branches lead from each choice of filling, and there are four choices of filling. Thus, the number of branch ends to the tree is the answer to the repeated addition $5 + 5 + 5 + 5$; that is, there are 4×5 possible branch ends to the tree. There are 20 possible choices for a sandwich.

Because the numbers are small in this example, it is easy to see that the number of possible sandwiches is 4×5. It would be more difficult if there were 48 fillings and 37 types of bread. It would also be difficult to draw a tree diagram for such a problem. However, one can *imagine* drawing a tree diagram and then concluding that there are 48×37 possible sandwiches. There is a general principle for this situation.

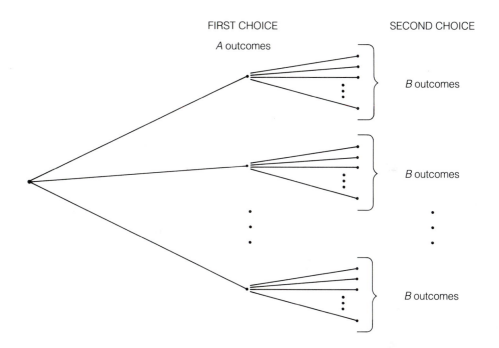

FIRST CHOICE   SECOND CHOICE

A outcomes

B outcomes

B outcomes

B outcomes

We will be using tree diagrams in later chapters.

A Solution to the Sandwich Problem Using the Cartesian Product of Two Sets

Another way to solve the sandwich problem is to make a table like the one shown.

KIND OF BREAD

		WHITE	FRENCH	ONION ROLL	RYE	WHOLE WHEAT
	TURKEY					
TYPE OF FILLING	TUNA SALAD					
	CHEESE					
	EGG SALAD					

The table has rows and columns. Each row is labeled with a type of filling; each column is labeled with a type of bread. In the empty space where a column and row intersect, write the label of the row and label of the column. For example,

	Rye
	•
	•
	•
Turkey	Turkey, rye

After filling in the whole table this way, we obtain an array of all the possible sandwiches.

KIND OF BREAD

TYPE OF FILLING	WHITE	FRENCH	ONION ROLL	RYE	WHOLE WHEAT
TURKEY	Turkey, white	Turkey, French	Turkey, onion roll	Turkey, rye	Turkey, whole wheat
TUNA SALAD	Tuna, white	Tuna, French	Tuna, onion roll	Tuna, rye	Tuna, whole wheat
CHEESE	Cheese, white	Cheese, French	Cheese, onion role	Cheese, rye	Cheese, whole wheat
EGG SALAD	Egg salad, white	Egg salad, French	Egg salad, onion roll	Egg salad, rye	Egg salad, whole weheat

Each possible sandwich is listed once—and only once—in this array. We know that the number of elements in the array is

Number of rows × number of items in each row,

which is the same as

Number of fillings × number of breads.

If $F = \{$turkey, tuna salad, cheese, egg salad$\}$ is the set of possible fillings and $B = \{$white, French, onion roll, rye, whole wheat$\}$ is the set of possible breads, then the table we have constructed is a way to list all ordered pairs (f,b) where f is an element of F and b is an element of B. One such pair is (turkey, rye).

DEFINITION OF CARTESIAN PRODUCT

The set of all ordered pairs (f,b) with $f \in F$ and $b \in B$ is called the *cartesian product* of F and B. It is denoted by $F \times B$.

What we have just shown is an instance of the next rule.

NUMBER OF ELEMENTS IN A CARTESIAN PRODUCT

The number of elements in $F \times B$ is equal to the number of elements in F times the number of elements in B. In other words,

$$n(F \times B) = n(F) \times n(B).$$

EXERCISES

25. When you buy a Lemonmobile GT you have a choice of four exterior colors: red, blue, white, and beige. You also have a choice of six interior colors: red, blue, black, brown, beige, and green. These are your only choices. How many choices of Lemonmobile GT are there? Solve this problem in two ways: (1) Draw a tree diagram to organize the possible choices of Lemonmobile GT in stages and (2) make a table listing the elements of the cartesian product $E \times I$, where E is the set of exterior colors and I is the set of interior colors.

26. City Diner is under new management. Now, when you order a sandwich, in addition to a choice of filling and choice of bread (as listed in the sandwich problem), you also have a choice of one spread: mayonnaise, mustard, and ketchup. How many different kinds of sandwiches can you now order? (Solve this by "extending" the tree diagram drawn earlier. The resulting tree will have three sets of branches to correspond to three stages of your choice of sandwich.)

5.4   EXTENDING THE IDEAS: ESTIMATING PRODUCTS

Suppose you are working a problem and must calculate a certain product. At the moment you are not interested in the exact answer, just a ballpark estimate. The following example suggests a way to find out what the answer should be, roughly.

To get a rough idea of what 14×23 should be, think this way:

1. 14 is larger than 10 and 23 is larger than 20. So 14×23 should be larger than 10×20. 10×20 is easy to figure out: It's 200. So 14×23 is larger than 200.

2. Similarly, 20 is larger than 14 and 30 is larger than 23. So 20×30 is larger than 14×23. 20×30 is easy to figure out: It's 600. So 600 is larger than 14×23.

3. *Conclusion:* 14×23 is a number smaller than 600 and larger than 200. In other words, $200 < 14 \times 23 < 600$. The picture illustrates the conclusion.

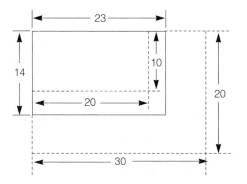

The general law is

LAW RELATING MULTIPLICATION WITH ORDER

If A, B, C, and D are whole numbers and if $A < B$ and $C < D$, then $AC < BD$. If also C is not zero, then $AC < BC$.

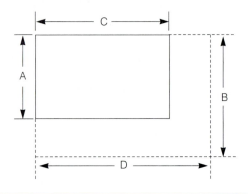

Why is the phrase "C is not zero" included in the statement of the law?

EXERCISE 27. Use the law relating multiplication with order to estimate the following products, by placing each product between two other products easy to calculate.

(a) 58×64 (b) 127×345 (c) 567×679 (d) 3471×5984

5.5   LOOKING AHEAD: MULTIPLICATION AND ALGEBRA

In this chapter, just as in the chapter on addition and subtraction of whole numbers, we used algebraic symbols to state laws for arithmetic. For example, we expressed the distributive property of multiplication over addition this way: For all numbers A, B, and C, $A \times (B + C) = A \times B + A \times C$.

It is easy to give specific instances of this law, such as $7 \times (8 + 6) = 7 \times 8 + 7 \times 6$. But the law is more than just this instance; it says something for *all* triples of whole numbers. Without the use of algebraic symbols, the law might be expressed:

> Take three numbers. The product of the first with the sum of the other two is the same as the product of the first with the second plus the product of the first with the third.

More print is used to produce this verbal description than the one using algebraic symbols, and some people may feel that therefore the verbal description takes more energy to absorb than the algebraic one. In any case, both descriptions are common and have their uses. There is a certain economy of expression in the use of algebraic symbols.

Everybody who uses algebraic symbols agrees to use certain rules. One such rule is assumed in interpreting the expression $A \times (B + C) = A \times B + A \times C$ in the statement of the distributive law. It is a rule for the *order of operations* that we have referred to in chapters 1 and 4.

RULES FOR ORDER OF OPERATION

When there are no parentheses, multiplications are carried out before additions. When there are parentheses, the operation inside the parentheses is carried out first.

A convention that we will frequently follow is the replacement of the sign $\times$ by a blank. If there is no confusion, instead of $A \times B$ we may write AB. With this convention, the distributive law for multiplication over addition looks like this: For all whole numbers A, B, and C, $A(B + C) = AB + AC$. Replacing 23×46 by 2346 would be confusing; the convention is not used in this case. However, replacing 23×46 by $(23)(46)$ is common.

THE TRUCK PROBLEM

Try solving the problem yourself.

John and Sally are truck drivers who work for the Merchandise Transport Company. They are driving separate trucks and have stopped at a truck stop for dinner. After dinner Sally says, "I think I'll take a little rest. John, you go on ahead. I'll catch up with you later." John leaves the truck stop at 8 P.M., driving his usual 50 mph. Sally wakes up later and leaves, driving her usual 60 mph. It's 10 P.M. when Sally leaves the truck stop. Sally wants to know when, and in how many miles, she will meet John again.

A Partial Solution to the Truck Problem

Sally thinks this way: "The number of hours from now until when we meet again and the number of miles from here to where we meet again are related. I travel 60 miles in an hour. In 2 hours I would travel twice that. In 3 hours 3 times that. In general, 'If I travel H hours, then the distance I go is 60 times H. In other words, the distance I travel is $60H$.'

"A similar fact is true for John. The distance John travels is equal to 50 times the number of hours traveled. If I travel for H hours, then, since he started 2 hours before me, he will have been traveling $H + 2$ hours. The distance he will have traveled is $50(H + 2)$. When we meet, his distance and mine will be the same, or $50(H + 2) = 60H$.

"The $=$ says that the two distances are the same. But that's at the time when we meet. There must be a special H that makes that equation work.

"To find an 'unknown' number H so that $50(H + 2) = 60H$, maybe I can rewrite those expressions. By the distributive law,

$$50(H + 2) = 50H + 50 \times 2 = 50H + 100.$$

So

$$50H + 100 = 60H.$$

"Now the problem is to find a number H that satisfies this equation. Maybe I can rephrase the problem again. I notice that $60 = 50 + 10$, so the equation can be rewritten as

$$50H + 100 = (50 + 10)H$$

or, after another use of the distributive law,

$$50H + 100 = 50H + 10H.$$

This last equation says that if I add 100 to a number ($50H$), I get the same thing as if I added $10H$ to that same number ($50H$). It must mean that 100 and $10H$ are themselves the same, or $100 = 10H$. The number that works in the equation is $H = 10$. We will meet in 10 hours! I will have traveled $60 \times 10 = 600$ miles in that time. John will have been traveling for $10 + 2 = 12$ hours and will have gone $50 \times 12 = 600$ miles."

The Mathematical Idea: Cancellation Laws, Unknowns, and Solving Equations

In the next to the last step in her solution to the truck problem, Sally had the situation

$$A + 100 = A + 10H.$$

(For Sally, $A = 50H$.) Sally concluded from this that $100 = 10H$. This is an instance of the cancellation law for addition discussed in chapter 4. There is a similar law for multiplication.

CANCELLATION LAW FOR MULTIPLICATION

If A, B, and C are whole numbers, if A is not zero, and if $AB = AC$, then it must follow that $B = C$.

(Why is the phrase "A is not zero" included in the statement of the law?)

We may have used this law to find a number H such that $100 = 10H$. We know from our multiplication facts that $100 = 10 \times 10$. From that we can conclude that $10 \times 10 = 10 \times H$, and from that, that $10 = H$. The cancellation law is obvious. But identifying when to use it doesn't always seem that straightforward when numbers are replaced by symbols.

In solving the truck problem, Sally didn't know exactly what the number of hours would be (before meeting John) so she gave it a temporary name H. After some thinking, she concluded that the number H has the property $50(H + 2) = 60H$. Then she used the rules of grammar that we have been discussing to find a number H having that property.

We have seen other instances of giving a number a temporary name. For example, we may want to find a number N such that $43 + N = 78$. We called the problem of finding a number N having this property a *missing addend* problem.

In the next chapter, we will be interested in finding a number F such that $23F = 437$. This is called a *missing factor* problem.

EXERCISES   28. Use the rules of algebra to solve each of the following problems. For each problem, justify every step with a rule.
(a) Find a whole number A such that $A + 7 = 12$.
(b) Find a whole number B such that $3B + 5 = 17$.
(c) Find a whole number C such that $8C = 7(C + 1)$.
(d) Find a whole number D such that $2(2D + 3) = 3(D + 4)$.
(e) Find a whole number E such that $3E + 6 = 2(E + 8)$.

29. Consider the rule that multiplication is distributive over subtraction, in which given whole numbers *A, B,* and *C* such that $B > C$, then $A(B - C) = AB - AC$. For example, $5(7 - 4) = 5 \times 7 - 5 \times 4$. Use the diagram to show why this law must be true.

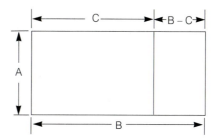

30. Dutch tulip bulbs cost $52 per 100, while domestic bulbs cost only $38 per 100. The director of Public Gardens needs 1600 bulbs for fall planting and has budgeted $720 for their purchase. She wants to buy as many of the higher quality Dutch bulbs as she can. Bulbs are sold by the hundred, and she wants to know how many hundred of each kind she should order. (*Hint:* Solve this in the same way that the truck problem was solved. Give the number of hundreds of Dutch bulbs to be purchased a name, such as *H*. Find an expression for the number of hundreds of domestic bulbs to be purchased if 100 *H* Dutch bulbs are to be purchased. What is the cost of the Dutch bulbs? What is the cost of the domestic bulbs? The sum of these two costs must equal $720. This gives you an equation involving the unknown *H*. Find the number *H* such that this equation holds.)

5.6   CALCULATORS AND COMPUTERS: MULTIPLICATION

It's easy to have a calculator or a computer calculate the product of two numbers. For example, if you want to multiply 74 times 87 with a calculator, you use the key sequence 74 [×] 87 [=]. For a microcomputer, you type PRINT 74*87.

Exactly how the calculator/computer finds the answer we are not told. (It probably uses a version of the standard method.) We know that 74×87 is what you get when you add 87 to itself 74 times. This is the basic meaning of 74*87, and the standard method is an alternative (shorter) way to find the number. We can get the calculator and the computer to obtain an answer using the basic meaning, the long way, and in such a way that we can see what is going on. This might be a useful thing to be able to do if you are trying to show young children that the standard method and the long way yield the same answer. You could also use the calculator or computer to multiply the long way *before* developing the standard method.

REPEATED ADDITION BY CALCULATOR   Take the problem 74×87. We can use the constant, or K, feature to add 87 repeatedly to itself 74 times. Here's how.

FOR A CALCULATOR WITH A [K] KEY		
KEYING SEQUENCE	DISPLAY	MATHEMATICAL EXPRESSION
87 [+] [K]	87	1×87
[=]	174	2×87
[=]	261	3×87
[=]	348	4×87
[=]	435	5×87

FOR MOST OTHER CALCULATORS		
KEYING SEQUENCE	DISPLAY	MATHEMATICAL EXPRESSION
87 [+]	87	1×87
[=]	174	2×87
[=]	261	3×87
[=]	348	4×87
[=]	435	5×87

(Your calculator may differ from both of these. If one of these key sequences doesn't work, check the manual for your calculator.) So, for both kinds of calculators, after having keyed [=] 73 times you will get 74×87, or 6438, and you will see all the intermediate additions as you go. Try it!

REPEATED ADDITION USING BASIC The continual addition of 87 to an accumulating sum suggests that we use a loop. In BASIC this involves the use of the FOR . . . NEXT statements. In the program let's use the variable S for the accumulating sum; the value of S will change as the program progresses. To S we will keep adding 87 and we will do this 74 times. The LET command will enable us to change the value of S by adding 87 at each step of the loop:

```
LET S = S + 87
```

This statement says, "Take the present value of S and add 87 to it. The result is the new value of S." Here is a program, with loop, using this command.

```
10 FOR I = 1 TO 74
20 LET S = S + 87
30 NEXT I
100 END
```

We must assign a value to the variable S to begin the program. This is called *initializing*. We want S to begin with the value 0, so we type an additional line

```
5 LET S = 0
```

The full program is

```
5 LET S = 0
10 FOR I = 1 TO 74
20 LET S = S + 87
30 NEXT I
100 END
```

Type and run the program above. What happens?
Nothing happens that you can see. To see something happen, you have to tell the computer to print something on the screen. So you type

```
25 PRINT S
LIST
5 LET S = 0
10 FOR I = 1 TO 74
15 PRINT S
20 LET S = S + 87
30 NEXT I
100 END
```
Run this revised program. What happens?

31. Alter the program above so that in addition to multiplying 74 times 87, it will multiply any pair of numbers by repeated addition. This alteration will allow you to see what is happening when the program is run. You can do this by including two INPUT statements at the beginning of the program to assign values to the variables A and B; then the remainder of the program would multiply A times B using repeated addition.

5.7 SUMMARY OF IMPORTANT IDEAS AND TECHNIQUES

- The product of whole numbers A and B; the definition of *multiplication*
- An array as a rectangular arrangement of objects; the number of items in an array with A rows and B items is the product $A \times B$
- Items used to develop the standard method for multiplication

  The multiplication tables (or elementary multiplication facts): the products $A \times B$ for A and B between 1 and 10, inclusive

  The properties of multiplication: commutative, associative, and distributive over addition

  Multiplication by powers of 10
- Stages leading up to the standard method for multiplication of several-digit numbers

  (For two-digit numbers) an array with dots, dashes, and squares

  Sketch of an array using expanded form, the distributive law, and partial products

  The method of partial products with zeros

  The standard method
- The Egyptian method of multiplication
- New paradigms for multiplication: tree diagrams and cartesian product of sets
- Estimating products using the law relating multiplication with order
- Rules for the use of algebraic symbols; the cancellation law for multiplication; solving equations with unknowns
- Using calculators and computers to simulate repeated addition

PROBLEM SET

PRACTICING
SKILLS

1. You are the catering manager for a large hotel and need to know how many tables can fit into the grand ballroom. A table is to be placed inside each little square in the picture of the grand ballroom shown on page 228. You know how to add three- and four-digit numbers, but you know nothing about multiplication. How would you solve this?

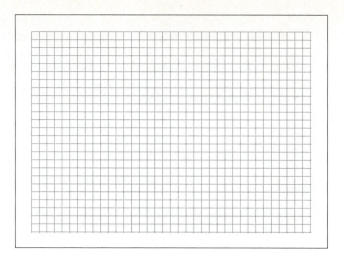

2. Without actually counting all the trees, figure out the number of trees in the orchard.

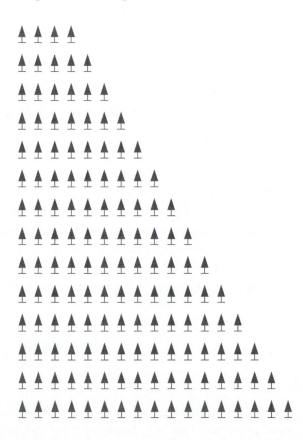

3. Joanna is in the third grade. Help her find the product 738 × 10 using (a) stones on a counting board and (b) place value blocks.

4. You know the associative property of multiplication, the multiplication tables, and how to multiply any number by 10. Use these to find the product 9 × 60.

5. Explain to Jaime how to multiply 1,000,000 × 879 so that he will know and understand how to multiply any number by 1,000,000. Why would Jaime want to be able to do this?

6. Find the product 73×86 by
   (a) Drawing a picture of the product as an array on graph paper using dots, dashes, and squares to organize the array.
   (b) Using partial products with zeros; show clearly how each partial product corresponds to a portion of the array in (a).

7. Find the product 675×49.
   (a) Sketch an array and organize it using expanded form and the distributive law.
   (b) Use the method of partial products with zeros. Show clearly how each partial product corresponds to a portion of the sketched array in (a).

8. Solve the problem using the doubling/halving Egyptian method: 94×87.

9. Use the rules for algebra to solve each of the following problems. Justify each step with a rule.
   (a) Find a whole number A such that $A + 8 = 20$.
   (b) Find a whole number B such that $4B + 3 = 31$.
   (c) Find a whole number C such that $5C = 4(C + 2)$.
   (d) Find a whole number D such that $3(2D + 5) = 7(D + 1)$.

10. The secretary of the school district needs to order paper for the office for the school year. Lower quality sulfite paper costs $6 per ream (500 sheets), while higher quality bond paper costs $9 per ream. The budget will allow her to spend $720 on paper. She knows from last year that she will need 90 reams and she wants as much bond paper as possible. How many reams of each kind should she buy?

11. Grant and Adam live 77 mi apart on opposite ends of a long country road. Both being avid bicyclists, they decide to bike toward each other and meet for lunch. Both will leave home at exactly 9 A.M. Grant bikes at an average pace of 15 mph, while Adam travels at an average pace of 18 mph. At what time will they meet for lunch? How far will each have traveled?

12. Use the law relating multiplication with order to estimate the products (by placing each product between two easily computable products).
    (a) 73×59 (b) 267×523 (c) 4577×6938

13. Sean and Sarah are buying a new condominium. They must choose colors for the living room carpet and the kitchen tile. They have six choices for the carpet: gray, beige, peach, blue, brown tweed, and off-white. There are five tile choices: yellow pattern, blue pattern, green pattern, solid tan, solid yellow. From how many color combinations do they have to choose? Solve this problem with (a) a tree diagram and (b) a table listing the elements of the cartesian product $C \times T$, where C is the set of carpet colors and T is the set of tile choices.

14. Help Mina complete the stick numeral multiplication table.

×	十	卄	卅	卌	十|
十					
卄					
卅			卄卄		
卌					
十|					

For each of the remaining problems, document your solution as clearly and completely as you can. Include in your documentation the steps you took, the problems and solutions that gave you ideas, and the problem-solving strategies that you used. You may want to organize all this before writing your final report.

15. Without actually counting all the seats, figure out the number of seats in the auditorium.

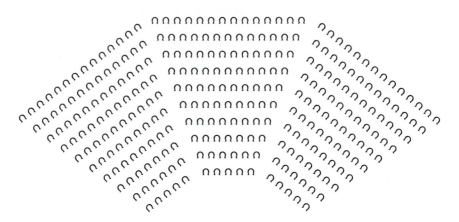

16. Without actually counting all the lots, figure out the number of lots in the housing development and explain how you did it.

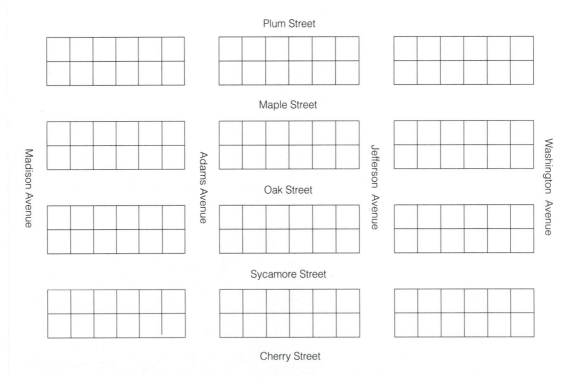

17. Consider the multiplication problem 453 × 57. Solve it three ways.
    (a) Sketch an array and organize it using expanded form and the distributive property.
    (b) Use the method of partial products with zeros. Show how each partial product corresponds to a portion of the array in (a).

(c) Use the standard method. Show how the steps you take here correspond to those in (b) and point out which steps are shortcuts for those in (b).

18. To figure out the product 34 × 256, you could sketch an array and organize it this way.

	200	50	6
30	30 × 200	30 × 50	30 × 6
4	4 × 200	4 × 50	4 × 6

It would be cumbersome to use just the units, flats, and longs from a set of place value blocks (or dots, dashes, and squares in a picture) to organize the array in the way shown on page 208 of the text. However, a collection of place value blocks has large cubes worth 1000 units in addition to the units, longs, and flats.

Figure out a way to organize the 34 × 256 array using this full set of place value blocks (or pictures of them) so that the partial products are clearly evident.

19. Mina knows the stick numeral multiplication tables (see prob. 14). She knows the distributive property and she knows the connection between a product and an array. Use what she knows to find the product ╪╪ × ╪╪ .

20. Mina must solve this stick numeral multiplication problem: ╪│ × ╪ ╪ ╪. Use a base 5 counting board to show her how to figure out the answer.

21. Mina knows her stick numeral multiplication table (see prob. 14); the commutative, associative, and distributive properties of multiplication; and how to multiply by ╪│. Help her figure out the number of trees in this orchard.

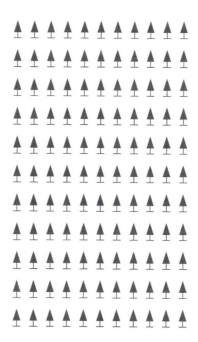

22. Using sticks, Mina organized an array of stones as shown.

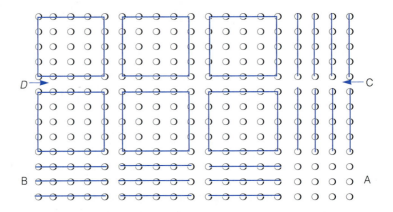

She was trying to figure out the product ╪╪ × ╪╪ . Each stick covers ┼│ stones. Each arrangement of 4 sticks in a square fences in ┼│| stones. This organizes the big array into 4 sub-arrays. She calculated the number of stones in each array and added them up.

SUB-ARRARY	NUMBER OF STONES		
A	╪ × ╪	=	╪╪
B	(╪ × ╪) × ┼│	=	┼╪ │
C	(╪ × ╪) × ┼│	=	┼╪ │
D	(╪ × ╪) × ┼||	= ┼ ┼ │ │
	Total		┼╪╪╪

(a) Use this method to figure out the product ╪╪ × ╪╪ by drawing the array, organizing it into sub-arrays using sticks, calculating the product for each sub-array, and adding them up.

(b) Eventually, Mina has learned to calculate products using the method of partial products with zeros. For example, she now does the preceding problem this way:

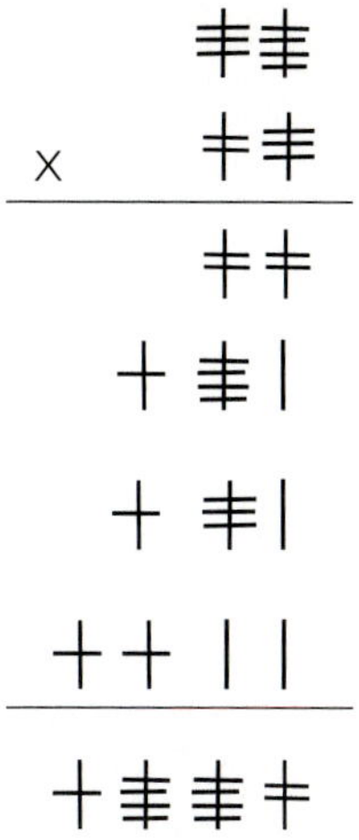

$$
\begin{array}{r}
丰丯 \\
\times\quad 丯丰 \\
\hline
丯丰 \\
十丰| \\
十丰| \\
十十|| \\
\hline
十丰丰丯
\end{array}
$$

Calculate the product of the next problem using the method of partial products with zeros.

$$
\begin{array}{r}
丰\ 丯 \\
\times\ 十\ 丰
\end{array}
$$

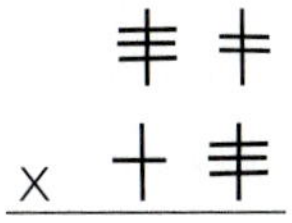

23. Solve the stick numeral multiplication problem 丰丯 × 十丰 in three ways.
   (a) Draw a picture of the product as an array on graph paper. Use dots, dashes, and squares to organize the array.
   (b) Use the method of partial products with zeros (as in prob. 22); show clearly how each partial product corresponds to a portion of the array in (a).
   (c) Use the standard method adapted to stick numbers; point out the shortcuts being taken in the standard method that were not being made in (b).

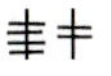

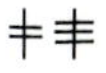

24. There is a way of multiplying called front-end multiplication.

$$
\begin{array}{r}
325 \\
\times\ 421 \\
\hline
1400 \\
650 \\
325 \\
\hline
146{,}825
\end{array}
$$

Do the following multiplication problem using the same method.

$$
\begin{array}{r}
645 \\
\times\ 832 \\
\hline
\end{array}
$$

Does it give you the right answer? Why or why not?

25. You discover this multiplication problem on a worn piece of paper at the bottom of an old trunk. Some of the digits are legible, but most are smudged. (A smudge is represented by a ◆.) Reconstruct the original problem.

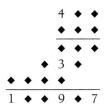

26. Café La Tour has a menu with 8 appetizers and 12 entrees.
    (a) Jacques, the proprietor, wants to know how many appetizer-entree meals are possible for a client. Draw an appropriate array and find the answer.
    (b) Café La Tour also has 5 dessert options. How many appetizer-entree-dessert meals are available at the restaurant? What appropriate geometric device (corresponding to the array for part [a]) could be used to display the meals and illustrate the answer?

27. A realtor claims that the house he is selling will double in price in a year and will triple in price in the two years after that. Thus he promises that the price in three years will be 2 × 3 = 6 times what it is now. How would you illustrate this situation in order to justify that 2 × 3 is the correct solution? (You could draw a 2 by 3 array. But an array of what?)

28. The Furniture Company makes one type of chair and one type of table. The owner wants to know how many chairs and how many tables she should produce each day. She has two workers, Able and Baker. They each have different skills and tools. To complete a finished chair, Able works on it for 2 hrs and Baker for 1. To complete a finished table, Able works on it for 1 hr and Baker for 2. Neither Able nor Baker will work more than 12 hr a day. There is a ready market for all that The Furniture Company produces. The owner wants to have as large a profit as she can. She makes a profit of $16 on each table and a profit of $12 on each chair. (*Hint:* Make a chart.)

29. We were off on our first trip ever to Europe. Our plane left at noon, but the travel agent told us to be at the airport an hour ahead of time. So we all left the house at 10 A.M. to drive the 40 mi to the airport. However, for some reason, there was very heavy traffic, and my father could only average 20 mph for the first 30 min. Both of my parents were getting more and more nervous before we got onto the freeway and the traffic cleared out. My mother asked me how fast we would have to go to get to the airport on time. What should my reply have been?*

30. Consider the base 8 multiplication problem $43_{\text{eight}} \times 57_{\text{eight}}$. Solve it three ways in the base 8 system.
    (a) Sketch an array and organize it using expanded notation (in the base 8 system) and the distributive property.
    (b) Use the method of partial products with zeros as adapted to the base 8 system. Show how each partial product corresponds to a portion of the array in (a).
    (c) Use the standard method as adapted to the base 8 system. Show how the steps you take here correspond to those in (b) and point out which steps are shortcuts for those in (b).

---

* From Carol Meyer and Tom Sallee, *Make It Simpler,* Addison-Wesley, Reading, Mass., 1983, p. 261.

31. A popular method for multiplying whole numbers in the Renaissance was called the *jalousie method*. You do your calculations on a grating, or jalousie. The two numbers to be multiplied—for example, 4672 and 83—are written at the top and right side of the grating.

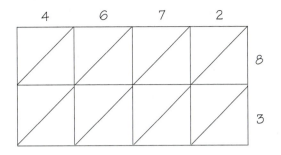

The products of pairs of digits in the two numbers are written in the squares of the grating. The numbers are added along the diagonals (upper right to lower left) to form the product of the two numbers. The product is written along the left and bottom of the grating.

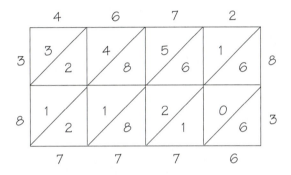

Draw a jalousie and find the product 643 × 895 using the jalousie method.

32. Why does the Egyptian method for multiplication work? (*Hints:* Think about the method for converting a number to a standard base 2 numeral. Think about the standard method of multiplication adapted to base 2 numerals.)

33. (a) To calculate 367,189 × 982,478, sketch an array and organize it as follows.

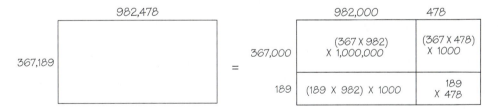

Then use a calculator to calculate the products 189 × 478, 189 × 982, 367 × 478, 367 × 982. Finally, use what you get to calculate the partial products and add them all up to get the answer to the original problem.

(b) Use the same method to calculate 470,987 × 872,395.

DIVISION OF WHOLE NUMBERS

C H A P T E R

In this chapter we will introduce division of whole numbers and discuss the evolution of a method for carrying out the operation when the numbers involved are "large." We will begin with several simple problems the solutions of which are, for us, clearly obtained by division. To somebody who hasn't had experience with division, it takes work to show that all these problems can be solved using the same technique.

We shall show, at a basic level, how solutions to these problems can be connected. At the same time, just as with addition, subtraction, and multiplication, the methods for dividing will evolve from the solutions to simple problems. As it turns out, the methods for division of "small" numbers versus "large" numbers are closely connected with different types of simple problems.

6.1   WHAT IS DIVISION OF WHOLE NUMBERS?

THE ROSE GARDEN PROBLEM

Please try this first.

A donor has given 63 rose bushes to Monroe School. The students in the third grade want to plant the bushes in a garden having 7 rows, with the same number of bushes in each row. They want to know how many bushes will be in each row. The students have had no experience with division. How would they solve this?

A Solution to the Rose Garden Problem

The students draw a picture of the 7 rows:

_____

_____

_____

_____

_____

_____

_____

"If we were to fill in all the bushes in these rows, we'd have an array of 63 bushes with 7 rows, so that 7 times the number of items in each row would equal 63. The problem will be solved if we can find a number Q such that $7 \times Q = 63$. Seven times what number equals 63? We know from the multiplication tables that $7 \times 9 = 63$. The answer is 9; there will be 9 items in each row; there will be 9 rose bushes planted in each of the 7 rows."

The Mathematical Idea: Division as the Solution to a Missing Factor Problem

To solve the rose garden problem, the students found a number Q so that $7 \times Q = 63$. They found a *missing factor* in a multiplication problem. At some point after doing a number of missing factor problems, a third grader will be told that finding the missing factor is called *division*. Thus, finding Q such that $6 \times Q = 48$ is gotten by "dividing 48 by 6," and the answer is written as $48 \div 6 = 8$. Similarly, the answer to the rose garden problem is $63 \div 7 = 9$. This gives rise to a definition of division.

DIVISION

Given two whole numbers A and B, with $B \neq 0$, if there is a whole number Q such that $B \times Q = A$, then Q is the result of *division* of A by B, and we write $A \div B = Q$.

Notice that if $B = 0$ and $A \neq 0$, there is no solution to $B \times Q = A$. If $B = 0$ and $A = 0$, then any Q is a solution to $B \times Q = A$. Thus division by 0 is not considered.

A third or fourth grader can solve the division problems

$$35 \div 5$$
$$56 \div 7$$
$$2350 \div 10$$

by solving the respective missing factor problems

$$5 \times Q = 35$$
$$7 \times Q = 56$$
$$10 \times Q = 2350.$$

He can solve the first two without too much trouble because he knows the multiplication tables. He shouldn't have too much trouble with the third one, either, provided he knows that multiplication by 10 appends a zero. After a while, he will begin to remember directly the solutions to simple division problems closely related to the multiplication tables, such as $35 \div 5 = 7$ and $56 \div 7 = 8$. Such simple statements are the *elementary division facts*.

EXERCISES

1. Use the multiplication tables and other basic multiplication facts about stick numerals to solve these division problems.

    (a) ╪╪ ÷ ╪   (b) ╪ ÷ ╪   (c) ╪╪ ÷ ╪

2. Use multiplication tables and other base 8 multiplication facts to solve the problems.
    (a) $52_{eight} \div 6_{eight}$ (b) $20_{eight} \div 4_{eight}$ (c) $5470_{eight} \div 10_{eight}$
    (d) $123{,}000_{eight} \div 1000_{eight}$

THE SCIENCE BOOK PROBLEM

Try this yourself.

The third grade at Monroe Elementary has been given \$63 to replace some of the science books, which are in poor condition. Each new replacement costs \$7. The students want to know how many new books they can buy. The third graders have had limited experience with division. Help them solve this.

A First Solution to the Science Book Problem

One third grader suggests, "Take the \$63 in separate dollar bills. Put them into piles of 7 each, one pile for each book, until we use up all the 63 bills. Then we count the number of piles we get. This will be the number of books we can buy."

A Second Solution to the Science Book Problem

A second third grader says, "I could put the 63 dollars into piles of 7 dollars each—one pile for each book. That would take a lot of work. Instead I *imagine* putting them into piles. For the first pile I would take \$7 from the \$63. I would have $63 - 7 = 56$ left. I would take away \$7 from that to make the second pile and have $56 - 7 = 49$ left. Each time I form a pile, I would subtract \$7 from what's left. The number of books we can buy is the same as the number of times I can subtract 7 from 63. Here goes.

$$
\begin{array}{r}
63 \\
-\;7 \\
\hline
56 \\
-\;7 \\
\hline
49 \\
-\;7 \\
\hline
42 \\
-\;7 \\
\hline
35 \\
-\;7 \\
\hline
28 \\
-\;7 \\
\hline
21 \\
-\;7 \\
\hline
14 \\
-\;7 \\
\hline
7 \\
-\;7 \\
\hline
0
\end{array}
$$

I was able to subtract 7 from 63 nine times. We can buy 9 books."

A Third Solution to the Science Book Problem A third offers, "You don't have to do all that subtraction! Just *suppose* you subtracted 7 from 63 a certain number of times. What that would mean is that if you added 7 to itself that certain number of times

$$7 + 7 + 7 + \cdots$$

you would get 63. That means that $7 \times$ that certain number $= 63$. In other words, you want to find a number Q so that $7 \times Q = 63$. From the 7s multiplication table, $7 \times 9 = 63$. So the answer is 9."

The Mathematical Idea: Division as Repeated Subtraction

The second third grader was clever to notice that the science book problem could be solved by *repeated subtraction* of 7 from 63. The third student was equally clever to notice that a repeated subtraction problem could be turned into a missing factor problem, that is, into a division problem, a type of problem that he had had a lot of experience with. We have, then,

---

DIVISION AND REPEATED SUBTRACTION

Given whole numbers A and B, with $A \geq B > 0$, if Q is a whole number such that $B \times Q = A$, then Q is also the number of times that B can be subtracted repeatedly from A.

To calculate $A \times B$ you *add* B repeatedly A times and to calculate $A \div B$, you count the number of times you can *subtract* B repeatedly from A.

EXERCISE

3. Sarah is in the third grade and has been selling boxes of saltwater taffy for her class trip in the spring. She has sold \$42 worth of the taffy, but she can't remember how many boxes she sold. She does know that each box sells for \$6. How would she figure out how many boxes she sold?

THE CABBAGE PATCH
PROBLEM

Try this yourself.

Carlos is planting cabbages in his garden. He has purchased 60 plants and plans to plant them in 8 rows, with the same number of cabbages in each row. He wants to know how many plants he should plant in each row. How can he solve this problem? (Carlos is in the third grade. He knows his multiplication tables. He has solved many missing factor division problems.)

A Solution to the Cabbage
Patch Problem

Here is Carlos's solution: "Let me *draw a picture* of what my cabbage patch should look like.

```
❋ ❋ ❋ ❋ ❋ ❋ ❋ · · ·
❋ ❋ ❋ ❋ ❋ ❋ ❋ · · ·
❋ ❋ ❋ ❋ ❋ ❋ ❋ · · ·
❋ ❋ ❋ ❋ ❋ ❋ ❋ · · ·
❋ ❋ ❋ ❋ ❋ ❋ ❋ · · ·
❋ ❋ ❋ ❋ ❋ ❋ ❋ · · ·
❋ ❋ ❋ ❋ ❋ ❋ ❋ · · ·
❋ ❋ ❋ ❋ ❋ ❋ ❋ · · ·
```

It should be a rectangular array of cabbage plants with 8 rows. Every row should have the same number Q of cabbage plants. So 8 times Q should equal 60: $8 \times Q = 60$, or $60 \div 8 = Q$. I know from the multiplication tables that $8 \times 7 = 56$ and $8 \times 8 = 64$ and that any other numbers would give me a product smaller than 56 or larger than 64. There's no answer! Wait, I have cabbage plants to plant. I don't have enough to plant 8 in each row. But I could plant 7 plants in each row, use up 56 of the plants, and have $60 - 56 = 4$ plants left over. I'll figure out something to do with the 4 extra plants . . ."

The Mathematical Idea: Division with Quotient and Remainder

For a given pair of whole numbers A and B there is not always a whole number Q such that $B \times Q = A$. However, as in the solution to the cabbage patch problem, we may still want to find a whole number Q so that $B \times Q$ is *close* to A. In fact, we will write $60 \div 8 = 7$ with a remainder of 4, to mean that 7 is the largest whole number Q such that $8 \times Q$ is no bigger than 60 and that $60 - 8 \times 7 = 4$. In other words, $60 = 8 \times 7 + 4$.

Similarly, $25 \div 3 = 8$ with a remainder of 1 means that 3 can be subtracted from 25 no more than 8 times and that when you do this, you will have 1 left over. In other words, $25 = 8 \times 3 + 1$. In general,

---

DIVISION WITH REMAINDER

Suppose that A and B are whole numbers with $B \neq 0$. If there are whole numbers Q and R such that $A = B \times Q + R$ and $0 \leq R < B$, then we write $A \div B = Q$ with a remainder R. Q is called the *quotient*, B the *divisor*, A the *dividend*, and R the *remainder*.

Notice that this definition includes the possibility that R, the remainder, be zero. When $R = 0$, then there is a whole number Q such that $A = B \times Q$. Thus, this definition includes the one given earlier.

Having remainders makes division different from addition, subtraction, and multiplication. Given two whole numbers, for each of those three operations there is associated a single third number—the sum, the difference, and the product, respectively. For division, given two whole numbers (the divisor and the dividend), there are associated two whole numbers—the quotient and the remainder. (Sometimes, when the remainder is zero, it is not mentioned.)

EXERCISES

4. Julie is having a birthday party. She and her mom have decided to give each friend who comes to the party a special favor. Her mom says: "Julie, here is $25 to buy the favors." Julie knows that each favor costs $3. She wonders how many favors she can buy because that will tell her how many friends she can invite. How can Julie solve this problem?

5. Solve the problems using only basic multiplication facts.
   (a) $1234 \div 10$ (b) $143,628 \div 100$

6. Using only the base 8 multiplication tables and basic multiplication facts, solve the problems.
   (a) $47_{eight} \div 6_{eight}$ (b) $50_{eight} \div 7_{eight}$ (c) $1234_{eight} \div 10_{eight}$
   (d) $143,627_{eight} \div 100_{eight}$

6.2   THE STANDARD METHOD OF LONG DIVISION

THE LOAVES OF BREAD PROBLEM

You have 65 loaves of bread, which you intend to share equally with 7 families. You want to know how many loaves each family will get. You have not had much experience with division; however, you have solved the rose garden problem and the science book problem. Here's the solution you come up with.

You line up the 7 families and begin handing out the loaves of bread 1 at a time: a loaf to the first family, a loaf to the second family, and so on, until you give a loaf to the seventh family. Then you make another pass through the families giving a second loaf to the first family, a second loaf to the second family, and so on, to the 7 families. You make as many passes through the families as you can until you can't make a complete pass. There may be some loaves left over. You keep track of the number of complete passes you make through all the families. The number of complete passes is the number of loaves each family has.

The Mathematical Idea: Division as Equal Distribution

We know that the loaves of bread problem can be solved by dividing 65 by 7. But, at first glance, the problem does not appear to be a missing factor problem or a repeated subtraction problem. After some thought, you can see that each pass in the solution corresponds to subtracting 7 from 65 and the number of passes you make is equal to the number of times you can subtract 7 from 65. In this way you turn the solution into the solution to a repeated subtraction problem. The loaves of bread problem is an *equal distribution* problem.

EQUAL DISTRIBUTION PROBLEM

Suppose that A and B are whole numbers such that $B \neq 0$. A problem in which A objects are to be distributed equally into B piles is called an *equal distribution* problem.

EXERCISES

7. Carlos has invited 8 friends to his birthday party. His mother has given him 70 pieces of candy to distribute equally among his friends as favors. Carlos wants to know how many pieces of candy each of his friends will get. Show that this is an equal distribution problem.

8. You have 43_{six} bottles of soda that you want to divide up equally among 7 friends coming to a party. How many bottles will each friend get? (A nice way of thinking of 43_{six} bottles of soda is 4 six-packs and 3 loose bottles.)

The Standard Method of Long Division with Single-Digit Divisor

Most versions of the standard method of long division are based on thinking of division as the solution to an equal distribution problem. We will show this using a single-digit divisor.

Consider the division problem 928 ÷ 7. First *we make a model* of 928 using place value blocks.

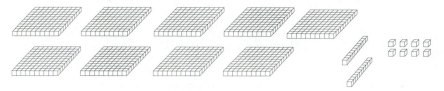

We want to put 928 items into 7 equal piles. Start with the flats. Distribute the 9 flats into 7 equal piles. Each pile gets 1 flat, and there are 2 left over: 9 ÷ 7 = 1 with remainder 2.

The 7 piles:

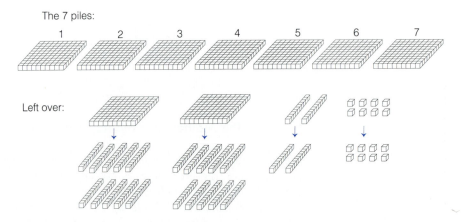

Left over:

Trade the 2 leftover flats for longs, making 22 longs in all. Then, distribute the 22 longs equally into the 7 piles. Each pile gets 3 longs, and there is 1 left over: 22 ÷ 7 = 3 with remainder 1.

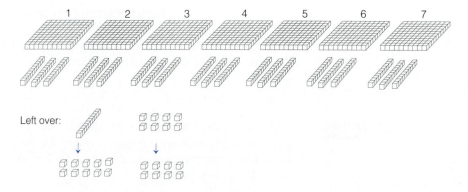

Left over:

Trade the 1 leftover long for units, making 18 units in all. Finally, distribute the 18 units equally into the 7 piles. Each pile gets 2 units with 4 left over: 18 ÷ 7 = 2 with remainder 4.

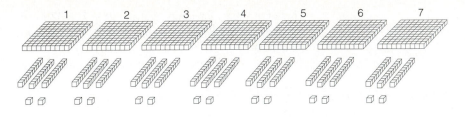

Left over: ⬚ ⬚ ⬚ ⬚

We have finished; as many as possible of the place value blocks have been used. Each of the 7 piles has 1 flat, 3 longs, and 2 units; there are 4 units left over. Thus, $928 \div 7 = 132$ with remainder 4.

Let's consider a second example. This time we will show the pencil and paper work for the standard method along with maneuvering place value blocks. The problem is $4371 \div 8$.

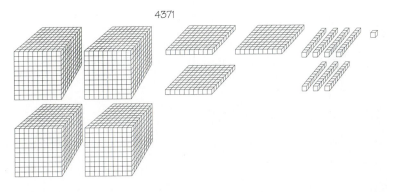

Since $4 \div 8 = 0$ with remainder 4, we trade the cubes for flats obtaining 43 flats in all.

Then we distribute the 43 flats equally into 8 piles. Each pile gets 5 flats, with 3 flats left over: $43 \div 8 = 5$ with remainder 3.

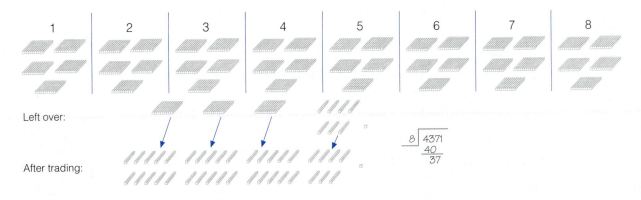

Trade the 3 flats for longs, getting $30 + 7 = 37$ longs in all. Distribute the 37 longs equally into the 8 piles. Each pile gets 4 longs, with 5 left over: $37 \div 8 = 4$ with remainder 5.

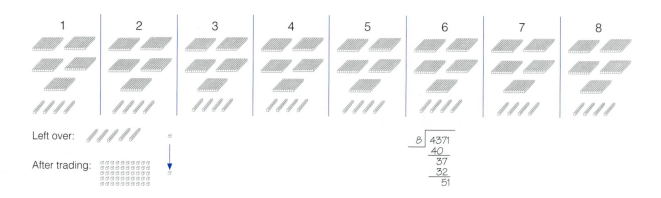

Left over:

After trading:

$$
\begin{array}{r}
8\,\overline{)\,4371} \\
\underline{40} \\
37 \\
\underline{32} \\
51
\end{array}
$$

Trade the 5 longs for units getting $50 + 1 = 51$ units in all. Distribute the 51 units equally into the 8 piles. Each pile gets 6 units, with 3 left over: $51 \div 8 = 6$ with remainder 3.

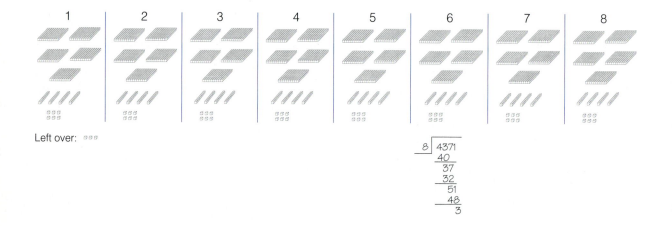

Left over:

$$
\begin{array}{r}
8\,\overline{)\,4371} \\
\underline{40} \\
37 \\
\underline{32} \\
51 \\
\underline{48} \\
3
\end{array}
$$

We're finished. All the blocks have been accounted for. There are 5 flats, 4 longs, and 6 units in each of the piles with 3 left over: $4371 \div 8 = 546$ with remainder 3.

EXERCISES

9. Use the method just demonstrated with place value blocks (or pictures of them) to solve the division problems.
   (a) $1542 \div 5$ (b) $2364 \div 5$
   Draw in the steps of the standard method in parallel.

10. Use base 8 place value blocks (or pictures of them) to solve $542_{\text{eight}} \div 6_{\text{eight}}$ in the same way.

11. Solve $6072_{\text{eight}} \div 5_{\text{eight}}$ using the standard method adapted to base 8 numerals.

6.3   THE SCAFFOLD METHOD OF DIVISION

Now we turn to division problems in which the divisor has two digits.

THE SCIENCE EXPERIMENT KIT PROBLEM

Please try this yourself.

The principal of Elena's school has given $742 to her third grade class for the year's science supplies. The class decides to use the money to buy a Science Experiment Kit for each member of the class. Each kit costs $35. Elena has been put in charge of purchasing these kits and wants to know how many kits she can buy with $742. How would Elena solve this problem? (She has solved division problems as missing factor problems using the multiplication tables; she has also solved division problems in which the remainders are not zero and in which quotients can be gotten from the multiplication tables.)

A Solution to the Science Experiment Kit Problem

Elena thinks, "If I bought 1 kit, it would cost $35. I'd have this much left:

$$\begin{array}{r} 742 \\ -35 \\ \hline 707 \end{array}$$

Then I can buy another one and have this much left:

$$\begin{array}{r} 707 \\ -35 \\ \hline 672 \end{array}$$

I just keep subtracting 35 from whatever I have left. The number of times I can do this will be the number of kits we can buy. That's a repeated subtraction problem, so that it's also the division problem $742 \div 35 = Q$ with remainder R, or $35 \times Q + R = 742$.

"But I don't know the 35s multiplication table. I could try multiplying 35 times a lot of numbers to see if I could get 742. That sounds a little hit or miss. Let me go back to subtracting 35s.

$$\begin{array}{r} 742 \\ -35 \\ \hline 707 \\ -35 \\ \hline 672 \\ -35 \\ \hline 637 \\ -35 \\ \hline 602 \end{array}$$

"Maybe there's an easier way. Every time I subtract 35 twice, it's the same as subtracting 35 + 35 = 70. Why don't I just subtract 70s from what I have left? I could also subtract 140s from what's left: That's two 70s, or four 35s. Let me try that and at the same time let me *organize what I have* by making a column on the right to keep track of the number of 35s I subtract.

NO. OF
35s SUBTRACTED

602	
− 140	4
462	
− 140	4
322	
− 140	4
182	
− 140	4
42	

I can't subtract any more 140s. But I can subtract one more 35.

NO. OF
35s SUBTRACTED

42	
− 35	1
7	

"Now let me figure out how many 35s I subtracted in all.

NO. OF
35s SUBTRACTED:

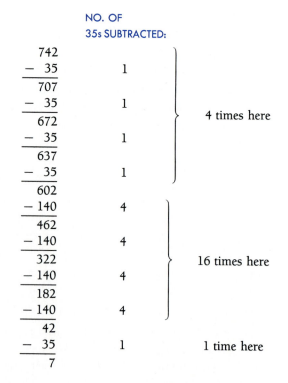

742		
− 35	1	
707		
− 35	1	4 times here
672		
− 35	1	
637		
− 35	1	
602		
− 140	4	
462		
− 140	4	
322		16 times here
− 140	4	
182		
− 140	4	
42		
− 35	1	1 time here
7		

"Let's see. That's $4 + 16 + 1 = 21$ times. That means we could buy 21 kits, and there would be $7 left over! I should check this answer. I was able to subtract 35 from 742 exactly 21 times, and there was 7 left over. Let me multiply 35 by 21.

$$\begin{array}{r} 35 \\ \times\ 21 \\ \hline 35 \\ 70 \\ \hline 735 \end{array}$$

and then add 7

$$\begin{array}{r} 735 \\ +7 \\ \hline 742 \end{array}$$

It checks."

EXERCISES

12. You are in the third grade. You have had no experience with division except where the multiplication tables apply. You discover that you have $137 in your savings account. You want to know how many $17 Cabbage Patch Dolls you can buy with this amount. How would you find out?

13. Solve the problem in the base 8 system using only what you know about base 8 addition, subtraction, and division and the base 8 multiplication tables: $253_{\text{eight}} \div 32_{\text{eight}}$.

14. Solve the stick numeral problem using only what you know about base 5 stick numeral addition, subtraction, and division and the stick numeral multiplication tables: ╪╪╪ ÷ ╪╪.

THE ORPHANAGE PROBLEM

John's third grade class has raised $4762 from a raffle to buy clothing and school supplies for the children in a local orphanage. The class wants to divide the proceeds equally among the 29 children, and it wants John to figure out how much each child will get. John has had no experience with division except for problems solved by elementary division facts and with Elena, helping her solve the Science Experiment Kit problem. He knows how to multiply a number by a power of 10.

Here is John's solution to this problem: "If I give every child $1, that would use up $29, and I would have

$$\begin{array}{r} \$4762 \\ -\$\ \ 29 \\ \hline \$4733 \end{array}$$

left. If I give every child another dollar, that would use up $29 again, and then I'd have

$$\begin{array}{r} \$4733 \\ -\$\ \ 29 \\ \hline \$4704 \end{array}$$

left. It's like the *solution to a similar problem*, the Science Experiment Kit problem: You deal out dollars to the kids. Each time you deal out a dollar to everybody, you subtract 29 from what you have left. The number of times you can subtract 29 from

$4762 will be the number of dollars each child gets. But if I keep subtracting like this, it's going to take a long time. Let me give each child a bunch of dollars each time, like maybe $4. That would be $4 × 29 = $116 in all that I would have to subtract. That still wouldn't make much of a dent. Let me think of something bigger to give the kids and something easier to multiply times 29. How about $10 for each child? That's a bigger number and also easy to multiply with: $10 × 29 = $290. Multiplication by 10 is easy; so is multiplication by 100. Let me try that. It might be too big, but it's worth a try. $100 × 29 = $2900. It's not too big at all. Starting from the beginning with $4762, we'd have

$$\begin{array}{r} \$4762 \\ -\ \$2900 \\ \hline \$1862 \end{array}$$

left. Can I subtract another 100 × 29? No, but I could subtract 10 × 29 = 290. Let me *organize what I have* to keep track of the number of times I subtract 29 from 4762.

	NO. OF SUBTRACTIONS OF 29
4762	
− 2900	100
1862	
− 290	10
1572	
− 290	10
1282	
− 290	10
992	

I can keep subtracting 10 × 29 until I can't do it any more. But 290 is a little less than 300 and 3 × 300 = 900. So I ought to be able to subtract 3 × 290 (or 30 × 29) from what's left.

992	
− 870	30
122	

Now I can't subtract any 10 × 29s. Since 29 is close to 30 and 3 × 30 = 90, it looks as if I could subtract three 29s.

122	
− 87	3
35	
− 29	1
6	

I'm finished. Let me count the number of 29s I subtracted.

```
      4762
    − 2900                    100
    ───────
      1862
    −  290                     10
    ───────
      1572
    −  290                     10
    ───────
      1282
    −  290                     10
    ───────
       992
    −  870                     30
    ───────
       122
    −   87                      3
    ───────
        35
    −   29                      1
    ───────
         6 (remainder)        164 (total no. of 29s subtracted)
```

"So each child will be given $164 worth of clothing and school supplies, and there will be $6 left over."

The Mathematical Idea: The Scaffold Method of Division

The solutions to the orphanage and science experiment kit problems took a long time. (Someone who knows the "standard" way of doing long division could do these problems more quickly.) However, they are accessible to people having little experience with division, and we can turn the solutions to these two problems into a method very close to the "standard" way of dividing called the *scaffold method*.

We will illustrate the method with the following problem: divide 79,783 by 24. To solve this, we will not think of the problem as a missing factor problem but as a repeated subtraction problem: How many times can we subtract 24 from 79,783? And how much will be left after subtracting 24 as much as we can?

We think of the *similar problems* we have just solved: From the original number 79,783 we want to subtract multiples of 24 that are easy to calculate. In fact, an important part of the method is to find the largest of 10 × 24 or 100 × 24 or 1000 × 24 or ... that can be subtracted. Since 10,000 × 24 = 240,000 is larger than 79,783, and 1000 × 24 = 24,000 is smaller than 79,783, the latter must be the largest we can subtract. So we start by subtracting 1000 × 24 = 24,000.

Another feature of the scaffold method is the way we *organize our work.*

We keep track of the number of 24s subtracted in this column.

We write down the dividend and divisor here, as usual.

We subtract 1000 × 24 here. ⟶

Here is what is left after ⟶ subtracting 1000 × 24.

```
        24 | 79,783
             − 24,000          1000
             ─────────
               55,783
```

We have 55,783 left. Now we want to know how many more 24s we can subtract from 55,783. Starting with the latter number, we think the same way as before: What's the largest of 10 × 24, 100 × 24, 1000 × 24, . . . that we can subtract from 55,783? We can see by now that we can subtract another 1000 × 24. We do that and continue on in this fashion. Here's our work and our thinking along the way.

24	79,783		
	− 24,000	1000	
	55,783		
	− 24,000	1000	
	31,783		
	− 24,000	1000	
Can't subtract 1000 × 24 but can subtract 100 × 24.	7783		
	− 2400	100	
	5383		
	− 2400	100	Subtract another 100.
	2983		
	− 2400	100	And another 100.
Can't subtract 100 × 24 but can subtract 10 × 24.	583		
	− 240	10	
	343		
	− 240	10	And another 10.
Can't subtract 10 × 24 but can subtract 1 × 24.	103		
	− 24	1	
	79		We'll be bold and
	− 48	2	subtract two 24s at
	31		once.
	− 24	1	
We can't subtract any more 24s. This must be the remainder!	7	3324	

This is the sum of all the numbers in the column above it. It is the total number of times 24 can be subtracted from 79,783.

Thus, 79,783 ÷ 24 = 3324 with a remainder of 7.

As you experience using it, you learn to make shortcuts; you begin to replace two or more steps by one step. For example, at the first step, you might have thought, "I know I can subtract 1000 × 24 from 79,783; but I can do more: I can subtract

3000 × 24 from 79,783." So the beginning of your work might look like

$$
\begin{array}{r}
24 \overline{\smash{)}\ 79{,}783} \\
-\ 72{,}000 \quad 3000 \\
\hline
7783
\end{array}
$$

instead of

$$
\begin{array}{r}
24 \overline{\smash{)}\ 79{,}783} \\
-\ 24{,}000 \quad 1000 \\
\hline
55{,}783 \\
-\ 24{,}000 \quad 1000 \\
\hline
31{,}783 \\
-\ 24{,}000 \quad 1000 \\
\hline
7783
\end{array}
$$

When all the calculations for the problem have been shortened in this way, then the method looks a lot like the "standard" method of long division. Here they are side by side.

$$
\begin{array}{r}
24 \overline{\smash{)}\ 79{,}783} \\
-\ 72{,}000 \quad 3000 \\
\hline
7783 \\
-\ 7200 \quad 300 \\
\hline
583 \\
-\ 480 \quad 20 \\
\hline
103 \\
-\ 96 \quad 4 \\
\hline
7 \quad 3324
\end{array}
\qquad
\begin{array}{r}
3324 \\
24 \overline{\smash{)}\ 79{,}783} \\
72 \\
\hline
77 \\
72 \\
\hline
58 \\
48 \\
\hline
103 \\
96 \\
\hline
7
\end{array}
$$

For someone learning how to divide, the scaffold method may have some advantages over the standard method. With the scaffold method you can be leisurely and make conservative guesses; with the standard method each "guess" must be exact (unless you want to do a lot of erasing of "poor" guesses). With the scaffold method it should be clear what you are doing at each step: You are always subtracting the divisor a certain number of times from what is left after previous subtracting. When you are finished, it is obvious that your answer is equal to the number of times you have subtracted the divisor.

EXERCISES

15. Solve the division problems using the scaffold method.
    (a) 60,983 ÷ 87   (b) 57,041 ÷ 263
    In solving these problems, take advantage of the features of the scaffold method. Don't try to mimic either the steps or the thinking associated with the standard method.

16. Solve the division problems using the scaffold method as adapted to base 8 numerals.
    (a) $653_{\text{eight}} \div 7_{\text{eight}}$ (b) $3054_{\text{eight}} \div 41_{\text{eight}}$

6.4 LOOKING BACK: DIVISION—ITS DEFINITION, WAYS OF THINKING ABOUT IT, AND METHODS FOR CARRYING IT OUT

The Definition of *Division*

Let's summarize the information given in this chapter in a formal definition of *division*.

DEFINITION OF *DIVISION*

Suppose that A and B are whole numbers such that $B \neq 0$. If whole numbers Q and R are such that $A = B \times Q + R$ and $0 \leq R < B$, then Q is called the *quotient* and R is called the *remainder* of A *on division by B*, and we write $A \div B = Q$ with remainder R.

It is worth having a look at this definition for several specific cases.

Case 1 Suppose that A is any whole number and that $B = 1$. What do you get when you divide A by 1? You get a quotient of A and a remainder of 0: $A = 1 \times A + 0$. If you think of $A \div 1$ as the solution Q to the missing factor problem $1 \times Q = A$, then $Q = A$ works. If you think of $A \div 1$ as the number of times you can subtract 1 from A, then $Q = A$ is the answer—and the remainder is 0.

Case 2 Suppose that A and B are whole numbers and that $A < B$. What happens when you divide A by B? Some might say "You can't divide A by B when B is bigger than A!" However, in the definition of division of whole numbers, the number 0 can play the role of quotient, and the number A the role of remainder: $A = B \times 0 + A$. If you think of $A \div B$ as the number of times you can subtract B from A, then 0 is the answer—with a remainder of A.

Case 3 Suppose $A = 0$ and that B is any nonzero whole number. What happens when you divide 0 by B? This is a special instance of case 2. You divide 0 by B and get a quotient of 0 with a remainder of 0: $0 = B \times 0 + 0$, or $0 \div B = 0$.

Case 4 We have already seen that $B = 0$ in the definition is either impossible ($A \neq 0$) or undesirable ($A = 0$). Thus, the possibility $B = 0$ is left out of the definition entirely.

Finally, the following theorem summarizes what the methods we have developed in this chapter do for us, something that we all have known (deep down); namely, in a division problem where the divisor is not zero, there always is a quotient and a remainder.

DIVISION THEOREM

Suppose that A and B are whole numbers and $B \neq 0$. Then there are whole numbers Q and R such that $A = QB + R$, $0 \leq R < B$.

Ways of Thinking about Division and Methods for Dividing

The formal definition of division evolved from several real problems, in the solutions of which division is used. From some of these solutions evolved the methods for actually finding the quotient and remainder, given the divisor and dividend. We can summarize the ways of thinking about division that these solutions suggest and how they relate to the methods for division.

MISSING FACTOR WAY OF THINKING ABOUT DIVISION

Suppose that A and B are whole numbers such that $B \neq 0$. If there is a whole number Q such that $B \times Q = A$, then Q is called A *divided by* B and is written $Q = A \div B$.

A person learning division for the first time thinks of it this way. Since there is not always a whole number Q such that $B \times Q = A$, the person next learns another way of thinking about division.

MISSING FACTOR WITH REMAINDER

Suppose that A and B are whole numbers such that $B \neq 0$. The largest whole number Q such that $B \times Q \leq A$ is called the *quotient of A divided by B*. If $R = A - B \times Q$, then we write $A \div B = Q$ with *remainder R*.

For $B \leq 10$ and most $A \leq 100$, the method of finding $A \div B$ is based on the missing factor way of thinking about division: To find the largest number Q such that $B \times Q \leq A$, look in the B's multiplication table for the Q that works; the remainder R is what's left over ($R = A - B \times Q$). This way of thinking is also useful when solving a problem in which the divisor B is a power of 10.

EQUAL DISTRIBUTION WAY OF THINKING ABOUT DIVISION

Suppose that A and B are whole numbers such that $B \neq 0$. Let S be a set with $n(S) = A$. Distribute the elements of S equally into B piles. The number of elements in each of the B piles is Q, the *quotient*. The number of items left over (i.e., not placed in one of the piles) is R, the *remainder*.

The standard method for dividing is based on this way of thinking about division. We developed this method in case the divisor B is a single-digit number.

The repeated subtraction way of thinking about division was the basis for the scaffold method of division normally used when the missing factor way of thinking isn't appropriate.

Division by Organizing an Array Using Place Value Blocks

There is a way of carrying out division using the missing factor way of thinking together with the way of organizing an array using place value blocks (or dots, dashes, and squares) from chapter 5. Consider the problem $524 \div 46$. Think: In a 46-row array, how many items should be in each row in order that the array have 524 items in all (or as nearly close to 524 items as possible)?

To solve this problem, *make a model* of 46 as (Recall that 1 long is worth 10 units $\square$.) Then arrange these blocks in a vertical column, making the left-hand border of an array that is yet to be filled in.

Next, *make a model* of 524 as

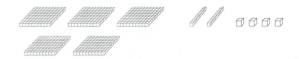

We want to arrange the latter blocks or their equivalent into the array drawn above having 46 on one side. When we finish, the array should look like the organized array for a multiplication problem; the answer to the division problem should appear horizontally on the top border of the array.

Let's start with the flats first. Four of them will go into an organized array.

Now what do we put under the flats in order to complete the column and still have it look like an organized array? First, place a long at the top as part of the horizontal border and a long beside each unit in the vertical border.

The 6 longs placed inside the array must come from the blocks for 524. How can this be? After using up 4 squares in 524, we have the following blocks left over.

To get the 6 longs for the array, we must exchange the last square in the leftover 524 pile for 10 longs, getting

in the leftover 524 pile.

After putting 6 longs in the array, we have a new leftover pile consisting of

Now the array looks like the last array picture above. What should we do next? We know that we won't be able to put another long along the top border, because there are no flats in the most recent leftover pile. Let's put a unit on the top border so that we have the array shown on the left and the leftover pile shown on the right.

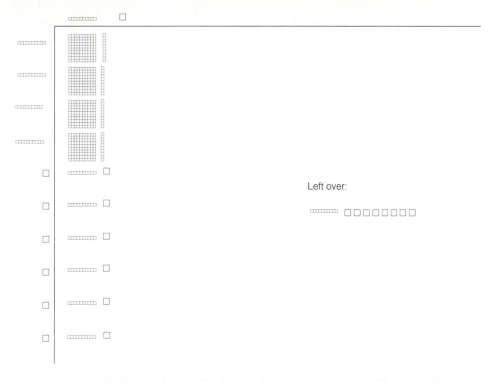

Left over:

Since the leftover pile has blocks worth less than 46, we're finished. The answer to the division problem 524 ÷ 46 is (11) with remainder (18).

EXERCISE 17. Use this method to solve the division problem 823 ÷ 37.

6.5 LOOKING AHEAD: DIVISION IN ALGEBRA

There are addition, subtraction, and multiplication properties of equality. There is also a division property of equality.

DIVISION PROPERTY OF EQUALITY

Suppose that A, B, and C are whole numbers and that $A = B$ and $C \neq 0$. Then $A \div C = B \div C$. (This last equation means that A and B have the same quotient and same remainder on division by C.)

Let's consider a situation where we might want to use this property.

THE COOLER PRODUCTION PROBLEM

Try this yourself, first.

The Cool Company makes coolers. It costs $1500 just to keep the company shop running each week. Beyond that, it costs the company $300 more to make each individual cooler. At the beginning of the week Cool Company has $5100 on hand from previous sales of coolers. With the $5100 what is the largest number of coolers the company can make that week?

You might solve the problem: "If I let N represent the number of coolers we make, then it will cost me $300N$ beyond costs to keep the shop running. We have $5100 available. When costs to keep the shop running are taken out of this, we will have $5100 − $1500 = $3600 left. The number N of coolers we make will be the largest possible when we use up all $3600. This happens when $300N = $3600.

"So I want to find a whole number N such that $300N = $3600. This is a missing factor problem, so the answer is $N = $3600 ÷ $300 = 12."

You might solve the problem somewhat differently: To find a number N such that $300N = $3600, you divide both sides of the equation by $300 to get

$$(\$300N) \div \$300 = \$3600 \div \$300 \qquad \text{or} \qquad N = 12$$

This solution also uses the fact that if A and B are whole numbers with $B \neq 0$, then $(AB) \div B = A$.

EXERCISES

18. You are the owner of Midtown Motel, which has an average occupancy of 20 rooms. You want to know how much to charge for each room per night. You have figured out that there are certain fixed costs for running the motel (electricity, water, upkeep, laundry, insurance, mortgage, etc.) no matter how many rooms are occupied. These costs come to $125 per day. You have also figured out that you need $100 per day for your own income. What is the minimum you should charge per room per night in order to cover fixed costs and your income requirements?

19. The Hampshire Hotel is catering a banquet for 412 people (including speakers and special guests). A special speakers' table will seat 20 people. Every other table in the banquet hall seats 8 people. The hotel staff wants to know how many ordinary tables to set up. Help the staff find out.

20. Sarah and Jim are two friends who like to bike. Sarah bikes at an average rate of 10 mph, and Jim bikes at the average rate of 15 mph. Both live on Route 10, Jim 7 mi east of City Center and Sarah 22 mi east of City Center. They plan the following bike trip for this Saturday: Both will get up, leave their homes at 8 A.M., and start biking east on Route 10. They want to know when they will meet and where. Help them find out.

21. Use the rules for algebraic symbols that we have developed so far to solve the following problems. Justify each step with a rule.
    (a) Find a whole number A such that $7A − 8 = 20$.
    (b) Find a whole number B such that $12B + 7 = 55$.
    (c) Find a whole number C such that $11C + 6 = 8C + 21$.
    (d) Find a whole number D such that $15D + 8 = 21D − 10$.
    (e) Find a whole number E such that $17E − 13 = 12E − 8$.

6.6   CALCULATORS AND COMPUTERS IN DIVISION

FINDING QUOTIENT AND REMAINDER USING A CALCULATOR   To divide 478 by 56 using a calculator, you use the keying sequence 478 [÷] 56 [=]. The calculator display will then read 8.535714286. The latter is an approximation of the fraction $\frac{478}{56}$ by a decimal fraction. Now $\frac{478}{56} = 8\frac{30}{56}$ so that $\frac{30}{56}$ is approximately equal to the decimal fraction .535714286. Also the whole number part of the display—8—is the quotient of 478 when divided by 56. (There will be more about fractions and division in chap. 8 and about approximating fractions by decimal fractions in chap. 10.)

How do you figure out the remainder from the calculator display? Since 8 is the quotient, we know that $478 = 8 \times 56 + remainder$. Thus, to find the remainder, you multiply 8 by 56 and subtract what you get from 478: $478 - 8 \times 56 = 478 - 448 = 30$. The remainder is 30. In general,

---

HOW TO FIND QUOTIENT AND REMAINDER
WHEN DIVIDING WITH A CALCULATOR

To divide A by B, use the keying sequence A [÷] B [=]. The whole number part of the calculator display is the quotient Q. To find the remainder R, multiply Q by B and subtract the product from A: $A - Q \times B = R$.

For example, to find $943 \div 47$, use the keying sequence 943 [÷] 47 [=], after which the calculator will display 20.06382979. So the quotient is 20. To find the remainder, multiply 20 by 47 to get 940 and subtract the latter from 943 to get a remainder of 3. Thus $943 \div 47 = 20$ with remainder 3.

SIMULATING DIVISION ON A COMPUTER   In chapter 5 we showed how a computer could multiply directly by repeatedly adding one of the factors. We can also get a computer to divide by repeatedly subtracting the divisor from the dividend. Consider the division problem encountered earlier: $478 \div 56$. We want to get the computer to subtract 56 repeatedly from 478 and count the number of times this can be done. To get the computer to subtract 56 repeatedly, a loop would be just the thing. However, with multiplication we add one of the factors to itself and the number of times we do this is equal to the other factor; with division we subtract the divisor from the dividend but we don't know how many times ahead of time—in fact, the number of times we subtract is what we are trying to find out. It will be convenient to use a new command—GOTO—in place of a FOR . . . NEXT loop. In BASIC, the GOTO command is always followed by a number, such as GOTO 30. When GOTO 30 is encountered in a program, the computer is instructed to "go to" line 30 and follow the program from there on. The following program carries out the division $478 \div 56$ using the GOTO command.

```
20 LET Q = 0 Initialization of Q
30 LET R = 478 Initialization of R
40 PRINT R, Q
50 LET R = R - 56
60 LET Q = Q + 1
70 GOTO 40
100 END
```

The variable R starts out having the value 478, then its value is $478 - 56$, then its value is what is left after another 56 is subtracted, and so on. The value of R changes and is what is left after successively subtracting 56. In line 50, after each subtracting of 56, you add 1 to the value of Q. Thus the variable Q "counts" the number of times 56 has been subtracted from 478.

There is a problem with this program. (It can be fixed!) Type it into your microcomputer and run it. What happens? It keeps going on and on and on and . . . To stop the computer, hold down the CONTROL key and push C; or if your computer has a

BREAK key, push that. (Consult your BASIC manual or your computer expert if neither works.)

Your screen should look something like this.

```
RUN

478        0
422        1
366        2
310        3
254        4
198        5
142        6
86         7
30         8
-26        9
-82        10
-138       11


BREAK
```

The computer has negative numbers, and the computer doesn't hesitate to subtract whole number B from whole number A, even though B is larger than A. However, we want the computer to stop when R "gets too small." To get the computer to stop, we add the new line

```
45 IF R < 56 THEN GOTO 100
```

Line 45 involves the IF . . . THEN . . . command, which has two parts. The first part—what is typed between the IF and the THEN—is a statement involving one or more of the variables in use in the program. (In the example, the statement is R < 56.) The second part is typed after the THEN and is another command in BASIC. (In the example, the command is GOTO 100.)

Here is how IF . . . THEN . . . works: If the statement between IF and THEN is true, the computer carries out the command following THEN. If the statement is not true, the computer passes to the next line of the program.

In the example, if R < 56 is true (no more 56s can be subtracted), the command GOTO 100 is carried out (the computer "skips over" lines 50 through 70). If R < 56 is false (i.e., $R \geq 56$ and at least one more 56 can be subtracted), the computer moves on to line 50, and the "loop" continues.

We now type LIST to obtain the complete, revised program.

```
LIST

20 LET Q = 0
30 LET R = 478
40 PRINT R, Q
45 IF R < 56 THEN GOTO 100
50 LET R = R - 56
60 LET Q = Q + 1
70 GOTO 40
100 END
```

22. Run the preceding program. How does the printout tell you what the quotient and remainder are when 478 is divided by 56?

23. Revise the preceding program, which starts with the pair 478 and 56 and repeatedly subtracts the latter from the former, so that it will accept any pair of whole numbers *A* and *B* (via INPUT commands) with *A* bigger than *B*, then repeatedly subtract *B* from *A* and determine the quotient and remainder when *A* is divided by *B*. (*Hint:* Look at exercise 31 in chap. 5.)

6.7   SUMMARY OF IMPORTANT IDEAS AND TECHNIQUES

- Division as the solution to a missing factor problem; introduction of terms *quotient*, *divisor*, and *dividend*
- Using the multiplication tables and facts about multiplication by powers of 10 for solving many missing factor problems
- Division as the solution to a repeated subtraction problem
- Division with quotient and remainder
- Division by zero not allowed
- Division as the solution to an equal distribution problem
- Division as the solution to equal distribution problems leading to the standard method
- Division as the solution to a repeated subtraction problem leading to the scaffold method of division
- The division property of equality as a rule for working with algebraic symbols

PROBLEM SET

PRACTICING
SKILLS

Problems 1 and 2 below are "primitive" division problems. To solve them, use the pairing of elements in two sets; do not count or use standard numerals in any way. Identify each as either a missing factor problem, a repeated subtraction problem, or an equal distribution problem.

1. The stones on the left represent the horses Ugboo would like to sell. The stones on the right represent the sheep Lagor would like to use for buying horses from Ugboo. The price is ○ ○ ○ ○ ○ sheep for each horse.

Horses   Sheep

Lagor will buy as many horses as he can with the sheep that he has. Show diagrammatically (for example, with arrows and circles) the horses Lagor is able to buy and the sheep he uses to buy them. Label clearly the sheep Lagor has left over after buying as many horses as he can; similarly, label the horses he is unable to buy.

2. Ugboo has loaves of bread represented by the stones on the left. The village warriors are represented by the stones on the right. Ugboo wants to distribute as many of the loaves as he can to the warriors so that all the warriors have the same amount. The loaves that are left over he will give to the chief and his family. Show how Ugboo would distribute the loaves. Indicate clearly the loaves the chief and his family get.

○ ○ ○ ○ ○   ○ ○ ○
○ ○ ○ ○ ○   ○ ○ ○
○ ○ ○ ○ ○   ○ ○ ○
○ ○ ○ ○ ○   ○ ○ ○
○ ○ ○ ○ ○   ○
○ ○ ○ ○ ○

Loaves   Warriors

3. Charlie returns to his lemonade stand, where Lucy has been taking care of things. She won't tell him how many glasses of lemonade she has sold in his absence, but she has made 72¢. Each glass of lemonade sells for 9¢. Charlie, who has no experience with division, wants to figure out how many glasses Lucy has sold. Help Charlie do this.

4. A new subdivision is to have four small neighborhood parks planted by the developer. Luis's father, who is in charge of planning these parks, has purchased 31 trees to be planted in the parks. Luis has no experience with division yet wants to help his father figure out how many trees should be planted in each park. Help Luis do this.

5. Joanna's third grade class has been given $1585 to spend on furniture for their classroom. The class decides they need new chairs. Each chair costs $56. How can Joanna find out how many chairs they can buy? She understands repeated subtraction.

6. Solve the following division problems as missing factor problems; do not carry out the long division.
   (a) $51 \div 8$ (b) $67 \div 7$ (c) $247 \div 10$ (d) $3562 \div 100$ (e) $81,704 \div 1000$

7. Solve the division problems using the scaffold method.
   (a) $6862 \div 78$ (b) $57,290 \div 59$ (c) $1,873,402 \div 428$

8. Solve the division problems using place value blocks (or pictures of them) and thinking of division as the solution to an equal distribution problem.
   (a) $472 \div 6$ (b) $3702 \div 8$ (c) $9064 \div 7$

9. Jill and her friends are going to the Burger Boy for Jill's eighth birthday. Including Jill, there will be 9 children in the party. Jill's father tells her she can spend up to $50 at the Burger Boy. Help Jill determine how much each child can spend by thinking of it as an equal distribution problem.

10. Monica leaves home at 6 A.M. for a long walk. At 7 A.M. Monica's husband, Robert, leaves home for a run. He follows the exact same route as Monica. Monica walks at 4 mph; Robert runs at 8 mph. At what time will Robert catch up to Monica?

11. You are in charge of a tutoring center. Your budget for this year is $15,700. You will need $2500 to cover nonpersonnel costs (paper, photocopying, telephone, etc.). Each tutor will be paid $1200. How many tutors can you hire?

12. The gardener has 392 flowers to plant. He selects 32 of the best plants to be placed in a circular planter in the center of the garden. How many flowers can be placed in each of the remaining 15 planters so that each planter has the same number of flowers?

13. Use the rules for algebra to solve the following problems. Justify each step of your solution with a rule.
    (a) Find a whole number A such that $8A + 5 = 37$.
    (b) Find a whole number B such that $12B - 7 = 5B$.
    (c) Find a whole number C such that $15C + 4 = 9C + 22$.
    (d) Find a whole number D such that $12D + 20 = 19D - 22$.
    (e) Find a whole number E such that $21E - 21 = 17E - 9$.

14. Use a calculator to find the quotient and remainder for each division problem.
    (a) $123{,}456 \div 406$ (b) $809{,}372 \div 7451$ (c) $1{,}298{,}347 \div 4572$

USING IDEAS   *For each problem remaining, document as clearly and completely as you can your solution to the problem. Include the steps you took to solve the problem, mention the problems or solutions from the text that gave you ideas, and include the problem-solving strategies you used. You might want to outline and organize these details before assembling your final report in the form of an essay.*

15. Ugboo wants to trade as many blankets as he can for Lagor's sheep. They agree to trade | | | blankets for ○ ○ ○ ○ sheep.

  ○ ○ ○ ○
  ○ ○○ ○ ○○
○ ○ ○ ○ ○
○ ○ ○ ○○
○ ○ ○ ○○

Ugboo's blankets   Lagor's sheep

Without counting or using standard numerals, figure out what will be left after all the trading has taken place.

16. Here are the single-digit multiplication tables for stick numerals.

Working entirely within the stick numeral system, solve the stick numeral division problems as missing factor problems.

(a) ⟨stick⟩ ÷ ⟨stick⟩   (b) ⟨stick⟩ ÷ ⟨stick⟩   (c) ⟨stick⟩ ÷ ⟨stick⟩

(d) ⟨stick⟩ ÷ ⟨stick⟩   (e) ⟨stick⟩ ÷ ⟨stick⟩   (f) ⟨stick⟩ ÷ ⟨stick⟩

(g) ⟨stick⟩ ÷ ⟨stick⟩   (h) ⟨stick⟩ ÷ ⟨stick⟩

17. Solve the division problems in two ways: (1) use place value blocks while thinking of division as a solution to an equal distribution problem (use pictures to describe your solution) and (2) use the standard method. Show how each step of the solution in (1) is related to a step in the solution to (2).

(a) $584 \div 9$ (b) $908 \div 7$ (c) $7603 \div 8$

18. Solve the stick numeral division problems in two ways: (i) use base 5 place value blocks and the equal distribution way of thinking; and (ii) the standard method as adapted to stick numerals. Show how each step of the solution in (i) is related to a step in the solution to (ii). (Compare prob. 17.)

(a)   ⟨stick⟩ ÷ ⟨stick⟩   (b)   ⟨stick⟩ ÷ ⟨stick⟩   (c)   ⟨stick⟩ ÷ ⟨stick⟩

19. Here is an example of a stick numeral division problem worked by the scaffold method.

Remainder   Quotient

Solve the stick numeral division problems using the scaffold method.

(a) ╪╪|╪ ÷ ╪╪   (b) ╪╪|╪╪ ÷ ╪╪

20. Use the method of division by organizing an array (using place value blocks) to solve $1521 \div 43$.

21. Solve the division problem $784 \div 37$ in two ways.
    (a) Use the missing factor approach to division together with our way of organizing an array using place value blocks. As in problem 20, set up an array with 37 rows that must be filled in with as close to 784 items as possible. Make a model of 37 in place value blocks, arrange along the left-hand border of the array, and go from there.
    (b) Use the scaffold method.
       Show how each stage of the scaffold method corresponds to what you do with the place value blocks in (a).

22. Below are two decimal division problems completed using the standard method. However, some of the digits have been erased (these are indicated by *s). Reconstruct the erased digits.

(a)
```
          * *
   5 * ) 1 * * *
       * 5 *
       * * *
       4 0 0
```

(b)
```
          9 * *
   3 * ) * 4 * 9 *
       * 1 *
       * * *
       * 1 *
       2 * 5
       2 * 5
```

23. You are the owner of Downtown Café. You want to serve a different soup-and-sandwich combination for each of the weekdays in the year. You want to know how many different kinds of sandwiches you will have to make in order to do this. Here are some clues:

    There are 261 weekdays in the year.
    You have a repertoire of 14 different soups.

24. The cost of janitorial supplies over an 8-month period has been $943.80. Projected over an entire year, what should the cost be?

25. An express train leaves Green City at 3 P.M. and arrives in Brownville at 6 P.M. In the same afternoon a slow train leaves Brownville at 1 P.M. and arrives in Green City at 6 P.M. The engineers of the two trains need to know within a minute when the two trains will be passing. Help them find out. Each train travels at a constant speed.

26. Here is another division problem solved by the standard method. Practically all the digits are missing. Find them.

```
              * * 8 * *
   * * * ) * * * * * * * *
           * * *
           * * * *
           * * *
             * * * *
             * * * *
```

27. Captain Spydyk was worried. A stray meteor had hit the *Star Quest* and severely damaged most of the air recycling system so that the carbon dioxide that the crew exhaled was slowly building up instead of being converted back into oxygen. Usually the equipment could convert 900 liters per hour of carbon dioxide back to oxygen, but now it was only possible to provide 150 liters of fresh oxygen per hr, while the crew needed almost 500 liters.

    Captain Spydyk knew there were 6500 liters of oxygen in reserve tanks and probably another 500 just now in the interior of the ship. He also knew that if the total oxygen inside the ship were less than 200 liters, there would not be enough to breathe. According to his computer, the nearest planet with breathable air was 17 hr away. Could he get there safely?*

28. Consider the following base 8 division problems. Some of them can be solved treating them as missing factor problems and using base 8 multiplication tables and other basic multiplication facts; others can be solved using the scaffold method adapted to base 8 numerals. Decide which method is appropriate and solve each of these completely within the standard base 8 numeral system. Justify the method you use.

    (a) $64_{eight} \div 7_{eight}$ (b) $573_{eight} \div 26_{eight}$

    (c) $4372_{eight} \div 100_{eight}$ (d) $4035_{eight} \div 6_{eight}$

29. Consider the division problem $753_{eight} \div 6_{eight}$. Make a model of 753 using place value blocks and solve the problem while thinking of division as the solution to an equal distribution problem.

30. The digits in a base twelve numeral system are 0,1,2,3,4,5,6,7,8,9,A,B. $A_{twelve} = 10$ and $B_{twelve} = 11$. Solve the following division problem completely within the base 12 system: $40A1B_{twelve} \div 5A_{twelve}$. Describe the method you use.

---

* From Carol Meyer and Tom Sallee, *Make It Simpler,* Addison-Wesley, Reading, Mass., 1983, p. 263.

MULTIPLE-
CHOICE
QUESTIONS

For each multiple-choice question several possible answers are given. Circle the letter just to the left of the item that best answers the problem.

1. Here is the beginning of the solution to a division problem using the scaffold method.

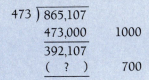

The number where the ? is written should be
(a) 61,007   (b) 3311   (c) 331,100   (d) 3784   (e) 378,400

2. The solution to the following stick numeral missing factor problem +||| × ? = ‡≢|‡‡
is

(a) ‡ with remainder ‡|‡   (b) ‡+‡ with remainder ‡‡

(c) ‡ with remainder ‡+‡   (d) ‡‡ with remainder +‡

(e) ‡‡| with remainder +‡

3. Roga has coconuts and Norum has blankets and have agreed to trade as much as possible according to the following scheme ○○○○○ coconuts will be traded for ||| blankets. After all the trading has taken place, what will be left over?

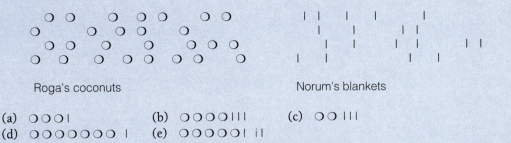

Roga's coconuts   Norum's blankets

(a) ○○○| (b) ○○○○|||| (c) ○○ |||
(d) ○○○○○○○ | (e) ○○○○○| i|

4. Consider the two following collections of base 4 place value blocks:

Their sum is

(a)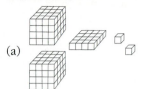

(b)

(c)

(d)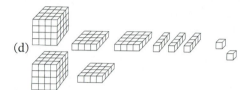

(e)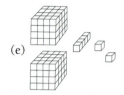

5. Here is a subtraction problem using expanded notation on a counting board.

8	3	4
3	7	8

$$\begin{array}{r} 834 \\ -\ 378 \\ \hline \end{array}$$

A next step using the method of equal additions might be

(a)

8	2	14
3	7	8

(b)

7	12	4
3	7	8

(c)

8	3	14
3	17	8

(d)

8	13	4
3	7	18

(e)

8	3	14
3	8	8

6. The merchant Neevil sold three rugs for ＋|╪, ╪╪╪, and ╪＋, respectively. His total earnings from the three rugs were
   (a) ＋|╪╪   (b) ╪╪╪   (c) ╪╪   (d) ╪＋╪   (e) ＋╪╪

7. Septipolis has the following coinage system

   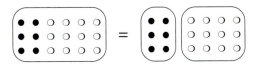

   You want to buy a chariot and give the merchant the coin ⓖ. The chariot costs Ⓡ ⓎⓎⓎⓎ.
   Your change will be
   (a)   ⓎⓎ ⓇⓇⓇⓇ   (b)   ⓖ Ⓡ ⓎⓎⓎⓎⓎ   (c)   ⓎⓎ ⓇⓇⓇⓇⓇ
   (d)   Ⓨ ⓇⓇⓇⓇ   (e)   Ⓨ ⓇⓇⓇⓇⓇ

8. The diagram illustrates an instance of which property of multiplication of whole numbers?

   (a)   associative   (b)   commutative
   (c)   distributive over addition   (d)   multiplication by a power of 10

9. To illustrate the product ╪╪ × ╪╪ of stick numerals, you draw the following array using dots, dashes, and squares:

   The partial product ╪| × ╪ corresponds to which part of this array?
   (a) A   (b) B   (c) C   (d) D

10. In the stick numeral subtraction problem some of the digits have been replaced by the letters P, Q, and R.

   $$
   \begin{array}{r}
   +|\ P\ + \\
   -\ \ Q\ ╪╪ \\
   \hline
   +\ R
   \end{array}
   $$

   What should the digit P be in order to make a correct solution?
   (a) | (b) ＋   (c) ╪   (d) ╪   (e) ╪

For each of the remaining problems, document your solution carefully in the form of an essay.

11. Use the scaffold method to solve the following division problem. Explain all your steps in such a way that it is evident that you are subtracting the divisor from the dividend a lot of times, that the quotient is the number of times you can subtract the divisor from the dividend, and that the remainder is what is left over after doing all of the subtracting.

$$87\,\overline{)\,25{,}701}$$

12. Consider the multiplication problem 35×42. Solve it in three ways.
    (i) Think of the product as the number of items in a 35 by 42 array. Organize the array using dots, dashes, and squares.
    (ii) Use the method of partial products with zeros.
    (iii) Use the standard method.
    With these solutions, (a) show clearly how each of the partial products of (ii) correspond to portions of the array in (i), and (b) explain clearly how and where the standard method of (iii) is a shortcut to (ii).

13. The land of Octavia uses base 8 place value blocks for its monetary system. You are visiting Octavia and purchase two items.

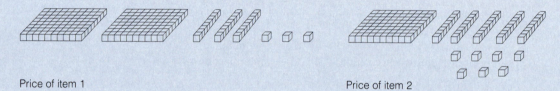

Price of item 1   Price of item 2

You have in Octavian currency:

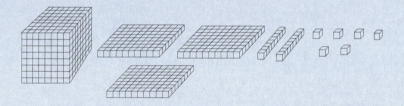

You want to know how much you will have left over after you make your purchase. Show how you figure this out. What you have left over should involve the fewest possible coins.

14. Consider the division problem $852 \div 34$. Solve it (a) using the scaffold method, (b) using the standard method, and (c) using the missing factor method with place value blocks as in the problem set. Compare these methods and show how they relate.

MULTIPLES, DIVISORS, AND PRIMES

CHAPTER 7

Grade school children learning multiplication tables notice curiosities in numbers, such as $8 \times 7 = 7 \times 8$ (7 added to itself 8 times is the same as 8 added to itself 7 times) and $6 \times 3 = 3 \times 6$. These turn out to be instances of a more general relationship expressed as the commutative property of multiplication of whole numbers. We have also described other relationships in the associative and distributive properties and used them to develop methods for multiplying large numbers.

In this chapter we will discuss properties of numbers that are related to their multiples and divisors. We will use these properties to solve problems and to help us understand how numbers work. Also, we will join others who, over the years, have looked for new patterns in numbers and are amazed and delighted at what they find.

7.1 COMMON MULTIPLES AND DIVISORS OF TWO NUMBERS

THE HOUSE PAINTER PROBLEM

Try it!

Gert and Joe are house painters. They plan to paint a house together and want to know how long it will take them. Joe estimates that it would take him 56 hr if he were painting alone. Gert estimates that it would take her 42 hr if she were painting alone. Help them solve this problem.

A Solution to the House Painter Problem

Gert: "Let me *solve a simpler problem.* If I could paint a house in 42 hours and you could paint the same house in 84 hours, then—if we started together painting identical houses—in 84 hours you'd paint one house and I'd paint two houses or we'd paint three houses together. If we worked together and painted three houses in 84 hours, then we could paint one house together in $84 \div 3$ hours. That's 28 hours.

"The numbers 42 and 56 are not as nice. If we worked together painting identical houses, I wonder how many hours we would have to paint for both of us to paint a whole number of houses? If we knew the answer to that, solving the problem would be a lot easier. Let's *solve a similar problem* having smaller numbers. Suppose there's a house you know you can paint in 3 hours and I know I can paint in 2 hours. Let me *draw pictures*—time lines—for each of us.

Gert:
```
  •  —  •  —  |  —  •  —  |  —  •  —  |  —  •  —  |  —  •  —  |  —  •  —  |  —  •  —
  0     1     2     3     4     5     6     7     8     9    10    11    12    13
```
Joe:
```
  •  —  •  —  •  —  |  —  •  —  •  —  |  —  •  —  •  —  |  —  •  —  •  —  |  —  •  —
```

I've marked the points where each of us completes a whole number of houses. In 6 hours we both complete houses: In 6 hours I paint 3 houses and in the same time you paint 2. Painting together, we could paint $2 + 3 = 5$ of them in 6 hours.

"Painting together, we could paint one in how long? One hour has 60 minutes, 6 hours has $6 \times 60 = 360$ minutes. So $360 \div 5 = 72$—72 minutes to complete the house if we were working together."

Joe: "What about the house we *are* going to paint together?"

Gert: "Let's try my idea with 42 and 56 instead of 2 and 3. After how many hours will we have both painted a whole number of houses? For the 3-hour house, you complete a whole number of houses after 3 hours, 6 hours, 9 hours, and so on—all multiples of 3. Then for the 2-hour house, I complete a whole number of houses after 2 hours, 4 hours, 6 hours, and so on—all multiples of 2. And 6 is the smallest (nonzero) common multiple of 2 *and* 3. The same thing should work with 42 and 56: You complete one house after 56 hours, 2 houses after 112 hours, 3 houses after 168 hours, and so on—all multiples of 56. It's similar for me: I will complete a whole number of houses when the number of hours are multiples of 42. To figure out when a multiple of 56 is equal to a multiple of 42, let's *organize* our multiples *in a chart to look for a pattern*.

	1	2	3	4	5
Multiple of 56	56	112	(168)	224	280
Multiple of 42	42	84	126	(168)	

"From this we can see that 168 is a multiple of 42 *and* a multiple of 56: $168 = 3 \times 56 = 4 \times 42$. Joe, you would paint 3 houses in 168 hours; I would paint 4; working together, we'd paint 7 houses. To paint one house working together it would take $168 \div 7 = 24$ hours."

The Mathematical Idea: Common Multiples

Gert noticed that the number of hours she has been painting when she completes a whole number of identical houses is a *multiple* of 42, that is, $42 \times M$ for some whole number M. Similarly for Joe: The number of hours he has been painting when he completes a whole number of houses is a multiple of 56 hr.

Gert solved the house painter problem by looking for a number that was not only a multiple of 42 but also a multiple of 56. She looked for a nonzero *common multiple* of 42 and 56. To find one, she listed the multiples of 42 and the multiples of 56 and found the common multiple 168 on both lists: $56 \times 3 = 168 = 42 \times 4$. This problem solution illustrates a general method for finding a (nonzero) common multiple of two natural numbers: List the (nonzero) multiples of the two numbers until you find a number on both lists.

You will always find a nonzero common multiple on these two lists since, given two nonzero whole numbers A and B, the whole number $A \times B$ is a common multiple of A and B.

In case $A = 42$ and $B = 56$, the guaranteed common multiple is $42 \times 56 = 2352$, a big number. A smaller common multiple is 168. In fact, 168 is the smallest (nonzero) common multiple of 42 and 56; it is called the least common multiple and abbreviated LCM.

A method for finding the LCM of two numbers is to list the nonzero multiples of the two numbers as in the solution to the house painter problem; the first (smallest) number to occur on both lists is the LCM.

An easy way to find the nonzero multiples of a number is to use the constant feature of a calculator. For example, to find the multiples of 56 using a calculator without a K key, the key sequence is 56 [+] [K] [=] [=] [=] .... Using a calculator with a constant feature, the key sequence may be 56 [+] [=] [=] [=] ... or perhaps 56 [+] [+] [=] [=] [=] .... If none of these works for your calculator, check the user's manual.

EXERCISES

1. Find the LCM of 12 and 15.

2. Find the LCM of 9 and 11.

3. Use a calculator to list the nonzero multiples of 72 and 39. Use the lists to find the LCM of 72 and 39.

4. Sarah can scan the day's X-rays in 45 min and Carlos can scan them in 36 min. If they work together, how long will it take them?

Multiples and Divisors

When you learned the multiplication tables, you also learned about multiples. For example, the nonzero multiples of 4 are

$$1 \times 4 = 4, \quad 2 \times 4 = 8, \quad 3 \times 4 = 12, \quad 4 \times 4 = 16, \quad 5 \times 4 = 20, \ldots$$

Similarly, you learned about the smaller multiples of 2 through 9. Before that, you learned all about the multiples of 2, 5, and 10 through skip counting.

Skip counting by 2s—2, 4, 6, 8, 10, 12, . . .
Skip counting by 5s—5, 10, 15, 20, 25, 30, . . .
Skip counting by 10s—10, 20, 30, 40, 50, 60, . . .

The issue of whether or not a given whole number A was a multiple of another whole number B became important when you began to divide. C divided by B has no remainder if C is a multiple of B. Note some common terminology connecting multiples with division.

MULTIPLES AND DIVISORS

Suppose that A and B are nonzero whole numbers. The following statements all mean the same thing.

1. A is a nonzero *multiple* of B.

2. B is a *divisor* of A.

3. A is *divisible* by B.

4. There is a nonzero whole number M such that $A = B \times M$.

A fifth grader knows at a glance that the numbers 6, 12, 18, 24, 30, 36, 42, 48, 54, 60 are all divisible by 6 and that all other nonzero whole numbers less than 60 are *not* divisible by 6. She knows this because she knows her 6s multiplication table. For numbers bigger than 60, she may not know at a glance whether a number is divisible by 6. Numbers such as 600 or 6000 or 1200 would be exceptions. For other large numbers she will have to carry out long division to find out whether or not it is divisible by 6.

Divisibility by 2 is another story. From experience with skip counting one can tell at a glance whether or not a given number is divisible by 2.

TEST FOR DIVISIBILITY BY 2 (AT A GLANCE)

A whole number is divisible by 2 if and only if the units digit is 0, 2, 4, 6, or 8.

The situation is the same for divisibility by 5 or by 10: A glance is all that is necessary.

TESTS FOR DIVISIBILITY BY 10 AND 5 (AT A GLANCE)

A whole number is divisible by 10 if and only if the units digit is 0. A whole number is divisible by 5 if and only if the units digit is 0 or 5.

What we have just described are *tests for divisibility by 2, 5, and 10.* Are there tests for divisibility by other numbers? Is there a way to decide easily—using its digits—whether a number is divisible by 3? by 4? by 6? by 7? by 8? by 9? In the language of multiples, is there a way to tell easily from its digits whether a number is a multiple of 3? Of 4? Of 6? Of 7? Of 8? Of 9?

The answer to each of these questions is yes. In the discussion to come we will describe tests for divisibility by 4 and by 9. We will also show how each test is created and why it works. This should give you some good ideas for constructing your own tests for divisibility by other numbers. Showing why the tests work will also reveal interesting features about whole numbers and the numerals that represent them.

A Test for Divisibility by 4

One important idea that we shall use for constructing a test for divisibility by 4 is expanded form, or some variation on expanded form. For example, we can write the number 6972 as

$$6972 = 69 \times 100 + 72$$

$$\underbrace{}_{\text{Digits ``above'' 10s and 1s}} \quad \underbrace{}_{\text{10s and 1s digits}}$$

This expresses the number as the sum of two numbers, each of which incorporates the digits of the original number in some simple way.

We are interested in knowing whether or not this number (or any other number similarly expressed) is divisible by 4. The part of the expansion that is independent of the specific digits is the number 100. We notice that $100 = 4 \times 25$ so that 100 is divisible by 4. This also means that 69×100 is also divisible by 4. The same is true for 85×100 and 193×100: The part of the expansion incorporating digits higher than the 10s and 1s digits is *always* divisible by 4. Thus we have written our number 6972 as a sum of two numbers.

$$6972 = 69 \times 100 + 72$$

$$\underbrace{}_{\text{Multiple of 4}} \quad \underbrace{}_{\substack{\text{Number formed from} \\ \text{units and ten's digits}}}$$

Here are some more examples:

$8563 = 85 \times 100 + 63$
$19{,}314 = 193 \times 100 + 14$
$376 = 3 \times 100 + 76$

Any number is a sum of a multiple of 4 plus the number formed from its 1s and 10s digits.

To describe a test for divisibility by 4, take a number N and write it as a multiple of 4 (call this $4A$ for some number A) plus the number formed from its 1s and 10s digits (call the latter B): $N = 4A + B$. Now if B is a multiple of 4 (this should be easy to decide since B is small), then N is also a multiple of 4.

If $B = 4C$, then

$$N = 4A + 4C$$
$$= 4(A + C) \quad \text{(by the distributive property)}$$
$$= \text{a multiple of 4.}$$

Thus, if the number B formed by the 1s and 10s digits is divisible by 4, then so is the original number N. Conversely, if N is divisible by 4 ($N = 4D$ for some number D), then $N = 4D = 4A + B$.

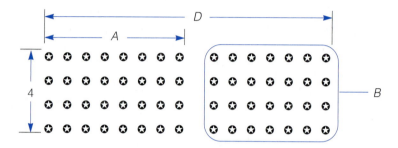

This means that B must also be a multiple of 4. We can summarize this discussion.

TEST FOR DIVISIBILITY BY 4

A whole number N is divisible by 4 if and only if the number formed by the 10s and 1s digits of N is also divisible by 4.

In our original example, the number formed by the 10s and 1s digits of 6972 is 72. Since 72 is divisible by 4, so is 6972.

For another example, take $N = 3722$. The number formed by the 10s and 1s digits is 22, which is *not* divisible by 4. The test says that 3722 is also *not* divisible by 4. You may want to check this conclusion with long division.

EXERCISE 5. Use the test for divisibility by 4 to determine which numbers are divisible by 4.
    (a) 13,987,624   (b) 9,820,000,746   (c) 28,967,015,736,508
    (d) 1,111,111,111,111,111,111,111,111,104   (e) 9,876,543,213,762

A Test for Divisibility by 9

Constructing a test for divisibility by 9 is similar to constructing a test for divisibility by 4. The main idea is to find a method for writing any number N as a multiple of 9 plus a small number.

$$N \quad = \quad 9R \quad + \quad S$$
(Any number)   (Multiple of 9)   (Small number)

Furthermore, we want to be able to determine S easily from the digits of the number N. Just as in the argument for the test for divisibility by 4, if B is a multiple of 9, so is N; if B is not a multiple of 9, neither is N.

To find a test for divisibility by 9, we will have to be much more clever than we were in finding one for 4. We will use expanded form to find the multiple of 9 and the small number S. We start with the number 6784. Then

$$6784 = 6 \times 1000 + 7 \times 100 + 8 \times 10 + 4.$$

Here's the clever part: Rewrite 1000, 100, and 10 as

$1000 = 999 + 1$
$100 = 99 + 1$
$10 = 9 + 1$

so that then

$$\begin{aligned}
6784 &= 6 \times 1000 + 7 \times 100 + 8 \times 10 + 4 \\
&= 6(999 + 1) + 7(99 + 1) + 8(9 + 1) + 4 \\
&= 6 \times 999 + 6 \times 1 + 7 \times 99 + 7 \times 1 + 8 \times 9 + 8 \times 1 + 4 \\
&\qquad\qquad\qquad\qquad \text{(By the distributive law)} \\
&= (6 \times 999 + 7 \times 99 + 8 \times 9) + (6 + 7 + 8 + 4) \\
&= (6 \times 9 \times 111 + 7 \times 9 \times 11 + 8 \times 9) + (6 + 7 + 8 + 4) \\
&= 9(6 \times 111 + 7 \times 11 + 8) + (6 + 7 + 8 + 4).
\end{aligned}$$

$\underbrace{\qquad\qquad}_{\text{Multiple of 9}}$ $\underbrace{\qquad\qquad}_{\text{Sum of digits of original}}$

What is exciting about this expression for 6784 is that you can do the same thing with *any* number: You can write it as the sum of a multiple of 9 plus the sum of its digits. The sum of the digits of 6784 is $6 + 7 + 8 + 4 = 25$, which is not divisible by 9. Consequently, 6784 is *not* divisible by 9. On the other hand, the sum of the digits of 26,784 is $2 + 6 + 7 + 8 + 4 = 27$, which *is* divisible by 9. So 26,784 is also divisible by 9. You should check both of these conclusions by long division. Here is a summary of what we have done.

TEST FOR DIVISIBILITY BY 9

A whole number N is divisible by 9 if and only if the sum of its digits is also divisible by 9.

EXERCISES

6. Use the tests to decide whether or not each number is divisible by 4, by 5, by 9, or by 10.
   (a) 1,230,948,780   (b) 978,513,246   (c) 101,023,344
   (d) 234,897,525   (e) 1,010,101,010,101,010,101

7. Use the ideas used in constructing the tests for divisibility by 4 and 9 to (a) construct a test for divisibility by 3 and (b) construct a test for divisibility by 8.

7.3   PRIME NUMBERS AND FACTOR TREES

Arrange the numbers from 1 to 100 in a 10 by 10 square array. Color in all the multiples of 2, except 2 itself. Then, on the same array, color in all the multiples of 3 that haven't been colored, except 3 itself. And so on: For each whole number successively, color in all the multiples of that whole number that haven't been colored yet; don't color the whole number itself if it hasn't been colored previously.*

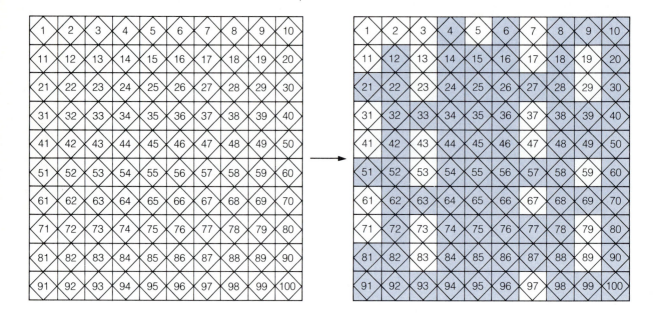

A number that hasn't been colored is a number that is a multiple of no other number except itself (and, of course, 1). Put another way, except for the number 1, a number that hasn't been colored has exactly two divisors: 1 and itself. A whole number with exactly two divisors is called a *prime* number. (The number 1 has only one divisor and is excluded from being a prime. There are also historical and practical reasons why the number 1 is not a prime, but we won't go into them here.) Here is a list of all the primes less than 100:

2, 3, 5, 7, 11, 13, 17, 19, 23,
29, 31, 37, 41, 43, 47, 53, 59,
61, 67, 71, 73, 79, 83, 89, 97.

The method we used to obtain the list of primes between 1 and 100 is sometimes called the *sieve of Eratosthenes,* after the Greek mathematician-astronomer of around 200 B.C.

EXERCISE 8. List the prime numbers between 100 and 200. (Hold on to the list for later use.)

Composite Numbers and Factor Trees

A whole number greater than 1 that is not a prime number is called a *composite* number. Take a composite number. It must have a divisor not equal to itself or 1. For example, 120 is a composite number; it is divisible by 12. In fact, $120 = 12 \times 10$. We can express this fact by drawing a tree diagram.

---

* A larger copy of this square array, suitable for coloring, appears in the lab manual designed to accompany this text.

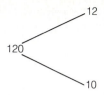

We look at the two factors 12 and 10 and see if we can write each one as a product of two other whole numbers (both greater than 1): $12 = 4 \times 3$ and $10 = 2 \times 5$. We record these facts on the tree as shown.

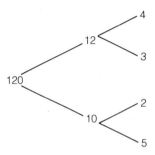

The numbers at the ends of the branches are 5, 2, 3, and 4. The numbers 5, 2, and 3 are prime numbers and cannot be written as the product of two other whole numbers. We leave them alone. We notice that $4 = 2 \times 2$ and add that fact to the tree.

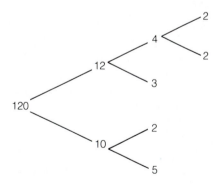

What we now have is a factor tree for the number 120. The numbers on the tips of the branches—2, 2, 3, 2, 5—are all prime numbers. Moreover, if we multiply all these prime numbers together we get the original number: $2 \times 2 \times 3 \times 2 \times 5 = 120$.

The expression $2 \times 2 \times 2 \times 3 \times 5$ is called a *prime factorization* of 120. We have used the factor tree to find this prime factorization, that is, to write the number as a product of prime numbers.

This device works for any composite number. In general, you take a whole number N that is not a prime and write the number as a product $N = A \times B$ so that neither

A nor *B* is equal to 1. (This is called *factoring N* into the product of *A* and *B*.) Begin the factor tree for *N*.

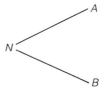

Continue in the same fashion with *A* and *B* as you did with *N*: Factor *A*, if you can, and record the factors on the tree. Factor *B*, if you can, and record the factors on the tree. If *A* can't be factored, leave it alone; if *B* can't be factored, leave it alone. Keep doing this with the numbers on the tips of the tree's branches until all the numbers on the tips are prime numbers. The original number *N* is then equal to the product of all the prime numbers that appear on the tips of branches.

You may have noticed that a given number can have more than one factor tree. For example, in addition to the factor tree for 120 given previously, there is also

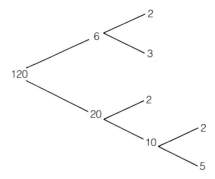

The two trees for 120 are different, but the primes on the tips of the branches of the two trees are the same and the number of occurrences of each prime is the same. (The primes that occur in the first tree are 2, 2, 3, 2, 5 in that order from top to bottom; the primes that occur in the second are 2, 3, 2, 2, 5. In both there are three 2s, one 3, and one 5.) This is an instance of the following fact about whole numbers bigger than one.

THE FUNDAMENTAL THEOREM OF ARITHMETIC

For any whole number *N* bigger than 1, the primes that occur in one prime factorization for *N* must be the same as those that occur in any other prime factorization for *N*. Moreover, the number of occurrences of a prime in one factorization must be equal to the number of occurrences of that prime in the other factorization.

Because of the fundamental theorem of arithmetic, we speak of *the* prime factorization of a whole number bigger than 1.

9. Construct three *different* factor trees for 360. For each tree write down the primes that appear and the number of occurrences of each prime. How do the results for one tree compare with the results for another? Find the prime factorization of 360.

10. Construct a factor tree for 9900 and use it to find the prime factorization of 9900.

A Test for Divisibility by 6

If a whole number is divisible by 6, then it is also divisible by 2 and by 3. On the other hand, if a whole number N is divisible by 2, then a factor tree for N starts this way

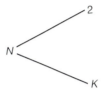

for some whole number K. If N is also divisible by 3, then we can start out a factor tree for N like this

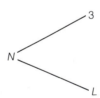

for some whole number L. By the fundamental theorem of arithmetic both 2 and 3 must appear in the prime factorization of N. So $N = 2 \times 3 \times M$ for some whole number M. That means that N is divisible by 6. This gives us a test for divisibility by 6 using tests for divisibility that we may already know for smaller numbers.

TEST FOR DIVISIBILITY BY 6

Let N be a whole number greater than 1. Ask (a) is N divisible by 2? and (b) is N divisible by 3? N is divisible by 6 if and only if the answers to (a) and (b) are *both* yes.

---

11. Use the test to determine which of the following numbers are divisible by 6.
   (a) 11,111,111,111,112   (b) 222,222,222,222   (c) 19,837,656
   (d) 111,111,111,111   (e) 3,030,303

12. The test for divisibility by 6 suggests that the following is a test for divisibility by any composite number.

> To test a whole number for divisibility by N, factor N into the product of two smaller numbers A and B greater than 1. Test the whole number for divisibility by A and by B. If both tests are positive, then the number is divisible by N; otherwise, it is not divisible by N.

Experiment with this idea for the following choices for N, A, and B.
(a) $N = 4$, $A = 2$, $B = 2$ (b) $N = 8$, $A = 4$, $B = 2$
(c) $N = 15$, $A = 3$, $B = 5$ (d) $N = 12$, $A = 2$, $B = 6$
(e) $N = 12$, $A = 4$, $B = 3$
What do you conclude from these experiments? When does the test work and when doesn't it?

13. Find a test for divisibility by 15.

14. Find a test for divisibility by 18.

7.4 THE LEAST COMMON MULTIPLE (LCM) OF TWO NUMBERS

THE GEAR TIMING PROBLEM

You have a machine that has two gears engaged. You want to know how fast the gears turn when the machine is running. You do know that one gear has 420 teeth and that the other has 198 teeth.

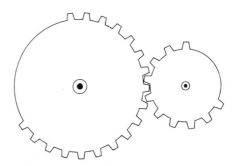

Beginning of a Solution to the Gear Timing Problem

To solve this problem, you decide to paint 1 tooth of the 420-tooth gear a bright color. You plan to turn the machine on and count the number of times per minute the bright tooth returns to its starting position. This will tell you the number of revolutions the 420-tooth gear makes in 1 min. You turn the machine on and soon realize that the gear is turning so fast that it's impossible to count the number of times the painted tooth returns to its starting position. You think: "I must find something that passes by much more slowly. What about *two* painted teeth, one on each gear? Let me turn the 420-tooth gear so that the painted tooth comes in contact with the 198-tooth gear. On the 198-tooth gear paint the indentation opposite the painted tooth.

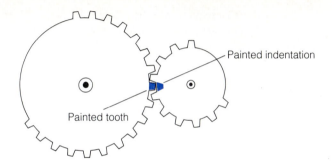

Painted indentation

Painted tooth

"*Two* brightly painted *touching* spots should be easier to see than one. When I set the machine going, I can observe the moments when the two spots come together. Those moments should be less frequent than those for one spot.

"Before I turn on the machine and determine the number of seconds between a pair of meetings of the two spots, I ought to figure out what I can do with this information. The spot on the 420-tooth gear passes the 'meeting point' (where both spots eventually meet) many times. Between two consecutive passes, a single revolution of the 420-tooth gear occurs, and 420 teeth of each gear go by the meeting point.

"The spot on the 198-tooth gear also passes the meeting point. Between two consecutive passes, a single revolution of the 198-tooth gear occurs, and 198 teeth of each gear go by the meeting point.

"So, between meetings of the *two* spots, a multiple of 420 teeth goes by the meeting point; a multiple of 198 teeth also goes by it. In fact, the number of teeth (of each gear) that go by the meeting place—between meetings of the two painted teeth—is *a common multiple of* 420 and 198. Since the two spots will meet after *any* common multiple of 420 and 198 have gone by, the two spots first meet after the LCM of 420 and 198 teeth have gone by.

"Let me figure out the LCM of 420 and 198 first. Then I'll come back and figure out what else I need to do to solve the problem."

Finding the LCM of 420 and 198

The numbers 420 and 198 are large. To find the LCM of the two numbers, it would be tedious to list the multiples of both numbers and then find the smallest number common to both lists. An alternative procedure uses their prime factorizations. Start with their factor trees.

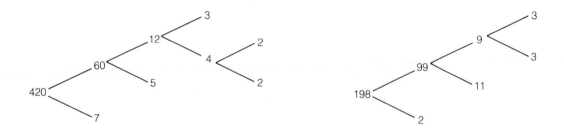

Consequently, $420 = 2 \times 2 \times 3 \times 5 \times 7$ and $198 = 2 \times 3 \times 3 \times 11$. A multiple N of 420 is of the form $N = 420 \times K$ and could have a factor tree that starts out

Continuing with the 420 branch, we'd get the primes 2 (twice), 3 (once), 5 (once), 7 (once) at the tips of the final branches; additional primes would come from the K branch. By the fundamental theorem of arithmetic, N (the multiple of 420) will always have at least two 2s, one 3, one 5, and one 7 in its prime factorization.

Similarly, N must be a multiple of 198 and any multiple of 198 will always have at least one 2, two 3s, and one 11 in its prime factorization. Any common multiple of 420 and 198 must satisfy both these conditions: It must have at least two 2s, two 3s, one 5, one 7, and one 11 in its prime factorization. What is the least number that satisfies these conditions? The number that has exactly two 2s, two 3s, one 5, one 7, one 11, and no more satisfies these conditions and is the smallest such number. It is $2 \times 2 \times 3 \times 3 \times 5 \times 7 \times 11 = 13{,}860$.

Completion of the Solution to the Gear Timing Problem

You have just calculated the LCM of 420 and 198, which gives you the number of teeth that go by between consecutive meetings of the two spots. Knowing that the LCM is a multiple of 420, you divide the LCM by 420 to obtain the number of revolutions the 420-tooth gear makes between occurrences. Since

$$\text{LCM of } 420 \text{ and } 198 = 13{,}860$$
$$= 2 \times 2 \times 3 \times 3 \times 5 \times 7 \times 11$$
$$= (2 \times 2 \times 3 \times 5 \times 7) \times 3 \times 11$$
$$= 420 \times 3 \times 11,$$

it follows that the LCM (13,860) divided by 420 is 33: The 420-tooth gear makes 33 revolutions between consecutive meetings of the two spots. Next you measure the time T (in seconds) between consecutive meetings and conclude that the 420-tooth gear makes 33 revolutions in T sec.

EXERCISES

15. You turn the machine on and find that the time between consecutive meetings of the two spots is 11 sec. How many revolutions does the 420-tooth gear make in 1 sec? How many revolutions does it make in 1 min? How many revolutions does the 198-tooth gear make in 1 sec? How many revolutions does it make in 1 min?

16. Two gears are engaged. One has 72 teeth; the other has 50 teeth. You paint adjacent spots on the two gears as in the gear timing problem. You set the gears in motion and find that there are 18 sec between consecutive meetings of the two spots. How many revolutions does the 50-tooth gear make in 1 min? How many revolutions does the 72-tooth gear make in 1 min?

The Mathematical Idea: A Method for Computing the LCM

We found the LCM of 420 and 198 first by finding the prime factorization of the two numbers. Then we used these to find the prime factorization of the LCM.

The general method is this: Let N and M be the two numbers the LCM of which you want to find. Find the prime factorizations of N and M and list the *distinct* primes that occur in one or the other (or both). These are the distinct primes that will occur in the prime factorization of the LCM. The number of occurrences of one of these primes in the prime factorization of the LCM is calculated by finding the number of its occurrences in the prime factorization of N and finding the number of its occurrences in the prime factorization of M; the larger of these two numbers is its number of occurrences in the prime factorization of the LCM.

For example,

$$N = 2 \times 5 \times 5 \times 5 \times 13, \qquad M = 2 \times 3 \times 3 \times 5 \times 7 \times 11.$$

The distinct primes that occur in the prime factorizations of N or M or both are 2, 3, 5, 7, 11, and 13. We *make a chart to organize the data we have.*

		PRIME					
		2	3	5	7	11	13
No. of occurrences of prime in prime factorization of	N	(1)	0	(3)	0	0	(1)
	M	1	(2)	1	(1)	(1)	0
	LCM of N and M	1	2	3	1	1	1

For one of the primes, the larger of the two numbers in its column and in the N's and M's rows has been circled. The circled number is also the number in the LCM's row. Thus, the LCM of N and M is the product of one 2, two 3s, three 5s, one 7, one 11, and one 13. In other words,

$$\text{LCM of } N \text{ and } M = 2 \times 3 \times 3 \times 5 \times 5 \times 5 \times 7 \times 11 \times 13.$$

EXERCISES
17. Find the LCM of $2 \times 3 \times 3 \times 3 \times 5 \times 5 \times 13$ and $2 \times 2 \times 5 \times 7$.

18. Find the LCM of $2 \times 2 \times 2 \times 3 \times 5 \times 7 \times 7$ and $3 \times 3 \times 3 \times 5 \times 7 \times 7 \times 7 \times 11$.

7.5 THE GREATEST COMMON DIVISOR (GCD) OF TWO NUMBERS

THE SECOND GEAR TIMING PROBLEM

You have a machine in which two gears are engaged. You know that one gear is supposed to rotate at 60 rpm (revolutions per minute) and that the other gear is supposed to rotate at 80 rpm. You want to check that the gears actually rotate the required number of times per minute. You know nothing about the number of teeth each gear has.

You remember the *solution to a similar problem,* the first gear timing problem, and decide to paint a spot on each gear, at a point where the two gears are engaged. You plan to turn the machine on and count the number of times per minute that the two spots meet. You will compare this with the number of times the spots should meet if the mechanism works as it is supposed to.

First, you must figure out what the latter number is. You think: "If the machine is working correctly and I start the clock at an instant when the spots meet, then I know that when the spots meet again, each gear will have made a whole number of revolutions. In fact, suppose that at the first instant they meet, the 80-rpm gear will have made M revolutions and the 60-rpm gear will have made N revolutions. Each successive instant the spots meet, the 80-rpm gear will have made M more revolutions and the 60-rpm will have made N more. Since the gears are supposed to make a whole number of revolutions in a minute, I know that one of these instances is exactly a minute after I start the clock.

"Now suppose that T is the number of times the two spots meet during the minute (including the last instance but not the first). Adding M to itself T times should equal 80 and adding N to itself T times should equal 60: $MT = 80$ and $NT = 60$.

"Let me *organize this information in a chart.*

INSTANCES SPOTS MEET AFTER CLOCK STARTS					
	1st	2d	3d	...	Tth
No. of revolutions of 80-rpm gear after clock starts	M	$2M$	$3M$		$TM = 80$
No. of revolutions of 60-rpm gear after clock starts	N	$2N$	$3N$		$TN = 60$
Time elapsed after clock starts					1 min

"So T is a common divisor of 80 and 60. Which common divisor of 80 and 60 is it? If D is any common divisor of 80 and 60, then I know that there must be whole numbers K and L such that $KD = 80$ and $LD = 60$.

"Let me divide up the minute into D equal pieces.

$$0 \quad 1 \quad 2 \quad 3 \quad \bullet \quad \bullet \quad \bullet \quad \bullet \quad \bullet \quad D$$

By the time point 1 is reached, the 80-rpm gear will have revolved K times and the 60-rpm gear L times. The two spots will meet at that point. And to get to point 2, there would be K more revolutions of the 80-rpm gear and L more revolutions of the 60-rpm gear. Consequently, I know that the two spots meet after $80 \div D$ revolutions of the 80-rpm gear and after $60 \div D$ revolutions of the 60-rpm gear for any common divisor D of 80 and 60. The *first* instance they meet corresponds to the largest of the common divisors of 80 and 60, because the largest divisor will give me the shortest period of time.

"To figure out the largest common divisor of 80 and 60 let me make a list of the divisors of each number.

Divisors of 60: 1, 2, 3, 4, 5, 6, 10, 12, 15, 20, 30, 60
Divisors of 80: 1, 2, 4, 5, 8, 10, 16, 20, 40, 80

The numbers common to both lists are

Common divisors of 60 and 80: 1, 2, 4, 5, 10, 20.

The largest of these is 20. That means that the two teeth should meet 20 times a minute."

The Mathematical Idea: How to Find the Greatest Common Divisor (GCD) of Two Numbers

The largest divisor common to two whole numbers A and B is called the *greatest common divisor* of A and B, abbreviated the GCD of A and B. The solution to the second gear timing problem demonstrates one method for finding the GCD:

1. Find the set of divisors of A and the set of divisors of B.

2. Find the intersection of the two sets; the elements of this intersection comprise the set of common divisors of A and B.

3. Find the greatest element in the set of common divisors.

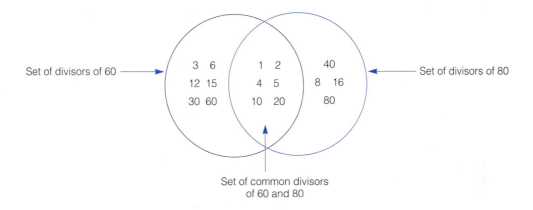

Set of divisors of 60

Set of divisors of 80

Set of common divisors of 60 and 80

EXERCISES 19. Using what you have learned,
(a) find the GCD of 36 and 42, (b) find the GCD of 32 and 45.

20. Adjacent spots are placed on each of two engaged gears as in the gear timing problems. One gear should rotate 45 rpm and the other 55 rpm. How many times per minute should the two spots meet?

Computing the GCD Using Prime Factorizations

Prime factorizations can be used to calculate the GCD of two numbers. We will illustrate this with the two numbers 420 and 198. We already have the prime factorization of these two numbers:

$$420 = 2 \times 2 \times 3 \times 5 \times 7$$
$$198 = 2 \times 3 \times 3 \times 11.$$

If D is a divisor of 420, then $420 = DK$ for some number K. One factor tree for 420 begins

A factor tree for D would be part of the tree for 420. The primes that occur on the tips of the branches for D are also primes that occur on the tips of the branches for 420 (but not necessarily all of them). Since $420 = 2 \times 2 \times 3 \times 5 \times 7$, the prime factorization of D must have at *most* two 2s, one 3, one 5, and one 7 (and no other prime).

Similarly, the prime factorization of a divisor of 198 must have at *most* one 2, two 3s, and one 11 (and no other prime). A *common* divisor of 420 and 198 must satisfy both these conditions. Thus, a common divisor of 420 and 198 must have at most one 2 and one 3 and no other primes in its factorization. The largest number with this property is 2×3. So $2 \times 3 = 6$ is the GCD of 420 and 198.

This method for finding the GCD of whole numbers N and M involves finding its prime factorization. First you find the prime factorizations of N and M and list the *distinct* primes that occur in both factorizations. These are the distinct primes that will occur in the prime factorization of the GCD. The number of occurrences of a prime on this list in the factorization of the GCD is calculated this way: Find the number of occurrences in the prime factorization of N and the number of occurrences in the prime factorization of M; the smallest of these is the number of occurrences in the prime factorization of the GCD.

Let's look at another example.

$N = 2 \times 3 \times 3 \times 3 \times 3 \times 5 \times 5 \times 5 \times 11 \times 13$
$M = 2 \times 2 \times 2 \times 3 \times 3 \times 5 \times 7 \times 11 \times 11$

The distinct primes occurring in the prime factorizations of both N and M are 2, 3, 5, 11. We *organize this data in a chart.*

		PRIME			
		2	3	5	11
No. of occurrences of prime in prime factorization of	N	①	4	3	①
	M	3	②	①	2
	GCD of N and M	1	2	1	1

For each one of the primes, the least of the two numbers in its column and in the N's and M's rows has been circled. The circled numbers are equal to the number of occurrences of the prime in the GCD. Thus, the GCD of N and M is the product of one 2, two 3s, one 5, and one 11; that is, the GCD is $2 \times 3 \times 3 \times 5 \times 11$.

21. Find the GCD of $2 \times 2 \times 2 \times 3 \times 3 \times 5 \times 5 \times 5 \times 5 \times 7 \times 11 \times 11$ and $2 \times 3 \times 3 \times 3 \times 5 \times 5 \times 7 \times 7$.

22. Find the GCD of $2 \times 3 \times 7 \times 7 \times 7 \times 7 \times 7 \times 13$ and $2 \times 3 \times 7 \times 7 \times 7 \times 7 \times 7 \times 7 \times 17$.

7.6   LOOKING BACK: EXPONENTIAL NOTATION AND PRIME FACTORIZATION IN STANDARD FORM

There is a way that we can write the prime factorization of a number in a more condensed fashion than we have seen so far. Recall that

$$2^1 = 2$$
$$2^2 = 2 \times 2$$
$$2^3 = 2 \times 2 \times 2$$
$$2^4 = 2 \times 2 \times 2 \times 2$$

and that, in general,

$$A^n = \underbrace{A \times \ldots \times A}_{n \text{ times}}.$$

Using this notational convention, we can write

$$2 \times 2 \times 2 \times 2 \times 3 \times 3 \times 3 = 2^4 \times 3^3,$$
$$2 \times 2 \times 2 \times 3 \times 3 \times 3 \times 3 = 2^3 \times 3^4,$$
$$2 \times 2 \times 2 \times 3 \times 5 \times 5 \times 11 \times 11 \times 11 \times 11 \times 11 = 2^3 \times 3^1 \times 5^2 \times 11^5.$$

Another convention is to write the primes that occur in order of size from left to right with the smallest prime on the left. We used this convention in the examples above. If these conventions are followed (putting primes in order and using exponential notation), then we say that the factorization is in *standard form*.

23. Rewrite the factorizations in standard form.
   (a) $5 \times 5 \times 5 \times 5$ (b) $7 \times 7 \times 7 \times 11 \times 11$
   (c) $3 \times 3 \times 3 \times 5 \times 5 \times 7 \times 7 \times 7 \times 7$ (d) $3 \times 5 \times 7 \times 11$

24. Find the GCD and LCM of the numbers (a) $2^3 3^7 5^1 11^3 17^4$ and (b) $3^2 7^8 11^1 17^3 19^1$.

7.7   EXTENDING THE IDEAS: CASTING OUT 9s

The test for divisibility by 9 can also be used to determine what the remainder is on dividing a number by 9. Take a number N. We know we can write N as the sum of a multiple of 9 and another number S, which is the sum of its digits, $N = 9R + S$. Now divide S by 9 and get a quotient of Q and a remainder of T so that $S = 9Q + T$. This means that

$$N = 9R + S$$
$$= 9R + 9Q + T$$
$$= 9(R + Q) + T \text{ (by the distributive law)}$$

Thus, if you divided N by 9, you'd get a quotient of $R + Q$ and a remainder of T. The number T, which is the remainder you get when you divide the sum of the digits by 9, is also the remainder you get when you divide the original number N by 9.

REMAINDER ON DIVISION BY 9

Take a number N, divide it by 9, and get a remainder T. Take the sum S of the digits of N, divide S by 9, and get a remainder of U. The two remainders are the same: $T = U$.

Not long ago schoolchildren were asked to check answers to arithmetic problems by using a technique called "casting out 9s." Today computers do the same sort of thing internally as "parity checks." Casting out 9s uses the method described above for finding the remainder of a number when you divide it by 9, but it simplifies things even more. To find the remainder of S (the sum of the digits) on division by 9, you can do this: Each time you see a combination of digits that adds up to 9 or a multiple of 9 you can "cast them out" and deal with just the remaining digits. For example, suppose that you want to find the remainder of 762,940,132 on division by 9. You know that this is the same as finding the remainder of

$$7 + 6 + 2 + 9 + 4 + 0 + 1 + 3 + 2$$

on division by 9. You notice that $7 + 2 = 9$ so that you can cast out the 7 and the 2.

$$\cancel{7} \quad 6 \quad \cancel{2} \quad \cancel{9} \quad 4 \quad 0 \quad 1 \quad 3 \quad 2$$

Looking at the remaining digits, you see that you can cast out the 9.

$$\cancel{7} \quad 6 \quad \cancel{2} \quad \cancel{9} \quad 4 \quad 0 \quad 1 \quad 3 \quad 2$$

Similarly, since $4 + 3 + 2 = 9$, you can cast out the 4, 3, and 2.

$$\cancel{7} \quad 6 \quad \cancel{2} \quad \cancel{9} \quad \cancel{4} \quad 0 \quad 1 \quad \cancel{3} \quad \cancel{2}$$

The remaining digits are 6, 0, and 1, which add to 7. Thus, the remainder of 762,940,132 on division by 9 is 7.

Here is how you use casting out 9s to check arithmetic problems. Take this multiplication problem, for example.

	REMAINDERS WHEN NUMBER IS DIVIDED BY 9
4567	4
× 385	7
22,865	
365,36	
1,360,1	
1,748,325	3

On the right we have written the remainders (4 and 7) of the two numbers being multiplied as well as the remainder (3) of the product as calculated. The claim is that the remainder of 4×7 (the product of the remainders of the two original numbers being multiplied) when divided by 9 will equal the remainder of the product of the original numbers when divided by 9. But $4 \times 7 = 28$ has a remainder of 1 when divided by 9. Since 1 is not equal to 3, there must be a mistake! (Can you find it [or them]?)

The technique works. Why? Take two numbers N and M that you intend to multiply together. Divide them both by 9, getting quotients P and Q and remainders S and T, respectively.

$$N = 9P + S$$
$$M = 9Q + T$$

Now multiply N and M together to get NM. Using an array, the product looks like

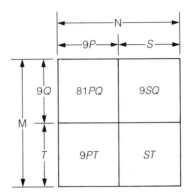

Thus, $NM = $ (multiple of 9) $ + ST = 9K + ST$.

If we divide ST by 9 and get a quotient of L and a remainder of U, then we'd have

$$NM = 9K + ST$$
$$= 9K + 9L + U$$
$$= 9(K + L) + U.$$

Consequently, NM has the same remainder when divided by 9 that the product ST has when divided by 9. The same idea works with addition.

Let's summarize what works with the whole number operations and remainders when you divide by 9.

1. Take two numbers N and M. Find the remainders S and T when you divide N and M by 9.

2. To find the remainder of NM when divided by 9, simply find the remainder of ST (a much smaller number) when divided by 9.

3. To find the remainder of $N + M$ when divided by 9, simply find the remainder of $S + T$ (a much smaller number) when divided by 9.

4. You can use casting out 9s with subtraction if you think of the answer to the subtraction problem as the missing addend in an addition problem, then use the technique for addition.

5. You can use casting out 9s with the division problem $N \div M$ if you think of the quotient Q and remainder R as satisfying the equation $N = MQ + R$ and then use the techniques for multiplication and addition.

1. *Multiplication problem*

$$
\begin{array}{r}
748 \\
\times\ 472 \\
\hline
353{,}056
\end{array}
\qquad
\begin{array}{l}
\text{Has remainder 1.} \\
\text{Has remainder 4.} \\
\\
\text{Has remainder 4.}
\end{array}
$$

Multiply the remainders (1 and 4) of the two factors together. Get 4. Cast out 9s and get 4 (still). This should be equal to the remainder of the product in the solution above. Since it is equal, no mistake in calculation has been detected.

2. *Multiplication problem*

$$
\begin{array}{r}
474 \\
\times\ 935 \\
\hline
443{,}290
\end{array}
\qquad
\begin{array}{l}
\text{Has remainder 6.} \\
\text{Has remainder 8.} \\
\\
\text{Has remainder 4.}
\end{array}
$$

Multiply the remainders (6 and 8) of the two factors together. Get 48. Cast out 9s and get 3. This should be equal to the remainder of the product in the solution above. The solution has a remainder of 4. There must be a mistake.

3. *Addition problem*

$$
\begin{array}{r}
7648 \\
+\ 9204 \\
\hline
16{,}852
\end{array}
\qquad
\begin{array}{l}
\text{Has remainder 7.} \\
\text{Has remainder 6.} \\
\\
\text{Has remainder 4.}
\end{array}
$$

Add the remainders (7 and 6) of the two addends together. Get 13. Cast out 9s and get 4. This should be equal to the remainder of the sum in the solution. It is, so no mistake in calculation has been detected.

4. *Addition problem*

$$
\begin{array}{r}
1235 \\
7642 \\
+\ 8064 \\
\hline
16{,}931
\end{array}
\qquad
\begin{array}{l}
\text{Has remainder 2.} \\
\text{Has remainder 1.} \\
\text{Has remainder 0.} \\
\\
\text{Has remainder 2.}
\end{array}
$$

Add the remainders (2, 1, and 0) of the three addends together. Get 3. Cast out 9s and get 3 (still). This should be equal to the remainder of the sum in the solution. Since it isn't, a mistake in calculation has been detected.

5. *Subtraction problem*
   (To check the calculation in the subtraction solution $8401 - 3578 = 4823$, we use casting out 9s to check the calculation in the addition solution $3578 + 4823 = 8401$.)

$$
\begin{array}{r}
8401 \\
-\ 3578 \\
\hline
4823
\end{array}
\qquad
\begin{array}{l}
\text{Has remainder 4.} \\
\text{Has remainder 5.} \\
\\
\text{Has remainder 8.}
\end{array}
$$

Add the remainders of the number being subtracted and the difference (5 and 8). Get 13. Cast out 9s and get 4. This should be equal to the remainder of the number being subtracted from. It is equal, and no mistake in calculation has been detected.

Some Final Remarks about Casting out 9s

If a use of casting out 9s detects a mistake, there really is a mistake. However, it is possible that a mistake occurred in a calculation even though the use of casting out 9s detected none. For example, consider:

$$
\begin{array}{rl}
29 & \text{Has remainder 2.} \\
\times 84 & \text{Has remainder 3.} \\
\hline
2526 & \text{Has remainder 6.}
\end{array}
$$

The remainder of 2526 when divided by 9 is 6, as it should be if the calculation is correct. Nevertheless, 2526 is not the right answer; the correct answer is 2436 (check it!). As it should, the correct answer also has a remainder of 6 when divided by 9.

EXERCISE　25. Use casting out 9s to check the calculations.

$$
\begin{array}{lll}
\text{(a)} \quad 7648 & \text{(b)} \quad 6043 & \text{(c)} \quad 675 \\
\quad\quad\; +\,9736 & \quad\quad\; -\,3291 & \quad\quad\; \times\,483 \\
\hline
\quad\quad 17,384 & \quad\quad\; 2852 & \quad 327,025
\end{array}
$$

(d) $6704 \div 78 = 85$ remainder 74

7.8　LOOKING BACK: THE DIVISIBILITY RELATIONSHIP

The whole number 51 is equal to $3 \cdot 17$. So 3 is a divisor of 51 and 51 is a multiple of 3. In general, if we have whole numbers A and B, then to say that A is a divisor of B means that there is some whole number M such that $B = AM$. The notation $A \mid B$ is frequently used to express this relationship between whole numbers A and B.

DEFINITION OF DIVISIBILITY RELATIONSHIP

If A and B are whole numbers and $A \neq 0$, then we write $A \mid B$ to mean that A is a *divisor* of B, that is, there is some whole number M such that $B = MA$.

Notice that $A \mid 0$ for every $A \neq 0$.

The notation $A \mid B$ is not to be confused with A/B. The former expresses a relationship between the two whole numbers; the latter is a fractional quantity related to division of the two whole numbers. (There will be more on this in the next chapter.)

To help us see how this notation may be used, there are some formal properties of $A\,|\,B$.

ADDITION PROPERTY OF DIVISIBILITY

Suppose that A, B, and C are whole numbers such that $A\,|\,B$ and $A\,|\,C$. Then also $A\,|\,(B+C)$. (In words: If A is a divisor of each of two numbers, then A is also a divisor of the sum of the two numbers.)

Here is an argument (or proof) for why this property is true. Start with the fact that $A\,|\,B$ and $A\,|\,C$. This means that there are whole numbers M and N such that $B = AM$ and $C = AN$. From this it follows that $B + C = AM + AN$. By the distributive law the latter is equal to $A(M+N)$ so that $B + C = A(M+N)$. This means that A is a divisor of $B + C$. In other words, $A\,|\,(B+C)$.

EXERCISES 26. There is another property of divisibility.

SUBTRACTION PROPERTY OF DIVISIBILITY

Suppose that A, B, and C are whole numbers with $B \geq C$ and such that $A\,|\,B$ and $A\,|\,C$. Then also $A\,|\,(B-C)$.

Show why this property of divisibility is true. (Use an argument similar to the one for the addition property of divisibility.)

27. Show why the third property of divisibility

MULTIPLICATION PROPERTY OF DIVISIBILITY

Suppose that A, B, and C are whole numbers such that $A\,|\,B$. Then also $A\,|\,(BC)$. (In words: If A is a divisor of B, then A is also a divisor of any multiple of B.)

---

is also true. (Use an argument similar to the one for the addition property of divisibility.)

28. Suppose that A and B are whole numbers and that $12\,|\,A$ and $B\,|\,12$. Which of the following statements are true?
   (a) $BM\,|\,12$ for any whole number M.   (b) $12\,|\,7A$
   (c) $12\,|\,A^8$ (d) $3\,|\,25A$
   (e) The only numbers that B can be are 1, 2, 3, 4, 6, or 12
   (f) $4\,|\,(9A-24)$ (g) $12\,|\,(A+B)$
   (h) $3\,|\,(A^7+17A)$ (i) $12\,|\,(14A-12B)$
   (j) $B\,|\,A$

The Test for Divisibility by 4 Revisited

Let's see how the derivation for the test for divisibility by 4 goes using the notation $A|B$ and the rules for divisibility.

Take a whole number $\underline{ABCDE}$. (What is meant by this is that the letters A, B, C, D, and E represent the digits of the number. Thus, the units digit of the number is E.) We can write this number as $\underline{ABCDE} = \underline{ABC} \times 100 + \underline{DE}$.

Since $4|100$, it follows by the multiplication property for divisibility that $4|\underline{ABC} \times 100$.

We are interested in knowing whether $\underline{ABCDE}$ is divisible by 4. Suppose that $4|\underline{DE}$. (In words: 4 is a divisor of the number formed by the 10s and 1s digits of the original number.) Thus, by the addition property,

$$4|(\underbrace{\underline{ABC} \times 100}_{\text{1st number}} + \underbrace{\underline{DE}}_{\text{2d number}}).$$

In other words, $4|\underline{ABCDE}$. This shows why the familiar test for divisibility by 4 actually detects multiples of 4.

Now we must show that the familiar test detects *all* multiples of 4. Suppose that 4 is a divisor of $\underline{ABCDE}$, that is, $4|\underline{ABCDE}$. Then also

$$4|(\underline{ABCDE} - \underline{ABC} \times 100) \text{ (subtraction property)} \qquad \text{or} \qquad 4|\underline{DE}.$$

In other words, if 4 is a divisor of the original number, then 4 is a divisor of the number formed by its 10s and 1s digits.

EXERCISES

29. Use the preceding ideas to find a test for divisibility by 16. (*Hint:* $2|10$, $4|100$, $8|1000$, . . .)

30. Use the preceding ideas to find a test for divisibility by 125.

A Test for Divisibility by 11

Now let's use some of these ideas to create a test for divisibility by 11. The test we are about to describe is very similar to the test for divisibility by 9. You recall that one reason why the test for divisibility by 9 works is that

$$10^n - 1 = \underbrace{99999 \ldots 9}_{n \text{ 9s}}$$

and $9|99999 \ldots 9$. To describe the test for divisibility by 11, note that all the following numbers are divisible by 11.

$10^2 - 1 = 100 - 1 = 99 = 11 \times 9$

$10^4 - 1 = 10,000 - 1 = 9999 = 11 \times 909$

$10^6 - 1 = 1,000,000 - 1 = 999,999 = 11 \times 90,909$

$10^1 + 1 = 10 + 1 = 11 = 11 \times 1$

$10^3 + 1 = 1001 = 11 \times 91$

$10^5 + 1 = 100,001 = 11 \times 9091$

$10^7 + 1 = 10,000,001 = 11 \times 909,091$

In general, we have: If n is an even number $(2|n)$, then $11|10^n - 1$. If n is an odd number (n is *not* divisible by 2), then $11|10^n + 1$.

Next, take a number $\underline{ABCDE}$ and write it using expanded form, as

$$\underline{ABCDE} = A \times 10^4 + B \times 10^3 + C \times 10^2 + D \times 10 + E$$
$$= A(9999 + 1) + B(1001 - 1) + C(99 + 1) + D(11 - 1) + E$$
$$= \underbrace{(9999A + 1001B + 99C + 11D)}_{N} + (A + C + E - B - D)$$

(*Note*: This equation in whole numbers assumes that $A + C + E \geq B + D$. If not, then write $\underline{ABCDE} = (9999A + 1001B + 99C + 11D) - (B + D - A - C - E)$ and replace $A + C + E - B - D$ by $B + D - A - C - E$ in the argument below.)

By the multiplication and addition properties of divisibility (used several times), $11|N$. Thus, if $11|A + C + E - B - D$, then $11|\underline{ABCDE}$. And, if $11|\underline{ABCDE}$, then also $11|A + C + E - B - D$. In general, we have the following test for divisibility by 11.

TEST FOR DIVISIBILITY BY 11

Form the *alternating sum* of the digits of a number by adding up every other digit and calculating the difference of that sum with the sum of the remaining digits. A number is divisible by 11 if and only if the alternating sum of its digits is divisible by 11.

For example, the alternating sum of the digits of 340,781 is $4 + 7 + 1 - (3 + 0 + 8) = 1$, which is not divisible by 11; so 340,781 is not divisible by 11. The alternating sum of the digits of 718,201 is $7 + 8 + 0 - (1 + 2 + 1) = 11$, which is divisible by 11; so 718,201 is also divisible by 11.

EXERCISES

31. Use the test to determine whether or not each number is divisible by 11.
    (a) 121   (b) 88   (c) 298,367   (d) 101,010,101
    (e) 1,010,101,010,101,010,101,010   (f) 9,762,489

32. The tests for divisibility that we have described utilize a number's base 10 digits. Other tests might utilize a number's digits when it written as a standard numeral in another base.
    (a) Use the ideas developed in this section to find a test for divisibility by 4 utilizing the base 5 digits of a number.
    (b) Find a test for divisibility by 7 that uses the base 8 digits of a number.
    (c) Can you generalize (a) and (b) and the base 10 test for divisibility by 9?
    (d) Find a test for divisibility by 6 that uses the base 5 digits of a number.

7.9   LOOKING AHEAD: NUMBER THEORY

The topics discussed in this chapter—divisibility, primes, GCDs, LCMs—are part of a major branch of mathematics called *number theory*. The beginnings of number theory are ancient. The subject was already well developed by the time of Euclid (around 300 B.C.).

Many unsolved problems of long standing are associated with number theory. One of these has to do with *perfect numbers,* a treatment of which appears in Euclid's *Elements.* Let's discuss perfect numbers here, because they have important present-day implications.

DEFINITION OF *PERFECT NUMBER*

A natural number is *perfect* if it is equal to the sum of all its divisors, except the number itself.

For example, the divisors of 6, except 6 itself, are 1, 2, and 3. Moreover, $1 + 2 + 3 = 6$. So 6 is a perfect number. The divisors of 8, except 8 itself, are 1, 2, and 4. Furthermore, $1 + 2 + 4 = 7$. So 8 is *not* a perfect number. The divisors of 28, except 28 itself, are 1, 2, 4, 7, and 14. Also, $1 + 2 + 4 + 7 + 14 = 28$. So 28 *is* a perfect number.

EXERCISE   **33.** Which of the following numbers are perfect? 12, 17, 72, 128, 253, 496, 512

Notice that

$$6 = 2 \times 3 = 2^1(2^2 - 1)$$
$$28 = 4 \times 7 = 2^2(2^3 - 1)$$
$$496 = 16 \times 31 = 2^4(2^5 - 1)$$
$$8128 = 64 \times 127 = 2^6(2^7 - 1)$$

(The numbers 496 and 8128 are also perfect.) These are all numbers of the form $2^{p-1}(2^p - 1)$ where $2^p - 1$ is a prime number. Euclid was able to show that every number of this form must be perfect and that every even perfect number must be of this form. One question comes to mind immediately: Are there any *odd* perfect numbers? So far, nobody knows.

FAMOUS UNSOLVED PROBLEM IN NUMBER THEORY

Is there an odd perfect number?

A second question is this: For which numbers p is $2^p - 1$ a prime number? We can answer the question in part: p must be a prime; otherwise, $p = mn, m \neq 1, n \neq 1$, and

$$2^p - 1 = 2^{mn} - 1 = (2^n - 1) \cdot (2^{n(m-1)} + 2^{n(m-2)} + \cdots + 2^n + 1),$$

which is not a prime number. But this doesn't solve the problem. Even though 11 is a prime, $2^{11} - 1 = 2047 = 23 \times 89$. We have an unsolved problem.

FAMOUS UNSOLVED PROBLEM IN NUMBER THEORY

For which prime numbers p is $2^p - 1$ also prime?

A prime number of the form $2^p - 1$ is called a *Mersenne prime,* after the monk Marin Mersenne (1588–1648), who corresponded with the well-known mathematicians of his time. Since the time of Mersenne, mathematicians have been interested in deciding whether $2^p -- 1$ is a prime number, and, if not a prime number, finding what its prime factors are. For the most part, number theorists are interested in doing this because it *is* interesting and, like climbing Mt. Everest, a challenge.

Recently, headway on this problem has turned out to have applications in cryptology, the study of the creation and breaking of secret codes. One secret code uses a whole number having 40 or more digits. Breaking the code involves finding the prime factors of the large number. These are known to the creators of the code but not to people from whom the code is to be kept secret. Typically, the large number is the product of two or more large prime numbers. One way to find big prime numbers is to find a prime number p such that $2^p - 1$ is prime. If p is moderately large, then $2^p - 1$ is humongous.

How do you tell whether a number is a prime? A number is prime if its only divisors are 1 and itself.

FIRST TEST FOR A PRIME NUMBER

Suppose that N is a natural number. If N is *not* divisible by M for all natural numbers M such that $1 < M < N$, then N is a prime number.

The way to use this test is to see if $M|N$ is true successively for $M = 2, 3, \ldots$. If $M|N$ for one of these numbers, then you know N is not prime. If $M|N$ never happens, you know N is prime. A calculator is a good tool to use in carrying out your investigation. A computer is even better.

After using this test for a while, you realize that you don't need to check whether $M|N$ for every M such that $1 < M < N$. You realize that if $N = MQ$ and $M > Q$, then you will have already found out that $Q|N$, hence, that N is not prime. This insight gives us an easier test.

SECOND TEST FOR A PRIME NUMBER

Suppose that N is a natural number. If M does not divide N for all natural numbers M such that $M^2 \leq N$ (i.e., $M \leq \sqrt{N}$), then N is a prime number.

Again, using a calculator or a computer is the best way to implement this test.

Finally, using this test systematically, you realize that, if $M|N$, then also $P|N$ for any prime factor of M. If $P < M$, then you would have found out earlier that $P|N$ and that N is not prime. This gives us a third test.

THIRD TEST FOR A PRIME NUMBER

Suppose that N is a natural number. If P does not divide N for all prime numbers P such that $P^2 \leq N$, then N is a prime number.

To test whether a very big number is prime, you would need to use methods more sophisticated and more efficient than these.

EXERCISE 34. Use a calculator, the list of primes between 1 and 200 that you gathered earlier, and the third test for a prime number to determine whether each number is prime.
(a) $2^{13} - 1 = 8191$ (b) $2^{13} + 1$ (c) $2^{15} + 1$
(d) 1003   (e) 11,111

7.10   COMPUTERS: SEARCHING FOR SOLUTIONS

THE POSTAGE STAMP PROBLEM

A storekeeper has a supply of 8¢ and 13¢ stamps. He regularly mails packages that require postage in varying amounts. He can use these stamps for some amounts of postage such as 8¢, 13¢, 16¢, and 21¢, but not for others such as 3¢, 9¢, and 15¢. For which amounts of postage can the storekeeper use the stamps he has on hand?

Here are some suggestions for how you might approach this problem.

First, *consider a simpler problem.* Suppose you want to know whether you can mail a package requiring 50¢ using the 8¢ and 13¢ stamps. If you can mail such a package, then so many (X) 8¢ stamps and so many (Y) 13¢ stamps will make up the required postage; in other words, $8X + 13Y = 50$. So you want to know whether there are whole numbers X and Y such that $8X + 13Y = 50$. You can have the computer "search" for solutions by having it try all possible pairs of whole numbers X and Y within a certain range. For example, X can't be any bigger than the quotient of 50 divided by 8; Y can't be any bigger than the quotient of 50 divided by 13 (why?). So we can search for solutions among all pairs of whole numbers (X,Y) such that $X \leq \frac{50}{8}$ and $Y \leq \frac{50}{13}$. The computer is ideally suited for such a search. The following program does the search.

```
10 FOR X = 0 TO 50/8
20 FOR Y = 0 TO 50/13
30 IF 8*X + 13*Y = 50 THEN GOTO 90
40 NEXT Y
50 NEXT X
60 PRINT ''NO SOLUTION''
70 GOTO 100
90 PRINT ''A SOLUTION IS'' X,Y
100 END
```

(You may have observed by now that the material inside quotation marks in a PRINT statement will appear on the screen exactly as typed while the *values* of variables typed outside the quotation marks will appear on the screen.)

Now, alter the program above so that the computer will search for solutions to $8X + 13Y = A$ for any whole number A between 8 and 100 inclusive and print out those values of A for which there is a solution. (There are no solutions when A is less than 8. Why? I chose 100 to be the largest value for A more or less arbitrarily.) Run the program. *Look for patterns.* What do you observe? Can you make any conclusions regarding which whole numbers A have solutions to $8X + 13Y = A$?

Number theorists are interested in finding whole number solutions to equations of the form $8X + 13Y = 50$. Such an equation is called a *Diophantine equation* (after the second century A.D. Egyptian-Greek mathematician Diophantus, who proposed—and solved—many problems involving such equations).

EXERCISES

35. In the postage stamp problem, replace 8¢ and 13¢ postage stamps by 4¢ and 7¢ postage stamps. Revise the computer program you wrote so that it will search for solutions to $4X + 7Y = A$, for various whole numbers A. What happens?

36. A manufacturer of ceramic products ships cartons that contain either 6 casserole dishes or 4 teapots; no partial cartons will be shipped. The wholesale prices of a casserole dish and a teapot are $3.50 and $4.50, respectively. A retailer has a $600.00 credit with the manufacturer, which she desires to take out in merchandise. She is interested in these two products only. What choices are available to her to use her credit exactly?

7.11 SUMMARY OF IMPORTANT IDEAS AND TECHNIQUES

- Multiples and divisors of a whole number
- Common multiple and least common multiple (LCM) of a pair of whole numbers
- Tests for divisibility by 2, 4, 5, 9, 10, and 11
- A prime number, a number with exactly two divisors
- A composite number, its factor tree and its prime factorization
- The fundamental theorem of arithmetic, that the primes occurring in one prime factorization of a number, and the number of times each occurs, must be the same as for any other
- A test for divisibility by 6: a use of the fundamental theorem of arithmetic to find a test for divisibility by a composite number
- Common divisor and greatest common divisor (GCD) of a pair of whole numbers
- Methods for computing the LCM of two whole numbers
  Listing the multiples of the two numbers and looking for the smallest number that occurs on both lists
  Using the prime factorizations of the two numbers
- Methods for computing the GCD of two whole numbers
  Listing the divisors of both numbers and looking for the largest that occurs on both lists
  Using the prime factorizations of the two numbers
- Writing the prime factorization of a number more efficiently using the standard form
- Extending the test for divisibility by 9 to give a method that tells easily what any number's remainder is on division by 9, a method used with casting out 9s to check the accuracy of calculations in arithmetic problems

- ■ Introduction of notation $A \mid B$ expressing the divisibility relationship and development of its formal properties; using it to create a test for divisbility by 11
- ■ Looking for number patterns historically: perfect numbers, Mersenne primes, unsolved problems, and cryptology

PROBLEM SET

PRACTICING
SKILLS

1. Use tests of divisibility to fill in the following table with X's in the appropriate boxes.

THE NUMBER BELOW	IS DIVISIBLE BY										
	2	3	4	5	6	8	9	10	12	15
316,200										
176,292										
175,820										
74,748,105										
1,111,111,111										

2. Draw factor trees for the numbers 132, 180, 210, 264, and 275.

3. Use the trees in problem 2 to find the
   (a) LCM of 132 and 275   (b) LCM of 210 and 264
   (c) GCD of 180 and 264   (d) GCD of 180 and 210

4. Construct three *different* factor trees for 190,400. Write the prime factorization of 190,400 in standard form.

5. It takes Keith an average of 45 min to prune 1 tree. Richard takes 70 min, on average, to prune 1 tree. The K-R Tree Pruning Service has the contract for pruning the 92 trees in The King's Arboretum. How long will it take them to prune all the trees?

6. It normally takes Kathy 4 hr to paint a house—trim excluded—in a housing development. Yesterday, Kathy got her friend Chris to help her. Together, they finished the job in 2.4 hr. How long would it take Chris, working alone, to paint the sides of a house?

7. I have 144 pens and 360 pencils left over at the end of the school year. Since we get a new shipment in the fall, I would like to distribute all these leftovers among my junior high students. Since my students have a highly developed sense of fairness, I must be careful that the number for each student is the same. If each student is to get some pens and some pencils, what is the largest number of students I can give pens and pencils to?

8. (a) Find a test for divisibility by 20.   (b) Find a test for divisibility by 36.

9. A machine has two engaged gears. One gear has 198 teeth; the other has 165. The gear with 198 teeth makes 100 rpm. How many revolutions per minute does the 165-tooth gear make?

10. A machine has two engaged gears. If the machine is operating normally, one gear should make 280 rpm and the other 168 rpm. To test this, you paint a spot on each gear at a point where the two gears are engaged, you turn on the machine, and count the number of times per minute the two spots meet. If the machine is operating normally, how many times should this be?

11. (a) Find the GCD and LCM of $2 \times 2 \times 3 \times 3 \times 3 \times 7 \times 11 \times 11 \times 13$ and $2 \times 3 \times 3 \times 7 \times 7 \times 11 \times 17$.
    (b) Find the GCD and LCM of $2 \times 5 \times 5 \times 5 \times 5 \times 5 \times 13$ and $3 \times 5 \times 5 \times 5 \times 5 \times 13 \times 19$.
    (c) Find the GCD and LCM of $2^2 3^3 5^5 7^7$ and $2^3 3^5 5^2 7^5$.
    (d) Find the GCD and LCM of $3^5 7^3 11^2 13^4$ and $5^8 7^2 11^3 17^5$.

12. Use casting out 9s to check the following calculations.

(a)	(b)	(c)	(d)
683	9204	35,924	760,213
× 597	× 3856	46,880	− 594,258
407,751	35,398,584	+ 76,917	166,965
		149,711	

    (e) $6076 \div 79 = 76$ remainder 72

13. Suppose that A and B are whole numbers and that $15 | A$ and $B | 30$. Which of the following statements are true?
    (a) $B | 30M$ for any whole number M (b) $15 | 5A$ (c) $15 | A^5$
    (d) $5 | 18A$ (e) $3 | 8A + 12B$ (f) $15 | 4A − 30B$ (g) $5 | A + B$

14. Use the test for divisibility by 11 to determine whether each of the following numbers is divisible by 11.
    (a) 638   (b) 7,153,684   (c) 83,623,892   (d) 2,020,202,020,202,020,202,020

15. We have established that the first four perfect numbers of the form $2^{p-1}(2^p − 1)$, where $2^p − 1$ is prime, are

$$6 = 2^1(2^2 − 1) \quad (p = 1)$$
$$28 = 2^2(2^3 − 1) \quad (p = 3)$$
$$496 = 2^4(2^5 − 1) \quad (p = 5)$$
$$8128 = 2^6(2^7 − 1) \quad (p = 7)$$

Use a calculator, a list of primes from 1 to 200, and the third test for a prime number to help you find the next perfect number of this form.

USING IDEAS *For each problem remaining, document as clearly and completely as you can your solution to the problem. Include the steps you took to solve the problem, mention the problems or solutions from the text that gave you ideas, and include the problem-solving strategies you used. You might want to outline and organize these details before assembling your final report in the form of an essay.*

16. An importer has obtained a large supply of small teak tiles that measure 32 mm by 52 mm. She wants to arrange quantities of them together to make larger square shapes for parquet floors. What are the possible dimensions for such shapes, and how many of the small tiles will be used in each?

17. For the gears shown on page 305, each turn of the shaft attached to A must produce a whole number of turns of the shafts attached to gears B and C. Also, space constraints limit A to at most 50 teeth.
    (a) How many teeth should gear A have?
    (b) If shaft A spins at 480 rpm, how fast will shaft B spin?
    (c) If shaft C spins at 500 rpm, how fast will shaft B spin?

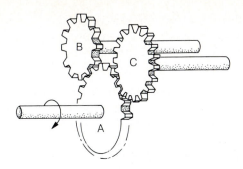

18. Joan can set the type for 1 chapter of a math book in 10 hr; Alice takes 12 hr for the same job. They are working together to set the type for a 22-chapter book. How long will it take them?

19. Larry and Mark are racing Go Karts. Larry's kart can complete 1 lap in 48 sec; Mark's kart can complete 1 lap in 40 sec. They start the race together. When does Mark catch up with and pass Larry? (In racing, this is called "lapping" someone, because when it happens, the faster car has covered 1 full lap more than the slower car.)

20. Sawzy-Dusties is packaged in 4-in by 6-in by 10-in boxes. You are to design a cubical crate for shipping these boxes of cereal. It is to hold no more than 1000 boxes, and there is to be no wasted space inside. What should the (inside) dimensions of the crate be, and how many boxes of cereal will each crate hold?

21. Of two neon signs, one blinks 80 times/min; the other blinks 60 times/min. The two signs are turned on at the same moment. How many times per minute will they blink together?

22. The planet Mars is closest to Earth when it is in a position such as is shown.

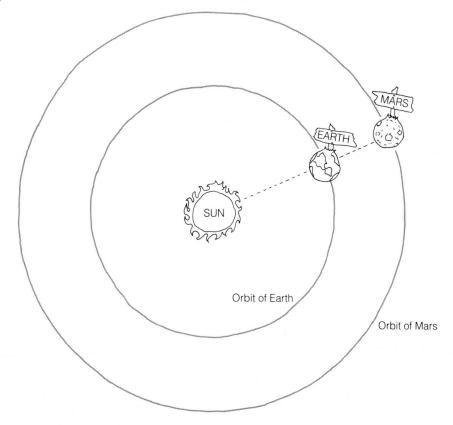

Such positions are good for observing features on Mars through telescopes on Earth. If such a position were to occur on a certain day, how many days would you have to wait for it to occur again? It takes Mars 687 (Earth) days to make one complete circuit of the sun, and the Earth 365 days.

23. (a) Find a test for divisibility by 5 for a stick numeral. The test must use the stick numeral digits, just as a test for divisibility for a standard decimal numeral uses the decimal digits.
    (b) Find a test for divisibility by 2 for a stick numeral.

24. Recall that $2^{64} = \underbrace{2 \times 2 \times .. \times 2.}$

    (Sixty-four 2s)

    The number 2^{64} has 20 digits when written out as a decimal numeral. Use casting out 9s to determine the remainder when this number is divided by 9.

25. At a light show, lights numbered from 1 to 1000 have been lined up in a row, in that order. A computer has been programmed to carry out the following steps. Step 1: All the lights are turned on; step 2: all the even-numbered lights are turned off; step 3: all the lights numbered by a multiple of 3 are "changed" ("changed" means an on light is turned off, and an off light is turned on); step 4: all the lights numbered by a multiple of 4 are changed. At step 5, multiples of 5 are changed, etc. There are 1000 steps in all. At the end of the thousandth step, which lights will be on?

26. In the diagram the circumference of pulley C is 5 ft and the circumference of pulley D is 4 ft.
    (a) How many revolutions for pulley C if D is turned 100 revolutions?
    (b) If pulley D moves at a rate of 50 rpm, at what rate does pulley C move?

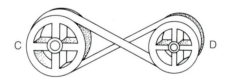

27. Shown is a drawing of a gear system for an automobile transmission. Gears ② and ③ are on a common shaft. Each gear has the number of teeth indicated in the picture. (Gear ① has 36 teeth, and so on.) Suppose that gear ① revolves 3000 times a minute. What happens to gear ④?

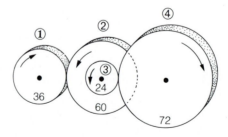

28. Each gallon of custom-mixed paint requires a certain amount of neutral base plus 18 g (grams) of chrome yellow and 12 g of cobalt blue. Tinting colors come in 90-g tubes. How many gallons of the custom mix can be prepared so that there will be no wasted tinting colors? (After a tube of tinting color is opened, the amount that has not been used is considered waste.)

29. Generalize the postage stamp problem and exercise 35 of the text: You want to see if you can say something about those amounts of postage that can be paid using B¢ and C¢ stamps, for any pair of whole numbers B and C. Use the data gathered in the postage stamp problem and exercise 35; get the computer to gather more data. Alter the program in the postage stamp problem so that you can input B and C, then have it search for solutions. Try several new pairs (B,C). Look for patterns in the values of A for which there are solutions.

30. Look at problem 23 from chapter 1. There are several solutions to the problem. Use the search method described in the postage stamp problem above to find *all* the solutions.

31. A concert hall has 1000 seats. For an upcoming concert, prices for tickets are $10 and $15. For the management to break even, not all tickets need be sold, but the total ticket sales must be at least $11,000. If X denotes the number of $10 tickets sold and Y the number of $15 tickets, what must a pair X, Y be in order to break even? There are many solutions. Use the computer to search for them.

INTRODUCTION TO FRACTIONS AND RATIOS

CHAPTER

In this chapter we will show that · there is a need to provide names for quantities that are parts of whole things, thereby introducing the idea of fraction. We will discuss how to compare fractions, what adding and subtracting fractions mean, and how to attach a fraction to the result. Along the way we will deal with a variety of issues: mixed numbers, improper fractions, and the connection of fractions with the division of whole numbers. We will introduce equality of fractions: two fractions are equal when they represent the same quantity. This notion will enable us to reduce problems of comparing, adding, and subtracting fractions to corresponding whole number problems.

We will also introduce the notion of ratio, discuss some of the connections between the notions of ratio and fraction, and point out some areas of possible confusion. Finally, we will reintroduce the number line, a convenient device with which to visualize the relative sizes of fractions.

8.1

WHAT ARE FRACTIONS AND
WHAT ARE THEY GOOD FOR?

THE APPLE PROBLEM

Try solving this problem.

The fourth grade teacher bought two bags of apples for a picnic for his class. He gives one bag to one group of eight students to divide up equally among the members of the group, and the other bag to another group to do the same. The first group opens its bag and counts the apples to find that there are 29 apples for the eight of them. Help them figure out how many apples each person will get. (They don't know much about fractions.)

A Solution to the Apple Problem

Here's how the students might tackle the problem. Sue says: "Let's see. This is a division problem. Divide 29 by 8 to figure out how many apples each of us will get."

John adds: "Yes, you're right. 29 divided by 8 is 3 with a remainder of 5. Everybody gets 3 apples."

Olivia: "Well, that's fine; but what do we do with the 5 apples left over?"

Luis: "Cut them up into pieces."

Marie: "How do we do that so everybody gets the same amount?"

Sam: "I know. There are 8 of us, right? Cut up every one of the 5 apples into 8 equal pieces. Then everybody take 1 of the 8 pieces from each apple."

Alice: "Since you cut each apple into 8 *equal* pieces, each piece must be an eighth of an apple. Everybody takes 5 of the pieces. That makes 5 eighths of an apple for everybody. So everybody gets 3 whole apples plus 5 eighths of an apple."

EXERCISE

1. There are six people in the other group going on the picnic. This group's bag of apples contains 22 apples. The 22 apples are to be divided equally among the six. Help the group figure out how many apples each person will get.

The Mathematical Idea: Concept of Fraction

You have a set whose elements you want to distribute equally among so many persons. You carry out the division and you get a quotient and a remainder. What do you do with the remainder? The apple problem is such a situation. And the idea of a fraction of an apple is one solution. The idea is this: You cut up an apple into 8 equal pieces. You call one of these pieces *an eighth* of an apple. It is then natural to call 5 of these pieces *five-eighths* of an apple. The idea is so useful in other situations as well that the phrase "five eighths" is frequently replaced by the symbol $\frac{5}{8}$. The quantity of apple is called a *fractional quantity* and the name—$\frac{5}{8}$—for the quantity is called a *fraction*.

What is a fraction made up of? There is a *unit,* a set or an item or a whole thing, a portion of which will be named by the fraction. The unit is divided into a nonzero whole number B of equal parts. The portion of the unit in question consists of A of the B equal parts. The whole number A is called the *numerator* and B is called the *denominator.*

For example, for the fraction $\frac{5}{8}$, the unit is an apple, 8 is the denominator, and 5 is the numerator. Let's look at some other fractions with various numerators, denominators, and units.

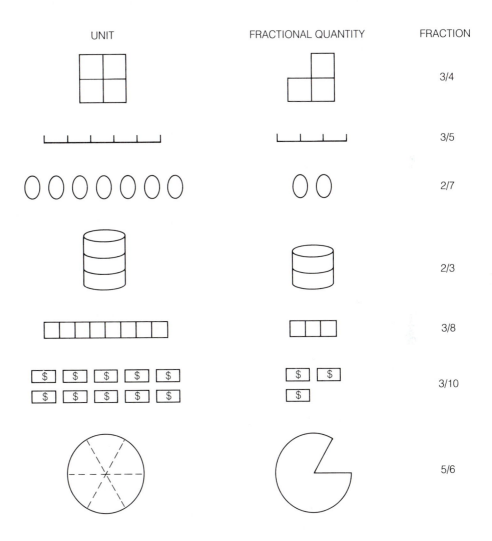

UNIT	FRACTIONAL QUANTITY	FRACTION
		3/4
		3/5
		2/7
		2/3
		3/8
		3/10
		5/6

The Mathematical Idea: Mixed Numbers

The answer to the first apple problem was 3 whole apples plus $\frac{5}{8}$ of an apple. This is usually written $3\frac{5}{8}$ apples and said as "three and five-eighths apples"; it is called a *mixed number.*

Paul, another member of the group of eight, kept quiet while the others were discussing how to divide up the apples. Now, as they are about to cut the apples, he speaks up: "Wait! I get another answer! Cut each of the extra 5 apples into halves.

That gives you 10 halves. Then give each of the eight people a half. Now everybody would have 3 apples plus $\frac{1}{2}$ an apple. Take the remaining 2 halves and cut each one into 4 equal pieces.

That would give you 8 little pieces all the same size. Give everybody one of those. Then everybody would have 3 whole apples plus half an apple plus one of those little pieces.

See? Isn't that right?"

Alice: "Yes, you are right—and so are the others. I'm going to draw a picture of your solution, Paul, and the solution the others came up with. I'll show only the part beyond 3 whole apples.

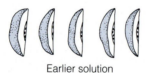

Earlier solution

Paul's solution

These two are the same quantity of apple."

Paul: "How could that be? My solution has 2 pieces; theirs has 5 pieces."

Alice: "It's not the number of pieces that counts; it's the amount of apple that's important. Look, if I gave John this whole apple and you these 2 halves, who would have more apple?"

Paul: "Well, we'd both have the same amount of apple. But we wouldn't have the same thing. I mean having 2 halves is not the same thing as having a whole apple."

Alice: "I agree. But the real issue is whether the two *amounts* of apple are the same. You agree that 2 halves is the same amount of apple as a whole apple. So we could write $1 = \frac{2}{2}$. Now, let me cut each of the halves in half. That would give me 4 quarters of an apple. Then we would have $1 = \frac{4}{4}$ and $\frac{1}{2} = \frac{2}{4}$. We're almost done. Next, I want to cut each of the quarters in half giving me 8 eighths of an apple. We would have

$$1 = \frac{8}{8} \qquad \frac{1}{2} = \frac{4}{8} \qquad \frac{1}{4} = \frac{2}{8}.$$

Let's go back to your solution. You had $\frac{1}{2}$ plus $\frac{1}{8}$. That's the same amount as $\frac{4}{8}$ plus $\frac{1}{8}$, or $\frac{5}{8}$."

Paul: "You're right."

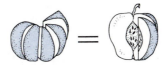

The Mathematical Idea: Equal Fractions

If we have a whole thing cut up into 5 equal pieces and we take 3 of them, then we have $\frac{3}{5}$. But, if each of the 5 equal pieces is in turn cut up into 4 smaller, equal pieces, then this would cut up the whole thing into $4 \times 5 = 20$ equal pieces. Originally we took 3 of the 5 pieces; to take the same amount now, we'd have to take $4 \times 3 = 12$ pieces or $\frac{12}{20}$ of the whole thing.

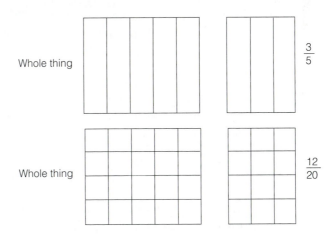

The fractions $\frac{3}{5}$ and $\frac{12}{20}$ represent the same quantity of apple. We call $\frac{3}{5}$ and $\frac{12}{20}$ *equal fractions* and write

$$\frac{3}{5} = \frac{4 \times 3}{4 \times 5} = \frac{12}{20}.$$

In reconciling the two solutions to the apple problem we encountered the pairs of equal fractions so that we can write

$$\frac{1}{2} = \frac{2 \times 1}{2 \times 2} = \frac{2}{4}$$

$$\frac{1}{2} = \frac{4 \times 1}{4 \times 2} = \frac{4}{8}$$

$$\frac{1}{4} = \frac{2 \times 1}{2 \times 4} = \frac{2}{8}.$$

More examples of equal fractions follow.

1. $\dfrac{5}{6} = \dfrac{3 \times 5}{3 \times 6} = \dfrac{15}{18}.$

2. $\frac{3}{5} = \frac{21}{35}$

because $\dfrac{3}{5} = \dfrac{7 \times 3}{7 \times 5} = \dfrac{21}{35}.$

3. $\frac{21}{35} = \frac{12}{20}$

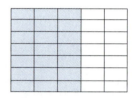

because $\dfrac{21}{35} = \dfrac{7 \times 3}{7 \times 5} = \dfrac{3}{5} = \dfrac{4 \times 3}{4 \times 5} = \dfrac{12}{20}.$

(This one is trickier!)

FIRST DEFINITION OF *EQUAL FRACTIONS*

That two fractions A/B and C/D are *equal* means that they represent the same quantity and we write $A/B = C/D$.

How do we decide when two fractions represent the same quantity? The examples we have seen suggest that A/B and MA/MB are equal fractions for any nonzero whole number M.

$$\frac{A}{B} = \frac{MA}{MB}.$$

What if we want to know whether $A/B = C/D$ and C is not a multiple of A (as in example 3 above)? Let's replace the two fractions by equal fractions with the same denominator. One denominator that will work is BD. Since $\dfrac{A}{B} = \dfrac{AD}{BD}$ and $\dfrac{C}{D} = \dfrac{CB}{DB}$, then $\dfrac{A}{B} = \dfrac{C}{D}$ means that $\dfrac{AD}{BD} = \dfrac{CB}{DB}$, which (since the two latter fractions have the same denominator) in turn means $AD = CB$, and vice versa. This gives us a more operational definition of equal fractions.

> ## SECOND DEFINITION OF *EQUAL FRACTIONS*
>
> Suppose that A/B and C/D are fractions. Then $\dfrac{A}{B} = \dfrac{C}{D}$ if and only if $AD = CB$.

In the second definition of equal fractions the phrase "if and only if" between the two statements $\dfrac{A}{B} = \dfrac{C}{D}$ and $AD = CB$ means that both the following statements must be true:

1. From $\dfrac{A}{B} = \dfrac{C}{D}$ it follows that $AD = CB$.

2. From $AD = CB$ it follows that $\dfrac{A}{B} = \dfrac{C}{D}$.

EXERCISE

2. Decide which of the following pairs of fractions are equal:
   (a) $\frac{1}{5}$ and $\frac{1}{6}$ (b) $\frac{3}{4}$ and $\frac{15}{20}$ (c) $\frac{10}{12}$ and $\frac{15}{18}$

8.2　COMPARING THE SIZES OF FRACTIONS

THE APPLE COMPARISON PROBLEM

Solve this yourself, first.

The other group going on the picnic has six people and 22 apples. This group divided the 22 apples equally among 6 people and got $3\frac{2}{3}$ apples per person. The first group, hearing of this, wanted to know which was the bigger quantity $3\frac{5}{8}$ or $3\frac{2}{3}$. How will they decide? (The students all know what fractions are by now and what equal fractions are. But that's all.)

A Solution to the Apple Comparison Problem

The group figures out that the question boils down to: Which is the larger amount of apple, $\frac{5}{8}$ or $\frac{2}{3}$? The members of the group realize that if they were comparing $\frac{5}{8}$ apple with $\frac{7}{8}$ apple their job would be easy: $\frac{7}{8}$ is larger than $\frac{5}{8}$. The denominators of $\frac{5}{8}$ and $\frac{7}{8}$ are the same.

"How do you compare $\frac{1}{8}$ with $\frac{1}{3}$?" they ask. The eight students with the 29 apples think of how they reconciled the two solutions to their problem by replacing the fraction $\frac{1}{2}$ by an equal fraction $\frac{4}{8}$. Can they do something similar here? They realize that there is no way to turn eighths into thirds or vice versa; to carry out the program they must turn both into something else. They must change both $\frac{5}{8}$ and $\frac{2}{3}$ into two other fractions with the same denominator. They know that a fraction equal to $\frac{5}{8}$ must be of the form

$$\frac{5}{8} = \frac{5Q}{8Q}$$

and similarly for $\frac{2}{3}$:

$$\frac{2}{3} = \frac{2P}{3P}.$$

They wonder how to find numbers Q and P so that the two denominators 8Q and 3P would be equal, 8Q = 3P. They aren't sure how they could do this, but they notice that such a denominator would be a common multiple of 8 and 3.

Sue: "I know. 24 is a common multiple of 8 and 3."

John: "And then

$$\frac{5}{8} = \frac{5 \times 3}{8 \times 3} = \frac{15}{24} \quad \text{and} \quad \frac{2}{3} = \frac{2 \times 8}{3 \times 8} = \frac{16}{24}.$$

The numerator 16 is larger than the numerator 15 so the fraction $\frac{16}{24}$ is larger than $\frac{15}{24}$. Thus $\frac{2}{3}$ is larger than $\frac{5}{8}$. Each of them gets a little bit more apple than we do!"

The Mathematical Idea: Finding Common Denominators in Order to Compare Fractions

A solution to the apple comparison problem was found by replacing the given fractions by equal fractions having the same denominator and then comparing the numerators. Let's summarize what we did.

ORDER FOR FRACTIONS

1. For fractions with the same denominator:
   A/B is *less than* C/B, written $A/B < C/B$, if and only if $A < C$.

2. For fractions with different denominators:
   Take fractions D/E and F/G and replace them by equal fractions having the same denominator. Then use 1.

Fractions D/E and F/G always have the common denominator EG, in which case the equal fractions are

$$\frac{DG}{EG} \quad \text{and} \quad \frac{FE}{GE}$$

Thus, $D/E < F/G$ if and only if $DG < FE$.

What we know about equal fractions and order on fractions gives us the following useful and general method for deciding whether two fractions are equal and if not which is greater.

GENERAL METHOD FOR DECIDING ORDER AND EQUALITY OF FRACTIONS

1. $A/B = C/D$ if and only if $AD = CB$.
2. $A/B < C/D$ if and only if $AD < CB$.
3. $A/B > C/D$ if and only if $AD > CB$.

The problem of comparing fractions has been reduced to a problem of comparing whole numbers.

EXERCISE 3. For each of the following pairs of fractions, decide which of the two is greater.

(a) $\frac{2}{3}$ or $\frac{5}{7}$ (b) $\frac{2}{3}$ or $\frac{7}{11}$ (c) $\frac{7}{12}$ or $\frac{5}{8}$

8.3   ADDING AND SUBTRACTING FRACTIONS

THE RECIPE PROBLEM

Try this yourself, first.

John is cooking. One dish he is making calls for $\frac{2}{3}$ of a cup of milk; another dish calls for $\frac{1}{4}$ of a cup of milk. He wants to know how much milk he will need in all for both dishes. John is in the fifth grade, knows about equal fractions and has had experience comparing fractional quantities. How would he solve this?

A Solution to the Recipe Problem

John might think like this: "Let me *solve a simpler, similar problem*. If one dish used $\frac{3}{8}$ of a cup of milk and the other used $\frac{1}{8}$ of a cup, then the two dishes together would use $\frac{1}{8} + \frac{3}{8} = \frac{4}{8}$ of a cup. The problem is easy to solve when the two fractions have the same denominators. Can I turn the original problem into an easier one where the denominators are the same? When we were trying to decide whether $\frac{5}{8}$ apples or $\frac{2}{3}$ apples was larger, we asked the same question. We solved it by replacing that problem by an easier one in which the fractions had the same denominators; we used equal fractions to do it. Let's try that here: Replace both $\frac{1}{4}$ and $\frac{2}{3}$ by equal fractions having the same denominator. We can use $4 \times 3 = 12$ as a common denominator.

$$\frac{1}{4} = \frac{1 \times 3}{4 \times 3} = \frac{3}{12} \quad \text{and} \quad \frac{2}{3} = \frac{2 \times 4}{3 \times 4} = \frac{8}{12}.$$

It's easy to add now.

$$\frac{1}{4} + \frac{2}{3} = \frac{3}{12} + \frac{8}{12} = \frac{11}{12}.$$

I will need $\frac{11}{12}$ of a cup of milk. That's a little less than a cup."

The Mathematical Idea: Adding and Subtracting Fractions

Given two quantities that are fractions of some unit, how much do you have when you put the two together? The answer is called the *sum* of the two fractions.

THE SUM OF TWO FRACTIONS

The *sum* of A/B and C/D is written $A/B + C/D$. A/B and C/D are called the *addends*.

Finding a fraction equal to the sum is called *addition* of fractions. If the two addends have the same denominator, then the sum is a fraction having the same denominator and having a numerator equal to the sum of the two original numerators. For example,

$$\frac{3}{11} + \frac{5}{11} = \frac{8}{11}.$$

In general, we arrive at a method.

HOW TO ADD FRACTIONS

1. For fractions with the same denominator:

$$\frac{E}{F} + \frac{G}{F} = \frac{E + G}{F}.$$

2. For fractions with different denominators: Replace fractions A/B and C/D by equal fractions having the same denominator and use method 1 to add the two equal fractions.

   As before, a common denominator that always works for fractions A/B and C/D is BD, in which case the equal fractions are

$$\frac{AD}{BD} \quad \text{and} \quad \frac{CB}{DB}$$

and the sum is

$$\frac{A}{B} + \frac{C}{D} = \frac{AD}{BD} + \frac{CB}{DB} = \frac{AD + CB}{BD}.$$

Similarly, if you have a fraction A/B of a unit and you remove from that a smaller fraction C/D of the same unit, you want to know what you have left. The answer is written $A/B - C/D$ and called the *difference* of A/B and C/D. Just as for whole numbers, the difference of A/B and C/D is the solution X to the missing addend problem $C/D + X = A/B$. Finding a fraction equal to $A/B - C/D$ is called *subtraction*. The method for doing this is similar to that for addition of fractions.

DEFINITION OF SUBTRACTION OF FRACTIONS

If $C/D < A/B$, then finding the missing addend X in $C/D + X = A/B$ is called *subtraction*, and we write $X = A/B - C/D$.

---

1. For fractions with same denominator:

$$\frac{E}{F} - \frac{G}{F} = \frac{E-G}{F}.$$

2. For fractions with different denominators: Replace fractions A/B and C/D by equal fractions having the same denominator and use method 1 to subtract the two equal fractions. Using the common denominator BD for these two fractions, you find that the equal fractions are

$$\frac{AD}{BD} \quad \text{and} \quad \frac{CB}{DB}$$

and the difference is

$$\frac{A}{B} - \frac{C}{D} = \frac{AD}{BD} - \frac{CB}{DB} = \frac{AD-CB}{BD}.$$

Just as the problem of comparing two fractions was reduced to the problem of comparing two whole numbers, so also the problems of finding the sum and difference of two fractions have been reduced to finding the sum and difference of two whole numbers.

EXERCISE   4. Given the two fractions $\frac{7}{15}$ and $\frac{9}{20}$, compare them, add them, and find their difference.

8.4   IMPROPER FRACTIONS

THE CREPE PROBLEM   John is cooking again. He wants to make 20 crepes and has a recipe for 10 crepes. He will have to double the amount of each ingredient called for by the recipe. The recipe calls for $\frac{3}{4}$ cup of flour. How much flour will he need for 20 crepes?

Please try this.

A Solution to the   John realizes that he will need $\frac{3}{4} + \frac{3}{4}$ cups of flour. He also knows that, since the two
Crepe Problem   fractions have the same denominator, the sum is easy: $\frac{3}{4} + \frac{3}{4} = \frac{6}{4}$. He is puzzled by the fraction $\frac{6}{4}$, since the numerator is larger than the denominator. "How can you divide something up into 4 equal pieces and take 6 of them?" He thinks a bit. "I know. If I had 2 cups of flour and divided each one of them up into 4 equal portions, it

would make sense to call each one of the 8 portions $\frac{1}{4}$ of a cup. Then I take 6 of those portions. That would make $\frac{6}{4}$ of a cup. That's one full cup plus $\frac{1}{2}$ of a cup.

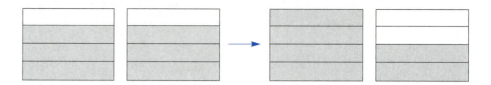

In other words, $1 + \frac{1}{2} = \frac{4}{4} + \frac{2}{4} = \frac{6}{4}$."

The Mathematical Idea: Improper Fractions

In the solution to the crepe problem, a fraction of the form A/B where A is larger than B arose naturally, and John was able to make sense of it. Such a fraction is called an *improper fraction*. (The choice of language is historical and is not meant to suggest the occurrence of some impropriety.) In the solution to the problem we also saw that $\frac{6}{4} = 1\frac{1}{2} = 1 + \frac{1}{2}$. As we have noted before, the fraction $1\frac{1}{2}$ is called a *mixed number*.

THE PIE PROBLEM John's family is having a picnic, and his mother plans to serve pie for dessert. She wants to know how much pie to order. She assumes that each pie will be cut into 8 equal pieces

and that each person will get one of these pieces. Twenty-nine people including the members of John's family will be at the picnic. John has been given the job of solving the problem of how much pie to order. Help him solve the problem.

A Solution to the John has been studying fractions in school and thinks, "Each pie will be divided up
Pie Problem into 8 equal pieces . . . . Each person will get 1 of these pieces . . . . Each person will get $\frac{1}{8}$ of a pie! So the amount of pie that we'll need is $\frac{1}{8}$ added up 29 times: $\frac{1}{8} + \frac{1}{8} + \frac{1}{8} + \cdots$. All those fractions have the same denominator so the sum must be $\frac{29}{8}$. That's $\frac{29}{8}$ of a pie. To figure out how many whole pies Mom will have to buy, I know that $\frac{8}{8}$ is 1 whole pie. Divide 29 by 8: $29 \div 8 = 3$ with remainder 5, or $29 = 3 \times 8 + 5$. So I have

$$\frac{29}{8} = \frac{3 \times 8 + 5}{8} = \frac{3 \times 8}{8} + \frac{5}{8} = \frac{3}{1} + \frac{5}{8} = 3\frac{5}{8}.$$

We need $3\frac{5}{8}$ pies. We'll have to buy 4 whole pies. We'll use up 3 whole ones and 5 pieces from the fourth one. That will leave us with $\frac{8}{8} - \frac{5}{8} = \frac{3}{8}$ of a pie left over."

The Mathematical Idea: A Fraction as an Answer to a Whole Number Division Problem

The fraction $\frac{29}{8}$ is an improper fraction equal to the mixed number $3\frac{5}{8}$. Seeing the two equations

$$\frac{29}{8} = 3\frac{5}{8} \quad \text{and} \quad 29 \div 8 = 3 \text{ with a remainder of } 5$$

suggests a strong connection of fractions with division of whole numbers. In certain cases one can think of the fraction A/B as an answer to the whole number division problem $A \div B$.

- Twenty-nine apples divided equally among 8 people is $\frac{29}{8} = 3\frac{5}{8}$ apples. Compare this with: $29 \div 8 = 3$ with remainder 5. (The answer is either "$3\frac{5}{8}$" or "3 with remainder 5," depending on whether you want to cut up the remainder of 5 apples.)

- Twenty-two apples divided equally among six people is $\frac{22}{6} = 3\frac{4}{6}$ apples. Compare this with: $22 \div 6 = 3$ with remainder 4.

- Thirty-seven pencils are distributed equally among five children. How many pencils does each child get? This is a division problem: $37 \div 5 = 7$ pencils with 2 pencils left over. Is $\frac{37}{5} = 7\frac{2}{5}$ pencils also an answer? What does $\frac{2}{5}$ of a pencil mean? Here a division problem interpreted as a fraction doesn't make much sense, because a fraction of a pencil doesn't make much sense for this problem.

- One hundred dollars has been allocated to buy math books for the third grade. Each math book costs \$7. How many books can be purchased? Again, this is a division problem: $100 \div 7 = 14$ books with \$2 left over. The corresponding fraction is $\frac{100}{7}$, which equals $14\frac{2}{7}$. Again, the fraction form of the division doesn't make sense—and for the same reason: A fraction of a book doesn't make sense for this problem.

WHOLE NUMBER DIVISION AND FRACTIONS

If A and B are whole numbers, $B \neq 0$, and $A \div B = Q$ with remainder R, then the fraction A/B is equal to the

$$\text{Mixed number } Q\frac{R}{B}$$

In some cases it is useful to write $A \div B = \dfrac{A}{B}$.

EXERCISES

5. Twelve pints of milk are to be evenly distributed to seven children. How much should each child get? Does it matter whether the answer is a fraction or a quotient with remainder? How would you measure out how much each child should get?

6. Fifty microcomputers are to be distributed equally to the eight elementary schools in the district. How many microcomputers should each school get? Does it matter whether the answer is a fraction or a quotient with remainder?

In describing its strength in Green City the Republican party has found out that the city has roughly 600,000 voters, among whom 200,000 are registered as Republicans. One way to describe the party's strength is as a fraction: The fraction of all registered voters consisting of Republicans is 200,000/600,000. Of course, this is equal to $\frac{1}{3}$, a fraction easier to understand.

The Republican party wants to compare its strength directly with the Democratic party, which has roughly 300,000 registered voters in Green City. (The remaining 100,000 registered voters are independents.) How can the party compare 200,000 directly with 300,000? The fraction 200,000/300,000 (equal to $\frac{2}{3}$) doesn't make sense because the 200,000 Republicans are not a part of the 300,000 Democrats. A way out is to say that the *ratio* of registered Republicans to Democrats in Green City is 200,000 to 300,000.

The benefits of this new language will become obvious when we figure out a way to compare ratios.

THE RATIO COMPARISON PROBLEM

The national Republican party has determined that the ratio of Republicans to Democrats in Green City is 200,000 to 300,000 and that the ratio of Republicans to Democrats in Brownsville is 150,000 to 250,000. Party officials would like to compare the strength of the Republicans versus Democrats in Green City against the strength in Brownsville; that is, they would like some way to compare ratios.

Someone points out that $200,000 = 2 \times 100,000$, $300,000 = 3 \times 100,000$ and that registered Republicans and Democrats in Green City can be arranged in an array like this:

```
R R     D D D
R R     D D D
R R     D D D     (100,000 rows)
: :     : : :
```

Suppose a smaller group of voters could be arranged in the array

```
R R     D D D     (11 rows)
R R     D D D
R R     D D D
R R     D D D
R R     D D D
R R     D D D
R R     D D D
R R     D D D
R R     D D D
R R     D D D
R R     D D D
```

Then you would say that this small group has the same strength of Republicans versus Democrats that Green City has. This group also has the same strength as

R R   D D D

R R   D D D

R R   D D D

as does this little group

R R   D D D.

We agree that the ratio of Republicans to Democrats is the same for all of these groups. The ratio of the last one is 2 to 3. For each of the groups there is a number N so that the number of Republicans is $2 \times N$ and the number of Democrats is $3 \times N$. Thus, we have agreed that a ratio of $2 \times N$ to $3 \times N$ is the same as a ratio of 2 to 3.

Using this agreement, we can simplify the ratio of 150,000 to 250,000. Since $150,000 = 15 \times 10,000$ and $250,000 = 25 \times 10,000$, the ratio of 150,000 to 250,000 is the same as the ratio of 15 to 25. Since $15 = 3 \times 5$ and $25 = 5 \times 5$, the ratio of 15 to 25 is the same as the ratio of 3 to 5. Thus the ratio of Republicans to Democrats in Brownsville is also 3 to 5. The Republicans and Democrats in Brownsville can be arranged in an array:

R R R   D D D D D   (50,000 rows)

R R R   D D D D D

R R R   D D D D D

⋮ ⋮ ⋮   ⋮ ⋮ ⋮ ⋮ ⋮

The relative strength of Republicans is the same for Brownsville as it is for this little group of voters:

R R R   D D D D D.

The Mathematical Idea: When Two Ratios Are the Same

Here is our agreement regarding the equality of ratios.

FIRST DEFINITION OF *EQUALITY FOR RATIOS*

The ratio of AN to BN is *equal* to the ratio of A to B.

THE RATIO COMPARISON PROBLEM, CONTINUED

The ratio of Republicans to Democrats in Green City is 2 to 3 and the ratio of Republicans to Democrats in Brownsville is 3 to 5. How can we compare these? Let's look at a simpler situation. If we were comparing a ratio of 2 to 5 to a ratio of 3 to 5, then we'd be comparing two groups that could be arranged in arrays as shown.

```
R R     D D D D D        R R R     D D D D D
R R     D D D D D        R R R     D D D D D
R R     D D D D D        R R R     D D D D D
: :     : : : : :        : : :     : : : : :
```

Certainly the strength of the Republican party is greater for the group on the right. So we agree that a ratio of 3 to 5 *is larger than* a ratio of 2 to 5.

In general,

FIRST DEFINITION OF *ORDER FOR RATIOS*

If A is larger than B, then the ratio of A to P ($\neq 0$) *is larger than* the ratio of B to P.

Returning to the harder problem of comparing the ratio of 2 to 3 with the ratio of 3 to 5, we could solve it if we were able to get the second of each pair of numbers to be the same. We know that the ratio of 2 to 3 is the same as a ratio of $2N$ to $3N$ (for any whole number N). And we know that the ratio of 3 to 5 is the same as a ratio of $3M$ to $5M$. Can we find whole numbers N and M so that $3N = 5M$? Whole numbers $N = 5$ and $M = 3$ will work. That means that a ratio of 2 to 3 is the same as a ratio of 2×5 to 3×5 (or 10 to 15), and a ratio of 3 to 5 is the same as a ratio of 3×3 to 5×3 (or 9 to 15). We've agreed that a ratio of 10 to 15 is larger than a ratio of 9 to 15 and that means that the strength of the Republican party relative to the Democrats is greater in Green City than in Brownsville.

The Mathematical Idea: Comparing Ratios; Ratios and Fractions

Suppose we want to compare two ratios A to B and C to D. We know that the ratio of AD to BD is equal to the ratio of A to B, and we know that the ratio of CB to DB is equal to the ratio of C to D. Thus, to compare ratio A to B with C to D is the same as comparing ratio AD to BD with CB to DB. Hence, to compare them, all we have to do is compare whole number AD with whole number CB. We can summarize.

SECOND DEFINITION OF *EQUALITY AND ORDER FOR RATIOS*

Suppose that $B \neq 0$ and $D \neq 0$.

1. Ratio A to B is *equal to* ratio C to D if and only if $AD = BC$.
2. Ratio A to B is *larger than* ratio C to D if and only if $AD > BC$.

Notice that the ratio A to B is equal to (respectively, larger than) the ratio C to D exactly when $A/B = C/D$ (respectively, $A/B > C/D$). To compare ratios, you compare fractions.

The connection of ratios with fractions is also apparent in the language used to talk about ratios. For example, the numbered statements all mean the same thing.

1. The ratio of Republicans to Democrats is 2 to 3.
2. For every 2 Republicans there are 3 Democrats.
3. The ratio of Republicans to Democrats is $\frac{2}{3}$.
4. There are $\frac{2}{3}$ as many Republicans as Democrats.

Ratios are frequently replaced by fractions and vice versa. For example, in Green City there are 200,000 registered Republicans among 600,000 registered voters. As we noted earlier, that means that the set of Republicans is $\frac{1}{3}$ of the set of all of the registered voters. One can use the language of ratios here and also say that the ratio of registered Republicans to all registered voters is 1 to 3. Thus, all the numbered statements mean the same thing.

1. The ratio of Republicans to all registered voters is 1 to 3.
2. One out of every three registered voters is a Republican.
3. The ratio of Republicans to all registered voters is $\frac{1}{3}$.
4. The fraction of Republicans among all registered voters is $\frac{1}{3}$.

The connection of ratios with fractions enlarges the number of situations in which fractions can be used. The reading contest problem points out that there are situations when this connection leads to confusion. You have to be careful!

THE READING CONTEST PROBLEM

The fourth grade students at Fort Lowell Elementary School were excited. The results of the current fourth grade reading contest had just been posted.

CLASS	NO. OF STUDENTS READING MORE THAN 25 BOOKS	TOTAL NO. IN CLASS
Mr. Jones	13	26
Ms. Eby	14	35
Ms. Ballentine	8	24

For each class they figured out the fraction of good readers out of the whole class.

Mr. Jones: $\frac{13}{26} = \frac{1}{2}$
Ms. Eby: $\frac{14}{35} = \frac{2}{5}$
Ms. Ballentine: $\frac{8}{24} = \frac{1}{3}$

They compared these fractions and found that $\frac{1}{2}$ was biggest so that Mr. Jones's class was the fourth grade winner for Fort Lowell as far as reading went. They also knew that, since the classes were of different sizes, they were comparing these fractions as if they were comparing ratios, not as if they were comparing fractions as "amount of class." Now they are interested in another question: Knowing that $\frac{1}{2}$ of Mr. Jones's class consists of good readers and that $\frac{1}{3}$ of Ms. Ballentine's class consists of good readers, what fraction of the *combined* two classes consists of good readers? How can they solve this?

Three students in the fourth grade offer solutions.

Fritz offers this solution: "The fraction of Mr. Jones's class that consists of good readers is $\frac{1}{2}$. The fraction of Ms. Ballentine's class that consists of good readers is $\frac{1}{3}$. The fraction of the combined classes that consists of good readers should be $\frac{1}{2} + \frac{1}{3}$

and, using equal fractions, I get $\frac{1}{2} + \frac{1}{3} = \frac{3}{6} + \frac{2}{6} = \frac{5}{6}$. So $\frac{5}{6}$ of the combined classes should consist of good readers."

Jane puts her hand in, saying: "No, that's all wrong. The unit is the set of students in the *two* classes, not the set of students in one class. The $\frac{1}{2}$ of Mr. Jones's class is really $\frac{1}{4}$ of the two classes and the $\frac{1}{3}$ of Ms. Ballentine's class is really $\frac{1}{6}$ of the two classes. Let me draw you a picture.

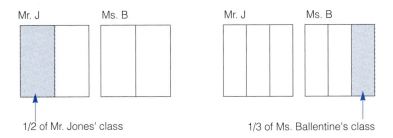

"So, to find out what fraction of the *two* classes consists of good readers, I add $\frac{1}{4}$ and $\frac{1}{6}$. Using equal fractions, I get $\frac{1}{4} + \frac{1}{6} = \frac{3}{12} + \frac{2}{12} = \frac{5}{12}$. That means that $\frac{5}{12}$ of the combined classes consists of good readers."

Antonio offers this solution: "If you don't mind my saying so, neither of you is right. You're treating all those ratios as if they were fractions, and you're getting some wrong answers. You're adding peaches to oranges and getting nonsense. Let's look at the data.

CLASS	NO. OF GOOD READERS	NO. IN CLASS
Jones	13	26
Ballentine	8	24
Total	21	50

As I see it, the combined class would have 50 students in it. Of those, 21 are good readers. Right? That means that the ratio of good readers to total number of students is 21 to 50, or $\frac{21}{50}$ of the students are good readers. Let's compare this with the fractions gotten by the other two methods.

$$\frac{21}{50} \text{ versus } \frac{5}{6}$$

$$\frac{21}{50} = \frac{21 \times 3}{50 \times 3} = \frac{63}{150} \qquad \text{versus} \qquad \frac{5}{6} = \frac{5 \times 25}{6 \times 25} = \frac{125}{150}$$

The two fractions $\frac{21}{50}$ and $\frac{5}{6}$ are not equal.

$$\frac{21}{50} \text{ versus } \frac{5}{12}$$

$$\frac{21}{50} = \frac{21 \times 6}{50 \times 6} = \frac{126}{300} \qquad \text{versus} \qquad \frac{5}{12} = \frac{5 \times 25}{12 \times 25} = \frac{125}{300}$$

The two fractions $\frac{21}{50}$ and $\frac{5}{12}$ aren't equal either. They're close, though!"

The Mathematical Idea: You Can't Add Ratios
in the Same Way You Add Fractions

Which of the three solutions above is correct? Fritz made an error about the unit for the fraction. He assumed that the unit was one class rather than two. Jane was a bit more subtle, but she assumed (erroneously) that all classes are the same size and wound up adding fractions of two different units. Antonio calculated the fraction directly, and his solution must be correct. The clue is that the fractions in question are fractions of different kinds. To compare them, you must compare them as ratios. Adding these ratios (as if they were fractions) doesn't make sense, as we have seen.

EXERCISE

7. Recall from earlier in the chapter that there are $\frac{2}{3}$ as many registered Republicans as Democrats in Green City and $\frac{3}{5}$ as many registered Republicans as Democrats in Brownsville. Figure out the ratio of registered Republicans to Democrats in the two cities combined. (To solve this, you may need to use information given in the ratio comparison problem.)

8.6   VISUALIZING FRACTIONS ON A NUMBER LINE

THE CITY-WIDE READING CONTEST PROBLEM

The fourth grade students at Fort Lowell Elementary have just seen the city-wide results for the fourth grade reading contest. Results for each class have been expressed as the fraction of the whole class consisting of good readers. Here are the fractions for the nine participating classes:

Fort Lowell: Jones $\frac{1}{2}$, Eby $\frac{1}{3}$, Ballentine $\frac{2}{5}$
Washington: Smith $\frac{4}{15}$, Garcia $\frac{3}{4}$, Hasselhoff $\frac{11}{30}$
Hughes: Thomas $\frac{3}{10}$, Schwartz $\frac{5}{12}$, Kopsky $\frac{3}{5}$

The students were trying to make sense of these scores. Each wanted to know how his or her class compared to all the other classes: How many were better? How many worse? The students in Mr. Jones's class—which did quite well city-wide—wanted to know how close their class was to its nearest competitors. The students in Ms. Ballentine's class—which didn't do well city-wide—wanted to know how close their score was to the lowest scores. They wanted a way to look at all the city scores so that they could answer these and similar questions easily. Can they find one?

One of the students *thought of a similar problem:* "A while ago, we were looking at the distances of the planets from the Sun and wanted to get some feeling for how everything was placed in the solar system. We *drew a picture,* a number line with the Sun at zero and each planet at the point on the line corresponding to its distance from the Sun. Those distances were all whole numbers. Now, we have fractions, but perhaps we could find a way to picture them on a number line."

Second student: "Let's draw a line. Since all of our fractions are less than 1, we can label one end 0 and the other 1.

|_____|
0   1

Let's start with the fraction $\frac{3}{4}$ (Garcia's score). Divide the unit length (between the points 0 and 1) into four equal lengths.

|_____|_____|_____|_____|
0   1

Each of the four equal lengths is $\frac{1}{4}$ of the unit length. If you start at 0 and measure off $\frac{1}{4}$, you get the first point. Label that point with $\frac{1}{4}$. Measure off a second $\frac{1}{4}$ from the first, getting a second point, which you label with $\frac{2}{4}$. Then measure off a third $\frac{1}{4}$ from the second point, getting a third point that you label with $\frac{3}{4}$.

|_____|_____|_____|_____|
0              $\frac{1}{4}$ $\frac{2}{4}$ $\frac{3}{4}$ 1

$\frac{4}{4}$

If you measure off a fourth $\frac{1}{4}$ from the third point, you get the point that is already labeled 1."

Third student: "The same idea will work with any fraction. Take $\frac{3}{5}$. Divide the unit length into 5 equal pieces. You'll get 4 points between 0 and 1. The third one from the left is the one corresponding to $\frac{3}{5}$.

|_____|_____|_____|_____|_____|
0         $\frac{1}{5}$ $\frac{2}{5}$ $\frac{3}{5}$ $\frac{4}{5}$ 1

$\frac{5}{5}$

Here's what it would look like on top of the picture with the $\frac{1}{4}$s."

|_____|__|_____|____|____|_____|__|_____|
0     $\frac{1}{5}$ $\frac{1}{4}$ $\frac{2}{5}$ $\frac{2}{4}$ $\frac{3}{5}$ $\frac{3}{4}$ $\frac{4}{5}$ 1

$\frac{5}{5}$

$\frac{4}{4}$

Fourth student: "It's beginning to look complicated. Is there a way to take what we have and add points for fractions without putting separate pictures together?"

Fifth student: "When we compare $\frac{3}{4}$ with $\frac{3}{5}$, we find a common multiple of 4 and 5—for example, 20. Then we convert $\frac{3}{4}$ and $\frac{3}{5}$ to $\frac{1}{20}$ths using equal fractions: $\frac{3}{4} = (3 \times 5)/(4 \times 5) = \frac{15}{20}, \frac{3}{5} = (3 \times 4)/(5 \times 4) = \frac{12}{20}$. Going from $\frac{1}{5}$s to $\frac{1}{20}$s amounts to dividing up each of the $\frac{1}{4}$s into 5 equal pieces. Let's do that and see what we get.

0 $\frac{1}{20}$ $\frac{2}{20}$ $\frac{3}{20}$ $\frac{4}{20}$ $\frac{5}{20}$ $\frac{6}{20}$ $\frac{7}{20}$ $\frac{8}{20}$ $\frac{9}{20}$ $\frac{10}{20}$ $\frac{11}{20}$ $\frac{12}{20}$ $\frac{13}{20}$ $\frac{14}{20}$ $\frac{15}{20}$ $\frac{16}{20}$ $\frac{17}{20}$ $\frac{18}{20}$ $\frac{19}{20}$ 1

$\frac{20}{20}$

$\frac{1}{5}$ $\frac{1}{4}$ $\frac{2}{5}$ $\frac{2}{4}$ $\frac{3}{5}$ $\frac{3}{4}$ $\frac{4}{5}$ $\frac{4}{4}$

$\frac{5}{5}$

You get different labels for the same point. See, $\frac{15}{20}$ and $\frac{3}{4}$ label the same point. The reason is that they are equal fractions."

Sixth student: "Now take $\frac{1}{3}$. A common denominator of $\frac{1}{3}$ and $\frac{1}{20}$ is 60. Using equal fractions, we have $\frac{1}{3} = (1 \times 20)/(3 \times 20) = \frac{20}{60}$. To add the $\frac{1}{60}$ths to the picture, we will have to divide each of the $\frac{1}{20}$ths into 3 equal pieces, dividing the unit length into 60 equal pieces. Here's the picture."

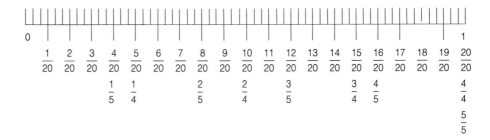

Seventh student: "I just noticed that it's easy to put the other fractions in the picture because they're all equal to fractions with the denominator 60. When all the fractions have the same denominator, then to picture them on the number line, all you have to do is line up the numerators as whole numbers."

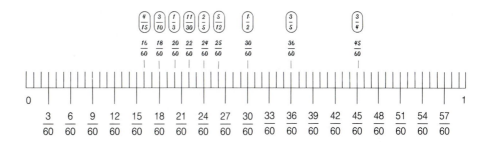

Eighth student: "Let's see how the various classes in the city did in the reading contest. The scores are spread between $\frac{4}{15}$ and $\frac{3}{4}$. Also, the winners did a lot better than Mr. Jones's class did—even though his class was third in the city. A lot of the scores are clustered very close to the score of Ms. Ballentine's class and those that are close are below it, so her kids shouldn't feel too bad."

The Mathematical Idea: Fractions on a Number Line

As you can see from the solution to the city-wide reading contest problem, it is useful to be able to associate a fraction with a point on a number line. It is especially useful when you have a set of fractions the relative sizes of which you want to compare: You do this by comparing their relative *positions* on the line. There is a conceptual bonus in associating fractions with points: You can observe that different labels for a point correspond to a fraction's different disguises amounting to equal fractions.

The use of the number line in the solution to the city-wide reading contest problem involved fractions between 0 and 1 only—so-called proper fractions. There is no difficulty in associating improper fractions with points on the number line; the idea is the same.

	$\frac{1}{4}$	$\frac{1}{2}$	$\frac{3}{4}$		$\frac{5}{4}$	$\frac{3}{2}$	$\frac{7}{4}$		$\frac{9}{4}$	$\frac{5}{2}$	$\frac{11}{4}$
0				1				2			

In a later chapter, we will use the number line a lot in working with decimal fractions.

EXERCISE 8. Here are some fictitious ratios—treated as fractions—of registered Republicans to Democrats in several southwestern states: Arizona: $\frac{2}{3}$; New Mexico: $\frac{2}{5}$; California: $\frac{5}{4}$; Nevada: $\frac{4}{5}$; Utah: $\frac{3}{2}$; Colorado: $\frac{5}{6}$. Place these fractions on a number line. On your line indicate the strongest and weakest Republican states in this group of states.

8.7 LOOKING BACK: GCDs, LCMs, AND FRACTIONS

From what we know about equal fractions, a given fractional quantity has several names. For example, $\frac{2}{3}$, $\frac{4}{6}$, $\frac{6}{9}$, $\frac{22}{33}$, $\frac{106}{159}$, and 10,000/15,000 are all names for the same quantity. Of all these names, $\frac{2}{3}$ is the most familiar, perhaps because its denominator is the smallest of all the fractions shown. There is no fraction equal to $\frac{2}{3}$ with a denominator smaller than 3. The reason for this is that the GCD of 2 and 3 is equal to 1. Indeed, if A/B is a fraction equal to $\frac{2}{3}$, i.e., $A/B = \frac{2}{3}$, then you know that $3A = 2B$. By the fundamental theorem of arithmetic you know that A must be a multiple of 2 and B must be a multiple of 3: $A = 2M$, $B = 3P$. In fact, $M = P$ and $A = 2M$, $B = 3M$. Any fraction equal to $\frac{2}{3}$ must have a denominator bigger than or equal to 3.

The same argument works for any fraction C/D that has the property that the GCD of C and D is equal to 1. (Two nonzero whole numbers the GCD of which is 1 are called *relatively prime*.)

A FRACTION IN LOWEST TERMS

Suppose that the GCD of C and D is 1. Then of all fractions equal to C/D, the fraction C/D has the smallest denominator. We call the fraction C/D a fraction *in lowest terms*.

Consider the fraction $\frac{54}{72}$. One reason it is not in lowest terms is because both 54 and 72 have a common divisor bigger than 1. In fact, $54 = 3 \cdot 18$, and $72 = 4 \cdot 18$, so that

$$\frac{54}{72} = \frac{3 \cdot 18}{4 \cdot 18} = \frac{3}{4}.$$

Since the GCD of 3 and 4 is 1, the fraction $\frac{3}{4}$ is in lowest terms. Since the number 18 is the GCD of 54 and 72, this suggests a general method, given a fraction E/F, for finding a fraction equal to E/F and in lowest terms.

REDUCING A FRACTION TO LOWEST TERMS

If E/F is a fraction, one method for finding a fraction equal to it that is in lowest terms is as follows. If E and F are relatively prime, then you are finished: E/F is in lowest terms. Otherwise, E and F have a common divisor $G > 1$. Then there are whole numbers J and K such that $E = JG$ and $F = KG$. Thus,

$$\frac{E}{F} = \frac{JG}{KG} = \frac{J}{K}.$$

If J and K are relatively prime, then you are finished. Otherwise, J and K have a common divisor bigger than 1, and you proceed as before. Eventually you will wind up with an equal fraction in lowest terms.

For example, to reduce $\frac{48}{72}$ to lowest terms, you notice that the 48 and 72 have 2 as a common divisor so

$$\frac{48}{72} = \frac{2 \times 24}{2 \times 36} = \frac{24}{36}.$$

But then 24 and 36 also have 2 as a common divisor.

$$\frac{24}{36} = \frac{2 \times 12}{2 \times 18} = \frac{12}{18}.$$

This time the numerator and denominator have 6 as a common divisor.

$$\frac{12}{18} = \frac{6 \times 2}{6 \times 3} = \frac{2}{3}.$$

You are finished, because 2 and 3 have no common divisor bigger than 1. Thus $\frac{48}{72} = \frac{2}{3}$.

EXERCISE 9. Reduce the fractions to lowest terms.
(a) $\frac{4}{18}$ (b) $\frac{21}{35}$ (c) $\frac{16}{88}$ (d) $\frac{96}{168}$ (e) 50,000/150,000

LCMs and Common Denominators

To add (or subtract or compare) $\frac{5}{6}$ with $\frac{3}{4}$, you replace each of $\frac{5}{6}$ and $\frac{3}{4}$ by an equal fraction, so that both of the replacements have the same denominator. This *common denominator* is a common multiple of the two initial denominators, in this case a common multiple of 6 and 4. To keep the common denominator small, a good choice is the LCM (least common multiple) of the two initial denominators. In the example, the LCM of 6 and 4 is 12.

$$\frac{5}{6} = \frac{5 \times 2}{6 \times 2} = \frac{10}{12} \quad \text{and} \quad \frac{3}{4} = \frac{3 \times 3}{4 \times 3} = \frac{9}{12}.$$

This LCM is the smallest possible common denominator, sometimes called the *least common denominator*. Using the LCM may help you keep fractions from getting too unwieldy. Here is a summary of the method.

FINDING COMMON DENOMINATORS USING THE LCM

Suppose that A/B and C/D are fractions and that you want to replace them by equal fractions having the *least common denominator*. Find the LCM of B and D and denote it by L. Find whole numbers N and M so that $L = BN = DM$. Then

$$\frac{AN}{BN} \quad \text{and} \quad \frac{CM}{DM}$$

are the two equal fractions having the least common denominator.

For example, to find fractions equal to $\frac{11}{15}$ and $\frac{7}{12}$ and having the least common denominator, you find that the LCM of 15 and 12 is 60. You also know that $15 \times 4 = 60$ and $12 \times 5 = 60$ (4 and 5 are the N and M in the description of finding common denominators using the LCM). Thus,

$$\frac{11}{15} = \frac{11 \times 4}{15 \times 4} = \frac{44}{60} \quad \text{and} \quad \frac{7}{12} = \frac{7 \times 5}{12 \times 5} = \frac{35}{60}.$$

The least common denominator is 60, and the two fractions are $\frac{44}{60}$ and $\frac{35}{60}$.

EXERCISE 10. For each pair find the least common denominator and replace each fraction by an equal fraction with that denominator.
(a) $\frac{7}{9}$ and $\frac{5}{12}$ (b) $\frac{3}{20}$ and $\frac{7}{8}$ (c) $\frac{4}{25}$ and $\frac{8}{15}$ (d) $\frac{16}{45}$ and $\frac{73}{150}$

8.8   LOOKING AHEAD: FORMAL PROPERTIES OF ADDITION OF FRACTIONS

If you add two fractions with the same denominator,

$$\frac{A}{B} + \frac{C}{B} = \frac{A + C}{B},$$

then—since whole number addition is commutative—$A + C = C + A$ and

$$\frac{A}{B} + \frac{C}{B} = \frac{C}{B} + \frac{A}{B}.$$

This means that fractions with the same denominator satisfy the commutative property of addition. When we add fractions, we replace them by equal fractions with the same denominator. Thus, we have the commutative property of addition of fractions.

COMMUTATIVE PROPERTY OF ADDITION OF FRACTIONS

Suppose that A/B and C/D are fractions. Then $A/B + C/D = C/D + A/B$.

Similarly, because addition of whole numbers is associative, we have the associative property of addition of fractions.

ASSOCIATIVE PROPERTY OF ADDITION OF FRACTIONS

Suppose that A/B, C/D, and E/F are fractions. Then $(A/B + C/D) + E/F = A/B + (C/D + E/F)$.

A fraction A/B is designated by two whole numbers A and B where $B \neq 0$. The fraction $0/B$ has a special property.

ADDITIVE IDENTITY FOR ADDITION OF FRACTIONS

Suppose that C/D is a fraction and that B is any nonzero whole number. Then $C/D + 0/B = C/D$. The fraction $0/B$ is called the *zero fraction*. For any nonzero whole number A, $0/A = 0/B$.

If N is a whole number, then the fraction $N/1$ is really the whole number N in disguise. The fraction $0/B = 0/1$ is an instance of this: The fraction $0/B$ is another name for the whole number 0. These facts are summarized in the following statement.

RELATIONSHIP BETWEEN WHOLE NUMBERS AND FRACTIONS

The set of whole numbers is a subset of the set of fractions.

8.9   EXTENDING THE IDEAS: ORDER, ADDITION, AND SUBTRACTION OF FRACTIONS ON A NUMBER LINE

We already know what the order relationship $A/B < C/D$ means for two fractions. Also, we have seen how a fraction can be identified with a point on a number line and that this gives us a way of visualizing the order relationship between fractions.

In this section we want to use the number line to visualize addition and subtraction of fractions and to explore connections between the order relationship and addition and subtraction of fractions, much the way we did earlier for whole numbers.

Fractions with the same denominator appear on a number line much as whole numbers do. For example, to place the fractions with denominator 12 on a number line you place $\frac{0}{12}, \frac{1}{12}, \frac{2}{12}, \frac{3}{12}, \ldots$ in order with the same space between them. (The space between consecutive twelfths is exactly $\frac{1}{12}$th the space between consecutive whole numbers!)

Comparing fractions with the same denominator on a number line is like comparing whole numbers. Given fractions A/B and C/B, the larger fraction is the one with the larger numerator and is the one that corresponds to the rightmost point on the number line.

Since adding (or subtracting) fractions with the same denominator amounts to adding (or subtracting) their whole number numerators, the *add-subtract slide rule* works for these fractions just as it did with whole numbers. For example, to add $\frac{7}{12}$ to $\frac{11}{12}$ you position the two slides like this

Then you find the sum as shown.

Since you normally change an addition (or subtraction or comparison) problem into one where the denominators are the same, addition (or subtraction or comparison)

of any two fractions on a number line can be carried out just as if those two fractions had the same denominator, hence, just as if they were two whole numbers.

COMPARISON OF FRACTIONS ON THE NUMBER LINE

If A/B and C/D are two fractions and $A/B < C/D$, then the two corresponding points on a number line should look like this.

ADDING AND SUBTRACTING FRACTIONS ON THE NUMBER LINE
USING THE ADD-SUBTRACT SLIDE RULE*

To find the sum $A/B + C/D$ on a number line, set the 0 of bottom line and the A/B of top line at the same position. Find the C/D of bottom line. Just above it on top line will be $A/B + C/D$.

If $C/D \leq A/B$, then to find the difference $A/B - C/D$ on the number line, set the 0 of bottom line on the A/B of top line at the same position. Find the C/D of top line. Just below it on bottom line will be $A/B - C/D$.

---

* An add-subtract slide rule to cut out and use can be found in the lab manual to accompany this text.

Because fractions and whole numbers behave in similar ways on a number line with respect to order, addition, and subtraction, fractions share many formal properties with whole numbers. We can summarize.

ORDER PROPERTIES OF FRACTIONS

TRICHOTOMY

For two fractions A/B and C/D, exactly one of the following must be true: $A/B < C/D$, $A/B = C/D$, or $C/D < A/B$.

DEFINITION OF ORDER OF FRACTIONS USING ADDITION

For fractions A/B and C/D, $A/B \leq C/D$ means that there is another fraction E/F such that $A/B + E/F = C/D$.

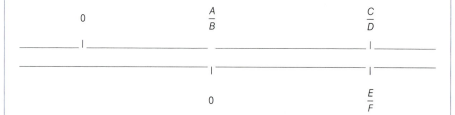

ORDER PROPERTIES OF ADDITION AND SUBTRACTION

Suppose that A/B, C/D, E/F, and G/H are fractions such that $A/B < C/D$ and $E/F < G/H$. Then also $A/B + E/F < C/D + G/H$. If, moreover, $G/H < A/B$, then also $A/B - G/H < C/D - E/F$.

EXERCISES

11. Draw pictures of points on a number line showing why the order properties of addition and subtraction are true. (*Hint:* Look at the solution to a similar problem: what was done in chap. 5 for order and whole number addition and subtraction.)

12. Draw pictures to show why the following property of order of fractions is true.

TRANSITIVITY OF ORDER OF FRACTIONS

Suppose that A/B, C/D, and E/F are fractions such that $A/B < C/D$ and $C/D < E/F$. Then also $A/B < E/F$.

Density of Fractions on a Number Line

Fractions and whole numbers on a number line have many properties in common, especially as related to order, addition, and subtraction. There is one way (at least) in which the set of fractions differs fundamentally from the set of whole numbers. It has to do with the number of whole numbers between a pair of whole numbers versus the number of fractions between a pair of fractions. Let's explore this idea a bit for some pairs of distinct whole numbers. Here is *a chart organizing what we get.*

PAIR OF WHOLE NUMBERS	NUMBERS BETWEEN THEM	HOW MANY NUMBERS BETWEEN THEM
3 and 5	4	1
3 and 10	4, 5, 6, 7, 8, 9	6
10 and 20	11, 12, 13, 14, 15, 16, 17, 18, 19	9
3 and 4	None	0
10 and 11	None	0

Here we see that between one pair of numbers there is 1 number, between another 6 numbers, and between yet another 0 numbers.

EXERCISES

13. Given whole numbers A and B with $A > B$. What is the relationship between the number of numbers between A and B and the numbers A and B themselves?

14. Given a whole number M, can you find a pair of whole numbers C and D such that the number of whole numbers between C and D is equal to M?

Now let's take a pair of fractions and look for the fractions between them. To be specific, take $\frac{1}{4}$ and $\frac{1}{2}$. What are the fractions between $\frac{1}{4}$ and $\frac{1}{2}$? One of them ought to be $\frac{1}{3}$: $\frac{1}{3} = \frac{4}{12}$, $\frac{1}{4} = \frac{3}{12}$, $\frac{1}{2} = \frac{6}{12}$ and $\frac{3}{12} < \frac{4}{12} < \frac{6}{12}$.

So $\frac{1}{3}$ is between $\frac{1}{4}$ and $\frac{1}{2}$. The inequality we just wrote suggests another: $\frac{3}{12} < \frac{4}{12} < \frac{5}{12} < \frac{6}{12}$.

That means that $\frac{5}{12}$ is also between $\frac{1}{4}$ and $\frac{1}{2}$. Using equal fractions, we can write this last inequality as $\frac{6}{24} < \frac{8}{24} < \frac{10}{24} < \frac{12}{24}$ so that also $\frac{6}{24} < \frac{7}{24} < \frac{8}{24} < \frac{9}{24} < \frac{10}{24} < \frac{11}{24} < \frac{12}{24}$.

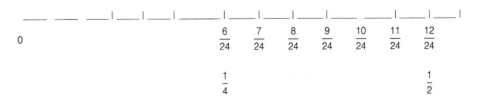

This gives us even more fractions between $\frac{1}{4}$ and $\frac{1}{2}$, namely, $\frac{7}{24}$, $\frac{9}{24}$, and $\frac{11}{24}$. What's going on here? We could do the same thing again (using equal fractions) to get

$\frac{12}{48} < \frac{14}{48} < \frac{16}{48} < \frac{18}{48} < \frac{20}{48} < \frac{22}{48} < \frac{24}{48}$, then by "filling in the spaces" get the following new fractions between $\frac{1}{4}$ $(= \frac{12}{48})$ and $\frac{1}{2}$ $(= \frac{24}{48})$: $\frac{13}{48}, \frac{15}{48}, \frac{17}{48}, \frac{19}{48}, \frac{21}{48}, \frac{23}{48}$. As a matter of fact, we could do it again and again and again and . . . We could continue the process forever and obtain infinitely many fractions between $\frac{1}{4}$ and $\frac{1}{2}$. This could never happen if you use just whole numbers. What we did can be done with any pair of distinct fractions. This property of the set of fractions is called its *density* in the number line.

DENSITY PROPERTY OF FRACTIONS

Given fractions A/B and C/D such that $A/B < C/D$, there is a third fraction E/F such that $A/B < E/F < C/D$. Here is a way to find such a third fraction when the denominators are the same: If $A/B < C/B$, then also $2A/2B < 2C/2B$ and

$$\frac{2A}{2B} < \frac{2A + 1}{2B} < \frac{2C}{2B}$$

So $\dfrac{2A + 1}{2B}$ is a fraction between A/B and C/D.

A way to find a third fraction when the denominators are *not* the same is to replace the two fractions by equal fractions with common denominators and use the method just given.

Once you have found a fraction A between X and Y, then you can find another B between X and A, then C between X and B, and so on.

EXERCISES

15. Find a fraction between $\frac{3}{4}$ and $\frac{7}{8}$.

16. Find a fraction between $\frac{37}{124}$ and $\frac{48}{201}$.

17. Find three distinct fractions between $\frac{7}{8}$ and 1.

8.10   SUMMARY OF IMPORTANT IDEAS AND TECHNIQUES

- That two fractions representing the same quantity are called *equal*
- Of all fractions equal to a given fraction, how to find the one with the smallest denominator by reducing it to lowest terms
- Addition and subtraction of fractions
- The ease of comparing, adding, and subtracting fractions when they have common denominators
- Methods for finding fractions A/B and C/D equal to these and having common denominators:
  Using BD as common denominator
  Using LCM of B and D as common denominator
- Special types of fractions: improper fractions and mixed numbers; special fractions: zero fraction; whole numbers as fractions

- The utility of expressing the answer to a whole number division problem as a fraction:
  $A \div B = A/B$
- Commutative and associative properties of addition of fractions; 0 as an additive identity
- How ratio and fractions are related
- When two ratios are equal
- When one ratio is larger than another
- Alternate expressions for the same ratio
- That ratios can't always be added as if they were fractional quantities
- Visualizing fractions on the number line
- Visualization of order relation between fractions
- Visualization of addition and subtraction of fractions using add-subtract slide rule
- Formal order properties of fractions with respect to addition and subtraction
- A way in which the set of fractions and the set of whole numbers differ: density of fractions on the number line

PROBLEM SET

PRACTICING
SKILLS

1. Which of the following pairs of fractions are equal?
   (a) $\frac{5}{6}$ and $\frac{15}{18}$ (b) $\frac{15}{20}$ and $\frac{24}{32}$ (c) $\frac{0}{3}$ and $\frac{0}{1}$ (d) $\frac{3}{4}$ and $\frac{3}{5}$

2. Which of the two fractions in each pair is larger?
   (a) $\frac{3}{4}$ or $\frac{5}{7}$ (b) $\frac{2}{9}$ or $\frac{3}{11}$ (c) $\frac{5}{6}$ or $\frac{8}{9}$ (d) $\frac{17}{30}$ or $\frac{13}{24}$

3. Convert the following improper fractions to mixed fractions.
   (a) $\frac{57}{3}$ (b) $\frac{12}{2}$ (c) $\frac{5721}{1000}$ (d) $\frac{5721}{100}$

4. Convert the following mixed fractions to improper fractions.
   (a) $2\frac{3}{4}$ (b) $5\frac{1}{3}$ (c) $3\frac{7}{10}$ (d) $5\frac{721}{1000}$

5. Add the following fractions.
   (a) $\frac{1}{5} + \frac{1}{6}$ (b) $\frac{1}{6} + \frac{11}{18}$ (c) $\frac{5}{9} + \frac{8}{15}$ (d) $\frac{5}{28} + \frac{5}{24}$ (e) $\frac{3}{11} + \frac{0}{8}$

6. Subtract the following fractions.
   (a) $\frac{2}{5} - \frac{1}{3}$ (b) $\frac{13}{24} - \frac{3}{8}$ (c) $\frac{7}{12} - \frac{7}{18}$ (d) $\frac{5}{36} - \frac{4}{45}$

7. You know that you have $1\frac{1}{2}$ rolls of high quality white paper in stock. You have three printing jobs today that will require you to use this paper. One job requires $\frac{1}{4}$ roll, the second requires $\frac{2}{5}$ of a roll, and the third requires $\frac{2}{3}$ of a roll. Will you have enough paper for the three jobs? If you do, how much paper will be left? If you don't, how much more paper will you need?

8. You take a metal strip 45 in long from inventory. From this you cut three smaller strips having lengths $12\frac{3}{4}$ in, $15\frac{1}{8}$ in, and $11\frac{2}{3}$ in. You waste $\frac{1}{8}$ in of the strip for each cut. You return what is left to inventory. You must record on an inventory form the length of the strip that you return. What do you record?

9. (a) You are going to give 56 turkeys equally to 6 shelters. How many turkeys should each shelter receive?

   (b) The third grade class has collected $9.00 to purchase pumpkins to decorate their classroom for Halloween. Pumpkins cost $ .70 apiece. How many pumpkins can they buy?

   (c) The Gonzales family purchased 12 small rosewood bushes to plant along a straight stretch of the southern boundary of the family's property. The stretch is 75 ft. They plan to plant them so that they are equally spaced and with a bush at each extreme end of the row. The family wants to know how many feet should be between each bush. What is it?

10. A current flu strain seems to be particularly prevalent among young grade school children. The health department is comparing the strength of the epidemic among first graders in two schools at opposite ends of town. Here are the results.

SCHOOL	INFECTED	HEALTHY
Northside	54	99
Southside	44	110

   (a) Find the ratio of infected to healthy for each school.
   (b) Which school has the greater ratio of infected to healthy?
   (c) Find the ratio of infected to healthy for the two schools combined.

11. In the first month of the season, Joe was at bat 20 times and made 11 hits, so his batting average for that month was $\frac{11}{20}$. In the second month he was at bat 15 times and made 7 hits, so his average for the second month was $\frac{7}{15}$. Which was his better month? What was his batting average for the two months?

12. (a) If there are $\frac{3}{4}$ as many boys as girls in a class, and there are 12 boys, how many children are in the class?

   (b) At a concert, there are $\frac{2}{3}$ as many boys as girls and $\frac{3}{4}$ as many girls as adults. If 48 adults are at the concert, how many children are there?

   (c) Ms. Jones reports that there are $\frac{4}{5}$ as many girls as boys in the school choir, and she requests that 8 more girls be added to equalize the sexes. How large will the equalized choir be?

13. For nine Midwestern schools suppose that the following are ratios of the number of students enrolled in a undergraduate liberal arts program, such as mathematics or French, to the number enrolled in a nonliberal arts undergraduate program, such as engineering or nursing:
   Ohio State: $\frac{5}{4}$; University of Wisconsin: $\frac{2}{1}$; Indiana University: $\frac{2}{3}$; University of Illinois: $\frac{5}{6}$; University of Iowa: $\frac{7}{6}$; University of Nebraska: $\frac{3}{5}$; University of Minnesota: $\frac{4}{5}$; University of Michigan: $\frac{7}{3}$; Michigan State: $\frac{7}{12}$.

   (a) Put these fractions (ratios) on a number line.
   (b) What is the smallest ratio? The largest ratio?
   (c) What school is closest to being evenly balanced in the liberal arts/nonliberal arts enrollment?

14. Reduce each fraction to its lowest terms.
   (a) $\frac{21}{27}$ (b) $\frac{24}{56}$ (c) $\frac{84}{108}$ (d) $\frac{12,000}{32,000}$

15. Replace each pair of fractions by an equal pair having the least common denominator.
   (a) $\frac{5}{12}$ and $\frac{8}{15}$ (b) $\frac{25}{42}$ and $\frac{7}{24}$ (c) $\frac{16}{33}$ and $\frac{30}{121}$ (d) $\frac{10}{21}$ and $\frac{18}{26}$

16. (a) Find a fraction between $\frac{1}{3}$ and $\frac{2}{9}$.
   (b) Find a fraction between $\frac{31}{116}$ and $\frac{32}{115}$.
   (c) Find three distinct fractions between $\frac{63}{32}$ and 2.

17. Each of the following is a sentence involving a fraction and pictures. Fill in the missing part to each sentence.

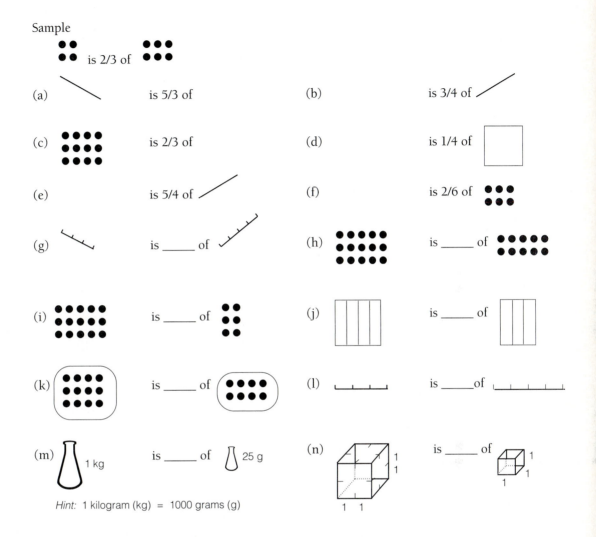

Sample

••
•• is 2/3 of •••
 •••

(a) ⟍   is 5/3 of   (b)   is 3/4 of ⟋

(c) ••••   is 2/3 of   (d)   is 1/4 of ☐

(e)   is 5/4 of ⟋   (f)   is 2/6 of •••

(g) ⟍   is ____ of ⟋   (h)   is ____ of

(i)   is ____ of   (j)   is ____ of

(k)   is ____ of   (l)   is ____ of

(m) 1 kg   is ____ of 25 g   (n)   is ____ of

Hint: 1 kilogram (kg) = 1000 grams (g)

USING IDEAS   *For each of the remaining problems, describe as clearly and completely as you can your solution to the problem. Include the steps you took to solve the problem, mention the problems or solutions from the text that gave you ideas, and include the problem-solving strategies you used. You might want to outline and organize these details before assembling your final description in the form of an essay.*

18. In each of the following a unit and a pair of fractions (of that unit) is given. For each, draw an appropriate picture showing why the two fractions (of that unit) are equal.
   (a) $\frac{3}{4}, \frac{9}{12}$, pie   (b) $\frac{10}{15}, \frac{8}{12}$, mile
   (c) $\frac{3}{8}, \frac{6}{16}$, cup of milk   (d) $\frac{6}{10}, \frac{9}{15}$, square yard

19. A wheat farmer has 5 dairy cows to supply the family's needs for dairy products. Whatever is left over is sold to the local dairy. Here is last week's production: Cow 1 produced $6\frac{3}{4}$ gal of milk; 2 produced $5\frac{1}{3}$ gal; 3 produced $5\frac{2}{3}$ gal; 4 gave $5\frac{1}{4}$ gal; and 5 produced $3\frac{5}{6}$ gal. The farmer saves out 3 qt per day for her family. How much milk did she sell to the dairy last week?

20. In a load of 264 tons of ore there is only $\frac{3}{8}$ as much iron (by weight) as there is waste. How much iron is in the load?

21. A box of firecrackers is $\frac{1}{8}$ duds. There are 120 more good firecrackers than duds. How many duds are in the box?

22. Two-thirds of the people in Switzerland speak German, $\frac{7}{12}$ speak French, and $\frac{1}{4}$ speak Italian.
    (a) What is the smallest fraction of the population that could speak all three languages?
    (b) What is the largest fraction of the population that could speak all three languages?*

23. In a cross-country motorcycle race across Avra Valley, it is 70 mi to the flag and 70 mi back. Alice averages 80 mph going out, but then with clutch trouble can only manage 60 mph coming back. Sally can only manage 70 mph but maintains this for the entire race. Who wins the race?

24. A fishery biologist wants to estimate the number of bass fish in a lake. To do this, he takes a sample of 250 bass from the lake, marks them, and returns them to the lake. In 2 weeks' time, he assumes that the marked bass have pretty much evenly distributed themselves around the lake. He takes another sample of 160 bass and finds that 25 of them have been marked. His method of estimating the whole population is this: He assumes that the ratio of the total number of marked fish (250) to the whole population is the same as the ratio of marked fish in his sample (25) to the total number of fish in the sample (160). What is his estimate of the whole population of bass fish in the lake?

25. Wires carrying electricity are often placed in a protective steel pipe called *conduit*. A wiring job calls for 32 pieces of conduit $7\frac{1}{2}$ ft long, 3 pieces $7\frac{3}{4}$ in. long, 8 pieces $13\frac{1}{4}$ in long, and 6 pieces $9\frac{5}{8}$ in long.
    (a) Conduit comes in standard lengths of 10 ft. How many such lengths are needed for this job?
    (b) How should the 10-ft lengths in part (a) be cut in order that there be as little waste as possible? Pieces of less than 2 ft in length are considered waste. Try to cut the 10-ft lengths so that there are as few pieces left with length less than 2 ft as possible.†

26. Find the length of a bolt that will go through a piece of tubing with $\frac{1}{2}$ in outside diameter, a washer $\frac{1}{16}$ in thick, a piece of tubing with $\frac{3}{4}$ in outside diameter, another washer, and a nut $\frac{3}{16}$ in thick.

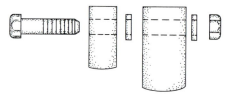

27. You want to frame a matted photograph measuring 16 by 20 inches, using framing material the cross section of which is as shown. You plan to add an additional $\frac{1}{16}$ inch to length and width to permit the photograph to fit easily into the frame.
    (a) What should the finished outside dimension of the frame be?

* From Deborah Hughes Hallett, *The Math Workshop: Algebra*, Norton, New York, prob. 41, p. 41.
† From D. Bushaw et al., *A Sourcebook of Applications of School Mathematics,* National Council of Teachers of Mathematics, Reston, Va., prob. 1. 17, p. 26.

(b) Is an 80-in piece of frame material long enough? (Each cut your saw makes eats up $\frac{1}{8}$ in of the length.)

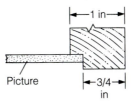

Picture

28. To "push" Kodak Tri-X (ASA rating of 400) film to an ASA rating of 800, you can use 1 part AGFA Rodinal developer and 50 parts water. How much developer will you need to make 240 ml of working solution?

29. A painter has formed a light pink by mixing 4 parts white with 1 part red. There are 2 liters of a darker pink that is half red and half white. How much white should be added to the darker pink to convert it to the lighter pink?

MULTIPLICATION AND DIVISION OF FRACTIONS

C H A P T E R **9**

In this chapter we will look at several problems in which fractions occur but which call for different types of solutions than those that appeared in the previous chapter. At first glance, the problems in this chapter seem to be unrelated. After a while some similarities appear— similarities in the ways the problems are solved. These similarities lead to the notions of multiplication and division of fractions. Since it is important to know how and when to use these concepts in solving problems, it is helpful to be aware of the problems that gave birth to the concepts in the first place. It is also important to remember that the concepts serve the problems rather than the other way around: The problems are not just examples of the uses of the concepts.

We will also continue the discussion of ratios begun in chapter 9, expanding on the situations in which the notion of ratio can be useful and connecting it with the multiplication and division of fractions discussed in the rest of the chapter.

MULTIPLICATION OF FRACTIONS

Please try this first.

The students in the sixth grade are making simple packs out of lightweight canvas for carrying books and other school items. Each pack requires $\frac{3}{4}$ yd of the canvas material. The students have been given the problem of finding the total length of canvas material needed for making 27 packs, one for each person in the class. The students have had experience comparing, adding, and subtracting fractions. Help them solve this problem.

A Solution to the
Book Pack Problem

The students quickly realize that the answer can be gotten by the repeated addition of $\frac{3}{4}$ twenty-seven times and that, since all the fractions being added are the same, they also have the same denominator. They deduce from this that the answer is a fraction the numerator of which is 3 added to itself 27 times and the denominator of which is 4; that is, the fraction is $(27 \times 3)/4$. From this they carry out the following computations to get the answer they want: $(27 \times 3)/4 = \frac{81}{4} = 20\frac{1}{4}$ (yd).

The Mathematical Idea: Repeated Addition of Fractions

The book pack problem was solved by repeated addition of the fraction $\frac{3}{4}$ twenty-seven times. The answer is $(27 \times 3)/4$. The general rule is the following.

REPEATED ADDITION OF FRACTIONS

If A/B is a fraction and N a whole number, then

$$\underbrace{\frac{A}{B} + \frac{A}{B} + \cdots + \frac{A}{B}}_{N \text{ times}} = \frac{NA}{B}.$$

Because repeated addition of whole numbers corresponds to multiplication of whole numbers, we can define the product of a whole number with a fraction.

MULTIPLICATION OF A FRACTION BY A WHOLE NUMBER

The *product* of whole number N with fraction A/B is written $N\left(\dfrac{A}{B}\right)$ and is equal to $\dfrac{NA}{B}$.

---

1. A certain recipe for a single cake calls for $\frac{2}{3}$ cup of milk. You are organizing a banquet at which 16 cakes will be needed. How much milk will you need for all these cakes?

During an orientation program at the beginning of the school year, the seventh graders were told that of all seventh graders who had entered the school in the past only $\frac{8}{15}$ eventually graduated. The students were interested in answering this question: If that trend were to continue, how many of the 135 students present at the program would eventually graduate? Help them solve this problem.

A Solution to the Graduation Prediction Problem

To solve this, the students realize that they must divide the set of 135 students up into 15 (disjoint) subsets with the same number of students in each and then take the union of 8 of those 15 subsets. Dividing 135 by 15, they get 9. That means that $\frac{1}{15}$ of 135 is 9. Taking 8 of these $\frac{1}{15}$ths, they get $8 \times 9 = 72$. So 72 of the 135 would eventually graduate if the trend continues.

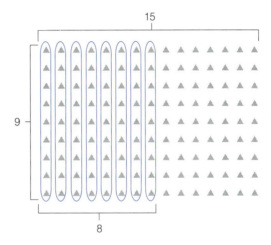

The Mathematical Idea: A Fraction of a Whole Number

The students solved this problem: If a set with 135 elements is the unit, what is $\frac{8}{15}$ of the unit? To solve it, you first find $135 \div 15$ and then you take 8 of what you get; that is, you repeatedly add $\frac{135}{15}$ eight times. The answer is $8 \times \left(\frac{135}{15}\right)$.

A FRACTION OF A WHOLE NUMBER

If the unit is a whole number quantity N, then the fraction A/B of the unit is $N(A/B) = (NA)/B$.

EXERCISE

2. It is estimated that $\frac{2}{3}$ of the owners of your town's businesses are Republicans. In a certain service club there are 96 members. If the club's makeup reflects that of all business owners in the town, how many of its members should be Republicans?

In the restoration of an antique picture frame a small rectangular area must be recovered with gold leaf. The cost of gold plating is $30 per square inch of surface. The rectangle measures $\frac{3}{4}$ by $\frac{2}{5}$ in. You want to know how much the gold leaf will cost you. You know about fractions, equivalent fractions, and how to add, subtract, and compare fractions. But that's all.

A Solution to the Gold Leaf Problem

You figure out that you must find the area of the rectangle. Toward this end you *draw a picture.*

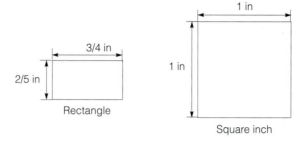

Your idea is to find out what fraction the area of the rectangle is of the square inch. You think: "If the rectangle had half the area of the square inch, then the cost would be half as much, or $15; if the rectangle had the area of $\frac{1}{3}$ square inch, then the cost would be $\frac{1}{3}$ as much, or $10.

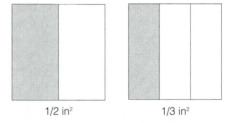

One of the sides of the rectangle is $\frac{3}{4}$ in. Let's divide a square inch up into $\frac{1}{4}$s like this

and then mark the width of the rectangle.

The other side of the rectangle is $\frac{2}{5}$ in. I can divide the square inch into $\frac{1}{5}$s in the other direction, then mark the length of the other side of the rectangle.

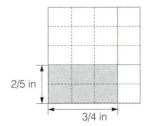

I can see the rectangle sitting inside the square inch. The lines I've drawn turn the square inch into a 5 by 4 array of little rectangles. All the little rectangles have the same area, and there are $5 \times 4 = 20$ of them, so each one must have an area of $\frac{1}{20}$ square inch. Now, all I have to do is count the number of little rectangles that appear in the rectangle. The lines divide the rectangle up into a 2 by 3 array of the same little rectangles, each one $\frac{1}{20}$ square inch. There are $2 \times 3 = 6$ of them in the rectangle. So the area of the rectangle is $\frac{6}{20}$ square inch."

EXERCISE   3. Complete the solution to the gold leaf problem by computing the cost of the gold leaf covering the rectangle.

THE ALCOHOL/TOBACCO CONSUMPTION PROBLEM

It is estimated that $\frac{2}{7}$ of the parents of school-age children smoke. It is also estimated that $\frac{4}{5}$ of those who smoke also consume alcohol. You want to know what fraction of the parents do both: smoke *and* consume alcohol. You know about fractions, equivalent fractions, and how to add, subtract, and compare fractions. You have also solved the gold leaf problem. But that's all. Can you solve this?

You think: "Maybe I can *use the solution to another problem.* I solved the gold leaf problem by showing how the rectangle fit into the square inch, the unit. Now the unit is the collection of all parents. Let me *draw a picture* of this unit—representing it by a square—and try to solve the problem as we did the gold leaf problem.

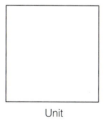

Unit

Some part of this square should represent the parents who smoke. I know that they amount to $\frac{2}{7}$ of the unit. Let me divide the unit into seven equal pieces, two of which represent the parents who smoke.

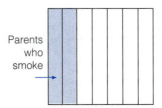

Parents who smoke

I'm interested in $\frac{4}{5}$ of those folk. Just as in the solution to the gold leaf problem, let's divide up the unit horizontally into five equal strips.

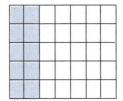

The horizontal lines also divide the smoking parents into five equal pieces. I'm interested in four of those. This represents a part of the unit corresponding to the parents who smoke *and* drink. That's the doubly shaded part of the picture.

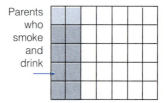

Now, to determine what fraction the doubly shaded part is of the whole square (the unit), I notice that the vertical and horizontal lines divide the unit into a 5 by 7 array of equal pieces. It divides the part representing parents who smoke *and* drink into a 4 by 2 array of those same equal pieces. Each one of those equal pieces is $1/(5 \times 7) = \frac{1}{35}$ of the unit. Parents who smoke *and* drink make up $2 \times 4 = 8$ of these $\frac{1}{35}$ths, or $\frac{8}{35}$ of all the parents (the unit)."

The Mathematical Idea: Multiplication of Fractions

Consider the two problems we have just worked:

- The gold leaf problem: The area of a rectangle of size $\frac{3}{4}$ by $\frac{2}{5}$ in equals $(3 \times 2)/(4 \times 5)$ square inch.

- The alcohol/tobacco consumption problem: $\frac{4}{5}$ of $\frac{2}{7}$ of a unit (that is, all the parents) equals $(4 \times 2)/(5 \times 7)$ of the unit.

What we observed were instances of two general rules:

1. The area of a rectangle of width A/B of an inch and length C/D of an inch is $\dfrac{AC}{BD}$ square inch.

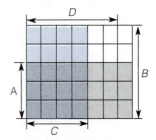

2. Given a fraction A/B of a unit, then the fraction C/D of A/B is the following fraction of the unit: $\dfrac{AC}{BD}$.

Because $(AC)/(BD)$ is the answer to so many problems that include the fractions A/B and C/D as part of their data, we make the following definition.

DEFINITION OF MULTIPLICATION OF FRACTIONS

$(AC)/(BD)$ is the *product* of A/B and C/D. We write

$$\frac{A}{B} \times \frac{C}{D} = \left(\frac{A}{B}\right)\left(\frac{C}{D}\right) = \frac{A}{B} \cdot \frac{C}{D} = \frac{AC}{BD}.$$

We also say that $(AC)/(BD)$ is the result of *multiplying A/B times C/D*.

This definition of multiplication is consistent with the multiplication of a fraction by a whole number, provided we make the following agreement. We have already included whole numbers as fractions: $1 = \frac{2}{2}$, $3 = \frac{12}{4}$, and so on. One can also think of a whole number N as the fraction $N/1$ so that, for example, $1 = \frac{1}{1}$ and $3 = \frac{3}{1}$. This is consistent with the fraction $N/1$ being the answer to the whole number division problem $N \div 1$. Agreeing to write $N = N/1$ enables us to rewrite the equation

$$N\left(\frac{A}{B}\right) = \frac{NA}{B}$$

as

$$\left(\frac{N}{1}\right)\left(\frac{A}{B}\right) = \frac{N \times A}{1 \times B}$$

and thus to see that multiplication of a fraction by a whole number is an instance of the multiplication of two fractions.

The book pack and the graduation prediction problems can be solved using multiplication of fractions, thusly:

- The book pack problem: Repeated addition of $\frac{3}{4}$ twenty-seven times equals $(27 \times 3)/4 = (27 \times 3)/(1 \times 4) = \left(\frac{27}{1}\right)\left(\frac{3}{4}\right)$.
- The graduation prediction problem: The unit is the set of 135 individual students; $\frac{8}{15}$ of the unit consists of $(8 \times 135)/15$ individual students. What is more, $(8 \times 135)/15 = (8 \times 135)/(15 \times 1) = \left(\frac{8}{15}\right)\left(\frac{135}{1}\right)$.

Here is another problem in which some of these ideas are used.

Your car gets $15\frac{2}{3}$ mi/gal. You have just put $5\frac{3}{4}$ gal of gasoline into an empty tank. You want to know how far you can go on that amount of gas. You know all about multiplication of fractions. How would you solve this?

Try this.

A Solution to the Gas Tank Problem

You think: "Each gallon will enable me to go $15\frac{2}{3}$ miles. So 5 gallons should enable me to go $5 \times 15\frac{2}{3}$ miles. I know how to figure that out:

$$5 \times 15\tfrac{2}{3} = 5 \times \frac{47}{3} = \frac{5 \times 47}{3} = \frac{235}{3} = 78\tfrac{1}{3} \text{ (miles)}.$$

"But what about that extra $\frac{3}{4}$ gallon? If I can go $15\frac{2}{3}$ miles with 1 gallon, then I should be able to go $\frac{3}{4}$ of $15\frac{2}{3}$ miles with $\frac{3}{4}$ gallon. How do I figure out $\frac{3}{4}$ of a unit when the unit is an improper fraction? Let me *draw a picture.*

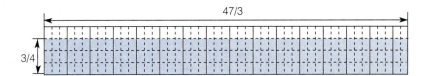

"Each teeny rectangle in the picture represents $\frac{1}{12}$ gallon. There are $3 \times 47 = 141$ of these teeny rectangles in the part of the picture that represents $\frac{3}{4}$ of $\frac{47}{3}$. Thus $\frac{3}{4}$ of $\frac{47}{3}$ equals $\frac{141}{12}$. Moreover,

$$\frac{141}{12} = \frac{3 \times 47}{4 \times 3} = \frac{3}{4} \times \frac{47}{3}.$$

Multiplication of fractions is appropriate even when the fractions are improper.
"The complete answer to the problem is this:

$$\frac{235}{3} + \frac{141}{12} = \frac{235 \times 4}{3 \times 4} + \frac{141}{12}$$

$$= \frac{940}{12} + \frac{141}{12}$$

$$= \frac{1081}{12}$$

$$= 90\frac{1}{12}$$

I can go $90\frac{1}{12}$ miles with $5\frac{3}{4}$ gallons of gasoline."

The Mathematical Idea: Some Properties of Multiplication of Fractions

The solution to the gas tank problem could have been solved directly this way: The answer is just the product of the fraction $15\frac{2}{3}$ and the fraction $5\frac{3}{4}$,

$$15\frac{2}{3} \times 5\frac{3}{4} = \frac{47}{3} \times \frac{23}{4} = \frac{47 \times 23}{3 \times 4} = \frac{1081}{12} = 90\frac{1}{12}.$$

Jim, who was the person solving the problem, may have hesitated to use this solution because he felt more comfortable *breaking the problem up into smaller ones* (not at all a bad strategy) or he was not sure that the rules for multiplication of fractions applied to mixed numbers. Indeed, the examples that led up to the definition of fraction multiplication involved factors neither of which were mixed numbers. In any case, Jim's solution shows that repeated addition of $15\frac{2}{3}$ five times is

$$5 \times \frac{47}{3} = \frac{5}{1} \times \frac{47}{3}$$

and that $\frac{3}{4}$ of $15\frac{2}{3}$ is the same as

$$\frac{3}{4} \times \frac{47}{3}.$$

Jim then added these two together to get the answer. We now know that the sum of these two is just $5\frac{3}{4} \times 15\frac{2}{3}$. In other words,

$$\left(5\frac{3}{4}\right)\left(15\frac{2}{3}\right) = \left(\frac{5}{1} + \frac{3}{4}\right)\frac{47}{3} = \left(\frac{5}{1}\right)\left(\frac{47}{3}\right) + \left(\frac{3}{4}\right)\left(\frac{47}{3}\right).$$

From the chapter on multiplication of whole numbers, you recognize that the latter equation is an instance of the distributive law for fractions.

MULTIPLICATION OF FRACTIONS DISTRIBUTES OVER ADDITION OF FRACTIONS

For all fractions A/B, C/D, and E/F,

$$\left(\frac{A}{B} + \frac{C}{D}\right)\frac{E}{F} = \left(\frac{A}{B}\right)\left(\frac{E}{F}\right) + \left(\frac{C}{D}\right)\left(\frac{E}{F}\right).$$

There are two more rules that are useful in working with fractions.

MULTIPLICATION OF FRACTIONS IS COMMUTATIVE

For all fractions A/B and C/D,

$$\frac{A}{B} \cdot \frac{C}{D} = \frac{C}{D} \cdot \frac{A}{B}.$$

MULTIPLICATION OF FRACTIONS IS ASSOCIATIVE

For all fractions A/B, C/D, and E/F,

$$\left(\frac{A}{B} \cdot \frac{C}{D}\right)\frac{E}{F} = \frac{A}{B}\left(\frac{C}{D} \cdot \frac{E}{F}\right).$$

EXERCISES

4. A certain kitchen counter-top material is sold by the square foot. How many square feet are there in a piece of material $1\frac{2}{3}$ by $3\frac{3}{4}$ ft?

5. Market researchers claim that $\frac{3}{8}$ of all adults use Fluorana regularly. Dental researchers claim that of all adults who use Fluorana regularly $\frac{2}{5}$ experience significant reduction in tooth decay. What fraction of the adult population experiences significant reduction in tooth decay while using Fluorana?

6. A woman who hikes at the rate of $2\frac{1}{3}$ mph has been hiking for $3\frac{5}{6}$ h (or 3 h and 50 min). How far has she hiked during that time?

9.2   DIVISION OF FRACTIONS

Four Partially Solved Missing Factor Problems

Each of the following four problems has an incomplete solution. To complete each, one must find a fraction (?) satisfying an equation of the form $\dfrac{A}{B} \times (?) = \dfrac{C}{D}$.

1. THE SHIRT PROBLEM

The Hathaway Shirt Company has $5\frac{2}{3}$ yd left of a special oxford cloth. The foreman in charge wants to know how many shirts the company can make with this material. Each shirt requires $\frac{3}{4}$ yd of the material. Help the foreman solve this problem.

A Partial Solution to the Shirt Problem

The foreman realizes that if N is the number of shirts that can be made, then N is the number of times that $\frac{3}{4}$ can be subtracted from $5\frac{2}{3}$. From this he concludes that $5\frac{2}{3} = \frac{3}{4} \times N$ plus whatever is left over (less than $\frac{3}{4}$ yd).

2. THE FENCE PROBLEM

The fence in your backyard needs to be painted. You have a gallon of fencing paint. The label on the can says 1 gal will paint 100 ft^2 of fence. Your fence is $5\frac{3}{4}$ ft high. How many feet along the fence can you paint with the 1 gal?

A Partial Solution to the Fence Problem

You *draw a picture* of your fence.

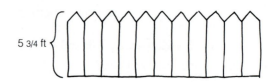

5 3/4 ft

You think: If I can paint (?) feet along the fence, then I know that the area I paint will be equal to 100 square feet. That means $5\frac{3}{4} \times$ (?) $= 100$.

3. THE BILINGUAL PROBLEM   It is estimated that $\frac{3}{8}$ of the population of the city speak both Spanish and English. It is also estimated that $\frac{9}{10}$ of those who speak Spanish also speak English. You want to know what fraction of the population speaks Spanish.

A Partial Solution to the Bilingual Problem   You *draw a picture* (a square) of the unit, the entire population of the city.

Inside the square you draw a circle representing the fraction $\frac{3}{8}$ of the population.

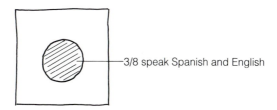

—3/8 speak Spanish and English

You want to indicate the fraction S of the population who speak Spanish. You know that this part must include the $\frac{3}{8}$ who speak *both* Spanish and English. You draw a larger circle inside the square that encloses the smaller one you have just drawn.

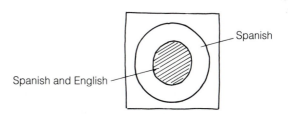

Spanish

Spanish and English

Now you look at the other piece of information that you have: $\frac{9}{10}$ of the Spanish-speaking population also speaks English. *That* would be the $\frac{3}{8}$ you've got drawn in. So if S is the fraction in the larger circle, then

$$\frac{9}{10} \text{ of } S = \frac{3}{8} \quad \text{or} \quad \frac{9}{10} \times S = \frac{3}{8}.$$

4. THE ARTICHOKE PROBLEM   You know that a $7\frac{3}{4}$-oz jar of marinated artichoke hearts costs $\$6\frac{1}{2}$. You are comparison shopping and you want to know how much 1 oz costs.

You figure out that if the answer were C dollars, then C times $7\frac{3}{4}$ would equal $6\frac{1}{2}$.

$$7\frac{3}{4} \times C = 6\frac{1}{2}.$$

The Mathematical Idea: Solving Missing Factor Problems

The solution to all four of these problems can be cast in this form: Given fractions A/B and C/D, find a fraction S such that

$$\frac{A}{B} \times S = \frac{C}{D}.$$

Such a problem is called a *missing factor* problem, in which the product and one of the factors of a multiplication problem are given. Such situations arise often enough that it would be nice to have a general technique for solving them. We have already seen the analogous problem for whole numbers: For whole numbers N and M find a whole number Y such that $NY = M$. We know that the solution to this equation (when it has a whole number solution) can be gotten by division: $Y = M \div N$. This suggests that, if the equation

$$\frac{A}{B} \times S = \frac{C}{D}$$

has a solution S, then perhaps it can be obtained by division of fractions:

$$S = \frac{C}{D} \div \frac{A}{B}.$$

This begs the question: What is

$$\frac{C}{D} \div \frac{A}{B}?$$

Now *we* know the answer to this. But how do we arrive at the answer using only the knowledge of fractions that has been developed so far? Let's try to solve the artichoke problem with what we have developed so far. We want to find a fraction S so that $7\frac{3}{4} \times S = 6\frac{1}{2}$ or, what is the same, $\frac{31}{4} \times S = \frac{13}{2}$.

To get a clue, let's try to *solve a simpler problem.* How about $\frac{31}{4} \times T = 1$? To solve this, replace T with A/B so that

$$\frac{31}{4} \times \frac{A}{B} = 1.$$

Then multiply it out:

$$\frac{31A}{4B} = 1.$$

In order that $(31A)/(4B) = 1$, the whole numbers $31A$ and $4B$ must be the same: $31A = 4B$. Numbers A and B that make this last equation work are $A = 4$ and $B = 31$: $31 \times 4 = 4 \times 31$. A solution to

$$\frac{31}{4} \times \frac{A}{B} = 1$$

is $A/B = \frac{4}{31}$ so that

$$\frac{31}{4} \times \frac{4}{31} = 1.$$

Will that help us with the original problem

$$\frac{31}{4} \times S = \frac{13}{2}?$$

Since

$$\frac{31}{4} \times \frac{4}{31} = 1 \qquad \text{and} \qquad 1 \times \frac{13}{2} = \frac{13}{2},$$

$$\left(\frac{31}{4} \times \frac{4}{31}\right) \times \frac{13}{2} = \frac{13}{2}.$$

Using the associative property to write the left-hand side of the last equation another way, we have

$$\frac{31}{4} \times \left(\frac{4}{31} \times \frac{13}{2}\right) = \frac{13}{2}.$$

The fraction

$$\frac{4}{31} \times \frac{13}{2} = \frac{52}{62} = S$$

is what we are looking for. This means 1 oz of marinated artichokes costs $\$\frac{52}{62}$!

Reciprocals and Division of Fractions

The general problem is: Given A/B and C/D, find a fraction S so that

$$\frac{A}{B} \times S = \frac{C}{D}.$$

The major breakthrough in solving $\frac{31}{4} \times S = \frac{13}{2}$ was in *solving a simpler problem* $\frac{31}{4} \times T = 1$ with $T = \frac{4}{31}$. To solve the general equation

$$\frac{A}{B} \times T = 1 \qquad \text{with } A \neq 0 \text{ and } B \neq 0,$$

we notice that

$$\frac{A}{B} \times \frac{B}{A} = 1$$

so that $T = B/A$. This solution is so important that we make the following definition.

DEFINITION OF RECIPROCAL

For $B \neq 0$ and $A \neq 0$ the fraction B/A is called the *reciprocal* of the fraction A/B. It has the property $A/B \times B/A = 1$.

So $\frac{4}{31}$ is the reciprocal of $\frac{31}{4}$. How do we go from knowing this, that

$$\frac{A}{B} \times \frac{B}{A} = 1$$

to solving

$$\frac{A}{B} \times S = \frac{C}{D}?$$

Since $1 \times \frac{C}{D} = \frac{C}{D}$, we have

$$\left(\frac{A}{B} \times \frac{B}{A} \right) \times \frac{C}{D} = \frac{C}{D},$$

which, using the associative property of multiplication, we can rewrite as

$$\frac{A}{B} \times \left(\frac{B}{A} \times \frac{C}{D} \right) = \frac{C}{D}.$$

The fraction $\dfrac{B}{A} \times \dfrac{C}{D}$ is our answer. Using the commutative property of multiplication we can also write the answer as

$$\frac{C}{D} \times \frac{B}{A}.$$

We can summarize this.

DIVISION OF FRACTIONS

If $A \neq 0$ and $B \neq 0$, the *division of* fraction C/D by fraction A/B is denoted by

$$\frac{C}{D} \div \frac{A}{B}$$

and is equal to

$$\frac{C}{D} \times \frac{B}{A}.$$

It is the solution S to

$$\frac{A}{B} \times S = \frac{C}{D}.$$

To check an answer to a fraction division problem, you remember that the answer is supposed to solve a missing factor problem—the last equation in the box. Plug your answer into the equation. If it works, you have the right answer. If not, you have a wrong answer.

We now know that the four problems with the partial solutions can be solved by division of fractions.

Something to Watch Out For in Division of Fractions

You recall that the solution to the shirt problem was reduced to: Find a whole number N and a fraction C/D such that $5\frac{2}{3} = \frac{3}{4} \times N + C/D$, where C/D is a fraction that is less than $\frac{3}{4}$.

Let's carry out the division of fractions to find the answer to the missing factor problem $5\frac{2}{3} = \frac{3}{4} \times [?]$.

$$5\frac{2}{3} \div \frac{3}{4} = \frac{17}{3} \div \frac{3}{4} = \frac{17}{3} \times \frac{4}{3} = \frac{68}{9} = 7\frac{5}{9}.$$

This means that, by the distributive law,

$$5\frac{2}{3} = \frac{3}{4} \times 7\frac{5}{9} = \frac{3}{4}\left(7 + \frac{5}{9}\right) = \frac{3}{4} \times 7 + \frac{3}{4} \times \frac{5}{9}.$$

Consequently, the company can make $N = 7$ shirts out of the $5\frac{2}{3}$ yd. The amount of material that will be left over (and wasted) is

$$\frac{3}{4} \times \frac{5}{9} = \frac{15}{36} = \frac{5}{12} \text{ yd.}$$

Notice that $C/D = \frac{5}{12}$. It is not $\frac{5}{9}$ yd that is left over but $\frac{5}{12}$ yd. (However, $\frac{5}{12}$ yd is $\frac{5}{9}$ the amount of material needed to make a whole shirt.) Division of fractions will find N, the whole number part of the answer but not the fractional leftover as was asked for in the original problem. You have to do a little additional work as we did in the preceding solution.

EXERCISES

7. A social worker has $15\frac{3}{4}$ lb of surplus cheese that he wants to divide equally among four families. He wants to know how much each family should get. Find out.

8. A garden row $15\frac{1}{2}$ m (meter, meters) long is to be planted with cabbage plants. The plants must be planted with a space of $\frac{2}{5}$ m between them. How many cabbage plants will be planted in the row?

9. You are an outdoor painter. One job you do is put protective coating on wooden fences. You estimate that you can coat about 75 ft^2 of fencing in an hour. A prospective customer has a fence that is $5\frac{2}{3}$ ft high. What length of this fencing can you coat in 1 hr?

10. If $\frac{5}{8}$ of the children in Norway are blue-eyed blonds, and $\frac{9}{10}$ of the blond children in Norway have blue eyes, what fraction of the children in Norway are blond?

11. You drove your car 153 mi and used $10\frac{3}{4}$ gal of gas. If this were typical driving for you, how many miles could you drive on 1 gal?

9.3 MORE ON RATIOS: SCALE DRAWINGS AND RATIOS OF LENGTHS

Here are two photographs.

A

B

Photo A is a *reduction* of photo B. Equivalently, photo B is an *enlargement* of photo A. One is a *scale drawing* of the other. This means that the ratio of the height of A to the height of B is the same as the ratio of the width of A to the width of B. It also means that the ratio of any other pair of corresponding lengths in the two photos is the same as the ratio of the height of A to the height of B. Let's see how all this works with some specific measurements.

A

B

In the case of these particular photos the ratio of the width of A to the width of B is 3 to 5. Here are some phrases that mean the same thing.

■ The width of A is $\frac{3}{5}$ the width of B.
■ The width of A is $\frac{3}{5}$ times the width of B.
■ The ratio of the width of B to the width of A is 5 to 3.
■ The width of B is $\frac{5}{3}$ the width of A.
■ The width of B is $1\frac{2}{3}$ the width of A.
■ The width of B is $1\frac{2}{3}$ times the width of A.

Let's look at a problem involving ratios and scale drawings.

THE ENLARGEMENT
PROBLEM

Roberto lives in Santa Fe. He is in the sixth grade and is working on a project having to do with agricultural uses of land in New Mexico. He has a small copy of the map of the state but needs to make a much larger version on which he can record all his accumulated data. The map he wants to enlarge is shown below.

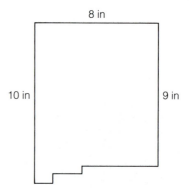

8 in

10 in   9 in

Solve this yourself, first.

He has decided that he wants the length of the northern boundary of the state for the larger version to be 20 in. He wants to know what the lengths of the other sides should be in order that the enlarged map be a scale drawing of the smaller one. He knows about ratios. Help him solve this.

A Solution to the Enlargement
Problem

Roberto measures the northern boundary of the small map and finds that it is 8 in long. He thinks: "The northern boundary of the larger map is 20 in and that of the smaller map is 8 inches. That means that 20 in in the larger corresponds to 8 inches in the smaller map. That's a ratio of 20 to 8. So the length of the larger is $\frac{20}{8}$ of the smaller. But $\frac{20}{8} = \frac{5}{2} = 2\frac{1}{2}$. So the larger is $2\frac{1}{2}$ times the length of the smaller. That means that when I measure the western side of the smaller map, the length of the western side of the enlarged map should be $2\frac{1}{2}$ times as large. The ratio of the length of the western side of the large map to the length of the western side of the small map should be $\frac{5}{2}$ or 5 to 2. Let's see, the length of the western side of the small map is 10 inches.

"That means that the western side of the enlarged map should be 10 in × $\frac{5}{2}$ = 25 in. That solves the problem."

EXERCISE

12. What should the eastern boundary of the state in the large version be?

Scale Drawings: The Choice of the Unit Length

For the two photos we saw earlier, the ratio of the widths was easy to figure out. The width of A was marked off into 3 pieces of equal length and the width of B was marked off into 5 pieces of the same length. The ratio of the width of A to the width of B was 3 to 5.

In the case of the two maps, the ratio of lengths was also easy to figure out. The northern boundary of the large map was 20 in, and the northern boundary of the small map was 8 in: The ratio of the larger to the smaller was 20 to 8.

In both these situations a *unit of length* was found so that the two lengths in question were equal to a whole number of those units. In the case of the photos the unit of length was not given a name but was suggested by the markings in the picture.

A

B

For the maps, the unit length was equal to an inch.

In the next problem the choice of unit length is not obvious.

A RATIO OF LENGTHS PROBLEM You know that the distance from *A* to *B* is $5\frac{3}{4}$ ft and that the distance from *C* to *D* is $9\frac{2}{3}$ ft.

A ———————————————————————————— B
C ———————————————————————————————————— D

You want to find the ratio of the length of *AB* to the length of *CD*. How can you solve this?

You know that if the distance from A to B were 4 ft and the distance from *C* to *D* were 10 ft, then the ratio of the length of *AB* to the length of *CD* would be 4 to 10 or $\frac{4}{10}$. The problem is to chop up the $5\frac{3}{4}$ and the $9\frac{2}{3}$ into lengths of equal size; the problem is to find a suitable unit of length. You think: "Let's look at those fractional lengths a little more closely: $5\frac{3}{4} = \frac{23}{4}$ and $9\frac{2}{3} = \frac{29}{3}$. If I had fractions $\frac{23}{4}$ and $\frac{29}{4}$ instead, then there would be no problem: a natural common unit would be $\frac{1}{4}$ foot and the ratio would be $\frac{23}{29}$.

"What I need to do is find a common denominator for the fractions $\frac{23}{4}$ and $\frac{29}{3}$, and use equal fractions. A common denominator is $4 \times 3 = 12$ and

$$\frac{23}{4} = \frac{23 \times 3}{4 \times 3} = \frac{69}{12} \quad \text{and} \quad \frac{29}{3} = \frac{29 \times 4}{3 \times 4} = \frac{116}{12}.$$

I can use $\frac{1}{12}$ of a foot as my unit of length. Then the ratio of the smaller to the longer of the two lengths is 69 to 116, or $\frac{69}{116}$."

The Mathematical Idea: Ratios of Lengths and Division of Fractions

Suppose you have two lengths: A/B units of length and C/D units of length. You are interested in the ratios of the first length to the second. The preceding solution suggests a general method for figuring out this ratio, namely, find a common denominator and use equal fractions. For these two fractions one common denominator is BD, so that

$$\frac{A}{B} = \frac{AD}{BD} \quad \text{and} \quad \frac{C}{D} = \frac{CB}{DB}.$$

A common unit of length is $1/BD$ and the ratio of the first length to the second is AD to CB or $(AD)/(CB)$. But the latter fraction is just $(AD)/(BC)$, which is equal to

$$\frac{A}{B} \div \frac{C}{D}.$$

We can make a statement about the situation.

RATIOS AND FRACTION DIVISION

The ratio of length A/B units to length C/D units is the fraction

$$\frac{A}{B} \div \frac{C}{D}.$$

EXERCISE

13. A photograph that is $5\frac{3}{4}$ by $8\frac{3}{8}$ in is to be reduced to a picture having its shorter side equal to $2\frac{1}{2}$ in. What is the ratio of the length of the reduced side to the length of the original? What should the other dimension of the reduced picture be?

9.4 LOOKING BACK: FORMAL PROPERTIES OF MULTIPLICATION AND ORDER OF FRACTIONS

Order and the operations on fractions have several properties in common with order and the operations on whole numbers. In this section we would like to compare these features of the two sets, explore their similarities, and point out their differences.

In chapter 8 we noted that addition of fractions is commutative and associative and that addition of fractions possesses an additive identity, namely, 0. In this chapter we used the facts that multiplication is associative and commutative and multiplication distributes over addition. There is an additional property of multiplication.

MULTIPLICATION OF FRACTIONS HAS AN IDENTITY

For any fraction A/B,

$$\frac{1}{1} \times \frac{A}{B} = \frac{A}{B}.$$

The fraction $1 = \frac{1}{1}$ is called a *multiplicative identity*.

We also noted in chapter 8 that the relationship between order, addition, and subtraction is the same for fractions as it is for whole numbers. Here is a rule describing the relationship between order and multiplication of fractions.

LAW RELATING MULTIPLICATION TO ORDER OF FRACTIONS

Suppose that A/B, C/D, E/F, and G/H are fractions such that $A/B < C/D$ and $E/F < G/H$. Then it follows that

$$\frac{A}{B} \times \frac{E}{F} < \frac{C}{D} \times \frac{G}{H}.$$

If, in addition $E/F \neq 0$, then

$$\frac{A}{B} \times \frac{E}{F} < \frac{C}{D} \times \frac{E}{F}.$$

So far, whole numbers and fractions look alike, if viewed in these formal ways. One difference was mentioned in chapter 8, namely, the density property of fractions. Another difference is that every nonzero fraction A/B has a reciprocal, what is sometimes called a *multiplicative inverse* and denoted $(A/B)^{-1}$. Thus, $(A/B)^{-1} = B/A$. The existence of multiplicative inverses also means that a missing factor problem with fractions always has a solution that is a fraction. If $A/B \neq 0$, then $(A/B)S = C/D$ has the solution $S = (C/D)(A/B)^{-1}$. The difference between fractions and whole numbers here is that a missing factor problem involving *whole numbers* does not always have a *whole number* for a solution. For example, $3S = 7$ does not have a whole number solution; viewed as an equation in fractions, it does have the solution $S = \frac{7}{3}$.

Solving Equations Involving Fractions

We know how to solve a missing factor problem such as

$$\frac{7}{4}X = \frac{9}{11}.$$

"Finding the missing factor X" is sometimes expressed as "solving the equation for X (or for the 'unknown' X)."

We can solve other equations in addition to those of this type. For example, suppose we want to find a number Y such that

$$\frac{7}{4}Y + \frac{2}{5} = \frac{9}{11};$$

that is, we want to solve the latter equation for Y. The strategy is to *turn the problem into one we've solved before*. In this case we turn the equation into one that has the same solution but that we've solved before, namely, an equation associated with a missing factor problem. To do this, we think of the equation

$$\frac{7}{4}Y + \frac{2}{5} = \frac{9}{11}$$

as a missing addend problem in which the missing addend is

$$\frac{7}{4}Y.$$

Solving the missing addend problem, we get

$$\frac{7}{4}Y = \frac{9}{11} - \frac{2}{5}, \qquad \text{or} \qquad \frac{7}{4}Y = \frac{23}{55}.$$

This is now a missing factor problem. Its solution is

$$Y = \frac{23}{55} \times \frac{4}{7} = \frac{92}{385}.$$

EXERCISE   14. Solve the equations.

(a) $\dfrac{2}{5}V + \dfrac{5}{12} = \dfrac{8}{9}$ (b) $\dfrac{5}{4}Z + \dfrac{2}{3} = \dfrac{7}{8}$ (c) $\dfrac{4}{7}W + \dfrac{5}{9} = \dfrac{6}{5}.$

Using the Rules to Estimate Answers to Fraction Problems

Multiplying $8\frac{3}{4}$ by $12\frac{5}{6}$ involves a few steps. Suppose you just want to get a rough idea of what the answer is, quickly, but without calculating the answer exactly. Here is one way. First, you know that

$$8\frac{3}{4} < 9 \qquad \text{and} \qquad 12\frac{5}{6} < 13.$$

By the law relating multiplication to order, you get $(8\frac{3}{4}) \times (12\frac{5}{6}) < 9 \times 13 = 117$. Also, you know that

$$8 < 8\frac{3}{4} \qquad \text{and} \qquad 12 < 12\frac{5}{6}$$

so that, by the same law, $96 = 8 \times 12 < (8\frac{3}{4}) \times (12\frac{5}{6})$. To put it another way, $96 < (8\frac{3}{4}) \times (12\frac{5}{6}) < 117$. The product you are interested in is between 96 and 117.

Next, suppose that you are interested in the quotient $25\frac{3}{4} \div 4\frac{7}{8}$. We know that the answer is $(25\frac{3}{4}) \times (4\frac{7}{8})^{-1}$ and that $25 < 25\frac{3}{4} < 26$ and $4 < 4\frac{7}{8} < 5$. To use the same idea that we used for estimating a product of fractions, we need to know something about inequalities and *reciprocals* of fractions. Here is a useful fact.

PROPERTY OF ORDER AND RECIPROCALS

Suppose that A/B and C/D are fractions such that $0 < A/B < C/D$. Then also $D/C < B/A$; that is, if $A/B < C/D$, then $(C/D)^{-1} < (A/B)^{-1}$.

For example, you know that $\frac{2}{3} < \frac{3}{4}$. From the property of order and reciprocals, $\frac{4}{3} < \frac{3}{2}$. (Check it!)

The reason the property is true in general can be shown using the law relating multiplication of fractions to order. If $0 < A/B < C/D$, it follows that

$$\frac{A}{B} \times \frac{B}{A} < \frac{C}{D} \times \frac{B}{A}, \qquad \text{or} \qquad 1 < \frac{C}{D} \times \frac{B}{A}.$$

From this last inequality, we have

$$1 \times \frac{D}{C} < \left(\frac{C}{D} \times \frac{B}{A}\right) \times \frac{D}{C}.$$

Using the commutative and associative properties, we can rewrite the latter inequality as

$$\frac{D}{C} < \frac{B}{A}.$$

This is just what we wanted to show.

Now, back to our problem. We want to get a rough idea of the size of $25\frac{3}{4} \div 4\frac{7}{8} = (25\frac{3}{4}) \times (4\frac{7}{8})^{-1}$. We know that $25 < 25\frac{3}{4} < 26$ and $4 < 4\frac{7}{8} < 5$. Using our new law relating order with reciprocals, we find that from the last pair of inequalities we obtain the pair

$$\frac{1}{5} < \left(4\frac{7}{8}\right)^{-1} < \frac{1}{4};$$

thus,

$$25 \times \frac{1}{5} < \left(25\frac{3}{4}\right)\left(4\frac{7}{8}\right)^{-1} < 26 \times \frac{1}{4}$$

or

$$5 < \left(25\frac{3}{4}\right)\left(4\frac{7}{8}\right)^{-1} < 6\frac{1}{2}.$$

In other words, the answer to $25\frac{3}{4} \div 4\frac{7}{8}$ lies between 5 and $6\frac{1}{2}$.

EXERCISE   15. Use the methods we have just presented to estimate the answers to the fraction problems.
(a) $(12\frac{7}{12})(5\frac{3}{7})$ (b) $(8\frac{3}{5})(9\frac{2}{11})$ (c) $48\frac{5}{6} \div 8\frac{3}{5}$ (d) $79\frac{3}{5} \div 20\frac{7}{8}$

9.5   LOOKING AHEAD: GENERALIZED AND ALGEBRAIC FRACTIONS

If A and B are whole numbers, then A/B denotes the fraction with numerator A and denominator B. Of course, this fraction can also be interpreted as the answer to the whole number division problem $A \div B$. The notation P/Q is also used when P and Q are not whole numbers. When P and Q are fractions (and $Q \neq 0$), then we define P/Q to mean

$$\frac{P}{Q} = P \div Q.$$

Of course, since whole numbers are fractions, P and Q can also be whole numbers. We sometimes call the expression P/Q a *generalized fraction* with *numerator* P and *denominator* Q, even though P and Q may be themselves ordinary fractions. The terminology *algebraic fraction* is used instead when numerator or denominator are denoted by variable letters. Generalized and algebraic fractions satisfy many of the same rules satisfied by ordinary fractions.

RULES FOR GENERALIZED AND ALGEBRAIC FRACTIONS

Suppose that P, Q, R, S, and M are fractions with M, Q, and $S \neq 0$. Then (the symbol $\pm$ means "+ or −")

1. $\dfrac{P}{Q} \pm \dfrac{R}{Q} = \dfrac{P \pm R}{Q}$ (if $P \geq R$).

2. $\dfrac{PM}{QM} = \dfrac{P}{Q}$.

3. $\dfrac{P}{Q} \pm \dfrac{R}{S} = \dfrac{PS \pm RQ}{QS}$ (if $P/Q \geq R/S$).

4. $\dfrac{P}{Q} \times \dfrac{R}{S} = \dfrac{PR}{QS}$.

5. $\dfrac{P}{Q} \div \dfrac{R}{S} = \dfrac{P/Q}{R/S} = \dfrac{P}{Q} \times \dfrac{S}{R}$ (if $R \neq 0$).

Other rules apply as well, such as the commutative, associative, and distributive laws for addition and multiplication. Let's look at some situations where these rules are used.

Rule 1: $\quad\quad \dfrac{\frac{2}{3}}{\frac{3}{10}} + \dfrac{\frac{7}{8}}{\frac{3}{10}} = \dfrac{\frac{2}{3} + \frac{7}{8}}{\frac{3}{10}}$

Rule 2: $\quad\quad \dfrac{a^2 b}{ab^2} = \dfrac{a(ab)}{b(ab)} = \dfrac{a}{b}$

Rule 3: $\quad\quad \dfrac{x^2}{y} - \dfrac{y}{x} = \dfrac{x^3 - y^2}{yx}$

Rule 3: $\quad\quad \dfrac{x+1}{x} + \dfrac{x}{x-1} = \dfrac{(x+1)(x-1) + x^2}{x(x-1)}$

Rule 4: $\quad\quad \left(\dfrac{pq}{q+1}\right)\left(\dfrac{p^3}{p+1}\right) = \dfrac{p^4 q}{(q+1)(p+1)}$

Rule 5: $\quad\quad \dfrac{\frac{3}{4}}{\frac{5}{8}} = \dfrac{3 \times 8}{4 \times 5} = \dfrac{24}{20}$

EXERCISES

16. For each expression, find the fraction equal to it.

(a) $\dfrac{\frac{3}{4}}{\frac{3}{5}} + \dfrac{\frac{2}{3}}{\frac{7}{8}}$
(b) $\dfrac{\left(\frac{3}{4}\right)\left(\frac{3}{5}\right)}{\left(\frac{3}{5}\right)\left(\frac{7}{8}\right)}$
(c) $\dfrac{\left(\frac{3}{4}\right)\left(\frac{4}{3}\right)}{\left(\frac{9}{7}\right)\left(\frac{7}{9}\right)}$

17. Use rule 2 to reduce each algebraic fraction to "lowest terms." (The expression "simplest form" is sometimes used instead of "lowest terms.") (*Hint:* For (b) use the distributive law.)

(a) $\dfrac{35a^2 b^2}{28ab^2}$
(b) $\dfrac{(c+d)^2}{3c+3d}$
(c) $\dfrac{x^2 y}{x}$
(d) $\dfrac{a^2 + ab}{a+b}$

Examples

One use for algebraic fractions occurs with formulas. For example, if a car is driven for h hr at an average speed of s mph, then the distance d the car covers in h hr is given by the formula $d = sh$. The power of such an expression is that it yields the distance traveled *no matter what values for the speed (s) and hours (h) traveled are.* There are other situations where formulas are used and where knowing rules for algebraic fractions is helpful.

EXAMPLE 1   The formula for the volume V of a cube with side s is

$$V = s^3.$$

The formula for the surface area A of a cube with side s is

$$A = 6s^2.$$

The ratio R of the surface area of the cube of side s to its volume is

$$R = \frac{A}{V} = \frac{6s^2}{s^3}.$$

(If you think of the cube as a cereal box, then R is roughly the amount of container material needed per unit volume. There will be more on this in later chapters.) Using the rules for algebraic fractions, we obtain the following simpler formula:

$$R = \frac{6}{s}.$$

EXERCISE   18. The volume V of a cylinder of height h and radius r is $V = \pi r^2 h$. The surface area A of the cylinder (including top and bottom) is $A = 2\pi rh + 2\pi r^2$. (Recall that π is a number approximately equal to $3\frac{1}{7}$.) As in example 1, find a formula for the ratio of A to V in terms of r and h and use the rules to simplify it.

EXAMPLE 2   The Machine Manufacturing Company purchases 30,000 #3Q5 bolts to use in its yearly production. It must worry about the inventory cost I for the bolts. If the company purchased the 30,000 bolts all at one time, it would have to make arrangements for storage, which would be expensive. So the company makes smaller purchases periodically during the year. However, purchasing in too many small quantities is also expensive. So the company developed a formula for I. Inventory cost I is the sum of two parts—the purchasing cost P and the storage cost S. If the company makes X equal purchases of bolts each year and each purchase costs the company $320, then $P = 320X$. The company estimates S as

$$S = \frac{10{,}000}{X}.$$

Since $I = P + S$,

$$I = 320X + \frac{10{,}000}{X}.$$

19. Use rule 3 for algebraic fractions to find an alternative formula for the inventory cost *I* that is a single algebraic fraction (instead of the sum of two, as it is above).

EXAMPLE 3 Suppose that two resistances of *R* ohms and *S* ohms are hooked up in parallel in an electric circuit.

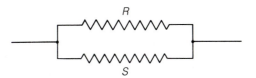

The effect of these two resistances is the same as a single resistance of *T* ohms placed where indicated in the circuit.

The resistances *R*, *S*, and *T* are related by the following formula.

$$\frac{1}{T} = \frac{1}{R} + \frac{1}{S}.$$

This is a formula for the *reciprocal* of *T* in terms of *R* and *S*. It might be more convenient to have a formula expressing *T* directly in terms of *R* and *S*. Let's do that.

$$\frac{1}{T} = \frac{1}{R} + \frac{1}{S}$$

Rule 3:

$$\frac{1}{T} = \frac{S + R}{RS}$$

Thus,

$$T = \frac{RS}{S + R}.$$

EXERCISE 20. For an optical lens, the focal length *F*, the distance *D* of an object from the lens, and the distance *T* of the image from the lens are related by the formula

$$\frac{1}{F} = \frac{1}{D} + \frac{1}{T}.$$

Use the rules to find a formula for *F* (instead of 1/*F*) in terms of *D* and *T*.

We have labeled lots of points on the number line with fractions. Imagine labeling all the points of the number line that correspond to fractions (all infinity of them). Is there a point on the number line that is not labeled with a fraction?

We know what the answer would be if we replaced "fractions" by "whole numbers." Between any two consecutive whole numbers—such as 2000 and 2001 there is a "hole," a space between the two points labeled 2000 and 2001.

Points labeled by fractions differ from points labeled by whole numbers. In the last chapter we discussed the density property of fractions: Between any two different fractions there must be a third fraction, different from the other two. That means that between any two points corresponding to different fractions on the number line, *no matter how close the two fractions are,* there is always a third point strictly between the two corresponding to a fraction. In fact, we have seen that there are infinitely many fraction points between even very close fractions.

It seems reasonable that if you select any point on the number line, you will always find a fraction to which it corresponds. This is what the Pythagoreans, a Greek sect from around 500 B.C., assumed. Their worldview was built on the assumption that everything could be reduced to fractions (*ratio* was the term they used). Here is a story about the Pythagoreans and the difficulties this assumption about fractions and points on the number line brought them.

On the interval from 0 to 1 on the number line, the Pythagoreans built a square.

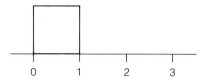

Then they cut the square into halves along a diagonal.

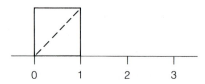

After that, they took one of the half squares and lay the diagonal side on the number line, with one end at 0, like this:

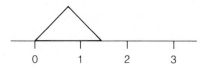

The other end of the diagonal side touches a point of the number line, and so corresponds to a fraction A/B.

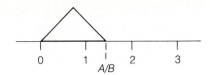

The Pythagoreans wanted to know what the fraction A/B was; they wanted to know its numerator and its denominator. To keep things specific, they decided that A/B should be a fraction reduced to lowest terms, that is, the GCD of A and B should be 1. Then they gathered some more information about A/B. First of all, they knew that A/B was the length of the diagonal of the original square. After some playing around, they took two copies of the original square, cut them along their diagonals, and arranged them like this.

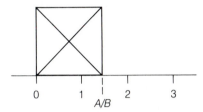

The four pieces formed a larger square! Immediately, the Pythagoreans sought to determine what new insight this fact would give them as to the identity of the fraction A/B. The first thing they noted was that the large square, having A/B for a side, had area equal to $(A/B)^2$ units. Next, they noted that the original smaller square, having a length of 1 for each side, had area 1 unit². Thus, two of the smaller squares put together would have 2 units². At the same time, the two smaller squares—cut up and the pieces rearranged—make the large square.

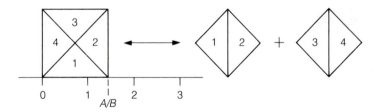

The large square has area 2 and also area $(A/B)^2$. Thus,

$$2 = \frac{A}{B} \times \frac{A}{B} = \frac{A^2}{B^2}.$$

They were excited. They were getting somewhere. They stared at the equation

$$2 = \frac{A^2}{B^2}$$

a bit and realized that they could multiply both sides by B^2 and arrive at the equation in whole numbers $2B^2 = A^2$.

At this point they realized they could use all they knew about multiples and divisors of whole numbers. First they recalled that the GCD of A and B is 1. Since $2 | 2B^2$, $2 | A^2$ also. And, since $2 | A^2$, it must also be that $2 | A$ (how could it be otherwise?). So $A = 2C$, for some whole number C, and $2B^2 = (2C)(2C) = (2)(2)C^2$.

Consequently (the excitement was rising), $B^2 = 2C^2$.

Then, noticing that the latter equation is similar to the original equation in whole numbers $2B^2 = A^2$, they used the same argument to get that $B = 2D$. At this point they stopped dead in their tracks, horrified at what they saw. Here's what they had: GCD of A and B is 1; $2 | A$; $2 | B$.

"Something must be wrong!" someone shouted. "A and B can't both have 2 as a common divisor and at the same time have a GCD equal to 1." They went back and looked again at everything they had done. Everything was O.K. Every conclusion they had reached—assuming that the point on the number line corresponded to fraction A/B—was correct. The only thing that could be wrong was the initial assumption itself. They were forced to conclude that the point on the number line does not correspond to a fraction!

This discovery—that some points on the number line do not correspond to fractions, that labeling points on a number line with fractions leaves holes—shattered the worldview of some leaders of the Pythagoreans and threatened to challenge the influence of the religious sect. The story goes that people who breathed a word of this discovery would be put to death.

Of course, we know the story in the following shortened (and dull) form: "If X is the length of the diagonal of a square of side one, then $X^2 = 2$; that is, X is the square root of 2. The square root of 2 is known to be *irrational* (meaning, 'not a ratio,' 'not a fraction')."

Many other points on the number line do not correspond to fractions. Numbers that correspond to such points are called *irrational numbers*. The totality of all numbers corresponding to the points of our number line to the right of zero are called the *positive real numbers*. There will be more on the real numbers in a later chapter.

EXERCISES

21. Suppose length X is not a fraction. Show that length $X + 1$ is also not a fraction.

22. If length X is not a fraction, show that length $5X$ is not a fraction.

23. Use the ideas and results from exercises 21 and 22 to show that there are infinitely many irrational numbers.

24. Suppose that Y is a length such that $Y^2 = 3$. Is Y a fraction or isn't it? Why or why not?

25. Suppose that Z is a length such that $Z^2 = 4$. Is Z a fraction or isn't it? Why or why not?

9.7   SUMMARY OF IMPORTANT IDEAS AND TECHNIQUES

- Multiplication of fractions: $\dfrac{A}{B} \times \dfrac{C}{D} = \dfrac{AC}{BD}$

- Division of fractions: $\dfrac{A}{B} \div \dfrac{C}{D} = \dfrac{A}{B} \times \dfrac{D}{C}$

- Properties and ideas associated with operations with fractions: distributive, commutative, and associative properties satisfied by multiplication of fractions, 1 as multiplicative identity
- That a nonzero fraction A/B has a multiplicative inverse (or reciprocal) equal to B/A, enabling every missing factor problem involving fractions to have a solution that is also a fraction
- Similarity between multiplication of whole numbers and multiplication of fractions in satisfying a law relating it to the order of fractions
- Using the properties to solve equations involving unknown fractions and to estimate fraction products and quotients
- Use of operations with ratios
- Definitions of generalized and algebraic fractions, their properties
- Irrational numbers

PROBLEM SET

PRACTICING
SKILLS

1. A metal alloy company has received an order for 175 lb of an alloy that is $\frac{4}{7}$ aluminum. How much aluminum will be needed to make this much of the alloy?

2. A certain rug material costs $15/yd². How much will a rug that measures $1\frac{3}{4}$ by $2\frac{2}{3}$ yd cost?

3. About $\frac{2}{5}$ of the student body smokes. Roughly $\frac{3}{4}$ of those who smoke also consume alcohol. What fraction of the student body smokes and drinks alcohol?

4. Sam runs at a rate of $9\frac{3}{5}$ mph. He has been running for 42 min. How far has he run?

5. A textile worker makes vests out of a manufactured leatherette fabric. She has $3\frac{1}{2}$ yd of the material on hand. Each vest uses $\frac{5}{8}$ yd of the leatherette. How many vests can she make? How much fabric will she have left over?

6. An electronics technician can assemble a microcomputer in $1\frac{1}{3}$ hr. How many can he assemble in a 35-hr work week?

7. The height of a row of bricks is $2\frac{5}{8}$ in. Mortar between each row is $\frac{3}{4}$ in. How many rows of bricks will be needed to build a wall 5 ft high?

8. The circumference of a circle (the distance around the circle) is about $\frac{22}{7}$ times its diameter. How big must the diameter of a circle be if the circumference is to be $5\frac{3}{4}$ ft?

9. A farmer raises chickens, geese, and goats. There are $\frac{2}{3}$ as many chickens as geese and $\frac{4}{5}$ as many chickens as goats. She raises 80 goats. How many chickens and geese does she raise?

10. A photograph that is $3\frac{1}{4}$ by $7\frac{5}{16}$ in is to be enlarged to a picture having its longer side equal to $15\frac{1}{2}$ in. What is the ratio of the length of the enlarged side to the length of the original? What should the other dimension of the enlarged picture be?

11. Solve the following equations. Express your answer in simplest terms.
   (a) $(\frac{3}{5})A + \frac{8}{15} = \frac{5}{6}$ (b) $(\frac{3}{16})B + \frac{3}{4} = \frac{6}{7}$ (c) $(\frac{2}{7})C + \frac{5}{8} = \frac{10}{9}$

12. Estimate the answers to the following fraction problems. Give upper and lower bounds for each.
   (a) $(11\frac{5}{9}) \times (6\frac{2}{5})$ (b) $(7\frac{8}{15}) \times (4\frac{12}{13})$ (c) $(53\frac{3}{4}) \div (10\frac{7}{12})$ (d) $(86\frac{6}{7}) \div (8\frac{1}{6})$

13. For each of the following expressions, find the fraction equal to it. Your answer should be in lowest terms.

(a) $\dfrac{\frac{5}{2}}{\frac{7}{6}} + \dfrac{\frac{1}{3}}{\frac{10}{9}}$

(b) $\dfrac{\frac{1}{8}}{\frac{3}{5}} + \dfrac{\frac{1}{6}}{\frac{5}{2}}$

(c) $\dfrac{(\frac{5}{2} \times \frac{1}{3})}{(\frac{7}{6} \times \frac{10}{9})}$

(d) $\dfrac{(\frac{3}{4} \times \frac{3}{8})}{(\frac{12}{5} \times \frac{3}{16})}$

14. Express each of the following algebraic fractions in simplest terms.

(a) $\dfrac{56a^3b}{64ab}$

(b) $\dfrac{25(c+d)^2}{5c+5d}$

(c) $\dfrac{x^3y^2}{x^2y}$

(d) $\dfrac{w+wy}{(1+y)^2}$

15. Solve for r_1 in terms of R and r_2 if

$$\frac{1}{R} = \frac{1}{r_1} + \frac{1}{r_2}.$$

USING IDEAS *For each of the remaining problems, document as clearly and completely as you can your solution to the problem. Include the steps you took to solve the problem, mention the problems or solutions from the text that gave you ideas, and include the problem-solving strategies you used. You might want to outline and organize these details before assembling your final report in the form of an essay.*

16. Indicate which fraction product the doubly shaded portion of each picture illustrates.

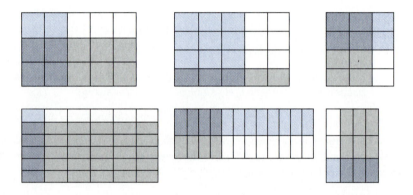

17. Draw a picture, similar to those in problem 16, illustrating each of the following fraction products.

(a) $\dfrac{2}{3} \times \dfrac{4}{7} = \dfrac{8}{21}$

(b) $\dfrac{3}{4} \times \dfrac{2}{5} = \dfrac{6}{20}$

(c) $\dfrac{1}{3} \times \dfrac{1}{3} = \dfrac{1}{9}$

18. A water purification plant works by passing the dirty water through two filters in turn. The first takes out all but $\frac{1}{4}$ of the dirt in the water and the second leaves $\frac{1}{5}$ of the dirt reaching it. What fraction of the dirt is left in the water after it has gone through the plant?

19. Four of five criminal cases are misdemeanors. The remainder are felonies. Two-thirds of all felony cases are solved, but $\frac{2}{3}$ of all misdemeanors are not solved. What is the fraction of all crimes that are solved?

20. You are building a cabinet that is to be 33 in high. It is to have a 4-in-thick base and a $2\frac{1}{2}$-in top. Four equally sized drawers must fit in the remaining space, with $1\frac{1}{4}$ in between drawers. You want to know what the height of each drawer should be.

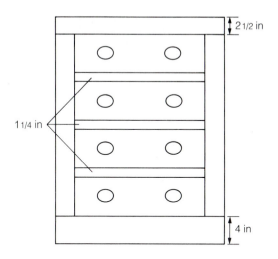

21. An old and very finicky natural gas compressor in an oil field burns a fuel mixture that must be precisely $\frac{2}{3}$ gasoline and $\frac{1}{3}$ oil. After the cranky machine failed to operate, the head roustabout took a look at the fuel tank and discovered that some of the gas had evaporated, leaving 4 gal of evenly mixed oil and gas. How much gas should the roustabout add to the tank to satisfy the compressor?*

22. The doctor prescribes a 1000-ml (milliliter, milliliters) intravenous bottle to be given to a patient over an 8-hr period. The nurse must set the drip rate of the bottle. Each milliliter contains 15 drops. How many drops per minute should there be?†

23. Before the active ingredient in a well-known nose drops medicine is sold over the counter, it is diluted with distilled water. One solution is made for children and another for adults. For children, the active ingredient is $\frac{1}{5}$ the solution. For adults, the active ingredient is $\frac{1}{2}$ the solution. A pharmacist is temporarily out of the solution for children and out of the pure active ingredient. He does have sufficient supplies of the adult solution, and he has lots of distilled water. He needs to dispense 100 ml of the child's solution. How can he do that?

24. A metallurgist has two tin-copper alloys. Alloy A is $\frac{1}{4}$ tin; alloy B is $\frac{1}{2}$ tin. He wants to make 40 lb of a tin-copper alloy that is $\frac{1}{3}$ tin by melting certain amounts of alloy A and B and mixing them together. How much of alloy A and B should he melt?

25. A martini is made with 5 units of gin and 1 unit of vermouth. You want to know what fraction of a martini is alcohol. You know that gin is $\frac{2}{5}$ alcohol and vermouth is $\frac{1}{6}$ alcohol.

---

* From Deborah Hughes Hallet, *The Math Workshop,* Norton, New York, prob. 30, p. 271.
† From Hal Saunders, *When Are We Ever Gonna Have to Use This?*, HMS Publications, Santa Barbara, Calif., 1981, prob. 23, p. 4.

26. A porch is 3 ft 8 in above the sidewalk. You are building a stairway leading from the sidewalk to the porch. You know that the stair treads are $1\frac{1}{8}$ in thick and that the height of all risers should be equal and be between 5 and 7 in. You want to know how many risers there should be and the height of each.

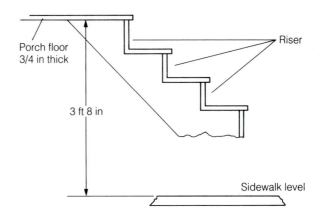

Porch floor
3/4 in thick

3 ft 8 in

Riser

Sidewalk level

27. One-twelfth of the money paid into the state lottery in the form of ticket sales actually returns to the citizens in the form of winnings. This amount is $\frac{3}{4}$ of what's left over after the expenses are taken out for running the lottery. What fraction of the lottery ticket sales goes for these expenses?

28. A new alloy is to be formed out of three other metal alloys. The new alloy will be made up of 4 parts of alloy X, 3 parts of alloy Y, and 1 part of alloy Z. Each of the three ingredients has a fraction of lead in it: $\frac{1}{12}$ of alloy X is lead, $\frac{1}{6}$ of alloy Y is lead, and $\frac{1}{4}$ of alloy Z is lead. You want to know what fraction of the new alloy is lead.

29. An enlargement with a longest edge of 7 in is to be made from a slide that is 24 × 35 mm.
    (a) How wide will the enlargement be?
    (b) An enlargement is to be made from the same slide in such a way that with a minimum of trimming it will just fill an 8- by 10-in frame. How large should the enlargement be before trimming?

MULTIPLE-
CHOICE
QUESTIONS *For each question, several possible answers are given. Circle the letter just to the left of the item that best answers the problem.*

1. The number 6,850,342,170 is evenly divisible by several numbers. Which of the following is not only a set of divisors of this number but also the most complete (has the most elements)?
   (a) {2,3,4,5,6,9,10,12,18}   (b) {2,4,5,9,10,18,20}
   (c) {2,3,5,6,9,10,15,18,45}   (d) {2,3,4,5,6,9,10,12,15}
   (e) {2,3,5,6,10,12,15,18}

2. The GCD of $2^2 3^3 5^3 7^1$ and $2^2 3^4 5^1 7^2 11^1$ is
   (a) $2^2 3^3 5^1 7^1$ (b) $2^2 3^4 5^3 7^2 11^1$ (c) $2^4 3^7 5^4 7^3 11^1$
   (d) $2^1 3^1 5^1 7^1 11^1$ (e) $2^2 3^4 5^3 7^2$

3. Two engaged gears are shown in the picture. When the motor is turned on, gear 1 makes 70 rpm. How many revolutions per minute does gear 2 make?

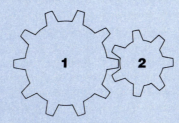

   (a) 700   (b) 7   (c) 10
   (d) 70   (e) 100

4. Before ordering campaign literature for a mailing, you must decide how many households there are among all registered voters. A rule of thumb is that there are $\frac{2}{3}$ as many households as registered voters. How many copies of a mailer should be ordered for a district in which there are 142,500 registered voters?
   (a) 47,500   (b) 95,000   (c) 71,250
   (d) 213,750   (e) 190,000

5. Which of the following is a test for divisibility by 24?
   (a) Use the tests for divisibility by 4 and 6. If these tell you that the number is divisible by both 4 and 6, then the number is divisible by 24.
   (b) See if the number formed by the first three digits is divisible by 24. If it is, then the entire number is divisible by 24.
   (c) Add up all the digits of the number and see if it is divisible by 24. If it is, then the original number is divisible by 24.
   (d) Use the tests for divisibility by 3 and 8. If these tell you that the number is divisible by both 3 and 8, then the number is divisible by 24.
   (e) Use the tests for divisibility by 12 and 2. If these tell you that the number is divisible by both 2 and 12, then the number is divisible by 24.

6. Among people aged 18 to 25, the ratio of smokers to nonsmokers is 3 to 7. The fraction of nonsmokers in the same age group is

   (a) $\frac{3}{7}$ (b) $\frac{4}{7}$ (c) $\frac{3}{10}$ (d) $\frac{4}{10}$ (e) $\frac{7}{10}$

7. Which of the following fractions is the largest?

   (a) $\frac{3}{4}$ (b) $\frac{4}{5}$ (c) $\frac{5}{6}$ (d) $\frac{7}{10}$ (e) $\frac{23}{30}$

8. In a recent election, $\frac{2}{5}$ of those citizens of the city living north of the river favored recharge of the water table using water coming from a new federal irrigation canal, while $\frac{1}{3}$ of those living south of the river favored the recharge. What fraction of the citizens in the entire city favored the recharge?

   (a) $\frac{11}{15}$ (b) $\frac{11}{30}$ (c) $\frac{3}{8}$ (d) $\frac{5}{6}$ (e)   not enough information to decide

9.

The diagram best illustrates which of the following fraction problems?

   (a) $\dfrac{3}{4} \times \dfrac{2}{5}$ (b) $\dfrac{3}{5} \times \dfrac{2}{4}$ (c) $\dfrac{3}{4} + \dfrac{2}{5}$ (d) $\dfrac{3}{5} + \dfrac{1}{4}$ (e) $\dfrac{3}{5} \times \dfrac{1}{4}$

10. A cabinet $10\frac{1}{2}$ ft long must have five doors of equal size. There must be stiles between the doors and at both ends. Each stile must be $2\frac{1}{2}$ in wide.

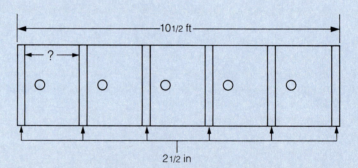

What must the width of each door be?

   (a)   15 in   (b)   111 in   (c) $22\frac{1}{5}$ in   (d) $\frac{37}{20}$ in   (e) $9\frac{1}{4}$ in

ESSAY QUESTIONS   *For each remaining problem, document your solution carefully in the form of an essay.*

11. Three-fifths of the faculty members at the university bike to work. One-fourth of the rest walk. What fraction of the faculty come to work by some means other than biking or walking, such as car, bus, glider, or camel?

12. (a) A 264-tn (ton, tons) load of copper ore has arrived at the San Carlos smelter from the copper mine in Garlic. It is known that ore from Garlic has $\frac{3}{5}$ as much copper (by weight) as waste. How much copper is in the load?

   (b) A 215-tn load of ore has arrived at San Carlos from Goldenbell. It is known that $\frac{3}{10}$ of Goldenbell ore is copper (by weight). How much copper is in the load?

   (c) What is the ratio of copper to waste in the two loads combined?

13. A machine has three colored lights each of which flashes on for an instant at regular intervals. The yellow one flashes on 15 times/min, the blue one flashes on 9 times/min, and the red one flashes on 12 times/min. You watch the machine and see all three lights flash on simultaneously. How much longer must you wait before the three lights flash on again simultaneously?

14. In Washington County, $\frac{2}{3}$ of all registered voters are Democrats; the rest are Republicans. Four-fifths of all the Republicans voted in the last election, but $\frac{3}{10}$ of the Democrats did not vote. What fraction of the registered voters did vote in the last election?

DECIMAL FRACTIONS AND PERCENTS

CHAPTER 10

In this chapter we will work with fractions with denominators of 10, 100, 1000, . . .—powers of 10. We will see that calculating with these fractions is much like calculating with whole numbers. We will develop the usual notation for decimals and the traditional methods used for adding and subtracting them. From knowing how to multiply ordinary (common) fractions, we will also develop the familiar rule for multiplying decimals.

When calculating with common fractions, we frequently replace them with decimal approximations—fractions with denominators a power of 10 that are "close to" the fractions. (When we use a calculator, the machine does this for us automatically.) Since common fractions arise naturally, we will discuss how to find decimal approximations in a process that is usually called *conversion of common fractions to decimal fractions.* Along the way we will highlight those fractions that are easy to convert and those that aren't. The method of conversion of common fractions to decimals will also help us to develop the familiar method for dividing decimal fractions.

10.1   ADDITION AND SUBTRACTION OF FRACTIONS WITH DENOMINATORS OF POWERS OF 10

THE HEIGHT PROBLEM   Juanita and Jorge are studying the heights of the students in their fifth grade class. One of the questions they want to answer is: What is the *average* height of all the students? They know that to answer this, they will have to add up all the heights and divide this quantity by the total number of students. They are making their measurements in metric, are using meter sticks, and are a little nervous about being able to add up all the heights. How can they feel confident about what they are doing?

The meter stick they are using looks like the picture.

0   1/10

To obtain finer measurements, the meter length has been divided into 10 equal lengths: The large markings on the meter stick correspond to these tenths of a meter. Then each of the tenths has been divided further into 10 equal lengths: The medium-sized markings within each tenth on the meter stick correspond to these tenths of tenths. Each of these smaller lengths is $\frac{1}{10}$ of $\frac{1}{10}$ m, or $\frac{1}{100}$ m. Finally, each one of these $\frac{1}{100}$s is divided even further into 10 equal lengths, corresponding to the smallest markings on the meter stick. These smallest lengths are $\frac{1}{10}$ of $\frac{1}{100}$ m, or $\frac{1}{1000}$ m.

Juanita and Jorge are ready to do the measuring of the heights of the students. They use a device such as the one in the picture: a vertical stick 2 m long with a horizontal sliding rod.

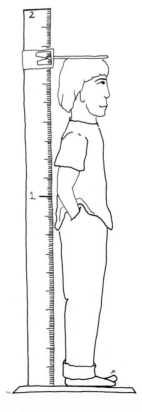

They figure that this should be adequate since everybody in their class has a height less than 2 m. The 2-m stick has been marked with $\frac{1}{10}$, $\frac{1}{100}$, and $\frac{1}{1000}$ m as described. The position of the first person they measure is shown in the picture.

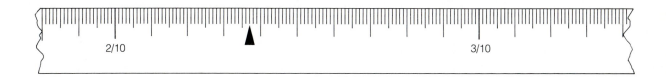

Jorge: "The height of this person is 1 meter plus a fraction. The fine marks are in $\frac{1}{1000}$s. So the fraction is a certain number of $\frac{1}{1000}$s. The arrow points to $\frac{7}{1000}$ after $\frac{3}{100}$ after $\frac{2}{10}$ after 1 meter. Using equivalent fractions, I get $\frac{3}{100} = \frac{30}{1000}$ and $\frac{2}{10} = \frac{200}{1000}$. That gives me

$$1 + \frac{200}{1000} + \frac{30}{1000} + \frac{7}{1000} = \frac{237}{1000}.$$

So the height of this person is $1\frac{237}{1000}$ meters."

Juanita: "There might be an easier way. There are 10 tenths in a meter, there are 10 hundredths in a tenth, and 10 thousandths in a hundredth.

"These fractions behave just like stones on a counting board. Let me set up a counting board so that besides units, 10s, 100s, and so on, going from right to left, there will also be tenths, hundredths, thousandths, and so on, going from left to right.

100s	10s	1s	1/10s	1/100s	1/1000s

A stone in the $\frac{1}{10}$ column represents a tenth of a meter, a stone in the $\frac{1}{100}$ column means a hundredth of a meter, and so on. A stone in a column is worth 10 stones in the column just to its right. This is just like a regular counting board. We can easily record the measurement we just made on this counting board."

1s	1/10s	1/100s	1/1000s
○	○ ○	○ ○ ○	○ ○ ○ ○ ○ ○ ○

Juanita: "This should help us a lot. We won't have to convert everything to $\frac{1}{1000}$s. We won't have to use stones, either. We can use numerals, just as with expanded notation on the counting board."

1s	1/10s	1/100s	1/1000s
○	○ ○	○ ○ ○	○ ○ ○ ○ ○ ○ ○
1	2	3	7

Jorge: "What about adding the measurements up?"

Juanita: "We can do *exactly* the same thing here as we did when we used the counting board for adding and subtracting whole numbers. The rules are the same: 1 stone in a given column is worth 10 in the column to the right. Let's try adding two measurements.

1s	1/10s	1/100s	1/1000s
1	2	3	7
1	4	1	5
2	6	5	2

At the same time, let's add the fractions normally. We've already noticed that

$$\frac{2}{10} + \frac{3}{100} + \frac{7}{1000} = \frac{237}{1000}.$$

Also,

$$\frac{4}{10} + \frac{1}{100} + \frac{5}{1000} = \frac{4 \times 100}{10 \times 100} + \frac{1 \times 10}{100 \times 10} + \frac{5}{1000}$$

$$= \frac{400}{1000} + \frac{10}{1000} + \frac{5}{1000}$$

$$= \frac{415}{1000}.$$

Now let's add the two quantities:

$$1\frac{237}{1000} + 1\frac{415}{1000} = 2 + \frac{237 + 415}{1000} = 2\frac{652}{1000}.$$

That's what we got on the counting board."

Jorge: "I think I can see why we got the same thing. In adding the fractions in the normal way, we found a common denominator and added the whole number numerators. The digits of these numerators are what appeared on the counting board."

Note different column headings.

100s	10s	1s
2	3	7
4	1	5
6	5	2

1/10s	1/100s	1/1000s
2	3	7
4	1	5
6	5	2

Adding whole number numerators   Adding fractions

The Mathematical Idea: Using a Counting Board to Add Certain Fractions

The scheme that Jorge and Juanita have devised can be used to add any number of fractions with denominators $\frac{1}{10}$, $\frac{1}{100}$, $\frac{1}{1000}$. But even more columns on the right are possible. If a stone in a given column equals 10 stones in the column to its right, then a column to the right of the $\frac{1}{1000}$ column should be labeled $\frac{1}{10,000}$, and the column to the right of that should be labeled $\frac{1}{100,000}$, and so on.

1s	1/10s	1/100s	1/1000s	1/10,000s	1/100,000s	. . . .
						. . . .

This *extended counting board* enables us to add with ease any number of fractions with denominators 10, 100, 1000, 10,000, 100,000, . . .—fractions with denominators of powers of 10. Knowing that the fraction $\frac{345}{1000}$ equals $\frac{3}{10} + \frac{4}{100} + \frac{5}{1000}$, one can enter it in the counting board as

1/10s	1/100s	1/1000s
3	4	5

A fraction, possibly the answer to an addition—or subtraction—problem, can be read easily from the counting board.

1s	1/10s	1/100s	1/1000s	1/10,000s
7	2	5	8	3

$\longrightarrow$ $7\dfrac{2583}{10{,}000}$

To write the fraction represented on the counting board, the rightmost column in which there is a nonzero digit tells you what the denominator is (it's the name of the column). The sequence of digits in the columns tells you what the numerator is.

10s	1s	1/10s	1/100s	1/1000s	1/10,000s
		1	0	2	3
			4	7	□
	8	0	2	1	
4	7	5	0	0	3

$\longrightarrow \dfrac{1023}{10{,}000}$

$\longrightarrow \dfrac{47}{1000}$ or $\dfrac{470}{10{,}000}$

$\longrightarrow 8\dfrac{21}{1000}$

$\longrightarrow 47\dfrac{5003}{10{,}000}$

EXERCISES

1. Use a counting board to compare, add, and find the difference of fraction A and B where

$$A = 3 + \frac{5}{100} + \frac{7}{1000} + \frac{2}{10000} \qquad \text{and} \qquad B = 3 + \frac{2}{10} + \frac{7}{1000} + \frac{5}{10000}.$$

2. Add, compare, and find the difference of the two quantities shown on the counting board. Use a counting board to do this.

1/10s	1/100s	1/1000s	1/10,000s
1	□	4	9
	9	9	

From Counting Board to Decimals

Since it is easy to add and subtract with fractions having denominators a power of 10, it is not surprising that there is a less cumbersome way of writing these fractions. The common way of writing these fractions can be derived from the way the fractional quantity is represented on an extended counting board: Write the sequence of digits from the counting board and place a period between the units digit and the $\frac{1}{10}$s digit.

10s	1s	1/10s	1/100s	1/1000s	
2	0	1	4	3	→ 20.143
	9	2	5		→ 9.25
			4	3	→ 0.043

The resulting fraction is called a *decimal fraction*. The period is called the *decimal point* of the fraction. Notice that the decimal point separates the whole number part from the proper fractional part of the mixed number. The positions where the digits appear to the right of the decimal point are called the *decimal places*. The fractions A/B that we have been discussing up until now are called *common fractions*, to distinguish them from decimal fractions.

The representation of these decimal fractions on an extended counting board demonstrates the standard conventions for decimals:

- Zeros to the right of the decimal point and on the far right can be eliminated: 5.300 = 5.30 = 5.3.

- Other zeros must be left alone because they are *place holders*:

1s	1/10s	1/100s	1/1000s	1/10,000s	1/100,000s	
	3	0	0	4	5	→ .30045
	0	0	5			→ .005

The first statement is analogous to the convention for whole numbers that allows 0034 to equal 34; the second statement is analogous to the convention for whole numbers that says that 304 is not equal to 34.

- When several decimals are being added—or one decimal is being subtracted from another—then the decimal points must be lined up.

10s	1s	1/10s	1/100s	1/1000s	
2	7	4	2		→ 27.42
	9	0	7	5	→ 9.075

Here are a few more examples of decimals and their representations on an extended counting board.

100s	10s	1s	1/10s	1/100s	1/1000s	1/10,000s	1/100,000s	
1	2	3	4					⟶ 123.4
	1	0	2	3	4			⟶ 10.234
	1	2	0	0	3	4		⟶ 12.0034
	1	0	2	0	3	0	4	⟶ 10.20304
			1		2	3	4	⟶ .10234

EXERCISES

3. Here are two decimal fractions: 30.572 and 32.075. Compare them, add them, and find their difference.

4. Write the numbers represented on the counting board as decimal fractions.

1000s	100s	10s	1s	1/10s	1/100s	1/1000s	1/10,000s
	5		6		7		8
5	6	7				8	
	5			6	7		8

5. Represent the following decimal fractions on an extended counting board: .00036, 3.5609, 21.0607.

6. Solve the problem on a counting board: 203.12 + 3.024 + 10.203.

7. Solve the problem on a counting board: 203.07 − 47.903.

10.2   MULTIPLICATION OF DECIMAL FRACTIONS

Addition and subtraction of decimal fractions are easy because, once you keep in mind the simple procedures we've just discussed, the computations are just like addition and subtraction of whole numbers. You also know that multiplication of decimal fractions is just like the multiplication of whole numbers, except for determining the position of the decimal point. We should try to understand why this is. First, let's consider some simple multiplications.

Multiplication by 10 and $\frac{1}{10}$

To multiply the decimal fraction 234.56 by 10, enter it on a counting board.

100s	10s	1s	1/10s	1/100s
2	3	4	5	6

From our study of multiplication of whole numbers, we know that to multiply a number on a counting board by 10, you move all the digits one column to the left. This action comes from the rule that 1 stone in a given column represents 10 stones in the column to its right. The same rule holds for the extended counting board.

Ten times 234.56 on the counting board is what you get by moving every digit one column to the left.

	1000s	100s	10s	1s	1/10s	1/100s
This →		2	3	4	5	6
multiplied by 10 is this →	2	3	4	5	6	

Moreover, moving every digit one column to the left on the counting board is the same as moving the decimal point one place to the right. Thus we have a rule.

MULTIPLICATION OF A DECIMAL BY 10

To multiply a decimal fraction by 10, move the decimal point one place to the right, for example, $234.56 \times 10 = 2345.6$.

Knowing how to multiply a decimal fraction by 10, we conclude that to multiply a decimal fraction by 100, we move the decimal point *two* places to the right. For example, $736.209 \times 100 = 73,620.9$. Similarly, we can conclude that to multiply a decimal fraction by 1000, we move the decimal point *three* places to the right, for example, $9.49078 \times 1000 = 9490.78$. The general property is the following.

MULTIPLICATION OF A DECIMAL BY 10^n

To multiply a decimal fraction by 10^n, move the decimal point n places to the right.

Notice how this compares with our previous rule for multiplying a whole number by 10. Before, we would say $10 \times 534 = 5340$. Now, if we give 534 a decimal point and write $534 = 534.00$, then our new rule says $10 \times 534.00 = 5340.0$. Of course, the two rules are really saying the same thing.

From the rule for multiplication by 10, we also obtain a rule for multiplication by $\frac{1}{10}$. Knowing that $234.56 \times 10 = 2345.6$ also means that $234.56 = \frac{1}{10} \times 2345.6$. Another way of writing this is

$$234.56 = .1 \times 2345.6.$$

So we have a familiar rule.

MULTIPLICATION OF A DECIMAL BY .1

To multiply a decimal fraction by $.1 = \frac{1}{10}$, move the decimal point one place to the left, for example, $.1 \times 782.93 = 78.293$.

Similar reasoning suggests the following general rule.

MULTIPLICATION OF A DECIMAL BY $\dfrac{1}{10^n}$

To multiply a decimal by

$$\underbrace{.000 \cdots 001}_{n-1 \text{ zeroes}} = \frac{1}{10^n},$$

move the decimal point n places to the left.

Look at the examples.

$$.01 \times 409.34 = 4.0934$$
$$\text{TWO places}$$

$$.001 \times 5378.2 = 5.3782$$
$$\text{THREE places}$$

$$.000001 \times 005378.2 = .0053782$$
$$\text{SIX places}$$

EXERCISE 8. Multiply the decimal fraction 2.305

    (a) by 10   (b) by 100   (c) by .1   (d) by .01   (e) by .00001

The school district maintenance department estimates that it costs $26.75 to redo each square meter of flooring in the district schools. The principal of Jefferson Elementary figures that 3.285 m² must be redone. Jorge and Juanita have been given the job of figuring out how much all this will cost the school. They know what decimal fractions are, how to add them, and how to multiply them by powers of 10 and their reciprocals, and how to multiply common fractions. But that's all. Help them solve this.

A Solution to the
Floor Repair Problem

Jorge: "Each square meter of flooring will cost $26.75 and there are 3.285 square meters to redo. To get an answer, we have to multiply 3.285 times 26.75. Do you know how to do that?"

Juanita: "Yes and no. I don't know an easy way, like the neat way we learned to add decimal fractions. But I do know how to multiply common fractions."

Jorge: "We could treat the decimal fractions as common fractions and then multiply them as common fractions."

Juanita: "Let's rewrite the decimal fractions:

$$26.75 = 26\frac{75}{100} = \frac{2675}{100} \quad \text{and} \quad 3.285 = 3\frac{285}{1000} = \frac{3285}{1000},$$

then multiply the two fractions.

$$\frac{2675}{100} \times \frac{3285}{1000} = \frac{2675 \times 3285}{100 \times 1000}$$

The denominator is easy to calculate; it's $100 \times 1000 = 100,000$. The numerator is a mess.

$$\begin{array}{r} 3285 \\ \times\ 2675 \\ \hline 8{,}787{,}375 \end{array}$$

The answer is 8,787,375/100,000—the same as 1/100,000 × 8,787,375. There are five zeros in 100,000. So to express the answer as a decimal fraction, move the decimal point in 8787375.00 five places to the left. The final answer is $87.87375. That's about $87.87."

Jorge: "That's not bad. To solve the problem, we multiplied the two decimal fractions as if there were no decimal points. (That's what we did when we multiplied 3285 times 2675.) To figure out where the decimal point would go, we counted the number of zeros in the denominator 100,000. The number of zeros in the denominator is just the sum of the number of zeros in the denominators of the original factors: 100 and 1000. The number of zeros in 100 is the same as the number of decimal places in 26.75 and the number of zeros in 1000 is the number of decimal places in 3.285. That means that the number of decimal places in our answer is the sum of the number of decimal places of the two factors."

The Mathematical Idea: Easy Multiplication of Decimal Fractions

The solution to the floor repair problem shows that the multiplication of decimal fractions is as easy as the multiplication of two whole numbers. Notice that Jorge and

Juanita's discovery of the method depended on knowing how to multiply a decimal by $\frac{1}{10}$ (and $\frac{1}{100}$ and ...) and knowing how to multiply two common fractions.

MULTIPLICATION OF DECIMAL FRACTIONS

To multiply two decimal fractions, (1) ignore the decimal points in the two fractions and multiply the two resulting whole numbers together; and (2) in this whole number product, locate the decimal point so that the number of decimal places is equal to the sum of the number of decimal places of the two original factors.

EXERCISE

9. Multiply the two decimals 234.6 and 1.34 in two ways: (1) using the rule above and (2) by writing them as common fractions and then using the rule for multiplying common fractions. Compare your answers.

10.3   FINDING A DECIMAL FRACTION "CLOSE TO" AN ORDINARY FRACTION

THE KITCHEN CABINET PROBLEM

Jefferson Elementary is designing and making cabinets for its kitchen. June and Sam, fifth graders, are making life-size drawings of a typical cabinet. Other students in the class have figured out that each cabinet must be $\frac{3}{4}$ m high and $1\frac{1}{6}$ m wide. June and Sam want to know how to make these measurements using a meter stick. How can they do this?

Sam: "Let's see. Our meter stick has marks for $\frac{1}{10}$s, $\frac{1}{100}$s, and $\frac{1}{1000}$s of a meter. How can we mark off $\frac{3}{4}$ of a meter on our paper? Is $\frac{3}{4}$ equal to so many $\frac{1}{10}$s or $\frac{1}{100}$s or $\frac{1}{1000}$s? If it were, we could find out by using equal fractions: Find whole numbers P and Q so that

$$\frac{3}{4} = \frac{3P}{4P} = \frac{Q}{10}.$$

We can't find P and Q because 10 is not a multiple of 4. Let's try a denominator of 100: Find whole numbers P and Q so that

$$\frac{3}{4} = \frac{3P}{4P} = \frac{Q}{100}.$$

We can do this because $4 \times 25 = 100$. $P = 25$ and $Q = 75$ work. That means that

$$\frac{3}{4} = \frac{3 \times 25}{4 \times 25} = \frac{75}{100}.$$

This tells us how to mark the height of our drawing using a meter stick. Now for the width, $1\frac{1}{6}$ of a meter."

June: "We can measure the 1 meter all right, but how are we going to measure $\frac{1}{6}$ of a meter? While you were working on $\frac{3}{4}$, I was trying to figure out $\frac{1}{6}$ by the same method. I can show that there is no number we can multiply 6 by to get either 10 or 100 or 1000: 10, 100, and 1000 are not multiples of 6. In fact, using our test for divisibility by 6, no power of 10 is a multiple of 6. But I also thought of fractions on the number line. Let me *draw a picture*.

This shows tenths. Think of these as tenths of a meter. To put sixths in the picture, divide each of the spaces between tenths into six equal pieces.

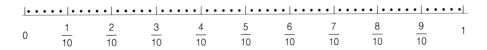

Each of those smaller lengths is a $\frac{1}{60}$th and $\frac{1}{6} = \frac{10}{60}$. So $\frac{1}{6}$ is between $\frac{1}{10} = \frac{6}{60}$ and $\frac{2}{10} = \frac{12}{60}$."

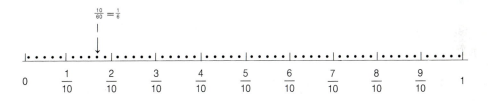

Sam: "You have a great idea. Let's do the same thing again. Let's look at the length from $\frac{1}{10}$ to $\frac{2}{10}$ divided up into 10 equal pieces—that would be $\frac{1}{100}$s of the original meter. Then we can try to zero in on the $\frac{1}{6}$."

June: "In my last picture $\frac{1}{6}$ is $\frac{2}{3}$ of the way from $\frac{1}{10}$ to $\frac{2}{10}$."
Sam: "Then we divide each of the spaces between $\frac{1}{100}$s into three equal lengths.

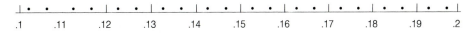

Each one of those small lengths is $\frac{1}{30}$ of the distance from .1 to .2. The point $\frac{1}{6}$ is $\frac{2}{3} = \frac{20}{30}$ the distance from .1 to .2.

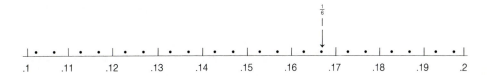

That places $\frac{1}{6}$ between the .16 and .17: $.16 < \frac{1}{6} < .17$."

June: "We've got $\frac{1}{6}$ squeezed between .16 and .17. Let's try to squeeze it between a couple of $\frac{1}{1000}$s. First draw this.

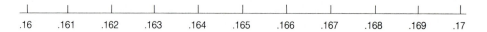

From the last picture, we know that $\frac{1}{6}$ is $\frac{2}{3}$ of the way from .16 to .17. So divide each $\frac{1}{1000}$ into thirds and put $\frac{1}{6}$ in the picture.

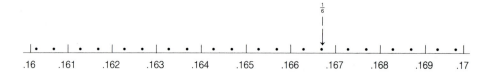

That places $\frac{1}{6}$ between .166 and .167; it's closest to .167. The distance between .166 and .167 is .001, less than the thickness of a saw blade. Isn't .167 close enough?"

EXERCISE

10. Use the method in the solution to the kitchen cabinet problem (fractions on a number line) to find the nearest $\frac{1}{100}$th to the fraction $\frac{2}{7}$.

The Mathematical Idea: Decimal Fractions Can Do a Lot of the Work for All Fractions

In the kitchen cabinet problem, June and Sam discovered that given a common fraction, there is a decimal fraction as close to the common fraction as you like. (June and Sam wanted their decimal fraction to be within a saw blade's width of $\frac{1}{6}$.) This is important to know: There are *enough* decimal fractions around to do a lot of what we want all common fractions to do. Besides, they are easy to work with: Comparing, adding, subtracting, and multiplying decimal fractions are very much like doing the same things with whole numbers.

Common fractions arise naturally, but decimal fractions are frequently used for computational purposes (for example, in hand-held calculators). For a given common fraction we need to be able to find a decimal fraction equal to it or as close to it as the particular use for the common fraction requires. That's what June and Sam were doing. The measuring and drawing tools they had limited them to measuring out $\frac{1}{10}$, $\frac{1}{100}$, and $\frac{1}{1000}$ m. They wanted to know how to measure $\frac{3}{4}$ m and $\frac{1}{6}$ m. The fraction $\frac{3}{4}$ was easy: They found a decimal fraction equal to it. The fraction $\frac{1}{6}$ was not as easy: There is no decimal fraction equal to it. But they found one close enough for their purposes. There is a relatively easy method for finding a decimal fraction "close to" a given common fraction. Let's talk about how it works and why.

Common Fractions Equal to Decimal Fractions

It was easy for June and Sam to find a decimal fraction close to $\frac{3}{4}$ because $\frac{3}{4}$ is equal to a decimal fraction:

$$\frac{3}{4} = \frac{3 \times 25}{4 \times 25} = \frac{75}{100} = .75.$$

What other fractions are equal to decimal fractions? In addition to fractions "obviously" equal to decimal fractions—3/10, 7/100, 13/1000, . . .—a few more come to mind.

$$\frac{1}{2} = \frac{1 \times 5}{2 \times 5} = \frac{5}{10} = .5$$

$$\frac{1}{4} = \frac{1 \times 25}{4 \times 25} = \frac{25}{100} = .25$$

$$\frac{3}{8} = \frac{3 \times 125}{8 \times 125} = \frac{375}{1000} = .375$$

$$\frac{7}{20} = \frac{7 \times 5}{20 \times 5} = \frac{35}{100} = .35$$

$$\frac{4}{25} = \frac{4 \times 4}{25 \times 4} = \frac{16}{100} = .16$$

Can you tell ahead of time from the way it is written whether a given common fraction is equal to a decimal fraction or not? If it is equal, how do you write the decimal fraction it's equal to? Take a fraction A/B. Assume that it is in lowest terms (that is, the GCD of numerator and denominator is equal to 1) and write down what it means for A/B to be equal to a fraction with denominator a power of 10.

CONDITION FOR A COMMON FRACTION
TO BE EQUAL TO A DECIMAL FRACTION

Suppose that A and B are nonzero whole numbers the GCD of which is 1. Then the fraction A/B is equal to a decimal fraction if and only if there are whole numbers Q and some power of 10—10^n—such that $BQ = 10^n$. Moreover, if $BQ = 10^n$, then

$$\frac{A}{B} = \frac{AQ}{BQ} = \frac{AQ}{10^n}.$$

Thus, given A/B, we seek a whole number Q such that BQ is a power of 10. In other words, we want to know when there is a power of 10 divisible by B. The key is the prime factorization of the powers of 10.

$$10 = 2 \times 5$$
$$100 = 2 \times 2 \times 5 \times 5$$
$$1000 = 2 \times 2 \times 2 \times 5 \times 5 \times 5$$
$$10,000 = 2 \times 2 \times 2 \times 2 \times 5 \times 5 \times 5 \times 5$$
$$\vdots$$

If we are successful in finding a whole number Q so that $BQ = $ power of 10, it must be that primes in the prime factorization of BQ must be the same as the primes in the factorization of the power of 10. Since the primes in the factorization of the power of 10 are 2 and 5, the primes in the factorization of BQ must also be 2 and 5.

This also means that the prime factorization of B itself involves only the primes 2 and 5. This explains the following list of equations.

$$\frac{1}{2} = .5 \text{—denominator of } \frac{1}{2} \text{ is } 2$$

$$\frac{1}{4} = .25 \text{—denominator of } \frac{1}{4} \text{ is } 2 \times 2$$

$$\frac{3}{8} = .375 \text{—denominator of } \frac{3}{8} \text{ is } 2 \times 2 \times 2$$

$$\frac{7}{20} = .35 \text{—denominator of } \frac{7}{20} \text{ is } 2 \times 2 \times 5$$

$$\frac{4}{25} = .16 \text{—denominator of } \frac{4}{25} \text{ is } 5 \times 5$$

This also explains why June and Sam were not successful in finding a decimal fraction equal to $\frac{1}{6}$: The prime factorization of 6 is 2×3. We can summarize.

> ### HOW TO TELL IF A COMMON FRACTION CAN BE REWRITTEN AS A DECIMAL FRACTION
>
> A common fraction A/B in lowest terms is equal to a decimal fraction provided the prime factorization of B consists only of 2s and 5s.

All this suggests a way to convert such a fraction into a decimal fraction. If you take a power of 10, you will notice that the number of 2s in its prime factorization is equal to the number of 5s in its prime factorization. Now take a denominator with a prime factorization consisting only of 2s and 5s. Three things can happen:

1. The number of 2s is equal to the number of 5s. In this case, the denominator is already a power of 10!

2. The number of 2s is greater than the number of 5s. In this case, multiply the numerator and denominator successively by enough 5s to equalize the number of 2s and 5s in the denominator.

3. The number of 2s is less than the number of 5s. In this case, multiply the numerator and denominator successively by enough 2s to equalize the number of 2s and 5s in the denominator.

Let's look at some examples.

EXAMPLE 1

Fraction: $\frac{1}{8}$.
Factorization of denominator: $8 = 2 \times 2 \times 2$.
Three 2s; no 5s.
Multiply numerator and denominator by $5 \times 5 \times 5$:

$$\frac{1}{8} = \frac{1 \times 5 \times 5 \times 5}{8 \times 5 \times 5 \times 5} = \frac{125}{1000}.$$

EXAMPLE 2

Fraction: $3/(2 \times 2 \times 5 \times 5 \times 5 \times 5)$.
Denominator has two 2s and four 5s.
Multiply numerator and denominator by 2×2:

$$\frac{3}{2 \times 2 \times 5 \times 5 \times 5 \times 5} = \frac{3 \times 2 \times 2}{2 \times 2 \times 2 \times 2 \times 5 \times 5 \times 5 \times 5} = \frac{12}{10,000}.$$

EXERCISE

11. Which of the fractions are equal to a decimal fraction?
    (a) $\frac{6}{15}$ (b) $\frac{7}{17}$ (c) $5/(2 \times 2 \times 2 \times 5 \times 5 \times 5)$ (d) $\frac{13}{500}$ (e) $\frac{1}{12}$
    For those that are, find the equal decimal fraction. For those that are not, explain why not.

Common Fractions That Are Not Equal to Decimal Fractions

As June and Sam discovered, not every fraction is equal to a decimal fraction. The fraction $\frac{1}{6}$ is one of those. The solution to the kitchen cabinet problem illustrates one method for finding the tenth nearest to $\frac{1}{6}$, the hundredth nearest to $\frac{1}{6}$, the thousandth nearest to $\frac{1}{6}$, and so on. Each of these is a decimal fraction *approximation* to the common fraction $\frac{1}{6}$. The solution is a little tedious: Imagine having to go through that process with *every* fraction. The next problem begins the search for a better way.

THE FRACTION APPROXIMATION PROBLEM June and Sam have discovered that $\frac{3}{7}$ is not equal to a decimal fraction. They are trying to find decimal fractions close to $\frac{3}{7}$. In particular, they want to find the nearest tenth, the nearest hundredth, and the nearest thousandth to the fraction $\frac{3}{7}$. How can they solve this?

June: "You know, we could solve this just like we solved the kitchen cabinet problem. But there must be an easier way. Let's look at the first problem: Squeeze $\frac{3}{7}$ between tenths. In symbols, the problem is to find a whole number N such that

$$\frac{N}{10} < \frac{3}{7} < \frac{N+1}{10}.$$

This means that N is the *largest* whole number such that $N/10 < \frac{3}{7}$. Let's replace the fractions in this inequality by equal fractions having the same denominator,

$$\frac{N}{10} = \frac{N \times 7}{10 \times 7} = \frac{7N}{70} \quad \text{and} \quad \frac{3}{7} = \frac{3 \times 10}{7 \times 10} = \frac{30}{70}.$$

In place of $N/10 < \frac{3}{7}$, we have

$$\frac{7N}{70} < \frac{30}{70}.$$

Thus, N is the largest whole number such that $7N < 30$. To find N, you divide 30 by 7: $30 \div 7 = N$ with remainder R. The answer is $N = 4$; $R = 2$.

"Here's what we have so far: $\frac{3}{7}$ is squeezed between $\frac{4}{10}$ and $\frac{5}{10}$: $\frac{4}{10} < \frac{3}{7} < \frac{5}{10}$. Which one is it closer to? Let's make denominators the same so that $\frac{4}{10} < \frac{3}{7} < \frac{5}{10}$ becomes $\frac{28}{70} < \frac{30}{70} < \frac{35}{70}$. The difference between 30 and 28 is 2 (that's the remainder, remember?), and the difference between 35 and 30 is 5. That means that $\frac{3}{7}$ is closer to $\frac{4}{10}$."

Sam: "The same idea will work for hundredths, too. Suppose this time that N is the largest whole number such that $N/100 < \frac{3}{7}$. Using $100 \times 7 = 700$ as a common denominator, $N/100 < \frac{3}{7}$ becomes $(7N)/700 < \frac{300}{700}$ so that N is the largest whole number such that $7N < 300$. In this case, $300 \div 7 = 42$ with remainder 6. Our number N is 42: $\frac{42}{100} < \frac{3}{7} < \frac{43}{100}$. Which is $\frac{3}{7}$ closer to? Common denominators again:

$$\frac{42 \times 7}{700} < \frac{300}{700} < \frac{43 \times 7}{700} \qquad \text{or} \qquad \frac{294}{700} < \frac{300}{700} < \frac{301}{700}.$$

The answer is clear: The difference between 300 and 294 is 6 (that's the remainder), and the difference between 300 and 301 is just 1. So it's closer to $\frac{301}{700} = \frac{43}{100} = .43$."

June: "The remainder is the key to telling you which it's closest to. The difference between 301 and 294 is 7. (This is no surprise because the difference between $\frac{301}{700}$ and $\frac{294}{700}$ is just $\frac{7}{700}$, which is equal to $\frac{1}{100}$.) The difference between 300 and 294 is 6, the remainder. The difference between 6 and 7 is 1. That means that if the remainder is bigger than half the denominator, the fraction is closer to the decimal on the right. Otherwise, it's closer to the decimal on the left. This agrees with what happened in looking for the nearest tenth: The remainder was 2—less than half of 7—and $\frac{3}{7}$ is closer to the tenth on the left."

Sam: "To find the closest $\frac{1}{1000}$th is to find the largest whole number N such that

$$\frac{N}{1000} < \frac{3}{7} \qquad \text{or} \qquad \frac{7N}{7000} < \frac{3000}{7000} \qquad \text{or} \qquad 7N < 3000.$$

Now $3000 \div 7 = 428$ (N) with remainder 4. That means $\frac{428}{1000} < \frac{3}{7} < \frac{429}{1000}$. It also means that

$$\frac{7 \times 428}{7000} < \frac{3000}{7000} < \frac{7 \times 429}{7000} \qquad \text{or} \qquad \frac{2996}{7000} < \frac{3000}{7000} < \frac{3003}{7000}.$$

The middle fraction is closer to the fraction on the right. At the same time, the remainder 4 is bigger than half of 7. The nearest thousandth to $\frac{3}{7}$ is .429."

The Mathematical Idea: The Standard Method for Approximating a Common Fraction by Decimal Fractions

June and Sam's procedure is very close to the standard method for approximating a common fraction by a decimal fraction. To compare, let's show the work for their three solutions all at once.

JUNE AND SAM'S PROCEDURE			
LAYOUT FOR STANDARD METHOD	NEAREST .1	NEAREST .01	NEAREST .001

.428
7) 3.000
  2 8
  ‾20
  14
  ‾60
  56
  ‾4
  ⋮
	4
	7) 30
	  28
	  ‾2
		42
		7) 300
		  28
		  ‾20
		  14
		  ‾6
			428
			7) 3000
			  28
			  ‾20
			  14
			  ‾60
			  56
			  ‾4

	$\frac{3}{7}$ CLOSEST TO .4	$\frac{3}{7}$ CLOSEST TO .43	$\frac{3}{7}$ CLOSEST TO .427

The work for the three problems June and Sam solved is cumulative: The last problem includes the work for the previous two, and the second problem includes the work for the first one. The layout for the standard method takes advantage of this: You don't have to start over again to find the closest decimal for each new level of precision that interests you.

If the denominator for the common fraction happens to have only 2s and 5s in its prime factorization, then at some point in the division using the standard method there will be a remainder of zero. This is another way of saying that some power of 10 is divisible by the denominator. Thus, the standard method if carried out far enough will detect those common fractions that are equal to decimal fractions. Here are some examples illustrating this.

EXAMPLE 1

$$\frac{3}{50}$$

$$
\begin{array}{r}
.06 \\
50 \overline{) 3.000} \\
3\ 00 \\
\hline
0
\end{array}
$$

$$\frac{3}{50} = .06$$

EXAMPLE 2

$$\frac{5}{16}$$

$$
\begin{array}{r}
.3125 \\
16 \overline{) 5.0000} \\
4\ 8 \\
\hline
20 \\
16 \\
\hline
40 \\
32 \\
\hline
80 \\
80 \\
\hline
0
\end{array}
$$

$$\frac{5}{16} = .3125$$

EXAMPLE 3

$$\frac{33}{125}$$

$$
\begin{array}{r}
.264 \\
125\overline{\smash{\big)}33.000} \\
\underline{25\,0} \\
8\,00 \\
\underline{7\,50} \\
500 \\
\underline{500} \\
0
\end{array}
$$

$$\frac{33}{125} = .264$$

EXERCISE

12. For each of the common fractions, find the nearest hundredth to it.

    (a) $\frac{3}{25}$ (b) $\frac{2}{11}$ (c) $\frac{5}{9}$ (d) $\frac{17}{20}$

10.4   DIVISION OF DECIMALS

THE ALLOY PROBLEM

Try this yourself, first.

To cast a small metal sculpture, 11.667 lb of tin and 15.750 lb of copper are melted and then mixed to create an alloy. The makers of the sculpture now need to know what fraction of the alloy (by weight) consists of copper. They have enlisted the aid of Sam and June who know how to add, subtract, and multiply decimal fractions, and how to approximate common fractions by decimal fractions. But that's about all they know. Help them solve this problem.

A Solution to the Alloy Problem

Sam: "There are 15.750 pounds of copper. I want to know what fraction this is of the total amount of metal there is. The alloy is made from 11.667 pounds of tin and 15.750 pounds of copper. When those are mixed, there are 11.667 + 15.750 pounds altogether—a total of 27.417 pounds. We want to find 15.750 ÷ 27.417. To divide these decimal fractions, we can rewrite them as common fractions:

$$
\begin{aligned}
15.75 \div 27.417 &= \frac{1575}{100} \div \frac{27417}{1000} \\[2mm]
&= \frac{1575}{100} \times \frac{1000}{27417} \\[2mm]
&= \frac{1575 \times 1000}{100 \times 27417} \\[2mm]
&= \frac{1575}{27417} \times \frac{1000}{100}.
\end{aligned}
$$

The $\frac{1000}{100}$ part is easy; it's a power of 10. To find an approximation of $\frac{1575}{27417}$ by a decimal fraction, I use the standard long division layout.

$$
\begin{array}{r}
.057 \\
27417 \overline{\smash{)}1575.000} \\
137085 \\
\overline{204150} \\
191919 \\
\overline{12231}
\end{array}
$$

Then I multiply the .057 by $\frac{1000}{100}$—the latter is equal to 10—and get .57. So copper, by weight, is .57 of the alloy."

The Mathematical Idea: Division of Decimals

The method for dividing decimal fractions in the solution to the alloy problem is so close to the standard method that it is useful to place the layouts for the two solutions side by side.

METHOD IN SOLUTION
TO ALLOY PROBLEM

$$
\begin{array}{r}
.057 \\
27417 \overline{\smash{)}1575.000} \\
137085 \\
\overline{204150} \\
191919 \\
\overline{12231}
\end{array}
$$

$$.057 \times \frac{1000}{100} = .57$$

STANDARD METHOD

$$
\begin{array}{r}
.57 \\
27.417 \overline{\smash{)}15.75000} \\
137085 \\
\overline{204150} \\
191919 \\
\overline{12231}
\end{array}
$$

EXERCISE

13. Solve the problems below in two ways: (1) using the method in the solution to the alloy problem and (2) using the standard method.
   (a) $.003 \div 1.05$ (b) $1.05 \div .003$
   (c) $.1002 \div .001002$ (d) $100.2 \div 0.001002$

10.5   ROUNDING AND CALCULATORS

We have already discussed finding the nearest tenth (or hundredth, or thousandth, or ...) to a given fraction. Suppose that you already know that the fraction is equal to 34.5847. Then finding the nearest .1, .01, or .001 to the decimal fraction 34.5847 is also called *rounding* to one, two, and three decimal places, respectively. Here are the results.

1. The nearest .1 to 34.5847 is 34.6, which is 34.5847 rounded to one decimal place. To see this, you might think this way: $34.5 = 34.5000 < 34.5847 < 34.6000 = 34.6$, and 5847 (ten-thousandths) is closer to 6000 (ten-thousandths) than it is to 5000 (ten-thousandths).

2. The nearest .01 to 34.5847 is 34.58, which is 34.5847 rounded to two decimal places. To see this, you note that $34.58 = 34.5800 < 34.5847 < 34.5900 = 34.59$, and 5800 is closer to 5847 than it is to 5900.

3. The nearest .001 to 34.5847 is 34.585, which is 34.5847 rounded to three decimal places.

Consider another example. Suppose that we want to round .185 to two decimal places. We know that .18 = .180 < .185 < .190 = .19. In this case, .185 is exactly half way between .18 and .19. When this happens, the larger value is chosen by convention. Thus .185 rounded to two decimal places is .19.

These examples suggest a general method.

TO ROUND OFF A DECIMAL FRACTION TO *N* PLACES

1. If the digit in the $N + 1$ place is 5 or larger, eliminate all digits beyond the Nth place and add 1 to the digit in the Nth place.

2. If the digit in the $N + 1$ position is less than 5, eliminate all digits beyond the Nth place and leave everything else alone.

For example, to round the decimal fraction 7.89403558 to four places, look at the digit in the fifth position.

$$7.89403558$$
$$\uparrow$$

Digit in fifth position is 3 (< 5).

So 7.89403558 rounded off to four places is 7.8940. To round off 7.89403558 to five places, look at the digit in the sixth position.

$$7.89403558$$
$$\uparrow$$

Digit in sixth position is 5 (≥ 5).

Thus, 7.89403558 rounded off to five places is 7.89404.

A common situation where you might want to round is when a decimal fraction appears on your calculator display as the answer to some problem. For example, suppose you want to find the nearest .001 to 4/17 using a calculator. Your key sequence will be 4 [÷] 17 [=], and the display will show 0.2352941. The latter rounded to the nearest .001 is .235, which is also the nearest .001 to $\frac{4}{17}$.

As another example, suppose you want to find 24.32 ÷ 7.67 to two decimal places. On the calculator, your key sequence will be 24.32 [÷] 7.67 [=], and the display will show 3.1707953. The latter rounded to the nearest .01 is 3.17.

EXERCISES
14. Round each of the following decimal fractions as indicated.
   (a) 5.1234 to two decimal places   (b) 354.190 to two decimal places
   (c) 0.5555 to three decimal places   (d) 1.4003 to two decimal places

15. Use a calculator to find decimal fractions that approximate each of the following and round each one to three decimal places.
   (a) $\frac{3}{8}$ (b) $\frac{27}{23}$ (c) 4.17 × 5.89   (d) 67.102 ÷ 17.871

16. Round each of the following fractions to four decimal places.
   (a) .12392   (b) .12397   (c) .12997   (d) .19997   (e) .99997
   For each of these, the rounded fraction should be the closest .0001 to the original. Is it? How should the rules for rounding be clarified to account for situations such as these?

PERCENT AND THE LANGUAGE OF FRACTIONS IN THE MARKETPLACE

Fractions occur in real life most often as percents. In this section we will review the language of percents and how to convert fractions to decimals to percents and back. We will also solve many problems of interest to consumers, in which percents appear as rates of increase, rates of decrease, rates of interest, rates of inflation, and so on.

World production of coffee expected to drop 14 percent

WASHINGTON (AP)—The world coffee crop for 1986-87 is forecast at 82.9 million bags, down 14 percent from last season's revised production of 96.4 million bags, the Agriculture Department said.

Brazil, the world's largest producer, is expected to harvest 16.5 million bags, half of last year's production, the department's Foreign Agricultural Service said Wednesday in its first global coffee forecast of the new season.

In a special report in February, the Agriculture Department also forecast Brazil's crop at 16.5 million bags because of drought in major producing areas.

A bag of green, unroasted coffee weighs 60 kilograms, or about 132 pounds.

Overall, South American coffee production was indicated at 33.8 million bags, a drop of 16 million bags from 1985-86 and the smallest output since 1977-78. However, larger crops were forecast in Colombia, up 3 percent from last season's 12 million bags, and in Ecuador, up 2 percent to a record crop of 2 million bags.

Percent: Fractions in the News

Fractions occur frequently in common discourse, but they occur most often in the form of a special fraction, the *percent*. One percent is the fraction $\frac{1}{100}$ and is denoted 1%; 17 percent is the fraction $\frac{17}{100}$ and is denoted 17%. 5% means $\frac{5}{100}$, 57% means $\frac{57}{100}$, 5.7% means $\frac{5.7}{100}$, and $33\frac{1}{3}$% means $33\frac{1}{3}/100$. The word *percent* is short for the Latin phrase *per centum*, meaning "out of 100." The use of 5%—instead of $\frac{5}{100}$ or 0.05—is traditional.

Percents are equal to decimal fractions as well as to common fractions.

$$5\% = \frac{5}{100} = .05$$

$$57\% = \frac{57}{100} = .57$$

$$5.7\% = \frac{5.7}{100} = .057$$

$$570\% = \frac{570}{100} = 5.70$$

$$\frac{3}{4}\% = .75\% = \frac{.75}{100} = .0075$$

$$33\frac{1}{3}\% = \frac{33\frac{1}{3}}{100} = \frac{1}{3} \approx .3333$$

or

$$33\frac{1}{3}\% \cong 33.33\% = \frac{33.33}{100} = .3333. \text{ (The symbol } \cong \text{ means "approximately equal.")}$$

Since percents are in common use, it is useful to be able to move easily from common fractions to decimals to percents and back. We have already discussed approximating common fractions by decimal fractions and converting a decimal fraction to a common fraction. Here is a review of the methods for converting decimals to percents and back.

CONVERTING DECIMALS TO PERCENTS

To convert a decimal fraction to a percent, move the decimal point two places to the right, and add the percent sign (%) on the right, for example,

$$0.785 = 78.5\% \left(\text{since } .785 = \frac{78.5}{100} \right),$$

$$3.03 = 303\% \left(\text{since } 3.03 = \frac{303}{100} \right), \quad \text{and}$$

$$0.0025 = 0.25\% \left(\text{since } .0025 = \frac{.25}{100} \right).$$

CONVERTING PERCENTS TO DECIMALS

To convert a percent to a decimal fraction, move the decimal point two places to the left and delete the percent sign; for example,

$$75\% = .75,$$

$$.04\% = .0004, \quad \text{and}$$

$$110.5\% = 1.105.$$

Since percents are fractions, the language of fractions is used wherever percentages occur. Thus, 30 is 75% of 40 means:

$$30 \text{ is } \frac{75}{100} \text{ of } 40 \quad \text{or} \quad 30 \text{ is } \frac{3}{4} \text{ of } 40 \quad \text{or} \quad 30 = \frac{3}{4} \times 40.$$

In a sentence of the form A is p% of B, p is the *percent* and sometimes the amount A is called the *percentage*, as in "the salesperson gets 10% of sales. John sold $500 worth of merchandise. His *percentage* is $50. ($50 = .10 × $500)."

Questions often arise in dealing with percents. How can you answer them?

1. To answer "What percent is 25 of 35?" (that is, 25 is what percent of 35?), you first answer, "25 is what fraction of 35?" (answer: $\frac{25}{35}$), then convert the answer to a percent: $\frac{25}{35} \cong .714 = 71.4\%$. So 25 is 71.4% of 35.

2. To answer "What is 120% of 58?" you convert the percent to a fraction (120% = 1.2) and answer the question, "What is 1.2 of 58?" (answer: $1.2 \times 58 = 69.6$). So 69.6 is 120% of 58.

3. To answer "35 is 42% of what number?" you convert the percent to a fraction (42% = .42) and answer the question, "35 is .42 of what number?" or "What is N if $35 = .42 \times N$? (answer: $N = 35/.42 = 83.33$). So 35 is 42% of 83.33.

The use of percents occurs in several contexts that we explore in the remainder of the section.

EXERCISES

17. 154 is what percent of 125?

18. What is 78% of 545?

19. 48 is 20% of what?

THE MEDICATION PROBLEM

Try this yourself, first.

A pharmacist needs 50 ml of a 1% solution of a certain medication. On the shelf he has a large bottle of a solution consisting of 1 part of the medication and 19 parts of distilled water. He wants to know if adding distilled water to part of the shelf solution would get him what he wants and, if so, he wants to know how much water to add.

A Solution to the Medication Problem

The pharmacist thinks that he ought to figure out—for the shelf solution that he has—what percent of the total solution the medication is. He thinks: "When the solution was made, 1 unit of pure medication was mixed with 19 units of distilled water. The total solution has 20 units in all, 1 of which is pure medication. That means that $\frac{1}{20}$ of the solution is pure medication. Now $\frac{1}{20} = 5\%$. So my shelf solution is 5% pure medication. That's too strong. I should add more distilled water to what I have. But how much? Let's see. I need 50 ml of 1% solution. In that 50 ml, 1% would be pure medication, or $.01 \times 50 = .5$ ml. The rest—49.5 ml—would be distilled water. How much of the shelf solution will give me exactly .5 ml? Let me *make a guess*: In 20 ml of the shelf solution there would be 1 ml of pure medication and 19 ml of distilled water. Take half of that, 10 ml; there would be .5 ml of pure medication and 9.5 ml of distilled water. Add 40 ml of distilled water to the 10 ml of shelf solution, and I'd have 50 ml of a 1% solution."

THE MONEY INVESTMENT PROBLEM

Please try this yourself.

Mr. Jones and Ms. Smith are discussing the earnings they have received from their investments. A year ago Mr. Jones put $1200 into a savings account at his bank. Without adding anything to the account since then, there is now $1283 in the account. At the same time a year ago, Ms. Smith put $545 in her credit union account and now, without adding anything to it since then, there is $589 in the account. They want to know which account is better.

A Solution to the Money Investment Problem

Mr. Jones: "The problem is to find a way to compare the two accounts. To measure the earning power of an account, look at the ratio of amount earned to amount invested. So consider the following fraction:

$$\frac{\text{Amount earned}}{\text{amount invested}}.$$

These fractions for the separate investments are the following.

Mr. Jones: $\dfrac{\text{Amount earned}}{\text{amount invested}} = \dfrac{\$83}{\$1200} = .069 = 6.9\%.$

Ms. Smith: $\dfrac{\text{Amount earned}}{\text{amount invested}} = \dfrac{\$44}{\$545} = .081 = 8.1\%.$

Ms. Smith, your ratio is bigger. That means that $\$44 = 8.1\%$ of $\$545$. If I had invested my money in an account in your credit union, then I would have earned 8.1% of $\$1200 = .081 \times \$1200 = \$97.20$."

The Mathematical Language: Principal, Interest, and Interest Rates

The method for comparing investments described in the solution to the money investment problem is standard, and there is some terminology associated with it. The amount of money invested is called the *principal*. The amount of money the principal earns is called the *interest*. The fraction

$$\frac{\text{Interest}}{\text{principal}} = \frac{\text{amount earned}}{\text{amount invested}}$$

is called the *interest rate,* or *rate of interest.* The rate of interest is usually expressed as a percent. Thus, the interest rate for Mr. Jones's bank account is 6.9%, that for Ms. Smith's account, 8.1%.

Time is another factor in financial investments. The money in Mr. Jones's account and in Ms. Smith's account stayed there for a year. To be precise, the interest rates for the two accounts should really be called the *annual interest rate.* Just as it is assumed that double the principal will produce double the interest, it is also assumed that double the time will produce double the interest, half the time will produce half the interest, and so on. For example, in Mr. Jones's account, $1200 with 6.9% annual rate will earn interest of

$$.069 \times \$1200 = \$83 \text{ after 1 yr,}$$
$$2 \times .069 \times \$1200 = \$166 \text{ after 2 yr, or}$$
$$.5 \times .069 \times \$1200 = \$41.50 \text{ after } \tfrac{1}{2} \text{ yr.}$$

This describes a type of interest called *simple interest.* (Another type, *compound interest,* will be discussed in a later chapter.)

EXERCISES

20. Mountain Bank promises that $1000 deposited in one of its savings accounts will be worth $1075 a year later. What is the savings account's annual rate of interest?

21. Suppose the pharmacist in the medication problem wants 50 ml of 2% solution. How would he make that up?

22. A pharmacist wants to make 50 ml of a 5% solution of treatment X. She has a solution that is 100% pure treatment X. How much distilled water and how much pure treatment X should be mixed to make the desired mixture?

23. A pharmacist wants to make 50 ml of a 10% solution of treatment Y. She has a solution that is 25% pure treatment Y. How much distilled water and how much of the 25% pure solution should be mixed to make the desired mixture?

The Southwest Products Company manufactures two brands of toothpaste, Fluorina and Minta. The company plans to discontinue one of these brands. The company will choose the single brand it will manufacture on the basis of which is more profitable. Here are the company's figures on the two toothpastes.

PROFITS VS. INVESTMENTS		
Brand	1986 investment in brand	1986 profits from brand
Fluorina	$1,125,000	$45,000
Minta	610,000	28,000

Which brand is more profitable?

A Solution to the Toothpaste Profit Problem

How does one decide which brand is the most profitable? Profit for a manufacturer is analogous to interest for a financial investment. To decide which financial investment is better, one compares the "interest rates." For a manufacturer the notion analogous to rate of interest is *rate of profit over investment*—the ratio of profit to investment. Here are the rates for the two toothpastes.

$$\text{Rate of profit over investment for Fluorina} = \frac{\text{profit}}{\text{investment}} = \frac{\$45,000}{\$1,125,000} = .04 = 4\%.$$

$$\text{Rate of profit for Minta} = \frac{\text{profit}}{\text{investment}} = \frac{\$28,000}{\$610,000} \cong .046 = 4.6\%.$$

So Minta has the higher rate of profit over investment.

THE BOOK PRICE INCREASE PROBLEM

The local school board is determining its budget for next year. One item they need to budget for is textbooks. They don't know what the price of textbooks will be a year from now, but they do have some figures.

YEAR	COST OF TEXTBOOKS PER STUDENT
1986	$57.85
1987	$68.70
1988	?

How can these figures be used to help predict what the cost of textbooks per student will be in 1988?

Solutions to the Book Price Increase Problem

One way to predict the cost for 1988 would be to see how the cost for 1986 and 1987 changed and then predict the cost for 1988 so that the change from 1987 to 1988 would be the same as the change from 1986 to 1987. One way to describe the change from 1986 to 1987 is to look at the *difference* in costs: $68.70 − $57.85 = $10.85. Using this way to describe the change in costs, you predict that the 1988 cost will be $68.70 + $10.85 = $79.55. (Is this a "good" prediction?)

Another way to describe the change is to find the ratio of the increase in cost from 1986 to 1987 to the 1986 cost.

$$\frac{\text{Increase in cost from '86 to '87}}{\text{'86 cost}} = \frac{\$10.85}{\$57.85} = 0.187 = 18.7\%.$$

The percentage 18.7% is called the *rate of increase*. If we assume that the increase in cost from 1987 to 1988 would also be 18.7% of the 1987 cost, then the actual increase would be

$$18.7\% \text{ of } 1987 \text{ cost} = .187 \times \$68.70 = \$12.85.$$

Using this method of prediction, we find that the predicted cost is $68.70 + $12.85 = $81.55.

EXERCISE 24. Discuss the pros and cons of each method of prediction in the solution to the book price increase problem.

THE WATER HEATING BILL PROBLEM

Try this yourself.

Mr. Jones and Mr. Smith are discussing their water heating bills. A year ago Mr. Jones installed a solar water heater. His bill for the year before installation was $127; his bill for the year after installation was $105. Mr. Smith has an annual water heating bill of $82. He is wondering what the bill would be if he had a solar water heater.

A Solution to the Water Heating Bill Problem

Mr. Smith assumes that the ratio of the amount of decrease in his water bill to the amount of his present water bill would be the same as the ratio of the amount of the decrease in Mr. Jones's water bill to the amount of his (Mr. Jones's) bill before installation of the solar water heater:

$$\frac{\text{Decrease in Jones's bill}}{\text{Jones's previous bill}} = \frac{\text{anticipated decrease in Smith's bill}}{\text{Smith's present bill}} \quad \text{or}$$

$$\frac{\$22}{\$127} = \frac{\text{Smith's anticipated decrease}}{\$82}.$$

Since $22/$127 = .173 = 17.3%, Smith's anticipated decrease should be 17.3% of $82, or .173 × $82, which is equal to $14.19. Mr. Smith's new bill should be $82 − $14.19 = $67.81.

The Mathematical Language: Rates of Increase and Decrease

In the solution to the book price increase problem the second method describes the change in price as a percent of the original price. This is called the *percent increase* (or the *rate of increase*) in price. In the water heating bill problem the change in the bill is expressed as a percent of the bill before the change occurred. This is called the *percent decrease* (or the *rate of decrease*) in cost. In both cases change is described as a percent of the price or cost before the change took place. Rates of increase or decrease of prices or costs are also indicated with other terms.

- A store *marks an item up by* 5%. This means the store increases the price of the item by 5%. The rate of increase of the price is 5%.

- A store *marks an item down by* 20%, meaning the store decreases the price of the item by 20%.

- A store gives a *discount of* 35% on an item, which means the store decreases the price of the item by 35%.

EXERCISE 25. After a good summer leading to a surplus in milk production, the Milk Commission decided on a 6% markdown on milk prices. What is the new price (to the nearest cent) of a quart of milk that used to cost 50¢?

THE CAR SALESMAN PROBLEM

Two salesmen working for different car dealers are comparing what they earn on the basis of new cars they have just sold. Salesman 1 has just sold a new car for $7200. He earned $414 on that sale. Salesman 2 just sold one for $8700; his earnings on this were $457. Which salesman has the better job, financially?

A Solution to the Car Salesman Problem

In terms of their most recent sales, salesman 2 earned more money than salesman 1. You might expect salesman 2 to earn more because he sold something more valuable. To help decide which job is better, we ought to answer the question "What would salesman 1 have earned if he had sold a car for the same amount as salesman 2?" We can answer this if we assume that the ratio of amount earned to value of sale is the same from one sale to another for each salesman. If we assume this, then for salesman 1,

$$\frac{\text{Amount earned}}{\text{value of sale}} = \frac{\$414}{\$7200} = 0.0575 = 5.75\%.$$

For salesman 2,

$$\frac{\text{Amount earned}}{\text{value of sale}} = \frac{\$457}{\$8700} = 0.525 = 5.25\%.$$

If our assumption is correct that the ratio of amount earned to value of sale is the same from one sale to another, then salesman 1 would always earn 5.75% of the value of any sale. That means that if he were to sell a car for $8700, he would earn .0575 × $8700 = $500.25.

EXERCISE 26. Can you say now which job is better financially?

The Mathematical Language: Rate of Commission

For a salesperson it is not unusual for the ratio of the amount the salesperson earns to the value of the sale to be the same from sale to sale. This ratio is called the *rate of commission* and is usually expressed as a percent. In a given sale the salesperson earns the rate of commission times the value of what is sold. The amount actually earned is called the *commission*.

27. Jane is a salesperson whose rate of commission is 4.67% on all washing machines she sells. She has just sold a washing machine for $432. What is her commission on this sale?

Each year the government figures what a "typical" individual purchases in a year and computes the ratio

$$\frac{\text{Increase in the cost of purchases from last year to this year}}{\text{cost of purchases last year}}.$$

Try it!

This ratio, expressed as a percent, is called the *rate of inflation*. Management wants each employee's salary for next year to be increased by the current rate of inflation. If an employee's current salary is $13,500 and the current rate of inflation is 5.3%, what will that person's salary be next year?

**A Solution to the Employee
Raise Problem**

The increase is salary should be 5.3% of $13,500. This is

$$0.053 \times 13500 = \$715.50.$$

The person's salary next year should be

$$\$13,500 + \$715.50 = \$14,215.50.$$

The Mathematical Language: Depreciation

A new automobile purchased now will have a resale value in a year considerably less than the purchase price. The difference between purchase price and resale value is called the amount of *depreciation*. The *percent rate of depreciation* is the ratio—expressed as a percent—

$$\frac{\text{Depreciation}}{\text{purchase price}}.$$

28. New automobiles tend to depreciate at a rate of 30% by the end of the first year of purchase. A new automobile is purchased for $9380. What is its resale value a year later?

29. The Lemonmobile dealer pays the manufacturer $6000 for a Lemonmobile with standard options. John just bought one of these for $7700. He must pay a sales tax of 7% on this price. The dealer, on the other hand, must pay taxes on the profit: a federal tax of 22% and a state tax of 11%. Taxes from the purchaser and the dealer amount to how much?

10.7 LOOKING BACK: REPEATING DECIMALS

We know that $\frac{3}{4} = .75$ and $\frac{7}{25} = .28$. These are not approximations, they are exact equations. The common fractions $\frac{3}{4}$ and $\frac{7}{25}$ are *equal* to the decimal fractions .75 and .28, respectively. In fact, fractions (in lowest terms) the denominators of which have prime factors consisting only of 2 or 5 (or both) are equal to decimal fractions. Conversely, every decimal fraction is equal to a fraction the denominator of which has only 2 and 5 as possible prime factors.

Now let's look at some common fractions that are not equal to decimal fractions. Take $\frac{1}{3}$ and $\frac{2}{7}$, for example. To find decimal fractions close to these, we use the standard layout.

$$
\begin{array}{r}
.3333\ldots \\
3\overline{)1.0000\ldots} \\
9 \\
\overline{10} \\
9 \\
\overline{10} \\
9 \\
\overline{1} \\
\vdots
\end{array}
$$

$$
\begin{array}{r}
.2857\ldots \\
7\overline{)2.0000\ldots} \\
14 \\
\overline{60} \\
56 \\
\overline{40} \\
35 \\
\overline{50} \\
49 \\
\overline{1} \\
\vdots
\end{array}
$$

The use of ellipses points . . . for each fraction means that we can keep going, to any level of exactness we want. The sequence of digits to the right of the decimal point is called the *decimal representation* of the fraction. Thus .3333 . . . is the decimal representation for $\frac{1}{3}$, and .2857 . . . is the decimal representation for $\frac{2}{7}$. Normally we write

$$\frac{1}{3} = .3333\ldots$$

$$\frac{2}{7} = .2857\ldots$$

The decimal fractions .3, .33, .333, .3333, . . . are *decimal approximations* to $\frac{1}{3}$. Similarly, the decimal fractions .2, .29, .286, .2857, . . . are decimal approximations to $\frac{2}{7}$.

The sequences of digits in the decimal representations of $\frac{1}{3}$ and $\frac{2}{7}$ will go on forever because these common fractions are not equal to decimal fractions. The decimal representations for such fractions are called *nonterminating decimals*. (A common fraction equal to a decimal fraction, such as $\frac{3}{4}$, is said to have a *terminating decimal* representation.) For a given fraction, can we predict anything about the sequence of digits in the decimal representation?

For example, if we look at the standard layout for finding the decimal representation (and the decimal approximations) for $\frac{1}{3}$, it seems clear that the digit 3 will keep repeating indefinitely. At each stage in carrying out the long division, a remainder of 1 always occurs, producing the same result at the next stage.

$$
\begin{array}{r}
.3333\ldots \\
3\,\overline{)\,①.0000\ldots} \\
9 \\
\hline
①0 \\
9 \\
\hline
①0 \\
9 \\
\hline
① \\
\vdots
\end{array}
$$

Remainders are circled.

This exact feature doesn't occur for $\frac{2}{7}$. But can we predict what subsequent digits of $\frac{2}{7}$ might be? Let's look at the remainders in other examples to *see if we can find a pattern*.

$\dfrac{5}{6}$

$$
\begin{array}{r}
.8333\ldots \\
6\,\overline{)\,⑤.0000\ldots} \\
4\ 8 \\
\hline
②0 \\
1\ 8 \\
\hline
②0 \\
1\ 8 \\
\hline
②0 \\
1\ 8 \\
\hline
② \\
\vdots
\end{array}
$$

Remainders are circled.

$\dfrac{4}{11}$

$$
\begin{array}{r}
.3636\ldots \\
11\,\overline{)\,④.0000\ldots} \\
3\ 3 \\
\hline
⑦0 \\
6\ 6 \\
\hline
④0 \\
3\ 3 \\
\hline
⑦0 \\
6\ 6 \\
\hline
④ \\
\vdots
\end{array}
$$

Remainders are circled.

$\frac{5}{37}$

Remainders are circled.

```
       .1351 . . .
   37 |(5).0000 . . .
       3 7
       (1 3)0
       1 1 1
        (1 9)0
         1 8 5
           (5)0
            3 7
           (1 3)
             :
```

Let's analyze each example one by one.

In the layout for $\frac{5}{6}$ the second remainder (the first remainder is the numerator itself) and all subsequent remainders is 2, producing the same result for each successive stage of the division.

```
       .8333 . . .
    6 |(5).0000 . . .
       4 8
       (2)0
        1 8
        (2)0
         1 8
         (2)0
          1 8
          (2)
           :
```

The digits in the decimal representation for $\frac{5}{6}$ will keep repeating 3 indefinitely: $\frac{5}{6} = .83333333\ldots$

The situation with $\frac{4}{11}$ is not the same. Nevertheless, something intriguing seems to be happening. The remainders alternate back and forth, 4 and 7, 4 and 7, . . .

```
       .3636 . . .
   11 |(4).0000 . . .
       3 3
       (7)0
        6 6
        (4)0
         3 3
         (7)0
          6 6
          (4)
           :
```

(It is useful to think of the numerator 4 of the fraction as the first remainder.) This in turn produces a periodic alternation of the digits 3 and 6 in the decimal representation of $\frac{4}{11}$. So we have this decimal representation: $\frac{4}{11} = .36363636\ldots$

For the fraction $\frac{5}{37}$, we know that its decimal representation begins with .1351. Can you predict what subsequent digits in the decimal representation will be? From the other examples we've looked at, it seems that the remainders at each stage give important clues. The remainders are: 5, 13, 19, 5.

$$
\begin{array}{r}
.1351\ldots \\
37\overline{)\,⑤.0000\ldots} \\
3\ 7 \\
\overline{1\ 30} \\
1\ 11 \\
\overline{190} \\
185 \\
\overline{⑤0} \\
3\ 7 \\
\overline{1\ 3} \\
\vdots
\end{array}
$$

But the first and the fourth remainders are the same. That means that the work for stages four, five, and six will be the same as the work for stages one, two and three.

$$
\begin{array}{r}
.135135\ldots \\
37\overline{)\,5.000000\ldots} \\
3\ 7 \\
\overline{1\ 30} \\
1\ 11 \\
\overline{190} \\
185 \\
\overline{50} \\
37 \\
\overline{130} \\
111 \\
\overline{190} \\
185 \\
\overline{5} \\
\vdots
\end{array}
$$

This pattern of the remainders will keep repeating cyclically and the digits in the decimal representation will repeat as well: $\frac{5}{37} = .135135135135\ldots$

In all these examples, once a remainder repeats an earlier remainder, all subsequent remainders will repeat as well, and the corresponding digits in the decimal representation will also repeat. Once a repetition occurs, you can predict the subsequent digits of the decimal representation.

What happens in general? Given a fraction, will there be a later remainder that repeats an earlier remainder? (Will this happen for $\frac{2}{7}$, the fraction we considered earlier?) Consider the remainders of a typical fraction A/B in lowest terms. In the division layout for calculating the decimal representation for A/B, what are the possible remainders? In the layout for $\frac{2}{7}$, the first five remainders are 2, 6, 4, 5, and 1. Without actually calculating, in *any* layout for division by the whole number 7, the possible remainders are 0, 1, 2, 3, 4, 5, 6. In our layout, the remainder 0 can't occur, because $\frac{2}{7}$ has a nonterminating decimal representation. So the possible remainders are 1, 2, 3, 4, 5, and 6. In general, here's what happens.

POSSIBLE REMAINDERS IN STANDARD LAYOUT
FOR DETERMINING DECIMAL REPRESENTATION

If fraction A/B in lowest terms has a nonterminating decimal representation, then the possible remainders are $1, 2, 3, 4, \ldots, B - 1$.

If the possible remainders for $\frac{2}{7}$ are $1, 2, 3, 4, 5, 6$, then among the first seven remainders in the standard layout two remainders must be the same; that is, some later remainder must repeat an earlier one. Let's continue the calculations for $\frac{2}{7}$ and see if this reasoning is correct.

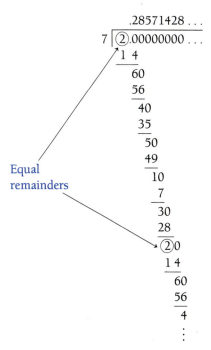

Yes! The seventh and the first remainders are the same. The same thing should happen in general.

DUPLICATION OF REMAINDERS IN THE STANDARD LAYOUT FOR A/B

In the standard layout for calculating the nonterminating decimal representation for fraction A/B (in lowest terms), two remainders among the first through the Bth must be the same. Thus the digits in the decimal representation start repeating by the Bth place.

Every fraction A/B is either equal to a decimal fraction or has a nonterminating repeating decimal representation. The *repeating part* must begin by the Bth decimal place in the representation and the number of decimal places in the repeating part (its *length*) is at most $B - 1$. For example,

Repeating part begins here, at first decimal place.
↓

$$\frac{2}{7} = .\underline{285714}285714285714\ldots$$

↑

Repeating part is six digits long.

Repeating part begins here, at third decimal place.
↓

$$\frac{9}{44} = .20\underline{45}45454545\ldots$$

↑

Repeating part is two digits long.

Repeating part begins here, at second decimal place.
↓

$$\frac{5}{6} = .8\underline{3}33333\ldots$$

↑

Repeating part is one digit long.

Frequently, the repeating part is written only once and a bar is drawn over it. Thus

$$\frac{2}{7} = .\overline{285714}$$

$$\frac{9}{44} = .20\overline{45}$$

$$\frac{5}{6} = .8\overline{3}$$

$$\frac{1}{3} = .\overline{3}$$

EXERCISE 30. Find the decimal representations of the following fractions. Indicate the repeating part and where it starts.

(a) $\frac{2}{3}$ (b) $\frac{6}{7}$ (c) $\frac{4}{9}$ (d) $\frac{1}{12}$ (e) $\frac{1}{13}$

(f) $\frac{7}{11}$ (g) $\frac{4}{15}$ (h) $\frac{11}{30}$ (i) $\frac{3}{70}$

Decimal Representation Corresponding to a Length

Using the technique developed earlier in the chapter, we can now find a decimal representation corresponding to any length L. Here's how. Given length L with $0 < L < 1$, follow the procedure given.

1. Find the largest digit A such that $.A \leq L$.
2. Find the largest digit B such that $.AB \leq L$.
3. Find the largest digit C such that $.ABC \leq L$.
4. Find the largest digit D such that $.ABCD \leq L$, and so on.

Then the decimal representation for L is $L = .ABCDEFG \ldots$

This procedure can be followed for the irrational length we encountered in the previous chapter, the length d of the diagonal of the square of side one. If you do this, you will get $d = 1.4142135 \ldots$ Since we might like to know the subsequent digits in the decimal representation of d, it would be convenient for the decimal representation to repeat from some point on. However, the following theorem says why it can't happen.

THEOREM: REPEATING DECIMAL REPRESENTATIONS

If a length has a repeating decimal representation, then that length corresponds to a fraction.

Since the length d isn't a fraction (it's irrational, remember?), it can't have a repeating decimal representation.

To see why the theorem is true, let's analyze a couple of examples. We will use this fact: An infinite decimal representation (i.e., one that doesn't terminate) can be treated just like a decimal fraction in the sense that multiplication by 10^n moves the decimal point n digits to the right. Thus $10 \times .894572402 \ldots = 8.94572402 \ldots$ and $1000 \times .8989898989 \ldots = 898.989898989. \ldots$ The examples of repeating decimals below will suggest a general method for converting a repeating decimal into a fraction.

EXAMPLE 1 Suppose that $R = .\overline{1234} = .123412341234. \ldots$ Then

$$10{,}000R = 1234.\overline{1234};$$

that is,

$$10{,}000R = 1234 + R,$$

or

$$10{,}000R - R = 1234,$$

or

$$9999R = 1234,$$

or

$$R = \frac{1234}{9999}.$$

EXAMPLE 2 Suppose that $S = .5\overline{61234}$. Then

$$100S = 56.\overline{1234} = 56 + .\overline{1234}.$$

In example 1, we found that $.\overline{1234} = \frac{1234}{9999}$. Thus, we have

$$100S = 56 + \frac{1234}{9999} = \frac{56 \times 9999 + 1234}{9999} = \frac{561178}{9999},$$

so that

$$S = \frac{561{,}178}{9999} \times \frac{1}{100} = \frac{561{,}178}{999{,}900}.$$

EXERCISES 31. For each of the repeating decimal representations, find the common fraction equal to it.
    (a) $.\overline{7}$ (b) $.\overline{54}$ (c) $.\overline{207}$ (d) $.8\overline{7}$ (e) $.315\overline{4}$ (f) $.123\overline{07}$

32. The method of rounding a fraction given by its repeating decimal representation is the same as for a decimal fraction. Thus .43157157157 ... rounded to four decimal places is .4316, to five decimal places is .43157, and to six decimal places is .431572. Notice also that the latter are (respectively) the nearest .0001, .00001, and .000001 to the fraction.
    Round each of the following fractions to four places.
    (a) $.6666$ (b) $.66666$ (c) $.\overline{6}$ (d) $.8\overline{53}$
    (e) $.\overline{8532}$ (f) $.\overline{1234}$ (g) $.34\overline{52}$ (h) $.34\overline{25}$

10.8   CALCULATORS AND COMPUTERS: EXPLORING REPEATING DECIMALS

You might think of using a calculator to find the decimal representation of a fraction, but there are difficulties with the obvious use. A calculator will display a decimal approximation to a fraction to within a limited number of decimal places, usually fewer than twelve. For example, I have a calculator that gives me an approximation to seven places. That would be no help for the fraction

$$\frac{1}{19} = 0.\overline{052631578947368421}.$$

When I enter the key sequence 1 [÷] 19 [=] on this calculator, the display reads 0.0526316, giving me no clues about the length of the repeating part or when the repeating part begins.

    You can use a calculator to find the decimal representation of a fraction by doing other things. However, it is more efficient to use a computer. Let's look at a program in BASIC that does this.

```
10 INPUT R          R is the fraction's numerator.
20 INPUT B          B is the fraction's denominator.
30 PRINT "FRACTION = "R"/"B
40 PRINT "REMAINDER","DIGIT", "PLACE"
50 FOR I = 1 TO B
```

```
 60 LET Q = INT(10*R/B)      For a discussion of INT(X), see following text.
 70 PRINT R,Q,I
 80 LET R = 10*R - Q*B
 90 NEXT I
100 END
```

[If X is a number, then INT(X) is the whole number part of X; for example, INT(74.025) = 74, INT(37) = 37 and INT(0.54) = 0.]

Type this program into your computer. When you run this program, you will be asked to input first the numerator then the denominator of the fraction. (Make sure the numerator is smaller than the denominator and that the fraction is in lowest terms.) The computer will then print out the remainder, the resulting digit in the quotient, and the decimal place. (The first remainder printed will be the fraction's numerator; the first digit printed will be for the first decimal place.) It will do this for the first B decimal places. Here is what happens for the fraction $\frac{2}{7}$.

```
RUN


? 2
? 7
FRACTION = 2/7
REMAINDER      DIGIT      PLACE
    2            2          1
    6            8          2
    4            5          3
    5            7          4
    1            1          5
    3            4          6
    2            2          7
```

$$
\begin{array}{r}
.2857142 \\
7\overline{)2.0000000} \\
1\,4 \\ \hline
60 \\
56 \\ \hline
40 \\
35 \\ \hline
50 \\
49 \\ \hline
10 \\
7 \\ \hline
30 \\
28 \\ \hline
20
\end{array}
$$

Notice that you can read off the decimal digits in succession in the DIGIT column and you can read off the successive remainders in the REMAINDER column. You know that in general a repetition of remainders will occur in the REMAINDER column. The first time a repetition occurs will give you information about when the repeated part of the decimal representation begins and the length of the repeated part.

EXERCISES

33. Use the computer program above to find decimal representations of the fractions.
    (a) $\frac{1}{13}$ (b) $\frac{1}{17}$ (c) $\frac{1}{21}$ (d) $\frac{1}{23}$ (e) $\frac{1}{26}$

34. Which fractions have decimal representations with a repeating part that begins immediately, at the first digit? Use the computer to help you in an "exploration" of the decimal representations of several fractions by having the foregoing program find them. Put these with the decimal representations of fractions given in the text and the results of exercises 30 and 33. Organize them all in a chart. Look for patterns.

10.9   SUMMARY OF IMPORTANT IDEAS AND TECHNIQUES

- Comparing, adding, and subtracting fractions with denominators having a power of 10 using the extended counting board
- Definition of decimal fraction and common fraction; rules for adding, subtracting and multiplying decimal fractions
- Finding decimal fractions close to a given common fraction; approximating a common fraction by decimal fractions
- How to tell if a common fraction is equal to a decimal fraction
- Standard method for division of decimal fractions
- The decimal representation of a fraction
  The correspondence of finite, or terminating decimals, to common fractions and decimal fractions
  The correspondence of infinite, or nonterminating decimals, to common fractions that are not equal to decimal fractions
  The terminating or repeating feature of the decimal representation of a fraction
  The nonrepeating feature of the decimal representation of an irrational length
- Method for converting a repeating (infinite) decimal representation to a common fraction
- Rounding of decimal fractions and decimal representations
- Percent; converting percents to decimal fractions and vice versa
- Rates of change
  Percent rate of interest on principal invested
  Annual rate of interest; simple interest
  Percent rate of profit over cost
  Percent rate of increase/decrease in price
  Percent rate of markup/down
  Percent rate of discount
  Percent rate of commission
  Percent rate of inflation
  Percent rate of depreciation

PROBLEM SET

PRACTICING
SKILLS

1. (a) Represent the following decimals on an extended counting board: .0028, 4.10307, 65.9802.
   (b) Solve on a counting board: 4.308 + 29.057 + 405.78.
   (c) Solve on a counting board: 310.02 − 98.706.

2. Multiply 32.00508 by 100, by 1000, by .001, and by .000001.

3. Multiply the decimal 642.08 by 7.3 using the following two methods:
   (a) The standard method.
   (b) First convert the decimals to common fractions; then use the rule for multiplying common fractions.

Compare the answers you obtained in (a) and (b).

4. (a) Use June and Sam's method of placing fractions on the number line to find the nearest $\frac{1}{100}$th to the fraction $\frac{3}{11}$.

   (b) Use any method to find the nearest $\frac{1}{100}$th to the common fractions $\frac{7}{12}$, $\frac{4}{19}$, $\frac{11}{30}$, $\frac{9}{50}$, $\frac{3}{16}$, $\frac{9}{150}$.

5. Which of the following are equal to a decimal fraction? For each one that is, find the decimal fraction equal to it.

   (a) $\frac{17}{800}$ (b) $\frac{5}{28}$ (c) $\frac{7}{24}$ (d) $\frac{8}{35}$

   (e) $\frac{6}{625}$ (f) $\frac{9}{16}$ (g) $\frac{11}{80}$ (h) $\frac{25}{600}$

6. Consider the decimal division problem $28.63 \div 7.09$. Solve this in two ways:

   (a) The standard way.

   (b) Convert the decimals to common fractions and divide as in the solution to the alloy problem.

7. While figuring out how many square meters the floor plan of a house has, a real estate agent has produced a picture of a room:

4.62 m

3.79 m

What is the area of this room in square meters?

8. Answer the percent questions.

   (a) What is 64% of 388?   (b) 36 is 40% of what?

   (c) 180 is what percent of 150?

9. Many stocks pay a dividend to the shareholder. Since the dividend represents a certain dollar amount per share of stock, it is difficult to compare dividend returns to each other or to the returns of other investments. For this reason the stockbroker will often convert the dividend into a percent of the price of the stock.

   (a) Which would produce a better return, a passbook savings account paying 5.5% or a stock selling for $20 per share and paying a dividend of $1.15 per share?

   (b) Which produces a higher percent return, a stock selling for $24.825 and paying a $1.84 dividend per share or a stock selling for $15.75 and paying a $1.20 dividend?

10. A taillight cover retails for $12.50 and wholesales for $7.22. One store offers the cover to the mechanic at a 35% discount off the retail price, while another source offers the same cover at a 25% markup over the wholesale price. Which is the better deal?

11. Management wishes to know how rapidly it is spending the budget for one of its projects. With 6 wk left on the 18-wk project, it has used $45,000 of a $62,000 budget. Compute the percent of time remaining on the project as well as the percent of the project's budget remaining.

12. The wholesale price of a certain luxury item is $100. A retailer intends to sell the item at a 80% markup from the wholesale price. However, the item does not sell, so the retailer marks his retail price down 45%. This time the item does sell. What is the retailer's profit (or loss) on the item?

13. The reject rate on parts at the plant is normally 5%. Last week 47 parts were inspected and, of these, 3 were rejected. Was the rate last week higher or lower than normal and by how much?

14. (a) Find the decimal representations of the following fractions. Indicate the repeating part and where it starts.

    (i) $\frac{5}{12}$ (ii) $\frac{9}{14}$ (iii) $\frac{11}{15}$ (iv) $\frac{2}{17}$

    (v) $\frac{5}{18}$ (vi) $\frac{4}{35}$ (vii) $\frac{13}{60}$ (viii) $\frac{49}{90}$

    (b) For each of the following repeating decimal representations, find the common fraction equal to it.

    (i) $.\overline{8}$ (ii) $.\overline{35}$ (iii) $.\overline{412}$ (iv) $.5\overline{7}$ (v) $.16\overline{92}$ (vi) $.249\overline{42}$

15. Round off each of the following fractions to four places:

    (a) $.77\overline{777}$ (b) $.\overline{7}$ (c) $.6\overline{29}$ (d) $.\overline{6297}$

    (e) $.48\overline{36}$ (f) $.4\overline{863}$ (g) $.34694$ (h) $.34696$

    (i) $.34996$ (j) $.39999$ (k) $.999956$

USING IDEAS   *For each remaining problem, write an essay with the purpose of communicating clearly and completely the solution to the problem. Mention the steps you took in solving the problem, other problems or solutions that gave you ideas, and the strategies you used.*

16. The standard sizes for drill bits in the United States are widths of the form $\frac{1}{2}$ in, $\frac{1}{4}$ in, $\frac{1}{8}$ in, $\frac{3}{8}$ in, $\frac{3}{16}$ in—all fractions of an inch with the denominator of the fraction being a power of 2—2, 4, 8, 16, 32. . . . You want to drill a hole of width $\frac{1}{3}$ in. You want to find the "closest" drill size to $\frac{1}{3}$ in. To keep your options open about what you mean by "closest," you decide to find the following fractions:

    ■ One with denominator 2 closest to and $\leq \frac{1}{3}$

    ■ One with denominator 4 closest to and $\leq \frac{1}{3}$

    ■ One with denominator 8 closest to and $\leq \frac{1}{3}$

    ■ One with denominator 16 closest to and $\leq \frac{1}{3}$

    What are these fractions?

17. The results of this year's citywide reading contest have been reported as the following three-place decimal fractions:

    (a) .700   (b) .254   (c) .333   (d) .635   (e) .378

    (f) .430   (g) .478   (h) .509   (i) .719

    Place these scores on a copy of the number line below. Indicate the smallest score, the largest score, and the score closest to $\frac{1}{2}$.

.1   .2   .3   .4   .5   .6   .7   .8

18. What is the best buy of the following?
    (a) Eight 4-oz bottles of grape juice for $1.69
    (b) A 12-oz bottle of grape juice for $.50
    (c) An 8-oz bottle of grape juice for $.33

19. A scale drawing is to be made from the floor plan shown. In the scale drawing the length of the longer side is to be .37 m. What is the ratio of a length in the scale drawing to a length in the real room? What should the length of the shorter side of the scale drawing be?

3.79 m

4.62 m

20. A county commissioner made the following statement at a public hearing: "Since 16.3% of the county is privately owned and since the eastern part of the county makes up 42% of the whole county, then only 6.8% of the eastern part of the county is privately owned."
What do you think of this statement?

21. Mr. Yenom is considering the purchase of a solar water heater for his home. The manufacturer claims that Mr. Yenom's electric bills will be reduced by 16% if he uses such a device.
(a) Mr. Yenom's electric bills now average $95/mo. If the manufacturer's claim is correct, what would an average monthly bill be with a solar water heater?
(b) The cost of the solar heater is $327.60. How long would it take for the savings on the monthly bill to pay for the heater?

22. Of the state's electorate, 70% live in urban areas; the rest live in rural districts. If a candidate gets 60% of the urban vote in the state, what percent of the rural vote must she receive to have a majority of votes in the state?

23. In Green City, 80% of those who enter high school eventually graduate. Of those who graduate from high school, 70% do not go to college. Of those who enter college, 60% eventually obtain a college degree. What percent of those entering high school eventually get a college degree?

24. The Consumer Price Index (CPI) is set so that 100 represents the price level existing in 1967. For example, if the same goods purchased in 1967 for $10.00 now cost $14.40, the CPI is 144.
(a) If prices increased by 7.8% in 1968, what was the CPI for that year?
(b) If the CPI last year was 188 and it went up 26 points (to 214) this year, what was the percent of the increase? (This percent increase is the year's annual rate of inflation.)
(c) "Double digit inflation" means that the CPI has gone up more than 10% from one year to the next. If the CPI is presently 188, what is the maximum level the CPI can reach next year in order to avoid double digit inflation?

25. A customer has a $5000 certificate of deposit account that must be left intact for 1 yr to earn the 8.5% annual rate. If he were to withdraw the money sooner than 1 yr, he would receive 7% annual interest for all but 90 days of the time the money was in the account. For the remaining 90 days the money would earn no interest. After 6 mo he needs $5000. He then has two choices: (1) He can withdraw the money immediately and take the penalty or (2) he can take out a loan at 10% annual interest and pay it off in 6 mo when his certificate matures. Which choice is better?

26. The librarian at City Library is planning the amount of new shelf space that will be needed for next year. He decides to look at some data—the number of volumes in City Library for the last 5 yr:

1985	37,150
1986	41,263
1987	45,920
1988	50,835
1989	56,695

(a) The librarian decides to find the yearly percent of growth in number of volumes for each year in this period. What are they?

(b)   Then the librarian decides to average the percents obtained in (a). What is this figure?

(c)   Finally, the librarian uses the percent obtained in (b) to predict the number of volumes the library will have in 1990. What is this predicted number?

27.   A survey of undergraduates asked the following two questions: Are you taking a mathematics course? Are you taking a language course? Results of the survey revealed that

- 70% of those surveyed answered yes to at least one of the questions
- 20% of those surveyed answered yes to both questions
- The same percentage of those surveyed answered yes to the first question as to the second

From these results, answer the questions:

(a)   What percentage of those surveyed are taking a language course?

(b)   What percentage of those surveyed answered yes to only one of the questions?

(c)   What percentage of those surveyed are taking neither type of course?

28.   The university has recently come under fire for its failure to hire minority faculty members. In fact, the federal government is withholding funds for student loans until a recently implemented affirmative action program brings the number of minorities to 15% of the total number of faculty members. There are currently 150 minority members in a total faculty of 2000. If new faculty members are hired so that 2 minority members are hired for every nonminority member, how many new faculty members must be hired before federal student loan funds start flowing again? (Assume there are no retirements, resignations or deaths.)

29.   A recent medical study reported that 3 of every 10 smokers have a certain lung disease and that only 1 of 8 nonsmokers has it. Smokers make up 20% of the population. What percent of the general population has the disease?

30.   For some time, Diddle's department store made a healthy profit selling Idaho Digital (I.D.) calculators, the only brand on the market with graphing capabilities. Recently, however, Federal Analog (F.A.) has introduced an identical unit that is becoming increasingly popular with the public. Both I.D. and F.A. models cost Diddle's $200 apiece. The store still has 1000 I.D.'s in stock, which it must sell at a 15% loss to sell them at all. If the store can make a 10% profit on each F.A., how many F.A.'s must it sell in order to break even on the two brands of calculators?*

31.   Problem 28 can be solved easily using computers. Here is a start.

```
10 LET M = 150      M = number of minorities
20 LET N = 1850     N = number of nonminorities
30 PRINT M,N,M+N,M/(M+N)
40 IF M/(M+N) >= .15 THEN GO TO 80
50 LET M = M + 2
60 LET N = N + 1
70 GOTO 30
80 PRINT ''MUST HIRE ''M + N - 2000'' NEW FACULTY''
90 END
```

(The expression >= in line 40 means "greater than or equal to.")

Type this program into your computer and run it. Does it work? What is it doing that makes it work? How does the computer solution compare with the solution you completed by hand?

---

* Adapted from Deborah Hughes Hallet, *The Math Workshop,* Norton, New York, prob. 3, p. 247.

32. Some fractions are equal to decimal fractions, and the others have repeating decimal representations. We can unify the discussion of the relation between common fractions and decimals by agreeing that a decimal fraction is really a repeating decimal.

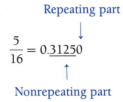

$$\frac{5}{16} = 0.31250$$

In this case the repeating part consists of 0s. In this way, every fraction has a repeating decimal representation. For common fractions whose repeating part consists of 0s, what can you say about the length of the nonrepeating part? (This is an "exploration" problem: Find the decimal representation for several common fractions equal to decimal fractions. Make a chart organizing your results. Look for patterns.)

33. Use the computer program given in the text and the results of exercise 34 (text) and problem 32 to explore the decimal representations of several fractions. You are looking for answers to the following sorts of questions:

    (a) For a fraction that does not repeat immediately, what is the length of the nonrepeating part?

    (b) For two fractions in lowest terms having the same denominator, how do the lengths of the repeating parts compare? How do the lengths of the nonrepeating parts compare?

    (c) You know that the length of the repeating part is less than the size of the denominator. Can you say anything else about this length? (You might want to answer this question first for fractions the decimal representations of which repeat immediately, then for fractions the decimal representations of which don't repeat immediately.)

    (d) Can you think of some interesting questions to ask about repeating decimal representations?

EXTENDING THE NUMBER LINE: POSITIVE AND NEGATIVE NUMBERS

CHAPTER 11

In this chapter we will look at several situations in which a quantity is of two kinds; having "plus" and "minus" qualities: asset and debt, favorable and unfavorable, above sea level and below sea level, and so on. For such a quantity it is useful to extend the number line to the left of zero. One of the two kinds (in our example, asset, favorable, above sea level) can correspond to the points to the right of zero and will be called positive numbers; the other can correspond to points on the left of zero and will be called negative numbers.

We will define an order to numbers on this extended line that naturally extends the order of whole numbers and of fractions. Similarly, we will extend the definition of addition and subtraction of whole numbers and fractions using the add-subtract slide rule. We will also extend multiplication of whole numbers and fractions to these new numbers.

Finally, we will look at the formal properties of these numbers and see how working with them makes doing algebra conceptually simpler.

THE HOUSEHOLD ASSETS PROBLEM

The sixth graders at Washington Middle School were studying household finances and thought it might be interesting to look at the value of the household for each member of the class and then compare the values. It wasn't the value of a particular household that interested the class but the values for all the households and how they compared. To avoid embarrassment to anyone, the class decided that each student would submit the value of his or her household to the teacher anonymously. The class devised a scheme for determining the value of a household.

1. The following tables were to be completed first.

ASSET (item owned by household)	VALUE OF ASSET
House(s), land, or other real estate	_____
Stocks and bonds	_____
Savings accounts	_____
Certificates of deposit	_____
Checking accounts	_____
Household items	_____
Other articles of value	_____
Total assets	_____

DEBT (item owed by household)	AMOUNT OWED
Mortgage balance	_____
Loan balance(s)	_____
Credit card balance(s)	_____
Other amounts owed	_____
Total debts	_____

2. Then, if the figure for total assets turned out to be larger than that for total debts, the difference would be written on a piece of paper with the word *Asset*. If the figure for total debts were larger than that for total assets, this difference would be written on a piece of paper with the word *Debt*.

    Some of the results are shown.

Asset:	$5500
Debt:	$22,000
Debt:	$3300
Asset:	$35,000
Asset:	$12,000
Asset:	$7000

Don't forget to try this yourself first.

Debt: $6500
Debt: $13,000
Debt: $2500

The students want to know how they can compare these figures. Help them solve this problem.

A Solution to the Household Assets Problem

The students *remembered a previous problem*—the city-wide reading contest problem in chapter 8—in which they had a list of quantities they wanted to compare. In that problem they used a number line. They think about using that device here.

"We could put asset quantities on a number line easily enough.

But what do we do with the debt quantities? The household with asset $7000 is better off financially than the household with asset $5500. On the number line this is expressed by the fact that 7000 is *to the right of* 5500.

Certainly, all the households with asset are better off financially than those with debt. So we should place all the asset quantities to the right of all the debt quantities. That would mean that all the debts should be to the left of zero on the number line.

I wonder what point to the left of zero should be associated with a given debt quantity? For example, where should we put debt $3300? We ought to match the situation with assets in which a better-off household appears to the right of a less fortunate one. The household with debt $3300 is better off than the household with debt $22,000, so debt $3300 should appear to the right of debt $22,000. Debt $1000 should be to the right of debt $2000, which should be to the right of debt $3300.

So we should label the number line to the left of zero as shown.

We can now place the debt quantities on this extended number line."

The Mathematical Idea: The Extended Number Line

The sixth grade students found it useful to label and use the points on the number line to the left of zero. The same device is used in other common situations. For example, a thermometer is marked with a number line. Temperatures above (or warmer than) zero are recorded to the right of zero on the line. Temperatures below (or colder than) zero are recorded to the left of zero on the line. (For a Celsius thermometer, zero is the temperature at which water freezes. For a Fahrenheit thermometer, zero is the temperature of equal quantities—by weight—of snow and common salt.) To distinguish points to the left of zero from those on the right, points on the left of zero are traditionally labeled, moving left from zero: $^-1$, $^-2$, $^-3$, $^-4$, and so on. (This symbolism is read as "negative one," "negative two," etc.).

Notice that, of two points on this number line, the point corresponding to the warmest temperature is to the right of the other.

A third situation in which points on the number line to the left of zero are used is in measuring elevation above sea level. The point zero corresponds to the level of the sea itself. Points to the right of zero correspond to elevations above sea level; points to the left of zero correspond to elevations below sea level.

Of two points on this number line, the point corresponding to the greatest distance from the center of the Earth is to the right of the other point.

In each of these three situations the quantities are of two kinds: assets and debts, temperatures above zero and temperatures below, elevations above sea level and elevations below. In each case it was useful to associate one kind of quantity with points to the right of zero, called *positive numbers,* and the other kind with points to the left of zero, called *negative numbers.* In so doing we created an *extended number line.* We can summarize.

THE EXTENDED NUMBER LINE

Numbers corresponding to points on an extended number line to the right of zero are called *positive numbers;* those to the left, *negative numbers.*

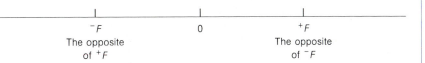

A nonzero fraction F in this context is frequently denoted ^+F. Its *opposite,* the point symmetrical to it with respect to zero, is denoted ^-F. The *opposite* of ^-F is ^+F.

The numbers . . . $^-3$, $^-2$, $^-1$, 0, $^+1$, $^+2$, $^+3$, . . . are called *integers.* The numbers $^+1$, $^+2$, $^+3$, . . . are the *positive integers.* The numbers $^-1$, $^-2$, $^-3$, . . . are the *negative integers.*

$$^-6 \quad ^-5 \quad ^-4 \quad ^-3 \quad ^-2 \quad ^-1 \quad 0 \quad ^+1 \quad ^+2 \quad ^+3 \quad ^+4 \quad ^+5 \quad ^+6$$

Negative | Positive

The set of integers and their opposites is called the *rational numbers.*

In each of the three situations, you can compare a pair of quantities. In the first you can say which of two household values is better financially; in the second you can say which of two temperatures is warmer; in the third you can say which of two elevations is farther from the center of the earth. For each of these situations there is an *order* on the quantities. For temperatures, *greater* means warmer. For household values, *greater* means financially better off. For elevations, *greater* means farther away from the center of the earth. The following definition of *greater* on the extended number line conveys these other senses of *greater.*

ORDER ON THE EXTENDED NUMBER LINE

When there are two numbers A and B on the extended number line, the right-most one is *greater than* the other.

If B is greater than A, we write $B > A$.

Another situation in which the extended number line is useful is in indicating changes. For example, if you look on the financial page of a newspaper you can find the change in the value of a share of stock in the course of a day. If the stock has increased in value, the change is indicated by a positive number. If the stock has decreased in value, the change is indicated by a negative number. For example, if one share of National Oil is worth $25 at the beginning of the day and $27 at the end, the change is $^+$$2. On the other hand, if it is worth $30 at the beginning of the day and $27 at the end, the change is $^-$$3. The possible changes in the value of a share correspond to points on the extended number line.

BCells	1.60e	7		$15\ 13\frac{3}{8}+\frac{1}{8}$	Disney	.48	22	1306	$93\frac{7}{8}-\frac{3}{4}$	HarBrJ			630	$14\frac{3}{8}-\frac{1}{8}$
BostEd	1.82	9	x2961	$17\frac{1}{8}$	DEI	1.52	11	713	$27\frac{1}{4}-\frac{1}{8}$	HarBJ pf	1.621		541	$11\frac{3}{8}$
BosE pf	8.88		y300	$87\frac{1}{2}+\frac{3}{4}$	Divrsin		14	19	$5\frac{1}{2}$	Harind	.68	16	372	$23\frac{1}{4}$
BosE pr	1.46		296	$15-\frac{1}{8}$	DomRs	3.20	11	429	$43\frac{7}{8}-\frac{1}{4}$	Harley		8	130	$27+\frac{3}{8}$
Bowatr	1.12	6	303	$27\frac{7}{8}+\frac{5}{8}$	Domtar	.50		7	$12\frac{1}{2}-\frac{1}{8}$	Harman		11	82	18
Brazil	.80e		175	$9\frac{1}{2}-\frac{1}{8}$	Donald	.38	10	1	$16\frac{3}{4}$	Harnish	.20	27	1856	$17\frac{5}{8}+\frac{1}{4}$
BrigSl	1.60	35	52	$26-\frac{3}{8}$	Doolley	.88	16	878	$43\frac{5}{8}+\frac{1}{4}$	Harris	.88	17	287	$32\frac{1}{8}$
BristMy	2	16	1997	$48\frac{3}{8}+\frac{1}{2}$	Dover s	.68	15	295	$31\frac{7}{8}-\frac{1}{8}$	Harsco	1.20	21	191	$24\frac{1}{4}+\frac{1}{4}$
BritAir	1.42e	8	8	$32\frac{7}{8}+\frac{1}{2}$	DowCh	3.20	6	2289	$84\frac{3}{4}+\frac{3}{4}$	Hartmx	1.20	14	86	$24\frac{1}{2}-\frac{1}{8}$
BritGas	1.63e	11	77	$31\frac{1}{8}+1$	Dow Jns	.72	11	124	$35\frac{1}{4}+\frac{3}{8}$	HattSe	1.56a	11	6	$15\frac{7}{8}+\frac{1}{8}$
BritPt	4.10e	15	284	$57\frac{3}{8}+1\frac{1}{4}$	Downey	.40	7	115	$26\frac{5}{8}+\frac{1}{2}$	HawEl	2.04	11	66	33
BritPwt			466	$6\frac{7}{8}+\frac{1}{4}$	Dravo		25	60	$18\frac{3}{8}-\frac{3}{8}$	HltRhb	1.12	12	31	$8\frac{7}{8}$
BriStt pp	1.03e		859	$11\frac{5}{8}+\frac{5}{8}$	Dresr	1	19	533	$40\frac{3}{4}-\frac{1}{8}$	HlthCP	2.73e	18	196	$29\frac{7}{8}+\frac{1}{8}$
BritTel	1.92e	10	272	$40+\frac{1}{8}$	Dreshr	.16	13	18	$4-\frac{1}{8}$	HeclaM	.05e	44	309	$12\frac{5}{8}-\frac{1}{4}$
Broadln	.10		795	$10\frac{7}{8}+\frac{1}{2}$	Dreyfus	.52	13	1456	$27\frac{1}{2}-\frac{5}{8}$	Heilig	.40	12	11	$18\frac{3}{4}$
Broad pf	1.50		12	$32+1$	DryStrt	.78a		197	$10\frac{3}{4}$	Heinz	1.44	16	402	$53\frac{1}{2}+\frac{1}{2}$

The order of points on the number line also reflects a natural order in the changes in price of a share. Suppose that two points on the number line correspond to changes in the price of a share of some stock that you own. The rightmost point corresponds to a change that is *more favorable* (to you, of course) than the change corresponding to the leftmost point.

More favorable change

EXERCISES

1. In each of the following pairs of integers, which is the greater integer?
   (a) $^+$10 and $^-$1,000,000 (b) $^-$1,000,000 and $^-$1,000,000,000
   (c) $^+$1,000,000 and $^-$10 (d) $^+$10 and $^+$1,000,000

2. For which stock, in the stock quotation given, did the largest dollar change in the price of stock occur? The smallest? What were the changes in price as rational numbers?

11.2   ADDITION ON THE EXTENDED NUMBER LINE

THE SHARES OF STOCK PROBLEM

Try this yourself, please.

Mr. Jones is a stock market analyst. He has been observing the changes in price of shares of various stocks. He has kept a daily record of these changes for several years that he might observe trends in them. He has discovered that weekly changes in the price of a share are more useful for this purpose than the daily changes. For a certain week the daily changes in the price for one stock were $^+$$3, $^+$$1, $^-$$2, $^-$$4, $^+$$5. He wants to know what the change in price for that week was. Help him solve this problem.

Mr. Jones thinks: "The changes the first two days were $^+\$3$ and $^+\$1$, respectively. So I know the change in price from the beginning of the first day to the end of the second was an increase of $\$3 + \$1$, or $\$4$. You just add the two price increases. Here is what is happening on the number line.

"Now, the change the third day was $^-\$2$. Since the change up to the beginning of the third day was $^+\$4$—an increase of $\$4$—this means that the change from the beginning of the week up to the end of the third day was $\$2$ less than this: You subtract the $\$2$ from the $\$4$ to get $\$2$. I can show this on the number line.

I can indicate positive changes as arrows to the right and negative changes as arrows to the left.

"During the fourth day the price changed $^-\$4$. That means it decreased $\$4$. An increase of $\$2$ followed by a decrease of $\$4$ would mean a net decrease of $\$2$ from the beginning of the week. That means a change of $^-\$2$ from the beginning of the week to the end of the fourth day.

"Another copy of the extended number line underneath the one I have might help to show what is going on. I'll put the zero of the bottom line just below the change in price by the beginning of the fourth day. I'll register the change during the fourth day on the bottom line as well. Just above that point on the upper line will be the total change in price by the end of the fourth day.

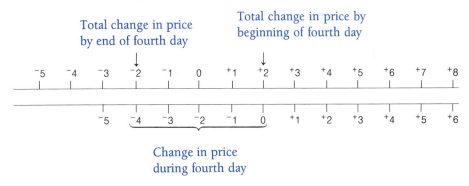

"I can do the same thing to figure out what happens on the fifth day.

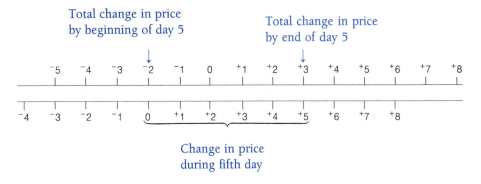

So the change in the price of a share from the beginning of the week to the end was $^+\$3$, an increase of $3."

The Mathematical Idea: Addition on the Extended Number Line

A change in price of $^+\$3$ followed by a change in price of $^+\$1$ is the same as a single change in price of $^+\$4$. The answer is gotten by ordinary whole number addition: $\$3 + \$1 = \$4$ (all quantities are increases). This is the sum of the first two days' increases. The procedure suggests that we call what we did to find the total increase for the first three, four, and five days "addition" of signed numbers. The two copies of the extended number line were used to find these total increases, just as the add-subtract slide rule was used to add whole numbers. We now have a way to define addition of integers and rational numbers that extends addition of whole numbers and fractions.

DEFINITION OF ADDITION OF NUMBERS ON THE EXTENDED NUMBER LINE

To find the sum of A and B on the extended number line, take an add-subtract slide rule and slide the *bottom line* so that the 0 of the *bottom line* and the A of the *top line* are in the same position.

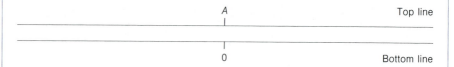

Point B on the *bottom line* and point $A + B$ on the *top line* are now in the same position.

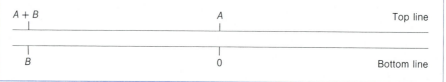

Here are four examples of addition of integers using our definition.

1. $^+3 + {}^+4 = {}^+7$

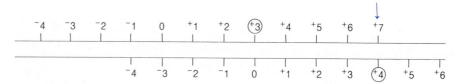

2. $^-3 + {}^+4 = {}^+1$

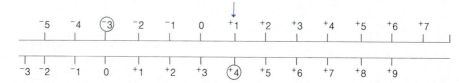

3. $^+3 + {}^-4 = {}^-1$

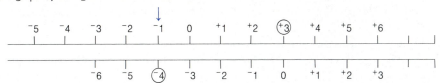

4. $^-3 + {}^-4 = {}^-7$

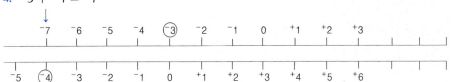

From our definition we arrive at the following sums:

$$^+3 + {}^+4 = {}^+7$$
$$^-3 + {}^+4 = {}^+1$$
$$^+3 + {}^-4 = {}^-1$$
$$^-3 + {}^-4 = {}^-7$$

EXERCISES

3. Calculate the sums of integers.
   (a) $^+22 + {}^+73$ (b) $^-22 + {}^+73$ (c) $^-22 + {}^-73$ (d) $^+22 + {}^-73$

4. Suppose that A and B are whole numbers and that A is bigger than B. Consider the integer problems.
   (a) $^+A + {}^+B = ?$ (b) $^-A + {}^+B = ?$
   (c) $^-A + {}^-B = ?$ (d) $^+A + {}^-B = ?$
   Describe a rule for calculating the answers in terms of the whole numbers A and B, whole number operations, and the opposite of a whole number. For example, $^+A + {}^-B = A - B$.

5. Mr. Berkowitz has assets totaling \$134,000 and mortgages, loans due, and bills totaling \$153,000. He wants to know the net value of his holdings. Interpret his assets and debts as signed numbers and show that addition of signed numbers can tell him what he wants to know.

THE TEMPERATURE PROBLEM

From February 1 to February 2 of last year, Juanita remembers that the high temperatures of the two days changed $^+10°$. And then, from February 2 to February 3, the high changed a record amount of $^-30°$. This year on February 1, the high is 12°. Juanita wants to know what the high on February 3 would be if the pattern of temperature changes that occurred last year also occurs this year.

Juanita knows that if the high on February 1 is 12° and the temperature changes $^+10°$, then she could get the temperature on February 2 by adding the whole numbers 12 and 10: $12 + 10 = 22$. She also knows that if the temperature changes $^-30°$ from February 2 to February 3, she can obtain the projected temperature on February 3 by adding the signed numbers $^+22$ and $^-30$ to get $^-8°$:

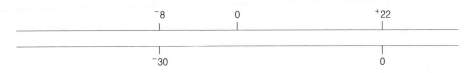

The Mathematical Idea: Situations in Which Addition of Integers and Rational Numbers Can Be Used

It is possible to solve the shares of stock problem and the temperature problem by thinking of the quantities in question as positive or negative numbers and then using addition on an extended number line. In the shares of stock problem the quantities are changes in stock prices. In the temperature problem one quantity is a temperature, and the other is a change in temperature. Although it is useful to think of both quantities as numbers on the extended number line, the "signs" means different things. A negative temperature means a temperature so many degrees *below* zero on the scale, while a negative change in temperature means a *drop* of so many degrees in temperature. However, it is useful to be able to add the two different quantities as numbers on the extended number line.

EXERCISES

6. Mr. Jones has made a list of his assets:

    $^+$$12,300
    $^-$$1250
    $^+$$2475
    $^+$$23,820
    $^-$$17,370

    What is the value of his holdings?

7. Here are the temperature changes for this week's weekdays. (These are the changes in the daily low temperature.)

M	T	W	T	F
$^+$7	$^+$2	$^-$5	$^+$6	$^-$10

    On Sunday, the low temperature was 25°. What was the low temperature on the following Friday?

8. Another situation in which positive and negative numbers are frequently used is describing motion along a straight line. Distances traveled in one direction are the positive distances while those traveled in the opposite direction are the negative distances. Position (relative to a given point, zero, on the straight line) is also indicated by positive and negative numbers: Points in the positive direction from zero are positive positions; those in the opposite direction are negative positions.

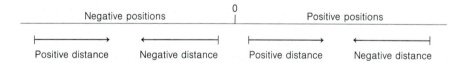

Notice that the signs for positions and distances traveled mean different things, a situation similar to that encountered in the temperature problem.

In the problem we are working on now, suppose the straight line is along a river and that distances in the down-river direction are positive while distances in the up-river direction are negative. You are on a boat trip on this river and start your trip at the point zero. Interpret and solve the following problems using addition on the extended number line. Draw appropriate pictures.

(a) Before lunch on the first day you travel 12 mi up river. After lunch you travel 14 mi more up river. How many miles do you travel on the first day? What is your distance from the starting point at the end of the day? What is your position at the end of the day?

(b) The next day in the morning, you travel 9 mi up river. In the afternoon, you travel 12 mi down river. How many miles do you travel on this day? What is the distance you travel on this day? What is your position at the end of the day?

(c) The third day before lunch, you travel 15 mi down river. Then after lunch you travel 13 mi more down river. How many miles do you travel on this day? What is the distance you travel on this day? What is your position at the end of the day?

(d) On the last day of the trip you travel 10 mi upstream. What is the distance you travel on this day? What is your position at the end of the day?

11.3 SUBTRACTION OF NUMBERS ON THE EXTENDED NUMBER LINE

THE SECOND TEMPERATURE PROBLEM

The sixth graders at Washington Middle School are keeping track of the daily temperatures in their city. They are interested in the highest temperature and the lowest temperature recorded each day and in the difference between the two. They construct a table.

DATE	HIGH	LOW	HIGH AND LOW DIFFERENCE	CHANGE IN HIGH FROM PREVIOUS DAY
2/3	33	10	23	—
2/4	28	8	20	⁻5
2/5	25	⁻3		⁻3
2/6	15	⁻10		⁻10
2/7	⁻2	⁻20		
2/8	10	⁻5		
2/9	20	⁻2		

Try this yourself.

They have no trouble figuring out the difference in cases where the high and low temperatures are temperatures *above* zero. They are having difficulty when one or more of the temperatures is *below* zero. They are also having trouble figuring out the change in daily high. Help them out.

A Solution to the Second Temperature Problem

The students think this way: "To find the temperature difference when the two temperatures are positive, you subtract the smaller from the larger as whole numbers. So 33 − 10 = 23. But we also know that 23 is the answer to the missing addend problem 10 + ? = 33.

"We know how to add numbers on the extended number line. To find the difference between $^+25$ and $^-3$ is the same as finding the solution to the missing addend problem $^-3 + ? = {}^+25$."

"We should be able to solve this by using the add-subtract slide rule in reverse, just as we did earlier with whole numbers and fractions. Place the 0 of the *bottom line* right under the $^-3$ of *top line*. On the *top line* look for the 'sum,' $^+25$, from the missing addend addition problem. The 'missing addend' should be right below $^+25$ but on the *bottom line*.

The answer is $^+28$.

"Let's do the others: $^-10 + ? = {}^+15$, or $^+15 - {}^-10 = ?$.

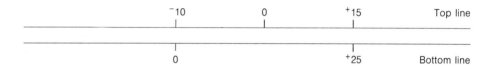

So $^+15 - {}^-10 = {}^+25$.

"Let's look at $^-20 + ? = {}^-2$, or $^-2 - {}^-20 = ?$.

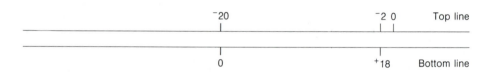

So $^-2 - {}^-20 = {}^+18$, and the rest are similar: $^+10 - {}^-5 = {}^+15$ and $^+20 - {}^-2 = {}^+22$.

"Subtracting on the extended number line should also help us figure out the change in daily high since

$$\text{Yesterday's high} + \text{change in highs} = \text{today's high}.$$

For example, in our chart, the high on February 3 is $^+33$, the high on February 4 is $^+28$, the change in highs is $^-5$, and $^+33 + {}^-5 = {}^+28$. On February 6 the high was $^+15$, and on February 7 it was $^-2$. To find the change, we want to solve the missing addend problem $^+15 + ? = {}^-2$, or $^-2 - {}^+15 = ?$.

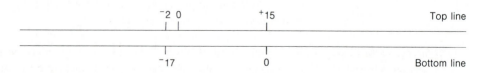

The answer is $^-2 - {}^+15 = {}^-17$."

The remaining entries in the chart can be completed similarly. The completed chart follows.

DATE	HIGH	LOW	HIGH AND LOW DIFFERENCE	CHANGE IN HIGH FROM PREVIOUS DAY
2/3	33	10	23	—
2/4	28	8	20	$^-5$
2/5	25	$^-3$	28	$^-3$
2/6	15	$^-10$	25	$^-10$
2/7	$^-2$	$^-20$	18	$^-17$
2/8	10	$^-5$	15	$^+12$
2/9	20	$^-2$	22	$^+10$

The Mathematical Idea: Subtraction on the Extended Number Line

For whole numbers we know that the answer to $A - B = ?$ is the same as the answer to the missing addend problem $B + ? = A$. Knowing how to add on the external number line thus suggests the following definition.

DEFINITION OF SUBTRACTION ON THE EXTENDED NUMBER LINE

For given numbers S and T on the extended number line, the number $S - T$ is the solution to the missing addend problem $T + ? = S$.

To compute $S - T$ using the add-subtract slide rule, place the zero of the *bottom line* just below the point for T on the *top line*. Find the point for S on the *top line*. The number on the *bottom line* just below S is the number $S - T$.

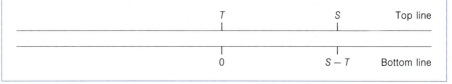

The latter is the method used in solving the second temperature problem.

The relationship between addition and subtraction of integers (respectively, rational numbers) is similar to that between addition and subtraction of whole numbers (respectively, fractions). However, there is a major difference. For whole numbers A and B, in order for $A - B$ to make sense, A must be bigger than B. For example, $20 - 33$ makes no sense for whole numbers; there is no whole number solution to the problem $33 + ? = 20$. However, $^+20 - {^+33}$ makes sense for integers; $^-13$ is a solution to $^+33 + ? = {^+20}$.

9. Solve the subtraction problems with integers.

(a) $^-73 - {}^-22$ (b) $^-22 - {}^-73$ (c) $^-22 - {}^+73$

(d) $^+73 - {}^-22$ (e) $^+73 - {}^+22$ (f) $^+22 - {}^+73$

10. Suppose that A and B are whole numbers and that A is bigger than B. Find rules for computing the following integer subtraction problems in terms of whole numbers A and B and whole number operations. You will want to use the traditional convention that $^+C = C$ for any whole number C.

(For example, the answer to $^+B - {}^+A = ?$ is the opposite of whole number $A - B$; that is, $^+B - {}^+A = {}^-[A - B]$.)

(a) $^+A - {}^+B = ?$ (b) $^+B - {}^+A = ?$ (c) $^-A - {}^-B = ?$

(d) $^-B - {}^-A = ?$ (e) $^+B - {}^-A = ?$ (f) $^-B - {}^+A = ?$

11. Complete the temperature chart.

DATE	HIGH	LOW	HIGH AND LOW DIFFERENCE	CHANGE IN HIGH FROM PREVIOUS DAY
2/10	28	10		$^+8$
2/11	40	25		
2/12	45	30		
2/13	38	18		
2/14	22	7		
2/15	10	$^-5$		
2/16	$^-5$	$^-10$		
2/17	$^-3$	$^-5$		

12. The Redondo family kept track daily of its elevation (above sea level) on a recent automobile trip in the Far West. They recorded the high and low elevation for each day and wanted to figure out the difference between the high and low as well as the change in highs from one day to the next. Here is the beginning of their chart.

DATE	ELEVATIONS: HIGH	LOW	DIFFERENCE OF HIGH AND LOW	CHANGE IN HIGH FROM PREVIOUS DAY
7/6	8700	5200		10,100
7/7	6300	2500		
7/8	3100	600		
7/9	800	$^-100$		
7/10	$^-50$	$^-200$		
7/11	$^-100$	$^-250$		
7/12	1000	$^-150$		
7/13	3200	500		

Complete the two empty columns on the right.

13. Ms. Chevalier has a checking account that can be overdrawn (up to a limit of $3000). On page 443 is a table showing the balance in this account at the beginning

of several months. Negative numbers are used to indicate an overdrawn amount and positive numbers indicate money in the account.

MONTH	BALANCE	CHANGE IN BALANCE FROM PREVIOUS MONTH
Jan.	$^+\$1234.75$	$^+\$573.20$
Feb.	$^-\$125.33$	
Mar.	$^-\$971.89$	
Apr.	$^-\$608.20$	
May	$^+\$537.44$	
June	$^+\$1084.58$	

She is interested in the change in her balance from month to month. Fill in the amounts in that column.

14. In an earlier exercise distances traveled along a straight line were treated as numbers on an extended number line. Distances traveled in one direction are positive numbers; distances traveled in the opposite direction are negative numbers.

   You can also think of the speed of an object traveling along a straight line as a number on an extended number line. If an object is traveling in the positive direction, then its speed is positive. If an object is traveling in the negative direction, then its speed is negative. Usually the term *velocity* is used instead of *speed* when speed can be positive or negative.

   In this exercise we assume the straight line is at an elevation of 25,000 ft running north and south. Distances in the northerly direction are positive; distances in the southerly direction are negative. An airplane traveling along this line in the northerly direction has positive velocity; an airplane traveling in the southerly direction has negative velocity.

   Answer the questions about this situation using positive and negative numbers.

   (a) You are traveling along the line in an airplane that can fly a maximum of 150 mph with no wind. Today you are traveling north. A wind is blowing at 20 mph in the northerly direction. What are the possible velocities for the airplane?

   (b) The next day you are traveling north again in the same airplane. This time there is a wind blowing in the southerly direction at 30 mph. What are the possible velocities for the airplane this day?

   (c) The third day you are traveling south in the airplane, and there is still a wind blowing in a southerly direction, now at 10 mph. What are the possible velocities for the airplane?

   (d) The fourth day you are still traveling south in the airplane. On this day there is a wind blowing in a northerly direction at 40 mph. What is the maximum velocity of the airplane?

11.4 MULTIPLICATION OF POSITIVE AND NEGATIVE NUMBERS

THE RESERVOIR PROBLEM The managers of City Reservoir use positive and negative numbers in three ways. The first is to indicate the rate of flow of water in and out of the reservoir. The rate is a positive number if water is flowing in and negative if it is flowing out. Secondly, they use positive and negative numbers to indicate the change in the amount of water in the reservoir: The change is positive if the amount of water in the reservoir has increased (during the interval of time under consideration), and negative if the amount of water has decreased. Finally, they use positive and negative numbers to indicate directed time: Time measured from now to a moment in the future is positive; time measured from now to a moment in the past is negative. For example, "3 hr from now" is positive time ($^+3$ hr) and "3 hr ago" is negative time ($^-3$ hr).

The managers know that if the water is flowing into the reservoir at the rate of 1000 gal/min and it continues at that rate, then in 30 min the quantity of water in the reservoir will be $1000 \times 30 = 30{,}000$ gal more than it is now. This uses the familiar formula rate $\times$ time $=$ quantity. In integers, this can be expressed as $^+1000 \times {}^+30 = {}^+30{,}000$.

The managers have other situations where the rate and directed time are given, but both are not positive; and they need to know a quick method for calculating the change in the quantity of water in the reservoir.

Don't forget to try this first.

A Solution to the Reservoir Problem

Given the rate of water flow (a number on the extended number line) and a time (another number on the extended number line), the managers want to know the change in quantity of water (a third number on the extended number line). The answer when rate and time are positive is given by multiplication of whole numbers or fractions. The managers are looking for a way to "multiply" numbers on the extended number line. To get some clues, the managers look at the following situations.

1. Water has been flowing for some time into the reservoir at the rate of 1000 gal/min. How much more or less water was in the reservoir 30 min ago than there is now?

$$^+1000 \times {}^-30 = ?$$

2. Water is flowing out of the reservoir at the rate of 1000 gal/min. If it continues flowing at that rate, how much more or less water will be in the reservoir in 30 min than there is now?

$$^-1000 \times {}^+30 = ?$$

3. Water is flowing out of the reservoir at the rate of 1000 gal/min and has been doing so for some time. How much more or less water was in the reservoir 30 min ago than there is now?

$$^-1000 \times {}^-30 = ?$$

How do the managers answer these problems?

1. Thirty minutes ago there were 30,000 gal less water than now. That's a change of $^-30{,}000$ from the present quantity: $^+1000 \times {}^-30 = {}^-30{,}000$.

2. Thirty minutes from now 30,000 gal of water will have flowed out of the reservoir. That's a change of $^-30{,}000$ from the present quantity: $^-1000 \times {}^+30 = {}^-30{,}000$.

3. Thirty minutes ago there must have been 30,000 gal more of water than there are now. That's a change of $^+30{,}000$ from the present quantity: $^-1000 \times {}^-30 = {}^+30{,}000$.

The Mathematical Idea: Multiplication of Integers and Rational Numbers

The solution to the reservoir problem suggests a definition of multiplication of integers and rational numbers.

DEFINITION OF MULTIPLICATION OF INTEGERS AND RATIONAL NUMBERS

To multiply rational numbers (integers) A and B, ignore the signs and multiply the fractions (whole numbers). Attach a sign to the product according to the following rule:

$$^+ \times {}^+ = {}^+$$
$$^- \times {}^+ = {}^-$$
$$^+ \times {}^- = {}^-$$
$$^- \times {}^- = {}^+$$

For example,

$$^+1000 \times {}^+30 = {}^+30{,}000.$$
$$^-1000 \times {}^+30 = {}^-30{,}000.$$
$$^+1000 \times {}^-30 = {}^-30{,}000.$$
$$^-1000 \times {}^-30 = {}^+30{,}000.$$

It is useful to compare the definition of multiplication of integers to that for whole numbers. For whole numbers 7 and 9, the product is defined

$$7 \times 9 = \underbrace{9 + 9 + 9 + 9 + 9 + 9 + 9.}_{7 \text{ times}}$$

Multiplication of whole numbers is defined in terms of addition of whole numbers. Can the same thing be done with integers?

For integers $^+7$ and $^-9$, it would be natural to define their product

$$^+7 \times {}^-9 = \underbrace{{}^-9 + {}^-9 + {}^-9 + {}^-9 + {}^-9 + {}^-9 + {}^-9.}_{7 \text{ times}}$$

We can do this because we know how to add integers and because we think of a positive integer ($^+7$) as a whole number (7). There is no problem here, and the answer is $^+7 \times {}^-9 = {}^-63$, just as in our definition.

However, for integers $^-7$ and $^+9$, a definition of multiplication in terms of addition doesn't make sense:

$$^-7 \times {}^+9 = \underbrace{{}^+9 + {}^+9 + {}^+9 + {}^+9 + \cdots ???}_{^-7 \text{ times ???}}$$

In other words, the number of times you do something (such as add numbers together) is a whole number—a positive integer. We must resort to something else in this case to define multiplication.

In the reservoir problem, we know that rate of flow, time, and change in quantity are related by multiplication when the numbers are whole numbers or fractions:

$$\text{Rate} \times \text{time} = \text{quantity.}$$

We *defined* multiplication of integers and rational numbers in order that the same relationship holds. Our definition is a good one if it preserves such relationships in other situations in which multiplication of whole numbers or fractions, and positive and negative numbers occur.

THE PHYSICIST'S PROBLEM A physicist wants to describe the motion of a car traveling back and forth along an east-west road. She specifies that velocity (directed speed) and distance traveled in the eastward direction are positive. As in the reservoir problem, time is also directed. The physicist knows that the velocity, time traveled, and distance traveled are related by the formula

$$\text{Velocity} \times \text{time} = \text{distance}$$

Try this yourself, first.

when the three quantities are positive numbers. She wants to know whether this relationship holds when the quantities are numbers on the extended number line.

A Solution to the Physicist's Problem

To solve this problem, the physicist looks at three situations.

1. A car travels east at 40 mph. Where was it 2 hr ago compared to where it is now?

$$^{+}40 \times {}^{-}2 = ?$$

Two hours ago the car must have been 80 mi west of where it is now and $^{+}40 \times {}^{-}2 = {}^{-}80$.

2. A car travels west at 40 mph. Where will it be in 2 hr compared to where it is now?

$$^{-}40 \times {}^{+}2 = ?$$

In 2 hr the car will be 80 mi west of where it is now and $^{-}40 \times {}^{+}2 = {}^{-}80$.

3. A car travels west at 40 mph. Where was it 2 hr ago compared to where it is now?

$$^{-}40 \times {}^{-}2 = ?$$

Two hours ago the car must have been 80 mi east of where it is now and $^{-}40 \times {}^{-}2 = {}^{+}80$.

The relationship

$$\text{Velocity} \times \text{time} = \text{distance},$$

which holds when the quantities are positive, seems to hold with any integers. So far our definition of multiplication of integers and rational numbers is proving to be satisfactory.

EXERCISE

15. Boats travel up and down the river. An observer stands on a dock on the river. Distances and velocities downstream are positive, and times into the future are positive. Use multiplication of integers and rational numbers to answer the questions.
    (a) One boat is traveling downstream at 10 mph and will reach the dock in 3 hr. Where is it now relative to the observer?
    (b) A second boat passed the observer 2 hr ago traveling upstream at 8 mph. Where is it now?
    (c) Another boat traveling upstream at 11 mph will reach the observer in 4 hr. Where is it now?
    (d) A fourth boat traveling downstream at 9 mph passed the observer 5 hr ago. Where is it now?

The physicist, who has been studying the motion of a car along an east-west road, has some questions.

1. A car passes me traveling east at 30 mph. In how many hours is it 90 mi east of here?

$$^+30 \times ? = {}^+90$$

2. How many hours does it take for the same car to be 90 mi west of here?

$$^+30 \times ? = {}^-90$$

3. A car traveling west stops to ask me directions. The driver says that in the last 2 hr she covered 100 mi. What was the car's velocity?

$$? \times {}^+2 = {}^-100$$

4. Another car, this time traveling east, stops and the driver reports that 2 hr ago he was 100 mi away. What was the car's velocity?

$$? \times {}^-2 = {}^-100$$

Try this yourself, first.

How can she solve these problems?

The physicist realizes that since velocity, time, and displacement are related by the formula

$$\text{Velocity} \times \text{time} = \text{displacement},$$

her four problems are really just missing factor problems.

1. $^+30 \times ? = {}^+90$
2. $^+30 \times ? = {}^-90$
3. $? \times {}^+2 = {}^-100$
4. $? \times {}^-2 = {}^-100$

To multiply two integers, you first drop the signs and multiply as if they were whole numbers; then you add a sign to the answer according to the rule for signs. So, to solve a missing factor problem with integers, you first drop the signs and solve (if you can):

1. $30 \times \underline{3} = 90.$
2. $30 \times \underline{3} = 90.$
3. $\underline{50} \times 2 = 100.$
4. $\underline{50} \times 2 = 100.$

Then you insert a sign according to the rules for multiplication, for each problem, respectively,

$$(^+ \times {}^+ = {}^+): 30 \times \underline{3} = 90 \rightarrow {}^+30 \times {}^+\underline{3} = {}^+90$$
$$(^+ \times {}^- = {}^-): 30 \times \underline{3} = 90 \rightarrow {}^+30 \times {}^-\underline{3} = {}^-90$$
$$(^- \times {}^+ = {}^-): \underline{50} \times 2 = 100 \rightarrow {}^-\underline{50} \times {}^+2 = {}^-100$$
$$(^+ \times {}^- = {}^-): 50 \times 2 = 100 \rightarrow {}^+\underline{50} \times {}^-2 = {}^-100$$

The Mathematical Idea: Division of Integers and Rational Numbers

For whole numbers and fractions, finding the solution to a missing factor problem is called *division*; thus, we make the following definition for integers and rational numbers.

> **DEFINITION OF DIVISION OF INTEGERS AND RATIONAL NUMBERS**
>
> Given integers (rational numbers) S and T with $T \neq 0$, the *division* of S by T is denoted $S \div T$ and is the integer (rational number) solution X to the missing factor problem $TX = S$ (if such a solution exists).

The discussion in the solution to the physicist's second problem suggests the following method for dividing two integers or rational numbers.

> **METHOD FOR DIVIDING INTEGERS AND RATIONAL NUMBERS**
>
> For integers (rational numbers) S and T, to find $S \div T$, drop the signs and divide as whole numbers (fractions) and add a sign to the result according to the following scheme:
>
> $$^+ \div\ ^+ =\ ^+$$
> $$^+ \div\ ^- =\ ^-$$
> $$^- \div\ ^+ =\ ^-$$
> $$^- \div\ ^- =\ ^+$$

Notice that if A and B are integers and $A \neq 0$, then $AX = B$ may not have a solution X that is also an integer. For example, there is no integer X such that $^-4X = {}^+7$. However, the rational number $^-7/4$ is a solution.

EXERCISES

16. Carry out the divisions of integers.
    (a) $^+40 \div {}^+8$ (b) $^-120 \div {}^+6$ (c) $^-99 \div {}^-11$
    (d) $^+150 \div {}^-25$ (e) $^-221 \div {}^+13$

17. An observer watches airplanes traveling along a north-south route. (North is the positive direction.) Solve the following problems using positive and negative numbers.
    (a) You observe an airplane traveling north at 250 mph. How many hours from now will it be 500 mi south of you?
    (b) You observe an airplane traveling south at 300 mph. How many hours from now will it be 600 mi south of you?
    (c) An airplane traveling south radios to you: "In the last 3 hours I covered 450 miles. What is my velocity?"
    (d) Another airplane traveling north radios to you: "Four hours ago, I was 480 miles from here. What is my velocity?"

11.6   LOOKING BACK: MORE ON RATIONAL NUMBERS

In this chapter, we have discussed several situations in which it is useful to use the extended number line. In most situations we used integers.

Since we can talk about $78\frac{3}{4}°$ above zero and of $9\frac{2}{3}°$ below zero, we should also be able to talk about temperatures of $^+78\frac{3}{4}°$ and $^-9\frac{2}{3}°$. Also, since we can talk of assets of \$230.73 and debts of \$3457.24, we should also be able to talk of assets of $^+\$230.73$ and of $^-\$3457.24$. We can talk of speeds of $37\frac{3}{5}$ mph going north (the "positive" direction) and 53.42 mph going south (the "negative" direction), so we should also be able to talk of velocities $^+37\frac{3}{5}$ mph and $^-53.42$ mph. The *opposite* of $^+\frac{5}{4}$ is $^-\frac{5}{4}$, and the opposite of $^-47/8$ is $^+47/8$. The numbers on the extended number line corresponding to fractions and their opposites are the *rational numbers*.

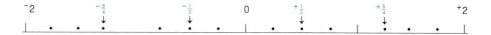

Notice that the set of integers is a subset of the set of rational numbers.

We have already discussed how the operations of addition, subtraction, multiplication, and division can be extended from whole numbers and fractions to integers and rational numbers.

For example, to add rational numbers $^+\frac{3}{4}$ and $^-\frac{7}{3}$, you take two copies of the extended number line, place the 0 of the *bottom line* just below the $^+\frac{3}{4}$ of the *top line* and look for $^-\frac{7}{3}$ on the *bottom line*. The answer is just above the latter on the *top line*.

EXERCISES

18. Replace the subtraction problems for rational numbers by missing addend problems.
    (a) $^+\frac{3}{4} - {}^+\frac{1}{2}$ (b) $^-\frac{3}{8} - {}^-\frac{1}{3}$ (c) $^-\frac{4}{5} - {}^+\frac{2}{3}$ (d) $^+\frac{5}{12} - {}^-\frac{5}{6}$

19. Find the sum in each problem.
    (a) $^-\frac{7}{8} + {}^+\frac{4}{3}$ (b) $^+\frac{1}{2} + {}^-\frac{2}{3}$ (c) $^-\frac{1}{3} + {}^-\frac{5}{12}$ (d) $^+\frac{1}{4} + {}^-\frac{3}{8}$

You recall that to multiply two rational numbers, you first ignore the signs and multiply the two fractions. Then you give the product a sign according to the following rule:

$$^+ \times {}^+ = {}^+,$$
$$^- \times {}^- = {}^+,$$
$$^+ \times {}^- = {}^-,$$
$$^- \times {}^+ = {}^-.$$

Thus, we have, for example,

$$^+\frac{3}{4} \times {}^+\frac{2}{3} = {}^+\frac{1}{2}.$$

$$^-\frac{3}{4} \times {}^-\frac{2}{3} = {}^+\frac{1}{2}.$$

$$^-\frac{3}{4} \times {}^+\frac{2}{3} = {}^-\frac{1}{2}.$$

$$^+\frac{3}{4} \times {}^-\frac{2}{3} = {}^-\frac{1}{2}.$$

Division of rational numbers is also worth spelling out again.

DEFINITION OF DIVISION OF RATIONAL NUMBERS

If R and S are rational numbers and $S \neq 0$, then the *quotient of R by S* (or *R divided by S*) is denoted by R/S, or $R \div S$ and is the solution X to the missing factor problem $SX = R$.

To find R/S: Ignore the signs of R and S, divide the two fractions, and assign the quotient of fractions a sign according to the rule

$$^+ \div {}^+ = {}^+,$$
$$^- \div {}^- = {}^+,$$
$$^+ \div {}^- = {}^-,$$
$$^- \div {}^+ = {}^-.$$

For example,

$$^+\frac{3}{4} \div {}^+\frac{2}{3} = {}^+\frac{9}{8}.$$

$$^-\frac{3}{4} \div {}^-\frac{2}{3} = {}^+\frac{9}{8}.$$

$$^+\frac{3}{4} \div {}^-\frac{2}{3} = {}^-\frac{9}{8}.$$

$$^-\frac{3}{4} \div {}^+\frac{2}{3} = {}^-\frac{9}{8}.$$

By contrast with integers, the missing factor problem $SX = R$ for rational numbers S and R with $S \neq 0$ always has a rational number solution X.

EXERCISE

20. Carry out the indicated operations on rational numbers.
(a) $^+\frac{3}{4} \times {}^-\frac{8}{11}$
(b) $^-\frac{5}{6} \times {}^-\frac{12}{4}$
(c) $^-\frac{12}{5} \div {}^-\frac{7}{10}$
(d) $^+\frac{23}{4} \div {}^-\frac{2}{5}$
(e) $^-5.32 \times {}^+3.41$
(f) $^-17.002 \div {}^+1.302$
(g) $^-35.03 + {}^+4.115$
(h) $^-7.004 - {}^-1.23$

LOOKING BACK: FORMAL PROPERTIES OF INTEGERS AND RATIONAL NUMBERS

In earlier chapters we discussed the formal properties of whole numbers and of fractions as they relate to the operations of addition and multiplication. We now have two new sets with these operations, integers and rational numbers. We will point out that many of the properties satisfied by whole numbers and fractions hold for integers and rational numbers as well. Before doing this, we should point out that both integers and rational numbers have a property the others don't.

INTEGERS AND RATIONAL NUMBERS HAVE ADDITIVE INVERSES

Suppose that M is an integer. Then there is always an integer solution N to the equation $M + N = 0$. In fact, $N = {}^-M$, the opposite of M, is the solution; ${}^-M$ is also called the *additive inverse* of M.

Similarly, suppose that R is a rational number. Then there is always a rational number solution S to the equation

$$R + S = 0.$$

In fact, $S = {}^-R$, the opposite of R, is the solution; ${}^-R$ is also clled the *additive inverse* of R.

Before, given fraction $A \neq 0$, we were not able to find a fraction solution for B in the equation $A + B = 0$.

A chart comparing whole numbers, fractions, integers, and rational numbers with respect to certain properties may be helpful.

PROPERTY	SET OF NUMBERS			
	Whole Numbers	Fractions	Integers	Rationals
Addition				
Equality	×	×	×	×
Commutative	×	×	×	×
Associative	×	×	×	×
Identity	×	×	×	×
Inverse			×	×
Multiplication				
Equality	×	×	×	×
Commutative	×	×	×	×
Associative	×	×	×	×
Identity	×	×	×	×
Inverse*		×		×
Distributive property of multiplication over addition	×	×	×	×

* The multiplicative inverse (or reciprocal) of the rational number ${}^-A/B$ ($A \neq 0$) is ${}^-B/A$. (Try it!)

Among the sets considered in the chart, the set of rational numbers is the only one that satisfies all the properties listed. A set having two operations and satisfying all these properties is called a *field*. So the rational numbers form a field. Another set that forms a field is the set of *real numbers*. The set of real numbers corresponds to all points on the extended number line. The real numbers include all rational numbers and numbers corresponding to irrational lengths (such as the irrational length we met in chap. 10) and their opposites.

Order Properties of the Rational Numbers

The order relation of the whole numbers and fractions also extends to the rational numbers.

DEFINITION OF ORDER FOR RATIONAL NUMBERS

If A and B are unequal rational numbers on the number line and the rightmost number is B, then B is *greater than* A, and we write $B > A$ (or $A < B$).

We also have the following alternative, a formal definition.

ALTERNATIVE DEFINITION OF ORDER FOR RATIONALS

If A and B are distinct rational numbers, then $A < B$ means that there is a positive rational number C such that $A + C = B$.

Order also cooperates with addition and multiplication of rational numbers.

PROPERTIES OF ORDER FOR RATIONAL NUMBERS

ADDITION

If R, S, T, and U are rational numbers such that $R < S$ and $T \leq U$, then $R + T < S + U$.

MULTIPLICATION

If R, S, and T are rational numbers such that $R < S$ and $0 < T$, then $RT < ST$.

OPPOSITES

If R and S are rational numbers such that $R < S$, then $^-R > {}^-S$.

Let's look at some examples of these properties.

EXAMPLE 1 Since $-\frac{3}{4} < \frac{1}{2}$ and $^-1 < {}^-\frac{1}{4}$, by the addition property, it follows that $-\frac{3}{4} + {}^-1 < \frac{1}{2} + {}^-\frac{1}{4}$. In other words, $^-1\frac{3}{4} < \frac{1}{4}$. (Notice that we have adopted the usual convention and dropped the $^+$ from positive rational numbers.)

EXAMPLE 2 Since $-\frac{3}{4} < {}^-\frac{1}{2}$ and $0 < \frac{3}{8}$, by the multiplication property, it follows that $(\frac{3}{8})({}^-\frac{3}{4}) < (\frac{3}{8})({}^-\frac{1}{2})$. In other words, $^-\frac{9}{32} < {}^-\frac{3}{16}$.

EXAMPLE 3 Since $-\frac{3}{4} < {}^-\frac{1}{2}$, by the opposites property, it follows that $^-({}^-\frac{3}{4}) > {}^-({}^-\frac{1}{2})$. In other words, $\frac{3}{4} > \frac{1}{2}$.

Notice that the rational numbers have features of order that fractions and whole numbers don't. One of these is the relationship between order and opposites. A second is that if R, S, T, and U are rational numbers such that $R < S$ and $T < U$, then it isn't always the case that $RT < SU$. For example, $^-4 < {}^-3$ and $2 < 3$. But $(^-4)(2) < (^-3)(3)$ is not true; in fact, $^-9 < {}^-8$.

EXERCISES

21. Draw pictures of rational numbers on the number line showing why the "opposites" property of order for rational numbers is true.

22. If R, S, T, and U are rational numbers such that $R < S$ and $T < U$, what additional conditions can you put on R, S, T, and U to guarantee that $RT < SU$?

11.8   LOOKING AHEAD: RATIONAL NUMBERS AND ALGEBRA

Having the integers and rational numbers provides a common language for dealing with temperatures above and below zero, assets and debts, favorable and unfavorable changes in stock prices, and other situations in which quantities come in two kinds and can be identified with the left and right ends of the number line. There is another very favourable aspect to rational numbers (and the operations that go with them). Rational numbers make dealing with algebraic expressions much simpler than it would be otherwise. For example, to subtract fraction A from fraction B, you must know that $A \leq B$ (even though A and B may be some *unknown* expression involving fractions). For rational numbers A and B, $A - B$ is always another rational number.

Another advantage to the rational numbers is that subtraction can be interpreted as addition. To help you make sense of this, think about how subtraction works on the extended number line.

SUBTRACTION OF RATIONAL NUMBERS IN TERMS OF ADDITION

If R and S are rational numbers, then $R - S = R + {}^-S$. Thus, $R - S$ is the same as the sum of R and the opposite of S.

We have also considered an expression such as $A - B + C$ and asked how it should be interpreted: Is it equal to $(A - B) + C$, or is it equal to $A - (B + C)$? (In general, the two expressions are not the same. For example, try $A = 4$, $B = 2$, $C = 1$.) If A, B, and C are rational numbers (which means that they could also be whole numbers), then—since addition is associative and since subtraction can be interpreted as addition $(A - B = A + {}^-B)$—there is no ambiguity in $A - B + C$: It is equal to $A + {}^-B + C$. Putting the parentheses in one way, we get $(A + {}^-B) + C = (A - B) + C$; putting them in another way, we get $A + ({}^-B + C) = A + (C - B)$. Thinking of whole numbers as rational numbers and remembering that the rational numbers satisfy all those nice properties *helps you keep track of what the rules are for working with whole numbers.*

As a third example of the benefits of having rational numbers, suppose the expression

$$12A - 4(7A - 3B) + 5B$$

occurs in a problem you are working on. (You may want to think of A and B as whole numbers the identity of which is unknown to you at this stage in solving the problem.) How can you deal with this expression? It would be nice if you could replace it by a simpler, equivalent expression. One solution is to treat it as an expression involving rational numbers. Then we can use the formal properties of rational numbers. Useful properties that follow from these are the properties of opposites.

PROPERTIES OF OPPOSITES

If A and B are rational numbers, then

$$^-A = (-1)A, \qquad {}^-(AB) = ({}^-A)B = A({}^-B), \qquad ({}^-A)({}^-B) = AB.$$

If A/B denotes AB^{-1} where $B \neq 0$, then

$$\frac{^-A}{B} = {}^-\!\left(\frac{A}{B}\right) = \frac{A}{^-B}, \qquad \text{and} \qquad \frac{^-A}{^-B} = \frac{A}{B}.$$

For this reason, we adopt the stated convention.

CONVENTION

For rational numbers A and B we write $^-A = -A$ and $-(AB) = -AB$.

Using all this, we get

$$12A - 4(7A - 3B) + 5B = 12A + (-4)[7A + (-3)B] + 5B$$

(Replace subtraction of whole numbers by addition of integers; use convention above.)

$$= 12A + (-4)7A + (-4)(-3)B + 5B$$

(Distributive property.)

$$= 12A + {}^-28A + 12B + 5B$$

(Properties of opposites.)

$$= (12 + {}^-28)A + (12 + 5)B$$

(Distributive law.)

$$= -16A + 17B$$

(Addition of integers.)

Of course, there are shortcuts for all this. But the steps in the derivation above give you the basic idea. To do algebra, you really need the rational numbers and their properties.

EXERCISES 23. Find the integer equal to each expression.
   (a) $-3(12 - 7)$ (b) $-10(-5 + -7)$
   (c) $25 + -4(12 - 43) + -5$ (d) $-3(-4 - -3)(12 + -5)$
   (e) $-(-5)(-6)(15 + -27)$

24. Simplify each expression, explaining each step you use by an appropriate rule.
   (a) $5C + 2(6C - 3)$ (b) $7D - 2(10 - 3D)$
   (c) $27 + 4(8E - 6)$ (d) $-2G(12 - 5G)$
   (e) $(7F - 9)(3F + 2)$ (f) $15A - 7(2A - 4B) - 10B$

Solving Equations

Having the rational numbers around also makes it easier to solve certain equations. For example, suppose you want to find a rational number X such that $3X - 12 = 7X + 10$. The strategy for solving such an equation is to *turn it into a simpler problem*—in fact, a missing factor problem—using the rules to replace the equation with an equation involving X that has the same solution. You want the end result to look like $AX = B$ for some particular rational numbers A and B. Your strategy is to isolate the terms involving X on one side of the equation,

$$\mathbf{3X} - 12 = \mathbf{7X} + 10.$$
$$\uparrow \qquad\qquad \uparrow$$
Terms involving X

To do this, we use the equals property of addition of rational numbers and "add" $-7X$ (the additive inverse of $7X$) to both sides of the equation:

$$3X - 12 + -7X = 7X + 10 + -7X.$$

This simplifies as shown.

$$3X - 12 + -7X = 7X + 10 + -7X:$$
$$3X + -7X - 12 = 7X + -7X + 10 \text{ (Commutative property of addition)}$$
$$3X + -7X - 12 = 0 + 10 \text{ (Additive inverse)}$$
$$(3 + -7)X - 12 = 10 \text{ (Distributive property)}$$
$$-4X - 12 = 10 \text{ (Addition of integers)}$$
$$-4X - 12 + 12 = 10 + 12 \text{ (Property of addition and equality)}$$
$$-4X = 22 \text{ (Additive inverse, addition of integers)}$$
$$\left(-\frac{1}{4}\right)(-4)X = \left(-\frac{1}{4}\right)22 \text{ (property of multiplication and equality)}$$
$$X = -\frac{22}{4}.$$

In this solution we used the property of addition and equality twice (in both cases, what we added to both sides of the equation was carefully chosen to "make" the equation simpler) to arrive at a missing factor problem. From there, we used the property of multiplication and equality to "solve" the equation.

EXERCISE

25. Find the rational number solution to each equation.
    (a) $-4Y + 2 = 3Y - 10$ (b) $7Z + 4 = 3Z + 8$
    (c) $-3W - 10 = -2W + 5$ (d) $-2V + 7(6 - 4V) = V + 10$
    (e) $U - 2(3U - 5) + 11 = 0$

Simplifying Inequalities

Some sets of rational numbers can be described by inequalities.

EXAMPLE 1 S is the set of all rational numbers X such that $X < 53$.
The shaded portion of the picture corresponds to the set S.

EXAMPLE 2 T is the set of all rational numbers X such that $-\frac{72}{11} < X$.
The shaded portion of the picture corresponds to the set T.

EXAMPLE 3 U is the set of all rational numbers X such that $-21 < X < \frac{3}{4}$.
The shaded portion of the picture corresponds to the set U.

We can use the formal properties of rational numbers to help us find alternate, simpler descriptions to sets of rational numbers described by inequalities. For example, consider the set V of all rational numbers X such that $3X - 4 < -2X + 5$.

Let's see what we can do. First note that if X is a number such that $3X - 4 < -2X + 5$, then by the addition property of order for rational numbers, X is also a number such that $3X - 4 + 4 < -2X + 5 + 4$, or, after simplifying, $3X < -2X + 9$. Conversely, if X is a number such that $3X < -2X + 9$, then X is also a number such that $3X - 4 < -2X + 9 - 4$, again by the addition property of order (in this case, addition of -4 to both sides of the inequality). Thus, we have the following equalities of sets:

$$V = \text{the set of all } X \text{ such that } 3X - 4 < -2X + 5$$
$$= \{X: 3X - 4 < -2X + 5\}$$
$$= \{X: 3X < -2X + 9\}.$$

By similar reasoning we can obtain the following chain of equalities of sets:

$$V = \{X: 3X - 4 < -2X + 5\}$$
$$= \{X: 3X < -2X + 9\} \text{ (Addition property of order)}$$
$$= \{X: 3X + 2X < -2X + 9 + 2X\} \text{ (Addition property of order)}$$
$$= \{X: 5X < 9\} \text{ (Distributive property, additive inverse)}$$
$$= \left\{X: \left(\frac{1}{5}\right)5X < \left(\frac{1}{5}\right)9\right\} \text{ (Multiplication property of order)}$$
$$= \left\{X: X < \frac{9}{5}\right\}.$$

Here is a picture of V:

EXERCISE 26. As in the foregoing example, find a simpler description for each set of rational numbers. Draw pictures of the set in each case.
(a) $\{X: 5X + 10 < 7X - 4\}$ (b) $\{X: -7X + 3 < 4X - 2\}$
(c) $\{X: 2X - 8 < 9X - 4\}$ (d) $\{X: .5X + 1.15 < .75X - 3.2\}$
(e) $\{X: 2X - 3 < 4X + 7 \text{ and } -3X + 2 < 4X - 3\}$
(f) $\{X: 7X + 4 < 2X + 1 \text{ and } X + 3 < 2X - 1\}$

11.9   SUMMARY OF IMPORTANT IDEAS AND TECHNIQUES

- The extended number line, positive and negative numbers
  The opposite of a positive or negative number
  Integers
  Rational numbers

- Order of numbers on the extended number line, extending the order of fractions and whole numbers

- Addition and subtraction of numbers on the extended number line, using the add-subtract slide rule

- Multiplication and division of integers and rational numbers, extending the operations on whole numbers and fractions

- The formal properties of rational numbers and integers as related to addition, multiplication, and order
  Definitions of additive and multiplicative inverses
  The definition of field

- The use of formal properties to simplify algebraic expressions, to solve certain equations, and to simplify inequalities

PROBLEM SET

PRACTICING SKILLS Use integers and rational numbers in all the exercises wherever appropriate.

1. Represent each set of integers on an extended number line.
   (a) $\{^-7, ^+3, ^+6, 0, ^-2, ^-1\}$ (b) $\{^-10, ^+8, ^-11, ^-13, ^+2, ^+9\}$

2. An object 5 ft above ground level drops into a well 49 ft deep. How far will it travel by the time it hits the bottom of the well?

3. In the early morning the temperature reading was $-14°$F. By 2 P.M. it had risen $25°$F. What was the temperature at 2 P.M.?

4. The Oakland ("Crunch") Raiders were on their opponent's 20-yd line. The next four plays ran as follows: $^+7, ^-10, ^-4, ^+18$. What was the total gain for the four plays? Did the Raiders make a first down? (A *first down* means a total of $^+10$ in four plays.)

5. A student has $83 in her checking account. If she writes checks for $21, $39, and $13, deposits $30, and then writes another check for $42, what positive or negative number represents the resulting status of her checking account?

6. In a recent cold spell the temperature registered $8°$F at the beginning of the week and then dropped $2°$F each day for seven consecutive days. What was the temperature reading at the end of the week?

7. A stockbroker discovered that his stock had a gain of $^-$$2 a share each day for eight days. If he held 100 shares, what was his total gain for those eight days?

8. Frank's Diner has been losing $12/day for the past 30 days and has a net worth right now of $^-$$150. What was its net worth 30 days ago?

9. Metro Tower has 40 floors above ground and 5 levels below ground for car parking. The elevator control panel shows numbers 1 to 40 and G1, G2, G3, G4, and G5 for the five garage levels.
   (a) Assuming that G1 is the level just below the ground floor, renumber and order the elevator control panel using integers.
   (b) Joe's office is on the twenty-first floor and his car is parked on G5. How many floors away from his car is Joe's office?
   (c) Mary's building does not have a floor numbered 13. If Mary has an office on the floor numbered 33 and is parked on G2 how many floors away from her car is her office?

10. Bob delivers messages and packages within the Metro Tower building. In a span of 2 hr he takes messages from 2244 (room 44 on floor 22) to Acme Printers 3 floors below, from Point Systems 7 floors above Acme Printers to Lazee Employment Offices 2 floors below Point Systems, and from Dog Daze Calendars 15 floors below Point Systems up to Cat Heir 5 floors from the top. Assume Bob goes directly from 2244 to Acme to Point Systems to Lazee to Dog Daze to Cat Heir with no detours.
    (a) Make a list of integers representing each segment of his trip.
    (b) What floor is the Cat Heir office on?
    (c) What is the net change in floors for Bob; that is, how many floors above or below 2244 is the Cat Heir office? (Use an integer for your answer.)

11. You play the following game with a friend. You roll an ordinary die. If a 6 turns up, you pay your friend three pennies. If any other number turns up, your friend pays you one penny.
    (a) The following sequence of rolls occurs as you begin playing the game: 6, 5, 2, 1, 4, 6, 3. Indicate as an integer how much money you have won by the end of each roll.
    (b) Roll a die 10 times and calculate your winnings (as an integer) by the end of each roll.

12. Jill played five games in a golf tournament. Her scores were reported on TV as 2 below par, 3 above par, 5 below par, 4 below par, and 4 above par.
    (a) Express these scores as integers.
    (b) If par for the course is 72, what were Jill's scores? Use integer addition.
    (c) Katrina played in the same tournament and had scores of $68, 75, 65, 72,$ and 70. List Katrina's scores relative to par using integers.
    (d) The winner of the tournament is the person scoring the fewest number of strokes. Who is doing the best, Jill or Katrina? (Answer this by adding the lists of integers relative to par.)

13. Bob, the courier in Metro Tower, reported that 5 times during the day he went down 8 floors, and 8 times he went up 12 floors, and that these were all his movements between floors. Is this possible?

14. The town of Blue Valley has a leak in its water tower at the rate of 12,500 gal/day.
    (a) How many gallons has the town lost in the last 3 days because of the leak?
    (b) The tank now has 1,500,000 gal of water in it, and the town normally uses 15,000 gal/day. Also, during this season 9000 gal flow into the tank each day. How much water did the tank have 3 days ago?
    (c) How much water will be in the tank in 10 days?
    (d) When will the tank be empty?

15. The temperature of a liquid in cold storage is dropping $5°$/hr.
    (a) How much colder will it be in 3 hr?
    (b) If it has been cooling for 5 hr and its temperature is $25°F$, how cold was it 5 hr ago?
    (c) If it has lost $35°F$ temperature, how many hours has it been in the cooler?

16. Place each set of numbers on a number line.

    (a) $\left\{\frac{1}{2}, \frac{-1}{3}, \frac{3}{4}, \frac{-7}{8}, \frac{-4}{3}, \frac{2}{3}\right\}$ (b) $\{2.3, -4.5, -1.2, -1.9, 2.6, 3.2\}$

    (c) $\left\{\frac{5}{16}, \frac{-13}{8}, -1\frac{3}{4}, \frac{9}{22}, \frac{-27}{16}, \frac{8}{9}\right\}$

17. Of each pair below, which is larger?

    (a) $-\frac{2}{3}, -\frac{3}{5}$ (b) $-\frac{4}{7}, \frac{5}{8}$

18. A tank containing 100 gal of water has a maximum capacity of 200 gal. The tank has a slow leak of 3 gal/hr. Water is being pumped in at a rate of 15 gal/hr.
    (a) Find a formula for the quantity of water in the tank in terms of t, where t is the number of hours that has passed. (*Think*: Water in tank plus water going in [positive] plus water loss [negative].)
    (b) How many hours will it take to fill the tank?

19. At noon an 8000-gal tank has 3000 gal of water in it. It is leaking at a rate of 70 gal/hr. At 5:00 P.M. water begins flowing in at a rate of 150 gal/hr. When will the tank be filled?

20. If water is pumped into a 10,000-gal tank at a rate of 160 gal/hr but it takes 75 hr to fill it, what is its leakage rate?

21. At 8:00 P.M. Flatman leaves home and drives toward Metro City at a rate of 75 mph in the Flatmobile. Andrew, his butler, realizes Flatman has forgotten to take his grappling hook and leaves with it at 8:15. He must overtake Flatman before he reaches the city 20 mi away.
    (a) How fast will Andrew need to drive to catch Flatman in 15 mi? Write an equation using S to represent Andrew's speed.

(b) If Andrew drives 10 mph faster than Flatman, how long will it take to catch him? Find formulas for the distances the two men have traveled in terms of T where T represents time elapsed from Flatman's departure.

22. Sonya wants a CD player that costs $599. She has started working at a job 40 hr/wk and saving her money after expenses. Although the job pays $5.25/hr, she figures that her expenses are about $1.20/hr. After 2 wk on this job she decides she isn't saving fast enough and takes on a second job in which she earns $4.85/hr and works 12 hr/wk. How many weeks will she need to work before she can buy the CD player? Find a formula for the amount of money Sonya saves in terms of W, the number of weeks she works.

USING IDEAS *For each remaining problem, write an essay the purpose of which is to communicate clearly and completely the solution to the problem. Mention the steps you took in solving the problem, other problems or solutions that gave you ideas, and the strategies you used.*

23. The dial of a combination lock contains 40 notches equally spaced, including a notch marked 0. Assume that a clockwise turn (R) is positive and a counterclockwise turn (L) negative. Determine the final position, relative to 0, for the following combination: Start at 0, then R 24 notches, L 30 notches, R 8 notches.

24. On a 150-question test, a student's score was to be determined by subtracting the number of wrong answers from the number of right answers. Unanswered questions would not be counted either way. One student answered 69 questions correctly and left 9 answers blank. What was his score on the test?

25. A teller at State Bank had $1000 in his cash drawer at the beginning of the day. Determine the amount of cash in his drawer after each of the following transactions.
    (a) $325 was deposited.
    (b) $37 was withdrawn.
    (c) A check for $145 was cashed, $50 of which was deposited.
    (d) A check for $75 was cashed.
    (e) $112 was withdrawn from a savings account at the bank.
    (f) At the end of the day the teller must have the amount of money he started with plus what he has taken in, less what has been withdrawn. The money must balance with the books. When he counted his money, he had $1118 in his drawer. Does this agree with your figures?

26. The hardware store took in $^+$$125 on its opening day business, $^-$$250 (because of a theft) on its second day, and $^+$$175 on the third day.
    (a) If the store started with $^+$$150 cash on hand on opening day, how much did it have at the end of the third day?
    (b) At the end of the fourth day of business the store had $75 more than it had at the beginning of the first day. What was the outcome of the fourth day of business?

27. Ken made the following trips in succession on Interstate 10, an east-west road where easterly directions are positive: $^+$150 miles, $^-$170 miles, $^-$20 miles, $^+$43 miles.
    (a) At the end of the fourth trip, is Ken east or west of his starting point?
    (b) How far must Ken go to return to his starting point?

28. Two gears are shown in the diagram on the next page. Gear A has 45 teeth and gear B has 30 teeth. Use negative numbers for clockwise turns and positive numbers for counterclockwise turns to answer the questions.
    (a) How many revolutions for B if A is turned $^+$8 revolutions?
    (b) How many revolutions for A if B is turned $^-$12 revolutions?

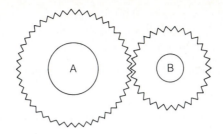

29. Two pulleys are shown in the diagram. Pulley C has $\frac{5}{4}$ the circumference of pulley D. Answer the questions using negative numbers for clockwise revolutions and positive numbers for counter-clockwise revolutions.
    (a) How many revolutions for pulley C if D is turned $^+100$ revolutions?
    (b) If pulley C is turned R revolutions and, as a result, pulley D moved S revolutions, how are R and S related?
    (c) If pulley D moves at a rate of $^+50$ rpm, at what rate does pulley C move?

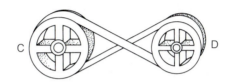

30. Using the convention that a positive distance is an ascent and a negative distance is a descent, a submarine logs the following maneuvers (in feet): $^+50$, $^-158$, $^-232$, $^+120$, $^-320$, $^+95$, $^-1124$, $^-225$, $^+430$. Where is the submarine now relative to where it was before the maneuvers began? If the depth of the submarine is 1400 ft below the surface of the sea when these maneuvers are completed, what was its depth before they began?

31. Discuss why temperatures offer a poor illustration for multiplication of positive and negative numbers.

32. Flying into the wind, a plane can go 190 mph. Flying with the wind, it can go 220 mph. What is the wind's speed? How fast can the plane go in still air?

33. Celsius temperatures (C) are related to Fahrenheit temperatures (F) by the equation $C = (\frac{5}{9})(F - 32)$.
    (a) Find the Celsius temperature corresponding to these Fahrenheit temperatures: (i) 104°F (ii) 212°F (iii) 14°F (iv) −40°F
    (b) Find the Fahrenheit temperatures corresponding to these Celsius temperatures: (i) 20°C (ii) 0°C (iii) −10°C (iv) 120°C

34. During one day's trading a speculator in stocks bought and sold shares in companies A, B, and C in the amounts and prices shown in the table. Her expenses (brokerage fees and so on) amount to 1% of total sales made. What was her net gain or loss for the day?

COMPANY	NUMBER OF SHARES	BOUGHT AT	SOLD AT
A	150	67	64
B	200	31	33
C	100	45	46

35. The owner of an eight-player, semipro basketball team has expenses of $1130 per player per game and $1425 per game for the coach. Costs for renting the arena and paying the custodian, ticket

seller, and so on, come to $850 per game. The team plays a 20-game schedule before an average crowd of 575 fans. The owner receives $20 for each ticket sold. What should his profits (as a positive or negative number) be by the end of the season?

36. A Reno blackjack dealer reports that one evening she had twenty customers. Eight of them won ⁻$15 apiece, three won ⁻$18 apiece, six won ⁺$4 apiece, one won ⁺$50, and the other two broke even.
    (a) What was the dealer's net gain (as an integer)?
    (b) What was the average gain to the dealer per customer?

37. You are standing at a train station beside a track that runs east-west. Using the conventions that a position to the east of you, a velocity in the easterly direction, and a time after an observation (by you) are all positive, answer each question using a rational number.
    (a) A train is traveling from west to east at 10 mph, and it will reach you in 3 hr. Where is it now?
    (b) A train passed you 2 hr ago traveling east to west at 18 mph. Where is it now?
    (c) A train traveling from east to west at 27 mph passed you 5 hr ago. Where is it now?
    (d) A train traveling from west to east at 13 mph passed you 5 hr ago. Where is it now?
    (e) A train 60 mi east of you will pass you in 3 hr. What is its velocity?
    (f) A train 24 mi east of you is traveling from east to west at 8 mph. When does it pass you?
    (g) A train 42 mi west of you is traveling west at 14 mph. When does it pass you?
    (h) A train passed you 2 hr ago and is now 36 mi west of you. What is its velocity?

38. Recall that Quabbin Reservoir supplies most of the water for the Boston area. The water from Quabbin is pumped into three holding reservoirs in the immediate vicinity of Boston; Boston and its suburbs draw from these holding reservoirs. At the end of each day Quabbin refills the holding reservoirs, replacing exactly the water drawn during the day. You work for Quabbin and want to know the contents of Quabbin at the end of the week's activities. Here's what you know already.

    ■ At the beginning of the week Quabbin contained 12,000 million gal of water.
    ■ Holding reservoir A starts with 300 million gal each day.
    ■ Holding reservoir B starts with 250 million gal each day.
    ■ Holding reservoir C starts with 150 million gal each day.
    ■ Boston takes 137 million gal each day from C.
    ■ Cambridge and Watertown each take 125 million gal daily from A.
    ■ Newton, Roxbury, and Waltham each take 25 million gal from B daily.
    ■ On Monday there was a particularly bad fire causing Boston to draw an extra 5 million gal from reservoir A.
    ■ On Tuesday and Wednesday it rained, adding 400 million gal to Quabbin.
    ■ At the beginning of the day on Thursday, holding reservoir B sprung a leak, which wasn't fixed until 6 P.M. Friday night. It leaked at the rate of 50,000 gal/hr.

    Think of a flow into Quabbin as positive and a flow out as negative to help figure out the contents of the reservoir at the end of the week.

39. A calculator can be used to perform integer and rational number arithmetic. For example, to calculate the expression 26 + −42, you use the key sequence 26 [+] 42 [+/−] [=]. The display will show −16. (The key [+/−] changes a displayed number to its opposite. Thus if −16 is displayed and [+/−] pushed, 16 will then be displayed.) To calculate the expression −26 − −42, you use the sequence 26 [+/−] [−] 42[+/−] [=].
    Use your calculator to calculate the following expressions:
    (a) 35.41 + −37.02 + 22.33 + −17.89   (b) −(46 − 75) + (−34 + −13)
    (c) −12 + −35 − 56 − −23

EXPONENTS, LARGE NUMBERS, AND THE ART OF ESTIMATION

12

CHAPTER

News item: January 30, 1990. President Bush proposes a budget of $1,230,000,000,000.

That's over a TRILLION dollars. How much is that? And how do you work with such a number?

In this chapter we will discuss ways to deal with large numbers such as 1 trillion, including ways to write them compactly and ways to do arithmetic with them. We will also be interested in getting a feel for a large quantity by relating it to something close to home. (If a trillion dollars were split up evenly among everyone in this country, how much would you get?)

In addition to knowing that it's the number of dollars in the 1990 federal government budget, we know something else about 1 trillion if we focus on the number in numeral form: It's a 1 followed by 12 zeros, and it's

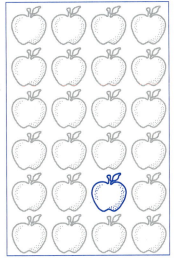

$$\underbrace{10 \times 10 \times \cdots \times 10}_{12 \text{ times}} = 10^{12}.$$

We know less about other numbers, for example, the number of mature trees growing in the continental United States or the number of hairs growing on the average person's head. We know that these are large numbers, but we haven't got a clue about what they are or how big. Is the number of trees close to the number of dollars in the federal budget? Is it a lot bigger? Smaller? How much bigger? Smaller?

We probably cannot know the large numbers in question exactly. But we don't need to know this. What we can know that is often useful to know is an *estimation* of the number. (Incidentally, President Bush did not propose that the government spend exactly $1,230,000,000,000. The figure is an estimate, a number close enough to the figure he expected the government to spend for purposes of discussion in Congress.) Showing how to understand and work with large numbers is one purpose of this chapter; a second is to discuss methods for making good estimations.

THE BACTERIA CULTURE PROBLEM

Mark and Judy are experimenting with growing bacteria in a dish. They have been told that a single bacterium is a simple animal and that, if it is provided with a sufficient amount of food and the right temperature and humidity, each bacterium will divide into two bacteria in 1 min. For their experiment, they plan to add gelatin (the food) to the dish, put a teeny bit of culture (a drop of water with live bacteria in it) on the gelatin, and set the dish in a warm, moist environment. Then they will observe how long it takes for the bacteria to cover the dish. To get some idea of what to expect, Mark and Judy decide to figure out, if they start with a single bacterium, how many bacteria there will be after 1 hr.

Judy: "After 1 minute there will be two bacteria. Then each of those will divide in two. That would make *four* bacteria after 2 minutes. Let me make a tree diagram showing what happens at each minute.

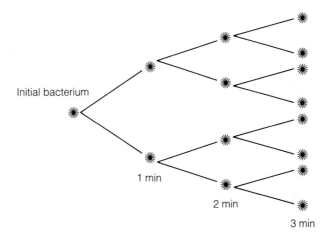

There will be *eight* bacteria after 3 minutes. The numbers are getting bigger."

Mark: "Let's make some more calculations and *organize the results in a chart.*

NO. OF MINUTES	NO. OF BACTERIA
0	1
1	2
2	4
3	8
4	16
5	32
6	64
7	128
8	256
9	512
10	1024
11	2048

Each number in the chart doubles the number that precedes it."

Judy: "After the first minute, there are two bacteria. After 2 minutes there are twice that: 2×2. After 3 minutes that is doubled: $2 \times 2 \times 2$. Let me put all this in our chart.

NO. OF MINUTES	NO. OF BACTERIA
0	1
1	$2 = 2$
2	$4 = 2 \times 2$
3	$8 = 2 \times 2 \times 2$
4	$16 = 2 \times 2 \times 2 \times 2$
5	$32 = 2 \times 2 \times 2 \times 2 \times 2$
6	$64 = 2 \times 2 \times 2 \times 2 \times 2 \times 2$
7	$128 = 2 \times 2 \times 2 \times 2 \times 2 \times 2 \times 2$
8	$256 = 2 \times 2 \times 2 \times 2 \times 2 \times 2 \times 2 \times 2$
9	$512 = 2 \times 2 \times 2 \times 2 \times 2 \times 2 \times 2 \times 2 \times 2$
10	$1024 = 2 \times 2 \times 2 \times 2 \times 2 \times 2 \times 2 \times 2 \times 2 \times 2$
11	$2048 = 2 \times 2 \times 2 \times 2 \times 2 \times 2 \times 2 \times 2 \times 2 \times 2 \times 2$

Let's see. In 10 minutes there will be

$$\underbrace{2 \times 2 \times 2 \times 2 \times 2 \times 2 \times 2 \times 2 \times 2 \times 2}_{\text{Ten 2s}}$$

bacteria. In 60 minutes there will be

$$\underbrace{2 \times 2 \times \cdots \times 2.}_{\text{Sixty 2s}}$$ "

Mark: "There's a shorthand way of writing those numbers:

$$2^1 = 2$$
$$2^2 = 2 \times 2$$
$$2^3 = 2 \times 2 \times 2$$
$$2^{60} = \underbrace{2 \times 2 \times \cdots \times 2}_{\text{Sixty 2s}}$$

We used that shorthand earlier to write 10, 100, 1000, 10,000, and so on, as 10^1, 10^2, 10^3, 10^4, respectively."

Judy: "Let's try to get a rough idea of what 2^{60} is. I remember from our chart that $2^{10} = 1024$, which is roughly 10^3. Let's use that."

Mark: "The number we're interested in is 2^{60}. That's 2 times 2 times 2—60 times. We can rewrite that as

$$2^{60} = \underbrace{(2 \times \cdots \times 2)}_{\text{Ten 2s}} \times \underbrace{(2 \times \cdots \times 2)}_{\text{Ten 2s}} \times \underbrace{(2 \times \cdots \times 2)}_{\text{Ten 2s}}$$
$$\times \underbrace{(2 \times \cdots \times 2)}_{\text{Ten 2s}} \times \underbrace{(2 \times \cdots \times 2)}_{\text{Ten 2s}} \times \underbrace{(2 \times \cdots \times 2)}_{\text{Ten 2s}}$$
$$= 2^{10} \times 2^{10} \times 2^{10} \times 2^{10} \times 2^{10} \times 2^{10}$$

Each 2^{10} is roughly 10^3, so that would make 2^{60} roughly equal to $10^3 \times 10^3 \times 10^3 \times 10^3 \times 10^3 \times 10^3$."

Judy: "You wrote $2^{60} = 2^{10} \times 2^{10} \times 2^{10} \times 2^{10} \times 2^{10} \times 2^{10}$. The exponents add! So

$$10^3 \times 10^3 \times 10^3 \times 10^3 \times 10^3 \times 10^3$$

$$= (10 \times 10 \times 10) \times (10 \times 10 \times 10) \times (10 \times 10 \times 10) \times (10 \times 10 \times 10)$$
$$\times (10 \times 10 \times 10) \times (10 \times 10 \times 10)$$

$$= 10^{18} = \underbrace{1000000000000000000}_{\text{Eighteen zeros}}$$

$$= 1{,}000{,}000{,}000{,}000{,}000{,}000.$$

That's 1 quintillion. That's a lot of bacteria."

The Mathematical Idea: Properties of Exponents

Mark and Judy figured that the number of bacteria present an hour after a single bacterium was placed in a nourishing environment would be 2^{60} and that this is roughly 10^{18}. They expressed the quantities using *exponential notation*. The quantity 2^{60} is read "two to the sixtieth power," or sometimes simply "two to the sixtieth." The numbers 2^1, 2^2, 2^3, 2^4, and so on, are called *the powers of* 2. Likewise, the numbers 10^1, 10^2, 10^3, 10^4, and so on, are *the powers of 10*. The powers of other numbers are referred to in the same way.

To account for the possibility that an exponent might be the whole number zero, we adopt a convention.

CONVENTION FOR A ZERO EXPONENT

If c is any nonzero number, then c^0 is defined to be

$$c^0 = 1.$$

For example, $2^0 = 1$ and $10^0 = 1$. (Why have we made the restriction $c \neq 0$ in this convention?)

Mark's and Judy's conclusion that

$$10^{18} = 10^3 \times 10^3 \times 10^3 \times 10^3 \times 10^3 \times 10^3$$

was based on the observation that if c is a number and N and M are positive whole numbers, then

$$c^N \times c^M = \underbrace{(c \times c \times \cdots \times c)}_{N \text{ times}} \times \underbrace{(c \times c \times \cdots \times c)}_{M \text{ times}}$$

$$= \underbrace{c \times c \times \cdots \times c}_{N + M \text{ times}}$$

$$= c^{N + M}.$$

Thus we have the first property of exponents.

If c is any nonzero number and N and M are whole numbers, then $c^N c^M = c^{N+M}$.

Mark and Judy could also have noticed that

$$\underbrace{10^3 \times 10^3 \times 10^3 \times 10^3 \times 10^3 \times 10^3}_{10^3 \text{ six times}} = (10^3)^6.$$

In fact, for any number c we have that

$$\underbrace{c^N c^N \dots c^N}_{M \text{ times}} = (c^N)^M$$

and, since the left-hand side of the foregoing expression is equal to c^{NM}, we have the second property of exponents.

PROPERTY 2 OF EXPONENTS

If c is any nonzero number and N and M are whole numbers, then $(c^N)^M = c^{NM}$.

EXERCISE 1. Use the laws of exponents to obtain alternate, simpler expressions for each expression given.
  (a) $3 \times 3 \times 3 \times 3 \times 3 \times 3$ (b) $7^4 \times 7^8$ (c) $5^4 \times 5^6 \times 5^{11}$
  (d) $8^7 \times 8^7 \times 8^7 \times 8^7$ (e) $2^4 \times 32^3$

Names for the Powers of 10

The chart lists the names in common use in the United States for some of the powers of 10.

POWER OF 10	COMMON NAME
10^1	Ten
10^2	Hundred
10^3	Thousand
10^6	Million
10^9	Billion
10^{12}	Trillion
10^{15}	Quadrillion
10^{18}	Quintillion
10^{21}	Sextillion
10^{24}	Septillion
10^{27}	Octillion

Mark and Judy have been told that the initial drop of water they added to their dish contained roughly 4,800,000 live bacteria. They want to know how many bacteria in all will be in their dish after 1 hr.

They remember that a single bacterium and all its offspring result in roughly 10^{18} bacteria in 1 hr.

Judy: "If each bacterium reproduces just like that single bacterium did, then we should multiply the number of bacteria in the drop by 10^{18}: $4,800,000 \times 10^{18}$. How can we carry out that multiplication? I know one way. We could convert the 10^{18} to a standard numeral, then multiply:

$$4,800,000 \times 1,000,000,000,000,000,000 = 4,800,000,000,000,000,000,000,000.$$

That's 4 septillion 800 sextillion. Big number!"

Mark: "There must be a better way. It would be nice if 4,800,000 were also a power of 10. Then we could multiply the two numbers easily using the property of exponents. Since 4,800,000 has a lot of zeros, we have

$$4,800,000 = 48 \times 100,000$$
$$= 48 \times 10^5.$$

So 4,800,000 is the product of a small number times a power of 10. Using the properties of exponents, we get

$$4,800,000 \times 10^{18} = 48 \times 10^5 \times 10^{18}$$
$$= 48 \times 10^{23}.$$

It's a small number times a power of 10. Since $48 = 4.8 \times 10$, our number could also be written as $4.8 \times 10 \times 10^{23} = 4.8 \times 10^{24}$. That's a number between 1 and 10 multiplied times 10^{24}. Our number is somewhere between 10^{24} and 10^{25}."

The Mathematical Idea: Scientific Notation

Powers of 10 written in exponential notation are compact and easy to multiply. This is especially true when the numbers are large. Mark and Judy discovered that something similar to exponential notation exists for a number that is not a power of 10: The number can be written as a product of a "small" number times a power of 10, thus, $4,800,000 = 4.8 \times 10^6$. In this case, the small number is between 1 and 10. This provides us with a definition of scientific notation.

DEFINITION OF SCIENTIFIC NOTATION

A number written as the product of two numbers, one between 1 and 10 and the other a power of 10, is written in *scientific notation*.

Note: The number between 1 and 10 may be *equal* to 1 but must be *less* than 10.

Thus, 1×10^5 is written in scientific notation, while 10×10^4 is not. The following number is also expressed in scientific notation:

$$4.8 \times 10^6.$$

Number between 1 and 10   Power of 10

Let's look at some more examples of numbers written in scientific notation.

NUMBER IN STANDARD FORM	NUMBER EXPRESSED IN SCIENTIFIC NOTATION
578,000	5.78×10^5
1,000,000	1×10^6
458	4.58×10^2
78,000,000,000,000	7.8×10^{13}

As an example of conversion from standard notation to scientific notation, consider the last number in the chart. To get the 7.8, move the decimal point of 78,000,000,000,000 (or, what is the same, 78,000,000,000,000.0) to just before its leftmost digit. The number of places moved, 13, is the exponent of 10:

$$7\,8\,,0\;0\;0\,,0\;0\;0\,,0\;0\;0\,,0\;0\;0.0 \; = 7.8 \times 10^{13}$$

13 12 11 10 9 8 7 6 5 4 3 2 1

Number of places moved   = Exponent of 10

To go from scientific notation to standard notation, reverse the procedure. Thus, 4.8×10^{24} in standard form is

$4.8 \times 10^{24} =$

4 8 0 0 0 0 0 0 0 0 0 0 0 0 0 0 0 0 0 0 0 0 0 0 0,

1 2 3 4 5 6 7 8 9 10 11 12 13 14 15 16 17 18 19 20 21 22 23 24

It is clear that the larger the number, the greater the advantage to writing it in scientific notation.

EXERCISES

2. An astronomer uses a unit of distance called a light-year, which is about 5,880,000,000,000 mi. It is the distance a photon of light travels in a vacuum in 1 yr. Express this number in scientific notation.

3. A chemist figures that an ounce of gold contains approximately 8.65×10^{21} atoms. Express this number in standard form.

4. Can the number 0 be expressed in scientific notation? Why or why not?

Doing Arithmetic with Numbers in Scientific Notation

Mark and Judy multiplied two numbers in scientific notation. There are other situations in which you would want to do the same. For example, a certain telescope can detect a star that is 3.4×10^3 light-years away. You want to know how many miles this is. Since a light-year is 5.88×10^{12} miles, the number we are interested in is $(3.4 \times 10^3) \times (5.88 \times 10^{12})$. By the commutative and associative laws for multiplication of numbers, this is equal to

$$\underbrace{(3.4 \times 5.88)}_{\substack{\text{Product of the} \\ \text{small numbers}}} \times \underbrace{(10^3 \times 10^{12})}_{\substack{\text{Product of the} \\ \text{powers of 10}}},$$

which, on carrying out the two multiplications, is equal to 19.992×10^{15}, since $19.992 = 3.4 \times 5.88$ and $10^{15} = 10^3 \times 10^{12}$. In scientific notation, our number is equal to 1.9992×10^{16}. This suggests a general procedure.

MULTIPLICATION OF NUMBERS IN SCIENTIFIC NOTATION

If $C \times 10^N$ and $B \times 10^M$ are two numbers expressed in scientific notation, then to find the expression for $(C \times 10^N) \times (B \times 10^M)$ in scientific notation, first compute $C \times B$ and express the result in scientific notation as $A \times 10^P$. The product written in scientific notation is then $A \times 10^{P+M+N}$. (Note that $P = 0$ or 1.)

THE GASOLINE PROBLEM

In 1970 there were about 81,000,000 cars in use in the United States. Gasoline stations estimate that during the same year 62,000,000,000 gal of gasoline were sold. You want to know on the average how many gallons of gasoline each car used during the year (in other words, if all cars used the same amount of gasoline, you want to know how much each car would use).

You realize that the answer is the number of gallons of gasoline sold during the year divided by the number of cars in use during the year. You decide to write each of these numbers in scientific notation:

$$81,000,000 = 8.1 \times 10^7$$
$$62,000,000,000 = 6.2 \times 10^{10}.$$

The number you are interested in is thus the following number:

$$\frac{6.2 \times 10^{10}}{8.1 \times 10^7}.$$

You realize that this is equal to

$$\frac{6.2}{8.1} \times \frac{10^{10}}{10^7}.$$

You look at these two numbers and realize that you know that $10^{10}/10^7 = 10^3$. Next you compute:

$$\frac{6.2}{8.1} = .765$$

(to the nearest .001). So your answer is $.765 \times 10^3$. To obtain your answer in scientific notation, you notice that

$$.765 = 7.65 \times \frac{1}{10}$$

so that

$$.765 \times 10^3 = 7.65 \times \frac{1}{10} \times 10^3 = 7.65 \times 10^2.$$

The Mathematical Idea: Division of Numbers Expressed in Scientific Notation

The solution to the gasoline problem suggests that there is a general method for division of numbers expressed in scientific notation. First let's consider dividing one power of 10 by another. For example, to divide 10^8 by 10^5 we form the fraction

$$\frac{10^8}{10^5} = \frac{10 \times 10 \times 10 \times 10 \times 10 \times 10 \times 10 \times 10}{10 \times 10 \times 10 \times 10 \times 10}$$

$$= 10 \times 10 \times 10$$

$$= 10^3.$$

This suggests another property of exponents.

PROPERTY OF EXPONENTS 3

If c is a nonzero number and N and M are whole numbers such that $N \geq M$, then

$$\frac{c^N}{c^M} = c^{N-M}.$$

In particular, $10^N/10^M = 10^{N-M}$. (We will consider the case $N < M$ later.)
 Here are two examples in which you want to express a quotient in scientific notation.

Example 1

$$\frac{7.5 \times 10^5}{2.3 \times 10^3} = \frac{7.5}{2.3} \times \frac{10^5}{10^3} \approx 3.3 \times 10^2.$$

Example 2

$$\frac{3.4 \times 10^5}{8.1 \times 10^3} = \frac{3.4}{8.1} \times \frac{10^5}{10^3} \approx .42 \times 10^2 = (4.2 \times \tfrac{1}{10}) \times 10^2 = 4.2 \times 10^1.$$

These examples suggest the a general method for expressing the quotient of two numbers in scientific notation.

If $C \times 10^N$ and $D \times 10^M$ are two numbers expressed in scientific notation and $N > M$, then to find the expression in scientific notation for

$$\frac{C \times 10^N}{D \times 10^M},$$

first compute C/D.

1. If $C > D$, then $A = C/D$ is a number less than 10 and greater than or equal to 1. The expression you are seeking is $A \times 10^{N-M}$.

2. If $C < D$, then $C/D = B \times \frac{1}{10}$, where B is less than 10 and greater than or equal to 1. The expression you seek is $B \times 10^{N-M-1}$.

EXERCISE

5. For this exercise use the figures in the gasoline problem for the total number of cars and the total number of gallons of gasoline used in 1970.
   (a) It is estimated that the average car travels 12,000 mi/yr. How many miles did all the cars in the United States travel in 1970?
   (b) What is the average number of miles per gallon of gasoline obtained for cars in 1970?

12.3   ROUNDING WHOLE NUMBERS; CALCULATORS AND SCIENTIFIC NOTATION

In solving the gasoline problem we saw how useful it was to be able to express the given numerical data in scientific notation. It was also nice that the number of cars—81,000,000—and the number of gallons of gasoline—62,000,000,000—turned out to be such "simple" numbers. Initially we might have been put off by the size of the numbers, but now we have a way—scientific notation—to deal with large numbers fairly easily. What would we have done if the numbers had been, instead (for example), 81,279,431 and 61,907,009,874? We might have given up, not because they are too large (they're about the same size as the numbers in the original version) but because it looks like the amount of computation involved wouldn't be worth the effort. (Even with the numbers in scientific notation—8.1279431×10^7 and $6.1907009874 \times 10^{10}$—we would still have to carry out the division $6.1907009874/8.1279431$.) A number such as 81,279,431 is more difficult to grasp than 81,000,000: There is too much information in 81,279,431 for us to take in all at once.

On the other hand, we might look at the numbers 81,000,000 and 62,000,000,000 in the original problem and ask whether 81,000,000 is *really* the number of cars manufactured in 1970. Exactly 81,000,000? Neither 81,000,001 nor 80,999,999 but *exactly* 81,000,000? Of course not. The number 81,000,000 is the nearest number in millions to the exact number. The process of going from the exact number to the nearest number in millions is called *rounding to the nearest million*. Whoever did the rounding *knew* that we might be overwhelmed by the amount of information included in the exact number. (In fact, it's possible that the exact number was not easy to determine and that 81,000,000 is actually an *estimate*. More about estimates later.)

Rounding is a general process. We can specify the degree of rounding; that is, we can round to the nearest hundred, we can round to the nearest thousand, we can round to the nearest billion, and so on. In fact, we can round to the nearest 10^n for any n. We were already doing this sort of thing when we were finding decimal fractions close to a given fraction. For example, the nearest $\frac{1}{100}$ to $\frac{1}{3}$ is 0.33; the nearest $\frac{1}{1000}$ to $\frac{5}{9}$ is 0.556. In situations such as those we are *forced* to make a choice of nearest hundredth, nearest thousandth, or whatever because there are no decimal fractions exactly equal to them.

What would be some examples of rounding for a certain number?

	NUMBER IN STANDARD FORM	NUMBER IN SCIENTIFIC NOTATION
An Eight Digit Number:	$81{,}279{,}431 = 8.1279431 \times 10^7$	
Rounded to the nearest 10^1	$81{,}279{,}430 = 8.127943 \times 10^7$	
Rounded to the nearest 10^2	$81{,}279{,}400 = 8.12794 \times 10^7$	
Rounded to the nearest 10^3	$81{,}279{,}000 = 8.1279 \times 10^7$	
Rounded to the nearest 10^4	$81{,}280{,}000 = 8.128 \times 10^7$	
Rounded to the nearest 10^5	$81{,}300{,}000 = 8.13 \times 10^7$	
Rounded to the nearest 10^6	$81{,}000{,}000 = 8.1 \times 10^7$	

The original number and each of the quantities to which the number has been rounded have been written in scientific notation in the table. For example, $81{,}279{,}000 = 8.1279 \times 10^7$. The power of 10 is the same for all of them but, because of rounding, the factors between 1 and 10 are different. One way in which these factors differ is in the number of digits each has. This number of digits is called the *number of significant digits* in the number obtained by rounding. For example, the number 8.1279 has five digits so that 81,279,431 rounded to five significant digits is $81{,}279{,}000 = 8.1279 \times 10^7$. The number 81,279,431 rounded to two significant digits is $81{,}000{,}000 = 8.1 \times 10^7$.

There is ambiguity in rounding a number such as 81,500,000 to the nearest million since it lies exactly halfway between 81,000,000 and 82,000,000. The usual convention in this case and other, similar, cases is to choose the larger of the two possibilities. Thus, 81,500,000 rounded to the nearest million is 82,000,000.

(*Warning:* The number 81,487,123 rounded to the nearest 10^5 is 81,500,000. The number 81,487,123 rounded to the nearest 10^6 is 81,000,000. The latter is *not* the same as rounding the number 81,500,000 to the nearest 10^6.)

One reason for rounding a number is for ease of calculation. Another is to make it easier to understand. But how *much* should you round? You round to the nearest given power of 10, but *which* power of 10? There are many answers, each depending on the situation, how the numbers are obtained, your audience, how precise you want the results of your computations to be, and so on. When we were finding the nearest decimal fractions to $\frac{1}{6}$ meter, we stopped at the nearest thousandth because we knew that a saw couldn't be more precise than a thousandth of a meter.

In the bacteria problem—when we were trying to figure out something about 2^{60}— we noticed that $2^{10} = 1024$ and that the latter is roughly 10^3. What does *roughly* mean here? It means that compared to 1000, 24 doesn't amount to much, and we may choose to ignore it in estimating 2^{60}—especially since we may not be interested in figuring out what 2^{60} is exactly. The fact that 2^{10} rounded to the nearest hundred is 10^3 and 2^{10} rounded to the nearest thousand is also 10^3 should also convey the feeling that 1024 is "roughly" equal to 10^3.

6. Round the number 56,487,503 to the (a) nearest 10, (b) nearest 100, (c) nearest 1000, (d) nearest 10,000, (e) nearest 100,000, (f) nearest 1 million, (g) nearest 10 million.

Calculators and Scientific Notation

If your calculator has an [EXP] key or something similar, you can use it to make calculations when the numbers, or rounded versions of them, are expressed in scientific notation. For example, to enter the number 4.2×10^{12} into a calculator, you key in the sequence 4.2 [EXP] 12. The display should show 4.2 ^{12} or perhaps 4.2 E 12. Now to multiply 4.2×10^{12} by 3.7×10^9, you key in 4.2 [EXP] 12 [x] 3.7 [EXP] 9 [=], and the display should show something like 1.554 E 22, meaning 1.554×10^{22}.

To calculate the quotient, $4.2 \times 10^{21} \div 3.7 \times 10^9$, you key in 4.2 [EXP] 21 [÷] 3.7 [EXP] 9 [=], and the display should show something like 1.135135135 E 12, meaning $1.135135135 \times 10^{12}$. (A calculator has a limit on the number of significant digits to which it will compute. My calculator will compute answers to 10 significant digits. If the exponent of 10 in the answer is less than this number of significant digits, then the calculator may display it in standard form rather than in scientific notation. Experiment with your calculator to find out what it does.)

EXERCISE

7. Use a calculator with an [EXP] key to carry out the calculations in scientific notation.
(a) $(7.3 \times 10^{12}) \times (9.8 \times 10^{34})$ (b) $(9.8 \times 10^{34}) \div (7.3 \times 10^{12})$
(c) $(4.8 \times 10^{24}) \div (6.3 \times 10^{12})$ (d) $(9.8 \times 10^4) \times (7.3 \times 10^5)$
(e) $(4.8 \times 10^{19}) \div (6.3 \times 10^{12})$

12.4 THE ART OF ESTIMATION

THE BACTERIA PROBLEM, CONTINUED

Mark and Judy were pleased that they were able to figure out that 2^{60} is about 10^{18}. However, they didn't have much feeling for the size of 10^{18}. To get some idea, they decided to figure out how long it would take to count to 10^{18}. They realize that to do this they will have to gather a certain amount of information. They figure first that they can comfortably count about 3 numbers a second. They remember that there are 60 sec in a minute and 60 min in an hour so that they would count

$$3 \times 60 \times 60 = 3 \times 6 \times 10 \times 6 \times 10$$

numbers in an hour.

Judy: "That's 108×10^2, or 1.08×10^4 numbers. Let's round that off to 1.1×10^4. Looks like we'll be counting for days, years even. Let's see, there are 24 hours in a day and 365 days in a year. So we could count about

$$1.1 \times 10^4 \times 2.4 \times 10$$

numbers in a day. That's $(1.1 \times 2.4) \times 10^5$, or 2.64×10^5 numbers in a day. Let's round that to 2.6×10^5. Then we could count about $2.6 \times 10^5 \times 365$ numbers in a year. That's $2.6 \times 10^5 \times 3.65 \times 10^2$. Let's round the 3.65 to 3.7. That would give us about $(2.6 \times 3.7) \times 10^7$, or 9.62×10^7 numbers each year."

Mark: "Let's figure out how many years it would take us to count to 10^{18}. The number of years it would take us would be about $10^{18}/(9.62 \times 10^7)$ years. That would be $(1/9.62) \times (10^{18}/10^7)$ years, or $.104 \times 10^{11}$ years, or 1.04×10^{10} years, which, rounding off, is about 1.0×10^{10} years. That is 10,000,000,000 years. So we estimate that it would take us 10 billion years to count to 10^{18}."

The Mathematical Idea: Estimating

To get some feeling for the size of 2^{60}, Mark and Judy decided to see if they could figure out how long it would take to count to 2^{60}. They were not particularly interested in knowing *exactly* how long it would take; they wanted to know *roughly* how long it would take. In other words, they wanted to find an *estimate* for how long it would take. Let's describe the features they used to obtain their estimate. First, they *broke the problem into simpler problems:*

1. How many numbers can be counted in a second?
2. How many seconds in a minute?
3. How many minutes in an hour?
4. How many hours in a day?

They eventually decided to figure out how long it would take in years. They figured they would also need to know the answer to the question

5. How many days in a year?

The answers to 2, 3, 4 and 5 are common knowledge. The answer to 1 they had to *estimate* from their own experience.

The second thing they did was to round each of these numbers to two significant digits as well as each other number obtained at intermediate stages of the computation. They also used scientific notation at all stages of the computation. They did both of these things in order to keep the arithmetic easy and under control. All this rounding also introduced error, but then they did not expect to obtain particular accuracy in their answer.

In the next problem and the one following it we will estimate certain quantities using these same ideas. The solutions to the problems that follow will differ from the one above in the extent to which the numbers in the computations are common knowledge. For many of these quantities an exact expression is not commonly known, and we will have to estimate it from our own experience; other quantities vary over time, and it will be necessary to estimate averages for them.

EXERCISE

8. Carry out all the calculations in the bacteria problem, part II, using a calculator and without rounding. Compare the two results and discuss the two methods.

THE BACTERIA PROBLEM, PART III

After estimating how long it would take to count to 2^{60}, Mark and Judy were still not satisfied that they had a good understanding for how big 2^{60} is. They decided to try something else.

Mark: "I've got an idea. Suppose we had 2^{60} peas and we decided to spread all those peas evenly over the United States. To make things easier, we can assume that the United States is relatively flat. Let's figure out how deep the peas would be.

"To get started, we know that there are roughly 10^{18} peas. Next, let's *break the problem into simpler problems.* First let's figure out how many peas there would be in a single layer spread over the United States."

Judy: "To do that, let's estimate how many peas there are in a square inch, then figure out how many square inches there are in the United States. *Let's make a plan for solving the problem.*

Main problem   Spread the peas evenly over the United States. How deep are the peas?

Small problem   How many peas in a single layer?

To solve small problem, first solve these   How many peas in a square inch? How many square inches in the United States?
Let's solve 'How many peas in a square inch?' first."

Mark: "I don't think that's something we can do in our heads. Here's a picture of a pea and a square inch.

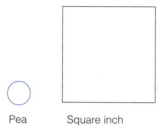

Pea   Square inch

To figure out how many peas will fit in a square inch, let's draw some in the square inch, side by side and squeezed together.

It looks as if 16 peas to the square inch is a good estimate."

Judy: "The next question is 'How many square inches in the United States?' I think we could *break that problem into smaller problems* by asking two questions:

How many square miles in the United States?
How many square inches in a square mile?

We can figure out how many square inches in a square mile pretty easily because we know about inches, feet, and miles. But how can we figure out how many square miles in the United States? We could look that up in an atlas."

Mark: "I think we could get a good enough estimate without doing that. Here's a rough map of the United States.

Let's not include Alaska and Hawaii. Let me draw a rectangle over the map like this.

Most of the country is inside the rectangle. The pieces that hang out can be tucked into the empty spaces of the rectangle.

So the area of the United States is roughly the same as the area of the rectangle. Let's see. It's about 3000 miles from New York to San Francisco. So the rectangle is about 3000 miles long. It's about 1500 miles from New York to Miami. So the rectangle is about 1500 miles tall. That means that the area of the continental United States is about 3000×1500 square miles. In scientific notation that's $3 \times 10^3 \times 1.5 \times 10^3$ square miles, or 4.5×10^6 square miles."

Judy: "We can also *break the problem* of figuring out how many square inches in a square mile *into smaller ones:*

How many square inches in a square foot?
How many square feet in a square mile?

There are 12 inches in a foot. Here's a square foot showing the square inches.

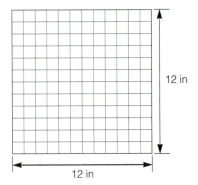

So there are 12 × 12 = 144 square inches in a square foot. There are 5280 feet in a mile. Here's a picture of the square mile but without the square feet drawn in.

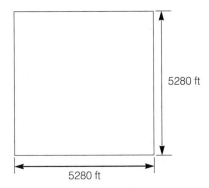

That makes 5280 × 5280 square feet in a square mile. With a little rounding and use of scientific notation that's $5.3 \times 10^3 \times 5.3 \times 10^3$ square feet or 28.09×10^6 which is roughly 2.8×10^7 square feet.

"It's time to see what kind of progress we are making in solving the main problem:

- 4.5×10^6 square miles in the United States without mountains and valleys
- 2.8×10^7 square feet in a square mile
- 1.4×10^2 square inches in a square foot
- 16 peas in a square inch

We can estimate the number of peas in a single layer by multiplying all four of these numbers together:

$$(1.6 \times 10^1) \times (1.4 \times 10^2) \times (2.8 \times 10^7) \times (4.5 \times 10^6)$$
$$= (1.6 \times 1.4 \times 2.8 \times 4.5) \times 10^{16}.$$

That's roughly 2.8×10^{17} peas in a single layer spread all over the country."

Mark: "All we need to do now is figure out how many layers of peas there would be. There are 10^{18} peas in all and 2.8×10^{17} peas in a single layer. The number of layers would be 10^{18} divided by 2.8×10^{17}. That's $(1/2.8) \times 10$, or about 4 layers. That's about an inch deep!"

Estimating: What's Involved

In estimating how deep the peas would be if 10^{18} of them were spread evenly over the continental United States, Judy and Mark did several things.

1. They *broke the main problem into smaller problems.* Then they broke these smaller problems into even smaller ones until the small problems could be solved. The answers to the smallest problems were used together to find solutions to the problems on the next level up, and so on, until the final problem was solved. It was important in this solution to *make a plan* (the plan involved how to break the problems into parts) *and to revise it* as work progressed (they needed to keep track of how the parts were broken into yet smaller parts).

2. They expressed the quantities obtained at each stage of the computation in scientific notation and used two significant digits. (The number of significant digits will vary with the problem.)

3. They used various kinds of estimates to obtain answers to the basic, smallest parts of the problem.
   (a) *Estimation as finding an average.* For example, in finding the number of peas in a square inch, you are aware that all peas are not the same size and that not every square inch will have the same number of peas in it. The answer to this question is not known precisely. However, the number they came up with is pretty good as an *average* for the number of peas in a square inch.
   (b) *Estimation made to keep calculations simple.* Number of square miles in the United States: A more exact expression for this quantity than they eventually obtained could have been found in an almanac or atlas. For their purposes, it was easier to replace the odd shape of the United States with a rectangle of roughly the same area and having an area they could calculate easily. This estimate was made in the same spirit as the use of two significant digits in the rest of the problem: to keep the calculations simple.

4. They used precise quantities when they were known. For example, in determining the number of square inches in a square mile, no estimating was necessary since all the information—number of inches in a foot, number of feet in a mile—is known precisely. Rounding was used, however, to estimate the answer to this part of the problem.

EXERCISES

9. Here is another idea for getting a feeling for how big 10^{18} is. Imagine you have 10^{18} square-inch postage stamps that are strung together in a roll. You are wrapping this roll of stamps around the equator of the earth as many times as it will go. How many times would this be?

10. In the bacteria problem, part III, instead of rounding, use a calculator in the scientific notation mode wherever possible. Compare the two answers and the methods.

THE TOOTHPASTE MARKETING PROBLEM

A company is considering the manufacture of a new brand of toothpaste. To help the company decide whether it should manufacture the new brand, the company will need to estimate the total annual retail dollar sales of toothpaste in the United States. Help the company do this.

A Solution to the Toothpaste Marketing Problem

You think: "There are 220 million people in the country. I assume they all brush their teeth. I don't know how much each person uses, but I know how much I use. I use a 5-ounce tube every 2 months, and I think I'm pretty normal. Anyway, I can't be too far off with that. That's six tubes per person per year. That's a total of $6 \times 2.2 \times 10^8$, or about 1.3×10^9 5-ounce tubes sold each year. What does each tube cost? About $1.50, I think. That makes a retail market of $1.5 \times 1.3 \times 10^9$ dollars, or about 2×10^9 dollars. That's *2 billion dollars!*"

An Estimation Strategy: Start at Home

An important feature of the solution to the toothpaste marketing problem is that in estimating how much toothpaste a typical citizen of the United States uses you started with yourself, you considered your own behavior, and you generalized this behavior to other people in the country. (There are dangers with this procedure: You might have false teeth and use no toothpaste at all!)

THE MEAT BUYING PROBLEM

A certain luxury liner is to make a trip from Rotterdam to New York City. The chief steward wants to know how much meat he must order for this one-way trip. He knows that the ship will have a crew of 741 and passengers numbering 1249. The trip is scheduled to take 8 days crossing the Atlantic. Help him solve this problem.

A Solution to the Meat Buying Problem

You figure that if you know how much a typical person eats in a day you can figure out how much meat to buy.

Total amount of meat = amount of meat a typical person eats in a day
$\times$ 8 days $\times$ number of persons eating

You wonder how much meat a typical person eats in a day and think of yourself: a quarter pound at dinner, less at lunch, not much at breakfast. Maybe half a pound a day? You go with that:

$$\text{Total amount of meat} = \tfrac{1}{2} \times 8 \times 1990$$
$$= 4 \times 1990$$
$$= 7960 \text{ lb.}$$

EXERCISE

11. Conservationists are interested in knowing whether the forested lands in the United States can supply the country's needs for newsprint for the next decade. They need an estimate of how many pounds of newsprint are used in this country each year. Help them find it.

12.5 LOOKING BACK: ERROR IN ROUNDING

In making estimations involving rounding, such as in estimating 2^{60}, we don't expect to obtain exact expressions. We can expect that error will be introduced into the calculations. To get some idea of how much error we might expect, let's look at our estimation for 2^{60}, in which we rounded 2^{10} to the nearest thousand, 10^3.

We know that $2^{10} > 10^3$ so that

$$2^{60} = 2^{10} \times 2^{10} \times 2^{10} \times 2^{10} \times 2^{10} \times 2^{10} > 10^3 \times 10^3 \times 10^3 \times 10^3 \times 10^3 \times 10^3$$
$$= 10^{18};$$

that is, $2^{60} > 10^{18}$.

On the other hand, $2^{10} = 1024 < 1.1 \times 10^3$ so that

$$2^{60} < (1.1 \times 10^3) \times (1.1 \times 10^3) \times (1.1 \times 10^3) \times (1.1 \times 10^3)$$
$$\times (1.1 \times 10^3) \times (1.1 \times 10^3) = (1.1)^6 \times 10^{18}$$

by using the laws of exponents and repeated applications of the rule for multiplying numbers expressed in scientific notation.

Multiplying $(1.1)^6$ with a calculator, we get $(1.1)^6 = 1.771561$, which is less than 1.78; thus, we have

$$1 \times 10^{18} < 2^{60} < 1.78 \times 10^{18}.$$

This tells us that the number 2^{60} lies between two large numbers. The difference between these two large numbers is $.78 \times 10^{18} = 7.8 \times 10^{17}$, or 780 quadrillion. My calculator tells me that 2^{60} is roughly 1.15×10^{18}. (There's error in *that* calculation, too! See Sec. 12.8, on using a calculator to calculate powers.) The amount of error in these estimates and calculations may be in the hundreds of quadrillions! That is the bad news. The good news is that the error can't be any more than 780 quadrillion. For example, it can't be as big as a quintillion.

EXERCISE   **12.** You are to estimate the product of the two numbers 486,543 and 384,318,000. To obtain your estimate, you decide first to round each number to two significant digits, getting 4.9×10^5 and 3.8×10^8, then multiply the latter two numbers together: $4.9 \times 10^5 \times 3.8 \times 10^8 = 18.62 \times 10^{13} = 1.862 \times 10^{14}$. Use the ideas in the previous discussion to figure what your error might be in rounding.

12.6 EXTENDING THE IDEAS: NEGATIVE EXPONENTS AND VERY SMALL NUMBERS

For most of this chapter we have been looking at situations in which large numbers occur and discussing ways to represent large numbers. With scientific notation, we can conveniently express any number bigger than $1 = 1.0 \times 10^0$. What about numbers smaller than 1? Here are some small numbers that might interest us:

■ Size of a virus: .000000914 cm long
■ Wave length of a gamma ray: .0000000000003048 m
■ Weight of a single bacterium: .000000000002 g
■ Time it takes a certain computer to do an addition problem: .0000044 sec.

Is there a convenient way to express these numbers? We know from our experience from decimals that

$$.000000914 = 9.14 \times \left(\frac{1}{10}\right)^7.$$

$$.0000000000003048 = 3.048 \times \left(\frac{1}{10}\right)^{13}.$$

$$.000000000002 = 2.0 \times \left(\frac{1}{10}\right)^{12}.$$

$$.0000044 = 4.4 \times \left(\frac{1}{10}\right)^6.$$

This suggests that every number less than 1 can be written as a product of two numbers, one of which is a number between 1 and 10 and the other of which is a power of $\frac{1}{10}$. The general statement is this:

Suppose a decimal d is less than 1 and that the first nonzero digit of d occurs at the nth decimal place, then there is a number e such that $d = e \times \left(\frac{1}{10}\right)^n$ and $1 \leq e < 10$.

Numbers of the form $e \times \left(\frac{1}{10}\right)^n$ are similar to those expressed in scientific notation earlier; both involve the product of a number between 1 and 10 times a power of a number. Nevertheless, they differ; the former uses powers of $\frac{1}{10}$, and the latter uses powers of 10. When we have two numbers bigger than 1 expressed in scientific notation and we are to multiply them, then we know what to do using the rules. What do we do when we have two numbers to multiply, one bigger than 1 expressed in scientific notation, the other less than 1 expressed as $e \times \left(\frac{1}{10}\right)^n$? We can get by, of course, but the following observations will enable us to unify the two kinds of expressions and obtain nice rules for doing arithmetic with them.

Suppose that N and M are whole numbers such that $N \geq M$. Then

$$10^N \left(\frac{1}{10}\right)^M = \frac{10^N}{10^M} = 10^{N-M} \quad \text{and} \quad 10^M \left(\frac{1}{10}\right)^N = \frac{10^M}{10^N} = \left(\frac{1}{10}\right)^{N-M}.$$

At some point in the history of mathematics, someone looked at these expressions and thought this way: "Take two whole numbers N and M with $N \geq M$. You multiply 10^N times 10^M you get 10^{N+M}: The exponents add. When you multiply 10^N times $\left(\frac{1}{10}\right)^M$, you get 10^{N-M}—10 to a power equal to the difference of the two exponents. In other words, *the power you get is the sum of the integers* ^+N *and* ^-M. *Multiplication of the two numbers is related to the addition of integers.* To take advantage of this situation, we can adopt the convention that 10^{-M} is equal to $\left(\frac{1}{10}\right)^M$ for any positive whole number M.

"There are some benefits to doing this: *Every number not equal to zero* can be written in the form $e \times 10^K$ for $1 \leq e < 10$ and K an integer. Secondly, the rules for multiplying integer powers of 10 are just like the rules for whole number powers of 10."

Let's formalize and generalize this.

DEFINITION OF NEGATIVE EXPONENTS

Let c be any nonzero number and N a positive whole number. Then define c^{-N} as

$$c^{-N} = \left(\frac{1}{c}\right)^N = \frac{1}{c^N}.$$

This definition is consistent with and justifies the notation defined earlier for the *reciprocal* of a fraction: $(A/B)^{-1} = 1/(A/B) = B/A$.

This tells us what c^K means for any integer K. If K is not negative, then we think of K as a whole number, and our previous rule tells us what c^K means. If K is negative, then the definition just given tells us what c^K means. What about c^0? Earlier in the chapter we adopted the convention $c^0 = 1$. We are now in a position to explain *why* we adopted this convention. We want the rule $c^K c^J = c^{K+J}$ to hold for all integers. In particular, for positive whole number N we *want* $c^N c^{-N} = c^0$. But $c^N c^{-N} = 1$. So we define (i.e., adopt the convention that) $c^0 = 1$.

Now that we know what c^K means for every integer K, we can list some properties that these powers satisfy. (Notice that we are not allowing c to be equal to zero. Why is this?)

PROPERTIES OF INTEGER EXPONENTS

Suppose that c is a nonzero number and that K and J are integers. Then

1. $c^K c^J = c^{K+J}$
2. $(c^K)^J = c^{KJ}$

   In particular, $(c^K)^{-1} = c^{-K}$.

The addition of exponents K and J on the right-hand side of property 1 is addition of integers; the multiplication of exponents K and J on the right-hand side of property 2 is multiplication of integers. It seems as if integers could have been created just to deal with the arithmetic of powers and exponents.

Finally, look at an extension of our earlier definition of scientific notation that encompasses all positive numbers.

DEFINITION OF SCIENTIFIC NOTATION

A positive number S is expressed in *scientific notation* if it is written as a product $S = e \times 10^n$ for some integer n and some number e such that $1 \le e < 10$. Every positive number can be expressed in scientific notation.

Thus, for the original numbers in this section, we have

$$.000000914 = 9.14 \times 10^{-7}.$$
$$.0000000000003048 = 3.048 \times 10^{-13}.$$
$$.000000000002 = 2.0 \times 10^{-12}.$$
$$.0000044 = 4.4 \times 10^{-6}.$$

13. Express each number in scientific notation.
    (a) .9   (b) .034   (c) .00000245   (d) .000000001
    (e) .000000001012   (f) .000000000000000057

14. The following numbers are expressed in scientific notation. Rewrite them in ordinary decimal form.
    (a) 3.04×10^{-1} (b) 8.9×10^{-8}
    (c) 5.78×10^{0} (d) 7.006×10^{-10}

15. The properties of integer exponents follow from the definitions of integer exponents and from the properties of whole number exponents. Show why this is so. (*Hint:* Break the problem into smaller problems that are possible to do. For example, to show $(c^N)^M = c^{NM}$, you may want to consider various cases: N positive, M negative; N negative, M negative, etc.)

16. Use the properties of integer exponents to simplify the expressions.
    (a) $10^8 \times 10^{-12}$ (b) $10^{12} \times 10^{-8}$ (c) $2^{60} \times 32^{-5}$
    (d) $10^7 \times (1000)^{-3}$ (e) $(2^3 2^{-5})^{-7}$ (f) $(-2x^2)^3$
    (g) $x^4 y^3 x^2$ (h) $5x^2 + (5x)^2$ (i) $(x^2 y^3)^3$

    (j) $x^3 x^{-3}$ (k) $\dfrac{a^5}{a^2}$ (l) $\dfrac{x^3}{x^{-3}}$

    (m) $\dfrac{x^{-3}}{x^3}$ (n) $\left(\dfrac{x}{y}\right)^{-3}$ (o) $\dfrac{a^2}{a^5}$

17. Carry out the indicated operations and express the answers in scientific notation.
    (a) $(3.4 \times 10^{-7}) \times (1.7 \times 10^{-3})$
    (b) $(3.4 \times 10^{7}) \times (1.7 \times 10^{-3})$
    (c) $(3.4 \times 10^{-7}) \times (1.7 \times 10^{3})$
    (d) $(3.4 \times 10^{-7}) \div (1.7 \times 10^{-3})$
    (e) $(3.4 \times 10^{7}) \div (1.7 \times 10^{-3})$
    (f) $(3.4 \times 10^{-7}) \div (1.7 \times 10^{3})$

18. The operations in exercise 17 can be carried out on a calculator using the [EXP] key. For example, to enter 3.4×10^{-7}, you use the key sequence: 3.4 [EXP] 7 [+/−]. Use a calculator with an [EXP] key to calculate the expressions in exercise 17.

19. A microscopic plant is 2.4×10^{-14} cm in diameter. If its diameter grows at a rate of 1.6×10^{-15} cm/sec, what will the diameter of the plant be after 5 sec?

20. The *Landsat* is a satellite used to study the earth's resources. Without sunlight, a detector in the satellite produces a current of 2×10^{-12} A (ampere or amperes). For each watt of reflected sunlight that lands on it the detector produces an additional 0.5 A of electrical current. How many watts must land on the detector to give a current 100 times greater than what the detector produces without sunlight?

21. Light travels about 3×10^8 m/sec. The diameter of a hydrogen atom is about 10^{-10} m. How long does it take light to travel the diameter of a hydrogen atom?

12.7   LOOKING BACK: EXPONENTIAL GROWTH

In the bacteria problem we obtained the table shown.

MINUTE	NO. OF BACTERIA PRESENT
0	1
1	2
2	2^2
3	2^3
4	2^4
5	2^5

To figure out how many bacteria will be around during a minute you multiply 2 times the number of bacteria present during the previous minute. This is an example of *exponential growth*. In exponential growth a quantity (in this example, the number of bacteria) is observed at successive moments of time (successive years, days, minutes, for example). To compute the quantity observed at one moment, you multiply the quantity observed at the previous moment by a fixed number. (In the bacteria example, the fixed number is 2.) Here is another example.

THE INVESTMENT PROBLEM

Carlos has saved $5000 and plans to invest it in a certificate of deposit. His banker tells him that he can buy a certificate from the bank for $5000 that will earn 6.5% interest each year. The bank assumes that Carlos will leave the amount of interest earned in his account so that in subsequent years the bank will pay interest on the total amount in Carlos account. (This is called *compound interest.*) Carlos wants to know what his investment will be worth in 10 yr.

Carlos thinks: "If I buy a certificate of deposit now, what will it be worth in 1 year? My banker says it will earn 6.5% interest in 1 year. That's .065 × $5000 = $325. So there will be $5000 + $325 = $5325 in my account at the beginning of the second year. In other words, the value of my investment will be $5325 at the end of 1 year. What will its value be at the end of 2 years? Since the interest is compounded, the interest for the second year will be 6.5% of $5325 or .065 × $5325. So, at the end of the second year the value of my investment will consist of that interest plus $5325: (.065)($5325) + $5325. However, from the distributive law, that's just ($5325)(.065 + 1) = $5671.13. At the close of the third year, the value will be (.065)($5671.13) + $5671.13, or ($5671.13)(.065 + 1), or $6039.75.

"To figure what the value of my investment will be at the end of a year, all I have to do is multiply .065 + 1 times what it was worth at the end of the previous year. Here is what this process looks like for several years.

YEAR	VALUE OF INVESTMENT AT BEGINNING OF YEAR
1	5000
2	(5000)(1 + .065)
3	(5000)(1 + .065)(1 + .065)
4	(5000)(1 + .065)(1 + .065)(1 + .065)

We can use exponents to simplify some of those expressions:

$$(1 + .065)(1 + .065) = (1 + .065)^2,$$
$$(1 + .065)(1 + .065)(1 + .065) = (1 + .065)^3$$

so that our table now has a slightly different look.

YEAR	VALUE OF INVESTMENT AT BEGINNING OF YEAR
1	5000
2	$(5000)(1 + .065)$
3	$(5000)(1 + .065)^2$
4	$(5000)(1 + .065)^3$
5	$(5000)(1 + .065)^4$
6	$(5000)(1 + .065)^5$

At the end of 10 years I'll have $(\$5000)(1.065)^{10} = \$9385.69$.

The Mathematical Language: Compound Interest

An investment that earns compound interest is one in which you place an initial amount of money in an account. The money in the account earns a certain *rate R* (usually given as a percentage) of interest at the end of each year. The interest earned is left in the account, and in subsequent years interest will be calculated on the total amount in the account. The type of interest such an investment earns is called *annual compound interest* (*annual* because the interest is calculated once a year). Carlos's calculations and observations suggest the following method for computing the value of such an investment (the amount in the account).

VALUE OF INVESTMENT AT END OF Y YEARS
WHEN INVESTMENT EARNS ANNUAL COMPOUND INTEREST
AT THE RATE OF R% PER YEAR

$$\text{Value} = (\text{initial amount invested}) \times \left(1 + \frac{R}{100}\right)^Y.$$

Annual compound interest is an example of exponential growth. The quantity observed every year is the money in the account. The quantity at the end of 1 yr is equal to $(1 + R/100)$ times the quantity observed at the end of the previous year.

22. You are considering making an initial investment of $1500 in a program that yields 5.5% interest, compounded annually. You plan to keep the money in the program for 8 yr. Find out what your investment will be worth at the end of that period.

Frequent Compounding of Interest on Investments

Typically, investment institutions such as banks compound interest on investments more than once a year. It favors the investor to have interest compounded often. The following summary should clarify the procedures that are commonly used and illustrate the advantage to the investor of more frequent compounding. In the table the annual rate is 8% for each account, and an initial deposit of $1000 has been made.

TYPE OF ACCOUNT	WHEN INTEREST IS PAID	RATE OF INTEREST PAID EACH TIME	VALUE OF ACCOUNT AT END OF YEAR
Compounded annually	Once a year	.08	$1080.00
Compounded semiannually	Twice a year	08/2 = .04	1081.60
Compounded quarterly	Four times a year	.08/4 = .02	1082.43
Compounded monthly	12 times a year	.08/12 = .0067	1083.43
Compounded daily	360 times a year	.08/360 = .00022	1084.48

When interest is paid more than once a year, a fraction of the annual rate is paid each time. Generally, this fraction is equal to the annual rate divided by the number of payments made each year. The exception is when interest is being paid daily, in which case the annual rate is divided by 360 rather than 365. This continues the procedure of an earlier day when there were no sophisticated computing machines and dividing by 360 was easier than dividing by 365.

There is a formula for the value of such an investment after a certain number of pay periods similar to the formula when interest is compounded annually. Here is a chart showing some formulas when the annual rate is r (= a decimal fraction), and the initial investment (the *principal*) is P.

NO. OF TIMES PER YEAR WHEN INTEREST IS PAID	RATE PAID EACH TIME	VALUE OF INVESTMENT AFTER N PAY PERIODS
1	r	$P(1 + r)^N$
2	$r/2$	$P(1 + r/2)^N$
4	$r/4$	$P(1 + r/4)^N$
12	$r/12$	$P(1 + r/12)^N$
365	$r/360$	$P(1 + r/360)^N$

Thus, if a type of investment pays interest M times a year, in Y years the investment will make YM payments. The value of the investment will be $P(1 + r/M)^{YM}$ (except in the case $M = 365$). Here is a chart for the cases we've seen.

NO. OF TIMES PER YEAR WHEN INTEREST IS PAID	VALUE OF INVESTMENT AT END OF Y YEARS
1	$P(1 + r)^Y$
2	$P(1 + r/2)^{2Y}$
4	$P(1 + r/4)^{4Y}$
12	$P(1 + r/12)^{12Y}$
365	$P(1 + r/360)^{365Y}$

EXERCISE

23. You make an investment of $1000 at an annual rate of 9.5%. Use a calculator to figure out the value of your investment at the end of 3 yr for the types of investment given.

(a) annual   (b) semiannual   (c) quarterly
(d) monthly   (e) daily

12.8 CALCULATORS AND COMPUTERS: POWERS AND EXPONENTIAL GROWTH

RAISING A NUMBER TO A POWER USING A CALCULATOR To compute 37^{12} using a calculator with a [y^x] key, you can use the keying sequence: 37 [y^x] 12 [=]. The display should read something like 6.582952006^{18}, or perhaps 6.582952006 E 18, meaning $6.582952006 \times 10^{18}$, which is 37^{12} in scientific notation. The same keying sequence can be used for exponents that are integers. For example, to compute 37^{-2} you use the sequence 37 [y^x] 2 [+/−] [=], and the display should read 0.00073046. (As before, to enter the negative number $^-2$ you use the key sequence 2 [+/−].)

ALTERNATE METHOD FOR RAISING A NUMBER TO A WHOLE NUMBER POWER If A and B are whole numbers, then

$$A^B = \underbrace{A\,A\,A \ldots A.}_{B \text{ times}}$$

The number A^B is obtained by multiplying A repeatedly B times, just as AB is obtained by adding A repeatedly B times. Just as we used the K key or constant feature to add repeatedly, we can use it to multiply repeatedly as well. For example, to calculate 12^8, you can use the following keying sequence.

FOR CALCULATORS WITH A K KEY

KEYING SEQUENCE	DISPLAY	MATHEMATICAL EXPRESSION
12 [x] [K]	12	12^1
[=]	144	12^2
[=]	1728	12^3
[=]	20736	12^4
[=]	248832	12^5
[=]	2985984	12^6
[=]	35831808	12^7
[=]	429981696	12^8

FOR CALCULATORS WITHOUT A K KEY

KEYING SEQUENCE	DISPLAY	MATHEMATICAL EXPRESSION
12 [x]	12	12^1
[=]	144	12^2
[=]	1728	12^3
[=]	20736	12^4
[=]	248832	12^5
[=]	2985984	12^6
[=]	35831808	12^7
[=]	429981696	12^8

(If neither of these schemes works with your calculator, check the calculator manual.)

EXERCISES

24. Use your calculator to compute the expressions.
    (a) 3^{10} (b) 3^{125} (c) 10^9 (d) $10^{.75}$ (e) $1237^{.5}$ (f) 2^{64}

25. When food is present, a bacterium divides itself into 2 bacteria; then each of those divides into 2; and so on. Starting with a single bacterium, how many divisions will it take to arrive at a collection of at least 10 million bacteria?

USING A CALCULATOR TO COMPUTE TABLES OF EXPONENTIAL GROWTH With a slight variation on the preceding method, we can use a calculator to make a table for exponential growth.

For example, suppose the fixed number to multiply (for exponential growth) is 1.04, and the number for the initial time period is 20,000. Here are the keying sequences and the steps for the two types of calculators.

CALCULATOR WITH K KEY

KEYING SEQUENCE EXPRESSION	DISPLAY	MATHEMATICAL EXPRESSION
1.04 [x] [K] 20000 [=]	20800	1.04×20000
[=]	21632	$(1.04)^2 \times 20000$
[=]	22497.28	$(1.04)^3 \times 20000$
[=]	23397.1712	$(1.04)^4 \times 20000$

CALCULATOR WITH CONSTANT FEATURE

KEYING SEQUENCE EXPRESSION	DISPLAY	MATHEMATICAL EXPRESSION
20000 [x] 1.04 [=]	20800	1.04×20000
[=]	21632	$(1.04)^2 \times 20000$
[=]	22497.28	$(1.04)^3 \times 20000$
[=]	23397.1712	$(1.04)^4 \times 20000$

Once again, one or the other set of instructions will work for most calculators. If neither works on yours, check the instruction manual.

26. You invest $10,000 in an account that yields 8.25% annual interest, compounded annually. You want to know when your account will double in value. Use a calculator to find out.

RAISING A NUMBER TO A POWER USING A COMPUTER To calculate 37^{12} in BASIC, you type

```
PRINT 37^12
```

27. Write a program using the BASIC operation ∧ described above that will accept a pair of numbers A and B as input, calculate A^B, and print out the result.

USING A COMPUTER TO PRINT OUT A TABLE OF EXPONENTIAL GROWTH If B is a whole number, you can also get a computer to simulate the calculation of A^B by multiplying A times itself B times and printing out the successive powers, A^1 through A^B. *We solved a similar problem* in chapter 5 when we wrote a program to add 87 to itself repeatedly 74 times in order to simulate the multiplication 74×87. Here is that program.

```
5 LET S = 0      Initialize sum.
10 FOR I = 1 TO 74
20 LET S = S+87
30 PRINT S
40 NEXT S
100 END
```

And here is an adaptation of it, simulating 87^{74}.

```
5 LET S = 1      Initialize product.
10 FOR I = 1 TO 74
20 LET S = S*87
30 PRINT S
40 NEXT I
100 END
```

28. Type the foregoing program into your computer, run it, and see what happens.

Now, let's revise the program to accept a pair A and B as input, where A is any number and B is a positive whole number, then print out the successive whole number powers of A ending up with A^B.

```
2 INPUT A
4 INPUT B
5 LET S = 1
10 FOR I = 1 TO B
20 LET S = S*A
30 PRINT S
40 NEXT I
100 END
```

29. Type this program into your computer, run it for some pairs, and see what happens. Here are some suggested pairs.

(a) $A = 12, B = 4$ (b) $A = .5, B = 20$ (c) $A = 0, B = 50$

(d) $A = 523, B = 1$ (e) $A = 1, B = 1$

We can revise the program once again to have the computer print out a table of exponential growth. This time we want to be able to input three numbers: $A =$ the fixed number by which you multiply the observed quantity at each successive moment in time; $B =$ the power (the number of successive moments of time), and $S =$ the initial (observed) quantity. Here is the revised program.

PROGRAM FOR EXPONENTIAL GROWTH

```
2 INPUT A
4 INPUT B
5 INPUT S
10 FOR I = 1 TO B
20 LET S = S*A
30 PRINT I, S      Moments of time printed, too
40 NEXT I
100 END
```

30. Use the program for exponential growth (immediately preceding) to provide an alternate solution to exercise 25. (You will have to make some guesses for B.)

31. You invest $10,000 at an annual rate of 8%, and interest is compounded annually. You would like to know how many years it will take for your initial investment to triple. Use the program for exponential growth to solve this.

12.9 EXTENDING THE IDEAS: MORE ON EXPONENTIAL GROWTH

Many phenomena besides compound interest express exponential growth. One general phenomenon is population growth, an example of which is the bacteria problem. We will look at two others, inflation and radioactive decay.

INFLATION   A high rate of inflation is a particular worry to individuals whose incomes cannot be expected to increase each year. The statement "The annual rate of inflation is 5%" means that the average cost of purchases made at the end of a year are 5% above the cost of the same purchases made at the beginning of that year. A consumer would expect that maintaining the same standard of living will cost 5% more money. If such a rate of inflation persists over several years, inflation can have an alarming effect on prices.

To get an idea of what can happen, suppose that the annual rate of inflation from 1980 to 1990 is 5% and that the price of a loaf of bread in 1980 is $ .90. Let's figure out what the price of bread should be in 1990. To do this, we start with the price in 1980 and add 5% of that to get the price for 1981; for each successive year we add on 5% of the price for that year to get the price for the next year. Look at the chart showing our results and note the repeated use of the distributive law.

YEAR	AVERAGE COST OF A LOAF OF BREAD
1980	$ .90
1981	$.90 + .05(.90) = .90(1 + .05)$
1982	$.90(1 + .05) + .05(.90)(1 + .05) = .90(1 + .05)^2$
1983	$.90(1 + .05)^2 + .05(.90)(1 + .05)^2 = .90(1 + .05)^3$
1984	$.90(1 + .05)^4$

The trend is this: The average price of a loaf of bread in a given year is 1.05 times the price in the previous year; thus, this is an example of exponential growth. Seeing the pattern, we estimate that in 1990, 10 yr after 1980, the average cost of a loaf of bread will be $ .90(1 + .05)^{10}$, or, roughly, $1.47.

EXERCISES

32. Use the program for exponential growth (p. 491) to print out a table of the price of a loaf of bread from 1980 through 1990. Use the figures in the example above.

33. If the cost of a quart of milk is $1 in 1985 and the annual inflation rate is 8% from 1985 to 1995, what will the cost of a quart of milk be in 1995?

34. How many years will it take for the average cost of a loaf of bread in the example above to be more than double what it was in 1980? (The program for exponential growth is a good tool for this problem.)

35. The population of Canada in 1980 was 24 million. If the population grows at an annual rate of 2%, how many years will it take for the population of Canada to double?

RADIOACTIVE DECAY   With compound interest, the value of your investment increases. With inflation the average price of a loaf of bread increases. In these examples, the quantity increases. There are examples of exponential growth in which the quantity decreases. Radioactive decay is one of these. A radioactive element emits particles that change it into another element in a predictable fashion. The change in the amount of the radioactive element present in any item is described in terms of its *half-life*, the amount of time it takes for the amount of the radioactive element to decrease to half its original mass. Different radioactive elements have different half-lives.

For example, the radioactive isotope carbon-14 has a half-life of 5600 yr. This means that if some item contains 20,000 g of carbon-14, then 5600 yr later it will contain 10,000 g (10,000 of the original 20,000 having changed into another element); 5600 yr after that (total of 11,200 yr) it will contain 5000 g, and so on. Here is a chart in which time is measured in terms of number of half-lives.

NO. OF HALF-LIVES	NO. OF YEARS	GRAMS OF C-14 CONTAINED IN ITEMS
0	0	(20,000)
1	5600	$.5(20,000)$
2	11,200	$.5(.5)(20,000) = (.5)^2 20,000$
3	16,800	$.5(.5)^2 20,000 = (.5)^3 20,000$
4	22,400	$.5(.5)^3 20,000 = 1250$

This property of carbon-14 and the fact that the element is present in living things enables anthropologists and geologists to estimate the age of fossils.

How does one measure the amount of carbon-14 present in a substance? When one atom of carbon-14 disintegrates and changes into another element, it emits 1 beta ray. Beta rays can be counted with a Geiger counter. A living body radiates approximately 918 rays/g (of total body mass)/hr. One can measure the number of beta rays per gram per hour emitted by the fossil to estimate how long it has been dead.

To see how this is done, suppose that you find a fossil in a cave and with a Geiger counter you determine that it is giving off 7 beta rays/g/hr from carbon-14. You want to find out how old the fossil is. You know that the decrease in beta rays emitted is the result of the decrease in the amount of carbon-14 in the fossil. In fact, every 5600 yr the number of rays per gram emitted each hour decreases by a factor of .5. You want to see how many years are required to decrease 918 rays to 7 rays. Here is a chart setting the number of rays against the age of the fossil.

AGE OF FOSSIL	RAYS EMITTED PER GRAM PER HOUR
0	918
5600	$(.5)918$
11,200	$(.5)(.5)918 = (.5)^2918$
16,800	$(.5)^3918$
22,400	$(.5)^4918$
$5600n$	$(.5)^n918$

You want to find the whole number n that makes $(.5)^n918$ equal to 7. This is the same as finding the number of times you must multiply 918 by .5 to get 7. Using the program for exponential growth yields the following results.

```
LIST

2 INPUT A
4 INPUT B
5 INPUT S
10 FOR I = 1 TO B
20 LET S = S*A
30 PRINT I, S
40 NEXT I
100 END

RUN

? .5
? 15        This is a guess.
? 918
1        459
2        229.5
3        114.75
4        57.38
5        28.69
6        14.34
7        7.17        Close to 7 rays/g/hr.
```

8	3.59
9	1.79
10	0.90
11	0.49
12	0.22
13	0.11
14	0.06
15	0.03

The best whole number estimate for n, the number of half-lives, is 7. The age of the fossil must be about 7×5600 or 39,200 yr.

EXERCISES

36. You have found a fossil. It weighs 10 g. With a Geiger counter, you find that the number of beta rays emitted per hour from the fossil is 570. Estimate the age of the fossil.

37. There are 10 g of a radioactive element in a laboratory. One day later only 9.5 g of the element remain. Assume that this rate of decay continues and use a calculator or computer to complete the chart.

TIME ELAPSED	NO. OF GRAMS REMAINING
0 days	10
1 day	9.5
2 days	
3 days	
4 days	
5 days	

Use the chart, extended if necessary, to find the half-life of the element.

38. The radioactive isotope carbon-11 decays (i.e., changes into another element) at the rate of 0.6%/min. If you start with 100 g of carbon-11, find an expression for the number of grams remaining m min later. Find the half-life of carbon-11 accurate to the nearest minute.

12.10 LOOKING AHEAD: RATIONAL EXPONENTS

In chapter 10 we encountered a number X that has the property that $X^2 = 2$. Of course, another name for X is the *square root of* 2, or $X = \sqrt{2}$. If we were to have fractional exponents and we wanted the rule $(a^r)^s = a^{rs}$ to hold for fractions r and s, then also $(2^{1/2})^2 = 2$; that is, it should be that $2^{1/2} = \sqrt{2}$.

In general, if n is a positive whole number, then a number Y such that $Y^n = 2$ is normally written $Y = \sqrt[n]{2}$ (read "nth root of 2"). But again, if we want fractional exponents and the multiplication rule $(a^r)^s = a^{rs}$ to hold for fractions r and s, then we would also want $(2^{1/n})^n = 2$ so that $2^{1/n} = \sqrt[n]{2}$. This suggests the following definition.

DEFINITION OF RATIONAL EXPONENTS

Suppose that c is any positive real number and that n and m are positive whole numbers. Then $c^{1/n}$ is defined to be the number

$$c^{1/n} = \sqrt[n]{c}.$$

Furthermore, $c^{m/n}$ is defined to be the number

$$c^{m/n} = (c^{1/n})^m.$$

Finally, $c^{-m/n}$ is defined to be the number

$$c^{-m/n} = \frac{1}{c^{m/n}}.$$

The definition provides a meaning for c^r for any positive real number c and any rational number r. We were guided in making this definition by a desire to have the properties of exponents—which we know hold for integers—hold similarly for rational numbers. Here are the properties of rational exponents.

PROPERTIES OF RATIONAL EXPONENTS

Suppose that c is a positive real number and that r and s are rational numbers. Then

$$c^r c^s = c^{r+s} \qquad \text{and} \qquad (c^r)^s = c^{rs}.$$

Some novelties in these definitions are worth discussing. One novelty is that we have been talking about the nth root (n, a positive whole number) $\sqrt[n]{c}$ of a positive number c as if it were obvious that there *is* a number whose nth power is c. It isn't obvious, but there is such a real number. It is not, in general, rational. If n is even, then there are two such numbers; one is the opposite of the other. By convention, to avoid ambiguity, $\sqrt[n]{c}$ refers to the positive one.

A second novelty is that c, the number we raise to a rational power, is a *real* number. This is the first time we have really used real numbers, the numbers that correspond to *all* points on the number line. I thought that this would be a good place for a definition in which real numbers occur. After all, if $\sqrt[n]{c}$ can be irrational when c is rational, why not allow for c to be irrational as well, provided everything works? Everything does work, but an explanation would take us beyond the scope of this book. Of course, the set of real numbers has the set of rational numbers as a subset, so the definition also works for rational numbers.

A third novelty is that c be *positive*. (For whole number exponents, the only restriction on c was that it be *nonzero*.) The major reason to require that c be positive is the following. Suppose that c is a negative number. Then $c^{1/2}$ would have the property that $(c^{1/2})^2 = c$. The square of a real number is negative. That can't be. Real numbers behave as rational numbers do with respect to the multiplication of positive and negative numbers. So $c^{1/2}$ makes no sense if c is negative. In general, if n is even and c negative, then $c^{1/n}$ makes no sense as a real number.

On the other hand, if n is odd and c negative, then $c^{1/n}$ might make sense. For example, we might want to write $(-1)^{1/3} = -1$ because $(-1)^3 = -1$. However, there are difficulties with this if you also assume that the properties of rational exponents hold for such numbers. For example, what do you make of

$$-1 = (-1)^{1/3} = (-1)^{2/6} = ((-1)^{1/6})^2?$$

The number on the far right is the square of a real number; it is equal to the number on the far left, which is a negative number. Ugly, eh?

(Additional subtleties and extensions of these ideas are beyond the scope of this book. For example, it is standard to write $(-1)^{1/3} = -1$. When this is done, certain properties of rational exponents can no longer be expected to hold. You must make a choice!)

EXERCISE

39. Use rational exponents to simplify the expressions.

(a) $(\sqrt{6})^2$ (b) $(\sqrt{6})^{-2}$ (c) $(\sqrt[3]{8})^2$

(d) $(\sqrt{32})^{6/5}$ (e) $(4/9)^{-3/2}$ (f) $2^{3/4}2^{5/4}$

(g) $(a^6b^9)^{1/3}$ (a and $b > 0$)   (h) $(x^4y^{12})^{3/4}$ (x and $y > 0$)

Calculating Rational Exponents with a Calculator

To compute $37^{1.2}$, use the sequence: 37 [y^x] 1.2 [=], and the display should read 76.18019305.

Whenever you use the [y^x] key and the first number you key in is negative, the display may indicate an error. For example, the sequence 2 [+/−] [y^x] .5 [=] will result in an error display since the expression $(-2)^5$ doesn't make sense as a real number. However, on some (but not all) calculators the sequence 2 [+/−] [y^x] 2 [=] will also result in an error display even though $(-2)^2$ does make sense. Know your calculator and exercise care!

Raising a number to the power $\frac{1}{2}$ can be accomplished in more than one way using a calculator. Since $37^{1/2} = \sqrt{37}$ and since most calculators have a square root key— [$\sqrt{x}$]—to calculate $37^{1/2}$, you can use the keying sequence 37 [$\sqrt{x}$], and the display will show 6.08276253.

EXERCISE

40. Use a calculator to evaluate the expressions.

(a) $\sqrt{67.42}$ (b) $1.08^{3.45}$ (c) $47^{3/4}$

12.11   SUMMARY OF IMPORTANT IDEAS AND TECHNIQUES

■ Powers of a number; exponents

■ Names for the powers of 10

■ Laws for exponents

$$c^N c^M = c^{N+M},$$
$$(c^N)^M = c^{NM},$$
$$\frac{c^N}{c^M} = c^{N-M}$$

- Scientific notation
- Multiplication and division using scientific notation
- Rounding a whole number to the nearest power of 10
- Significant figures
- Techniques for estimating numbers
  Breaking main estimation into smaller ones
  Keeping "small" estimations familiar and close to home
  Allowing some estimations to be averages
  Using scientific notation
  Keeping numbers "simple" by rounding
- Errors created when rounded numbers are used in computations
- Integer exponents; scientific notation for small numbers
- Examples of exponential growth, situations in which exponents are used: population growth, compound interest, inflation, and radioactive decay
- Using calculators and computers to construct tables of exponential growth
- nth roots and rational exponents

PROBLEM SET

PRACTICING
SKILLS

1. Which is the largest number: $1,000^5$, $10,000^4$, or $100,000^3$?

2. Write each expression in exponential form. *Sample:* $10^3 \times 10^8 = 10^{11}$
   (a) $6^8 \times 6^{10}$ (b) $(6^8)(6^8)$ (c) $(6^8)^3$ (d) $2^4 \times 4^2$

3. In each blank write $<$, $>$, or $=$ to make a true statement.
   (a) 4^3 _____ 3^4 (b) 2^7 _____ 7^2
   (c) 5^6 _____ 6^5 (d) $(2 + 5)^4$ _____ $2^4 + 5^4$
   (e) 2^{3+5} _____ $(3 + 5)^2$ (f) 2^{3+5} _____ $2^3 + 2^5$
   (g) 3^5 _____ 15 (h) 10^{100} _____ 100^{10}
   (i) 1.3×10^{12} _____ 8.5×10^9

   Solve the problems.
4. (a) By conservative estimate, the human brain has 10^{11} nerve cells, or neurons. Write this number in standard form.
   (b) In 1987 Americans owed $613,000,000 in all forms of installment credit. Write this number in scientific notation.

   Solve the problems.
5. (a) The 1980 Census counted approximately 226,500,000 people in the United States. The land area of the United States is approximately 3,600,000 mi^2. Use scientific notation to find the number of people per square mile in the United States in 1980.
   (b) Astronomers estimate that the Milky Way is about 3×10^4 parsecs across. How many miles is this? A parsec equals 1.924×10^{13} mi.

   Solve the problems.
6. (a) In 1987 the average per capita consumption of ice cream in the United States was 18.1 gal. Use scientific notation to determine how many gallons of ice cream Americans consumed in 1987. The U.S. population in 1980 was about 2.27×10^8.
   (b) The U.S. public debt in 1987 was 2.35×10^{12}. How much was this per person? The U.S. population in 1987 was about 2.44×10^8.

7. During one summer it is possible for a couple of houseflies to become parents and ancestors of 1.9×10^{20} flies. Suppose the Swindle Swatter Company decides to improve its business prospects by placing 5×10^9 pairs of houseflies in strategic locations all over the country at the beginning of the summer. How many flies could theoretically be raised during the summer?

8. Round the number 465,926,385 to the
   (a) nearest 100
   (b) nearest 10,000
   (c) nearest 1 million
   (d) nearest 100 million

9. You want to estimate the product of the two numbers 762,671,327 and 3,483,394,440.
   (a) Find an estimate of this product by first rounding each number to two significant digits.
   (b) Without computing the product exactly, what could the error due to rounding be for the estimated product you found in part (a)?

10. Moscow's Red Square is used for ceremonial occasions, parades, and strolling. The "square" is 700 m long and 130 m wide. How many people would it take to fill Red Square edge to edge?

11. Solve the problems.
    (a) There are approximately 9.96×10^{-11} g of radium present in each metric ton of sea water. Write this number in standard form.
    (b) A suspended atmospheric particle .000002–.000005 m in diameter and smaller is considered especially harmful to humans because particles of this size are believed to be able to penetrate the body's natural defense mechanisms and reach most deeply into the lungs. Write these numbers in scientific notation.

12. Neuroscientists estimate that the size of each neuron (nerve cell) in the human brain is no more than 100 micrometers in diameter. A micrometer is a thousandth of a millimeter. Write this number in scientific notation, with meter as the unit of measure.

13. Use the properties of integer exponents to simplify the expressions.
    (a) $10^{10} \times 10^{-8}$
    (b) $10^{-10} \times 10^8$
    (c) $100^5 \times (10000)^{-4}$
    (d) $3^{24} \times (27)^{-3}$
    (e) $(5^4 5^{-3})^6$
    (f) $(x^4 y^{-4})^3$
    (g) $x^4 x^{-4}$
    (h) y^8 / y^5
    (i) x^2 / x^{-2}
    (j) x^{-4} / x^4
    (k) $(x/y^2)^{-3}$
    (l) y^4 / y^7

14. Express your answers to the problems in scientific notation.
    (a) $(4.7 \times 10^{-5}) \times (2.1 \times 10^{-4})$
    (b) $(3.2 \times 10^6) \times (2.6 \times 10^{-2})$
    (c) $(2.9 \times 10^{-8}) \times (2.8 \times 10^3)$
    (d) $(7.92 \times 10^{-7}) \div (3.3 \times 10^{-5})$
    (e) $(9.28 \times 10^8) \div (5.8 \times 10^{-2})$
    (f) $(8.61 \times 10^{-9}) \div (4.1 \times 10^3)$

15. To manufacture computer chips a thin film of conducting material is deposited on a ceramic base by vacuum evaporation or cathode sputtering at a thickness of 10^{-5} m per deposit. If the thickness of film must be approximately 1.5×10^{-2}, how many deposits are necessary?

16. Use rational exponents to simplify the expressions.
    (a) $(\sqrt{5})^2$
    (b) $(\sqrt{7})^{-2}$
    (c) $(\sqrt[4]{16})^3$
    (d) $(27)^{5/3}$
    (e) $(5^{-2/5})^{5/2}$
    (f) $(2^{3/2})(2^{5/2})$
    (g) $(a^4 b^6)^{3/2}$ (a and $b > $ zero)
    (h) $(x^3 y^{12})^{1/3}$ (x and $y > $ zero)

17. If you invest $24,000 at the rate of 8%/yr and leave the money in the program for 7 yr to be compounded annually, how much money will you have?

18. You invest $20,000 at an interest rate of 11%. Find the value of your investment after 5 yr if the interest is paid
    (a) annually   (b) semiannually   (c) quarterly   (d) monthly   (e) daily
    Which way of payment of interest would you choose for your investment?

For each remaining problem, communicate clearly and completely the solution to the problem in the form of an essay. Mention the steps you took in solving the problem, other problems or solutions that gave you ideas, and the strategies you used.

19. It takes light a year to travel 6×10^{12} mi. (Consequently, 6×10^{12} mi is called a light-year.) Some scientists estimate that the universe has existed for about 4.6 billion yr. Based on these figures, if we were to see now an event happening (an explosion?) during the early life of the universe, estimate the distance from us of the location of the event.

20. Estimate, without really counting much, the number of dots in the figure below. Write your answer in scientific notation.

21. A telephone cable across the Atlantic Ocean connects Newfoundland with Scotland. To keep the sound loud enough to hear, 51 amplifiers are spaced fairly evenly along its length. Each one of these amplifiers increases the signal strength by about a million times to make up for the fading of the signal along the cable. From the time it leaves Newfoundland and before it reaches Scotland, by how many times has the strength of the signal been increased along the length of the cable?

22. A school wants to know how much a lighting system for its football field will cost. There are 4 poles each containing 16 fixtures of 1500 w (watt) apiece and 4 poles each containing 8 fixtures of 1650 w apiece. The school plans to use the lights about 120 hr/yr. It costs 11¢/kwh (kilowatt-hour) to run the lights. Use scientific notation to figure out the school's total yearly cost for running the lights.

23. A publisher is ordering paper for a new set of encyclopedias he is publishing. Each set has 100 volumes, and each volume will contain approximately 1300 pages. He knows that the paper for one page weighs .1 g. He calculates the total weight of paper needed for 100,000 sets of the encyclopedia as follows.

$$\text{Weight} = (.1 \times 1300) \times 100 \times 100,000 \text{ g}$$
$$= 130 \times 100 \times 100,000 \text{ g}$$
$$= 1.3 \times 10^2 \times 10^2 \times 10^5 \text{ g}$$
$$= 1.3 \times 10^{2 \times 2} \times 10^5 \text{ g}$$
$$= 1.3 \times 10^4 \times 10^5 \text{ g}$$
$$= 1.3 \times 10^{4 \times 5} \text{ g}$$
$$= 1.3 \times 10^{20} \text{ g}$$
$$= 1.3 \times 10^{17} \text{ kg}$$

(A kilogram is 1000 g, or about 2.2 lb.)

Is this a reasonable answer? Is there an error in the publisher's thinking? Where would it be?

24. The rate of inflation for real estate in a certain large metropolitan area is 8%/yr. How many years will it take for the cost of a home now costing $60,000 to double?

25. A fossil weighing 15 g emits beta rays at the rate of 450/hr. Estimate its age.

26. If 12 g of a radioactive substance weighs only 11.2 g one day later, find its half-life, assuming that the rate of decay is constant.

27. Use a calculator or computer to complete the tables.
    (a) Microcomputer sales are increasing at the rate of 4% annually.
    (b) The population of the Mt. Graham red squirrel is decreasing at the rate of 1% annually. How many years will it take for the population to decrease to half what it was in 1990?

YEAR	ANNUAL SALES
1990	1,200,000
1991	
1992	
1993	
1994	

YEAR	POPULATION
1990	100
1991	
1992	
1993	
1994	

(c) The rate of gasoline consumption in the United States is decreasing at the rate of .5%/yr.

YEAR	GASOLINE CONSUMPTION (MILLIONS OF GALLONS)
1990	16,000
1991	
1992	
1993	
1994	

In your essay/solution to each remaining problem, describe in detail how you arrive at each estimation. Include descriptions of any intermediate guesses and estimates you may make. List sources of information that you use, such as almanacs, atlases, or encyclopedias.

28. Every year each of us contributes a little more junk to the environment. Estimate the total yearly accumulation of junk in the United States for (a) junked cars, (b) cans, and (c) bottles.

29. (a) Estimate the lifetime consumption of cigarettes for the average person who smokes. Estimate the value of these cigarettes.
    (b) Estimate the total annual consumption of cigarettes in the United States. Estimate the retail value of all these cigarettes.

30. Estimate the number of people in the United States whose last name is Smith.

31. Estimate the number of needles on an averaged-sized pine tree.

32. You are thinking about opening a microcomputer repair shop and need to know something about your market. Estimate the number of microcomputers that are not working right now in a metropolitan area the size of Phoenix, Ariz. (around 1.5 million people).

33.

> ## Udall bill seeks end to Indian water suit
>
> U.S. Rep. Morris K. Udall, D-Ariz., introduced legislation yesterday to try to resolve an Indian water-rights lawsuit involving up to 17,500 Southern Arizona well owners.
>
> Udall's bill seeks to settle years of litigation between the Papagos and major water users in the Upper Santa Cruz basin. The bill would authorize delivery of up to 180,000 acre feet of water annually to four separate areas of local Indian reservations at the expense of the federal government.
>
> *(Arizona Daily Star,* June 24, 1980)

How many typical families could have their annual domestic water needs provided by 180,000 acre-feet of water?

34. Some people claim that it will soon be impractical to convey information by the printed page because there will not be enough trees around for making newsprint.
    (a) If all trees in the United States were cut up, how many pounds of newsprint would they make?
    (b) How many pounds of newsprint are needed each year to print the country's newspapers?

For each one, several possible answers are given. Circle the letter just to the left of the item that best answers the question.

1. Which number is largest?
   (a) 1.67   (b) 1.098   (c) $\frac{5}{3}$ (d) $1\frac{3}{5}$ (e) $1\frac{5}{9}$

2. Standard sizes for drill bits have widths in fractions with a denominator of 32. You want to drill a hole $\frac{1}{5}$ in in diameter into a piece of wood; thus, you want to know the standard bit size that is closest to $\frac{1}{5}$ in but also less than $\frac{1}{5}$. Which standard size is it?
   (a) $\frac{4}{32}$ in   (b) $\frac{5}{32}$ in   (c) $\frac{6}{32}$ in   (d) $\frac{7}{32}$ in   (e) $\frac{8}{32}$ in

3. A gold pendant originally sells for $20.00. It is marked up 80% for the Christmas holiday. After New Year's, the holiday price is marked down 80%. What is the price of the pendant after New Year's?
   (a) $20.00   (b) $1.00   (c) $7.20   (d) $16.00   (e) $28.80

4. The temperature has been rising 6°C each hour and is now 9°C. What was it 4 hr ago?
   (a) 24°C   (b) −24°C   (c) 33°C   (d) −15°C   (e) 15°C

5. On Monday morning a certain stock was selling for $52.25 a share. During the week the following changes in the stock price were recorded: $+2$, $-3\frac{1}{8}$, $-1\frac{1}{4}$, $+2\frac{1}{2}$, and -1. What was the selling price for a share of the stock on Friday evening?
   (a) $4.50   (b) −$5.38   (c) −$0.88   (d) $51.38   (e) $53.13

6. The add-subtract slide rule as set up below illustrates the solution to several integer arithmetic problems. Which of the problems listed does it *not* illustrate?

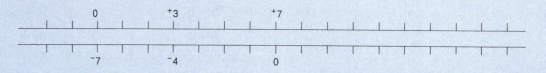

   (a) $^+7 + {}^-4 = {}^+3$ (b) $^-7 + {}^-3 = {}^-10$ (c) $^+5 - {}^+7 = {}^-2$
   (d) $^-7 + {}^+7 = 0$ (e) $^+3 + {}^-4 = {}^-1$

7. The national debt for the United States in 1987 was $2,350 billion. The population at that time was 244.6 million. Estimate the debt per person.
   (a) 1×10^4 (b) 5.8×10^5 (c) 9.6×10^1
   (d) 5.8×10^{20} (e) 9.6×10^2

8. According to the *Reader's Digest Almanac,* the area of Alaska is 586,412 mi^2. This figure rounded to three significant figures is
   (a) 412   (b) $.590 \times 10^6$ (c) 5.86×10^5
   (d) 586   (e) 586.4×10^3

9. Which of the following numbers is largest?
   (a) 4×10^3 (b) 2^{12} (c) $(6^2)^3$ (d) 8^4 (e) 2^{6+2}

10. In a telephone survey of a sample of the city's population, HiFi, Inc., found that 70% of the respondents have cassette tape players, 20% have compact disc players, and 25% have neither. What percent of the respondents have both a cassette tape player and a compact disc player?
    (a) 5%   (b) 10%   (c) 15%   (d) 35%   (e) 55%

11. $5000 is invested at 8.25% interest compounded annually. In 10 yr what amount will have accumulated in the account?
    (a) $4125.00   (b) $2.05 \times 10^6   (c) $7303.14
    (d) $9125.00   (e) $11047.12

ESSAY QUESTIONS *For each remaining problem, document your solution carefully in the form of an essay.*

12. Lumber companies reseed forests after they have cut down the mature trees that are used in making lumber. Of the seeds planted 20% never germinate, and of all seedlings (young trees not ready to be cut for lumber) 25% never become mature trees. If a paper company harvests 18,000 trees, how many seeds must it plant to ensure that it will be able to return to the same area some years later and harvest another 18,000 trees?

13. An east-west track passes through River City. Positions east of the River City terminal are positive; positions west are negative; the position of the terminal itself is zero. A time before zero hour is negative; a time after zero hour is positive. A train going -55 mph passes through the terminal at $+1$ hr. Find its position at the following times: $+3$ hr; -2 hr.

14. Many people leave the water running each time they brush their teeth.
    (a) Estimate the amount of water a person with such a habit would waste in a year.
    (b) If $\frac{1}{10}$ of the population of the United States were to have this habit, how much water would be wasted?

INTRODUCTION TO MEASUREMENT: LENGTH, POSITION, AND SHAPES

13

Measurement is important in many activities. To teachers, homeowners, farmers, carpenters, plumbers, engineers, and architects, among others, a mastery of the mathematics and the techniques of measurement is essential. This is the first of several chapters devoted to measurement, and length is the first topic.

How do you tell when two lengths are the same? If they are not the same, which one is longer? We will discuss simple methods for answering these questions and, from there, proceed to more sophisticated methods, close to the ones with which we are familiar. Along the way we will describe the two modern systems of standardized units for measuring length, the traditional (so-called English) and metric systems.

The need to measure length arises in a variety of situations. One may be interested in finding a perimeter of a plane shape, or in measuring a length associated with a shape in space, or in determining a length that cannot be measured directly. To respond to these situations, we will introduce some language for talking about shapes in the plane, create flat patterns for three-dimensional shapes, and discuss scale drawings.

THE MOLDING PROBLEM

The Joneses are remodeling their living room and are installing new molding along the baseboard of one of the walls. They have a piece of the molding material and want to know if it will be enough for the whole wall and, if it is enough, whether they will have to cut the molding.

A Solution to the Molding Problem

One way to solve this problem is to use a yardstick to measure the length of the wall and the length of the molding and then compare the two. A simpler (perhaps more sensible) method is to lay the molding along the baseboard of the wall with one end of the molding at one end of the wall. If the molding extends exactly to the other end of the baseboard, then the wall's baseboard and the molding *have the same length,* and no cut will be necessary. If the molding extends beyond the other end, then the baseboard is *shorter in length* than the piece of molding, and a cut in the molding will be needed. If the molding doesn't extend to the corner, then the baseboard is *longer in length* than the piece of molding, and the piece of molding will not be enough.

THE PATIO FORM PROBLEM

The O'Briens are building the forms for a concrete slab that will make a kidney-shaped patio that they have marked out in their backyard.

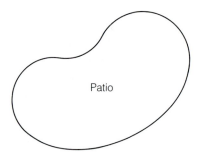

Patio

Try this before reading on.

To make the forms for the concrete, they will bend a piece of metal stripping and hold it in place with wooden stakes. A local hardware store has a roll of metal stripping from which they will purchase a piece for the job. The O'Briens want to know how much to have cut from the roll. In the meantime Mr. O'Brien seems to have misplaced the one tape measure the family ever owned. Help them solve this problem.

A Solution to the Patio Form Problem

If we had a metal tape measure long enough, we could lay it on edge along the path where the form is to be. But we don't. An alternative is to use a large spool of string: Fix the beginning of the string at some point along the path where the form is to go; draw string from the spool and lay it out along this path until you traverse it entirely, reaching the beginning of your path again; cut the string from the spool right at that point. The metal form and the piece of cut string should have the same length. Take the piece of string to the hardware store and ask for a piece of metal stripping the same length as the string.

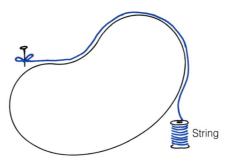

String

The Mathematical Idea: Determining Length without Measuring Tools or Numbers

The molding and patio form problems are problems of length, and we solved them without recourse to tools, such as rulers or tape measures, or to numbers, such as number of inches, feet, or centimeters.

Many other problems having to do with deciding whether one length is shorter (or longer) than another can be solved similarly—without the use of measuring tools. If you want to know whether a couch will fit along a certain part of a wall, you can move the couch to that part of the wall and see. If you want to know if a certain piece of rope can be used as a clothesline to be hung between two hooks, you can take the rope, attach one end of it to one hook, and see if it stretches to the other. If it doesn't, it's not long enough. If it does, it *is* long enough. These two problems and the molding problem are problems of Which length is longer? and are solved by taking one length and placing it next to the other.

The patio form problem was similar: Cut from one length a length equal to another length. For that problem, however, it was not convenient to place either length next to the other. An intermediary length was used: A piece of string equal in length to the edge of the curved form was created, and the string was then placed next to the length of metal stripping.

There are many situations in which some sort of intermediary length—a simple measuring device—is convenient, and often essential, for solving problems of length. You want to surround your pasture with fencing and go to the hardware store to buy some. You want to put molding along the baseboards of all of your bedrooms and go to the lumberyard to buy the right amount. You plan to make drapes for your living room windows and go to the fabric store to buy the right length of drape material. You have an old garage and want to know whether the car you are considering buying—now in a downtown showroom—will fit.

EXERCISE

1. Show how you would solve each of the problems in the preceding paragraph without using modern tools of measurement or modern units of measurement.

Evolution of Techniques for Measuring Length

When modern tools are not available, string may be convenient for determining length. When string is not available, you can *pace* along the path where the fence for your pasture is to go and *count* the number of paces it takes you to cover the whole path, then pace along the fencing the hardware store has for the same number of paces.

You can walk around the baseboards in your bedroom toe-heel-toe-heel and *count* the number of *feet* you use to walk along all the baseboards, then go to the lumberyard and walk along the molding in the same fashion, counting out the same number of feet. For smaller lengths you can use *hand spans* or *thumb widths*. The number of such lengths can be written down and easily carried from place to place. For many lengths, string does not have this convenience.

We still use such methods for comparing and replicating lengths. They make up the first steps in the evolution of length-measuring techniques.

1. Put a number of equal, small lengths end to end to cover another (longer) length, and *count* the *number* of small lengths that you get. (If it doesn't come out "even," estimate the fractional part of the small length left over.)

2. For the small lengths in 1 use "1s" that we "carry" with us (foot, thumb width [inch], hand, tip of nose to tip of outstretched finger [yard]).

To primitive people the foregoing methods may have been the only ones. Some next steps would have been the following.

3. Groups of people agree to use common *units* (foot, thumb, hand) for purposes of public commerce. The exact length of the unit used may vary depending on the person whose foot or thumb or hand is used.

4. One person's foot may not have the same length as another's. In a situation of controversy, whose foot shall we use to determine the length of that field? A solution to this and other similar problems is to *standardize* the units.

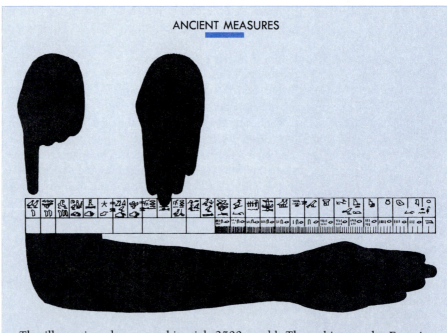

ANCIENT MEASURES

The illustration shows a cubit stick 3500 yr old. The cubit was the Egyptian standard unit of length and was equal to the distance from a man's elbow to the tip of his longest finger. The cubit was divided into smaller units, called digits, each the width of a finger. A larger unit, the palm (or hand), was equal to 4 digits. Seven palms, or 28 digits, was equal to 1 cubit.

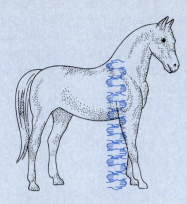

1 hand

A horse that is 16 hands tall

The hand (palm) was used as a basic unit of measure by nearly all ancient civilizations and is still used in this country to measure the heights of horses. The height of a horse is the number of hand breadths from the ground to the horse's shoulders.

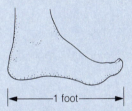
1 foot

In Roman times the foot was a basic unit of length and was divided into 12 equal parts, each one called an *uncia* (from *unus,* "one"). The English adopted the Roman system and *uncia* became "inch." The yard was established by royal decree in the twelfth century by King Henry I as the distance from his nose to his thumb.

5. An easy way is arrived at to "convert" from one standardized unit to another, to enable the length of something measured using one unit (such as a foot) to be compared to the length of something measured in another unit (such as a thumb).

6. Measuring devices (foot ruler, yardstick, etc.) that convey the standard units and that also help to count the number of units are created.

EXERCISE 2. Measure the cover of this book using your thumb. Compare the number of thumbs you get with the numbers from other classmates.

13.2 STANDARD UNITS OF LENGTH

The Traditional System and the Metric System

Two systems of the kind just described, the traditional system and the metric system, are commonly in use in the United States. The *traditional system* finds its origin in the Roman system, which itself emerged from the use of units of length associated with the human body (in ways mentioned earlier). Until the creation of the metric system, this was the only broadly used system of standardized units.

The traditional system's familiar units of length are the inch, the foot, the yard, and the mile. Here are their conversion factors:

    1 foot = 12 inches
    1 yard = 3 feet
    1 mile = 5280 feet = 1760 yards

The *metric system* was created by the French government in the 1790s after the French Revolution. This system has conversion factors that mesh nicely with the decimal place value system for representing numbers.

The basic unit of length in the metric system is the meter, longer than the traditional yard by a few inches. The conversion factors for other units relative to the meter are powers of 10. In addition to the meter, the most common units of length are the millimeter, the centimeter, and the kilometer. Here are their conversion factors:

    1 millimeter = .001 meter
    1 centimeter = 10 millimeters = .01 meter
    1 meter = 100 centimeters
    1 kilometer = 1000 meters

Throughout the whole metric system—there is more to it than length—the prefix *kilo-* means "thousand," *centi-* means "hundred*th*," and *milli-* means "thousand*th*.")

Converting from Traditional to Metric and Vice Versa

In this text, as in real life, it is not usually necessary to convert measurements made in units of the metric system into measurements from the traditional system and vice versa. For most situations all measurements are in a single system, and there is no need to translate from one to another. However, those of us not familiar with the metric system will need to relate its units to human scale. We want to know more than facts such as 1 meter = 100 centimeters. We want to have the same familiarity with the metric system as we do with the traditional system that enables us to say, "Oh, he's pretty tall, about 6′1″"; "She lives about 10 miles from here"; or, "I think I'll need about a yard and a half of that material." Of course, the best way to get comfortable with the system is to use it—and we will. In the meantime, here are some comparisons between the two systems, some "rough," some more precise. Abbreviations for the units are also given. For the most part, as you will have noticed, I use abbreviations in this text.

UNIT (ABBREVIATION)	ROUGH COMPARISON	PRECISE COMPARISON
1 millimeter (mm)	Thickness of a dime; a bit longer than $\frac{1}{32}$ inch	.039 inch
1 centimeter (cm)	Width of fingernail on little finger; a little less than half an inch	.39 inch
1 meter (m)	Half the height of an average door; a little longer than a yard	39.37 inch
1 kilometer (km)	A little more than half a mile; .6 of a mile	.62 mile
1 inch (in)	2.5 centimeters	2.54 centimeters
1 foot (ft)	30 centimeters	30.48 centimeters
1 yard (yd)	90 centimeters; almost a meter	.9144 meter
1 mile (mi)	1.6 kilometers, a little over $1\frac{1}{2}$ kilometers	1.60 kilometers

EXERCISE **3.** In the metric system, estimate the (a) width and length of the cover of this book, (b) height from the ground to a chair seat, (c) distance from New York City to San Francisco, (d) thickness of a nickel, (e) diameter of a quarter.

13.3   PERIMETER

THE FENCING PROBLEM Mr. Ortega is building a corral for his cattle, shown in a bird's-eye view.

Try this before reading on. He plans to buy the fencing that he needs from a hardware store. He wants to know how much fencing he will need to buy. Help him solve this problem.

To solve the problem, he thinks: "How much fencing will I need in all? When I install the fencing, I'll start at one corner, run the fencing to an adjacent corner, bend it, run it to another corner, bend it again, and so on, until I get back to where I started. So the amount of fencing I'll need is the same as if I 'unfolded' the corral to get one length.

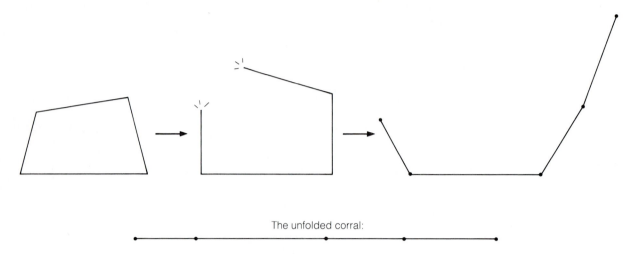

The unfolded corral:

Pacing off that one length would tell me how much fencing I would need; but if I were to pace off each side of my corral separately, the sum of the paces for the separate sides should add up to the number of paces for that one length."

So Mr. Ortega paced off each of the sides of the corral to be built and obtained the numbers indicated.

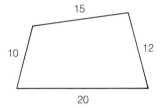

"Each of my paces is about 1 meter, so the figures tell me how much fencing I will need for each side in meters. How much will I need in all? Add all those figures up: 10 meters + 20 meters + 12 meters + 15 meters = 57 meters. Add in a few meters for error to get 60 meters."

The Mathematical Idea: Perimeter

In the fencing problem, Mr. Ortega was interested in finding out the "length around" his proposed corral, that is, the total length the sides would make if they were placed end to end. This length is called the *perimeter* of the corral. In general, the perimeter of a shape is the length of fencing needed to fit around it snugly. While figuring out his problem, Mr. Ortega made a discovery.

PERIMETER

The *perimeter* of a shape having straight sides is equal to the sum of the lengths of those sides.

His principle was simple.

PRINCIPLE FOR LENGTH

A single length broken into pieces is equal to the sum of the lengths of the pieces.

Here are some bird's-eye views of rooms, corrals, gardens, pastures, and backyards that need fencing or molding fitted snugly around them. To get an exact fit, you have to determine the perimeter of each. The length of each straight side has been measured and is shown in the picture, and the perimeter is calculated using the method just described.

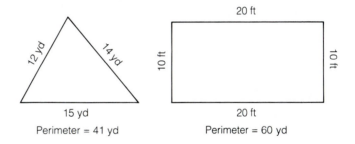

Perimeter = 41 yd   Perimeter = 60 yd

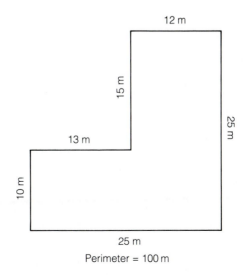

Perimeter = 100 m

In the patio problem, we were interested in the length of metal stripping needed to fit around the shape snugly; thus, we were interested in the perimeter of the patio. However, the method we used for finding the perimeter for the corral and other shapes will not work for finding the perimeter of the patio: The edge of the patio is curvy, whereas the other shapes have straight sides. A closed, flat shape with straight sides is called a *polygon*. A string is one way to measure the perimeter of a shape that is not a polygon. We will discuss other ways in chapter 16.

Look at some examples of flat shapes that are polygons, and some that aren't.

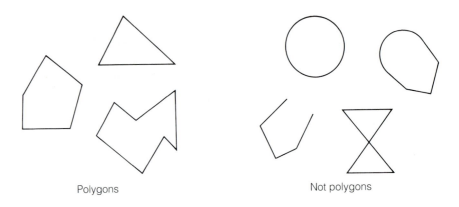

Polygons   Not polygons

EXERCISE   4. Find the perimeters of the polygons. The lengths of the straight sides have been written in.

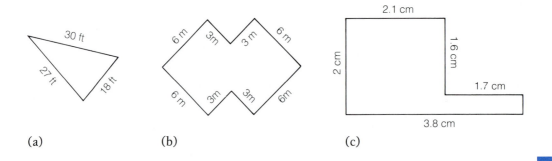

(a)   (b)   (c)

THE TABLE MOLDING PROBLEM   The Joneses are covering a table with Formica. After the Formica has been glued on the table top they will finish the sides of the table with protective metal molding. The molding must be ordered in advance, and they need to find out how much of it they need. Here is a bird's-eye view of the table top.

The Joneses figure that they must measure the lengths of the sides of the table, then add them up to find the perimeter. Mr. Jones first measures one side and then another:

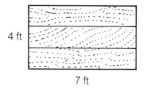

As he is about to measure a third side, Mrs. Jones interrupts him: "You don't need to measure the other two sides. The shape of the table top is a rectangle. Opposite sides are equal.

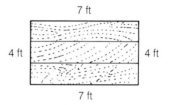

Here are the four lengths: 4 feet, 7 feet, 4 feet, and 7 feet. Add them up: $4 + 7 + 4 + 7 = 22$ feet."

The Mathematical Idea: Shapes, Formulas, and Terminology

The Joneses discovered that to figure out the perimeter of a rectangle, all you have to do is measure *two* adjacent sides. The lengths of the two unmeasured sides can be determined from the lengths of the measured sides. For a rectangle only *half* the sides have to be measured.

There is a condensed prescription for calculating the perimeter of a rectangle.

THE PERIMETER OF A RECTANGLE

If the lengths of two adjacent sides of a rectangle are H and B, then the *perimeter* of the rectangle is $H + H + B + B = 2(H + B)$.

The two lengths H and B are sometimes called the *height* and *base,* respectively, of the rectangle. The shorthand expression

$$\text{Perimeter of a rectangle} = 2(H + B)$$

is our first *formula,* the power of which is that it can be used for *any* rectangle.

The rectangle is one of many flat shapes that are frequently used in our culture and must be measured. Let's review some terminology for describing these shapes. First of all, a line segment is a piece of a line with a beginning and an end. A line extends indefinitely in both directions.

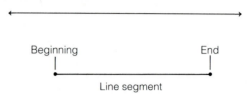

Loosely, if you assemble a bunch of line segments together with the end point of one to the beginning point of another to make a closed shape, you obtain a *polygon*.

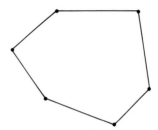

A point at which exactly two sides of a polygon meet is called a *vertex* (plural: *vertices*). Two sides of a polygon meeting in a vertex are called *adjacent* sides.

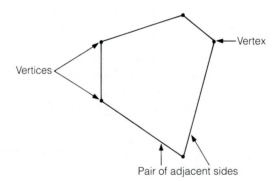

A *ray* is a piece of a line with a beginning point but no ending.

A configuration consisting of two rays joined at their beginning points is called an *angle*. The two rays are called the *sides* of the angle. The point at which the two rays meet is call the *vertex* of the angle.

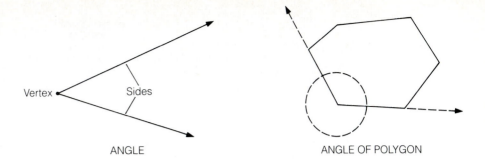

ANGLE   ANGLE OF POLYGON

You can think of two line segments that meet at a point as an angle by extending the ends of the segments that don't meet and making them into rays. In this sense, a polygon has many angles.

A rectangle has four sides, four vertices, and four angles. Many polygons have this property, but the distinguishing feature for the rectangle is that its four angles are "equal" in a certain sense.

CONGRUENT ANGLES

Two angles are *congruent* if the two sides and the vertex of a copy of one fit exactly on the two sides and the vertex of the other. (The actual drawn lengths of the sides of the angles are not important in determining whether the angles are congruent.)

Congruent   Not congruent

The four congruent angles of a rectangle have a special property: They completely fill in the space around a point without overlapping, as shown.

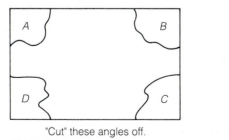

"Cut" these angles off.   Rearrange this way.

So the four angles of a rectangle are right angles.

In a rectangle, a pair of sides that aren't adjacent are called *opposite* sides. A pair of opposite sides extended in both directions never meet. Two lines in a plane that never meet are called *parallel;* thus, opposite sides of a rectangle are parallel.

Pair of parallel lines:

_____

_____

EXERCISES

5. When the two lengths H and B of a rectangle are equal, then the rectangle is also a *square*. All four sides of a square are equal. There is a particularly nice formula for the perimeter of a square. What is it?

6. Find the perimeters of the polygons.

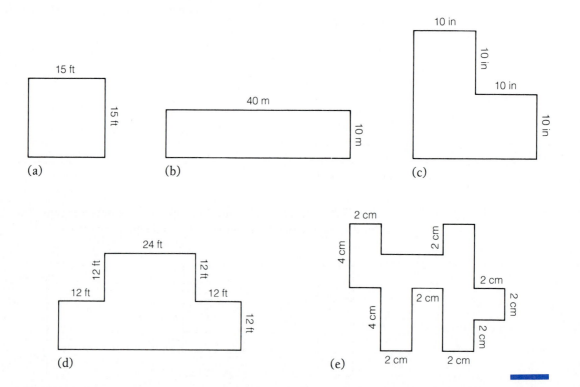

(a) (b) (c)

(d) (e)

Obregon is repaving all the numbered streets between Columbus St. and Washington St. To figure out the cost of this, engineers must figure out the total amount of paving. A map of the town is provided. All the streets in the city are the same width. Help the engineers solve this problem.

Try this yourself.

**A Solution to the Street
Paving Problem**

Realizing that the blocks in the town form rectangles, the city engineers conclude that the length of paving on one numbered street is the same as the length of paving of another—because these are lengths of opposite sides of a rectangle. All they have to do, then, is figure out the length of one cross street and multiply it by the number of cross streets to obtain the total length of paving for the project.

The Mathematical Idea: Using Rectangles to Measure Indirectly

The town engineers didn't have to measure the length of a numbered street several blocks away. All they had to do was measure the length of one nearby numbered street and use the fact that the other length was the opposite side of a rectangle and thus equal in length to the one nearby.

EXERCISE

7. You are replacing the cornice at the top of a several-story building. You need to know the length of the top of the building to estimate the cost of replacement. When you look at the picture of the building, can you think of an easy way to solve this problem?

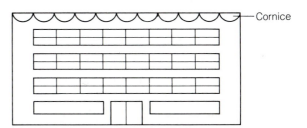

THE WATER PIPE PROBLEM

The Jones family is planning to add a new bathroom to their house. One of the items that will affect the cost of this project is the water line. To estimate the cost of the water line and its installation, they figure they must know its projected length.

Mr. Jones cannot measure the length easily because there is no clear path from the present water source to its destination in the new bathroom: The water line must pass under several rooms. Mr. Jones decides to make a scale drawing of that part of the house and then measure the length of the line on the scale drawing. He decides on a scale: Every centimeter of length in the scale drawing will represent 1 m in the house. The rooms are all rectangular, so the scale drawing is not difficult. Here it is.

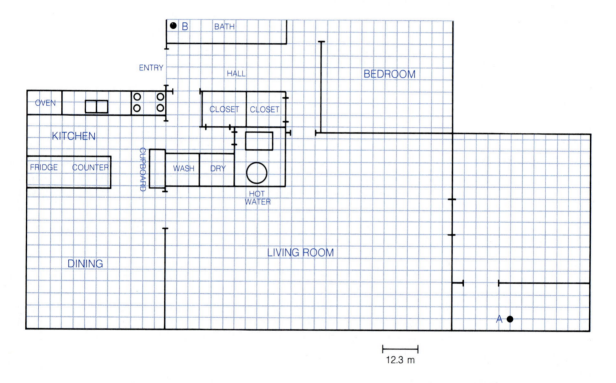

12.3 m

The bathroom will need water at point A; the water pipes nearest to this are at point B. On the scale drawing Mr. Jones measures the distance from A to B and finds it to be 12.3 cm. This represents 12.3 m in real life. This is Mr. Jones's estimate of the length of the new water line.

The Mathematical Idea: Using a Scale Drawing to Measure Length

When you reduce the size of a rectangular photograph, the ratio of one side in the original to the corresponding side in the reduction is equal to the ratio of the other side in the original to the other corresponding side in the reduction.

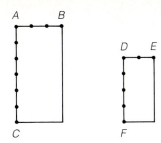

The ratio of the length of *AB* to the length of *DE* is 3 to 2, or $\frac{3}{2}$. The ratio of the length of *AC* to the length of *DF* is also 3 to 2.

You also expect any other length in the original photograph to be reduced using the same ratio. (One says that the lengths are in the *same proportion*.)

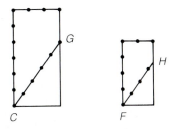

The ratio of the length of *CG* to the length of *FH* is 5 to $3\frac{1}{3}$, or $\frac{3}{2}$.

In the solution to the water pipe problem the ratio of a length from the original to the corresponding length in the scale drawing is 100 to 1, or $\frac{100}{1}$. The ratio of a length in the scale drawing to the corresponding length in the original is 1 to 100, or $\frac{1}{100}$. The latter is called the *scale factor* for a scale drawing. Frequently, a scale is given in which the two lengths have different units, for example, 1 cm represents 2 m. In this case the scale factor is *not* 1 to 2, or $\frac{1}{2}$. Since a centimeter is .01 m, the scale factor is .01 to 2, or $\frac{1}{200}$.

As in the solution to the water pipe problem, scale drawings can be used to measure lengths indirectly. There will be more on scale drawings in chapter 15.

EXERCISE

8. Water from the Colorado River is scheduled to arrive in Tucson, Arizona, in late 1989, thanks to the Central Arizona Project (CAP). Some water will arrive by open canal at the northwestern corner of the city. A cluster of industries at the southeastern corner of the city is considering the use of some of the unprocessed water because of the potential low cost per gallon. The city would have to tunnel a water main from the one corner to the other to get this water to the industries. To estimate the cost of the water main, the city needs to know the length of the main. A map (a scale drawing) of the city showing the two corners A and B is provided (page 522). Help the city solve this problem.

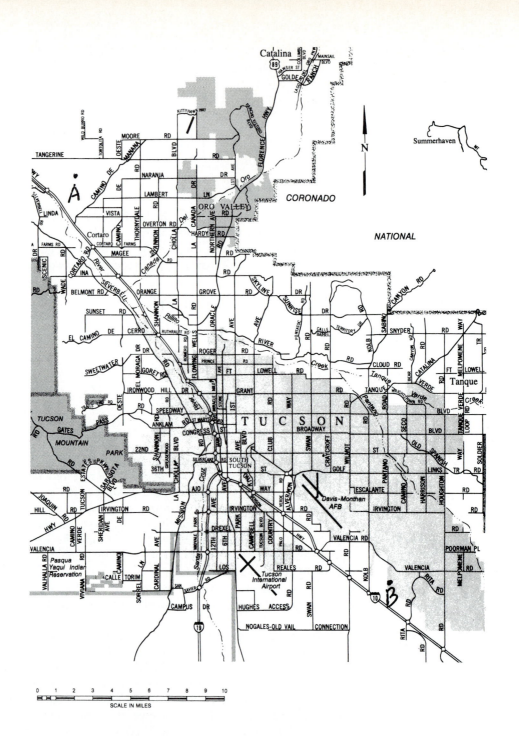

The Joneses have a house that was built around 1900. Many of the rooms had molding that went all around the baseboards, up all the corners of the rooms, and around the edges of the ceiling where the side walls and ceiling meet. They are planning to restore the molding in the room shown.

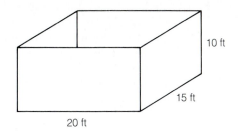

The room is a box. The floor is a rectangle 15 by 20 ft, and the ceiling is 10 ft from floor to ceiling. The Joneses need to know how much molding they will need so they can estimate the cost of this restoration. Molding is sold by the foot. Help them find the answer.

A Solution to the Room
Molding Problem

Mrs. Jones draws another picture of the room.

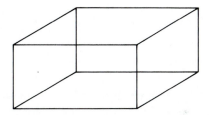

"This is a skeleton of the room," she says. "All those lines drawn correspond to pieces of molding. To solve our problem we must find the total length of all those lines.

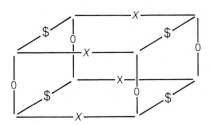

"The 4 pieces marked with an X are each 20 feet long. The 4 pieces marked with O are each 10 feet long. The 4 pieces marked with $ are each 15 feet long.

"There are 12 pieces in all. That makes 4 × 10 feet + 4 × 15 feet + 4 × 20 feet or 180 feet of molding in all."

EXERCISE

9. The Jones' house once had ornate trim all along the outside roof line. This has long since disappeared, but the Joneses are now planning to restore the trim on the front of the house to its original elegance. Such trim is sold by the foot; thus, the Joneses will need to determine the total length of trim on the front of the house in order to estimate the cost of their project. Below is a picture of the front of their house with measurements of the roof line marked in. Find the total amount of trim they will need.

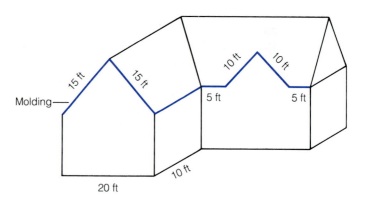

THE SPEAKER WIRING PROBLEM

John was lying in bed one morning listening to his stereo and imagining how nice it would be if he could place one of the speakers up near the ceiling in the corner opposite his turntable and amplifier. The latter were on a table in the corner just to his right where he could turn the stereo on easily without getting out of bed. He was wondering how much wire he would need to connect the speaker to his amplifier. He knew that his room was shaped like a cube: A square floor 9 by 9 ft and a ceiling 9 ft high. He figured that the speaker wire connection on the amplifier was 3 ft up from the floor in the corner and that the wire would attach to a point in back of the speaker exactly 3 ft down from the ceiling in the opposite corner. Help John figure out how long the wire should be if it takes the shortest route along the walls and floor of his room.

Try this yourself, first.

A Solution to the Speaker Wiring Problem

John decides to draw a picture of his room, marking on it the two ends of the wire.

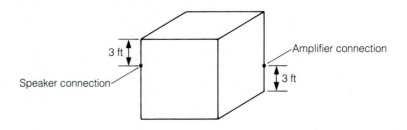

He thinks: "One way to do it would be to run the wire straight down the corner from the amplifier to the floor, across the floor diagonally, and up the opposite corner to the speaker.

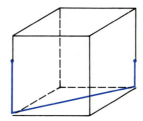

Is that the shortest way? I know that if the wire were to run on a flat surface, I could figure out the shortest way: I'd just draw a line between the two ends. Then I'd measure along the line from one end to the other to figure out the length. But my room is not flat! Is there a way I could make it flat? The ceiling, floor, and walls are flat themselves. It's the corners that mess things up. What if I were to 'cut' the room along the corners and flatten it out? I'd snip along the edges of the ceiling and bend it back, like this.

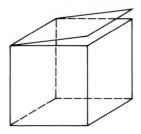

Then I'd snip along the corners from the ceiling to the floor, like this.

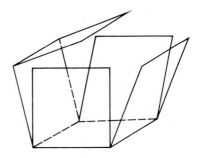

Then, I'd flatten it out. It would look like this.

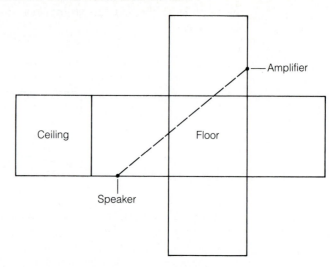

Then I could mark the two ends of the speaker connection and draw a straight line between the two points. Let me make a scale drawing of what I would get. From that I should be able to approximate pretty closely what the length of the wire should be. I'll get some graph paper and make the width of each little square on the graph paper represent a foot in the room. I won't have to include the ceiling.

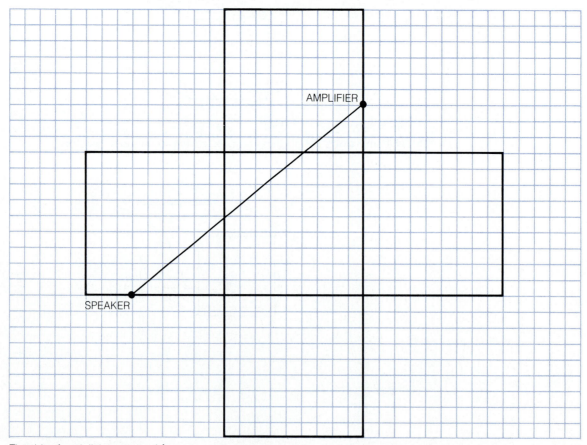

The side of each little square = 1 ft.

"On my scale drawing I've marked where the two ends of the wire will be and drawn the line between them. To measure the length of that line I'll take another piece of graph paper and use it to count the number of square-widths that will just fit along the line.

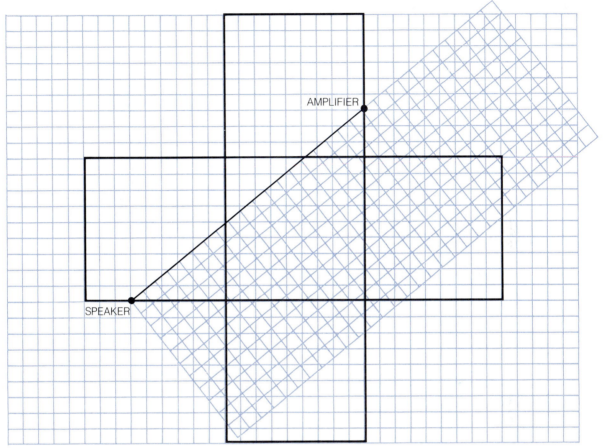

The side of each little square = 1 ft.

A little more than 19 squares. That represents a length of a little more than 19 feet in my room."

EXERCISE   10. Think some more about John's situation.
  (a)   The speaker can be located on the scale drawing differently than it is in our drawing. Find the way and draw the line between it and the amplifier. What is the length of the corresponding wire?
  (b)   Use the scale drawing to estimate the length of the wire John would need if he followed his original idea of running the wire down one corner from the speaker, across the room diagonally, and then up the other corner to the amplifier.

The Mathematical Idea: Making a Flattened Pattern
for a Three-Dimensional Shape

To measure the length of the speaker wire for his room John found it useful to "flatten the room out." He obtained a flat shape that if folded and taped together in the right places could be reassembled into the original room, or, in John's case, a scale model of the room. We call this flat shape a *(flat) pattern* for the three-dimensional shape.

Another example follows. In this case we have an open trough, shown on the left, and its pattern, shown on the right.

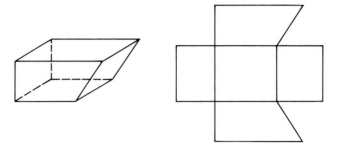

11. Create a flat pattern for the shape.

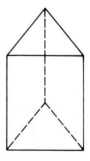

12. Trace a copy of the pattern below and assemble it. What do you get? (Fold on solid lines.)

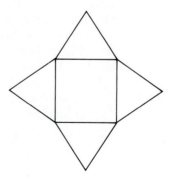

13. The Steins are installing a light in the cathedral ceiling of their living room. Here's a picture of the room and where they want to put the light.

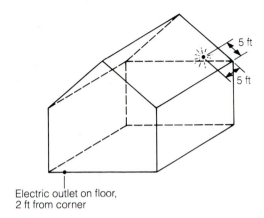

Electric outlet on floor,
2 ft from corner

The nearest electrical outlet is near the floor on the opposite side of the room. How should they run the wire from the outlet to the light in order to use the least amount of wire?

13.5   MEASURING POSITION USING COORDINATE GEOMETRY

Typically we measure length to see if something will fit or to replicate a length, as in figuring the right amount of fencing to buy. We also use length to measure position along a path. Mileposts along a road tell us how far we have traveled or how far the next town is; knowing how far can help us plan our time on a trip. A car's odometer tells how far the car has traveled; this is, effectively, the car's "age." An altitude marker indicates the distance of a certain location above sea level; this can tell us something to expect about the weather, the air pressure, and the amount of oxygen at the location.

These uses of length give a position along a straight line or path. Length can also be used to specify one's position on a plane or flat surface. The location of a hidden treasure, for example, can be described this way: "Walk 10 paces due east from the edge of the stone well, where you will come to a metal marker in the ground; then 7 paces due north from the marker you will come to a hollow oak tree. In the hollow is the treasure."

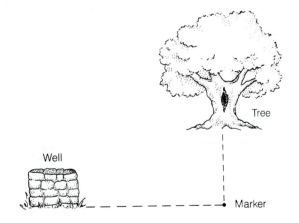

A starting place (the well), a direction (due east) and a length (10 paces), and another direction (due north) and length (7 paces) pinpoint the position of the hidden treasure exactly. These are the basic ingredients for establishing a *coordinate system* for a plane.

To create a coordinate system, select a point on the plane called the *origin* (a starting point). Through the origin draw a line (corresponding to the east-west directions). Mark lengths on this line, creating a number line with 0 at the origin. (The negative numbers are lengths in the opposite direction.) This line is called the *horizontal axis*.

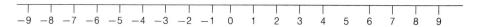

Draw a second line through the origin, making a right angle to the first and create a second number line out of this with the origin as the 0 of the new number line. This line is called the *vertical axis*.

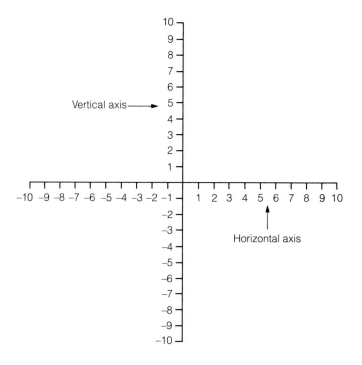

Once having drawn the two lines and marked the numbers on them, you are ready to give an "address" to every point in the plane. Take a point P and draw two lines through it, the first one parallel to the vertical axis and the second parallel to the horizontal axis.

Where the first line (parallel to the vertical axis) intersects the horizontal axis is the *horizontal coordinate* of the point; where the second line (parallel to the horizontal axis) intersects the vertical axis is the *vertical coordinate* of the point. These two numbers are the *coordinates* of the point. The *address* of the point is the ordered pair (A,B) where A is the horizontal (or *first*) coordinate and B is the vertical (or *second*) coordinate. The address of the point P in the diagram on the next page is (6,4). In the hidden treasure example, if we think of the origin as the well, the horizontal axis as the east-west direction (east to the right, west to the left), and the vertical axis as the north-south direction (with north up, south down), then the address of the hidden treasure is (10,7).

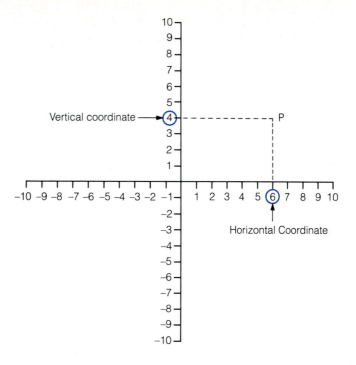

Here are some more points with their addresses.

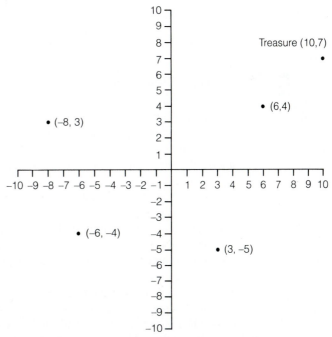

The two axes and the method of assigning coordinates to points is called a *coordinate system*. In working with points and their coordinates there are two basic jobs: (1) to determine the coordinates of a given point and (2) to find (*plot*) a point having a given pair of coordinates. Both these jobs are easy when a grid of lines parallel to the two axes is provided. Ordinary graph paper is designed with this in mind. If you have to construct on paper a coordinate system and then work with it to do these jobs, graph paper is the best thing to use.

14. On graph paper draw a coordinate system and plot the points with these addresses: $(3,4)$, $(-3,4)$, $(0,-4)$, $(5,0)$, $(3,-4)$, $(-3,-4)$. Make sure the points are labeled with their addresses.

15. On the coordinate system provided, find the address of each of the points A, B, C, D, E, and F.

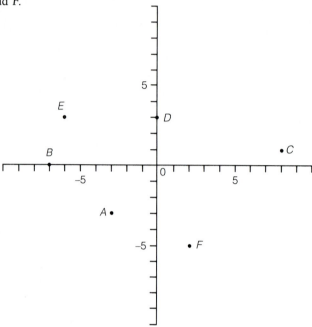

13.6   LOOKING BACK: MORE GEOMETRIC TERMINOLOGY

Special terms are used to describe many of the shapes that we see, that we measure, that we use to measure other shapes, and that we build with. You are familiar with many of these and some of them, such as rectangle and angle, have already been discussed in the chapter. The most basic of these are *point* and *line* and *plane*. *Point* is an abstraction conveying the common properties of the sharpened tip of a pencil, the pointed end of a needle, and the tip of the Washington Monument, among other things. *Line* captures the common properties of a string stretched tautly, the horizon of a western sky, and a single rail of a railroad track. *Plane* is an abstraction of the smooth surface of a table top or a floor. A line is meant to extend indefinitely in both directions; a plane is meant to extend indefinitely in all its directions. For us a point is often a tiny dot made by a pencil on a piece of paper, a line is the trace made by streaking a pencil along the edge of a ruler, and a plane is the piece of paper itself. In formal geometry the terms point and line and plane are *undefined*. Everything else is described in terms of them. Let's look at some more terms and what they describe.

TERM	ILLUSTRATION
A *line segment* is a subset of a line between (and including) two points A and B on that line. The two points are called the *end points* of the line segment.	$\bullet\!\!\!\!\!\!\!\!\rule[0.5ex]{8em}{0.4pt}\!\!\!\!\!\!\!\!\bullet$ $A \qquad\qquad\qquad\qquad B$

A *ray* is a subset of a line consisting of a point *P* and all the points of the line on one side of it.

Two distinct lines having a point *P* in common *intersect* at point *P*. Two such lines have only the point *P* in common.

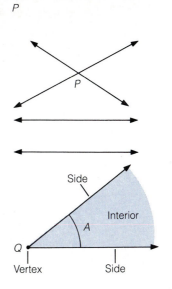

Two lines in a plane are *parallel* if they have no points in common; that is, they do not intersect.

An *angle A* is the union of two rays with a common end point Q and the space between the two rays. The two rays are the *sides* of the angle. The common end point Q is the *vertex* of the angle. The space between the two rays is called the angle's *interior*. (Informally, one talks about an angle formed by two line segments with a common end point.)

Angle *A* is *smaller* than angle *B* if a copy of *A*, its vertex in common with *B*'s, lies in the interior of *B*.

An *acute angle* is an angle that is smaller than a right angle.

An angle the two sides of which lie on the same straight line is called a *straight angle*.

An *obtuse angle* is an angle larger than a right angle and smaller than a straight angle.

A *polygon* is a collection of line segments, called *sides*, joined together in a plane at their end points. These points are called the *vertices* of the polygon. Every end point is a vertex, and at every vertex two and only two segments meet. A pair of sides may intersect only at vertices. Two sides that meet at a vertex form an *angle* of the polygon.

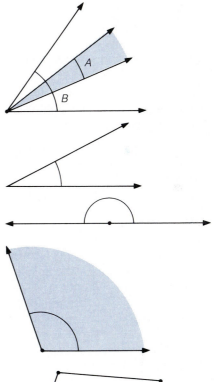

Polygons occur frequently, and special terms are used to classify them. One set of terms is related to the number of sides (or vertices) a polygon has.

TERMS FOR POLYGONS ACCORDING TO NUMBER OF SIDES	
NO. OF SIDES	TERM FOR POLYGON
3	Triangle
4	Quadrilateral
5	Pentagon
6	Hexagon
7	Heptagon
8	Octagon
9	Nonagon
10	Decagon
n	n-gon

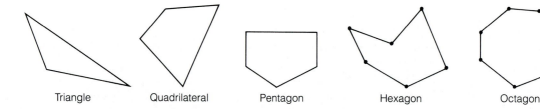

Triangle   Quadrilateral   Pentagon   Hexagon   Octagon

A polygon all the sides of which have the same length and all the angles of which are congruent is called a *regular polygon*. All the shapes shown are regular polygons.

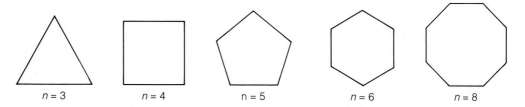

$n = 3$ $n = 4$ $n = 5$ $n = 6$ $n = 8$

Two vertices of a polygon that are end points of a single side are called *adjacent* vertices. A *diagonal* of a polygon is a line segment joining two nonadjacent vertices. A polygon partitions the plane in which it sits into three pieces, the polygon itself, the *interior* of the polygon (the finite or bounded part), and the *exterior* of the polygon. A polygon is convex if every diagonal can be drawn in the interior of the polygon; otherwise, the polygon is *concave*.

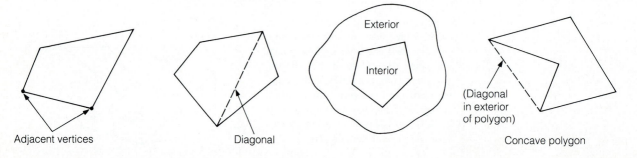

Adjacent vertices   Diagonal   Exterior / Interior   (Diagonal in exterior of polygon)   Concave polygon

Finally, since 3-gons and 4-gons are the most frequently occurring polygons, there are special terms classifying them.

TERMS FOR 3-GONS AND 4-GONS		
TERM	DESCRIPTION OF POLYGON	ILLUSTRATION
Right triangle	Triangle with one right angle; a little square in an angle will always mean right angle	
Acute triangle	Triangle with all angles acute	
Obtuse triangle	Triangle with one obtuse angle	
Equilateral triangle	Regular triangle (all sides and all angles equal)	
Isosceles triangle	Triangle with at least two sides equal	
Scalene triangle	Triangle with no two sides equal (a triangle that is not isosceles)	
Trapezoid	Quadrilateral with one and only one pair of parallel sides	
Parallelogram	Quadrilateral with two pairs of parallel sides	

(*continued*)

(Continued)

TERMS FOR 3-GONS AND 4-GONS		
TERM	DESCRIPTION OF POLYGON	ILLUSTRATION
Rectangle	Quadrilateral with all angles equal	
Square	Rectangle with all sides equal	
Rhombus	Parallelogram with all sides equal	

EXERCISES   16. Label each polygon with all the terms in the preceding chart that apply.

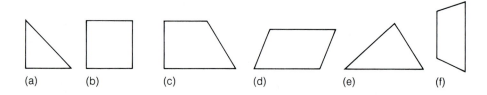

(a)   (b)   (c)   (d)   (e)   (f)

17. According to the preceding definitions, every square is also a rectangle. That means that the set *S* of all squares is a subset of the set *R* of all rectangles.

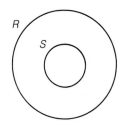

Draw a similar, *single* picture expressing the relationship among the listed sets.

$$T = \text{set of all trapezoids}$$
$$P = \text{set of all parallelograms}$$
$$R = \text{set of all rectangles}$$
$$S = \text{set of all squares}$$
$$Rh = \text{set of all rhombi}$$
$$Q = \text{set of all quadrilaterals}$$
$$Re = \text{set of all regular 4-gons}$$

18. As in exercise 17, draw a single picture expressing the relationship among the sets.

$$R = \text{set of right triangles}$$
$$Re = \text{set of regular 3-gons}$$
$$I = \text{set of isosceles triangles}$$
$$A = \text{set of acute triangles}$$
$$O = \text{set of obtuse triangles}$$
$$E = \text{set of equilateral triangles}$$
$$S = \text{set of scalene triangles}$$

Symmetry

Shapes can be described in ways other than by how many lines or angles are used to make them and the comparative sizes of these lines and angles. One of these ways is through the *symmetry* the shape possesses.

One type of symmetry is called *mirror* (or *bilateral*) *symmetry*. Take a shape and draw a line L through it. Place a mirror perpendicular to the paper along this line. Part of the shape will be in front of the reflecting surface of the mirror. Part of the shape will be in back of the reflecting surface of and covered up by the mirror. If the image in the mirror recreates the part covered up, then the shape has *mirror symmetry along line L*. Here are some examples.

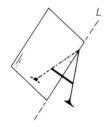
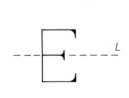

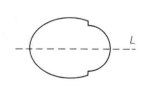

Some shapes have mirror symmetry along several lines.

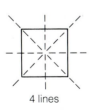

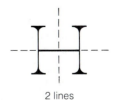

4 lines   3 lines   2 lines   Infinitely many lines

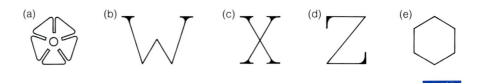

(a) (b) W (c) X (d) Z (e)

Mirror Symmetry and Transformational Geometry

The mirror symmetry of a plane object can also be accounted for by subjecting the entire plane to a certain *transformation,* or *motion.* The pumpkin face shown, below, has line L of mirror symmetry. Imagine that the line is a "spit" with which you have "speared" the plane; then, holding the spit fixed, slowly "turn the plane over." When you have done this, the pumpkin face appears as if it has not been changed. This would not have happened if the pumpkin had not had mirror symmetry in line L. The transformation—turning the plane over using "spit" L—is sometimes called a *flip about L.* A shape has mirror symmetry at line L if the flip about L leaves the shape unchanged in how it looks.

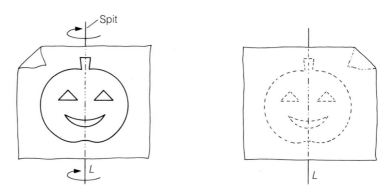

A way to express the fact that the tree below has mirror symmetry along line L is to trace a copy of the tree (with the line L, too) on a separate piece of paper. Flip the piece of paper over and lay the traced L over the original L, with each traced point of the line lying over the original point. The traced tree should fit exactly over the original tree.

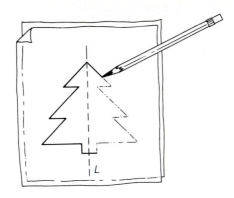
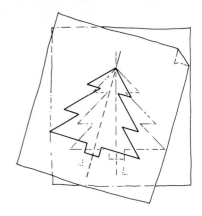

EXERCISE **20.** Make a tracing of each of the following. Then use the criterion demonstrated with the tree and the pumpkin face to test for the mirror symmetry of the object along line L.

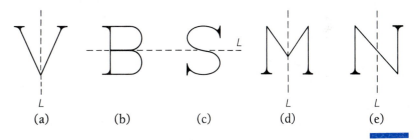

(a) (b) (c) (d) (e)

13.7 SUMMARY OF IMPORTANT IDEAS AND TECHNIQUES

- The evolution of length measurement
  Without modern tools
  Using an intermediate device
  Using convenient units
  Using standard units in the traditional system and metric system
- Perimeter of polygon; formula for perimeter of rectangle
- Measurement of length indirectly
  Using a rectangle
  Using a scale drawing
  Using a flat pattern of a three-dimensional model
- Basic terminology used to describe shapes
  Point, line, plane, parallel, angle, polygon
  Vertices and sides of angles and polygons
  Special terminology for angles, right angles
  Special terminology for polygons, especially triangles and quadrilaterals
  Symmetry of an object along line L
- Using length to describe position via a coordinate system

PROBLEM SET

1. Find the amount of fencing needed to fence in each pasture shown.

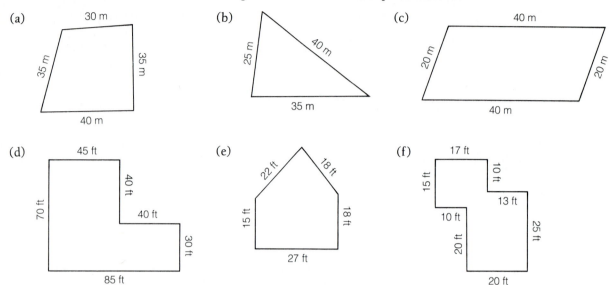

(a) 30 m, 35 m, 35 m, 40 m

(b) 25 m, 40 m, 35 m

(c) 40 m, 20 m, 20 m, 40 m

(d) 45 ft, 40 ft, 70 ft, 40 ft, 30 ft, 85 ft

(e) 22 ft, 18 ft, 15 ft, 18 ft, 27 ft

(f) 17 ft, 15 ft, 10 ft, 13 ft, 10 ft, 20 ft, 25 ft, 20 ft

2. You want to buy molding to place around the top of the wall in your living room, just next to the ceiling and above all doors and windows. You know that the room is a 10-ft-long by 15-ft-wide rectangle. How much molding do you need?

3. The owner of a small motel knows that all his rooms are identical. He wants to know the dimensions of room 18 at the end but has lent out the key to a carpenter who will not return until tomorrow. How can he find out the dimensions now?

4. Name five commonly used scale drawings. [*Hint:* look in the glove compartment of your car and at your owner's manuals.]

5. A housing contractor is building a tract of 20 homes each on same-size lots as in the picture. He wishes to buy fencing to fence in three sides of each lot; the side of each lot facing Grape, Apple, and Pear streets are to be left unfenced. How much fencing must he buy?

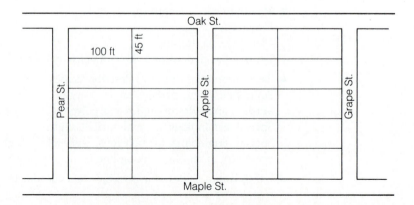

6. The contractor in problem 5 must also install curbing along both sides of all five streets shown. Each street is 15 ft wide, and each lot will have an 8-ft-wide break in the curbing to leave room for a driveway. What is the total length of curbing he must install?

7. Solve the speaker and wiring problem if your room is 12 ft by 15 ft with 8-ft ceilings, using John's method with a scale drawing and ruler.

8. Draw a flat pattern for each shape.

(a)  (b)  (c)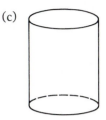

9. For each of the following prescriptions draw a polygon if you can. (If there is no polygon that fits the prescription, explain why not.)
   (a) a scalene right triangle   (b) an isosceles right triangle
   (c) an obtuse right triangle   (d) an equilateral right triangle
   (e) a regular rectangle   (f) a regular triangle
   (g) a regular trapezoid

10. Draw in all the lines of mirror symmetry for each shape.
    (a) 8   (b) B   (c) @
    (d) $ (e) H   (f) !
    (g) *   (h) +   (i) =

    (j) [rectangle]   (k) [heart]   (l) [wheel]

11. On a piece of graph paper, draw horizontal and vertical axes and plot the points the coordinates of which are as follows.
    (a) (2,−1)   (b) (3,8)   (c) (−2,1)   (d) (2,1)
    (e) (−2,−1)   (f) (−3,−8)   (g) (0,−2)   (h) (−2,0)

12. Find the coordinates of each of the plotted points.

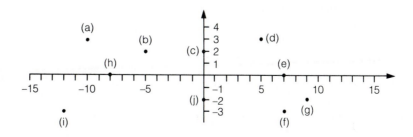

13. You have a drawing $2\frac{1}{2}$ by $3\frac{1}{2}$ in that you want to enlarge to make a poster 4 ft tall. You want to know how wide the poster will be.

14. On an interior decorator's drawing, $\frac{1}{4}$ in represents 1 ft. On the drawing, a certain rug is 2 by 3 in. What are the dimensions of the real rug?

15. Use the map below to estimate the distance by air between the following pairs of cities.
    (a) Cincinnati and Chicago   (b) Santa Fe and Kansas City
    (c) New York and Austin   (d) Salt Lake City and Fargo
    (e) Seattle and Bangor   (f) Helena and Washington, D.C.
    (g) Denver and Miami   (h) New Orleans and Los Angeles

USING IDEAS   *For each remaining problem, write an essay to communicate clearly and completely the solution to the problem. Mention the steps you took in solving the problem, other problems or solutions that gave you ideas, and the strategies you used.*

16. In certain parts of the country drainage pipes must be laid around the periphery of a house to carry away rainwater that drips from the roof and to keep water away from the foundations and from getting into the basement. The house shown at the upper left is an example in which the pipe appears as a dotted line about 1.5 ft from the foundation. What is the length of piping that will be needed for each house indicated? (Only certain measurements have been provided. You must infer the rest from those that are given. A pair of sides that *look* parallel *is* parallel!)

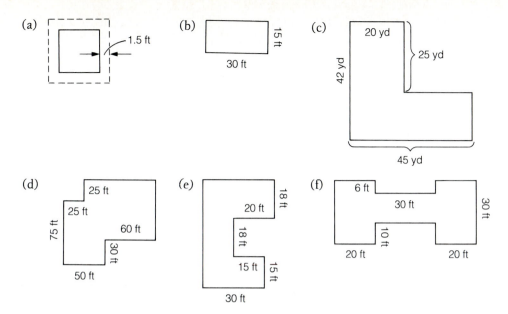

17. Below is the design for a rather unusual hand mirror. You plan to put a thin silver molding around its edge and want to know how much silver molding you will need. You decide to solve this in two ways:
    (a) Using string as in the text
    (b) Approximating the curved edge with a lot of short, straight lines (you draw them in), measuring the straight lines, and adding up their lengths.
    What do you get with each of these methods?

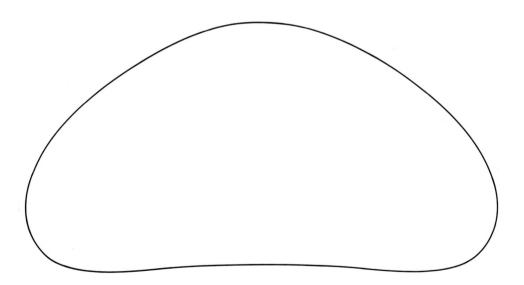

18. You work for the Perfect Packaging Company. Your supervisor tells you, "A large rush order has just come in, and we need to send out 140 cartons as soon as possible. I'd like you to fill the cartons and tape them up. Before doing that you will need to pick up enough tape from the store room." "How much tape will I need?" you ask. The reply: "The cartons are 65 centimeters long, 25 centimeters wide, and 10 centimeters thick; and we tape them twice around the long way and use two strips across the top." How much tape will you need? (See illustration on page 544.)

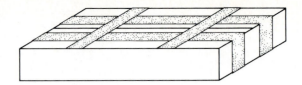

19. Below is the floor plan of your kitchen and dining nook. The whole room is a rectangle. You have laid linoleum tile on those parts of the floor that are not shaded in. (The shaded parts of the diagram correspond to items that are permanently fixed to the floor.) Now you plan to install protective rubber molding around the perimeter of the new linoleum. What length of rubber molding will you need?

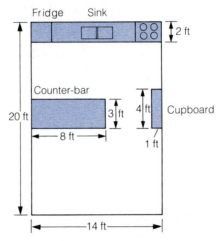

20. Here is some information regarding the planting of bush beans:

   ■ The distance between plants should be from 4 to 6 in.
   ■ 1 lb of seed will seed 100 row-feet.
   ■ 100 row-feet has an expected yield of 50 lb beans.

   (a) How many row-feet are necessary to bring an expected yield of 300 lb?
   Bush beans, like other vegetables, may benefit from being grown in a rectangular block rather than in one long row. In block planting, leaves shade the soil, keeping it moist and reducing the growth of weeds. Plants grown in this way are equally spaced in the directions of width and length of the block. To make weeding easier, it is best to make the block no more than 2 ft wide. The length of the block can then be adjusted to provide the desired yield.
   (b) If bush beans are planted in blocks 2 ft wide and at the minimum distance of 4 in, how long must the block be in order to yield 300 lb?
   (c) How many pounds of seed are required for this planting?*

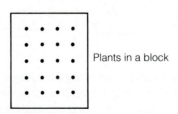

Plants in a block

---

* With thanks to D. Bushaw et al., *A Sourcebook of Applications of School Mathematics,* National Council of Teachers of Mathematics, Reston, Va., 1980, prob. 1.14, p. 24.

21. A photograph is to be reduced in size so that it can be mounted on an $8\frac{1}{2}$- by 11-in sheet of paper. The photograph now measures 12 by 20 in. When mounted, the reduced photo should have a margin of at least $1\frac{1}{4}$ in all around. You'd like to have the reduced photo be as large as it can be, given these restrictions. What is the size of the reduced photo? What is the scale factor?

22. Adam and his sixth grade friends decide to lay out a scale model of the solar system in the school gymnasium. They decide that all nine planets should be included and that each orbit should be a circle with a radius equal to the planet's average distance from the Sun. Since the gym is 180 ft wide, this means that Pluto's circular orbit will also have a diameter of 180 ft. Using a calculator and the information provided, figure out what the diameters of the other planets' orbits should be.

PLANET	AVERAGE DISTANCE FROM SUN (IN MILLIONS OF MILES)
Mercury	36
Venus	67
Earth	93
Mars	142
Jupiter	484
Saturn	884
Uranus	1789
Neptune	2809
Pluto	3685

23. You are about to purchase an old upright piano. You want to put it in your living room but are worried about whether you can get it there through the rest of your house. Scale models of the floor plan of your house and of the piano are shown. Can you do it? If you can, how? If you can't, why?

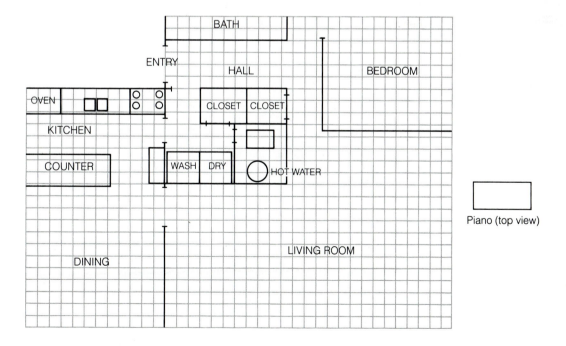

Piano (top view)

24. You have a rectangular garden surrounded by fencing. You plan to enlarge it by extending the rectangle 1 m in all directions as in the picture. You plan to take the fencing from the present garden and use it as fencing for the new garden. You will need some additional fencing, however. How much?

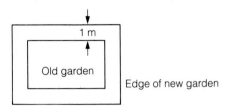

1 m

Old garden

Edge of new garden

25. You have just purchased the ranch shown in the map. You have decided to replace all the existing fencing (marked on the map by a heavy dashed line). You want to know how much it will cost and how long it will take you to complete the job. Fencing costs $3.75/linear ft (including posts). It takes about 30 min to install each 10 linear ft.

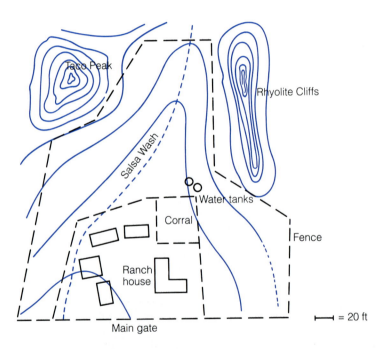

Taco Peak

Rhyolite Cliffs

Salsa Wash

Water tanks

Corral

Fence

Ranch house

Main gate

⊢──┤ = 20 ft

26. In this problem you will construct a scale model of a room using graph paper. (If you can, use graph paper with squares 2 cm on a side; otherwise, use graph paper having squares 1, .5, or .25 cm on a side.) The scale model will look like the one shown in the picture.

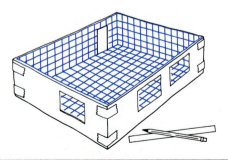

First, tape four sheets of paper together to make one piece, at least 17 by 22 cm.

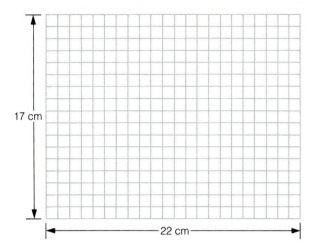

17 cm

22 cm

Next, draw a flattened pattern for the room on these sheets using certain requirements.
(a)   Use a scale of 2 cm represents 1 yd (3 ft).
(b)   The floor is a rectangle 50 by 32 ft.
(c)   The ceiling is 8 ft off the floor.
(d)   There are three windows, each 3 by 6 ft.
(e)   There is one door, 4 by 7 ft.
Proceed as shown in the drawings.

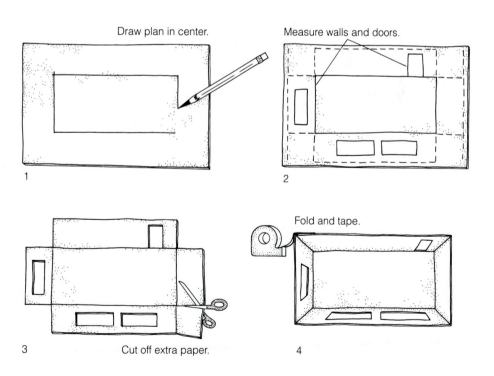

Draw plan in center.

Measure walls and doors.

1

2

3

Cut off extra paper.

Fold and tape.

4

You plan to install wooden molding trim around the door, all the windows, the baseboards, and on the ceiling at the tops of all the walls. Molding is sold by the (linear) foot. You want to know how much molding you will need. (Save this model for use in later problems.) *

27. Below are three views of the same cube. List the pairs of letters that appear on opposite faces of the cubes.

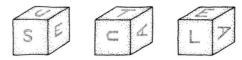

28. Below is a picture of a room. You want to install a light fixture right in the middle of the ceiling. You plan to run a wire from the fixture to the nearest electrical outlet, which is at the baseboard as shown. Use a dressmaker's pattern for the room to find the shortest route for the wire to take and find the length of the route.

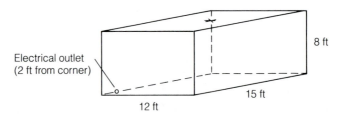

29. You, Officer Garcia, and your assistant, Officer O'Reilly, are needed as soon as possible to help capture criminals at the Wheeler Warehouse, corner of 11th and Wilson. You and O'Reilly are in your patrol car at 5th and Jefferson. You have two choices. You can drive there in your patrol car at an average speed of 60 mph, or you can go there by helicopter, which can travel at an average speed of 200 mph, with 5 additional min for takeoff and 5 min for landing. Of course, to use the helicopter, you must get to the police station and into the helicopter. You can radio ahead to have the helicopter waiting for you when you arrive. Once you arrive at the station, based on past experience it'll take you 6 min to park your car, get out, and get to the helicopter. Below is a map of the city showing the location of the warehouse and the police station with heliport. (Each city block is a mile square.) What should your choice be, helicopter or patrol car?

* With thanks to Sherry Fraser, *Spaces: Solving Problems of Access to Careers in Engineering and Science,* Lawrence Hall of Science, Berkeley, Calif., 1982, pp. 9–11.

	Main	Washington	Jefferson	Adams	Franklin	Monroe	Jackson	Grant	Columbus	Wilson	Roosevelt
12th St.											
11th St.											
10th St.											
9th St.											
8th St.											
7th St.											
6th St.											
5th St.											
4th St.											
3rd St.		■ ←Police									
2nd St.											
1st St.											

30. Which are flattened patterns for cubes?

(a)

(b)

(c)

(d)

(e)

(f)

(g)

(h)

(i)

(j)

(k)

(l)

GRAPHING

CHAPTER 14

Many times we have used the problem-solving strategy **make a chart**. For some problems charts were used to organize guesses and consequences of these guesses in order to zero in on a solution. (See problems in chap. 1 especially.) In other problems we made guesses at regular intervals and set these numbers up in the leftmost column of a chart in order to look for a particular number or observe a pattern in the quantity in the rightmost column. (See especially problems in chaps. 1, 2, and 12.) We tried to figure out something about the relationship between the quantities in the leftmost column and those in the rightmost column to use that information to solve the problem. In this chapter we will go one step further and discuss *graphing,* which is a way to associate a picture with such a two-column chart of numbers. Graphing is an additional tool for observing trends or patterns, that is, for observing relationships between two particular quantities that label columns of a chart.

We will pay particular attention to straight-line graphs and to those associated with exponential growth.

14.1   THE GRAPH ASSOCIATED WITH A TABLE

THE SOLAR PANEL PROBLEM

Try this before reading on.

Southwest Sun company makes solar energy collector panels. The company is small, and the number of panels it makes each month varies. The cost of materials (copper and Plexiglas) is $375 per panel. However, no matter how many panels are ordered, rent and salaries must be paid. Each month those fixed costs amount to $5000. Every month the company must decide, on the basis of how much cash it has on hand, how many panels it can manufacture. For example, this month Southwest Sun has only $30,000 to spend for manufacturing panels. The company would like to know how many panels it can make this month. Also, to help in future decisions, the company wants to know generally how many panels it can make in a month given the amount of money it has in the bank. Help it solve this problem.

A Solution to the Solar Panel Problem

Mr. Stein plans the company's monthly production. He thinks: "If I know how many panels are to be made in a month, it should be easy to figure out the total cost to the company that month. Let me make a table of monthly costs relative to the number of panels the company manufactures that month.

NO. OF PANELS MANUFACTURED IN MONTH	TOTAL COST OF COMPANY FOR THE MONTH
0	$5000
1	$5375
2	$5750
3	$6125
4	$6500

It might help if I could *see* how the company's total costs are related to the number of panels. Although I could place the total costs on a number line by themselves, it's really the pairs (0,5000), (1,5375), (2,5750),... that I want to see. I can think of

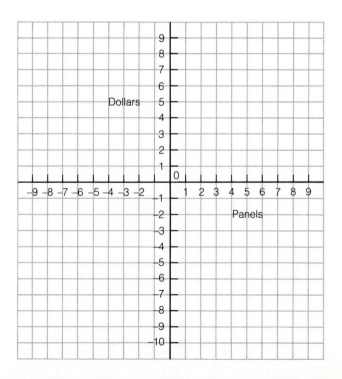

those pairs as points in a coordinate system. The first coordinate will be the number of panels, and the second, the number of dollars. We can identify the points along the horizontal axis with the number of panels and the points along the vertical axis with dollars. (See figure on page 552.)

"If the unit on the vertical axis is a dollar, I'm in trouble. I would need a very large piece of graph paper to graph a point the second coordinate of which is 5000. Let me change the unit to $500. Also, I don't think I'll be needing the negative parts of the axes. Here are the redrawn axes.

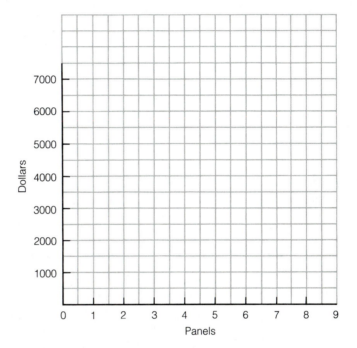

Now let me plot the points corresponding to the rows of my chart.

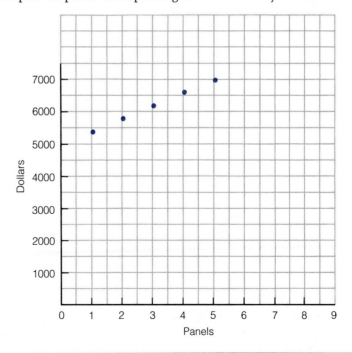

It looks as if the plotted points all lie on a straight line. If the plotted points corresponding to more than 4 panels also lie on that line, then I'd have a graph something like the next one.

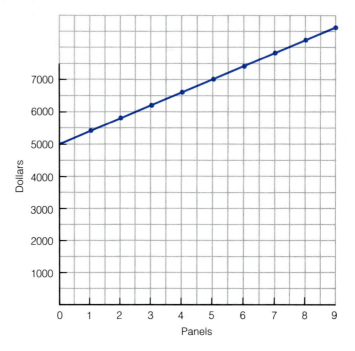

"If all the points do in fact lie on a straight line, I *can* figure out how many panels we can manufacture given that we have so much cash on hand. For example, we have $30,000 this month. First I'll find $30,000 on the vertical axis and draw a horizontal line through it. This horizontal line will intersect the line passing through the plotted points. Then I'll look at the 'shadow' of the point of intersection on the horizontal axis below it. (The shadow of P is also the first coordinate of P placed on the number line of the horizontal axis.)

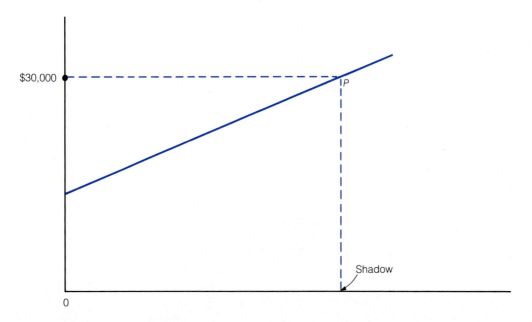

"To be more accurate, I'll need a bigger piece of graph paper. I'll also need smaller units on the axes. Let me change the vertical unit again, to $1000, also the horizontal unit, to 5 panels.

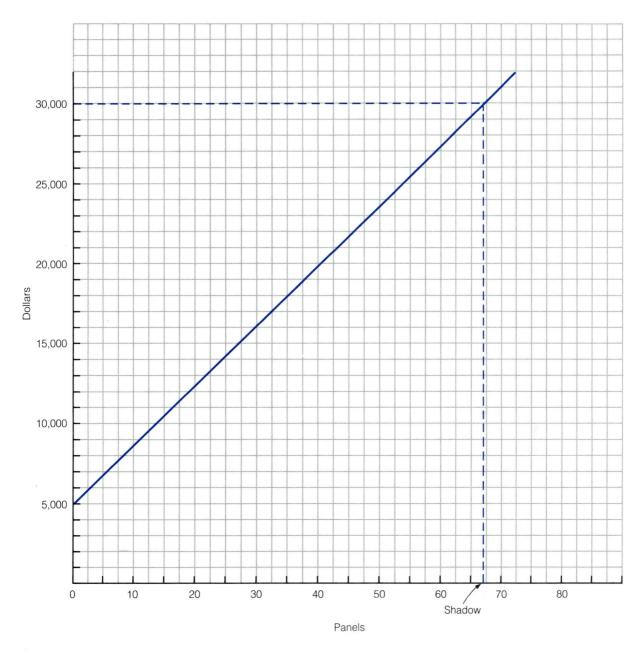

The 'shadow' on the horizontal axis appears to lie between the values 65 and 70. If my reasoning and my assumptions are correct, we should have enough money to manufacture at least 66 panels.

"Let me check that: 66 panels at $375 makes 66 × $375 = $24,750. That plus $5000 overhead makes $29,750. That would leave $250 left over. There would not be enough to make an additional panel. Using coordinates works; we can use it every month."

Mr. Stein started to solve the solar panel problem by making a chart.

NO. OF PANELS MANUFACTURED IN MONTH	TOTAL COST TO COMPANY FOR THE MONTH
0	$5000
1	5375
2	5750
3	6125
4	6500

Although he may have felt that he could solve the problem by continuing with the chart, he thought there might be a way to *see* what was happening with the numbers in the chart. He moved from thinking of each row of the chart as a pair of numbers to thinking of each row as a point in a coordinate system. By plotting these points he formed the graph corresponding to the chart. From the graph he was able to observe *visual trends* (*look for a pattern*). In his case he observed that the points all lay on a single straight line. Then, assuming that this visual trend would persist, he used the graph to predict the number of panels that would achieve a "target" of $30,000.

Many times in this book we have used charts to help solve problems. Drawing the graph associated with such a chart gives us another tool for solving the problem, just as we have used it to solve the solar panel problem. Let's look at a couple of examples of such charts (from chap. 1) and the graphs that correspond to them.

THE COFFEE BLEND PROBLEM   Recall that Max's Coffee Mill wants to make 50 Ib of a blend of inexpensive Costa Rican coffee (selling for $4.50/Ib) and expensive mocha coffee (selling for $7.00/Ib). He wants the blend to cost $5.20/Ib. He needs to know how many pounds of Costa Rican (C.R.) and how many pounds of mocha he will need to do this. He has calculated that, at $5.20/Ib, 50 Ib of the desired blend should cost $260.00. (The latter is what we called the target cost.) Here is the table he created.

C.R. (POUNDS)	MOCHA (POUNDS)	COST OF C.R.	COST OF MOCHA	TOTAL COST	TARGET COST OF BLEND
30	20	$135	$140	$275	$260
40	10	180	70	250	
35	15	157.50	105	262.50	

This chart has more than two columns. Since what we are really interested in is how many pounds of Costa Rican will produce a 50-lb blend costing $260.00, we are really interested in a condensed chart.

C.R. (POUNDS)	TOTAL COST OF BLEND
10	$325
20	300
30	275
40	250
35	262.50

The graph corresponding to this chart is the following.

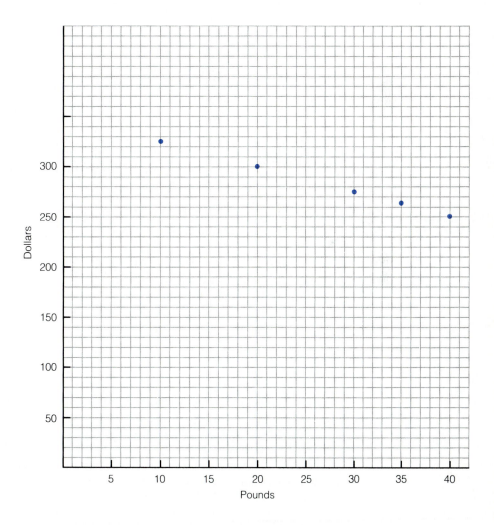

The five points lie on a straight line; so, assuming that points plotted for other amounts of Costa Rican lie on this same line, we can use the "shadow" technique used by Mr. Stein in the solar panel problem to find out how many pounds of Costa Rican will achieve a target cost of $260.00.

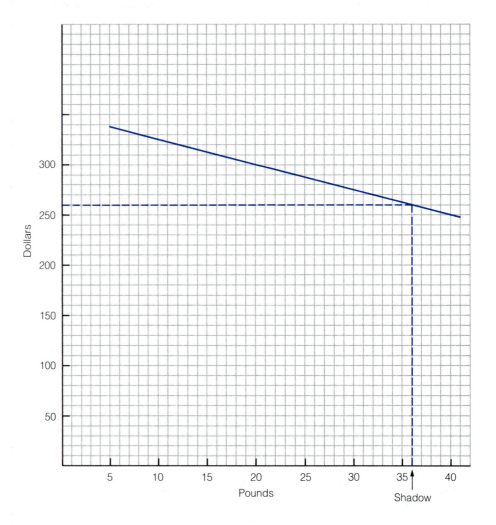

This technique suggests that around 36 lb of Costa Rican would achieve the target cost. This is the solution to the problem that we got in chapter 1.

THE BEST-PRICE PROBLEM   Recall that a gift shop chain selling miniature cactus gardens for $20 each is considering changing the price of each. At the present price the chain sells 200 of them every week. For each decrease of $1 in the present selling price, it can sell 5 additional gardens above the 200; and for each $1 increase in the selling price, the chain will sell 5 gardens less than the 200. The chain wants to know what the selling price should be in order that its total income from the gardens be as large as possible.

To help solve this problem, the following chart was begun. We have added a few more rows.

PRICE EACH	TOTAL SALES
20	$4000
21	4095
22	4180
23	4255
24	4320
25	4375
26	4420
27	4455
28	4480
29	4495
30	4500
31	4495
32	4480
33	4455
34	4420
35	4375
36	4320
37	4255
38	4180
39	4095
40	4000

Here is the graph corresponding to the chart:

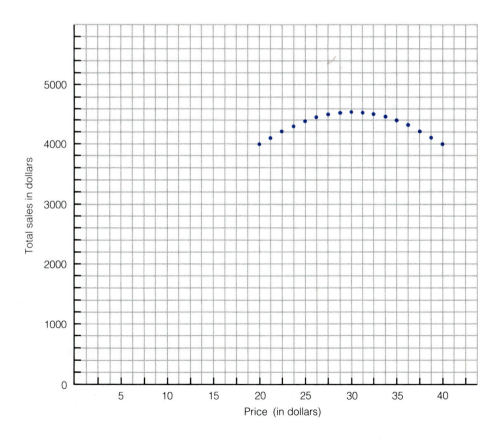

In this problem we want to know which price will achieve the highest total sales. From the graph, the price that does this appears to be $30. It's true that this conclusion can be reached from the chart itself, but the graph adds visual support.

14.2   TIPS ON DRAWING A GRAPH

For each of the foregoing charts the number in the left-hand column determines the other number in the same row in the right-hand column. The numbers in the left-hand column are called *inputs* and correspond to the points on the horizontal axis of the graph; those in the right-hand column are called *outputs* and correspond to points on the vertical axis of the graph.

NO. OF PANELS MANUFACTURED IN MONTH (INPUTS)	TOTAL COST TO COMPANY FOR THE MONTH (OUTPUTS)
0	$5000
1	5375
2	5750
3	6125
4	6500

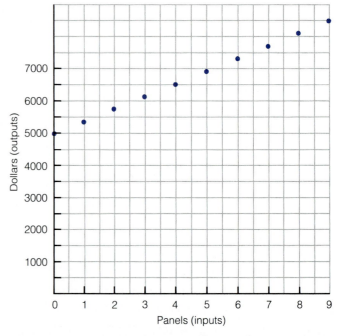

CHOOSING THE UNITS FOR HORIZONTAL AND VERTICAL AXES   Plotting the points corresponding to the rows of a chart is as easy as plotting points in a coordinate system. In fact, it is plotting points in a coordinate system, with one difference: In setting up a coordinate system, the numbers on the axes represented so many *units* of length, and the scale for both axes is therefore the same. For a graph the numbers on the horizontal axis represent so many of the input units (miles, pounds, years, etc.), and the numbers on the vertical axis represent so many of the output units, typically different from the input units. The scales for the two axes can be quite different. For a graph the difficulty comes in choosing the units for the two axes in such a way that you can plot all the points you need to on the piece of graph paper you happen to have.

The numbers in your chart are your first clues. For example, in the solar panel problem each output was in thousands of dollars (not ten thousands, but thousands). So it seemed reasonable to make $500 the unit. It also seemed reasonable to make a single panel the unit for an input. After having plotted the points using these units, we wanted to use the graph to find out how many panels could be manufactured in order to use up the target amount of $30,000. We needed a graph that would allow for an output of $30,000. Since the graph we had wouldn't do this, we redrew it, using $1000 as the unit for the vertical axis. From the "shape" of the graph (a straight line going off in a certain direction) we also got the impression that the input unit would have to be larger as well; so we made the new unit on the horizontal axis equal to 5.

In the case of the coffee blend problem the outputs are in the hundreds of dollars, so we chose the unit for the vertical axis to be $10. In the case of the best-price problem the largest output is $4500, and we chose the unit for the vertical axis to be $200.

Following is another example of a chart with rows the management of Computer Chip Manufacturing might want to plot.

NO. OF COMPUTER CHIPS MANUFACTURED (INPUTS)	COST OF MANUFACTURING EACH INDIVIDUAL CHIP (OUTPUTS)
1000	$1.00
2000	.80
3000	.50
4000	.20
5000	.10
6000	.05
7000	.02
8000	.01

In this case the inputs are in the thousands, and I choose the unit for the horizontal axis to be 250. The outputs range from $.01 to $1.00, so I choose the unit for the vertical axis to be $.05. These choices are dictated somewhat by the fact that the graph paper I am using is about 40 spaces high and 25 spaces wide. The graph is shown.

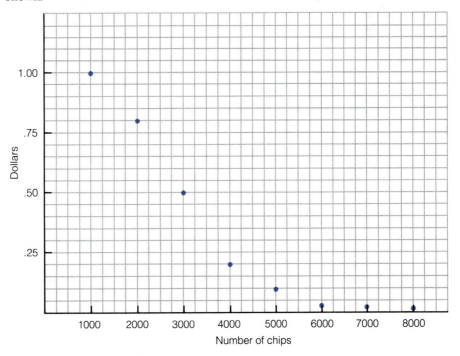

EXTENDING THE CHART AND PLOTTING MORE POINTS   In both the coffee blend and best-price problems we inserted rows in the charts that weren't in the original charts. We *extended* the old charts to make larger ones. Although this gave us more points to plot, more points gave us a greater opportunity to observe visual trends. In the case of the coffee blend problem we know that the number of pounds of Costa Rican in the blend can range from 0 to 50. Thus, the numbers on the horizontal axis will never be greater than 50 in any extension of the table, so we choose the horizontal unit accordingly.

STEPS USED IN GRAPHING   In the examples above, the steps used to create a graph from a chart are typical. Here is a summary of these steps along with some additional suggestions.

1. Be prepared to make several attempts at choosing good units for the axes. Have lots of graph paper on hand. Use a full sheet of graph paper for each try.

2. Try to figure out what the *range* of useful values for the inputs will be for the problem at hand. For the coffee blend problem the range of values is 0 to 50. You will not always know ahead of time what this range will be. You may have to make a guess and see what happens, then try again if your guess doesn't pan out.

3. Based on the range you have come up with, figure out the value of a unit on the horizontal axis. One way to do this is to think of the length of the side of a square on your graph paper as representing a unit; count the number of squares of the graph paper that occur along the horizontal axis; then divide this number into the largest of the range of values (in this chapter you can assume that the smallest value for an input is zero). Round this up to some nice, convenient number to obtain the value of your unit. For the coffee blend problem, the number of squares along the horizontal axis was 28. Dividing 50 (largest possible input) by 28 you get 1.79. Round this up to 2.5, a convenient quantity for the problem.

4. Do the same thing for the vertical axis that you did for the horizontal axis: Determine the *range* of useful values for the outputs (you may have to guess as before) and figure out a unit for the vertical axis.

5. Frequently, the table you wind up graphing is not the one you start with. You may find it useful to extend the original table and plot the additional points for greater visual effect.

EXERCISES   1. Draw a graph corresponding to each table.

(a)

MONTHLY RENT FOR EACH APARTMENT	NO. OF APARTMENTS RENTED (OUT OF POSSIBLE 200)
$300	200
350	190
400	180
450	170
500	160

(b)

PRICE PER POT	PROFIT FROM ALL POTS SOLD
$18	$960
19	990
20	1000
21	990
22	960
23	910

(c)

NO. OF POUNDS MOCHA IN BLEND (OUT OF POSSIBLE 50 LB)	COST OF BLEND PER POUND
10	$5.20
20	5.40
30	5.60
40	5.80
50	6.00

2. The firm of White & Riley manufactures high-quality notebook binders. The firm does a market study to find out what effect the selling price of the binder (minus production cost) has on total monthly sales. The study results in the following graph of monthly sales against the unit price of a binder. (Individually plotted points have been connected to make a "smooth" curve.)

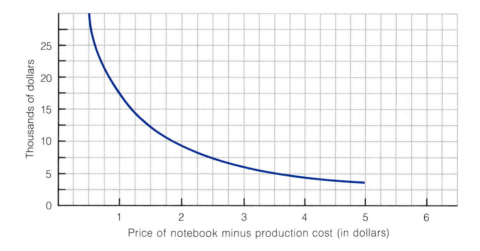

Thousands of dollars

Price of notebook minus production cost (in dollars)

The company must have monthly sales of $15,000 to make a reasonable profit. What must the range of the unit selling price for a binder be in order that the company make a profit?

3. Gasohol is a mixture of gasoline and alcohol that can be used instead of pure gasoline to run automobiles. It creates less pollution than pure gasoline. Gasoline now costs $1.10/gal and alcohol costs $1.75/gal. You operate an automobile service station and want to offer gasohol to your customers at a price you think the market will take: $1.25/gal. You decide to try selling 500 gal of such a mixture. The total price to the customers of the 500 gal would be (500)($1.25) = $625.00. To figure out how many gallons of gasoline and how many gallons of alcohol should go into the mixture, you make a chart and obtain the following graph that corresponds to it. Individually plotted points have been connected to make a smooth curve.

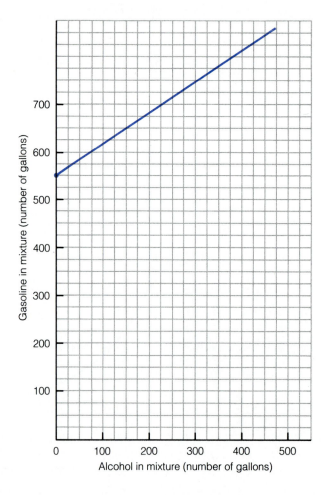

Use the graph to estimate the number of gallons of alcohol and of gasoline that should go into the mixture in order to achieve the target cost.

4. Here is a situation in which negative values on the horizontal and vertical axes will be needed for plotting a chart. The following chart shows the relationship between temperature and altitude at noon on a certain day and at a specific location on earth.

ALTITUDE (FEET)	TEMPERATURE (°C)
−1000	20
0	18
1000	16
2000	14
3000	12
4000	10
5000	8
6000	6
7000	4
8000	2
9000	0
10,000	−2
11,000	−4

Plot the graph corresponding to this chart.

14.3 STRAIGHT-LINE GRAPHS

When Do the Points from a Table All Lie on a Line?

For two of the graphs above, the plotted points all lie on a straight line. In each case this suggested that points not yet drawn—corresponding inputs not yet included in the table—would also lie on the same straight line. It would be nice to be able to predict when the points corresponding to all possible inputs lie on a straight line. For some clues about how we might be able to tell, let's look at a graph with all points lying on a straight line.

Consider the sequence of (equally spaced) values of the inputs along the horizontal axis. Suppose these numbers are 0, 1, 2, 3, ... As you move from 0 to 1 the output increases by a certain amount.

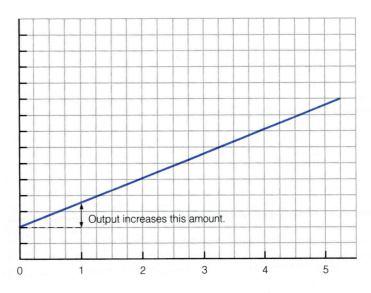

Output increases this amount.

Now move from 1 to 2 along the horizontal axis and see how much the output increases. It increases the same amount as it did before. The same thing happens as you move from any whole number to the next larger whole number: The increase in the output is the same as it was going from 0 to 1.

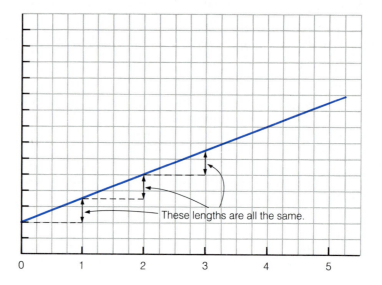

The output increases by the same amount whether you go from 3 to 4 or from 17 to 18. The same should be true when the input increases by any interval. For example, if the input goes from 3 to 7 (interval of 4), the output should increase the same as if the input went from 5 to 9 (interval of 4). In other words, the outputs increase *at a steady rate.*

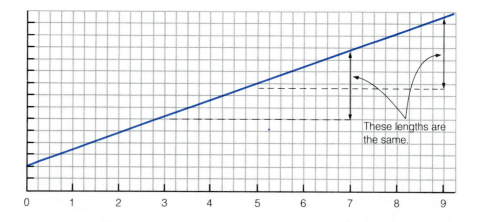

For the solar panel problem each increase of 1 panel increases the total cost by $375. (We knew that!) This increase is the same whether you go from 3 to 4 panels or from 17 to 18 panels. The total cost increases at a steady rate, and the graph corresponding to a table for the solar panel problem is a straight line.

For the coffee blend problem the line appears to be going in the other direction: The outputs decrease as the inputs increase. In fact, for each increase of 10 lb of Costa

Rican the total cost of the blend changes by the amount

$$10 \quad (\$4.50) \quad - 10 \quad (\$7) \quad = -\$25.$$

	Cost of		Cost of
	10 lb more		10 lb less
	Costa Rican		mocha

In other words, there is a steady decrease in the total cost as the number of pounds of Costa Rican increases. What we have discovered suggests a general rule.

TABLE WITH PLOTTED POINTS ALL LYING ON A STRAIGHT LINE

If the outputs increase (or decrease) at a steady rate, then the points of the graph all lie on a straight line. Conversely, if all the points of a graph lie on a straight line, then the outputs increase (or decrease) at a steady rate.

The explanations and descriptions we have given add plausibility to the rule. Although we have not given a rigorous proof of it, we will accept the rule as valid.

If all the points of a graph lie on a straight line, then we say that *the graph is a straight line*. There are several advantages to having a graph be a straight line. One is that it is easy to draw. Another is that once the straight line has been drawn, points corresponding to other inputs need not be plotted. A third advantage to a straight-line graph results from the fact that two points determine a line. To draw the graph corresponding to a table when you know the graph is a straight line, you plot just two points and then draw the unique line that joins them.

EXERCISES

5. Without actually drawing the graphs, determine which of the tables will yield a graph with all points lying on a straight line.

(a)

INPUT	OUTPUT
10	100
20	81
30	64
40	49
50	36

(b)

INPUT	OUTPUT
1	2
2	4
3	6
4	8
5	10

(c)

INPUT	OUTPUT
1	3
2	5
3	7
4	9
5	11

(d)

INPUT	OUTPUT
1	2
2	4
3	6
4	4
5	2

6. Assume that you know that the graph corresponding to each of the following tables is a straight line. Draw the graph for each table.

(a)

INPUT	OUTPUT
1	2
2	5
3	8
4	11
5	14

(b)

INPUT	OUTPUT
10	$5300
20	5600
30	5900
40	6200
50	6500

(c)

INPUT	OUTPUT
1000	$11,500
2000	11,000
3000	10,500
4000	10,000
5000	9,500

7. Guy Calvert owns a small fishing boat. Fishing for a day costs him $90 in wages, diesel oil, and incidental expenses. Any fish he catches he can sell for $1.30/lb. Make a table with one column the number of pounds of fish caught (the inputs) and the other column the amount of money he sells the fish for (the outputs). Draw a graph corresponding to this table and use it to figure out how much fish he should catch in order to break even.

8. Mr. and Mrs. Cheng have an 8-year-old daughter who, they assume, will go to college when she is 18. Anticipating that they will need $50,000 for her college expenses, they decide to invest some money now. They are considering an investment program that pays 7% interest compounded annually (check sec. 12.7 for a review of what this means). They want to know how much their initial investment should be in order that it be worth $50,000 in 10 yr. They decide to solve this by making some systematic guesses and organizing them in a chart. Here is the chart together with their first guess.

INITIAL INVESTMENT	VALUE OF INVESTMENT IN 10 YR
$4000	$(\$4000)(1.07)^{10} =$

Then they decided they would draw the graph corresponding to the chart. Show that the graph should be a straight line. Draw the graph and solve the problem for the Chengs.

9. You plan to retire in 20 yr. You are considering an investment program that offers 8.75% interest compounded annually. You want to know how much you should invest now in the program in order that the value of your investment be $100,000 at the time you retire. (*Hint:* See exercise 8.)

THE CAR RENTAL PROBLEM

Please try the problem yourself, first.

Northwest Manufacturing Company frequently has an out-of-town visitor who needs a car for getting around town. Northwest obtains a car for the visitor by making use of local rent-a-car agencies. However, the two agencies the company does business with have different rates. The Cheap Car Rental Company charges an initial $32.00 and then $.27/mi. Rent-a-Lemon, Inc., charges $28.00 and then $.30/mi. The company is trying to come up with a policy to decide when it would be cheaper to use one agency and when it would be cheaper to use the other. Help them solve this problem.

A Solution to the Car Rental Problem

Ms. Lopez, who is in charge of the study for the company, thinks: "Usually we know in advance roughly how many miles the car will be driven. If the car will not be driven very many miles, we should rent from Lemon. But if the car is going to be driven a lot, then we should rent from Cheap. But how much is a lot? And how much is a little? Where is the cutoff point? Let me make a table.

NO. OF MILES DRIVEN	COST OF RENTING FROM LEMON	COST OF RENTING FROM CHEAP
1	$28.30	$32.27
2	28.60	32.54
3	28.90	32.81
4	29.20	33.08

As the number of miles gets larger, the costs get bigger, but Rent-a-Lemon's cost is still less. Let me try some more numbers.

NO. OF MILES DRIVEN	COST OF RENTING FROM LEMON	COST OF RENTING FROM CHEAP
1	$28.30	$32.27
2	28.60	32.54
3	28.90	32.81
4	29.20	33.08
10	31.00	34.70
100	58.00	59.00
200	88.00	86.00

"It looks as if Cheap's cost becomes less than Lemon's somewhere between 100 and 200 miles. It seems to me there ought to be some way to *see* when Rent-a-Lemon gets to be more expensive than Cheap. Let me try graphing. I'll draw two graphs. The inputs for both will be the number of miles driven. The outputs for one will be Lemon's costs; for the other, Cheap's costs.

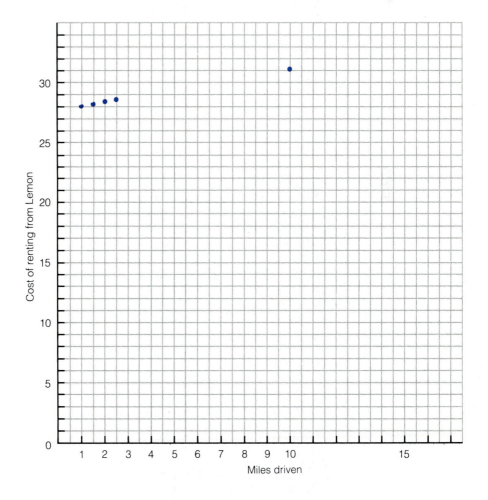

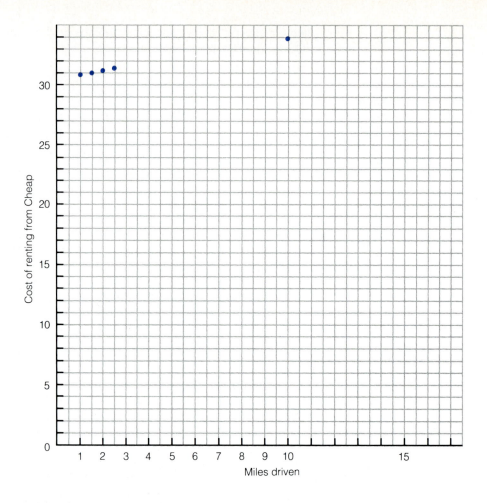

"It looks as if both graphs are straight lines. That makes sense because for each increase of a mile, Lemon's cost goes up $.30 and Cheap's goes up $.27. Both outputs grow at a steady rate. Since they are straight lines, all I have to do is plot two points for each graph—using inputs 10 and 100, say—and connect them with a straight line. For another thing, I think it would be easier to compare Cheap with Rent-a-Lemon if I graphed the two charts on the same coordinate system.

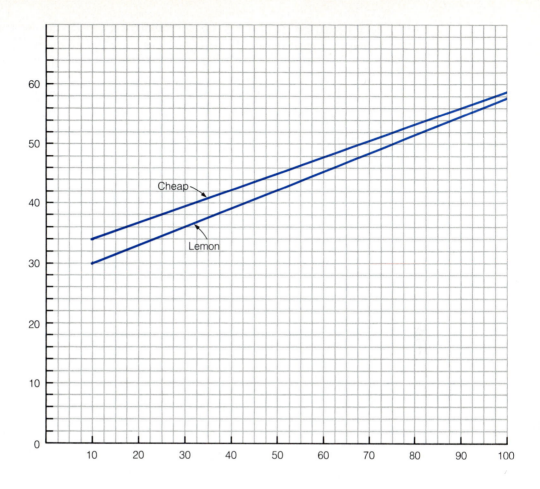

"It looks as if the two lines are getting closer together and will intersect if I extend them far enough. As the lines get closer together, the costs for the two rental agencies get closer as well. In fact, the point where the two lines meet should tell me the number of miles for which the costs are the same. Here is a sketch of what that would look like.

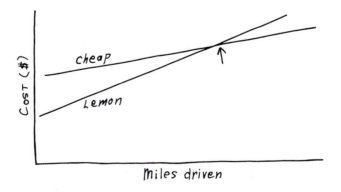

If I could get my picture to look like the sketch, I'd have my problem solved. Let me choose a new unit for the horizontal axis and redraw the graph.

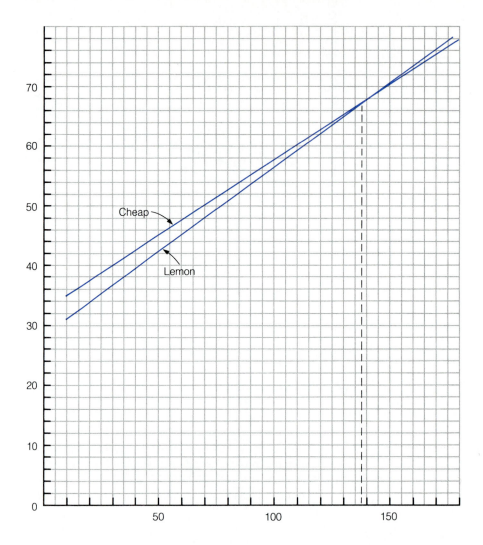

"The two lines appear to intersect at a point above the interval between 130 miles and 140 miles on the horizontal axis. We can check this with our costs.

NO. OF MILES DRIVEN	COST OF RENTING FROM LEMON	COST OF RENTING FROM CHEAP
130	$28 + ($.30)(130) = $67.00	$32 + ($.27)(130) = $67.10
131	$67.30	$67.37
132	$67.60	$67.64
133	$67.90	$67.91
134	$68.20	$68.18

At 133 miles, Lemon is cheaper by $.01 than Cheap. At 134 miles Cheap is cheaper by $.02 than Lemon. Since the graph is a straight line, Cheap will be cheaper than Lemon for any number of miles driven above 134 miles. By the same token, Lemon is the better deal when the number of miles driven is 133 or less. That solves our problem; we have a way to decide when to use Lemon and when to use Cheap."

EXERCISES

10. A well-known criminal was spotted at 8:10 leaving St. Mary's. She was traveling south on Route 18 and going 90 mph. Officer Levitz leaves Brookville, 30 mi south of St. Mary's, 5 min later and travels north on Route 18 in an attempt to intercept the criminal. He is traveling at 60 mph. Two graphs, one for the distance of the criminal (from St. Mary's) and one for the distance of the officer versus the time elapsed since 8:10, are plotted on the same coordinate system.

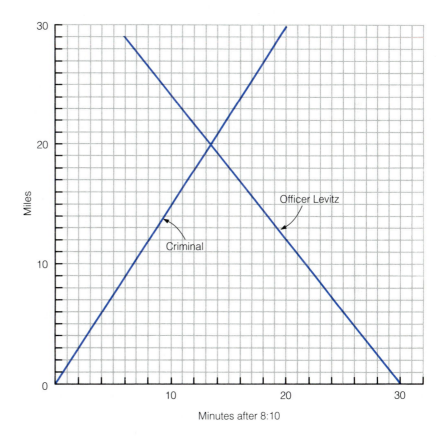

Minutes after 8:10

(Why are the two graphs straight lines?) Officer Levitz wants to know when he will be within 2 mi of the criminal's car in order to set up a road block. When will that be?

11. An employee from an outlet in a distant city pays a visit to Northwest Manufacturing. The company offers her a rental car for her stay in town. At the moment, funds for such purposes are low, and the company can allot her only $100 for the rented car. However, the company will allow her to choose the rental agency, either Cheap Car Rental Company or Rent-a-Lemon, Inc. With $100 how many miles can she travel using each agency? Which agency should she choose? (See the car rental problem and its solution for help in doing this exercise.)

12. A salesman's earnings depend on the volume of business he can do. He is offered a choice by his employer: a weekly wage of $250 plus a commission of 1% of the dollar value of his sales or $100 in wages plus a 2.3% commission. Make a table and graph of earnings versus dollar sales for each choice. Use these to help analyze which plan is better for him for various sales volumes.

13. A bank offers two checking account plans. For plan 1 the monthly charges are $3 plus .5% of the month's transactions. For plan 2 the charges are .6% of the month's transactions. Which plan is better for various total monthly transactions? (Draw graphs showing what the charges would be for various total monthly transactions.)

14. You are about to go into business renting cars and wish to set your rates so as to be cheaper than both Lemon and Cheap for all trips between 50 and 200 mi. What should your initial fee and mileage charge be?

14.4   EXTENDING THE IDEAS: GRAPHS FOR EXPONENTIAL GROWTH

Recall that the bacteria problem of chapter 12 was an instance of exponential growth. Here is a shorthand version of the table we obtained.

MINUTE	NO. OF BACTERIA PRESENT
1	1
2	2
3	2^2
4	2^3
5	2^4
6	2^5

To figure out how many bacteria will be around during a particular minute, you multiply 2 times the number of bacteria present during the previous minute. Here is the graph corresponding to this table.

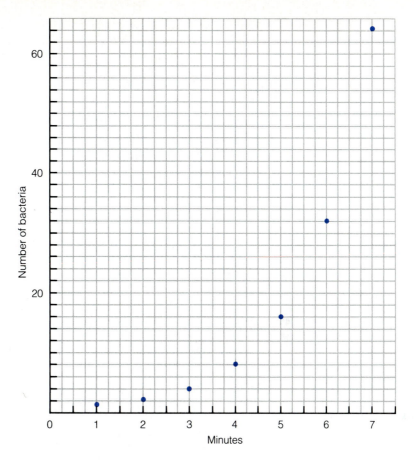

(In the bacteria problem, the number 2 is called the *fixed multiplier.*)

Let's look at charts and corresponding graphs for two more examples of exponential growth.

EXAMPLE 1. VALUE OF INVESTMENT   Fixed multiplier is 1.08. (See graph on page 576.)

YEAR	VALUE OF INVESTMENT AT BEGINNING OF YEAR
1	$1000
2	1000 (1.08)
3	1000 $(1.08)^2$
4	1000 $(1.08)^3$
5	1000 $(1.08)^4$

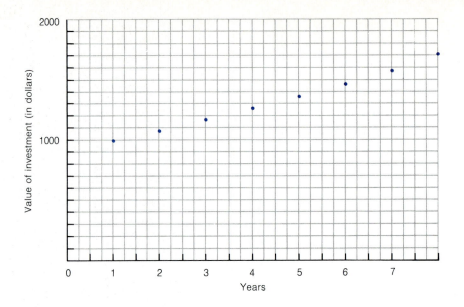

EXAMPLE 2. POPULATION DECLINE   Fixed multiplier is .85.

YEAR	POPULATION OF BLUE VALLEY
1950	20,000
1960	20,000 (.85)
1970	20,000 $(.85)^2$
1980	20,000 $(.85)^3$
1990	20,000 $(.85)^4$

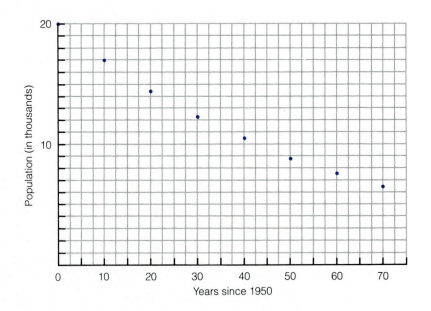

In general, when its points are connected by smooth curves, a graph for exponential growth has the shape of one of the following two graphs.

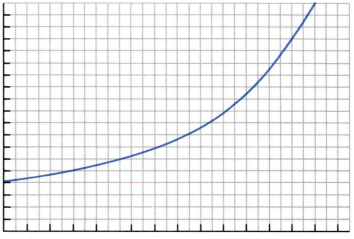

0   Graph for exponential growth when fixed multiplier is greater than 1

0   Graph for exponential growth when fixed multiplier is less than 1

The salary increase problem uses a graph for exponential growth.

THE SALARY INCREASE PROBLEM

Please try before reading on.

Sarah Bernstein has just been offered two jobs. Apart from the salaries, both jobs appear equally attractive. Her decision about which offer to accept will depend on which company offers her the best salary package. Company 1 offers a starting salary of $20,000 with a potential increase of $1000 at the beginning of each subsequent year on the job if her job performance is satisfactory. Company 2 offers a starting salary of $20,000 with a potential 4% increase in salary at the beginning of each year if job performance is satisfactory.

Sarah wants to know which salary package is best. Help her find out.

Sarah decides to make a table of what her salaries would be from the two companies.

YEAR ON THE JOB	SALARY FROM COMPANY 1 DURING THE YEAR	SALARY FROM COMPANY 2 DURING THE YEAR
1	$20,000.00	$20,000.00
2	21,000.00	20,800.00
3	22,000.00	21,632.00
4	23,000.00	22,497.28

"Let me draw the two graphs that go with this chart. Since the salary from company 1 increases by the same amount ($1000) each year, the points on the graph for company 1 should all lie on a straight line. Because both salaries start at $20,000, I won't need the part of the vertical axis between 0 and $20,000. I'll put ⋁⋀ to indicate the gap in the vertical axis. Here is the graph for company 1.

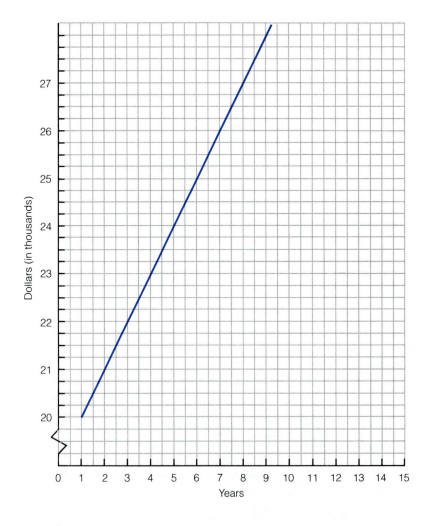

"For company 2 I know that the salary for year 2 is $20,800 = 20,000 (1.04)$ and that the salary for year 3 is $21,632 = 20,800 (1.04) = 20,000 (1.04)^2$. That's exponential growth with a fixed multiplier of 1.04. Such a graph for exponential growth curves upward. Perhaps the graphs for the two companies' salaries will look something like the following.

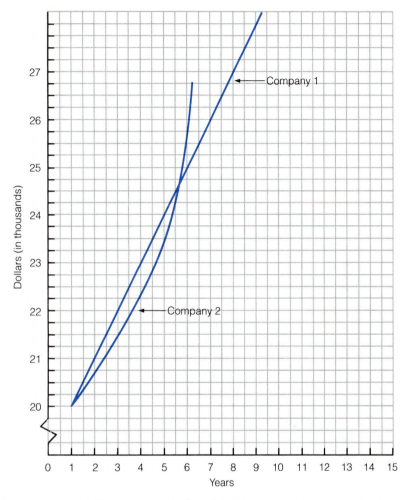

"Let me *use a calculator* to extend the table for company 2 to see what happens.

YEAR ON THE JOB (INPUTS)	SALARY FROM COMPANY 2 (OUTPUTS)
1	$20,000.00
2	20,800.00
3	21,632.00
4	22,497.28
5	23,397.17
6	24,333.06
7	25,306.38
8	26,318.64
9	27,371.38
10	28,466.24
11	29,604.89
12	30,789.08
13	32,020.64
14	33,301.47

Here are the corresponding points plotted on graph paper.

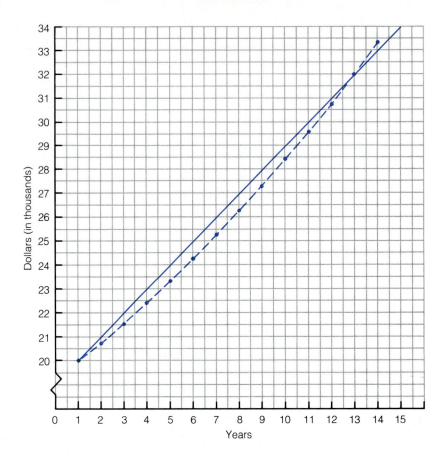

"I was right. In 13 years company 2's salary will surpass company 1's salary—and because it's an example of exponential growth, company 2's salary will continue to surpass company 1's for all the years after 13."

EXERCISES 15. At the last moment a third company offers Sarah a starting salary of $18,000 with a 6% increase in salary at the beginning of each year. Make a table giving the salaries Sarah would earn from this company for the first 14 yr. Draw the graph corresponding to this table. Compare the salaries from this company with those offered by company 1 and company 2.

16. The annual rate of inflation in 1989 was 3%. That means that items costing $100 at the beginning of 1989 cost $100 + .03 × $100 = $100 × (1.03) = $103 on January 1, 1990. Assuming that this inflation rate continues through 1999, draw the graph showing how much these same items would cost on each January 1 through the year 2000.

17. Use the solution to the salary increase problem to discuss which job Sarah should take.

14.5   LOOKING BACK: FUNCTIONS

In this chapter as well as in other parts of the book we have encountered charts such as the one shown.

NO. OF MILES DRIVEN	COST OF RENTING FROM LEMON
1	$28.30
2	28.60
3	28.90
4	29.20

There are two columns to this chart, and the numbers in the second column are related to the numbers in the first column. It is understood that we can extend this chart by placing a whole number *n* in the left-hand column and, in the right-hand column and in the same row, the cost of renting a car from Lemon and driving it for *n* mi. We called the possible numbers in the left-hand column the *inputs* and those in the right-hand column the *outputs*. We also know that there is a *rule* that tells us what the number in the right-hand column should be given the number in the left-hand column. This rule is called a *function*.

One can think of a function as a machine into which one places an input. After turning a crank, the machine produces an output. The machine is consistent: Each time you place the same input in the machine, it produces the same output.

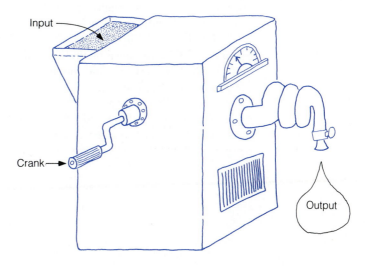

One can then make a chart with inputs in the left column and corresponding outputs in the right column. We've done this for the Lemon rental cost function.

LEMON RENTAL COST FUNCTION	
INPUT: NO. OF MILES DRIVEN	OUTPUT: COST OF RENTING FROM LEMON
1	$28.30
2	28.60
3	28.90
4	29.20

The corresponding function machine can be described "Input certain number of miles; turn crank; output the Lemon rental costs."

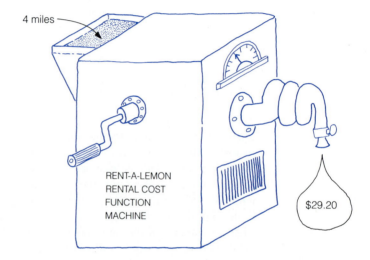

4 miles

RENT-A-LEMON
RENTAL COST
FUNCTION
MACHINE

$29.20

In the language of functions, one says, "The cost of renting a car from Lemon is a function of the number of miles the car is driven." One also says, "Lemon rental cost function expresses the relationship between the number of miles the car is driven and the cost of renting the car."

The set of possible inputs is called the *domain* of the function. The set of possible outputs is called the *range* of the function. The domain of the Lemon rental cost function is the set of all nonnegative numbers. The range is the set {28.30,28.60,28.90,29.20, . . .}.

Consider another example of a function. You are putting together 50 lb of coffee made of a blend of mocha and Colombian. Mocha costs $6.00/lb, and Colombian costs $5.00/lb. You are interested in the function that tells you the cost of the blend per pound given the total number of pounds of mocha in the blend.

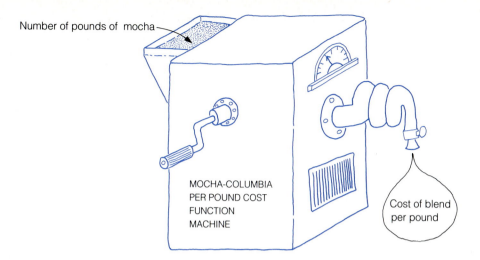

Number of pounds of mocha

MOCHA-COLUMBIA
PER POUND COST
FUNCTION
MACHINE

Cost of blend per pound

The chart associated with this function:

MOCHA IN BLEND (POUNDS)	COST OF A POUND OF BLEND
0	$5.00
10	5.20
20	5.40
30	5.60
40	5.80
50	6.00

shows you that the domain for this function is the set of all numbers between 0 and 50 inclusive.

Describing Functions

Functions have appeared many times in this book. Almost every time we have used a chart, a function was standing behind it. The four ways we are using in this text to describe a particular function are: verbally, using a chart, using a graph, and using a formula.

VERBAL DESCRIPTION One way to describe a function is *verbally*. The function above tells me "the cost of a pound of blend given the number of pounds of mocha in the blend."

USING A CHART Another way to describe a function is by using a *chart*. A chart can be an incomplete description of a function in that it normally includes only a few of the many possible input values. You may notice a pattern to the outputs in the chart that *suggests* output values associated with inputs not in the chart. However, the pattern you notice may not persist.

USING A GRAPH A third way to describe a function is by a *graph*. In this chapter we first constructed a chart for the function and from that the graph of the function. In many of our examples the graph seemed to incorporate more inputs than the table did by *extrapolation*, by guessing what the shape of the remainder of the graph would be based on the points gotten by plotting those from the table. For example, the graph corresponding to the chart on cost of blend per pound looks as shown on page 584.

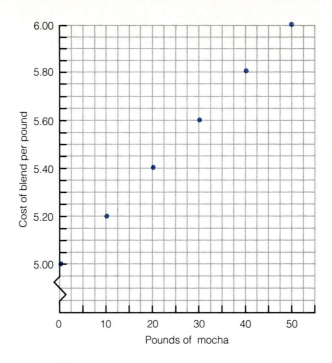

On the basis of these few plotted points we might extrapolate the following, more complete graph of the function.

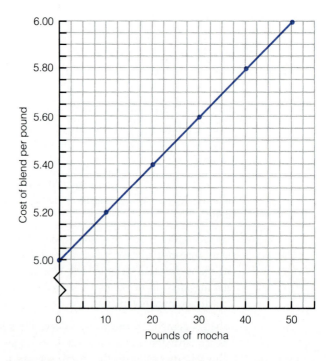

Just as a table for a function can be incomplete—in the sense that more inputs could be listed than are given—so also can a graph be incomplete. Sometimes we are sloppy in calling an incomplete graph the "graph of the function." This informal language is common.

In another instance, we added more points that were meant to help us see rather than to add more to the graph. We drew a line connecting the plotted points of the graph of the Lemon rental cost function.

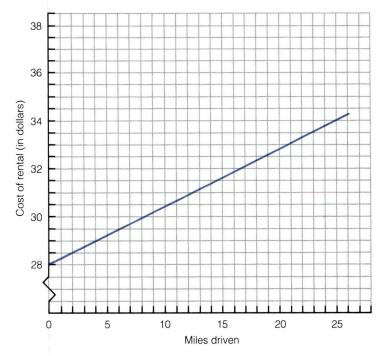

This suggests that 23.78 mi would be a possible input to the function and that driving the rent-a-car 23.78 mi would result in a cost somewhere between the 23-mi cost and the 24-mi cost. In reality, the company likely rounds 23.78 *up* to 24 mi, the next whole number bigger than the number, so that the graph should look like this if fractional inputs are allowed.

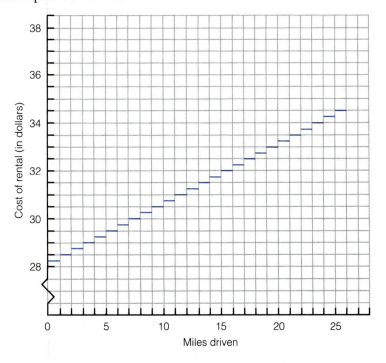

Alternatively, one could limit the inputs to whole numbers so that the graph would look like the one shown next. (The points of the dotted line are not points of the graph. The line is drawn to show that the points of the graph all lie on the line.)

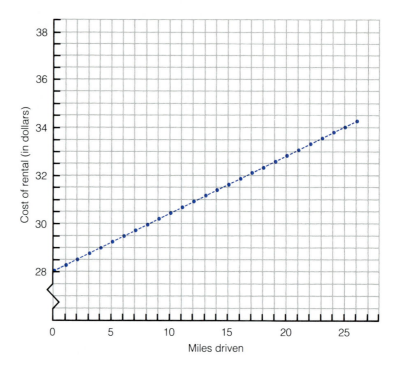

USING A FORMULA   A fourth way to describe a function is by a *formula*. For example, we know that to figure the cost of renting a car from Lemon, you multiply the number of miles driven (rounded up to the nearest whole mile) by $ .30 and add this to $28.00. Thus, if M is the number of miles (rounded up), the cost is $.30M + 28$. If $S(M)$ is the rental cost, then we have the formula

$$S(M) = .3M + 28.$$

Describing a function by a formula involves assigning one letter to represent a typical input, then producing an expression containing the letter to yield the corresponding output. The letter representing a typical input is called the *independent variable.* If M is the *independent variable,* then the output for input M is represented by $S(M)$, the *dependent variable.* The notation $S(M)$ for the dependent variable is suggestive: $S(M)$ *depends on* M. The notation $S(M)$ does not mean "S times M"; it is shorthand for "the cost of renting a car that has been driven M miles." The expression $S(M)$ is read "the function S of M."

Let's find a formula for the cost (in dollars) per pound of the mocha-Colombian coffee blend. To do this, we first let P stand for the number of pounds of mocha in the blend. Next we must figure out the cost of a pound of the blend with P pounds of mocha in it. *A simpler problem* is to figure out the cost of all 50 lb of the blend. The blend has P pounds of mocha at \$6.00/lb and $50 - P$ lb of Colombian at \$5.00/lb. So we have

$$\text{Cost (in dollars) of 50 lb of blend} = 6P + 5(50 - P)$$
$$= 6P + 250 - 5P \text{ (Distributive law)}$$
$$= (6 - 5)P + 250 \text{ (Distributive law)}$$
$$= P + 250.$$

The cost of 1 lb of this blend is this last expression divided by 50.

$$\text{Cost of blend per pound} = \frac{P + 250}{50}.$$

Thus if $C(P)$ denotes the per pound cost of a blend with P pounds of mocha in it, then we have the formula

$$C(P) = \frac{P + 250}{50}.$$

EXERCISES

18. Find a formula for the cost of renting a car from Cheap Car Rental in terms of (i.e., as a function of) the number of miles the car is driven.

19. In the solar panel problem, the Southwest Sun Company makes solar collectors. Find a formula for the function relating the total cost to the company for the month with the number of panels manufactured during the month.

14.6 LOOKING AHEAD: FORMULAS FOR STRAIGHT-LINE AND EXPONENTIAL GROWTH

The formula for Lemon rental costs is $S(M) = .3M + 28$. If you drive the car M mi, then your cost is $.3M + 28$. If you drive 1 mi more, then you will have driven $M + 1$ mi and your cost will be $S(M + 1) = .3(M + 1) + 28 = .3M + .3 + 28$—\$ .30 more than the cost for driving M mi. For each increase in the value of M by 1 the value of $S(M)$ increases by \$ .30. This is what makes the graph of Lemon rental costs a straight line.

The formula for the cost of the mocha-Colombian blend per pound is

$$C(P) = \frac{P + 250}{50} = \frac{P}{50} + \frac{250}{50} = .02P + 5.$$

If the blend has P pounds of mocha, then its cost per pound is $.02P + 5$. If the blend has 1 lb more of mocha, or $P + 1$ lb, then the cost of the blend will be $C(P + 1) = .02(P + 1) + 5 = .02P + .02 + 5/\text{lb}$—$.02$ more than the cost when the blend has P pounds of mocha. For each increase in the value of P by 1 the value of $C(P)$ increases by $.2$ (or $\$.20$). This means that the graph of the cost per blend function is a straight line. We call this a *straight-line* function.

We already know that the graph of the Lemon rental costs is a straight line. Its formula is $S(M) = .3M + 28$. The formula for the cost of mocha-Colombian blend is $C(P) = .02P + 5$. Both formulas are of the *form*

$$F(X) = mX + b$$

where X is the independent variable and m and b are fixed numbers. If $F(X) = mX + b$ is the formula for a function, then each time X is increased by 1, $F(X)$ increases by m. The graph of $F(X)$ is a straight line.

FORMULA FOR A STRAIGHT-LINE FUNCTION

A straight-line function has a formula of the form

$$F(X) = mX + b$$

where X is the independent variable and m and b are fixed numbers.

In the salary increase problem, Sarah's salary from company 2 in the Yth year on the job is

$$S(Y) = 20{,}000(1.04)^Y.$$

In the bacteria problem, after M min have passed, the number of bacteria present is

$$N(M) = 2^M.$$

Both of these are examples of *exponential-growth functions.*

FORMULA FOR EXPONENTIAL-GROWTH FUNCTIONS

An exponential-growth function has a formula of the form

$$F(T) = cd^T$$

where T is the independent variable and c and d are fixed numbers.

In case the formula for exponential growth is $F(T) = cd^T$, each time T is increased by 1 the value of $F(T)$ is *multiplied* by d. The number d is the fixed multiplier.

20. You invest $5500 in an account that yields 7.5% interest compounded annually. Find a formula for the value of your investment after Y years.

21. Find a formula for the function giving the number of beta rays emitted by 1 g of carbon-14/hr at the end of H half-lives. Draw the graph of this function. (Include values of H through 10.)

14.7 LOOKING AHEAD: MOTION ALONG A STRAIGHT LINE AND QUALITATIVE GRAPHING

When a spaceship is sent aloft, it is important to be able to predict its position and speed for a given instance in time. The motion of a spaceship is complicated, but we can consider a simpler kind of motion, motion along a straight line. For example, a ball is thrown straight up into the air, an object is dropped from the top of a tall building, a piston moves back and forth, an elevator moves up and down.

For each of these situations there are questions we might like to answer. For the ball thrown into the air, we might like to know the answer to the questions, How far up will the ball go? How fast will it be going when it hits the ground? For the object thrown from the building, How long will it take for it to hit the ground? For the piston, How long will it take for the piston to go back and forth just once?

Think of other situations where an object travels approximately along a straight-line path, a car on the road or an airplane en route between two cities, for example. To see how one might describe the motion of an object along a straight line, take a trip yourself. "Draw" a line somewhere—through your backyard, along a sidewalk, across a room. Fix a reference point on the line (at the edge of the backyard, at a point on the wall of the room, say) and take a trip on your line. Do a variety of things during your trip: Start, stop, turn around, speed up, slow down, stand still, and so on.

How might you describe your trip completely, in full detail?
A good description should provide, among other points of information,

- How fast you were going (at any time)
- At what times you turned around
- How long your trip took
- How far you are from the reference point (at any time)
- The farthest you got from the reference point (and when)

There is a method for creating a description. Set up a coordinate system (see the accompanying figure). The numbers along the horizontal axis represent the time (in seconds) elapsed during your trip. The point 0 represents the time at which you start your trip. The numbers along the vertical axis represent the possible positions (in feet) along the line measured from the reference point. The point 0 represents the reference point. For each instant t in time during your trip, you plot the point (t,d) where d is the distance you are from the reference point at that time.

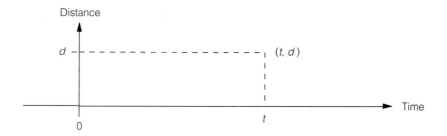

Using this scheme, you might come up with a picture such as shown.

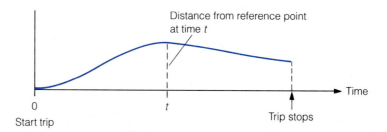

(For the moment we do not assume that this is an *exact* picture of a trip, that all the times and distances are given exactly. We assume that it is a good *qualitative* picture of the trip, that it captures many of the features of the trip. If you are trying this for yourself, you should not try to be too precise.)

Some important features of these trip pictures are marked on the next pictures.

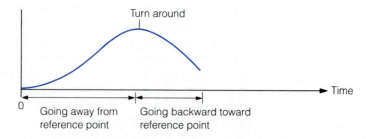

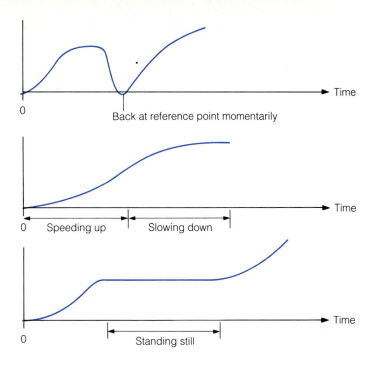

Back at reference point momentarily

Speeding up   Slowing down

Standing still

EXERCISES

22. Here is a picture of a trip.

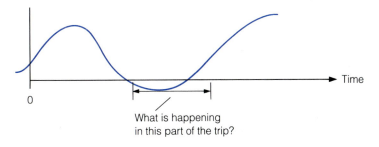

What is happening
in this part of the trip?

23. Here is a picture of a trip.

Describe what is happening here.

10

0

24. Here is a picture of a trip.

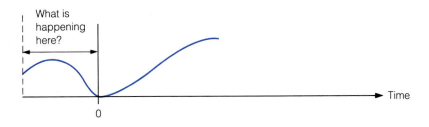

What is
happening
here?

0

25. Is the following a picture of a possible trip? Why or why not?

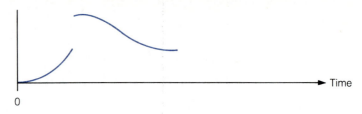

Comparing Trips

You can use pictures to compare two trips. Here is a picture of John's trip, for example.

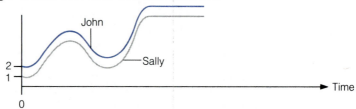

Sally's trip is just like John's except that she is always 1 ft behind him. (They might be doing a routine with straw hats and canes . . .)

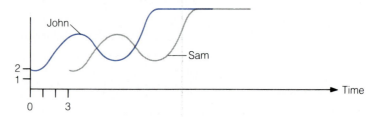

Sam's trip is also like John's except that he starts out 3 sec after John does.

EXERCISES   **26.** Here is a picture of Marco's trip along a straight line.

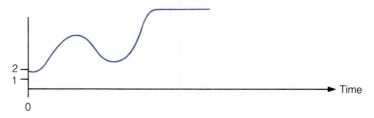

Label the points on the picture that represent instances where

Marco stops
Marco is at the reference point
Marco turns around
Marco is walking back toward the reference point
Marco is farthest from the reference point

27. Using the picture for Marco's trip in exercise 26, draw trip pictures for

Bert, who is always exactly 3 ft behind Marco
Joan, whose trip is the same as Marco's but she starts 5 sec later
Ellena, whose trip is the same as Marco's but she starts 4 sec earlier

Even though we have not set up a table of inputs and outputs, a trip picture is really the graph of a function. A typical input is a time t of seconds elapsed during the trip; the corresponding output is the distance d from the reference point at time t.

14.8   CALCULATORS AND COMPUTERS: GRAPHING

If you want to obtain a graph for a function and you have a formula for the function, then you may want to use a calculator with graphics capabilities. Consult the calculator's manual for instructions on how to use its graphics features.

A second way to take advantage of technological advances in helping you to graph is to use one of the graphing software packages available for a microcomputer. Some of these are commercially available (for example, Eureka and the IBM Mathematics Exploration Tool Kit) and some are in the public domain (for example, Gnuplot).

A third way is to use a microcomputer spreadsheet with graphing capabilities (for example, AS-EASY-AS). An activity in which such a spreadsheet is used to create graphs appears in the Lab Manual designed to accompany this text.

14.9   SUMMARY OF IMPORTANT IDEAS AND TECHNIQUES

■ The use of graphing for visualizing numbers in a chart and for solving problems
Inputs and outputs related to them
Constructing a graph; determining the scales on the two axes

■ The definition of function
Function machine
The domain of a function, the set of possible values for the inputs; the range of a function, the set of possible values for the outputs
Describing a function using a chart, a graph, and a formula

■ Straight-line and exponential-growth functions and formulas

■ Qualitative graphing

PROBLEM SET

1. Draw a graph corresponding to each table.

(a)
NO. OF POUNDS	TOTAL PRICE PAID
5	$ 2.50
8	4.00
11	5.50
14	7.00
17	8.50
20	$10.00

(b)
NO. OF GALLONS OF GAS USED	MILES DRIVEN
5	85.0
10	200.0
25	550.0
40	920.0
55	1237.5
75	1725.0

(c)
NO. OF HOURS WORKED	MONEY EARNED
5	$ 26.25
8	42.00
12	63.84
20	110.0
25	138.75

(d)
NO. OF FEET OF PAPER	TOTAL COST
3	$3.30
8	3.80
12	4.20
15	4.50
20	5.00

2. Of the graphs in problem 1, which ones have the property that all its points lie on a straight line?

3. A store is buying giftwrap for its customer courtesy gift-wrapping service. It can buy paper from manufacturer A at $10 delivery cost plus $ .25/ft ordered. Company B charges $12 to deliver but only $ .22/ft. How many feet of paper would the store have to use in order to make company B the better paper supplier? Solve this by making tables and graphs as in the solution to the car rental problem.

4. Do the points on either graph in problem 3 lie on a straight line?

5. Without drawing the graphs determine which of the following tables will yield graphs with all points lying on a straight line.

(a)
INPUT	OUTPUT
1	35
2	70
3	105
4	140
5	175

(b)
INPUT	OUTPUT
12	22
14	25
16	28
18	31
20	34

(c)
INPUT	OUTPUT
3	7
5	10
7	14
9	19
11	24

(d)
INPUT	OUTPUT
5	2
7	3
9	5
11	8
13	13

6. For each table in problem 5 with plotted points lying on a straight line, construct the corresponding graph.

7. You must choose between two job offers. Company A offers a beginning salary of $23,000 with a 6% yearly increase, while company B offers a starting salary of $25,000 with a yearly 5.5% increase. For each offer, make a table showing the salary for several different years on the job and draw the corresponding graph. Will company A's salary eventually be higher than company B's salary? If so, after how long?

8. You plan to buy a home in 10 yr and will need a down payment of $35,000. You are considering investing in a plan that offers 10% interest compounded annually. How much money will you need to invest?

9. For each company in problem 3 above, find a formula for the function relating the total cost of the paper to the number of feet used.

10. The rate of inflation for real estate in a certain large metropolitan area is 8%/yr. Your home in the area is now worth $50,000. Find a formula for the function relating the value of this home to the number of years Y into the future.

11. A bacteria population of 1500 grows at a rate of 3%/hr. Find a formula for the function relating population of bacteria to the number H of hours from now.

12. Draw the graph corresponding to each chart.

(a)

LENGTH	AREA OF SIDE
2	4
3	9
5	25
8	64

(b)

AVERAGE TEMP. OF MONTH	HEATING AND AIR-CONDITIONING BILL
85°	$ 75
75°	50
70	35
65°	75
50°	100
30°	120

(c)

INPUT	OUTPUT
3	−5
2	0
1	3
0	4
−1	3
−2	0
−3	−5

(d)

INPUT	OUTPUT
−2	6
−1	3
0	2
1	3
2	6

13. From the trip picture describe what is happening in the interval of time between each pair of consecutive letters.

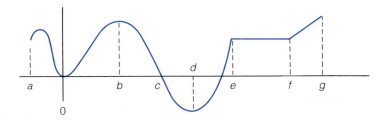

14.　Below is a picture of Dale's trip.

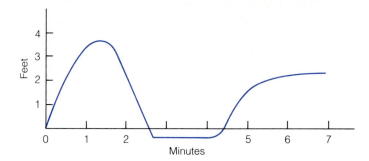

Draw trip pictures for Jean, Bob, and Sandra.
(a)　Jean who is 2 ft behind Dale but otherwise does the same thing
(b)　Bob who takes the same trip as Dale but starts 3 min before Dale does
(c)　Sandra who takes the same trip as Bob but starts 2 min after Bob does

USING IDEAS　*For each problem that remains, write your solution in the form of an essay communicating clearly and completely the steps you took. Mention other problems or solutions that gave you ideas and the strategies you used.*

15.　You are investing $1000 in bonds that will pay interest of 9%/yr. Draw a graph of the function giving the value of your investment for several years after the initial investment. Use this to figure out when you will double your money. (This is a particularly good problem with which to use a graphics calculator or graphics software on a microcomputer.)

16.　A saleswoman's earnings depend on the volume of business she can accomplish. She is offered a choice by her employer: a weekly wage of $250 plus a commission of 1% of the dollar value of her sales, or $100 in wages plus a 2.3% commission. For each choice, make a table relating her earnings (output) to her total sales (input). Next, construct the graph corresponding to one of the choices; then, on the same paper and with the same axes, construct the graph corresponding to the other. Each graph should be a straight line. (Why?) Use these graphs to discuss the desirability of one plan over the other.

17.　A vacation in England costs $920 for round-trip air fare and $85 for each day you stay there. Construct the graph relating the total cost of the trip (output) to the number of days you stay (input). (Why should the graph be a straight line?) Use the graph to answer the questions.
(a)　How much will a 2-wk vacation cost?
(b)　If you have $2100 to spend, how long can your vacation in England be?

18.　A jet airplane uses a fixed quantity of kerosene for a combined takeoff and landing and, when in the air, a certain quantity per mile. If you were to graph the kerosene consumption (output) of the airplane for a trip versus the length of the trip (input) in miles, the graph should be a straight line. Why? Use this and the following information to construct the graph: A 400-mi trip requires 1455 gal and a 260-mi trip uses 1077 gal. Use the graph to answer the questions.
(a)　How much fuel is used for the combined takeoff and landing?
(b)　How much fuel will be needed for a 1230-mi trip?

19.　The profit a movie theater makes in a week depends on the number of customers. Why is it reasonable to assume that the graph of a week's profits versus the number of customers is a straight line? In a week when there are 1372 customers the profit is $1790; when there are 1115 customers, there is a profit of $1310. Use this information plus the fact that the graph is a straight line to construct the graph of the week's profit versus the number of customers. Then use the graph to answer the questions.

(a) Estimate the profit in a week with 2000 customers.

(b) Find the break-even point, that is, the number of customers the theater needs in order to begin making a profit.

20. You are an investment broker. A customer has requested that you invest her $130,000 in a combination of high-risk securities that pay 15.4% annually and low-risk securities that pay 9.1%. The customer requests that the investment yield an annual income of $14,000. You want to know how the money should be invested in order to obtain this income and to do so at minimum risk. To solve the problem, start by continuing the table.

AMOUNT INVESTED AT 15.4%	AMOUNT INVESTED AT 9.1%	YIELD FROM COMBINATION
$10,000	$120,000	$12,460

Then graph the yield versus the amount invested at 15.4%. The points of the graph should lie on a straight line. Why?

21. Dutch tulip bulbs cost $52.50 per 100, domestic bulbs, only $38.00 per 100. The director of the Public Garden needs 1600 bulbs for fall planting and has budgeted $700 for their purchase. She wishes to buy as many of the better Dutch bulbs as possible. She wants to know how many of each kind she should order. She makes a table.

NO. OF DUTCH BULBS	NO. OF DOMESTIC BULBS	TOTAL COST
100	1500	$622.50
200	1400	637.00

She continues to fill in the values in the left-hand column in increments of 100 and then figures out the corresponding quantities in the other two columns of the table. (Do this yourself.) After a while she observes, "If I graph total cost versus the number of Dutch bulbs, I should get a straight line." (Why does she say this?) Construct the graph yourself and use it to solve her problem.

22. A 12% alcohol solution is mixed with a 36% alcohol solution to produce 30 gal of a new solution. Here is the beginning of a table showing the amount of alcohol in various solutions.

NO. GALLONS OF 12% SOLUTION	NO. GALLONS OF 36% SOLUTION	GALLONS ALCOHOL IN MIXTURE
5	25	$.12 \times 5 + .36 \times 25 = 9.6$
10	20	$.12 \times 10 + .36 \times 20 = 8.4$

Fill in two more rows of the table, in which the number of gallons of 12% solution increases by an increment of 5 gal from one row to the next.

Notice in your table that the number of gallons of alcohol in the mixture *decreases* by 1.2 gal from one row to the next. Why should this be? The graph of the number of gallons of alcohol in the mixture versus the number of gallons of 12% solution in the mixture should be a straight line. Why is this? Draw this graph and use it to figure out how much 12% solution and how much 36% solution should be mixed in order to have 30 gal of solution consisting of 22% alcohol.

23. The Johnson Company has need for 12,000 units of product X each year. The company can order all these items once a year. However, since the use of product X is spread throughout the year, the cost of keeping a year's supply of product X in stock is expensive. One way to keep this cost (called *carrying cost*) down is to order smaller amounts of product X more often. Since the process of ordering itself has a fixed cost, ordering smaller amounts *too* often is also expensive. Inventory costs for product X for the year are equal to the sum of the carrying costs for the year plus ordering costs for the year. The company wants to know how many times a year it should order product X to minimize this inventory cost. A graph of inventory cost versus number of orders for product X per year is shown. (Individually plotted points have been connected with a smooth curve.) Use this graph to carry out the tasks.

(a) If the company makes two orders per year, find out what the inventory costs will be.

(b) Figure out how many orders of product X the company should make each year in order to minimize the inventory costs for product X.

24. Here are descriptions of possible graphs:

(a) a graph of the average daily temperature in Boston versus the day of the year, for a whole year

(b) a graph of the number of cookies in a cookie jar versus the length of time since the cookies left the oven

(c) a graph of the cost (in dollars per mile) of driving a car versus the age of the car

(d) a graph of the price of heating oil versus the amount of heating oil you buy

(e) a graph of the value of a house versus the age of the house

Six graphs are shown below. The labels for the axes are missing; individually plotted points have been connected with a smooth curve. Match each description above with a graph below. Label the axes for inputs and outputs with their units and, where possible, put reasonable scales on the axes.*

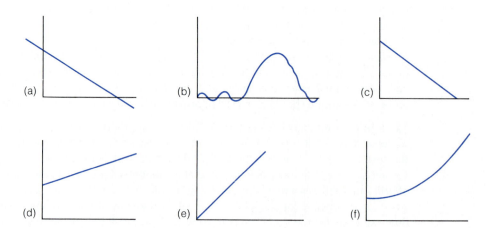

___

* Adapted from Ethan D. Bolker, *Using Algebra*, Little, Brown, Boston, 1983, prob. 6, p. 85, and fig. 7.1, p. 86.

25. An express train leaves New York at 3:00 P.M. and arrives in Boston at 6:00 P.M. In the same afternoon a slow train leaves Boston at 1:00 P.M. and arrives in New York at 6:00 P.M. The engineers of the two trains need to know within a minute when the two trains will be passing. Each train travels at the same speed at all times. Help them find out by graphing. First graph the distance the express train is from New York versus the time it has been traveling. This graph should be a straight line. (Why?) On the same paper, using the same horizontal and vertical axes, graph the distance of the slow train from New York versus time that has passed after 3:00 P.M. This second graph should be a straight line, too. (Why?)

26. After a business meeting in Los Angeles John unwittingly drives off to San Francisco with Sarah's briefcase. Discovering this 15 min later, Sarah leaves in her own car to pursue John. Sarah knows that John is not a fast driver. (In fact, he averages 50 mph.) Sarah, wanting to catch John as soon as possible but not wanting to speed too much, drives at 65 mph. Use graphing to figure out when she will intercept John.

27. A bacteria population decreases from 2500 to 2200 in 1 hr. Assuming that the population continues to decrease at this rate, what is the half-life of this population? (*Hint:* Try graphing, especially with a graphics calculator or software.)

28. Below is shown the graph of the population of Central City versus the year. (Individually plotted points have been connected with a smooth curve.)

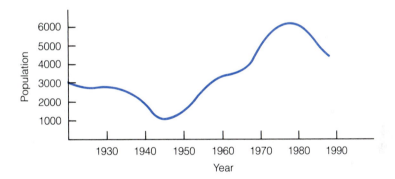

Use the graph to estimate the quantities.
(a) the population in 1960
(b) the year(s) when the population was 5000
(c) the year when the population was a minimum (What was the population during that year?)
(d) the year when the population was a maximum (What was the population during that year?)
(e) the change in the population from 1960 to 1970
(f) the change in the population from 1980 to 1990

29. Recall the following program in BASIC from chapters 5 and 12 that adds 87 to itself repeatedly 74 times. (It is a simulation of the multiplication 74 × 87.)

```
5 LET S = 0      Initialize sum.
10 FOR I = 1 TO 74
20 LET S = S+87
30 PRINT S
40 NEXT I
100 END
```

With a few alterations, we can get the program to compute the costs for the Lemon car rental agency.

```
5 LET S = 28
10 FOR I = 1 TO 150
20 LET S = S+.30
30 PRINT I, S
40 NEXT I
100 END
```

Think of the initial value of S as the initial charge for Lemon ($S = \$28$); in the loop think of I as the number of miles driven and S as the total cost of renting a car that has been driven I miles. Type this program into your computer, run it, and see what happens.

Revise this last program so that it will simultaneously compute the total cost T of renting a car from Cheap that has been driven I miles. When the program runs, you want it to print out I, S, and T in parallel columns. You will have to initialize T.

Use this program and its printout to give an alternate solution to the car rental problem. Compare the methods used in the two solutions.

MEASURING LENGTH INDIRECTLY

CHAPTER 15

It is impractical to measure directly the height of a mountain or the distance across a lake, yet it is often important to have such measurements. Throughout history techniques have been developed for gaining them indirectly. Some of these techniques rely on scale drawings made of triangles in clever ways and are based on the relationship of a scale drawing to the original formation.

In this chapter we will explore this relationship using the concepts of scale drawing, parallel lines, the angles and vertices of a triangle, and the congruence of two angles as discussed in chapter 14. We will also use ratios as developed in chapters 8 and 9.

By the end of the chapter we will have used methods of measuring length that are crude versions of more sophisticated methods used by land surveyors. However, when used carefully, our methods can be very powerful.

INDIRECT MEASUREMENT USING A SCALE DRAWING OF A TRIANGLE

The tiny, remote town of Santa Catalina has a water problem. It can no longer rely on its system of underground wells and is investigating the possibility of piping in water from Don Spring, a good source about 25 miles from town by road. Since the town cannot afford to build an aqueduct along the road, the town council is looking for an alternative route. The route by road is not very direct; it skirts Mount Manlo, a large hill that lies on a straight line between the spring and the city. The council feels that it might be cheaper to build a tunnel for the aqueduct through the hill. Council members use a sketch to begin their deliberations.

Please try this before reading on.

To decide whether a tunnel would be feasible, the council needs to find out what the length of the aqueduct would be if it passed through the hill. Normally, some of this information could be gotten from a map, but no existing map shows the location of Don Spring. How can the council find this length?

A Solution to the Santa Catalina Aqueduct Problem

Lupita, a member of the council, suggests that they construct their own map of the region. Here is her thinking.

"On the road between here and Don Spring there is a fork called Three Points. The right road of the fork goes to Don Spring. From Three Points (*T*), you can sight both the church steeple (*S*) in Santa Catalina and also Don Spring (*D*). We know the distances from the church steeple to Three Points and from Don Spring to Three Points, and the two roads are straight. I'll draw a bird's-eye sketch of this."

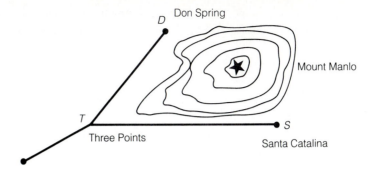

So we know the lengths of *ST* and *DT*. We want to know the length of *SD*. Points *S*, *T*, and *D* make the vertices of a triangle. Let's make a scale drawing of that triangle."

Another council member asks, "But, Lupita, how can you make a scale drawing if you only know the lengths of two sides?"

Lupita: "Let's try a little experiment. Here's a triangle I've drawn on graph paper.

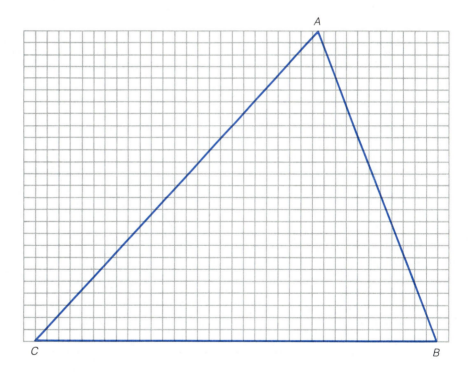

Then what you do, with another sheet of graph paper, is make a scale drawing of the triangle using the width of two squares to represent 5.

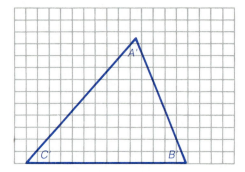

"When you've finished, take some scissors and cut out the little triangle, which is a scale drawing of the bigger triangle. Label the vertices of both triangles so that you can talk about them and place the smaller triangle on the larger triangle.

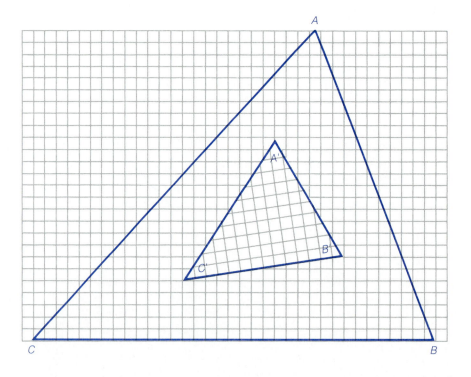

"Vertices A', B', and C' of the little triangle correspond to vertices A, B, and C, respectively, of the big triangle; and $A'B'$, $A'C'$, and $B'C'$ are the scale drawings of the line segments AB, AC, BC, respectively, using the same scale factor. Put the little triangle in the middle of the big one with A' pointing to A, B' to B, and C' to C. Move the little triangle so that A' lies on top of A and the straight line segment $A'B'$ lies on top of as much of the straight-line segment AB as it can.

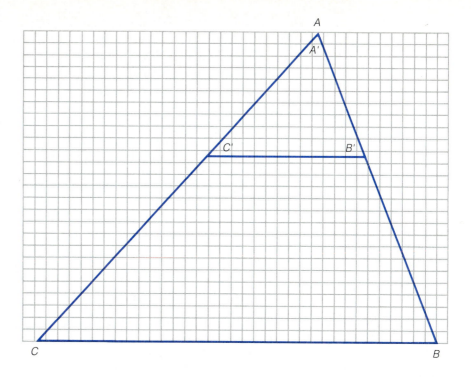

"Here is what happens. The side A'C' also lies on top of AC. The angle at A' coincides with the angle at A. The two angles are congruent. This is not surprising, since you'd expect a scale drawing to have the same shape as the original.

"We have just constructed a scale drawing where we can measure all the sides of the original triangle, and we can make copies of all the angles. The difficulty with constructing a scale drawing of the Mount Manlo triangle is that we know only two of its sides and the angle between them. However, as it turns out, that's *all* we need to know to make a scale drawing."

A third council member interjects, "Whoa! Back up, Lupita. How do we know this angle?"

Lupita: "Later."

ONE WAY TO MAKE A COPY OF AN ANGLE

To use Lupita's solution to the Santa Catalina aqueduct problem, you need to be able to make a copy of the angle at Three Points, the angle at vertex *T* of triangle *STD*. It would be difficult to "trace" this angle as Lupita suggests, since triangle *STD* hasn't even been drawn; only the three vertices of the triangle have been given. However, with a *transit,* an ancient device used for measuring angles, tracing the angle is easy. To make and use a simple transit, you will need a piece of $8\frac{1}{2}$- by 11-in paper and a flat piece of corrugated cardboard, roughly the same size as the paper. You will also need a drinking straw and a pin. Tape the paper

(continues on next page)

(*continued from page 605*)

on the cardboard and pin the middle of the straw to the middle of the paper. With the cardboard parallel to flat ground (it might be helpful to have a small portable table on which to place the cardboard and a level to make the table flat in case the ground isn't) and with the pin above the vertex *T* of the angle you want to copy, sight the vertex *C* of the big triangle through the straw. Keeping straw, paper, and cardboard rigid, draw a line along the side of the straw. Then, without moving the paper and cardboard, rotate the straw and sight the third vertex *S* of the triangle through the straw. Again keeping straw, paper, and cardboard rigid, draw a line along the edge of the straw. The two lines you have drawn will form the two sides of the desired copy of the angle at *T*.

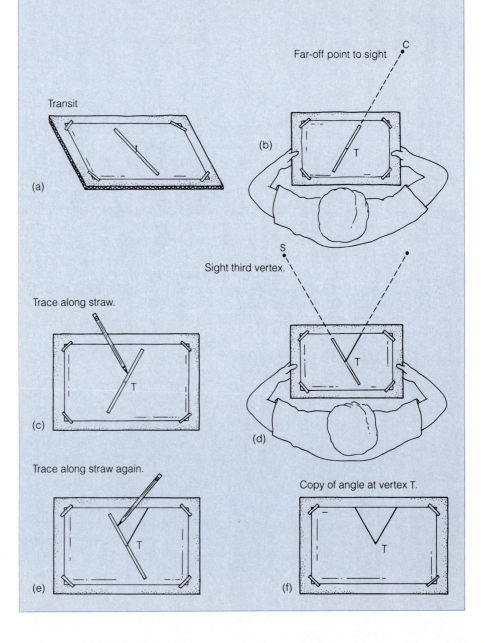

Far-off point to sight   C

Transit

(a)

(b)

S
Sight third vertex.

Trace along straw.

(c)

(d)

Trace along straw again.

Copy of angle at vertex T.

(e)

(f)

Lupita continues: "Now we know how to copy the angle at *T*—Three Points. (I got it using the method in the box.) We also know *TS* (the distance from Three Points to Santa Catalina) and *TD* (the distance from Three Points to Don Spring.)

"To make a scale drawing of a triangle knowing two sides and the angle between them, take the big triangle on the graph paper again. Suppose we know the lengths of sides *AB* and *AC* and the angle between them but don't know length *BC* nor the angles at *B* and *C*. What can we do?"

Make a copy of the angle at *A* with tracing paper (call the traced angle *A'*) and construct scale drawings of the two sides we know and mark their end points here

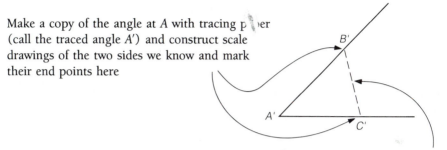

Then connect the two end points.

"We obtain a little triangle. It's the same triangle we would have gotten if we had known *everything* about the original and constructed the scale drawing. This little triangle must *be* a scale model! We can use this idea to figure out the length of the proposed aqueduct."

FILLING IN THE FINAL STEPS OF LUPITA'S SOLUTION   Here are the measurements the town council made: *TD* = distance from Three Points to Don Spring = 10 mi; *TS* = distance from Three Points to Santa Catalina = 15 mi. The accompanying figure shows a copy of the angle at vertex *T* of triangle *STD*. (See the aside, "One Way to Make a Copy of an Angle.") Use this information to construct a scale model of triangle *STD* using Lupita's method, then find *DS* = straight-line distance from Don Spring to Santa Catalina.

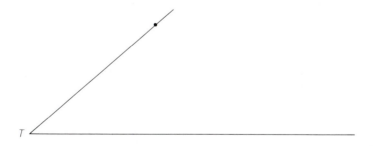

FINISHING LUPITA'S SOLUTION   Take pencil and paper and follow along. Make a copy of the angle at vertex *T*, preceding, to construct the scale drawing. (Use tracing paper or waxed paper.) Label the vertex of the copied angle *T'*. The scale drawing will have vertices *T'*, *S'*, and *D'*. Use the convenient scale $\frac{1}{4}$ in represents 1 mi. Since the length of *TD* = 10 mi, the length of *T'D'* (the scaled version of *TS*) will be $10 \times \frac{1}{4}$ in = $\frac{10}{4}$ in = $2\frac{1}{2}$ in. Measure $2\frac{1}{2}$ in along one side of the angle, using *T'* as one end and labeling the other end with *D'*.

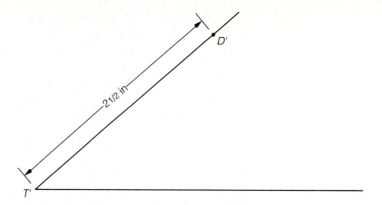

Similarly, the length of $T'S'$ (the scaled version of TS) will be $15 \times \frac{1}{4}$ in $= \frac{15}{4}$ in $= 3\frac{3}{4}$ in. Measure $3\frac{3}{4}$ in along the other side of the angle, using T' as one end and labeling the other end with S'.

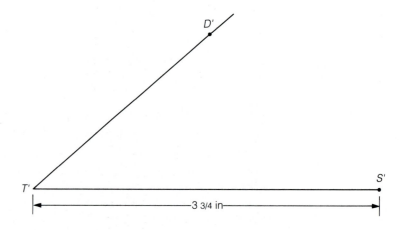

Finally, connect S' and D' with a straight line and measure the length of $S'D'$.

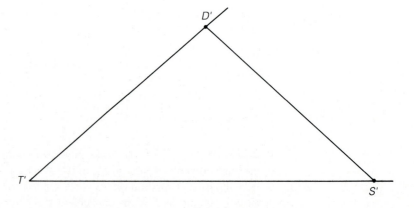

You find that the length of $S'D'$ is about 3 in. In the scaled version $\frac{1}{4}$ in represents 1 mi. That means that 1 in represents 4 mi. Thus, 3 in represents $3 \times 4 = 12$ mi.

The Mathematical Idea: Method 1 for Constructing a Scale Drawing of a Triangle

Lupita solved a seemingly insoluble problem. To find a distance that would be impractical to measure directly, construct a scale drawing of a triangle. How the scale drawing was made was also clever. Let's summarize the method.

CONSTRUCTING A SCALE DRAWING OF A TRIANGLE KNOWING TWO SIDES AND THE ANGLE BETWEEN

To make a scale drawing of triangle ABC, take one of the vertices of the original triangle (A, say). Make a copy of the angle at A and call the copied vertex A'. Then, along the two sides of this copied angle, using A' as one end point, make scale drawings of AB and AC using B' and C' as the other end points, respectively. Then connect B' and C' with a line segment. Triangle $A'B'C'$ is a scale drawing of ABC.

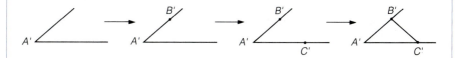

Alternatively, instead of making a copy of angle A, use the original angle A and mark off the scale drawing of AB along AB, starting at A and ending at B'. Similarly, mark off the scale drawing of AC along AC, starting at A and ending at C'. Then connect B' with C' with a line segment.

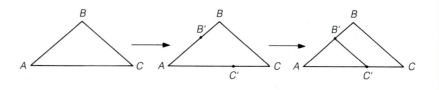

EXERCISE 1. There are other situations where one might use the idea of making a scale drawing to find an unknown distance.

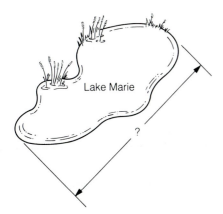

Let's look at Lake Marie as an example. You are interested in finding the distance across Lake Marie and think of using method 1. You have already found a place *A* where you can sight both ends of the lake at *B* and *C* and where you can measure *AB* and *AC*. You measure *AB* and *AC* and record what you get, as shown in the sketch.

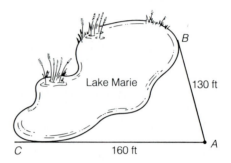

(The angle at *A* in the sketch is a copy of the real angle at *A*. But the lengths in the sketch are not scale drawings of the original.) Make a scale drawing of triangle *ABC* and find the distance *BC* across the lake.

THE TREE PROBLEM

STOP

Try this yourself, first.

You are about to cut down a tree. You need to know how tall it is in order to determine where you should make it fall. How do you figure out how tall it is before cutting it down?

A Solution to the
Tree Problem

This is another situation where you need to measure a length, but you can't measure it directly (unless you are a monkey!). It's like the Santa Catalina aqueduct problem or the Lake Marie exercise, and you think: "Maybe I can solve this by making a scale drawing of some big triangle. Which big triangle? In the previous problems, the big triangle had one side of unknown length and two sides that could be measured. The top of the tree could be *C* and its base *B*; the unknown length would be *CB*.

I could measure the distance from any point *A* on the ground to the base *B* of the tree. So *AB* and *CB* would be two sides of a triangle. The third side would have to be

AC, the line gotten by connecting the top of the tree *C* with the point *A* on the ground. I couldn't measure *that* length directly because it's in the air.

"Perhaps there's another way to make a scale drawing. Let me look at Lupita's two triangles *ABC* and *A'B'C'*. Here is one of the things she did with the two triangles.

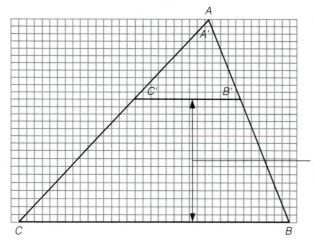

The angle at *A'* is equal to the angle at *A*.

Also, the remaining "nontouching" sides *C'B'* and *CB* are parallel.

The same thing happens when I match the angles at vertices *B'* and *B* (instead of *A'* and *A*) and, similarly, with the angles at vertices *C'* and *C*. The pairs of "nontouching" sides are always parallel. This suggests a new method for making a scale drawing of a (big) triangle *ABC*. Choose a vertex (*A*, say); then move down one of the sides adjacent to *A* and draw a line parallel to the side opposite *A*. (The side opposite *A* is *BC*.)

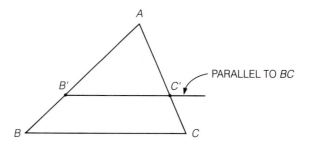

PARALLEL TO *BC*

The parallel line meets the sides adjacent to angle *A* in points *B'* and *C'*. The point *B'* is on the line *AB* and *C'* is on the line *AC*. Then triangle *AB'C'* is a scale model of triangle *ABC*.

"To use this method to solve the tree problem I need a big triangle *ABC*, a vertex *A* of the big triangle, and a line parallel to the side opposite angle *A*. Let me look at my previous picture.

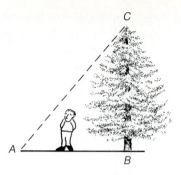

One side (*BC*) of *ABC* is the tree, a second side (*AB*) is along the ground, and a third side (*AC*) is in the air. The line from the top of my head to my feet is parallel to the tree. I must choose a point *A* on the ground so that I can take advantage of this. Let *A* be the tip of the tree's shadow on the ground. Then I go and stand in the shadow of the tree so that the tip of the *tree's* shadow and the tip of my shadow (or, rather, the tip of the shadow I would have if there were no tree in the way) are the same—at *A*. Then my feet *E*, the very top of my head *D*, and point *A* form the three vertices of a little triangle *ADE*. The line segment *DE* (me standing) is parallel to *CB* (tree). So triangle *ADE* is a scale drawing of triangle *ABC*."

EXERCISE 2. Complete the solution to the tree problem using the measurements shown in the picture.

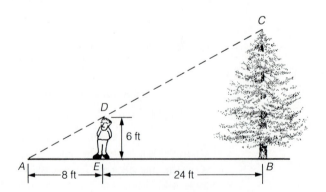

The Mathematical Idea: Method 2 for Constructing a Scale Drawing of a Triangle

The method for constructing a scale drawing used in finding the height of the tree differs significantly from Lupita's method. We can summarize.

To construct a scale model of triangle *ABC*, pick a vertex (say, *A*). On side *AB* pick a point *B'* different from *A*. The side *AB'* will be the scale drawing of *AB*.

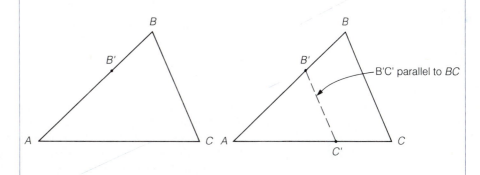

Draw a line through *B'* parallel to *BC*. This line will intersect *AC* at a point *C'*. Triangle *AB'C'* is then a scale model of triangle *ABC*.

EXERCISES 3. You are to find the height of the building shown. You measure the shadow of the building along the ground and find that it is 75 ft. Then you take a 3-ft-high stick, measure its shadow, and find that it is 5 ft. Use this to find the height of the building.

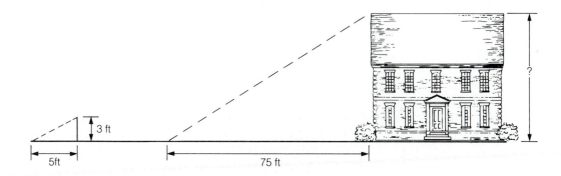

4. You need to find the height of the electric pole shown. A guy wire is strung from the top of the pole to the ground. You stand so that the tip of the guy wire just touches your head and make the measurements shown. Find the height of the pole.

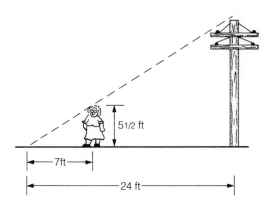

5 1/2 ft

7ft

24 ft

THE SWAMP PROBLEM

Please try this before reading on.

The Colonial Development Company is considering the building of a subdivision at the edge of town. As shown in the accompanying picture, the proposed subdivision would lie alongside a highway, separated from the highway by a swamp. An access road, to be built from the highway to the subdivision, is indicated by dashed lines. The company must bear the cost of this, and, to estimate its cost, it must determine the length of the proposed road. The swamp makes it impractical to measure this length directly. How can the company measure the length of the road?

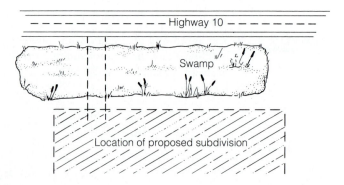

Highway 10

Swamp

Location of proposed subdivision

A Solution to the Swamp Problem

This problem seems to be similar to the Santa Catalina aqueduct problem. You think of A and B, end points of the line segment you want to measure, as two vertices of a triangle. Then you want to find a point C, the third vertex of your triangle, from which you can measure directly the straight-line distances, CA and CB.

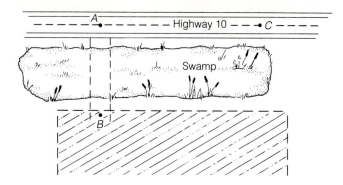

If the point C is on the highway as in the picture, then you can measure the length of CA directly, but not CB—because of the intervening swamp. However, there is something else in triangle ABC you could measure that might help. You know the directions of lines AB and CB because you can *sight* B from A and B from C. With a transit you can make copies of the angles of triangle ABC at vertices A and C.

You try to construct a scale drawing of ABC using this information. Returning again to Lupita's pair of triangles—ABC and scale drawing $A'B'C'$—you remember that the angle at A' is congruent to the angle at A, the angle at B' is congruent to the angle at B, and the angle at C' is congruent to the angle at C. You make $A'C'$ a scale drawing of AC, copy angle A at A', and copy angle C at C'. You then have something like what's shown.

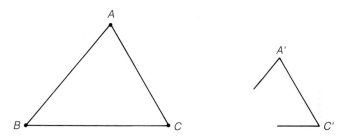

It is the beginning of a scale drawing of ABC. To complete it, you extend the two lines from A' and C' that don't yet intersect until they *do* intersect at some point B'. $A'B'C'$ will then be a scale drawing of ABC.

EXERCISE 5. Complete the scale drawing for the swamp problem as started. From the drawing measure the lengths of $A'B'$ and $A'C'$. From that figure out the length of AB. (The distance from A to C on Highway 10 is 200 ft.)

The Mathematical Idea: Method 3 for Constructing a
Scale Drawing of a Triangle

The solution to the swamp problem suggests the following technique.

CONSTRUCTING A SCALE DRAWING OF
A TRIANGLE KNOWING TWO ANGLES

Start with a triangle *ABC*.

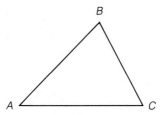

Trace the angle at *A*. Call the traced vertex *A'*. Then choose a scale. As in method 2, along the tracing of *AB* mark the scale drawing *A'B'* of *AB*, starting with *A'*.

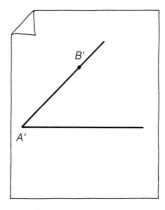

Now move the tracing paper so that *B'* lies on top of *B*, and segment *A'B'* lies on top of as much of *AB* as it can.

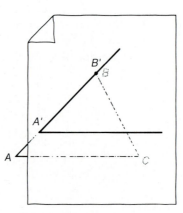

(continues)

(Continued)

Then trace the angle at *B* using *A′B′* as one of its sides. This new line, if extended, will meet the tracing of *AC* at a point (call it *C′*). *A′B′C′* will be a scale drawing of *ABC*.

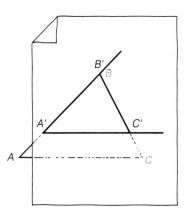

EXERCISE   6. Get a piece of tracing paper (or waxed paper) and use method 3 to construct a scale drawing of triangle *ABC* shown. The length of *AB* is 2 in. Use the scale $\frac{1}{2}$ in represents 1 in.

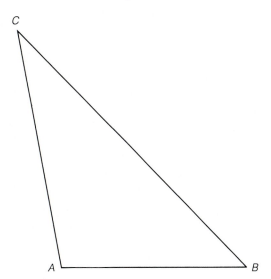

15.2   SCALE DRAWINGS AND SIMILAR TRIANGLES

We have just solved several problems using a scale drawing of a triangle. The power of this kind of scale drawing is that we are able to construct it with seemingly incomplete information. All three methods that we used were the result of our experimentation with and observation of the properties of a pair of triangles, one of which is a scale drawing of another.

In a formal course in geometry, certain language is used.

DEFINITION OF SIMILAR TRIANGLES

Of two triangles ABC and $A'B'C'$, if

$$\frac{\text{Length of } AB}{\text{Length of } A'B'} = \frac{\text{length of } BC}{\text{length of } B'C'} = \frac{\text{length of } AC}{\text{length of } A'C'},$$

then ABC is *similar* to $A'B'C'$ and sides AB, BC, and AC *correspond to* sides $A'B'$, $B'C'$, and $A'C'$ respectively. The common ratio of lengths is called the *scale factor* relating ABC with $A'B'C'$. In other words, if one triangle is a scale drawing of another, then the two triangles are called *similar*.

In formal geometry courses, the properties of similar triangles that we observed in our small sample are proved generally and rigorously from basic principles. Eventually, a careful study of similar triangles leads to a study of trigonometry, with the help of which the sorts of measurements we have been making can be made with greater precision than we have been able to obtain with our methods.

Precise measurements cannot be made without sophisticated measurement tools. The transit that we described earlier is primitive in comparison to the tools used today for careful land surveying. Nonetheless, however primitive and prone to error our methods and tools, with a little care they can be very powerful.

How to Recognize Similar Triangles

Earlier, when we were trying to find the height of a tree, we created a scale drawing of a triangle without knowing ahead of time what the scale factor would be. Somehow we knew that the two triangles were similar. We figured out the scale factor later by measuring the length of the two shadows.

From the methods we know for creating a scale drawing of a triangle, there are ways of recognizing when two triangles are similar without knowing what the scale factor is that relates the two triangles.

1. Take a pair of triangles. Suppose one angle of the smaller is equal to an angle of the larger, and you fit the smaller triangle into the larger at this angle. In this position, suppose the sides of the two triangles not touching are parallel. Then the two triangles are similar.

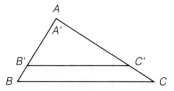

2. Take a pair of triangles. If the angles of one triangle are equal to the angles of the other, then the two triangles are similar. (Actually, we have seen earlier that all

we need is for *two* angles of one to be equal to two angles of the other. Why is this?)

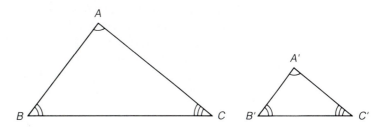

To find out what the scale factor is in both cases, measure a pair of corresponding sides. For example, in the diagram above, the scale factor is the ratio

$$\frac{\text{Length of } BC}{\text{Length of } B'C'}.$$

THE FLAGPOLE PROBLEM

Try this yourself.

The rope that is used to raise and lower the flag on a flagpole has disappeared, and the owner wants to replace it. To find the length of the replacement rope, he needs to know how high the flagpole is. Help him find out.

Solution 1 to the Flagpole Problem

To figure this out, the owner makes a triangle $A'B'E'$ out of stiff material (such as plywood, Masonite, or heavy cardboard) and takes it to a position from which he can sight the top of the flagpole, as in the picture. The angle at A' is a right angle, and sides $A'E'$ and $A'B'$ have lengths equal to 40 cm and 20 cm, respectively. He places the triangle so that $A'E'$ is parallel to the ground and E' is at his eye.

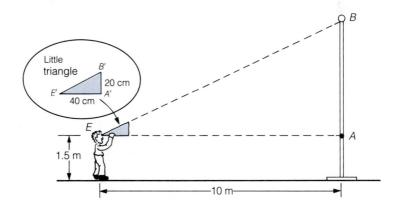

From the diagram it looks as if the little triangle and triangle EAB are similar. (The point $E = E'$ is the owner's eye, B is the tip of the flagpole, and A is a point on the flagpole the same distance from the ground as E.) Let's see if this is the case. The angle at A' is equal to the angle at A, and the angle at E' is equal to the angle at E. (Except for knowing a scale, it looks as if $E'A'B'$ could have been created from EAB using method 3.) By criterion 2, stated earlier, the two triangles are similar.

Since $E'A'$ corresponds to EA, and $E'A'$ is 40 cm, we would know a scale factor once we know the length of EA. We measure EA and find that it is 10 m. So the scale is 40 cm represents 10 m. Stated another way, the scale factor relating the big triangle to the smaller one is the ratio 10 to .40.

From the diagram the distance from E to the ground is 1.5 m, which is equal to the distance from A to the ground. Thus, if we find the length of AB, we can add that to 1.5 m to get the distance from B to the ground—the height of the flagpole. The side AB of triangle ABE corresponds to side $A'B'$ in the scale drawing of $E'A'B'$, and the length of $A'B'$ is 20 cm or .20 m. Since the scale factor is 10/.4, or 25 to 1, we must have

$$\frac{\text{Length of } AB}{\text{Length of } A'B'} = \frac{25}{1} = 25.$$

If we let X represent the length of AB, we have

$$\frac{X}{.2} = 25.$$

Solving for X, we obtain $X = (.2)25 = 5$ m. The height of the flagpole is 5 m + 1.5 m = 6.5 m.

Solution 2 to the Flagpole Problem

Solution 1 uses the scale factor—the fact that the ratio of lengths of a pair of corresponding sides is the same as the ratio of lengths of another pair of corresponding sides. There is another way to think about the flagpole problem. You know that triangle $E'A'B'$ is similar to triangle EAB and that $E'A'$ and EA are corresponding sides of lengths 40 cm and 10 m, respectively. You want to find the length of AB; the corresponding side of the small triangle is $A'B'$ with length 20 cm. You think: "20 cm is half of 40 cm. The ratio of $A'B'$ to $E'A'$ is 20 to 40, or $\frac{1}{2}$. The ratio of the length of AB to the length of EA should also be $\frac{1}{2}$; in other words, the length of AB should be half of length EA. Thus, the length of AB should be 5 m, and the height of the flagpole 5 m + 1.5 m = 6.5 m."

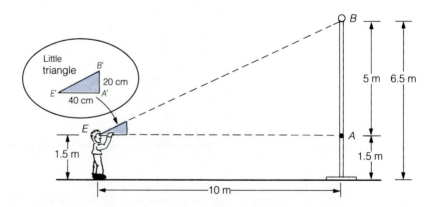

The Mathematical Idea: Ratio, Proportion, and Similar Triangles

Both solutions to the flagpole problem used ratios and proportions, that is, equations involving proportions.

For example, the equation

$$\frac{\text{Length of AB}}{.2} = \frac{25}{1}$$

is a proportion.

Solution 1 used the proportions given in the definition of similar triangles. Let's have a look at the definition once again. Suppose that you are given the pair of similar triangles shown, in which one triangle ABC has sides of lengths x, y, and z, and the other $A'B'C'$ has corresponding sides of lengths X, Y, and Z.

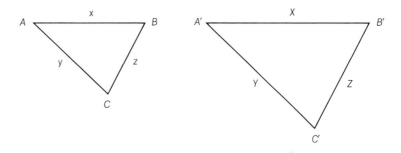

A restatement of the definition of similar triangles can be given in terms of proportions.

Solution 2 to the flagpole problem used another ratio property.

Suppose we have two similar triangles such that two sides of the smaller triangle are 2 cm and 4 cm, and the scale is 1 cm represents 12 m. Then the corresponding two sides of the big triangle are 2×12 m and 4×12 m, respectively.

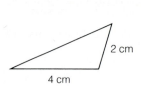

2 cm

4 cm

The ratio of these two sides is

$$\frac{2}{4}$$

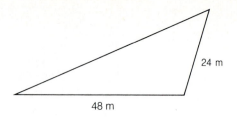

24 m

48 m

The ratio of these two sides is

$$\frac{2 \times 12}{4 \times 12}$$

The two ratios are the same.

Here's another example. Take a pair of similar triangles in which two sides of the smaller are 3 in and 7 in, and the scale is 1 in represents 5.7 ft. Thus, the corresponding sides of the big triangle are 3 × 5.7 ft and 7 × 5.7 ft, respectively.

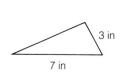

3 in

7 in

The ratio of these two sides is

$$\frac{3}{7}$$

3 x 5.7 ft

7 x 5.7 ft

The ratio of these two sides is

$$\frac{3 \times 5.7}{7 \times 5.7}$$

The two ratios are the same.

In a third example, the three sides of the smaller triangle are 3.8 cm, 7.9 cm, and 5.2 cm, and the scale is 1 cm represents 5.6 m. The big triangle should have these measurements: 3.8 × 5.6 m, 7.9 × 5.6 m, 5.2 × 5.6 m. The ratios of corresponding sides are equal.

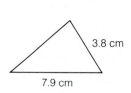

3.8 cm

7.9 cm

The ratio of these two sides is

$$\frac{3.8}{7.9}$$

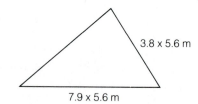

3.8 x 5.6 m

7.9 x 5.6 m

The ratio of these two sides is

$$\frac{3.8 \times 5.6}{7.9 \times 5.6}$$

The two ratios are the same.

The second ratio property follows from the first ratio property algebraically. Let us show why. Suppose that two triangles ABC and $A'B'C'$ are similar so that $x/X = y/Y = z/Z$.

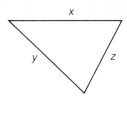
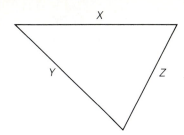

Working with the equation $x/X = y/Y$, we multiply both sides of this equation by X/y to obtain

$$\frac{x}{X}\frac{X}{y} = \frac{y}{Y}\frac{X}{y}.$$

After simplifying both sides of the equation, we obtain

$$\frac{x}{y} = \frac{X}{Y}.$$

This is the first equation of the second ratio property. In the same manner, starting with the equation $x/X = z/Z$, you can deduce $x/z = X/Z$; and starting with $y/Y = z/Z$, you can deduce $y/z = Y/Z$.

TREE PROBLEM 2   Suppose the measurements in the tree problem are as given in the drawing.

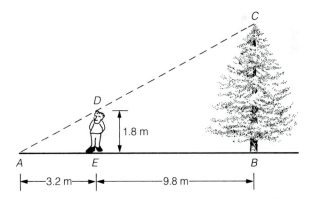

Please try solving this yourself.   Find the height of the tree.

Solutions to Tree Problem 2   Let's solve this using the first ratio property of similar triangles. The scale factor relating the larger triangle to the smaller is the ratio of the length of AB to the length of AE, or 13 m to 3.2 m, or 13/3.2. (*Note:* 13 m = 9.8 m + 3.2 m.) If X represents the length of CB, then we have the proportion

$$\frac{13}{3.2} = \frac{X}{1.8}.$$

Solving for X, we obtain

$$X = \frac{(1.8)(13)}{3.2} = 7.3125.$$

Now let's solve it using the second ratio property of similar triangles. The ratio of the lengths of two sides DE and AE of the small triangle ADE is 1.8/3.2. The ratio of the lengths of the corresponding two sides of the big triangle must be the same,

$$\frac{1.8}{3.2} = \frac{\text{length of } CB}{\text{length of } AB}.$$

The length of AB is 13 m so that if X represents the length of CB again,

$$\frac{1.8}{3.2} = \frac{X}{13}.$$

Solving for X, we obtain

$$X = \frac{(1.8)\,13}{3.2} = 7.3125.$$

EXERCISE 7. Alternative measurements for the flagpole problem are given in the drawing. Find the length of AB in two different ways: (1) using the first ratio property of similar triangles and (2) using the second ratio property of similar triangles. (Which method is easiest? Why?)

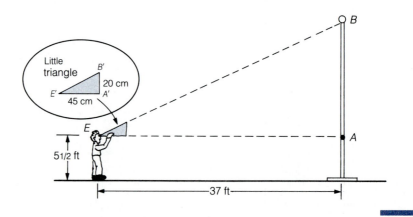

"Scale" and "Scale Factor"

Earlier in the chapter, when we were creating a scale drawing (small) of a triangle (large), we established a "scale." This was our way of specifying what some small unit of length (the side of one small square of the graph paper, for example) in the scale drawing corresponded to (or "represented") in the large triangle. The term *scale* is related to the term *scale factor* in a certain way. If the scale factor is the ratio $\frac{3}{5}$, then we might have stated the scale in a number of different ways:

3 ft represents 5 ft.
3 in represents 5 in.
6 m represents 10 m.
1 in represents $1\frac{2}{3}$ in.
1 cm represents approximately 1.67 cm.

Notice for each statement of the scale that the ratio of numbers in the pair is equal to the scale factor $\frac{3}{5}$ and that *the units of length for both numbers in the pair are the same*.

Earlier we had an example where the scale was given as $\frac{1}{4}$ in represents 10 ft. In this case, the two units are different. To figure out the scale *factor*, we must make the units for the two lengths the same. Since $\frac{1}{4}$ in $= \frac{1}{4} \times \frac{1}{12}$ ft $= \frac{1}{48}$ ft, the scale is $\frac{1}{48}$ ft represents 10 ft. The scale factor relating the smaller triangle to the larger is $\frac{1}{48}/10$, or $\frac{1}{480}$.

We may have chosen the scale to be $\frac{1}{4}$ in represents 10 ft because $\frac{1}{4}$ in was a convenient unit in our scale drawing. If we measure a length in our scale drawing and find that it has length L of these units, the corresponding length in the original has length $10L$ ft. This is really a use of the second ratio property:

$$\frac{L}{1} = \frac{10L}{10}.$$

15.3   EXTENDING THE IDEAS: CONGRUENCE OF GEOMETRIC SHAPES AND DEDUCTIVE GEOMETRY

The method we have described in this chapter for measuring a length difficult to measure directly is very powerful. A single application of the method is simple: It involves the creation of a scale drawing of a triangle. There can be problems with the method, however. One problem has to do with the accuracy of tools. If you want your lengths to be accurate to a certain level of precision, you will need tools that can make measurements with the same accuracy. A second problem is related to situations in which you must use the method many times. In such situations, you want the method to be practical and feasible for repeated use. Error that may be negligible with a single use can accumulate and become significant with many uses.

Here is an example in which the method we have described is used many times. In 1669–1670, the Abbé Picard initiated the first accurate survey of France by laying down a chain of triangles on the Paris meridian. In addition to helping map makers create accurate maps, the survey also enabled him to measure a segment of the meridian's arc—a necessary factor in calculating the earth's size. (See chap. 16.) He used the *triangulation method* in which one length (the *baseline*) is carefully made. From both ends of this length surveyors then measure angles by sighting on some distant object. A triangle results, and from the methods of this chapter the lengths of the new sides are determined. From these sides, more triangles can be laid out and their sides determined with the same methods. By using sophisticated tools Picard was able to avoid significant errors. For example, he used telescopic sights in his sighting tools. A sample of his work is shown on accompanying map.

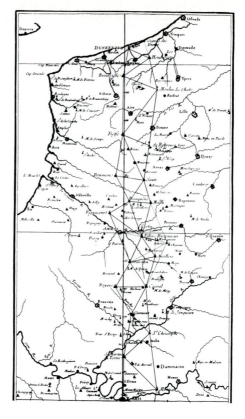

What about constructing more precise tools of measurement? On a small scale (such as drawings on paper) we used tracing to copy an angle. When possible to do so and when done with care, this method can be reasonably accurate. Alternative small-scale methods for copying an angle are with the use of a protractor or with the use of straightedge and compass (which we discuss in the next chapter). On a large scale (such as for surveying), we described the use of a transit to copy an angle. Our transit is crude. However, modern, high-tech versions of the transit are very precise.

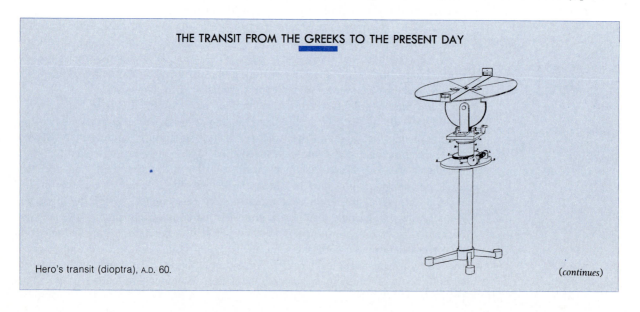

THE TRANSIT FROM THE GREEKS TO THE PRESENT DAY

Hero's transit (dioptra), A.D. 60.

(continues)

(*Continued*)

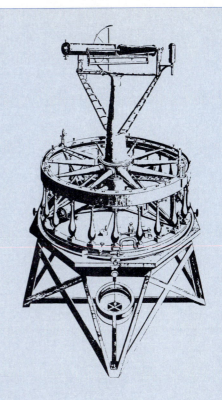

Jesse Ramsden's theodolite ("Transit"), built for the Royal Society, made possible the first accurate triangulation of England (eighteenth century).

Modern theodolite connected to a computer interface that inputs measurements directly. The keyboard is for entering additional information such as "oak tree," etc.

(*continues*)

(*Continued*)

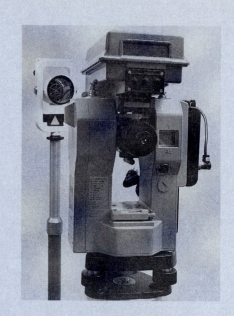

Modern theolodite with an electronic distance measuring instrument (EDMIR) attached on top. At the left of the picture is a retro-reflector. This reflects back the infrared signal from the EDMIR. This operation can be done up to 10 miles in one measurement. At 10 miles however, three retro-reflectors would have to be used to bounce back the signal. Since it is so difficult to focus the EDMIR at that distance, these operations are frequently done at night. The person with the three retro-reflectors flashes a strobe light, which is bright enough to be seen by the EDMIR operator, giving him or her a target to aim at. The strength of the signal is then recorded by the EDMIR, allowing fine-tuning of the aim.

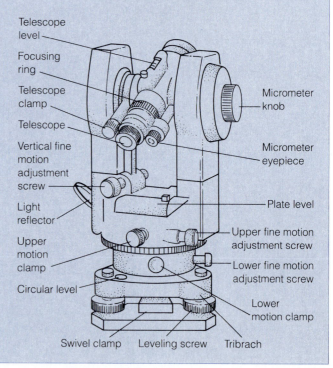

Controls layout on typical modern theodolite

Another way to make more accurate measurements is to develop more sophisticated methods for creating scale drawings of triangles using theoretical, as opposed to physical, tools. Theoretical tools can also be used to make measurements more efficiently.

A simple example of the sort of tool we mean can be illustrated with the Lake Marie exercise. You want to find the distance from *B* to *C*.

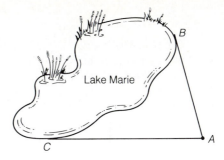

Extend the two lines of sight through A and let C' be a point on one of these extensions. At C' copy angle ACB as in the next sketch. The side of angle C' that is not one of the extensions will meet the other extension at a point B'.

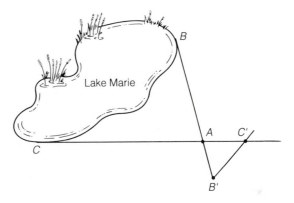

It can be shown that triangle $AB'C'$ is similar to triangle ABC. Then the length of BC can be found easily by measuring one known side of triangle ABC, measuring sides of $AB'C'$, and solving a proportion. Most of the work in measuring can be minimized if we make triangle $AB'C'$ small. How do we know, however, that triangles $AB'C'$ and ABC are similar? First, a theoretical tool tells us that angles BAC and $B'AC'$ *are* congruent (not just that they *look* congruent—we're interested in precision, right?); second, we constructed angles at C and C' to be equal; third, we know from what we did earlier in the chapter that this is all we need to have the two triangles similar.

The theoretical tool mentioned above is the knowledge that a certain pair of angles are congruent. (The specific theoretical tool is discussed in the next section "Vertical Angles.") Our methods for detecting a pair of similar triangles are also theoretical tools. (For example, a method of detection says that if we know that two angles of one triangle are congruent to two angles of another, we know the two triangles are similar.) There are other situations in which one can identify two angles as congruent and then use this fact to construct a pair of similar triangles. A large part of what we call plane geometry was created in order to identify such situations. In the next section we will discuss some of the methods of plane geometry and some of the theoretical tools for measurement obtained from it. This look at geometry should also help to make more precise and give new meaning to many of the ideas in the chapter.

Vertical Angles

Before discussing the theoretical tool used in the solution to the Lake Marie exercise, we need to introduce some helpful terminology.

An angle may be identified by its vertex *P*:

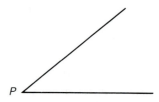

When several lines meet at a vertex, identifying an angle by its vertex is ambiguous. Which angle is meant by angle *P* in the following diagram?

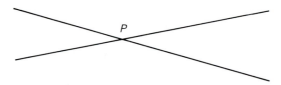

To avoid this ambiguity, an angle can be identified by its vertex *P* and two other points *A* and *B*, one on each of its sides:

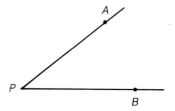

We refer to this angle as "angle *APB*" or ∠*APB*. (The vertex of the angle in "angle *APB*" is always the middle letter.) We refer to its two sides as *AP* and *BP*. The region between the two sides is the interior of the angle:

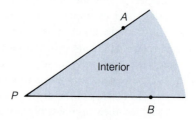

Sometimes, if there is no confusion, an angle can be referred to by a symbol drawn near its vertex in the angle's interior:

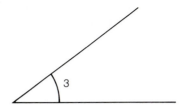

Two angles that share a vertex and a side but the interiors of which do not overlap are called *adjacent angles:*

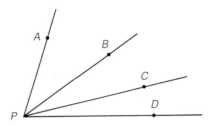

∠*APB* and ∠*BPC* are adjacent. ∠*BPC* and ∠*CPD* are also adjacent. ∠*APB* and ∠*APC* are *not* adjacent, because their interiors overlap. ∠*APB* and ∠*CPD* are *not* adjacent, because they do not share a common side.

Of two shapes (two angles, two line segments, two polygons, etc.), if one can be made to coincide with the other when one is placed on top of the other (as in a tracing), then the two shapes are called *congruent.*

NOTATIONAL CONVENTION

Shorthand for "shape *S* is congruent to shape *R*" is $S \cong R$.

The *sum* of two angles *APB* and *CQD* is a third angle formed the following way: Using *P* as a vertex and *PA* as one of its sides, copy ∠*CQD* to make an angle adjacent to ∠*APB* and congruent to ∠*CQD*.

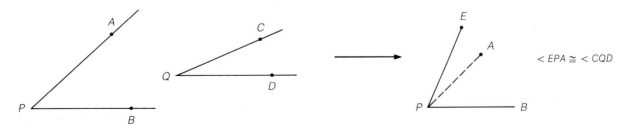

∠*EPA* is then congruent to ∠*CQD*. Then ∠*EPB* is the *sum* of ∠*APB* and ∠*CQD*.

The drawings show examples of sums of angles.

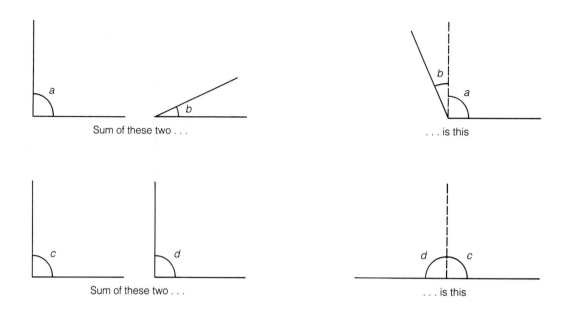

Sum of these two . . .

. . . is this

Sum of these two . . .

. . . is this

The sum of two angles is commutative and satisfies a cancellation law.

CANCELLATION LAW FOR THE SUM OF TWO ANGLES

If the sum of angles 1 and 2 is congruent to the sum of angles 3 and 2, then $\angle 1$ is congruent to $\angle 3$.

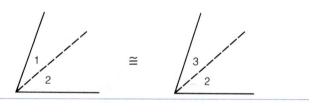

Now we are ready to describe the new theoretical tool. Two lines intersecting at point P form four angles labelled 1, 2, 3, and 4.

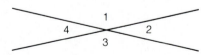

Of the four angles, any nonadjacent pair is called a pair of *vertical angles*. There are two pairs of vertical angles: angles 1 and 3 and angles 2 and 4. The new tool is the theorem that vertical angles are congruent.

The two angles in a pair of vertical angles are congruent.

Thus, in the diagram, $\angle 1$ is congruent to $\angle 3$, and $\angle 2$ is congruent to $\angle 4$.

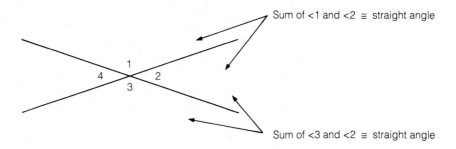

This theorem is true because: The sum of $\angle 2$ and $\angle 1$ is a straight angle; likewise, the sum of $\angle 2$ and $\angle 3$ is a straight angle. Thus, the sum of $\angle 2$ and $\angle 1$ is congruent to the sum of $\angle 2$ and $\angle 3$. By the cancellation law, $\angle 1$ is congruent to $\angle 3$. Similarly, $\angle 2$ is congruent to $\angle 4$.

Corresponding Angles

If along side AB of triangle ABC you select a point B' and draw a line through it parallel to BC, then the new line will intersect BC at a point C', and the triangle $AB'C'$ will be similar to the original triangle ABC.

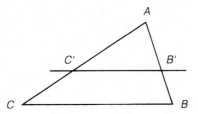

In particular, $\angle ABC$ is congruent to $\angle AB'C'$. This can be put another way: Take a pair of parallel lines and a third line that intersects both of them. This third line is called a *transversal* to the two parallel lines.

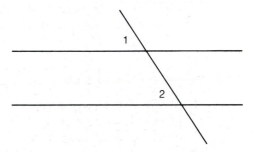

Angles 1 and 2 are called *corresponding angles*. By the preceding argument concerning similar triangles, they are congruent.

PROPERTY: CORRESPONDING ANGLES ARE CONGRUENT

Corresponding angles formed by a transversal intersecting two parallel lines are congruent.

This property seems reasonable just as the property of similar triangles on which it is based seems reasonable. In this book we will accept it as a basic fact of geometry. One can provide an argument for it using an even more basic fact of geometry, an axiom, called the *parallel postulate:* Given a line L, through any point not on the line there is one single line L' parallel to the given line.

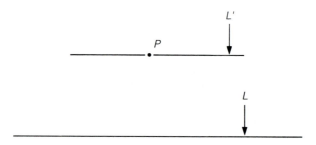

From the theorem concerning vertical angles and the property concerning corresponding angles follows another fact about angles. Take two parallel lines and a transversal:

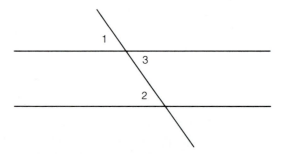

Angles 2 and 3 are called *alternate interior angles*. (The two angles are on opposite sides of the transversal, and they lie between the two parallel lines.)

THEOREM: ALTERNATE INTERIOR ANGLES ARE CONGRUENT

Alternate interior angles formed by a transversal to two parallel lines are congruent.

An argument for this is as follows: In the diagram angles 1 and 2 are corresponding angles so $\angle 1 \cong \angle 2$. Also, angles 1 and 3 are vertical angles so $\angle 1 \cong \angle 3$. It follows that $\angle 2 \cong \angle 3$.

EXERCISES

8. A parallelogram is a quadrilateral such that opposite (i.e., nonadjacent) sides are parallel. Suppose that one of the angles of a parallelogram is congruent to a right angle. Show that all the angles of the parallelogram must therefore be congruent to a right angle, that is, that the parallelogram is a rectangle. (*Hint:* Think of one pair of opposite sides as transversals to the other pair of opposite sides. Then use the theorem that alternate interior angles are congruent.

9. Consider the statement that alternate *exterior* angles are congruent. In the following diagram lines L and L' are parallel, and a transversal to these is drawn. Give an argument showing why angles 1 and 2 must be congruent.

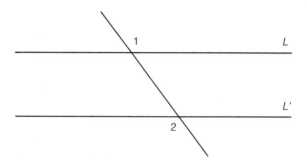

Sum of the Angles in a Triangle

One of the ways to conclude that two triangles are similar is to look solely at their angles: If the three angles of one are congruent in pairs to the three angles of the other, then the two triangles are similar. In fact, in the early part of this chapter it appeared that having two of the three pairs congruent forced the two triangles to be similar.

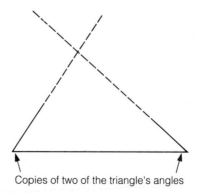

Copies of two of the triangle's angles

This suggests that, given two angles of a triangle, the third can be determined from it. This is a fact that can also be derived from the following theorem, which itself follows from the theorem relating alternate interior angles.

THEOREM: THE SUM OF THE ANGLES OF A TRIANGLE
IS CONGRUENT TO A STRAIGHT ANGLE

Given the three angles of a triangle, their sum is congruent to a straight angle.

What is the argument for this theorem? Take a triangle *ABC* with angles 1, 2, and 3. Through *C* draw a line *L* parallel to *AB*.

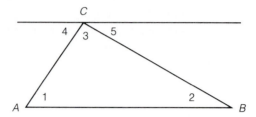

Since *AC* is a transversal to the two parallel lines, alternate interior angles are congruent; that is, $\angle 1 \cong \angle 4$. Also, since *BC* is a transversal to the two parallel lines, its alternate interior angles are congruent. So we also have $\angle 2 \cong \angle 5$. The sum of angles 3, 4, and 5 is congruent to a straight angle. Therefore, the sum of angles 1, 2, and 3 is also congruent to a straight angle.

Thus, if you know two angles of a triangle, there is only one choice for the third angle.

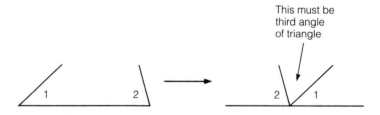

This must be third angle of triangle

EXERCISES 10. For each of the following pairs of angles, find a third angle that will make a triangle. (Some of these may be impossible. Which ones and why?)

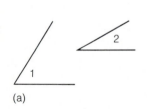

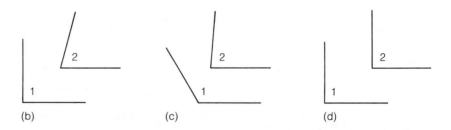

(a)   (b)   (c)   (d)

11. In the following picture the angles 1, 2, and 3 are called the *exterior angles* of a triangle. (To avoid confusion, in this context the angles of a triangle that we have been discussing up to now are called the *interior angles*.) Show that if a triangle

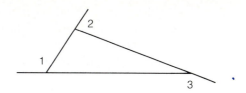

has vertices *A*, *B*, and *C*, then the exterior angle at *A* is congruent to the sum of the interior angles at *B* and *C*.

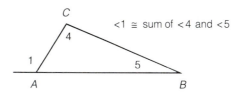

$<1 \cong$ sum of <4 and <5

12. Recall that a parallelogram is a quadrilateral such that opposite (i.e., nonadjacent) sides are parallel. Show that the sum of two adjacent angles of a parallelogram is a straight angle.

Constructing Parallel Lines

One method for making a scale drawing calls for constructing a line *M* through a point *P* parallel to a given line *L*. (The parallel postulate presented earlier says that such a line always exists.)

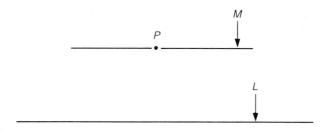

Here is one way to construct the parallel line. Draw a line *N* through *P* intersecting line *L*.

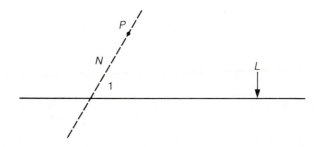

You know that the line M through P parallel to L will make corresponding angles congruent. You know one of the angles; it's ∠1. Accordingly, make a congruent copy of ∠1 having vertex P and one side line N. The other side will then be the line M passing through P and parallel to L.

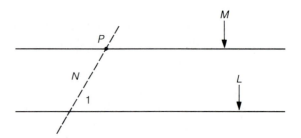

There is an important consequence of this discussion.

CONDITION FOR PARALLEL LINES

Suppose that you have two lines L and M. Suppose also that a third line N intersects L and M at points P and Q, respectively. If the corresponding angles at P and Q are equal, then lines L and M are parallel.

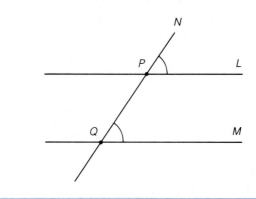

EXERCISES 13. Use the foregoing method to draw a line through point P parallel to line L in the diagram.

P •

L _____

14. Use the foregoing method to construct a line through point *C* parallel to line *AB* in the diagram below.

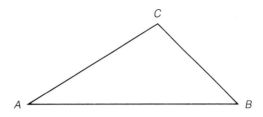

Deduction

The theorems we have stated so far provide us with situations in which we can conclude that two angles are congruent. We can then try to recreate one of these situations in order to make a pair of similar triangles. The theorems themselves are powerful theoretical tools because of their generality: Whenever such and such a situation occurs, then such and such a conclusion can be drawn. There is another, different kind of theoretical tool lurking behind the statements of these theorems. The tool is called *deduction*. This is the tool we use when we provide arguments for the theorem, arguments that connect certain ideas with certain other ideas. Using the theorem concerning alternate interior angles, an argument enabled us to conclude the theorem about the sum of the angles of a triangle. This argument is frequently called a *proof*. Proofs not only show how ideas are connected (they give structure or organization to a set of ideas), but they also provide us with some certainty: If we use theorem A to prove theorem B and we are very certain about A, then we can also be certain about B.

Of course, the edifice of certainty that we build for these ideas depends on the certainty of our initial assumptions about geometric objects. These initial assumptions are the postulates or axioms, such as the parallel lines postulate previously mentioned. The certainty we have about these basic assumptions is not the result of deduction but is forged out of our experience with the world. This certainty is reinforced as the consequences we prove from these basic assumptions continue to fit our real-world experience of geometry.

Congruent Triangles

A pair of congruent triangles is a special case of similar triangles and a common situation in which to identify pairs of congruent angles. We have already defined congruence for a pair of shapes. Here is a alternative definition for a pair of line segments.

This definition of congruence of line segments is more workable than the "tracing paper" definition given earlier. To give an equivalent and also more workable definition for a pair of triangles, we need some more terminology.

In our discussion we will abbreviate *triangle ABC* as $\triangle ABC$.

If $\triangle ABC$ and $\triangle DEF$ are two triangles and the one-to-one correspondence between the two sets of vertices $\{A,B,C\}$ and $\{D,E,F\}$ is

$$A \leftrightarrow D,\ B \leftrightarrow E,\ \text{and}\ C \leftrightarrow F,$$

then we say that the *corresponding angles* of the two triangles are the pairs *BAC* and *EDF*, *ABC* and *DEF*, and *ACB* and *DFE*; and the *corresponding sides* are the pairs *AB* and *DE*, *AC* and *DF*, *BC* and *EF*.

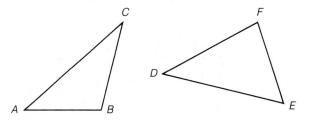

CONGRUENCE OF TRIANGLES

Two triangles $\triangle ABC$ and $\triangle DEF$ are *congruent* if and only if there is a one-to-one correspondence between the two sets of vertices $\{A,B,C\}$ and $\{D,E,F\}$ such that corresponding angles are congruent and corresponding sides are congruent.

For example, in the following diagram $\triangle ABC \cong \triangle DEF$ because $\angle ABC \cong \angle DEF$, $\angle BCA \cong \angle EFD$, $\angle CAB \cong \angle FDE$, $AB \cong DE$, $BC \cong EF$, and $CA \cong FD$.

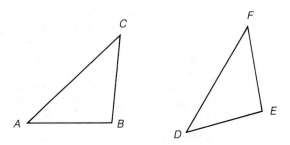

Thus, if you know that two triangles are congruent, you can conclude that a corresponding pair of angles is also congruent. Let us consider how useful this idea is. Suppose that you have two angles, one an angle of $\triangle ABC$ and the other an angle of $\triangle DEF$. You are trying to show that the two angles are congruent. You decide to do this by first showing that $\triangle ABC \cong \triangle DEF$. But, according to the definition of congruent triangles, you need to know that the two angles are congruent before you can conclude that the two triangles are congruent. That's not nice—unless there is a way to show the two triangles congruent without knowing ahead of time our two angles are congruent.

According to the definition, congruence of a pair of triangles involves six pieces of information. Perhaps it is possible that knowing fewer than six of them will guarantee the rest. For example, if we know that the three pairs of corresponding sides and *two* pairs of corresponding angles are congruent, then all six conditions are satisfied— because knowing two angles of a triangle uniquely determines the third angle; the sixth bit of data follows from the other five. Can we do better? What is the minimum information we need to know about two triangles to guarantee that they are congruent?

Suppose that we know about $\triangle ABC$ the lengths of two sides AB and AC and the angle $\angle BAC$ formed by the two sides.

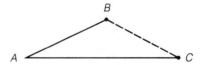

From these data only one triangle can be made: Draw the line segment between the points B and C to complete the triangle. If we had another $\triangle DEF$ with two sides (DE, DF) and the angle $\angle EDF$ between them congruent to the two sides and angle of $\triangle ABC$, we could trace a copy of $\angle EDF$ and its two sides, then fit the tracing over $\angle BAC$ so that the two angles and two pairs of corresponding sides coincide. The line connecting E and F will lie right over the line connecting A and C. The two triangles would be congruent.

SIDE-ANGLE-SIDE (SAS) CONGRUENCE PROPERTY

If two sides and the angle they make in one triangle are congruent to two sides and the angle they make in a second triangle, then the two triangles are congruent.

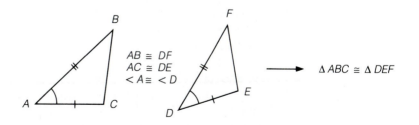

The following theorem is an example of how SAS can be used.

THEOREM: BASE ANGLES OF AN
ISOSCELES TRIANGLE ARE CONGRUENT

Take an isosceles triangle, that is, a triangle two sides of which are congruent. Then the two angles at either end of the triangle's third side (called the *base* of the isosceles triangle) are also congruent. (The two congruent angles are called the *base* angles.)

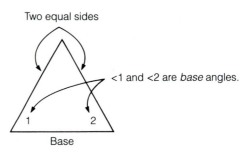

Two equal sides

<1 and <2 are *base* angles.

1   2

Base

To show why this theorem is true, suppose that the two sides of equal length are *AB* and *AC*, as in the next diagram. Draw a line through vertex *A* that meets the opposite side at point *D* such that the $\angle BAD \cong \angle DAC$. We then claim that $\triangle BAD \cong \triangle DAC$. First of all, $\angle BAD \cong \angle DAC$. Second, *AB* is congruent to *AC* (because $\triangle ABC$ is isosceles), and *BD* is congruent to *AD*. By SAS our claim is proved: $\triangle BAD \cong \triangle DAC$, thus, also $\angle ABC \cong \angle ACB$ because they are corresponding angles in congruent triangles.

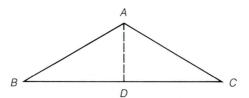

EXERCISE

15. What can you say about a triangle if you know the following information: the length of two of its sides and an angle but not the angle formed by the two sides? Explore the possibilities with straws or toothpicks as the two sides and a stiff, bent wire as the angle.

The SAS congruence property says that a certain three pieces of data are sufficient to guarantee the congruence of two triangles. Are there other "small" subsets of the set of the six basic conditions (three corresponding angles congruent, three corresponding sides congruent) that would guarantee the congruence of the two triangles? Two similar triangles have the three angles of one congruent to the three angles of the other but the triangles themselves may not be congruent. So the congruence of *three angles* of one triangle and three angles of another does *not* guarantee that the two triangles are congruent.

Consider another possibility. Suppose that two angles and the common side of one triangle are congruent to two angles and the common side of another triangle.

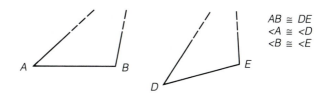

$AB \cong DE$
$<A \cong <D$
$<B \cong <E$

For each of these, the two remaining sides will intersect at one point and the tracing of one triangle will fit exactly over the other triangle. This gives us the following theorem.

ANGLE-SIDE-ANGLE (ASA) CONGRUENCE PROPERTY

If two angles and the common side of one triangle are congruent to two angles and the common side of another triangle, then the two triangles are congruent.

EXERCISES

16. Recall that a parallelogram is a quadrilateral such that opposite (i.e., nonadjacent) sides are parallel. Show that a diagonal divides the parallelogram into two congruent triangles. (*Hint:* Consider the diagonal as a transversal to both sets of parallel lines. In each case you can use the theorem that states alternate interior angles to be congruent. Then use ASA.)

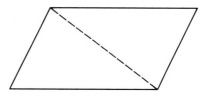

17. Use exercise 16 to show that opposite sides of a parallelogram have equal length.

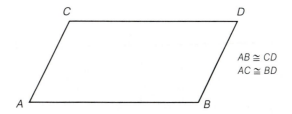

$AB \cong CD$
$AC \cong BD$

18. Show that the two diagonals of a rectangle are equal.

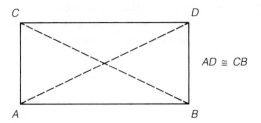

$$AD \cong CB$$

Another "small" subset of the set of six basic data will also guarantee the congruence of two triangles.

SIDE-SIDE-SIDE (SSS) PROPERTY OF CONGRUENCE

If the three sides of one triangle are equal in length to the three sides of another triangle, then the two triangles are congruent.

To see why this is true, suppose that the three sides of $\triangle ABC$ are congruent to the three sides of $\triangle A'B'C'$, as in the diagram.

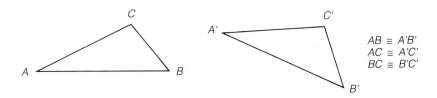

$$AB \cong A'B'$$
$$AC \cong A'C'$$
$$BC \cong B'C'$$

Make a copy of $\triangle A'B'C'$ underneath $\triangle ABC$, as in the following diagram, so that $\triangle ADB \cong \triangle A'B'C'$ ($AB \cong A'B'$, $AD \cong A'C'$, and $\angle B'A'C' \cong \angle DAB$).

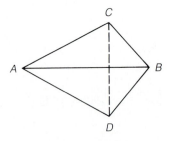

Then draw the line joining C with D. Thus, $\triangle ACD$ is an isosceles triangle. Consequently, $\angle ACD \cong \angle ADC$. Similarly, $\angle DCB \cong \angle BDC$. From these two sets of angle congruences we get that $\angle ACB$ (the sum of $\angle ACD$ and $\angle DCB$) is congruent to $\angle ADB$ (the sum of $\angle ADC$ and $\angle BDC$). By SAS (AC, CB, and $\angle ACB$ in $\triangle ABC$; AD, BD, and $\angle ADB$ in $\triangle ADB$), $\triangle ABC \cong \triangle ADB$. Since $\triangle ADB \cong \triangle A'B'C'$, we also have that $\triangle ABC \cong \triangle A'B'C'$.

19. Suppose you know that two sides of one triangle are congruent to two sides of another triangle. What can you conclude about the two triangles?

20. Suppose you know that two sides and two angles of one triangle are congruent to two sides and two angles of another triangle. What can you conclude about the two triangles?

Thus, once you know the lengths of the three sides, you know the triangle: There is only one with sides of these three lengths. Following is an illustration of a method for constructing a triangle the sides of which are three given lengths. Suppose the three lengths are 4, 5, and 6 units. To construct a triangle with these three lengths, set out the longest length:

Next, attach one shorter side at *A* and pivot it about *A*. The end not attached to *A* will trace out an arc of a circle.

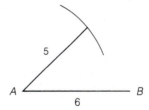

Attach one end of the other shorter side from *B* and do the same thing. The end not attached to *B* will trace out an arc of a circle.

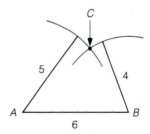

The two traced arcs will intersect at a single point *C* above the line *AB* so that △*ABC* is the desired triangle. (The two circles if drawn completely will also intersect at a point *D* below the line *AB* and △*ABC* ≅ △*ABD*.)

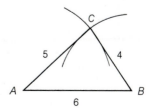

21. For each of the following sets of lengths (the unit length is an inch), construct a triangle having the three lengths as sides: {3,4,6}, {2,3,4}, {4,4,5}, {1,2,3}, {2,3,6}. (Some of these might not work. Which ones? Why?)

22. What can you say about the length of the third side of a triangle the other two sides of which have lengths 4 in and 3 in? (Use straws of lengths 4 in and 3 in to explore triangles two of the sides of which are 3 in and 4 in.)

23. Not every set of three lengths corresponds to the three sides of a triangle. (See exercises 22 and 23.) What can you say in general about three lengths that do correspond to the sides of a triangle?

24. Suppose you have a parallelogram the two diagonals of which are equal. Prove that the parallelogram must be a rectangle. (*Hint:* You know that the sum of the adjacent angles of a parallelogram is congruent to a straight angle. If you can show that two adjacent angles are equal, then you will be finished. [Why?] To show that two adjacent angles are equal, show that certain pairs of triangles are congruent using SSS.)

25. Suppose that opposite sides of a quadrilateral are equal. Show that the quadrilateral must be a parallelogram.

15.4   LOOKING AHEAD: DESCRIBING STRAIGHT LINES USING COORDINATES

René Descartes (1596–1650) was one of the first to exploit the possibilities of a coordinate system for points in a plane. (In fact, the coordinates of a point are sometimes called *Cartesian coordinates,* after Descartes.) One of his goals was to use coordinates to describe geometric shapes, such as lines and circles. For example, take the horizontal line *L* in the coordinate system shown.

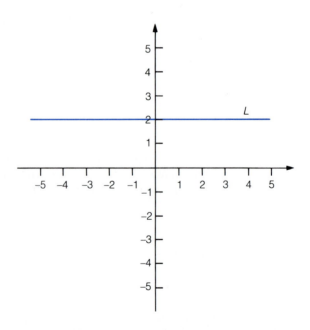

Using coordinates, we can describe the line L as the set of all points the second coordinate of which is 2, that is,

$$L = \{(x,y): y = 2\}.$$

Traditionally, the coordinates of a variable point are indicated by (x,y); the horizontal axis is called the *x axis*, and the vertical axis, the *y axis*. The description of the line L given above is traditionally abbreviated by the expression "the line $y = 2$."

We would like to find descriptions of other lines using coordinates. In chapter 14, it seemed plausible that the formula for a function the graph of which is a straight line should be of the form $y = mx + k$, where x is a typical input and y is the corresponding output. The discussion in this section should provide verification and new understanding of what before was merely plausible.

Let's start with a typical line L passing through the origin and moving from the lower left to the upper right:

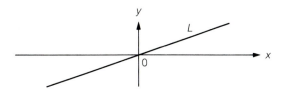

Take two points P and Q on line L to the right of and above the origin O. The lines through these points parallel to the vertical axis meet at points R and S (respectively) on the horizontal axis. These lines also make right angles with the horizontal axis.

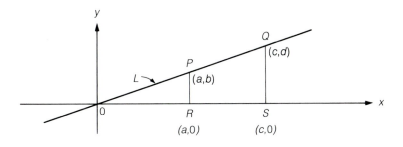

Now $\triangle OPR$ is similar to $\triangle OQS$. Thus,

$$\frac{PR}{OR} = \frac{QS}{OS}.$$

If the coordinates of P and Q are (a,b) and (c,d), respectively, this last equation means that

$$\frac{b}{a} = \frac{d}{c}.$$

You will notice that for a point (e,f) on the line to the left and below the origin, the ratio f/e is also equal to b/a.

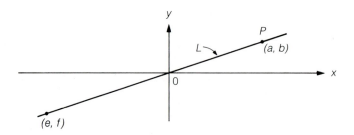

In fact, if (x,y) is any point on the line, then

$$\frac{y}{x} = \frac{b}{a} = \frac{d}{c} = \frac{f}{e} = m.$$

This common number m is called the *slope* of the line.

Finally, if (g,h) is a point such that $h/g = m$, then we claim that (g,h) is also a point on the line L. To show this, let (g,k) be the address of the point that is the intersection of the line through $(g,0)$ on the horizontal axis and the line L.

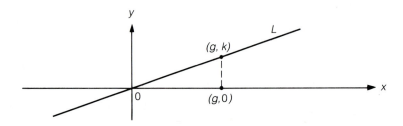

Then we know that $k/g = m$. Since $h/g = m$ also, it follows that $h = k$ and the point (g,h) is on the line.

Thus, the line L can be described

$$L = \{(x,y): y/x = m\},$$

or, what is the same,

$$L = \{(x,y): y = mx\}.$$

The latter is the more traditional description. It is usually abbreviated by the expression "the line $y = mx$."

A similar argument shows that for a line M through 0 and moving from the upper left to the lower right, there is a number k such that $y/x = k$ for every point (x,y) on the line and, conversely, if a point (p,q) satisfies $q/p = k$, then (p,q) is a point on the line. Thus, we can write

$$M = \{(x,y): y = kx\}.$$

For the line M, k is also called the slope; but in this case the slope k is *negative*. (For lines that go from lower left to upper right, the slope is positive.) The slope of a horizontal line, y = fixed number, is defined to be 0. A vertical line has no slope; the slope of the line x = a fixed number is *not defined*.

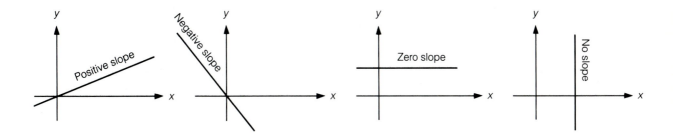

So far we have a description in terms of coordinates for every line through the origin and every horizontal and vertical line. Let's describe the remaining lines. Take a line K that does not pass through the origin and is neither vertical nor horizontal. It must intersect the vertical axis in a point $(0,b)$, and it must be parallel to a line L given by $y = mx$.

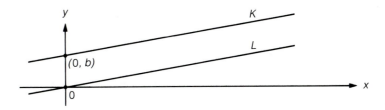

Now take a point P with coordinates (x,y) on the line K. The vertical line through P intersects the line L at a point Q with coordinates $(x, y - b)$.

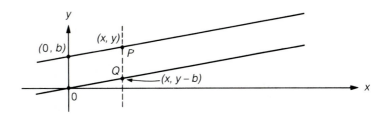

But, since Q is a point on the line L,

$$y - b = mx, \quad \text{or} \quad y = mx + b.$$

Furthermore, any point (p,q) such that $q = mp + b$ must be a point on the line K. Thus, we can write

$$K = \{(x,y): y = mx + b\}.$$

The number m is the slope of the line K also. There is a common definition of the slope of any line drawn in a coordinate system.

TWO-POINT DEFINITION OF THE SLOPE OF A NONVERTICAL LINE

To calculate the slope of a line that is not vertical, take two distinct points (c,d) and (e,f) on the line.

Then $\dfrac{f-d}{e-c}$ is the slope of the line.

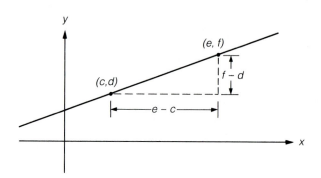

THE EQUATION OF A LINE

Given a nonvertical line L in the plane, there are numbers m and b such that $L = \{(x,y): y = mx + b\}$. The line's slope is m, the line's *vertical intercept* is (O,b), and the line's *equation* is $y = mx + b$.

Given a vertical line M, there is a number b such that $M = \{(x,y): x = b\}$. Its *equation* is $x = b$.

EXERCISES   26. Some lines are drawn on graph paper. For each line find the slope, vertical intercept (if it has one), and equation.

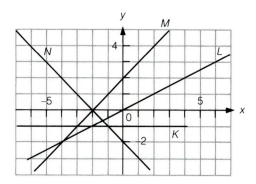

27. Here are some equations for lines. Draw each of the lines on graph paper.
   - (a) $y = x$
   - (b) $y = 2x$
   - (c) $y = 2x + 1$
   - (d) $y = 2x - 1$
   - (e) $y = .5x$
   - (f) $y = -x$
   - (g) $y = -2x$
   - (h) $y = -2x + 1$
   - (i) $y = -2x - 1$
   - (j) $y = -.5x$

Graphs Corresponding to Trips

Recall the scheme devised in chapter 14 for picturing a trip taken along a straight line. The picture is the graph of the function the input of which is the amount of time (positive or negative) that has elapsed since time zero and the output of which is the distance (positive or negative) from a fixed reference point at that time. Suppose that you are taking a trip along a straight line and that throughout the trip you travel at the same (constant) speed of 30 ft/sec. If at time zero you are at the reference point, then your distance d from the reference point t sec later will be $30t$. A formula for the function relating distance to time is thus $d = 30t$.

The graph of this function is a straight line! In general, if you travel the same speed of s ft/sec throughout your trip and you start at the starting point, then a formula for the function is $d = st$.

If your speed is the same as this throughout the trip but you are f ft from the reference point at time zero, then the formula is $d = st + f$.

The two graphs are parallel! Two trips with the same speed should have parallel graphs.

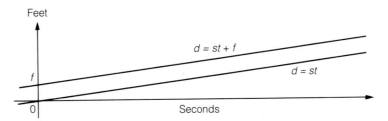

EXERCISES 28. Graphs for several trips are given. For each trip: Find the speed during the trip; find the distance of the traveler from the reference point at time zero; and find the formula for the corresponding function.

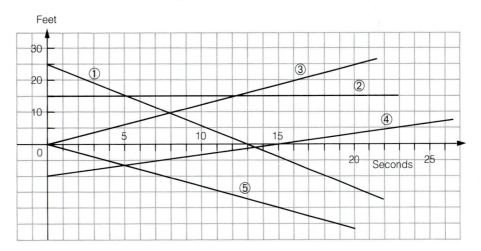

29. Draw the graphs corresponding to the following trips. (Distances and speeds are in positive direction unless otherwise noted. Also, all trips begin at time $t = 0$.)
    (a) Speed a constant 15 ft/sec; start trip 10 ft from reference point
    (b) Speed a constant 15 ft/sec in negative direction; start trip 10 ft from reference point

(c) Speed a constant 15 ft/sec; start trip 10 ft from reference point in negative direction

(d) Speed a constant throughout trip; at 2 sec the distance from reference point is 10 ft; at 10 sec the distance from reference point is 74 ft

15.5 SUMMARY OF IMPORTANT IDEAS AND TECHNIQUES

- How to make a scale drawing of a triangle
  Using definition of scale drawing from earlier chapters
  Copying an angle and making scale drawings of its two sides
  Making a scale drawing of one side and copying the angles at both ends
- The use of tracing paper and a transit for copying angles
- Definition of *similar triangles* and *corresponding sides*
- Criteria for recognizing similar triangles
- Scale factor between similar triangles; relationship to scale
- Using ratios and proportions to solve problems related to similar triangles
- Deductive geometry
  Congruence of two shapes
  The congruence of vertical angles
  The congruence of corresponding angles and alternate interior angles associated with a transversal to a pair of parallel lines
  Congruence of two triangles using the side-angle-side (SAS), angle-side-angle (ASA), and side-side-side (SSS) properties
  Applications of these ideas to isosceles triangles, parallelograms, and rectangles
- Describing straight lines using coordinates
  Slope, vertical intercept, and equation of a straight line
  Trip on a straight line with a picture also a straight line

PROBLEM SET

PRACTICING
SKILLS

1. An electricity pole is to be supported by a guy wire running from a position 15 ft up the pole to a point on the ground 10 ft from its base. A total of 3 ft of extra wire will be needed to wrap the guy wire around the pole and secure it to the ground. How much wire will be needed in all? (Solve this using a scale drawing.)

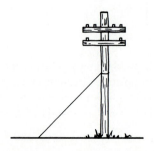

2. Make a scale drawing of an equilateral triangle each side of which is 20 ft. You choose the scale.

3. You are a lumberjack and need to know the height of the tree shown. Because you are unable to measure the tree directly, you measure the shadows of the tree and also your 1.8-m-tall assistant. These shadows are 16 m and 1.2 m, respectively.

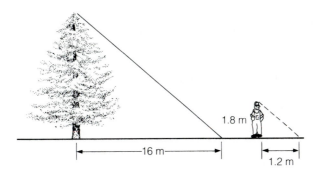

4. The distance from the point T where the guy wire is attached to the ground and the base of the light pole is 20 ft. The distance from the man's feet to T is 5 ft. How tall is the pole?

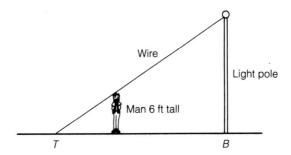

5. To find the distance across a lake, surveyors sighted $\triangle ABC$ and $\triangle ADE$ and found certain distances to be as indicated in the picture. Find the distance across the lake. ($\angle ABC \cong \angle ADE$.)

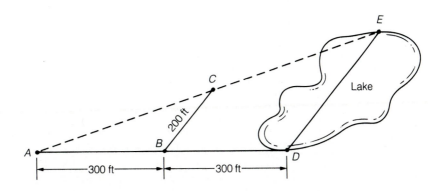

6. Enlarge each triangle so that each side *AB* is 3 in long.

(a) 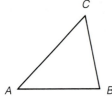 (b)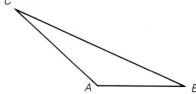

7. A scale drawing of a triangle has sides of length 11, 12, and 13 cm, and the scale is 1 cm representing 2.3 ft. Find the lengths of the sides of the large triangle.

8. Find the lengths of the missing sides *x*, *y*, *z*, and *w* in the picture.

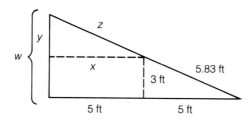

9. Assume *AB* is parallel to *CD* in the drawing. Find side *AB*.

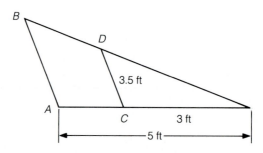

10. Find side *AB* in the drawing.

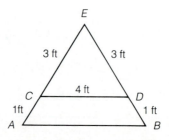

11. Give an argument based on theorems and definitions from section 15.3 showing why △ABC, below, is similar to △ADE if we know that side DE is parallel to side BC.

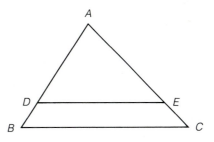

12. Give an argument showing why the following angles are congruent if you know that lines L and L' are parallel and that lines L' and L'' are parallel.
   (a) $\angle 1$ and $\angle 12$
   (b) $\angle 10$ and $\angle 3$
   (c) $\angle 9$ and $\angle 4$

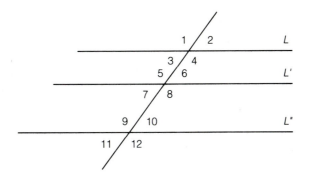

13. Show that the sum of $\angle 1$ and $\angle 2$ of the trapezoid must be a straight angle.

14. Show that $\angle 1$ and $\angle 2$ in the parallelogram are congruent. (*Hint:* Use a diagonal of the parallelogram.)

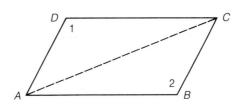

15. Assume that *ABCD* is a rectangle. Show that △*ABM* is congruent to △*DCM*.

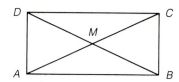

16. Suppose that *DE* is parallel to *AB*, *E* is the midpoint of *BC*, and *D* is the midpoint of *AC*. Show that △*FEB* is congruent to △*DCE*.

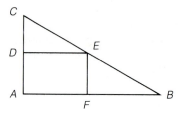

17. Show that the diagonals of a rectangle meet at their midpoints.

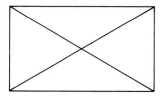

18. If *AC* ≅ *BC* and *AD* ≅ *EB*, show that *CD* ≅ *CE*.

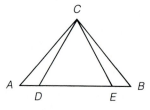

19. If *AE* and *BC* are parallel and *AD* ≅ *DC*, show that △*ADE* is congruent to △*CDB*.

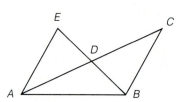

20. If lines *AB* and *CD* bisect each other at *E*, show that △*AEC* is congruent to △*BED*.

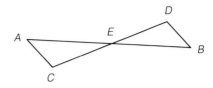

21. Construct triangles with sides of the given lengths.
    (a) 3, 4, 5 in   (b) 2, 4, 5 in   (c) 3, 5, 7 in

22. Find its equation and draw (on graph paper) each line.
    (a) The line with slope 1/2 passing through the point (0,0)
    (b) The line with slope −1/2 passing through the point (0,0)
    (c) The line with slope 2 passing through the point (0,0)
    (d) The line with slope −2 passing through the point (0,0)

23. Find its equation and draw each line.
    (a) The line with slope 3 passing through (0,0)
    (b) The line with slope 3 passing through (0,−1)
    (c) The line with slope 3 passing through (2,0)
    (d) The line passing through points (0,2) and (3,2)
    (e) The line passing through points (2,0) and (0,3)
    (f) The line passing through points (−1,0) and (3,2)
    (g) The line passing through points (5,3) and (5,−1)
    (h) The line passing through points (−1,l) and (−l,4)
    (i) The line passing through points (−1,1) and (3,1)
    (j) The line with slope 2/3 passing through the point (4,5)
    (k) The line with slope −2/3 passing through the point (4,5)
    (l) The line with slope 3/2 passing through the point (4,5)
    (m) The line with slope −3/2 passing through the point (4,5)

24. Draw the lines described by the equations.
    (a) $y = -2x + 3$ (b) $y = 2x + 3$ (c) $y = 5$
    (d) $x = 2$ (e) $y = 3x$ (f) $y = \frac{1}{2}x + 1$
    (g) $y = -\frac{1}{2}x + 1$ (h) $y = 2x + 1$ (i) $y = -2x + 1$

USING IDEAS   *For each remaining problem, write an essay in which you communicate clearly and completely the solution to the problem. Mention the steps you took in solving the problem, other problems or solutions that gave you ideas, and the strategies you used.*

25. A surveyor needs to find the length of a planned bridge extending across a canyon. The drawing on page 658, a bird's-eye view, shows the situation from the air. Unable to measure from *A* to *B* directly (*A* and *B* are eye-level features of the landscape), the surveyor uses a masonite right triangle (also shown): He walks along the canyon (the path makes a right angle with the planned bridge) until he reaches a point *C* where he can sight *B* along the unmeasured side of his triangle and at the same time sight *A* along the 40 cm side of the triangle. (The triangle is shown in this position. The 25-cm side of the triangle is parallel to the line joining *A* and *B*, and the plane of the triangle is level.) Find the distance from *A* to *B*.

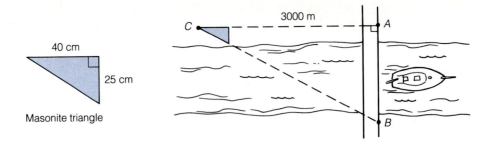

Masonite triangle

26. You are updating the map of a certain mountainous region. From the top of a mountain you sight, in the valley below, an interesting rock formation that is not on the existing map but should be. You know that the mountain you are standing on lies 2000 m above the valley. Also, as you sight it, another peak 1450 m above the valley is in line with the rock formation. The existing map includes the mountain and the intervening peak and indicates that the distance from the mountain on which you are standing to the peak is 2200 m. To add the rock formation to your map, you need to know the distance from the mountain to the rock formation. What is it?

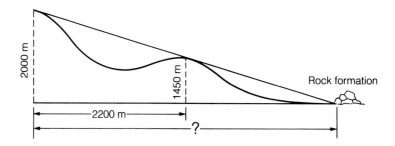

27. You are an architect and must make a scale drawing of the plot for a house. The plot is triangular with sides 100 ft, 80 ft, and 70 ft. You decide on a scale of 1 in for 10 ft. Construct the scale drawing and describe how you did it.

28. Part of a highway realignment program is to replace the present bridge over a river by another one. Surveyors, needing to determine the length of the proposed bridge AB, have decided to make a scale drawing and have measured CB and CA as indicated. They have also sighted the angle at C and have traced it, as shown. Complete the scale drawing of △ABC, and from it figure out the length of AB.

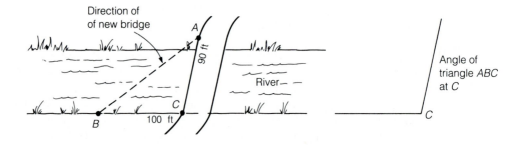

29. The highway builder for problem 28 proposes to build a bridge over a gorge to carry the realigned highway. To figure out how long the bridge BC will be, surveyors measured the length of AB

along one side of the gorge, found it to be 75 ft and traced two angles of △*ABC* as shown. Complete the scale drawing and figure out the length of *BC* from it.

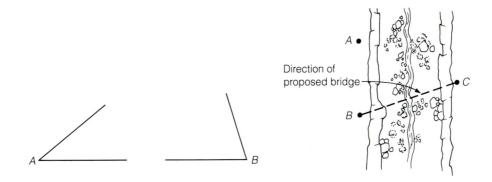

30. You are a forest ranger with a job at a fire lookout tower. You have just spotted a fire. You need to pinpoint the location of the fire exactly so that firefighters can be directed to it. Quickly you radio Jane, the ranger in the other lookout tower of the range. (A map of the two lookout towers and the surrounding environment is provided.) You tell Jane the approximate location of the fire and ask her to sight the fire in her viewfinder and tell you the angle the line of sight makes with the line *AB* joining the two towers. She does this and communicates to you the angle shown. You figure out the angle your line of sight to the fire makes with the line *AB* and mark it on the map as shown.

    (a) On this map complete the scale drawing (of a triangle) two of the vertices of which are *A* and *B* and two of the sides of which are already drawn. The missing line is gotten by tracing Jane's angle at *B*; the missing vertex will be the point at which your and her two sight lines meet—at the location of the fire!

    (b) What directions for finding the fire will you give over the radio to the firefighters?

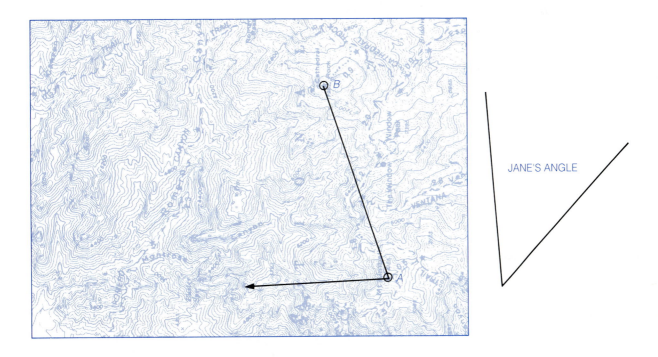

31. One of the triangles is a scale drawing of the other. Find the length of the side marked ?. How do the perimeters of the two triangles compare?

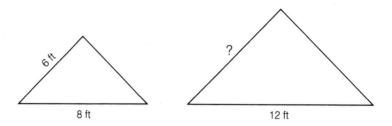

32. How tall is the tree?

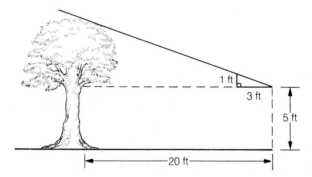

33. A farmer is estimating the size of one of his fields. The field has been freshly plowed, and the furrows are shown in the picture below as parallel lines spaced equally across the field. To estimate the length of one side *RS* of the field, she stands at point *A* in one furrow and sights *R* and *S*. In another furrow she has her assistant put stakes at *P* and *Q*, which lie in her line of sight from *A* to *R* and from *A* to *S*, respectively. The assistant measures the distance from *P* to *Q* and finds that it is 40 m. Use this information to help the farmer find the distance from *R* to *S*.

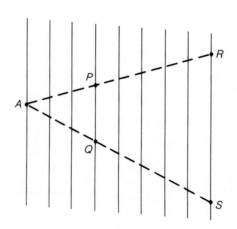

34. You plan to build a highway by making a cut through an existing hill, shown in the sketch. To estimate its cost, you need to know (among other things) how long the highway will be. You decide to create a scale drawing and have found a position C from which you can sight both ends A and B of the proposed section of highway. You are able to measure CA and CB and find that they are 2.8 mi and 1.5 mi, respectively. You have traced the angle between the sight lines CA and CB, shown. Find the length of the proposed highway AB.

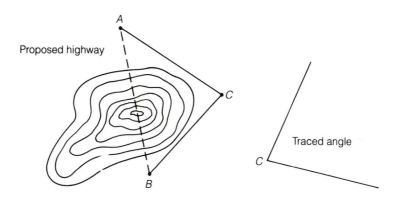

35. You are the manager of Deep Snow Ski Resort. Business is great, and you plan to propose to the owner that he build an additional ski lift. To make your case, you need an estimate of the cost, and for that you need to know the length of the proposed ski lift. Deciding to make a scale drawing, you sight the top T of the lift-to-be from two points P (the base of the lift) and Q (another point at the bottom of the mountain). You measure the length of PQ and figure out the angles of △TPQ at P and Q. The results are shown. Use this information to construct the scale drawing and figure out the length of TP.

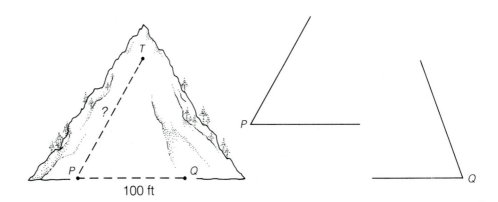

36. The results of exercises 24 and 25 in the text can be used by construction workers to make sure that the foundation of a house, which is supposed to be rectangular, really is a rectangle. The following is an illustration of the method. Suppose the foundation is to be a rectangle 20 by 30 ft.

Pound in a stake at *A*, where you want one corner to be; pound in another stake at *B* 30 ft away, where you want another corner to be.

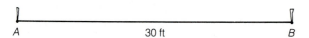

A   30 ft   B

Tie a string to the stake at *A*; 20 ft along this string attach another stake; 30 ft from there attach a second stake; continue the string along for 20 ft more and attach it to the stake at *B*. Tautly stretch the string with the two additional stakes. You will get something like this:

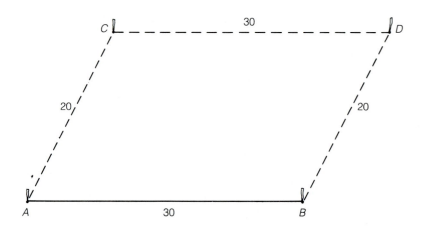

The additional stakes are at *C* and *D*.

(a) Why should this figure be a parallelogram?

The idea is to keep the string taut but to move the stakes at *C* and *D* until a rectangle is formed. The workers take more string to measure the length from *C* to *B* and from *A* to *D*. When these two lengths are the same, they claim they have a rectangle and pound in stakes *C* and *D*.

(b) Why does this method guarantee that the string and stakes form a rectangle?

37. (a) Draw a pair of noncongruent quadrilaterals each having the property that all four sides have length 3 in.

(b) Draw a pair of noncongruent quadrilaterals each having the property that two opposite sides have lengths 3 in and the other two have lengths 2 in.

(c) Draw a pair of noncongruent quadrilaterals each having the property that one side has length 2 in, a second length 3 in, a third 4 in, and the fourth 5 in.

(d) Sometimes a set of three lengths will make a triangle and sometimes not. Will a set of four lengths always make a quadrilateral?

(e) For a triangle, once you know the lengths of its three sides, then you know the triangle. (This is SSS.) What can you say about a quadrilateral once you know its four sides?

(f) You know a quadrilateral if you know the lengths of its four sides and you know its four angles, a total of eight items of information. Can you determine a quadrilateral with fewer than eight items? Which combinations of items will do this?

38. Take some strips of stiff paper around 3/4 in wide and from 8 to 12 in long and some brass fasteners. Punch holes near the ends of the strips, just large enough for the ends of the fasteners to fit through. Use these to make the flat frameworks shown in the pictures.

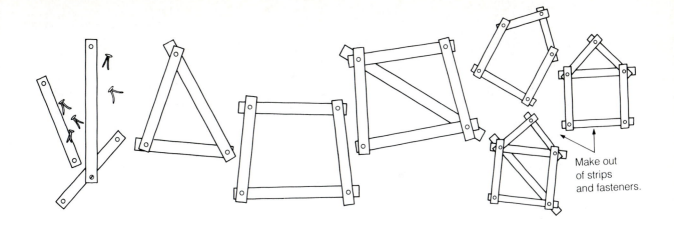

(a) Keep each framework flat on top of the table and try to alter its shape. Some will keep their shape, and some won't. For example you can "flex" a square as shown.

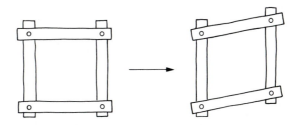

Which frameworks are *rigid*, that is, will not flex? What does the SSS property of congruence of triangles say about the rigidity (i.e., nonflexibility) of a triangle? What does the *triangulation* of bridges and scaffolding mean, and why is it done?

(b) Is there such a thing as a rigid quadrilateral?

39. Show that if the diagonals of a quadrilateral bisect each other the figure is a parallelogram.

40. Show that if the diagonals of a rectangle are perpendicular to each other the figure is a square.

41. Show that joining the midpoints of adjacent sides of a parallelogram *ABCD* forms another parallelogram *A'B'C'D'*.

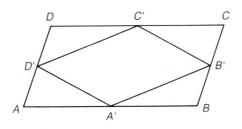

REVIEW TEST FOR CHAPTERS 13, 14, AND 15

For each multiple-choice question, circle the letter to the left of the most appropriate response.

1. The state department of environmental quality allows small energy facilities to burn oil with a sulfur content no greater than 2.2%. Clean oil contains 1.2% sulfur; dirty oil contains 4.8% sulfur. The graph shows the amount of sulfur in a 100-gal mixture of the two oils versus the amount of the mixture that is dirty oil.

Find the largest amount of dirty oil in the mixture that would satisfy the requirements of the department of environmental quality for sulfur level.
   (a) 4.8 gal   (b) 21 gal   (c) 1.2 gal   (d) 30 gal   (e) 70 gal

2. Which of the following sets of lengths will *not* assemble to make a triangle?
   (a) 3, 4, 5 in   (b) 2, 2, 3 in   (c) 1, 2, 4 in   (d) 5, 5, 5 in   (e) 2, 5, 6 in

3. A picture $2\frac{1}{2}$ in wide by $3\frac{3}{4}$ in tall is to be enlarged to make a poster 4 ft tall. The width of the poster will be
   (a) 6 ft   (b) $2\frac{2}{3}$ ft   (c) $\frac{4}{15}$ ft   (d) $1\frac{1}{2}$ ft   (e) $\frac{2}{5}$ ft

4. A cattle rancher wants to know when she should sell her herd of beef cattle. Although each animal gains weight daily, the price per kilogram of cattle is decreasing daily and it costs a certain amount to feed each animal daily. The graph shows the selling price of the herd (minus additional cost of feeding) versus the number of days from the present. To make the most money, the rancher should sell her cattle how many days from now?
   (a) 54 days   (b) 28 days   (c) 78 days   (d) 0 days   (e) 14 days

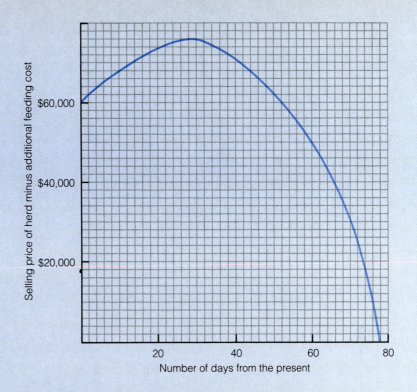

5. Which of the following figures has the smallest perimeter?

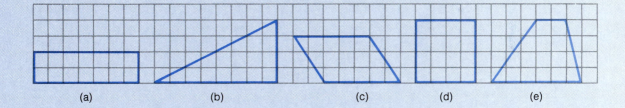

(a)   (b)   (c)   (d)   (e)

6. Which of the following patterns is *not* a dressmaker's pattern for the tent shown? (The tent has a bottom.)

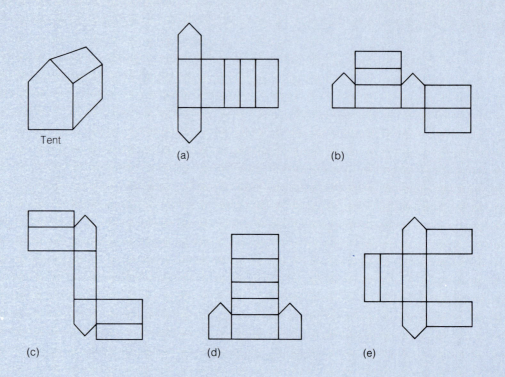

Tent

(a)   (b)

(c)   (d)   (e)

7. Two forest rangers in different fire lookout towers *A* and *B* are trying to pinpoint the location *F* of a fire (indicated in the diagram, left). They know the distance between the two towers and are able to sight the angles of the triangle at *A* and *B*. This enables them to construct the scale drawing, right.

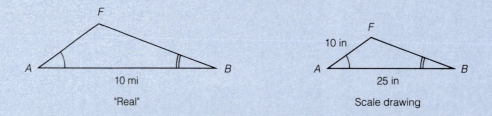

"Real"

Scale drawing

From this the forest rangers can conclude that the distance from *A* to fire *F* is how far?
(a) 10 mi   (b) 4 mi   (c) 2.5 mi   (d) 25 mi   (e) 40 mi

8. To find the distance across a lake, surveyors sighted $\triangle ABC$ and $\triangle ADE$ and found certain distances to be as indicated in the picture. What is the distance *DE* across the lake? ($\angle ABC \cong \angle ADE$.)
(a) 1216 ft   (b) 576 ft   (c) 528 ft   (d) 225 ft   (e) 475 ft

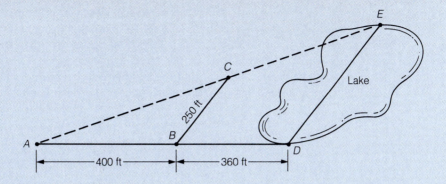

ESSAY
QUESTIONS *For each remaining problem, express your final solution carefully in the form of an essay.*

9. You are in charge of a large diplomatic reception at which you plan to serve champagne. You figure you will need 100 bottles. You want to serve French champagne, which costs $12 a bottle, rather than domestic, which costs $7 a bottle. However, you have budgeted only $900 for the champagne. You decide to buy 100 bottles of champagne and make as many of them French as you can and still keep within your budget. Figure out how many French and domestic bottles you will buy. Do this by graphing the cost (output) of an order of 100 bottles versus the number (input) of bottles of French in the order. (Start with a table.)

10. You are installing a new fence for your barnyard and garden, as shown in the scale drawing. Of course, you will not need fencing where the buildings and gates are. How much fencing will you need?

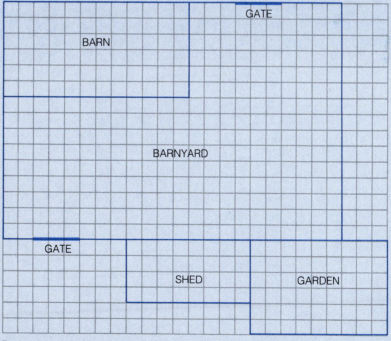

Each square in grid = 1 m²

11. To measure the distance from *D* to *E* across a lake, a point *C* is located so that points *D* and *E* can be seen from *C*, the distance from *C* to *D* can be measured, and a copy of the angle at *D* can be made. The straight line from *D* to *C* is then extended to a point *B* at which the angle at *B* is constructed equal to the angle at *D*. The straight line from *E* to *C* is also extended, and the following diagram results. You find that the length of *BC* is equal to 100 m, the length of *AB* is equal to 80 m, and the length of *CD* is equal to 1500 m. What is the length of *DE*?

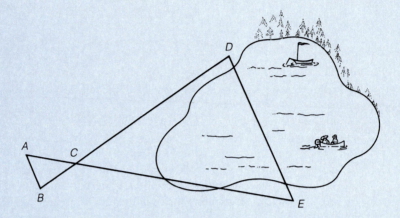

CIRCLES AND ANGLES

C H A P T E R

Circles, like rectangles, are a prevalent shape in the environment and in our culture. A circle is the shape of the sun and the full moon in the sky, of a cross section of grapefruit, of the opening of a pot, of a ring, and, of course, of the wheel.

In this chapter, we want to solve two problems having to do with circles. One of these is the problem of finding an efficient and accurate way of measuring a circle's perimeter (circumference). We will do this by combining some ideas from chapters 13 and 15.

The second is the problem of finding a convenient way to communicate the size of an angle, a problem hinted at in chapter 15. The solution is to create a unit of angle measurement and a device for doing the measuring. The circle is intimately involved in this solution.

We will use both of these solutions to solve a third problem, finding the circumference of the earth.

You are a forest ranger working at a fire lookout tower. When you spot a fire, one of your jobs is to pinpoint its location precisely so that firefighters can be directed to the fire quickly. One method for doing this was sketched in chapter 15; we'll summarize it again here.

There are two towers. You are in charge of one. Jane is in charge of the other. You have a map of the region on which is drawn a line joining the two towers. You sight Jane's tower and the fire and copy on the map the angle made by the two lines of sight. Jane sights the fire and your tower and gives you enough information by radio so that you can create a copy of the angle made by her two lines of sight. You copy this angle on your map and determine the exact location of the fire on the map.

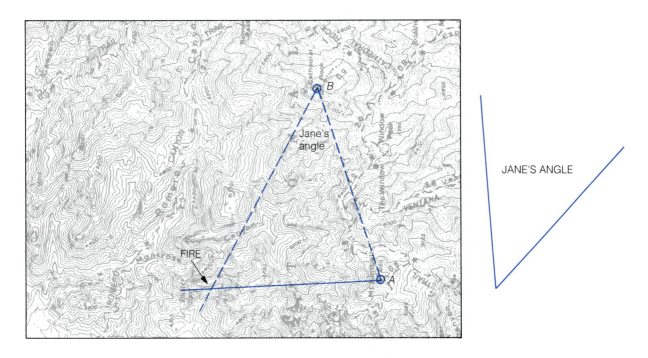

JANE'S ANGLE

Think about this.

What information can Jane give you over the radio so that you can make a copy of the angle formed by her two lines?

A Solution to the
Fire Lookout Problem

Think of the *solution to a similar problem.* When information about the length of an object has to be transported a long distance, it may be inconvenient to carry a "duplicate" of the length with you, in the form of a piece of string, say. One solution to this recurring problem is to create standardized units of length and measuring devices (rulers) so that a number can be attached to a length and carried about easily.

The angle problem is similar. How does one communicate the size of an angle without making an exact copy of it and carrying it to where it is needed? The historical solution to the angle problem has been similar to the solution of the length problem: to create units of angle measure and a measuring device to determine the number of units to associate with a given angle.

We will create a temporary basic unit and a measuring device. We choose a "small" angle as the basic unit:

As a primitive measuring device, cut a copy of this "unit" angle out of heavy cardboard. Now take an angle you want to measure.

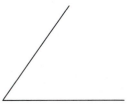

Place the vertex of the cardboard angle on the vertex of the angle you want to measure so that the right-hand sides of the two angles coincide.

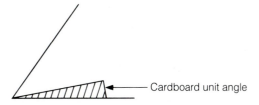

Cardboard unit angle

On the angle you want to measure, trace the left-hand side of the basic measure.

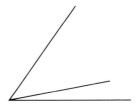

Move the basic angle measure up to that line and do the same thing again.

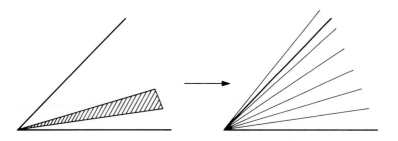

Keep doing this until you are just beyond the left-hand side of the angle you want to measure. Count the number of times you have to do this. In our example it is roughly $5\frac{1}{2}$ times. So the measure of our angle is roughly $5\frac{1}{2}$ of our basic units.

The Mathematical Idea: Development of Units and Devices for Measuring Angles

Measuring angles this way is a primitive method. It is like measuring things with our thumb. We need something for measuring angles that corresponds to rulers and tape measures for measuring length. To construct a ruler, one takes a straight stick and marks thumb widths (or some other unit of length of our choice) on it, then numbers the marks 1, 2, 3, and so on. It's not so obvious what device for angle measurement could correspond to a straight stick for length measurement.

At some ancient time someone who was very interested in this problem thought of using a circle for solving the problem.

DEFINITION OF A CIRCLE

Take a point C on a piece of paper and a length R. The set of all points on the paper that have distance R from C form a *circle*. The point C is the *center* of the circle. The length R is the *radius* of the circle.

HOW TO DRAW A CIRCLE OF RADIUS R AND CENTER C

Take a piece of string. Tie one end to a pin and the other to a pencil. Push the pin in the paper and, keeping the string taut, trace out a circle with the pencil. The center of the circle is the point where the pin punctures the paper; the radius is the distance from the pin to the pencil along the taut string.

To get back to our problem of creating a device for measuring angles, draw a circle on a piece of cardboard. Make sure its center is clearly indicated. Choose a point on the circle itself and mark it with *S* for "start." Draw a line joining the center and *S* and extend it to intersect the circle at a point *E* opposite from *S*. Place the basic unit (the cardboard angle you cut out earlier) with its vertex on the center of the circle and its right-hand side intersecting the circle at *S*.

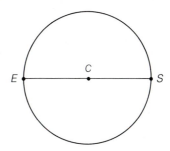

Mark the point *A* on the circle where the left-hand side of the basic unit intersects it.

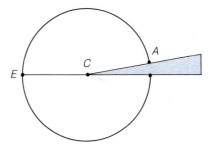

Keeping its vertex at the center of the circle, move the basic unit so that its right-hand side intersects the circle at *A*.

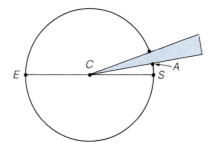

Again, mark the new point on the circle where the left-hand side of the basic unit intersects it. Keep doing this. Move the basic unit and mark points on the circle until you reach the point *E* on the circle opposite the starting point (or a point beyond it). Now, starting with *S* labeled as 0, label the marked points in succession with numerals.

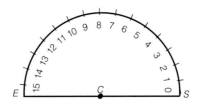

Cut along the line from *E* to *S*; then cut out the semicircle with the marks on it. This is your measuring device.

To use it, take the angle you want to measure and place *C* on top of the vertex of your angle. Make the line from *C* to *S* lie on top of the right-hand side of your angle. Look at the point at which the left-hand side of your angle intersects the semicircle and read off the number of "angle units" from the marked semicircle. That number is the measure of your angle in terms of the unit we created.

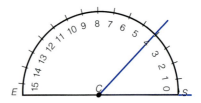

Degrees and Protractors

A common basic unit for measuring angles is the *degree,* and the common measuring device is the *protractor.* The angle unit of a degree works just like the unit we created earlier. The protractor, with degrees marked on it, is also a semicircle that works like the semicircular measuring device we constructed. The only difference is the choice of unit. The degree was created by the Babylonians over three thousand years ago. It has the property that the measure of a straight angle in degrees is 180; thus, there are 180 marks on the semicircle:

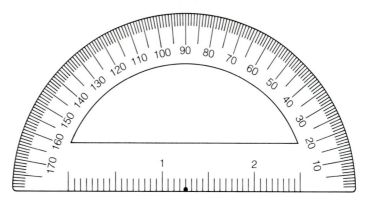

If the markings were to continue around the entire circle, there would be 360 markings. One says, "There are 360 degrees in a circle." It is likely that the choice of the degree as a unit for measuring angles has something to do with the fact that 360 is close to the number of days in a year and also that 360 is closely related to the base for the Babylonian system of numerals. (A cardboard protractor to cut out and use can be found in the lab manual designed to accompany this text.)

EXERCISE 1. Use a protractor to measure the number of degrees in each angle.

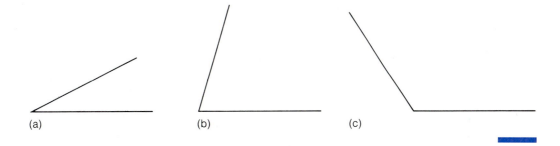

(a)   (b)   (c)

16.2   THE CIRCUMFERENCE OF A CIRCLE

THE WHEEL MANUFACTURING PROBLEM

The Wagon Wheel Company manufactures wagon wheels of all sizes. One part of the process of wheel making is to make the metal outer rim of the wheel. To figure out the length of this metal strip, the company must measure the distance around the wheel—the perimeter of the wheel's circular shape. Until now the company's staff has been doing this by wrapping a piece of string exactly once around the wheel where the outer rim should go and then measuring the string. This is satisfactory for wheels that are already made. It is not satisfactory for wheels that are at the design stage. The staff would like to be able to compare the costs of the outer wheel rims for various-sized wheels, and it is not very easy or accurate to figure out the perimeter of a circle with a string when the only information they have to work from is a scale drawing. The company is looking for another way to figure out the perimeter of a circle.

Diego, the head designer for the Wagon Wheel Company, thinks: "Let's *consider a simpler problem* for clues. Let's look at shapes whose perimeters are easy to measure.

For these, all you have to do is measure the sides, then add them up. The circle doesn't have any sides. We could get a rough idea of the perimeter of a circle by measuring the straight sides of a shape that is close to a circle.

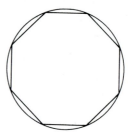

That's not a bad idea."

EXERCISE

2. Try Diego's idea for measuring the perimeter of the circle on the circle immediately preceding and on the shapes shown: "Approximate" each shape by a polygon, measure the sides of the polygon, and add the lengths.

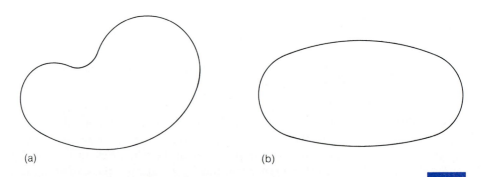

(a)   (b)

Jocelyn, Diego's assistant, has been looking over his shoulder. "It seems like a lot of work to do it that way. You have to draw a lot of 'sides' and then measure them.

"Take a square. It's easy to figure out its perimeter. All you need to do is measure *one* of its sides S, and you've got the whole perimeter: $4S$. If only there were a *single*, easy measurement to make on a circle that we could use to figure out its perimeter. One measurement of length we use when we draw a circle is the radius. It would be nice if knowing the radius of a circle would enable us to figure out its perimeter.

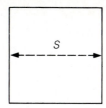

Perimeter = 4 *S*

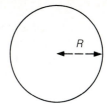

Permeter = ?

"Let's play around with your idea of approximating the perimeter of the circle with a lot of straight sides and with my idea of using the radius.

"We design wheels and know that the length of each spoke is a radius. If we connect the points where these spokes touch the circle with straight lines, then we'll have a polygon whose perimeter approximates that of the circle

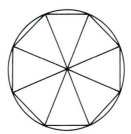

What happens if we do the same thing with a circle that has a different radius? Keep the same center, make a circle with larger radius, extend the spokes of the smaller circle to the perimeter of the larger circle, and connect the points again.

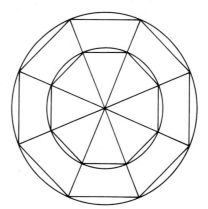

"The sum of the lengths of the sides of this larger polygon is an approximation of the perimeter of the larger circle. Let's compare the two approximations, the one for the larger circle with the one for the smaller circle. On the small circle two adjacent spokes and a connecting side make a little triangle. The extended spokes and the new connecting side also make a triangle. Furthermore, the two triangles are similar. [Why?] That means that the ratio of the length of one connecting side to its radius is the same as the ratio of the length of the other connecting side to its radius.

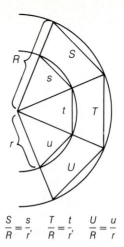

$$\frac{S}{R} = \frac{s}{r}, \quad \frac{T}{R} = \frac{t}{r}, \quad \frac{U}{R} = \frac{u}{r}$$

The ratio of the sum of all the lengths approximating the smaller circle to its radius is the same as the ratio of the sum for the larger circle to its radius:

$$\frac{s}{r} + \frac{t}{r} + \frac{u}{r} + \cdots = \frac{S}{R} + \frac{T}{R} + \frac{U}{R} + \cdots$$

or

$$\frac{s + t + u + \cdots}{r} = \frac{S + T + U + \cdots}{R}.$$

This will be the case no matter what the radii are and no matter how many spokes there are. Furthermore, the closer together the spokes, the better the approximation.

"For spokes really close together,

$$\frac{\text{Perimeter of small circle}}{r} \underset{\uparrow}{\cong} \frac{s + t + u + \cdots}{r},$$
$$\text{is roughly}$$
$$\text{equal to}$$

and

$$\frac{\text{Perimeter of large circle}}{R} \cong \frac{S + T + U + \cdots}{R}.$$

Thus,

$$\frac{\text{Perimeter of small circle}}{r} \cong \frac{\text{perimeter of large circle}}{R}.$$

"This suggests that the ratio of the perimeter of one circle to its radius is actually equal to the ratio of the perimeter of *another* circle to *its* radius."

We won't do it here, but it is possible to provide a rigorous proof of this fact.

THEOREM RELATING PERIMETERS OF TWO CIRCLES

Given one circle of radius r and another of radius R, then the following equation holds:

$$\frac{\text{Perimeter of circle of radius } r}{r} = \frac{\text{Perimeter of circle of radius } R}{R}.$$

Diego: "It's the same with squares. A square with a side 5 ft has perimeter 4×5 ft = 20 ft; the ratio of its perimeter to its side is $\frac{20}{5}$, or 4. A square with a side 7 ft has perimeter 4×7 ft; the ratio of its perimeter to its side is $\frac{28}{7}$, or 4. The ratios of perimeter to side are the same. No matter what the side of the square is, the ratio is 4. What is the ratio for circles? If we knew what it was, then we could figure out the perimeter of a circle whenever we know its radius. With a square, if we know the length S of its side, then its perimeter is $4S$. If the ratio for the circle is K, then we know

$$\text{Perimeter of circle/radius of circle} = K,$$

from which it follows that

$$\text{Perimeter of circle} = K \times \text{radius of circle.}"$$

Jocelyn: "That formula looks just like the one for a square:

$$\text{Perimeter of square} = 4 \times \text{side of square.}$$

For a square, the magic number is 4. For a circle the magic number is K. All we have to do is figure out what K is!"

The Mathematical Idea: The Circumference of a Circle and a Formula for Finding It

Traditionally, the perimeter of a circle has been called its *circumference,* and the number K—which figures in the formula for the circumference of a circle in terms of its radius—is usually written as 2π, where the Greek letter π (pi) represents a second number $(\pi = [\frac{1}{2}]K)$.

TRADITIONAL FORMULA FOR THE CIRCUMFERENCE OF A CIRCLE

Circumference of circle of radius $R = 2\pi R$.

For the formula to be useful to Diego and Jocelyn and others, we need to know something about the value of the number π.

The formula above has three numbers in it: the circumference, the number 2π, and the radius. If we know any two of the three numbers, we can find the third. In particular, if we know the radius and circumference of *one single circle,* then we can determine 2π (and, from that, π itself). From then on the formula will be useful for *all other circles.*

To find the radius and circumference of a single circle, think about how we figured out the circumference of a circle earlier: We took a string, wrapped it around the circle, and measured the part of the string that fit around the circle exactly. That would give us the circumference of the circle. (Of course, our result would be subject to the imprecision associated with any kind of measuring.) That gives us the value of the left-hand side of the formula. Next we measure the radius of our special circle. At this point, we know the values of two numbers—the circumference and the radius of a single circle. From these two measurements we can estimate 2π using the formula

$$\text{Circumference of circle/radius of circle} = 2\pi.$$

Our work is cut out for us. All we need to do is find a circle, measure its circumference with a string, then measure its radius.

EXERCISE   3. Let's practice with some of these ideas.
  (a) Use a string to measure the circumference of the circle. Measure the radius of the circle as well. Compute the ratio of your two measurements, circumference of circle/radius of circle.

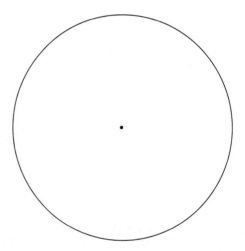

  (b) Do the same thing for a *large* circle of your choosing, say, the top of a circular wastebasket or a cross section of a large drainage pipe. Compare what you get with the results of (a).

The Mathematical Idea: The Value of π

Having made the measurements above and calculated the ratio, we estimated a value for 2π. We feel a little uncertain about this, a feeling that we do not have with the number 4 in the formula for the perimeter of a square. The closeness of our estimate to the actual value of 2π depends on how carefully we make our measurements. In contrast, we know ahead of time—from the nature of a square—that the number in the formula must be 4, *exactly* 4.

Some people have made it their business to calculate the value of π to a high degree of precision. To the nearest 1/100,000 these people have determined that the value is 3.14159; at the same time, they can also show that π is not even a rational number. This means that π (for the circle) is not as "nice" as 4 is (for the square). Another approximation to π is $\frac{22}{7}$.

The length of a line segment from one point on a circle to another and passing through the center of a circle is called a *diameter*. Its length is twice the radius of the circle. We have another formula for the circumference of a circle.

ALTERNATIVE FORMULA FOR CIRCUMFERENCE OF CIRCLE

Circumference of circle of diameter $d = \pi d$.

EXERCISES

4. Use either formula to calculate the circumferences of the circles.

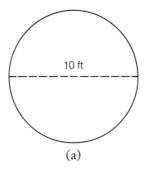 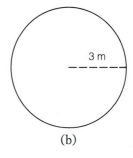

(a) (b)

5. Get out your calculator.
   (a) Use it to compare $\frac{22}{7}$ and 3.14159.
   (b) Many calculators have a special key $[\pi]$ that can be used instead of entering 3.14 or $\frac{22}{7}$ as an approximation of π. For example, to calculate the circumference of a circle of radius 7 m, you could use the key sequence 2 $[\times]$ $[\pi]$ $[\times]$ 7 $[=]$, and the display would show 43.98229715. Use a calculator and the $[\pi]$ key to calculate the circumferences of the circles in exercise 4.

You have designed a gear for an automobile that when engaged with the car's axle can make it spin up to 1000 rpm. You would like to know how fast the car would be going (miles per hour) if the axle were spinning at this speed.

**A Solution to the Wheel
Speed Problem**

You know that each revolution of the axle makes each wheel of the car go around exactly once and that the car travels the circumference of the wheel during that time. So you figure out the circumference of a wheel.

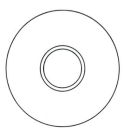

You measure a wheel of your car and find that its diameter is 2 ft. Its circumference is thus about 3.14×2 ft $= 6.28$ ft. For each revolution of the axle, the car travels 6.28 ft; with 1000 revolutions, the car travels 1000×6.28 ft or 6280 ft. Since a mile equals 5280 ft, that means that the car would travel more than a mile a minute. To be more exact, it would travel $\frac{6280}{5280} \sim 1.19$ mi/min, or $60 \times 1.19 = 71.4$ mph.

EXERCISE

6. You find that you can pedal your bike a maximum of 180 rpm. If each of these "pedal-revolutions" makes the wheel go round exactly once (i.e., there are no intervening gears), what will the ground speed of your bicycle be if you pedal your maximum?

THE LAMPSHADE PROBLEM

You are making a cylindrical lampshade like the one shown in the picture. You want it to be 40 cm high and 35 cm across. You want to know what a flattened-out pattern for the lampshade would be.

40 cm

35 cm

You realize that the first thing you need to do is figure out the general shape of a pattern for such a lampshade. You think: "With a completed lampshade, what would happen if I were to make a vertical cut as indicated

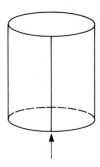

and then flatten it out? I'd get a rectangle!

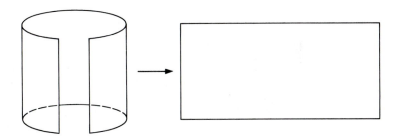

My pattern will be a rectangle. To make the rectangle, I need to know the lengths of two of its adjacent sides. The side I cut along is the height of the lampshade and is 40 centimeters. The other side is the circumference of the circle that forms the base of the lampshade.

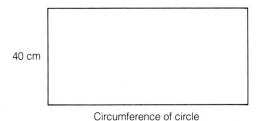

40 cm

Circumference of circle

"I know that the diameter of the circle is the width of the base of the lampshade, which is 35 centimeters. Here's a picture of the lampshade viewed from the top (or bottom).

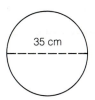

35 cm

If the diameter of the circle is 35 centimeters, the circumference must be about 3.14 × 35 centimeters = 109.9 centimeters. My rectangular pattern must be 40 by 109.9 centimeters."

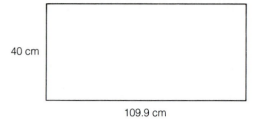

40 cm

109.9 cm

THE TRUNDLE WHEEL PROBLEM You are making a device for measuring length. It is a wheel with a handle that you use to guide the wheel as it rolls along the ground. People who pave city streets use such a device.

The wheel will have a circumference the length of which is equal to 1 m, with decimeters (ten*ths* of a meter) marked along the circumference. You place the "zero point" of the wheel at the beginning of the path you want to measure. Then you roll the wheel along the path. Each time you pass a meter—that is, each time the wheel makes a full revolution—the wheel makes a clicking noise. You count the number of clicks. When you reach the end of the path, you note the number of decimeters indicated by the position on the wheel that rests on the end point of the path. The length of the path is the number of clicks in meters plus this last amount in decimeters. This device, called a *trundle wheel,* is particularly useful for measuring paths that are long, not very straight, or are relatively inaccessible. People who repair roofs also use this device for making cost estimates.

Please try first.

To construct such a measuring device, you need to know the radius of the wheel. What is it?

A Solution to the Trundle Wheel Problem

The problem is to make a circle with circumference 1 m. You want to know what its radius should be. You know the formula for the circumference of a circle in terms of its radius, and you write, accordingly, $1 \text{ m} = 2\pi R \cong 6.28R$, where R stands for the unknown radius. You realize that this is a missing factor problem. The answer is about

$$\frac{1}{6.28} \text{ m,}$$

which is roughly .16 m.

16.3   THE LENGTH OF AN ARC OF A CIRCLE

THE SECOND TRUNDLE WHEEL PROBLEM

You also realize that you need to mark the decimeters on the circumference of the wheel. What is a good way to do this?

Try this first, please.

A Solution to the Second Trundle Wheel Problem

You think: "The circle will have a circumference of 1 meter. Each decimeter (tenth of a meter) should account for a tenth of the way around the circle. How can I measure that? I know that there are 360 degrees in a circle; therefore, each degree marked on a protractor should mark off a distance along the circle that is $\frac{1}{360}$ of the total distance around the circle, or $\frac{1}{360}$ of the circumference. Two sides of an angle of 1 degree with vertex at the center of a circle should intercept a piece of the circle whose length is exactly $\frac{1}{360}$ of the circumference! The sides of an angle of 2 degrees should intercept $\frac{2}{360}$ of the circumference. I want $\frac{1}{10}$ of the circumference. I would need $\frac{1}{10}$ of 360, or 36 degrees. An angle of 36 degrees would intercept $\frac{1}{10}$ of the circumference. I can use my protractor to mark decimeters on the trundle wheel!"

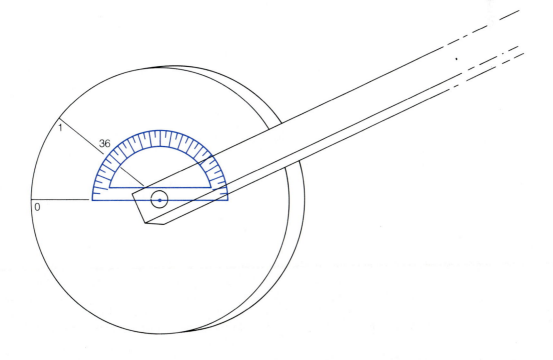

The Mathematical Idea: Using Degrees to Measure the Length of an Arc of a Circle

A piece of a circumference of a circle is called an *arc* of the circle. The solution to the second trundle wheel problem suggests a general method for measuring the length of an arc using degrees and a protractor.

MEASURING THE LENGTH OF AN ARC OF A CIRCLE

Suppose you have an arc of length L on the circumference of a circle. Suppose that the two sides of an angle of Q degrees, the vertex of which is at the center of the circle, intercepts the circle in this arc. Then the ratio of Q to 360 should be the same as the ratio of L to the circumference of the whole circle. In other words,

$$\frac{Q}{360} = \frac{L}{\text{circumference of whole circle}}.$$

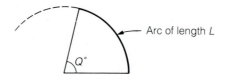

Arc of length L

$Q°$

An eighteenth-century trundle wheel (perambulator)

If you know Q (using a protractor) and the circumference of the circle (by measuring the radius and using the formula provided earlier), then you can find the length L. Similarly, if you know L and the circumference (as we did in the second trundle wheel problem), then you can find Q.

EXERCISE   7. The planetarium has a spherical ceiling on which during a show various designs and devices are projected. The light from one projector, located at the center of the sphere, projects light in an angular swath that measures $10°$. The projectionist wants to know the length of the image on the ceiling from this projector. The sphere has a radius of 12 m. Help the projectionist solve this problem.

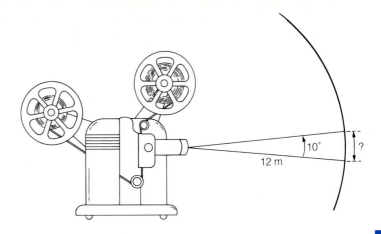

Measuring the Size of the Earth

The ancient Greeks hypothesized that the earth was spherical and, based on that, the Alexandrian mathematician Eratosthenes carried out a scheme for estimating the circumference of the earth. The scheme depends on the relationship between arc length and angle measure that we have discussed and on a couple of other ideas that we will introduce now.

First we need to introduce some terminology and facts about a sphere. A *sphere* is a shape in space analogous to a circle in a plane: It is the set of all points the same distance (the *radius* of the sphere) from a fixed point (the *center* of the sphere). A plane containing the center of the sphere will intersect the sphere in a circle, called a *great circle*. A *north-south meridian* on the spherical earth is a great circle passing through the North and South poles. If you were to slice the earth into two pieces along this circle, the cut would pass through the center of the earth and cut the earth into two equal hemispheres. The earth's equator is another great circle. We are interested in the circumference of a great circle on the spherical earth.

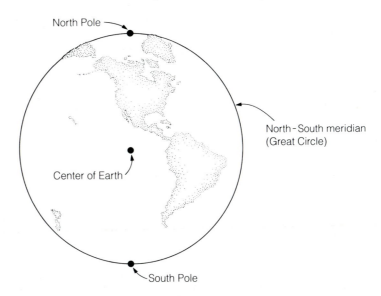

We will also need a fact about angles and parallel lines that we discussed in chapter 15. Taking an angle, through a point on one side of the angle draw a line parallel to the other side of the angle.

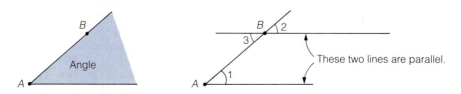

You will recognize angles 1 and 2 as *corresponding angles* created by a *transversal* to a pair of parallel lines. They are congruent. Also, angles 2 and 3 are congruent. (*Vertical angles* are congruent.) Thus, angles 1 and 3 are congruent. (*Alternate interior angles* are congruent.)

The idea Eratosthenes had for measuring the circumference of the earth is to find an arc of a great circle of the earth; measure the length of that arc; measure the angle with vertex at the center of the earth that intercepts that arc; put these measurements in the formula we developed previously and figure out the circumference of the earth. This may sound simple, but how do you measure an angle with a vertex at the center of the earth? The trick is to measure an angle that is *congruent* to it.

Eratosthenes had discovered that two cities in Egypt, Alexandria and Syene, were on a north-south meridian and that it was easy to measure the distance between them along this great circle. It was also well known that at noon on the day of the summer solstice the sun's rays shine directly to the bottom of a certain well in Syene; thus, at noon on June 21 the sun is directly over the well.

He conceived of the following scheme for measuring the angle corresponding to the arc of the great circle from Syene to Alexandria: "At noon on June 21 the sun's rays and the great circle from Alexandria to Syene look like this.

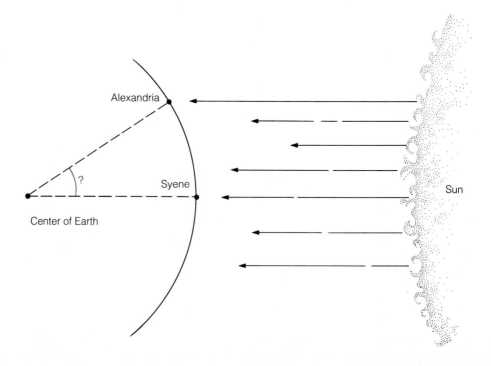

Since the sun is so far away from the earth and is so big, its rays are essentially parallel. That means that the angle I want to measure is equal to this one:

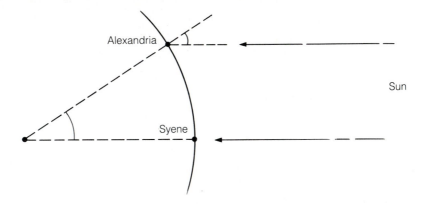

To measure that angle, I will place a stick perpendicular to the ground at Alexandria. Then the rays of the sun will make an angle with the stick, and that's the angle I want to measure. To measure that, I measure the shadow the stick makes on the ground. The stick, the shadow, and the line joining the tip of the shadow and the top of the stick form a triangle.

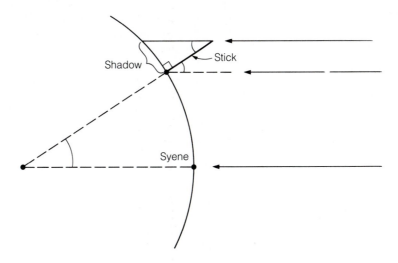

The angle formed by the stick and the shadow along the ground is a right angle; the angle at the top of the stick is the one I want to measure. I make a scale drawing of the triangle. I know two sides and the angle between (a right angle). That's all I need to know. I'm off to Alexandria next June 21!"

Eratosthenes did measure the angle and got 7.2°. The distance from Alexandria to Syene was found to be about 575 mi. Plugging these numbers into our formula, we have

$$\frac{7.2}{360} = \frac{575 \text{ mi}}{\text{circumference of great circle}},$$

or

$$\frac{360}{7.2} = \frac{\text{circumference of earth}}{575},$$

or

$$\frac{360}{7.2} \times 575 = \text{circumference of earth},$$

or

Circumference of earth = 28,750 mi.

With more recent and careful measuring, the circumference of the earth has been found to be close to 24,900 mi.

16.4   EXTENDING THE IDEAS: GEOMETRIC CONSTRUCTIONS

A convenient device for drawing a circle is a *compass*. You open the compass so that the distance from the sharp point to the tip of the pencil is the radius of the circle you want to draw. You place the sharp point at the point where you want the center. Then you rotate the compass about the sharp point, and the pencil traces out a circle of desired center and radius.

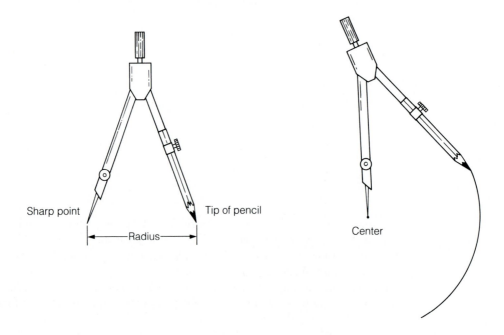

Sharp point   Tip of pencil

Radius

Center

From this description of how to draw a circle, it is clear that a circle is the set of all points a fixed distance (the radius) from a fixed point (the center).

8. Use a compass to draw a circle with *C* as a center and radius of length *AB*.

When *two* circles are drawn in a plane, three things can happen: (1) The two circles do not intersect; (2) the two circles intersect at a point; or (3) the two circles intersect at two points.

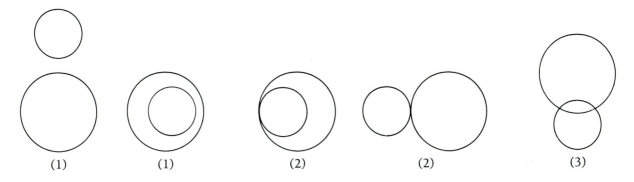

(1)   (1)   (2)   (2)   (3)

Similarly, if a circle and a line are drawn in a plane, three things can happen: (1) The line and the circle do not intersect; (2) the line and the circle intersect at a single point; or (3) the line and the circle intersect at two points. These happenings, the definition of a circle, and some of the geometric ideas discussed in the previous chapter are the basis for making certain geometric constructions using ruler and compass.

CONSTRUCTION 1: COPYING A LINE SEGMENT

Problem   Given a line segment *AB*, a line *L*, and a point *P* on *L*, to find a point *Q* on *L* such that $AB \cong PQ$

Open the compass to length *AB*.

A   B

With the sharp point of the compass at *P*, draw a circle of radius *AB*. The circle will intersect the line *L* at two points. Choose one and call it *Q*. Then *PQ* ≅ *AB*.

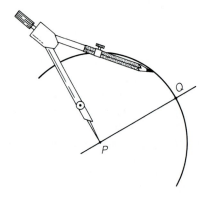

EXERCISE   9. On line *L* below, with *P* as one of the end points, use a compass to construct a copy of segment *AB*.

                  P

—————————————————————

               L

                A   *B*

              •————————————•

CONSTRUCTION 2: GIVEN THE THREE SIDES OF A TRIANGLE, MAKE A COPY OF IT

Problem   Given the three sides *AB*, *BC*, and *AC* of a triangle, line *L*, and point *P* on *L*, find point *Q* on *L* and point *R* not on *L* so that *PQ* ≅ *AB* and △*ABC* ≅ △*PQR*.

A ————— B

B —————— C

A ——————— C

Solution   Copy AB on line L as in construction 1 so that $AB \cong PQ$.

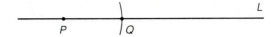

Open the compass to length AC. With the point of the compass at P, draw a circle of radius AC.

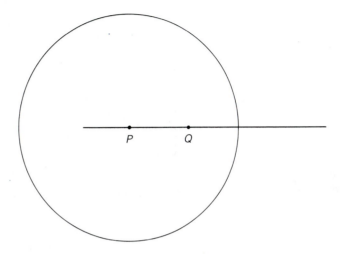

Open the compass to length BC. With the point of the compass at Q, draw a circle of radius BC.

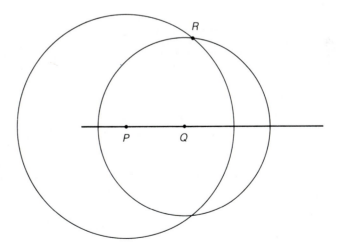

The two circles will intersect at two points. Choose one of these and call it *R*. Then △*PQR* ≅ △*ABC*.

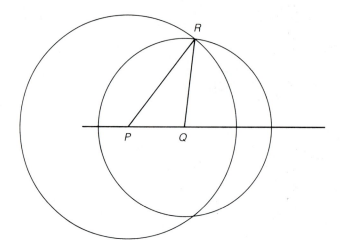

EXERCISES

10. Use ruler and compass to construct a triangle the sides of which are congruent to the given segments.

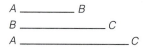

11. Construction 2 will work if you start with lengths that are the sides of a triangle. What happens in construction 2 if you happen to start out with lengths that do not make a triangle?

CONSTRUCTION 3: COPYING AN ANGLE

Problem   Given ∠*A*, line *L* and points *P* and *S* on *L*, find a point *Q* such that ∠*SPQ* ≅ ∠*A*.

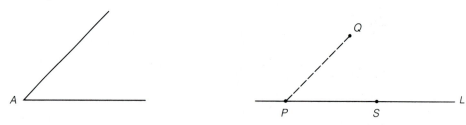

Solution   Open the compass to length *PS*. With the point of the compass at *A*, draw an arc that intersects both sides of ∠*A*. Call these points of intersection *B* and *C*.

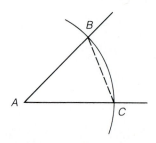

Starting with $AB \cong PS$ already complete, use construction 2 to copy $\triangle ABC$ so that $\triangle PQS \cong \triangle ABC$. Then $\angle A \cong \angle CAB \cong \angle SPQ$.

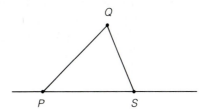

This construction works because, first of all, $\triangle PQS \cong \triangle ABC$. Then because corresponding angles are congruent, $\angle CAB \cong \angle SPQ$. (*Note:* This is but one of many ways to make a copy of an angle.)

EXERCISE   12. Use ruler and compass to copy $\angle A$ so that its vertex is P and one side is the ray from P through Q.

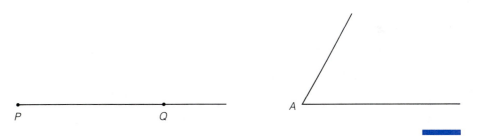

CONSTRUCTION 4: CONSTRUCTING A LINE PARALLEL TO A GIVEN LINE

Problem   Given a line L and a point P not on L, construct the line M through P parallel to L.

Solution   Draw a line through P and a point Q on L.

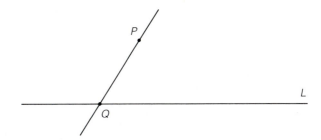

The idea of the construction is this: You know that if a transversal to two lines creates equal corresponding angles, then the two lines are parallel. In our case, think of the line through P and Q as the transversal. We want to construct an angle at P congruent and corresponding to $\angle RQP$ where R is another point on line L.

Select a point S on the line through P and Q so that P is between S and Q. With the ray from P through S as one side, with P as its vertex, find a point T on the same side of the line through P and Q as R is and such that $\angle SPT \cong \angle PQR$.

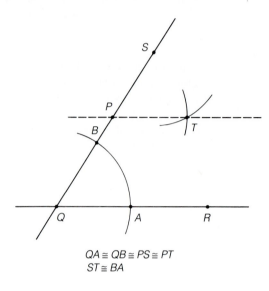

$QA \cong QB \cong PS \cong PT$
$ST \cong BA$

EXERCISE   13. Use ruler and compass to construct a line through P parallel to the line L.

$P \bullet$

L

CONSTRUCTION 5: BISECTING AN ANGLE

Problem   Given $\angle BAC$, find a point P interior to the angle such that $\angle PAB \cong \angle PAC$.

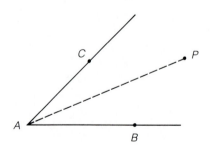

Solution   Open the compass to length *AB*. With the point of the compass at *A*, draw a circle with radius of length *AB*. The circle will intersect the ray from *A* through *C* at a point. Call it *D*.

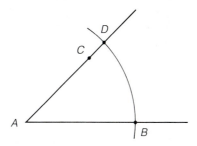

With radius of length equal to that of *BD*, place the point of the compass at *D*, and then at *B*, and construct intersecting arcs interior to ∠*BAC*. Call the point of intersection *P*. Then ∠*PAB* ≅ ∠*PAD*.

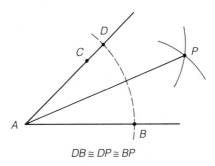

DB ≅ *DP* ≅ *BP*

The reason this construction does what it says is that we have constructed △*PBA* to be congruent to △*PBD*. This is true by the SSS congruence property. Then the two angles in question are corresponding angles of two congruent triangles.

EXERCISE   14. Use ruler and compass to bisect angle *A*.

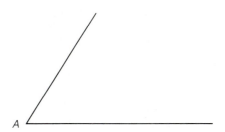

CONSTRUCTION 6: CONSTRUCTING THE PERPENDICULAR BISECTOR OF A LINE SEGMENT

Problem   Given line segment *AB*, find a point *P* and a line *L* through *P* such that *AP* ≅ *BP* and *L* is *perpendicular* to *AB*, that is, such that *L* and *AB* form four right angles at *P*.

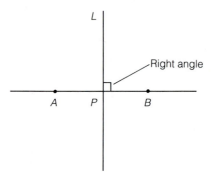

Solution   With the point of the compass at *A*, draw a circle with radius the same length as *AB* (or any radius of length bigger than half length *AB*). Then, with the point of the compass at *B*, draw a circle with radius of length *AB*. The two circles will intersect at two points; call them *C* and *D*.

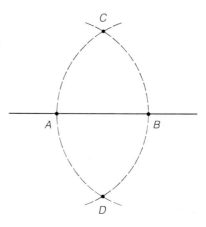

Draw the line joining *C* and *D*. This line will intersect the line segment *AB* at a point; call it *P*. Then *AP* ≅ *BP*, and *CD* is perpendicular to *AB*.

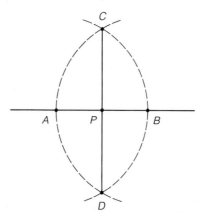

This construction is one of many methods for creating a right angle. Why it works involves showing that two separate pairs of triangles are congruent and then using this to conclude that certain corresponding angles and sides are congruent.

To sketch the argument, first, $\triangle ACD \cong \triangle BCD$ by the SSS congruence property and by the way we obtained the points C and D in our construction.

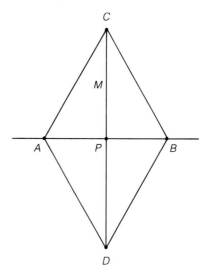

Thus, also $\angle ACP \cong \angle PCB$, because they are corresponding angles of congruent triangles.

Second, $\triangle ACP \cong \triangle BCP$ by the SAS congruence property. Consequently, $AP \cong BP$ and $\angle APC \cong \angle BPC$, because they are corresponding sides and angles of congruent triangles. The congruence of segments says that P bisects the segment AB; the congruence of angles says that the line CD is perpendicular to AB.

EXERCISE 15. Copy the segment and use ruler and compass to construct its perpendicular bisector.

CONSTRUCTION 7: CONSTRUCTING A LINE PERPENDICULAR
TO A LINE THROUGH A POINT ON THAT LINE

Problem Given a line L and a point P on L, construct a line M through P such that M is perpendicular to L.

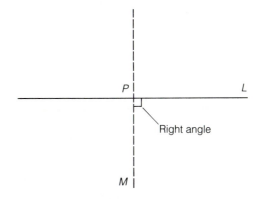

Solution   With the point of the compass at *P*, draw a circle. The circle will intersect line *L* at two points; call them *A* and *B*.

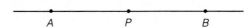

Since *AP* ≅ *PB*, you can now use construction 6 to construct the perpendicular bisector *M* of segment *AB*. The line *M* will pass through *P*. This does the job.

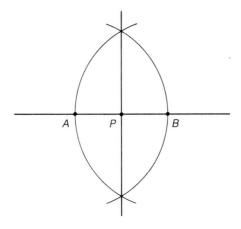

EXERCISE   16. Use ruler and compass to construct the line through point *P* perpendicular to the line *L*.

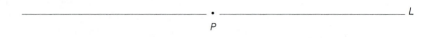

CONSTRUCTION 8: CONSTRUCTING A LINE PERPENDICULAR TO A LINE THROUGH A POINT NOT ON THAT LINE

Problem   Given a line *L* and a point *P* not on *L*, construct a line *M* through *P* that is also perpendicular to *L*.

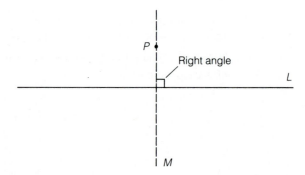

Solution   With the point of the compass at *P* and open to a radius larger than the distance of *P* to *L*, draw a circle. The circle will intersect line *L* at two points; call them *A* and *B*.

With the compass open to length *PA*, use construction 6 to construct line *M*, the perpendicular bisector of *AB*. The point *P* will lie on the line *M*. Line *M* does the job.

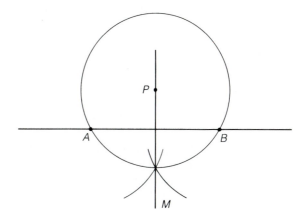

EXERCISES   17. Use ruler and compass to construct the line through point *P* perpendicular to the line *L*.

18. Use ruler and compass to construct a triangle with one side congruent to the segment on the left and with the other two sides congruent to the segment on the right.

19. Use ruler and compass to construct an equilateral triangle with all sides congruent to the segment.

20. Use ruler and compass to construct a square with a side of length AB.

A.———————————— •B

21. (a) Construct a circle one of the diameters of which is the segment AB.

A.———————————— •B

(b) Through the center C of the circle constructed in (a), construct a line L perpendicular to AB.

(c) The line L intersects the circle at points D and E. Connect A to D, A to E, B to D, and B to E with line segments. Show that the quadrilateral ADBE is a square.

16.5 LOOKING BACK: GRAPHS CORRESPONDING TO FORMULAS FOR PERIMETER AND CIRCUMFERENCE

You can think of the formula $P = 4S$ for the perimeter of a square as the formula for a function the inputs of which are possible sides S and the corresponding output P of which is the perimeter of a square of side S. Similarly, $C = 2\pi R$ is the formula for a function with inputs R possible radii of circles and with output C the circumference of a circle of radius R. From chapter 15 we know that the graphs of both these functions are straight lines.

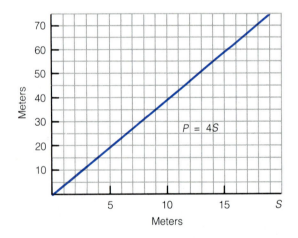

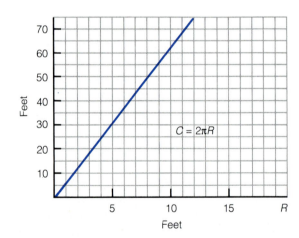

As in chapter 14, we can use the graph of $C = 2\pi R$ to solve the following type of problem: If a circle has a circumference of 20 cm, what is its radius? To solve it using a graph, you draw the horizontal line through 20 cm on the vertical axis. This line intersects the graph at a point P. The vertical line through P intersects the horizontal axis at a point Q. The number corresponding to Q is the radius you are looking for.

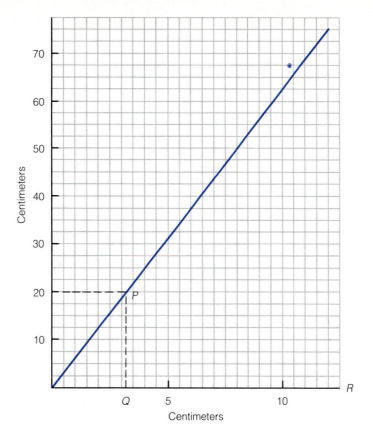

EXERCISE

22. You have a circle of circumference 10 m. The formula $L = \frac{1}{36}Q$ relates the length L of an arc of this circle to the number of degrees Q in the angle having vertex at the center of the circle and intercepting the arc. Draw the graph of this function.

16.6   LOOKING AHEAD: ROTATIONAL AND TRANSLATIONAL SYMMETRY

Rotational Symmetry

You recall from chapter 13 we found that one way to tell that a shape has mirror symmetry in line L is to flip the entire plane about line L. If this leaves the shape unchanged to the eye, then the shape has mirror symmetry in line L; otherwise, not. The flip is called a *transformation of the plane*.

The shape shown has no mirror symmetries.

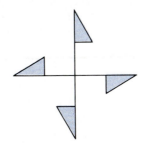

However, it has another kind of symmetry that we can also describe using a transformation of the plane. To do this, imagine a line perpendicular to the plane of the shape passing through the "center" *C* of the slope; then, using this line as a "spit" as before, turn the plane through an angle of 90°. After you have done this, the shape appears as if it has not changed.

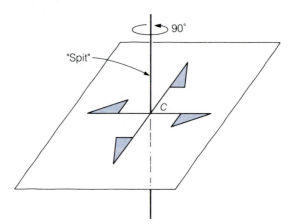

The transformation to which we have subjected the plane is called a *rotation*. A figure that remains unchanged after this transformation has taken place has *rotational symmetry*. A rotation (and the rotational symmetry that goes with it) is characterized by its *center* (the point that remains fixed, the point the spit passes through) and the *angle* through which the plane is turned. The shape preceding has rotational symmetry with center *C* and angle 90°.

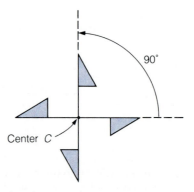

We can also using tracing paper to describe rotational symmetry. On a separate piece of paper, trace a copy of the shape. Keep the traced copy over the original, point for point. Put a pin through the tracing paper and into the original at point *C*. Then, keeping the pin fixed, turn the tracing paper 90° clockwise. The traced shape should fit exactly over the original.

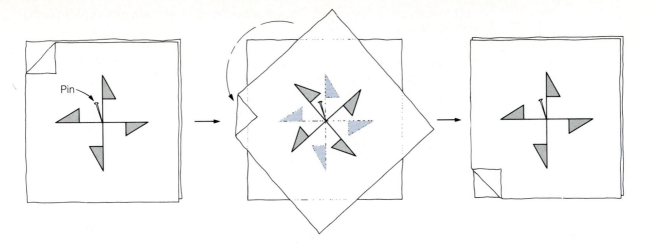

A rotational symmetry is identified by a point (the center of rotational symmetry) and by an angle (the angle of rotational symmetry). In addition to having rotational symmetry with center C and angle $90°$, this shape also has rotational symmetry with center C and angle $180°$.

EXERCISES

23. Investigate the rotational and mirror symmetries of each shape by tracing a copy of it on another sheet of paper. You may want to identify points on the original and on the traced copy to carry out the activities described in the text.

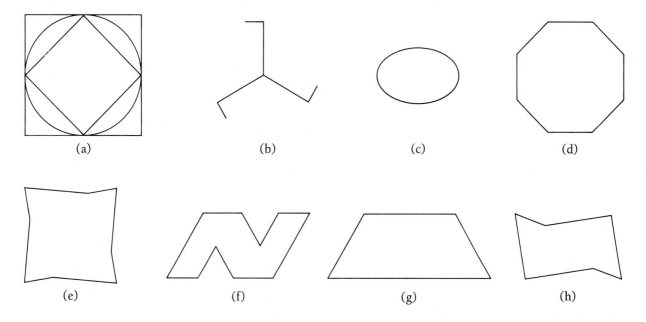

24. Every shape has rotational symmetry with center any point and angle $360°$. Why is this? (Such a symmetry is sometimes called a *trivial* symmetry. Other symmetries are *nontrivial*.)

25. In addition to rotational symmetries with angles 90 and $180°$ (center C), what other rotational symmetries does the shape discussed in the text have?

26. List all the rotational symmetries of each shape. Identify each rotational symmetry by its center and angle.

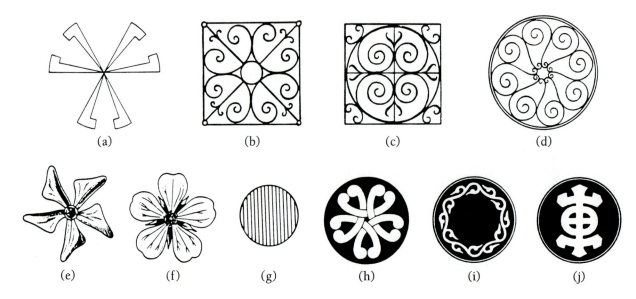

(a)   (b)   (c)   (d)

(e)   (f)   (g)   (h)   (i)   (j)

27. Indicate the mirror symmetries of each shape in exercise 26. Do you observe any patterns in the mirror and rotational symmetries of a shape?

28. Triangles can be classified according to the symmetries they possess. Which triangles have exactly one mirror symmetry? Which triangles have exactly three mirror symmetries? Which triangles have nontrivial rotational symmetry? (See exercise 24 for an explanation of this terminology.)

29. Quadrilaterals can also be classified by the symmetries they possess. Use terms other than those having to do with symmetry to describe each set of quadrilaterals:
(a) The set of quadrilaterals having exactly one mirror symmetry and no nontrivial rotational symmetries
(b) The set of quadrilaterals having exactly two mirror symmetries and one nontrivial rotational symmetry
(c) The set of quadrilaterals having exactly one nontrivial rotational symmetry and no mirror symmetries
(d) The set of quadrilaterals having exactly four mirror symmetries and three nontrivial rotational symmetries

Translational Symmetry

Consider a design suggested by the picture.

The entire design extends indefinitely in both directions—to the left and to the right. The entire design has neither mirror symmetry nor rotational symmetry. It has a symmetry called *translational symmetry,* which means that the shape does not change when the entire plane undergoes a transformation called a *translation.* To describe this transformation, consider the arrow A in the next diagram and the distance d between two like elements of the design.

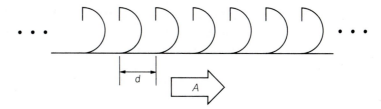

Now slide the plane in the direction of the arrow for a distance d. The design should appear as if it has not changed. The sliding transformation is called the *translation in the direction of the arrow through distance d.*

Another way to describe the translational symmetry is to trace a copy of the design on a separate piece of paper. Then, starting with the tracing placed over the original design point for point, slide the tracing in the direction of the arrow for a distance d. The tracing should now fit exactly over the original.

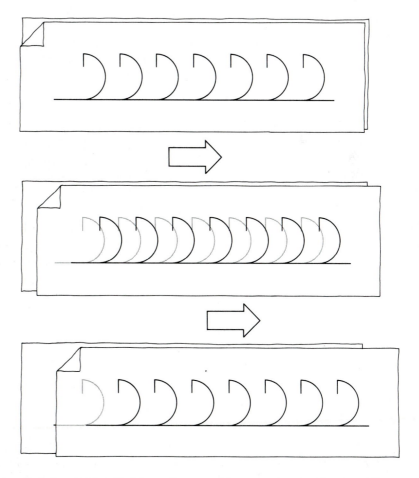

A translation is identified by a direction (the arrow) and a distance (d).

30. The design we have been working with has other translational symmetries in addition to the one described. What are they? (A different translation could have the same direction as the one described but a different distance. A different translation might also have a different direction but the same distance.) Trace a copy of the design on a separate sheet of paper to illustrate the translation described in the text and to help you seek out these additional translations.

31. Describe the translational symmetries of each shape. (It is possible that a shape has no translational symmetry.)

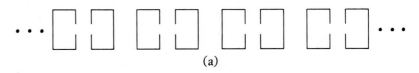

(a)

(b)

(c)

(d)

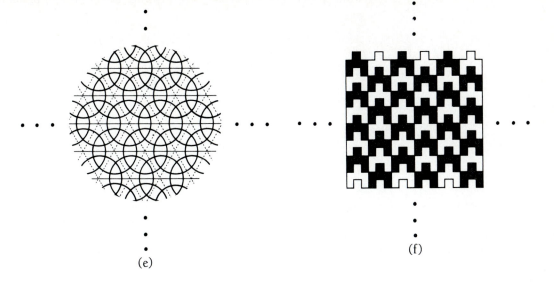

(e)   (f)

32. Describe the rotational and mirror symmetries of each shape in exercise 31.

16.7   COMPUTERS: LOGO AND GEOMETRY

Besides BASIC, another computer programming language in wide use is Logo. We have written programs in BASIC to get the computer to make many calculations and provide us with lists of numbers. In this section we will show how to write programs in Logo to get the computer to draw pictures. In the schools Logo is primarily used to learn and reinforce geometric ideas.

When the microcomputer is set up for programming in Logo, a *turtle* appears in the center of the screen. Some versions of Logo use a triangle rather than a turtle. In any case, the turtle's head (or the triangle's most acute angle) will be pointing up, or North, on the screen.

When you program in Logo, you give instructions to the computer to move the turtle about the screen and have it draw things as it moves. For example, if you type

```
forward 50 {return}
```

you will see the turtle move 50 turtle steps up the screen (North) drawing a line as it goes.

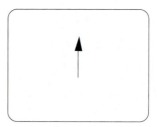

If you type

right 30 {return}

you will see the turtle turn right 30°. The turtle's head is now pointed 30° East of North.

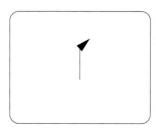

If you now type

forward 50 {return}

you will see the turtle travel 50 turtle steps in the direction it has been pointed.

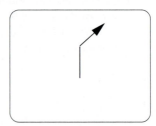

You can also make the turtle turn left,

left 90 {return}

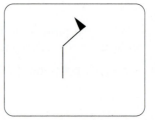

and you can make the turtle go backward.

```
back 50 {return}
```

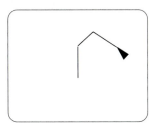

Then you can get the turtle to return to its original position, pointing North, by typing

```
home {return}
```

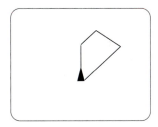

Finally, to start over with a new set of instructions, you can clear the graphics the turtle has made by typing

```
cg {return}
```

EXERCISE

33. Have the turtle draw a triangle with sides 20 and 30 and the angle between them 50°.

Abbreviations; The Repeat Command

The turtle *commands forward, back, right, left* can be abbreviated "fd," "bk," "rt," and "lt," respectively. Each of these commands must be followed by a whole number: fd 30 tells the turtle to move forward (in the direction its head is pointing) 30 turtle steps; lt 40 means the turtle is to turn 40° to the left from the direction its head is now pointing. Pushing {return} has the effect of executing what has just been typed (much like RUN in BASIC). Several commands can be typed in one line. Typing

```
fd 50 rt 90 fd 50 rt 90 {return}
```

results in

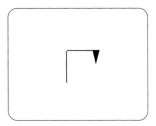

You can get the turtle to repeat a sequence of moves using the *repeat* command. For example, after typing `cg` {return}, type

```
repeat 4 [fd 50 rt 90]  {return}
```

and you will see this:

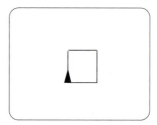

The repeat command must be followed by a number that tells the turtle the number of times to repeat the sequence of commands placed in the square brackets.

EXERCISES

34. Use the repeat command to get the turtle to draw an equilateral triangle.

35. Use the repeat command to get the turtle to draw a regular hexagon.

36. Use the repeat command to get the turtle to draw the five-pointed star shown.

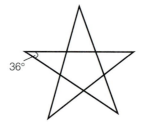

37. What does the turtle do when given the following sequence of commands?

```
repeat 18 [fd 50 bk 50 lt 10]  {return}
```

Pen Up, Pen Down

You can get the turtle to move without drawing. You do this by typing `penup` (abbreviated `pu`). To get the turtle to start drawing again, you type `pendown` (abbreviated `pd`). To see how this works, type

```
pu fd 20 pd fd 20 pu fd 20   {return}
```

and you will see

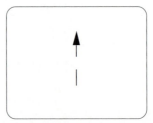

PROCEDURES   If you type

```
repeat 4 [fd 50 rt 90] {return}
```

the turtle will draw a square. If we want the turtle to draw several squares, then, instead of typing the sequence of commands above several times, we can define a *procedure*. A procedure in Logo is the closest thing to a program in BASIC. To define a procedure for drawing a square you type

```
to square     to followed by name of procedure
repeat 4 [fd 50 rt 90]    Sequence of commands (this may take several lines)
end      Signifies end of procedure
```

Then if you type

```
square {return}
```

the turtle will draw a square as before. If you type

```
pu rt 90 fd 60 lt 90 pd square
```

the turtle will draw the same square but translated 60 turtle steps to the right.

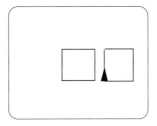

You can also type

```
pu lt 30 fd 20 rt 30 pd square
```

and you will get

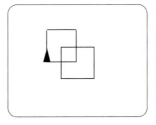

In this way you can get Logo to carry out a translation.

EXERCISE   38. Write a procedure in Logo to draw an equilateral triangle and end up at home (pointing North). Call the procedure "triangle." Type `triangle {return}`. Then type a sequence of commands including `triangle` that translates the original triangle 30° South of East 40 turtle steps.

Logo and Rotational Symmetry

We can also use the procedure "square" to produce a figure having rotational symmetry. Type

```
repeat 12 [square lt 30] {return}
```

and the turtle will draw

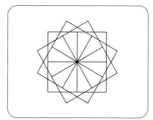

What the turtle drew has rotational symmetry with center the turtle's home and angle 30°.

EXERCISES

39. Use the procedure "triangle" to get the turtle to create a shape having rotational symmetry with center the turtle's home and angle of 72°.

40. Type the following sequence of commands.

    ```
    lt 90 fd 140 rt 90 repeat 4 [square rt 50] {return}
    ```

    What happens?

41. Define the following procedure.

    ```
    to blade
    fd 50 lt 90 fd 10 lt 150 home
    end
    ```

    Then type in the following sequence of Logo commands.

    ```
    repeat 4 [blade rt 90] {return}
    ```

    What happens? What sort of symmetry does the shape have?

42. Use the procedure "blade," defined in exercise 41 to get the turtle to create a windmill having six blades.

43. Get the turtle to produce a triangle having these specifications: an angle of 45°, an angle of 30°, and a side common to these two angles of 30 turtle steps.

This discussion is meant to give you just a taste of Logo and the things it can do. It can handle lots that we haven't mentioned, such as arithmetic, variables, conditional statements, and recursive procedures. Check a Logo manual or books on Logo in a library for the possibilities.

16.8 SUMMARY OF IMPORTANT IDEAS AND TECHNIQUES

- Definition of a circle and its center, radius, diameter, and circumference
- Measurement of angles
- Degree as a unit for measuring angles
- Protractor as a tool for measuring degrees
- A formula for the circumference of a circle
- Finding the value of π
- Measuring the length of an arc of a circle using angle measurement and the formula for the circumference of a circle
- Measuring the circumference of the earth
- Using a compass and ruler to make certain geometric constructions
  Drawing a circle
  Copying a line segment
  Constructing a triangle, given its three sides
  Copying an angle
  Constructing a line through a point parallel to a given line
  Bisecting an angle
  Constructing the perpendicular bisector of a line segment
  Constructing a line perpendicular to a given line through a given point
- Graphs of the functions relating the perimeter of a square to the length of a side and relating the circumference of a circle to its radius
- Transformations of the plane—rotations and translations; rotational and transformational symmetry of shapes

PROBLEM SET

PRACTICING
SKILLS

1. The protractor is marked at 5° intervals and its center is at *M*. Rays with end points at *M* are lettered.

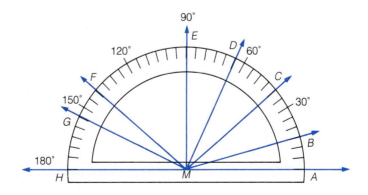

(a) Complete the sentences.
    (i)   The number of degrees in angle *FMG* is _____.
    (ii) The number of degrees in angle *AMB* is _____.
    (iii) The number of degrees in angle *AMG* is _____.
    (iv) The number of degrees in angle *FMH* is _____.

(b) Complete the sentences.
    (i)   An angle in the picture the measure of which is 40° is _____.
    (ii) An angle in the picture the measure of which is 25° is _____.
    (iii) An angle in the picture the measure of which is 90° is _____.
    (iv) An angle in the picture the measure of which is 115° is _____.

2.   Use a protractor to measure the number of degrees in each angle.

(a)   (b)   (c)

3.   Use a protractor to measure each angle of each triangle. Add up the degrees for each triangle. What is the sum in each case?

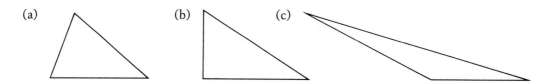

(a)   (b)   (c)

4.   Use a piece of string to measure the perimeter of the shape. Then construct straight lines between the points to approximate the perimeter with a polygon. Measure the lengths of these lines and add them. Compare this sum to the length of your string.

5.   Calculate the circumference of each circle using a formula.

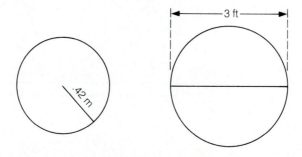

6. You have designed a gear for your car that when engaged with the car's axle can make it spin up to 1200 rpm. How fast can your car go with the axle spinning at this speed? Assume a wheel diameter of 2 ft.

7. You have a new bicycle with a wheel diameter of 16 in. You find you can pedal a maximum of 200 rpm, and each pedal revolution turns the wheel once. What is your maximum speed?

8. You have an old wagon wheel that has 18 spokes radiating from the center to the outside rim, dividing the circle into equal parts. The diameter of the wheel is 48 in. The wheel has a metal rim around the outside that has rusted through in the space between 2 spokes. A blacksmith has agreed to fix it by cutting out the rusted part and replacing it with new metal. What is the length of the piece of metal he will need? (If you had the real wheel in front of you, what would be the most efficient way to answer the question?)

9. You have an 8-in.-high lampshade you want to mail home. You know the shade has a circumference of 36 in. Find the dimensions of the mailing box you will need.

10. Use a compass to draw a circle with radius 1 in. Using the same center, draw circles with radii 1.5 in. and 2 in.

11. On line *L* and with *P* as one of the end points, use a compass to construct a copy of line segment *AB*.

12. Use a ruler and compass to construct triangles with the side lengths (a) 3 cm, 4 cm, and 5 cm, and (b) all sides 2 cm.

13. Use a ruler and compass to copy angle *A* on line *L* with its vertex at point *P*. Several possible configurations can result from doing this. What are they?

14. Use a ruler and compass to construct a line through *P* parallel to *L*.

15. Use a ruler and compass to bisect angle *A* of the triangle *ABC*.

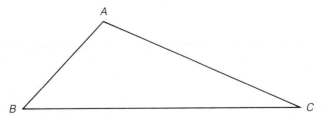

16. Use a ruler and compass to bisect side *AB* of the triangle.

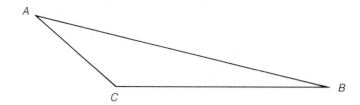

17. Use a ruler and compass to construct a rectangle with base length 4 cm and height 6 cm. Start by drawing a long line, marking points *P* and *Q* on the line 4 cm apart, then construct perpendicular lines through *P* and *Q*.

18. Use a ruler and compass to construct a circle of diameter 2 in. Then construct a diameter and a perpendicular through this diameter at the center, dividing the circle into four equal parts.

19. Use a ruler and compass to construct a square with sides 2 in. in length. Bisect a pair of opposite sides. With the line segment joining these bisection points as diameter, construct the circle inscribed in the square.

20. Use the construction in problem 19 to draw a square inscribed in a circle by joining the end points of the diameters with straight lines. (First draw a second diameter perpendicular to the first.)

21. Using the graph in section 16.5 for $C = 2\pi R$, what should R be if $C = 35$ cm?

USING IDEAS   *For each remaining problem, communicate its solution in the form of an essay. Mention the steps you took in solving the problem, other problems or solutions that gave you ideas, and the strategies you used.*

22. The diagram shows several angles, some of which have been measured and the degrees indicated.

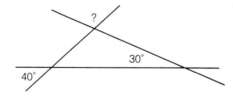

Find the measure of the angle marked with ? from the information given without actually measuring the angle.

23. Use a protractor to measure each angle of each quadrilateral. Add up the degrees for each quadrilateral. What is the sum in each case? Do you see a pattern? Make a conjecture about the sum of the angles in *any* quadrilateral. Try to prove your conjecture.

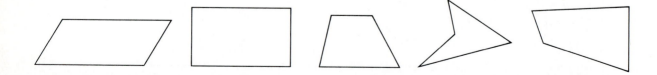

24. You are to use four different methods to estimate the circumference of the circle.

(a) *Method 1:* Use a string. The length of string that just fits around the circle is your approximation using this method.

(b) *Method 2:* Make a copy of the circle on a piece of paper. Approximate the circumference of your traced circle by a polygon, as shown. (You may want to use a polygon with more sides than this one has.) With a ruler measure the lengths of all the sides and add them up. The sum is your approximation using this method.

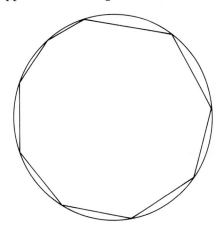

(c)   *Method 3:* Make a copy of the circle on a piece of cardboard or stiff paper and cut it out. Next take a large piece of paper (such as a double page of newspaper) and draw a long, straight line on it. Mark a point at the end of the line. Mark a point on the circumference of the circle on the stiff paper and stand the circle on end so that the point on the circle and the point on the line touch. Roll the circle along the line until the marked point on the circle touches the line again. Mark the point on the line where this happens and measure the distance between the two marked points on the line. This distance is your approximation using this method.

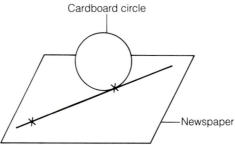

(d)   *Method 4:* Measure the radius of the circle and use the formula for the circumference of the circle in terms of the radius. This is your approximation using this method.

(e)   Compare the approximations you get in parts (a), (b), (c), and (d). Which approximation do you think is best? Why?

25.   A piece of glass having the shape shown must be edged with metal molding before it can be inserted into a window frame. You want to know what length of metal molding you will need.

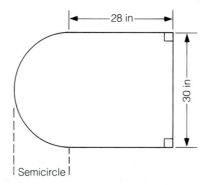

26.   City Park has a plan for its central plaza. Each of the gardens (the shaded areas) must be surrounded by fencing. To figure out the cost of their project, park officials want to know how much fencing will be needed. Help them find out.

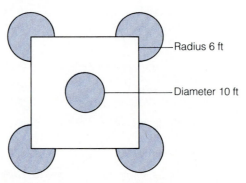

27. (a) You own a circular flower bed that you plan to enlarge by 1 yd all the way around. The present flower bed has fencing that you plan to remove and use for the expanded flower bed. You will need additional fencing. How much?

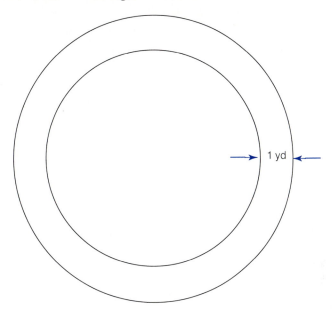

(b) You order a piece of string 24,900 mi long, which you assume is just long enough to encircle the globe exactly, at the equator. You take this string and fit it snugly around the earth, over oceans, deserts, and jungles. Unfortunately, you find that there has been a slight error: The string is just a yard too long! To overcome the mistake, you decide to distribute the extra 36 in evenly over the entire 24,900 mi by propping it up equally at all points on the equator. Naturally, it will never be noticed, but you are interested in how far the string will stand off from the ground at each point. How much do you figure?

28. Which of the following two flower beds needs the most fencing, the one with a "figure eight" border on the left or the one with a simple circular border on the right? Give reasons for your choice.

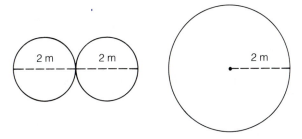

29. Consider the following problems.
(a) A truck has wheels that are 3 ft in diameter. How many revolutions will each wheel make on a 1-mi trip?
(b) An automobile's speedometer measures the rate at which the drive shaft of the car is rotating, and, through the differential, the rate at which the wheels are turning. The speedometer is calibrated to be accurate when the tires are new (9/32-in. tread depth) and the air pressure is 30 lb/in². Now, the 14-in. diameter tires have worn to 1/16-in. tread depth. With the air pressure still at 30 lb/in², what is the error in a speedometer reading of 30 mph?

30. A track for field events has been constructed as shown in the diagram. (The diameter of the small semicircle is 30 m.) You want to know the distance around the inside border of the track. You also want to know what fraction of a kilometer that is.

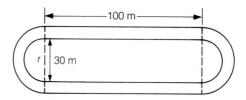

31. Cylindrical kegs often have a thin metal band around the middle of the outside surface that helps them retain their shape. A company that makes kegs would like to know how many meters of this metal they need in order to finish 1000 kegs of the size indicated in the diagram. How many feet will they need within the nearest meter?

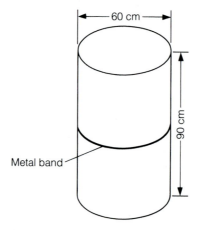

32. You have a large ball with circumference 75 cm. You are giving it to a friend and wish to put it in a gift box. How long will the sides of the box have to be?

33. You want to build a trundle wheel that measures yards and inches; you want the circumference of the wheel to have length 1 yd, and you want to mark inches around the circumference. To build the wheel, you will need to know two things. Figure them out.
    (a) The diameter of the wheel
    (b) The angle, measured from the center of the wheel, between consecutive inches on the circumference

34. The hand mirror shown is in the shape of a sector of a circle. To finish it, the maker will put silver molding along its perimeter. Find out the length of molding (in inches) that will be needed.

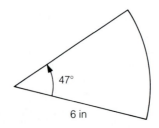

35. You design and make lampshades. One such lampshade is shown.

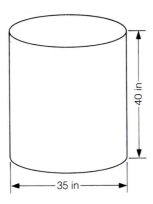

(a) Sketch a flattened pattern for this lampshade. On the pattern mark in the dimensions needed for assembling it. The pattern should allow for a 1-in. overlap when gluing the pattern together.
(b) You plan to add trim to the top and bottom rims of the lampshade. What length of trim will you need?

36. Adam, a student at Hughes Elementary, validated Eratosthenes' measurement of the circumference of the earth with a little help from his friends. A well, such as the one at Syene, into which the sun directly shines at summer solstice was not necessary. He found two locations on the same north-south meridian and measured the distance between the two locations using the scale of a map. One morning, he and a friend drove to one location; two other friends drove to the other location. Exactly at solar noon (when the sun is at its highest point in the sky), each team, using a stick perpendicular to the ground, measured the angle of the rays of the sun at that location. A diagram showing the details of this experiment is shown.

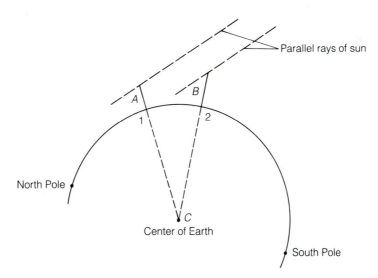

(a) Adam claims that angle A minus angle B is equal to angle C. Why is this?
(b) From his measurements Adam finds that angle C measures about 2° and from the map that the distance from location 1 to location 2 along the north-south meridian is about 133 mi. Based on these measurements, what is the circumference of the earth?

INTRODUCTION TO AREA

17
C H A P T E R

Let's look at a new set of problems: What is the crop yield of that plot of land? How many tiles will I need to tile that floor? How much paint will I need to paint that wall? How much will I have to pay for a rug that fits my floor? We have already discussed the measurement of length and the measurement of angles. These new problems lead us to create a new concept, the area of a planar shape. Part of working with this concept is developing techniques for measuring area.

We start with rectangles, the areas of which, of all shapes, are easiest to find. From there we move to simple shapes with areas more difficult to determine: triangles, parallelograms, trapezoids. To help us find the areas of these shapes, we discuss some basic principles concerning the measurement of area. We also use these principles to devise strategies for measuring the areas of more complicated shapes.

Using these principles and strategies, we will develop a formula for the area of a circle, a shape of particular interest to us. From this we can find the area of a sector, a piece of a circle bounded by an arc and two radii.

We will also consider the efficiency of shapes. We shall attempt to answer two types of questions.

■ You have a certain amount of fencing for a rectangular pasture. What should the dimensions of the rectangle be in order that the animals have the most grazing area?

■ You want your rectangular patio to have a certain area. What should its dimensions be in order to minimize the cost of the wall you plan to build to enclose it?

17.1

WHAT IS AREA?

THE GARDEN PLOT PROBLEM

The Smith family has a plot of land on which they grow potatoes. In the accompanying scale drawing of this plot, each of the little squares is a meter on a side.

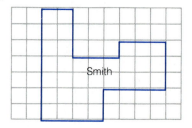

Try this yourself before reading on.

The local agricultural extension agent has told the Smiths that they can expect a yield of $7 worth of potatoes from each square. Help the family figure out what the value of their whole potato crop would be.

A Solution to the Garden Plot Problem

The members of the Smith family realize that if they are to solve the problem they must first figure out the number of small squares in their plot. They count them and get 33 squares. At $7 per square, that's $7 \times 33 = \$231$.

THE FLOOR TILING PROBLEM

The Jaworskis are planning to tile their kitchen floor. They know that each square tile, a foot on a side, will cost them $3. They want to know what all the tiles for the kitchen will cost them. They have made a scale drawing of their kitchen, shown, in which each square represents a tile. Help them solve this problem.

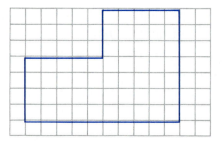

Please try to solve this first.

A Solution to the Floor Tiling Problem

The Jaworskis, like the Smiths, realize that to figure out the cost of the tiles for their kitchen, they must count the number of squares in the scale drawing. They do this and get 55 squares. At $3 per tile, that makes $3 \times 55 = \$165$.

The Mathematical Idea: Area

In the garden plot problem, the Smiths wanted to know how many squares, a meter on a side, covered their plot. In the floor tiling problem, the Jaworskis wanted to know how many squares, a foot on a side, covered their kitchen floor.

Common units of area are squares with sides of common units of length: inch, foot, yard, mile, centimeter, meter, and kilometer. The units of area are usually called the *square inch, square foot, square yard, square mile, square centimeter, square meter, and square kilometer,* respectively.

THE SECOND GARDEN PLOT PROBLEM

The Ronstadts have planted their garden plot, sketched below, in cotton. To figure out what their yield will be, they need to know what the area of their plot is in square yards.

Please try this before reading the solution.

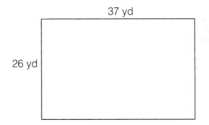

A Solution to the Second Garden Plot Problem

The Ronstadts realize that they must figure out how many squares, a yard on a side, exactly cover their garden plot. They decide to draw a scale drawing of their plot on graph paper, with each square representing a square yard.

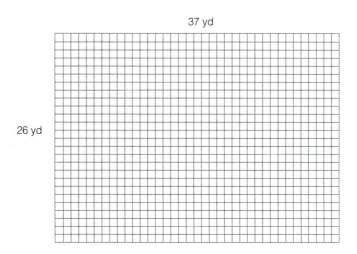

This turns their rectangular plot, 26 by 37 yd, into a 26 by 37 array, in which each item is a square yard. *Thinking of similar problems* involving arrays, they know that they don't have to count all the items: The number of items is the product of the number of rows (26) times the number of items in each row (37). Thus, they find that their plot has $26 \times 37 = 962$ yd² in it (yd² is a shorthand way of writing *square yards;* the superscript ² with any unit of measure means "square" or "squared").

The Mathematical Idea: A Formula for the Area of a Rectangle

The solution to the second garden plot problem suggests a shortcut for determining the area of a region that happens to be a rectangle with sides a whole number of unit lengths. If these lengths are L and W units, then we can cover the rectangle with an L by W array of square units. The rectangle then has area LW square units. It would be tedious to have to count the square yards in the Ronstadt plot to determine its area. This formula represents a considerable saving in effort.

What about rectangles with sides that are not whole number lengths? We'll begin our investigation with a problem similar to one we did in chapter 9.

THE GOLD-PLATING PROBLEM

A dear friend has given you an antique rectangular medallion. The front needs to be gold plated. The cost of gold plating is \$12/in² of surface. The medallion measures $1\frac{1}{4}$ by $2\frac{2}{3}$ in. You want to know how much the gold plating will cost you.

Try this first.

A Solution to the Gold Plating Problem

You figure out that you must find the area of the rectangular medallion. Toward this end you draw a picture.

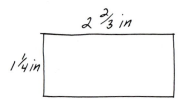

You *think of similar problems* involving area and decide to try turning the rectangle into an array of pieces all the same size. Then you will determine the number of pieces and figure out the area of just one of them. You decide to express the lengths of the sides as improper fractions, which enables you to divide up the rectangle naturally:

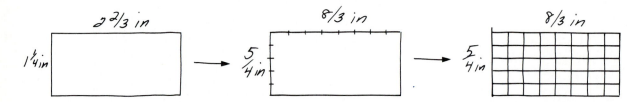

Your rectangle is now a 5 by 8 array of smaller, equal rectangles, each of which is $\frac{1}{4}$ by $\frac{1}{3}$ in. The area of the latter times 40 ($= 5 \times 8$) will give you the area of your medallion.

To figure out the area of the $\frac{1}{4}$ by $\frac{1}{3}$ in, you take a square inch, mark fourths on one side and thirds on the other. This, in turn, divides the square inch naturally into smaller rectangles each one of size $\frac{1}{4}$ by $\frac{1}{3}$ in.

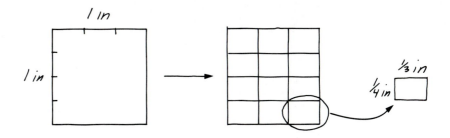

This makes the square inch into a 4 by 3 array of rectangles of size $\frac{1}{4}$ by $\frac{1}{3}$ in. A square inch has thus been cut up into $4 \times 3 = 12$ equal pieces. Each of the pieces must be $\frac{1}{12}$ in^2.

To complete the problem, we remember that the original medallion was divided into an 5 by 8 array of small rectangles. We have just shown that each small rectangle has area $\frac{1}{12}$ in^2. Thus,

$$\text{Area of medallion} = \frac{40}{12} = \frac{5 \times 8}{4 \times 3} = \frac{5}{4} \times \frac{8}{3} = 1\frac{1}{4} \times 2\frac{2}{3}$$

$$= 3\frac{4}{12} = 3\frac{1}{3} \text{ in}^2.$$

The Mathematical Idea: Fractions and Area

An important concept in the solution to the gold-plating problem is fractional area. The square inch is divided into 12 pieces of the same size and shape. It is assumed that each of these pieces has area equal to $\frac{1}{12}$ in^2. Thus, the rectangle of size $\frac{5}{4}$ by $\frac{8}{3}$ in has area $\frac{40}{12}$ in^2.

This suggests that the formula for the area of a rectangle with whole number sides works when the two sides are any fractional lengths. We can summarize this.

AREA OF A RECTANGLE

The *area* of a rectangle with sides of length L and W is equal to LW.

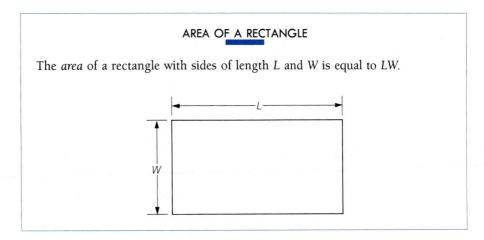

1. Find the areas of the rectangles.

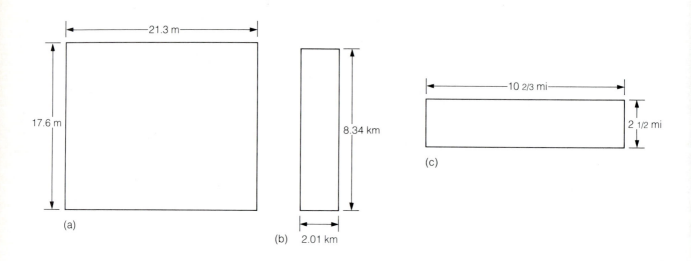

(a) 21.3 m, 17.6 m

(b) 2.01 km, 8.34 km

(c) 10 2/3 mi, 2 1/2 mi

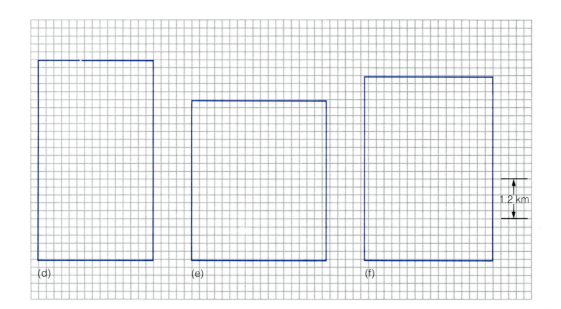

(d) (e) (f) 1.2 km

17.2 FORMULAS FOR AREA

THE THIRD GARDEN PLOT PROBLEM

The Joneses have a (right) triangular plot on which they grow alfalfa. A scale drawing of the plot, drawn on graph paper, is shown. Each square on the graph paper represents a square yard.

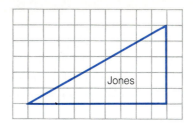

Please try this before reading on.

Like the Smiths and the Jaworskis, the Joneses are interested in the value of the yield from their plot. Help them solve this problem.

A Solution to the Third Garden Plot Problem

The Joneses realize that if they are to solve the problem they must figure out the area of their plot. Unfortunately, their plot does not have the shape of a rectangle with an easily determined area. Furthermore, it is not easy to count the square yards one by one, because the plot as shown on the graph paper has many little pieces of square yards that are not themselves rectangles.

Tom Jones has an idea: "Our plot is not a rectangle. Is there any way we can solve our problem by *solving a simpler problem* with rectangles? Look, our plot is sitting inside a larger rectangular plot.

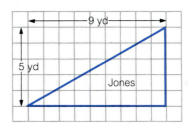

The area of that rectangle is 45 square yards. I notice that the rectangle is made up of two triangles, one of which is our plot and the other of which is congruent to our plot.

"The area of the other triangle is the same as the area of our plot. And the two equal areas should add up to the area of that rectangle. That means that the area of our triangular plot is half the area of the rectangle or $22\frac{1}{2}$ square yards."

The Mathematical Idea: Principles for Area and a Formula for the Area of a Triangle

In solving the third garden plot problem, Tom Jones used two facts (or principles) about area that we will find useful in solving other area problems. Both principles were also used to extend the formula for the area of a rectangle with whole-number sides to encompass rectangles with fractional sides.

TWO AREA PRINCIPLES

1. Two regions that are congruent also have the same area.

2. If a region is broken up into two or more small pieces, then the area of the whole region is equal to the sum of the areas of the pieces.

Using these principles, Tom Jones showed that

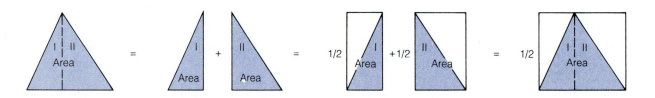

Consider two more examples in which these principles can be used to find areas.

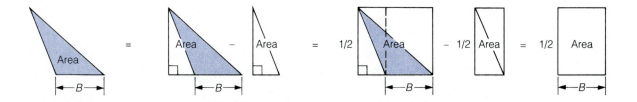

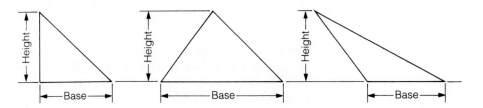

These three examples suggest a formula for finding the area of a triangle. First, a bit of terminology. Take a triangle, choose one of its sides, and place it along a horizontal line.

Call this side the *base* of the triangle. Draw a vertical line from the opposite vertex perpendicular to the horizontal line. The length of this line is called the *height* of the triangle relative to this base. Notice that the base and the height of the triangle depend on the choice of the side that is to function as the base.

FORMULA FOR THE AREA OF A TRIANGLE

Choose a side of the triangle to be its base. Call the length of this side *B*. Measure the height of the triangle relative to this base. Call this length *H*. Then the area of the triangle is equal to $\frac{1}{2}BH$.

EXERCISES 2. Find the areas of the triangles.

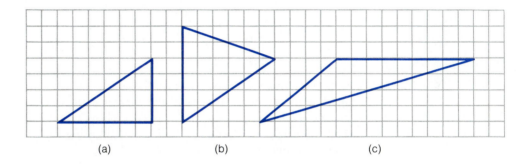

(a)   (b)   (c)

3. Use the principles and the formulas to find the areas of the shapes.

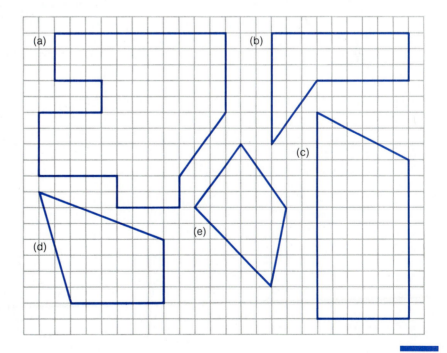

The Area of a Parallelogram

A *parallelogram* is a four-sided polygon such that pairs of opposite sides are parallel.

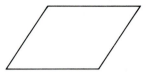

A rectangle is a special case of a parallelogram. There is a way to find the area of the illustrated parallelogram using the area of a rectangle *(a simpler problem)* and the principles for area presented earlier.

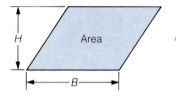 = 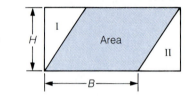 − =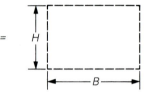

First find the length of one side of the parallelogram, calling this side the *base* of the parallelogram and orienting it horizontally. Then find the length of a vertical from the opposite side perpendicular to this horizontal, calling this length the *height* above the base. This information gives you a formula.

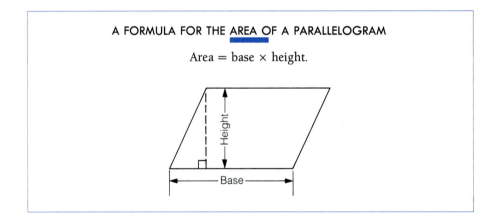

A FORMULA FOR THE AREA OF A PARALLELOGRAM

Area = base × height.

EXERCISE   4. Find the areas of the parallelograms.

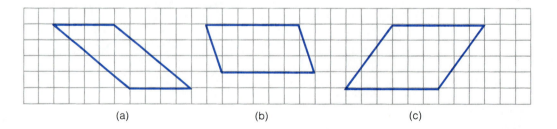

(a)   (b)   (c)

The Area of a Trapezoid

A *trapezoid* is a four-sided polygon having one pair of sides that is parallel and another pair that isn't.

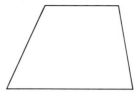

There is a way to find the area of a trapezoid using the area of a triangle and the principles for area.

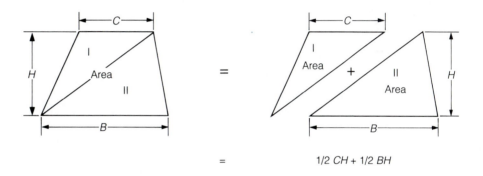

$$= \quad 1/2\ CH + 1/2\ BH$$

This gives us a formula for the area of a trapezoid.

FORMULA FOR THE AREA OF A TRAPEZOID

If the lengths of the two parallel sides of the trapezoid are B and C and the (vertical) distance between these two parallel sides is H, the *height* of the trapezoid, then

$$\text{Area of trapezoid} = \frac{1}{2}\,H(B + C).$$

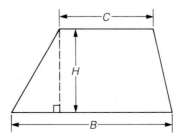

---

5. Find the areas of the following trapezoids.

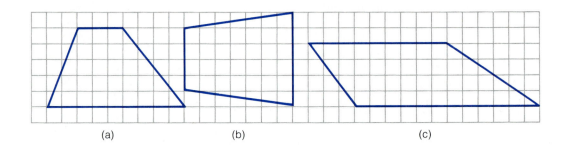

(a) (b) (c)

6. Use the principles and the formulas to help you find the areas of the shapes.

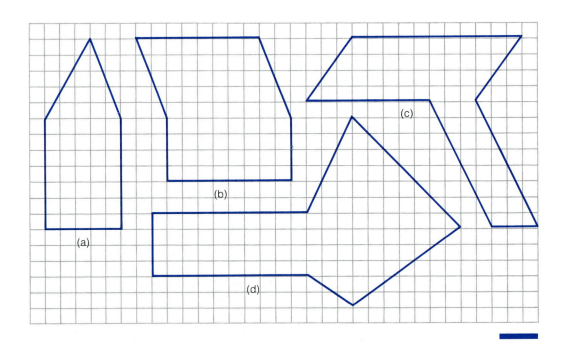

Look at the scale drawing of the Andrews' garden plot. Each square in the drawing represents a square yard. They want to find the area of their plot in square yards. Help them do this.

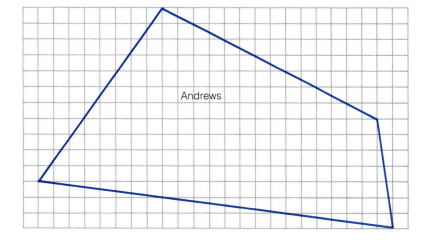

Try this yourself, first.

A Solution to the Fourth
Garden Plot Problem

The Andrews family members quickly realize that their plot has a shape for which there is no area formula, no formula that they know of, in any case. Sally Andrews thinks of the principles for area and of how she can *break the problem up into simpler problems*. She divides the area up into two pieces.

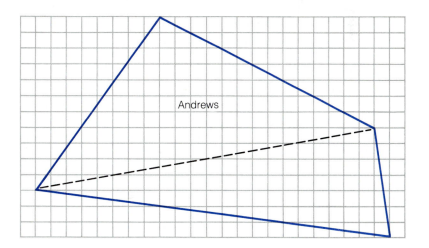

She thinks: "Each of those pieces is a triangle. I know how to find their areas. The area of the plot will be the sum of the areas of the two triangles. I will need to use another piece of graph paper to measure a base for each triangle and to measure the height on each base. Since the lines I will be measuring don't lie along horizontal or vertical lines of the graph, these measurements will be estimates.

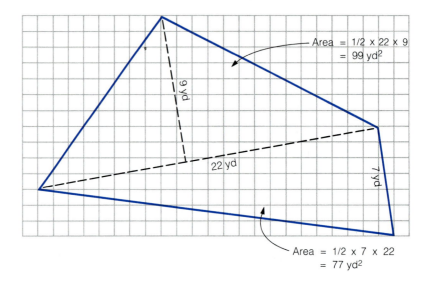

The areas of the two triangles are about 99 square yards and 77 square yards. So the area of our plot is about 176 square yards."

Arthur Andrews has been looking on and suggests an alternative solution: "I have an idea for a solution that doesn't involve as much estimation. My idea is to put the scale drawing of our plot inside a rectangle with sides of lengths easy to figure out.

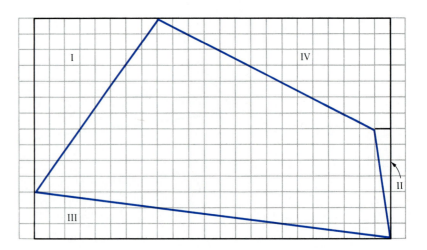

Since the sides of the rectangle are 14 yards and 23 yards, its area is 322 square yards. The area of the rectangle is also equal to the area of our plot plus the area of the three triangles and a trapezoid—labeled I, II, III, and IV, respectively. It's easy to figure out the areas of the triangles and trapezoid.

$$\text{Area of triangle I} = \frac{1}{2} \times 8 \times 11 = 44 \text{ yd}^2$$

$$\text{Area of triangle II} = \frac{1}{2} \times 1 \times 7 = 3\frac{1}{2} \text{ yd}^2$$

$$\text{Area of triangle III} = \frac{1}{2} \times 23 \times 3 = 34\frac{1}{2} \text{ yd}^2$$

$$\text{Area of trapezoid IV} = \frac{1}{2}(1 + 15)7 = 56 \text{ yd}^2$$

"Thus, we have the sums

$$\text{Area of rectangle} = 322 \text{ yd}^2$$
$$\text{Sum of areas of I, II, III, and IV} = 44 + 56 + 34.5 + 3.5 = 138 \text{ yd}^2$$

and can conclude

$$322 \text{ yd}^2 = 138 \text{ yd}^2 + \text{area of our plot},$$

or

$$\text{Area of our plot} = 322 \text{ yd}^2 - 138 \text{ yd}^2 = 184 \text{ yd}^2.$$

That's a little different from what you got. But then I didn't have to do any estimating by eye."

The Mathematical Idea: Strategies for Finding Areas

We have used several strategies to find formulas for areas and to solve other area problems.

STRATEGY 1   *Break the problem up into simple problems.* Take a complicated area and break it up into "simple" pieces, pieces with areas you already know how to find.

STRATEGY 2   Add pieces to the region you are interested in to create a larger region. Do this so that the areas of the pieces you add as well as the area of the large region are easy to find. This strategy is a second way to *turn the original problem into a bunch of simpler problems.*

STRATEGY 3   Break the region you are interested in into pieces and rearrange the pieces into another region that has an area you know how to find. This strategy is a third way to *turn the original problem into a bunch of simpler, previously solved problems.*

STRATEGY 4   Use combinations of strategies 1 through 3. Use the principles for area, too.

7. Find the areas of the shapes using the strategies.

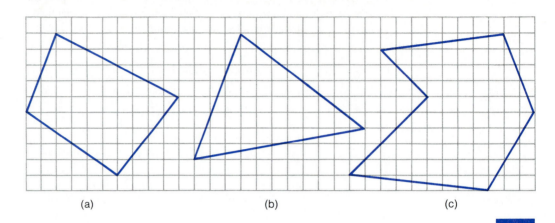

(a)   (b)   (c)

THE RUG PROBLEM

Try this yourself.

The Gonzales family is planning to have wall-to-wall carpeting laid in their living room. The members of the family have measured the living room floor and calculated its area to be 433.5 ft². They are now out looking in rug stores for ideas and prices and find that rugs are sold by the square yard. They realize that they need to know what the area of the floor is in square yards. Help them solve this.

A Solution to the Rug Problem

The members of the family figure that one way to solve the problem is to remeasure the living room in yards and from that calculate the area in square yards. If they can remember the measurements of the living room in feet, they can convert feet to yards and go from there.

Bernice Gonzales thinks out loud: "We know how many square feet the living room floor has: 433.5. What about a square yard? A yard is 3 feet in length. Here's a picture of a square yard.

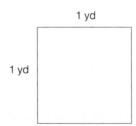

I can divide the square yard into square feet easily.

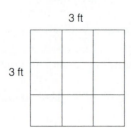

There are $3 \times 3 = 9$ square feet in a square yard. We've got 433.5 square feet. The number N of square yards in our living room floor times 9 should equal 433.5:

$$9N = 433.5.$$

The number we are looking for is $N = 433.5/9$, or about 48.17 square yards."

The Mathematical Idea: Area Conversions

Problems such as the rug problem arise when an area is calculated using one unit of area and you need to know what the area is in some other unit. These are problems of *conversion of units*.

One way to solve the Gonzales problem was suggested: Remeasure the room with the other units of length (yards) or convert one unit of length to the other (if you happen to know it). Here is a sketch of the Gonzales living room floor.

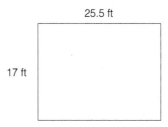

Since 1 yd = 3 ft, these measurements in yards are

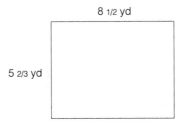

Thus, the area in square yards is $5\frac{2}{3} \times 8\frac{1}{2} \sim 48.17$ ft^2. This is what Bernice got.

The solution that Bernice used involved converting the units of area directly. She found that $1 \text{ yd}^2 = 9 \text{ ft}^2$.

We can give more examples of conversions from one unit of area to another.

$$1 \text{ ft}^2 = 144 \text{ in}^2 \quad (1 \text{ ft} = 12 \text{ in}; 12^2 = 144)$$

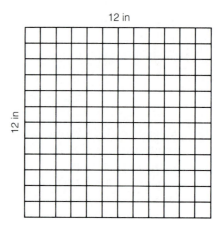

$$1 \text{ mi}^2 = 27{,}878{,}400 \text{ ft}^2 \quad (1 \text{ mi} = 5280 \text{ ft}; 5280^2 = 27{,}878{,}400)$$

$$1 \text{ m}^2 = 10{,}000 \text{ cm}^2 \quad (1 \text{ m} = 100 \text{ cm}; 100^2 = 10{,}000)$$

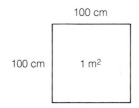

$$1 \text{ km}^2 = 1{,}000{,}000 \text{ m}^2 \quad (1 \text{ km} = 1000 \text{ m}; 1000^2 = 1{,}000{,}000)$$

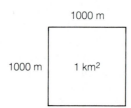

These conversions are not meant to be memorized! They are meant to give you a sample of typical conversions and how they are calculated.

8. An acre is a unit of area having the property that there are 640 acres in a square mile. How many square feet are there in an acre?

9. An average urban residential lot in the United States is $\frac{1}{4}$a. How much is this in square feet?

10. The area of 433.5 ft^2 is equal to how many square inches?

11. The area of 15,742,432 m^2 is equal to how many square kilometers?

12. The area of 5,350 in^2 is equal to how many square yards?

17.3   THE AREA OF A CIRCLE

THE CIRCULAR GARDEN PLOT PROBLEM

The Cohens own and operate a farm near Phoenix, Arizona. Because there is so little rainfall there, they must irrigate all cultivated land. They use a system that involves a long pipe to which nozzles that spray water are intermittently attached. One end of the pipe is fixed to a water source, while the rest of the pipe is on wheels and rotates about the fixed end.

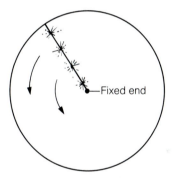

The Cohen farm consists of several of these circular fields. The family is interested in comparing the yield of their fields with the yields of other farms in Arizona and in other parts of the country. Yield is typically measured in so many pounds per square yard. The family knows their yield from last summer, and they know how many circular fields they had under cultivation. What they need to know is the area of each circular field.

A Solution to the Circular Garden Plot Problem

Tom Cohen thinks: "Is there some way we could *break up the circle into simple pieces?* I cut up a circle every time I cut up a pie. Let me draw a picture of that.

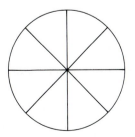

That breaks the circle up into a lot of wedges that are almost triangles. Then the area of the circle is equal to the sum of the areas of all the triangularlike wedges. Let me cut out those wedges to see if I can rearrange them into some nice, simple shape.

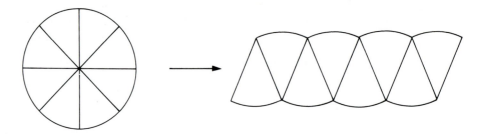

"That's sort of a parallelogram. If I had cut the circle up into many more, smaller, wedges, then the shape would be even more like a parallelogram. A parallelogram is a shape with an area I know how to find:

Area of parallelogram = length of base × height.

The "base" of this "parallelogram" is half the circumference of the original circle. The "height" of this "parallelogram" is a radius of the original circle. That leads me to

Area of the circle = area of "parallelogram" $\cong$ half the circumference × radius of circle.

"Since

Circumference of circle of radius $R = 2\pi R$,

Half the circumference of circle of radius $R = \pi R$.

That means that

Area of circle of radius $R \cong \pi RR$,

or

Area of circle of radius $R \cong \pi R^2$.

That should be pretty useful!"

The Mathematical Idea: A Formula for the Area of a Circle

The solution to the circular garden plot problem suggests that there is a formula for finding the area of a circle once you know its radius R.

FORMULA FOR THE AREA OF A CIRCLE

Area of circle of radius $R = \pi R^2$.

As the wedges in Tom Cohen's argument become smaller and smaller, the "parallelogram" becomes more and more like a "real" parallelogram, and it becomes increasingly plausible that the formula is a true formula for the area of a circle. With more advanced techniques, such as those of calculus, a more rigorous argument justifying this formula could be provided; but that is beyond the scope of this book. We will accept this as the formula for the area of a circle.

Now let's make the formula work for us. Recall that we used angle measure and the formula for the circumference of a circle to find the length of an arc of a circle. We can also use angle measure and the formula for the area of a circle to find the area of a pie-shaped piece of a circle, a shape formed by two radii and an arc.

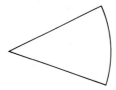

Such a piece is called a *sector* of a circle. If you measure the angle formed by the two radii and find that it measures $1°$, then you would agree that the area of the sector is $\frac{1}{360}$ the area of the whole circle. If the angle, called the *angle of the sector,* measured $10°$, then the area of the sector would be $\frac{10}{360}$ of the area of the whole circle.

FORMULA FOR THE AREA OF A SECTOR OF A CIRCLE

For a sector of angle D degrees in a circle of radius R,

$$\text{Area of sector} = \frac{D}{360}\pi R^2.$$

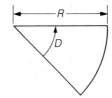

For example, suppose you have a sector with an angle of $15°$ in a circle of radius 10 ft, then from the formula

$$\text{Area of the sector} = \left(\frac{15}{360}\right)\pi\,10^2 \cong .0417 \times 3.14 \times 100 = .0417 \times 314 = 13.09 \text{ ft}^2.$$

EXERCISES 13. Find the areas of the circles and sectors of circles.

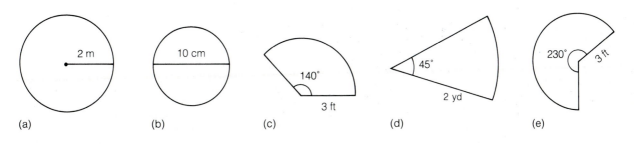

(a) (b) (c) (d) (e)

---

14. Roofing material is sold by the square foot. Roofing material is needed for each flat roof indicated. Find the area of each roof.

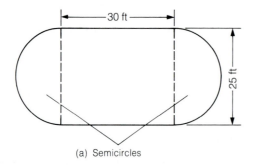

(a) Semicircles

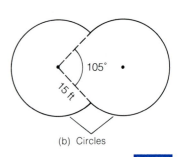

(b) Circles

EFFICIENT SHAPES

THE GARDEN FENCING PROBLEM

Try this yourself.

You are planning to dig a garden. Because of the rabbits and squirrels that live nearby, you must surround the garden with a fence. You have purchased 160 ft of fencing, which is all you can afford. The garden is to be in the shape of a rectangle. You are wondering what the length and the width of the rectangle should be. You want the area of the garden to be as large as possible, of course, but as long as you make a rectangle using up all the fencing, will the dimensions of the rectangle make a difference? And if this does make a difference, what should the dimensions of the rectangle be in order to have the largest possible area?

A Solution to the Garden Fencing Problem

You decide to begin by *making some guesses*. You think: "Suppose my garden has a width of 10 feet. I've got 160 feet of fencing. One side will use up 10 feet; the opposite side will use up 10 feet. That leaves me 160 feet − 20 feet = 140 feet for the other two sides. I could use up only a part of the 140 feet. For example, I could make each of the other two sides 20 feet, which would then use up 40 of the 140 feet.

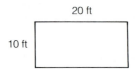

But certainly I would have a larger area if I use up *all* of the 140 feet. If I were to use all the 140 feet on the other two sides, then each side would have to be 70 feet.

70 ft

10 ft

The area of this garden is 10 feet × 70 feet = 700 square feet. Is that the largest area I can get? Let me try another width: 15 feet. That and the opposite side would use up 30 feet of the fencing, leaving 130 feet for the other two sides. If I use up all this remaining fencing (which I must), then the *other* two sides must have length 65 feet each.

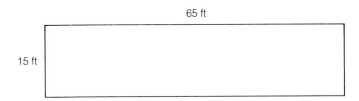

"The area of *this* garden is 15 feet × 65 feet = 975 square feet. That's a greater area than the other garden. That means that the dimensions of the rectangle do have an effect on the area—even when all the fencing is used up! Let me *make a chart* showing what I know already.

WIDTH	LENGTH	PERIMETER (MUST = 160 FT)	AREA
10 ft	70 ft	160 ft	700 ft^2
15 ft	65 ft	160 ft	975 ft^2

Let me try some more choices.

WIDTH	LENGTH	PERIMETER (MUST = 160 FT)	AREA
10 ft	70 ft	160 ft	700 ft^2
15 ft	65 ft	160 ft	975 ft^2
20 ft	60 ft	160 ft	1200 ft^2
25 ft	55 ft	160 ft	1375 ft^2
30 ft	50 ft	160 ft	1500 ft^2
35 ft	45 ft	160 ft	1575 ft^2
40 ft	40 ft	160 ft	1660 ft^2

"The next width to consider would be 45 feet. That would mean a length of 35 feet. A rectangle of width 45 feet and length 35 feet is really the "same" as a rectangle of width 35 feet and length 45 feet (it's just tilted on its side). That rectangle is already considered on the chart. When the width is equal to 40 feet, the width and the length are the same. For every rectangle with a width bigger than 40 feet (and thus with a length less than 40 feet) there is an "equal" rectangle with width less than 40 feet. It's enough to look at rectangles with widths 40 feet or less.

"If I'm going to add more to the chart, I should add guesses between the values I've already got. Before doing that, let me *look for patterns.* One thing I see is that as widths increase from 10 feet to 40 feet, the areas increase as well. Does the rectangle with width of 40 feet have the greatest area? Maybe between a rectangle of width 35 feet and one of 40 feet the area gets larger, then smaller. Let me try a few values.

WIDTH	LENGTH	PERIMETER (MUST = 160 FT)	AREA
35 ft	45 ft	160 ft	1575 ft^2
40 ft	40 ft	160 ft	1600 ft^2
37 ft	43 ft		1591 ft^2
39 ft	41 ft		1599 ft^2

"It looks as if the pattern persists: As widths increase to 40 feet, areas increase, too. So it appears that a rectangle of width 40 feet and length 40 feet is my best bet. That's a square!"

The Mathematical Idea: Efficient Shapes

According to the solution to the garden fencing problem, it seems that if you set out to make a rectangular garden with a fixed amount of fencing, then the best you can do is to split up the fencing into four equal pieces and make a square garden. The square is the *most efficient* rectangle for this situation. It will give you the most area for your fencing. We arrived at this conclusion by *making guesses and organizing them into a chart*. We might be even more convinced if we *made a graph* of area versus width. We add a few widths to the previous table to make the table of values we want to plot yield a more effective graph.

WIDTH (FEET)	AREA (SQUARE FEET)	WIDTH (FEET)	AREA (SQUARE FEET)
5	375	45	1575
10	700	50	1500
15	975	55	1375
20	1200	60	1200
25	1375	65	975
30	1500	70	700
35	1575	75	375
40	1600		

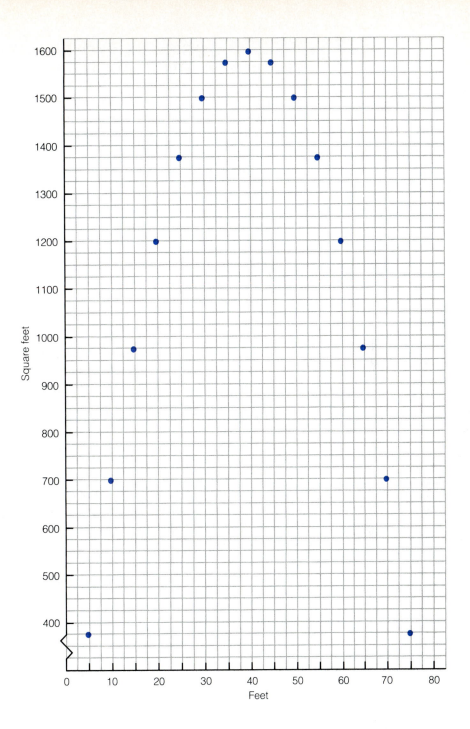

15. You are building an outdoor storage area for lumber and tools. You want the area to be in the shape of a rectangle having 900 ft². You want to know what dimensions of the rectangle would minimize the cost of the fencing that will surround it. Will the dimensions of the rectangle make any difference as long as the rectangle has an area of 900 ft²? (*Warning:* This is not the same as the garden fencing problem, in which the *perimeter* was fixed. In this problem, the *area* is fixed.)

LOOKING AHEAD: GRAPHS RELATED TO QUADRATIC FUNCTIONS

In chapter 16 we thought of the formula $P(S) = 4S$ for the perimeter of a square as the formula for a function with inputs possible sides S and with output of $P(S)$ corresponding to S, the perimeter of a square of side S. The graph of this function is a straight line.

In a similar way, we can think of the formula $A(S) = S^2$ for the area of a square as the formula for a function with typical input a possible side S and corresponding output the area $A(S)$ of square of side S. There are other formulas for functions that are consequences of what we have done in this chapter.

INPUT	OUTPUT	FORMULA FOR OUTPUT IN TERMS OF INPUT
Side S of square	Area $A(S)$ of square	$A(S) = S^2$
Radius R of circle	Area $A(R)$ of circle	$A(R) = \pi R^2$
Width W of rectangle	Area $A(W)$ of rectangle with length twice its width	$A(W) = 2W^2$
Base B of triangle	Area $A(B)$ of triangle with height half its base	$A(B) = .25B^2$

The formula for each function involves the square of the input. These are examples of *quadratic functions,* which we will define completely later. For the time being, we would like to find the graphs of these functions.

We start with the graph of $A(S) = S^2$. If S is the side of a square, then any $S \geq 0$ is an input. To get a good idea of what the graph looks like, we will take liberties and allow any S (positive, negative, and zero). So $A(S) = S^2$ is no longer interpreted as the formula for the area of a square but as the formula for a function with input any number S and output S^2. To obtain some representative points for the graph, we construct a table.

INPUT S	OUTPUT $A(S) = S^2$
0	0
1	1
2	4
3	9
4	16
5	25
−1	1
−2	4
−3	9
−4	16
−5	25

The graph corresponding to the table looks like this.

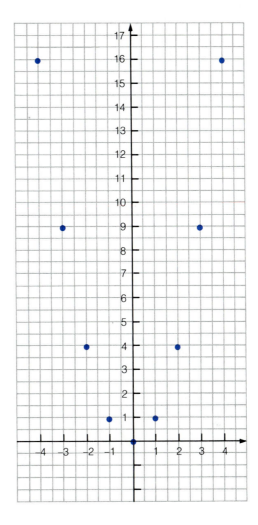

We have something new: The plotted points suggest that the graph of $A(S) = S^2$ is neither a straight line nor a graph of exponential growth. To get a better indication of the shape of the graph of $A(S) = S^2$, we choose several more possible inputs and calculate the corresponding outputs.

INPUT S	OUTPUT $A = S^2$
.5	.25
1.5	2.25
2.5	6.25
3.5	12.25
−.5	.25
−1.5	2.25
−2.5	6.25
−3.5	12.25

Including the points corresponding to this table in our graph, we obtain an expanded graph.

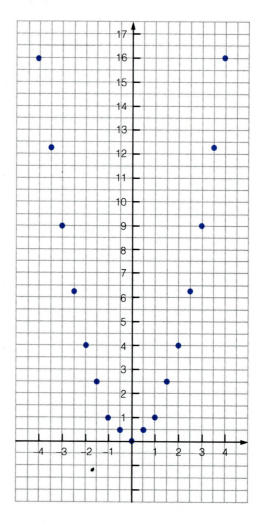

The points of the graph above seem to suggest that the shape of the graph of $A(S) = S^2$ for all possible inputs S looks like the following.

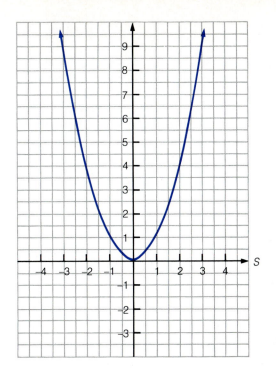

The part of the graph appropriate for sides and areas of squares is the following ($S \geq$ zero).

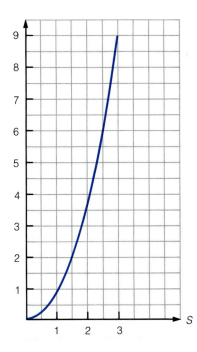

The graphs of the other functions listed in the chart will emerge from the following discussion.

Qualitative Graphing and Trips, Revisited

In chapters 14 and 15 we considered trips along a straight line and looked at the graphs of functions associated with such trips. For such a function an input T is the time elapsed from time $T = $ zero (usually the start of the trip), and the corresponding output $D(T)$ is the distance the person is from the reference point at time T. Now, instead of starting with a picture, let's start with a formula for a trip function. We'll start with a trip that Alvarez takes. Let's assume that Alvarez's trip is described by the formula $D(T) = T^2$, that is, her distance from the reference point at T seconds is T^2. From the discussion in the previous paragraphs we know that the picture of her trip is the following

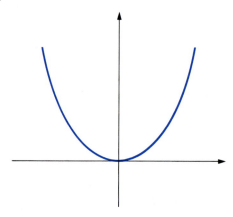

From this picture, we can obtain the graphs corresponding to many other related trips using some of the ideas explored in chapter 14. At the same time, we will be able to draw some connections between the graphs of functions and formulas for the functions. To see this, we start with the function for Alvarez's trip and its graph. Then we will describe trips other people take *in terms of* Alvarez's trip and obtain formulas and graphs for them as well.

1. Berger's trip is just like Alvarez's except that he is always 3 ft ahead of Alvarez. Here are the graph and the formula.

Graph:

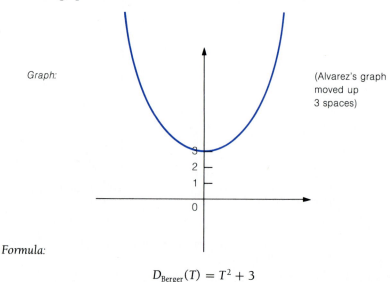

(Alvarez's graph moved up 3 spaces)

Formula:

$$D_{\text{Berger}}(T) = T^2 + 3$$

2. Cromwell's trip is just like Alvarez's except that she's twice as far as Alvarez is from the reference point at all times. Here are her graph and formula.

Graph:

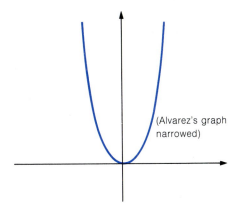

(Alvarez's graph narrowed)

Formula:

$$D_{\text{Cromwell}}(T) = 2T^2$$

3. Duval's trip is just like Cromwell's trip except that he's always 8 ft behind Cromwell.

Graph:

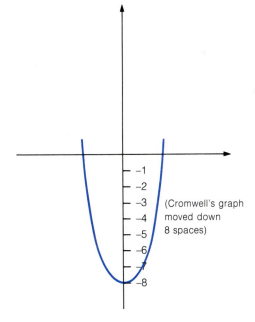

(Cromwell's graph moved down 8 spaces)

Formula:

$$D_{\text{Duval}}(T) = 2T^2 - 8$$

4. Ericson's trip is just like Alvarez's except that at a given time Ericson is always where Alvarez was 3 sec earlier. In other words, Ericson's trip is just like Alvarez's but delayed by 3 sec.

Graph:

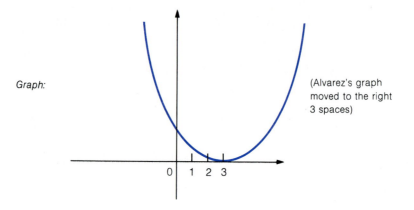

(Alvarez's graph moved to the right 3 spaces)

Formula:

$$D_{\text{Ericson}}(T) = (T-3)^2$$

[Ericson's distance at time T is the same as Alvarez's distance 3 sec earlier, i.e., at time $T-3$. Alvarez's distance at time $T-3$ is $(T-3)^2$. So we have that $D_{\text{Ericson}}(T) = (T-3)^2$.]

5. Fan's trip is just like Duval's except that she's 6 sec ahead of Duval: Her distance at time T is just what Duval's will be 6 sec later—at time $T+6$. Since Duval's distance at time $T+6$ is $2(T+6)^2 - 8$, we have

Graph:

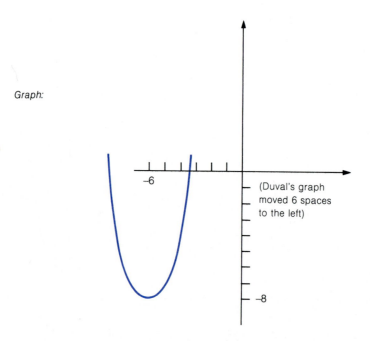

(Duval's graph moved 6 spaces to the left)

Formula:

$$D_{\text{Fan}}(T) = 2(T+6)^2 - 8$$

6. For Gertz's trip all we know is a formula: $D_{\text{Gertz}}(T) = 4(T - 3)^2 - 10$. To figure out the graph corresponding to this function, we can build it up as follows.

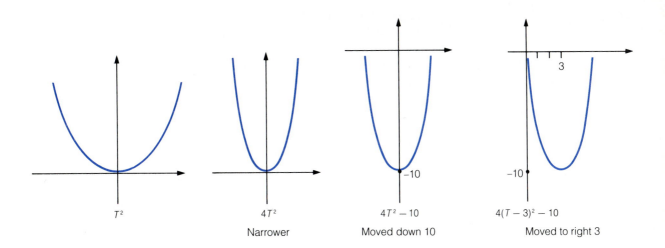

T^2	$4T^2$	$4T^2 - 10$	$4(T - 3)^2 - 10$
	Narrower	Moved down 10	Moved to right 3

The graph for Gertz's trip is a narrower T^2 graph moved around. We got the graph for Gertz's trip not by constructing a table but by using the graph for $D(T) = T^2$ (for which we *did* construct a table) and altering it.

Using the distributive law several times, you will notice that

$$D_{\text{Gertz}}(T) = 4(T - 3)^2 - 10$$
$$= 4(T^2 - 6T + 9) - 10$$
$$= 4T^2 - 24T + 36 - 10$$
$$= 4T^2 - 24T + 26$$

and that

$$D_{\text{Fan}}(T) = 2(T + 6)^2 - 8$$
$$= 2(T^2 + 12T + 36) - 8$$
$$= 2T^2 + 24T + 36 - 8$$
$$= 2T^2 + 24T + 28.$$

Thus, all the functions in examples 1 through 5 are instances of a quadratic function.

DEFINITION OF *QUADRATIC FUNCTION*

A function with input T and corresponding output $D(T)$ such that $D(T) = aT^2 + bT + c$ (for some fixed numbers a, b, c) is called a *quadratic function*.

It turns out that the graph of any quadratic function can be obtained from the graph of the function $D(T) = T^2$ by a sequence of one or more of the following changes: flipping upside down, narrowing or widening, moving up or down, and moving right or left.

16. Draw the graph of $D(T) = -T^2$. (Remember that $-T^2$ means first square the number T, then take the negative of your answer.) Do this by starting with the graph for $D(T) = T^2$ and thinking of how the graph for $D = -T^2$ should be related to it.

17. Start with the graphs for $D(T) = T^2$ and $D(T) = -T^2$ (from the text and exercise 16) and, in the manner of the preceding discussion, use them to graph the functions.

(a) $D(T) = 3T^2$

(b) $D(T) = (T - 1)^2$

(c) $D(T) = 3(T - 1)^2$

(d) $D(T) = 3T^2 + 4$

(e) $D(T) = (T - 1)^2 + 4$

(f) $D(T) = 3(T - 1)^2 + 4$

(g) $D(T) = 3(T - 1)^2 - 4$

(h) $D(T) = -3(T - 1)^2 - 4$

(i) $D(T) = 3(T + 1)^2 + 4$

(j) $D(T) = .25T^2$

(k) $D(T) = -.25(T - 1)^2 + 4$

Returning to the functions we met at the beginning of this section (related to area), we can use the techniques we have developed in this section to draw the corresponding graphs.

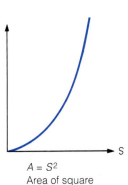

$A = S^2$
Area of square

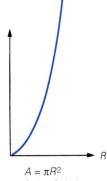

$A = \pi R^2$
Area of circle

$A = 2W^2$
Area of rectangle
with $L = 2W$

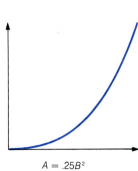

$A = .25B^2$
Area of triangle
with $H = .5B$

We can also use the techniques of this section to solve the garden fencing problem by graphing alone. Recall that you plan to make a rectangular garden, having width W and length L.

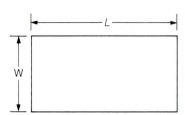

Also, the perimeter of the garden is to be 160 ft, the amount of fencing you have purchased. Thus, $160 = 2L + 2W$. Subtracting $2W$ from both sides, you can rewrite the latter equation as $2L = 160 - 2W$. Then, dividing both sides by 2, you obtain

$$L = \frac{160 - 2W}{2}, \quad \text{or} \quad L = 80 - W.$$

Now the area of the garden, which you want to be as big as possible, is given by the formula $A = LW$. But, since $L = 80 - W$, $A = LW$ can be replaced by $A = (80 - W)W$, or $A = -W^2 + 80W$.

This means that $A = A(W) = -W^2 + 80W$ is a quadratic function, and we know what the graph of a quadratic function looks like, roughly. To figure out what it looks like exactly, we do some algebra on the formula.

$$\begin{aligned} A(W) &= -W^2 + 80W \\ &= -(W^2 - 80W) \text{ (distributive property)} \\ &= -(W^2 - 80W + 1600) + 1600 \text{ (add 0)} \\ &= -(W - 40)^2 + 1600 \text{ (distributive property).} \end{aligned}$$

The graph of the function can thus be obtained from the graph of W^2 by first flipping it upside down (see exercise 16), then moving it to the right 40 units, and finally moving it up 1600 units. Using this information and observing that when $W = 80$, $A = 0$ and that when $W = 0$, $A = 0$ (the latter bits of information tell us that the graph intersects the horizontal axis at points $(0, 0)$ and $(80, 0)$, we obtain the following graph of $A = -W^2 + 80W$.

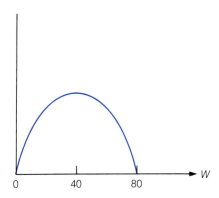

It is pretty clear from the graph that the area A is biggest when $W = 40$. (The graph of a quadratic has mirror symmetry in a vertical line through its "peak"; 40 is halfway between 0 and 80, the two places touched by the graph on the horizontal axis.) This coincides with the solution obtained earlier in the chapter. At this point, the second solution may seem no easier than the first. However, it does provide some understanding of the fact that the graph of any quadratic looks like the graph of W^2 "moved around."

A third way to solve the garden fencing problem is also by way of graphing, this time through the graph plotting software mentioned in chapter 14. The software avoids the use of algebra. A fourth method for solving the garden fencing problem is described in the next section.

17.6   COMPUTERS: FINDING EFFICIENT SHAPES

The first solution to the garden fencing problem involves making a table. We have seen before that the computer is ideally suited for solving problems in that way. Let's get the computer to solve the problem. The beginning of the table we want the computer to print is shown.

WIDTH (FT)	LENGTH (FT)	AREA (FT^2)
5	75	375
10	70	700

If we let W be width, L, length, and A, area, then we know that $W + L = 80$ (half the perimeter) and $WL = A$. Here is a program that completes the table.

```
10 PRINT ''WIDTH'', ''LENGTH'', ''AREA''
20 FOR W = 5 TO 80 STEP 5
30 LET L = 80-W
40 LET A = W*L
50 PRINT W, L, A
60 NEXT W
100 END
```

Next, we run the program.

```
RUN

WIDTH   LENGTH   AREA
5       75       375
10      70       700
15      65       975
20      60       1200
25      55       1375
30      50       1500
35      45       1575
40      40       1600
45      35       1575
50      30       1500
55      25       1375
60      20       1200
65      15       975
70      10       700
75      5        375
80      0        0
```

From this printout it appears that the area is biggest when the width is 40. We can investigate this further by looking at the values of W that we have missed on either side of 40.

```
10 PRINT ''WIDTH'', ''LENGTH'', ''AREA''
20 FOR W = 35 TO 45
30 LET L = 80-W
40 LET A = W*L
50 PRINT W, L, A
60 NEXT W
100 END

RUN
```

WIDTH	LENGTH	AREA
35	45	1575
36	44	1584
37	43	1591
38	42	1596
39	41	1599
40	40	1600
41	39	1599
42	38	1596
43	37	1591
44	36	1584
45	35	1575

We can continue in the same fashion and test values of W as close to 40 as we like.

```
10 PRINT  ''WIDTH'',  ''LENGTH'',  ''AREA''
20 FOR W = 39 TO 40 STEP .1
30 LET L = 80-W
40 LET A = W*L
50 PRINT W, L, A
60 NEXT W
100 END

RUN
```

WIDTH	LENGTH	AREA
39	41	1599
39.1	40.9	1599.19
39.2	40.8	1599.36
39.3	40.7	1599.51
39.4	40.6	1599.64
39.5	40.5	1599.75
39.6	40.4	1599.84
39.7	40.3	1599.91
39.8	40.2	1599.96
39.9	40.1	1599.99
40	40	1600

EXERCISE   18. Write a program to solve exercise 15 (this chapter).

Take a lot of squares of the same size.

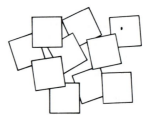

You can arrange these squares as shown.

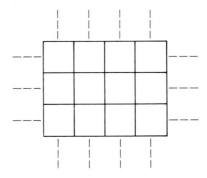

If you had enough of these squares, you could extend this arrangement and *tile* the entire plane; that is, you could cover the plane completely with these squares with no overlaps. It's like tiling your kitchen with square linoleum or ceramic tiles, except that the plane goes on forever in all directions; it needs infinitely many tiles for a complete covering. This covering of the plane by many copies of a single shape is called a *tessellation*. Some shapes other than the square will also form a tessellation. Other shapes won't. An equilateral triangle is another example of a shape that will.

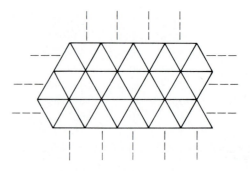

It is perhaps due to its ability to tile the plane that a square has been chosen to be the unit for measuring the area of shapes in the plane. One could just as well have chosen an equilateral triangle as the unit, except for the fact that we seem to be prejudiced toward rectangles in our culture, and a rectangle with whole-number sides can itself be "tiled" with unit squares, the number of them being its area. At the same time, no rectangle can be tiled with equilateral triangles, unless you allow for pieces of triangles around the edge. Look what happens.

Unit

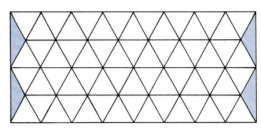

Trying to tile a rectangle with
unit equilateral triangles

Here are some shapes that can be tiled with whole numbers of "unit" equilateral triangles. (If the equilateral triangle were our unit of measure, would the floor plans of houses be shapes like these?)

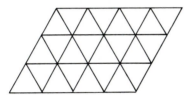

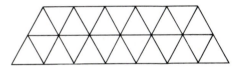

EXERCISES   **19.** A number of quadrilaterals are shown. Make several copies of each. Try to make a tiling with each of the shapes. Which of the quadrilaterals will tile the plane? What can you say in general about a quadrilateral that can tile the plane?

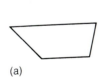
(a)

(b)

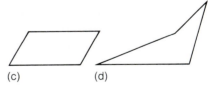
(c)

(d)

(e)

20. A number of triangles are shown below. Make several copies of each of them. Try to make a tiling with each of the triangles. Which of the triangles will tile the plane? What can you say in general about a triangle that can tile the plane?

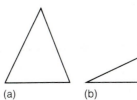
(a)   (b)   (c)

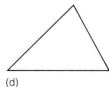
(d)

21. Regular 3-gons (equilateral triangles) and regular 4-gons (squares) will tile the plane. What other regular polygons will tile the plane? A regular pentagon, regular hexagon, and regular septagon are shown. Make several copies of each. Which of these three shapes will tile the plane? What can you say in general about regular polygons that can tile the plane?

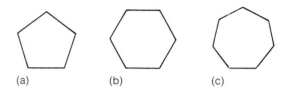

(a)   (b)   (c)

22. A number of shapes are shown. Which will tile the plane? You may want to make several copies of each to find out.

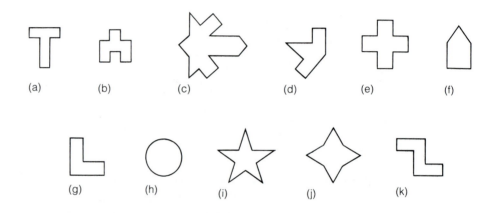

(a)   (b)   (c)   (d)   (e)   (f)

(g)   (h)   (i)   (j)   (k)

23. Tilings are the basis for interesting floor patterns in patios, kitchens, bathrooms, and large public places. The tilings we have seen consist of the repetition of a single shape. A tiling can also consist of the repetition of several single shapes in combination. Below is a familiar tiling pattern made up of squares and regular octagons.

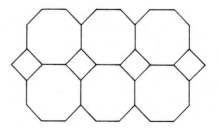

Several interesting tiling patterns can be made by combining two or more of the following shapes. Make several copies of each. Explore. See what tiling designs you can make from combinations of these shapes.

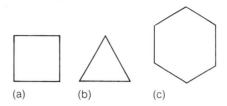

(a)   (b)   (c)

17.8   SUMMARY OF IMPORTANT IDEAS AND TECHNIQUES

- The area of a rectangle with whole-number sides
- The area of a rectangle with fractional sides
- A formula for the area of any rectangle
- Development of formulas for areas of triangles, parallelograms, and trapezoids
- Useful principles and strategies for finding areas
- Formula for the area of a circle
- Formula for the area of a sector of a circle
- Efficient rectangular shapes: with fixed perimeter, the rectangle having the greatest area; with fixed area, the rectangle having the least perimeter
- Constructing graphs of quadratic functions
- Tiling patterns

PROBLEM SET

PRACTICING SKILLS

1. Find the areas of the rectangles: (a) length $3\frac{1}{4}$, width $2\frac{1}{3}$ and (b) length 2, width $3\frac{2}{3}$.

2. Use an argument similar to that found in "Solution to the Gold Plating Problem" to show that a rectangle $3\frac{5}{8}$ by $2\frac{1}{3}$ has area $\frac{203}{24}$.

3. Find the areas of the right triangles: (a) length of base 2, height $3\frac{1}{2}$ (b) length of base $3\frac{1}{3}$, height $2\frac{1}{2}$.

4. Use an argument similar to that found in "Solution to the Third Garden Plot Problem" to show that a right triangle with a base $3\frac{1}{3}$ cm long and height $2\frac{1}{2}$ cm has an area $\frac{50}{6}$ cm.

5. Find the areas of the pastures. Each square in the grid has sides equal to 1 ft.

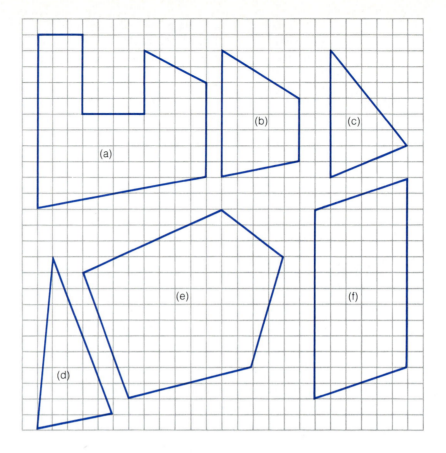

6. How many square yards are in a square mile?

7. If the area of a room is 108 yd², what is its area in square feet? In square inches?

8. If the area of a garden is 218 ft², what is its area in square yards?

9. Find the areas of the circles and sectors of circles.

(a) 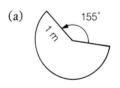 (b) 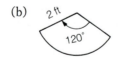 (c) 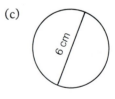 (d)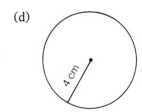

10. Find the area of the window.

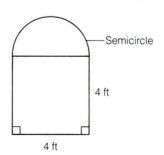

11. Find the dimensions of the rectangle of least perimeter with area 625 ft².

12. Find the rectangle of largest area with perimeter 12 ft.

13. Graph the functions.
    (a) $D(T) = T^2$
    (b) $D(T) = 5T^2$
    (c) $D(T) = 5(T - 1)^2$
    (d) $D(T) = (T + 1)^2$
    (e) $D(T) = 5(T + 1)^2 + 3$
    (f) $D(T) = 5(T - 1)^2 + 3$
    (g) $D(T) = 5(T + 1)^2 - 3$
    (h) $D(T) = 5(T - 1)^2 - 3$

14. Graph the functions.
    (a) $D(T) = -T^2$
    (b) $D(T) = -2T^2$
    (c) $D(T) = -2(T - 1)^2$
    (d) $D(T) = -2(T + 1)^2$
    (e) $D(T) = -2(T - 1)^2 + 2$
    (f) $D(T) = -2(T - 1)^2 - 2$
    (g) $D(T) = -2(T + 1)^2 + 2$
    (h) $D(T) = -2(T + 1)^2 - 2$

15. Write a program in BASIC to solve problem 11.

16. Write a program in BASIC to solve problem 12.

USING IDEAS *Write the solution to each remaining problem carefully and clearly in the form of an essay. In it mention the steps you took to solve the problem, the principles, tools, or formulas you used, other problems or solutions that gave you ideas, and the problem-solving strategies you found helpful.*

17. Here is the western end of a house that is to be stuccoed. To determine the cost of the stuccoing, you need to know the area. What is it?

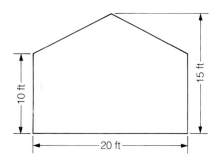

18. It ought to be possible to determine the area and perimeter of a region by figuring out the area and perimeter of a scale drawing of the region.
    (a) Find the area and perimeter of each square and compare them.

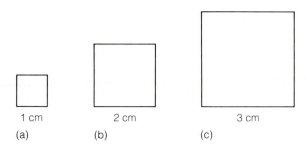

1 cm   2 cm   3 cm
(a)   (b)   (c)

(b) Find the area and perimeter of each rectangle and compare them.

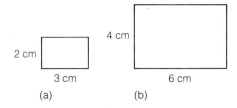

(a)   (b)

(c) Find the area and perimeter of each triangle and compare them.

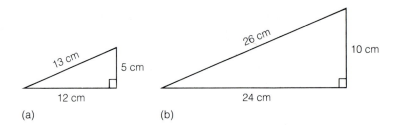

(a)   (b)

(d) Suppose the ratio of lengths of an original to a scale drawing is 5 to 3. Suppose the perimeter of the scale drawing is 21 ft. What is the perimeter of the original? Suppose the area of the scale drawing is 12 ft². What is the area of the original?

(e) Find a general rule for comparing the perimeter of a scale drawing with the perimeter of the original. Find a general rule for comparing the area of a scale drawing with the area of the original.

19. A store sells two types of gift wrapping paper. Type A has four rolls in each package, each roll is 75 by 150 cm, and the package costs $5.98. Type B has a single roll that is 88 by 500 cm and costs $6.38. Which choice gives you more paper for the money?

20. Your backyard has a pool and patio. You are thinking of tiling your patio with mosaic tiles. To figure out how much it would cost, you need to know its area. Find it.

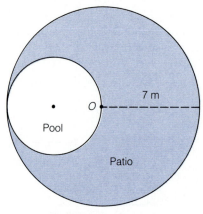

Point *O* is the center of
the larger circle.

21. In a park there is a circular garden of diameter 26 ft. Maintenance personnel will be building a circular sidewalk 3.5 ft wide to surround the garden. To figure out how much concrete they will need, they need to know the surface area of the sidewalk. What is it?

22. For tax purposes, buildings are assessed at a rate of $189/m².

    Rectangular: 8 m by 13.75 m
    L-shaped: 8.7 by 11 m plus 8 by 9.5 m

    The tax rate is $52 for every $1000 of assessment. What must the owners of each of these houses pay in real estate taxes?

23. Here is a picture of your house and the lot on which it is situated. You plan to sow grass everywhere on the lot except where the house is. You will need 1 lb of grass seed for every 100 ft² of ground to be covered. How many pounds of grass seed will you need?

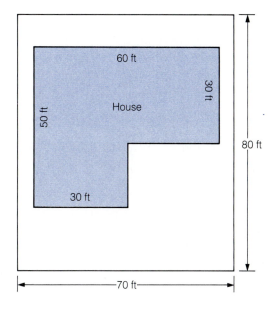

24. Which of these two pasture has the largest area, (a) or (b)? Which needs the most fencing?

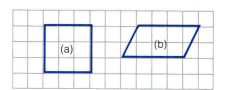

25. The floor plan of your kitchen and eating room shows that the whole room is a rectangle. You plan to lay new linoleum on the parts of the floor not shaded in. Using the measurements given, find the area in square feet of the part to be covered with linoleum.

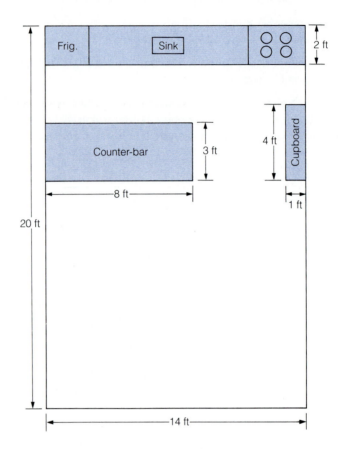

26. You plan to paint a bedroom with a square-shaped floor 12 ft on a side and a ceiling that slopes from a height of 9 ft 6 in on one side to 7 ft on the other. The room has a 30 in by 6 ft 8 in doorway, a 5 by 6 ft closet opening, and a 40 by 60 in window opening. About how much paint will be needed to paint the walls of this room with two coats, if 1 qt of paint covers about 110 ft²? Do the door, window, and closet openings significantly affect the calculation of how much paint to buy?

27. A chair with thin legs can be tough on floors when it is tilted back. To see why, suppose the legs of a chair are round with a bottom diameter of 1 in and suppose the chair is occupied by a person weighing 200 lb.
    (a) What is the pressure (in pounds per square inch) exerted on the floor when the person is sitting squarely and all four legs of the chair are on the floor?
    (b) What is the pressure on the floor when the person is tilted back and only $\frac{1}{10}$ of the two rear legs of the chair have contact with the floor?

28. You plan to build a pen for your goat. It will be a rectangular pen with area 25 m². One side of the pen will be an existing wall of your house. What length and width of the pen will require the smallest amount of fencing? How much fencing material will you need in this case?

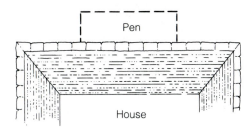

29. You and a neighbor are planning to plant gardens side by side as in the picture, with fencing all around and dividing the two plots. The two of you together can afford a total of 100 ft of fencing. What should the dimensions of the big plot be in order that area of the two gardens be as large as possible?

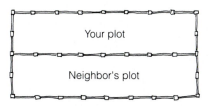

30. Trees lose moisture through their leaves. The amount of moisture lost is directly related to the total surface area of a tree's leaves. Estimate the area of the leaf below. Assume that each square in the grid is $\frac{1}{4}$ in on a side.

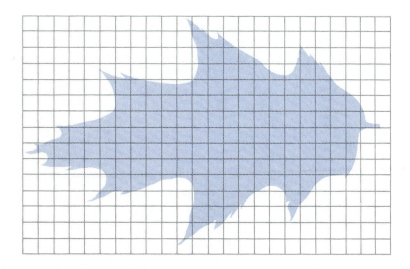

31. A scale drawing of the Palm Grove subdivision is shown.

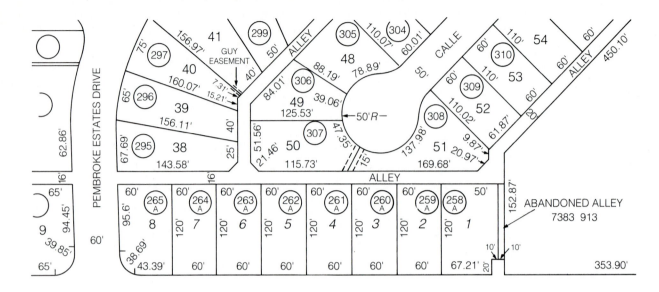

You are thinking of purchasing lot number 308. If you buy it, you will place mobile homes on the lot and rent them out. The county requires an area of 350 ft^2 for every mobile home. To determine what your income from the lot would be, you want to know how many mobile homes you can place on the lot. Thus, you need to find the area of the lot. Since the lot has an irregular shape, this requires some ingenuity. You decide to: (a) enlarge the scale drawing of the lot using a fancy photo copier, (b) trace the outline of the lot onto graph paper, (c) estimate the number of squares that would cover the enlargement, (d) figure out the area of each of these squares in real life, and (e) multiply the answer in (d) by the answer in (c).

We've done (a). Carry out the rest of the procedure to estimate the area of the lot and determine the number of mobile homes allowed on it.

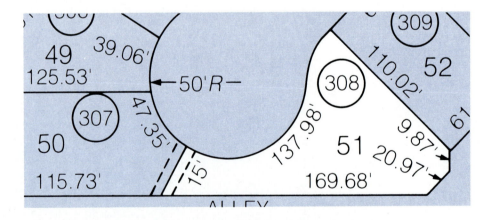

APPLICATIONS OF AREA

18 CHAPTER

In this chapter we will discuss two major topics related to area. The first, the Pythagorean theorem, is a striking fact about right triangles that follows from the basic principles of area that we developed in the last chapter. The primary use of the Pythagorean theorem, a statement about area, is in the measurement of length!

The second topic has to do with surface area. We will want to be able to answer questions such as

- How much cardboard (measured in square inches) will you need to make a certain box?

- How much metal (measured in square centimeters) will you need to make a certain can?

- How much paint will you need to paint a certain three-dimensional shape?

THE RIGHT-ANGLE PROBLEM

In the construction of a building, it is important that the ground floor be level. To ensure that it is, carpenters use what is called a *carpenter's level*. (See illustration: The long side can be placed on any surface to see if the surface is level. If it is, an air bubble appears between two cross hairs in the middle of the tube (which is partly filled with a liquid). If the surface is not level, the bubble is not centered.)

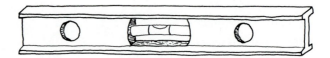

Normally, the walls of a building are constructed to be at a right angle to any level, horizontal line. To ensure "verticality," carpenters use a plumb line, which is a long string with a heavy piece of metal attached to one end. The metal piece—the plumb *bob*—is typically shaped as in the illustration. When the bob is suspended freely, the string makes a line forming a right angle with the horizon. This line is then compared to the line formed by the side of a building to see if the building is vertical or not.

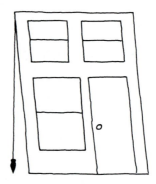

For most buildings the shape of the foundation is a rectangle (or a composition of rectangles), a shape that involves a lot of right angles. It is important that these angles be accurate. How can one create an accurate right angle on a level place?

The ancient Egyptians discovered a clever way to create a "true" right angle: Take a rope and tie a knot near one end. Tie 12 more knots so that the distances between any 2 adjacent knots on the rope are the same. This gives 13 equally spaced knots.

Place the 2 end knots together at the point where you want to create a right angle and drive a nail or tack through them (1 in the illustration). This will give you a loop of rope with 12 equal spaces between knots. The idea is to turn this loop into a right triangle.

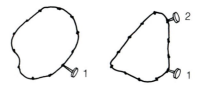

The nail will be the vertex of the right angle. To make one of the sides, count out 3 knots from the vertex. Pull the rope tight and drive a nail through that knot (2 in the illustration). This is the second vertex of the triangle. Go back to the right-angle vertex again and count out 4 knots from there in the other direction. This knot will become the third vertex of the triangle. Pull the rope so that all three sides are taut and drive a nail in this knot (3 in the illustration). You now have a right triangle, with the right angle at the first nail.

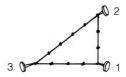

The Mathematical Idea: An Observation about Right Triangles

The triangle created by the Egyptians, as we have described, has sides of length 3, 4, and 5 units. Besides noticing that this triangle is a right triangle and using it to create right angles, the Egyptians and the Greeks after them also noticed another feature of the triangle.

Let's construct squares on the three sides of the triangle having 3, 4, and 5 sides.

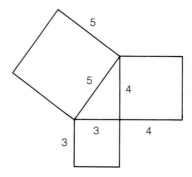

Look at the areas of these squares: 9 square units, 16 square units and 25 square units. Notice that $9 + 16 = 25$. The sum of the areas of the squares on the two sides forming the right angle, called the *legs* of the right triangle, is equal to the area of the square on the opposite side, called the *hypotenuse* of the right triangle.

There is another naturally occurring right triangle: Take a square and draw in one of its diagonals.

The diagonal and two adjacent sides of the square form a right triangle (shaded in the illustration). Now make a copy of this triangle and four copies of the original square and cut them out. Split two of these squares along their diagonals and arrange the four pieces in a new square.

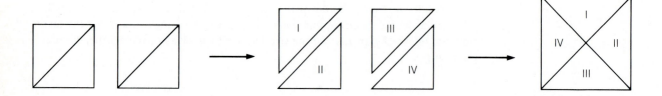

The area of the large square is equal to the sum of the areas of the two small squares. Place this large square and the two remaining smaller squares around the right triangle as shown.

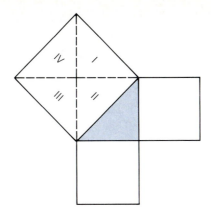

The sum of the areas of the squares on the two legs is equal to the area of the square on the hypotenuse!

Many ancient peoples observed this same relationship for many other right triangles. There is an argument to explain this fact that uses only cleverness and the principles we know for area. The fact has come to be known as the *Pythagorean theorem*.

AN INSTANCE OF THE PYTHAGOREAN THEOREM IN 400 B.C. CHINA

The illustration of a Chinese manuscript of around 400 B.C. It shows why a right triangle having legs of lengths 3 and 4 units must also have a hypotenuse equal to 5 units.

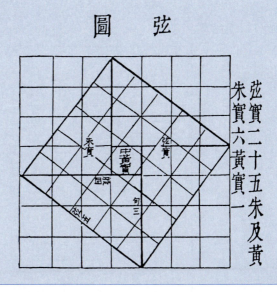

A Proof of the Pythagorean Theorem

Draw a right triangle and three squares, each having a side equal to one of the three sides of the triangle, as shown.

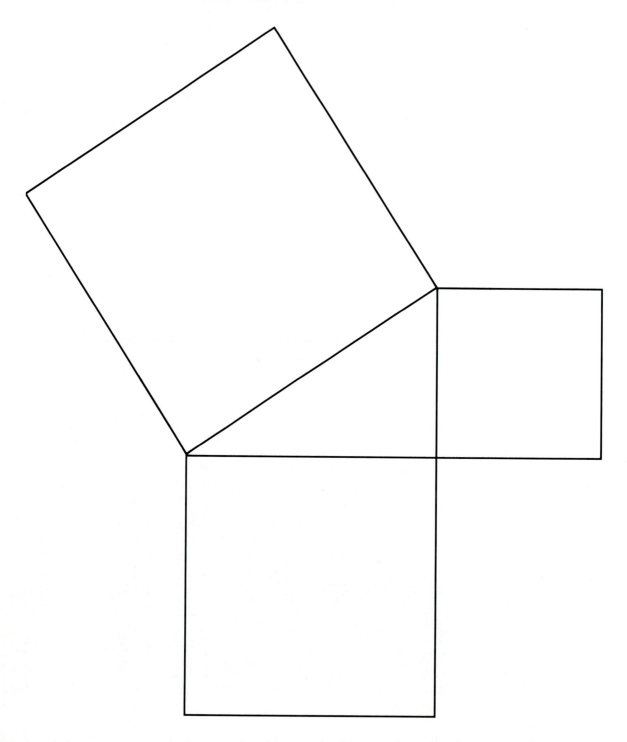

Make a copy of the drawing and cut out the pieces: the three squares and the triangle.

Take the two smaller squares, the squares on the legs of the right triangle, and tape them together.

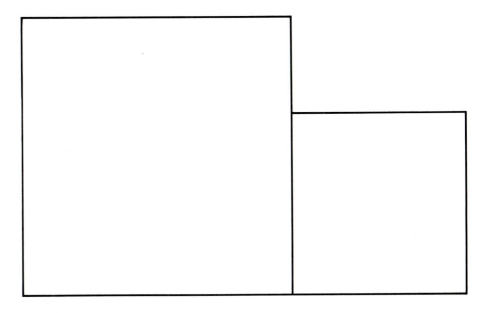

Next we want to take the shape consisting of the two smaller squares, cut *it* up into pieces, and rearrange them into another (surprising) shape. Using the area principles, the area of this new shape will be equal to the sum of the area of the two small squares. Here's how to cut up this shape. Trace a copy of the original triangle in two places:

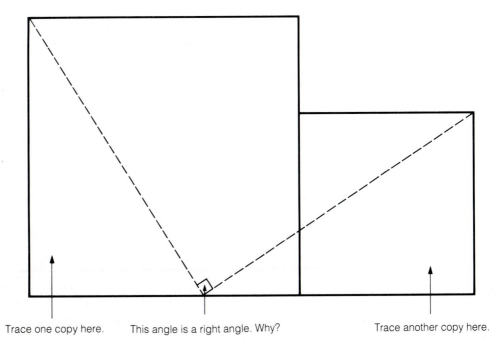

Trace one copy here.   This angle is a right angle. Why?   Trace another copy here.

Cut the shape consisting of the two squares up into three pieces: the two triangles and the rest (an unusual sort of figure).

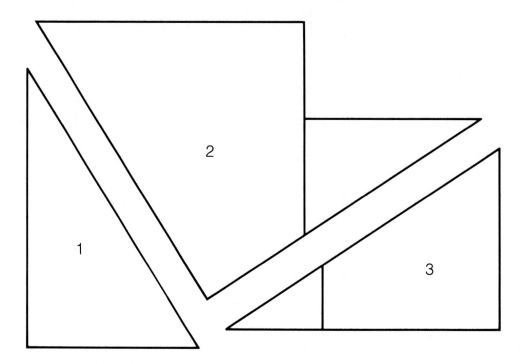

Then rearrange the three pieces.

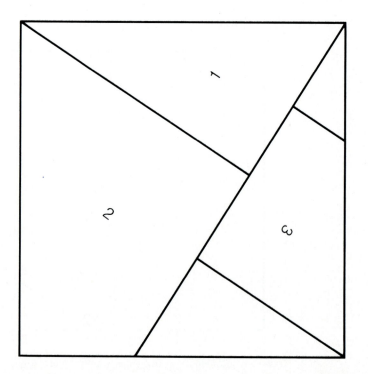

This new shape is a square with side equal to the hypotenuse of the original triangle. We conclude that the area of the large square is equal to the sum of the areas of the smaller squares, the squares that made the shape before it was cut.

We can summarize.

THE PYTHAGOREAN THEOREM

Construct squares on the sides of a right triangle. The sum of the areas of the smaller squares (those with sides equal to the two legs) is equal to the area of the largest square (the one with side equal to the hypotenuse).

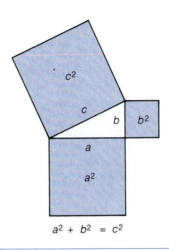

$$a^2 + b^2 = c^2$$

EXERCISE   1. The proof of the Pythagorean theorem we have given is one of many. There is another one that involves cutting out shapes and rearranging them.

(a) Make four copies of the right triangle, below.

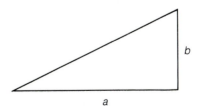

(b) The two legs have lengths *a* and *b*. Draw a square having sides equal to *a* + *b* and place the four copies of the original triangle in it as in the illustration.

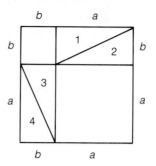

(c) Next rearrange the four triangles in the square as indicated.

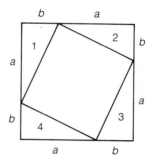

(d) What do you conclude from (b) and (c)?

THE NEW-BRIDGE PROBLEM A new road has been built to the river, and you are in charge of determining the length of a new bridge. The location of the river and the new and old bridges and some measurements you have made are given in the picture.

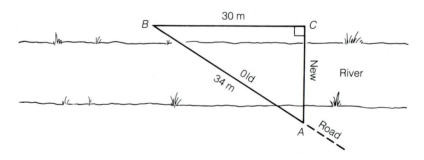

Try solving this yourself before reading on.

How will you find the length of the new bridge?

You think: "Points *A*, *B*, and *C* form the vertices of a triangle. If I knew the angle at *B*, then I could construct a scale drawing of the big triangle and from that figure out the distance from *A* to *C*. But since the angle at *C* is a right angle, maybe I can use the Pythagorean theorem. Let me construct the squares on the sides.

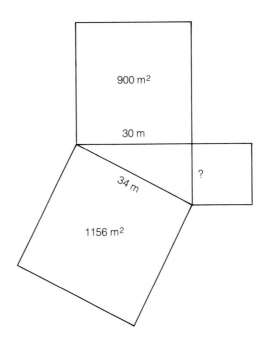

The area of the big square is 34 × 34 m = 1156 m²; the area of one of the small squares is 30 × 30 m = 900 m². I don't know the area of the other small square because its side is the length I'm trying to find. The Pythagorean theorem says that

$$1156 \text{ m}^2 = 900 \text{ m}^2 + \text{area of square with unknown side},$$

or

$$\text{Area of square with unknown side} = 1156 \text{ m}^2 - 900 \text{ m}^2 = 256 \text{ m}^2.$$

The area of the square with the unknown side is 256 m², so the length of the unknown side squared is equal to 256. A number that squared is equal to 256 is 16: 16 × 16 = 256. The unknown side is 16 m. The length of the new bridge should be 16 m."

The Mathematical Idea: Measuring Length Indirectly Using the Pythagorean Theorem

In the solution to the new-bridge problem, you knew two sides of a right triangle and were able to find the third side using the Pythagorean theorem. Even though we presented it as a statement about areas, the Pythagorean theorem is most frequently used to find the length of the third side of a right triangle when you know the lengths of the other two sides.

In chapter 13 we solved a problem involving speaker wiring. We can use the Pythagorean theorem to provide an alternative solution to that problem.

A Solution to the Speaker Wiring Problem Using the Pythagorean Theorem

Here again is the scale drawing of a pattern for John's room indicating the position of the speaker wire across the walls and floor.

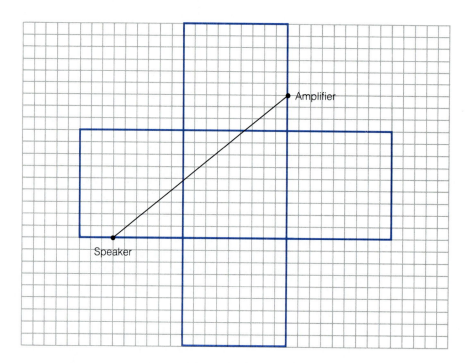

In chapter 13 we were interested in the length of the wire, and in our solution there we measured its length using another piece of graph paper. This time, since the path of the wire forms the third side of a right triangle, let's use the Pythagorean theorem. We draw in the squares and compute the areas that we know.

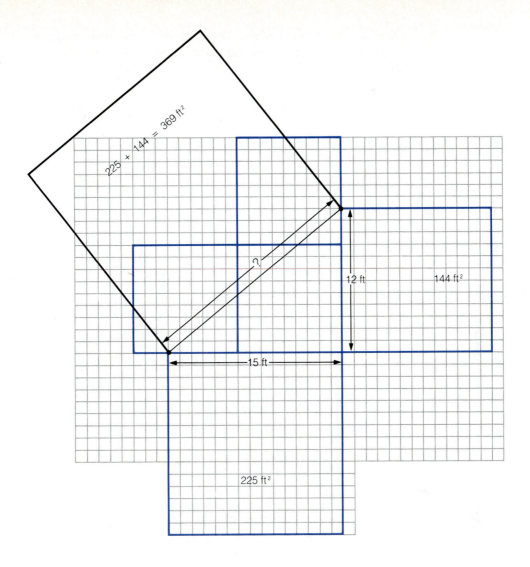

$225 + 144 = 369\ \text{ft}^2$

?

12 ft

144 ft²

15 ft

225 ft²

We know the areas of the squares on the legs because we know the lengths of their sides; we use these two areas together with the Pythagorean theorem to figure out the area of the square on the hypotenuse, shown in the scale drawing.

Now we are interested in finding the length of the side of a square with an area 369 ft². We want to find a number that squared is 369. Let's *make some guesses and organize them in a table.*

SIDE OF SQUARE IN FEET (GUESS)	AREA OF SQUARE IN SQ FT	TARGET AREA: 369 FT²
20	400	Too much.
15	225	Too little.
17	289	Closer, but still too little.
18	324	Still too little.
19	361	Much closer.
19.5	380.25	Too much this time.
19.25	370.56	Very close, but too much.
19.2	368.64	Very close, too little: Answer must be between 19.2 and 19.25.
19.22	369.41	Closer yet: Answer must be between 19.2 and 19.22.
19.21	369.02	Isn't this close enough?

Since 19.21 ft is too big and 19.2 ft is too small, the answer must lie between. But the difference between the two is .01 ft, less than $\frac{1}{8}$ in! So 19.21 ft is close enough.

The Mathematical Idea: Finding Square Roots

As we have mentioned in an earlier chapter, a number N with square equal to 369 is called the *square root* of 369. The difficulty in finding N in the speaker wiring problem comes from the fact that there is no whole number with square 369. However, we were able to solve the problem by *making guesses, organizing them in a chart,* and then zeroing in on a number close enough for all practical purposes. The method for zeroing in is this: If a guess A is too big and guess B is too small, then the length we are looking for must be between A and B. A good choice for the next guess might then be a number halfway between A and B.

With a calculator you can find the square root of a number very easily. You key in 369 [$\sqrt{x}$], and the display shows 19.20937271, quite a precise result. The method we used got us very close to that. Although our method is more tedious than using a calculator, it can be used to estimate square roots as well as make sense of a calculator's "magic" outcome.

2. You are trying to find the distance from one end of a lake to the other. On dry land you have created two legs of a right triangle. The hypotenuse is the length you want to measure. You measure the two legs of the right triangle and get 120 m and 90 m. What is the distance you are trying to find?

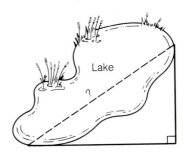

3. You are installing a guy wire support for a utility pole. You want to know how long the guy wire will be. One end will be attached to the top of the 25-ft pole and the other to a stake on horizontal ground 15 ft from the base of the pole. Solve this problem.

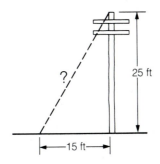

18.2 SURFACE AREA OF THREE-DIMENSIONAL SHAPES

THE BOX MANUFACTURING PROBLEM

You manufacture boxes. One particular box you have been asked to make is shown.

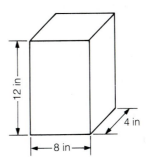

Find a real box and try solving this before reading on.

It is a metal box in which linseed oil is sold. One item of expense in manufacturing the box is the cost of the metal used in making it. The metal used is sold by the square inch. You want to know what the area of the metal for each box will be.

You think: "The box has a top, a bottom, and four sides. I must figure out the area of each of these and add those areas together. That will be the total area of metal used in making the box."

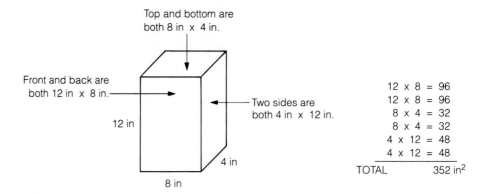

Top and bottom are
both 8 in × 4 in.

Front and back are
both 12 in × 8 in.

12 in

Two sides are
both 4 in × 12 in.

4 in

8 in

```
12 x 8  =  96
12 x 8  =  96
 8 x 4  =  32
 8 x 4  =  32
 4 x 12 =  48
 4 x 12 =  48
TOTAL       352 in²
```

You have an afterthought: "It would have been the same thing to flatten out the box into a pattern and then figure out the area of the pattern.

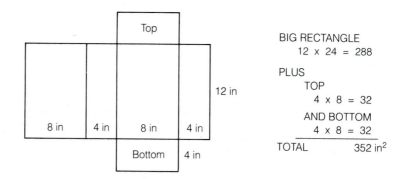

Top

8 in   4 in   8 in   4 in

12 in

Bottom   4 in

BIG RECTANGLE
12 × 24 = 288

PLUS
   TOP
     4 × 8 = 32

AND BOTTOM
     4 × 8 = 32

TOTAL   352 in²

That's a little easier."

The Mathematical Idea: Surface Area
of Three-Dimensional Shapes

In the solution to the box manufacturing problem we took all the flat pieces that made up the box, computed their areas, and added them up. This sum of the areas that make up the shell (or "skin") of a three-dimensional shape (in this case, the box itself) is called the *surface area* of the shape. The surface area of a three-dimensional shape is the analogue of the perimeter of a flat plane shape. The solution suggests two ways to calculate the surface area of a shape: (1) Calculate the areas of the separate flat pieces that make up the shell of the shape and add them up; (2) calculate the area of a pattern for the shape's shell.

EXERCISE   4. You are being asked to manufacture a metal storage bin.

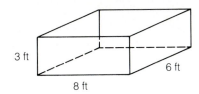

3 ft   8 ft   6 ft

The bin has a bottom and four sides but no top. You want to know the area of the metal needed to manufacture this bin.

THE TIN CAN MANUFACTURER'S PROBLEM

You manufacture tin cans in which food is preserved and sold in grocery stores. Here is a picture of one tin can you are being asked to manufacture.

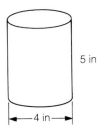

5 in

← 4 in →

Grab a soup can and try this yourself, please.

This shape is called a (*right-circular*) *cylinder*. The top and bottom are circles of the same size. As with the metal box for the linseed oil, one of the major expenses in manufacturing this can is the amount of metal that goes into making it. Again, this metal is sold by the square inch. You want to know how much metal is needed for each can.

A Solution to the Tin Can Manufacturer's Problem

You think: "I need to figure out the area of the various flat pieces of metal that go into making this tin can. I can handle the top and the bottom, but what about the curved sides? A *similar problem* is the box manufacturing problem, which I solved by making a pattern. To make a pattern for the tin can, I can cut the can from top to bottom here,

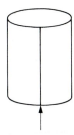

then cut around the top and bottom here,

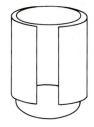

then flatten the whole thing out into something like this:

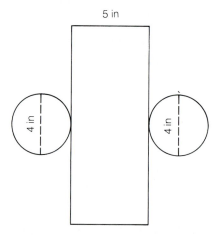

There are three areas to figure out: two circles and a rectangle. To figure out the areas of the circles, I measure the diameter of one and use the formula I know. To figure out the area of the rectangle, I need to measure the length of the horizontal side in the picture; that's the height of the tin can. I also need to measure the length of the other side of the rectangle. That length just fits around a circular end. It's the circumference of the circular end! That's π times the diameter, or about 12.57 inches. I'll draw a picture showing my calculations.

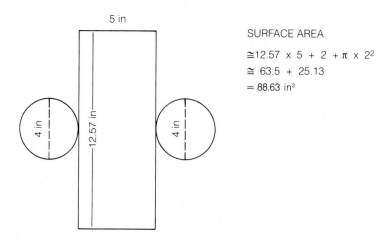

SURFACE AREA

$\cong 12.57 \times 5 + 2 + \pi \times 2^2$

$\cong 63.5 + 25.13$

$= 88.63 \text{ in}^2$

"That does it."

5. If you had tuna fish for lunch, (a) will be easy.
    (a) Find a tuna fish can, measure it, and figure out how much metal is used in making it.
    (b) Do the same with a Quaker Oats oatmeal box.

6. You are building a grain elevator. Your plan is, first, to construct a frame (in the shape shown) out of lightweight steel beams and, second, to cover the top and sides of this frame with thin panels of a lightweight aluminum-steel alloy. This paneling is sold by the square foot. You want to know how much of it you will need.

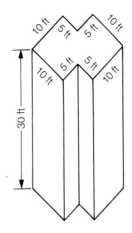

THE ROCKET NOSE CONE PROBLEM

You have been asked to manufacture nose cones of rockets. Each nose cone is in the shape of the cone shown. You will be responsible for the outer shell only, but it must be made to withstand the extremely high temperatures that occur when the rocket leaves the earth's atmosphere at high speeds; thus, the shell of the nose cone must be made of an expensive alloy of rare metals. To estimate the cost of the metal in this shell, you will need to figure out its area. At the same time, you need a flat pattern for the shell because you plan to make the shell from a flat sheet, then bend it into the final shell. Solve this problem.

Find a paper cone and try this.

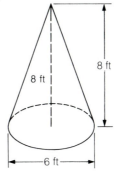

A Solution to the Nose Cone Problem

You figure that finding a pattern for the cone may also help you to find its area. (This strategy has worked before in *solving similar problems*.) But you are not sure what a pattern for a cone should be. You decide to look around for a cone to cut up. You think of a paper cone drinking cup that comes in a dispenser. You find one and make a cut from bottom to top, as indicated.

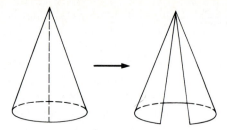

You flatten it out. (You are a little surprised that it *does* flatten out!)

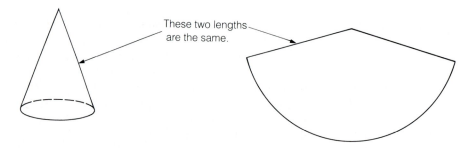

You think, "It flattens out into a sector of a circle!" You know that figuring out its area will be easy if you can find out the length of the radius of the circle and the angle of the sector. You start with the radius. You discover that it's a certain length on the original (uncut) cone.

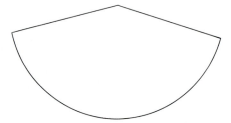

These two lengths are the same.

Next you figure out this length, called the *slant height:* The circle on the bottom of the cone has radius 3 ft. Since the height of the cone is 8 ft, the square of the length of the cone's slant height is equal to $8^2 + 3^2 = 73$. The square root of the latter is about 8.54. The length of the slant height is about 8.54 ft.

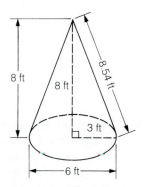

8 ft

8 ft

8.54 ft

3 ft

6 ft

What about the angle of the sector? You know that

$$\frac{\text{Angle of sector}}{360} = \frac{\text{length of arc of sector of radius 8.54 ft}}{\text{circumference of circle of radius 8.54 ft}}.$$

You also know that

$$\frac{\text{Angle of sector}}{360} = \frac{\text{area of sector of radius 8.54 ft}}{\text{area of whole circle of radius 8.54 ft}},$$

which means

$$\frac{\text{Length of arc of sector}}{\text{Circumference of circle}} = \frac{\text{area of sector}}{\text{area of circle}}.$$

All circles in this equation are of radius 8.54 ft.

"The length of the arc of the sector of radius 8.54 ft is equal to the circumference of the circle forming the bottom of the original, uncut cone. The circumference of that circle (of radius 3 ft) is about 2×3 ft $\times 3.14 = 18.85$ ft. There is no need to find the angle of the sector since in the last equation I wrote, I can figure out three of the pieces of information, then solve for the fourth:

Length of arc of sector of radius 8.54 ft $\cong$ 18.85 ft

Circumference of circle of radius 8.54 ft $\cong 2 \times 3.14 \times 8.54$ ft $= 53.66$ ft

Area of circle of radius 8.54 ft $\cong 3.14 \times 8.54^2 = 229.12$ ft^2

So

$$\text{Area of cone} = \text{area of sector} \sim 229.12 \times \frac{18.85}{53.66} = 80.49 \text{ ft}^2.$$

Very nice!"

EXERCISE 7. A funnel is basically a cone. One factor in the cost of manufacturing a funnel is the amount of metal used in making it. The metal is sold by the square meter. Find the surface area of the large cone shown.

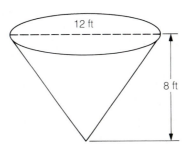

LOOKING AHEAD: USING COORDINATES TO FIND DISTANCES AND TO CREATE AN EQUATION FOR A CIRCLE

Distance

If a coordinate system has been set up and you know the coordinates of two points, then it is easy to calculate the distance between the two points. Let's look at several cases, starting with the easiest ones first.

DISTANCE BETWEEN POINTS ON THE EXTENDED NUMBER LINE   The distance from 0 to 3 is 3. The distance from 0 to -5 is 5.

ABSOLUTE VALUE

The distance from 0 to a number N on the extended number line is also called the *absolute value* of N and is denoted $|N|$.

Thus $|3| = 3$ and $|-5| = 5$. The distance between points 3 and 7 is 4. The distance between points -5 and 12 is 17.

In both cases, we can find distance by calculating the difference of the two numbers and then ignoring the sign. We can make a general statement about this.

DISTANCE BETWEEN POINTS ON THE NUMBER LINE

If A and B are two points on the extended number line, then the distance between A and B is also $|A - B|$.

Let's check this fact with some pairs of points.

■ The distance between 3 and 7 is 4. Also,
$$|3 - 7| = |-4| = 4.$$

■ The distance between points -5 and 12 is 17. Also
$$|-5 - 12| = |-17| = 17.$$

■ The distance between points 3 and -7 is 10. Also

$$|3 - (-7)| = |3 + 7| = |10| = 10.$$

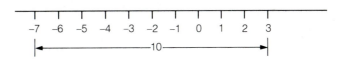

DISTANCE BETWEEN TWO POINTS ON A LINE PARALLEL TO ONE OF THE COORDINATE AXES The distance from $(2,3)$ to $(2,7)$ is 4. The distance from $(2,-5)$ to $(2,12)$ is 17. The distance from $(3,-1)$ to $(-7,-1)$ is 10.

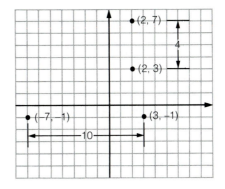

The information can be stated in a general rule.

DISTANCE BETWEEN TWO POINTS ON A LINE PARALLEL TO A COORDINATE AXIS

The distance between (A,B) and (A,C) is $|B - C|$.
The distance between (D,E) and (F,E) is $|D - F|$.

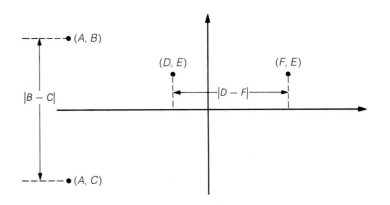

DISTANCE BETWEEN ANY TWO POINTS   Suppose points P and Q have coordinates $(1,5)$ and $(4,9)$, respectively.

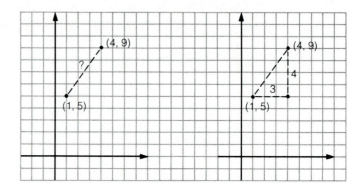

Then, using the Pythagorean theorem, the square of the distance from point P to point Q is

$$(1 - 4)^2 + (5 - 9)^2.$$

Note that $(|A|)^2 = A^2$, so that

$$\text{Distance from } (1,5) \text{ to } (4,9) = \sqrt{(1 - 4)^2 + (5 - 9)^2}$$
$$= \sqrt{3^2 + 4^2}$$
$$= \sqrt{25}$$
$$= 5.$$

The general statement of the distance between two points in a plane is as follows.

DISTANCE BETWEEN TWO POINTS IN THE PLANE

The distance between two points whose coordinates are (A,B) and (C,D) is
$$\sqrt{(A - C)^2 + (B - D)^2}.$$

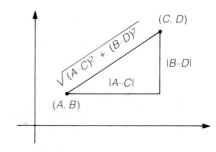

EXERCISES   **8.** Evaluate each expression:

    (a) $|10|$ (b) $|10 - 3|$ (c) $|3 - 10|$ (d) $|-3 + 10|$

    (e) $|3| - |10|$ (f) $-|3 - 10|$ (g) $|-(10 - 3)|$

9. Find the distance between each pair of points.
   (a) $(0,0)$ and $(0,7)$ (b) $(0,7)$ and $(0,-3)$
   (c) $(2,12)$ and $(2,23)$ (d) $(-3,-2)$ and $(-14,-2)$
   (e) $(7,0)$ and $(-5,0)$ (f) $(4,3)$ and $(3,4)$
   (g) $(-1,-3)$ and $(2,1)$ (h) $(-7,2)$ and $(2,-10)$

Equation for a Circle

In chapter 15 we showed that a line that isn't vertical is the set of all points in the plane with coordinates (x,y) such that $y = mx + b$ where m is the line's slope and b is the point of intersection of the line with the vertical axis. The equation of the line is $y = mx + b$. We can also find an equation for a circle. To do this, we will use the method we have developed for finding distance between points in terms of their coordinates.

A circle is determined by two aspects, its center and its radius. Suppose a certain circle has radius 5 and center at the point $(1,3)$.

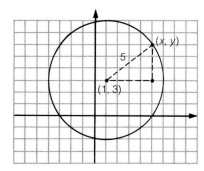

If (x,y) is a point on this circle, its distance to the center must be 5. We can express this fact using the distance formula by the equation

$$\text{Distance from } (x,y) \text{ to } (1,3) = \sqrt{(x-1)^2 + (y-3)^2} = 5,$$

or, squaring both sides of the last equation,

$$(x-1)^2 + (y-3)^2 = 5^2.$$

This equation must be true for any point (x,y) on the circle in question. Furthermore, any point for which this equation holds must be a point on the circle. Thus we have

The circle of radius 5 with center at $(1,3) = \{(x,y): (x-1)^2 + (y-3)^2 = 5^2\}$.

EQUATION FOR A CIRCLE

The circle of radius R with center (A,B) is the set of all points (x,y) such that

$$(x-A)^2 + (y-B)^2 = R^2.$$

---

10. Find the equation for each circle.

(a) center (1,2), radius 2   (b) center (0,0), radius 3

(c) center (−2,−3), radius 4   (d) center (−1,2), radius 1.5

18.4 SUMMARY OF IMPORTANT IDEAS AND TECHNIQUES

- Egyptian rope construction of a right angle
- Explanation of Pythagorean theorem from area principles
- Use of Pythagorean theorem to measure length indirectly
- Using guesses and charts to find square roots
- Surface area of some three-dimensional shapes
- Flat patterns for cylinder and cone
- Surface area of cylinder and cone
- Distance between two points with known coordinates
- Equation for a circle in terms of coordinates

PROBLEM SET

PRACTICING SKILLS

1. Use a calculator to find the third side of each right triangle.

(a)

(b)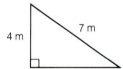

(c)

2. Find the square root of 162 using the guessing method. Obtain an answer accurate to one decimal place. Compare this with what you get when you use the square root key on a calculator.

3. How far apart (to the nearest tenth of a mile) are the two long-distance relay stations shown in the picture?

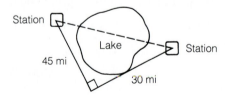

4. Find the surface area of each rectangular box.

(a)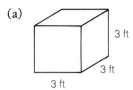
3 ft
3 ft
3 ft

(b)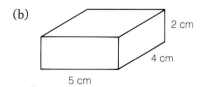
2 cm
4 cm
5 cm

(c)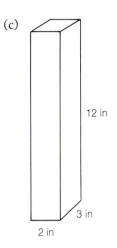
12 in
3 in
2 in

5. Find the surface area of each can.

(a)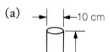
10 cm
1 m

(b)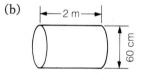
2 m
60 cm

(c)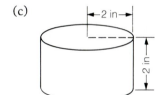
2 in
2 in

(d)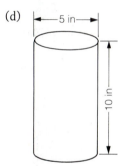
5 in
10 in

6. Find the surface area of each cone.

(a)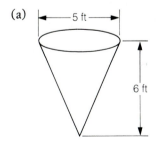
5 ft
6 ft

(b)
1 m
30 cm

(c)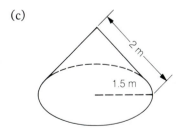
2 m
1.5 m

7. You manufacture circular potato chips. All chips have a diameter of 1.5 in. You plan to package them in a tube 5 in high and need to know the cost of the container. The material out of which a container is made costs 27¢/in^2.

8. You are a farmer and are constructing a metal corncrib in the shape of a cone. A picture of the crib is shown. How much metal do you need? (The crib has a bottom, too.)

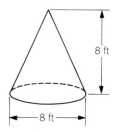

9. Find the distance between the points on the number line.
   (a)   3 and 5   (b)   −2 and −8   (c)   −3 and 14   (d)   5 and −8

10. Evaluate each expression.
    (a) $|-10|$ (b) $|8-5|$ (c) $|2-16|$
    (d) $|-4-18|$ (e) $|-10+3|$ (f) $|-(-3+5)|$

11. Find the distance between the points.
    (a)   (5,0) and (−8,0)   (b)   (−3,2) and (8,2)
    (c)   (2,16) and (2,−7)   (d)   (−5,−4) and (18,−4)

12. Find the distance between the points.
    (a)   (2,3) and (5,4)   (b)   (−2,4) and (8,−2)
    (c)   (−5,−1) and (7,2)   (d)   (1,−3) and (−2,7)
    (e)   the two points on the graph

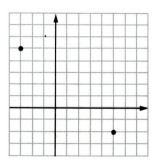

13. Find the equation for each circle.
    (a)   circle with center (0,0) and radius 4
    (b)   circle with center (2,1) and radius 2
    (c)   circle with center (−1,3) and radius 5
    (d)   circle with center (−1,0) and radius 3

14. Find the equation for each circle.
    (a) circle with center $(-1,-2)$ and diameter 8
    (b) circle with center $(0,0)$, passing through the point $(4,3)$
    (c) circle with diameter having ends at $(1,1)$ and $(-1,-1)$
    (d) circle with diameter having ends at $(0,0)$ and $(6,0)$
    (e) circle on the graph

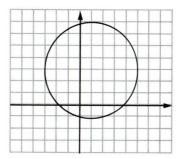

USING IDEAS   *Write the solution to each remaining problem carefully and clearly in the form of an essay. In it mention the steps you took to solve the problem, the principles, tools, or formulas you used, other problems or solutions that gave you ideas, and the problem-solving strategies you found helpful.*

15. Sally is interested in walking to work, and she wants to evaluate two alternative routes. Her problem is that she is always in a rush.
    (a) How much *distance* will she save by cutting across (as opposed to walking along the edges of) a park that is 1 km on a side?

    (b) How much *time* would Sally save if she walks 1 km in 12 min?

16. The inside measurements of a piece of luggage are length 60 cm, height 54.5 cm, width 15.5 cm. What is the maximum length of a long, rigid object (such as a violin bow), disregarding the thickness, that can be placed into the luggage?

17. The Soup Factory is covering the lateral surface of 50,000 cans of soup with labels. The cylindrical cans each have a radius of 4 cm and a height of 15.5 cm. The label on each can overlaps about 2 cm. How many square centimeters of paper will be needed for the 50,000 cans? (The *lateral surface* of a cylinder is that part of the surface excluding the two circular ends.)

18. Sketch a flat pattern for the tent and figure out how much nylon (in square feet) would be used to make it. Label the pattern with all the relevant dimensions. The tent has a bottom.

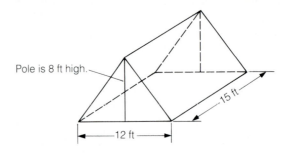

Pole is 8 ft high.

15 ft

12 ft

19. You want to have a metal trough built. The top is to be open, and both ends are trapezoids of the same size. To figure out how much metal will be used in its construction, you need to know its surface area. What is it?

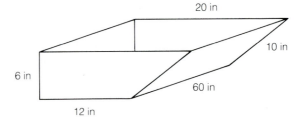

20 in

10 in

6 in

60 in

12 in

20. The ability of the human body to cool itself is directly related to its surface area. Estimate the surface area of your body, assuming that your head, torso, arms, and legs are cylinders (roughly).
    (a) Estimate the radii and heights of these cylinders.
    (b) Find the surface areas of the appropriate parts of these pieces and add them up.

21. Muffin papers are sold in a box. The sketch shows a pattern for the box. To determine the amount of material used in making it, you need to figure out its surface area. What is it? To determine how much shelf space one of these boxes will take, you need to figure out the dimensions of the assembled box. What are they?

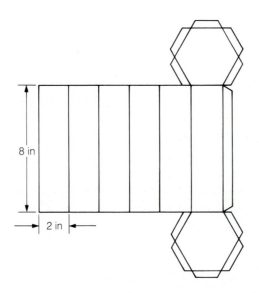

8 in

2 in

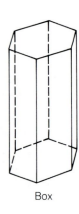

Box

22. A lampshade and a scale model of the pattern for it are shown. To determine the amount of material used in making the lampshade, you need to figure out its surface area. What is it? You plan to put braid trim along the two rims of the lampshade. What length of braid will you need? You want to know the size of the finished lampshade. How tall will the lampshade be? What will the diameter of the top be? What will the diameter of the bottom be?

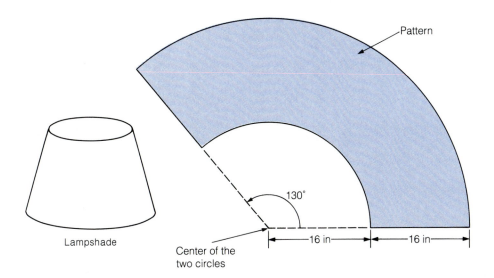

Pattern

130°

16 in ── 16 in

Lampshade

Center of the two circles

23. The sides and roof of the silo are to be reshingled. To estimate the cost of this project, you need to know the area of the surface to be reshingled. What is it?

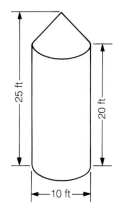

25 ft

20 ft

10 ft

24. The floor plan of your living-dining area, which you are remodeling, is given. The ceilings are 9 ft high. Except for a door 6 by 7 ft and a window 6 by 4 ft, there are no other openings in the wall. Your intentions are

■ To retile the floor at a cost of $1.50/ft²
■ To tile the ceiling with acoustical tile at a cost of $2.25/ft²
■ To panel the walls with teak paneling at a cost of $5.00/ft²
■ To replace the molding around the baseboard and around the door and window at a cost of $ .75/ft(linear)

You want to know what the total cost of these renovations will be.

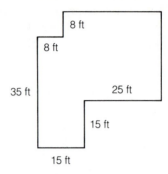

25. You are building a grain elevator. You have already constructed its frame out of lightweight steel beams. Now you plan to cover the frame (top and sides) with thin panels of some lightweight steel and aluminum alloy. You want to know how much of this paneling you will need.

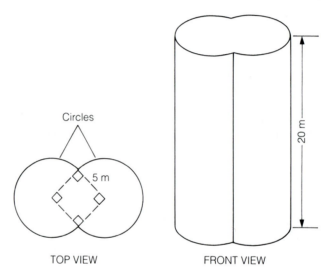

26. Recall the scale model you made in problem 26 of chapter 13.
    (a) Assume that this is a possible scale model of a one-room storage shed you are planning to build. The floor will be dirt. The roof and walls will be constructed of prefabricated corrugated iron paneling sold by the square foot. To estimate the cost of the shed, you need to know how many square feet of paneling you will need. What is it?
    (b) You are getting serious about building your shed. Your basic requirements are that it be a rectangular box with 1600 ft^2 of floor space, that it have one door (4 by 7 ft) and three windows (each 3 by 6 ft), ceiling 8 ft off the ground, flat roof, and walls and roof made of prefabricated corrugated iron paneling. (All these requirements are satisfied by the shed the scale model of which you were looking at in [a].) The primary cost of the shed is for materials. Here are the unit costs:

Door	$30
Windows	$15 each
Paneling	$5/ft^2

How much would the materials cost for the shed you considered in (a)?

(c) You mull over the cost of materials for the shed represented by the scale model you built and wonder if there were another shed you could build that would satisfy your requirements and cost even less. You think about the requirement of 1600 ft² and realize that 1600 is just the product of 32 and 50, the width and length of the cabin. You ask yourself: "Is there another pair of numbers with product 1600?" "Of course," you answer, "10 and 160 will work. So will 16 and 100, 8 and 200, 80 and 20. There are other possibilities: 25 and 32, 5 and 320, 40 and 40." Figure out the cost for building two more sheds: one with floor dimensions 20 ft and 80 ft; the other with floor dimensions of 40 ft and 40 ft; and fill in the table.

DIMENSIONS OF FLOOR	COST OF MATERIALS FOR SHED
50 by 32 ft	
80 by 20 ft	
40 by 40 ft	

What do you notice?

Of *all possible* pairs of dimensions for the rectangular floor of the shed, which one(s) will have the least cost of materials? (Why?)

27. Construct a full-sized pattern for the conical lampshade.

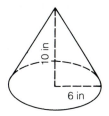

10 in

6 in

REVIEW TEST FOR CHAPTERS 16, 17, AND 18

For each question, circle the letter to the left of the most appropriate response.

1. The measure of angle A, below, is

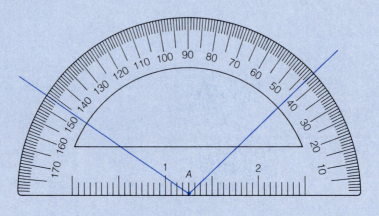

   (a) 104°   (b) 42°   (c) 137°   (d) 33°   (e) 147°

2. Certain angles are given in the diagram. Find the missing angle.

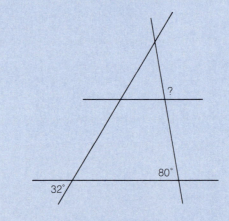

   (a) 102°   (b) 148°   (c) 100°   (d) 78°   (e) 80°

3. Which plot of land has the greatest area?

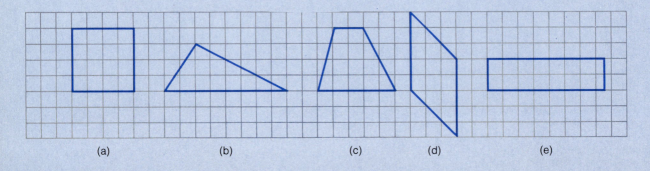

      (a)   (b)   (c)   (d)   (e)

4. The top and bottom rims of the lampshade are to be covered with trim. What length of trimming will you need (to the nearest inch)?

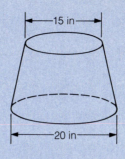

(a) 63 in   (b) 55 in   (c) 70 in   (d) 110 in   (e) 47 in

5. You want to surround your garden completely with fencing. The garden itself is a sector of a circle, two sides of which abut on a patio. Fencing is sold by the foot. How much fencing will you have to buy?

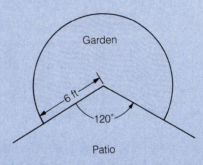

(a) 19 ft   (b) 46 ft   (c) 38 ft   (d) 26 ft   (e) 32 ft

6. A 15-ft ladder is leaning against a wall. The top of the ladder extends above the top of the wall by 2 ft. The base of the ladder stands at a point 5 ft away from the wall. What is the height of the wall?

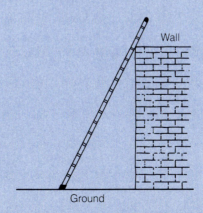

(a) 8 ft   (b) 12 ft   (c) 13.9 ft   (d) 14.1 ft   (e) 15.8 ft

7. You plan to redecorate your studio apartment, the floor plan of which is given, by paneling the walls with mahogany.

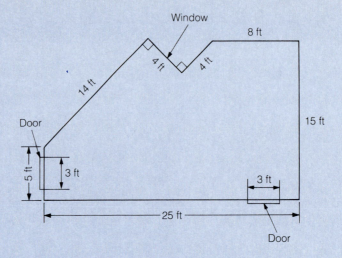

The window and doors begin at the floor and rise 7 ft above it. The height of the ceiling is 9 ft. How many square feet of mahogany paneling will you need?

(a) 675 ft²   (b) 605 ft²   (c) 385 ft²   (d) 495 ft²   (e) 525 ft²

8. A tunnel designer has drawn a sketch to figure out how much ceramic tile will be needed to cover the surface of the front side of a tunnel. (The tunnel opening is half a circle.) What will the surface area of the front side of the tunnel be approximately?

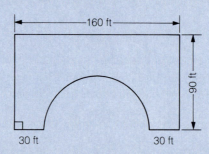

(a) 14,400 ft²   (b) 18,327 ft²   (c) 10,473 ft²   (d) 6546 ft²   (e) 22,254 ft²

ESSAY QUESTIONS

For each remaining problem, express your solution carefully and clearly in the form of an essay.

9. Sketch a flat pattern for the tent and figure out how much nylon (in square feet) would be needed to make it. The tent has a top and a bottom, and both are square. Each side of the tent is a trapezoid.

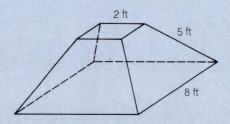

10. You are designing an oval running track. The requirements are these: The two ends of the track are to be half circles; the length of the track must be 10 km; and half the running must take place on straight track. What must the radius of the two circles be in order to accomplish this?

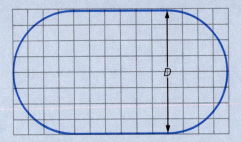

11. Find the area of the pasture.

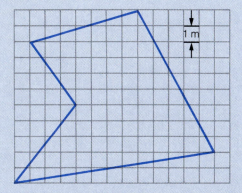

12. The Jones family and the Garcia family are planning to share a rectangular garden. One side of the garden will be for the Jones family and the other for the Garcia family. The total area of the garden is to be 600 ft². The two sides are to have equal areas. The families want to buy fencing to enclose the large plot and to separate the two gardens. Find the dimensions of the large plot that uses the least amount of fencing. Solve this by making guesses and organizing them in a chart.

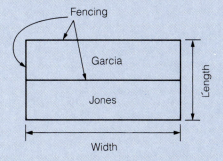

WIDTH OF PLOT (FEET)	LENGTH OF PLOT (FEET)	AREA OF PLOT	TOTAL AMOUNT OF FENCING
60	10	600 ft²	200 ft

INTRODUCTION TO VOLUME

19
C H A P T E R

In chapter 18 we looked at the outsides of various three-dimensional shapes and asked: How much paint will be needed to paint it? How much metal will be needed to cover it? These questions were answered by determining the surface areas of the shapes. In this chapter we are interested in the "insides" of three-dimensional shapes. How much air does that house contain? How much rice will that bin hold? How much metal is in that bracelet? These questions will be answered by determining the volume of the shape.

As with area, we will begin the study of volume with simple shapes—rectangular boxes—and move to shapes that are more complicated—triangular prisms, cylinders, and other prisms. We will find formulas for the volumes of some of these shapes. As with area, we will also develop strategies for finding volumes of complicated shapes.

We will also discuss liquid displacement, a method for estimating the volume of irregular shapes. This method has no analogue for area.

Finally, we will discuss an analogy with area. In chapter 17 we solved problems having to do with which shape was the most efficient. For example, we were building a rectangular pasture of fixed area that we would eventually surround with fencing. We wanted to know which particular rectangle having this area would need the least amount of fencing. An analogous problem for volume is to construct a rectangular box, out of cardboard (say), with fixed volume. We want to know the particular rectangular box that will use the least amount of cardboard.

THE QUARRY PROBLEM   You are a quarrier. You cut stone from a stone quarry in large blocks. When these large blocks have been removed from the quarry area, they are cut into smaller pieces for use as building materials. Each of the large blocks is in the shape of a cube 1 m on a side.

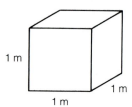

Experience tells you that the large rock formation from which these blocks are cut is roughly in the shape of a large rectangular box with dimensions you estimate to be 9 by 10 by 6 m.

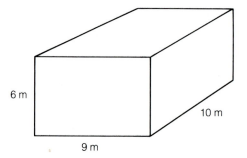

Please try this yourself.   You want to know how many of the smaller cubical stone blocks can be cut from this rock formation. Solve this problem. (You don't know any formulas for finding volume.)

A Solution to the   You imagine how you would cut stone blocks from the 9- by 10- by 6-m rectangular
Quarry Problem   shape. You would remove a block out of one corner, then another right next to it, and so on, until you get to the end of the row. Then you would start cutting again a meter back and move along a row again, and so on, until you have sliced a layer 1 m thick from the top of the of the whole large rectangular shape. You *draw a picture* of the layer, marking the blocks to be cut out.

You know how many blocks there are in this layer because this is a 9 by 10 array of blocks: There are 9 × 10 of them. After cutting all the blocks in the first layer, you would start on the second layer. You realize that the second layer (and all subsequent layers) would look just like the first layer; each layer would have 9 × 10 blocks in it. You realize that you will have your final answer if you know the number of layers in the large rectangular shape. Each layer is 1 m thick, and the block is 6 m tall. That makes 6 layers. That means 6 × 9 × 10 blocks in all. That's 540 blocks, each one a cube having a side length of 1 m.

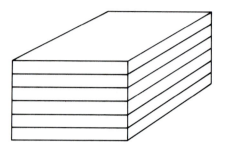

EXERCISE   1. You are building a monument out of cubical blocks of stone, 1 ft on each side. The monument is to be solid stone in the shape of a large box. Here is a picture of it.

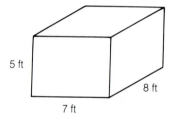

You want to know how many stone blocks you will need. Solve this problem. (One of your few experiences with volume is with the quarry problem.)

THE GRANARY STORAGE PROBLEM   You have a large bin in which you plan to store grain. You know that a 5 yd² plot planted with grain yields 1 cubical box of grain, 1 ft on a side.

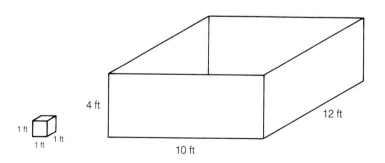

Try this yourself, first.

You want to know how many of the small boxes full of grain will fill the bin. Solve this problem. (Your only experiences with volume are with the quarry problem and the problem of building a monument in exercise 1.)

A Solution to the Granary Storage Problem

One way to solve this problem is to fill a cubical box (with side length 1 ft) with grain, pour it into the bin, fill the box again, pour it into the bin, and so on, until the bin is full, then count the number of times you filled the cubical box. However, you would like to know *ahead of time* how many times you can do this. You try to *imagine* pouring full boxes of grain into the bin and counting them. You realize that, for this exercise to be successful, you must pour the full boxes into the bin in some clever way. You think: "What if I had a *lot* of boxes, filled them up with grain, and— instead of pouring them into the bin—placed the full boxes themselves into the bin (leaving no empty spaces between them)? Let me try that.

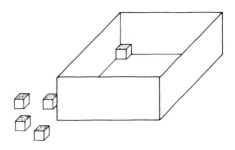

Let me place one box in a corner, then one right next to it—leaving no space—until I fill out a whole row along one side. That side is 10 ft wide, so there must be 10 boxes in that row. After that, I can start another row.

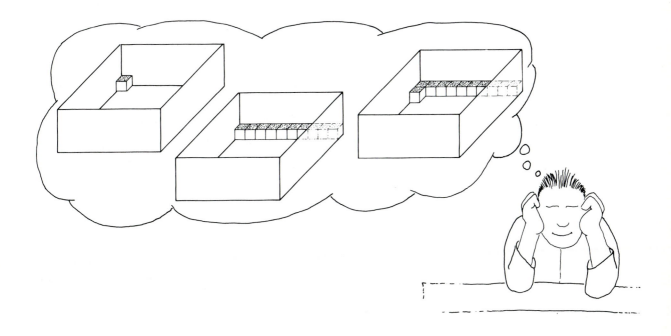

"I'm building an array of boxes. I know how many will be in each row—10. To figure out how many rows there will be, I can place boxes along this other side. The number I can put there will tell me. That side is 12 ft long. I can put 12 boxes there. There are 12 rows with 10 boxes in each row, so there are 10 × 12 boxes in the layer.

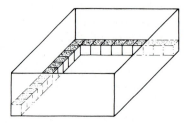

"I can cover the bottom of the bin completely with an array of boxes. On top of that layer, I can place another array of full boxes. That layer will have the same number as the bottom layer does. I know how many boxes were in the first layer. The same number is in the second layer. I keep filling the bin with layer after layer of full boxes. Each layer will have the same number of boxes as the first layer has. All I need to do is figure out how many layers there would be. I can do that by stacking boxes in one corner. The bin is 4 ft deep, so I should be able to stack 4 boxes in the corner.

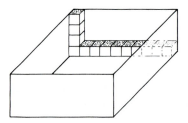

There are 4 layers with 10 × 12 boxes in each layer. There would be 4 × 10 × 12 boxes in the bin. If I were to fill boxes full of grain and pour them into the bin, I would have to do it 4 × 10 × 12 times in order to fill up the bin. That solves the problem."

EXERCISE 2. The tank pictured below is full of heating oil. The amount of oil to fill the small cubical container is enough to heat your house for a day during the winter months. To determine whether you have enough oil for the winter, you need to know how many small containers full of oil can be drawn from the large tank. Solve this problem.

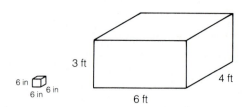

6 in 6 in 6 in

3 ft

4 ft

6 ft

The Mathematical Idea: Solid Content, Liquid Capacity, and Volume

In the quarry problem we were interested in how many small blocks of stone could be cut out of a large block of stone. In exercise 1 we were interested in how many small blocks of stone would be needed to make a large, box-shaped monument. In each case we imagine the large shape to be made up of the smaller blocks and want to know how many of the smaller blocks there are. The number of cubical blocks that make up the large shape is called the *solid volume* of the shape. Just as for area, we require that the cubical blocks fit together to make up the shape completely and without overlaps. The small cubical block, many of which make up the larger shape, is called a *unit* of volume. A common unit of volume is a cube, with all sides a common unit of length, such as an inch, foot, yard, centimeter, or meter. The corresponding units of volume are called the *cubic inch, cubic foot, cubic yard, cubic centimeter,* and *cubic meter.* The large block of stone in the quarry measured 9 by 10 by 6 m. The unit we used to *measure the volume* of this large block was the cubic meter. We found that the large block was made up of $9 \times 10 \times 6 = 540$ of these cubic meters. So the volume of the large block is 540 cubic meters, which we will express in our text as 540 m^3.

In the granary storage problem we were interested in how many times we have to fill a small box full of grain and pour it into the bin in order to fill up a bin. In exercise 2 we were interested in how many small containers full of oil could be drawn from a full tank. In both cases we had a large container and a small container. We solved the first problem by imagining how many of the smaller containers full of grain would fit together to fill up the larger. The second problem involved oil instead of grain. The number of small, full cubical containers we must pour into a large container to fill it up is called the *liquid volume (or capacity) of the (large) container.* The small cubical container, many copies of which are used to fill the larger container, is called a *unit* of liquid volume.

Liquid volume measures liquid matter, which takes its total shape from the container it's placed in; and solid volume measures solid matter, which maintains its own shape. There is a strong connection between the two notions of volume: If you have a grain bin of size 9 by 10 by 6 m and you use a cubical container 1 m on a side, then the liquid volume of the grain bin would be 540 of these containers, the same number of cubic meters as in the large rock block of the same size.

In the metric system the differences between the two notions are minimized. The common units of liquid volume are cubical containers with sides common units of metric length: the centimeter, the decimeter (1/10m), and the meter. The corresponding units of liquid volume are called the cubic centimeter (also called a *milliliter*), the cubic decimeter (also called, more commonly, the *liter*), and the cubic meter.

In the traditional (English) system, the difference between the two kinds of volume is exaggerated because of the common units used for liquid volume. As with metric units based on units of length, the cubic foot and cubic yard are common units for measuring liquid volume in the traditional system. Typically, these units are used for measuring the volume of air in a building or the volume of natural gas used for heating a house in a month. However, in some situations other units are used. Liquids such as water and milk are measured in gallons. Many dry goods, such as grain, are measured in bushels. Sugar, flour, water, and milk can all be measured in cups. You do not measure solid rock or wood by the cup or by the gallon or by the bushel.

In this book we will use only liquid volume units based on units of length. Because of this, we will use the single term *volume* to mean either liquid volume or solid volume. The context should tell you which notion we are referring to.

A Second Mathematical Idea: A Formula for the Volume of a Rectangular Box

The solutions to the quarry and granary storage problems suggest a shortcut to finding the volume of a rectangular box when its sides have whole-number units of length. If the lengths of the sides of the box are L, W, and H—whole numbers of units— then the solid can be made up of H layers each of which is an L by W array of cubes. Thus, there are LW cubes in each layer and HLW cubes in all. The box has a volume of HLW cubic units. (The cubic unit corresponds to the unit of length used to measure the sides of the box.) This formula is analogous to the formula for the area of a rectangle.

What about volumes of boxes the sides of which do not all have whole-number lengths? Consider the following problem.

THE GRANITE BLOCK PROBLEM The illustrated monument, in the shape of a rectangular box, is made of a single block of granite. Workmen, who are to move the monument, need to know how much it weighs. They know that a cubic foot of granite weighs 100 lb.

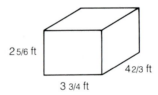

2 5/6 ft

4 2/3 ft

3 3/4 ft

The workmen *think of a similar problem,* the gold leaf problem (in chap. 9 and chap. 17): "Let's change the mixed fractions into improper fractions.

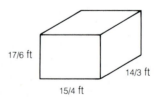

17/6 ft

14/3 ft

15/4 ft

Let's *draw a picture* showing how we might slice the block.

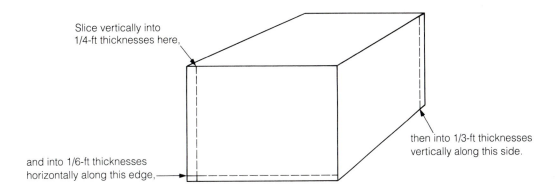

Slice vertically into
1/4-ft thicknesses here,

then into 1/3-ft thicknesses
vertically along this side.

and into 1/6-ft thicknesses
horizontally along this edge,

That would cut the whole block up into little blocks all the same size.

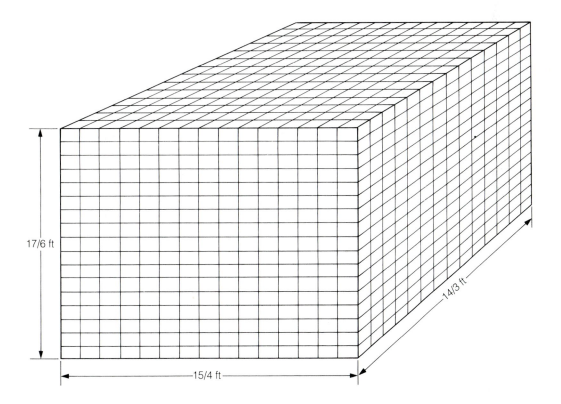

17/6 ft

14/3 ft

15/4 ft

"Next, let's count the little blocks. We can find out how many there are by doing what we did in another *similar problem*—the quarry problem. There are $17 \times 15 \times 14$ of them. If we knew the volume of each of the little blocks, we could multiply that volume times $17 \times 15 \times 14$ to get the volume of the large block.

"Let's have a look at one of the little blocks.

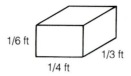

Let's see how it fits in a cubic foot.

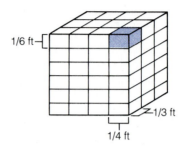

We can slice the cubic foot up into little blocks the same size as *our* little block.

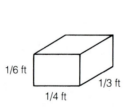

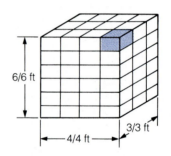

This cuts the cubic foot up into $6 \times 4 \times 3 = 72$ little pieces, all the same size. So they must all have the same volume, and each piece must have volume equal to $\frac{1}{72}$ ft³. That means that our little block also has volume equal to $\frac{1}{72}$ ft³.

"The big block consists of $17 \times 15 \times 14$ of these little blocks. So

$$\text{Volume of big block} = \frac{17 \times 15 \times 14}{72}$$

$$= \frac{17 \times 15 \times 14}{6 \times 4 \times 3}$$

$$= \frac{17}{6} \times \frac{15}{4} \times \frac{14}{3}$$

$$= 2\frac{5}{6} \times 3\frac{3}{4} \times 4\frac{2}{3}.$$

That's just the area of the front $(2\frac{5}{6} \times 3\frac{3}{4})$ times the depth $(4\frac{2}{3})$."

The Mathematical Idea: Volume Principles and the Volume of a Rectangular Box

The solution to the granite block problem suggests a rule for calculating the volume of a rectangular box, regardless of whether the lengths of the sides are whole numbers or fractions.

VOLUME OF A RECTANGULAR BOX

Suppose the dimensions of a rectangular box are L, W, and H. Then

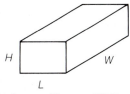

Volume of box $= LWH.$

In solving the granite block problem the workmen used two principles about volume, which we will also find useful.

TWO VOLUME PRINCIPLES

1. Two three-dimensional objects that have the same size and shape have the same volume.

2. If a solid three-dimensional object is broken up into smaller pieces, then the volume of the larger object is the sum of the volumes of the pieces.

The volume principles are analogous to the area principles we have already discussed in an earlier chapter. The area principles were used to find the areas of complicated shapes. Similarly, the volume principles will be used to find the volumes of complicated three-dimensional shapes.

EXERCISE 3. Find the volumes of the shapes. All measurements shown are in centimeters.

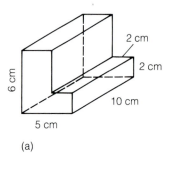

(a)

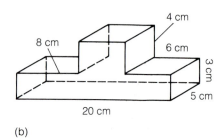

(b)

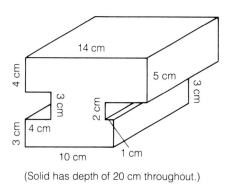

(Solid has depth of 20 cm throughout.)

(c)

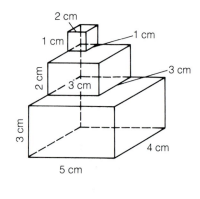

(d)

19.2

VOLUME FORMULAS

THE BIN PROBLEM

You work for a supermarket and have designed the bin shown for holding bulk goods, such as nuts, rice, candy, and grain.

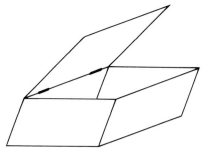

Try this yourself before reading on.

From these bins customers can help themselves to the quantity of bulk goods they want. For inventory purposes you need to know what the volume of the bin is.

You notice that two of the sides of the bin are parallelograms. You think of a *solution to a similar problem,* where you were able to figure out the area of a parallelogram by cutting a triangle off of one end and rearranging the two pieces to make a rectangle.

You imagine that you cut up your bin similarly.

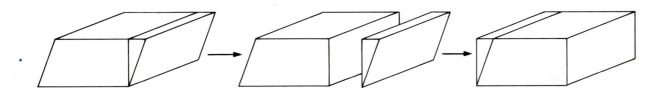

The principles for volume tell you that the sum of the volumes of the two pieces is equal to the volume of the original bin. You put them together to make a rectangular box. Again, the principles tell you that the rectangular box has volume equal to the volume of the bin. "That's it!" you exclaim. "The volume of the bin is equal to the volume of the rectangular box:

Volume of bin = base (of parallelogram) × height (of parallelogram) × width of bin.

I could rewrite that equation as

Volume of bin = area of parallelogram × width of bin."

The Mathematical Idea: Volume of a Triangular Prism

From the solution to the bin problem we know how to find the volume of the *parallelogram bin.*

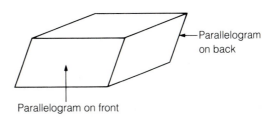

Parallelogram on back

Parallelogram on front

If you call one of the parallelogram faces the *base* and stand the bin on this face, then

Volume of parallelogram bin = area of parallelogram base × height of bin.

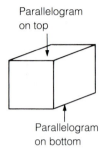

Parallelogram
on top

Parallelogram
on bottom

The workmen who solved the granite block problem also noticed that if you select one of the faces of a rectangular box as a base on which to stand it, then

Volume of rectangular box = area of base × height of box.

We can use our solution to the bin problem to find the volume of another bin, one shaped thusly.

This shape is called a *triangular prism*. Let's look at more triangular prisms.

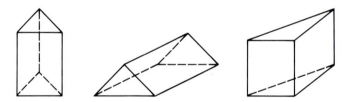

How can we find the volume of a triangular prism using what we know already? Take the triangular prism and an identical copy of it. By the volume principles we know that the volumes of the two prisms are equal. Put the two triangular prisms together to make a parallelogram bin.

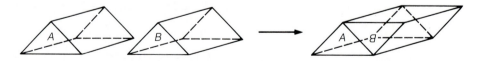

The volume principles say that the volume of the parallelogram bin is equal to the sum of the volumes of the two triangular prisms. Since the volume of the parallelogram bin is twice the volume of the original triangular prism, the volume of the triangular prism is one-half the volume of the parallelogram bin. Let's see what that gives us.

Volume of triangular prism $= \frac{1}{2} \times$ volume of parallelogram bin

$= \frac{1}{2} \times$ area of parallelogram $\times$ height of bin

$=$ area of triangle $\times$ height of bin.

We know this because the area of a triangle $= 1/2 \times$ area of parallelogram. We can summarize.

VOLUME OF TRIANGULAR PRISM

Stand the triangular prism on one of its triangles as a *base*. Then

Volume of triangular prism = area of triangular base × height.

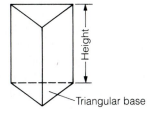

EXERCISES   4. Find the volumes of the triangular prisms.

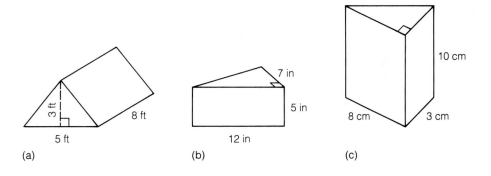

(a)   (b)   (c)

5. Find the volumes of the shapes

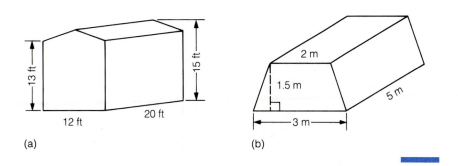

(a)   (b)

Working for the same supermarket, you have another problem. You have designed cylinder containers for storing the bulk goods. One of these is shown.

Try solving this from what we
know so far.

Again, to help the store keep an inventory of these goods, you need to find the volume of each of these cylindrical containers.

A Solution to the Cylindrical
Container Problem

You think: "I've solved the bin problem, and I know how to find the volume of a triangular prism, and I know some volume principles. Can I use what I know to find the volume of a cylinder? Can I break the cylinder up into pieces with volumes I can figure out? When we figured out the area of a circle we broke the circle up into sectors, pieces that were pretty close to triangles.

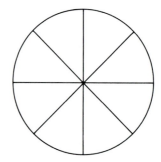

If I were to 'slice' the whole container vertically, through the lines that make those sectors in its circular base, I'd get something like this.

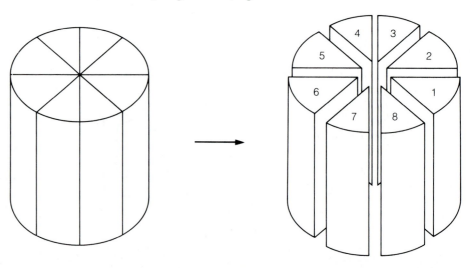

"That breaks the cylinder up into shapes that are roughly triangular prisms. The volume of the cylinder is the sum of the volumes of the triangularlike prisms. The volume of a triangular prism is the area of the triangle times the height of the prism. It seems reasonable to assume that the volume of each triangularlike prism is the area of the sector times the height of the prism. The height of all those triangularlike prisms is the same. I'll call the common height H. So it seems reasonable that

$$\text{Volume of cylinder} = \frac{\text{area of sector } 1 \times H + \text{area of sector } 2}{\times H + \text{area of sector } 3 \times H + \cdots}$$

By the distributive property the sum on the right-hand side is

(Area of sector 1 + area of sector 2 + area of sector 3 + $\cdots$)H.

That expression is equal to

Sum of areas of sectors × H.

But the sum of the areas of the sectors is just the area of the circular base of the cylinder. A reasonable conclusion is that

Volume of cylinder = area of circular base × height of cylinder.

That's neat!"

The Mathematical Idea: Volume of a Cylinder

The solution to the cylindrical container problem suggests a formula.

FORMULA FOR THE VOLUME OF A CYLINDER

Volume = area of base × height

$$= \pi R^2 H,$$

where R is the radius of the circular base and H is the height of the cylinder.

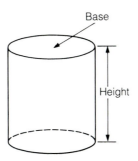

Base

Height

---

6. Find the volumes of the cylinder

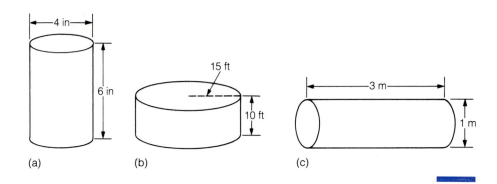

(a) (b) (c)

A Second Mathematical Idea: Volume of a General Prism

The solution to the cylindrical container problem also suggests a general method for finding the volume of shapes such as those shown.

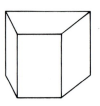 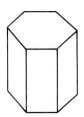 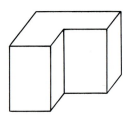

For each of these shapes, a horizontal, cross-sectional slice is congruent to the base of the shape.

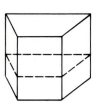 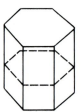 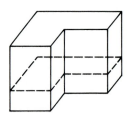

They also "stand upright." They don't lean as the next shape does.

Each side of an upright shape—a side along which the height could be measured—makes a right angle with the base. Thus, the upright shapes are called *right prisms*. (We will usually call them *prisms* for short.) The triangular prism, the rectangular box, and the (right circular) cylinder are all prisms. The formulas for the volumes of these three prisms have a similarity that we can take advantage of. Let's review the formulas.

Volume of triangular prism = area of triangular base × height

Volume of rectangular box = area of rectangular base × height

Volume of cylinder = area of circular base × height

These suggest a formula for the volume of any right prism.

FORMULA FOR THE VOLUME OF A RIGHT PRISM

Volume = area of base × height

To see why this general formula should be true, we use the method from the solution of the cylindrical container problem: We dissect the base of the prism into pieces that are triangular or roughly triangular, then break the whole prism up into triangular prisms, and use the volume and area principles. This is a use of the strategy *break the problem into simpler problems*. Here are a couple of examples.

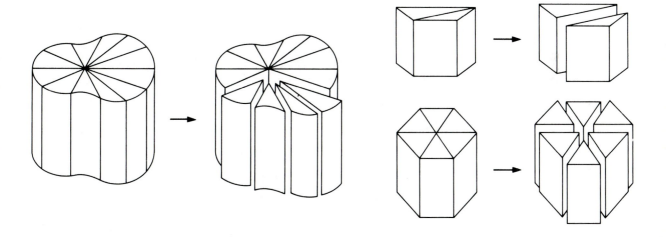

These examples add plausibility to the formula. A rigorous proof of the formula is beyond the scope of this book.

7. Find the volumes of the shapes.

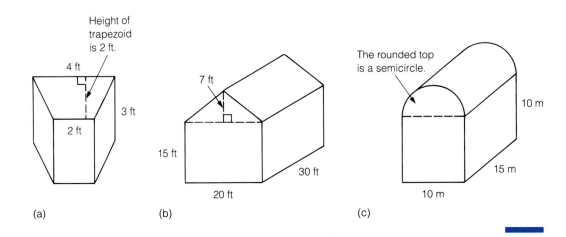

(a)   (b)   (c)

More Mathematical Ideas: Strategies for Finding Volumes

We used the volume principles mentioned earlier to find the volumes of rectangular boxes with fractional sides, of parallelogram bins, and of cylinders and other prisms. The ways in which we used these principles suggest some general strategies for finding the volumes of other, possibly more complicated, shapes.

In the bin problem we found the volume of a parallelogram bin, a right prism with parallelogram end. To do this, we dissected the bin into pieces. (Volume principle 2 says that the volume of the bin is equal to the sum of the volume of the pieces.) Then we rearranged the pieces to form a rectangular box, a shape for which we already knew how to find the volume. (Again, volume principle 2 says that the volume of the rectangular box is equal to the sum of the volumes of the pieces, which, in turn, is equal to the volume of the original bin.) Here is the strategy we used.

STRATEGY 1 FOR FINDING VOLUMES

Dissect the shape into pieces. Rearrange the pieces into a shape with a volume you already know how to find. Then

Volume of new shape = volume of original shape.

In finding the volume of a triangular prism, we took two copies of the prism. Volume principle 1 says that the volumes of the two copies are the same. We put the two prisms together to make a parallelogram bin, a shape with a volume we already knew how to find. Volume principle 2 says that the volume of the parallelogram bin is equal to the sum of the volumes of the two prisms. Since the parallelogram bin is dissected into two pieces of equal volume, the volume of one of those pieces, the original triangular prism, is equal to half the volume of the parallelogram bin. Here is the strategy we used.

STRATEGY 2 FOR FINDING VOLUMES

Make several copies of the shape you are interested in and rearrange them to form a shape with a volume you already know how to find.

In figuring out the volume of a cylinder, we dissected it into wedges that were approximately triangular prisms. By volume principle 2 we know that the volume of the cylinder is equal to the sum of the volumes of these triangularlike prisms. We also know how to figure out the volume of these triangularlike prisms, approximately. The strategy we used was this.

STRATEGY 3 FOR FINDING VOLUMES

Dissect the shape you are interested in into pieces, each with a volume you already know how to find.

There is one final strategy.

STRATEGY 4 FOR FINDING VOLUMES

Use combinations of strategies 1–3.

Note the similarity between the strategies for finding volumes and those for finding areas listed in chapter 17.

8. Use the volume strategies to find the volumes of the shapes.

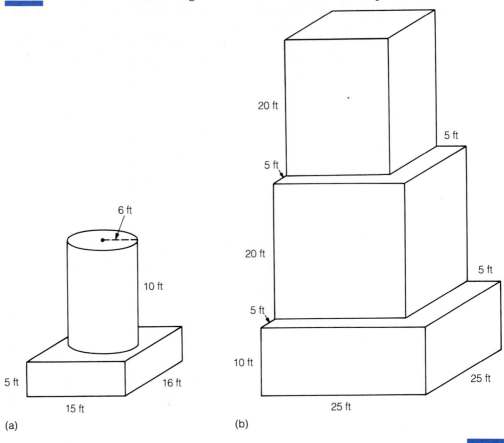

(a)

(b)

19.3   VOLUME BY DISPLACEMENT

You have just inherited a yellow gold bracelet, from an elderly aunt. You are not interested in wearing the bracelet, and an antique jewelry expert tells you that its design is not noteworthy. The expert suggests that the bracelet should be melted down and made into items of more use to you. Before doing this, however, you must determine the purity of the gold used to make the bracelet. The yellow gold used in making jewelry is an alloy of pure gold and copper. The purity of the gold in the bracelet is the percentage of gold in the alloy. How are you going to figure out what this percentage is?

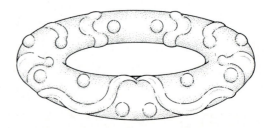

You figure that equal volumes of copper and gold should weigh different amounts. You consult your dictionary and find that a cubic centimeter of copper weighs 8.92 g and that a cubic centimeter of gold weighs 19.3 g. You also figure that a cubic centimeter of an alloy of gold and copper should weigh somewhere between 8.92 g and 19.3 g. You decide *to graph* the weight of a cubic centimeter of alloy as a function of the percentage of gold in the alloy. First, you *make a chart*.

PERCENT GOLD	WEIGHT OF COPPER	WEIGHT OF GOLD (GRAMS)	TOTAL WEIGHT
0	8.92	0	8.92
1	.99 × 8.92 = 8.8308	.01 × 19.3 = .193	9.0238
2	.98 × 8.92 = 8.7416	.02 × 19.3 = .386	9.1276
3	.97 × 8.92 = 8.6524	.03 × 19.3 = .579	9.2314

You think: "Each time I add a percentage point of gold I add .1038 g in weight. So the graph of total weight versus percent of gold must be a straight line. I only need to plot two points. Two good points would be where the percent of gold is zero—total weight 8.92 g—and where the percent of gold is 100—total weight 19.3 g. Here's the graph.

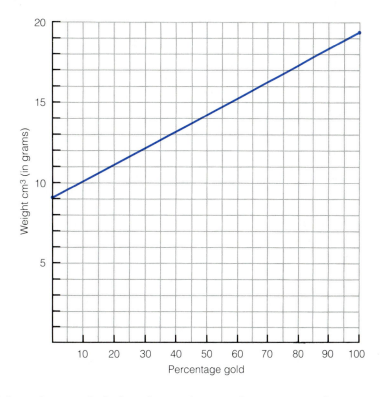

"If I know how much the bracelet weighs per cubic centimeter, then I can use the graph to figure out what percentage of gold is in the bracelet. The bracelet weighs 362.5 g. To figure out how much it weighs per cubic centimeter, I need to figure out its volume. I don't know a formula for a shape such as that one, and I can't think of how I might dissect it into pieces with volumes I know how to find. Perhaps I could make it *part* of a volume I know how to find.

"Let me put the bracelet in a measuring cup, add water to the cup until the bracelet is covered, then measure the volume of the contents of the cup. The volume of the contents will be equal to the volume of the water in the cup plus the volume of the bracelet. Then, when I remove the bracelet from the cup, I can measure the volume of the water alone.

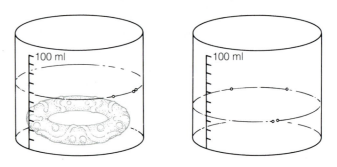

The volume of bracelet plus water is 60 ml. The volume of the water alone is 35 ml. The difference is 25 ml. So the volume of the bracelet is 25 ml. Recall that a milliliter is a cubic centimeter. The bracelet's weight is 362.5 g. That means that its weight per cubic centimeter is $\frac{362.5}{25} = 14.5$ g. Now I can use my graph to find out what percentage of the alloy in the bracelet is gold.

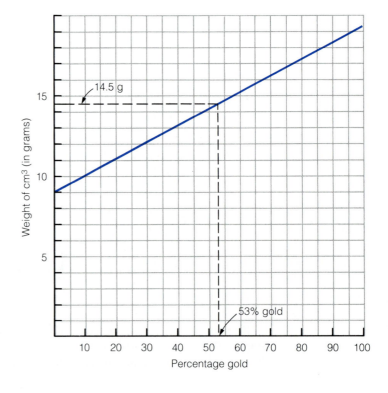

The alloy is 53% gold."

The Mathematical Idea: Measuring Volume by Displacement

The solution to the gold bracelet problem suggests a general method for finding the volume of an irregular shape that will sink in water, such as a stone. You will need a container for the stone and the water. You put the stone in the container, cover it with water, and measure the volume of the contents of the container. This is the volume of the stone plus the volume of the water. You remove the stone and measure the volume of just the water. You calculate the difference of the two volumes to get the volume of the stone.

To carry out this process, you will need a container such that the volume of its liquid contents is easy to determine. A box, a cylinder, or other right prism will do. In these instances, the volume of the contents is equal to the depth of the liquid times the area of the base of the prism. (These measurements must be on the inside of the container, not on the outside.) Of course, the ideal container for this job is a glass, professionally calibrated cylinder, on which the volumes of the liquid contents for various levels have been calculated and carefully marked.

A method for making your own calibrated cylinder is to take a clear glass cylindrical jar like the one shown (with the stone) and stick a piece of tape on the side. Find (or make) a small container with known volume.

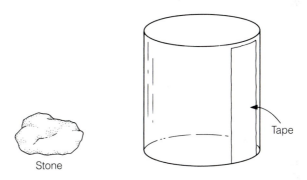

Stone   Tape

A small container with a volume of 50 ml is used in our illustrations. Fill the small container with water and pour its contents into the jar. Mark the water level on the tape. Repeat the procedure to create the scale shown.

50 cm3

Now to measure the volume of the stone. The water level of stone-plus-water is about 425 ml. When the stone is removed the water level is 300 ml. The volume of the stone is 425 ml − 300 ml = 125 ml.

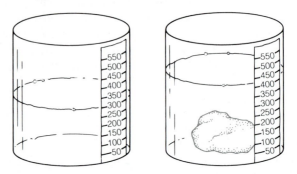

If the irregular object—the volume of which you are seeking—won't sink, you can attach a weight to it so that it will sink. You will then have to subtract the volume of the weight from the total volume displaced to obtain the volume of your irregular shape.

EXERCISES

9. Estimate the volume of a golf ball using the method of displacement we have described.

10. You have an aquarium. You want to make sure that you do not add too many fish to your aquarium. An aquarium guide suggests that, for the type and size of fish you plan to have, there be 3000 ml of water for each fish. You plan to have 5 cm of sand in the bottom of the aquarium, to fill the water in the tank to within 2 cm of the top, and to have rocks and decorative ceramic items on top of the sand in which (and behind which) the fish can hide. You use the displacement method to determine the volume of the rocks and ceramic items. When these are in the graduated cylinder, the water level registers 720 ml. When they have been removed from the graduated cylinder, the water level registers 250 ml. From all this information figure out how many fish you can have in your aquarium.

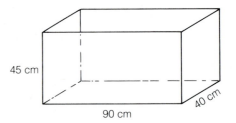

45 cm

90 cm

40 cm

19.4

EXTENDING THE IDEAS: EFFICIENCY OF THREE-DIMENSIONAL SHAPES

THE TEA BOX PROBLEM   You work for a company that manufactures packaging for grocery items. You are working on the design for a box to hold 1000 ml of bulk tea. The distributors of the tea would like the bottom and the top of the box to be square, for aesthetic reasons. The top and bottom of the box will also be made of reinforced cardboard costing

Try this before reading on.

$ .001/cm², and the sides of the box will be made with lighter cardboard costing $ .0005/cm². Since you want to minimize the cost of manufacturing the box, you would like to know what dimensions of the box would make the costs of the materials (used in making the box) as little as possible. How can you solve this problem?

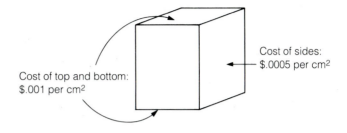

Cost of sides:
$.0005 per cm²

Cost of top and bottom:
$.001 per cm²

A Solution to the Tea Box Problem

To get some feeling for the problem, you *make a guess.* You know that the volume of the box is 1000 ml and that the top and bottom must be squares. A box 10 by 10 by 10 cm satisfies these conditions, and that is your guess. You figure the cost of the box this way.

10 cm Top 10 cm

10 cm

10 cm Bottom 10 cm

10 cm

Area of top plus area of bottom = 200 cm²

Cost of top and bottom = 200 × $ .001 = $ .20

Area of sides = 10 × 40 = 400 cm²

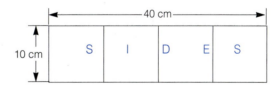

40 cm

10 cm

S I D E S

Cost of sides = 400 × $ .0005 = $ .20

Total cost = $ .40

You decide to try a box with other dimensions satisfying the conditions of square top and bottom and volume of 1000 ml. You think that since the materials for the top and bottom are more expensive, perhaps a box with a smaller top would be cheaper. A box with a top 5 by 5 cm and a height of 40 cm has a smaller top but still satisfies the requirements for the box. You figure out the cost as before.

Top

5 cm

5 cm

Bottom

5 cm

5 cm

Area of top plus bottom = 50 cm²

Cost of top and bottom = 50 × $ .001 = $ .05

Area of sides = 40 × 20 = 800 cm²

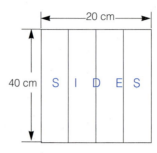

Cost of sides = 800 × $ .0005 = $ .40

Total cost = $ .45

You notice that this is more expensive than the first box. You decide to *make more guesses* and at the same time *organize their consequences in a table*. You plan to *look for a pattern* in the table. Here is your table. (You realize very soon that you need to use a calculator or computer.)

SIDE OF TOP/BOTTOM	HEIGHT	TOP + BOTTOM AREAS	AREA OF SIDES	COST TOP + BOTTOM	COST SIDES	TOTAL COSTS
(centimeters)		(square centimeters)			(dollars)	
10	10	200	400	.20	.20	.40
5	40	50	800	.05	.40	.45
9	12.35	162	444.44	.162	.222	.384
8	15.63	128	500	.128	.25	.378
7	20.41	98	571.43	.098	.285	.383
6	27.79	72	666.67	.072	.333	.405
11	8.26	242	363.64	.242	.182	.424
20	2.5	800	200	.40	.20	.60

You think: "My lowest cost is when the top is a square 8 cm on a side. It appears that the price goes up when I make the top a square bigger than 10 cm on a side. Let me try 8.5 and 7.5 as possible lengths for a side of the square top."

SIDE OF TOP/BOTTOM	HEIGHT	TOP + BOTTOM AREAS	AREA OF SIDES	COST TOP + BOTTOM	COST SIDES	TOTAL COSTS
(centimeters)		(square centimeters)			(dollars)	
8.5	13.84	144.5	470.56	.145	.235 (no improvement)	.380
7.5	17.78	112.5	533.4	.113	.267 (same cost as for 8-cm square top)	.378

It looks as if my best bet is to make a box with a top and bottom a square about 8 cm on a side and a height of 15.63 cm. The materials in the box would cost $ .378."

EXERCISES 11. Write a program that gets the computer to solve the tea box problem by having it print out a table that begins

Side of top (S)	Height (H)	Area top + bottom (A1)	Area sides (A2)	Cost top + bottom (C1)	Cost sides (C2)	Cost total (T)
1	1000	2	4000	.002	2.00	2.002
2	250	8	2000	.008	1.00	2.008

Using the variables written under the column headings, you will need to know that $H = 1000/(S*S), A1 = 2*S*S, A2 = 4*S*H, C1 = .001*A1, C2 = .0005*A2,$ and $T = C1 + C2$. Try to find a more accurate solution than the one in the text by getting the computer to "zero in." (See sec. 17.6, "Computers: Finding Efficient Shapes," chap. 17.)

12. You have a square piece of cardboard 50 cm on a side. You plan to cut equal squares out of each corner of the cardboard and fold the remaining cardboard into an open box as shown.

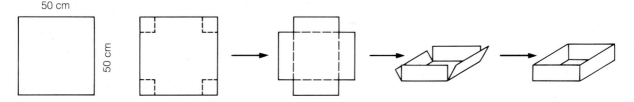

How can you do this so that the box you make will have the largest possible volume? (*Hint:* Make guesses and organize them into a table. Use a calculator or computer.)

19.5   LOOKING AHEAD: GRAPHS RELATED TO CUBIC FUNCTIONS

The formula $P = 4S$ is the formula for the function the input of which is the side S of a square and corresponding output of which is the perimeter P of the square. We know that the graph of this function is a straight line. The formula $A = S^2$ is the formula for the function the input of which is the side S of a square and the corresponding output of which is the area A of the square. In chapter 17, we drew the graph of the latter function and other quadratic functions. (One such function is $F = 6S^2$, where S is the side of a cube and F its surface area.) Now, from what we have done in this chapter, we know that $V = S^3$ is the formula for the function the input of which is the side S of a cube and the corresponding output of which is the volume V of the cube. This is an example of a *cubic* function. The graphs of the four functions mentioned are shown.

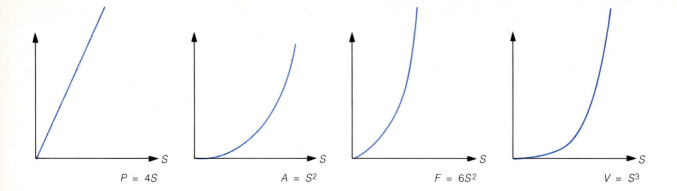

$P = 4S$ $A = S^2$ $F = 6S^2$ $V = S^3$

Since the inputs for these functions are lengths, we have $S \geq$ zero. Let's compare the preceding graphs with the graphs corresponding to the following: $D(T) = T$, $D(T) = T^2$, and $D(T) = T^3$—functions for trips in which there is no restriction on the input T.

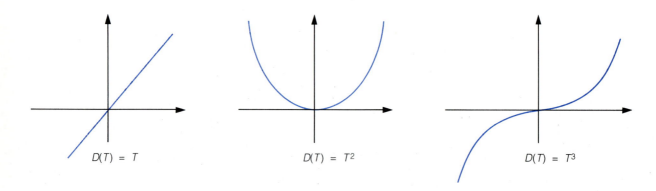

$D(T) = T$ $D(T) = T^2$ $D(T) = T^3$

The function $D(T) = T^3$ is an example of a cubic function. We can define the general cubic function.

DEFINITION OF CUBIC FUNCTION

A *cubic function* has a formula of the form

$$D(T) = aT^3 + bT^2 + cT + d,$$

where a, b, c, and d are fixed numbers.

Following are additional examples of cubic functions and their graphs.

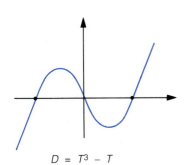

$D = T^3 - T$

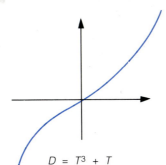

$D = T^3 + T$

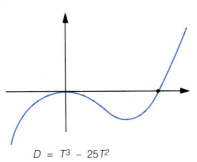

$D = T^3 - 25T^2$

EXERCISES 13. Use the preceding graphs and the ideas from the sections on graphing in chapters 14 and 17 to graph the functions having the following formulas.
(a) $D = (T - 1)^3$ (b) $D = T^3 + 1$ (c) $D = -T^3$
(d) $D = (T - 3)^3 - (T - 3)$ (e) $D = -T^3 + T$
(f) $D = (T - 1)^3 + 1$

14. Solve exercise 12 in the following way.
(a) Suppose the side of one of the squares cut from a corner is denoted by S. Find a formula for the volume V of the box as a function of S.
(b) Use graphing software to produce a graph of this function. Use it to estimate the dimensions of the open box of largest volume that can be made in the way prescribed.

19.6   SUMMARY OF IMPORTANT IDEAS AND TECHNIQUES

- Solid and liquid volume and the relationship between them.
- Volume units
- Formula for the volume of a rectangular box
- Volume principles
- Volumes of prisms: cylinder, triangular prism, parallelogram bin, and others
- General formula for the volume of a prism
- Strategies for finding volumes of complicated shapes
- The method of liquid displacement for finding volumes of irregular shapes
- Shapes that are more "efficient" than others
- Graphs of cubic functions

PROBLEM SET

PRACTICING
SKILLS

1. You are making a low fence of wood rails extended between posts made of brick. Each post will have a square base 3 bricks wide and be 5 bricks high. Each brick is also square and each post solid, without a hollow center. How many bricks will you need for each post?

2. You have a block of cheese which measures 5 by 3 by 2 in. You wish to make 1 in cubes of cheese for a snack tray and plan to put a toothpick in each cube as a handle. How many toothpicks will you need?

3. Sugar cubes come packed in a box in which there are 3 layers. Each layer has 6 rows, and each row has 14 cubes. How many cubes are in one box?

4. You have a cooler that is 12 soft drink cans wide by 6 long and 2 deep. How many cans of soft drinks can you stand in your cooler? What can you say about the volume of the cooler?

5. Wholesale Grocers has just purchased 4820 cartons of tomato paste that it wishes to stack in its warehouse. The warehouse foreman plans to stack them on the floor in a rectangle 13 cartons wide by 22 cartons long. How many cartons high will he need to stack the tomato paste?

6. Look at the floor plan of the living-dining room area that you are remodeling. The ceilings are 9 ft high. You want to install air conditioning for the room. To do this, you need to know how many cubic feet of air the room will hold. Find out.

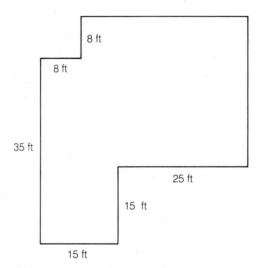

7. You wish to make a diving board platform in the shape of a set of 3 steps. The steps are 3 ft wide, 2 ft deep, and 1 ft high. The top of the platform must be 3 ft deep. How many cubic feet of concrete will you need to make the platform?

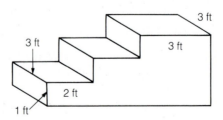

8. The Egyptian Monument Company has agreed to make a Rose Garden Monument Seat for the new City Central Park. The seat is to be shaped like a pyramid with a square base measuring 16 by 16 ft. Each layer is square and measures 4 ft less in each direction than the previous layer, making a 2-ft-deep step/seat on all four sides; that is, the second layer is 12 by 12 ft, the third layer is 8 by 8 ft, and the fourth layer is 4 by 4 ft. Each layer is 18 in high. What is the total volume of the pyramid seat?

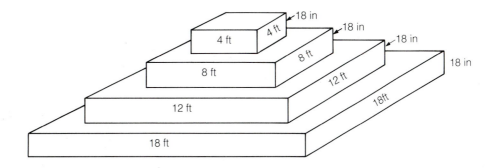

9. A syrup tin is made to look like a log cabin. The tin has a rectangular base that measures 3 by 4 in and is 5 in high on a side and 6 in high at the peak. How many cubic inches of syrup will it hold?

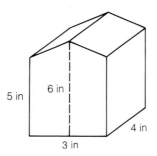

10. A hot-water heater is in the shape of a cylinder 60 cm in diameter and 150 cm high. How many milliliters of water will it hold?

11. Ohio Smith is caught in an airtight room in the Temple of Defeat, which is in the shape of a rhombus. The ceiling of the room is only 1.8 m above the floor. How many cubic meters of air does Ohio have? (Discount his bulk.)

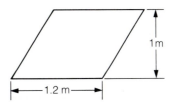

12. An irregularly shaped piece of amethyst submerged in a 2- by 3-ft tank of water raises the water level by 5 in. What is the volume of the amethyst in cubic feet?

13. Central Monument Company is making "mock" mini Grecian columns, cylinders with square blocks on each end. The cylinders are 4 ft high and 2 ft in diameter, and the end blocks are 2.5 by 2.5 by .5 ft. What is the total volume of a column?

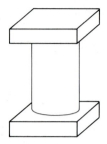

14. The cross section of a septic tank 5 ft deep is shown at left. Find the capacity of the tank in cubic feet.

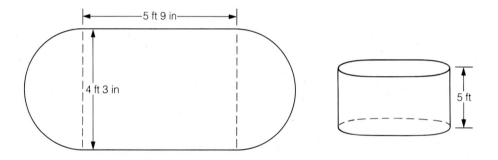

15. You have a rectangular piece of tin 90 by 120 cm that you want to make into a tool storage box, with no top. You do this by cutting out equal squares at the four corners and then folding up the sides. What should the size of squares (that you cut out) be in order that the tool box have maximum volume?

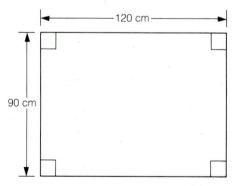

16. Write a program in BASIC to solve problem 15.

Write the solution to each remaining problem carefully and clearly in the form of an essay. In it mention the steps you took to solve the problem, the principles, tools, or formulas you used, other problems or solutions that gave you ideas, and the problem-solving strategies you found helpful.

17. A man has 700 cement blocks each of which is 6 by 6 by 3 in. He wants to stack them in a rectangularly based pile no more than 4 ft high. To ensure that the pile is stable, he decides to lay each block on its 6-by-6 side, that is, its largest side. He could make many differently shaped piles. What is the shape of the pile the base of which uses the least amount of area? What are its dimensions? (*Hint:* Make a table of possible solutions.)

18. You plan to desert-landscape your front yard. You will be covering the 30×20 ft rectangular area indicated in the picture with a 6-in layer of decomposed granite that costs $50/\text{yd}^3$. How many cubic yards will you need, and what will it cost you?

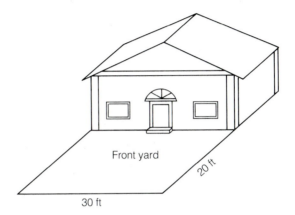

Front yard

20 ft

30 ft

19. In problem 26 of chapter 13 you built a scale model of a room. You are planning to install air conditioning in the room. Before doing this, you must determine how much air, in cubic feet, the room will hold. How much will it hold?

20. By the end of 1990, Americans had discarded 51 billion tons of paper and 180 million tons of plastic.
    (a) If all this could be compressed into cubes 1 ft on a side weighing 50 lb each, how many cubes would be created?
    (b) If all the cubes in (a) were stacked in the shape of a rectangular box, what would its dimensions be?

21. A cylindrical tank is to hold 100 l of gasoline. The circular base must have an area of 100 cm^2. What must the height of this cylinder be? (The "height" of this cylinder is a horizontal distance, since the cylinder in the illustration is lying on its side.)

22. Speedy Trucking Company has agreed to deliver a decorative arch to Central Park and needs to know its weight. The arch is made of two rectangular columns topped with a semicircular cap. The columns measure 4 by 6 in. by 8 ft. The outside diameter of the cap is also 8 ft. It weighs 50 lb/ft^3. What is its total weight?

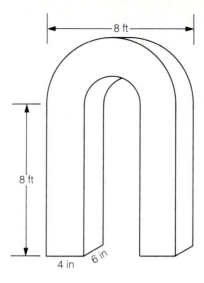

23. A grain elevator is shown in perspective on the left, below. A top view of the elevator is shown on the right. What is the volume of the grain elevator?

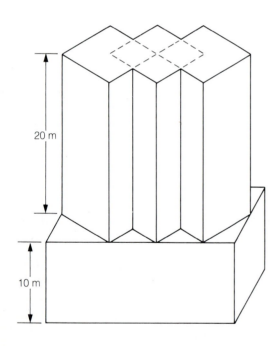

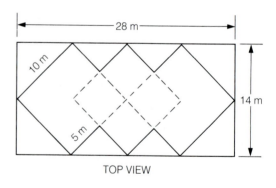

TOP VIEW

24. Dr. Roland, a dentist, has ordered an unusual fish tank (shown in the picture) for her treatment room. There will be an 8-cm layer of sand in the bottom of the tank.
    (a) How many liters of water will she need to fill the rest of the tank if she fills it to within 4 cm of the top?
    (b) Each fish living in the tank will need 3000 cm³ of living space if it is to get enough oxygen and nutrients from the water. What is the largest number of fish that can live together in the tank?

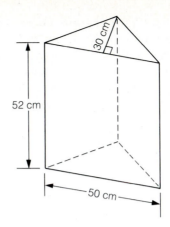

25. You are planning to build the swimming pool shown on the left. On the right is a top view of the swimming pool. (Each square of the grid is 1 m².) The cost of water is about $2/100 ft³. What will it cost to fill the pool?

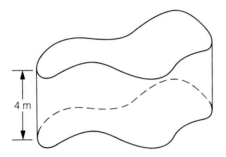

26. A section of cylindrical concrete drainage pipe is shown. Find the volume of the concrete used to make the section.

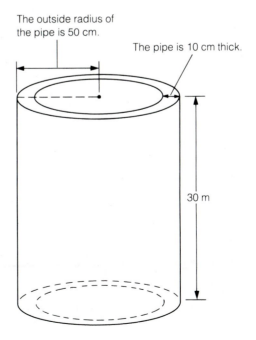

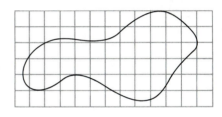

27. My sister and I got lost in the mountains but stumbled on an abandoned miner's shack. Out behind the shack was an old well built in the shape of a square 3 ft on a side. There was some water in the well, but it was 7 ft from the top, and we could only reach down about 3 ft. Luckily, my sister hit on the idea of dropping some bricks into the well to raise the water level to a point where we could reach it. Each brick was about $\frac{1}{4}$ ft^3 in volume. How many bricks did we have to throw in to raise the water level to where we could reach it?*

28. The mathematics department is planning to present a trophy to the outstanding graduating senior in mathematics. The department has engaged a sculptor to make a tiered base for the trophy, which is to be cast in bronze. The tiered base is shown. How much bronze will the sculptor need for this?

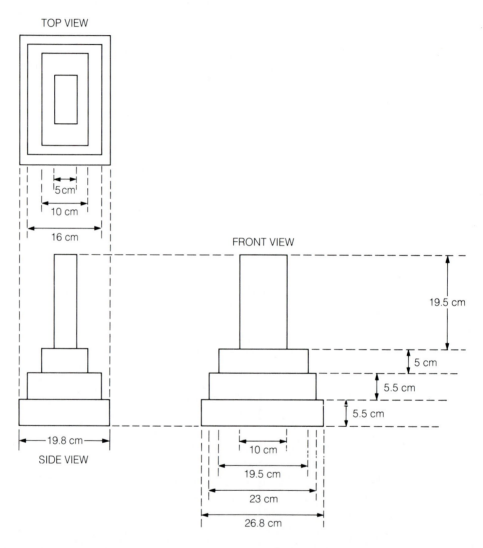

29. A shipping company will only handle packages that meet strict size requirements. A cylinder is measured by wrapping a tape rule across the diameter of one circular base and then along one side. This measurement, diameter plus height of cylinder, may not exceed 18 in. What are the

* From Carol Meyer and Tom Sallee, *Make It Simple*, Addison-Wesley, Reading, Mass., 1983, prob. 376, p. 269.

dimensions of the cylinder of largest volume that they will handle? (*Hint:* A cylinder the height plus diameter of which is less than or equal to 18 in with a maximum volume must have its height plus diameter *equal* 18 in. Why? Find a formula for the volume of a cylinder the diameter plus height of which equals 18 in. in terms of its diameter. Graph the function using graphics software and solve.)

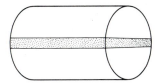

30. You are designing a rectangular cardboard cereal box that is to have a volume of 3000 cm³. The height is to be twice as big as the width of its front. The top, bottom, and one of the side panels will have a double thickness of cardboard. What should the dimensions of the carton be in order that a minimum amount of cardboard be used in making it? (*Hint:* Make a table. Use calculator or computer.)

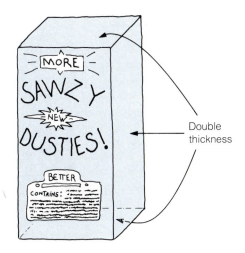

31. You are a contractor and are preparing a bid for the job of digging a hole for the foundation of an apartment building. The dimensions of the hole to be dug are 150 ft long, 90 ft wide, and 15 ft deep. In preparing the bid you have to take into account a variety of things, including the machinery needed, the salaries of the workers involved, and the time needed for each step.
   (a) You need to know how much dirt to remove. How much will it be, in cubic feet? In cubic yards?
   (b) A dump truck can carry 10 yd³ of earth. How many truck loads will have to be removed?
   (c) A digger operating a steam shovel can loosen and load 100 yd³ of earth in an hour. How long will it take the digger to dig and load all the dirt in the hole?
   (d) You have located a suitable dumping ground and you figure that a full truck can make the trip from the hole to the dumping ground, dump the load, and return in 30 min. How many hours of travel time will be needed to transport all the dirt from the hole to the dumping ground?
   (e) How many trucks can the digger fill in an hour? How long does it take to fill a single truck?

(f) To minimize the idle time for the truck drivers and for the digger, exactly how many trucks should there be? (You realize that once a truck is filled, it will be 30 min before it can be filled again.)

(g) Each truck driver is paid $10.50/hr. What will be the pay for a single truck driver for this project? What will be the total of all pay for truck driving?

(h) The shovel operator is paid $15.75/hr. What will be the total pay for the shovel operator?

(i) The foreman's salary is $18.95/hr. What will be his total pay?

(j) From past experience you figure that your overhead costs for any job should be about 25% of the labor costs. How much should your overhead for this job be?

(k) The cost of fringe benefits for the employees is 14% of their base salaries. What will be the total cost of fringe benefits for this project?

(l) What will be the total cost to you for completing the project?

(m) You figure that your profit for the project should be 10% of your total costs. What will this be?

(n) Your estimate for completing the job should be total cost plus profit. What is your estimate?

32. A certain kind of tea is to be sold in cylindrical tins. As in the tea box problem, it is to hold 1000 ml, the cost of material to make the top and bottom is $ .001/cm², and the cost of material to make the lateral side is $ .0005/cm². You want to know what the height and radius of the top should be to minimize the cost of materials for the tin. Modify the program from exercise 11 in the text to solve this problem.

APPLICATIONS OF VOLUME

CHAPTER 20

In this chapter we continue our discussion of volume. We start with the problem of finding the volume of a cone and, in trying to solve it, are led to finding the volume of a triangular pyramid, a pyramid having a triangle for a base. We use the solution to the latter to solve the former.

Finding the volume of a triangular pyramid also enables us to find the volume of a pyramid having any polygon for its base. Surprisingly, it enables us to find the volume of a sphere as well.

The success in finding the volumes of cones, pyramids, and spheres comes largely from exploiting analogies of volume with area: The vol-

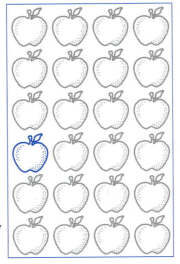

ume of a triangular pyramid is analogous to the area of a triangle; and the volume of a sphere is analogous to the area of a circle, in which the surface area of the sphere plays the role of the circumference of the circle.

Finally, we will compare a three-dimensional shape with a scale model of it. We will be interested in how the volume of the original compares with the volume of the scale model and how the surface area of the original compares with that of the scale model. We will discuss how these comparisons might affect the size and shape of living creatures.

THE PILE OF PEBBLES PROBLEM

You own a landscape supply house and sell small pebbles for use as a ground cover. You sell them by the cubic foot. One of your suppliers has just dumped a load of pebbles in your supply yard. The pile forms the conical shape shown in the next illustration. For inventory purposes, you need to know the volume of the pile of pebbles.

A Solution to the Pile of Pebbles Problem

You look at the pile of pebbles and think: "The pile forms a cone, and I need to find its volume. Since I'm always dealing with conical piles of rocks or sand or bark pieces, solving this problem should help me with other situations as well. Let me *draw some pictures* of a cone.

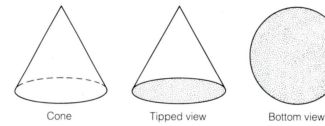

| Cone | Tipped view | Bottom view | Top view |

The cone has a circular base and, like an Egyptian pyramid, it comes to a point at the top. However, an Egyptian pyramid has a square base, whereas the cone has a circular base. Because it has a circular base, the cone also reminds me of a cylinder. How did we deal with the volume of a cylinder? We dissected the circular base into sectors (trianglelike shapes) and used the dissection to cut the cylinder up into triangularlike prisms.

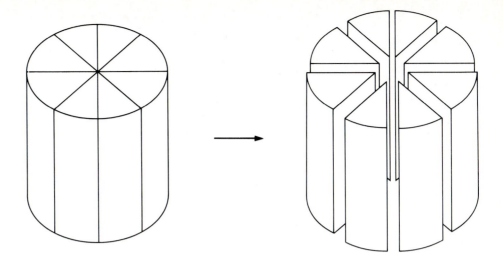

I could do a similar thing with the cone. Let me cut its circular base into sectors.

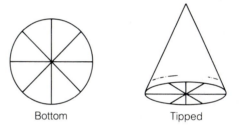

Bottom   Tipped

Now I'm going to dissect the cone vertically along the lines forming the sectors.

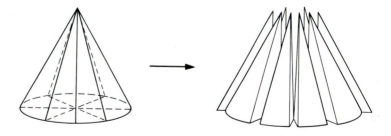

That gives me a bunch of odd shapes—pyramids with sectors of circles for bases.

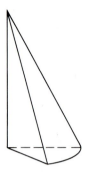

"If I knew how to figure out the volume of a triangular pyramid, then I could get a rough idea of the volume of one of those odd shapes, since each one is roughly a triangular pyramid. Then, to approximate the volume of the cone, all I would have to do is add up those volumes. Figuring out the volume of a triangular pyramid should be an easier problem than figuring out the volume of a cone."

THE TRIANGULAR-PYRAMID PROBLEM

You have a triangular pyramid and you want to find its volume.

A Solution to the Triangular-Pyramid Problem

You think of the strategies for finding volume. "Perhaps I can make the triangular pyramid part of a larger shape with a volume I know how to find. It looks as if a triangular pyramid would fit very neatly into a triangular prism.

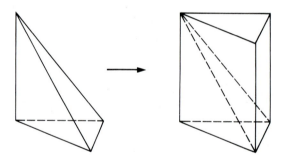

I know a formula for the volume of a triangular prism. I also know that the volume of the triangular prism is the sum of the volume of a triangular pyramid plus the volume of the 'rest' of the prism. To figure out what the 'rest' is in this case, let me draw a picture.

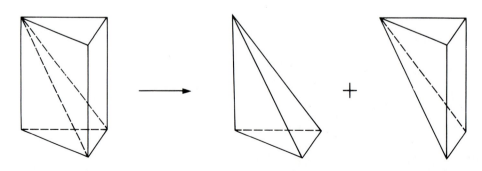

Hmmm. I don't know anything about the shape on the right. But, if I label its vertices and slice it in two pieces along the plane determined by points A, C, and D, then I get the pieces shown on the right (below).

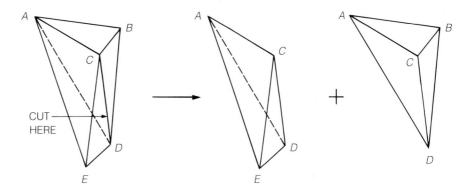

The volume of the triangular prism must be the sum of the volumes of the three shapes shown to the right.

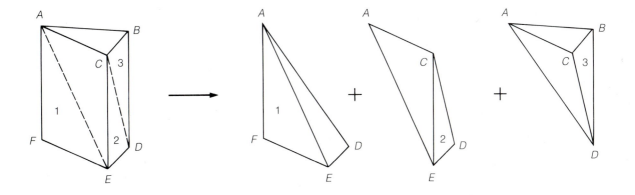

"I see that the three pieces I have cut from the prism have a property in common. The triangular pyramid has a triangular base and three triangular sides coming to a point at the top. The same is true of the other two shapes. Both of them sit on triangular bases; both of them have three triangular sides that come to a point at the top. All three shapes are triangular pyramids."

A Pause in the Solution to the Triangular Pyramid Problem

To follow the remainder of the solution to the triangular pyramid problem, you might want to have a real triangular prism that you can dissect into three triangular prisms. On the next two pages are patterns for the triangular prism and the three triangular pyramids. Copy them, cut them out, and assemble. (For each, cut out the pattern and fold away from you along each line drawn. Use the tabs to glue or tape each pyramid together.) Then fit the three assembled pyramids together to make a triangular prism.*

---

* Copies of these patterns, ready to cut out and assemble, are printed in the lab manual designed to accompany this text.

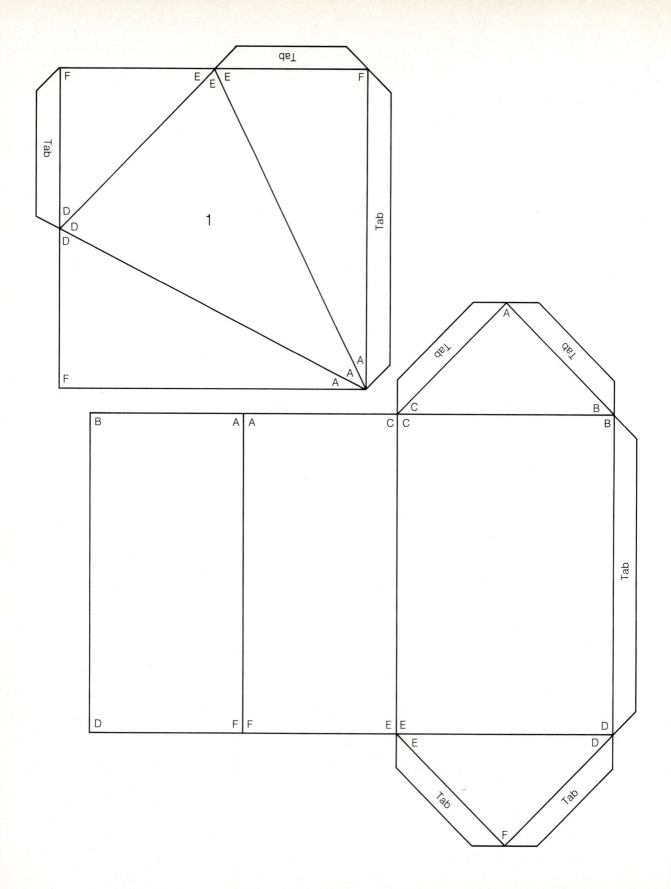

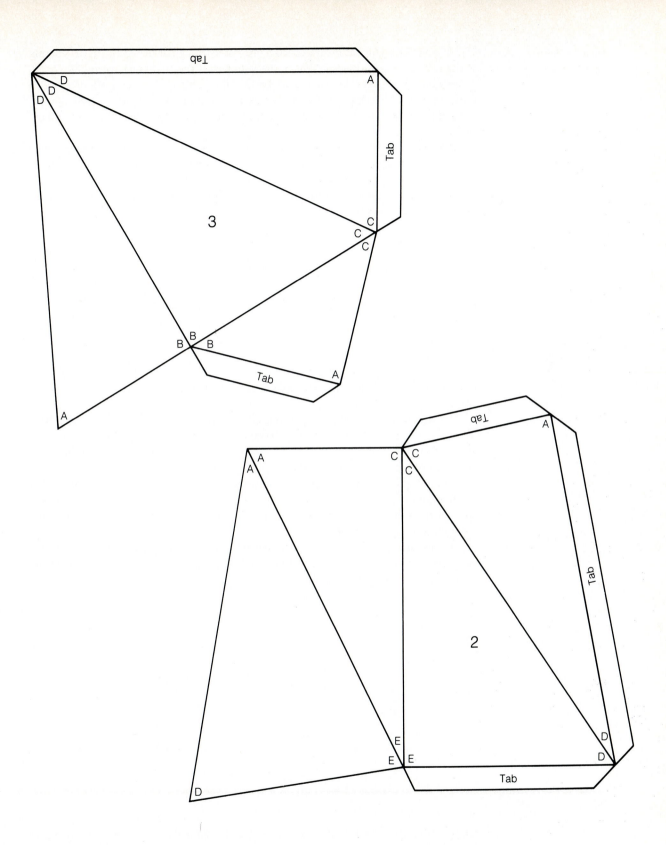

"The triangular prism has been dissected into three triangular pyramids. So the volume of the triangular prism is the sum of the volumes of the triangular pyramids.

"However, it seems a little circular: To find the volume of a triangular pyramid, I made it a part of a triangular prism (I know how to find that volume), which, in turn, is equal to the sum of the volumes of *three* triangular pyramids. But I don't know how to find those volumes.

"That reminds me of a *similar problem*—figuring out the area of a right triangle. We took the triangle and a copy of it and arranged the two triangles into a rectangle. We made the original triangle a part of a rectangle (whose area we could find), and the area of the rectangle was then equal to the sum of the areas of the two triangles. The areas of the two triangles were the same.

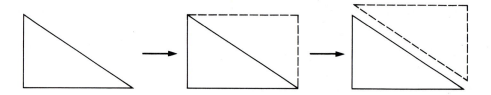

From this we concluded that the area of the original triangle was equal to half the area of the rectangle.

"The volume of the triangular prism is equal to the sum of the volumes of the three triangular pyramids. Could the three triangular pyramids have *equal* volumes? If the answer were yes, then the volume of the original triangular pyramid would be equal to one-third the volume of the triangular prism. That would be fantastic!

"Let me explore the possibility that the three pyramids have the same volume. With the triangle-rectangle problem, the two triangles have equal areas because one is a copy of the other. With the three pyramids, however, it doesn't look as if any one pyramid is a copy of another.

"Do the three pyramids have any properties in common? Pyramids 1 (the original) and 3 have the same base and the same height (the height is the distance of the 'peak' to the base along a perpendicular to the base).

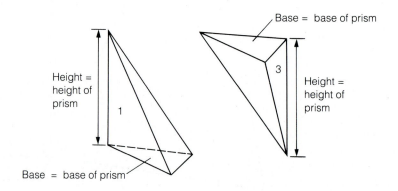

If I use different faces as bases, pyramids 2 and 3 have the same base and the same height above that base.

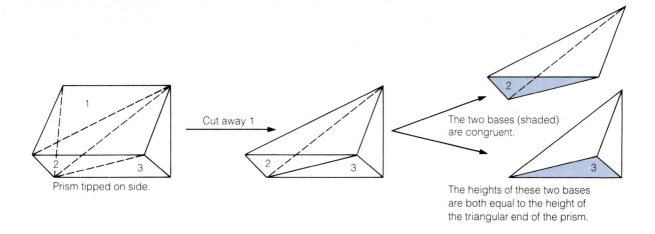

Prism tipped on side.

Cut away 1

The two bases (shaded) are congruent.

The heights of these two bases are both equal to the height of the triangular end of the prism.

"Triangles with the same base and height have the same areas. I wonder if two triangular pyramids with the same base and height have the same volume? If that were true, then the volume of all three pyramids would be the same."

20.2

THE VOLUME OF A TRIANGULAR PYRAMID USING CAVALIERI'S PRINCIPLE

A Solution to the Triangular-Pyramid Problem, Part III

"How could I *show* that two triangular pyramids with the same base and height have the same volume? It looks as if one pyramid in such a pair is a 'leaned on' version of the other. What do I know about two shapes, one of which is a 'leaned on' version of the other?

"I must be careful about what I mean by *leaned on*. If I take a rectangular frame made of tooth picks and lean on it, then the areas change."

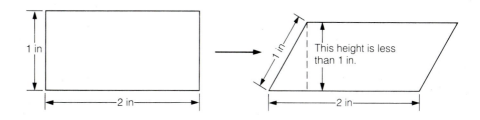

1 in

2 in

1 in

This height is less than 1 in.

2 in

Find out what happens when you try this with a rectangular frame of toothpicks. You'll discover, first of all, that the base of the parallelogram on the right is equal to the base of the rectangle, but the height of the parallelogram is shorter. Keep working along with the problem solver and see what develops.

"Let's see. For what I'm doing I want the base and the height to stay the same. Let me try something else. What if I imagine that the rectangle is made of a stack of thin strips and push sideways on the stack. I'd have this (see next page):

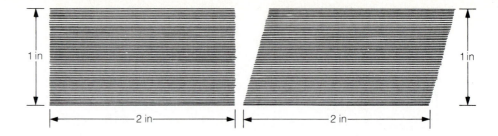

The height and base stay the same, and the area stays the same. (My friend, an expert on these matters, tells me that the parallelogram on the right is a *shear* of the rectangle on the left.) I can do the same thing with a triangle: I imagine that it is made of a stack of thin strips. I push on it sideways (shear it) and get a triangle with the same height and base.

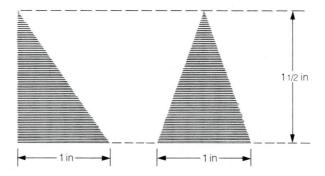

The areas of the two triangles are the same, too.

"Thinking of plane shapes as a stack of thin strips helps me to relate equal areas. I could think of solid shapes similarly and imagine that a rectangular box is a stack of thin layers, like a deck of cards.

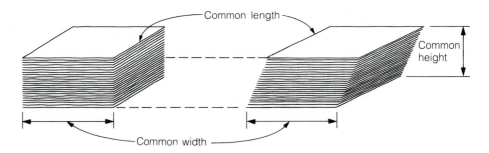

If I push sideways on this deck (shear the rectangular box), I get a second solid with the same base and height that has the same volume.

"Let me try the same thing with a triangular pyramid and imagine that it is made of layers, like a triangular deck of cards. I can push sideways on this solid in many ways to make other triangular pyramids that have the same height and base and volume as the original. In this way I can get any other triangular pyramid having the same height and base.

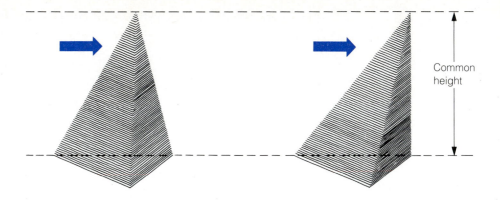

From this I can conclude that *any two triangular pyramids with the same base and height have the same volume*. That solves my problem!"

Thinking of a solid as a deck of cards and shearing it to obtain another shape with the same volume is a version of Cavalieri's principle, discussed in more detail later in the chapter.

THE SOLUTION TO THE PROBLEM OF THE TRIANGULAR PYRAMID, SUMMARIZED

1. Here's the triangular pyramid.

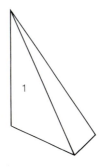

2. Here are the three pyramids that fit together to make the triangular prism.

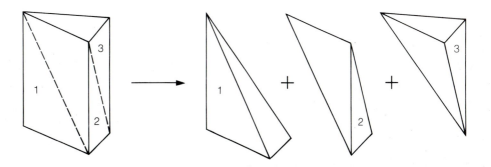

3. Here are pairs of the three pyramids having the same bases and heights.

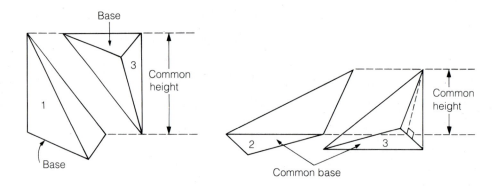

4. We showed that two pyramids with the same base and height have the same volume.

5. Consequently, pyramids 1, 2, and 3 have the same volume.

6. Consequently, the volume of each pyramid is one-third the volume of the prism.

7. Since we know the formula for the volume of a triangular prism, we have a new formula.

FORMULA FOR THE VOLUME OF A TRIANGULAR PYRAMID

$$\text{Volume} = \frac{1}{3} \times \text{area of base} \times \text{height on the base.}$$

EXERCISE **1.** Find the volumes of the triangular pyramids.

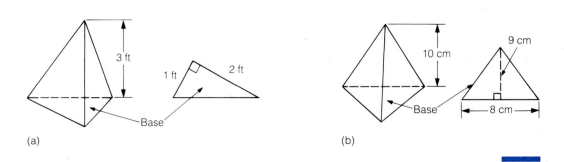

(a)   (b)

A Final Solution to the Pile of Pebbles Problem   You recall that to find the volume of the conical pile of pebbles, you dissected a cone into pieces, each of which was roughly a triangular pyramid. The volume of the cone is the sum of the volumes of these pieces.

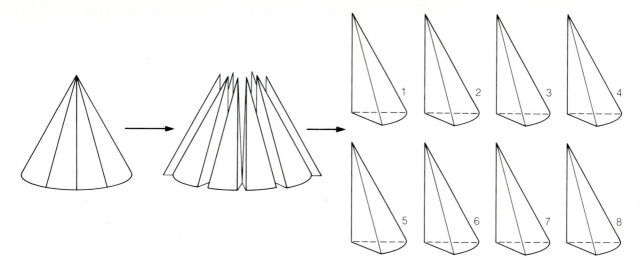

Then you found a formula for the volume of a triangular pyramid. We haven't proved it, but it seems reasonable to conclude that the volume of each pyramid with the sector of a circle as base is also

$$\frac{1}{3} \times \text{area of base} \times \text{height}$$

so that

$$\text{Volume of cone} = \text{volume of 1} + \text{volume of 2} + \text{volume of 3} + \cdots$$

$$= \frac{1}{3} \times \text{area of base of 1} \times \text{height of 1}$$

$$+ \frac{1}{3} \times \text{area of base of 2} \times \text{height of 2}$$

$$+ \frac{1}{3} \times \text{area of base of 3} \times \text{height of 3} + \cdots$$

But the height of all these pyramids is the same—the same as the height H of the cone on its base. So we have the following equation:

$$\text{Volume of cone} = \frac{1}{3} \times \text{area of base of 1} \times H + \frac{1}{3} \times \text{area of base of 2} \times H$$

$$+ \frac{1}{3} \times \text{area of base of 3} \times H + \cdots$$

Each term in the sum has $\frac{1}{3} \times H$ in it. By the distributive law, we can rewrite the last equation as

Volume of cone

$$= \frac{1}{3} H \, (\text{area of base of 1} + \text{area of base of 2} + \text{area of base of 3} + \cdots).$$

The sum of the areas of the bases of the pyramid is just the area of the base of the cone. This give us a nice formula.

FORMULA FOR THE VOLUME OF A CONE

$$\text{Volume} = \frac{1}{3} \times \text{height} \times \text{area of base}$$

It is assumed that the *base* of the cone is the circular part on which it sits and its *height* is the distance of the peak (or apex) of the cone to its base, along a line perpendicular to its base.

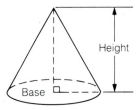

EXERCISE   **2.** Find the volumes of the cones.

(a)

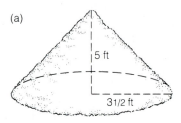

5 ft

3 1/2 ft

(b)

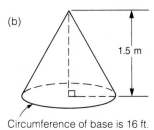

1.5 m

Circumference of base is 16 ft.

The Mathematical Idea: The Volume of Pyramids and Cones

We can use the formula for the volume of a triangular pyramid and the method that we used to find the volume of a cone to find the volume of other pyramids. For example, take the two pyramids in the next illustration.

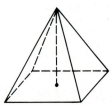

The method we will use to find the volume of a pyramid of this sort is to draw lines dissecting its base into triangles, then slice the pyramid along these lines up to its peak (or *apex*). This dissects the pyramid into triangular pyramids, each of which has the same height as the original pyramid.

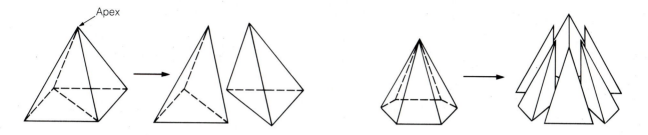

Thus, the volume of the pyramid is equal to the sum of the volumes of a bunch of triangular pyramids.

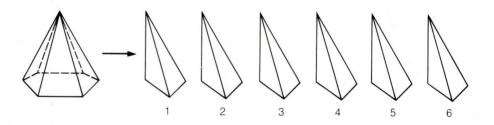

If the height of the original pyramid is H, then we have:

$$\text{Volume of original pyramid} = \frac{1}{3} \times H \times \text{area of base of 1}$$

$$+ \frac{1}{3} \times H \times \text{area of base of 2}$$

$$+ \frac{1}{3} \times H \times \text{area of base of 3} + \cdots$$

$$= \frac{1}{3} \times H \times (\text{area of base 1} + \text{area of base 2} + \cdots)$$

$$= \frac{1}{3} \times H \times \text{area of base of original pyramid.}$$

This translates into a formula for the volume of any pyramid.

FORMULA FOR THE VOLUME OF A PYRAMID

$$\text{Volume} = \frac{1}{3} \times \text{area of base} \times \text{height}$$

---

3. Find the volume of each shape.

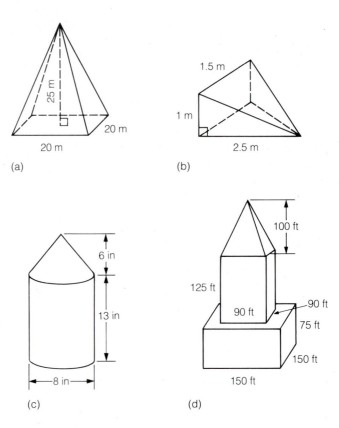

(a)

(b)

(c)

(d)

20.3   THE VOLUME OF A SPHERE

THE SPACE STATION
PROBLEM

You work in the space industry and are involved in a project to design a livable space station. You and the other members of your group are considering a variety of shapes for the main core of the station. One of the shapes you are considering is a large sphere. As part of your evaluation of this shape, you will need to figure out its volume—because you must know how much air is in the station at any time. Also, the outside of the space station must be covered with a sheet of an expensive metal alloy that can withstand the high heat from the sun and that is also relatively impervious to the bombardment of cosmic rays and other particles from space. You want to know how much of this expensive metal you will need. Since the metal sheeting is sold by the square foot, knowing the surface area of the sphere will tell how much sheeting you will need. So you have two problems: What is the volume of the sphere, and what is its surface area?

You think: "To find the volume of the sphere I could cut it up into pieces with volumes I already know how to find. *A similar problem* I've already solved is finding the area of a circle in a plane. To find the area of a circle, I cut it into sectors.

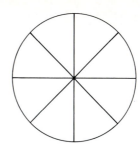

"The area of the circle is the sum of the areas of the sectors, and the area of each sector is roughly $\frac{1}{2} \times$ 'base' $\times$ 'height.' The height is the radius R of the circle, so I have the following:

Area of circle = sum of area of sectors

$$\cong \frac{1}{2} \times R \times \text{base of } 1 + \frac{1}{2} \times R \times \text{base of } 2 + \frac{1}{2} \times R \times \text{base of } 3 + \cdots$$

$$= \frac{1}{2} R \ (\text{base of } 1 + \text{base of } 2 + \text{base of } 3 + \cdots)$$

$$= \frac{1}{2} R \ (\text{sum of bases of sectors})$$

$$= \frac{1}{2} R \ (\text{circumference of circle})$$

$$= \frac{1}{2} R \ (2\pi R)$$

$$= \pi R^2.$$

The sectors of the circle are 'wedges' that meet in the circle's center. I could cut the sphere into little wedges that meet in its center.

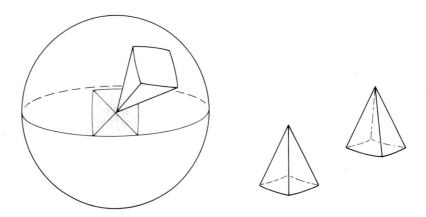

"Each wedge is roughly a little pyramid! The base of each wedge is rounded, unlike a real pyramid, which has a flat base. If I cut the sphere up into these pyramidal wedges, then the volume of the sphere will be the sum of the volumes of the wedges.

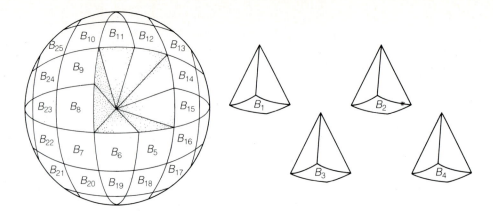

The volume of each pyramidal wedge is, roughly, $\frac{1}{3}$ × area of base × height. The height of each is the radius R of the sphere. I have, then,

$$\text{Volume of sphere} = \text{sum of volumes of wedges}$$

$$\cong \frac{1}{3} R \,(\text{area of base of 'pyramid' 1})$$

$$+ \frac{1}{3} R \,(\text{area of base of 'pyramid' 2})$$

$$+ \frac{1}{3} R \,(\text{area of base of 'pyramid' 3}) + \cdots$$

$$= \frac{1}{3} R \,(\text{area of base of 'pyramid' 1}$$

$$+ \text{area of base of 'pyramid' 2} + \cdots)$$

$$= \frac{1}{3} R \,(\text{sum of areas of bases of 'pyramids'}).$$

"Furthermore, the sum of the areas of the bases of all the 'pyramids' is the surface area of the sphere. That's exciting! Here's my formula for the volume of a sphere so far.

$$\text{Volume of sphere} = \frac{1}{3} R \,(\text{surface area of sphere}).\text{"}$$

This formula reinforces the analogy we have made between the circle and the sphere. In the analogy the area of a circle corresponds to the volume of the sphere, and the circumference of the circle corresponds to the surface area of the sphere. The formula

$$\text{Area of circle} = \frac{1}{2} R \,(\text{circumference of circle})$$

corresponds nicely to the formula for the volume of a sphere.

"Now wait a minute!" you say. "When I figured out the area of a circle in terms of its circumference, I knew the circumference of a circle. I don't know the surface area of the sphere. In fact, my other problem is to figure out the sphere's surface area. However, if I can solve one of the two problems, I'll have the other problem solved, too."

The Mathematical Idea: The Volume and the Surface Area of a Sphere

Although you were not able to solve the space station problem, you were able to show that the answers to the two problems—the volume of the sphere and the surface area of the sphere—were intimately connected.

You can perform an experiment to help solve the volume problem. Take a hollow hemisphere (call its radius R) and a hollow cone having the same radius R and height $2R$. (For suggestions on how to find such items, see laboratory activity 20 in the lab manual accompanying the text.) Fill the hollow cone with water and pour its contents into the hollow hemisphere.

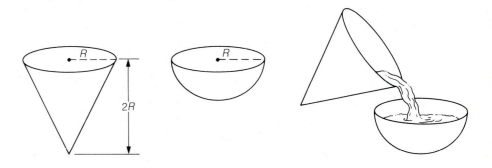

The water from the cone should fill up the hemisphere entirely, with none left in the cone and none spilled. Such a demonstration is not a proof, but it suggests that the volume of the cone is equal to the volume of the hemisphere:

Volume of hemisphere of radius R

$$= \text{volume of cone of height } 2R \text{ and base of radius } R.$$

Another argument justifying this equation is given in section 20.4.

Using the formula for the volume of a cone, we get

$$\text{Volume of hemisphere} = \frac{1}{3} \times \text{area of base of cone} \times \text{height of cone}$$

$$= \frac{1}{3} (\pi R^2)(2R)$$

$$= \frac{2}{3} \pi R^3.$$

Then, since the hemisphere is half the original sphere of radius R, we have the following formula.

Since we know how to find the volume of a sphere and know the relationship between the volume and the surface area of a sphere, we can now find a formula for the surface area of a sphere:

$$\text{Volume of sphere} = \frac{1}{3}R \text{ (surface area of sphere)},$$

or

$$\frac{4}{3}\pi R^3 = \frac{1}{3}R \text{ (surface area)},$$

or

$$\frac{1}{3}R\,(4\pi R^2) = \frac{1}{3}R \text{ (surface area)}.$$

That gives us another formula.

EXERCISE   4. Find the volumes and surface areas of the shapes.

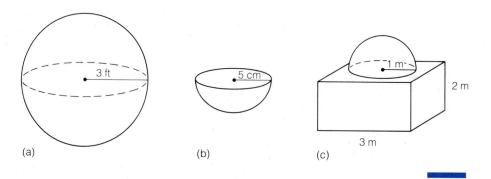

(a)   (b)   (c)

---

* An experiment for estimating the surface area of a sphere directly is described in James V. Bruni, *Experiencing Geometry,* Wadsworth, Belmont, Calif., 1977, pp. 249–251.

In finding the volume of a triangular pyramid we showed that two pyramids having equal heights and congruent bases also have equal volumes. To do this, we imagined one of the pyramids to be made of layers as if it were a deck of cards, then pushed sideways to form the other pyramid. From this, we concluded that the two pyramids have equal volumes. The Renaissance mathematician Bonaventura Cavalieri (1598–1647) generalized this idea.

CAVALIERI'S PRINCIPLE

Suppose that two solids sit on a plane. Any plane parallel to this will intersect each of the solids in a *cross section*. If the areas of the two cross sections are equal for every such parallel plane, then the volumes of the two solids are also equal.

In the case of the deck-of-cards box and the sheared deck-of-cards box, the two cross sections (obtained by intersecting the two solids with a plane parallel to their bases) are identical "cards" and so have the same areas.

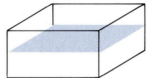 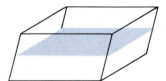

Similarly, two triangular pyramids with congruent bases and equal heights when intersected by a plane parallel to their bases have cross-sectional areas that are equal. By Cavalieri's principle, they also have equal volumes.

The same argument shows that an *oblique prism* (a right prism that has been sheared) has the same volume formula as a right prism.

FORMULA FOR THE VOLUME OF AN OBLIQUE PRISM

Volume of oblique prism = area of base × height

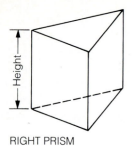

RIGHT PRISM

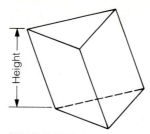

OBLIQUE PRISM

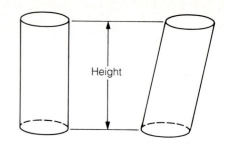

Height

To use Cavalieri's principle in calculating the volume of a solid, you find a second solid with a volume you know how to find and with a cross-sectional area equal to the cross-sectional area of the original solid for every plane parallel to the bases. Let's show how this works by finding the volume of a hemisphere in a new way. We assume that we want to find the volume of a hemisphere of radius R. We need a nice, friendly solid to compare it with.

Take a cylinder of radius R and height R. From the cylinder, hollow out a cone of radius R and height R with apex at the bottom of the cylinder and base at the top, as in the diagram.

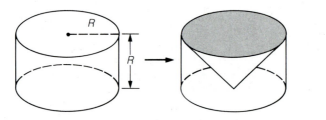
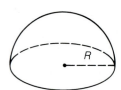

We will compare the hemisphere on the right with this hollowed-out cylinder. Note that we can figure out the volume of the latter.

Volume of hollowed-out cylinder = volume of cylinder of height R and radius R

$-$ volume of cone of height R and radius R

Place the hemisphere and the hollowed-out cylinder on a base plane, take a plane parallel to the base plane, and consider the two cross-sectional areas. Assume that the parallel plane is A units from the base plane, measured along a line perpendicular to the base plane.

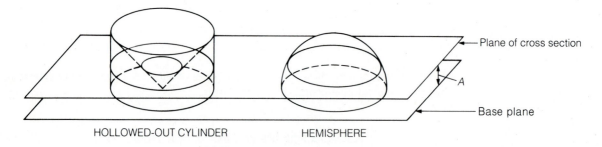

HOLLOWED-OUT CYLINDER   HEMISPHERE

Now we need to calculate the two cross-sectional areas. The diagram shows a side view and a top view of these areas.

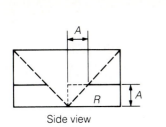

Side view

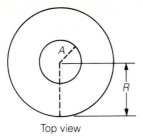

Top view

CROSS SECTION OF
HOLLOWED OUT CYLINDER

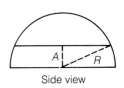

Top view

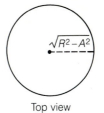

Side view

CROSS SECTION
OF HEMISPHERE

For the hollowed-out cylinder the cross section is a washer with outside radius R and inside radius A. The area of this washer is $\pi R^2 - \pi A^2$, or $\pi(R^2 - A^2)$. For the hemisphere, the shape is a circle with radius $\sqrt{(R^2 - A^2)}$. (This follows from the Pythagorean theorem.) Thus, the area of the cross section of the hemisphere is $\pi(R^2 - A^2)$. The areas of the two cross sections are the same! By Cavalieri's principle, the volumes of the two solids are the same.

Now let's finish calculating the volume of the hollowed-out cylinder:

Volume of hollowed-out cylinder = volume of cylinder of height R and radius R

$\qquad$ − volume of cone of height R and radius R

$$= \pi(R^2)R - \frac{1}{3}\pi(R^2)R$$

$$= \pi R^3 - \frac{1}{3}\pi R^3$$

$$= \frac{2}{3}\pi R^3.$$

This is equal to the volume of a hemisphere of radius R, which is what we got before. It is nice to have this verification, since previously we got the formula by pouring water.

EXERCISES 5. Find the volumes of the solids.

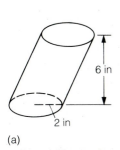

(a)

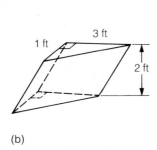

(b)

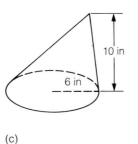

(c)

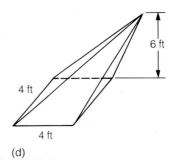

(d)

6. A soap manufacturer manufactures a spherical-shaped "bar" of soap that is packed in a box, 10 cm on a side, shown on the left. He is thinking of making eight smaller spherical soaps and packing them in the same-sized box. These are shown on the

right. What is the volume of soap in the box on the right? How does this compare with the volume of soap in the box on the left?

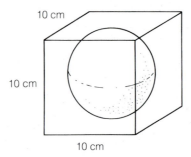

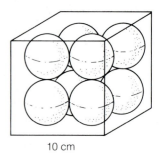

20.5
EXTENDING THE IDEAS:
VOLUME AND SCALE MODELS

THE SECOND SPACE STATION PROBLEM

You are still exploring different designs for a livable space station. You are considering a dumbbell shape.

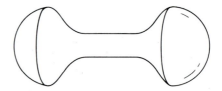

You have the same problem with this shape that you had with the spherically shaped station: You must determine its volume and surface area.

A Solution to the Second Space Station Problem

This time you try a different tactic for finding the volume and surface area of the shape. You *decide on the following plan*:

1. Build a scale model of the proposed space station.
2. Figure out the volume of the model by the water displacement method.
3. Use the volume of the model to figure out the volume of the full-sized station.
4. Figure out the surface area of the model. (You will figure out how much paint it takes to paint a wall 3 by 3 m. From this you will figure out how much paint it takes to paint 1 m². Then you will paint the surface of the scale-model space station and figure out how much paint you use. From this you will estimate the model's surface area.)
5. Use the surface area of the model to figure out the surface area of the full-sized station.

You decide to build a scale model $\frac{1}{20}$ the size of the proposed full-sized space station; that is, the length of the scale model is to be $\frac{1}{20}$ the length of the full-sized station, and all other lengths on the model are to be $\frac{1}{20}$ the corresponding lengths of the full-sized station. You realize that you must figure out how you will calculate the volume and surface area of the full-sized station using the volume and surface area of the model. Your first *guess* is that because the lengths on the model are $\frac{1}{20}$ the corresponding lengths of the full-sized station, both the volume and surface area of the model will be $\frac{1}{20}$ the volume and surface area of the full-sized station. Before you come to a final conclusion you decide to try out your guess on some shapes with volumes and surface areas you know how to calculate.

You choose three shapes to play the role of the full-sized station: a box, a cylinder, and a sphere. Then you make scale models of each, in which all the length measurements in the scale models are $\frac{1}{20}$ the lengths of the originals.

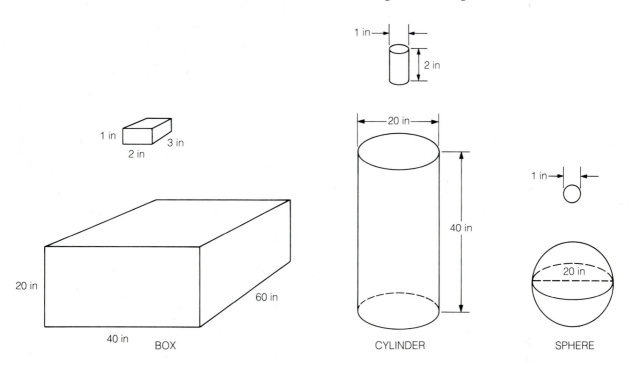

BOX   CYLINDER   SPHERE

Then you figure out the volumes and surface areas of each and tabulate your results.

SHAPE	VOLUME OF ORIGINAL (CUBIC INCHES)	VOLUME OF SCALE MODEL (CUBIC INCHES)	SURFACE AREA OF ORIGINAL (SQUARE INCHES)	SURFACE AREA OF SCALE MODEL (SQUARE INCHES)
Box	48,000	6	8800	22
Cylinder	12,566.37	1.57	3141.59	7.85
Sphere	4188.79	.52	1256.64	3.14

You think: "That's interesting. For each shape, the volume of the original is *not* 20 times the volume of the scale model. And the surface area of the original is *not* 20 times the surface area of the scale model. In fact, for the box, the volume of the original box is 8000 times the volume of the scale model; and the surface area of the original is 400 times that of the scale model. The same happens with the other shapes. The volume of the original is 8000 times the volume of the scale model, and the surface area of the original is 400 times that of the scale model. If the same relationship holds with the full-sized space station and its scale model (where the lengths of the scale model are $\frac{1}{20}$ those of the original), then the volume of the full-sized station will be equal to 8000 times the volume of the scale model, and the surface area of the full-sized station will be equal to 4000 times the surface area of the scale model."

The Mathematical Idea: Volume and Surface Area of Similar Shapes

In the second space station problem we looked at a pair of *similar* three-dimensional shapes (one shape is a scale model of the other) in which the ratio of a length in the larger shape to the corresponding length in the smaller is 20 to 1. We were interested in comparing the surface areas of the two shapes and also the volumes and concluded that the ratio of the surface area of the large shape to the small one is 400 to 1 and that the ratio of the volume of the large to the small is 8000 to 1. In general, for two similar three-dimensional shapes, how do the surface areas compare and how do the volumes compare?

To figure out an answer, take two similar shapes. Assume that the ratio of a length measured in the one to a corresponding length in the other is K to 1. (In the second space station problem $K = 20$; K could also be a number less than 1.) Thus, a length in the first is K times the corresponding length in the second. In fact, let's take a couple of pairs of similar shapes with the same ratio of lengths.

1. BOX

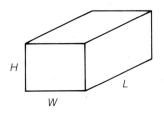

$$\text{Volume} = HWL$$
$$\text{Surface area} = 2HW + 2HL + 2WL$$

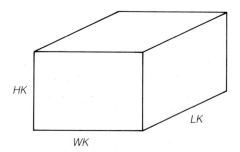

$$\text{Volume} = (HK)(WK)(LK)$$
$$= HWLK^3$$
$$\text{Surface area} = 2(HK)(WK) + 2(HK)(LK) + 2(WK)(LK)$$
$$= 2K^2(HW + HL + LW)$$

2. SPHERE

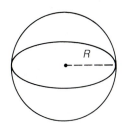

$$\text{Volume} = \frac{4}{3}\pi R^3$$

$$\text{Surface area} = 4\pi R^2$$

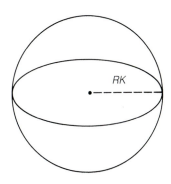

$$\text{Volume} = \frac{4}{3}\pi (RK)^3$$

$$= \frac{4}{3}\pi R^3 K^3$$

$$\text{Surface area} = 4\pi (RK)^2$$

$$= 4\pi R^2 K^2$$

These calculations suggest a rule.

RATIOS OF SURFACE AREAS AND VOLUMES FOR SIMILAR SHAPES

Take two similar three-dimensional shapes such that the ratio of corresponding lengths of one to the other is K to 1. Then the ratio of surface area of one to the other is K^2 to 1. The ratio of the volume of one to the other is K^3 to 1.

Notice that our calculations also suggest that something can be said about comparing the areas of two similar shapes in a plane.

THE HOUSE-HEATING PROBLEM

You work for the Environmental Research Center and are conducting an experiment on heat loss in residential homes. You are particularly interested in determining a house size and shape that will minimize loss of heat. You are performing experiments on a small, one-room house, pictured. You want to know what you can use from your results to predict heat loss for a larger house similar to your experimental house, with corresponding lengths double those of the experimental house.

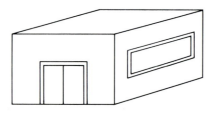

A Solution to the House-Heating Problem

You know that heat is measured in *calories,* 300 cal being the amount of energy needed to raise the temperature of 1 m³ of air 1°C. The output of a furnace or heater is also measured in calories per unit of time. The *heat content* of the building is

$$\text{(Temperature of air)} \times \text{(volume of building in m}^3) \times 300.$$

You also know that heat is lost through the walls (including the roof) of the building. For a given type of wall (thickness and material used will determine the type), *heat loss L* is so many calories per second for every square meter of wall surface.

Total heat loss for house $= L \times$ surface area (in m²) of outer walls of house

Finally, since you are looking at houses of different shapes and sizes, you are interested in *heat loss per cubic meter.* It is this last quantity that you want to make small. This quantity can be expressed as

$$\text{Heat loss per cubic meter} = \frac{\text{total heat loss for house}}{\text{volume of house}}$$

$$= \frac{L \times \text{surface area of outside walls of house}}{\text{volume of house}}.$$

You think: "Since L depends only on the nature of the wall, to make heat loss per cubic meter small, all I need to do is make the ratio of surface area to volume small. The better of two houses will be the one with the smaller ratio of surface area to volume. A house with lengths double the corresponding lengths of a similar experimental house has surface area 4 times that of the experimental house and volume 8 times that of the experimental house. So we have

$$\text{Heat loss per cubic meter} \atop \text{(for large house)} = \frac{L \times \text{surface area of walls of large house}}{\text{volume of large house}}$$

$$= \frac{L \times 4 \times \text{surface area of walls of small house}}{8 \times \text{volume of small house}}$$

$$= \frac{L \times \text{surface area of walls of small house}}{2 \times \text{volume of small house}}$$

$$= \frac{1}{2} \times \text{heat loss per m}^3 \text{ (for small house)}.$$

If I multiply the dimensions of the experimental house by K, the heat loss of the resulting building per cubic meter will be $1/K$ as much as the experimental house. That means: Build big for less heat loss per unit volume."

20.6   LOOKING AHEAD: ON BEING THE RIGHT SIZE

Since heat loss is also important for living creatures, the ratio of the surface area of a living creature to its volume is also an important quantity. There are other ways in which the volume and surface area of a creature and the cross-sectional area of the creature's bones or other structural elements are important for the creature's functioning and survival. Many of these are discussed in a provocative article by J. B. S. Haldane, "On Being the Right Size."*

- Weight (of the creature) is *proportional* to its volume; that is, weight = some fixed number × volume. Thus, a giant person all of whose length measurements are twice those of a normal person will have weight 8 times that of the normal person.

- A given bone can support so many pounds per square inch of cross-sectional area (think of a bone as a cylinder; its cross-sectional area is the area of a circular end). Bone material can support so many pounds per square inch. What a specific bone *can* support is proportional to its cross-sectional area. What the bone *must* support is the weight of the creature. The latter is proportional to the creature's volume. For example, suppose that a normal person 6 ft tall weighing 200 lb has a leg bone with diameter 2 in. The cross-sectional area of the bone would be 3.14 in². Suppose also that he can support at most 500 lb of additional weight before the bone caves in. Thus, the material in his leg bone supports a maximum of 223 lb/in². A giant person with all length measurements 4 times those of the normal person will have a leg bone with diameter 8 in and cross-sectional area 50.25 in². The giant's bone will support 50.23 × 223 ≈ 11,209 lb. However, the giant will weigh 12,800 lb— 64 times the normal person's weight. The giant's bone would be crushed by his own weight.

- The amount of water that clings to a creature after taking a "bath" is proportional to its surface area. The amount the creature is *able* to carry is proportional to its weight. For example, a normal adult person (weight 130 lb) getting out of the

---

* In J. R. Newman, ed., *The World of Mathematics,* Simon & Schuster, New York, 1956, pp. 952–957.

bathtub will be covered with a film of water about $\frac{1}{50}$ in thick. This film weighs about 1 lb. A midget person all of whose length measurements are $\frac{1}{200}$ the normal person's will weigh $130/200^3 \cong 0.000016$ lb and, on getting out of the bathtub, will be covered with a film of water weighing $1/200^2 = 0.000025$ lb. The weight of this film of water is almost twice the weight of the midget. It would be very difficult for the midget to get out of the tub!

■ For a creature that has lungs, the quantity of oxygen per breath that can be absorbed in its bloodstream is proportional to the surface area of its lungs. At the same time, the quantity of oxygen it needs is proportional to its weight. For example, a giant person whose linear measurements are 3 times those of a normal person will have 27 times as much blood as the normal person but will have lungs with only 9 times as much surface area. Thus the giant has $\frac{1}{3}$ the capacity of the normal person for absorbing oxygen into his bloodstream.

EXERCISE 7. What would happen if all a person's linear dimensions were to be doubled? Compare a giant person with a normal person in these aspects: ability to retain heat, ability to walk, and ability to supply oxygen to his blood.

20.7   SUMMARY OF IMPORTANT IDEAS AND TECHNIQUES

■ Comparing the volume of a triangular pyramid to the volume of a triangular prism of same height and base

■ Triangular pyramids with same base and height having the same volume

■ Formula for the volume of a triangular pyramid

■ Formula for the volume of triangular pyramid used to find formulas for the volumes of a cone and other pyramids and a formula relating volume and surface area of a sphere

■ Relationship of the volume of a cone to the volume of a hemisphere used to find a formula for the volume of a sphere

■ Formula for the surface area of a sphere

■ Cavalieri's principle for finding volumes

■ Relationship between volumes and surface areas of two similar three-dimensional shapes

■ Implications for living creatures of the effects of scale

PROBLEM SET

PRACTICING
SKILLS

1. A silo is a cylinder topped by a cone. If the cylinder is 5 ft high with a diameter of 4 ft and the cone has a height of 3 ft, what is its volume?

2. A monument honoring the town's veterans of the Vietnam War is to be erected in Central Square. It will be a rectangular column topped by a pyramid and will be built of reinforced concrete. The column will have a base 3 by 2 ft and be 15 ft high; the pyramid will have a height of 4 ft. What is the volume of concrete that will go into constructing the monument?

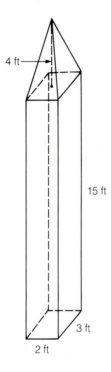

4 ft

15 ft

3 ft

2 ft

3. You are making concrete fence posts for a decorative fence around your lawn. There will be 10 posts, each a cylinder with a hemispherical top. (You will hang a large chain between each post.) Each post will be 90 cm tall and have a diameter of 45 cm. How many cubic meters of concrete will you need to make the fence posts?

4. An ice-cream manufacturer wants to market her new snack in an unusual shape. She has decided to make it in the shape of a sheared cone with a stick handle extending from the base. If the base is a circle of radius 2 in and she wants a total volume of approximately 12.6 in^3 of ice cream, what should the height of the cone be?

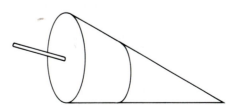

5. You have just received a shipment of 2- by 4-in boards of length 6 ft that has shifted from its original shape to form a sheared rectangular pile. The invoice says that the total amount of wood

in the pile should be 120 ft³. You want to check this. You can see that there are 18 horizontal layers of boards. How many 2 by 4s should there be in all and how many in each layer?

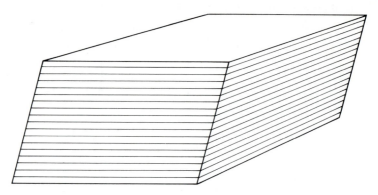

6. Ohio Smith is trapped in a watertight room in the Temple of Defeat with water being pumped into the room at ground level from a 100 ft³ tank that he knows is only half full. Quickly he measures the room. It has a square base 4½ ft on a side and is in the shape of a pyramid with one corner edge making a right angle with the floor. The room peaks 9½ ft up. Ohio can tread water and displaces 6 ft³ of water. Will he survive or will he drown?

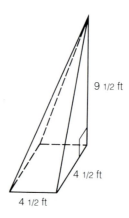

9 1/2 ft

4 1/2 ft

4 1/2 ft

7. A rectangular tank with base 3 by 4 ft and height 12 ft is filled with water to a depth of 4 ft. An iron ball with diameter of 2 ft is dropped into the tank.
   (a) What is the volume of the ball?
   (b) How much will the water rise?

8. You have a cylindrical bin 90 cm in diameter and 180 cm high in which you have been storing grain. Until now it has been adequate, but you anticipate that this year's crop will yield 3 times as much grain as the bin will hold. You want a new cylindrical tank that will hold this year's crop and have the same ratio of height to diameter as your present tank. What are the dimensions of the new tank?

9. A spherical balloon is being filled with helium. Find its volume when the radius is 8 cm. If the radius is increased to 24 cm, how many times larger is the volume than when the radius was 8 cm?

10. Prefab Crating Company constructed a shipping crate in the shape of a cube when it realized that someone had misread the dimensions of the requested crate. The constructed crate has side length 20 ft, but the invoice requested a crate of 2 ft. How many times too large in volume is the constructed crate?

11. In the local store, you find two different cans of juice, but the volumes are unmarked. You notice that the smaller can has a diameter two-thirds as big as the larger can, is the same height, and costs half as much. Which can of juice costs least per unit of volume?

12. A conical tank is filled with oil to the 1.5-m level. If the base of the tank is 2.4 m in diameter and the tank is 2.7 m tall, how much oil is in the tank?

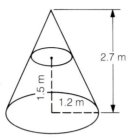

13. A conical reservoir, with apex in the ground, is filled with water to a depth of 8 ft. The tank itself has a depth of 10 ft and a radius of 5 ft. How much more water can be added to the tank?

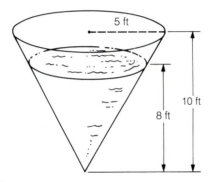

14. A bunch of the triangular prisms shown on the left (below) has been assembled to form the large prism in the middle. Each triangular prism has a volume of 15 m³.
    (a) What is the volume of the large prism?
    (b) The pyramid on the right has a base the same size and shape as the large prism and is the same height. What is its volume?

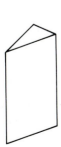 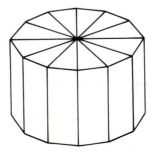 

Write the solution to each of the remaining problems carefully and clearly in the form of an essay. In it mention the steps you took to solve the problem, the principles, tools, or formulas you used, other problems or solutions that gave you ideas, and the problem-solving strategies you found helpful.

15. How much sand is there in a conical sandpile with a circumference at the bottom of 44 ft and with a height of 4 ft?

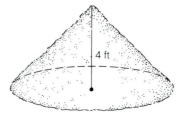

16. When the rain gauge is full, it indicates that 1 in of rain has fallen. It rained last night, and the gauge is filled up to the mark shown, which is halfway down the side of the gauge. How much rain fell last night?

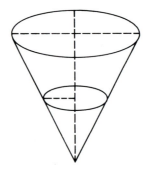

17. A serving dish, to be made out of stainless steel, is a cylinder with a hemisphere scooped out of the top. To find out how much stainless steel is used in the finished dish, you need to know its volume. Using the dimensions given, find out.

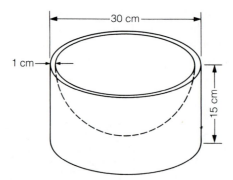

18. Each pattern assembles into a three-dimensional shape. Find the surface area and volume of each one. (You might want to trace copies of the patterns so that you can cut them out and assemble them.)

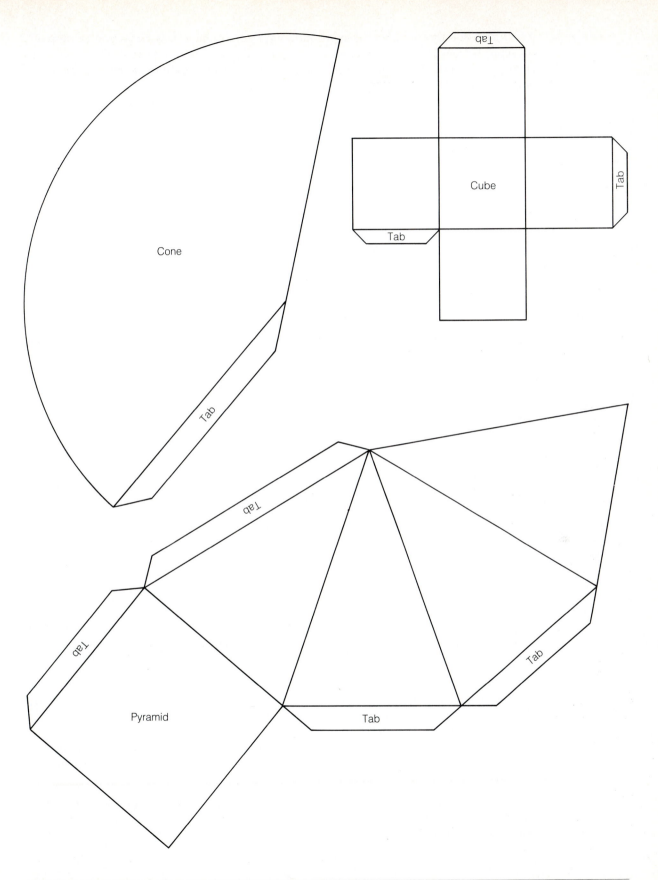

Cone

Cube

Tab

Tab

Tab

Pyramid

Tab

Tab

Tab

Tab

19. A bathysphere is used for deep-sea exploration. Typically, one person occupies this "submarine." Air supplied from a boat on the surface of the water fills the bathysphere through a hose. If the air hose were suddenly cut, how long could a person in a bathysphere survive? (A human being needs 3 ft³/min of air to survive.)

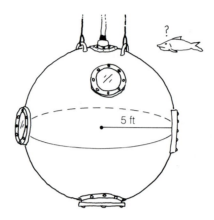

5 ft

20. Kitchenware, Inc., is considering manufacturing a new soup cooker.
     (a) A good serving of soup is 250 ml. How many servings of soup would the hemispherical soup cooker hold?

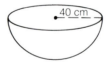

40 cm

     (b) The cost of the stainless steel sheeting to make the soup cooker is $10/100 cm². What would be the total cost of the sheeting needed to make the cooker?

21. An aluminum sphere for a liquified natural gas tanker has an inside diameter of about 36.6 m and an outside diameter of 37 m. What is the volume of aluminum used in making such a sphere?

22. Refer to section 20.6 as you work through this problem.
     (a) Estimate the surface area and the volume of your body. (You may want to make some simplifying assumptions in your estimation, for example, your arms and legs are cylinders and your head is a sphere.)
     (b) Calculate the surface area per pound weight for your body.
     (c) Suppose all the linear dimensions of your body were multiplied by 10. What would your surface area be? What would your weight be? What would the surface area per pound of weight be?

23. The Union 76 station has contracted you to paint its sign and pole. The sign is a sphere with a diameter of 6 ft on top of a pole 20 ft high and 1 ft in diameter. Estimate the total surface area you will have to paint.

24. Each model of a prefabricated storage shed has a large door (costing $20) and three windows (costing $10 each). Wall material costs $5/ft²; roofing material costs $7.50/ft². Find the cost of materials and the volume for each model. Find the cost of materials per unit volume for each model. Which shed is the most economical to build? Discuss.

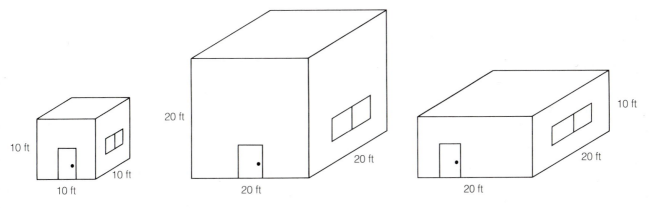

25. A cylindrical tank with diameter 1.2 m and height 3.6 m is filled with water to a depth of 1.2 m. An iron ball with diameter 0.9 m is dropped into the tank. How much will the water rise?

26. A playground toy is to be made in the shape of a cylinder with a hemisphere on each end. Children will climb on it and roll it. The cylinder will be 3 ft long and have a radius of 1 ft; each hemisphere will have a radius of 2½ ft.

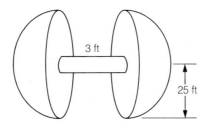

(a) The toy will be constructed out of resin. How much resin will be needed?

(b) The toy will also have to be painted. What will the surface area of the toy be?

27. Discuss the statement "Small cups of tea cool more quickly."

28. You have a madman for a science instructor. He has given you an assignment.

(a) Compare the area of the cross section of a cylindrical bone having a radius of r centimeters with that of a cylindrical bone of radius $r + 2$ cm. Compare the cross-sectional area of a cylindrical bone with radius r with that of a cylindrical bone of radius $2r$.

(b) The ability of a bone to support weight is proportional to the area of its cross section. If a youngster's bone has a radius r, to what radius must it grow so that it can support twice the weight that it can now?

(c) Imagine that all King Kong's linear dimensions are 10 times a normal ape's. Why is this King Kong not possible in real life?

(d) Why does an elephant require thicker legs (proportionally) than a flea?

29. You are designing a cone-shaped cup that is to hold 200 ml of a frozen custard dessert. You want to know what its dimensions (radius and height) should be to minimize the amount of material used to make the cone. This is a problem for a computer. It might be helpful to develop a formula for the surface area of a cone using ideas in the solution to the rocket nose cone problem from chapter 18.

PROBABILITY: MAKING DECISIONS IN THE FACE OF UNCERTAINTY

21

CHAPTER

Should you spend money to dig an oil well even though you know you might not strike oil? Should you pay money for an advertisement even though you are not sure how successful it will be? Should you undergo a certain treatment for your illness even though you know it might not be successful? These questions reflect the fact that the results of certain actions (digging a well, placing an ad, taking a treatment) are uncertain. In this chapter we will discuss a framework for dealing with actions the exact outcomes of which we cannot predict ahead of time. This framework involves the interplay of a set of interrelated concepts: the *experiment* and its set of *outcomes* and a number, called a *probability,* associated with the subset of outcomes satisfying a certain condition. All these concepts will be based on our own natural uses of the sentence, "The chances that such and such will happen are . . ."

For each dilemma—whether to dig the well, whether to place the ad, whether to take the treatment—the deciding factor may be the answer to a question such as one of these: What would I gain in the long run? How much would I lose in the long run? We will use the concept of *expected value* together with the concepts of experiment, outcome, and probability to answer such questions. The answers will be used to help decide which step to take,

even though the outcomes are not certain.

A type of experiment with uncertain result that we will deal with is one for which any one outcome is as likely as any other. Flipping a coin is a simple example of such an experiment; of its 2 outcomes—heads and tails—each is assumed to be just as likely to occur as another. Rolling a die is another example; of its 6 outcomes—1 spot, 2 spots, and so on—each is assumed to be just as likely to occur as another.

Flipping several coins is also an example of an experiment with uncertain result, but it doesn't seem to be an activity for which there is much interest, except perhaps with people who like to gamble. However, it turns out that other experiments with uncertain results are so very much like flipping coins that we say that flipping coins *models* those experiments. We will look carefully at the experiment of flipping several coins and describe its outcomes in such a way that one outcome is as likely as another outcome. Calculating probabilities for this experiment will require some clever counting. *Pascal's triangle* will help us with this.

Finally, we will use the fact that flipping several coins models several important experiments in order to create a second device for making decisions called *hypothesis testing.*

The governor has just set up a lottery and wants to use the revenues to help fund the state's educational system. In this lottery, every Saturday night, balls labeled from 1 through 1,000,000 are placed in a large barrel and thoroughly stirred. One ball is selected by the blindfolded governor, who reads the winning number for the week from the ball. All during that week, citizens of the state buy tickets entitling them to register guesses for the winning number at their local convenience store. It costs $1 for each ticket (and subsequent guess). If you guess the winning number, then you win $100,000 (minus the $1 you paid for the ticket). Otherwise you lose your dollar.

The governor wants to make sure that this scheme will actually bring in money to the state and has asked the lottery staff to figure out how much the state will earn. Members of the staff realize that the lottery's earnings will vary from week to week. In some weeks there may be no winner, in which case the lottery takes in all the money from the tickets; in other weeks several people may guess the winning number, and the lottery may take in less than it gives out. They decide that a reasonable measure of earnings would be the amount they earn per ticket or, rather—since the earnings for each ticket vary—the *average* earnings per ticket. Then, since they anticipate selling a lot of tickets, the lottery's total earnings would be the number of tickets sold times the average earnings per ticket.

To figure the average earnings per ticket, they think: "Suppose a person's guess is the number 1. In the barrel is the ball labeled 1. Since the balls in the barrel are stirred well, we assume that the governor would draw ball 1 from the barrel about once every million times. For this guess, .000001 of the time the lottery would lose $99,999 and .999999 of the time would gain $1. So, if the drawing were to take place many times, the earnings (to the lottery) of guess 1 would be

$$-(.000001)(\$99,\!999) + (.999999)(\$1) = -\$.099999 + \$.999999$$
$$= \$.90.$$

There is nothing special about guess 1. The same analysis would work for any other guess. That means that in the long run the lottery would earn $ .90 for every lottery ticket. That's not bad."

The Mathematical Idea: Experiments, Outcomes, and Simple Probabilities

In the lottery problem, a million balls are stirred and a blindfolded governor draws one of them. This *experiment* has a million possible *outcomes,* namely, the different balls with labels from 1 through 1,000,000. Which ball will she draw? You know that the outcome is uncertain. But the way the drawing takes place (thoroughly stirred balls, blindfolded governor) you say that *it is just as likely that she will draw one ball as it is that she will draw another.* Another way of saying this is that the ball is selected *at random.* Will the governor draw ball 1? You don't know for sure, but you say that the *chance* the governor will draw ball 1 is 1 in a million, meaning that, roughly, a millionth of the time she will draw ball 1. We also say that the *probability* of drawing ball 1 is the fraction 1/1,000,000. Here are more examples of experiments with uncertain but *equally* likely outcomes.

RAFFLE   The local Arts Consortium is having a raffle to raise money. The prize from the raffle is to be a new Chevrolet; the consortium has sold 1000 tickets. The ticket stubs have been placed in a hat. The *experiment* is to select a stub at random to determine the winner. The possible *outcomes* are the 1000 different stubs. Since a stub is selected at random, the 1000 possible outcomes are *equally likely*. The *probability* that your stub is selected is $\frac{1}{1000}$.

FLIPPING A COIN   The *experiment* is flipping a coin; the possible *outcomes* are heads and tails. You assume that the coin is an ordinary one that has not been tampered with so that the two outcomes are *equally likely*. (A coin that has not been tampered with is frequently called a *fair,* or *balanced,* coin.) The probability that the outcome is heads is $\frac{1}{2}$.

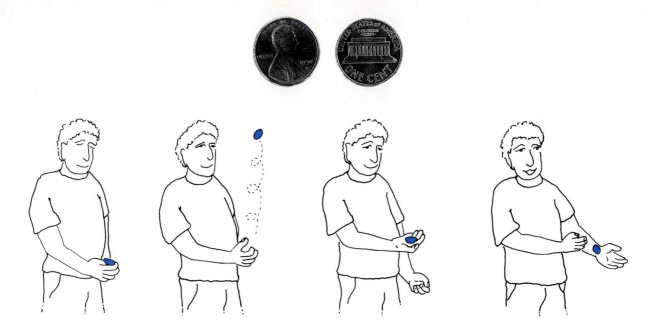

ROULETTE   The American roulette wheel illustrated has slots labeled from 1 through 36 plus slots labeled 0 and 00. When the wheel is spun, a ball emerging from the center of the wheel will eventually land in one of the 38 slots. The *experiment* is spinning the wheel, and the *outcomes* are the 38 different slots. We assume that the roulette wheel is "fair," or "balanced," so that it is as likely for the ball to land in any one of the 38 slots as it is for it to land in any other. The outcomes are *equally likely*. Thus, the probability that the ball lands in slot 17 is equal to the fraction $\frac{1}{38}$.

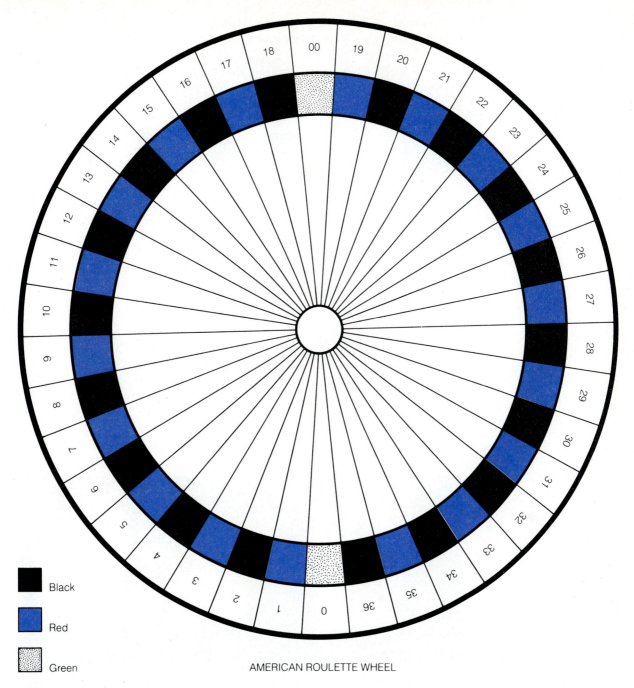

	Black
	Red
	Green

AMERICAN ROULETTE WHEEL

The general situation is the following.

PROBABILITY OF A SINGLE OUTCOME FOR AN EXPERIMENT
WITH EQUALLY LIKELY OUTCOMES

Suppose that an experiment has N equally likely outcomes. Then the *probability* that a particular outcome occurs is $1/N$.

---

1. The experiment is rolling a standard, balanced die (*die* is the singular form of *dice*). The outcomes are the 6 different faces that appear on top when the die comes to rest. (These are 1, 2, 3, 4, 5, or 6 spots.) *Balanced* means that these outcomes are equally likely. What is the probability that the outcome from a balanced die is 4 (spots)?

Faces of a standard die

Standard die

2. The experiment is drawing a card from a standard, well-shuffled, 52-card deck. What are the outcomes? By *well-shuffled* you mean that the outcomes are equally likely; that is, the draw is at random. What is the probability that you draw the ace of hearts from a well-shuffled deck? (A standard 52-card deck has four suits of 13 cards each. The suits are clubs, diamonds, hearts, and spades. Each suit consists of an ace (A), king (K), queen (Q), jack (J), 10, 9, 8, 7, 6, 5, 4, 3, and 2.)

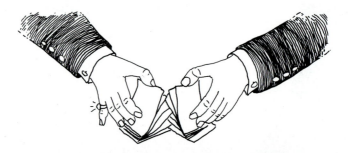

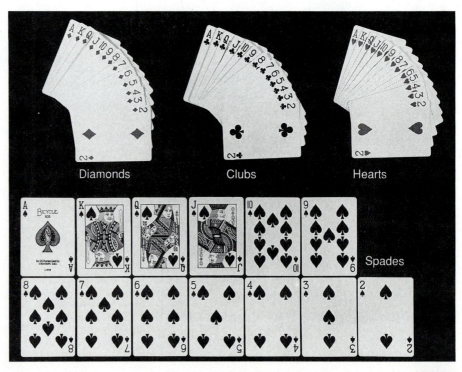

Diamonds   Clubs   Hearts

Spades

You know that the probability that your ticket will win the raffle described earlier is $\frac{1}{1000}$. You and some friends (20 in all) make a pact. You decide to buy 20 tickets and agree that if one of the 20 tickets wins, you will share the winnings equally among yourselves. This time you say that there are 20 chances in 1000 that one of the 20 stubs is drawn, meaning that if the experiment were repeated many times, roughly $\frac{20}{1000}$ of them would have an outcome consisting of the selection of one of the 20 stubs.

The Mathematical Idea: Probability That an Outcome Satisfies a Certain Condition

In the raffle problem, $\frac{20}{1000}$ of the time one of the 20 chosen stubs will be drawn. The fraction $\frac{20}{1000}$ is also called the *probability* that one of the 20 stubs will be drawn. Earlier we discussed the probability of a particular outcome—for example, the probability that *your* stub will be drawn in the 1000-ticket raffle. Now we are dealing with the probability that an outcome satisfies a more general condition. In the raffle problem the more general condition is that the outcome is one of the 20 stubs. The definition of such a probability is the following.

DEFINITION OF *EQUALLY LIKELY PROBABILITY*

If all the outcomes of an experiment are equally likely, then the *probability* that a given outcome will satisfy a certain condition is equal to the fraction

$$\text{\textit{Probability} that the condition is satisfied} = \frac{\text{number of outcomes that satisfy the condition}}{\text{number of possible outcomes to the experiment}}.$$

Notice that, from the definition, the smallest a probability can be is 0, and the largest it can be is 1.

Let's look at some examples of the uses of this definition.

LOTTERY You decide to buy 100 tickets (and make 100 different guesses). You want to know your chances for winning something. This is the same as the probability that one of your 100 guesses will be the winning number. The condition is "draw a number that is included in one of the 100 guesses." The probability can be calculated.

$$\text{\textit{Probability} that the condition is satisfied} = \frac{\text{number of outcomes that satisfy the condition}}{\text{number of possible outcomes to the experiment}}$$

$$= \frac{100}{1,000,000} = .0001.$$

CARDS You draw a card from a standard 52-card deck. You want to know the probability that you will draw an ace. The condition to be satisfied is "the card you have drawn is an ace." The outcomes that satisfy this condition are: ace of hearts, ace of clubs, ace of spades, ace of diamonds. Thus, 4 outcomes satisfy the condition. There are 52 outcomes in all. Consequently,

$$\text{Probability that the card drawn is an ace} = \frac{4}{52} \cong .077.$$

ROULETTE The croupier is about to spin the roulette wheel. You decide to place a bet on all the numbers 15, 16, 17, 18, and 19. You want to know the probability that the ball will land in a slot having one of these numbers. The condition is "the ball will land in one of slots 15 through 19." There are 38 outcomes in all. Thus,

$$\text{Probability that the ball will land in one of slots } 15\text{–}19 = \frac{5}{38} \cong .132.$$

EXERCISES 3. The experiment is rolling a standard, balanced die. What is the probability that the outcome is an even number of spots?

4. The experiment is drawing a card from a standard, well-shuffled, 52-card deck. What is the probability that you draw either an ace, a king, or a queen?

5. In the American roulette wheel the slots 1, 3, 5, . . . , 35 are colored red, and the slots 2, 4, 6, . . . , 36 are colored black. In a gambling casino you can bet on red (or on black). What is the probability that the ball will wind up in a red slot?

THE OIL WELL PROBLEM

An investment firm is reassessing its program of investing in oil wells in a certain part of the country. It knows that investing in a single well at a given location is always risky. Oil might be struck, and the firm would get a lot of money. On the other hand, there might be no oil at all, and the firm would lose all the money it invested in the well.

To help in its reassessment, members of the staff have gathered some data. It costs $100,000 to dig a well in this part of the country. If oil is struck, the well will yield oil worth $1,500,000. They have found that 120 wells have been drilled in the region and that only 12 of them produced oil.

A Solution to the Oil Well Problem

They reason in the following way. "The fraction of success in drilling wells has been $\frac{12}{120}$, or $\frac{1}{10}$. If that trend were to continue, then whenever we drilled a well, $\frac{1}{10}$ of the time we would earn $1,400,000 ($1,500,000 minus the initial investment of $100,000), and $\frac{9}{10}$ of the time we would lose $100,000. In the long run, if we invest in a lot of wells, we should earn the following amount for each well:

$$\frac{1}{10}(\$1,400,000) - \frac{9}{10}(\$100,000) = \$140,000 - \$90,000$$

$$= \$50,000.$$

That's not too bad: $50,000 per well. That's a return of 50%. But we'd have to invest in a lot of wells."

The Mathematical Idea: Estimated Probability

In the oil well problem the investment firm was interested in knowing the chances of success in drilling an individual well. To pursue the problem, it looked at past experience with wells and found that of 120 wells that had been drilled in the region 12 were producers. The ratio of successful to total wells was $\frac{12}{120}$, or $\frac{1}{10}$. The firm felt the wells it was considering drilling in the future to be no different from those in the past and that the chances for success of a future well should be no different from the chances of success for a past well. Twelve successes out of 120 would be what you'd expect if the probability of success were $\frac{1}{10}$. The fraction $\frac{1}{10}$ is what is called an *estimated probability*.

ESTIMATED PROBABILITY

Suppose you repeat an experiment N times and the outcomes of K of them satisfy a certain condition. Then

$$\textit{Estimated probability that the condition is satisfied} = \frac{K}{N}.$$

Notice that an estimated probability must be greater than or equal to 0 and less than or equal to 1.

Examples of estimated probabilities can be found in merchant advertising, medicine, and retail sales.

ADVERTISING   You are in business and are rethinking your policy of buying advertisements in the local paper. You know that a successful ad tends to increase your profits but also that when an ad is not successful you will be out the cost of the ad. To decide what your policy should be, you estimate the probability that an ad will be successful. You find that you have placed an ad 50 times in the local paper and that, of these, 30 were successful. The estimated probability that an ad will be successful is $\frac{30}{50}$, or $\frac{3}{5}$.

MEDICINE   You are a doctor. You treat patients with a certain disease. One treatment is not always successful. In fact, in a recent study 840 patients were treated, and for 168 of these the treatment was successful; for the other 672 the treatment was not successful. You estimate the probability that a particular use of the treatment will be successful to be $\frac{168}{840}$, or $\frac{1}{5}$.

MAKING PURCHASES   In a study of a sporting goods store, it was found that out of 348 customers who parked in the store's parking lot, 287 made at least one purchase, whereas of 518 customers who did not use the parking lot, 305 made purchases. You want to know the probability that a customer who uses the parking lot will make a purchase. Here the experiment is selecting at random customers who have used the parking lot. The condition is "making a purchase." Thus,

Estimated probability that a purchase will be
made by a customer using the parking lot

$$= \frac{\text{number of experiments with outcome satisfying condition}}{\text{total number of times experiment performed}}$$

$$= \frac{287}{348} \cong .82.$$

You may also want to know the probability that a purchase will be made by a customer not using the store's parking lot. In this case the experiment is selecting at random a customer not using the store's parking lot and the condition is the same as before—"making a purchase." Thus,

Estimated probability that a purchase will be
made by a customer not using the parking lot

$$= \frac{\text{number of experiments with outcome satisfying condition}}{\text{total number of times experiment performed}}$$

$$= \frac{305}{518} \cong .59.$$

EXERCISES
6. A county permits a limited amount of hunting of antelope in order that the size of the herd be controlled. Last year 1000 hunting licenses were issued, each hunter was permitted to kill only 1 antelope, and 160 antelopes were killed. Estimate the probability that a given hunter will kill an antelope.

7. A study of newspaper records indicates that snow has been on the ground on Christmas Day in a certain northern city in 60 of the past 75 years. Estimate the probability that the city will have a white Christmas this year.

21.2   EXPECTED VALUE

In the lottery problem we attached a value to each outcome of the experiment (of drawing a number from 1 through 1,000,000 at random): a loss of $99,999 (= amount paid out [$100,000] minus amount taken in [$1]) if the draw is the same as the ticket's guess and a gain of $1 if it isn't. The probability of a loss is 1/1,000,000, and the probability of a gain is 999,999/1,000,000, meaning that roughly 1/1,000,000 of the time the state will lose $99,999 and 999,999/1,000,000 of the time will gain $1. From this we figured that the average amount the state earns per ticket is

$$-(.000001)(\$99,999) + (.999999)(\$1) = -\$.099999 + \$.99999 = \$.90.$$

This is called the *expected value* of the experiment (from the point of view of the lottery, of course).

In the oil well problem we also attached a certain value in dollars to each outcome of the experiment (of drilling a well). For each well that is successful, we earn a net of $1,400,000 (= income minus cost of digging the well); for each well that is not successful we lose $100,000 (= cost of digging well). Since the (estimated) probability of a successful well is $\frac{1}{10}$ and the (estimated) probability of an unsuccessful well is $\frac{9}{10}$, we figured that if a lot of wells were drilled we should earn roughly the following amount for each well:

$$\frac{1}{10}(\$1,400,000) - \frac{9}{10}(\$100,000) = \$140,000 - \$90,000$$

$$= \$50,000.$$

Again, this is the *expected value* of drilling a well based on the estimated probabilities. This is the amount you expect to earn from each well, *on the average.*

The general situation is this. You have an experiment such that value A is assigned to some of the outcomes and value B to the rest.

The concept of expected value has relevance in a number of experiments.

ROULETTE   A standard way to play American roulette is to bet on a number (from 1 through 36). You pay $1 to play and win $37 if the ball lands in your slot; otherwise, you get nothing back. The value associated with your number is +$36 (what you win minus what you paid to play the game), and the value associated with any other number is −$1. The value +$36 occurs with probability $\frac{1}{38}$ and the value −$1 occurs with probability $\frac{37}{38}$. The expected value (to you) of this experiment is

$$\frac{1}{38}\,(\$36) + \frac{37}{38}\,(-\$1) \sim -\$.026.$$

This means that if you play the game a lot, you can expect to lose $.026 for every dollar you bet. From the point of view of the casino, it will sometimes make $1 and sometimes lose $36; but on the average for every dollar bet it will make $.026.

ADVERTISING   You are still rethinking your policy of buying advertisements in the local paper for your business. A successful ad tends to increase your income by $900. However, with an unsuccessful ad you will lose $400, the cost of the ad. You have estimated that the probability that an ad is successful is $\frac{3}{5}$. To help decide what your policy should be, you decide to calculate the expected value of taking out an ad, which should be the average income per ad in the long run. The value $500 (= income of $900 minus cost of ad [$400]) occurs with probability $\frac{3}{5}$, and the value −$400 occurs with probability $\frac{2}{5}$. Thus,

$$\text{Expected value of taking out an ad} = \frac{3}{5}\,(\$500) + \frac{2}{5}\,(-\$400)$$

$$= \$300 - \$160$$

$$= \$140.$$

Since the expected value is positive, it makes sense to take out the ad. You will either make $500 or lose $400 on each ad, but on the average you will make $140.

EXERCISES

8. In Monte Carlo roulette, the wheel has 37 slots (instead of 38 slots, as for American roulette). The slots are equally spaced and numbered from 0 through 36. If a player makes a $1 bet on a positive number and the ball comes to rest in this slot, the croupier pays her $36. What is the expected value of the game to the player?

9. In this exercise the experiment has three, rather than two, values assigned to it. If the values are A, B, and C, then the expected value of the experiment is

A × probability that outcome has value A

$+ B$ × probability that outcome has value B

$+ C$ × probability that outcome has value C.

An insurance company charges a woman a premium of $150 for an accident insurance policy for the coming year. The policy will pay for one accident. If the policyholder has a major accident during the year, the company estimates that it will pay her $5000, and if she has a minor accident, $1000. (If there is no accident during the year, the company does not return the premium of $150.) Based on past experience with its customers, the company estimates that the probability she will have a minor accident is .08, and the probability she will have a major accident is .005. Thus, the probability she will have no accident is .915. What is the expected value of the insurance policy to the company (for the year)?

21.3   COIN TOSSING

THE SAMPLING PROBLEM   The Sun Light Company makes light bulbs. It does not test all the bulbs coming off the assembly line because it is too expensive. Instead, members of the staff test only a few of the bulbs that are produced in a given hour. (This procedure is called *sampling*.) They select at random five of the bulbs from an hour's production. If one or more of the five bulbs is defective, the company will take further action, such as sample more of that hour's production, throw out that hour's lot, cease production, or look for malfunctions in the assembly line. On the other hand, if none of the five bulbs is defective, then it assumes the whole lot is pretty much OK and sends the bulbs in that lot out for packing. You are in charge of this procedure and wonder how effective it really is. You imagine the following terrible scene. One hour, unbeknownst to the company, a worker sabotages the assembly line so that half the bulbs coming off the line are defective. You want to know how likely is it that this sabotage will go undetected; that is, you want to know the probability that the sampling procedure that hour will reveal no defective bulbs.

A Solution to the   In solving this problem, you think: "Testing a bulb is just like flipping a coin. For the
Sampling Problem   bulb testing there are 2 outcomes: defective (D) and not defective (ND). For the coin flipping there are 2 outcomes: heads (H) and tails (T). Furthermore, with the testing the 2 outcomes are equally likely, just as with flipping the coin: $P(D) = \frac{1}{2}$ and $P(ND) = \frac{1}{2}$; $P(H) = \frac{1}{2}$ and $P(T) = \frac{1}{2}$. (We have used some abbreviations here. For example, $P(D)$ is short for "probability that the bulb is defective.") That means that the experiment of testing five bulbs is just like the experiment of flipping five coins in succession and, if I let the outcome H correspond to the outcome D, then the probability that five bulbs will be defective will be the same as the probability that five coins will turn up heads."

We'll complete this solution later after analyzing more closely the flipping of many coins.

THE TELEVISION   You own six vacation cottages that you rent out by the week. You supply television
SET PROBLEM   sets at extra cost to renters who request them. You estimate that the probability that a family who rents a cottage will want a television set is .5. You own four sets. In a week in which all the cabins are rented, you want to know the answer to the following question: What is the probability that you will have enough sets to supply all the families that want one?

You think: "Asking a family that arrives at the cottages whether it wants a television set is just like flipping a coin. There are 2 outcomes: The family says yes (Y); or the family says no (N). The 2 outcomes are equally likely:

$$P(Y) = \frac{1}{2} \quad \text{and} \quad P(N) = \frac{1}{2}.$$

When the cottages are full, there are six families. That means that I ask the question about the television set six times in succession. That's like flipping six coins. The probability that there will be enough TVs is the same as the probability that four or fewer of the answers to my question are Y's. And, if Y's correspond to H's in coin flipping, that's the same as the probability of getting four or fewer heads in six tosses."

We'll also complete the solution to this problem after a closer analysis of coin tossing.

The Mathematical Idea: Using Coin Tossing to Model Other Experiments

The sampling problem and the television set problem have not been solved. However, we can solve them if we solve some problems related to coin tossing. In the sampling problem, selecting a bulb at random and seeing whether it is defective is like flipping a coin and seeing whether it comes up heads. In the television set problem, asking a family whether it wants a television and waiting for a response is also like flipping a coin and seeing whether it comes up heads. In both cases, tossing a coin *models* the real situation. Tossing five coins and observing heads and tails models selecting five bulbs at random and observing the defective and nondefective status of each bulb. Tossing six coins and observing heads and tails models asking each of six families whether it wants a television and observing its yes or no.

Solving the sampling and television set problems has been reduced to solving problems about tossing several coins. Many other problems can also be reduced to problems about tossing coins. In what follows we will develop a framework for tossing coins that will enable us to find probabilities related to coin tossing. First, we will look at the experiment of tossing two coins; after that we will look at the experiment of tossing three coins; and so on. We want to specify the outcomes of each experiment so that all its outcomes are equally likely, because we know (at least theoretically) how to find probabilities in such a situation. After that, we will have to figure out ways to count outcomes in order to compute the probability associated with a given condition.

Tossing One Coin

The possible outcomes are heads (H) and tails (T). The 2 outcomes are equally likely.

Tossing Two Coins

Suppose the result of the first toss is H. Then toss a second coin. The possible results of the second toss are H and T, and these are equally likely. So the outcomes HH (H on first coin, H on second) and HT (H on first coin, T on second) are equally likely; their probabilities must be the same.

A similar situation holds if the result of the first toss is T. You toss a second coin. The possible results of the second toss—H and T—are equally likely. Thus, TH (T on first coin, H on second) and TT (T on first coin, T on second) are equally likely; their probabilities must be the same.

Finally, any one of TH or TT is as likely as HH or HT. Thus, the 4 possibilities HH, HT, TH, and TT are equally likely. Since these 4 possibilities also adequately describe what happens when two coins are tossed, we call these the outcomes of tossing two coins. We can summarize these nicely in a tree diagram.

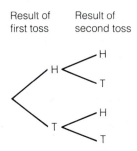

Result of first toss   Result of second toss

Each trip through the tree starting from its root (on the far left) and traveling along branches from left to right winds up at an end point of the tree. Think of the trip's highlights as the nodes of the branches, the results of tossing first one coin, then the next. Each end point of the tree corresponds to a different trip. If you keep track of the H's and T's that occurred on the trip (in order) and record what you get at the end, you will have written the symbol for an outcome of the experiment of tossing two coins.

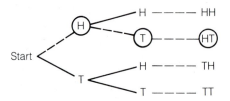

Now let's compute some probabilities using our previous definition of probability when the outcomes are equally likely.

■ Compute the probability that exactly one of the coins comes up H. The outcomes satisfying the condition are HT, TH. The 4 possible outcomes to the experiment are HH, HT, TH, and TT.

$$\text{Probability} = \frac{\text{number of outcomes satisfying condition}}{\text{number of outcomes to experiment}}$$

$$= \frac{2}{4} = \frac{1}{2}$$

■ Compute the probability that at least one of the coins is H. The outcomes satisfying the condition are HT, TH, and HH.

$$\text{Probability} = \frac{\text{number of outcomes satisfying condition}}{\text{number of outcomes to experiment}} = \frac{3}{4}$$

EXERCISES

10. Mr. and Mrs. Jones are now childless but plan to have two children. What is the probability that the two children will be the same sex? (Assume that having a male child is as likely as having a female child. Then model the sex of the two children by the toss of two coins.)

11. The Black Widows and the Tarantulas, evenly matched baseball teams, are playing a double-header. What is the probability that the Black Widows win both games? (*Evenly matched* means that each team is equally likely to win a game. Then model wins and losses for the Black Widows on the two games by the toss of two coins.)

Tossing Three Coins

As for two coins, we can draw a tree diagram for the experiment of tossing three coins.

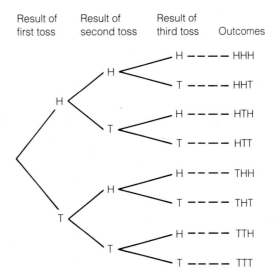

| Result of first toss | Result of second toss | Result of third toss | Outcomes |

Again, each end point of the tree corresponds to an outcome, and one outcome is as likely as another. Next to each end point we have listed the corresponding output symbolically. For example, the symbol HTT means H on the first coin, T on the second, and T on the third. Since there is a total of 8 outcomes, 8 will be the denominator when we compute a probability for three coins.

- Compute the probability that at least two of the coins come up H. The outcomes that satisfy the condition are HHH, HHT, HTH, and THH.

$$P(\text{at least two H}) = \frac{4}{8} = \frac{1}{2}$$

- Compute the probability that exactly one of the coins comes up H. The outcomes that satisfy the condition are HTT, THT, and TTH.

$$P(\text{exactly one H}) = \frac{3}{8}$$

EXERCISES

12. In the toss of three coins, what is the probability that at most two of the coins turn up heads?

13. Mr. and Mrs. Jones have changed their plans and now want to have three children. What is the probability that all three children will be the same sex? (*Hint:* Model this with the toss of three coins.)

14. Vila and Jensen are equally matched tennis players. In the first three sets of a match, what is the probability that no player wins all three? (*Hint:* Model this with the toss of three coins.)

Tossing Many Coins

To solve the sampling problem and the television set problem, we need to find the following probabilities associated with coin tossing: (1) probability that out of five coins tossed none is heads and (2) probability that out of six coins tossed four or fewer are heads.

To compute the first probability, we need to know

- The total number of outcomes to the experiment of tossing five coins.
- The number of outcomes satisfying the condition that none is heads.

To compute the second probability, we need to know

- The total number of outcomes in the experiment of tossing six coins.
- The number of outcomes satisfying the condition that four or fewer are heads.

We can calculate this last number in the following way:

Number of outcomes with four or fewer heads

= number of outcomes with exactly four heads

+ number of outcomes with exactly three heads

+ number of outcomes with exactly two heads

+ number of outcomes with exactly 1 head

+ number of outcomes with zero heads.

Thus, we can figure out both probabilities, provided we can figure out: the total number of outcomes to tossing N coins, and in tossing N coins, the number of outcomes with exactly M heads. To find this out, let's make a table showing what we know and what we can figure out from the trees we have drawn.

NO. OF COINS	TOTAL NO. OF OUTCOMES	NO. OF OUTCOMES WITH EXACTLY THIS MANY HEADS						
		0	1	2	3	4	5	6
1	2	1	1					
2	4	1	2	1				
3	8	1	3	3	1			
4	?	?	?	?	?	?		

The solution to one of our problems is easy. We can find the total number of outcomes for N tosses from the table and from the way we construct the tree diagrams.

TOTAL NUMBER OF OUTCOMES FOR N TOSSES

If N coins are tossed, then the total number of outcomes is 2^N.

Next, we must figure out the numbers in the other columns of our table.

Pascal's Triangle

Before figuring out the numbers in the other columns, let's make a few observations about the shape of the table we should obtain. First, in horizontal row 3 there are four numbers and in horizontal row 4 there are five numbers. In general, in row N there will be $N + 1$ numbers. Thus, the numbers in the table should form a triangle, called *Pascal's triangle*. The first three rows of Pascal's triangle are shown completed in the table.

Two numbers in each row of our table should be easy to figure out. If N coins are tossed, then the only outcome satisfying the condition of zero heads is

$$\underbrace{TTTTTTT \ldots T}_{N \text{ tails}}.$$

So the number of outcomes with zero heads is 1. Similarly, if N coins are tossed, the only outcome with N heads is

$$\underbrace{HHHHHH \ldots H}_{N \text{ heads}}.$$

So the number of outcomes with N heads is also 1. We can fill in more of the table.

NO. OF COINS	TOTAL NO. OF OUTCOMES	NO. OF OUTCOMES WITH EXACTLY THIS MANY HEADS						
		0	1	2	3	4	5	6
1	2	1	1					
2	4	1	2	1				
3	8	1	3	3	1			
4	16	1	?	?	?	1		
5	32	1	?	?	?	?	1	
6	64	1	?	?	?	?	?	1

Two additional numbers in each row are also easy to figure out. If N coins are tossed, the outcomes with exactly one head are

HTTTT ... T	H on the first toss
THTTT ... T	H on the second toss
TTHTT ... T	H on the third toss
⋮	
TTTT ... THT	H on the next-to-last $(N - 1)$ toss
TTTTT ... TH	H on the last (N) toss

There are N of these outcomes.

Similarly, if N coins are tossed the outcomes with exactly $N - 1$ heads are the same as the outcomes with exactly one tail. There are also N of these outcomes.

Thus we can fill in still more of the table.

NO. OF COINS	TOTAL NO. OF OUTCOMES	NO. OF OUTCOMES WITH EXACTLY THIS MANY HEADS						
		0	1	2	3	4	5	6
1	2	1	1					
2	4	1	2	1				
3	8	1	3	3	1			
4	16	1	4	?	4	1		
5	32	1	5	?	?	5	1	
6	64	1	6	?	?	?	6	1

To get a clue about how to figure out the other entries in the table, let's try to figure out the answer to the following question: Suppose four coins are tossed. How many outcomes with exactly two heads? Let's start making a list: HHTT, HTHT, HTTH, THHT, THTH, TTHH.

So far, 6 outcomes. Do we have them all? (How do we know the same outcome hasn't appeared twice? We can check this here, but it might be more difficult with a longer list.) We need to find a way we can figure out the outcomes with some assurance of completeness and of no duplication. Maybe we could figure out the *number* of outcomes without actually listing them all. Let's *break the problem up into simpler problems.* Look at the first coin tossed. There are 2 possibilities: Either the first coin tossed is H or the first coin tossed is T.

1. Suppose the first coin tossed is H. Then there are three coins left to toss, and there must be exactly one H in the three. The number of outcomes here is the same as the number of outcomes with one head in three tosses. Here they are.

$$\underline{H}HTT, \underline{H}THT, \underline{H}TTH$$

2. Suppose the first coin tossed is T. Then there are three coins left to toss, and there must be exactly two H's in the three. The number of outcomes here is the same as the number of outcomes with two heads in three tosses. Here they are:

$$\underline{T}HHT, \underline{T}HTH, \underline{T}THH$$

That means that the number of ways of getting two heads in four tosses is equal to the number of ways of getting one head in three tosses *plus* the number of ways of getting two heads in three tosses. We can find the number we want related to four tosses by adding together two numbers we already know for three tosses. We can now fill in the rest of the fourth horizontal row of our table.

NO. OF COINS	TOTAL NO. OF OUTCOMES	NO. OF OUTCOMES WITH EXACTLY THIS MANY HEADS						
		0	1	2	3	4	5	6
1	2	1	1					
2	4	1	2	1				
3	8	1	3	3	1			
4	16	1	4	6	4	1		

Breaking the problem into simpler, similar problems works in general. To count the number of outcomes with K heads in N tosses, you add together two numbers:

■ The number of outcomes with K heads in N tosses when the first toss is a head
■ The number of outcomes with K heads in N tosses when the first toss is a tail

The first of these two numbers is the same as the number of outcomes with $K - 1$ heads in $N - 1$ tosses:

$$N \text{ tosses with } K \text{ heads}$$
$$H * * * * \cdots * *$$
$$N - 1 \text{ tosses with } K - 1 \text{ heads}$$

The second of the two numbers is the same as the number of outcomes with K heads in $N - 1$ tosses:

$$N \text{ tosses with } K \text{ heads}$$
$$T * * * * \cdots * *$$
$$N - 1 \text{ tosses with } K \text{ heads}$$

Thus,

The number of outcomes with exactly K heads in N tosses

$$= \text{ the number of outcomes with exactly } K - 1 \text{ heads in } N - 1 \text{ tosses}$$
$$+ \text{ the number of outcomes with exactly } K \text{ heads in } N - 1 \text{ tosses.}$$

This gives us a method for filling in the Nth row of Pascal's triangle once the $N - 1$ row has been filled in.

NO. OF COINS	TOTAL NO. OF OUTCOMES	NO. OF OUTCOMES WITH EXACTLY THIS MANY HEADS		
		$\cdots$ $K - 1$	K	$\cdots$
$\vdots$		$\vdots$	$\vdots$	
$N - 1$	2^{N-1}	(*) +	(*)	
N	2^N		(*)	

Let's use this rule to figure out the numbers in the fifth row. To determine a number in a certain position of the fifth row, look at the two numbers in the fourth row just above and to the left of the position. Add these two numbers together to get your answer.

NO. OF COINS	TOTAL NO. OF OUTCOMES	NO. OF OUTCOMES WITH EXACTLY THIS MANY HEADS						
		0	1	2	3	4	5	6
1	2	1	1					
2	4	1	2	1				
3	8	1	3	3	1			
4	16	1	4	6	4	1		
5	32	1	5	10	10	5	1	

Continuing with this, we obtain Pascal's triangle through the sixth row.

NO. OF COINS	TOTAL NO. OF OUTCOMES	NO. OF OUTCOMES WITH EXACTLY THIS MANY HEADS						
		0	1	2	3	4	5	6
1	2	1	1					
2	4	1	2	1				
3	8	1	3	3	1			
4	16	1	4	6	4	1		
5	32	1	5	10	10	5	1	
6	64	1	6	15	20	15	6	1

EXERCISES

15. Use the rule and the first six rows of Pascal's triangle to calculate the seventh and eighth rows of Pascal's triangle.

16. Why are the following two statements true?

   ■ "The number of outcomes with exactly 5 heads in 50 tosses is the same as the number of outcomes with exactly 45 tails in 50 tosses."

   ■ "The number of outcomes with exactly 45 tails in 50 tosses is the same as the number of outcomes with exactly 45 heads in 50 tosses."

17. You will notice that the rows of Pascal's triangle we have filled in possess a certain symmetry: Reading a row backward is the same as reading it forward. Will this be true of a row we haven't filled in yet? Why or why not? (*Hint:* Look at exercise 16.)

A Solution to the Sampling Problem, Continued

We wanted to find $P(0$ heads in five tosses). Using Pascal's triangle, we get

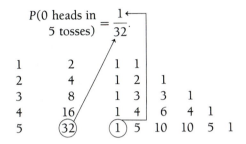

$$P(0 \text{ heads in 5 tosses}) = \frac{1}{32}.$$

1	2	1	1				
2	4	1	2	1			
3	8	1	3	3	1		
4	16	1	4	6	4	1	
5	32	1	5	10	10	5	1

Thus, the probability that if five bulbs are tested, none is defective is $\frac{1}{32} = .03125$.

A Solution to the Television Set Problem, Continued

We wanted to find P(four or fewer heads in six tosses). The number of outcomes corresponding to the condition of four or fewer heads is $1 + 6 + 15 + 20 + 15 = 57$.

1	2	1	1					
2	4	1	2	1				
3	8	1	3	3	1			
4	16	1	4	6	4	1		
5	32	1	5	10	10	5	1	
6	64	1	6	15	20	15	6	1

Thus, $P(4$ or fewer heads in 6 tosses$) = 57/64 \cong .89$.

Thus, the probability that four televisions will be sufficient for all the families that want them is about .89. (In other words, about 89% of the time, you will have enough televisions for your customers.)

EXERCISES

18. In the sampling problem, what is the probability that one or fewer light bulbs will be defective?

19. In the sampling problem, suppose you sample seven bulbs. If the probability that a single bulb is defective is $\frac{1}{2}$, use Pascal's triangle to find the probability that in your sample two or fewer are defective.

20. In the television set problem, you have decided to buy an additional television set. What is the probability that five televisions will be sufficient for all the families that want them?

21. In six matches between evenly matched tennis players Vila and Jensen, what is the probability that Vila will win four or more of the matches? (To solve this, assume that you can model the outcome of a match by coin tossing. Is this a realistic assumption?)

21.4   EXTENDING THE IDEAS: HYPOTHESIS TESTING

If you toss 30 coins, then you can use the thirtieth row of Pascal's triangle to calculate the probability of K heads:

$$P(K \text{ heads in 30 tosses}) = \frac{\text{number of outcomes for } K \text{ heads}}{2^{30}}.$$

The graph shows these probabilities.

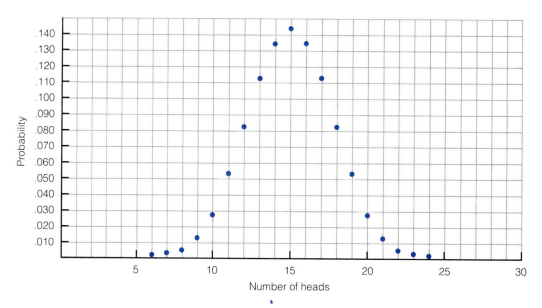

You notice that many of the probabilities are small. (The probabilities for 5 or fewer and 25 or greater are all .0001 or less.) When you toss 30 fair coins, you expect around 15 of the 30 to be heads. The probability that *exactly* 15 will be heads is about .144. However, the probability that the number of heads will be between 12 and 18 (inclusive) is about .800, and the probability that the number of heads will be between 10 and 20 (inclusive) is about .957. So 95.7% of the time, the number of heads should be greater than or equal to 10 and fewer than or equal to 20. Not so surprising. This also says that about 4.3% of the time, the number of heads will be fewer than 10 or greater than 20. It is possible that you could get fewer than 10 heads or greater than 20, but the occurrence is rare. Because of this, if you toss a coin 30 times and fewer than 10 of them come up heads, you begin to *suspect* that the coin is not a balanced one. This suspicion is the basis for the decision-making procedure described in the following problem.

THE ANTIHISTAMINE PROBLEM

You work for a pharmaceutical company. A consumer advocate group suspects that using your company's antihistamine increases a person's reaction time. This would make driving after taking the antihistamine dangerous. If the group can confirm these suspicions, then the group may bring suit against the company to cause it to cease distribution of the drug. How can you decide whether the consumer advocacy group's suspicions are warranted?

A Solution to the Antihistamine Problem

You come up with the following scheme for deciding, and the group agrees. An independent scientist will perform an experiment in which he will measure the reaction time of several human subjects twice. The scientist will measure each subject's reaction time once with the drug and once without. A set of reaction times for 30 subjects is shown in the table.

SUBJECT	REACTION TIME WITHOUT DRUG	REACTION TIME WITH DRUG	SIGN
1	1.05	1.10	+
2	.95	.93	−
3	.45	.65	+
4	.75	.80	+
5	.61	.70	+
6	.83	1.05	+
7	1.20	1.10	−
8	.47	.50	+
9	.98	1.31	+
10	.95	.97	+
11	.88	.95	+
12	1.03	.95	−
13	.78	.85	+
14	.83	.91	+
15	.89	.84	−
16	.68	.75	+
17	.97	.93	−
18	1.15	1.05	−
19	.88	.90	+
20	.74	.80	+
21	.64	.60	−
22	.67	.90	+
23	.98	.91	−
24	.76	.78	+
25	.81	.89	+
26	1.10	1.05	−
27	.95	1.02	+
28	.80	.94	+
29	.74	.91	+
30	.97	.99	+

The scientist marks a − (minus sign) in a row of the table when the reaction time is shorter with the drug than without and a + (plus sign) when the reaction time is longer with the drug than without. Your reasoning goes like this.

Under normal conditions (no drug used) a person's reaction time will certainly vary. In comparing two reaction times under normal conditions, it is reasonable to assume that it is just as likely for a + as a − to appear in the chart. If the drug has no effect, then the experiment (of recording +'s and −'s) should be just like tossing 30 coins.

How will you decide whether or not the antihistamine has an effect on reaction time?

You will tabulate the number K of +'s from the experiment. (In the table $K = 21$.) Then, assuming that the drug has no effect, you will calculate the probability that K or more +'s occur. This is equal to the probability that K or more heads occur in the toss of 30 coins.

If this probability is less than .05, then the decision will be that the drug *does* affect reaction time adversely. (You base this on the fact that if you assume the drug has no effect, the results of the experiment are very unlikely—less than 1 chance in 20. So you decide that your assumption is false.)

If the probability calculated is greater than .05, you and the consumer advocacy group let the assumption of no effect stand. Your decision in this case is that some variation in the number of + 's and − 's is reasonable. Of course, you and the group decide ahead of time on the level of unlikeliness you will not tolerate. In this case, it's the probability .05.

This method of making a decision is called *hypothesis testing.* (In the example you are testing the hypothesis that the drug has no effect.)

In the table, $K = 21$. From the graph, $P(21$ or more heads in 30 tosses$) \sim 0.022$. This is more unlikely than you will tolerate. You reject the hypothesis that the drug has no effect.

EXERCISES

22. Suppose that the number of + 's in the chart had been $K = 18$. What would the decision have been?

23. The Heroditus Pharmaceutical Company manufactures a treatment for a certain disease. The treatment leads to a cure in half the cases. (So coin tossing models the use of this treatment.) The research division of the company has come up with a new treatment that it claims improves on the old. The marketing division, however, doesn't want to sell it because it feels that it is no better (no worse, either) than the old treatment. To decide whether to believe the research division, the company will use hypothesis testing (to test the hypothesis that coin tossing models the new treatment): Of the people having the disease 30 will be given the new treatment, and the number K of cures will be noted. If the probability that K or more heads in 30 tosses is less than .1, then they will decide that the new treatment is sufficiently better and will market the new treatment. Otherwise, they will not market it. What should K be in order that the company market the new treatment?

21.5   LOOKING BACK: FORMAL PROPERTIES OF PROBABILITY

In this section we would like to take a more formal look at what we have done with probability. This will make it easier for us to extend what we have learned to other situations. Here is the framework we have been working with so far and some new terminology.

TERMINOLOGY AND PROPERTIES OF PROBABILITY

You conduct an *experiment* that has a set S of possible *outcomes.* To each outcome s in S is associated a positive number $P(s)$, called the *probability* of s. A subset E of S is called an *event.* (The subset of outcomes satisfying a certain condition is an event.) In case all the outcomes are *equally likely,*

$$P(s) = \frac{1}{n(S)} \quad \text{and} \quad P(E) = \frac{n(E)}{n(S)}.$$

In particular,

$$P(S) = 1 \quad \text{and} \quad P(\phi) = 0.$$

For example, for the experiment of tossing a balanced die, the set of outcomes is $\{1,2,3,4,5,6\}$. The condition "the number of spots is even" corresponds to the event $E = \{2,4,6\}$, and the probability that the number of spots is even $= P(E) = P(\{2,4,6\}) = \frac{3}{6} = \frac{1}{2}$. Sometimes $P(\{2,4,6\})$ is simplified to $P(2,4,6)$.

To see how we might extend this framework, let's look at an experiment in which the outcomes are not equally likely. For example, suppose we toss a die that is not balanced. In this case, the probability of an individual outcome will differ from outcome to outcome. For example, we might have $P(1) = \frac{1}{7}$ and $P(2) = \frac{1}{8}$. Each of the other 4 outcomes has a probability associated with it and the sum of all 6 probabilities must add up to 1:

$$P(1) + P(2) + P(3) + P(4) + P(5) + P(6) = 1.$$

For example, we might have

$$P(1) = \frac{1}{7}$$

$$P(2) = \frac{1}{8}$$

$$P(3) = \frac{1}{4}$$

$$P(4) = \frac{2}{7}$$

$$P(5) = \frac{1}{8}$$

$$P(6) = \frac{1}{14}$$

(Check that they add up to 1.)

Let's assume that the probabilities of individual outcomes are the numbers given and then figure out the probability that the number of spots is even. We might reason as follows: $\frac{1}{8}$ of the time the number of spots is 2; $\frac{2}{7}$ of the time the number of spots is 4; $\frac{1}{14}$ of the time the number of spots is 6. It seems reasonable that $P(\{2,4,6\}) = \frac{1}{8} + \frac{2}{7} + \frac{1}{14}$.

This argument motivates a definition.

DEFINITION OF *PROBABILITY OF AN EVENT*

Let S be the set of outcomes for an experiment. If $E \subset S$ is an event and $E = \{a,b,c, \ldots\}$, then $P(E) = P(a) + P(b) + P(c) + \cdots$

This more general definition coincides with the previous definition of probability, because when all outcomes are equally likely,

$$P(E) = \frac{n(E)}{n(S)} = \underbrace{\frac{1}{n(S)} + \frac{1}{n(S)} + \cdots + \frac{1}{n(S)}}_{n(E) \text{ times}}$$

$$= P(a) + P(b) + P(c) + \cdots$$

since

$$P(a) = P(b) = P(c) = \cdots = \frac{1}{n(S)}.$$

Because events are subsets, we can exploit what we know about sets to help in calculating probabilities. To get some idea of what we might be able to do, recall the experiment of tossing five coins where the set of outcomes has $2^8 = 32$ elements. To calculate the probability of the event E consisting of those outcomes in which one or fewer of the coins come up heads, we did the following:

$$n(E) = \text{number of outcomes in } E$$

$$= \text{number of ways of getting exactly zero heads}$$
$$+ \text{ number of ways of getting exactly one head}$$

$$= n(A) + n(B)$$

where A is the set of all outcomes with exactly zero heads and B is the set of all outcomes with exactly one head. In terms of probabilities this can be written

$$P(E) = \frac{n(E)}{n(S)} = \frac{n(A)}{n(S)} + \frac{n(B)}{n(S)} = P(A) + P(B).$$

In other words, $P(A \cup B) = P(A) + P(B)$, provided $A \cap B = \phi$. In the coin problem, finding $n(A)$ and $n(B)$ are easier problems than finding $n(E)$. In general, finding $P(A)$ and $P(B)$ may be easier than finding $P(A \cup B)$. We can describe this technique for finding probabilities.

PROBABILITY OF THE UNION OF DISJOINT EVENTS

Suppose that E is an event and that $E = A \cup B$ with $A \cap B = \phi$. Then $P(E) = P(A) + P(B)$.

More generally, if $E = A \cup B \cup \cdots \cup Z$ such that every pair of sets selected from $A, B, \ldots, Z$ has empty intersection, then $P(E) = P(A) + P(B) + \cdots + P(Z)$.

EXERCISE 24. Show that if event E has the property $E = C \cup D$, then $P(E) = P(C) + P(D) - P(C \cap D)$ regardless of whether C and D are disjoint. (*Hint:* Draw a Venn diagram for the subsets C and D of S. Use the diagram to express $C \cup D$ as a union of three disjoint subsets. Then use the fact about probability of the union of disjoint events.)

Let's return to the experiment of tossing five coins. Suppose that we are interested in calculating the probability of the event F that two or more of the coins come up heads. Earlier we computed the probability of the event G that one or fewer coins come up heads (it's $\frac{1}{32} + \frac{5}{32} = \frac{6}{32}$). The subset G is the complement of the subset F in the set S of all outcomes. G is the event that F doesn't happen. If $P(G)$ is the fraction a/b, then when we perform the experiment many times the event G should occur about a/b of the time. The event F should occur the rest of the time, or $1 - a/b$ of the time. In general, we have the following statement about the probability of complementary events.

PROBABILITY OF COMPLEMENTARY EVENTS

Suppose that S is the set of outcomes for some experiment and E an event. If E' is the complement of E in S, then $P(E') = 1 - P(E)$. The event E' is called the *complementary event* to E.

For example, for the experiment of tossing five coins,

$$P(2 \text{ or more heads}) = 1 - P(1 \text{ or fewer heads})$$

$$= 1 - \frac{6}{32}$$

$$= \frac{26}{32}.$$

It's easy to find the probability of an event when you know the probability of the complementary event. This suggests a strategy: If you are having trouble finding the probability of an event, try finding the probability of the complementary event and use the property we have stated.

The rule for computing the probability of a complementary event also follows from the rule governing the calculation of disjoint events and the fact that $P(S) = 1$. To see this, if E is an event, then $E \cup E' = S$, $E \cap E' = \phi$, and $1 = P(S) = P(E \cup E') = P(E) + P(E')$. Consequently, $P(E') = 1 - P(E)$.

EXERCISES
25. Describe the set of outcomes for each experiment.
   (a) A person is asked his month of birth.
   (b) An 8-sided die (with sides marked 1,2,...,8) is tossed.
   (c) A card is drawn from the 13-card suit of spades.

26. For the sets in exercise 25, describe as subsets the following events.
   (a) The person's birthday occurs in a solstice month.
   (b) The number that comes up is greater than 5.
   (c) The card drawn is a face card.

27. The experiment is tossing a standard die where the set of outcomes is $\{1,2,3,4,5,6\}$. Which of the following assignments of probabilities to individual outcomes are consistent with the properties of probability as described in this section?
   (a) $P(1) = .1$, $P(2) = .2$, $P(3) = .3$, $P(4) = .4$, $P(5) = .5$, $P(6) = .6$
   (b) $P(1) = P(2) = .1$, $P(3) = P(4) = P(5) = P(6) = .2$
   (c) $P(1) = P(2) = P(3) = P(4) = .3$, $P(5) = .2$, $P(6) = -.4$
   (d) $P(1) = P(3) = P(5) = .15$, $P(4) = .05$, $P(2) = P(6) = .25$

28. Suppose the probabilities for the individual outcomes in tossing a die are as in exercise 27(d). Find the probability that the number that comes up is greater than 4. Find the probability that the number that comes up is odd.

29. Suppose that the following probabilities have been estimated for what happens when you put a penny in a certain defective vending machine: The probability that nothing comes out is $\frac{1}{3}$; the probability that the penny is returned or peanuts come out (but not both) is $\frac{1}{6}$.

    (a)   What is a reasonable set of outcomes for this experiment?

    (b)   The probabilities of which events have been estimated? (Express the events as a subset.)

    (c)   Use the estimations given and the laws of probability to find the probability that peanuts come out and you get the penny back.

    (d)   What is the probability that you will get peanuts?

30. Suppose that A and B are events such that $A \subset B$. Show that $P(A) \leq P(B)$.

21.6   LOOKING AHEAD: PROBABILITY AND TREE DIAGRAMS

In the experiment of tossing many coins we used tree diagrams to help us list and count all the outcomes. We can also use tree diagrams to help compute probabilities directly in case the experiment in question can be accomplished in several successive stages. Here are some examples.

TOSSING THREE COINS   Tossing coins numbered 1, 2, and 3 can be done in three stages: stage 1—toss coin 1; stage 2—toss coin 2; stage 3—toss coin 3. At each stage, there are two results: H or T. Each occurs half the time. We put these probabilities on the appropriate branches of the tree as follows.

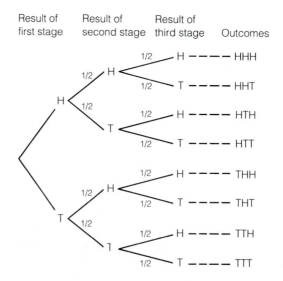

This is called the *probability tree* for the experiment. If you multiply the probabilities that occur along the branches associated with a particular outcome you obtain the probability of that outcome.

ROLLING A PAIR OF BALANCED DICE   In the game of craps you roll a pair of dice. Having the sum of the spots be 11 on the first roll is a winning combination. What is the probability that the sum of the spots is 11?

Rolling a pair of dice, one green and the other red, can be accomplished in two stages: first, roll the green die; second, roll the red die. There will be 6 results to the first stage, each occurring with probability $\frac{1}{6}$, and 6 results to the second stage, each occurring with probability $\frac{1}{6}$. Here is the probability tree.

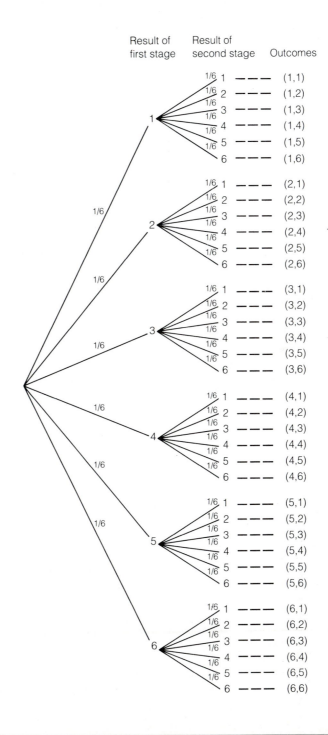

Each outcome is an ordered pair of numbers where the first number in the pair is the result of the first stage and the second number in the pair is the result of the second stage; thus, the outcome (6,4) means a 6 on the green die and a 4 on the red die.

$P[(6,4)]$ can be computed from the tree in the following manner: $\frac{1}{6}$ of the time the green die will come up with a 6; $\frac{1}{6}$ of that time the red die will come up with a 4. Thus $\left(\frac{1}{6}\right)\left(\frac{1}{6}\right)$ of the time will result in the outcome (6,4). In other words, $P[(6,4)] = \frac{1}{36}$. In general, the probability of an outcome is obtained by multiplying the probabilities on the path to that outcome.

The outcomes with sum of the spots equal to 11 are (6,5) and (5,6), each with probability $\frac{1}{36}$. Thus,

$$P(\text{sum of spots is 11}) = \frac{2}{36} = \frac{1}{18}.$$

FIRING TORPEDOES   You are firing torpedoes at an enemy ship. The probability that any one torpedo will sink the ship is $\frac{1}{3}$. You will be allowed to fire only four torpedoes before you are discovered by the enemy. What is the probability that you will sink the ship before you are discovered?

The experiment of firing torpedoes has four stages corresponding to the firing of each of the four torpedoes in succession. (Of course, if you sink the ship in less than four, you don't have to fire more.) The result at each stage is either sink (S) or not sink (NS). Here is the probability tree.

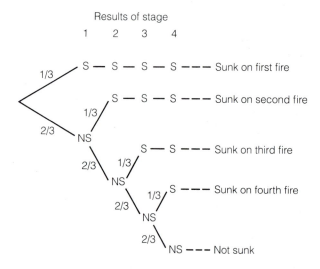

Again, the probability of a given outcome at an end point of the tree is the product of the probabilities that occur on the branches of the path to that outcome. Thus,

$$P(\text{sunk on first fire}) = \left(\frac{1}{3}\right)(1)(1)(1) = \frac{1}{3}$$

$$P(\text{sunk on second fire}) = \left(\frac{2}{3}\right)\left(\frac{1}{3}\right)(1)(1) = \frac{2}{9}$$

$$P(\text{sunk on third fire}) = \left(\frac{2}{3}\right)\left(\frac{2}{3}\right)\left(\frac{1}{3}\right)(1) = \frac{4}{27}$$

$$P(\text{sunk on fourth fire}) = \left(\frac{2}{3}\right)\left(\frac{2}{3}\right)\left(\frac{2}{3}\right)\left(\frac{1}{3}\right) = \frac{8}{81}.$$

Thus, also,

$$P(\text{sunk in four or fewer fires}) = \frac{1}{3} + \frac{2}{9} + \frac{4}{27} + \frac{8}{81} = \frac{65}{81}.$$

MAKING A SALE   A sales representative for a clothing manufacturer is planning to visit a department store. The representative estimates the probability that the store's head buyer will be in to be .40. If the head buyer is out, the representative must see an assistant buyer instead. The representative also estimates the probability of making a sale if the head buyer is in to be .50 but only .30 if the assistant buyer must be seen. The sales representative wants to know the probability of making a sale on his visit to the department store.

We can think of this situation as an experiment that can be accomplished in two stages. In the first stage the sales representative goes to the department store where the head buyer is in (I) or not in (NI). In the second stage the representative makes a sale (S) or no sale (NS). Here is the probability tree.

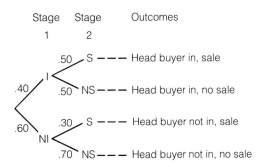

As before, the probability of an outcome at an end point of the tree is equal to the product of the probabilities that occur on the branches that make up the path to that end point. Consequently, we have the following:

$P(\text{head buyer in and sale}) = (.40)(.50) = .20$

$P(\text{head buyer not in and sale}) = (.60)(.30) = .18$

Thus,

$$P(\text{sale}) = P(\text{head buyer in and sale}) + P(\text{head buyer not in and sale})$$
$$= .20 + .18$$
$$= .38.$$

These examples suggest the following properties of probability trees.

PROBABILITY TREES

If an experiment can be carried out in several stages, then it can be represented by a probability tree in which each node is the result of one stage of the experiment and the branches attached to the node to its right are the results of the next stage.

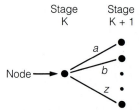

These branches are labeled with the probabilities $(a,b,c, \ldots ,z)$ of the various results of the next stage. The sum of these numbers must be equal to 1: $a + b + c + \cdots + z = 1$.

The outcomes of the experiment are associated with the end points of the tree: The probability of an outcome is equal to the product of all the probabilities on the path leading to the outcome.

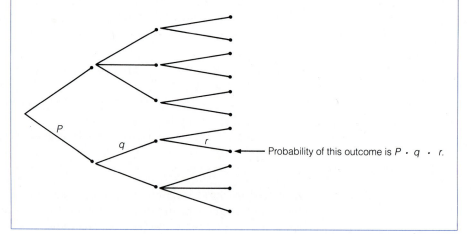

Probability of this outcome is $P \cdot q \cdot r$.

31. In the game of craps in which a pair of dice is rolled, the number 7 is also a winning combination. What is the probability that the sum of the spots is 7? What is the probability that the sum of the spots is 7 or 11?

32. In the torpedo example, suppose that you have time to fire five torpedoes. What is the probability that you sink the ship in five or fewer firings? (Solve this by extending the tree in the text from four stages to five.)

33. Alter the torpedo example in the following way. This time you know that a single torpedo has a probability $\frac{1}{2}$ of sinking a ship, probability $\frac{1}{4}$ of damaging it, and probability $\frac{1}{4}$ of missing it. You also know that two damaging shots sink the ship. For this situation, find the probability that four or fewer torpedo firings will sink the ship.

34. In women's tennis, the winner of a match is the first person to win two sets. (At most, three sets are played.) Here is the tree of possible outcomes for a match between Martina Navratilova (N) and Steffi Graf (G).

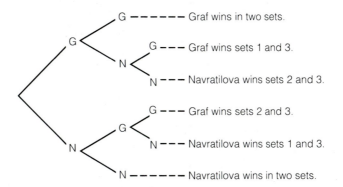

G ------ Graf wins in two sets.

G --- Graf wins sets 1 and 3.

N --- Navratilova wins sets 2 and 3.

G --- Graf wins sets 2 and 3.

N --- Navratilova wins sets 1 and 3.

N ------ Navratilova wins in two sets.

If the two players are evenly matched, then the probability that Graf will win a given match is $\frac{1}{2}$ and the probability that Navratilova will win is $\frac{1}{2}$. Use these probabilities to turn the tree above into a probability tree and calculate the probability that the match will end in two sets.

35. In exercise 34, if Graf will win a set with probability .4 and Navratilova with probability .6, draw the appropriate probability tree and calculate the probability that the match will end in two sets.

36. In men's tennis, the winner of a match is the first person to win three sets (and, at most, five sets are played). Draw the tree, similar to the one that appears in exercise 34, showing the possible outcomes for a match between Boris Becker (B) and Ivan Lendl (L). Turn the tree into a probability tree using .4 for the probability that Becker wins a given set and .6 for the probability that Lendl wins. Then calculate the probability that the match will end in three sets.

Suppose we toss a fair coin 20 times. Using Pascal's triangle, we can figure out the following probabilities:

P(exactly 0 heads)
P(exactly 1 head)
P(exactly 2 heads)

⋮

P(exactly 20 heads)

If we were interested in similar probabilities for tossing 50 coins, it would be trickier because we would need Pascal's triangle to be expanded to 50 rows. And that would be no fun.

However, with a computer we can estimate the probabilities by *simulation*. BASIC has a feature called a *random-number generator,* which randomly selects numbers between 0 and 1. It uses the command RND. The following program produces 100 of these numbers and prints them out:

```
10 FOR I = 1 TO 50
20 PRINT RND
30 NEXT I
40 END
```

Type this program and run it. Roughly a tenth of the numbers printed out should be between .1 and .2, a third should be between $\frac{2}{3}$ and 1, a fifth should be between .4 and .6, and so on. In general, the fraction of numbers that are between a and b—with $0 \le a < b \le 1$—should be $b - a$. Check this against the output from running the program. (You may need a copy of the output printed on paper. See your computer expert on how to do this.)

Now run the program again and see what happens. Compare the two sets of random numbers. If your computer is like many others, the string of random numbers generated the second time around is the same as the first time. This is no good. To avoid this, add the following statement to the program:

```
5 RANDOMIZE TIMER
```

This statement will guarantee that the random numbers generated will be different each time you run the program. To check this, run the program again with the new line added.

Since roughly half the numbers generated should be between 0 and $\frac{1}{2}$ and the other half between $\frac{1}{2}$ and 1, we can simulate the tossing of a fair coin by letting the computer produce a random number. When the number is bigger than $\frac{1}{2}$, then we say the coin comes up "heads", and if it is less than $\frac{1}{2}$, we say the coin comes up "tails." The following program, a modification of the preceding program, does just this for 50 "coins":

```
5 RANDOMIZE TIMER
10 FOR I = 1 TO 50
20 IF RND > .5 THEN GOTO 27
22 PRINT "TAILS"
24 GOTO 30
```

```
27 PRINT "HEADS"
30 NEXT I
40 END
```

Type this program into your computer and run it.

EXERCISES

37. An unfair coin has probability equal to .4 of coming up heads and .6 of coming up tails. Write a program to simulate the tossing of this coin 50 times.

38. Write a program to simulate the rolling of 100 balanced standard dice and print the outcome of each roll as 1, 2, 3, 4, 5, or 6.

Getting the Computer to Count and Make Several Experiments

Next let's modify the program above again to flip 100 fair "coins" and print out the number of heads that result. In the program below, H = number of heads.

```
5 RANDOMIZE TIMER
7 LET H = 0          Initialize H.
10 FOR I = 1 TO 100
20 IF RND > .5 THEN GOTO 27
24 GOTO 30
27 LET H = H+1
30 NEXT I
40 PRINT "THE NUMBER OF HEADS IS "H
100 END
```

If we want to estimate the probability that exactly 22 heads occur in the toss of 50 fair coins, we will want to simulate the experiment many times (for example, by running the program many times) and figure out the fraction of times there are 22 heads. Of course, we can run the program ourselves many times and do the tabulating. But to do that would be to underutilize the computer. Let's make it do the work. First, we can put the preceding program within another loop, a loop that has the computer repeat the tossing of 50 coins several times—300, say.

```
5 RANDOMIZE TIMER
6 FOR J = 1 TO 300
7 LET H = 0
10 FOR I = 1 TO 50
20 IF RND > .5 THEN GOTO 27
24 GOTO 30                          ←— New loop
27 LET H = H+1
30 NEXT I
40 PRINT "THE NUMBER OF HEADS IS "H
50 NEXT J
100 END
```

Make the modifications and run this. The computer will print out a string of numbers—the various values of H for the 300 different experiments of tossing 50 coins.

To figure out how many times 45 occurs as the number of heads, you have to go through the list of 300 numbers. Let's get the computer to do the work again. We can have it keep track of the number of times exactly 22 heads come up. To do this, we introduce another counter C, which starts at 0 and increases by 1 each time the number of heads is exactly 22. The program modification follows.

```
3 LET C = 0            Initialize C.
5 RANDOMIZE TIMER
6 FOR J = 1 TO 300
7 LET H = 0
10 FOR I = 1 TO 50
20 IF RND > .5 THEN GOTO 27
24 GOTO 30
27 LET H = H+1
30 NEXT I
40 IF H = 22 THEN LET C = C+1     Increase C by 1 when H = 45.
50 NEXT J
60 PRINT C, C/300
100 END
```

The outputs of this program (from line 60) are the number *C* of times that 22 heads occur in 300 repetitions of the experiment and the estimated probability *C*/300 that 22 heads will occur in 50 tosses of a fair coin.

RENUMBERING THE LINES OF A PROGRAM

At this point, anticipating even more modifications of the preceding program, I notice that many of the present line numbers of the program are close together. This may make future insertions difficult. The system command RENUMBER will help us out. RENUMBER will keep the order of the lines but renumber them to make a reasonable gap for insertion of new lines between two consecutive current lines. Here is how it works for the program.

```
RENUMBER
LIST
10 LET C = 0
20 RANDOMIZE TIMER
30 FOR J = 1 TO 300
40 LET H = 0
50 FOR I = 1 TO 50
60 IF RND > .5 THEN GOTO 80
70 GOTO 90
80 LET H = H+1
90 NEXT I
100 IF H = 22 THEN LET C = C+1
110 NEXT J
120 PRINT C, C/300
130 END
```

(Note: RENUMBER might not be the appropriate command for your version of BASIC. Check with your expert.)

Arrays in BASIC

The program we have been using tabulates how many times 22 heads occurred in 300 repetitions of the tossing of 50 fair coins. It would be nice if we could get the program to do the same thing for values other than 22—in fact, to do it for all possible numbers of heads that can occur in 50 tosses: $0, 1, 2, 3, \ldots, 50$. To do this, we need a counter for each of the 101 possibilities. Do we have to type in a line for each of these 51 counters? No. Such a repetitive activity is what a computer is designed for. There is a device in BASIC called an *array* and denoted C(I) which will keep track of the 51 counters. C(I) acts like a function with whole number inputs I. For us

$$C(I) = \text{number of times exactly } I \text{ heads occur.}$$

For example, $C(22)$ is the number of times exactly 22 heads occur in 50 tosses. Just as we initialized the counter C, we will have to initialize the array of counters C(I). We will also have to tell the computer to have 51 variable locations for the 51 values $C(0), C(1), \ldots, C(50)$. The latter is accomplished in what is called a *dimension* statement. The modification of our program follows.

```
4 DIM C(51) ←──────────── Dimension statement
5 FOR K = 0 TO 50 ←
10 LET C(K) = 0      ├── Initializing C(K)
15 NEXT K ←
20 RANDOMIZE TIMER
30 FOR J = 1 TO 300
40 LET H = 0
50 FOR I = 1 TO 50
60 IF RND > .5 THEN GOTO 80
70 GOTO 90
80 LET H = H+1
90 NEXT I
100 LET C(H) = C(H)+1
110 NEXT J
115 PRINT "# HEADS," "# TIMES," "EST. PROB."
120 FOR L = 0 TO 50 ←
130 PRINT L, C(L), C(L)/300    ├── Printing C(L)
140 NEXT L ←
150 END
```

This program is a great time saver. If we were to figure out exactly the probabilities that this program estimates, we would have to list Pascal's triangle out to the fiftieth row. No fun. We ought to check, however, that the program does arrive at reasonable estimations. To do this, we can modify the program once more so that, instead of tossing 50 coins, it tosses 16. (We *can* list Pascal's triangle out to 16 rows.) We need only make modifications in lines 50 and 120.

```
50 FOR I = 1 TO 16
120 FOR L = 0 TO 16
```

EXERCISES

39. Compare the output from the most recent program with probabilities determined by row 16 of Pascal's triangle. (These probabilities are the numbers in the sixteenth row all divided by 2^{16}.)

40. Modify the program just written to simulate 16 tosses of an unfair coin ($P(H) = .4$, $P(T) = .6$) 300 times. You want it to print out the number of times exactly I heads occur, for values of I between 0 and 16. You also want it to estimate the probabilities that exactly I heads occur for the same values. Compare the probabilities you get here with those that you get for a fair coin.

41. Write a program that will simulate the rolling of a pair of balanced dice and print out the sum of the spots.

42. Modify the program in exercise 41 so that it will estimate the probabilities of obtaining the various sums (2,3,4,5,6,7,8,9,10,11,12).

21.8   SUMMARY OF IMPORTANT IDEAS AND TECHNIQUES

- The framework for dealing with uncertainty: the experiment, the outcomes of the experiment, the probability that a certain condition occurs
- Experiments with all outcomes equally likely; formula for probability in this case
- Estimated probabilities
- Attaching values to the outcomes of an experiment; computing the expected value of the experiment
- Using the experiment of tossing several coins to model other experiments
- Describing the outcomes of tossing several coins using tree diagrams
- Using Pascal's triangle to compute probabilities associated with tossing several coins
- Using the experiment of tossing several coins as the basis for a decision-making procedure: hypothesis testing
- Generalizing the notion of probability to situations where all outcomes are not equally likely; computing probabilities of disjoint events; computing the probability of a complementary event
- Using probability trees for experiments that can be accomplished in several stages

PROBLEM SET

PRACTICING
SKILLS

1. You receive a letter in the mail saying "Congratulations! You have won one of the following prizes—a new car worth $12,000, a diamond ring worth $1000, or a camera worth $29." You are clever and search the fine print to find that the probability of winning the car is 1/1,750,000, the probability of winning the ring is 10/1,750,000, and the probability of winning the camera is 1,749,989/1,750,000.
   (a) How many cars are they giving away if we assume 1,750,000 letters were mailed?
   (b) How many rings are they giving away?
   (c) How many cameras?
   (d) What is the total value of the giveaway assuming every prize is claimed?

2. You draw a card from a shuffled standard 52-card deck of cards. Find the probabilities that the conditions are satisfied.

(a) You draw a face card.   (b) You don't draw a face card.

(c) You draw a diamond.   (d) You don't draw a diamond.

(e) You draw a black face card.   (f) You don't draw a black face card.

3. Your college has literacy in a foreign language as a prerequisite for graduation. You are taking your foreign language exam Tuesday. A study of college records shows that of 1820 students who took the exam in the last 5 yr, 850 passed it on the first try, 560 passed on the second, and 410 needed three or more tries.

    (a) If you are like the previous test takers, what is the estimated probability that you pass the exam on the first try?

    (b) Estimate the probability that you will need to take the exam twice.

4. In the last three years there have been 276 car accidents within the town limits of Erehwon. Of these, 183 occurred on the corner of Main and Vine. Sheriff Cook receives a call reporting an accident, but the caller is so upset he does not give the location of the accident. Estimate the probability that the accident is at Main and Vine.

5. At the Carnival a ball-toss game costs $1 for three balls. If you knock over a pyramid of six pins, you win a large stuffed bear (worth $40). If you knock over four or five of the pins, you win a small stuffed animal (worth $5). Otherwise, you lose. It is estimated that the probability of knocking over all six pins is $\frac{1}{10}$, and the probability of knocking over four or five pins is $\frac{3}{10}$. What is the expected value of the game to you? (Remember that even if you win one of the prizes, you must pay $1 initially to enter the game.) Is it profitable for you to play this game?

6. In problem 1, if you must reply by mail to win and a charge of $1 is required for shipping and handling, what is the expected value to you of entering the contest? Should you enter the contest?

7. At Muddy Track Raceway, your horse, Sloe Dancer, has a probability of $\frac{1}{10}$ of winning, a probability of $\frac{3}{10}$ of coming in second, and $\frac{1}{5}$ of coming in third. First place wins $5000, second place $1000, and third place $500. It costs you $250 to enter the race. What is the expected value of the race to you? Is it worthwhile for you to enter the race?

8. Three fair coins are tossed.

    (a) What is the probability that two are heads?

    (b) What is the probability that two or three are tails?

    (c) What is the probability that at least one is heads?

9. The probability of rain over the next 3 days is estimated to be $\frac{1}{2}$ for each day. Model rain or no rain for the 3-day period by the toss of three coins so that you can estimate the probabilities of the events.

    (a) Rain on all 3 days   (b) Clear weather all 3 days

    (c) Rain on at least 2 of the 3 days   (d) Rain on at least 1 of the 3 days

10. Using Pascal's triangle, answer the questions.

    (a) What is the probability of getting exactly three heads on six tosses of a coin?

    (b) What is the probability of getting three or fewer heads on six tosses of a coin?

    (c) What is the probability of getting four or more heads on six tosses of a coin?

11. The Cougars and the Bulldogs are evenly matched softball teams. They are playing a triple-header.

    (a) What is the probability that one team wins all three games?

    (b) What is the probability that one team wins two of the three games?

    (c) What is the probability that neither team wins two games?

12. You must take a biology test but hate questions that ask you to name specific muscles. The teacher gives you your choice of test A or B, and you choose the test by flipping a coin. The teacher will

then ask you to answer two questions from the test picked at random. Test A has three questions out of eight on muscles and test B has five out of nine questions on muscles.

(a) Draw a (reasonable) tree for this experiment.
(b) What is the probability that you are asked at least one question on muscles?
(c) What is the probability that both questions are on muscles?
(d) What is the probability that you are asked no questions on muscles?

13. The weather forecaster predicts that it will rain today with an 80% probability. If it does rain today, then he predicts rain tomorrow with probability only 10%. If it doesn't rain today, he predicts rain tomorrow with a probability of 50%.

(a) Draw a tree indicating the weather (rain or no rain) for both days.
(b) What is the probability of no rain either day?
(c) What is the probability it will rain at least one of the two days?
(d) What is the probability it will rain tomorrow?
(e) What is the probability that it will rain both days?

14. In a test of extrasensory perception, six cards, each from a different standard deck, are placed face down on a table and a "psychic" is asked to tell which suit each card is. He gets three correct out of the six. If a person guessed at random what suit each card was, the approximate probability of getting exactly k correct out of the six is given by the table.

k	0	1	2	3	4	5	6
P(k correct)	.18	.36	.30	.13	.03	.00	.00

What is the approximate probability that a person who guesses will do at least as well as the psychic did?

15. On a separate sheet of paper, complete the following table for Pascal's triangle up to 16 rows. Use the table to answer problems 16 and 17.

NO. OF COINS	TOTAL NO. OF OUTCOMES	NO. OF OUTCOMES WITH EXACTLY THIS MANY HEADS																
		0	1	2	3	4	5	6	7	8	9	10	11	12	13	14	15	16
1	2	1	1															
2	4	1	2	1														
3	8	1	3	3	1													
4	16	1	4	6	4	1												
5	32	1	5	10	10	5	1											
6	64	1	6	15	20	15	6	1										
7																		
8																		
9																		
10																		
11																		
12																		
13																		
14																		
15																		
16																		

16. Toss 16 fair coins.
    (a) What is the number of ways of getting exactly eight heads?
    (b) What is the probability of getting exactly eight heads?
    (c) What is the number of ways of getting six, seven, or eight heads?
    (d) What is the probability of getting six, seven, or eight heads?

17. Professor Smith gave a student a 15-question true-false exam. He suspects that the student didn't study and just guessed at the answers. The professor wants to be sure of his suspicions within a probability of .05. How many answers must the student have right to convince Professor Smith that he didn't guess?

USING IDEAS   *In essay form write the solution to each of the problems that remain. Mention the steps you took to solve the problem, the principles, tools, or formulas you used, other problems or solutions that gave you ideas, and the problem-solving strategies you found helpful.*

18. A man plays the following game. He draws a card at random from a standard 52-card deck. If it is an ace, he wins $5. If it is a jack, queen, or king, he wins $2. Otherwise, he loses $1. On the average, how much should he win (or lose) per play of the game?

19. Bigelow Light Bulb Company makes light bulbs. The estimated probability that a light bulb coming off the assembly line will be defective is $\frac{1}{100}$. The company makes no attempt to find out which bulbs are good or bad: All are sent to the stores. The company makes a profit of $ .50 for every bulb it sells, assuming no defective bulbs. However, each defective bulb costs the company $5 in replacement charges and in soothing the irate, dissatisfied customer. What profit does the company really make per bulb on the average?

20. You have $1000 to invest. The local bank offers two kinds of saving plans. Plan A has a fixed interest rate of 7%/yr while plan B has a variable interest rate (based on the market), which is now 6%. The interest is paid quarterly and not compounded. You plan to leave your money in for only two quarters. You know that plan B has a lower interest rate now, but rates are rising and a columnist in your paper's financial pages predicts that the variable interest rate will rise from 6% to 9% in just 1 mo. The columnist has predicted correctly 7 of the last 10 times. Which plan should you choose? (You cannot change plans between quarters but will get the higher interest rate for the second quarter if you choose plan B.)

21. You order a fruit tree from Shady Nursery. You haven't had much luck with this nursery, but no one else has the tree you want. You estimate the probability that the tree you receive will be the wrong tree and die to be $\frac{1}{3}$, that it will be the right tree and die to be $\frac{1}{9}$, and that it will be the wrong tree and grow to be $\frac{2}{9}$.
    (a) Draw a Venn diagram to picture the set of outcomes.
    (b) What is the probability that the tree will grow and be the right tree?
    (c) What is the probability that the tree you receive, right or wrong, grows?

22. The mortality table on page 930 is based on the lives and deaths of policyholders in several large insurance companies. The table starts, at age 0, with 10,000,000 persons born and follows them through to their seventieth birthday. For example, in the row for age 9, the table shows 9,817,749 of the original 10,000,000 still living. Of the 9,817,749 some 11,879 die during their ninth year.

MORTALITY TABLE

AGE	NUMBER LIVING	NUMBER DYING	AGE	NUMBER LIVING	NUMBER DYING
0	10,000,000	70,800	35	9,373,807	23,528
1	9,929,200	17,475	36	9,350,279	24,685
2	9,911,725	15,066	37	9,325,594	26,112
3	9,896,659	14,449	38	9,299,482	27,991
4	9,882,210	13,835	39	9,271,491	30,132
5	9,868,375	13,322	40	9,241,359	32,622
6	9,855,053	12,812	41	9,208,737	35,362
7	9,842,241	12,401	42	9,173,375	38,253
8	9,829,840	12,091	43	9,135,122	41,382
9	9,817,749	11,879	44	9,093,740	44,741
10	9,805,870	11,865	45	9,048,999	48,412
11	9,794,005	12,047	46	9,000,587	52,473
12	9,781,958	12,325	47	8,948,114	56,910
13	9,769,633	12,896	48	8,891,204	61,794
14	9,756,737	13,562	49	8,829,410	67,104
15	9,743,175	14,225	50	8,762,306	72,902
16	9,728,950	14,983	51	8,689,404	79,160
17	9,713,967	15,737	52	8,610,244	85,758
18	9,698,230	16,390	53	8,524,486	92,832
19	9,681,840	16,846	54	8,431,654	100,337
20	9,664,994	17,300	55	8,331,317	108,307
21	9,647,694	17,655	56	8,223,010	116,849
22	9,630,039	17,912	57	8,106,161	125,970
23	9,612,127	18,167	58	7,980,191	135,663
24	9,593,960	18,324	59	7,844,528	145,830
25	9,575,636	18,481	60	7,698,698	156,592
26	9,557,155	18,732	61	7,542,106	167,736
27	9,538,423	18,981	62	7,374,370	179,271
28	9,519,442	19,324	63	7,195,099	191,174
29	9,500,118	19,760	64	7,003,925	203,394
30	9,480,358	20,193	65	6,800,531	215,917
31	9,460,165	20,718	66	6,584,614	228,749
32	9,439,447	21,239	67	6,355,865	241,777
33	9,418,208	21,850	68	6,114,088	254,835
34	9,396,358	22,551	69	5,859,253	267,241

The table can be used to estimate probabilities in the following way: Suppose you want to estimate the probability that a person now 10 years old will live to be age 25. You look at row 10 and find 9,805,870 of the original 10,000,000 were living. Then you look at row 25 and find that of the 9,805,870 living in their tenth year 9,575,636 were still living. You estimate the probability of any person now 10 years old living to age 25 to be the same as the probability for one of the 9,805,870 persons living to age 25:

$$P(\text{10-year-old will live to age 25}) = \frac{9,575,636}{9,805,870} \cong .9765.$$

Use this method to estimate the following probabilities:
(a) The probability that a child born now will live to be 1 year old.
(b) The probability that a person born now will live to age 50.

(c)   The probability that a person of age 20 will live to age 65.
(d)   The probability that a person of age 60 will live to age 65.
(e)   If an insurance company has 7000 policyholders of age 28, how many death claims should it expect to pay before the 28-year-olds reach age 29?

23.   A manufacturer is considering the manufacture of a new product. She estimates the probability that the new product will be a success to be $\frac{2}{3}$. If successful, the product would produce profits of $84,000. The development costs for the product are $60,000. Should the manufacturer proceed with the plans for the new product? (Why or why not?)

24.   It will cost the Davidovskys $60,000 to buy a restaurant that can earn up to $200,000 a year if it survives. The estimated probability of survival for a restaurant is $\frac{2}{5}$. What is the expected value to the Davidovskys for buying the restaurant? Is it wise for them to buy the restaurant?

25.   An oil company executive estimates the cost of drilling a well at $200,000. He also estimates the probability of actually striking oil at $\frac{1}{10}$. What should the income from a successful well be in order to justify taking the risk of drilling?

26.   A detective feels he has a $\frac{1}{10}$ probability of recovering some stolen jewels. He estimates that his investigation costs will be $10,000. How large should his fee be so that, on the average, his costs will be covered? (He gets paid only if he recovers the jewels.)

27.   You are a doctor. For a certain disease you administer a treatment. You and other doctors have observed that the treatment cures the disease about half the time; thus, you estimate the probability that a given treatment will cure to be $\frac{1}{2}$. You would like to devise a method for improving the chances of curing the disease. You wonder: "If I were to repeat the treatment twice, what would the probability of cure be? Maybe I could repeat the treatment three times. What would the probability of cure be then?"
      You think: "There are 2 outcomes to the treatment: cure (C) or no cure (NC). Administering the treatment once is like flipping a coin. Administering the treatment twice is like flipping a coin twice. I want to know the probability that at least one of the two treatments produces a cure. If C corresponds to H, then that's the same as the probability of getting at least one head in two tosses of a coin. A similar analysis would work for three treatments."
(a)   Find the probability that two treatments will result in a cure.
(b)   Find the probability that three treatments will result in a cure.
(c)   How many treatments will be needed to make the probability greater than .99 that the treatments will result in a cure?

28.   Take an ordinary thumbtack, "toss" it 16 times, and record the number of times it lands point up (⤲) and the number of times its lands otherwise (➚). Call S the smaller of these two numbers and use Pascal's triangle (from problem 15) to compute the probability that if landing in these two positions is equally likely, you would get S or fewer of them (out of 16) landing in the position of the smaller number. What do you think about the hypothesis that the two positions are equally likely?

29.   On a 16-question true-false test, you guess each question. This is like tossing a coin: heads for correct, tails for incorrect. What is the probability that if you guess, you will get 75% or more correct?

30.   The sales manager of a large corporation believes that she will be chosen as vice-president of a new division of the corporation if the corporation opens the new division and if this year's sales are higher than last year's. She estimates the probability that the corporation will open the new division to be .90, that this year's sales will be higher than last year's to be .70, and that at least one of these will happen to be .98. What should be her estimate of the probability that she will become vice-president of the new division?

31. In the baseball World Series, the first team to win four games wins the series. (At most, seven games are played.)
    (a) Draw a tree indicating the possibilities for winning the series.
    (b) Suppose the two teams are evenly matched. What is the probability that the series will end in four games?
    (c) Suppose that in a game between the Yankees and the Dodgers, it is estimated that the Dodgers will win with probability .55. What is the probability that a series between these two teams would end in fewer than seven games?

32. While Mr. Jones is on a trip, he must leave his frail rose bush in the care of a lazy gardener. He estimates that the probability of the gardener's tending his plant is .3, the probability of the bush's surviving if cared for is .7, and the probability of the bush's surviving if not cared for is .2. Draw a tree to help figure out the probability of the rose bush's survival.

33. In his never-ending quest for new ways of tormenting his son, Mr. Jones has hit upon the following scheme: He plans to place four $20 bills and one hundred $1 bills in his hat each week. His son Billy is then allowed to reach into the hat and draw out one of the bills. The bill he draws will be his allowance for the week. Little Billy, quickly realizing that the probability of his drawing one of the $20 bills is only $\frac{1}{26}$, hits on the following counterscheme: He asks his father whether he could use two hats; Billy would select some of the 104 bills to place in one, and the rest would be placed in the other. Then picking a hat at random, Billy would draw at random from the bills in the selected hat.
    (a) If Daddy goes along with Billy's scheme, show that Billy can make the probability of getting a $20 bill considerably larger than $\frac{1}{26}$.
    (b) What is the expected value to Billy of Mr. Jones original scheme?
    (c) For Billy's scheme, what is the largest the expected value can be?

ORGANIZING, VISUALIZING, AND ANALYZING DATA

22

C H A P T E R

We collect data to help us understand what is going on in the world and make decisions for action. If we are to use a set of data efficiently, especially when there is a lot of it, we need ways to organize, summarize, and present it. This is particularly important when we are comparing two or more sets of data. In this chapter we will discuss ways of presenting data visually: bar graphs, pie charts, histograms, and box and whisker plots. All these involve organizing the data. One particularly useful device we will discuss is the stem and leaf plot. We will also discuss several numerical measures of a set of data, each one a single number that reveals an important feature of the data and that is often used to summarize the whole set of data. Two of these are measures of *central tendency*—the *mean* and the *median;* one is a measure of *spread—standard deviation.*

BAR GRAPHS AND PIE CHARTS

THE WORK-FORCE PROBLEM

The Council of Education is trying to get some idea of the kinds of careers for which the state should be preparing its high school graduates. The members of a committee set up to investigate this decide to have a look at how the U.S. work force is distributed and obtain the following data.

OCCUPATION	PERCENT OF WORK FORCE	
	1950	1987
White-collar workers	35.8	55.9
Blue-collar workers	40.1	27.6
Service workers	10.2	13.4
Farm workers	11.6	3.1
Other	2.3	0.1

Try this yourself, first.

The members of the committee would like to be able to see this data visually. How can they do this?

A Solution to the Work-Force Problem

The committee members think that if this were a table of inputs and outputs, they would visualize the data using a graph. They are familiar with tables in which the inputs and outputs are numbers. For this table, however, the outputs are numbers, but the inputs (occupations) are not. They decide to use part of the idea anyway, space the occupations equally along the horizontal axis, and plot the percentages vertically.

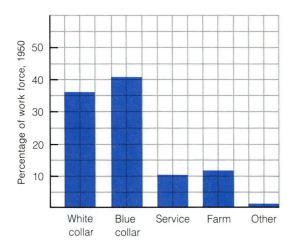
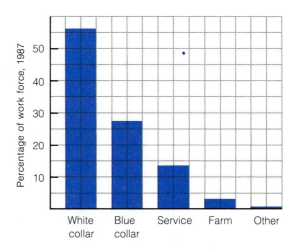

In this way they obtain two graphs, one for the distribution of workers in 1950 and one for the distribution in 1987.

They realize that the two graphs separately don't give them much idea of how the distribution changed from 1950 to 1987, so they decide to put them together, as shown.

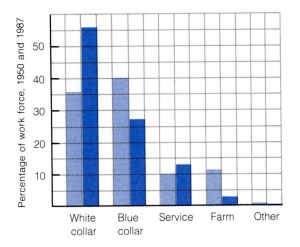

They are pretty happy with this as a device for comparing the distributions of 1950 and 1987 for each occupational group. Now, however, they want a better way to visualize the fraction each occupation takes from the whole work force compared to each of the others. For example, in the graph for 1987, they can see that white-collar workers constitute the largest group, but it is more difficult to see from the graph that they constitute over half the work force. (You have to focus on the numbers of the vertical axis in order to see this.) In the graph for 1950, they can see that while white-collar workers form the second largest group—greater than both service workers and farm workers—it is more difficult to see that white-collar workers are more than service and farm workers combined. They realize that they want a way to visualize fractional parts of a whole thing. They decide to represent the whole thing (the entire work force) as a circle (a pie) and each occupation as a piece of that pie. If an occupation constitutes x% of the entire work force, then it should be represented by x% of the pie. In this manner they obtain the following "graphs."

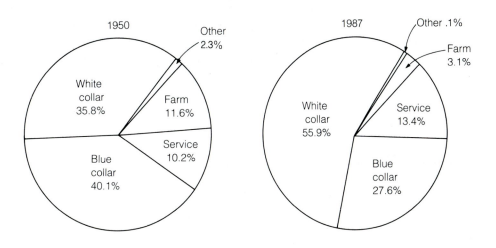

The Mathematical Idea: Bar Graphs and Pie Graphs

All the information about distribution of the work force is contained in the table. Why the interest in turning it into a picture, in visualizing it? Earlier in this book we constructed the graph associated with a table of inputs and outputs and used it to observe visual trends and patterns. It gave us a way to compare one table of inputs with another (as in comparing Cheap Rental with Rent-a-Lemon and comparing the salary from company 1 with that from 2). Even though the work-force distribution table hasn't got numbers for inputs as we had before, we have the feeling that a picture might be useful. With a picture we get to "see" all the information at once and can get beyond the individual pieces of information. Of course, to take full advantage of a picture, we have to learn how to read and interpret what we see.

The first device used for visualizing the work-force data is called a *bar graph*. Here are more examples of sets of data and bar graphs that go with them.

1. HUMAN BIRTH RATES OF THE WORLD, BY REGION

REGION	NO. OF BIRTHS PER 1000 POPULATION
Africa	47
Asia (excluding USSR)	38
Latin America	38
Oceania	25
Europe (excluding USSR)	18
North America	18
USSR	17
World	34

The bar graph that goes with this data follows.

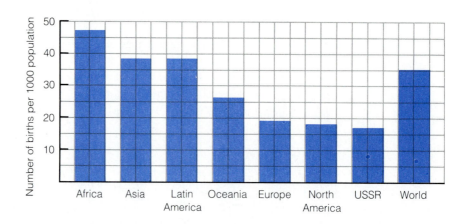

2. HUMAN DEATH RATES OF THE WORLD, BY REGION

REGION	NO. OF DEATHS PER 1000 POPULATION
Africa	20
Asia (excluding USSR)	15
Latin America	9
Oceania	10
Europe (excluding USSR)	10
North America	9
USSR	9
World	14

The bar graph for the death-rate data follows.

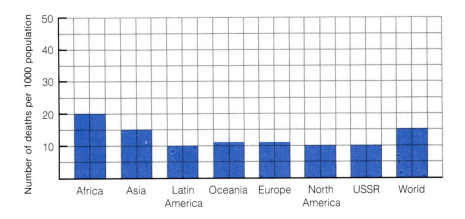

3. HUMAN BIRTH AND DEATH RATES COMPARED

If you are interested in population growth, then human birth and death rates are important items to consider. Population growth itself is really the difference between the two. A way to see all three is to superimpose the two bar graphs from 1 and 2 as in the combined graph, following.

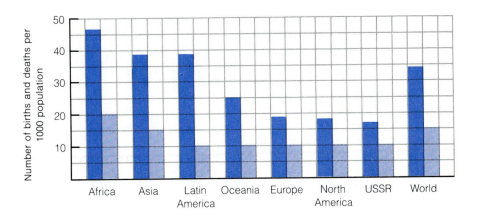

Annual population growth for a region is then indicated by the difference in the height of the corresponding pair of juxtaposed bars.

With the use of pictorial devices in place of bars, the world birth- and death-rate bar graph is transformed into the next graph. Both graphs are read in the same way.

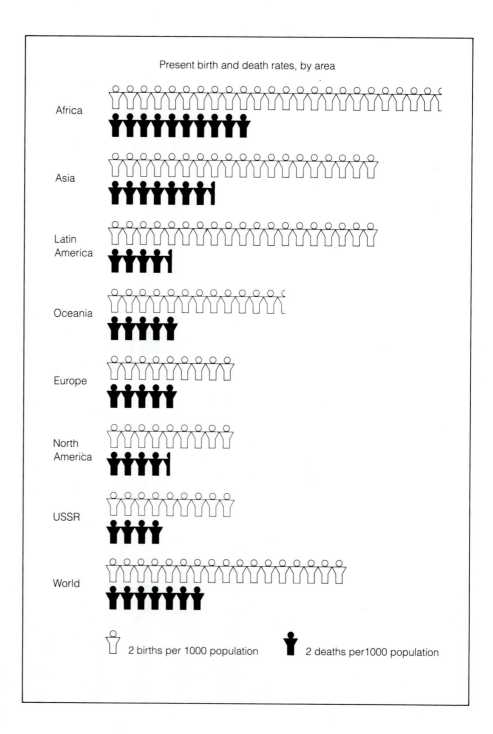

Present birth and death rates, by area

Africa

Asia

Latin America

Oceania

Europe

North America

USSR

World

2 births per 1000 population   2 deaths per 1000 population

The second device for picturing data involves cutting up a pie into pieces. The resulting picture is called a *pie chart* (or *pie graph*). Each piece of the pie is a fraction of the pie and corresponds to a row of the original table. The number in that row must itself be a fraction of some whole thing. For the preceding example, the whole thing is the work force and the number in a row is a fraction of a work force. The tables in examples 1 and 2 do not satisfy this condition and are not candidates for visualization by pie graph. Let's look at some examples that are.

4. WORLD POPULATION, BY REGION (1990)

REGION	POPULATION (IN MILLIONS)
Africa	645
Asia (excluding USSR)	3057
Latin America	453
Oceania	27
Europe (excluding USSR)	500
North America	275
USSR	291
World	5248

First, we construct a bar graph for this table.

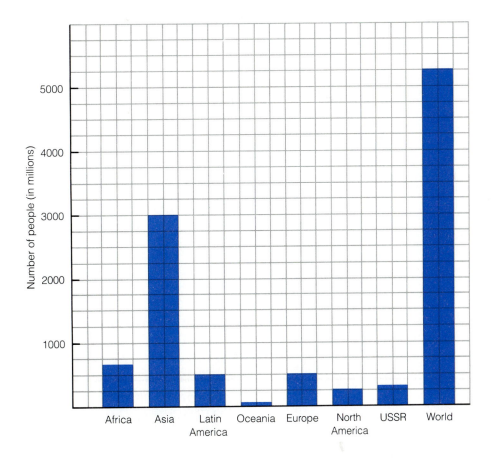

As it stands, we can't construct a pie graph for the table since the entries aren't fractions of some whole thing. However, assuming the world population to be the unit, we can convert the numbers in the table into fractions of this unit (this is easy using the constant, or K, feature of a calculator).

REGION	FRACTION OF WORLD POPULATION
Africa	.123
Asia (excluding USSR)	.583
Latin America	.086
Oceania	.005
Europe (excluding USSR)	.095
North America	.052
USSR	.055
World	1.000

From this we can construct the corresponding pie graph.

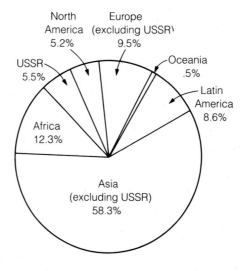

5. U.S. LAND USE

LAND USE	PERCENT OF TOTAL LAND
Urban areas	1.5
Forest	31.7
Grassland, pastures, and range	26.4
Cropland	20.5
Desert, marsh, and other areas of little use	13.3
Recreation and wildlife areas	3.9
Government installations, transportation areas	2.7

Since all the numbers in this table are percents (of the total land in the United States), we can construct a pie graph.

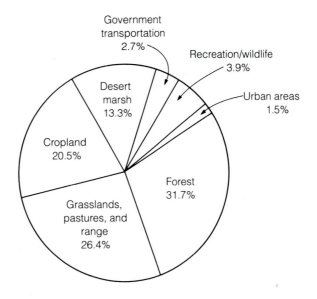

How to Construct a Pie Graph

If you are given a table of fractions (of some unit), it is not difficult to construct a pie graph. You will need a calculator, a compass, and a protractor. We will illustrate how it is done for the table in example 5.

Each piece of a pie graph is really just a sector of a circle. A sector of a circle is measured by the number of degrees in its determining angle.

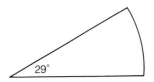

This piece of pie is the fraction of the whole pie

$$\frac{\text{Degrees in angle of sector}}{360}.$$

Now each fraction F in the original table must be converted to a sector of the circle so that

$$F = \frac{\text{degrees in angle of sector}}{360} \qquad \text{or} \qquad F \times 360 = \text{degrees in angle of sector}.$$

Of course, once you know the degrees in the angle of the sector, you can use a protractor to construct the sector corresponding to the fraction F in the table. So the first job is to multiply all the entries in the table by 360 using the constant, or K, feature of your calculator (see page 31 for a refresher on how to do this). For example, let's do this for example 4, the world population, by region. The first entry is Africa with a population the fraction .123 of the world's population. Since $(.123)(360) \sim 44$, Africa will be assigned a sector of the pie graph of 44°. The table gives the degrees corresponding to all the regions.

REGION	FRACTION OF WORLD POPULATION	DEGREES
Africa	.123	44
Asia (excluding USSR)	.583	210
Latin America	.086	31
Oceania	.005	2
Europe (excluding USSR)	.095	34
North America	.052	19
USSR	.055	20
World	1.000	360

Next use your compass to draw a circle (of whatever size you want for your graph). To get started, draw in a radius.

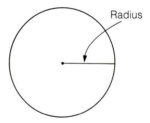

Then, starting with the radius drawn as one side of the first sector, use the protractor and the number in the degrees column in the table to locate the second side of the sector.

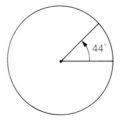

Move on to the next item of the table using the line just drawn as the first side of the sector and proceed as before.

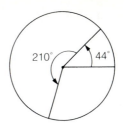

1. Draw a bar graph and a pie chart for the table.

ENERGY PRODUCTION (1987) IN THE UNITED STATES	
SOURCE	PERCENT
Natural gas	26.1
Crude oil	27.3
Coal	31.2
Nuclear electric	7.6
Hydroelectric and geothermal	4.4
Natural gas plant liquids	3.5

2. Make a table consisting of the months of the year listed in the left-hand column and in the right-hand column (for a given month) the number of births in the country during that month last year. (You will need to gather the data somehow. You may try estimating it by calling a local hospital and asking them for the number of births that occurred at their institution for each month of last year; or call your county's registry of births for similar information; or call the appropriate state agency.) Then make a bar graph corresponding to the table. Discuss what you see. Explain what you see, if you can. Discuss the feasibility and desirability of constructing a pie graph corresponding to the table.

3. Construct a bar graph for the table.

DEATH RATES FOR VARIOUS CAUSES FOR PEOPLE AGED 15–24.	
CAUSE	RATE OF DEATH PER YEAR PER 100,000
Heart diseases	2.9
Cancer	6.3
Strokes	1.0
Motor vehicle accidents	44.8
Other accidents	16.9
Suicide	12.3
Homicide	15.6
Birth defects	1.4
Other health-related causes	2.2

If it makes sense, convert the table, as in example 4, so that a pie graph can be constructed; then construct the pie graph.

4. Below is a pie chart showing the various components by weight of air pollution in a certain city.

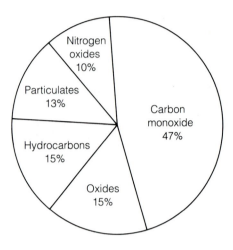

(a) Which item is the largest component of pollution?
(b) Which is the smallest?
(c) Particulates and hydrocarbons together are what percentage of total pollution by weight?

22.2   LINE PLOTS AND HISTOGRAMS

THE SUNSHINE PROBLEM

Please try this yourself before reading on.

The Chamber of Commerce of Boise, Idaho, is putting together a brochure to lure industries to its city. The members think that the city's favorable climate is one factor in getting a company to locate there, and they want to present the case for it. They have obtained data showing the percentage of possible sunshine observed in a variety of American cities and would like to display this data so that a potential client can easily see Boise's favorable position with regard to sunshine. How can they do this?

CITY	AVERAGE % POSSIBLE SUNSHINE OCCURRING	CITY	AVERAGE % POSSIBLE SUNSHINE OCCURRING	CITY	AVERAGE % POSSIBLE SUNSHINE OCCURRING
Montgomery, AL	59	Louisville, KY	57	Cleveland, OH	52
Juneau, AK	31	Shreveport, LA	64	Oklahoma City, OK	67
Phoenix, AZ	86	Portland, ME	58	Portland, OR	47
Little Rock, AR	63	Baltimore, MD	57	Philadelphia, PA	58
Los Angeles, CA	73	Boston, MA	59	Providence, RI	56
San Francisco, CA	67	Sault Ste. Marie, MI	48	Columbia, SC	63
Denver, CO	70	Minneapolis, MN	58	Rapid City, SD	62
Hartford, CT	57	Jackson, MS	64	Memphis, TN	64
Wilmington, DE	53	St. Louis, MO	58	Houston, TX	56
Washington, DC	57	Great Falls, MT	64	Salt Lake City, UT	70
Key West, FL	75	Omaha, NE	62	Burlington, VT	51
Atlanta, GA	61	Reno, NV	80	Richmond, VA	60
Honolulu, HI	68	Concord, NH	54	Seattle, WA	49
Boise, ID	67	Atlantic City, NJ	54	Parkersburg, WV	48
Chicago, IL	57	Albuquerque, NM	77	Milwaukee, WI	56
Indianapolis, IN	58	New York, NY	59	Cheyenne, WY	64
Des Moines, IA	59	Raleigh, NC	60	San Juan, PR	63
Wichita, KS	65	Bismark, ND	62		

A Solution to the Sunshine Problem   One member of the brochure committee suggests: "If we made a bar graph of this data, then a person could *see* where Boise fits in with respect to sunshine. Here's a start."

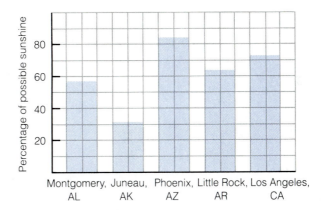

A second member of the committee comments: "That doesn't look very helpful at all. For one thing, all those names of individual cities makes it confusing. For another, we won't be able to see easily how Boise fits in the scheme of things. We need to arrange the data in order of size with smaller percentages first. In fact, why don't we just ignore the names and mark the percentages on a number line, like this?"

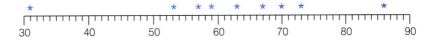

A third member joins in: "On the line you've marked the first nine percentages from our list. The next item is 57, for Washington, DC, and that number has already been marked on the number line (it's the percentage for Hartford, CT). I guess we can 'stack' the new item on top of the old."

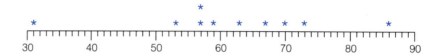

A fourth member adds: "Let's keep going like that and see what happens."

A fifth member exclaims: "It looks good! Let's see where Boise fits in this picture.

I think that diagram makes the city look quite favorable. Shall we print it in the brochure?"

The first member responds: "Before we decide, let's try a variation on what we just did. Instead of stacking individual percentages on the number line, it might be more effective for the brochure if we lump percentages together, stack all the percentages between 45 and 50 together (include 45 but not 50), stack all the percentages between 50 and 55 together (include 50 but not 55), stack all the percentages between 55 and 60 together, and so on. Then squeeze it together a little and mark Boise's position."

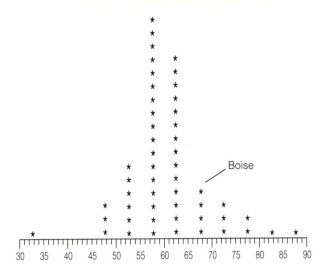

Second member again: "Not bad. I think it might be easier to grasp Boise's position from this last picture than from the earlier one."

The Mathematical Idea: Line Plots and Histograms

The first device the brochure committee used to picture the sunshine data is called a *line plot*. Let's consider another example, a table of data and a graphical presentation of it using a line plot.

PERCENT PHOSPHATES IN DETERGENTS	
DETERGENT	% PHOSPHATES
Ajax Laundry	25
Axion	43
Biz	40
Blue Cheer	22
Breeze	22
Calgon	76
Cold-Water All	10
Fab	22
Ivory Snow	0
Punch	26
Salvo	31
Spic & Span	23
Wisk	8

What are the distinctive features of this picture? When you look at the line plot, you see things that you might not have noticed in the table of data itself. You notice the points at the extreme ends of the line plot. These correspond to the *largest* and *smallest* values of the data in your table. The set of numbers lying between the largest and smallest values, inclusive, is frequently called the *range* of the set of data.

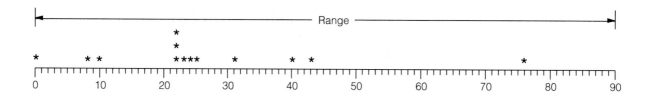

You notice points that are at the extreme ends of the line plot and are also isolated from other points. These points are called *outliers* and correspond to data values that are much bigger or smaller than the others.

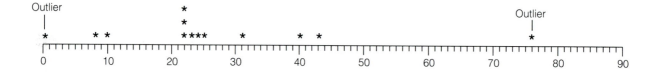

You notice *gaps,* large spaces between points on the lines.

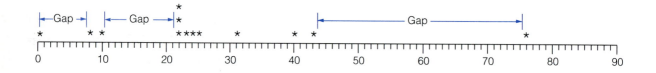

You notice where isolated groups of points, or *clusters,* occur, and you notice a part of the line where most of the points seem to be.

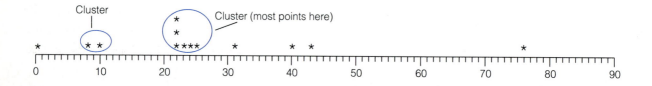

The same features can be identified in the line plot of sunshine percentages.

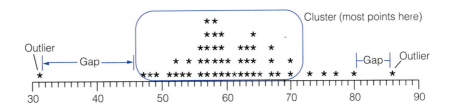

Let's look at another example of a set of data and its graphical presentation.

The table is of crime rates in 1987 for each of the 50 states. The "rate" for each state is actually the number of offenses known to the police for each 1000 persons in the state.

STATE	CRIMES PER 1000	STATE	CRIMES PER 1000	STATE	CRIMES PER 1000
Alabama	45	Louisiana	59	Ohio	46
Alaska	55	Maine	35	Oklahoma	60
Arizona	72	Maryland	55	Oregon	69
Arkansas	42	Massachusetts	47	Pennsylvania	32
California	65	Michigan	65	Rhode Island	53
Colorado	65	Minnesota	46	South Carolina	52
Connecticut	50	Mississippi	35	South Dakota	27
Delaware	49	Missouri	47	Tennessee	46
Florida	85	Montana	46	Texas	77
Georgia	58	Nebraska	41	Utah	56
Hawaii	58	Nevada	64	Vermont	43
Idaho	41	New Hampshire	34	Virginia	40
Illinois	54	New Jersey	53	Washington	70
Indiana	41	New Mexico	65	West Virginia	22
Iowa	41	New York	60	Wisconsin	41
Kansas	49	North Carolina	47	Wyoming	40
Kentucky	32	North Dakota	29		

Here is the line plot for this data.

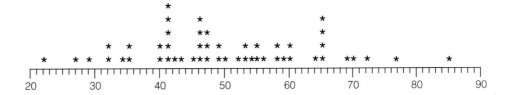

From this plot we see that the range of the data is between 22 and 85. We can also see some places where the points are clustered. The points seem to be pretty evenly spread out between the values of 40 and 60. At this point, it might be useful to do what we did with the sunshine percentage data and lump data together in groups and see what we get. This time, let's put all the values from 20 through 24 in one group, all the values from 25 through 29 in another, all the values from 30 through 34 in another, and so on.

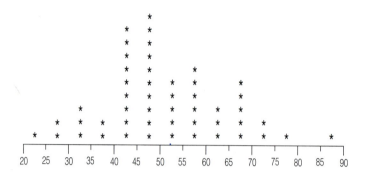

In this picture, the data do not appear to be as spread out as in the line plot. Furthermore, the data appear to become more concentrated as the values move from 25 to 45; then they taper off again as the values move from 45 to 70.

This picture, in which the values from the table are lumped together, is called a *histogram*. The groups into which the data are placed are called *class intervals*. In this case, the class intervals are the numbers from 25 through 29, 30 through 34, 35 through 39, 40 through 44, and so on. Since each interval can contain five possible values, it is called an interval of *size* (or *length*) 5. In a histogram all intervals must be the same size. The number of data items from the table that are lumped into a given class is called the *frequency* of the class. The frequency of the class 30 through 34 in the histogram above is 3, which can be determined by counting the number of *'s stacked there. Similarly, the frequency of the class 45 through 49 is 10. Often, each stack of *'s is replaced by a rectangle of the same height, and a vertical axis is drawn indicating the possible heights of the rectangles. This gives us a graph in which the class intervals are marked along the horizontal axis, and the class frequencies are marked on the vertical axis. Using these conventions, the preceding histogram looks like this.

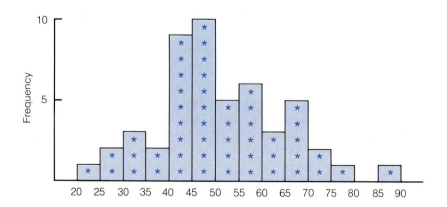

The class intervals we have been using are of size 5. Let's construct another histogram for the same data but with class intervals of size 10. The class intervals will be 20 through 29, 30 through 39, 40 through 49, 50 through 59 and 60 through 69. Here is the resulting histogram.

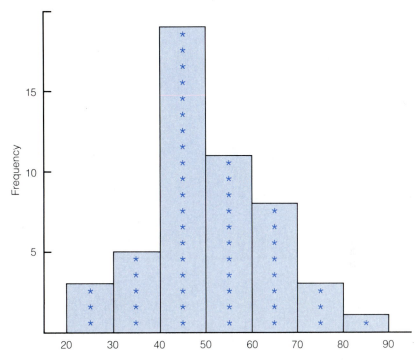

EXERCISES

5. Use the histograms for the crime rate data to begin answering the questions.
   (a) What would you say is the approximate average crime rate in the country? (How did you arrive at your answer?)
   (b) Can you say anything about the states with crime rates at the upper end of the range of data? (65 or more)?
   (c) Can you say anything about the states with crime rates at the lower end of the scale? (less than 35)?
   (d) Does the histogram suggest to you anything about where you might want to live?

6. Construct a line plot for the set of data. Point out the features of the data: its range, outliers (if any), gaps (if any), clusters (if any).

   20 11 31 19 22 19

   14 32 15 20 21 23

   20 26 15 24 18 23

7. From the line plot, construct a histogram for the same set of data with class-interval size of 4.

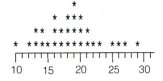

8. In the chart a set of data has already been organized into class intervals and the frequency of each class interval calculated. Construct the histogram that goes with this table.

CLASS INTERVAL	FREQUENCY
20–29	12
30–39	15
40–49	10
50–59	6
60–69	3

9. The set of data is arranged in numerical order. First construct a table of class intervals of size 25 and their frequencies. Then construct the histogram that goes with the table.

105 110 112 123 131 134 137 143 146 149
152 153 155 158 164 165 167 167 169 170
172 177 180 182 188 195 201 207 211

Getting Information from a Histogram

The histogram displays the starting salaries for the 1990 graduates of Eastern College.

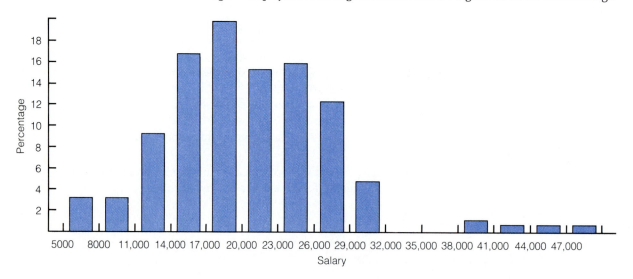

The salaries are shown along the horizontal axis and the percentage of salaries (=100[frequency/total number of salaries]) is shown along the vertical axis. You can obtain a lot of information from the histogram. As with a line plot, you can estimate the smallest salary and the largest salary of the graduates. The values between these two extremes make up the range of values of the set of data. The smallest salary is around $5000, and the largest is around $50,000. You also notice a *gap* and a *cluster* of salaries (between $5000 and $32,000). If you happened to be a graduate of Eastern

College in 1990, you could observe where your salary is relative to the other graduates. For example, suppose your starting salary were $25,900. Your position is shown in the histogram.

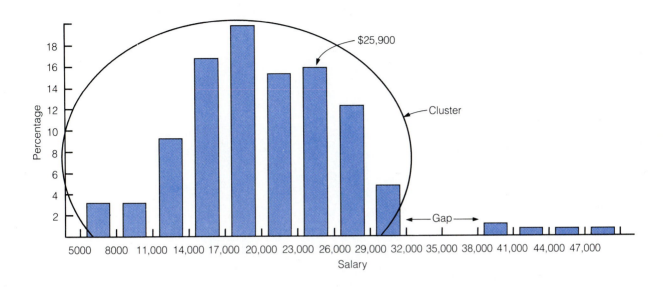

Knowing the position of your salary, you might be interested in other information. For example, you might like to know the percentage of graduates who earn a salary greater than yours. To determine this using the histogram, you must add up the percentages that correspond to the rectangles to the right of your salary. These rectangles are shaded in the next histogram and the percentages marked above each one. (The percentage corresponding to each rectangle can be read from the vertical scale, as in a graph.) So the percentage of people with salaries higher than yours is $12 + 4.5 + 1 + .5 + .5 + .5 = 19$. The number of your classmates starting out with a salary higher than yours amounts to 19%.

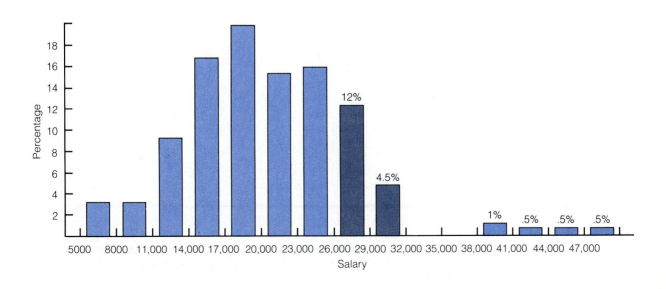

10. The number of children born to a group of women during their entire lives is described by the histogram.

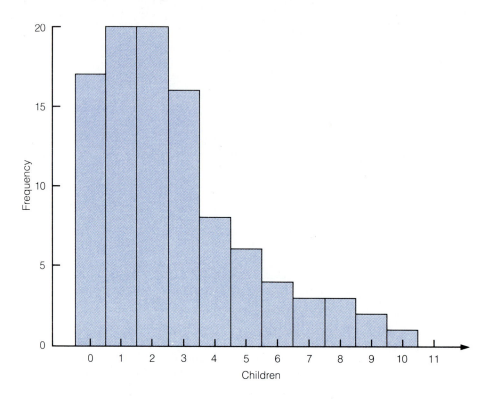

(a) How many women are in the group?
(b) How many women in the group had three or fewer children?
(c) What percentage of the women had seven or more children?

Shapes of Histograms

Often the shape of a histogram can give you information about the people or items being described. Many of the histograms we have created or discussed have features common to the following shapes.

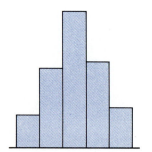 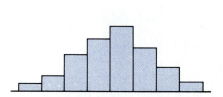 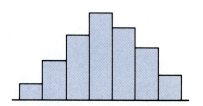

For each of these the heights of the rectangles increase from the left to a high point in the middle after which the heights decrease to the right. There is a "peak" in the middle, and the shape of the histogram is roughly symmetrical about a vertical line through this peak. Such a histogram is called *bell shaped* because, with the sharp edges smoothed off, it has roughly the same shape as one of the bell curves shown, following. (It is also called *normal*, loosely, because such a shape occurs frequently and is therefore normal in the usual English sense of the word. *Normal* also has a technical meaning beyond the scope of this book.)

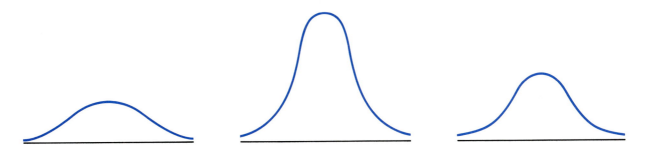

Another shape also occurs commonly.

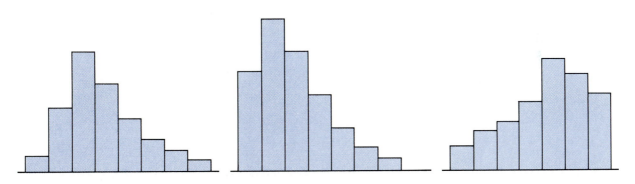

Each of these histograms has a peak, but it does not occur in the middle. For some the rectangles start on the left, rise very quickly in height to a peak, and then drop off slowly on the right with a long "tail." Note the next example, a histogram describing the age at which people start businesses, which illustrates this pattern.

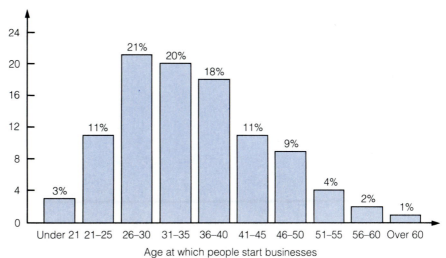

Age at which people start businesses

Source: National Federation of Independent Business.

For others, the peak starts almost immediately at the leftmost edge of the histogram, and the heights of the rectangles decrease as you move to the right along the horizontal axis. An example of such a histogram is given in exercise 10, describing the number of children born to a group of women.

Such histograms in which the heights of the rectangles rise quickly in one direction to a peak and trail off slowly in the other direction are called *skewed*. A skewed histogram in which the "tail" occurs on the left rather than the right is the following, which describes the grades of a group of students on an exam.

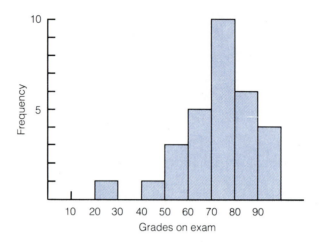

There is also a third shape. This histogram describes the starting salaries for graduates of Western University.

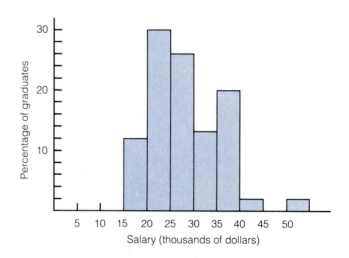

More histograms of similar shape are shown below.

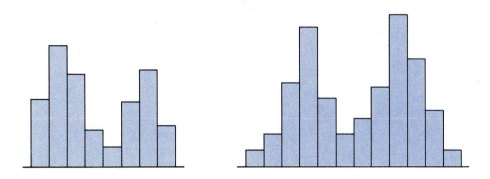

All these histograms share a common feature: Each has two peaks, not just one. Such a histogram is called *bimodal* (as opposed to *unimodal* for a histogram with one peak).

When you notice that one histogram has a shape different from another, it is natural to ask why this is. Why is the number of children histogram skewed to the left rather than bell shaped like the number of days of sunshine histogram? Why is the grades on the exam histogram skewed to the right? Why does the starting salaries for the Western University histogram have two peaks rather than the one peak that the starting salaries for the Eastern University histogram has?

You might begin to answer the question about the number of children histogram in the following way. "I think that the average number of children in a family is around two. Also, a woman cannot have fewer than zero children, so the range of values for the data begins with zero. Furthermore, there are a lot of women with no children, and there are a lot of women with just one child. So there is no gradual buildup from the number of women having zero children to those having two children."

Not every question has such an obvious answer. For example, why are there two peaks instead of one in the histogram of the starting salaries for graduates of Western University? The histogram will not tell you the answer. But you might guess that there are two types of students graduating from Western University and that the histogram describing the salaries for each type has a single peak. It turns out that Western has two undergraduate programs, a liberal arts program and an engineering program. Look at the histograms describing the starting salaries for the graduates from both programs.

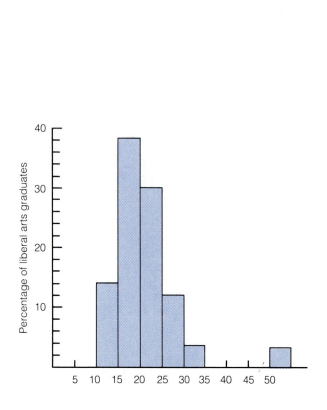

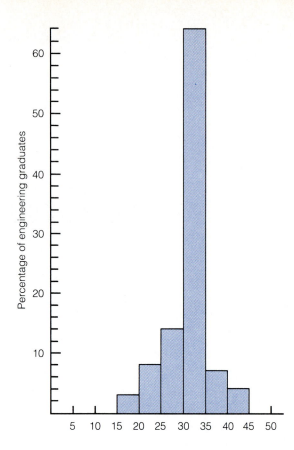

Why is the left-hand peak in the original, combined histogram higher than the right-hand peak? It turns out that Western graduates three times as many students from the liberal arts program as it does from its engineering program.

From these examples it is clear that a histogram can help you to formulate questions that may lead you to finding out more of what is happening behind the data.

11. Review the grades on the exam histogram.
    (a) Why is it skewed to the right?
    (b) What percent of students earned a grade of 90 or more on the exam?
    (c) What percent of students earned a grade of 60 or less?

12. The histogram shows the heights of the entering freshmen at Midwestern University.

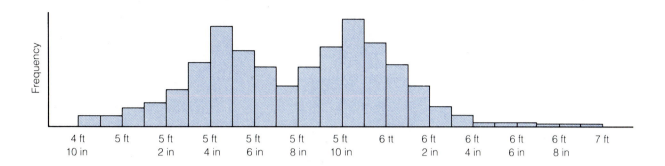

(a) Why does this histogram have two peaks?

(b) What percent of students are taller than 6 ft 6 in? What percent of students are shorter than 5 ft?

13. The histogram shows the adjusted gross annual income for individuals in the United States with income less than $30,000.

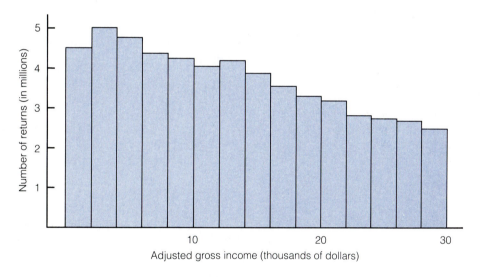

(a) Why is this histogram skewed to the left?

(b) What percent of the population has an income between $20,000 and $30,000?

Following are the average 1987 state and local taxes, as a percentage of income, paid by a family of four in 30 large U.S. cities. The income of each family was $35,000.

CITY	STATE AND LOCAL TAX AS % OF INCOME	CITY	STATE AND LOCAL TAX AS % OF INCOME	CITY	STATE AND LOCAL TAX AS % OF INCOME
Albuquerque, NM	7.4	Des Moines, IA	10.2	Norfolk, VA	7.9
Atlanta, GA	9.7	Detroit, MI	11.7	Omaha, NE	7.6
Baltimore, MD	10.8	Honolulu, HI	9.7	Philadelphia, PA	11.9
Bridgeport, CT	12.5	Indianapolis, IN	7.6	Portland, ME	8.7
Burlington, VT	7.7	Jackson, MS	7.7	Portland, OR	11.5
Charleston, WV	7.7	Louisville, TN	8.9	Providence, RI	11.0
Charlotte, NC	8.2	Memphis, TN	6.8	St. Louis, MO	7.4
Chicago, IL	8.1	Milwaukee, WI	13.3	Salt Lake City, UT	9.4
Cleveland, OH	9.3	Newark, NJ	13.5	Sioux Falls, SD	6.3
Columbia, SC	8.3	New York, NY	11.2	Washington, DC	10.8

Source: *Statistical Abstract of the United States 1989*, U.S. Department of Commerce, Bureau of the Census, Washington, D.C., 1989, no. 475, p. 291.

You are interested in constructing a histogram for this set of data. There is an easy way to do this.

First, designate a certain part of each number in the chart as its *stem* and the rest as its *leaf*. For this chart the stem will be the part of the number to the left of the decimal point, and the leaf will be the part of the number to the right of the decimal point. For the number 7.4 in the chart, its stem is 7 and its leaf is 4. The stem of 11.0 is 11 and its leaf is 0. The stem of 13.5 is 13 and its leaf is 5.

Next list all the possible stems for the data in a column, starting at the top with the smallest stem and continuing to the largest. (The smallest stem is 6, from Memphis and Sioux Falls; the largest is 13, from Milwaukee and Newark.)

STEMS
6
7
8
9
10
11
12
13

The next step is to place the leaf of each number in the chart to the right of its stem. For example, the first number in the chart is 7.4 (for Albuquersque). Its stem is 7. So you place its leaf, 4, next to the 7 as shown.

STEMS	LEAVES
6	
7	4
8	
9	
10	
11	
12	
13	

If you proceed in a similar fashion with all the other numbers in the chart, what you get looks like this.

STEMS	LEAVES
6	83
7	47767964
8	21397
9	7374
10	828
11	72950
12	5
13	35

This is what is called a *stem and leaf plot* of the original data. If you turn this plot on its side, you will get something closely resembling a histogram with interval size 1, like this.

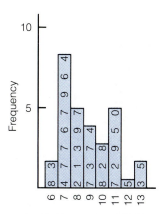

To make this turned-on-its-side stem and leaf plot into a familiar-looking histogram, all you have to do is replace each stack of digits with a rectangle,

Let's look at another example. This time we have a chart of the annual resident tuition for a selection of large public universities in the United States.

UNIVERSITY	ANNUAL RESIDENT TUITION (1989)	UNIVERSITY	ANNUAL RESIDENT TUITION (1989)	UNIVERSITY	ANNUAL RESIDENT TUITION (1989)
U. of Alabama	$1642	U. of Maryland		Ohio State U.	$2040
U. of Alaska	1332	(College Park)	$1906	U. of Oklahoma	1000
U. of Arizona	1446	U. of Massachusetts	2350	Oregon State U.	1604
U. of Arkansas	1290	Michigan State U.	4242	Penn State U.	
U. of Cal. (Berkeley)	1670	U. of Minnesota		(University Park)	3610
U. of Colorado	2000	(Minneapolis)	2412	U. of Rhode Island	2331
U. of Connecticut	2623	U. of Mississippi	1790	U. of South Carolina	2228
Delaware State College	1000	U. of Missouri (Columbia)	1801	U. of South Dakota	1804
U. of Florida	1144	Montana State U.	1343	U. of Tennessee	1456
U. of Georgia	1849	U. of Nebraska	1703	U. of Texas (Austin)	830
U. of Hawaii (Manova)	1230	U. of Nevada (Reno)	1280	U. of Utah	1517
U. of Idaho	1048	U. of New Hampshire	2767	U. of Vermont	3726
Northern Illinois U.	2072	Rutgers State U. of		U. of Virginia	3950
Indiana U. (Bloomington)	1887	New Jersey	2744	Washington State U.	1798
Iowa State U.	2739	U. of New Mexico	1222	West Virginia U.	1400
U. of Kansas	1355	SUNY (Albany)	1478	U. of Wisconsin (Madison)	1857
U. of Kentucky	1540	U. of North Carolina		U. of Wyoming	1003
Louisiana State U.	1814	(Chapel Hill)	876		
U. of Maine (Orono)	1970	U. of North Dakota	1472		

Source: From Otto Johnson, ed., *Information Please Almanac 1990,* Houghton Mifflin, Boston, 1989, pp. 846–871.

To construct a stem and leaf plot of this data, we first round the data to the nearest hundreds.

UNIVERSITY	ANNUAL RESIDENT TUITION (1989)	UNIVERSITY	ANNUAL RESIDENT TUITION (1989)	UNIVERSITY	ANNUAL RESIDENT TUITION (1989)
U. of Alabama	$1600	U. of Maryland		Ohio State U.	$2000
U. of Alaska	1300	(College Park)	$1900	U. of Oklahoma	1000
U. of Arizona	1400	U. of Massachusetts	2400	Oregon State U.	1600
U. of Arkansas	1300	Michigan State U.	4200	Penn State U.	
U. of Cal. (Berkeley)	1700	U. of Minnesota		(University Park)	3600
U. of Colorado	2000	(Minneapolis)	2400	U. of Rhode Island	2300
U. of Connecticut	2600	U. of Mississippi	1800	U. of South Carolina	2300
Delaware State College	1000	U. of Missouri (Columbia)	1800	U. of South Dakota	1800
U. of Florida	1100	Montana State U.	1300	U. of Tennessee	1500
U. of Georgia	1800	U. of Nebraska	1700	U. of Texas (Austin)	800
U. of Hawaii (Manova)	1200	U. of Nevada (Reno)	1300	U. of Utah	1500
U. of Idaho	1000	U. of New Hampshire	2800	U. of Vermont	3700
Northern Illinois U.	2100	Rutgers State U. of		U. of Virginia	4000
Indiana U. (Bloomington)	1900	New Jersey	2700	Washington State U.	1800
Iowa State U.	2700	U. of New Mexico	1200	West Virginia U.	1400
U. of Kansas	1400	SUNY (Albany)	1500	U. of Wisconsin (Madison)	1900
U. of Kentucky	1500	U. of North Carolina		U. of Wyoming	1000
Louisiana State U.	1800	(Chapel Hill)	900		
U. of Maine (Orono)	2000	U. of North Dakota	1500		

We specify the stem for each of the numbers in this chart to be the 1000s digit and the leaf to be the 100s digit. Because there will be too many leaves for some stems, we split each stem in two.

STEM	LEAF
2	
*	

After the 2 we will place the leaves 0, 1, 2, 3, 4, and after the *, the leaves 5, 6, 7, 8, 9. Here is the stem and leaf plot.

STEMS	LEAVES
0	
*	98
1	34301204332040
*	678958988755685589
2	01044032
*	6787
3	
*	67
4	20
*	

And here is the stem and leaf plot turned into a histogram.

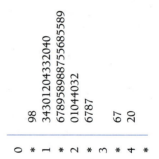

EXERCISES

14. Make a stem and leaf plot for the data in the sunshine chart. Designate the 10s digit of each number as the stem and the unit's digit as the leaf.

15. Here are the yields (in tons per acre) for the vineyards owned by a Sacramento Valley grape farmer in a certain recent year.

4.7	7.4	6.1	5.9	8.0	1.9	1.8	5.3	8.1	6.6	9.0
6.8	9.7	3.3	7.7	2.8	8.8	6.2	1.4	7.9	3.6	2.3
7.6	2.2	7.1	2.8	4.5	0.9	7.3	7.5	8.6	8.2	4.0
2.7	6.7	6.0	1.9	8.8	9.5	2.6	1.4	2.4	7.9	3.0
1.9	6.5	9.2	7.1	8.1	9.3	2.2	5.7	8.4	2.2	7.3

Make a stem and leaf plot of this data. Use the part of the number to the left of the decimal point as the stem and the part to the right as the leaf.

16. Use the stem and leaf plot for the tuition data to create a histogram for the data.

17. A company that is looking for a location in which to construct a new plant may be concerned with the living conditions for employees that must be transferred there. One condition for living in a given location is the size of the local tax bite. On the one hand, a large tax eats into an employee's income; on the other hand, a large tax may reflect the quality of local services, such as schools and transportation. Use the tax histogram we created earlier in the chapter to see if you can locate areas of the country where taxes are high and areas where they are low. Use it to estimate the typical local tax for a family of four having an annual income of $30,000 in the United States. If you think that high taxes occur in locations where schools are better, in what parts of the country is the quality of public education best? Discuss.

18. Use the tuition data stem and leaf plot (or the histogram from exercise 16) to look for answers to the questions.
    (a) What is the average annual tuition for a state university?
    (b) In what parts of the country is tuition lowest?
    (c) In what parts of the country is tuition highest?
    (d) How do you account for low tuition in some parts of the country and high tuition in other parts?

When to Use a Bar Graph, Pie Chart, or Histogram: Qualitative versus Quantitative Data

When you fill out a questionnaire, you provide various bits of information about yourself. Some of this information (data)—your name, nationality, sex, address, occupation—is called *qualitative data*. Other data about yourself—your height, weight, annual salary, age—are measured on numerical scales (or number lines) and are called *quantitative data*.

For the work-force problem, a survey was taken (questionnaires filled out!), the occupation (a qualitative category) of every individual noted, the number in each category counted, and the fraction of each category in the whole population of people surveyed calculated. We used a bar graph and a pie chart as ways of displaying this data visually. In our bar graph the qualitative categories occur along the horizontal axis, and the percentages or fractions are marked quantitatively along the vertical axis. (In some bar graphs the two axes are reversed. But every bar graph has at least one quantitative axis.) In a pie chart, each piece of the pie is simultaneously a fraction (a number) and is typically also labeled qualitatively.

To obtain the chart giving the human birth rates for regions of the world, a survey was taken, each individual "placed" in the region (a qualitative category) where he or she lives, the number in each category counted, the number in each category born that year counted, and the ratio of the latter to the former calculated. We used a bar graph to display the data visually. We did not use a pie chart because it was not appropriate to do so. The items in the table were not fractions (or percents) of some one whole thing. In the work-force problem, each quantitative item in the right-hand column of the table is the percent of the entire work force belonging to the qualitative category noted in the left-hand column. All the items in the right-hand column add up to 100%, as they should.

OCCUPATION	PERCENT OF WORK FORCE 1950	
White-collar workers	35.8 ⎫	
Blue-collar workers	40.1 ⎪	
Service workers	10.2 ⎬	All percents.
Farm workers	11.6 ⎪	
Other	2.3 ⎭	
Total	100.0	Numbers in column sum to 100.

In the sunshine problem we started with a table having cities of the United States (qualitative categories) listed in the left-hand column and percent of possible sunshine in the right-hand column. A bar graph would not provide us with a very useful picture. For one thing, there are too many categories. Instead, we created a histogram, in which the qualitative categories are ignored (the cities have been eliminated; only the percent of sunshine remains). The horizontal axis of a histogram plays the role of a real number line; in the sunshine problem, points on this axis represent percents of possible sunshine. The horizontal axis has been divided into class intervals, and along the vertical axis is indicated the possible numbers of items in the original table falling into each class interval.

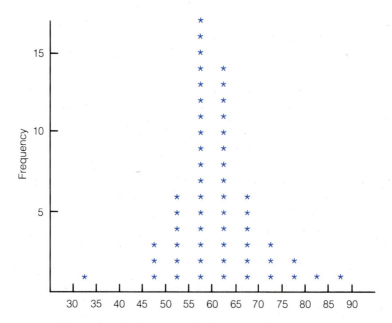

EXERCISE 19. For each table of data, decide which type or types of visual description would be useful—bar graph, pie chart, or histogram. For each table and each description, discuss how the visual description could be used.

(a) Per capita debts by state (1986)

STATE	STATE DEBT PER CAPITA ($)	STATE	STATE DEBT PER CAPITA ($)	STATE	STATE DEBT PER CAPITA ($)
Alabama	926	Louisiana	2329	Ohio	824
Alaska	13,085	Maine	1330	Oklahoma	1158
Arizona	449	Maryland	1213	Oregon	2643
Arkansas	458	Massachusetts	2030	Pennsylvania	656
California	745	Michigan	775	Rhode Island	3025
Colorado	612	Minnesota	892	South Carolina	1102
Connecticut	2292	Mississippi	451	South Dakota	1840
Delaware	4162	Missouri	741	Tennessee	449
Florida	486	Montana	1518	Texas	325
Georgia	402	Nebraska	819	Utah	796
Hawaii	2655	Nevada	1266	Vermont	1819
Idaho	657	New Hampshire	2321	Virginia	663
Illinois	1038	New Jersey	2216	Washington	800
Indiana	396	New Mexico	1445	West Virginia	1112
Iowa	562	New York	2044	Wisconsin	974
Kansas	143	North Carolina	412	Wyoming	1627
Kentucky	1103	North Dakota	1094		

(b) Lengths of the world's 10 longest highway tunnels

TUNNEL	LENGTH (MILES)
St. Gotthard (Switzerland)	10.01
Mont Blanc (France-Italy)	7.20
Great St. Bernard (Italy-Switzerland)	3.60
Viella (Spain)	3.10
Ahmed Hamdi (Egypt)	3.00
Mersey (England)	2.80
Kanmon (Japan)	2.10
Reboucas (Brazil)	1.80
Brooklyn-Battery (USA)	1.73
Eisenhower (USA)	1.70

(c) A state's expenditures (where the tax money goes . . .)

CATEGORY	AMOUNT (MILLIONS OF $)
Education	1056
Public welfare	118
Highways	300
Hospitals	76
Natural resources	35
Health	64
Insurance trusts	148
Total	2288

(d) Density of the planets in the solar system

PLANET	DENSITY (WATER = 1)
Mercury	5.13
Venus	5.26
Earth	5.52
Mars	3.94
Jupiter	1.33
Saturn	0.69
Uranus	1.56
Neptune	2.27
Pluto	4.00

22.4   LOOKING BACK: NUMERICAL MEASURES OF A SET OF DATA

Mean and Standard Deviation

Recall that a histogram is bell shaped if it has a single peak and if it is symmetrical about a vertical line passing through the peak. One way to distinguish one bell-shaped histogram from another is by the location of the peak. For example, in the bell-shaped histograms shown, the peaks are located at the values 45, 6.5, and 350 along the horizontal axes. It turns out that the approximate location of the peak can be calculated directly from the set of data without drawing the histogram. The number is called the *mean* of the set of data.

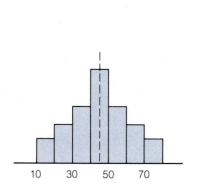

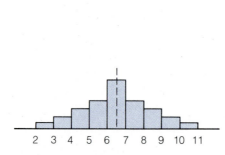

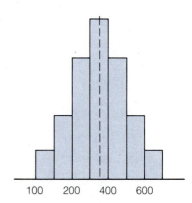

DEFINITION OF *MEAN OF A SET OF NUMBERS*

To calculate the *mean* of a set of numbers, add all the numbers, then divide by the number of elements in the set.

For example, to calculate the mean of the following set of numbers

$$\{8,7,3,12,20,4\},$$

add them: $8 + 7 + 3 + 12 + 20 + 4 = 54$. Then divide 54 by the number of elements (six) in the set: $54 \div 6 = 9$. The mean is 9.

As another example, to calculate the mean of the set of Fahrenheit temperatures

$$\{5, -6, -2, 0, -10, 8, 15, 0\},$$

add them—$5 + (-6) + (-2) + 0 + (-10) + 8 + 15 + 0 = 10$—and divide what you get by 8: $\frac{10}{8} = 1.25$. The mean is 1.25.

EXERCISES

20. Calculate the mean of the set of percents of phosphates in detergents (p. 947). Mark the location of the mean on a histogram describing this data.

21. Calculate the mean of the set of percents in the sunshine problem. Use a calculator.

The mean of a set of data can be calculated even if the histogram is not bell shaped. The location of the mean is marked on the horizontal axis of the next histograms.

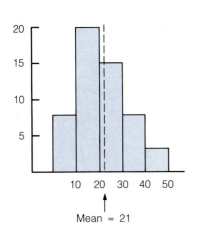

Mean ≈ 21

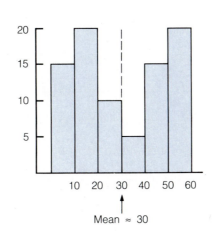

Mean ≈ 30

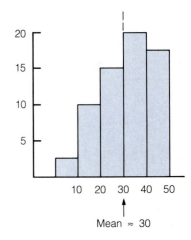

Mean ≈ 30

The mean occurs at the point on the horizontal axis where the histogram would balance if placed on a fulcrum.

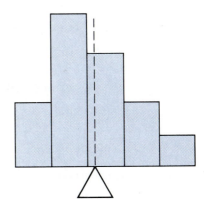

A second feature of a histogram that enables us to distinguish one bell-shaped histogram from another is its spread. Some bell-shaped histograms are flat and spread out; others are steep and narrow. A number that measures this aspect of the shape of a histogram is called a *measure of dispersion*.

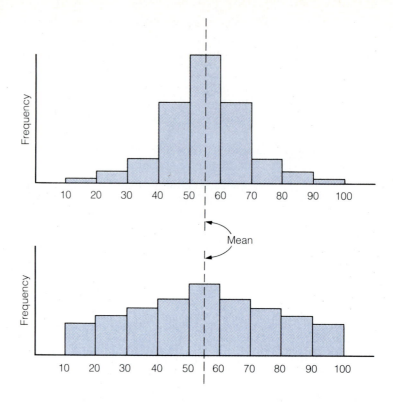

The measure of dispersion that is used most frequently is the standard deviation.

DEFINITION OF *STANDARD DEVIATION*

To calculate the *standard deviation* of a set S of data,

1. Calculate the mean m.
2. Subtract m from all the elements of the set S, obtaining a new set N.
3. Square all the elements of the set N and add them.
4. Find the average of the numbers in 3.
5. Take the square root of the number you get in 4.

   This last number is the standard deviation.

For example, take the set of data $\{8,7,3,12,20,4\}$. We calculated the mean earlier and got $m = 9$. Next subtract 9 from all the elements in the set:

$$8 - 9 = -1$$
$$7 - 9 = -2$$
$$3 - 9 = -6$$
$$12 - 9 = 3$$
$$20 - 9 = 11$$
$$4 - 9 = -5$$

Next square all the numbers in the new set:

$(-1)^2 = 1$
$(-2)^2 = 4$
$(-6)^2 = 36$
$3^2 = 9$
$11^2 = 121$
$(-5)^2 = 25$

Then add all the squares:

$$1 + 4 + 36 + 9 + 121 + 25 = 196.$$

Divide by the number of elements in the set:

$$\frac{196}{6} \cong 32.667.$$

Take the square root:

$$\sqrt{32.667} \cong 5.715.$$

The quantity 5.715 is the standard deviation of the set of data.

EXERCISE   **22.** Calculate the standard deviation for the set of Fahrenheit temperatures.

$\{5, -6, -2, 0, -10, 8, 15, 0\}$.

Roughly, the flatter and more spread out the histogram, the larger the value of the standard deviation. Here are some histograms with their standard deviations given. Again, a histogram needn't be bell shaped for the standard deviation to be calculated.

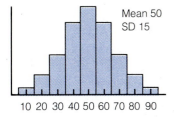

Mean 50
SD 15

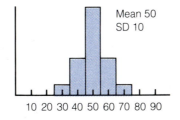

Mean 50
SD 10

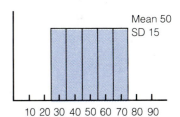

Mean 50
SD 15

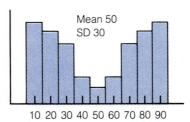

Mean 50
SD 30

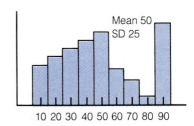

Mean 50
SD 25

The Median

The mean is sometimes used as a single number to summarize a set of data. The mean is a kind of average or typical value for the data. (In fact, in certain contexts *average* is synonymous with *mean*.)

However, you can sometimes be rushed in thinking of the mean as typical for a set of data. For example, suppose the annual salaries of the employees of a small company are: $9,000, $12,500, $15,800, $16,200, $21,000, $22,300, $65,000. The mean of this set of numbers is $23,114.29. Six of the seven salaries in the company are less than the mean! The mean hardly seems to be typical in this case.

Another choice for a single number to summarize the set of salaries would be the middle number (when the salaries are arranged in order from small to large). The middle number is $16,200 and is called the *median* of the set of data. Let's define *median*.

DEFINITION OF *MEDIAN OF A SET OF DATA*

To calculate the *median* of a set of data, arrange the data in order from large to small. If the number of elements in the set is odd, the median is the number in the middle. If the number of elements in the set is even, add the *two* middle numbers and divide by 2 to get the median.

For example, to calculate the median of the data 8, 7, 3, 12, 20, 4, arrange the numbers in order from small to large: 3, 4, 7, 8, 12, 20. Since the number of elements in the set is even, take the two middle numbers, 7 and 8, add them and divide by 2:

$$\frac{7 + 8}{2} = 7.5.$$

The median is 7.5.

As another example, to calculate the median of the test scores 37, 82, 90, 86, 77, first arrange them in order: 37, 77, 82, 86, 90. Then, since the number of elements in the set is 5, an odd number, you take the middle one, 82, which is the median.

The mean and the median are both used to summarize a set of data and act as "typical" elements of the set. For the set of annual salaries, there is *one* very large salary, compared to the others. In this case, the mean may be much larger than what we would want to consider as a typical salary. To see this, suppose we take a different set of salaries: {$9,000,$12,500,$15,800,$16,200,$21,000,$22,300,$25,100}. This is the same set that we had before, with one exception: The largest salary has been changed from $65,000 to $25,100. The median for this new set is the same as before—$16,200—while the mean is now $17,414.29—a considerable change but now more "typical." It seems that the mean is sensitive to extreme values. The addition of a few very large or very small values compared to the other numbers in the set can change the mean significantly, especially if the number of elements in the set of data is small. The median is not affected very much by such additions.

EXERCISES

23. Find the mean of the set of five test scores for which we calculated the median: {37,82,90,86,77}. Which value do you think is more typical of the set of test scores, the mean or the median? Discuss.

---

24. Find the mean and the median for the data given in the table.

GRADUATING CLASS GRADE POINT AVERAGES	
INTERVAL	FREQUENCY
2.0–2.2	42
2.2–2.4	37
2.4–2.6	33
2.6–2.8	28
2.8–3.0	19
3.0–3.2	12
3.2–3.4	11
3.4–3.6	8
3.6–3.8	5
3.8–4.0	3

25. The table gives certain information about the economy of some Middle African countries.

(a) Compute the mean and the median for the data given.

PER CAPITA GROSS NATIONAL PRODUCT (GNP) FOR MIDDLE AFRICAN COUNTRIES (1979)	
COUNTRY	PER CAPITA GNP (US$)
Angola	330
Cameroon	340
Central African Empire	250
Chad	130
Congo	500
Equatorial Guinea	340
Gabon	3730
Sao Tome & Principe	420
Zaire	130

(b) Which value is more typical, the mean or the median?

(c) How would you account for the fact that the 1979 *World Population Data Sheet* of the Population Reference Bureau gives $250 as the mean per capita GNP for all the people of Middle Africa?

26. San Pedro is a small, growing suburb of a large city. Here are the results of a recent survey of the families living in this town.

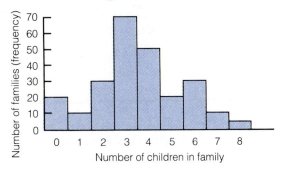

(a) Would you use the mean or the median of this data to describe the "typical" San Pedro family if you were the administrator of the county's only school trying to predict the number of children to expect in the fall based on the number of families in the town at that time and the number of children in a "typical" family?

(b) If you were a small land developer wanting to build one type of house designed for the "typical" family, what would the typical family be?

27. Complete the table so that the mean equals the replacement level (i.e., the mean should equal 2, the number of parents per family). There are many correct answers. (It might be interesting to compare various answers.)

CHILDREN DESIRED PER FAMILY	NO. OF FAMILIES
0	
1	
2	36
3	
4	
5	2
Total	100

22.5   EXTENDING THE IDEAS: BOX AND WHISKER PLOTS

Consider the scores on a test for the students from two different classes.

Class 1: 57, 60, 61, 63, 65, 68, 70, 70, 73, 74, 75, 78, 80, 82, 84, 86, 87, 89, 90, 92
Class 2: 55, 57, 60, 63, 68, 69, 70, 71, 73, 74, 75, 76, 76, 78, 79, 83, 85, 89, 92, 95

How do the two classes compare? We could calculate the means and the medians of the two sets and compare them.

Class 1: Median = 74.5; mean = 75.2
Class 2: Median = 74.5; mean = 74.4

The medians are the same; the means are almost the same. Based on these two measures, the two classes performed pretty much the same on the test.

There is another way to represent a set of data visually that may enable us to compare the two sets of test scores. It is easy to construct (easier than a histogram) and involves the median. The visual representation of the set of data is called a *box and whisker plot*. We will illustrate how to construct one using the test scores from class 1. First, we will need to determine or calculate five values associated with the set of data. Three of these values we already know: (1) the lowest score (57), (2) the highest score (92), (3) the median (74.5). The remaining two values are called the *lower quartile* and the *upper quartile*. (The idea is to divide the data roughly into fourths, or quarters. This is the origin of the word *quartile*.) To calculate the lower quartile, you take the lower half of the scores (not including the median, in case the number of original data is odd),

$$57, 60, 61, 63, 65, 68, 70, 70, 73, 74,$$

and find its median: $(65 + 68)/2 = 66.5$. This number (66.5) is called the *lower quartile* of the original set of scores. Similarly, to determine the upper quartile, you take the upper half of the scores (again, not including the median, in case the number of original data is odd), 75, 78, 80, 82, 84, 86, 87, 89, 90, 92, and find its median: $(84 + 86)/2 = 85$. This number (85) is called the *upper quartile* of all the scores. Next, place the five values along a number line.

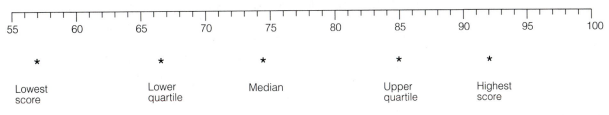

Then draw a box with the lower quartile at one side on the left and the upper quartile at the opposite side. In the box draw a line vertically through the median.

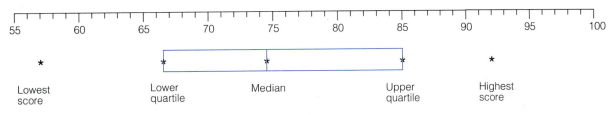

Finally, connect the lowest and highest scores to the box with a "whisker."

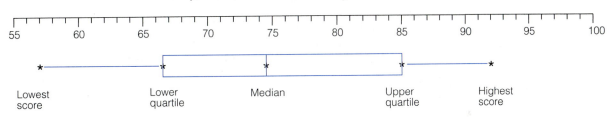

You see that the middle 50% of all the scores lie in the box; half of these lie to the right of the middle line and half to the left. The upper 25% lie along the upper (right) whisker; the lower 25% lie along the lower (left) whisker.

Let's construct a box and whisker plot for the scores for class 2 and see if we can see a difference. Here are the scores from the lower half: 55, 57, 60, 63, 68, 69, 70, 71, 73, 74. The lowest score is 55, and the lower quartile is 68.5. From the scores from the upper half, 75, 76, 76, 78, 79, 83, 85, 89, 92, 95, the upper quartile is 81, and the highest score is 95. Look at the box and whisker plot for class 2, set directly below the one for class 1:

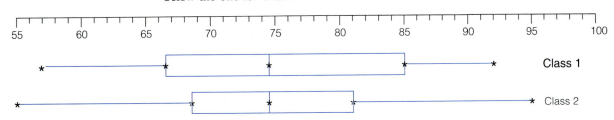

From the two box and whisker plots, we can see that while the range of scores for class 2 is larger, the scores for class 1 in the middle portion are more spread out than those of class 2. On the other hand, the scores for class 2 are more spread out at the upper and lower ends than those of class 1.

Here is the box and whisker plot for a third class, drawn directly below those for the other two.

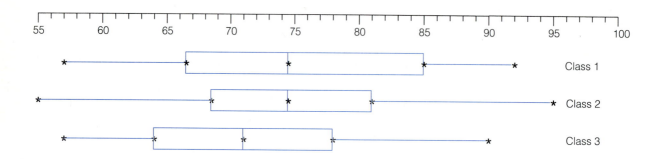

You can see that the median for the third class is lower than for the other two. At the same time, you can see that the scores for class 3 seem to be generally lower than those for the other two classes, at least in the middle range.

Here is a list of daily high temperatures in degrees Fahrenheit for 40 consecutive days in two different cities of the United States.

CITY 1

69 70 78 79 92 79 65 69 83 80
76 74 81 71 80 82 75 81 61 72
73 74 74 77 72 80 68 70 74 69
85 85 73 81 88 77 81 85 60 72

CITY 2

60 84 86 82 71 82 74 67 87 67
77 69 76 61 78 60 90 89 65 81
63 77 83 69 72 76 62 80 71 89
65 68 64 79 75 90 74 66 84 73

To compare the temperatures in these two cities, we would like to make box and whisker plots of the two sets of data. Let's start with the first city. First we must arrange the data in order. An easy way to do this is to make a stem and leaf plot of the data, then count in from the top and bottom to obtain the median and quartiles. It would be natural to use the 10s digits of the numbers as stems

6
7
8
9

and the units digits as leaves. A glance at the set of data suggests that some stems would have too many leaves. So we spread out the stem and leaf plot.

6
*
7
*
8
*
9
*

We will put the leaves 0, 1, 2, 3, 4 on the first line of each stem and 5, 6, 7, 8, 9 on the second.

CITY 1
6 01
* 58999
7 001222334444
* 5677899
8 000111123
* 5558
9 2
*

From this we find

Lowest value: 60
Lower quartile: 71.5
Median: 75.5
Upper quartile: 81
Highest value: 92

Then from this we obtain the box and whisker plot:

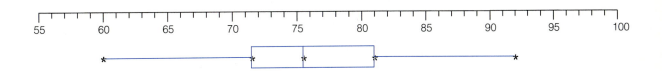

EXERCISES   28. (a) Construct a stem and leaf plot for the temperatures of city 2 and use it to make a whisker and box plot as we did for the temperatures of city 1.
(b) Look at the two whisker and box plots to see if they tell you anything about how the temperatures of the two cities compare.
(c) Look at the stem and leaf plots for the two cities for the same thing.
(d) Which of the two plots do you prefer for purposes of comparison?

29. Here are the average (over 30 yr) monthly high temperatures for five U.S. cities:

City	J	F	M	A	M	J	J	A	S	O	N	D
Tucson	64	67	72	80	89	99	99	96	94	84	72	65
San Diego	65	66	66	68	69	71	71	78	77	75	70	66
San Francisco	65	69	61	63	66	70	71	72	73	70	63	56
Miami	75	76	79	82	85	87	89	89	88	84	80	76
Seattle	45	50	53	58	65	69	75	74	69	60	51	47

(a) Make a box and whisker plot for each of the cities.
(b) Use the box and whisker plots to compare the weather in the five cities.
(c) What do the plots say about the quality of the weather in the five cities?

22.6   COMPUTERS AND THE ORGANIZATION OF DATA

You may be convinced that drawing a pie graph, a histogram, or a box and whisker plot can be very useful for understanding and analyzing a set of data. But you may not be happy at the prospect of having to construct one of these visual aids, especially if the data set is large. One way to deal with this situation is to use computer software that will create the visual presentation for you once you give it the set of data. One type of software that can be used just for this purpose is a spreadsheet. In the lab manual designed to accompany this text, LAB Activity 21 does just this.

22.7   SUMMARY OF IMPORTANT IDEAS AND TECHNIQUES

- Qualitative versus quantitative data
- Bar graphs and pie charts; when to use them and how to make them
- Line plots and their features: range, outliers, gaps, and clusters
- Constructing a histogram by dividing the data into class intervals of a certain size and calculating the class frequency
- Features of histograms: peaks, normal histograms, skewed histograms, bimodal and unimodal histograms
- An easy way to construct a histogram from a set of data: a stem and leaf plot
- Numerical measures of a set of data: mean, standard deviation, and median
- A final method for organizing and visualizing a set of data: box and whisker plot

PROBLEM SET

PRACTICING
SKILLS

1. Below is a table of the percentages of total municipal solid waste by weight for several categories in 1960 and 1984 in the United States.

CATEGORY	1960	1984
Paper and paperboard	32.1	37.1
Glass	8.4	9.7
Metals	13.7	9.6
Plastics	.5	7.2
Rubber and leather	2.2	2.5
Textiles	2.6	2.1
Wood	3.9	3.8
Food wastes	14.6	8.1
Yard wastes	20.3	17.9
Other	1.7	1.9

(a) Construct bar graphs corresponding to this table for the two years. Juxtapose the two graphs as in the work-force problem.

(b) What do the two graphs tell you about the change in the makeup of municipal waste in the United States from 1960 to 1984?

2. The table gives the voter participation in the Unites States for presidential elections between 1932 and 1988.

(a) Construct a bar graph corresponding to this table.

(b) In recent years many political observers have claimed that the American public is taking less and less advantage of its right to vote. What do you think of their claims?

VOTING FOR PRESIDENT					
	CANDIDATES	VOTER PARTICIPATION (% OF VOTING-AGE POPULATION)		CANDIDATES	VOTER PARTICIPATION (% OF VOTING-AGE POPULATION)
1932	Roosevelt-Hoover	52.4	1964	Johnson-Goldwater	51.2
1936	Roosevelt-Landon	56.0	1968	Humphrey-Nixon	50.9
1940	Roosevelt-Wilke	58.9	1972	McGovern-Nixon	55.2
1944	Roosevelt-Dewey	56.0	1976	Carter-Ford	53.5
1948	Truman-Dewey	51.1	1980	Carter-Reagan	54.0
1952	Stevenson-Eisenhower	51.8	1984	Mondale-Reagan	53.2
1956	Stevenson-Eisenhower	50.3	1988	Dukakis-Bush	50.0
1960	Kennedy-Nixon	42.3			
(Source: Federal Election Commission)					

3. Study the bar graph to answer the questions.

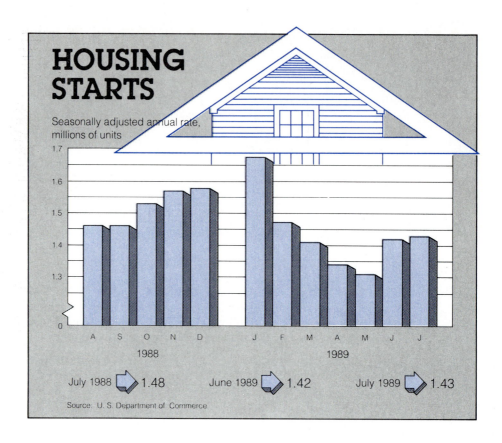

HOUSING STARTS

Seasonally adjusted annual rate, millions of units

July 1988 ⇨ 1.48   June 1989 ⇨ 1.42   July 1989 ⇨ 1.43

Source: U. S. Department of Commerce

(a) During which month of the year preceding August 1989 was the number of starts the least?
(b) During which month of the year preceding August 1989 was the number of starts the greatest?
(c) During which months did construction of more than 1,500,000 houses begin?

4. The bar graph shows the average monthly sales per shop for quick-print franchisees.
(a) How much did a typical Alphagraphics quick-print franchise shop sell during the whole year of 1988?
(b) When did an Alphagraphics franchise begin to make twice as much per month on the average as other quick-print franchises?

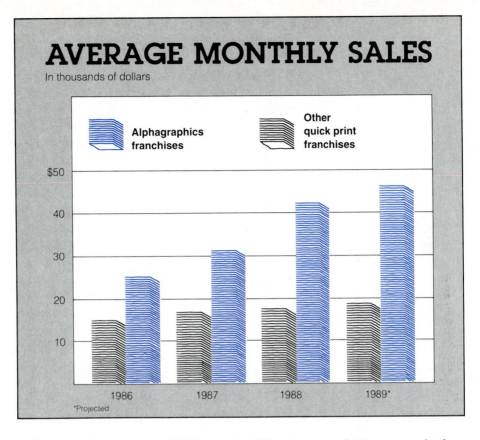

AVERAGE MONTHLY SALES

In thousands of dollars

Alphagraphics franchises

Other quick print franchises

$50
40
30
20
10

1986   1987   1988   1989*

*Projected

5. The earth's atmosphere consists of 21% oxygen, 78% nitrogen, and 1% argon and other gases. Make a pie chart of the earth's atmosphere.

6. The pie chart illustrates land ownership in Pima Country, Arizona.

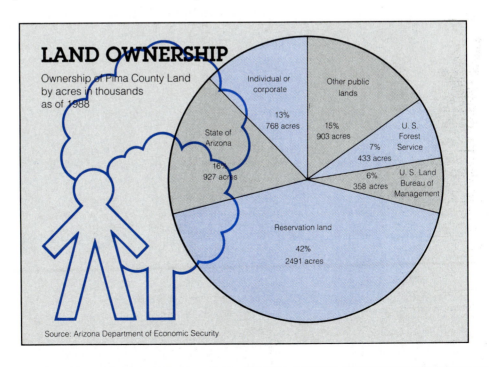

LAND OWNERSHIP

Ownership of Pima County Land by acres in thousands as of 1988

Individual or corporate
13%
768 acres

Other public lands
15%
903 acres

U. S. Forest Service
7%
433 acres

State of Arizona
16%
927 acres

U. S. Land Bureau of Management
6%
358 acres

Reservation land
42%
2491 acres

Source: Arizona Department of Economic Security

(a) What percentage of land in Pima County is owned by the U.S. government? (Reservation land is owned by Native Americans.)

(b) What percentage of land in Pima County is owned by governments at all levels?

7. The pie charts illustrate various data about the U.S. work force.

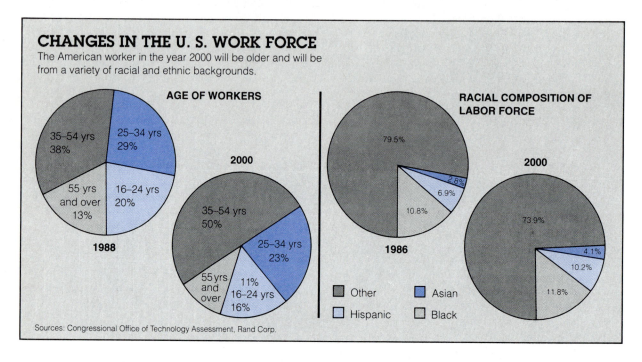

CHANGES IN THE U. S. WORK FORCE

The American worker in the year 2000 will be older and will be from a variety of racial and ethnic backgrounds.

AGE OF WORKERS

RACIAL COMPOSITION OF LABOR FORCE

35–54 yrs 38% 25–34 yrs 29% 55 yrs and over 13% 16–24 yrs 20%

1988

2000

35–54 yrs 50% 25–34 yrs 23% 55 yrs and over 11% 16–24 yrs 16%

79.5% 2.8% 6.9% 10.8%

1986

2000

73.9% 4.1% 10.2% 11.8%

☐ Other ☐ Asian
☐ Hispanic ☐ Black

Sources: Congressional Office of Technology Assessment, Rand Corp.

(a) Workers 35 or more years of age made up what percentage of the work force in 1988? Workers 35 or more years of age will make up what percentage of the work force in the year 2000?

(b) What do these charts tell you about the changes in the U.S. work force?

8. The table gives the miles of coastline and of shoreline for the states in the United States.

U.S. COASTLINE BY STATES					
STATE	COASTLINE[1]	SHORELINE[2]	STATE	COASTLINE[1]	SHORELINE[2]
Atlantic coast	2,069	28,673	Virginia	112	3,315
Connecticut	0	618	Gulf coast	1,631	17,141
Delaware	28	381	Alabama	53	607
Florida	580	3,331	Florida	770	5,095
Georgia	100	2,344	Louisiana	397	7,721
Maine	228	3,478	Mississippi	44	359
Maryland	31	3,190	Texas	367	3,359
Massachusetts	192	1,519	Pacific coast	7,623	40,298
New Hampshire	13	131	Alaska	5,580	31,383
New Jersey	130	1,792	California	840	3,427
New York	127	1,850	Hawaii	750	1,052
North Carolina	301	3,375	Oregon	296	1,410
Pennsylvania	0	89	Washington	157	3,026
Rhode Island	40	384	Arctic coast, Alaska	1,060	2,521
South Carolina	187	2,876	United States	12,383	88,633

(1) Figures are lengths of general outline of seacoast. Measurements were made with a unit measure of 30 minutes of latitude on charts as near the scale of 1:1,200,000 as possible. Coastline of sounds and bays is included to a point where they narrow to width of unit measure, and includes the distance across at such point. (2) Figures obtained in 1939-40 with a recording instrument on the largest-scale charts and maps then available. Shoreline of outer coast, offshore islands, sounds, bays, rivers, and creeks is included to the head of tidewater or to a point where tidal waters narrow to a width of 100 feet.

Source: NOAA, U.S. Commerce Department (statute miles)

(a) Make a stem and leaf plot for the miles of coastline.
(b) Make a stem and leaf plot for the miles of shoreline.

9. Turn the stem and leaf plots in problem 8 into histograms.
(a) How many states have a longer coastline than Maine? How many have a longer shoreline?
(b) How many states in the chart have a shorter coastline than Florida? How many have a shorter shoreline?
(c) How do you account for the differences?

10. Below is a stem and leaf plot giving the altitudes (in hundreds of feet) of selected volcanoes in the world.

```
 0 | 98766562
 1 | 97719630
 2 | 6998776654442211009850
 3 | 876655412099551426
 4 | 99988443319294333611107
 5 | 97666666554422210097731
 6 | 898665441077761065
 7 | 98855431100652108073
 8 | 653322122937
 9 | 377655421000493
10 | 0984433165212
11 | 4963201631
12 | 45421164
13 | 47830
14 | 00
15 | 676
16 | 52
17 | 92
18 | 5
19 | 39730
```

(a) How many volcanoes have an altitude higher than 10,000 ft?

(b) Describe the shape of the stem and leaf plot. (You might want to turn it into a histogram first.) How do you account for this shape?

11. Below is a table of population density by state for various years.

DENSITY OF POPULATION BY STATES (PER SQUARE MILE, LAND AREA ONLY)													
STATE	1920	1960	1970	1980	STATE	1920	1960	1970	1980	STATE	1920	1960	1970	1980
Ala.	45.8	64.2	67.9	76.6	La.	39.6	72.2	81.0	94.5	Ch.	141.4	236.6	260.0	263.3
Alas.*	0.1	0.4	0.5	0.7	Me.	25.7	31.3	32.1	36.3	Okla.	29.2	33.8	37.2	44.1
Ariz.	2.9	11.5	15.6	23.9	Md.	145.8	313.5	396.6	428.7	Ore.	8.2	18.4	21.7	27.4
Ark.	33.4	34.2	37.0	43.9	Mass.	479.2	657.3	727.0	733.3	Pa.	194.5	251.4	262.3	264.3
Cal.	22.0	100.4	127.6	151.4	Mich.	63.8	137.7	156.2	162.6	R. I.	566.4	819.3	902.5	897.8
Col.	9.1	16.9	21.3	27.9	Minn.	29.5	43.1	48.0	51.2	S. C.	55.2	78.7	85.7	103.4
Conn.	286.4	520.6	623.6	637.8	Miss.	38.6	46.0	46.9	53.4	S. D.	8.3	9.0	8.8	9.1
Del.	113.5	225.2	276.5	307.6	Mo.	49.5	62.6	67.8	71.3	Tenn.	56.1	86.2	94.9	111.6
D. C.	7,292.9	12,523.9	12,401.8	10,132.3	Mon.	3.8	4.6	4.8	5.4	Tex.	17.8	36.4	42.7	54.3
Fla.	17.7	91.5	125.5	180.0	Neb.	16.9	18.4	19.4	20.5	Ut.	5.5	10.8	12.9	17.8
Ga.	49.3	67.8	79.0	94.1	Nev.	.7	2.6	4.4	7.3	Vt.	38.6	42.0	47.9	55.2
Ha.*	39.9	98.5	119.6	150.1	N. H.	49.1	67.2	81.7	102.4	Va.	57.4	90.6	116.9	134.7
Ida.	5.2	8.1	8.6	11.5	N. J.	420.0	805.5	953.1	986.2	Wash.	20.3	42.8	51.2	62.1
Ill.	115.7	180.4	199.4	205.3	N. M.	2.9	7.8	8.4	10.7	W. Va.	60.9	77.2	72.5	80.8
Ind.	81.3	128.8	143.9	152.8	N. Y.	217.9	350.6	381.3	370.6	Wis.	47.6	72.6	81.1	86.5
Ia.	43.2	49.2	50.5	52.1	N. C.	52.5	93.2	104.1	120.4	Wy.	2.0	3.4	3.4	4.0
Kan.	21.6	26.6	27.5	28.9	N. D.	9.2	9.1	8.9	9.4					
Ky.	60.1	76.2	81.2	92.3						U. S.	*29.9	50.6	57.4	64.0

*For purposes of comparison, Alaska and Hawaii included in above tabulation for 1920, even though not states then

(a) Construct a stem and leaf plot for the year 1980.

(b) What does the shape of the plot say about the United States?

12. Use the data for problem 11 to find the answers.

(a) mean population density

(b) median population density

(c) standard deviation of the population densities

13. Use the data in problem 8 to find the answers.

(a) mean coastline length

(b) median coastline length

(c) standard deviation of coastline lengths

14. Below is a table of per capita tax revenues for selected countries in 1985.

TAX REVENUES, 1985	
COUNTRY	PER CAPITA (DOL.)
United States	$4,740
Australia	3,213
Austria	3,714
Belgium	3,854
Canada	4,621
Denmark	5,573
Finland	4,116
France	4,216
Greece	1,178
Italy	2,565
Japan	3,107
Netherlands	3,879
New Zealand	2,304
Norway	6,668
Portugal	676
Spain	1,226
Sweden	6,064
Switzerland	4,554
United Kingdom	3,025
West Germany	3,869

(a) Make a stem and leaf plot for the revenues.

(b) Use the stem and leaf plot to make a box and whisker plot.

(c) In both plots indicate the position of the United States.

(d) What is the percentage of countries shown that have per capita tax revenues less than that of the United States? Do the plots show this?

(e) How do the two visual displays of data compare for this set of data?

15. The box and whisker plots display the Nielsen ratings for prime-time television shows during the week of April 29–May 5, 1985. The plots indicate that the shows have ratings between 5 and 25. A show with rating of 15.5 means that out of 1000 houses with televisions, 155 were watching that show when it was on.

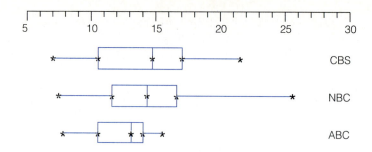

(a) Use the plots to estimate the median, quartiles, and range for NBC.
(b) Which network had the highest-ranking show?
(c) Which network had the largest median?
(d) Which network had the largest upper quartile?
(e) Write a description of the relative standings of the three networks for the week in question.

USING IDEAS   *In essay form write the solution to each of the problems that remain. Mention the steps you took to solve the problem, the principles, tools, or formulas you used, other problems or solutions that gave you ideas, and the problem-solving strategies you found helpful.*

16.   The table shows the number of bachelor degrees conferred in this country by subject for the years 1970–71 and 1985–86.

UNDERGRADUATE BACHELOR DEGREES CONFERRED		
DISCIPLINE	1970–71	1985–86
Agriculture, natural resources	12,672	16,823
Architecture, environmental design	5570	9119
Business, management, public affairs	121,117	252,038
Communications	10,802	43,091
Computer, information sciences	2388	41,889
Education	176,614	87,221
Engineering	50,046	95,953
Health sciences	25,190	64,535
Home economics	11,167	15,288
Humanities, general studies, languages	98,485	71,023
Natural sciences, mathematics	81,956	76,561
Social sciences, psychology	193,116	134,224
Visual, performing arts	30,394	36,949
Other	15,924	36,310
Total	835,441	981,024

Source: From Mark S. Hoffman, ed., *The World Almanac and Book of Facts 1989*, Pharos, New York, 1988, p. 253.

(a) Construct a bar graph corresponding to each of the two years. Juxtapose the graphs as in the work-force problem.

(b) Use the graph to discuss the changes from 1970–71 to 1985–86 in the pattern of degrees conferred. What questions for further research do these changes suggest?

17. Below is a table giving the number of persons employed by occupation and by sex in 1987.

NO. OF PERSONS EMPLOYED (THOUSANDS)		
OCCUPATION	MALE	FEMALE
Managerial and professional specialty	15,457	12,286
Technical, sales, and administrative support	12,378	22,704
Service occupations	5924	9130
Precision production, craft, and repair	12,416	1153
Operators, fabricators, and laborers	12,978	4508
Farming, forestry, and fishing	2954	554

Source: From Mark S. Hoffman, ed., *The World Almanac and Book of Facts 1989*, Pharos, New York, 1988, p. 152.

(a) Construct a pair of bar graphs, one for the number of males employed and another for the number of females and juxtapose these two graphs as in the work-force problem.

(b) Use the graphs to discuss the issue of the equality of opportunity for employment for men and women in various occupations.

18. The table shows how people in this country spend their money after taxes (1987).

CATEGORY	AMOUNT SPENT (BILLIONS OF $)
Food, beverages, and tobacco	562.1
Clothing and personal care	265.9
Housing and household operations	830.0
Medical care	403.2
Personal business	215.5
Transportation	378.9
Recreation and foreign travel	236.9
Private education	51.3
Religious and welfare activities	68.1

Source: From Mark S. Hoffman, *The World Almanac and Book of Facts 1989*, Pharos, New York, 1988, p. 146.

(a) Construct a pie chart corresponding to this table.

(b) What percentage of money is spent on food, clothing, and housing? Make some observations regarding personal spending in the United States. What additional data might be useful in studying this?

19. Below is a table showing the use of selected drugs among graduating high school students for the classes of 1975 and 1987.

PERCENT OF GRADUATES WHO EVER USED DRUG		
DRUG	CLASS OF '75	CLASS OF '87
Marijuana/hash	47	50
Hallucinogens	16	10
Cocaine	9	15
Heroin	2	1
Alcohol	90	92
Cigarettes	74	67

Source: From Mark S. Hoffman, ed., *The World Almanac and Book of Facts 1989,* Pharos, New York, 1988, p. 215.

(a) Construct a pair of bar graphs, one for 1975 and another for 1987. Juxtapose the two graphs.

(b) What sorts of trends in the use of drugs are suggested by a comparison of the two graphs?

20. Below is a table giving the average life spans of a large selection of mammals.

ANIMAL	AVERAGE LONGEVITY (YEARS)	ANIMAL	AVERAGE LONGEVITY (YEARS)
Ass	12	Hippopotamus	25
Baboon	20	Horse	20
Bear: black	18	Kangeroo	7
grizzly	25	Leopard	12
polar	20	Lion	15
Beaver	5	Monkey	16
Buffalo (American)	15	Moose	12
Camel	12	Mouse (meadow)	8
Cat (domestic)	15	Mouse (domestic)	8
Chimpanzee	20	Opossum (American)	7
Chipmunk	5	Pig (domestic)	10
Cow	15	Puma	12
Deer (white-tailed)	8	Rabbit (domestic)	5
Dog (domestic)	12	Rhinoceros (black)	15
Elephant (African)	25	Rhinoceros (white)	20
Elephant (Asian)	40	Sea lion (Californian)	12
Elk	15	Sheep (domestic)	12
Fox (red)	7	Squirrel	10
Giraffe	10	Tiger	16
Goat (domestic)	8	Wolf	5
Gorilla	20	Zebra	15
Guina pig	4		

Source: From Mark S. Hoffman, ed., *The World Almanac and Book of Facts 1989,* Pharos, New York, 1988, p. 258.

(a) Construct a stem and leaf plot from these data.

(b) Indicate the position of a human being in this plot and discuss.

21. The median prices of homes for selected U.S. cities in the first quarter of 1988 are shown in the table.

CITY		CITY	
Akron, OH	$ 57,100	Los Angeles, CA	$198,900
Albany, NY	82,800	Louisville, KY	51,100
Albuquerque, NM	79,700	Memphis, TN	77,800
Anaheim/Santa Ana, CA	185,800	Miami, FL	78,000
Baltimore, MD	83,600	Milwaukee, WI	72,500
Baton Rouge, LA	85,700	Minneapolis/St. Paul, MN	84,400
Birmingham, AL	73,100	Nashville, TN	77,800
Boston, MA	176,900	New Orleans, LA	73,000
Buffalo, NY	84,100	New York, NY	186,600
Charleston, SC	72,500	Oklahoma City, OK	56,500
Chattanooga, TN	61,200	Omaha, NB	58,300
Chicago, IL	82,800	Orlando, FL	78,700
Cincinnati, OH	87,000	Philadelphia, PA	81,400
Cleveland, OH	85,500	Phoenix, AZ	79,000
Columbus, OH	66,200	Pittsburgh, PA	80,900
Dallas/Fort Worth, TX	85,900	Portland, OR	82,900
Denver, CO	83,700	Providence, RI	123,300
Des Moines, IA	64,500	Rochester, NY	73,200
Detroit, MI	71,500	St. Louis, MO	74,100
El Paso, TX	67,300	Salt Lake City/Ogden, UT	85,300
Ft. Lauderdale, FL	78,500	San Antonio, TX	63,400
Grand Rapids, MI	65,400	San Diego, CA	134,400
Hartford, CN	166,400	San Francisco, CA	178,800
Honolulu, HI	195,400	Seattle/Tacoma, WA	85,100
Houston, TX	80,200	Syracuse, NY	65,100
Indianapolis, IN	61,800	Tampa, FL	60,200
Jacksonville, FL	86,900	Toledo, OH	56,500
Kansas City, MO	70,900	Tulsa, OK	63,500
Knoxville, TN	66,300	Washington, D.C.	132,400
Las Vegas, NV	75,700	W. Palm Beach, FL	94,500

Source: From Mark S. Hoffman, ed., *The World Almanac and Book of Facts 1989*, Pharos, New York, 1988, p. 799.

(a) Construct a stem and leaf plot from these data.

(b) Use the table and the plot to describe the geographic patterns of housing prices around the country. (You might want to include in your description those parts of the country where prices are particularly high and those parts where they are particularly low.)

22. The high school graduation rate by state in 1986 is given in the table.

STATE	%	STATE	%
Alabama	71.5	Montana	87.2
Alaska	67.3	Nebraska	88.1
Arizona	61.0	Nevada	86.2
Arkansas	78.0	New Hampshire	73.3
California	66.7	New Jersey	77.6
Colorado	73.1	New Mexico	72.3
Connecticut	68.8	New York	64.2
Delaware	70.7	North Carolina	70.0
District of Columbia	66.8	North Dakota	80.7
Florida	82.0	Ohio	80.4
Georgia	62.7	Oklahoma	71.6
Hawaii	70.8	Oregon	74.1
Idaho	73.0	Pennsylvania	78.5
Illinois	75.8	Rhode Island	67.3
Indiana	71.7	South Carolina	64.5
Iowa	87.5	South Dakota	61.5
Kansas	81.3	Tennessee	67.4
Kentucky	66.8	Texas	64.3
Louisiana	62.7	Utah	60.3
Maine	78.5	Vermont	77.6
Maryland	76.6	Virginia	73.2
Massachusetts	76.7	Washington	75.2
Michigan	67.8	West Virginia	73.2
Minnesota	81.1	Wisconsin	86.3
Mississippi	63.3	Wyoming	61.2
Missouri	75.6		

Source: From Mark S. Hoffman, ed., *The World Almanac and Book of Facts 1989,* Pharos, New York, 1988, p. 223.

(a) Construct a stem and leaf plot for these data.
(b) Use the plot and the table to see if you can detect any geographic patterns in the graduation rates. (Are there particular geographic regions where low/high rates occur? Are regions of industrialization/urbanization where low/high rates occur?) Discuss what you find.

23. Below is a table giving the monthly morning average (over 30 yr) relative humidity for Miami, New York, Los Angeles, and Seattle.

CITY	J	F	M	A	M	J	J	A	S	O	N	D
Miami	84	83	82	79	81	85	85	86	88	86	85	83
New York	65	65	66	66	70	72	72	75	75	73	71	68
Seattle	80	80	82	83	82	81	81	83	86	86	83	82
Los Angeles	63	71	74	78	81	85	84	84	78	76	61	62

(a) Construct a box and whisker plot for each city. Construct the plots on the same scale so that they can be compared.
(b) Describe the relative humidities of the cities using the plots you have made.

24. In place of a subdivided pie (where the whole pie represents 100%), a subdivided bar of a fixed length is often used instead.

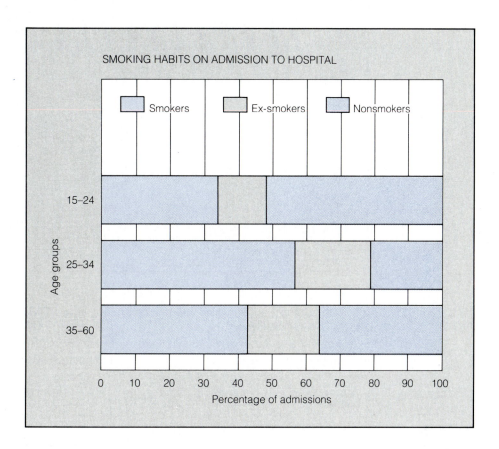

(a) Which age group has the largest percent of smokers?
(b) Which are group has the largest percent of non-smokers?

25. A *line graph* is often used in place of a bar graph, especially when the items in the left-hand column of the corresponding table of data are successive days, months, or years. In this case, the horizontal axis is treated as a number line (a "time line"), the rows of the table are plotted as points in the coordinate plane, and consecutively plotted points are connected with a line. (This is similar to a situation in chapter 14 where we constructed the graph associated with a table or a function.)

The example shows rates of unemployment in the United States for the months July 1988– July 1989.

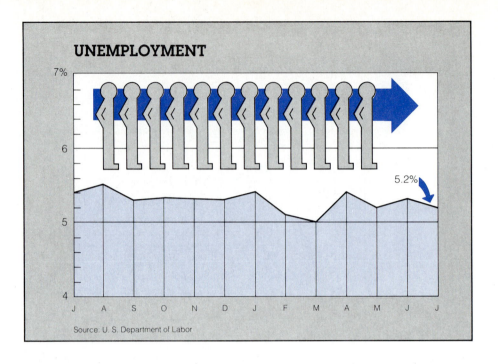

UNEMPLOYMENT

Source: U. S. Department of Labor

(a) During which month of this year was unemployment lowest? What was the rate of unemployment for that month?

(b) How did unemployment in July 1989 compare with that of July 1988?

(c) During the months of September 1988 through December 1988, employment was pretty steady. Estimate the rate of employment during those months.

26. Bar graphs can indicate negative as well as positive quantities.

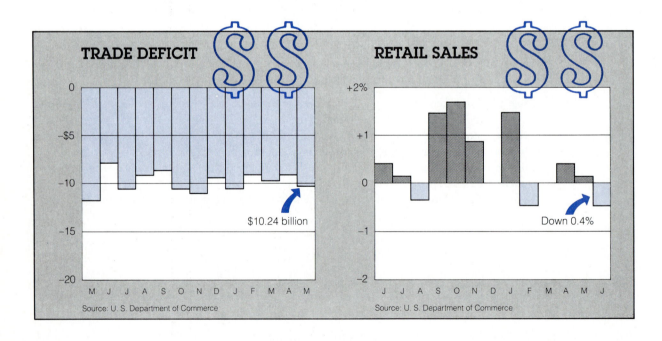

TRADE DEFICIT

$10.24 billion

Source: U. S. Department of Commerce

RETAIL SALES

Down 0.4%

Source: U. S. Department of Commerce

(a) In the trade deficit graph, the monthly (May 1988–May 1989) deficits are shown as negative numbers. During which month in this period was the deficit greatest? What was the deficit?

(b) In the retail sales graph for the months of June 1988 through June 1989, what do the "positive" and "negative" bars mean? (For example, the bar for June 1989 is a negative .4%. What does this mean?)

(c) A histogram can never indicate negative values on the vertical axis. Why not?

27. In the example of world human birth and death rates, we saw how pictorial devices can replace the use of bars.

(a) Here is another example:

Reprinted courtesy of *The Washington Post*.

The example of the shrinking dollar is misleading, however. The length of each dollar bill shown corresponds to its buying power, compared to the 1958 Eisenhower dollar. For example, the buying power of the 1968 dollar compared to the 1958 dollar is 83¢, so the length of the 1968 dollar shown is 83% of the length of the 1958 dollar. At the same time, the width of the 1968 dollar is also 83% of the width of the 1958 dollar. In addition to length and width a dollar also has area, and area is a strong visual feature of the dollar bills to be compared. However, the area of the 1968 dollar is only 69% of the area of the 1958 dollar. This misleading feature of the graph is quite evident with the 1978 dollar: In length it is 44% of the 1958 dollar; in area it is less than 20% of the 1958 dollar. What exactly are the areas of the 1963 and 1973 dollars compared to the area of the 1958 dollar?

(b)   Below is another graph that uses a pictorial device in place of a bar.

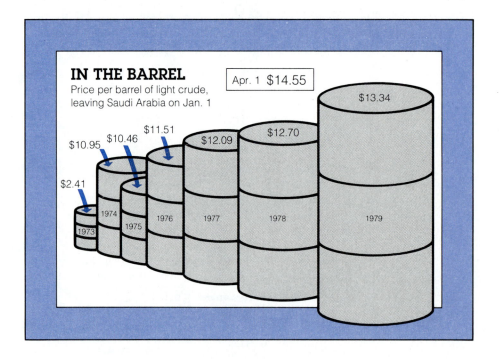

Volume is a strong visual feature of this graph. Discuss how it makes this graph misleading.

(c) Here is a third graph that uses pictorial devices in place of bars.

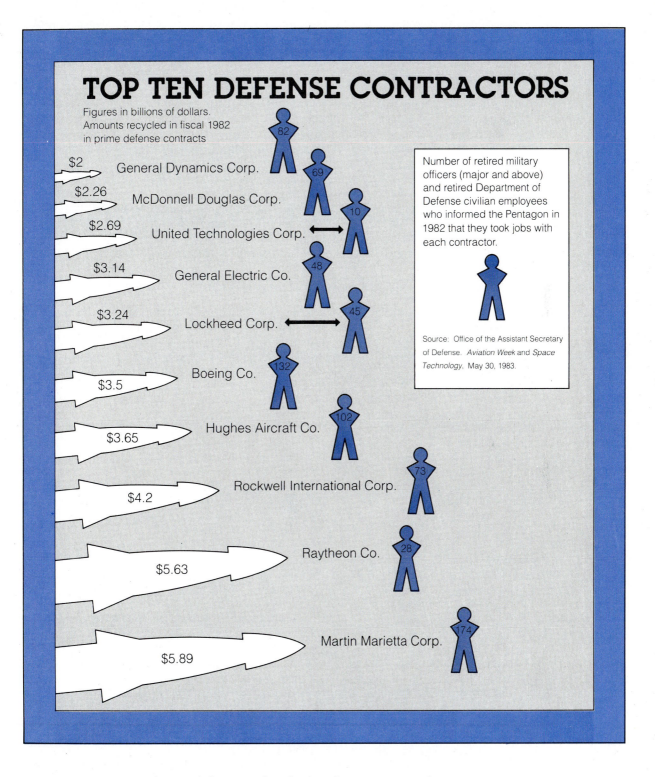

TOP TEN DEFENSE CONTRACTORS

Figures in billions of dollars.
Amounts recycled in fiscal 1982
in prime defense contracts

$2   General Dynamics Corp.   82

$2.26   McDonnell Douglas Corp.   69

$2.69   United Technologies Corp. ←→ 10

$3.14   General Electric Co.   48

$3.24   Lockheed Corp. ←→ 45

$3.5   Boeing Co.   132

$3.65   Hughes Aircraft Co.   102

$4.2   Rockwell International Corp.   73

$5.63   Raytheon Co.   28

$5.89   Martin Marietta Corp.   174

Number of retired military officers (major and above) and retired Department of Defense civilian employees who informed the Pentagon in 1982 that they took jobs with each contractor.

Source: Office of the Assistant Secretary of Defense. *Aviation Week* and *Space Technology*, May 30, 1983.

This graph has several misleading features. Discuss them.

28. The table below shows deaths because of major earthquakes.

DATE	PLACE	DEATHS	MAG.	DATE	PLACE	DEATHS	MAG.
526 May 20	Syria, Antioch	250,000	N.A.	1957 July 2	Northern Iran	2,500	7.4
856	Greece, Corinth	45,000	"	1957 Dec. 13	Western Iran	2,000	7.1
1057	China, Chihli	25,000	"	1960 Feb. 29	Morocco, Agadir	12,000	5.8
1268	Asia Minor, Cilicia	60,000	"	1960 May 21-30	Southern Chile	5,000	8.3
1290 Sept. 27	China, Chihli	100,000	"	1962 Sept. 1	Northwestern Iran	12,230	7.1
1293 May 20	Japan, Kamakura	30,000	"	1963 July 26	Yugoslavia, Skopje	1,100	6.0
1531 Jan. 26	Portugal, Lisbon	30,000	"	1964 Mar. 27	Alaska	114	8.5
1556 Jan. 24	China, Shaanxi	830,000	"	1966 Aug. 19	Eastern Turkey	2,520	6.9
1667 Nov.	Caucasia, Shemaka	80,000	"	1968 Aug. 31	Northeastern Iran	12,000	7.4
1693 Jan. 11	Italy, Catania	60,000	"	1970 Mar. 28	Western Turkey	1,086	7.4
1730 Dec. 30	Japan, Hokkaido	137,000	"	1970 May 31	Northern Peru	66,794	7.7
1737 Oct. 11	India, Calcutta	300,000	"	1971 Feb. 9	Cal., San Fernando Valley	65	6.5
1755 June 7	Northern Persia	40,000	"	1972 Apr. 10	Southern Iran	5,057	6.9
1755 Nov. 1	Portugal, Lisbon	60,000	8.75*	1972 Dec. 23	Nicaragua	5,000	6.2
1783 Feb. 4	Italy, Calabria	30,000	N.A.	1974 Dec. 28	Pakistan (9 towns)	5,200	6.3
1797 Feb. 4	Ecuador, Quito	41,000	"	1975 Sept. 6	Turkey (Lice, etc)	2,312	6.6
1811-12	New Madrid, Mo	—	"	1976 Feb. 4	Guatemala	22,778	7.5
1822 Sept. 5	Asia Minor, Aleppo	22,000	"	1976 May 6	Northeast Italy	946	6.5
1828 Dec. 28	Japan, Echigo	30,000	"	1976 June 26	New Guinea, Irian Jaya	443	7.1
1868 Aug. 13-15	Peru and Ecuador	40,000	"	1976 July 28	China, Tangshan	242,000	8.2
1875 May 16	Venezuela, Colombia	16,000	"	1976 Aug. 17	Philippines, Mindanao	8,000	7.8
1896 June 15	Japan, sea wave	27,120	"	1976 Nov. 24	Eastern Turkey	4,000	7.9
1906 Apr. 18-19	Cal., San Francisco	503	8.3	1977 Mar. 4	Romania, Bucharest, etc	1,541	7.5
1906 Aug. 16	Chile, Valparaiso	20,000	8.6	1977 Aug. 19	Indonesia	200	8.0
1908 Dec. 28	Italy, Messina	83,000	7.5	1977 Nov. 23	Northwestern Argentina	100	8.2
1915 Jan. 13	Italy, Avezzano	29,980	7.5	1978 June 12	Japan, Sendai	21	7.5
1920 Dec. 16	China, Gansu	100,000	8.6	1978 Sept. 16	Northeast Iran	25,000	7.7
1923 Sept. 1	Japan, Yokohama	200,000	8.3	1979 Sept. 12	Indonesia	100	8.1
1927 May 22	China, Nan-Shan	200,000	8.3	1979 Dec. 12	Colombia, Ecuador	800	7.9
1932 Dec. 26	China, Gansu	70,000	7.6	1980 Oct. 10	Northwestern Algeria	4,500	7.3
1933 Mar. 2	Japan	2,990	8.9	1980 Nov. 23	Southern Italy	4,800	7.2
1934 Jan 15	India, Bihar-Nepal	10,700	8.4	1982 Dec. 13	North Yemen	2,800	6.0
1935 May 31	India, Quetta	50,000	7.5	1983 Mar. 31	Southern Colombia	250	5.5
1939 Jan. 24	Chile, Chillan	28,000	8.3	1983 May 26	Japan, N. Honshu	81	7.7
1939 Dec. 26	Turkey, Erzincan	30,000	7.9	1983 Oct. 30	Eastern Turkey	1,300	7.1
1946 Dec. 21	Japan, Honshu	2,000	8.4	1985 Mar. 3	Chile	146	7.8
1948 June 28	Japan, Fukui	5,131	7.3	1985 Sept. 19-21	Mexico City	4,200+	8.1
1949 Aug. 5	Ecuador, Pelileo	6,000	6.8	1987 Mar. 5-6	NE Ecuador	4,000+	7.3
1950 Aug. 15	India, Assam	1,530	8.7				
1953 Mar. 18	NW Turkey	1,200	7.2	(*) estimated from earthquake intensity. (N.A.) not			
1956 June 10-17	N. Afghanistan	2,000	7.7	available.			

Source: From Mark S. Hoffman, ed., *The World Almanac and Book of Facts 1989,* Pharos, New York, 1988, p. 524.

(a) Construct a stem and leaf plot displaying deaths because of earthquakes occurring since 1925.

(b) Find the mean, median, and standard deviation of deaths from earthquakes since 1925.

(c) Construct a box and whisker plot of the data.

(d) What do the results of (a), (b), and (c) tell you about deaths from earthquakes? Is one plot more useful than another for displaying these data?

29. Below are two tables, one showing deaths because of notable tornadoes in the United States since 1925, the other showing deaths because of hurricanes, typhoons, blizzards, and other storms.

SOME NOTABLE TORNADOES IN U.S. SINCE 1925					
DATE	PLACE	DEATHS	DATE	PLACE	DEATHS
1925 Mar. 18	Mo., Ill. Ind	689	1958 June 4	Northwestern Wisconsin	30
1927 Apr. 12	Rock Springs, Tex.	74	1959 Feb. 10	St. Louis. Mo	21
1927 May 9	Arkansas. Poplar Bluff. Mo	92	1960 May 5,6	SE Oklahoma. Arkansas	30
1927 Sept. 29	St. Louis. Mo	90	1965 Apr. 11	Ind. Ill., Oh., Mich. Wis.	271
1930 May 6	Hill & Ellis Co., Tex.	41	1966 Mar. 3	Jackson. Miss.	57
1932 Mar. 21	Ala. (series of tornadoes)	268	1966 Mar. 3	Mississippi. Alabama	61
1936 Apr. 5	Miss. Ga	455	1967 Apr. 21	Ill., Mich	33
1936 Apr. 6	Gainesville. Ga	203	1968 May 15	Midwest	71
1938 Sept. 29	Charleston, SC	32	1969 Jan. 23	Mississippi	32
1942 Mar. 16	Central to NE Miss	75	1971 Feb. 21	Mississippi delta	110
1942 Apr. 27	Rogers & Mayes Co., Okla.	52	1973 May 26-27	South. Midwest (series)	47
1944 June 23	Oh., Pa. W. Va., Md.	150	1974 Apr. 3-4	Ala., Ga., Tenn., Ky., Oh	350
1945 Apr. 12	Okla-Ark	102	1977 Apr. 4	Ala., Miss., Ga	22
1947 Apr. 9	Tex., Okla. & Kan.	169	1979 Apr. 10	Tex., Okla.	60
1948 Mar. 19	Bunker Hill & Gillespie, Ill.	33	1980 June 3	Grand Island, Neb. (series)	4
1949 Jan. 3	La. & Ark.	58	1982 Mar. 2-4	South, Midwest (series)	17
1952 Mar. 21	Ark., Mo., Tenn. (series)	208	1982 May 29	So. Ill.	10
1953 May 11	Waco, Tex.	114	1983 May 18-22	Tex.	12
1953 June 8	Mich., Oh	142	1984 Mar. 28	N. Carolina: S. Carolina	67
1953 June 9	Worcester and vicinity, Mass.	90	1984 Apr. 21-22	Mississippi	15
1953 Dec. 5	Vicksburg, Miss.	38	1984 Apr. 26	Series Okla to Minn.	17
1955 May 25	Kan., Mo., Okla., Tex.	115	1985 May 31	N.Y., Pa., Oh., Ont. (series)	90
1957 May 20	Kan., Mo.	48	1987 May 22	Saragosa, Tex.	29

Source: From Mark S. Hoffman, ed., *The World Almanac and Book of Facts 1989,* Pharos, New York, 1988, p. 525.

(continued)

DATE	LOCATION	DEATHS	DATE	LOCATION	DEATHS
1926 Sept. 11-22	H., Fla., Ala.	243	1967 July 9	T. *Billie*, SW Japan	347
1926 Oct. 20	H., Cuba	600	1967 Sept. 5-23	H. *Beulah*, Carib., Mex., Tex.	54
1928 Sept. 6-20	H., So. Fla.	1,836	1967 Dec. 12-20	Blizzard, Southwest, U.S.	51
1930 Sept. 3	H., Dominican Rep.	2,000	1968 Nov. 18-28	T. *Nina*, Philippines	63
1938 Sept. 21	H., Long Island, N.Y., New		1969 Aug. 17-18	H. *Camille*, Miss., La.	256
	England	600	1970 July 30-		
1940 Nov. 11-12	Blizzard, U.S. NE, Midwest	144	Aug. 5	H. *Celia*, Cuba, Fla., Tex.	31
1942 Oct. 15-16	H., Bengal, India	40,000	1970 Aug. 20-21	H. *Dorothy*, Martaquo	42
1944 Sept. 9-16	H., N.C. to New Eng.	46	1970 Sept. 15	T. *Georgin.* Philippines	300
1952 Oct. 22	Typhoon, Philippines	0,300	1970 Oct. 14	T. *Sening*, Philippines	583
1954 Aug. 30	H. *Carol*, Northeast U.S.	68	1970 Oct. 15	T. *Titang*, Philippines	526
1954 Oct. 5-18	H. *Hazel*, Eastern, U.S., Haiti	347	1970 Nov. 13	Cyclone, Bangladesh	300,000
1955 Aug. 12-13	H. *Connie*, Carolinas, Va., Md.	43	1971 Aug. 1	T. *Rose*, Hong Kong	130
1955 Aug. 7-21	H. *Diane*, Eastern U.S.	400	1972 June 19-29	H. *Agnes*, Fla. to N.Y.	118
1955 Sept. 19	H. *Hilda*, Mexico	200	1972 Dec. 3	T. *Theresa*, Philippines	169
1955 Sept. 22-28	H. *Janet*, Caribbean	500	1973 June-Aug.	Monsoon rains in India	1,217
1956 Feb. 1-29	Blizzard, Western Europe	1,000	1974 June 11	Storm *Dinah*, Luzon Is., Philip.	71
1957 June 25-30	H. *Audrey*, Tex. to Ala.	390	1974 July 11	T. *Gilda*, Japan, S. Korea	108
1958 Feb. 15-16	Blizzard, NE U.S.	171	1974 Sept. 19-20	H. *Fifi*, Honduras	2,000
1959 Sept. 17-19	T. *Sarah*, Japan, S. Korea	2,000	1974 Dec. 25	Cyclone leveled Darwin, Aus.	50
1959 Sept. 26-27	T. *Vera*, Honshu, Japan	4,466	1975 Sept. 13-27	H. *Eloise*, Caribbean, NE U.S.	71
1960 Sept. 4-12	H. *Donna*, Caribbean, E. U.S.	148	1976 May 20	T. *Olga*, floods, Philippines	215
1961 Sept. 11-14	H. *Carla*, Tex	46	1977 July 25, 31	T. *Thelma*, T. *Vera*, Taiwan	39
1961 Oct. 31	H. *Hattie*, Br. Honduras	400	1978 Oct. 27	T. *Rita*, Philippines	c 400
1963 May 28-29	Windstorm, Bangladesh	22,000	1979 Aug. 30-		
1963 Oct. 4-8	H. *Flora*, Caribbean	6,000	Sept. 7	H. *David*, Caribbean, East. U.S.	1,100
1964 Oct. 4-7	H. *Hilda*, La., Miss., Ga.	38	1980 Aug. 4-11	H. *Allen*, Caribbean, Texas	272
1964 June 30	T. *Winnie*, N. Philippines	107	1981 Nov. 25	T. *Irma*, Luzon Is., Philippines	176
1964 Sept. 5	T. *Ruby*, Hong Kong and		1983 June	Monsoon rains in India	900
	China	735	1983 Aug. 18	H. *Alicia*, southern Texas	17
1965 May 11-12	Windstorm, Bangladesh	17,000	1984 Sept. 2	T. *Ike*, southern Philippines	1,363
1965 June 1-2	Windstorm, Bangladesh	30,000	1985 May 25	Cyclone, Bangladesh	10,000
1965 Sept. 7-12	H. *Betsy*, Fla., Miss., La.	74	1985 Oct. 26-		
1965 Dec. 15	Windstorm, Bangladesh	10,000	Nov. 6	H. *Juan*, SE U.S.	97
1966 June 4-10	H. *Alma*, Honduras, SE U.S.	51	1987 Nov. 25	T. *Nina*, Philippines	650
1966 Sept. 24-30	H. *Inez*, Carib., Fla., Mex.	293			

(a) Construct a stem and leaf plot and find the mean, median, and standard deviation for the data in each table.

(b) Use the calculations made in this problem and problem 28 to compare the effects of the three categories of natural disasters: earthquakes; tornadoes; and hurricanes, typhoons; blizzards, and other storms.

30. Construct box and whisker plots of the three sets of data given in problems 28 and 29. Use these to compare the effects of the three categories of natural disasters. Discuss the two types of visual presentation of data relative to their effectiveness in making comparisons.

31. Here is a table of crimes per 1000 population in each of the 50 states in 1983. Use any (or all) of the techniques we have discussed in this chapter to describe the change in the crime rate from 1983 to 1987. (The table for the latter appears in the text p. 949).

NUMBER OF CRIMES PER 1000 POPULATION BY STATE (1983)					
STATE	CRIMES PER 1000	STATE	CRIMES PER 1000	STATE	CRIMES PER 1000
Alabama	41	Louisiana	50	Ohio	45
Alaska	60	Maine	37	Oklahoma	49
Arizona	64	Maryland	54	Oregon	63
Arkansas	35	Massachusetts	50	Pennsylvania	32
California	67	Michigan	65	Rhode Island	50
Colorado	66	Minnesota	45	South Carolina	48
Connecticut	50	Mississippi	32	South Dakota	25
Delaware	55	Missouri	45	Tennessee	40
Florida	68	Montana	46	Texas	59
Georgia	45	Nebraska	38	Utah	51
Hawaii	58	Nevada	67	Vermont	41
Idaho	39	New Hampshire	34	Virginia	40
Illinois	52	New Jersey	52	Washington	61
Indiana	41	New Mexico	63	West Virginia	25
Iowa	39	New York	59	Wisconsin	43
Kansas	45	North Carolina	42	Wyoming	40
Kentucky	34	North Dakota	27		

Source: From Mark S. Hoffman, *The World Almanac and Book of Facts 1989*, Pharos, New York, 1988, p. 818.

For each question several possible answers are given. Circle the letter just to the left of the item that best answers the problem.

1. You want to find the volume of the unusual prism on the left.

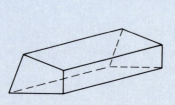 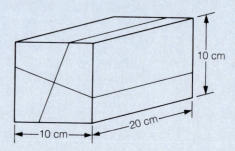

   Four copies of the prism fit together to form the rectangular solid on the right. What is the volume of the unusual prism?
   (a) 2000 cm³   (b) 8000 cm³   (c) 500 cm³   (d) 25 cm³
   (e) cannot be determined from the information given

2. It is raining. You have a cylindrical water cistern. At 8 A.M. you measure the depth of the water in the cistern and find it to be 25 cm. An hour later, you measure the depth and find that it is 30 cm. Approximately how much water entered the cistern between 8 and 9 A.M.?

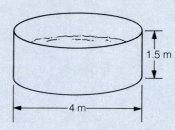

   (a) 630 l   (b) 3780 l   (c) 3150 l   (d) 18,900 l   (e) 15,120 l

3. You make estimates for a paint supplier. A sphere, 20 m in outside diameter, contains compressed ammonia in its interior. To aid in its insulation, the sphere must be painted with a special asphalt aluminum coating. The coating goes on at the rate of 1 gal per 2 m² and costs $6.50/gal. What is the total cost for coating the spherical tank?

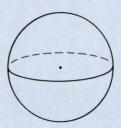

   (a) $8171   (b) $4084   (c) $628   (d) $16,336   (e) $2512

4. A meeting hall is to be built in the shape shown. The floor plan is square. Estimate the amount of air it will hold.

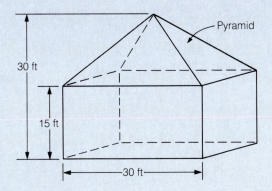

(a)   15,750 ft³   (b)   21,500 ft³   (c)   13,500 ft³   (d)   27,000 ft³   (e)   18,000 ft³

5. When sand is dumped from a hopper, it forms the shape of a cone with diameter twice its height. You measure the circumference of one such pile of sand and find that it is 54 ft. Approximately how many cubic feet of sand are in the pile?

(a)   665 ft³   (b)   1994 ft³   (c)   486 ft³   (d)   2572 ft³   (e)   322 ft³

6. An automobile insurance company has compiled some data concerning 1000 of its customers during the year 1991.

THIS MANY PERSONS	HAD THIS MANY ACCIDENTS DURING 1990.
742	0
122	1
58	2
35	3
43	4 or more

Based on these data and assuming that 1991 will be similar to 1991 as far as accidents go, estimate the probability that a customer will have at least one accident during 1990.
(a) .122   (b) .135   (c) .258   (d) .742   (e) .864

7. You take a 12-question true-false test and decide to guess on each question. If you get $\frac{2}{3}$ or more of the answers correct, you will pass the test. Otherwise you will fail. What is the probability that you fail? (Here is the twelfth row of Pascal's triangle: 1 12 66 220 495 792 924 792 495 220 66 12 1.)
(a) $3797/2^{12}$ (b) $794/2^{12}$ (c) $299/2^{12}$ (d) $495/2^{12}$ (e) $3302/2^{12}$

8. The pie graph shows how a family spends its money.

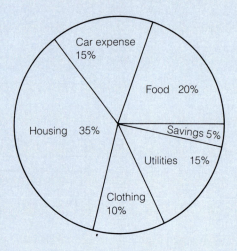

The family has a monthly income of $2400. How much does it spend on food and housing?
(a) $480   (b) $840   (c) $1080   (d) $1320   (e) $1920

9. The bar graph shows the annual production of various kinds of vegetable oil.

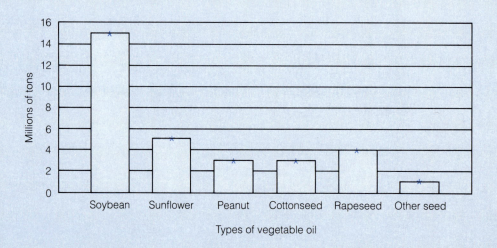

The production of sunflower oil is what percent of all the vegetable oil produced?
(a) 5.5%   (b) 17%   (c) 33%   (d) 55%   (e) 83%

10. Below is a histogram displaying checkout times for customers at a certain supermarket.

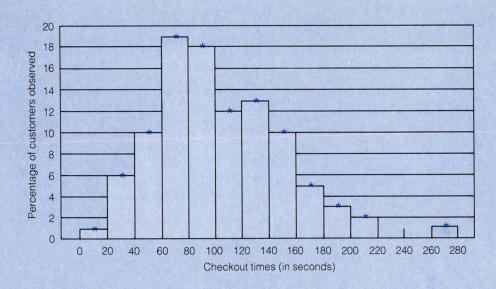

What percentage of persons in the survey had checkout times of 2 min or more?
(a) 32.5%   (b) 12.5%   (c) 20%   (d) 6%   (e) 50%

ESSAY   *For each remaining problem, express your solution carefully and clearly in essay form.*
QUESTIONS

11. A farmer wishes to build a rectangular water storage tank from cement. He wants its inner dimensions to be 2.5 m long, 2 m wide, and 1.5 m high with walls and floor 10 cm thick, and no top. How many cubic meters of cement will this require and how many liters of water will the finished tank hold?

12. An ice-cream container has the shape shown. You have an ice-cream scoop that always gives you a perfect sphere of ice cream $1\frac{1}{4}$ in in radius. Estimate the number of single-scoop ice-cream cones that can be obtained from the large container.

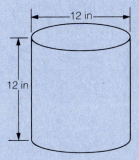

13. A venture capitalist is planning to invest $500,000 on a venture that has a .15 probability of success. If the venture is successful, it will return an amount of $4,000,000 to the venture capitalist. What is the expected value of this experiment to the venture capitalist? Is the venture worth it to her?

14. In the table are listed the highway estimates of miles per gallon for several 1985 European and Japanese model automobiles.

EUROPEAN		JAPANESE	
MODEL	MPG	MODEL	MPG
Alfa Romeo Spider	27	Datsun Nissan Pulsar	37
Audi 4000S	30	Honda Civic	42
BMW 3 series	29	Isuzu Impulse	28
Jaguar XJ	19	Mazda GLC	31
Rolls Royce Camargue	11	Mitsubishi Cordia	39
VW Scirocco	29	Subaru XT	32
Volvo 740/760	23	Toyota Corolla Diesel	47
		Toyota Celica	30

Construct box and whisker plots for the two sets of data. Use the plots to compare the two groups of foreign-made cars with respect to mileage.

SOLUTIONS TO SELECTED PROBLEMS

CHAPTER 1

Exercise Answers

1. 3 more days 2. 16 inches 3. walk about 4/5 mile, exact answer 45/56 mile 4. 10 or 11 order large dishes, there may be more answers 5. 1 boy 3/8 bottle/wk; 1 girl 4/15 bottle/wk; boys use 12/120 more/wk 8. 47 lb peanuts, 23 lb cashews 9. must sell 6 color 10. 10:17 pm 11. 5:36 am 12. 2 13. 2 14. 3 15. no 16. $23 17. (a) [2][+][5][×][2][0][=]
(b) [(][2][+][5][)][×][2][0][=] (c) [2][+][5][×][2][0][+][3][=] (d) [(][2][+][5][)][×][2][0][+][3][=]
(e) [(][2][+][5][)][×][(][2][0][+][3][)][=] (f) [2][+][5][×][(][2][0][+][3][)][=] 18. (a) [(][4][+][5][+][6][)][÷][3][=]
(b) [2][0][÷][(][4][+][6][)][=] (c) [(][1][0][+][1][2][+][1][6][)][÷][(][9][+][1][0][)][=]
19. (a) [1][7][×][(][1][3][×][(][2][3][+][5][9][)][−][5][7][)][+][2][9][=]
(b) [(][1][2][×][1][4][+][2][4][×][3][3][)][÷][(][3][7][×][4][2][+][5][7][)][=]
(c) [(][7][×][(][5][2][−][1][7][)][+][1][3][)][÷][(][8][3][−][3][5][)][=] 21. $106.80, $147.60, $78.00, $56.40
23. (a) prints N^2 (b) prints "This program will square a number. What number do you want to square? N^2"
(c) square all the numbers from 1 to 10 (d) prints all the numbers from 1 to 10 with their square (e) no difference
(f) open-ended loop, l, must be loaded in separately (g) increments p by 2 (h) prints headings for the columns

Practicing Skills Answers

1. Bill $4.50, Bryan $1.50 3. 2.5 hours, 3:30 am 5. $60.89 7. smaller, guess (a) 9. 16¢ 11. 6:40 a.m. 13. Chef Andres, Farmer Cohen, Teller Brown 15. yes

CHAPTER 2

Exercise Answers

1. (a) air-conditioning but no radio

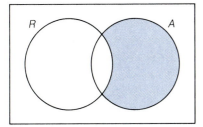

(b) at least one option

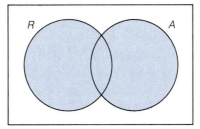

(c) no radio

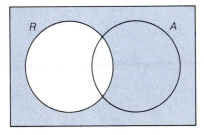

(d) radio or no air-conditioning

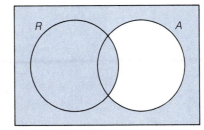

2. (a) large color TVs; large black and white TVs; small TV either black and white or color

(b) (i) all black and white

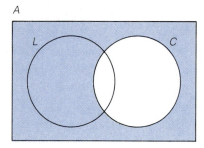

(ii) large black and white

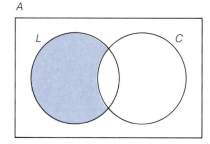

(iii) large colored TV

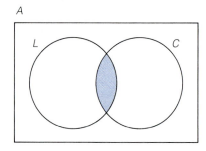

(iv) either colored or large

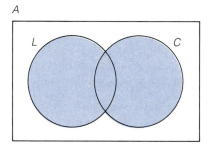

(c) 8 large colored TVs, 11 small TVs, total of 40 TVs

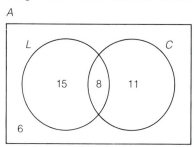

3. 976 in the survey; 345 agree with economic policy; 72 disagree with all three; 256 disagree with just one policy. **4.** (a) antigens A and Rh include A+ and AB+; (b) A or Rh or both include A−, A+, AB+, B+, and O+; (c) neither B nor A include O− and O+; (d) don't have A but do have Rh including O+ and B+ **5.** 48 **6.** $3 \le$ do both ≤ 7; $0 \le$ do neither ≤ 4 **7.** least number 8, largest number 21 **8.** (a) false (b) true (c) true (d) false **9.** (a) true (b) false (c) false (d) true (e) true (f) true (g) true (h) false (i) true **10.** (a) (babies) $B \subset I$ (illogical) (b) (politicians) $P \subset D$ (dishonest) (c) (squares) $S \subset R$ (rectangles) (d) (equilateral) $E \subset I$ (isosceles) **11.** $A = B$ **12.** $A \subset B$ **13.** $\{h,e,a,t\}, \{h,e,a\}, \{h,e,t\}, \{h,a,t\}, \{e,a,t\}, \{h,e\}, \{h,a\}, \{h,t\}, \{e,a\}, \{e,t\}, \{a,t\}, \{h\}, \{e\}, \{a\}, \{t\}, \emptyset$ **14.** $\{1,3,5\}$; $\{1,2,3,4,5,7,9\}$ **15.** $S \cap T$ is the set of all students at the university who are over 25 and smoke. $S \cup T$ is the set of all students who are either over 20 or who smoke. **16.** (a) k owns a computer (b) k is 22 years of age (c) k does not own a computer (d) k is 22 and owns a computer (e) k is either 22 or owns a computer (f) k is not 22 and does not own a computer (g) k is either not 22 or does not own a computer **17.** (a) B' (b) $(A' \cap B') \cup (A \cap B)$ (c) $A \cap B'$ (d) $(A \cap B') \cup (A' \cap B)$ There are other equivalent answers. **18.** (a) $\emptyset$ (b) $\{1,2,3,4,5,6\} = C$ (c) $\{1,3,5\}$ (d) $\{1,3,5\}$ (e) $\{10,11,12,\ldots\}$ (f) $\{1,2,3,4,\ldots\} = U$ (g) $\emptyset$ (h) U

19. (a) $(A \cap B) \cap C$

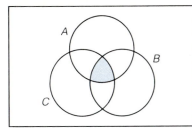

(b) $(A' \cup B) \cap C$

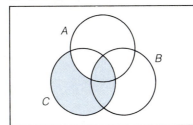

(c) $C \cup (B' \cap A)$

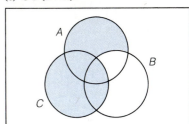

(d) $A' \cup (B \cup C)$

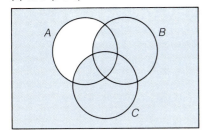

(e) $(A \cup B)' \cup C$

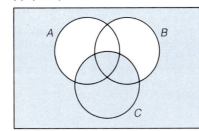

(f) $A' \cap (B' \cup C)$

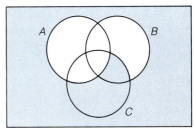

20. (a) B all babies; I illogical; $B \subset I$; (b) C manage crocodile; D despised; $C \subset D'$ (c) $I \subset D$

(d)

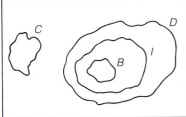

21. A ▨ and $B \cup C$ ▨ $A \cap (B \cup C)$ ▨

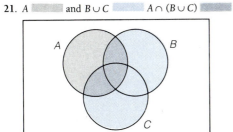

$A \cap B$ ▨ and $A \cap C$ ▨ $(A \cap B) \cup (A \cap C)$ all shaded

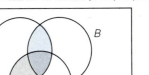

22. A' ▨ B' ▨

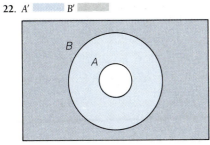

A' ▨ B' ▨ answer ▨

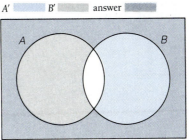

23. $(A \cup B)'$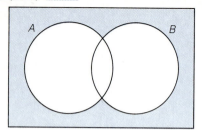

24. (a) use rule 6 twice   (b) use rule 1   (c) use rules 10 and 5
(d) use rules 8 and 10

Practicing Skills Answers

1. (a) all chiming clocks that are not digital   (b) all digital chiming clocks   (c) all clocks that neither chime nor are digital   (d) all nondigital clocks   (e) all chiming clocks   (f) either chiming digital clocks or nonchiming nondigital clocks.   **3.** (a) 6   (b) 25   (c) 37   (d) 85   **5.** (a) 5   (b) 15   **7.** (a) A (b) C, D (c) A, E (d) B, C, D (e) B (f) none
9. $\{C,3,P,0\}, \{C,3,P\}, \{C,3,0\}, \{C,P,0\}, \{3,P,0\}, \{C,3\}, \{C,P\}, \{C,0\}, \{3,P\}, \{3,0\}, \{P,0\}, \{C\}, \{3\}, \{P\}, \{0\}, \varnothing$
11. (a) k is a child in Ms. Wilson's class   (b) k is a child who is at least seven years old and not in Ms. Wilson's class   (c) k is a child who is either at least seven years old or is not in Ms. Wilson's class   (d) k is a child who is less than 7 years old and is in Ms. Wilson's class   (e) same as (d)   (f) k is a child who is either less than 7 years old or not in Ms. Wilson's class
13. $(A \cap B)'$ all shaded

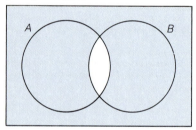

$A' \cup B'$ all shaded

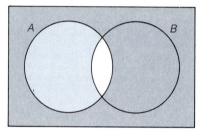

15. (a) use rules 10 and 5   (b) use rules 8, 9, 10, and 6

CHAPTER 3

Exercise Answers

3. more sheepskins than spears   **4.** 1 minute = 60 seconds; 1 hour = 60 minutes; 1 day = 24 hours; 1 week = 7 days; 1 year = 52 weeks   **5.** 1 cup = 8 ounces; 1 pint = 2 cups; 1 quart = 2 pints; 1 gallon = 4 quarts; 1 barrel = 42 gallons (This may vary.)   **6.** Farida has more than enough wheat.   **7.** 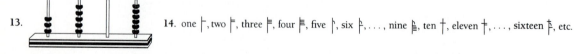   **8.** The larger number is on the left.   **9.** (a) $165 = 1 \times 100 + 6 \times 10 + 5$;
(b) $4073 = 4 \times 1000 + 0 \times 100 + 7 \times 10 + 3$;   (c) $17,078 = 1 \times 10,000 + 7 \times 1,000 + 0 \times 100 + 7 \times 10 + 8$;
(d) $245,673 = 2 \times 100,000 + 4 \times 10,000 + 5 \times 1000 + 6 \times 100 + 7 \times 10 + 3$ **10.** 2,542   **12.** 6304

13.   **14.** one ⊢, two ⊨, three ⊫, four ⊟, five ⊩, six ⊬, . . . , nine ⊯, ten †, eleven †, . . . , sixteen ⊹, etc.

15. ╫ │ ⧻   **16.** (a) ⧻ ⧻ │ ⧻ smaller than ⧻ ⧻ ╫ │ (b) ⧻ │ │ ⧻ larger than ╫ ⧻ ⧻ ⧻
(c) ⧻ ⧻ │ ╫ smaller than ⧻⧻╫ │   **17.** (a) 10^6 (b) 10^9 (c) 10^{12}

18. (a) $12,378 = 1 \times 10^4 + 2 \times 10^3 + 3 \times 10^2 + 7 \times 10 + 8$ (b) $508,122 = 5 \times 10^5 + 0 \times 10^4 + 8 \times 10^3 + 1 \times 10^2 + 2 \times 10 + 2$
(c) $89,142,693 = 8 \times 10^7 + 9 \times 10^6 + 1 \times 10^5 + 4 \times 10^4 + 2 \times 10^3 + 6 \times 10^2 + 9 \times 10^1 + 3$ **19.** 39,487   **20.** 203   **21.** 299
22. 10333_{six} **23.** 1707_{eight} **24.** 1111000111_{two} **25.** (a) 4201   (b) 25   (c) 1281   (d) 40,803   (e) 82,853

---

26. (a)  (b) (c)

27. The scale below is $\frac{1}{4}$ inch = 125 million miles

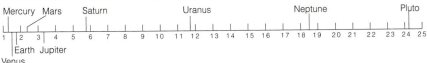

28. The following scale is $\frac{1}{4}$ inch = 500

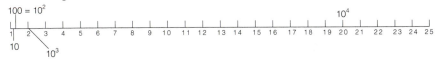

29. (a) $A \leq B$ (b) $A \leq B$ (c) $A > B$ (d) $A < B$

Practicing Skills Answers

3. (a) 2058 (b) 3000 (c) 1111 (d) 9109 **5.** The bottom one is larger. **7.** (a) 452 (b) 31 (c) 3,142

9. (a) 13,423 (b) 3021 **11.** (a) ┿│ (b) ┿╪┿╪ (c) ╪││ (d) ╪╪│ (e) ┿╪┿╪ (f) ┿╪│

13. (a) $4214 > 3124$ (b) $3210 < 31,320$ **15.** (a) 3243 (b) 437 (c) 115 (d) 714 **17.** (a) 50,593 (b) 3148

Review Test: Chapters 1, 2, 3

1. E **2.** C **3.** B **4.** B **5.** E **6.** D **7.** A **8.** E **9.** E **10.** B **11.** 12 **12.** 13°C **13.** no **14.** 46¢

CHAPTER 4

Exercise Answers

1. two camels extra **2.** 84 **3.** ╪┿ **4.** (a) 843 (b) 1315 **5.** ┿│╪╪ **6.** (a) 843 (b) 1315 **7.** ┿│╪╪ **8.** (a) 843

(b) 1315 **9.** ┿│╪╪ **10.** ┿│╪╪ **11.** $1 + 1 = 2, 1 + 2 = 3, 1 + 3 = 4, 1 + 4 = 5, 1 + 5 = 10, 2 + 2 = 4, 2 + 3 = 5,$

$2 + 4 = 10, 2 + 5 = 11, 3 + 3 = 10, 3 + 4 = 11, 3 + 5 = 12, 4 + 4 = 12, 4 + 5 = 13, 5 + 5 = 14, 15 - 5 = 10, 15 - 4 = 11,$
$15 - 3 = 12, 15 - 2 = 14, 15 - 1 = 14, 14 - 5 = 5, 14 - 4 = 10, 14 - 3 = 11, 14 - 2 = 12, 14 - 1 = 13, 13 - 5 = 4,$
$13 - 4 = 5, 13 - 3 = 10, 13 - 2 = 11, 13 - 1 = 12, 12 - 5 = 3, 12 - 4 = 4, 12 - 3 = 5, 12 - 2 = 10, 12 - 1 = 11, 11 - 5 = 2,$
$11 - 4 = 3, 11 - 3 = 4, 11 - 2 = 5, 11 - 1 = 10, 10 - 1 = 5, 10 - 2 = 4, 10 - 3 = 3, 10 - 4 = 2, 10 - 5 = 1, 5 - 1 = 4, 5 - 2 = 3,$

$5 - 3 = 2, 5 - 4 = 1, 4 - 1 = 0, 4 - 2 = 2, 4 - 3 = 1, 3 - 1 = 2, 3 - 2 = 1, 2 - 1 = 1$ **12.** 34 **13.** 47 **14.** ┿╪ **15.** 167

16. 267 **17.** ╪╪╪ **18.** (a) 348 (b) 2816 **19.** (a) 14_{six} (b) 1224_{six} **20.** (a) 348 (b) 2816 **22.** (a) 4049

(b) 32,338 (c) 4588 **23.** (a) 38 (b) 367 (c) 581 **24.** (a) $(a - b) + c \neq a - (b + c)$ (b) $(a + c) - b = a + (b - c)$
(c) $(a - b) - c \neq a - (b - c)$ (d) $a - (b + c) \neq (a - b) + c$ (e) $a - (b - c) \neq (a - b) - c$ (f) $(a + c) - b = a + (c - b)$
25. (a) 25 (b) 68 (c) 28 (d) 4 (e) 24 (f) 429 **26.** (a) 43 (b) 63 **29.** yes **30.** yes **31.** (a) 900 to 1100
(b) 4300 to 4500 (c) 60,100 to 60,300 (d) 400 to 600 (e) 4000 to 4200 (f) 16,000 to 18,000

1. yes   3. (a) 982   (b) 1605   7. (a) 194   (b) 6649   9. (a) 4584   (b) 2557   11. (a) 103   (b) 17

C H A P T E R   5

Exercise Answers

1. 962   2. ╪ ╪   3. 43$_{\text{eigl}}$ 4.

x	1	2	3	4	5	6	7
1	1	2	3	4	5	6	7
2	2	4	6	10	12	14	16
3	3	6	11	14	17	22	25
4	4	10	14	20	24	30	34
5	5	12	17	24	31	36	43
6	6	14	22	30	36	44	52
7	7	16	25	34	43	52	61

5. 54   6. 962   7. ╪ ╪ ╪ ╪   8. 120   9. 133$_{\text{eight}}$ 10. 270   11. 322$_{\text{eight}}$ 14. 560   18. 1440   19. 918   20. ╪ ╪ ╪ ╪

21. 25, 228   22. ╪ │ │ │ ╪   23. (a) 1702$_{\text{eight}}$ (b) 32,552$_{\text{eight}}$ 24. 3876   25. 24   26. 60   27. (a) 3000; 4200

(b) 30,000; 80,000   (c) 300,000; 420,000   (d) 15,000,000; 24,000,000   28. (a) 5   (b) 4   (c) 7   (d) 6   (e) 10   30. 8

31.
```
   1   LET A = ⎫
   2   LET B = ⎬ any numbers you choose.
   5   LET S = A
  10   FOR I = 1 to B
  15   PRINT S
  20   LET S = S + A
  30   NEXT I
 100   END
```

1. 962   7. 33,075   9. (a) 12   (b) 7   (c) 8   (d) 8   11. Grant 35 miles, Adam 42 miles   13. 30

C H A P T E R   6

Exercise Answers

1. (a) ╪   (b) ╪   (c) ╪   2. (a) 7$_{\text{eight}}$ (b) 4$_{\text{eight}}$ (c) 547$_{\text{eight}}$ (d) 123$_{\text{eight}}$ 3. 7   5. (a) $123 \times 10 + 4$

(b) $1436 \times 100 + 28$ 6. (a) $47_{\text{eight}} = 6_{\text{eight}} \times 6_{\text{eight}} + 3$ (b) $50_{\text{eight}} = 5_{\text{eight}} \times 7_{\text{eight}} + 5$ (c) $1234_{\text{eight}} = 123_{\text{eight}} \times 10_{\text{eight}} + 4$
(d) $143{,}627_{\text{eight}} = 1436_{\text{eight}} \times 100_{\text{eight}} + 27_{\text{eight}}$ 8. 3   9. (a) $1542 \div 5 = 308$ R2   (b) $2364 \div 5 = 472$ R4   10. $542_{\text{eight}} \div 6_{\text{eight}} = 73_{\text{eight}}$

11. $6072_{\text{eight}} \div 5_{\text{eight}} = 1162_{\text{eight}}$ 12. 8 dolls   13. $253_{\text{eight}} \div 32_{\text{eight}} = 6$ R17$_{\text{eight}}$ 14. ╪ ╪ ╪ ÷ ╪ ╪ = ╪ R ╪ │

15. (a) $60{,}983 \div 87 = 700$ R83   (b) $57{,}041 \div 263 = 216$ R233   16. (a) $653_{\text{eight}} \div 7 = 75_{\text{eight}}$ (b) $3054_{\text{eight}} \div 41_{\text{eight}} = 57_{\text{eight}}$ R35$_{\text{eight}}$
17. 22 R9   19. 49 tables plus speaker's table   20. 52 miles east of city center at 11 am   21. (a) 4   (b) 4   (c) 5   (d) 3   (e) 1
22. Last Q value, 8, is quotient and last R value, 30, is remainder
23.
```
  10   INPUT A,B
  15   IF A⟨B GOTO 100
  30   LET R = A
  45   IF R⟨B THEN GOTO 100
  50   LET R = R − B
```

Rest of program is unchanged.

Practicing Skills Answers

1. repeated subtraction **3.** repeated subtraction **5.** 28 chairs **7.** (a) $6862 \div 78 = 87$ R76 (b) $57,290 \div 59 = 971$ R1
(c) $1,873,402 \div 428 = 4377$ R46 **9.** $5 **11.** 11 **13.** (a) 4 (b) 1 (c) 3 (d) 6 (e) 3

Review Test: Chapters 4, 5, 6

1. C **2.** D **3.** C **4.** A **5.** E **6.** A **7.** A **8.** C **9.** B **10.** E **11.** 295 R36

12. (i)
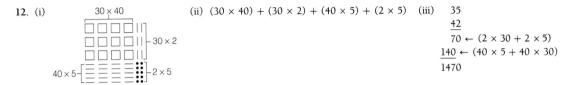
(ii) $(30 \times 40) + (30 \times 2) + (40 \times 5) + (2 \times 5)$ (iii)

$$
\begin{array}{r}
35 \\
42 \\
\hline
70 \leftarrow (2 \times 30 + 2 \times 5) \\
140 \leftarrow (40 \times 5 + 40 \times 30) \\
\hline
1470
\end{array}
$$

C H A P T E R 7

Exercise Answers

1. 60 **2.** 99 **3.** 1872 **4.** 20 minutes **5.** (a) yes (b) no (c) yes (d) yes (e) no **6.** (a) 4, 5, 10 (b) 9 (c) 4, 9
(d) 5, 9 (e) none **8.** 101, 103, 107, 109, 113, 127, 131, 137, 139, 149, 151, 157, 163, 167, 173, 179, 181, 191, 193, 197, 199
9. 2, 2, 2, 3, 3, 5 **10.** 2, 2, 3, 3, 5, 5 **11.** (a) yes (b) yes (c) yes (d) no (e) no **12.** (a) no (b) no (c) yes (d) no
(e) yes **15.** 420-tooth gear, 3 rev/sec, 180 rev/minute; 198-tooth gear, $6\frac{4}{11}$ rev/sec, $381\frac{9}{11}$ rev/minute
16. 50-tooth gear, 2 rev/sec, 120 rev/minute; 72-tooth gear, $1\frac{7}{18}$ rev/sec, $83\frac{1}{3}$ rev/minute **17.** $2 \times 2 \times 3 \times 3 \times 3 \times 5 \times 5 \times 7 \times 13$
18. $2 \times 2 \times 2 \times 3 \times 3 \times 3 \times 5 \times 7 \times 7 \times 11$ **19.** (a) 6 (b) 1 **20.** 5 **21.** $2 \times 3 \times 3 \times 5 \times 5 \times 7$
22. $2 \times 3 \times 7 \times 7 \times 7 \times 7 \times 7$ **23.** (a) 5^4 (b) $7^3 \times 11^2$ (c) $3^3 \times 2^2 \times 7^4$ (d) $3 \times 5 \times 7 \times 11$
24. LCM is $2^3 3^7 5^1 7^8 11^3 17^4 19^1$, GCD is $3^2 11^1 17^3$ **25.** (a) no error detected (b) error (c) error (d) no error detected
28. (a) false (b) true (c) true (d) true (e) true (f) true (g) false (h) true (i) true (j) true **31.** (a) yes (b) yes
(c) no (d) no (e) yes (f) yes **33.** 496 **34.** (a) 8191 prime (b) 8193 prime (c) 216 composite (d) 1003 composite
(e) 11,111 composite **36.** 12, 124; 48, 96; 84, 68; 120, 40; 156, 12

Practicing Skills Answers

1.

#	2	3	4	5	6	8	9	10	12	15
316,200	×	×	×	×	×	×		×	×	×
176,292	×	×	×		×		×		×	×
175,820	×		×	×			×			
74,748,105		×		×			×			×
1,111,111,111										

3. (a) 3300 (b) 9240 (c) 12 (d) 30 **5.** 42 hours **7.** 72 **9.** 120 **11.** (a) $2 \times 3^2 \times 7 \times 11$; $2^2 \times 3^3 \times 7^2 \times 11^2 \times 13 \times 17$
(b) $5^4 \times 13$; $2 \times 3 \times 5^5 \times 13 \times 19$ (c) $2^2 3^3 5^2 7^5$; $2^3 3^5 5^5 7^7$ (d) $3^5 7^2 11^2$; $3^5 5^9 7^3 11^3 13^4 17^5$ **13.** (a) true (b) true (c) true
(d) true (e) true (f) true (g) false **15.** $12^{12}(2^{13} - 1)$

C H A P T E R 8

Exercise Answers

1. 3 and 4 sixths **2.** (a) $\frac{1}{5} \neq \frac{1}{6}$ (b) $\frac{3}{4} = \frac{15}{20}$ (c) $\frac{10}{12} = \frac{15}{18}$ **3.** (a) $\frac{2}{3} < \frac{5}{7}$ (b) $\frac{2}{3} > \frac{7}{11}$ (c) $\frac{7}{12} < \frac{5}{8}$ **4.** $\frac{7}{15} > \frac{9}{20}, \frac{235}{300}, \frac{5}{300}$
5. 1 pt R5; 3 halfpints R3 or $27\frac{3}{7}$ oz. **6.** 6 R2 **7.** 7 to 11 **8.** strongest—Utah; weakest—New Mexico **9.** (a) $\frac{1}{3}$; (b) $\frac{3}{5}$;
(c) $\frac{2}{11}$; (d) $\frac{4}{7}$; (e) $\frac{1}{3}$ **10.** (a) 36; $\frac{28}{36}, \frac{15}{36}$ (b) 40; $\frac{6}{40}, \frac{35}{40}$ (c) 75; $\frac{12}{75}, \frac{40}{75}$ (d) 450; $\frac{160}{450}, \frac{219}{450}$ **13.** $A - B - 1$
14. C any number, $D = C + m + 1$ **15.** $\frac{13}{16}$ **16.** any x where $\frac{5952}{24,924} < x < \frac{7437}{24,924}$ **17.** $\frac{29}{32}, \frac{30}{32}$ and $\frac{31}{32}$

1. (a) $\frac{5}{6} = \frac{15}{18}$ (b) $\frac{15}{20} \neq \frac{24}{32}$ (c) $\frac{0}{3} = \frac{0}{1}$ (d) $\frac{3}{4} \neq \frac{3}{5}$ **3.** (a) 19 (b) 6 (c) $5\frac{721}{1000}$ (d) $57\frac{21}{100}$ **5.** (a) $\frac{11}{30}$ (b) $\frac{14}{18}$ (c) $\frac{49}{45}$ (d) $\frac{65}{168}$
(e) $\frac{3}{11}$ **7.** $\frac{11}{60}$ left over **9.** (a) 9 R2 (b) 12 (c) $6\frac{9}{11}$ **11.** 11 to 20; 18 to 35 **13.** (b) $\frac{7}{12}; \frac{7}{3}$ (c) $\frac{5}{6}$ or $\frac{7}{6}$ **15.** (a) $\frac{25}{60}; \frac{32}{60}$
(b) $\frac{100}{168}; \frac{49}{168}$ (c) $\frac{176}{363}; \frac{90}{363}$ (d) $\frac{260}{546}; \frac{378}{546}$ **17.** (g) $\frac{3}{4}$ (h) $\frac{3}{2}$ (i) $\frac{5}{2}$ (j) $\frac{4}{3}$ (k) $\frac{3}{2}$ (l) $\frac{3}{5}$ (m) $\frac{40}{1}$ (n) $\frac{8}{1}$

CHAPTER 9

Exercise Answers

1. $10\frac{2}{3}$ **2.** 64 **3.** \$9 **4.** $6\frac{1}{4}$ **5.** $\frac{3}{20}$ **6.** $8\frac{17}{18}$ **7.** $3\frac{15}{16}$ **8.** 38 **9.** $13\frac{4}{17}$ **10.** $\frac{25}{36}$ **11.** $14\frac{10}{43}$ **12.** $22\frac{1}{2}$ in **13.** $\frac{10}{23}; 3\frac{59}{92}$ **14.** (a) $\frac{17}{24}$
(b) $\frac{1}{6}$ (c) $\frac{203}{180}$ **15.** (a) 60; 78 (b) 72; 90 (c) $5\frac{1}{3}; 6\frac{1}{8}$ (d) $3\frac{16}{21}; 4$ **16.** (a) $\frac{169}{84}$ (b) $\frac{6}{7}$ (c) 1 **17.** (a) $\frac{5a}{4}$ (b) $\frac{c + d}{3}$ (c) xy
(d) a **18.** $\frac{2(1 + R)}{R}$ **19.** $\frac{320x^2 + 10,000}{x}$ **20.** $\frac{DT}{(T + D)}$ **25.** $z = 2$

Practicing Skills Answers

1. 100 **3.** $\frac{3}{10}$ **5.** 5 vests, $\frac{3}{8}$ yard left **7.** 18 **9.** 72 chickens, 108 geese **11.** (a) $\frac{1}{2}$ (b) $\frac{4}{7}$ (c) $\frac{245}{144}$ **13.** (a) $2\frac{31}{70}$ (b) $\frac{11}{40}$
(c) $\frac{9}{14}$ (d) $\frac{15}{104}$ **15.** $r_1 = \frac{Rr_2}{r_2 - R}$

Review Test: Chapters 7, 8, 9

1. C **2.** A **3.** E **4.** B **5.** D **6.** E **7.** C **8.** E **9.** A **10.** C **11.** 3/20 **12.** (a) 165 (b) 64.5
(c) 459 to 499 or about 9 to 10 **13.** 20 minutes **14.** 11/15

CHAPTER 10

Exercise Answers

1. $A < B$; $A + B = 6 + \frac{2}{10} + \frac{6}{100} + \frac{4}{1000} + \frac{7}{10,000}$; $B - A = \frac{1}{10} + \frac{5}{100} + \frac{3}{10,000}$ **2.** $1049 > 990$; $\frac{2}{10} + \frac{3}{1000} + \frac{9}{10,000}$; $\frac{5}{1000} + \frac{9}{10,000}$
3. $30.572 < 32.075$; 62.647; 1.503 **4.** 506.0708; 5670.008; 500.6708 **6.** 216.347 **7.** 155.167 **8.** (a) 23.05 (b) 230.5 (c) $.2305$
(d) $.02305$ (e) $.00002305$ **9.** 314.364 **10.** $.286$ **11.** (a) $\frac{6}{15} = .4$ (c) $\frac{5}{2 \times 2 \times 2 \times 5 \times 5 \times 5} = .005$ (d) $\frac{13}{500} = .026$
12. (a) $.120$ (b) $.182$ (c) $.556$ (d) $.850$ **13.** (a) $.002857$ (b) 350 (c) 100 (d) $100,000$ **14.** (a) 5.12 (b) 354.19
(c) $.556$ (d) 1.40 **15.** (a) 0.375 (b) 1.74 (c) 24.561 (d) 3.774 **16.** (a) $.1239$ (b) $.1240$ (c) $.1300$
(d) $.2000$ (e) 1.000 **17.** 123.2% **18.** 425.1 **19.** 240 **20.** 7.5% **21.** add 30 ml water to 20 ml original
22. 10 ml medication, 40 ml distilled water **23.** 20 ml of 25% soln. plus 30 ml water **25.** 47¢ **26.** #1 **27.** \$20.17
28. \$6570 **29.** \$539, \$374, \$187 **30.** (a) $.\overline{6}$ (b) $.\overline{857142}$ (c) $.\overline{4}$ (d) $.08\overline{3}$ (e) $.\overline{076923}$ (f) $.\overline{63}$ (g) $.2\overline{6}$
(h) $.3\overline{6}$ (i) $.0\overline{428571}$ **31.** (a) $\frac{7}{9}$ (b) $\frac{54}{99}$ (c) $\frac{207}{999}$ (d) $\frac{79}{90}$ (e) $\frac{347}{1100}$ (f) $\frac{1523}{12375}$ **32.** (a) $.6666$ (b) $.6667$ (c) $.6667$
(d) $.8539$ (e) $.8533$ (f) $.1234$ (g) $.3453$ (h) $.3425$ **33.** (a) $.\overline{076923}$ (b) $.08588235294117647$ (c) $.\overline{047619}$
(d) $.0434782608695652173913$ (e) $.0384615$

Practicing Skills Answers

1. (b) 439.145 (c) 211.314 **3.** 4687.184 **5.** (a) $\frac{17}{800} = .02125$ (e) $\frac{6}{625} = .0096$ (f) $\frac{9}{16} = .5625$ (g) $\frac{11}{80} = .1375$ **7.** 17.5098
9. (a) the stock (b) \$15.75 stock **11.** $33\frac{1}{3}\%$ time; 27.4% budget **13.** higher, 6.4% **15.** (a) $.7778$ (b) $.7778$ (c) $.6296$
(d) $.6298$ (e) $.4836$ (f) $.4864$ (g) $.3469$ (h) $.3470$ (i) $.3500$ (j) $.4000$ (k) 1.000

CHAPTER 11

Exercise Answers

1. (a) $^+10$ (b) $^-1,000,000$ (c) $^+1,000,000$ (d) $^+1,000,000$ 2. largest, Brit Pr, $^+1\frac{1}{2}$; smallest, 0, many companies 3. (a) $^+95$ (b) $^+51$ (c) $^-95$ (d) $^-51$ 5. $^-19,000$ (debt) 6. $^+\$19,975$ 7. $25°$ 8. (a) 26, $^+26$, $^+26$ (b) 21, $^-3$, $^+23$ (c) 28, $^-28$, $^-5$ (d) 10, $^+5$ 9. (a) $^-51$ (b) $^+51$ (c) $^-95$ (d) $^+95$ (e) $^+51$ (f) $^-51$ 10. (a) $^+(A-B)$ (b) $^-(A-B)$ (c) $^-(A-B)$ (d) $^+(A-B)$ (e) $^+(A+B)$ (f) $^-(A+B)$ 11. high/low difference, $^+18$, $^+15$, $^+15$, $^+20$, $^+15$, $^+5$, $^+5$, $^+2$; change in high, $^+8$, $^+12$, $^+5$, $^-7$, $^-16$, $^-12$, $^-15$, $^-2$ 12. difference in high/low, $^+3500$, $^+3800$, $^+2500$, $^+900$, $^+150$, $^+150$, $^+1150$, $^+2700$; change in high, $^+10,100$, $^-2400$, $^-3200$, $^-2300$, $^-850$, $^-50$, $^+1100$, $^+2200$ 13. $^+\$573.20$, $^-\$1360.08$, $^-\$846.56$, $^+\$363.69$, $^+\$1145.64$, $^+\$547.14$ 14. (a) 170 (b) 120 (c) 160 (d) 110 15. (a) $^-30$ (b) $^-16$ (c) $^+44$ (d) $^+45$ 16. (a) $^+5$ (b) $^-20$ (c) $^+9$ (d) $^-6$ (e) $^-17$ 17. (a) $^-2$ (b) $^+2$ (c) $^-150$ (d) $^+120$ 19. (a) $^+\frac{11}{24}$ (b) $^-\frac{1}{6}$ (c) $^-\frac{9}{12}$ (d) $^-\frac{1}{8}$ 20. (a) $^-\frac{6}{11}$ (b) $^+\frac{5}{2}$ (c) $^+\frac{24}{7}$ (d) $^-\frac{115}{8}$ (e) $^-18.1412$ (f) $^-13.058$ (g) $^-30.915$ (h) $^-5.774$ 22. S, T, and U positive 23. (a) $^-15$ (b) 120 (c) 144 (d) 21 (e) 360 24. (a) $17C-6$ (b) $13D-20$ (c) $32E+3$ (d) $-24G+10G^2$ (e) $21F^2-13F-18$ (f) $A+18B$ 25. (a) $\frac{12}{7}$ (b) 2 (c) -15 (d) $\frac{32}{31}$ (e) $\frac{21}{5}$ 26. (a) $\{X: X > 7\}$ (b) $\{X: X > \frac{5}{11}\}$ (c) $\{X: X > \frac{-4}{7}\}$ (d) $\{X: X > \frac{87}{5}\}$ (e) $\{X: X > \frac{7}{5}\}$ (f) no solution

Practicing Skills Answers

3. $11°F$ 5. $^-\$2$ 7. $^-\$1600$ 9. (b) 25 (c) 33 13. impossible 15. (a) $^-15°$ colder (b) $50°F$ (c) 7 hours 17. (a) $^-\frac{2}{3} < ^-\frac{3}{5}$ (b) $^-\frac{4}{7} > ^-\frac{5}{8}$ 19. $71\frac{7}{8}$ hours 21. (a) 300 m/hr (b) 2.125 hours = $2\frac{1}{8}$ hours

Exercise Answers

1. (a) 3^6 (b) 7^{12} (c) 5^{21} (d) 8^{10} (e) 2^{19} 2. 5.88×10^{12} 3. 8,650,000,000,000,000,000,000 4. no 5. (a) 9.72×10^{11} (b) 15.69 6. (a) 56,487,500 (b) 56,487,500 (c) 56,488,000 (d) 56,490,000 (e) 56,500,000 (f) 56,000,000 (g) 60,000,000 7. (a) 7.154E47 (b) 1.3424E22 (c) 7.619E11 (d) 7.154E10 (e) 7.619E6 8. 5.534×10^{24} 9. 6.3492×10^8 10. 5.94 11. 9.8×10^{10} pounds 12. max. error 8.7×10^{12} 13. (a) 9.0×10^{-1} (b) 3.4×10^{-2} (c) 2.45×10^{-6} (d) 1.0×10^{-9} (e) 1.012×10^{-9} (f) 5.7×10^{-17} 14. (a) .304 (b) .000000089 (c) 5.78 (d) .0000000007006 16. (a) 10^{-4} (b) 10^4 (c) 2^{35} (d) 10^{-2} (e) 2^{14} (f) $-8x^6$ (g) x^6y^3 (h) $30x^2$ (i) x^6y^9 (j) 1 (k) a^3 (l) x^6 (m) x^{-6} (n) $x^{-3}y^3$ (o) a^{-3} 17. (a) 5.78×10^{-10} (b) 5.78×10^4 (c) 5.78×10^{-4} (d) 2.0×10^{-4} (e) 2.00×10^{10} (f) 2.0×10^{-10} 19. 2.5165E -88 20. 3.96E -10 21. 3.33E -19 22. $2302.03 23. (a) $1312.93 (b) $1321.07 (c) $1325.34 (d) $1328.27 (e) $1334.99 24. (a) 59,049 (b) 3.948 (c) 1E9 (d) 5.6234 (e) 2.8963E15 (f) 1.8446E19 25. 24 26. 9 years
27. 10 INPUT A, B
    20 C=A∧B
    30 PRINT "A=", A, "B=", B, "A∧B=", C
    40 END
29. (a) output 12; 144; 1928; 20,736 (b) .5; .25; .125; .0625, etc. to 9.53674E -7 (c) all 0 (d) all 523 (e) all 1 31. 15 years 33. $2.16 34. 15 years 35. 36 years 36. 22,400 years 37. 9.025; 8.57; 8.145; 7.38; 14 years 38. 11 minutes 39. (a) 6 (b) $\frac{1}{6}$ (c) 4 (d) 8 (e) $\frac{27}{8}$ (f) 4 (g) a^2b^3 (h) x^3y^9 40. (a) 8.211 (b) 1.304 (c) 17.95

Practicing Skills Answers

1. $10,000^4$ 3. (a) $<$ (b) $>$ (c) $>$ (d) $>$ (e) $>$ (f) $>$ (g) $>$ (h) $>$ (i) $>$ 5. (a) 62.9 (b) 5.772×10^{17} miles 7. 9.5×10^{29} 9. (a) 2.66×10^{18} (b) 2.57×10^{16} 11. (a) .0000000000996 (b) 2.0×10^{-6}; 5.0×10^{-6} 13. (a) 10^2 (b) 10^{-2} (c) 10^{-6} (d) 3^{15} (e) 5^6 (f) $x^{12}y^{-12}$ (g) 1 (h) y^3 (i) x^4 (j) x^{-8} (k) $x^{-3}y^6$ (l) y^{-3} 15. 1500 17. $41,131.78

Review Test: Chapters 10, 11, 12

1. A 2. C 3. C 4. D 5. D 6. E 7. A 8. C 9. C 10. C 11. E 12. 30,000 13. 110 W; 165 E 14. (a) 1460 gal (b) 3.8×10^{10} gal

CHAPTER 13

Exercise Answers

3. (b) $\frac{1}{2}$ meter (c) 4160K (d) 2 millimeters (e) 3 centimeters **4.** 75 ft; 36 m; 11.2 cm **5.** $p = 4S$ **6.** (a) 60 ft (b) 100 m
(c) 80 inches (d) 144 feet (e) 48 centimeters **8.** 21 miles **9.** 70 ft **10.** (b) 21.7 feet

14.

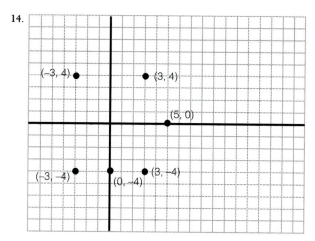
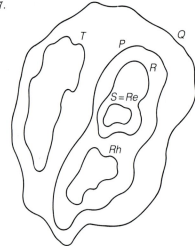

15. $A(-3,-3)$, $B(-7,0)$, $C(8,1)$, $D(0,3)$, $E(-6,3)$, $F(2,-5)$
16. isosceles right triangle; square; trapezoid; parallelogram; scalene triangle; trapezoid. All are convex.

17.

18.

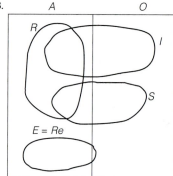

19. 5 lines; 1 line; 2 lines; none; 6 lines **20.** (a), (b), and (d) have mirror symmetry

Practicing Skills Answers

1. (a) 140 m (b) 100 m (c) 120 m (d) 310 ft (e) 100 ft (f) 130 ft **5.** 2850 feet **7.** 26 feet **9.** c, d, and g are not possible

11.

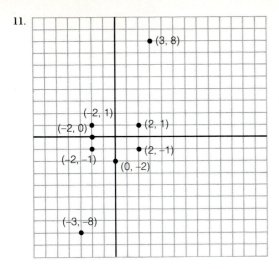

13. $34\frac{2}{7}$ in   **15.** (a) 250   (b) 650   (c) 1500   (d) 850   (e) 2450   (f) 1900   (g) 1700   (h) 1625

CHAPTER 14

Exercise Answers

1. (a)

(b)

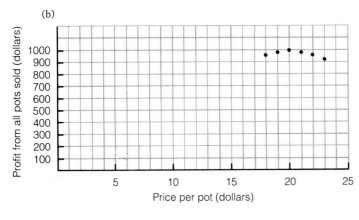

(c)

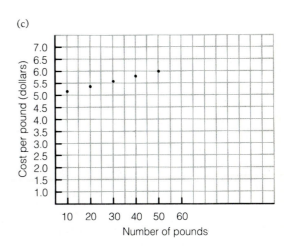

2. less than $1.30 each   **3.** 125 grams alcohol

4.

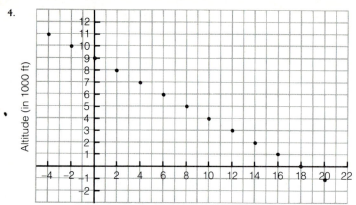

5. tables b and c

6. (a)

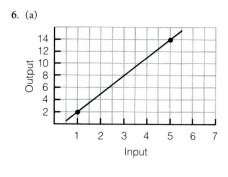

(b)

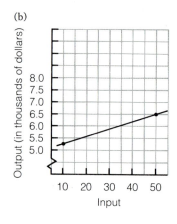

(c)

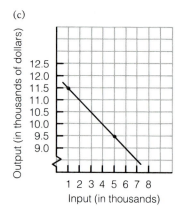

7. 70 pounds   **8.** $26,000   **9.** $19,000   **10.** 11 minutes   **11.** 240 miles with Lemon; 251.85 with Cheap   **14.** $28 + .27x   **15.** $19,080; $20,224.80; $21,438.88; $22,724.59; $24,088.06, $25,533.34; $27,065.35, $28,689.27; $30,410.62; $32,235.26; $34,169.37; $36,219.54; $38,392.71; $40,696.27   **16.** $103; $106.09; $109.27; $112.55; $115.93; $119.41; $122.99; $126.68; $130.48; $134.39; $138.42.   **18.** $C(M) = 32 + .27M$ **19.** $f(N) = 375N + 5000$ **20.** $f(y) = 5500(1.075)^y$ **21.** $f(H) = 918(.5)4$ **22.** movement in opposite direction   **23.** movement starting at a distance of 10 from reference point   **24.** movement before reference time   **25.** not possible

Practicing Skills Answers

1. (a)

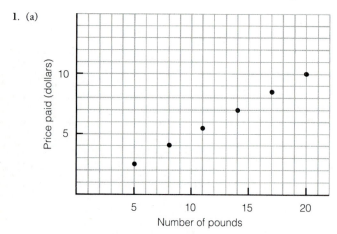

(b)

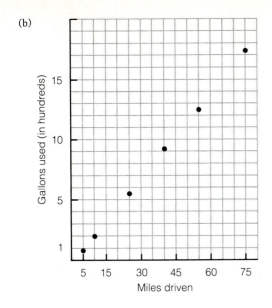

Gallons used (in hundreds) / Miles driven

(c)

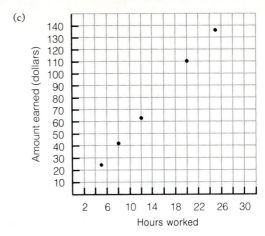

Amount earned (dollars) / Hours worked

(d)

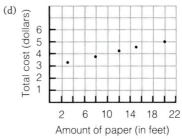

Total cost (dollars) / Amount of paper (in feet)

3. 67 feet **5.** (a) and (b) **7.** 18 years **9.** $c(x) = \$10 + \$.25x; c(x) = \$12 + \$.22x$ **11.** $T(H) = 15{,}000\,(1.03)^H$

CHAPTER 15

Exercise Answers

1. 180 feet **2.** 24 feet **3.** 45 feet **4.** $19\frac{1}{4}$ feet **5.** 110 feet **7.** $164\frac{4}{9}$ feet **10.** (c) and (d) and not possible **15.** 2 triangles exist
19. nothing **20.** congruent **21.** (1,2,3) impossible, (2,3,6) impossible **22.** more than 7 **26.** $K: m = 0, b = -1, y = -1;$
$L: m = \frac{1}{2}, b = 0, y = \frac{1}{2}x; M: m = 1, b = 2, y = x + 2; N: m = -\frac{3}{2}, b = -3, y = -\frac{3}{2}x - 3$ **28.** (1) $f = 25, s = -\frac{25}{13}, d = -\frac{25}{13}t + 25$
(2) $f = 15, s = 0, d = 15$ (3) $f = 0, s = 4, d = 4t$ (4) $f = -10, s = \frac{10}{15}, d = \frac{10}{15}t - 10$

Practicing Skills Answers

1. about 21 feet **3.** 24 m **5.** 600 feet **7.** 25.3; 27.6, 29.9 feet **9.** $5\frac{5}{6}$ ft **23.** (a) $y = 3x$ (b) $y = 3x - 1$ (c) $y = 3x - 6$
(d) $y = 2$ (e) $y = -\frac{3}{2}x + 3$ (f) $y = \frac{1}{2}x + 2$ (g) $x = 5$ (h) $x = -1$ (i) $y = 1$ (j) $y = \frac{2}{3}x - \frac{7}{3}$ (k) $y = -\frac{2}{3}x + \frac{23}{3}$
(l) $y = \frac{3}{2}x - 1$ (m) $y = -\frac{3}{2}x + 11$

Review Test: Chapters 13, 14, 15

1. D **2.** C **3.** A **4.** B **5.** B **6.** E **7.** B **8.** E **9.** 40 **10.** 66 m **11.** 1200 m

CHAPTER 16

Exercise Answers

1. $27°, 73°, 65°$ **3.** (a) $c \cong 9$ inches, $r \cong 1\frac{7}{16}$ so $r \approx 3.1304348$ **4.** 31.4159; 18.84954 **5.** (b) 31.415927; 18.849556 **6.** 14.458 m/hr

7. 1.047 meters

23.

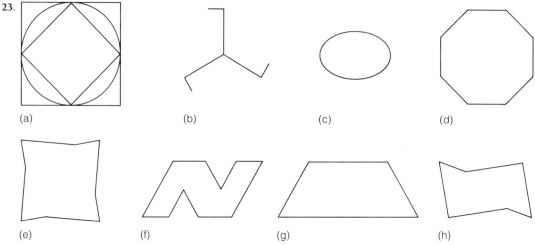

(a)   (b)   (c)   (d)

(e)   (f)   (g)   (h)

(a) 2 mirrors, 90°, 180°, 270°   (b) 120°, 240°   (c) 2 mirrors, 180°   (d) 8 mirrors, 45°, 90°, 135°, 180°, 225°, 270°, 315°
(e) 90°, 180°, 270°   (f) 180°   (g) 1 mirror   (h) 180°   25. 90°, 180°, 270°

26.

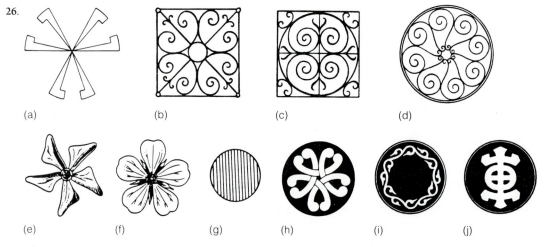

(a)   (b)   (c)   (d)

(e)   (f)   (g)   (h)   (i)   (j)

(a) 120°, 240°   (b) 90°, 180°, 270°   (c) 180°   (d) 45°, 90°, 135°, 180°, 225°, 270°, 315°   (e) 72°, 144°, 216°, 288°
(f) 72°, 144°, 216°, 288°   (g) 180°   (h) 72°, 144°, 216°, 288°   (i) 60°, 120°, 180°, 240°, 300°   (j) 180°

28. isosceles, equilateral, equilateral   29. (a) trapezoid   (b) rectangle   (c) parallelogram   (d) square

33. forward 20   34. repeat 3 [fd20 rt60]   35. repeat 6 [fd20 rt120]   36. repeat 5 [fd20 rt36]
    left 50
    forward 30
    home

38. to triangle   39. repeat 5 [triangle rt72]
    repeat 3 [fd20 rt120]
    end
    triangle
    pu rt120 fd40 Lf120 Pd triangle

42. repeat 6 [blade rt60]   43. fd50 rt135 fd30 rt150 fd50

Practicing Skills Answers

1. (a) (i) 15°, (ii) 15°, (iii) 155°, (iv) 40°   (b) (i) ∠AMC, (ii) ∠BMC, (iii) ∠AME, (iv) ∠CMG   3. (a) 68°, 72°, 40°
(b) 90°, 58°, 32°   (c) 154°, 15°, 11°   5. 2.6389; 9.4248   7. 9.52 miles/hr   9. 8 in × 11.5 in × 11.5 in   21. R = 5.6 cm

CHAPTER 17

Exercise Answers

1. 374.88 m; 16.7634 km; $26\frac{2}{3}$ mi; 21.6 km; 20.16 km; 20.5344 km   2. 12; 18; 18   3. 99; 33; 37.9; 27; 69   4. 16; 18; 24
5. 30; 35; 42   6. 47.5; 72; 68; 106   7. 47; 42; 74   8. 43,560   9. 10,890   10. 62,424   11. 15.742432   12. about 4.128
13. 4π; 25π; $\dfrac{7\pi}{2}$; $\dfrac{\pi}{2}$; $\dfrac{23\pi}{4}$ 14. 1240.87; 1207.5497   15. 30 × 30

18.
```
10 PRINT "WIDTH","LENGTH", "PERIMETER"
20 FOR W=5 TO 30
30 LET L=900/W
40 LET P=2*L+2*W
50 PRINT W,L,P
60 NEXT W
100 END
```
21. squares, equilateral triangles, hexagons

Practicing Skills Answers

1. (a) $\frac{91}{12}$ (b) $\frac{22}{3}$ 3. (a) $\frac{7}{2}$ (b) $\frac{25}{6}$ 5. 82; 30; 21; 27.5; 101; 72   7. 972 ft²; 139,968 in²   9. $\dfrac{41\pi}{72}$ m²; 12π ft²; 9π cm²; 16π cm²

11. 25 × 25   15.
```
10 PRINT "WIDTH", "LENGTH", "AREA"
20 FOR W=5 TO 25
30 LET L=625/W
40 LET P=2*L+2*W
50 PRINT W,L,P
60 NEXT W
100 END
```

CHAPTER 18

Exercise Answers

2. 150 m   3. 29.155 ft   4. 132 sq ft   5. (a) 219.91 cm² (b) 596.9 cm²   6. 1800 ft²   7. 17.51 m²   8. (a) 10 (b) 7 (c) 7 (d) 7
(e) −7 (f) −7 (g) 7   9. (a) 7 (b) 10 (c) 11 (d) 11 (e) 12 (f) $\sqrt{2}$ (g) 5 (h) 15   10. (a) $(x-1)^2 + (y-2)^2 = 4$
(b) $x^2 + y^2 = 9$ (c) $(x+2)^2 + (y+3)^2 = 16$ (d) $(x+1)^2 + (y-2)^2 = 2.25$

Practicing Skills Answers

1. (a) 1.414 ft (b) 5.74 m (c) 3.61 km   3. 54.1 miles   5. (a) 1050π cm² (b) $3.\pi$ m² (c) 16π in² (d) 62.5π in²   7. $7.32
9. (a) 2 (b) 6 (c) 17 (d) 13   11. (a) 13 (b) 11 (c) 23 (d) 23   13. (a) $x^2 + y^2 = 16$ (b) $(x-2)^2 + (y-1)^2 = 4$
(c) $(x+1)^2 + (y-3)^2 = 25$ (d) $(x+1)^2 + y^2 = 9$

Review Test: Chapters 16, 17, 18

1. A   2. C   3. A   4. D   5. C   6. B   7. B   8. C   9. 148 ft²   10. 5/(2π) ≐ 796 km   11. 79.5 m   12. 20′ × 30′

CHAPTER 19

Exercise Answers

1. 280   2. 576   3. (a) 220 (b) 420 (c) 2120 (d) 80   4. (a) 60 ft³ (b) 210 in³ (c) 120 cm³   5. (a) 3360 (b) 18.75
6. (a) 24π in³ (b) 2250π ft³ (c) $.75\pi$ m³   7. (a) 18 ft³ (b) 20,100 ft³ (c) 2678.1 m³   8. (a) 2330.97 ft³ (b) 18,750 ft³
9. 2.806 in³   10. 45 fish   12. $8\frac{1}{3}$; 9259.259 cm³

Practicing Skills Answers

1. 45   3. 252   5. 17   7. 35 ft³   9. 64 in³   11. 2.16 m³   13. 18.82 ft³   15. 17

Exercise Answers

1. (a) 1 ft³   (b) $26\frac{2}{3}$ cm³   2. (a) 64.14 ft³   (b) 33.42 ft³   3. (a) $3333\frac{1}{3}$ m³   (b) 1.25 m³   (c) 240π in³   (d) 2,970,000 ft³
4. (a) 36π ft³; 26π ft²   (b) $83\frac{1}{3}$π cm³; 50π cm²   (c) 20.094 m³; 57.14 m²   5. (a) 6π in³   (b) 3 ft³   (c) 120π in³   (d) 32 ft³
6. $\dfrac{500\pi}{3}$ cm³   7. 8 times as great

Practicing Skills Answers

1. 24π ft³   3. .417 m³   5. 360   7. (a) $\dfrac{4\pi}{3}$ (b) .34 in   9. 27 times   11. larger can   13. $40\frac{2}{3}$π ft³

Exercise Answers

1. $\frac{1}{6}$ 2. $\frac{1}{52}$ 3. $\frac{3}{6}$ 4. $\frac{12}{52}$ 5. $\frac{18}{38}$ 6. $\frac{4}{25}$ 7. $\frac{4}{5}$ 8. 0   9. −$32.25   10. $\frac{1}{2}$ 11. $\frac{1}{4}$ 12. $\frac{7}{8}$ 13. $\frac{1}{4}$ 14. $\frac{3}{4}$
15. eight row: 1; 8; 28; 56;70; 56; 28; 8; 1   17. yes   18. $\frac{1}{32}$ 19. $\frac{29}{128}$ 20. $\frac{63}{64}$ 21. $\frac{22}{64}$ 22. no effect   23. 23   25. (a) January through
December   (b) {1,2,3,4,5,6,7,8}   (c) A,2,3,4,5,6,7,8,9,10,J,Q,K of spades   26. (a) {June,December}   (b) {6,7,8}   (c) {J,Q,K}   27. (a) no
(b) yes   (c) no   (d) yes   28. .4; .45   29. (a) nothing, peanuts, penny, peanuts and penny
(b) {nothing}, {peanuts or penny} − {peanuts and penny}   (c) $\frac{1}{2}$ (d) cannot determine   31. $\frac{1}{6}$; $\frac{2}{9}$ 32. $\frac{211}{243}$ 33. $\frac{251}{256}$ 34. $\frac{1}{2}$ 35. .52
36. .28

Practising Skills Answers

1. (a) 1   (b) 10   (c) 1,749,989   (d) $50,771,681   3. (a) $\frac{850}{1820}$ (b) $\frac{560}{1820}$ 5. $4.50   7. $750   9. (a) $\frac{1}{8}$ (b) $\frac{1}{8}$ (c) $\frac{1}{2}$ (d) $\frac{7}{8}$
11. (a) $\frac{1}{4}$ (b) $\frac{3}{4}$ (c) 0   13. (b) .1   (c) .9   (d) .18   (e) .08   17. 11

Exercise Answers

4. carbon monoxide; nitrogen oxide, 28%   5. 50   6. range: 11 to 32; outliers: 11, 31, 32; gaps: 11 to 14, 15 to 18, 26 to 31; clusters: 18
to 24   10. (a) 100   (b) 73   (c) 9%   11. (b) $13\frac{1}{3}$%, $16\frac{2}{3}$%   12. (b) 4%; 4%   13. 14%   17. Milwaukee, Newark, Bridgeport
18. $1500 to $2000 or $1750   19. (a) bar graph   (b) histogram   (c) pie chart   (d) bar graph   20. 26.77   21. 60.5   22. 7.458C
23. 74.4   24. mean 2.6, median 2.5   25. (a) mean 685.56, median 340   (b) median   26. (a) mean 3.7, median 3   (b) 3
28. (a) median 74.5, lower quartile 67, upper quartile 82   (b) City 1 warmer   (c) City 2 more days in 60's
29.

City	Lower quartile	Median	Upper quartile
Tucson	69.5	82	97
San Diego	66	69.5	73
San Francisco	63	67.5	70.5
Miami	77.5	83	87.5
Seattle	50.5	59	69

Practicing Skills Answers

3. (a) May   (b) January   (c) Oct., Nov., Dec., Jan.   7. (a) 51%; 61%   (b) workforce aging   9. (a) 9, 3   (b) 20, 17
13. (a) 452.92   (b) 157   (c) 1074.95   15. (a) 14.3; 17.9; 11.8; 7 to 25.8   (b) NBC   (c) CBS   (d) NBC

Review Test: Chapters 19, 20, 21, 22

1. C   2. A   3. B   4. E   5. A   6. C   7. B   8. D   9. B   10. A   11. 1.8 m³; 7.5 m²   12. 166   13. $100,000   14. Japanese best

INDEX